HANDGUNS 2006

18TH EDITION

Edited by
Ken Ramage

Published by

Gun Digest® Books
An imprint of F+W Publications
700 East State Street • Iola, WI 54990-0001
715-445-2214 • 888-457-2873

Our toll-free number to place an order or obtain
a free catalog is (800) 258-0929.

Library of Congress Catalog Number: 2005906831

ISBN: 0-87341-662-7

Designed by Patsy Howell & Tom Nelsen

Edited by Ken Ramage

Printed in the United States of America

HANDGUNS Staff

EDITOR

Ken Ramage – Firearms & Gun Digest Books

CONTRIBUTING EDITORS

Holt Bodinson – Handgun Ammunition
John Malloy – Autoloading Pistols
Larry Sterett – Handloading
John Taffin – Revolvers & Single-Shot Pistols

ABOUT OUR COVERS

THE FRONT COVER:

Kimber's Desert Warrior in 45 ACP

The desert tan Desert Warrior, with the lighter tan G10 Tactical Grips, is one of Kimber's most striking pistols. Based on the pistol created for the elite Marine detachment assigned to U.S. Special Operations Command, the Desert Warrior is well-suited for personal defense as well as action-shooting competition.

The Desert Warrior is similar to the Warrior pistol. Both are full-size 1911-style 45 ACP pistols with Kimber's integral tactical rail for flashlight mounting and include traditional 1911 features like short guide rods for easy field-stripping, and internal extractors.

Unique Warrior features include lanyard loop, ambidextrous thumb safety, Tritium night sights, bumped and grooved beavertail grip safety and bumper pad on the magazine. Edges are slightly rounded with Kimber's new Service Melt treatment, similar to but less aggressive than the Carry Melt treatment.

THE BACK COVER:

S&W Model 1911 PD in 45 ACP

One of the newest members of S&W's growing family of 1911-style pistols, the 1911 PD is built in the traditional "Commander" configuration and accepts most after-market parts and accessories for that model.

The pistol carries a non-reflective black matte finish, and wears a desert-tan set of Crimson Trace Laser Grips. The medium-sized frame is of Scandium alloy. Other key features include an external extractor, Novak Lo-Mount carry sights and a full-length spring guide rod. The pistol comes with two magazines, and has an empty weigh of 28 ounces.

CONTENTS

PAGE 6

PAGE 44

PAGE 72

PAGE 86

PAGE 112

The "K-22"
Outdoorsman's Revolver
Sturdy as a Tractor -:- Accurate as a Watch
Designed for highest speed .22 long rifle ammunition; its recessed head space, a feature that will without doubt be widely copied later, protects the shooter from injury by burst cartridge heads and obviates possibility of the discharge of adjoining shells; while the chambers, burnished by our patented process, guarantee ease of extraction.
It is a faithful copy of the world famous .38 S. & W. Military and Police Target revolver with all its rugged honesty, unequalled balance, pre-war workmanship and beauty of finish, crisp unchanging trigger pull; and, above all else, accurate to the last degree. Its sturdy, adjustable, target sights with the Call Gold Bead front, make it the ideal arm for field, woods, or target range; while its weight, balance, and accurate, powerful, but inexpensive ammunition make it without peer for that unremitting practice needed to become a great revolver shot.
SMITH & WESSON
Springfield, Mass., U. S. A.
Send postal for full description and price

PAGE 132

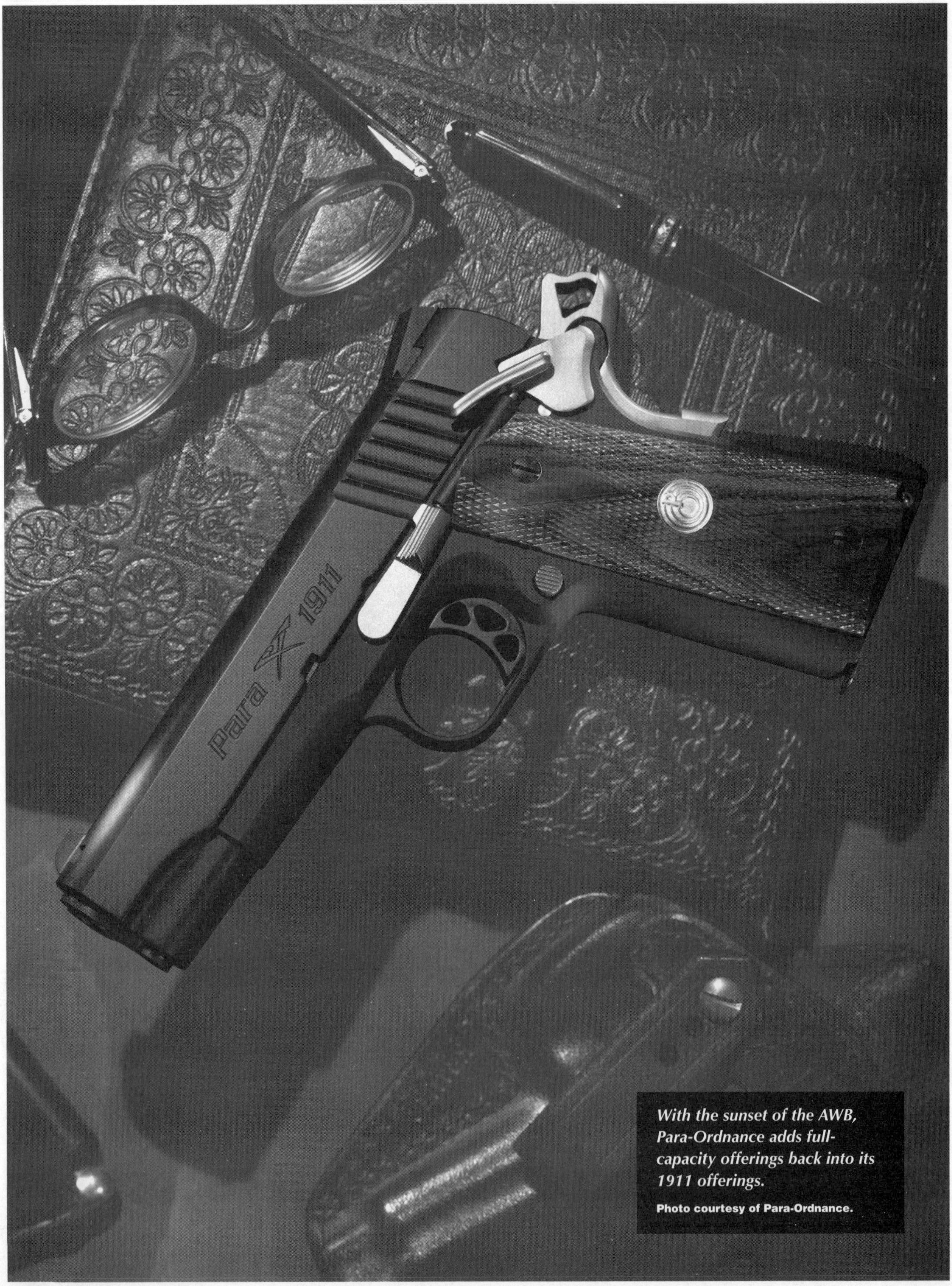

With the sunset of the AWB, Para-Ordnance adds full-capacity offerings back into its 1911 offerings.

Photo courtesy of Para-Ordnance.

NEW AUTOLOADERS

by John Malloy

The biggest recent news concerning the autoloading handgun scene was probably not mechanical, but political. As those with an interest in firearms know now, the so-called "Assault Weapons Ban" (AWB) was allowed to sunset at its appointed time on September 13, 2004. Then, George W. Bush was reelected President of the United States on November 4, 2004.

This report is not really a place for political commentary. However, some aspects of the political situation affect autoloading handguns directly, so it is perhaps appropriate to discuss them briefly here. The now-defunct AWB was thought by many to deal only with "assault" rifles. However, perhaps most of the effect was actually felt in relation to semiautomatic handguns.

The AWB banned the manufacture of 19 specific firearms, most of them rifles, guns that were deemed to be "assault weapons." Also, "copycat" models were banned if they had any two cosmetic features considered offensive, such as a flash suppressor or a bayonet mount. The false picture presented to the public by the major media was that the rifles that had been banned, such as the semiautomatic AR-15 and AK-47 clones, were really machineguns.

However, semiautomatic handguns, hardly mentioned by the major media, were addressed in greater detail in the law. Only two specific handgun models, the TEC-9 and the SWD M-10 (the "MAC-10") were specifically banned. However, manufacturers were prohibited from making any autoloading pistol that used a detachable magazine and had two or more arbitrary features. Such features included a magazine outside the pistol grip, a threaded muzzle that could accept various accessories, a shroud around the barrel, a weight of 50 ounces or more, or just being a semiautomatic version of a full-automatic firearm.

A major provision of the "Assault Weapon Ban" was the prohibition on the manufacture of "ammunition feeding devices" that held more than 10 rounds. This restriction most affected manufacturers of autoloading handguns. With most rifles that are designed to use extended magazines, the magazine protrudes below the lower line of the rifle. Thus, rifles designed for greater capacity magazines could just substitute a shorter 10-round magazine.

The overwhelming majority of automatic pistols, however, have the magazine contained within the pistol's grip frame. The frame is of a size and shape to accommodate a magazine of a certain size and shape. Thus, decreased-capacity pistol magazines had to be redesigned—not only to hold just 10 rounds and fit the pistol and work properly—but to prevent any efforts to later increase the capacity. The innovations in plugged and distorted magazines that resulted might make an interesting historical collection—one that should remind us never to let such legislation become the law of the land again.

It is good that this bad law, which was based largely on emotion, and without any support of facts or logic, has been allowed to sunset. However, the effect of the AWB is not completely gone. A number of laws in different areas essentially duplicated the federal law, and they are still in effect. Since the sunset, anti-gun

AMT is back, and the DAO Back Up pistols, in 380 and 45 ACP, are once again in production. The larger 45-size frame will also be offered in other calibers.

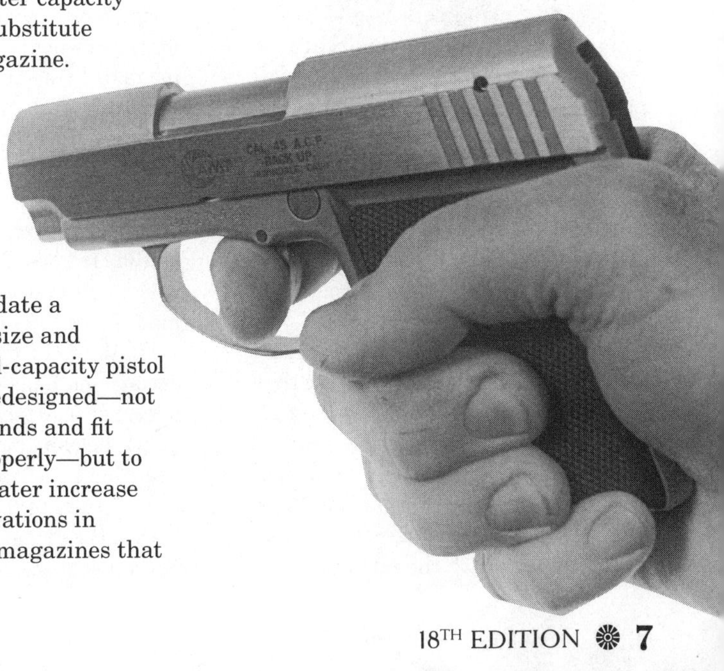

organizations have made an effort to introduce bills in state legislatures that would, in effect, reestablish the AWB in the affected states.

So, the issue has not gone away. Unfortunately, neither has the federal "Assault Weapons Ban." It was not deleted from federal law; it just remains on the books, dormant, because the sunset clause has removed from it the force of law. We can bet that the antis will continue their efforts to either strike out the sunset language or to write an even more restrictive bill. However, for the present, pistol shooters can legally acquire new magazines that were actually designed for their handguns, and can enjoy "politically-incorrect" features on new guns.

The failure of the anti-gun forces to prevent sunset of the AWB was a prelude to the elections of November 4, 2004. The gun rights issue had been a strong factor in the 2000 elections, and the Democrats' 2004 presidential candidate, John Kerry, made an effort to disguise his two-decade anti-gun voting record. He appeared in TV ads as a hunter and shooter. The facts of his record, coupled with his incredibly bizarre descriptions of his hunting experiences, worked against him. George W. Bush was reelected for a second term as president, and the number of reportedly pro-gun legislators in both the House and Senate increased.

The Bush administration is not perfect, but is basically in accord with firearms rights. The Bush Justice Department released an exhaustively-researched report concluding that the Second Amendment "secures an individual right to keep and bear arms." So, drastic federal anti-gun legislation seems unlikely within the next few years. However, efforts to continue and expand bans of certain firearms and "high-capacity" magazines can be expected to continue at state and local levels. Autoloading pistols always seem to be the objects of such proposed legislation.

Perhaps we should make an effort to dispense with the terminology that the anti-gun forces use. They use the term "high-capacity" as something sinister and evil. A 13-round magazine for a Browning Hi-Power is not really a "high-capacity" magazine—it is the magazine for which the pistol was designed. Thus, it is a "normal-capacity" or "full-capacity" magazine. The 10-round magazines we were forced to use for a decade were "reduced-capacity" or "restricted-capacity" magazines.

Now, then, as far as the guns themselves are concerned: the fighting in Iraq, the threat of terrorism and the continuing need for personal protection have kept interest in autoloading handguns high. Most autoloaders introduced recently are suitable for personal protection, or for police or military use. The 45 ACP cartridge seems still to be king of the hill as far as new introductions are concerned. Several companies have introduced new 45s for the first time.

The tried-and-true Colt/Browning 1911 still reigns as the most-used design. For each of the past few years, a company that had never before made a 1911 brought out its version of the classic design. This year we add another two companies, Taurus and United States Fire Arms.

Old names are returning, and it is good to see them back. To the Detonics and Whitney pistols reintroduced last year, we can now add AMT and AutoMag offerings. The Iver Johnson name is also back, offering, among other things, another new 1911 line!

State and local restrictions, no matter how illogical, have to be considered by the manufacturers. In order to sell their products in all states, some handgun makers have had to add internal locking devices, magazine disconnectors and other mechanical devices, and have to be able to supply restricted-capacity 10-round magazines for those who live in areas where magazine freedom has not reached.

Frame rails have become more popular. More organizations and more shooters seem to like the option of hanging various things from their pistols. With polymer-frame pistols, similar frames may be moulded with or without a rail, and some manufacturers offer both varieties.

Laser sighting devices have also become more popular. If a shooter does not want to attach a laser device to his pistol, he can opt for laser grips. Such grips have the batteries, switches and beam generators contained entirely within the grips. At least one American manufacturer, Smith & Wesson, now offers some handguns that are factory-equipped with laser grips.

As a reason to buy a new pistol, why not a commemorative model to celebrate an anniversary? A number of anniversary models—including anniversaries for pistols and companies and organizations—are offered this year.

Interest in pistol-caliber carbines continues to grow, and the option of larger magazine capacity has perhaps given that category of firearms special favor this year. The pistol-caliber carbines are generally not covered along with traditional hunting and target rifles, so we'll give them at least a little attention here.

Please keep all this in mind, and let's take a look at what the companies are doing:

ADCO

The 45 ACP ADCO TT45 was introduced last year, and it has now been joined by versions in 9mm and 40 S&W. The new pistols were introduced, logically so, as the Models TT9 and TT40. These polymer-frame pistols, made in the Czech Republic and based on the CZ 75 mechanism, weigh 26 ounces. With the federal magazine capacity restrictions lifted, the 9mm has 15+1 capacity, and the 40 holds 12+1. For those in states that still restrict magazine capacity, reduced-capacity 10-round magazines are available.

American Derringer

Almost unnoticed among the variety of derringers and other non-autoloading handguns made by this Texas company, a stainless-steel 25 auto has been in the line for some time. With the increased interest in 25-sized 32 autos, the company investigated revising the pistol into a 32. The prototype apparently worked well, but production of the 32 would have required extensive redesign of the pistol and tooling. A decision was made to drop the work on the 32. The 25, a stainless-steel pistol with wood grips, remains in the line.

AMT/Automag

To the disappointment of many shooters, AMT ceased production of its line of innovative stainless-steel pistols in late 2001. However, in 2004, the Crusader Group acquired the assets, and selected AMT pistols are once more being offered. By early 2005, the double-action-only (DAO) BackUp pistols had been returned to production. They are available in 380 and 45 ACP calibers. The original larger BackUp was also made in five other calibers (40 S&W, 9mm, 38 Super, 357 SIG, and 400 Cor-Bon), and smaller numbers of these additional chamberings are now in the works.

The AutoMag II, the first-ever production autoloading pistol for the 22 Winchester Magnum Rimfire (22 WMR), is now back in production, in three barrel lengths. Lengths offered are the original 6-inch, 4 1/2-inch and 3 3/8-inch variants. A new version in 17 Hornady Magnum Rimfire (17 HMR) was scheduled for late 2005. The AutoMag III, in 30 Carbine, is also being returned to production.

Parts and magazines for AMT and AutoMag pistols will be available, and will work with previously-made guns. Magazines will be available for all models and all calibers. (see also CRUSADER)

Armscor

Armscor offers a line of 45-caliber Philippine-made 1911 pistols, and has recently introduced some changes. All 1911 pistols made under the Armscor name now have external extractors and fully-supported barrels. Guns made under the Rock Island name have the original 1911 features.

Still considered prototypes *(although they made it into the 2005 catalog)* are two new 9mm pistols. Of CZ 75 style, one has a steel frame, and the other has a polymer frame.

Beretta

A number of companies have taken an established pistol design and used it as the basis for a pistol-caliber carbine. Beretta, on the other hand, has taken its successful Storm Cx4 carbine and, with that as a concept, has developed a companion Storm pistol. The new Px4 Storm pistol was shown for the first time at the January 2005 SHOT Show. The new Beretta pistol is a polymer-frame pistol that uses the same magazines as the Storm carbine. It is designed around what Beretta calls a "modular concept."

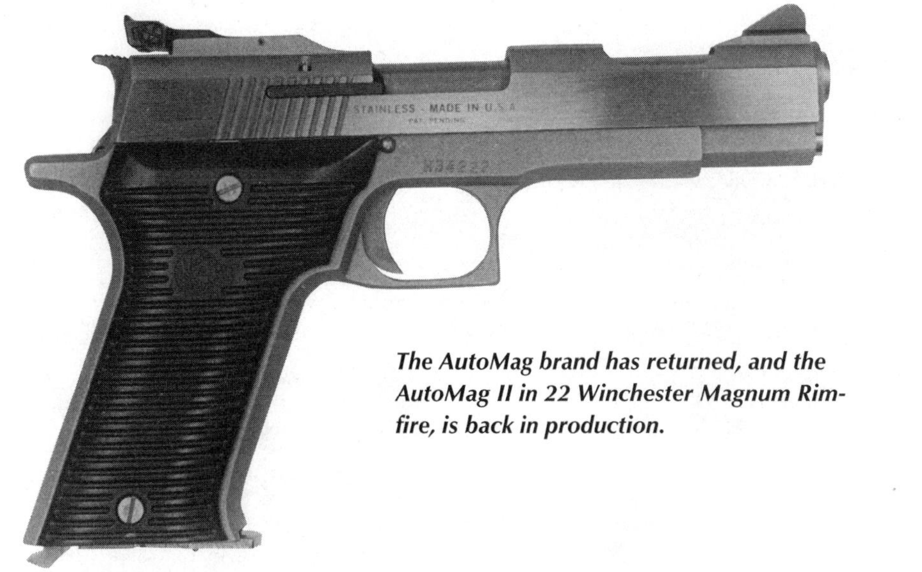

The AutoMag brand has returned, and the AutoMag II in 22 Winchester Magnum Rimfire, is back in production.

The emphasis toward potential law-enforcement acceptance is obvious. The Storm pistol can meet just about any specifications a department might have. To fit different hand sizes, the pistol has three interchangeable grip backstraps. Reversible magazine-release buttons—of different sizes—are included to further customize the gun to the shooter. The safety lever also comes in two different interchangeable sizes. Available at first as a conventional double-action (DA), Beretta's vision is that the trigger mechanism can be customized to include the options of conventional DA with or without a manual safety, and two types of double-action-only (DAO) mechanisms.

The locking system is a new rotary barrel arrangement, and the recoil spring is held captive. Takedown is simple, and the pistol frame has a Picatinny accessory rail moulded in. The new Storm pistol is available now in 9mm and 40 S&W, has a barrel length of 4 inches and an overall length of 7-1/2 inches. The 9 weighs 27-1/2 ounces and has 17+1 capacity. The 40 weighs 29 ounces, with 14+1 capacity. Rumors are that a 45-caliber version will also be introduced, and this seems logical, but there was no official confirmation.

Bersa

Bersa Thunder 9 and Thunder 40 double-action pistols were designed for larger-capacity magazines, but had to be sold with 10-round magazines. As of January 2005, the Bersa 9mms

The new Beretta Storm Px4 pistol has interchangeable grip backstraps and controls of different sizes to customize a pistol to the shooter's hand.

The action of Browning's Buck Mark rifles is essentially the same as that of the Buck Mark pistols.

The Browning Buck Mark target rifle has a heavy bull barrel and can use a variety of optical or electronic sights.

Browning's Buck Mark Sporter is an open-sight carbine based on the Buck Mark pistols.

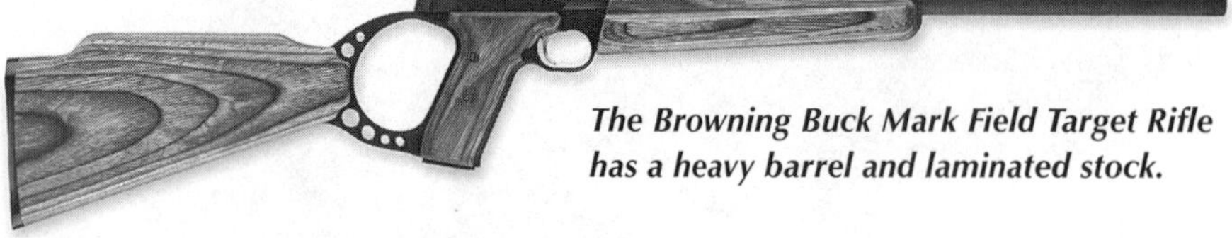

The Browning Buck Mark Field Target Rifle has a heavy barrel and laminated stock.

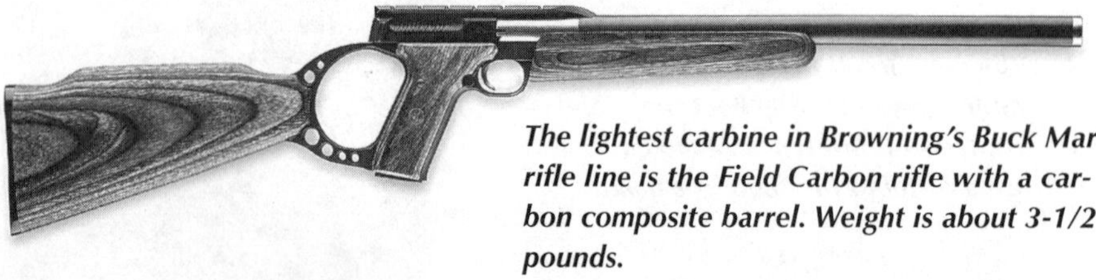

The lightest carbine in Browning's Buck Mark rifle line is the Field Carbon rifle with a carbon composite barrel. Weight is about 3-1/2 pounds.

will be shipped with 17-round, and 40s with 13-round magazines. Extra full-capacity magazines will be available as separate items. Bersa pistols are imported by Eagle Imports.

Browning

Browning has introduced a number of new variants of its popular 22-caliber Buck Mark pistol.

One version is called the Buck Mark Hunter. It features a round, heavy 7 1/4-inch barrel with an integral scope mount base. The pistol has a Pro-Target adjustable rear sight, and a fiber-optic Truglow front sight from Marble. Cocobolo target-type grips are furnished.

The Buck Mark Camper Stainless is a stainless-steel version of the existing Camper pistol, and has a 5 1/2-inch tapered bull barrel.

Two stainless-steel versions of the Buck Mark Standard pistol are now available, one with a flat-sided 5 1/2-inch barrel, and the other as a 4-inch-barrel "Micro" version.

The Buck Mark 5.5 Field pistol has a 5 1/2-inch bull barrel that sports target sights and a full-length mounting rail for optical or electronic sights. The 5.5 Target pistol is similar, and also has the front and rear sights hooded—a potential help when shooting in bright sunlight.

The 22-caliber carbines based on the Buck Mark pistol mechanism *(called "Buck Mark rifles" by Browning)* have proven popular. Several different variants are now available. There is a Sporter with open sights, and also Target and Field Target heavy-barrel variants. A lightweight rifle with a carbon composite barrel weighs only about 3-1/2 pounds. All Buck Mark rifles have 18-inch barrels.

Bushmaster

With the sunset of the "Assault Weapons Ban," Bushmaster is again able to offer models and features not available for a decade. Of interest to us here are the 223-caliber Carbon 15 pistols that Bushmaster offered for the first time last year, which are now freed from weight restrictions.

Recall that Bushmaster acquired Professional Ordnance last year, and thus became a pistol––as well as a rifle––company. Their Carbon 15

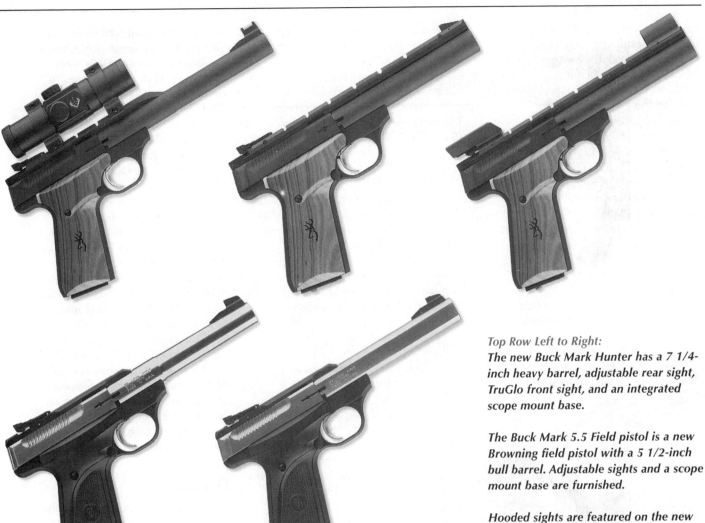

Top Row Left to Right:

The new Buck Mark Hunter has a 7 1/4-inch heavy barrel, adjustable rear sight, TruGlo front sight, and an integrated scope mount base.

The Buck Mark 5.5 Field pistol is a new Browning field pistol with a 5 1/2-inch bull barrel. Adjustable sights and a scope mount base are furnished.

Hooded sights are featured on the new Browning Buck Mark 5.5 Target pistol. A full-length scope mount base and hooded adjustable sights are standard.

Bottom Row Left to Right:

The Browning Camper Stainless pistol is a new field pistol with a 5 1/2-inch tapered bull barrel. Adjustable sights are standard.

The Buck Mark Standard pistol is now available in a stainless-steel version. The new Browning pistol has a 5 1/2-inch flat-sided bull barrel.

pistols feature the same controls as the Bushmaster AR 15-type rifles, but the upper and lower receivers are of Carbon 15 material, bringing the weight down substantially.

The Type 21 pistol, which has a 7 1/4-inch barrel, is now joined by the Type 21S. The new 21S has added a forend/handguard surrounding the barrel, and a full-length optics rail.

The Type 97, with a 7 1/4-inch fluted stainless-steel barrel, is now also offered as the 97S. This new version has a handguard, a full-length upper optics rail, and a lower accessory rail.

A conversion kit to upgrade Type 21 and Type 97 pistols to Type 21S configuration is also available.

Century

Century International Arms carries a line of new Bulgarian Arcus pistols *(based on the Browning "Hi-Power")* in 9mm chambering, and the Bulgarian Makarov pistols in 9x18mm. Century also carries the innovative line of Korean Daewoo "tri-fire" pistols, in 9mm and 40 S&W.

In addition to their newly-manufactured pistols, Century is handling surplus CZ 52 pistols, and has a limited stock of surplus German Lugers and P-38s.

The company recently dropped its line of Philippine-made 45-caliber 1911-type pistols.

Charles Daly

The ZDA pistol, announced by Charles Daly last year, is now a new catalog item. The Zastava-made conventional double-action pistols are available in 9mm or 40 S&W calibers.

The Ultra-X pistol, a very compact double-column polymer-frame 45 of 1911 style, was not approved for importation last year. Charles Daly hoped to have everything worked out so the Ultra-X would be available here by late 2005.

Ciener

Jonathan Arthur Ciener now has in production 22 Long Rifle (22 LR) conversion kits for the Browning Hi-Power pistol and its clones.

Interest in 22 LR conversions for centerfire pistols dates back to the Colt Ace units of the pre-WWII days. In the last fifteen years, Ciener has become a dominant force in such conversions, previously offering kits for 1911, Glock, Beretta and Taurus pistols, as well as for a number of long guns.

22 LR conversion kits obviously let a shooter shoot more for less money. The kits are not firearms, and can generally be purchased without restrictions and shipped directly to a buyer. Use of a conversion kit can extend the usefulness of a pistol in a location that may restrict the number of firearms a person may possess.

***Top:* 2005 was the 30th anniversary of the CZ 75 pistol, and the Czech company has brought out a special commemorative version with engraving, gold-plated parts and special grips.**
***Bottom:* The CZ 75 Compact pistol is now available in a new 40 S&W version.**

Ciener's new Browning kits are offered in two styles, Standard and Hi-Power Plus. The standard unit has fixed sights, while the Plus unit has adjustable sights. Finishes are matte black, gloss black and silver. The units work on both 9mm and 40-caliber Hi-Power pistols.

Cobra

Cobra Enterprises has made a subtle name change, and is now Cobra Enterprises of Utah, Inc. The company still offers pistols similar to those formerly marketed under the Davis, Lorcin, Republic and Talon names. New items now offered are holsters and rebuild kits for older pistols.

Colt

The original Colt 1911, made to World War I specifications, became a catalog item last year, and is now in full production.

The Series 70 pistol is now made in a lightweight Officer's version. The new variant has a 4 1/4-inch barrel, a short "officer's" grip and Novak sights.

A new heavy-barrel 38 Super is being offered. The barrel of the new 38 Super is the same diameter as that of the 45, and fits the 45's barrel bushing.

Crusader

The formation of this new group was announced in September 2004, and although the name may be new to some, to others, the name "Crusader" may evoke memories of the limited-production High Standard Crusader revolver of the late '70s and early '80s. Yes, High Standard is indeed part of the new Crusader Group, which also includes the resurrected AMT and AutoMag lines. Other companies included are Firearms International, Inc., and Arsenal Line Products. (see also AMT / AUTOMAG, and HIGH STANDARD)

CZ

2005 was the 30th anniversary of the CZ 75 pistol, which was introduced in 1975, when Czechoslovakia was still hidden behind the Iron Curtain. Reports of the new pistol at that time were vague, but some thought it to be the best new pistol design introduced. It does seem to have stood the test of time. To commemorate this 30-year milestone, CZ-USA offered a limited run of a special 30th anniversary edition.

The 30th Anniversary pistols will have special serial numbers from 1 to 1000. The pistols are special CZ 75B pistols, chambered for the 9mm cartridge, and featuring high-polish blue, special engraving, inlays, plated controls and blond-finish birch grips. A 15-round magazine comes with each gun.

It is nice to again have design-capacity magazine options, and CZ will now ship full-capacity magazines with the appropriate models.

CZ also introduced a new 40 S&W version of its CZ 75 Compact. The steel frame has an accessory rail, and the pistol has an ambidextrous manual safety. Magazine capacity is 10 rounds. The barrel on the new compact is 3.87 inches, and the gun weighs about 38 ounces.

Detonics

Detonics USA reintroduced the Detonics pistol last year, and the 45-caliber compact version, the CombatMaster, is now in production and has been shipping since February 2005. Detonics president Jerry Ahern says that a very few CombatMaster pistols will also be made in 357 SIG, 40 S&W, 38 Super and 9mm.

Eventually the "commander-size" ServiceMaster and then later, the full-size target-ready ScoreMaster will be added to the line.

Before then, though, Detonics had planned a surprise. The new Detonics StreetMaster was scheduled to debut during early 2005. Ahern, a leading authority on concealed carry, felt there was a niche that had not been addressed in the world of concealed carry and personal protection. The new StreetMaster has the same abbreviated frame as the compact CombatMaster, but has a 5-inch barrel and a full-length slide to match. In a number of situations, such a pistol would be easier to carry and conceal than many conventional pistols, while offering the advantages of the longer barrel. With spacers, full-length magazines can be used to offer a full-size grip. The new StreetMaster has been given the trademarked model number 9-11-01.

FNH USA

FNH expanded their FNP line of polymer-frame pistols with two new models in production. The FHP 40 is a 40-caliber pistol with a 4-inch barrel. It is available with 16-round or 10-round magazines, depending on the location of the sale. Interchangeable mainspring housings allow the gun to be fit to the shooter's hand. A rail is made as part of the frame, for attaching lights, lasers or other accessories. Action and controls are the same as the previously-introduced FNP 9.

There is also a new FNP 9. It is a compact version with a 3.8-inch barrel, and an overall length of 7 inches. Weight is about 25 ounces. As with the new 40-caliber pistol, 16- or 10-round magazines are available. The new polymer pistol line now has a magazine disconnector.

The interesting Five-seveN pistol is now available in a new model, the USG. The new refined version of this lightweight polymer pistol has a more traditionally-shaped trigger guard, reversible magazine release, and a textured grip. The pistol's 5.7x28 cartridge, originally designed for FN's P90 machinegun, had previously been available only to law enforcement. Now, a new sporting round, designated SS196, is available. Because of the small diameter of the cartridge, the magazine capacity is 20 rounds. A 10-round magazine is also available. It will be interesting to follow future sporting interest in this combination.

Glock

The 45 Glock Automatic Pistol (45 G.A.P.) cartridge was introduced two years ago and the Model 37 pistol in that new caliber went into production last year. It was seemingly just a matter of time before compact and subcompact 45 G.A.P. versions were introduced. That time came at the January 2005 SHOT Show, when the new Models 38 and 39 were announced. The compact Model 38 has 8+1 capacity, while the Model 39 subcompact holds 6+1.

Heckler & Koch

2005 was the 25th anniversary of HK's interesting squeeze-cocking P7 pistol. To celebrate, the company brought out a limited commemorative edition of the P7M8, with special engraving and checkered walnut grips. The guns are packaged in wood presentation cases, each with a special commemorative coin. Only 500 of the commemorative P7s will be made.

For 2005, the company offered some of the most popular HK pistols with tan, green or grey frames. These will be offered on a limited basis for five models—the USP 40, the USP 40 Compact, the USP 45, the USP 45 Tactical and the Mark 23.

High Standard

In September 2004, High Standard Manufacturing Company became part of the Crusader Group. Recall that the Crusader revolver was one of the last new products of the old High Standard company before its demise in 1984. Rejuvenated in 1993, High Standard continued its line of 22-caliber target pistols, and added 45-caliber pistols based on the 1911 design.

For 2005, the company has added several new 45s, and two now carry the Crusader name. The Crusader Model 1911 and Crusader Combat pistols are embellished 1911 pistols with 5-inch and 4 1/4-inch barrels, respectively. A shorter version, with a 3 7/8-inch barrel, will also be available. There is also a new military-specification Parkerized 45, the Model of 1911 USA.

One question is sure to be asked, so here is the answer: There is no official word as to whether or not the Crusader revolver will ever be put back into production. All we know is that it was not a possibility before, and there is at least some possibility now.

High Standard will incorporate the services of a company historian, and will offer factory letters for Hi-Standard pistols. (see also CRUSADER)

Hi-Point

Hi-Point Firearms offers a line of affordable pistols in 380, 9mm, 40 S&W and 45 ACP. The company also produces what is perhaps the most popular line of pistol-caliber carbines in America. Available in 9mm and 40, the carbines have been limited to 10-shot magazines. Now, with the AWB's magazine ban no longer in effect, Hi-Point plans to offer magazines of larger capacity, but none were yet available for inspection at the January 2005 SHOT Show.

The new Glock Model 38 is a new compact pistol chambered for the 45 G.A.P. cartridge. An accessory rail is molded into the polymer frame.

A new Glock subcompact pistol is chambered for the 45 G.A.P. cartridge. The small Model 39 does not have a rail incorporated into the frame.

Hornady

What is Hornady, a company involved with ammunition and components, doing in this report? Ah, it is here because Hornady has taken an interest in keeping surplus firearms shooting, and has offered a new line of rifle and handgun cartridges and components. The first autoloading pistol cartridge, just made available, is the 9mm Steyr. A lot of nice shootable old 1911/1912 Steyr pistols sit unused now, and fresh new ammunition can get them out and shooting. The new Hornady ammo is distributed by Graf & Sons.

Iver Johnson

The Iver Johnson name has returned, and the new company offers some interesting autoloading pistols. With the name dating back well over a century, Iver Johnson has been located in New England, in Arkansas, and now in Rockledge, Florida. The present company is connected with Essex Arms of Vermont, which acquired the tooling for the Arkansas-made Iver Johnson 30-caliber carbines. Because Essex already made 1911 slides and frames, it seemed a logical move to add complete 1911 pistols to the new Iver Johnson line of M1 carbines and other guns.

The Iver Johnson 1911s are offered in 45 ACP chambering, and also as 22-caliber pistols. 45-caliber guns are made with steel frames and slides, while the 22s have aluminum frames and slides. A pretty extensive line of pistols is offered, with adjustable- and fixed-sight variants, in 5-inch or 4 1/4-inch barrel lengths. Blue or stainless finishes are available, along with two-tone options. The guns are made in Vermont and shipped to Florida for distribution.

In addition, the nice little Iver Johnson X300 "Pony" 380 ACP pistol will be offered once again. Initial production was planned for late 2005. This 6+1 capacity 380 pistol goes back a long way, and it will be good to have it available again.

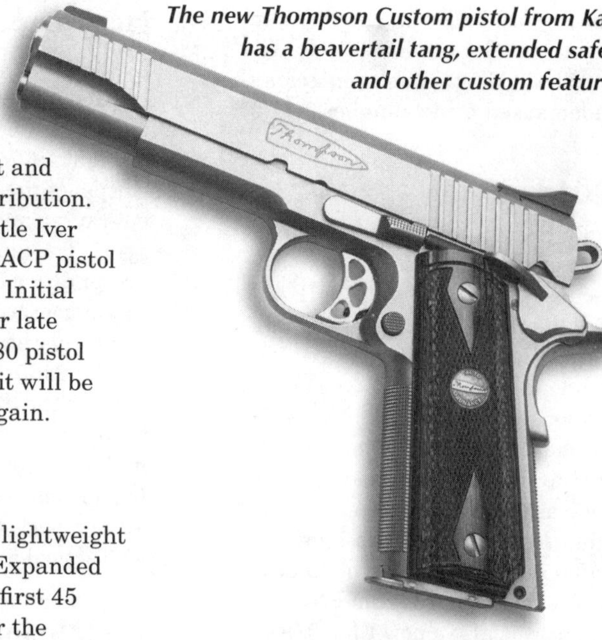

The new Thompson Custom pistol from Kahr has a beavertail tang, extended safety and other custom features.

Kahr

Kahr has expanded its lightweight polymer-frame DAO line. Expanded it up to 45-caliber! Kahr's first 45 ACP pistol to actually bear the Kahr name *(we won't count the Auto-Ordnance/Thompson 1911 45s that Kahr also makes)* weighs only a bit over 20 ounces, with magazine. It features a textured black polymer frame with a stainless-steel slide. The barrel is 3-1/2 inches long, and is polygonally rifled. The pistol feels good in the hand, and has a 7 1/2-pound trigger. Capacity is 6+1, and each P45 comes with two magazines.

Kahr also introduced a value-priced pistol to appeal to the concealed-carry market. The CW9 is a 9mm with a 3 1/2-inch barrel and has 7+1 capacity.

In the Thompson 1911 line, Kahr has introduced two new Custom models, one with a stainless-steel frame, and one with an aluminum frame. Both versions have stainless slides, adjustable triggers, beavertail tangs, extended manual safety levers and other features.

Pistol-caliber carbines are popular now, and Malloy tries out what is perhaps the most popular of all, the Hi-Point 9mm carbine. Magazines with capacity of more than 10 rounds are now legal for such carbines.

Kel-Tec

Kel-Tec continues its line of lightweight polymer-frame personal-protection pistols in 9mm, 380 and 32 ACP.

The company has a knack for coming up with interesting model designations for its firearms. Recall that their 380 ACP pistol is the Model P-3AT. I get a kick out of saying that aloud. Their 223 carbine is the SU-16, in which the SU represents a "Sport Utility" rifle.

The company's pistol-caliber carbine, the SUB 2000, has a number of interesting features. For one, it folds in half, with a folded overall length of 16 inches, which is also the barrel length. It is offered in 9mm and 40 S&W calibers. The carbine can be ordered with a number of different frames, to fit standard pistol magazines used in Smith & Wesson, Glock, Beretta, SIG, or Kel-Tec pistols. Thus, a shooter with a favorite 9mm or 40-caliber pistol of one of these types can have a Kel-Tec SUB-2000 carbine that uses the same ammunition—and the same magazines—as his pistol.

Kimber

Interest in 1911 pistols is strong, and Kimber addressed that

The pistol-caliber Kel-Tec SUB 2000 carbine can be folded to an overall length of only 16 inches.

situation with the introduction of a number of new 1911 variants. Here are some of them.

The 45-caliber LAPD "SWAT" pistol is now available in a stainless-steel version, as the Stainless TLE/RL.

The Stainless Target II is the same as the existing full-size stainless 45 ACP target pistol, but is available in 9mm and 10mm chamberings.

The Pro TLE/RL II in 45 ACP is a blued version with a 4-inch barrel. This shorter variant uses a bushingless barrel-to-slide arrangement. The frame is standard size and includes an accessory rail.

The Stainless Pro TLE/RL is a stainless-steel version of the above pistol.

The Tactical Pro II 9mm, except for caliber, is the same as the 45 ACP version, including lightweight aluminum alloy frame, checkered front strap, and laminated grips.

Two 38 Super pistols have joined the Kimber line. The Stainless II 38 Super is a full-size pistol with polished flats and fixed sights. The Stainless Target II 38 Super is the same basic pistol with adjustable sights.

Kimber claims to be the largest maker of 1911-style pistols. Their goal seems to be to make a variant that will appeal to every individual 1911 shooter, no matter what his preferences.

La Prade

Full-capacity magazines are finally again permissible for ordinary citizens to have, and a number of sources can provide them. Some, like La Prade, can also supply extended magazines. With the growing popularity of pistol-caliber carbines, these can be used to good effect with such carbines, as well as with pistols. The extended magazines can be useful for plinking, law enforcement, for some forms of competition, and for personal protection. La Prade offers Glock magazines in capacities of 33 rounds (9mm), 29 rounds (40 S&W, 357 SIG), 29 rounds (10mm) and 25 rounds (45 ACP). An extended magazine in a Mech-Tech, Kel-Tec or Olympic carbine designed to accept Glock magazines would make an impressive piece of equipment. They will work in the appropriate Glock pistols too, of course.

For those who need one, La Prade also has the last remaining supply of original Bren Ten magazines.

Les Baer

Les Baer Custom has been in business 25 years, and it seemed the appropriate time for a 25th Anniversary Model 1911. The guns will be engraved, and will feature real (legal) ivory grips. White gold inlays of the legend "25th Anniversary" and Baer's signature are on the slide. Only 25 pistols will be made.

A new addition to the Baer line is the "Recon" pistol. A 5-inch 1911 custom pistol, the frame is machined with a Picatinny rail. A SureFire X-200 light comes standard with the pistol.

Llama

The latest Llama catalog does not list any large-capacity pistols, but the Spanish gunmaker has supplied them in the past, and the importer has announced that they will again be available. In addition, normal-capacity magazines will be available for those large-capacity pistols previously sold with 10-rounders. The Llama Max-II pistols will be available with 13-round magazines for the 45-caliber Llama Max-II, and 17-rounders for the 9mm version. Import Sports, of New Jersey, imports Llama pistols.

Olympic

The Whitney Wolverine 22-caliber pistol, featured last year as a pre-production item, has advanced to the production stage. By February 2005, the first production run of 5000 pistols was well under way. Seven hundred Whitney pistols had been completed, but the supply of magazines had not kept up with pistol production. By the time you read this, the Wolverine may be on dealers' shelves.

The OA-93, Olympic's big 223-caliber pistol based on the AR-15 design, had been outlawed by the 1994 AWB because of its weight. In response, Olympic had brought out the OA-98, a pistol of similar design, but drastically lightened to get the weight under 50 ounces. The lightening included putting holes in every component possible, giving the big pistol an interesting

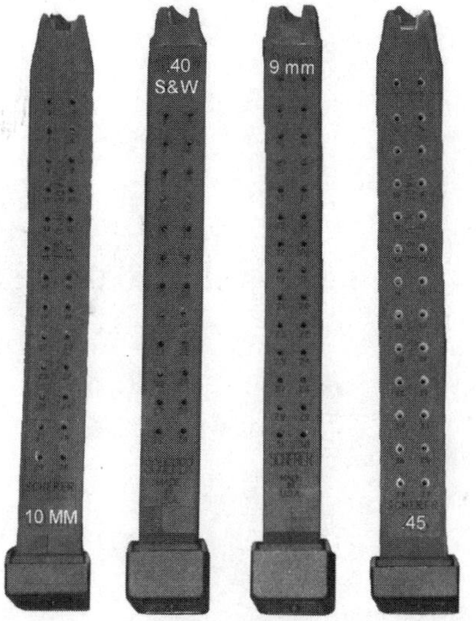

La Prade offers new extended Glock magazines that will hold 33 rounds (9mm), 29 rounds (40 or 357 SIG), 29 rounds (10mm) and 25 rounds (45 ACP).

ventilated appearance. Now, the original OA-93 and the light OA-98 will both be part of Olympic's product line. Barrel length for both pistols is 6-1/2 inches.

The company also makes a variety of pistol-caliber carbines in 9mm, 40, 10mm and 45 ACP. These guns are all based on the AR-15 design.

Para-Ordnance

Recall that Para-Ordnance was the leader in increased-capacity frames for 1911-type pistols. With the sunset of the AWB, Para adds full-capacity offerings back into its 1911 line.

The company can hardly be said to be lacking for new 1911 offerings. Para has introduced six new models of its PXT (Power Extractor) line. Variants are available with double-action (DA) or single-action (SA) triggers, and with high-capacity or single-column magazines. A Para-Ordnance communication states that the question now is not, "Do I want single-action or double-action, and do I want High Capacity or Single Stack?" but "Which Para do I want?" The company certainly does offer a variety. All the new pistols are in 45 ACP.

The OPS is a single-action, single-column compact pistol. Its 3 1/2-inch barrel gives it an overall length of 7 inches. In stainless steel, it has "Griptor" grasping grooves, other niceties, and Cocobolo stocks.

The stainless-steel Lt. Colonel (LTC) is a single-action, single-column pistol with a 4 1/4-inch barrel and length of 7-3/4 inches. Capacity is 7+1, and the weight is 35 ounces.

The "Hi-Cap LTC" is a similar pistol with a wider frame and 14+1 capacity.

The last of the single-action versions added is the S12.45 Limited. This pistol features a 3 1/2-inch barrel and what Para calls "Sterling" finish—all stainless steel with a black slide that has polished sides. Capacity is 12+1.

Two LDA (Light Double Action) pistols have been introduced. The Stealth Carry is a compact 30-ounce single-column pistol with a 3-inch barrel and a capacity of 6+1.

The Colonel is a high-capacity LDA pistol with a 4 1/4-inch barrel and a weight of 37 ounces. A full 14 + 1 capacity and lots of other niceties.

Para seems to have gone hog-wild with some of its nomenclature. Recall that the "Warthog," a small 10+1 45-caliber pistol with a 3-inch barrel, was introduced last year. This year, the "Nite Hawg" has been added, essentially a Warthog in covert black finish. The "Hawg 9" is a similar pistol in 9mm. The "Slim Hawg" is a new 3-inch 45 with a single-column magazine that gives 6+1 capacity.

Rohrbaugh

The little Rohrbaugh 9mm pistol has been standardized with a revised frame. Pistols with the new frames have fired 5000 rounds without a problem. Serial numbers for the revised-frame pistols now have an "R" prefix. The all-metal pistol weighs 12.8 ounces, and measures 5.2 x 3.7 inches. Carbon-fiber grips are now standard. Still, two models are offered, the Model R9 (without sights) and the Model R9S (with sights). With a capacity of 6+1, the Rohrbaugh is the smallest, lightest, flattest 9mm pistol made. Reportedly, it has received attention from troops going to Iraq—it can be carried inconspicuously and uses the military 9mm ammunition.

Top: ***Para's new LTC pistol is a stainless-steel single-column pistol with a 4 1/4-inch barrel.***
Middle: ***The Colonel is Para's 14+1 steel pistol with a 4 1/4-inch barrel and Para's LDA trigger.***
Bottom: ***The 10+1 Para Nite Hawg is a compact 24-ounce pistol.***

Ruger

Sturm, Ruger & Company slipped a mid-year model, the P345, in on us since the last edition. In 45 ACP, this new polymer-frame pistol is available in a blued-slide or stainless-slide manual-safety version, and a stainless-steel "decocker-only" version. The new Ruger 45s are slimmer than the company's previous offerings, and

Above: ***Ruger's new Mark III Hunter is in stainless steel, and has a long 6 7/8-inch fluted barrel.***
Below: ***The new Ruger P345 is available in a blued version with a manual safety.***
Bottom: ***A Ruger P345 with a stainless slide and a decocker is available.***

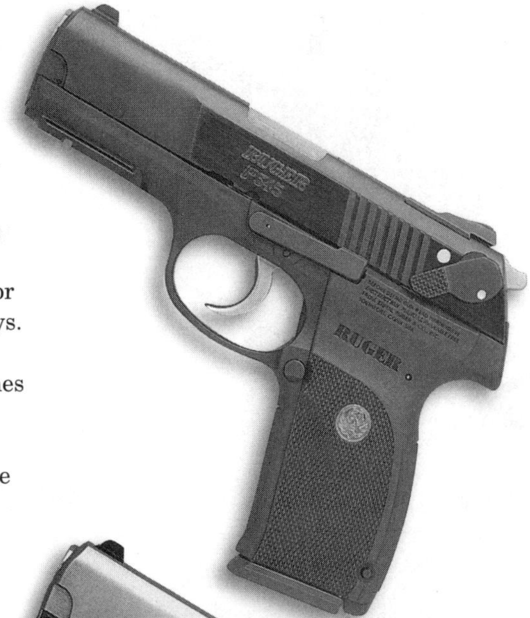

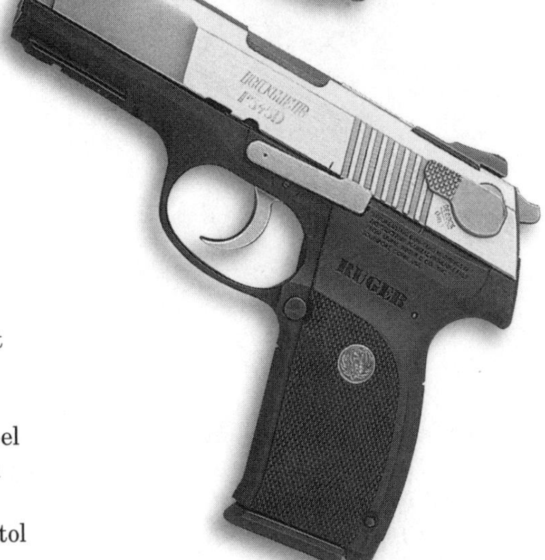

seem to feel good in most hands. With barrel lengths of 4.2 inches, the pistols are 7-1/2 inches in length. Weight for either variant is 29 ounces. Each pistol comes with two 8-round magazines.

The Mark III semiauto, in 22 Long Rifle, is the latest incarnation of the original Ruger Standard pistol of 1949. The magazine release has been moved from the butt to the left side of the frame, and a loaded chamber indicator is on the left side of the receiver. The Mark III series pistols come with Weaver-type scope adapters, as well as new internal locking devices and magazine safeties. A 17 Mach 2 version is now also available. The Mark III 22/45 variant has the controls in the same positions as the 1911-style pistols.

For 2005, the Mark III series offered a special version, the Mark III Hunter. It is of stainless steel, with a 6 7/8-inch barrel, and the barrel is fluted. It features adjustable sights that are a departure from the traditional square-notch type. The rear sight has a V-notch, and the front sight is a round "HiViz" light-gathering sight. Don't like the front-sight color? No problem. Six interchangeable "LitePipes" are included. A scope-mounting base is also included, for which the receiver is already drilled and tapped.

Ruger has made a number of subtle changes on a number of models. Internal locks, magazine disconnectors and other mechanical devices have been added to appropriate models. Such guns now meet the mishmash of state laws, and can now be sold in every state.

Ruger is proud that the company was able to fill a rush order from the U. S. Army for 9mm pistols. The pistols were needed in a hurry, and Ruger was able to deliver an order for 5000 9mm P95 pistols within 30 days.

Ruger 9mm pistols are now supplied with the 15-round magazines for which they were designed. Except, of course, where state or local regulations still limit magazine capacity. There, reduced-capacity magazines can be supplied.

Ruger's pistol-caliber carbines logically use Ruger pistol magazines. The 40-caliber version still comes with a 10-round magazine, but the 9mm variant now comes with a 15-round magazine.

Sigarms

Sigarms introduced a number of new pistols this year. One of the most noteworthy is the X-Five. Although SIG has an actual real 1911 in their line now, the X-Five is a stainless-steel P226 pistol modified for single-action firing, and with a 5-inch barrel and with 1911-style controls. The new pistol offers shooters the choice of 9mm or

40 S&W. Magazine capacities are 19 for the 9mm and 14 for the 40. The pistols have fired groups of under 2 inches in factory testing, and the pistol is suited for the Limited category of IPSC (International Practical Shooting Confederation) shooting.

The polymer-frame SP2022 is available in 9mm, 40 and 357 SIG. With slightly modified controls and a standard accessory rail, the pistol was accepted by a U. S. Army unit, which ordered 5000 of the new guns in 9mm chambering. Mechanism is conventional double action, and the standard magazine holds 12 rounds.

The new 22 LR Mosquito pistol was introduced at the January 2005 SHOT Show. With a polymer frame and standard rail, adjustable sights and new locking devices, the 22-caliber Mosquito is about 90 percent the size of the P226. Trigger mechanism is conventional double action. The new blowback 22 has several safety and lock features, and a 10-shot magazine is standard.

The P229 and P226 DAK pistols are double-action-only guns with a new trigger system. Pull is 6-1/2 pounds, and the mechanism allows second-strike capability in case of a misfire. These pistols were available to law enforcement last year, and are now available for commercial sales.

SIG 1911 "commander-size" and "officers-size" pistols will become available in the near future. To be called the GSC (Granite Series Compact) models, the new smaller guns will be made without the accessory rail of the full-size pistol.

Sigarms puts out a number of limited-edition arms each year. It certainly would seem to be a way to keep collectors happy, as they could get at least one new SIG every year. This year, a number of limited editions were offered. Perhaps the most eye-catching were the P239 and P232 pistols with multicolored "rainbow" titanium slides.

Smith & Wesson

All right, S&W brought out another big new headline-stealing revolver, the 460 S&W Magnum, but there were plenty of new items introduced in the autoloading pistol lines.

Three existing pistols are now offered with fitted Crimson Trace Lasergrips. The variants available with these laser grips are the 1911PD

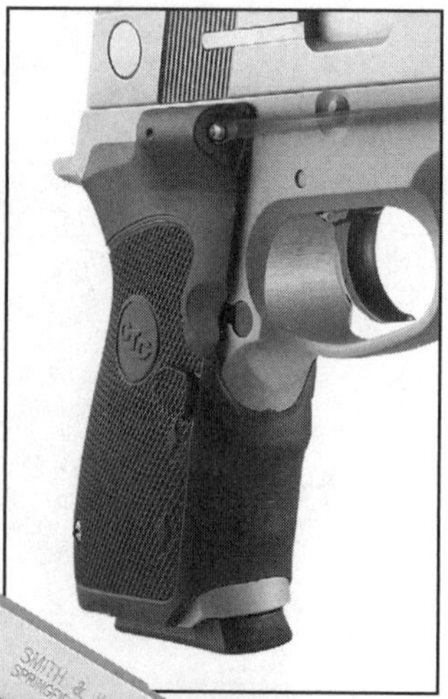

Top: The right side view of the Smith & Wesson 410 S.
Bottom: A new stainless-steel SW 1911 factory-equipped with Crimson Trace olive-drab Lasergrips.

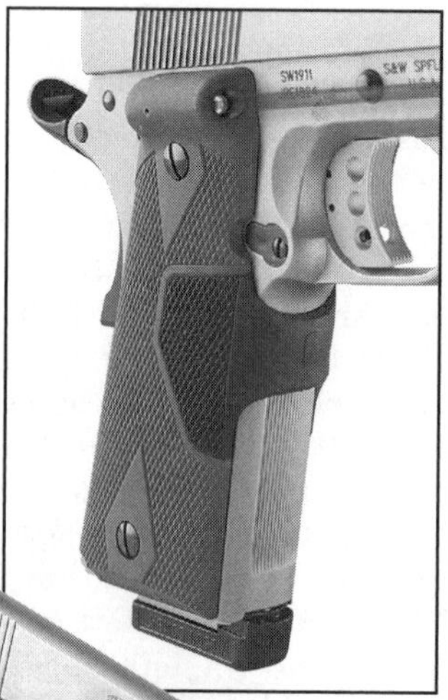

Top: 1911 with olive-drab Lasergrips, right view.
Bottom: The 40-caliber S&W 410 S comes from the factory with Crimson Trace Lasergrips.

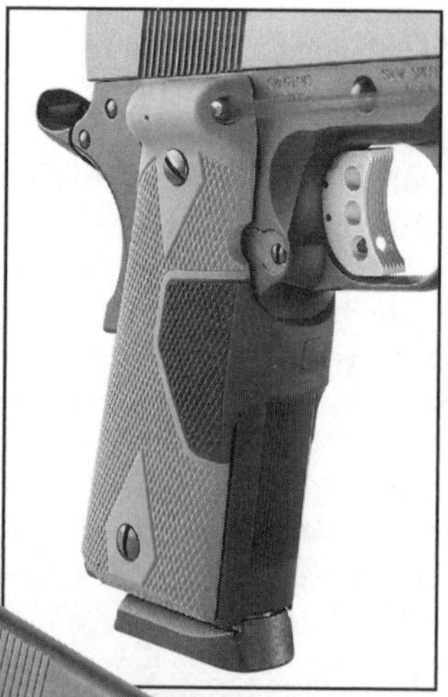

Top: The Lasergrip-equipped carbon-steel SW 1911 PD, right view.
Bottom: A carbon-steel SW 1911 PD, with a 4 1/4-inch barrel, is fitted with tan Lasergrips.

45 ACP with 4 1/4-inch barrel, the standard SW1911 stainless-steel full-size pistol, and the 410S, a double-action, double-column-magazine gun in 40 S&W caliber.

Smith & Wesson, once it decided to make 1911-style pistols, went into it in a big way. Six new 1911 models have now been added to the line. The 1911 scandium-frame full-size pistol with a 5-inch barrel is now available, a larger variant of the original scandium compact pistol that had been recently introduced. A new full-size pistol is now in the line, with frame and slide made of carbon steel, instead of stainless steel.

A special Doug Koenig variant has a blued carbon-steel slide on a stainless frame. Lots of the niceties that many shooters prefer are standard on this model.

A Doug Koenig variant in 38 Super is also available from the S&W Performance Center. This hand-built pistol may perhaps be the company's first handgun in the 38 Super chambering since its experimental big-frame revolver in that caliber back around 1929.

Two additional five-inch-barrel 1911 models are now available. They are similar to the Performance Center models introduced last year, but made of stainless steel. One has a satin finish over its entire surface. The other has the flats polished.

In the 22-caliber line, S&W had added a new Model 22A pistol, this variant with polished sides on the barrel and slide, and a "Hi-Viz" front sight.

Because the Walther PPK does not meet the arbitrary BATF standards for importation, Smith & Wesson, under license from Walther, is now making the PPK here, in 380 ACP. The new gun is smaller and about 3 ounces lighter than the PPK/S that previously replaced the PPK.

A Smith & Wesson 38 Super, the Doug Koenig Professional Series, is now available.

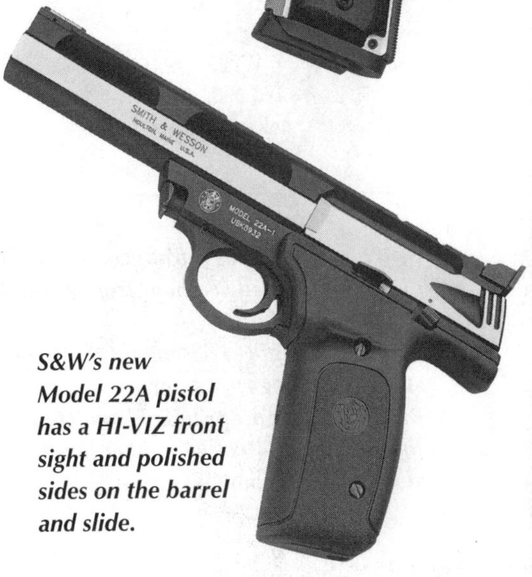

S&W's new Model 22A pistol has a HI-VIZ front sight and polished sides on the barrel and slide.

Springfield

Springfield's Parkerized military-style 45-caliber 1911-A1 pistols were well-received last year. Now, with the sunset of the AWB, the company has introduced a Parkerized GI-type full-size pistol with a "Hi-Cap" magazine. Specifications are essentially the same as the other military-style pistols, but the frame is wider to house a 13-shot magazine. Other high-capacity competition pistols have also been added to Springfield's line.

In addition, some additional models have been added to the company's line of single-column 45-caliber 1911-style pistols. Most, but not all, are competition variants.

With the acceptance of the 45 G.A.P. cartridge, Springfield last year chambered its XD polymer-frame pistol in that caliber. For 2005, the company thought that those with smaller hands might favor a 1911 with the grip scaled down for that shorter cartridge. The result was the new lightweight 1911 Defender pistol in 45 G.A.P. The new little pistol weighs only 23 ounces, with a grip 1/8-inch shorter front-to-back and 1/4-inch less in circumference.

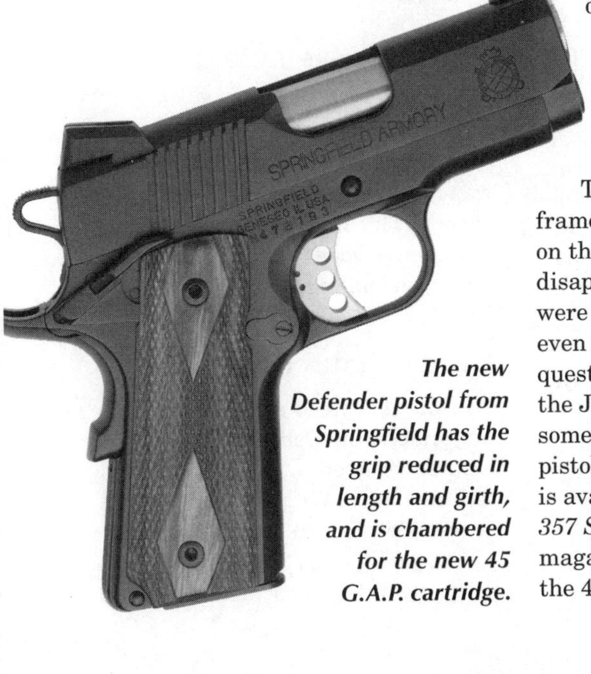

The new Defender pistol from Springfield has the grip reduced in length and girth, and is chambered for the new 45 G.A.P. cartridge.

Steyr

The striking-looking polymer-frame Steyr Model M pistol came on the scene several years ago, then disappeared. For some time, we were unable to learn whether it was even being made any more. This question has now been answered. At the January 2005 SHOT Show, the somewhat redesigned Steyr M-A1 pistol was displayed. The new pistol is available in 9mm and 40S&W *(and 357 SIG on request)*, with a 15-round magazine for the 9 and a 12-rounder for the 40 and 357. The new Steyr pistols still feature the interesting triangular sight system. Literature accompanying the new pistols listed only an Austrian address, so importation arrangements were still uncertain.

STI

2006 is the 30th anniversary of the International Practical Shooting Confederation (IPSC), and STI International is building special commemorative pistols to celebrate that occasion. Work on the pistols began in 2005 and was scheduled to continue into 2006. The pistols are made in 9mm, 40 S&W and 45 ACP. With 5-inch barrels, the two-tone guns will have "saber tooth" serrations on the slide, and special slide engraving for the IPSC 30th anniversary.

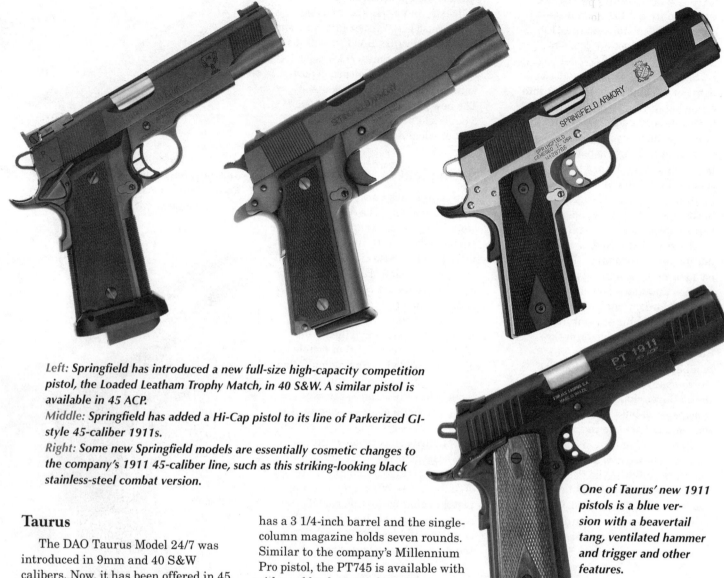

Left: ***Springfield has introduced a new full-size high-capacity competition pistol, the Loaded Leatham Trophy Match, in 40 S&W. A similar pistol is available in 45 ACP.***
Middle: ***Springfield has added a Hi-Cap pistol to its line of Parkerized GI-style 45-caliber 1911s.***
Right: ***Some new Springfield models are essentially cosmetic changes to the company's 1911 45-caliber line, such as this striking-looking black stainless-steel combat version.***

One of Taurus' new 1911 pistols is a blue version with a beavertail tang, ventilated hammer and trigger and other features.

Taurus

The DAO Taurus Model 24/7 was introduced in 9mm and 40 S&W calibers. Now, it has been offered in 45 ACP. The new polymer-frame 45 pistol is available with either a stainless or blued slide. The grip has ergonomic finger-indexing "Memory Pads" that aid in providing a consistent grip. Contrary to competition practice, the magazine release is recessed. The frame extends into an accessory rail that allows attachment of a light or laser. A manual safety lever (not common on a DAO pistol), a firing pin block, and the key-operated Taurus Security System are incorporated in the design. The 45-caliber 24/7 has a 12+1 round capacity. The earlier 9mm and 40 S&W pistols now are available in their full design capacity—17+1 for the 9 and 15+1 for the 40.

Taurus' new PT745 is a new lightweight 45 that comes in under 21 ounces. A polymer-frame pistol, it has a 3 1/4-inch barrel and the single-column magazine holds seven rounds. Similar to the company's Millennium Pro pistol, the PT745 is available with either a blued or stainless slide.

Another new 1911! Taurus displayed two variants of its brand-new PT 1911 at the January 2005 SHOT Show. At that time, the pistols were so new that the two displayed were the only two specimens in the United States. Taurus' new 1911 has the basic Colt/Browning mechanism, and includes other features. Both the blued steel and the stainless versions of the pistol exhibited similar features. Many of the niceties that seem to appeal to modern shooters, such as beavertail tang, ambidextrous safety, Heinie sights and lowered ejection port, are on the Taurus 1911 pistols. The exhibited pistols seemed to have trigger guards that were somewhat thicker than usual, and had rather shallow grasping grooves on both the front and rear of the slide.

The Taurus PT 922, which went through several incarnations and was finally standardized last year, is gone. The 22-caliber autoloader has been dropped from the line and is no longer being produced.

United States Fire Arms

United States Fire Arms Manufacturing Company has made a name for itself by recreating early Colt revolvers. With the continuing current interest in the 1911 semiauto pistol, would it not be logical for the company to pay some attention to the early Colt autoloading pistols? By early 2005, they had done just that.

Two new 45 automatics were introduced by the firm. Mechanically, they are 1911s, but they have a "retro" appearance that makes them look even earlier, and that ties in with the company's other products.

The first one was named the "Model of 1910 Commercial." It has the burr hammer of the older Colt Model 1905 pistol, and also has that earlier pistol's wide, flat walnut grips with small-head grip screws. It has a long trigger, the 1905–type tiny sights, and a commercial-grade high-polish finish. The markings are taken from the 1905, and the caliber is marked, "Calibre 45 Rimless Smokeless."

The "later" version was called the "Model 1911 Military," and has a number of features of the original Model 1911. The gun has a wide hammer spur and a short tang, as did the early 1911s. However, it also sported the 1905 walnut grips and the small grip screws. Each of these 1911 guns will come with a reprint of the 1917 manual, "Description of the Automatic Pistol, Caliber .45 Model of 1911."

The U. S. Fire Arms automatics do not really replicate any particular historical firearm. However, they capture the flavor of the old Colts made in the early days of the automatic pistol in our country.

Walther

The Walther PPK is back. The original PPK fell afoul of the arbitrary BATF point system, and could not be imported. It was replaced by the PPK/S, which was enough larger to be importable. However, many people liked the smaller, lighter PPK. In early 2005, Walther and Smith & Wesson announced that the little gun would be manufactured by S&W under license in the United States.

Also new in Walther's lineup is the Model P99QA with its polymer frame finished in desert sand color. Recall that QA stands for "Quick Action" and indicates the striker is partially pre-cocked by the movement of the slide, allowing a short 8-pound pull. The war in Iraq has created some interest in sand-colored pistols, and the new Walther addresses this interest. Strangely, it is available only in 40 S&W chambering. One might have expected it to also be in the NATO-standard 9mm, as are the other series P99QA pistols.

Wildey

The JAWS Viper pistol, a joint venture between Wildey and the country of Jordan, has finalized its design. Parts are now in production, and the initial production run has been sold, even before final production.

Several interesting things were on display by Wildey at the January 2005 SHOT Show. One was the actual pistol used in the "Death Wish 3" motion picture, which starred Charles Bronson.

A Wildey Colt was also displayed. About 5 years or so ago, a small number of Wildey pistols were made by the company for Colt and were so marked. These interesting pistols were reportedly made with three barrels each, for 45 Winchester Magnum, 45 Wildey Magnum and 475 Wildey Magnum. About seven pistols were left undelivered when the arrangement ended. These are interesting collectible items.

Selected Wildey arms, including the Wildey carbine, are now available with a muzzle brake. The 18-inch-barrel Wildey carbine is perhaps taking the concept of the pistol-caliber carbine to its logical extreme. Chambered for 44 AutoMag, 45 Winchester Magnum, 45 Wildey Magnum and 475 Wildey Magnum, it can certainly be considered suitable for a range of game hunting beyond the capability of most traditional pistol cartridges.

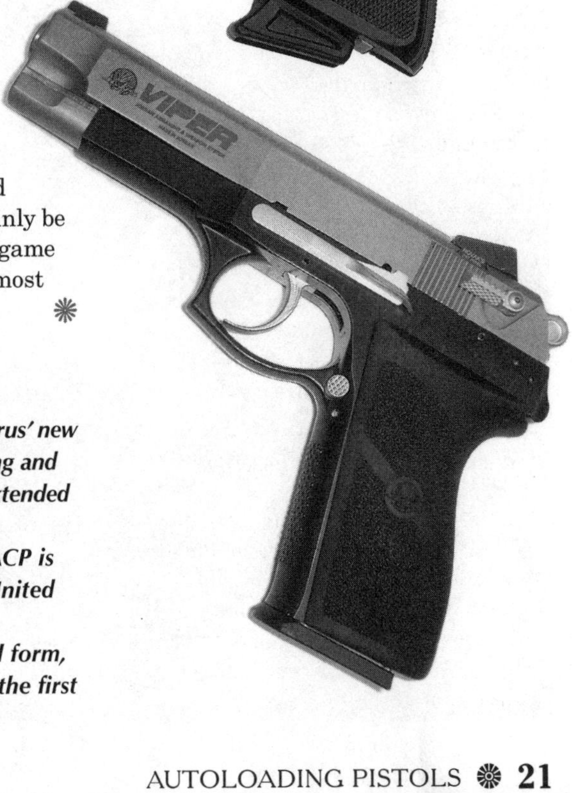

Top: A stainless-steel variant of Taurus' new 1911 pistol also has a beavertail tang and other special features, such as an extended manual safety.
Middle: The Walther PPK in 380 ACP is back, made under license in the United States by Smith & Wesson.
Bottom: The JAWS Viper is in final form, and parts are being produced for the first production run.

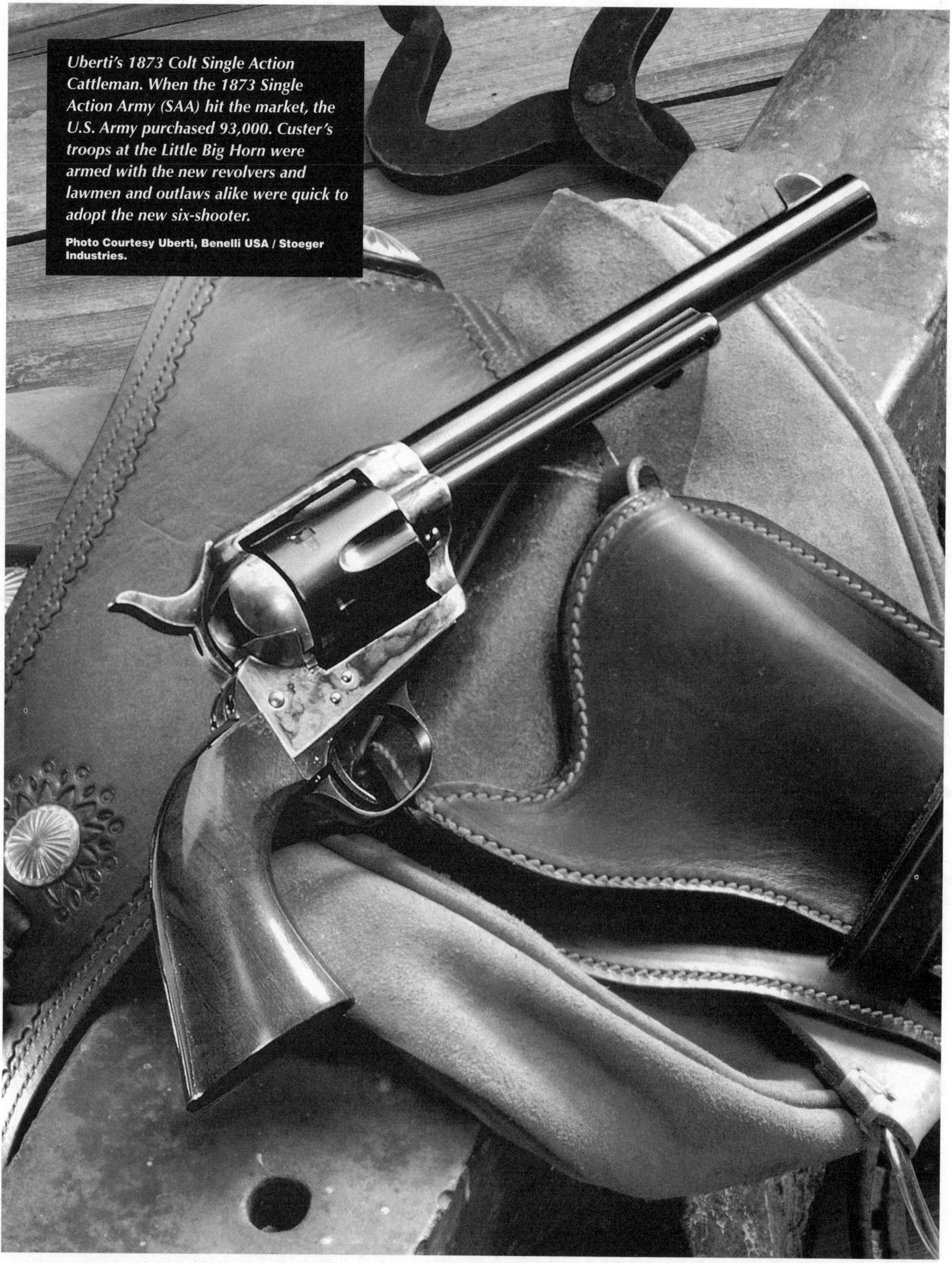

Uberti's 1873 Colt Single Action Cattleman. When the 1873 Single Action Army (SAA) hit the market, the U.S. Army purchased 93,000. Custer's troops at the Little Big Horn were armed with the new revolvers and lawmen and outlaws alike were quick to adopt the new six-shooter.

Photo Courtesy Uberti, Benelli USA / Stoeger Industries.

REVOLVERS, SINGLE-SHOTS & OTHERS

by John Taffin

Life used to be so simple! When McDonald's first opened up they had a walk-up window offering two choices: a hamburger or cheeseburger. The choice of the latter was usually predicated on whether one had the extra four cents or not. Today, one has to choose between the drive-through or walk-in, and then be faced with a menu board larger than the square footage in the floor plan of most houses. The same situation now applies to the firearms industry. In 1955, if one wanted a Ruger 357 Blackhawk, the situation was almighty simple; there was only one: blued, with a 4 5/8-inch barrel. One year later, shooters could have any 44 Magnum Blackhawk desired as long as it was a 6 1/2-inch version, also blued. The Super Blackhawk arrived in 1959 and, until well into the 1980s, it was only offered in a blued 7 1/2-inch model.

Over the years, most gun manufacturers have followed McDonald's lead. Ruger alone offers a total of 40 new choices this year, handguns and long guns combined. If we factor in all models from the rest of the major manufacturers I guess there are at least 100 new choices.

It's time to take our annual look at the state of handguns: single-action and double-action six-guns, as well as single-shot pistols.

Ruger

There is good news and bad news from Ruger this year. The bad news: After a dozen years of production and nearly three-quarters of a million units manufactured, the Vaquero has been removed from production. However, the greater good news is that the Vaquero is being replaced by an even better single-action six-gun: the New Vaquero. The original Vaquero was a virtually indestructible single-action six-gun built on the same frame size as the 44 Magnum Super Blackhawk. If there was any complaint about the Vaquero, it was its size and bulkiness. The New Vaquero addresses this "problem."

Several years ago Ruger's Bill Ruger, Jr., Steve Sanetti and Bob Stutler sat down for a brainstorming session and one of the results we are now seeing is the New Vaquero, a much improved, downsized version. The original Vaquero was larger than the traditional Single Action Army; the New Vaquero is basically the same size as the Colt Model P and its replicas. In addition to its smaller, easier-to-carry size, several other improvements have been made to the New Vaquero. The ejector rod head is now larger, allowing more comfort and positive action when ejecting spent shells, and the cylinder

Production Manager Bob Stutler, with Ruger's latest single action, the New Vaquero.

Above: Two great choices for the handgun hunter are Ruger's Bisley and Super Blackhawk 44 Magnum models.

now lines up correctly with the ejector rod. In the old Vaquero, the audible *click* as the cylinder was rotated told us we had gone too far and the cylinder had to be backed up slightly for the ejector rod to enter the chamber mouth; with the New Vaquero the *click* says we are there, and the cylinder is lined up correctly with the ejector rod.

When the first Ruger six-gun, the Single-Six 22, appeared in 1953 the grip frame was virtually identical in size and shape to the 1st Generation Single Action Army. This XR3 frame was carried over to the 357 Blackhawk of 1955 and the 44 Magnum version one year later. In 1963 the grip frame was changed to XR3-RED, allowing more room between the back of the trigger guard and the front of the grip strap. It has taken more than four decades to go back to the original; however, the New Vaquero has the 1950s XR3 size and shape.

The New Vaquero grip frame is also slightly narrower than the old and, combined with the checkered rubber grips, which are also slimmer than the original Vaquero's wooden grips, makes it feel awfully good in my hand. In fact, these are the best-feeling Ruger single-action factory stocks I've ever experienced and I've been shooting Ruger single-action six-guns exactly a half-century this year. Instead of the medallion found in all Ruger stocks since 1953, these new checkered rubber grips have the Ruger Eagle molded into the grip itself.

The New Vaquero will be initially offered in 357 Magnum and 45 Colt, in both blue/case-colored and stainless steel versions in barrel lengths of 4-5/8 and 5-1/2 inches, with the 45 Colt also offered in the longer 7 1/2-inch barrel length. They should be very popular not only with cowboy action shooters but with all six-gunners appreciating traditionally-sized and styled single actions. I certainly hope Ruger will eventually offer it in 44 Special. WARNING: These New Vaqueros are for standard 45 Colt loads only, not the "Heavy Ruger Loads" listed in many loading manuals and articles.

Ruger's other single-action offering, which will probably be sold out by the time you read this, is their 50th Anniversary Model of the 357 Blackhawk. Although it is built on the New Model action instead of the three-screw action of the original, this Anniversary version has the 4 5/8-inch barrel, Micro-style rear sight, and checkered hard rubber grips with a black eagle medallion as did the original Blackhawk in 1955, and it is also the same size as the New Vaquero,

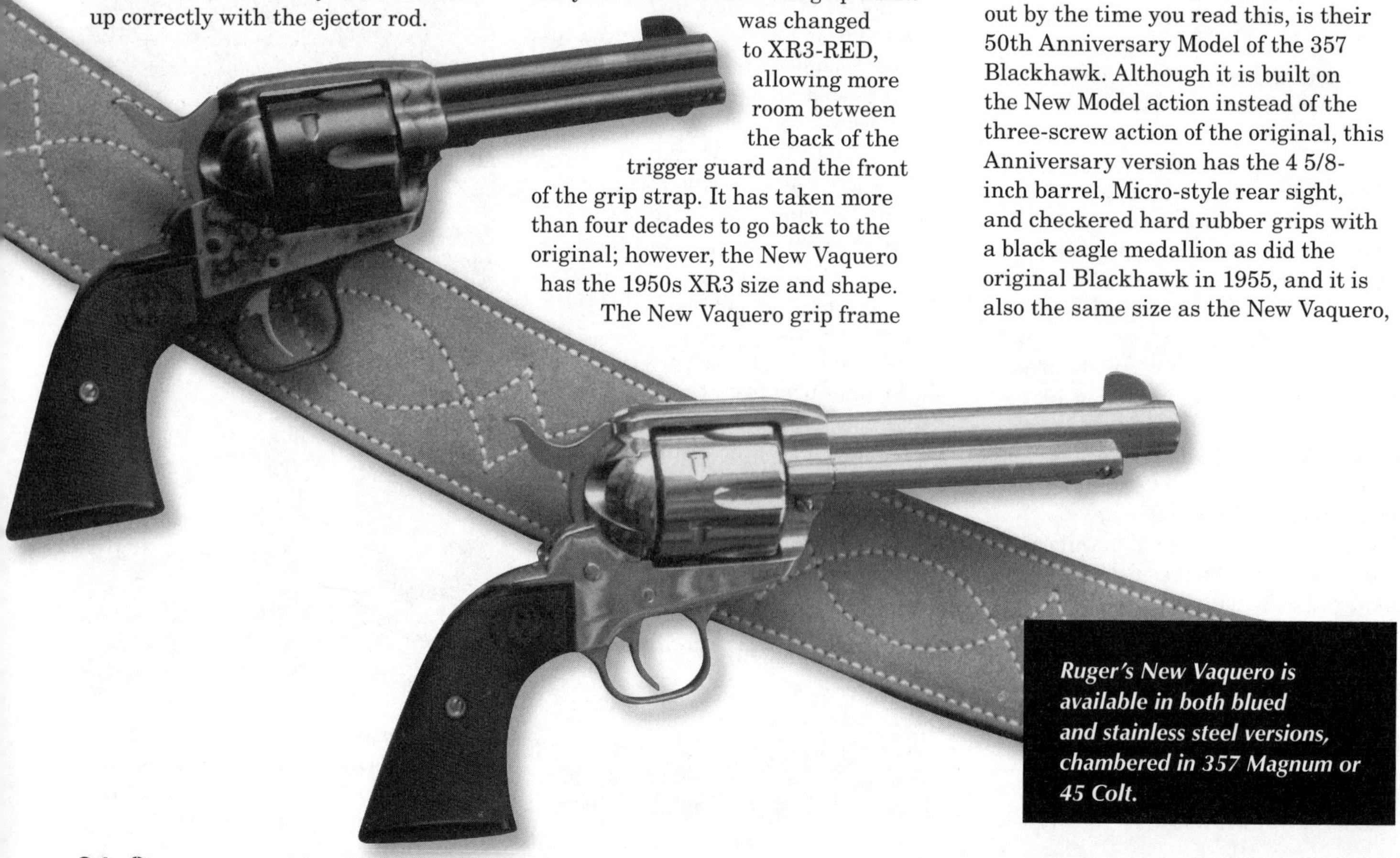

Ruger's New Vaquero is available in both blued and stainless steel versions, chambered in 357 Magnum or 45 Colt.

having the same old-style XR3 grip frame, and the capability of taking a lot of six-gunners back to their roots. This special Ruger is only to be offered for one year; however, in talking with Ruger President Steve Sanetti I was given hope this basic model could stay in the catalog and also be offered in other chamberings *(hint: 44 Special)* and barrel lengths. If you feel the same as I do, a short letter to Ruger would help to influence the decision.

One of the best bargains out there for the handgun hunter has been Ruger's Hunter Model. First introduced in 1992 in 44 Magnum with a 7 1/2-inch solid ribbed heavy barrel cut for Ruger's scope rings, this is a stainless steel six-gun made for heavy-duty outdoor use. Two years ago the Bisley Model version arrived with the Ruger Bisley Model grip frame, hammer, and trigger, and this was then followed one year later by a 22 Single-Six version with an extra cylinder chamber in 22 Magnum. Now for this year Ruger has added the fourth 7 1/2-inch stainless steel, scope-ready Hunter Model to the catalog chambered in 17HMR with an extra cylinder for the 17 Mach 2. With these four Hunter Models, Ruger has covered all the bases when it comes to hunting big game, small game, or varmints.

At the other end of the six-gun spectrum, Ruger is offering something special for those who like truly big-bore packin' pistols. Ruger's Super Redhawk, probably the most durable and strongest double-action revolver ever offered, is now cataloged in a much more convenient carrying version. Until this year the Super Redhawk, whether chambered in 44 Magnum, 480 Ruger or 454 Casull, was offered only in 7 1/2- and 9 1/2-inch barrel lengths, and scope-ready for the handgun hunter. This year Ruger has gone really radical by cutting the barrel even with the extended frame, for a barrel length of only 2-1/2 inches. Known as the Alaskan, this new Super Redhawk will have a rounded trigger guard and trigger, rubber Hogue Monogrip, no cuts in the frame for scope rings, and will be chambered in 480 Ruger and 454 Casull. I expect it to be very popular with those spending a lot of time outdoors and needing a very powerful but portable six-gun.

Top: The 22 LR/22 Magnum and bottom: the 17HMR/17 Mach 2 models have now joined the ranks of handgun hunting choices for hunters.

Smith & Wesson

Two years ago Smith & Wesson introduced the new "world's most powerful revolver" with the X-frame Model 500 chambered in 500 S&W Magnum. Now from S&W comes the second chambering in the X-frame: the 460XVR, or X-treme Velocity Revolver. While the 500 in its most powerful loading uses a 440-grain bullet at 1650 fps, the 460 becomes the factory-chambered big-bore revolver velocity king with a 200-grain 45-caliber bullet at 2300 fps.

Smith & Wesson notes this is the most powerful 45-caliber production revolver in the world, with over 2400 ft/lbs of muzzle energy (fpe) and "incredibly low perceived recoil." Several factors come together to help tame the 460 namely, a weight of 73 ounces, a compensated 8 3/8-inch barrel and special recoil-reducing grips made of a rubber-like substance called Sorbothane. One can well imagine what the recoil would feel like in a traditional-sized revolver of 48 ounces. In addition to the 200-grain load, Cor-Bon also offers a 250-grain bulleted load at "only" 1900 fps. The 460 will also accept 454 and 45 Colt loads.

The Model 460XVR comes drilled and tapped for a scope mount base, has a fully adjustable rear sight mated with a black blade front sight with a gold bead, and an interchangeable HI-VIZ green dot front sight is also included. Something new for Smith & Wesson in this revolver is gain-twist rifling, which means the twist becomes faster towards the muzzle. This is not a new

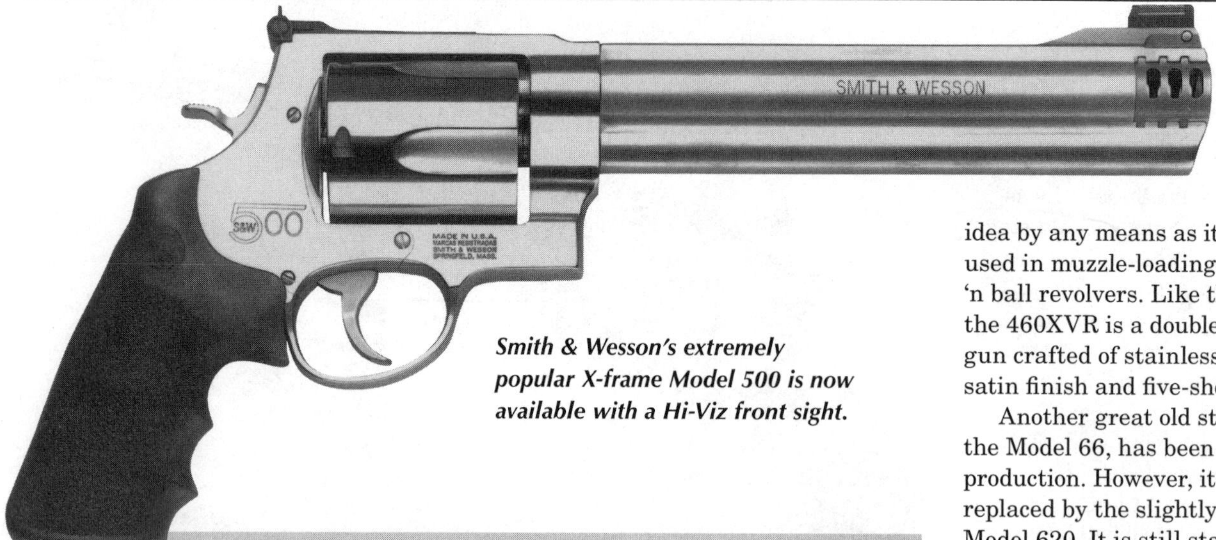

Smith & Wesson's extremely popular X-frame Model 500 is now available with a Hi-Viz front sight.

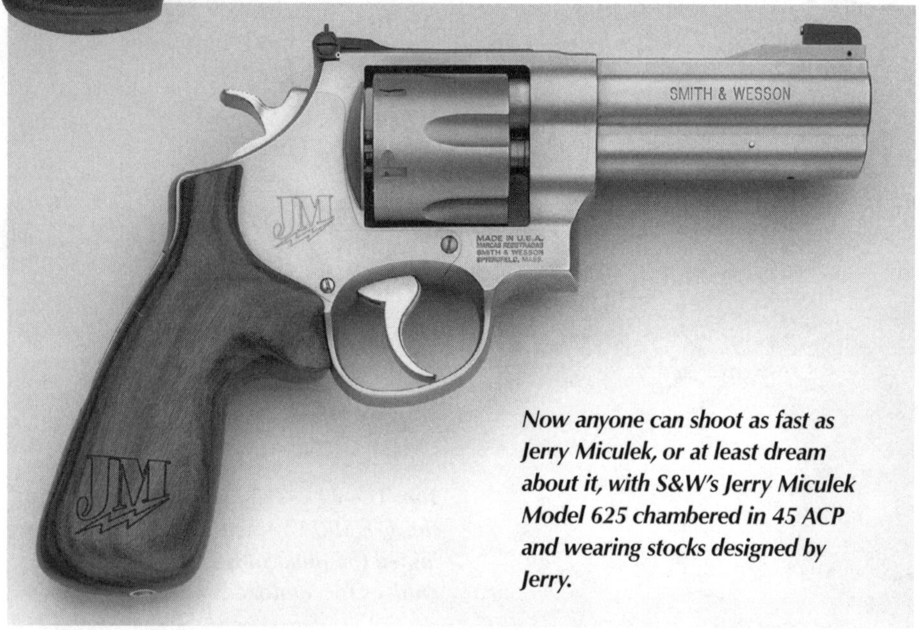

Now anyone can shoot as fast as Jerry Miculek, or at least dream about it, with S&W's Jerry Miculek Model 625 chambered in 45 ACP and wearing stocks designed by Jerry.

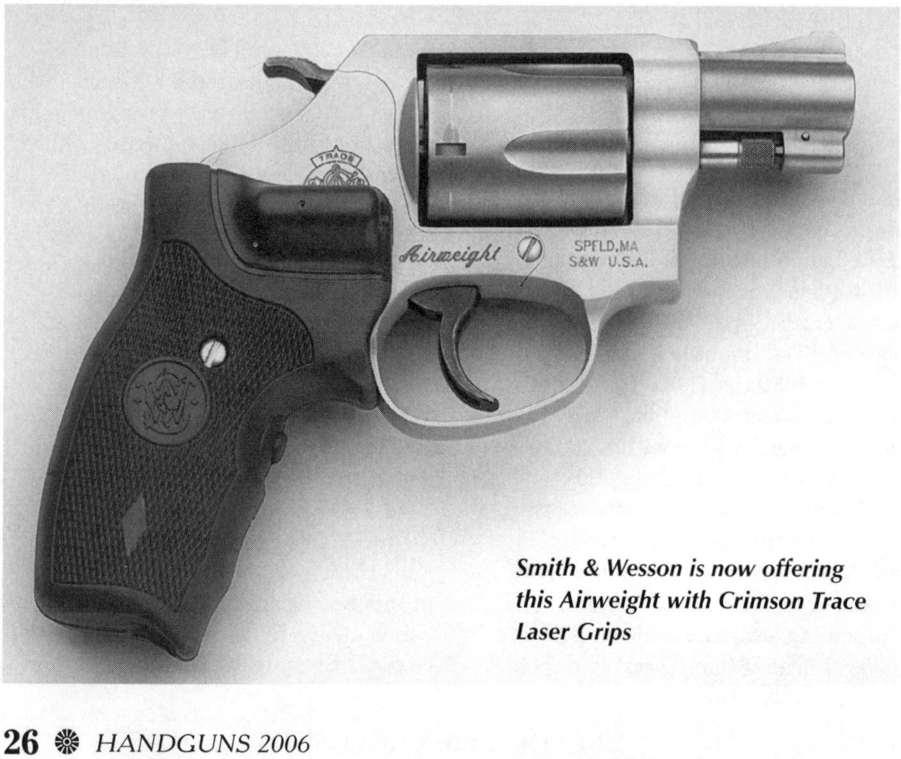

Smith & Wesson is now offering this Airweight with Crimson Trace Laser Grips

idea by any means as it has even been used in muzzle-loading rifles and cap 'n ball revolvers. Like the Model 500, the 460XVR is a double-action six-gun crafted of stainless steel with a satin finish and five-shot cylinder.

Another great old standby revolver, the Model 66, has been dropped from production. However, it has been replaced by the slightly larger L-frame Model 620. It is still stainless steel, with a Model 66-style barrel without the heavy underlug, and has a seven-shot cylinder. The Model 65 has also been upgraded to a fixed sight, seven-shot L-frame 357 Magnum, the Model 619, with a standard barrel without an enclosed ejector rod housing. Smith & Wesson's first stainless steel revolver, the Model 60, is available in a new version having a five-inch barrel with an enclosed ejector rod and adjustable sights. This 357 Magnum five-shooter should be a very popular, relatively lightweight trail gun.

Jerry Miculek, the "World's Fastest Revolver Shooter," a title he holds for such remarkable feats as 12 shots from one six-shot revolver in less than three seconds, now has his name on a standard production gun from Smith & Wesson, the Model 625 Jerry Miculek Professional Series. This is a stainless steel double-action revolver with a 4-inch heavy underlug barrel, adjustable rear sight paired with a gold bead/black post front sight, and chambered in 45 ACP (full-moon clips recommended). Also included are Jerry's specially designed wooden stocks and a wide Miculek Speed trigger.

The 44 Special is also back at Smith & Wesson with the Model 21-4 Thunder Ranch Special. This is the first fixed-sight, 4-inch, blued, six-shot 44 Special since the original Model 21 was dropped 40 years ago. Thanks to Clint Smith's collaboration with Smith & Wesson, we have a real no-nonsense, big-bore fighting six-gun in the Model 21-4. The original run of these "Special" 44 Specials have the Thunder Ranch gold logo on the right side; however, expect later

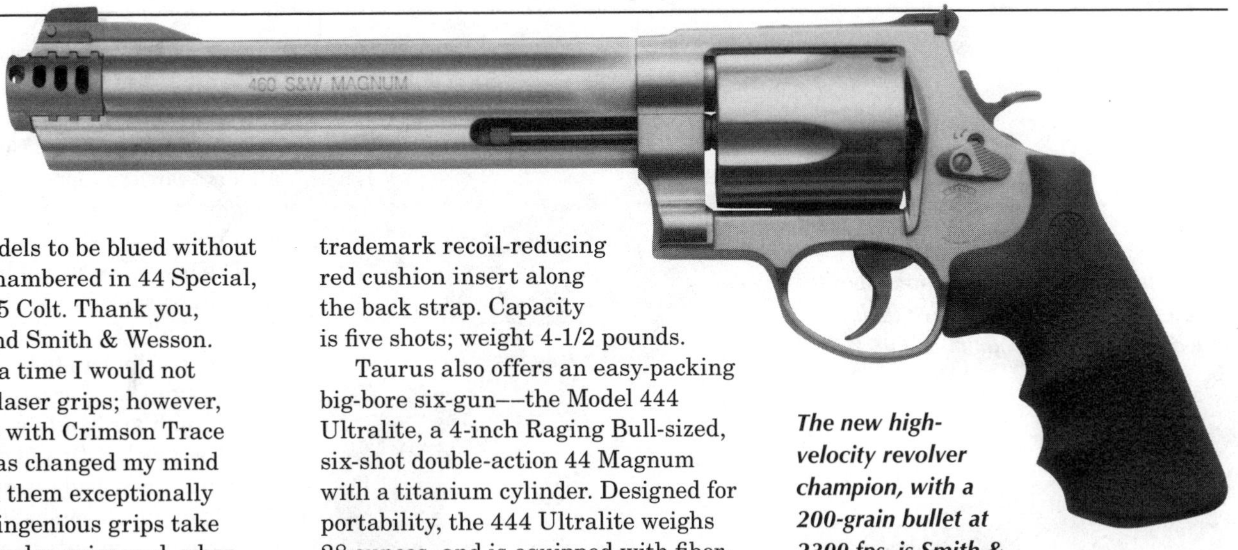

The new high-velocity revolver champion, with a 200-grain bullet at 2300 fps, is Smith & Wesson's 460XVR chambered in 460 S&W Magnum.

production models to be blued without the logo and chambered in 44 Special, 45 ACP, and 45 Colt. Thank you, Clint Smith and Smith & Wesson.

There was a time I would not even consider laser grips; however, my experience with Crimson Trace Laser Grips has changed my mind and I now find them exceptionally useful. These ingenious grips take the place of regular grips and, when a small button in the front strap of the grip is depressed as one takes a normal shooting grip, a small red beam appears on the target.

Now Smith & Wesson is offering two J-frame six-guns already equipped with Crimson Trace Laser Grips. The 15-ounce 38 Special stainless steel 2-inch Model 637 and the 13.5-ounce 32 Magnum black matte 2-inch Model 432PD both come with Crimson Trace Laser Grips already installed. For those having concealed weapon permits, especially women who do not shoot a lot, either one of these could be very useful.

Taurus

As usual, Taurus has a full line of new six-guns for this year. The single-action Gaucho was prematurely announced last year; however, by now it should be readily available in blue, blue/case-colored, and stainless steel versions. The Gaucho is offered in both 45 Colt and 357 Magnum and barrel lengths of 5-1/2 and 7-1/2 inches, all with fixed sights, black rubber grips, four-click action, half-cock loading notch, and a transfer bar safety. Those I have handled seemed exceptionally smooth.

The Taurus Raging Bull, chambered in 44 Magnum, 454 Casull, and 480 Ruger, has been popular with handgun hunters and big-bore revolver shooters for several years. Joining the lineup is the newest Bull, the 500 Magnum. This 10-inch version features a ported heavy-underlug barrel, adjustable rear sight mated with a black post front, smooth trigger and black rubber finger groove grips with the trademark recoil-reducing red cushion insert along the back strap. Capacity is five shots; weight 4-1/2 pounds.

Taurus also offers an easy-packing big-bore six-gun—the Model 444 Ultralite, a 4-inch Raging Bull-sized, six-shot double-action 44 Magnum with a titanium cylinder. Designed for portability, the 444 Ultralite weighs 28 ounces, and is equipped with fiber-optic sights, smooth trigger and Raging Bull cushioned-insert rubber grips. A

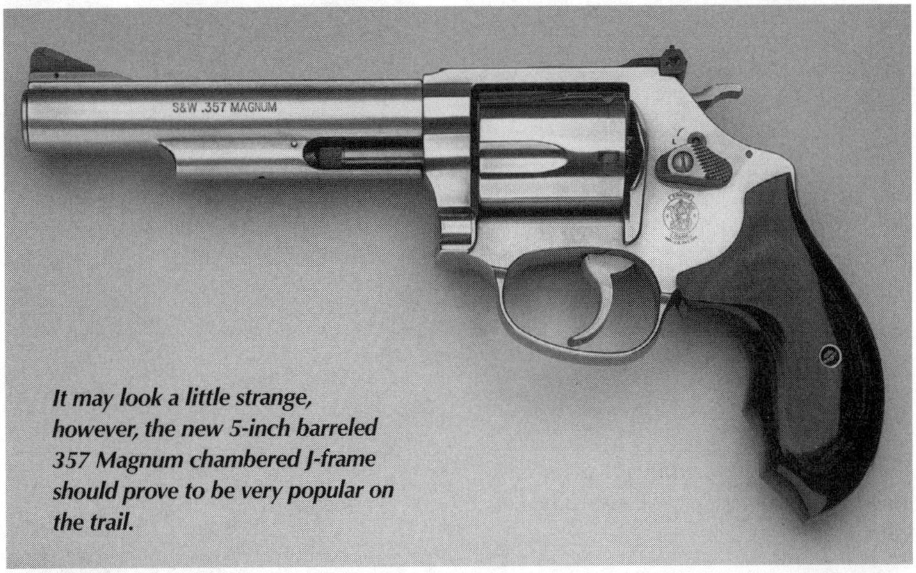

It may look a little strange, however, the new 5-inch barreled 357 Magnum chambered J-frame should prove to be very popular on the trail.

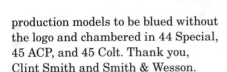

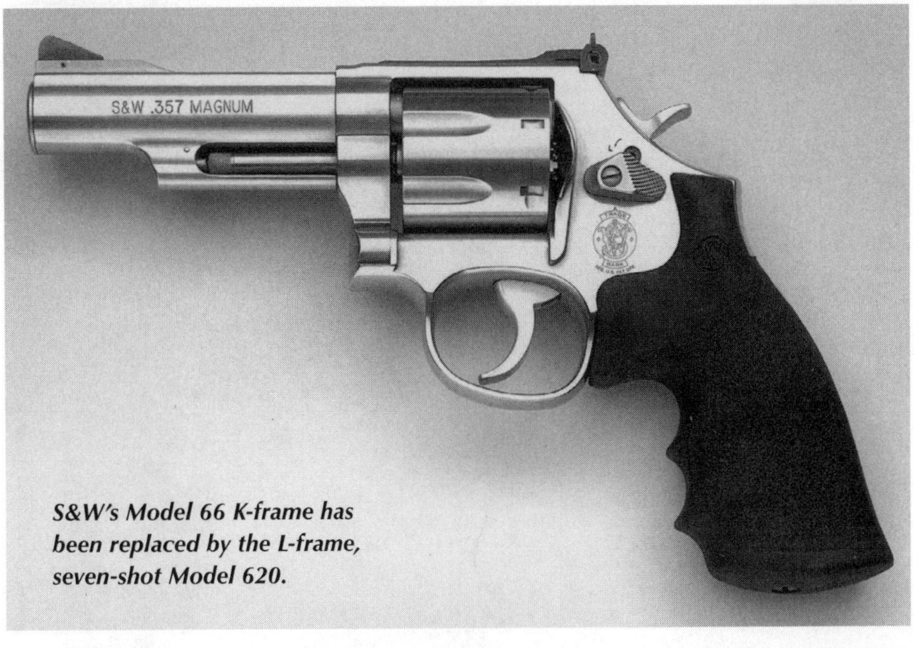

S&W's Model 66 K-frame has been replaced by the L-frame, seven-shot Model 620.

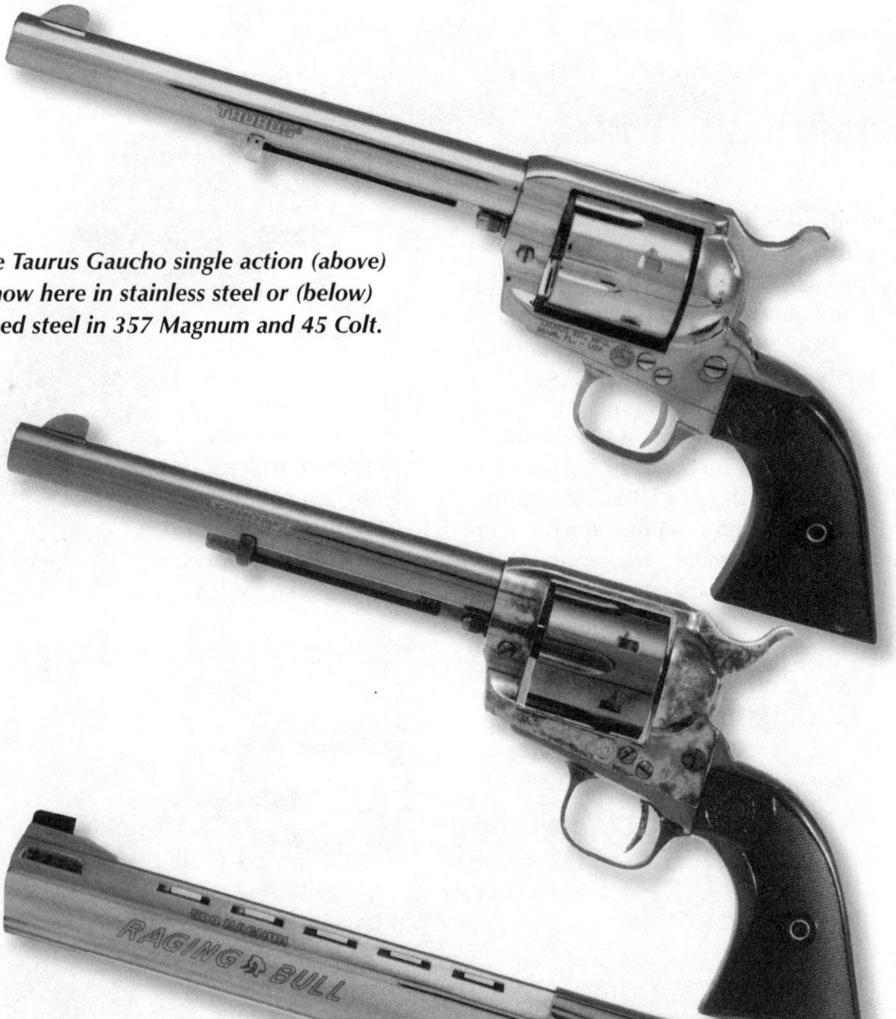

The Taurus Gaucho single action (above) is now here in stainless steel or (below) blued steel in 357 Magnum and 45 Colt.

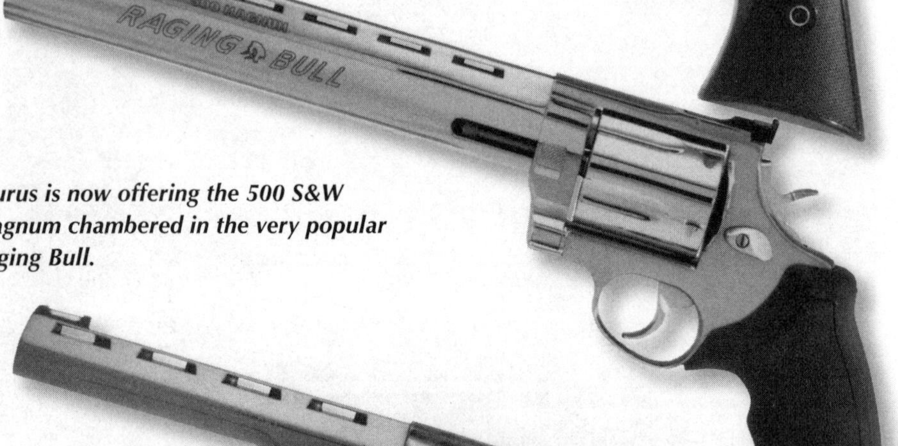

Taurus is now offering the 500 S&W Magnum chambered in the very popular Raging Bull.

Another Raging Bull offering from Taurus is the long-cylinder .410/44-40 revolver.

second 44 Magnum offered by Taurus is the slightly smaller five-shot Tracker with a 4-inch barrel, Ribber grips, and ported heavy-underlug barrel. Of all steel construction, the Tracker 44 weighs 34 ounces. Both models are offered in either blue or stainless steel.

The last two new big-bore revolvers from Taurus are the Model 44-Ten Tracker and 44-Ten Bull, featuring elongated cylinders to handle the .410 shotgun shell or 44-40 revolver round. Both are available in blue or stainless steel, with a fiber-optic front sight and cushioned insert grips. The Raging Bull version features a ventilated, ribbed barrel. Weights are 32 ounces for the Tracker version and 39 ounces for the Bull model.

Taurus also has several interesting little guns. The very popular 38 Special five-shot Model 85 is now available with Ribber grips, while the IB (Instant Backup) double actions are offered in both blue and stainless versions in either a five-shot 9mm or eight- shot 17 HMR. The Triad Model 85 takes 38 Specials, or 357s plus 9mms with a provided clip. There is also a larger Tracker Triad with a seven-shot cylinder.

All Ruger, Smith & Wesson and Taurus handguns either now have––or soon will have––internal locking devices, which are now required by many cities and states. This is a fact of life in today's society, and whether we like it or not, they are not going to go away.

Colt

What does the Colt Python have in common with the New Service, Official Police, Officers Model Match, Detective Special, King Cobra, and Anaconda? All are great six-guns and all, including the Python, are now gone. The Python arrived in 1955 and was soon regarded as the Cadillac of double-action revolvers. Now it is gone.

The only revolver left in the Colt catalog is the Single Action Army. It is now offered in barrel lengths of 4-3/4, 5-1/2 and 7-1/2 inches, blue/case hardened or nickel plating and in six chamberings: 32-20, 38 Special, 357 Magnum, 38-40, 44-40 and 45 Colt. The major question is whether or not Colt can continue to compete

***Left:* This eye-catching six-gun, the 444 Ultralite, is Taurus' entry into the lightweight 44 Magnum arena. The red cushion insert along the back strap really helps reduce felt recoil.**
***Middle:* The Taurus IB (Instant Backup) is available in both 17 HMR and 9mm.**
***Right:* The Taurus Tracker Triad, with felt recoil-reducing Ribber grips, handles 38 Specials, 357 Magnums, and 9mms—all from the same cylinder.**

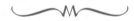

in the civilian handgun market, offering only the Single Action Army and the 1911 Government Model. They have a very small share of the latter market and must compete with imported replica single actions, as well as American-made single-action six-guns from United States Firearms and Ruger. Most six-gunners would truly be saddened to see Colt disappear from the civilian firearms scene; however, it seems pretty obvious Colt must do more to survive.

Freedom Arms

The single-action six-guns from Freedom Arms, whether a full-sized Model 83 or the mid-frame Model 97, are expensive––there is no doubt about that. However, I have yet to hear of any owner of a Freedom Arms revolver saying they are not worth the money.

All of Freedom Arms' six-guns are crafted of stainless steel, and the full-sized Model 83 is offered in both a bright, brushed Premier Grade or less expensive matte finished Field Grade. Whichever finish is chosen, both are built with the same materials and attention to detail and tight tolerances. Premier Grade Model 83s are offered in 475 Linebaugh, 454 Casull and 357, 41 and 44 Magnums, while the Field Grade comes in the same chamberings, plus the 22 Long Rifle. Both models feature adjustable sights with standard barrel lengths of 4-3/4, 6, 7-1/2 and 10 inches; other lengths and octagon barrels are offered on a custom basis. Currently the only fixed-sight Model 83 offered is the Premier Grade chambered in 454.

The Model 97 is available only in the Premier Grade with adjustable-sighted models chambered in 45 Colt, 44 Special, 41 Magnum––all with five-shot cylinders––while the 357 Magnum, 32 H&R Magnum, 22 Long Rifle and 17HMR all have six-shot cylinders. All versions are available with a 4 1/4-, 5 1/2-, or 7 1/2-inch barrel, with 10-inch barrels available on the latter three chamberings. Fixed-sight models are also available in 45 Colt, 357 Magnum, and 32 H&R Magnum.

Freedom Arms also offers auxiliary cylinders in 45 Colt, 45 ACP and 45

With these Freedom Arms Model 83s the handgun hunter can tackle anything, anywhere. Top guns are chambered in 454 Casull, while the bottom six-guns are both 475 Linebaughs.

Winchester Magnum for the Model 83 in 454 Casull; in 480 Ruger to fit the 475 Linebaugh, and 22 Magnum for the 22 Long Rifle Model 83. Optional cylinders for the Model 97 include 45ACP, 38 Special, 32-20, 22 Match, 22 Magnum and 17 Mach 2. All Freedom Arms' cylinders have been unfluted; however, they may now be ordered with flutes, and both the Model 83 and Model 97 are now offered with a rounded butt.

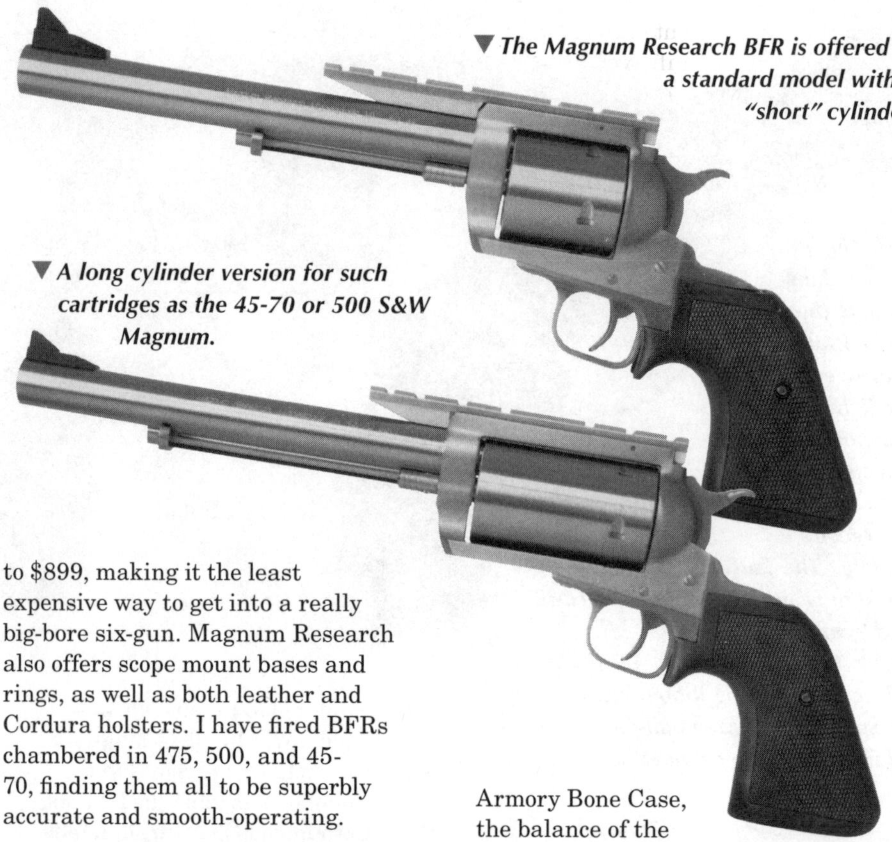

▼ *The Magnum Research BFR is offered in a standard model with a "short" cylinder.*

▼ *A long cylinder version for such cartridges as the 45-70 or 500 S&W Magnum.*

Magnum Research

This is the home of the 50 AE Desert Eagle semi-automatic pistol, however Magnum Research also offers the BFR *(Biggest, Finest Revolver)*, a stainless steel single-action six-gun offered in a variety of frame sizes and calibers. With standard "Short Cylinder" and frame, the BFR is found in 454 Casull, 475 Linebaugh/480 Ruger, 50 AE and 22 Hornet, while the Long version is chambered in 45-70, 444 Marlin, .410/45 Colt, 450 Marlin, 30-30, and even in the relatively new 500 S&W.

All BFRs are totally American-made featuring all stainless steel construction, cut-rifle barrels, free-wheeling 5-shot cylinders, adjustable sights, hand-filling grips––and the retail price has just been reduced to $899, making it the least expensive way to get into a really big-bore six-gun. Magnum Research also offers scope mount bases and rings, as well as both leather and Cordura holsters. I have fired BFRs chambered in 475, 500, and 45-70, finding them all to be superbly accurate and smooth-operating.

United States Firearms

USFA is putting out beautiful traditionally styled single-action six-guns! The main frame and the hammer are case-colored in what is described as Armory Bone Case, the balance of the six-gun is finished in a deep, dark Dome Blue color, and the standard grips are checkered hard rubber with a "US" molded into the top part of the grip. On all the USFA single actions I have examined, these stocks are perfectly fitted to the frame and feel exceptionally good in my hand.

The BFR 475 Linebaugh has proven to be an exceptionally accurate revolver.

One of the things I always look for in the fitting and finishing of single action six-guns is the radiusing of the lower part of the back of the hammer and the two "ears" formed by the backstrap where it screws into the mainframe on both sides of the hammer. A well-made single action will exhibit a smooth mating of the contours of all three. USFA six-guns are very nearly perfect in this area, and the same careful fitting can also be found where the top of the face of the hammer meets the top strap. The fit of the trigger guard to the bottom of the mainframe is so perfectly done one can run a finger over the area and not feel where one part begins and the other ends. The same is true where the backstrap meets the mainframe.

The front of the ejector rod housing as well as the cylinder are both beveled which not only looks good and feels good, it also provides for easier holstering. Markings on these six-guns include the serial number in three places: the butt, in front of the trigger guard and on the mainframe in front of the trigger guard screw. This is exactly as the original 19th-century single action armies were marked. Trigger pulls are set at three pounds. Cylinders lock up tight both in the hammer down or cocked position.

All USFA six-guns are totally American-made and available with a V-notch or square-notch rear sight perfectly filled in by a front sight that also has a square profile, rather than tapering to the top. Shooters also have a choice of a cross pin or screw-in "black powder" cylinder pin latch. Chamberings for USFA single actions include the 45 Colt, of course; however, other choices include 32 WCF (32-20), 41 Long Colt, 38 Special, 38 WCF (38-40), 44 WCF (44-40), 45 ACP, 44 Russian and 44 Special. The latter can be marked, and properly chambered as "RUSSIAN AND S&W SPECIAL 44" as early Colt single actions were marked, while 38 Specials can also be marked on the left side of the barrel with "COLT AND S&W SPECIAL 38" just as were early 20th-century revolvers.

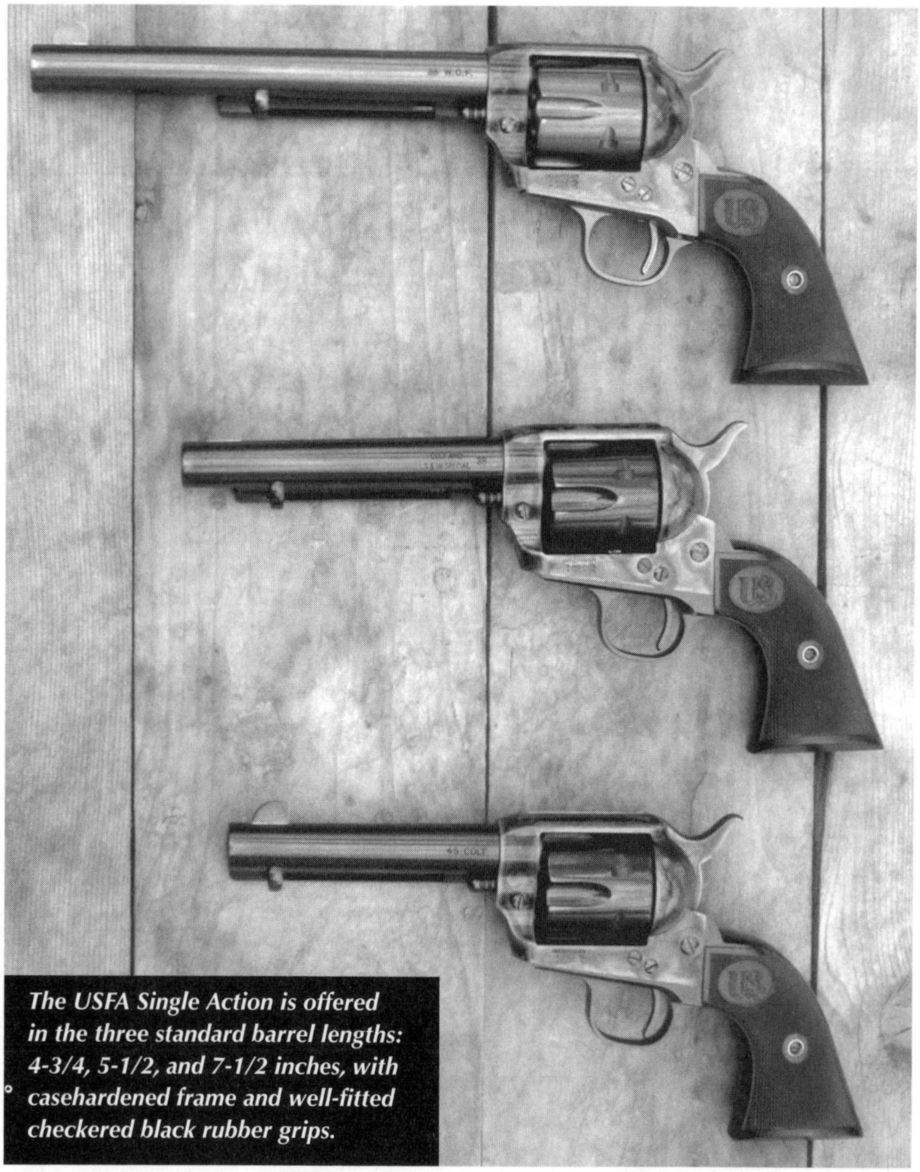

The USFA Single Action is offered in the three standard barrel lengths: 4-3/4, 5-1/2, and 7-1/2 inches, with casehardened frame and well-fitted checkered black rubber grips.

The less expensive Rodeo is the same basic six-gun as the Single Action Army except it comes with a matte blue finish instead of the beautiful finish of the standard revolver. The Rodeo has proven so popular it is now offered in several chamberings and all three standard barrel lengths. In addition to the Single Action Army that is also offered in an ejectorless Sheriff's Model, USFA offers a Flat-Top Target version patterned after the target models of the 1890s. The Omni-Potent is a special USFA single action with a grip frame reminiscent of the 1878 Colt Double Action. It is available in all calibers and barrel lengths as well as a target version, all with checkered wood grips and a lanyard ring, and what may be the ultimate belly gun—The Snubnose, with a 2-inch barrel *sans* ejector rod housing.

Hartford Armory

Hartford Armory began manufacturing their version of the Remington Models 1875 and 1890, chambered in 45 Colt and capable of handling +P+ loads, last year. As with any new endeavor it is always a slow process getting everything up and running smoothly, however the kinks have been smoothed out and Remingtons are now coming through regularly. These high-quality Remingtons are being produced on thoroughly

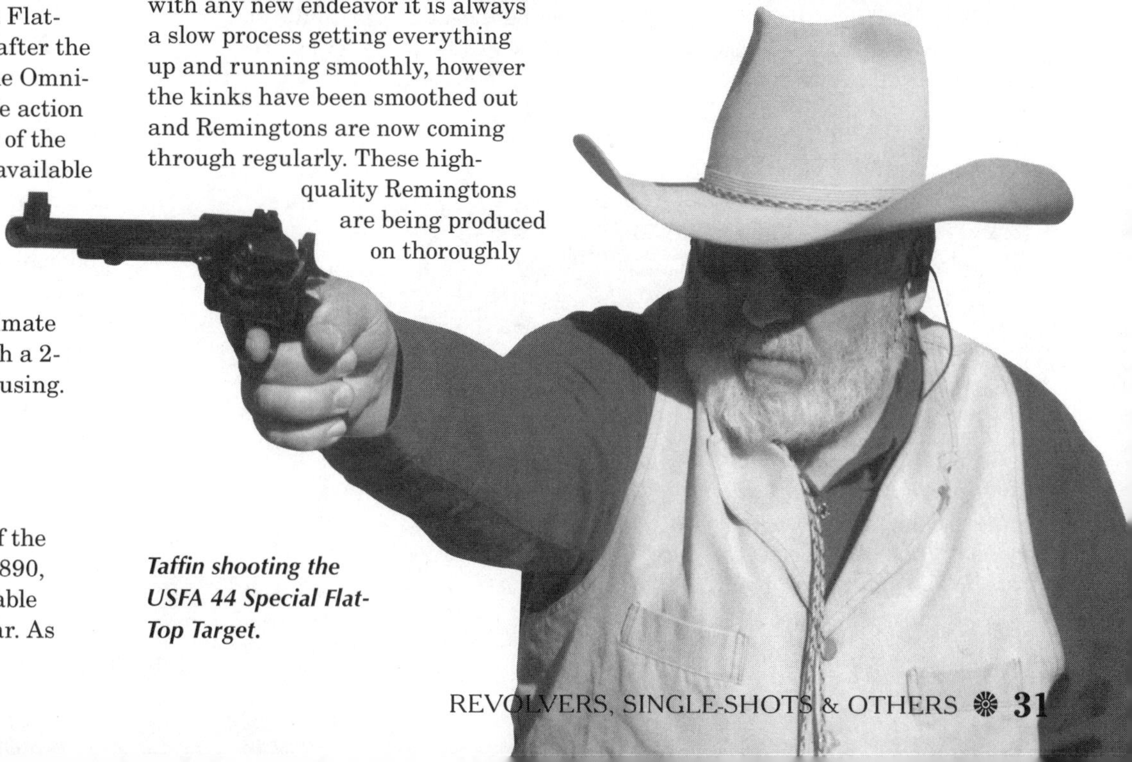

Taffin shooting the USFA 44 Special Flat-Top Target.

modern, totally up-to-date machinery using the finest American-made 4130 and 4140 steels with forged mainframes, not cast. Hartford Armory has deviated from the original design in only one way: making the cylinder approximately 1/8-inch longer to allow use of today's 45 Colt ammunition. The original Remington cylinders were even shorter than those in the Colt Single Action Army, and many of the modern rounds offered in 45 Colt are deliberately made long enough to preclude their being used in Colt Single Actions or replica Remingtons as they are simply are not strong enough to handle +P or Heavy Duty 45 Colt hunting loads. However, Hartford Armory's Remingtons are strong enough to handle any factory 45 Colt ammunition currently offered; even strong enough to be chambered in 44 Magnum.

The grip frame of the Remington raises the comfort level considerably when using heavy loads since the backstrap is slightly straighter and also comes up higher, much like the design found on the original Colt Bisley Model and the current Freedom Arms and Ruger Bisley model. Both the 1875 and 1890 Hartford Armory Remingtons come from the factory with smooth actions, easy-to-operate hammers and the trigger pull set at around three pounds. Both models feature a beautifully polished blue finish, with a case-hardened hammer and loading gate, as on the originals. Cylinder lockup is tight with no movement side-to-side or front-to-back. The barrel/cylinder gap will not accept the smallest feeler gauge I have, which is 0.002-inch. Hartford Armory Remingtons are available only through Taylor's & Co. They are available in blue or stainless steel, with 5 1/2- or 7 1/2-inch barrels and chambered in 45 Colt, 44 Magnum, 44-40 and 357 Magnum.

Gary Reeder

In the 1920s Elmer Keith set about to build the perfect six-gun, the result being his #5SAA, a 5 1/2-inch 44 Special. Gary Reeder is now offering six-guns, built on his frames, of the #5 Improved that is based on Elmer's #5 as it appeared in the 1929 *American Rifleman.* Reeder has made a few changes: better sights, a standard cross-pin cylinder pin latch and a transfer bar safety conversion combined with a standard single-action style action. For loading and unloading, the loading gate is opened and the hammer put on half-cock, even though it has a transfer bar safety.

Reeder's Deluxe Grade all-steel #5 in 44 Special is of polished stainless steel, fully engraved, with an octagonal barrel. Sights are fully adjustable with an interchangeable front sight feature, stocks are elephant ivory, and the grip frame is like no other. Keith had very small hands, which is evident in the design of his #5 grip frame. Reeder has maintained the same basic grip frame while making it more useable by adding 3/8-inch to the length.

The #5 Improved was designed around the 44 Special and will also be available in 45 Colt. The standard Field Grade #5 with walnut stocks has a base price of $1295, with full engraving, octagon barrel and custom stocks available.

As a companion piece to the #5 Improved, Reeder offers the Improved #6, which is nothing more than a slightly larger #5 Improved that can handle the 44 Magnum, as well as the 41 Magnum and a five-shot version in 454. The Deluxe Grade Improved #6 has a 5 1/2-inch octagon barrel, is also fully engraved, and is fitted with Mongolian stag stocks.

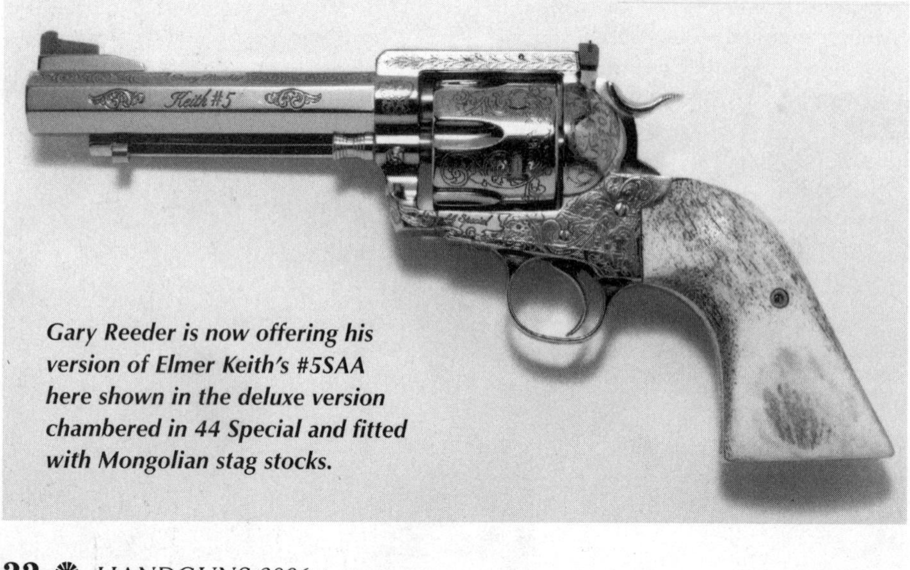

Gary Reeder is now offering his version of Elmer Keith's #5SAA here shown in the deluxe version chambered in 44 Special and fitted with Mongolian stag stocks.

Thompson/Center

For nearly four decades the T/C Contender has been the single-shot pistol by which all other single shots are measured. It was definitely the leading force in long-range silhouetting and remains one of the best choices for the handgun hunter. A few years back, a second version was added to the Thompson/Center lineup: the Encore. The Contender, now in its second stage as the easier-opening G2, handles most revolver and rifle cartridges up to 30-30 pressures, while the Encore is reserved for high-pressure cartridges such as the 454 Casull and the 308 Winchester.

Since the mid-1960s, the Contender has been offered in a long list of chamberings––including just about every six-gun, semi-automatic pistol, and levergun cartridge. It has been especially favored by handgun hunters in 30-30 and 44 Magnum. Current offerings include 22 Match, 22 Hornet, 357 and 44 Magnum, and 45 Colt/.410-bore with 12-inch barrels, while the selection with the Super 14 barrel includes 17HMR, 204 Ruger, 22 Match, 22 Hornet, 223 Remington, 7-30 Waters, 30-30, 375 JDJ, 44 Magnum, 45-70, and 45 Colt/.410. When I was participating in long-range silhouetting my favorite chamberings were the 357 and 30-30.

Encores are catalogued with 12-inch barrels in 223, 44 Magnum, 454 Casull, and 45 Colt/.410. The longer barrel Encore has a near-rifle length of 15 inches and is offered in a range of rifle cartridges including 204 Ruger, 22 Hornet, 223 Remington, 22-250, 243, 25-06, 270 Winchester, 7mm-08, 308, 30-06, 375 JDJ, 45-70, 45 Colt/.410. Both the Contender and Encore are offered with blued barrels and frames

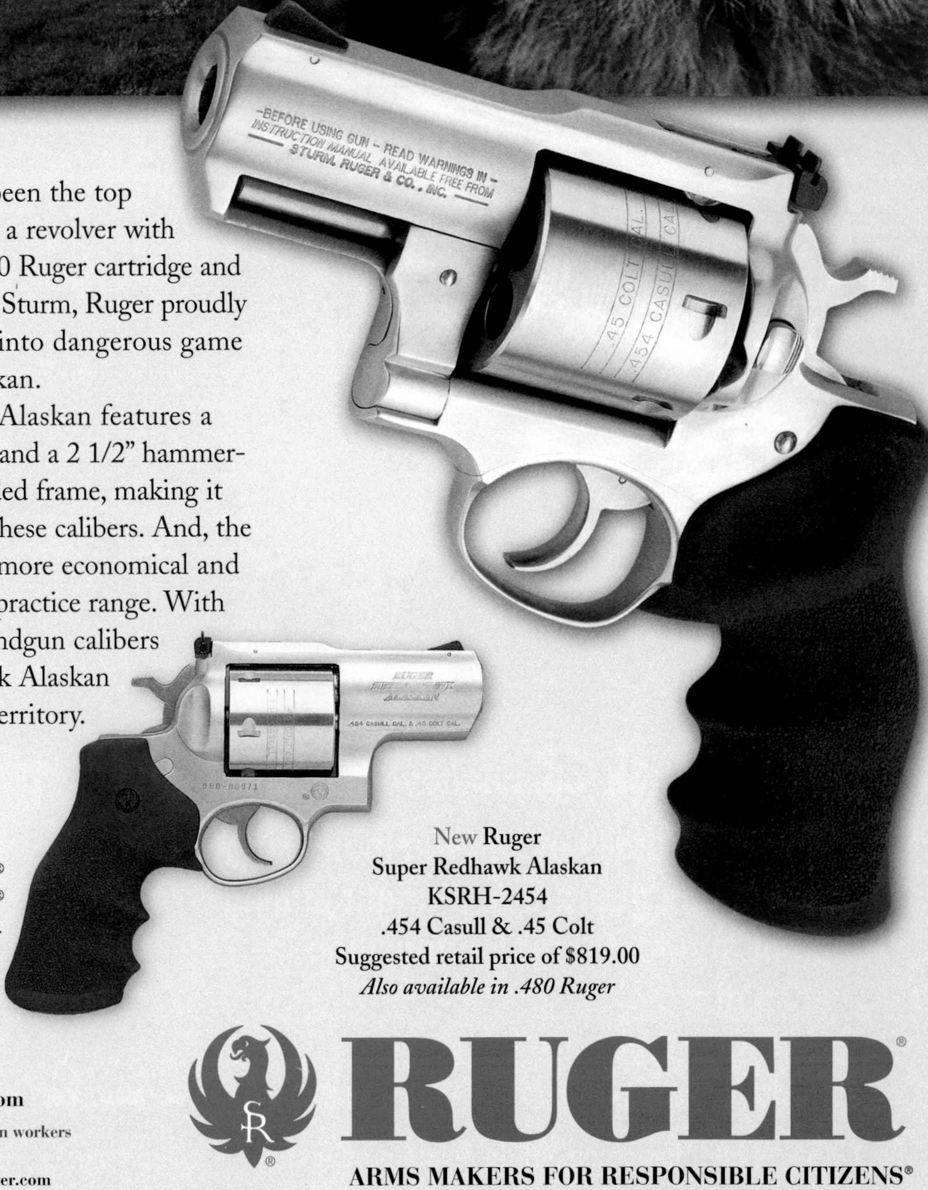

The Ruger Super Redhawk has always been the top choice among handgun hunters who want a revolver with the decisive power of the .454 Casull or .480 Ruger cartridge and the confidence of a six-shot cylinder. Now, Sturm, Ruger proudly introduces the perfect revolver for a trek into dangerous game country – the New Super Redhawk Alaskan.

The all-stainless-steel Super Redhawk Alaskan features a Hogue® Monogrip® to help cushion recoil and a 2 1/2" hammer-forged barrel fitted inside the sturdy extended frame, making it the most compact revolver ever offered in these calibers. And, the .454 Casull model allows you to shoot the more economical and lighter-recoiling .45 Colt cartridges at the practice range. With all the power of two of the most potent handgun calibers and a six-shot cylinder, the Super Redhawk Alaskan is essential for trips into dangerous game territory.

SHOOTING INDUSTRY 2005 ACADEMY OF EXCELLENCE
Manufacturer of the Year

New Hogue® Tamer™ Monogrip® helps cushion recoil.

New Ruger
Super Redhawk Alaskan
KSRH-2454
.454 Casull & .45 Colt
Suggested retail price of $819.00
Also available in .480 Ruger

STURM, RUGER & CO., INC.

Southport, CT 06890, U.S.A. • www.ruger.com

All Ruger firearms are designed and built with pride by American workers at Ruger factories in the United States of America.

FREE Instruction Manuals are available online at www.ruger.com

RUGER®

ARMS MAKERS FOR RESPONSIBLE CITIZENS®

with walnut stocks and forearms, while a few models are offered in stainless steel. The T/C rubber grip is a desirable addition for the harder-kicking Encores.

Thompson/Center has a new owner. Greg Ritz, who has been with T/C for quite a while and who may regularly be seen hunting on television, is a true shooter and should prove a very valuable asset not only to Thompson/Center but all shooters.

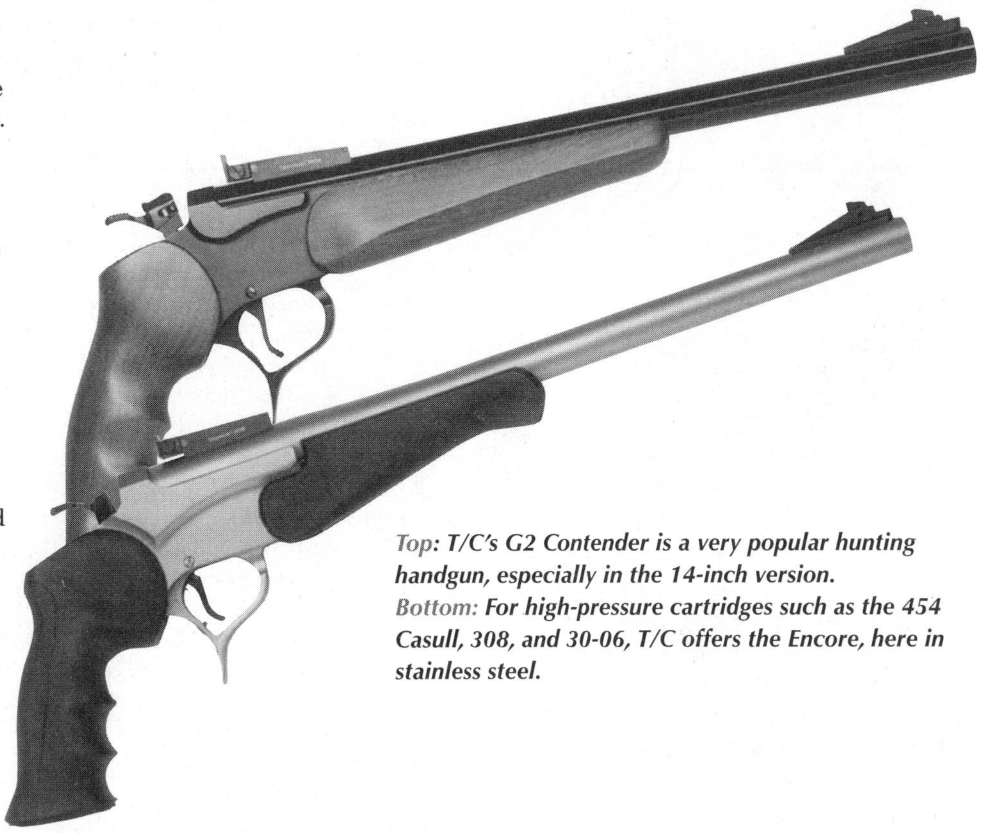

Top: T/C's G2 Contender is a very popular hunting handgun, especially in the 14-inch version. Bottom: For high-pressure cartridges such as the 454 Casull, 308, and 30-06, T/C offers the Encore, here in stainless steel.

SSK Industries

It is virtually impossible to mention Thompson/Center single-shot pistols without thinking of SSK Industries and the genius of J.D. Jones. J.D. is one of the world's top handgun hunters using custom SSK T/Cs to take virtually everything. I started handgun hunting with one of SSK's early efforts, the 430 JDJ, nearly 30 years ago; moved up to the 45-70, and then settled on the 375 JDJ for large game and the superb 6.5 JDJ for deer-size game. The latter is based on the 225 Winchester case expanded and blown out to 6.5mm. It kills all out of proportion to its paper ballistics, especially when loaded with the 120-grain Speer SP at 2400 fps.

With the coming of the Encore, SSK moved up a notch and offers custom barrels in any safe chamberings, including several wildcats such as the 6.5 Dreadnought based on the 30-06 case. Two of the most recent chamberings are the 500 S&W and 460 XVR. In addition to standard Encores chambered in 22-250, 308, and 7mm-08, I also use J.D.'s barrels chambered in the aforementioned Dreadnought and 500 S&W. If it can be done safely, SSK can provide a custom Encore barrel in virtually any rifle chambering. SSK also offers the ONLY scope mounting system for really hard-kicking handguns, the T'SOB. It works and is the only one I recommend for the heavy-hitters.

Mag-Na-Port

Even before J.D. Jones started SSK Industries, his good friend and hunting buddy, Larry Kelly, started helping shooters reduce recoil by the EDM process known as Mag-na-port. The little trapezoidal-shaped ports were cleanly cut into barrels electronically and reduced muzzle flip. Kelly soon began offering not only the Mag-na-port feature but also custom handguns design for the handgun hunter. The Stalker conversions were, and are, accomplished on big bore Ruger, Smith & Wesson, and Freedom Arm six-guns, with specially tuned actions, Mag-na-porting, sling swivels, and scopes mounted using SSK's T-SOB system.

Now Larry Kelly is retired and Mag-na-port is headed up by son Ken who offers several new packages for the new generation of six-guns.

Smith & Wesson's new line of revolvers are traveling in two directions: The 500 and 460 Magnums are two extremely powerful cartridges in very large and heavy revolvers; on the other hand S&W offers the 357 and 44 Magnum in very lightweight revolvers made of scandium and titanium. The answer to help tame recoil, especially on the very lightweight guns, is Mag-na-porting.

European American Armory

EAA has entered the single-shot market. Thor is the latest single-shot pistol from Tanfoglio, via EAA. Chambered in 45-70, the grip frame is 1911-shaped and Hogue's checkered rubber grips with finger grooves provide a very secure hold.

Thor is built heavy-duty with a 1/2-inch block of steel containing the firing pin. To open the action, the hammer is placed on half-cock, the 1911-style "magazine" release button is pushed in and the other hand pushes down on the top of the barrel. A cartridge is inserted, the receiver is pushed down into place and the action locks. To fire, the hammer is fully cocked. There is a thumb safety and grip safety; again, just as on a 1911.

Barrel length, including the entire cartridge, is 14 inches and the top of the massive receiver has a scope mount integrally machined. Thor is finished in matte black, appropriate for a gun with this name, and comes with a matching matte black Leupold M8-4x scope mounted in quick-release rings. Thor is also available in 444 Marlin and 308 Winchester.

Replica Single Actions

I've been hoping and watching for it since Navy Arms first introduced the Schofield Model in the early 1990s. I knew it had to be close when Navy

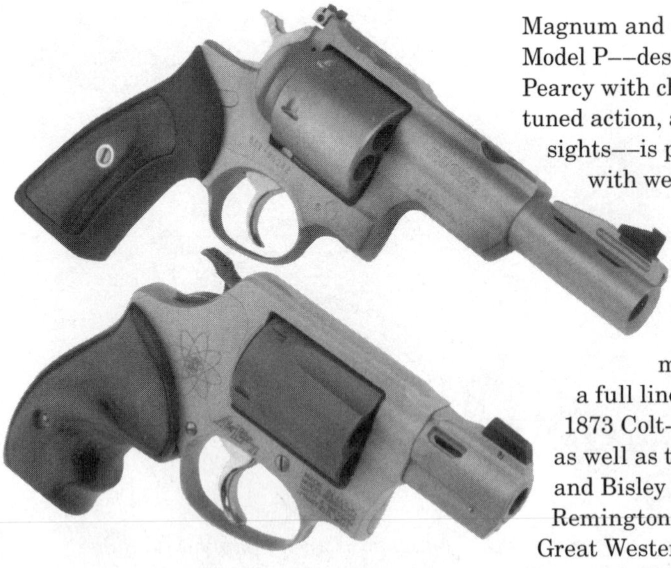

Top: The Ruger Super Redhawk becomes a much easier to pack six-gun with the Mag-Na-Port 480 Advantage conversion. Bottom: Some of the nastiest recoil imaginable is found in the 12-ounce S&W 360Sc 357 Magnum. Mag-na-porting helps tame the muzzle flip.

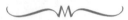

followed with the Model #3 Russian. Now it is here. ***Beretta/Uberti*** has announced the New Model #3––patterned after the original Smith & Wesson New Model #3 of the 1880s. The original was chambered in 44 Russian, a few in 44-40. For some reason, Beretta/Uberti chose to go with the 45 Colt. The prototype at the SHOT Show was a Target Model hurriedly finished in matte black; production models will be polished blue. It felt very good, with a smooth action, and I hope they chamber it for one of the original cartridges. Beretta/Uberti also displayed nickel-plated Bisley models looking very close to the originals of the 1890s.

By the time you read this, ***Cimarron Firearms*** hopes to have the cartridge conversion Model 1858 Remington complete with ejector rod housing. They continue to offer the Colt-style cartridge conversions with both the 1851 Navy and 1860 Army grip frame, as well as the 1871-72 Open-Top. The Model P is offered in blue/case-colored, nickel-plated and in a variety of calibers––as well as stainless steel––in all three standard barrel lengths, chambered in both 357 Magnum and 45 Colt. Their Evil Roy Model P––designed by Gene "Evil Roy" Pearcy with checkered wood stocks, tuned action, and easy-to-see square sights––is proving to be very popular with western action shooters.

EMF continues to offer the Great Western II in blue and nickel finishes and has now added stainless steel models. They also offer a full line of traditionally styled 1873 Colt-style Hartford Models as well as the Pinkerton, Buntline, and Bisley Models––plus the replica Remington Model 1875. EMF's Great Western II is produced by Pietta, which also manufactures the Heritage Single Action. The latter, with a 4 3/4-inch barrel, nickel plating, and well-fitted and shaped American walnut stocks, will retail for only $329.

Navy Arms, as mentioned was the first to offer an S&W single action: the Schofield, followed by the Model #3 Russian. The Schofield, in 45 Colt or 38 Special, is offered in the 7-inch Cavalry, 5-inch Wells Fargo, and 3 1/2-inch Hideout Models, while the Model #3 Russian is offered only in the traditional 6 1/2-inch, and chambered in 44 Russian. In addition to the standard 1873 Single Action, Navy also has The Gunfighter, specially tuned with checkered rubber grips, silver-plated backstrap and trigger guard, all three traditional barrel lengths and chambering choices of 45 Colt, 44-40, and 357 Magnum.

In addition to being the exclusive distributor of the American-made Hartford Armory Remingtons, ***Taylor's & Co.*** has a full line of traditional-styled 1873 single actions as well as the Bisley Model, round-butted Birdshead, stainless steel Outfitter, and the compact Stallion. New this year is the "TR Presidential" with enhanced photo engraving. Taylor's is the first to offer a specially tuned Ruger New Vaquero as the HandleBar Doc Signature Series. Taylor's also offers a full line of R&D drop-in cylinders to convert cap and ball revolvers to cartridge firing. These include 45 Colt to fit Uberti, Pietta, and ASM Remingtons and Ruger Old Armies as well as 38 Special cylinders for steel-frame Pietta or Uberti 36-caliber Remingtons.

Kenny Howell of ***R&D*** is also doing conversions and offering conversion kits on 1851/1861 and 1860 cap and ball six-guns. These conversions consist of a cartridge cylinder complete with loading gate and a lined barrel to 38LC/38 Special on all models or 44 Colt on the 1860. He is also offering a five-shot 45 Colt cylinder kit, which matches up with the existing barrel on the 1860. These are quality conversions all the way.

The latest entry into the single shot handgun field, here shown chambered in 45-70, is the EAA Thor with a break-open action and a 1911-style grip frame.

Custom Six-Guns On Old Model Ruger Blackhawks

Skeeter started it *(Skeeter Skelton, that is)* with an article in the April 1972 issue of *Shooting Times* about converting old model Rugers and the S&W Highway Patrolman to 44 Special. Skeeter went Home in 1988 and I have been doing my best to continue to spread the word about the wonders of the 44 Special in general––especially when chambered in a three-screw Ruger, whether it started life as Flat-Top or Old Model 357 Magnum. Unlike the New Model Ruger Blackhawk, which is built on the larger 44 Blackhawk frame, the three-screws manufactured from 1955-1972 all have Colt single action-sized frames. Bill Ruger expected to chamber his original Flat-Top Blackhawk in 44 Special; however, the arrival of the 44 Magnum changed all that and he instead brought out a larger-framed 44 Flat-Top in 1956.

Whether starting with a Highway Patrolman or three-screw Ruger for the conversion, it is necessary to re-chamber the cylinder and either re-bore the barrel or use an available 44 Special barrel. This was not a problem with the Smith & Wesson conversion thirty years ago when original 44 Special Model 24 barrels were still available. Today, they are nearly impossible to find. The Ruger conversion is much easier to accomplish since a Ruger 44 Magnum barrel can be used, or one may start with 44 barrel stock, which is much easier to fit to a single action than a double-action revolver requiring a cut-out and lock-up for the ejector rod.

Here then are ten 44 Special conversions on three-screw Rugers by five different gunsmiths, another custom 44 by a very special friend, and if you look closely you may even catch a glimpse of that other Special, the 41. Feel free to use any of these ideas, or better yet contact one of the four remaining six-gunsmiths, as Bill Grover has been called Home.

HAMILTON BOWEN: Pictured are four 44 Special Blackhawk conversions and one 41 Special Blackhawk with case-colored frame and hammer––all by Hamilton Bowen. Three of the 44s are on Flat-Tops, one on an Old Model, and the 41 on a Flat-Top frame. The latter has to be one of the most beautiful single-action six-guns in existence. Two of the 357 Flat-Tops

▲ ***Mike Harvey of Cimarron Firearms shows an engraved and nickel-plated 1871-72 Open-Top.***

▼ ***Some replica single actions available today are,*** *clockwise from top right,* ***EMF's Model 1875 Remington, Navy Arms Model #3 Russian, and two from Cimarron–an Original Finish Model P and an 1871-72 Open-Top***

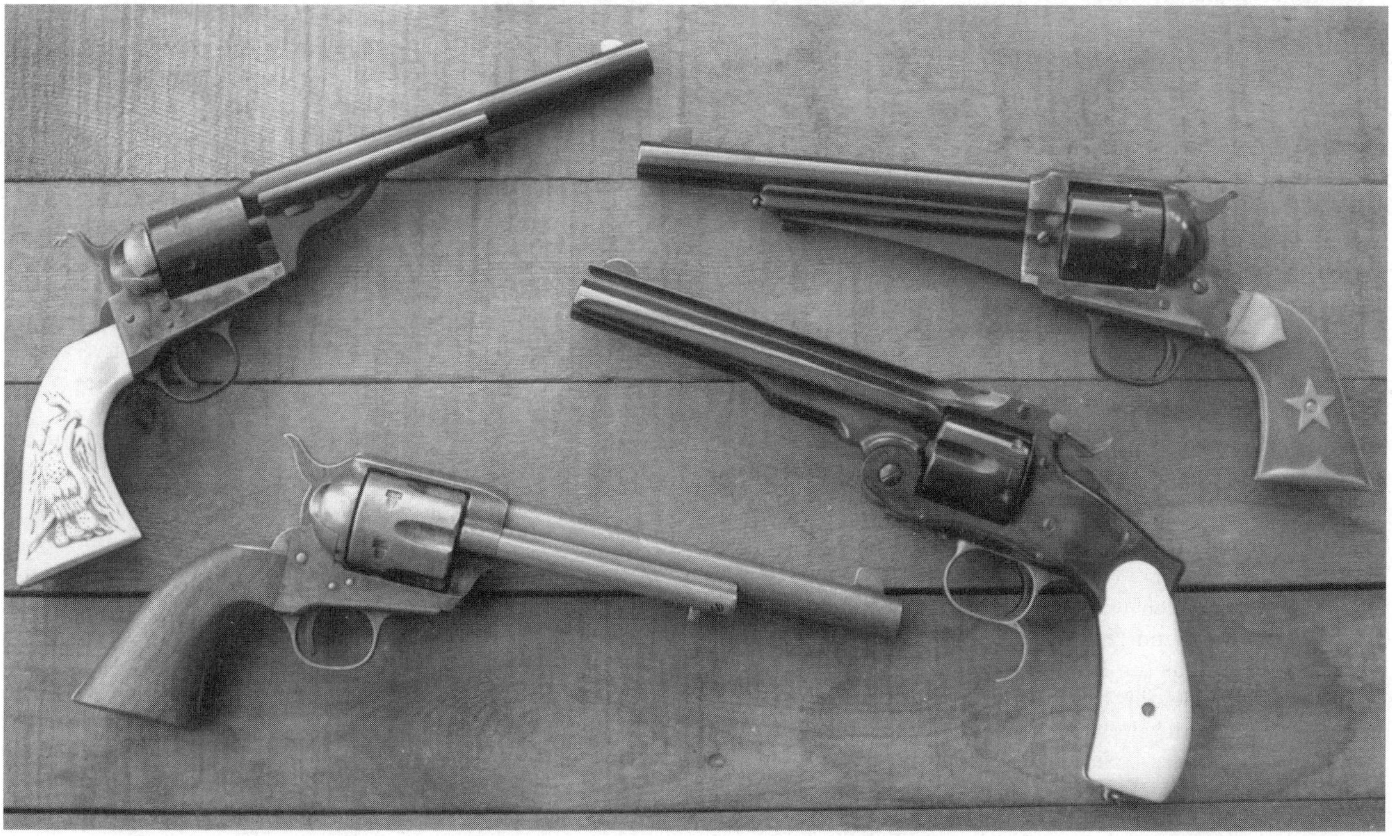

are now a matched pair of 4 5/8-inch bright blue 44 Specials with stag grips. The third one had been ridden hard and put up wet and although it was mechanically fine, the finish was pitted in places. This has been made into a real workin' 44 Special six-gun with a bead blasted finish. The final 44 Special conversion by Bowen on an Old Model frame is fitted with a 7 1/2-inch barrel, polished grip frame, and black micarta grips by Charles Able.

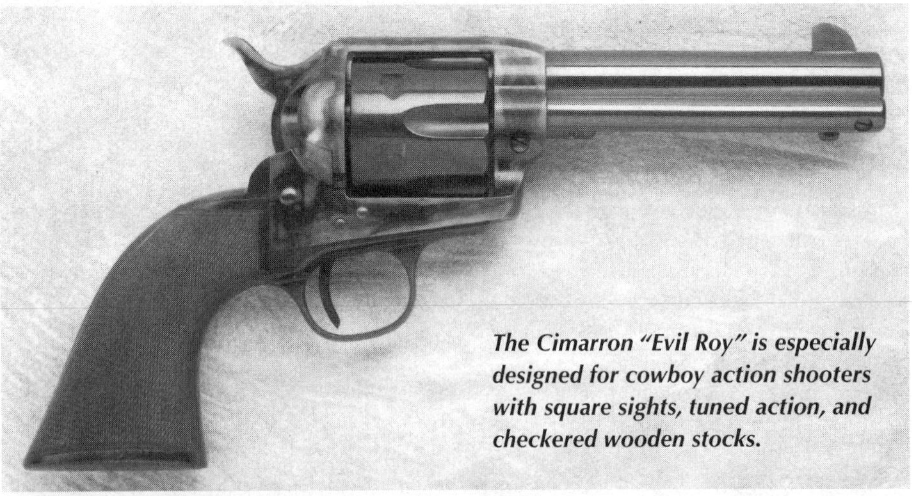

The Cimarron "Evil Roy" is especially designed for cowboy action shooters with square sights, tuned action, and checkered wooden stocks.

DAVID CLEMENTS: David Clements is another custom six-gunsmith building many big-bore New Model conversions, however, he also turns out some fine three-screw 44 Special six-guns.

BEN FORKIN: Ben Forkin of Montana began his gunsmithing career the right way, working under Hamilton Bowen. All of the custom three-screw Blackhawks mentioned thus far have 4 5/8- or 7 1/2-inch barrels. Using a recently purchased like-new 6 1/2-inch 44 Magnum Flat-Top barrel, we decided to do a 5 1/2-inch 44 Special complete with case hardened mainframe and hammer. Ben performed his usual action work: smoothing, tuning, and tightening; re-chambered the cylinder to 44 Special cutting it to use .430-inch Keith bullets; cut the 44 Magnum barrel to the proper length and fitted it with a post front sight mated with a Bowen adjustable rear sight. He finished off the package with one of Belt Mountain's #5 base pins.

BILL GROVER: In the late 1980s I saw a very special 44 Special on a Ruger Old Model. The barrel was 4-5/8 inches long, the grip frame was polished bright, and the grips were made from the horns of a bighorn sheep. This special six-gun was shown to me by Bart Skelton as it had belonged to his dad Skeeter before he died and then belonged to gunwriter John Wootters. Two three-screw 357 Blackhawks went off to Bill Grover of Texas Longhorn Arms.

Grover and I put our heads together on this one so a double influence can be seen. The cylinder has been re-chambered to 44 Special to allow the use of .429-inch diameter bullets, but kept to minimum dimensions for long case life. Barrel/cylinder gap was set at 0.0025-inch. The Ruger XR3 grip frame and steel ejector housing were

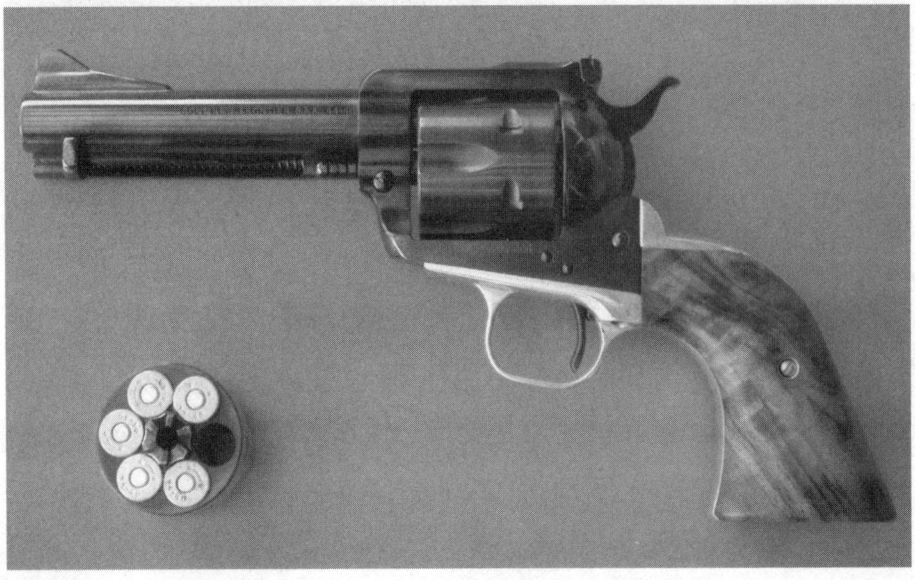

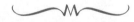

Middle Left: ***Taylor's & Co. now offers the R&D drop-in cylinder, chambered in 45 Colt, for the Ruger Old Army.***
Bottom Left: ***Not a New Frontier but rather a Ruger OM converted to 44 Special, with an auxiliary cylinder in 44-40 and a New Frontier barrel fitted by David Clements. Custom stocks are by Larry Caudill.***

Two easy-packing 44 Specials: the blued version by Andy Horvath and the nickel-plated "Baby" by R.G. Baer.

not discarded, but put back for use on the other 44 Special Grover was building. In their place Grover fitted steel Colt parts, a Colt backstrap and trigger guard, which now wears one-piece ivories, and a Colt ejector housing along with a bullseye-head ejector rod.

The second 44 Special six-gun from Grover was built with a 7 1/2-inch barrel using a 10 1/2-inch Ruger Super Blackhawk barrel. The XR3 grip frame of #SS4 now resides on this six-gun along with rosewood stocks. This long-range six-gun made to complement the #SS4 packin' pistol also wears a Number Five front sight and a Number Five base pin.

R.G. BAER: Bob Baer is not a working gunsmith but simply a special friend who likes to customize his own six-guns. An Old Model three-screw 357 Ruger Blackhawk was turned over to him with instructions to simply build me a special gun, his choice of style and caliber. Having seen, handled, and shot many of Baer's creations from short barrels to long barrels, from round butts to lanyard rings, from 22s to 357s to 44s, with all kinds of artistic touches, I knew I would not be disappointed.

Since Baer had a pretty good idea where my heart lies, the conversion is a 44 Special. The front and rear edge of the grip frame are tapered for greater comfort, with no sharp edges to emphasize recoil, and the fancy walnut grips have been expertly fitted to the bright polished aluminum grip frame. The aluminum ejector rod housing is also polished bright while the rest of Baby, as Baer dubbed it, is finished in satin hard nickel plating. To aid in the project, gunsmith Keith DeHart expertly re-chambered the cylinder and furnished the 3 1/4-inch barrel. The total package is a very easy to pack 30 ounces.

ANDY HORVATH: About 20 years ago Horvath was asked if he could do a round-butted, 4-inch barrel 44 built on a Ruger 357 three-screw Blackhawk, a real 44 Special packin' pistol. The answer came back affirmative and off went a 6 1/2-inch 357 three-screw Blackhawk, a 7 1/2-inch Super Blackhawk barrel, and some special items I had been saving for just such a project.

Recently I have had the pleasure of working with one of Horvath's latest 44 Specials. Starting with a Flat-Top 357 Blackhawk, Andy re-chambered it to 44 Special, fitted it with a full-ribbed heavy barrel from a S&W 44 Magnum with an undercut post front sight, re-contoured the front edge of the top strap to blend in perfectly with the ribbed barrel, then fitted it with an abbreviated style #5 base pin. The finish is a deep, high polished blue set off perfectly by a case hardened frame and hammer. It was very difficult to even consider returning this test gun––so I bought it.

Yes, thing were much simpler in the old days when so few choices were available. With so many options open to today's handgunner we can sincerely say that sometimes progress can be wonderful. Have a great six-gunnin' year!

The Lyman T-Mag II turret press (shown right) has been reengineered and upgraded to offer even more versatility and precision. Improvements include: a new hi-tech iron frame, a new turret handle and improved retention system for smoother indexing. With a detachable T-Mag Turret precise set-up with various loading dies (shown below) can be easily maintained while changing calibers.

HANDLOADING UPDATE

by Larry S. Sterett

Handloaders, particularly ones who have been loading for some years, or who reload a number of different calibers, always seem to be looking for new equipment and/or accessories to make the operation simpler, safer, faster––or all of the above. Such products are available and what follow are some of the newest.

Berry's Manufacturing

Berry's is known for their copper-plated swaged bullets, including two weights for the 50 S&W, but the firm also has a number of other products for handloaders. New are covered loading trays, or blocks. Available in three sizes to fit cases from the 9mm Parabellum and 223 up to cartridges with head sizes just under 0.625-inch, the trays hold 50 rounds and feature clear plastic covers. Other new items include powder funnel inserts to fit 17- and 50-caliber cartridges, and plastic 50-round ammo boxes in smoke and orange colors, in addition to the clear and blue colors previously available. *(Boxes holding 20 and 100 rounds are also available in smoke and orange colors.)* Ten sizes are available to fit most handguns and rifle cartridges from the 380 ACP to the 500 S&W and 50 A.E., including the various WSM and WSSM calibers.

Battenfeld Technologies, Inc.

Battenfeld has a couple of new items in their Frankford Arsenal line. First is a tumbler with up to 600-case capacity and Rotary-7 Media Separator. *(The Rotary 7 Media Separator is available separately, and includes the Separator, bucket adaptor, and a 3-1/2 gallon bucket. Polishing and cleaning media in the form of plain or treated corn cobs or walnut hulls is available in quantities from 4-1/2 to 18 pounds, depending on the type.)* An easy-to-use Overall Length Gauge to determine the optimum bullet seating depth for reloaded cartridges is also new. All a handloader needs is a cleaning rod of 1/4-inch diameter *(or less)*, calipers, a pencil, and the Frankford gauge, to determine the overall length of the reloaded cartridge so seated bullets just touch the rifling.

GSI International, Inc.

Even when using some progressive reloaders, it's necessary to perform a certain number of manual operations, such as inserting a bullet when loading metallic cartridges. GSI International, Inc. has made a portion of the reloading operation easier with their GSI Bullet Feed System for the Dillon XL650 loading press. The GSI System will accept standard 7/8 x 14 dies, and it slides right into the toolhead slot of the XL650 press. *(The Dillon powder system and powder checker fit right in on the GSI toolhead.)* After installation of the GSI System, a bullet is advanced with every pull of the press handle. As the handle moves down, one bullet moves into the seating station, directly above the cartridge case, and a detent ball holds the bullet. Completion of the handle stroke seats the bullet into the cartridge case, without the need to manually position the bullet on top of the case or guide it up to the seating die. Currently, the GSI System, which includes the toolhead, bullet guide, rotary feed wheel and a

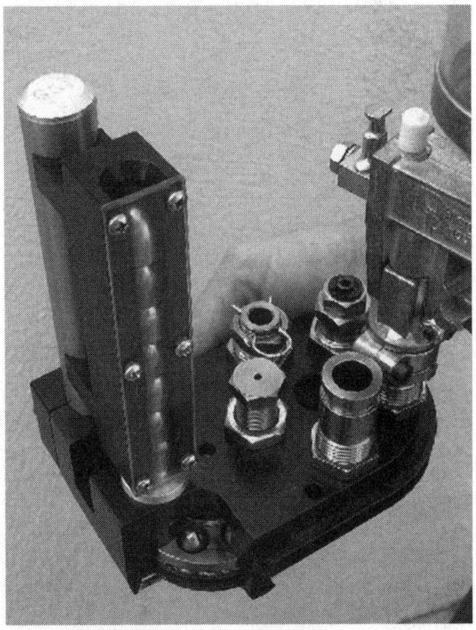

GSI International's Bullet Feed attached to a Dillon XL650 reloading press positions a bullet ready for seating on the downstroke of the press handle The feed, visible here in the center of the photo, slides into the toolhead slot of the XL650 press.

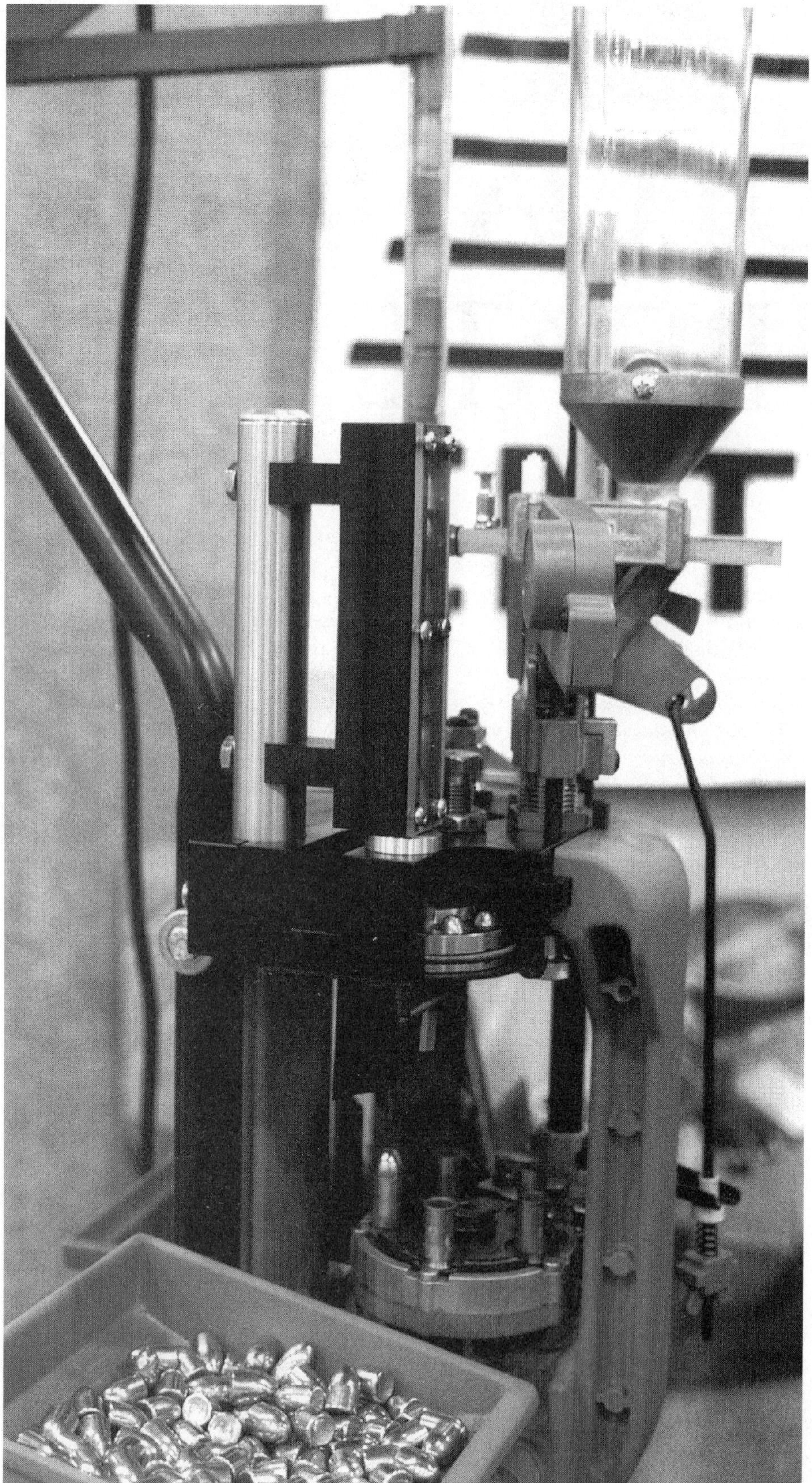

GSI International's Bullet Feed attached to a Dillon XL650 reloading press positions a bullet ready for seating on the downstroke of the press handle. The feed, visible here in the center of the photo, slides into the toolhead slot of the XL650 press.

specially machined seating stem for one caliber, is available in 38/357, 9mm, 40/10mm, 44 and 45 ACP handgun cartridges. *(Originally, the system was to also have been available to handle 223 Remington cartridges.)* It is necessary to keep the hopper filled with bullets.

Hornady Mfg. Company

Hornady always has some items for handloaders, and the latest include trimmer pilots for the 204 Ruger and 500 S&W cartridges, plus a 204 collet for the Cam Lock Bullet Puller. There are Custom-Grade Reloading Dies for the 460 S&W in the Series II Three-Die Pistol sets.

Huntington Die Specialties

Huntington, the firm founded by the late Fred Huntington, the R.C.B.S. man, has more standard and hard-to-find reloading products—presses, scales, trimmers, dies, components, bullet moulds, etc.—than any other firm in the business. If reloading dies are available for a specific cartridge, Huntington probably has them or can produce them. More than 500 different cartridges are available. It may take awhile for some of the exotics, but they can be obtained. The same comment applies to forming dies, with nearly 300 different ones available. *(More than fifty items, including collets, neck-sizers, die sets, etc., were added to the availability for 2005.)* Huntington currently carries 16 brands of bullets for reloading, and 23 brands of new brass cases, including HDS, Bertram, Norma, Horneber, and RWS.

Lee Precision

New Lee Precision products include Bottle Neck Pistol Factory Crimp Dies for the 30 Mauser/30 Tokarev, 30 (7.65m) Luger, 357 SIG, and 400 Cor-Bon cartridges. Lee loading dies for handgun calibers range from the 25 ACP to the 500 S&W Magnum, and include the 455 Webley Mark II, 45 GAP, 480 Ruger, 50 Action Express. Some die sets, such as the 41 A.E., 45

HP Italian, 7mm BR and 7mm TCU are no longer catalogued.

Lee Precision has dropped the wadcutter 208-grain mould for the 44 Special cartridge. New is a double mould to cast a 325-grain flat-nose gas check design for the 480 Ruger and 475 Linebaugh cartridges. Moulds are available to cast 440, 450, and 500-grain bullets for the 500 S&W and 50-70 Government cartridges.

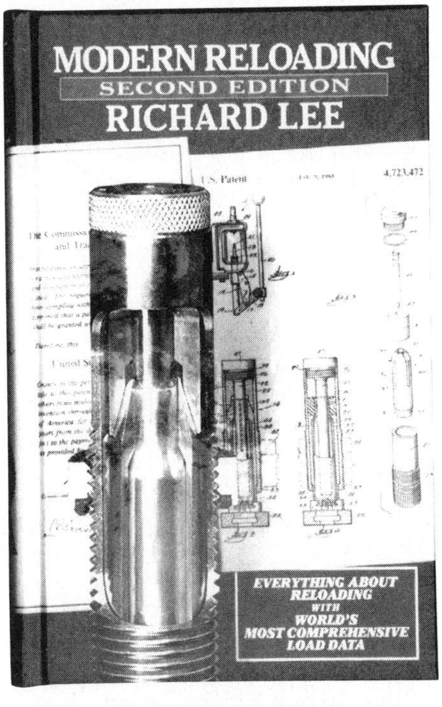

Lee Precision's **Modern Reloading** *manual contains load data for both cast lead and jacket bullets in handgun and rifle loads from the 17 Ackley Bee to the 50 BMG, and much more.*

Lee Carbide Dies are used in commecial loading machines that cycle four to five thousand times per hour. You can't wear them out with personal use.

Lyman Products Corporation

Lyman has three new electronic powder measuring devices for handloaders. The 1000 XP Compact has a 1000-grain capacity, and features a hinged fold-back cover, digital readout, and an AC adapter. The larger 1500 XP features a built-in powder trickler, 1500-grain capacity, fold-back dust cover, and a storage tray for scale accessories. Accurate to 0.1-grain, the scales will measure in grains or grams.

The top of the measuring line is the new 1200 DPS II Digital Powder System, with powder hopper and 100-load storage capacity. An optional PC interface is available to permit transfer

Lyman's 'top cat' is the 1200 DPS (Digital Powder System), which can store up to 100 loads.

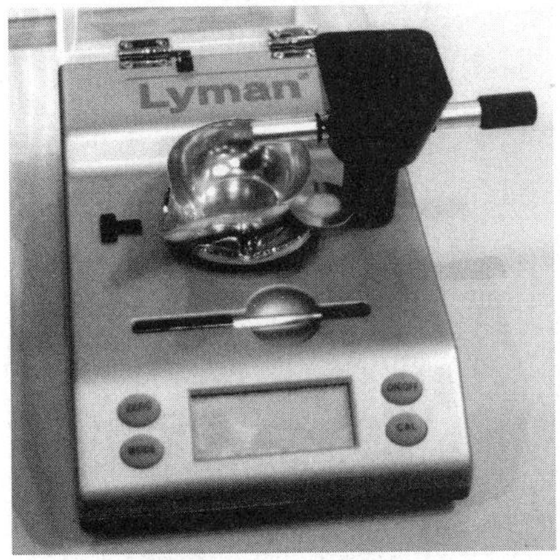

Lyman's new 1500 XP electronic powder measure with hinged cover. (The item to the right of the measure pan is a trickler.) The 1500 is battery or AC powered.

The Universal Powder Funnel Set was designed to meet the needs of serious reloaders who load multiple calibers. 7 Piece Set includes:
- *Small Mult-caliber Powder Funnel*
- *.22 to .45*
- *Patented Adapto Powder Funnel - 4 adapters and drop tube attach to this funnel.*
- *Adapter 1 = .17 to .22*
- *Adapter 2 = .22 to .29*
- *Adapter 3 = .30 to .45*
- *Adapter 4 = .22 to .50 Designed for WSM, WSSM and Rem Ultra Mags.*
- *4" Drop Tube*

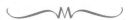

from, or storage of data on, a computer.

Two other new Lyman accessories include the E-ZEE Powder Funnel, which will handle cases from 22 to 50, and the E-ZEE Flo Universal Powder Trickler. The Trickler works with any beam or electronic scale and is adjustable, up or down, in or out.

MTM

MTM Case-Gard Company usually has something new for handloaders each year; this year is no exception. Their new Universal Powder Funnel Set will handle any case from the 17s to the 500s, and it's packed in a clear storage box. It features two funnels—small multi-caliber and an "Adapto" for use with adaptors and the five included drop tubes.

There never seem to be enough loading blocks of the right size available, but the new MTM Universal Loading Tray will handle handgun and rifle calibers from the 17s to the 500 Smith & Wesson, including the WSM, WSSM and Remington Ultra Mag cases. For bulk storage of empty cases or loaded ammunition, the polypropylene Ammo Can will provide 750 cubic inches of lockable storage. A new version of the R-100 Rifle Ammo Case, the R-100-MAG for reloaded ammunition, will handle the 460 and 500 S&W cartridges. The 64-round P-64-50-10 Ammo Box will handle the 50 A.E. and 502 Thunder Sabre cartridges, plus the 480 Ruger and 475 and 500 Linebaugh.

MTM has a number of other new items, including a new Predator Shooting Table to check out the results of their work. Standing 30 inches tall, the table folds down to less than four inches in thickness for carrying. It's ideal for handloaders wanting to check out the results of their work at the bench.

The RCBS ChargeMaster Combo combines the ChargeMaster Dispenser with the ChargeMaster 1500 Scale. It can store up to 30 loads in its memory and can dispense charges weighing from 2 to 300 grains with an accuracy of ±0.1 grain.

RCBS

RCBS, a division of ATK (Alliant Techsystems) has a new AmmoMaster 2 Single Stage reloading press, an improvement on the AmmoMaster, consisting of longer support columns and larger toggle block. It's set for standard 7/8 x 14 dies, but will accept 1-1/2 x 12 dies.

Standard Bullet Puller collets for the 475 and 500 are now available. Case trimmer pilots, reamers, and cutters now include 20 caliber sizes.

To make precision powder weighing easier, two new electronic scales, the RangeMaster 750 *(750-grain capacity)* and ChargeMaster 1500 *(1500 grain capacity)* have been introduced. Available in a choice of 110VAC or 220VAC models, either model will operate on a 9-volt battery. The scales are accurate to ±0.1 grain, and come equipped with two precision calibration/check weights.

For the ultimate weighing convenience, the new ChargeMaster Combo is available. This combines the ChargeMaster 1500 Scale with the ChargeMaster Dispenser. Fill the hopper with a pound+ of the desired powder, enter the desired charge data—in grains or grams—and press the dispense button. A 60-grain charge of smokeless powder will take approximately 20 seconds, and it will be accurate to ±0.1 grain. Up to 30 loads can be stored in the dispenser memory for easy recall, and loads can be from 2.0 to 300.0 grains of ball, flake, or extruded smokeless powder. (NO BLACKPOWDER)

A new Competition Powder Measure, for rifle or pistol/small rifle, is available. Based on the Uniflow Measure, but with a baffle and UPM micrometer adjustment screw, the new measure can drop charges weighing from 10 to 110 grains in the rifle size, and from 5 to 40 grains in the pistol size. The new measure is available separately or as a combo item with both drum sizes.

Special reloading dies may be available from RCBS, with a wait time involved and a no-return policy. Custom reloading and case-forming dies are no longer available from RCBS. However, with the specifications for more than a thousand different cartridge reloading and forming sets on file, chances are good RCBS has the one you want.

For those handloaders who cast their own bullets, RCBS has a new wooden mould mallet to help prevent mould damage, plus a new mould to cast a 400-grain SWC bullet for the 500 S&W cartridge.

Redding Reloading Equipment

Redding now owns Imperial Lubricants, developer and producer of Imperial Sizing Die Wax used to reduce resizing drag. Two container sizes of the wax, bearing the Redding name, plus an Imperial Action Wax syringe and Dry Neck Lube are available. A new Universal Decapping Die, available in small or large size, should be on every handloader's bench if several different caliber cartridges are reloaded. The small die will accept cases from 22- to 50-caliber up to 2.5 inches in length, with an optional 17- and 20-caliber rod available. The large die will handle cases up to three inches long with neck diameters 7mm or larger.

New Redding products include die sets for the 460 S&W and 500 S&W, with titanium carbide sets for the 45 GAP.

The T-7 Turret and Big Boss reloading presses have been improved. Both presses feature a ram stroke of 3.8 inches, and the Big Boss will accept 1-1/4 x 12 die sets. A slide bar automatic primer feeding system with a capacity of approximately a box of 100 primers will fit both the T-7 and Big Boss presses. *(Big Boss Pro-Paks with all the tools—press, dies, scale, lube, etc. —needed to reload a specific cartridge are available in a number of handgun calibers.)*

The TR-1400 Case Trimming Lathe has been made longer and stronger. It comes with a universal

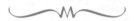

Redding's TR-1400 case trimming lathe in which the case turns against a stationary cutter. A universal collet, six pilots, two neck cleaning brushes, and two primer pocket cleaners are provided with each R-1400. (A hex-shaped power adapter is available as an option to allow the use of a cordless screwdriver.)

collet to fit all popular rifle and handgun case head sizes. Unlike most trimmers, the case in the TR-1400 turns against a stationary TiN (titanium nitride)-coated cutter. Featured accessories include six pilots, small and large primer pocket cleaners, and two neck-cleaning brushes that will handle 22- to 30-caliber cases. *(An optional 1/4-inch hex shaft adapter to permit powering with a cordless screwdriver is available.)*

In the SAECO line, Redding now has traditional bullet moulds available in calibers from 309 to 458. Weights range from 140 grains to 525 grains.

RUAG Ammotec USA Inc.

This company, distributor of Norma ammunition, powders, unprimed brass, and bullets, has a reloading manual that anyone using Norma powders should use. It features chapters on ballistics, powders, etc., plus loads for 73 calibers––from the 222 Remington to 505 Gibbs. Naturally, it's for Norma by Norma. (Norma ammunition and unprimed cases are available in calibers not readily available elsewhere.)

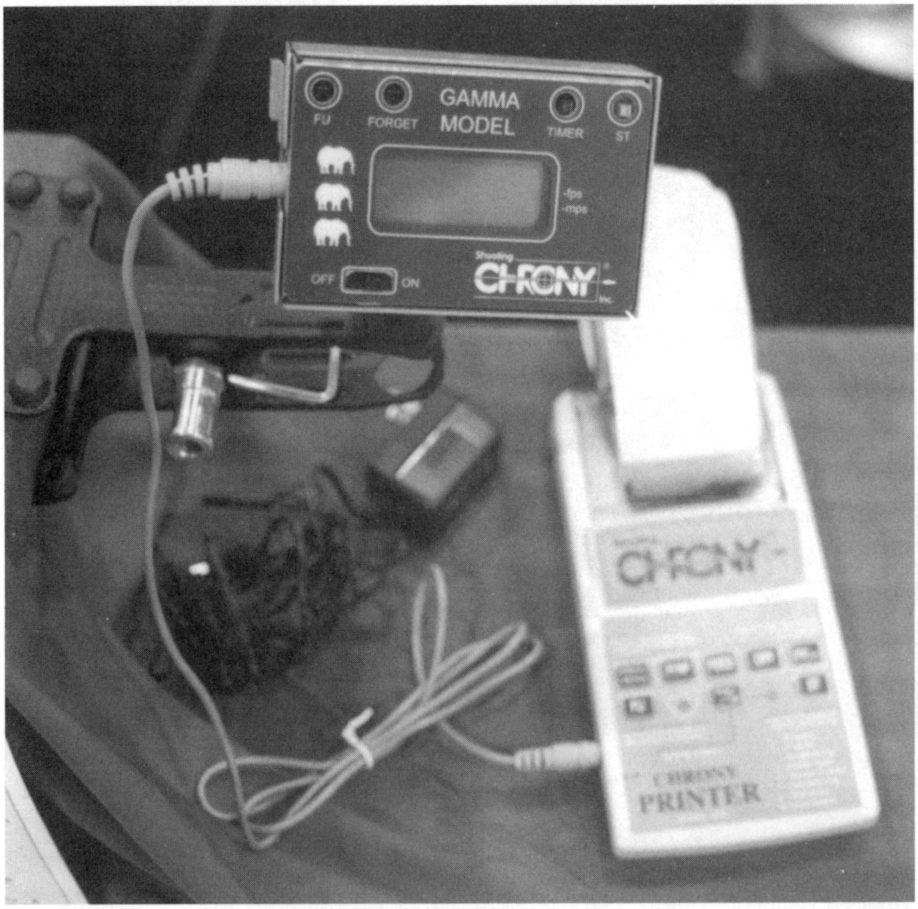

The Gamma Model Shooting Chrony (chronograph) can be attached to a printer to provide a hard copy of your chronographing results, for placement in your handloader's log.

Johnson Design Specialties

This company has a powder measure they claim can charge 100 cases in less than four minutes. Charging directly into the cartridge case, it is said to not cut powder and is simple to use. A powder scale should always be used to check the accuracy of the measure.

Rapine Bullet Moulds

This Pennsylvania company is said to have the world's largest selection of moulds, in a variety of styles, calibers and designs. Many of their current designs have been improved, and they also have a new graphite compound for use in mould preparation.

The Old Western Scrounger

Handloaders unable to find loading dies elsewhere for a specific caliber should check with OWS in Carson City, Nevada. This firm reloads for a number of obsolete cartridges, and handles reloading components and equipment.

Shooting Chrony, Inc.

Handloaders need to use a chronograph if they are to derive the most from their handloads. That 'boom and kick' big bore may be moving faster than you think, or that 'crack and whistle' wildcat may not actually whistle. Check out those handloads on a chronograph. Shooting Chrony has ten models available, from a low of under a C-note to just over two C-notes. They are capable of measuring even low velocity projectiles, such as paintballs, air gun pellets, and arrows. Accessories available include remote controls, indoor light sources, IBM/PC interfaces, and even protective shields—just in case. Some models store a reading until the next shot, others store a series, and readings can even be printed out.

Handloaders should always avail themselves of the loading data provided by the various powder companies every year. The small booklets are complimentary and usually have data on new cartridges long before similar data appears in the larger loading manuals. Check your local dealer for a copy.

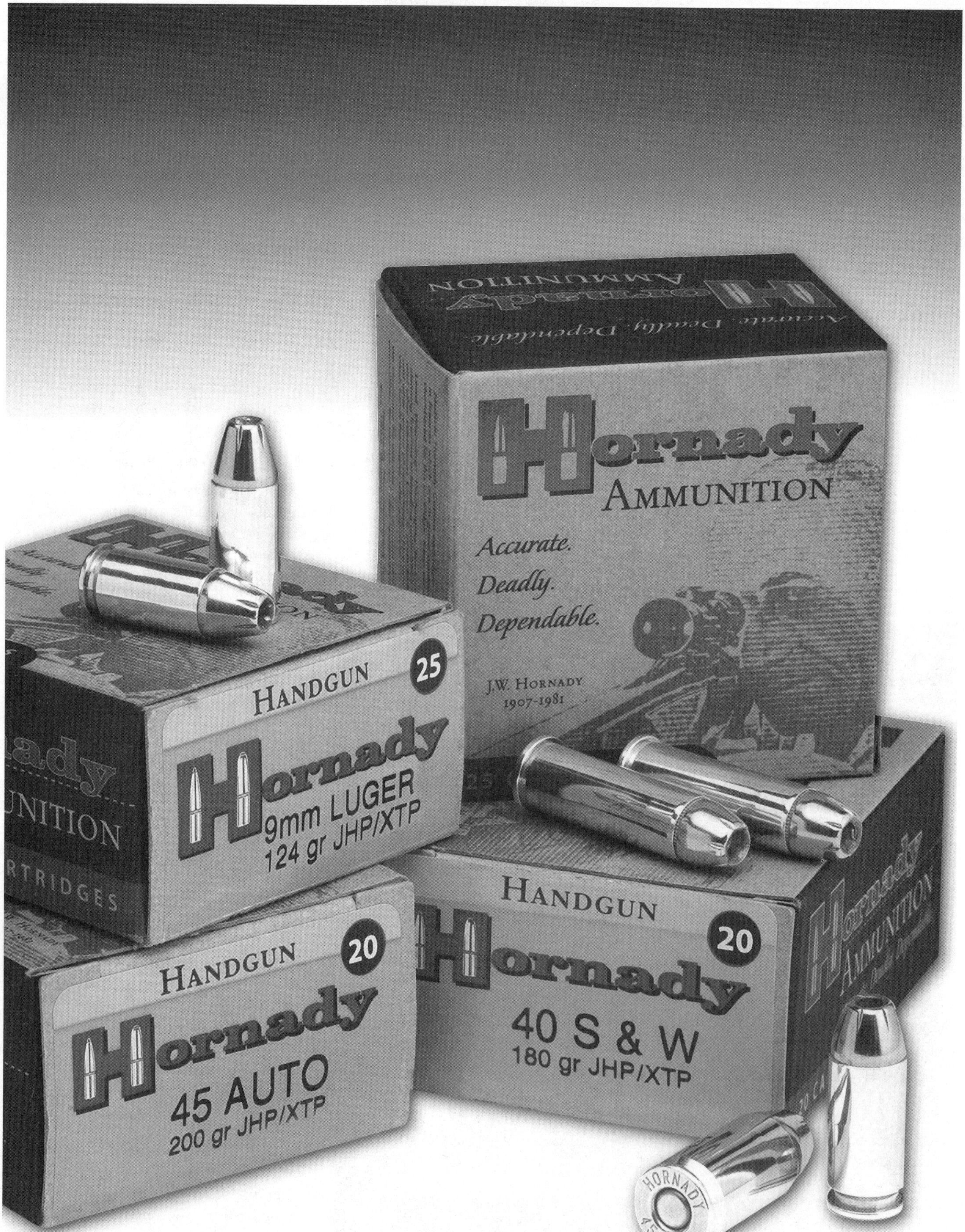
Hornady
AMMUNITION
Accurate.
Deadly.
Dependable.
J.W. HORNADY
1907-1981
HANDGUN
25
Hornady
9mm LUGER
124 gr JHP/XTP
HANDGUN
20
Hornady
45 AUTO
200 gr JHP/XTP
HANDGUN
20
Hornady
40 S & W
180 gr JHP/XTP
HORNADY
45 AUTO

AMMUNITION, BALLISTICS & COMPONENTS

by Holt Bodinson

It's been an active year for acquisitions and consolidations. Western Powder buys Accurate Arms. American Ammunition acquires Triton, and Powerbelt purchases West Coast Bullets.

We needed some new cartridges and we got them: S&W teamed up with Cor-Bon to roll out its "stomper," the 460 S&W.

Graf & Sons, teamed with Hornady, is giving the old warhorses a new lease on life with fresh components and loaded ammunition for the 9mm Steyr and 455 Webley.

It's been an innovative year indeed in the ammunition, ballistics and components business.

Accurate Arms Company

New owner. Western Powders Company, the largest master distributor of reloading powders in North America and originator of the Ramshot powders, has purchased Accurate Arms and moved it to its home base, Miles City, Montana. Western says the existing line of Accurate Arms powders will be maintained with no disruption of service or availability. www.accuratepowder.com

Aguila

No new products but a great new color catalog this year that is full of photographs and ballistic data. Aguila's 22 rimfire line continues to be outstanding with both the heaviest loading (60 grains) and the highest velocity (1700 fps) loading. www.aguilaammo.com

Barnes

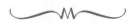

Anticipating the unveiling of the 460 S&W, Barnes is producing a new 200-grain 460 *(actually 0.451-inch)* spitzer boattail bullet in the XPB line. What's interesting is the adoption of the Barnes line by many of the major ammunition makes such as Federal, Cor-Bon, Black Hills, Sako and Sellier & Bellot. "Unleaded" may be the future! www.barnesbullets.com

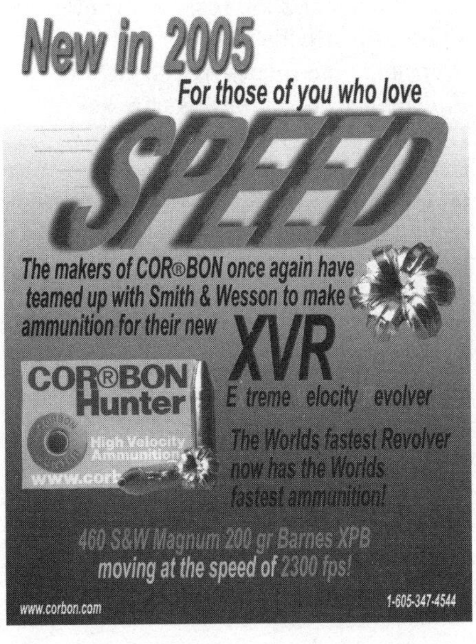

New in 2005
For those of you who love
SPEED
The makers of COR®BON once again have teamed up with Smith & Wesson to make ammunition for their new
XVR
E treme elocity evolver
COR®BON Hunter
The Worlds fastest Revolver now has the Worlds fastest ammunition!
460 S&W Magnum 200 gr Barnes XPB moving at the speed of 2300 fps!
www.corbon.com
1-605-347-4544

Black Hills Ammunition

The Black Hills are famous for gold, and the Black Hills Gold line is famous for being one of the greatest premium hunting ammunition lines ever assembled. Black Hills has just been awarded the U.S. Army contract for 9mm, 45 ACP and 223 match ammo, and continues to furnish the USMC Rifle Team with 77-grain molycoated MatchKing loads. You can buy the exact match load from Black Hills, so be sure to see their complete catalog at www.black-hills.com

Cor-Bon

The Cor-Bon/Smith & Wesson team has done it again. Last year it

Cor-Bon's "Hunting" ammunition line features proprietary Barnes X and Triple Shock bullets in a variety of rifle and handgun calibers.

was the development of the 500 S&W Magnum. This year it's the 460 S&W Magnum with a 200-grain bullet at 2300 fps. If the full-powered 500 S&W is a bit much, Cor-Bon has developed a light target load featuring a 350-grain FMJ at 1,200 fps. Child's play! Expanding their DPX (Deep Penetrating X) line utilizing proprietary Barnes X and Triple Shock bullets, Cor-Bon has added a new "Hunter" line that includes a variety of handgun and rifle calibers. The light-kicking "Pow'Rball" line offered under the Glaser label has been enhanced with a 165-grain bullet at 1075 fps for the increasingly popular 45 GAP, and oh, yes, the 45 GAP gets a 145-grain Glaser Safety Slug at 1325 fps, too. www.corbon.com

Fiocchi

Fiocchi's 40 S&W offerings have been updated with a 165-grain JHP at 1100 fps and a 165-grain truncated cone encapsulated-base projectile at 1140 fps. www.fiocchiusa.com

GOEX

GOEX is back in the non-corrosive, replica blackpowder business with the introduction of "Pinnacle Black Powder" in FFG and FFFG. We've missed the old Clear Shot brand. Pinnacle looks like blackpowder, shoots consistently with little fouling build-up and offers an indefinite shelf life. A new granulation called "Cowboy Action Cartridges" in GOEX's standard blackpowder line is designed specifically for 40-grain loads or less.

For the personal and home-defense market, Hornady is introducing a special line of handgun, rifle and shotgun ammunition under the "TAP" label.

Speaking about cowboy cartridges, GOEX is now marketing a complete line of blackpowder-loaded, SPG lubed, Black Dawge cartridges for rifle, pistol and scatterguns. Let the boom begin. www.goexpowder.com

Graf & Sons

There's no excuse for not shooting those old surplus rifles of any nationality. Loaded for them by Hornady, Graf now offers 9mm Steyr and 455 Webley ammunition at attractive prices, plus special Hornady runs of the component bullets to reload those calibers. Based on my testing, this is premium quality ammunition. Stock up while you can. www.grafs.com

Hodgdon Powder

After acquiring the IMR Powder Company last year, Hodgdon is refining the IMR line. The first improvement, which will prove to be a boon for handloaders, is a "super short-cut" version of IMR7828. Look for a new complimentary "IMR Smokeless Powder Guide" with updated data for the most recent cartridge introductions like the 204 Ruger and 25 WSSM. www.hodgdon.com

Hornady

Smith & Wesson's new 460 Magnum is getting a special 200-grain SST loading from Hornady. The polymer-tipped spitzer SST bullet is loaded to a velocity of 2250 fps, and when sighted-in 3 inches high at 100 yards, drops only 3.8 inches at 200 yards. Flat indeed! Look for lots of new Hornady component brass in all of the popular handgun calibers. Lots of new pistol additions to Hornady's "TAP" personal defense ammunition line. See them at www.hornady.com.

Huntington

Here's the one-stop source for common and oddball components for any cartridge you can imagine reloading plus all the RCBS products and parts. Don't miss their extensive reference catalog at www.huntington.com

Hodgdon is introducing its "short cut" technology to the IMR powder line.

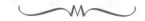

Liberty Shooting Supplies

Earlier this year, I was looking for an unplated lead bullet for the 8mm Nambu. Remembering that Liberty Shooting Supplies casts the most extensive array of bullet designs I know of, I went searching there and found exactly what I was looking for. If you enjoy shooting quality cast bullets, sized and lubricated to your specifications, take a look at their catalog. Liberty will also cast from your moulds. www.libertyshootingsupplies.com

Magtech

Magtech's "First Defense" line of 100-percent copper hollowpoint ammunition for law enforcement and personal defense is now available in 38 Special, 357 Magnum and 380 Auto—plus the same bullet technology has been carried over to a new "Hunting" line featuring the larger handgun calibers. For the cost-conscious plinkers, Magtech is offering its most popular handgun calibers in 250-round boxes. www.magtechammunition.com

Meister Bullets

This well-known brand of hard cast bullets is expanding this year to include a 330-grain 500 S&W bullet. www.meisterbullets.com

Northern Precision

I suspect those long, northern winters in upstate New York give Northern Precision the time to invent the most interesting array of bullets in the industry. This year it's a bonded-core spitzer for the 454 Casull. Call for their catalog at (315) 493-1711.

Old Western Scrounger

When Dangerous Dave states that "we carry the largest and finest inventory of obsolete ammunition, bar-none," you had better believe it. The Old Western Scrounger is the place to go. www.ows-ammunition.com

PMC

A big push is on at PMC to bring new calibers into its environmentally friendly PMC Green line featuring frangible copper-polymer bullets and primers made without any heavy metal compounds. Added this year is a 77-grain loading for the 380 Auto. The bullets are so frangible they disintegrate harmlessly when fired into steel plate only 3 inches from the muzzle. Over in the rimfire line are an ultra-quiet 22 Super Subsonic featuring a 20-grain bullet at 500 fps, a high-speed 22 Short, and the 17PMC outfitted with a 20-grain bullet at 1800 fps. www.pmcammo.com

Powerbelt

Big news! Powerbelt buys West Coast Bullets and will continue and expand the extensive West Coast cast line under the named "Accura." A few of the new introductions will be hollowpoints and new coatings on top of the standard copper-clad coating. The newer coatings, called "Black Pearl" and "Sterling," permit the use of the cast bullets in Glocks, yielding higher velocities, lower pressures and better accuracy. Also being introduced is a new 40- and 45-caliber frangible line featuring sintered, copper-plated bullets. www.powerbeltbullets.com

Speer's "Short Barrel" loads like this 135-grain/38 Special ammo are specifically designed for snubbies.

Remington

Keeping shooting affordable, Big Green is expanding its UMC lines with a 230-grain JHP and FMJ at 835 fps in the new 45 GAP.

Big Green is pushing its reloading components line. Watch for some snappy-looking plastic bags of Remington brass and bullets on your dealer's shelves.

Speer

Building on their successful introduction last year of a 38 Special Gold Dot HP loading for snubbies, Speer has expanded this much-needed concept with loads designed specifically for the short-barreled 9mm, 357 Magnum, 40 S&W, 44 Remington Magnum and 45 Auto. Guess what the line is called? "Short Barrel," of course! www.speer-bullets.com

SSK

JD Jones has finally outdone himself with the 620 JDJ. The new round for the T/C Encore is based on a shortened and fire-formed 577 Nitro case expanded to take a 600 Nitro bullet. JD is getting 1000 fps with a 1000-grain bullet from an Encore with a 12-inch barrel. T-Rex-grade ammunition! www.sskindustries.com

Triton

Whatever happened to Triton? It has been revived by American Ammunition, which recently acquired Triton's assets. Quik-Shok 9mm, 40 S&W and 45 ACP ammunition is once again available featuring the pre-stressed Quik-Shok core bullet that splits into three pieces upon impact. Triton Hi-Vel ammunition may be reintroduced by year's end. www.a-merc.com

Winchester continues to upgrade its 500 S&W offerings this year with a Platinum Tip.

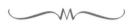

Ultramax

Producing quality reloaded ammunition at great savings to the consumer, Ultramax has added three new loadings for the 500 S&W this year. The Ultramax line now includes rifle, pistol and cowboy loadings. www.ultramaxammunition.com

Vihtavuori and Lapua

Vihtavuori and Lapua have expanded their website this year. See their products at www.vihtavuori-lapua.com.

Western Powders

Western Powders buys Accurate Arms! See the comments under Accurate Arms. www.westernpowders.com

Winchester Ammunition

The powerful 500 S&W is getting quite a play this year, so Winchester will be offering a 400-grain Platinum Tip HP at 1800 fps to the Supreme line for bone-crunching effectiveness.

It's been a busy year at Winchester Ammunition! www.winchester.com

CENTERFIRE HANDGUN CARTRIDGES — BALLISTICS & PRICES

Notes: Blanks are available in 32 S&W, 38 S&W and 38 Special. "V" after barrel length indicates test barrel was vented to produce ballistics similar to a revolver with a normal barrel-to-cylinder gap. Ammo prices are per 50 rounds except when marked with an ** which signifies a 20 round box; *** signifies a 25-round box. Not all loads are available from all ammo manufacturers. Listed loads are those made by Remington, Winchester, Federal, and others. DISC. is a discontinued load. Prices are rounded to nearest whole dollar and will vary with brand and retail outlet. † = new bullet weight this year; "c" indicates a change in data.

Cartridge	Bullet Wgt. Grs.	VELOCITY (fps)			ENERGY (ft. lbs.)			Mid-Range Traj. (in.)		Bbl. Lgth. (in).	Est. Price/ box
		Muzzle	50 yds.	100 yds.	Muzzle	50 yds.	100 yds.	50 yds.	100 yds.		
22, 25											
221 Rem. Fireball	50	2650	2380	2130	780	630	505	0.2	0.8	10.5"	$15
25 Automatic	35	900	813	742	63	51	43	NA	NA	2"	$18
25 Automatic	45	815	730	655	65	55	40	1.8	7.7	2"	$21
25 Automatic	50	760	705	660	65	55	50	2.0	8.7	2"	$17
30											
7.5mm Swiss	107	1010	NA	NA	240	NA	NA	NA	NA	NA	NEW
7.62mmTokarev	87	1390	NA	NA	365	NA	NA	0.6	NA	4.5"	NA
7.62 Nagant	97	790	NA	NA	134	NA	NA	NA	NA	NA	NEW
7.63 Mauser	88	1440	NA	NA	405	NA	NA	NA	NA	NA	NEW
30 Luger	93†	1220	1110	1040	305	255	225	0.9	3.5	4.5"	$34
30 Carbine	110	1790	1600	1430	785	625	500	0.4	1.7	10"	$28
30-357 AeT	123	1992	NA	NA	1084	NA	NA	NA	NA	10"	NA
32											
32 S&W	88	680	645	610	90	80	75	2.5	10.5	3"	$17
32 S&W Long	98	705	670	635	115	100	90	2.3	10.5	4"	$17
32 Short Colt	80	745	665	590	100	80	60	2.2	9.9	4"	$19
32 H&R Magnum	85	1100	1020	930	230	195	165	1.0	4.3	4.5"	$21
32 H&R Magnum	95	1030	940	900	225	190	170	1.1	4.7	4.5"	$19
32 Automatic	60	970	895	835	125	105	95	1.3	5.4	4"	$22
32 Automatic	60	1000	917	849	133	112	96			4"	NA
32 Automatic	65	950	890	830	130	115	100	1.3	5.6	NA	NA
32 Automatic	71	905	855	810	130	115	95	1.4	5.8	4"	$19
8mm Lebel Pistol	111	850	NA	NA	180	NA	NA	NA	NA	NA	NEW
8mm Steyr	112	1080	NA	NA	290	NA	NA	NA	NA	NA	NEW
8mm Gasser	126	850	NA	NA	200	NA	NA	NA	NA	NA	NEW
9mm, 38											
380 Automatic	60	1130	960	NA	170	120	NA	1.0	NA	NA	NA
380 Automatic	85/88	990	920	870	190	165	145	1.2	5.1	4"	$20
380 Automatic	90	1000	890	800	200	160	130	1.2	5.5	3.75"	$10
380 Automatic	95/100	955	865	785	190	160	130	1.4	5.9	4"	$20
38 Super Auto +P	115	1300	1145	1040	430	335	275	0.7	3.3	5"	$26
38 Super Auto +P	125/130	1215	1100	1015	425	350	300	0.8	3.6	5"	$26
38 Super Auto +P	147	1100	1050	1000	395	355	325	0.9	4.0	5"	NA
9x18mm Makarov	95	1000	NA	NA	NA	NA	NA	NA	NA	NA	NEW
9x18mm Ultra	100	1050	NA	NA	240	NA	NA	NA	NA	NA	NEW
9x23mm Largo	124	1190	1055	966	390	306	257	0.7	3.7	4"	NA
9x23mm Win.	125	1450	1249	1103	583	433	338	0.6	2.8	NA	NA
9mm Steyr	115	1180	NA	NA	350	NA	NA	NA	NA	NA	NEW
9mm Luger	88	1500	1190	1010	440	275	200	0.6	3.1	4"	$24
9mm Luger	90	1360	1112	978	370	247	191	NA	NA	4"	$26
9mm Luger	95	1300	1140	1010	350	275	215	0.8	3.4	4"	NA
9mm Luger	100	1180	1080	NA	305	255	NA	0.9	NA	4"	NA
9mm Luger	115	1155	1045	970	340	280	240	0.9	3.9	4"	$21
9mm Luger	123/125	1110	1030	970	340	290	260	1.0	4.0	4"	$23
9mm Luger	140	935	890	850	270	245	225	1.3	5.5	4"	$23
9mm Luger	147	990	940	900	320	290	265	1.1	4.9	4"	$26
9mm Luger +P	90	1475	NA	NA	437	NA	NA	NA	NA	NA	NA
9mm Luger +P	115	1250	1113	1019	399	316	265	0.8	3.5	4"	$27
9mm Federal	115	1280	1130	1040	420	330	280	0.7	3.3	4"V	$24
9mm Luger Vector	115	1155	1047	971	341	280	241	NA	NA	4"	NA
9mm Luger +P	124	1180	1089	1021	384	327	287	0.8	3.8	4"	NA
38											
38 S&W	146	685	650	620	150	135	125	2.4	10.0	4"	$19
38 Short Colt	125	730	685	645	150	130	115	2.2	9.4	6"	$19
39 Special	100	950	900	NA	200	180	NA	1.3	NA	4"V	NA
38 Special	110	945	895	850	220	195	175	1.3	5.4	4"V	$23
38 Special	110	945	895	850	220	195	175	1.3	5.4	4"V	$23
38 Special	130	775	745	710	175	160	120	1.9	7.9	4"V	$22

Centerfire Handgun Cartridges — Ballistics & Prices, continued

Notes: Blanks are available in 32 S&W, 38 S&W and 38 Special. "V" after barrel length indicates test barrel was vented to produce ballistics similar to a revolver with a normal barrel-to-cylinder gap. Ammo prices are per 50 rounds except when marked with an ** which signifies a 20 round box; *** signifies a 25-round box. Not all loads are available from all ammo manufacturers. Listed loads are those made by Remington, Winchester, Federal, and others. DISC. is a discontinued load. Prices are rounded to nearest whole dollar and will vary with brand and retail outlet. † = new bullet weight this year; "c" indicates a change in data.

Cartridge	Bullet Wgt. Grs.	VELOCITY (fps)			ENERGY (ft. lbs.)			Mid-Range Traj. (in.)		Bbl. Lgth. (in).	Est. Price/ box
		Muzzle	50 yds.	100 yds.	Muzzle	50 yds.	100 yds.	50 yds.	100 yds.		
38											
38 Special Cowboy	140	800	767	735	199	183	168			7.5" V	NA
38 (Multi-Ball)	140	830	730	505	215	130	80	2.0	10.6	4"V	$10**
38 Special	148	710	635	565	165	130	105	2.4	10.6	4"V	$17
38 Special	158	755	725	690	200	185	170	2.0	8.3	4"V	$18
38 Special +P	95	1175	1045	960	290	230	195	0.9	3.9	4"V	$23
38 Special +P	110	995	925	870	240	210	185	1.2	5.1	4"V	$23
38 Special +P	125	975	929	885	264	238	218	1	5.2	4"	NA
38 Special +P	125	945	900	860	250	225	205	1.3	5.4	4"V	#23
38 Special +P	129	945	910	870	255	235	215	1.3	5.3	4"V	$11
38 Special +P	130	925	887	852	247	227	210	1.3	5.50	4"V	NA
38 Special +P	147/150(c)	884	NA	NA	264	NA	NA	NA	NA	4"V	$27
38 Special +P	158	890	855	825	280	255	240	1.4	6.0	4"V	$20
357											
357 SIG	115	1520	NA	NA	593	NA	NA	NA	NA	NA	NA
357 SIG	124	1450	NA	NA	578	NA	NA	NA	NA	NA	NA
357 SIG	125	1350	1190	1080	510	395	325	0.7	3.1	4"	NA
357 SIG	150	1130	1030	970	420	355	310	0.9	4.0	NA	NA
356 TSW	115	1520	NA	NA	593	NA	NA	NA	NA	NA	NA
356 TSW	124	1450	NA	NA	578	NA	NA	NA	NA	NA	NA
356 TSW	135	1280	1120	1010	490	375	310	0.8	3.50	NA	NA
356 TSW	147	1220	1120	1040	485	410	355	0.8	3.5	5"	NA
357 Mag., Super Clean	105	1650									NA
357 Magnum	110	1295	1095	975	410	290	230	0.8	3.5	4"V	$25
357 (Med.Vel.)	125	1220	1075	985	415	315	270	0.8	3.7	4"V	$25
357 Magnum	125	1450	1240	1090	585	425	330	0.6	2.8	4"V	$25
357 (Multi-Ball)	140	1155	830	665	420	215	135	1.2	6.4	4"V	$11**
357 Magnum	140	1360	1195	1075	575	445	360	0.7	3.0	4"V	$25
357 Magnum	145	1290	1155	1060	535	430	360	0.8	3.5	4"V	$26
357 Magnum	150/158	1235	1105	1015	535	430	360	0.8	3.5	4"V	$25
357 Mag. Cowboy	158	800	761	725	225	203	185				NA
357 Magnum	165	1290	1189	1108	610	518	450	0.7	3.1	8-3/8"	NA
357 Magnum	180	1145	1055	985	525	445	390	0.9	3.9	4"V	$25
357 Magnum	180	1180	1088	1020	557	473	416	0.8	3.6	8"V	NA
357 Mag. CorBon F.A.	180	1650	1512	1386	1088	913	767	1.66	0.0		NA
357 Mag. CorBon	200	1200	1123	1061	640	560	500	3.19	0.0		NA
357 Rem. Maximum	158	1825	1590	1380	1170	885	670	0.4	1.7	10.5"	$14**
40, 10mm											
40 S&W	135	1140	1070	NA	390	345	NA	0.9	NA	4"	NA
40 S&W	155	1140	1026	958	447	362	309	0.9	4.1	4"	$14***
40 S&W	165	1150	NA	NA	485	NA	NA	NA	NA	4"	$18***
40 S&W	180	985	936	893	388	350	319	1.4	5.0	4"	$14***
40 S&W	180	1015	960	914	412	368	334	1.3	4.5	4"	NA
400 Cor-Bon	135	1450	NA	NA	630	NA	NA	NA	NA	5"	NA
10mm Automatic	155	1125	1046	986	436	377	335	0.9	3.9	5"	$26
10mm Automatic	170	1340	1165	1145	680	510	415	0.7	3.2	5"	$31
10mm Automatic	175	1290	1140	1035	650	505	420	0.7	3.3	5.5"	$11**
10mm Auto. (FBI)	180	950	905	865	361	327	299	1.5	5.4	4"	$16**
10mm Automatic	180	1030	970	920	425	375	340	1.1	4.7	5"	$16**
10mm Auto H.V.	180†	1240	1124	1037	618	504	430	0.8	3.4	5"	$27
10mm Automatic	200	1160	1070	1010	495	510	430	0.9	3.8	5"	$14**
10.4mm Italian	177	950	NA	NA	360	NA	NA	NA	NA	NA	NEW
41 Action Exp.	180	1000	947	903	400	359	326	0.5	4.2	5"	$13**
41 Rem. Magnum	170	1420	1165	1015	760	515	390	0.7	3.2	4"V	$33
41 Rem. Magnum	175	1250	1120	1030	605	490	410	0.8	3.4	4"V	$14**
41 (Med. Vel.)	210	965	900	840	435	375	330	1.3	5.4	4"V	$30
41 Rem. Magnum	210	1300	1160	1060	790	630	535	0.7	3.2	4"V	$33
41 Rem. Magnum	240	1250	1151	1075	833	706	616	0.8	3.3	6.5V	NA

CENTERFIRE HANDGUN CARTRIDGES — BALLISTICS & PRICES, *continued*

Notes: Blanks are available in 32 S&W, 38 S&W and 38 Special. "V" after barrel length indicates test barrel was vented to produce ballistics similar to a revolver with a normal barrel-to-cylinder gap. Ammo prices are per 50 rounds except when marked with an ** which signifies a 20 round box; *** signifies a 25-round box. Not all loads are available from all ammo manufacturers. Listed loads are those made by Remington, Winchester, Federal, and others. DISC. is a discontinued load. Prices are rounded to nearest whole dollar and will vary with brand and retail outlet. † = new bullet weight this year; "c" indicates a change in data.

Cartridge	Bullet Wgt. Grs.	VELOCITY (fps)			ENERGY (ft. lbs.)			Mid-Range Traj. (in.)		Bbl. Lgth. (in).	Est. Price/ box
		Muzzle	50 yds.	100 yds.	Muzzle	50 yds.	100 yds.	50 yds.	100 yds.		
44											
44 S&W Russian	247	780	NA	NA	335	NA	NA	NA	NA	NA	NA
44 S&W Special	180	980	NA	NA	383	NA	NA	NA	NA	6.5"	NA
44 S&W Special	180	1000	935	882	400	350	311	NA	NA	7.5"V	NA
44 S&W Special	200†	875	825	780	340	302	270	1.2	6.0	6"	$13**
44 S&W Special	200	1035	940	865	475	390	335	1.1	4.9	6.5"	$13**
44 S&W Special	240/246	755	725	695	310	285	265	2.0	8.3	6.5"	$26
44-40 Win. Cowboy	225	750	723	695	281	261	242				NA
44 Rem. Magnum	180	1610	1365	1175	1035	745	550	0.5	2.3	4"V	$18**
44 Rem. Magnum	200	1400	1192	1053	870	630	492	0.6	NA	6.5"	$20
44 Rem. Magnum	210	1495	1310	1165	1040	805	635	0.6	2.5	6.5"	$18**
44 (Med. Vel.)	240	1000	945	900	535	475	435	1.1	4.8	6.5"	$17
44 R.M. (Jacketed)	240	1180	1080	1010	740	625	545	0.9	3.7	4"V	$18**
44 R.M. (Lead)	240	1350	1185	1070	970	750	610	0.7	3.1	4"V	$29
44 Rem. Magnum	250	1180	1100	1040	775	670	600	0.8	3.6	6.5"V	$21
44 Rem. Magnum	250	1250	1148	1070	867	732	635	0.8	3.3	6.5"V	NA
44 Rem. Magnum	275	1235	1142	1070	931	797	699	0.8	3.3	6.5"	NA
44 Rem. Magnum	300	1200	1100	1026	959	806	702	NA	NA	7.5"	$17
44 Rem. Magnum	330	1385	1297	1220	1406	1234	1090	1.83	0.00	NA	NA
440 CorBon	260	1700	1544	1403	1669	1377	1136	1.58	NA	10"	NA
45, 50											
450 Short Colt/450 Revolver	226	830	NA	NA	350	NA	NA	NA	NA	NA	NEW
45 S&W Schofield	180	730	NA	NA	213	NA	NA	NA	NA	NA	NA
45 S&W Schofield	230	730	NA	NA	272	NA	NA	NA	NA	NA	NA
45 G.A.P.	185	1090	970	890	490	385	320	1	4.7	5	NA
45 G.A.P.	230	880	842	NA	396	363	NA	NA	NA	NA	NA
45 Automatic	165	1030	930	NA	385	315	NA	1.2	NA	5"	NA
45 Automatic	185	1000	940	890	410	360	325	1.1	4.9	5"	$28
45 Auto. (Match)	185	770	705	650	245	204	175	2.0	8.7	5"	$28
45 Auto. (Match)	200	940	890	840	392	352	312	2.0	8.6	5"	$20
45 Automatic	200	975	917	860	421	372	328	1.4	5.0	5"	$18
45 Automatic	230	830	800	675	355	325	300	1.6	6.8	5"	$27
45 Automatic	230	880	846	816	396	366	340	1.5	6.1	5"	NA
45 Automatic +P	165	1250	NA	NA	573	NA	NA	NA	NA	NA	NA
45 Automatic +P	185	1140	1040	970	535	445	385	0.9	4.0	5"	$31
45 Automatic +P	200	1055	982	925	494	428	380	NA	NA	5"	NA
45 Super	185	1300	1190	1108	694	582	504	NA	NA	5"	NA
45 Win. Magnum	230	1400	1230	1105	1000	775	635	0.6	2.8	5"	$14**
45 Win. Magnum	260	1250	1137	1053	902	746	640	0.8	3.3	5"	$16**
45 Win. Mag. CorBon	320	1150	1080	1025	940	830	747	3.47			NA
455 Webley MKII	262	850	NA	NA	420	NA	NA	NA	NA	NA	NA
45 Colt	200	1000	938	889	444	391	351	1.3	4.8	5.5"	$21
45 Colt	225	960	890	830	460	395	345	1.3	5.5	5.5"	$22
45 Colt + P CorBon	265	1350	1225	1126	1073	884	746	2.65	0.0		NA
45 Colt + P CorBon	300	1300	1197	1114	1126	956	827	2.78	0.0		NA
45 Colt	250/255	860	820	780	410	375	340	1.6	6.6	5.5"	$27
454 Casull	250	1300	1151	1047	938	735	608	0.7	3.2	7.5"V	NA
454 Casull	260	1800	1577	1381	1871	1436	1101	0.4	1.8	7.5"V	NA
454 Casull	300	1625	1451	1308	1759	1413	1141	0.5	2.0	7.5"V	NA
454 Casull CorBon	360	1500	1387	1286	1800	1640	1323	2.01	0.0		NA
460 S&W	200	2300	2042	1801	2350	1851	1441	0	-1.60	NA	NA
460 S&W	250	1900	1640	1412	2004	1494	1106	0	-2.75	NA	NA
460 S&W	395	1550	1389	1249	2108	1691	1369	0	-4.00	NA	NA
475 Linebaugh	400	1350	1217	1119	1618	1315	1112	NA	NA	NA	NA
480 Ruger	325	1350	1191	1076	1315	1023	835	2.6	0.0	7.5"	NA
50 Action Exp.	325	1400	1209	1075	1414	1055	835	0.2	2.3	6"	$24**
500 S&W	275	1665	1392	1183	1693	1184	854	1.5	NA	8.375	NA
500 S&W	400	1675	1472	1299	2493	1926	1499	1.3	NA	8.375	NA
500 S&W	440	1625	1367	1169	2581	1825	1337	1.6	NA	8.375	NA

Rimfire Ammunition — Ballistics & Prices

Note: The actual ballistics obtained with your firearm can vary considerably from the advertised ballistics. Also, ballistics can vary from lot to lot with the same brand and type load.

Cartridge	Bullet Wt. Grs.	Velocity (fps) 22-1/2" Bbl.		Energy (ft. lbs.) 22-1/2" Bbl.		Mid-Range Traj. (in.)	Muzzle Velocity
		Muzzle	100 yds.	Muzzle	100 yds.	100 yds.	6" Bbl.
17 Aguila	20	1850	1267	NA	NA	NA	NA
17 Hornady Mach 2	17	2100	1530	166	88	0.7	NA
17 HMR	17	2550	1902	245	136	NA	NA
17 HMR	20	2375	1776	250	140	NA	NA
22 Short Blank	—	—	—	—	—	—	—
22 Short CB	29	727	610	33	24	NA	706
22 Short Target	29	830	695	44	31	6.8	786
22 Short HP	27	1164	920	81	50	4.3	1077
22 Colibri	20	375	183	6	1	NA	NA
22 Super Colibri	20	500	441	11	9	NA	NA
22 Long CB	29	727	610	33	24	NA	706
22 Long HV	29	1180	946	90	57	4.1	1031
22 LR Ballistician	25	1100	760	65	30	NA	NA
22 LR Pistol Match	40	1070	890	100	70	4.6	940
22 LR Sub Sonic HP	38	1050	901	93	69	4.7	NA
22 LR Standard Velocity	40	1070	890	100	70	4.6	940
22 LR HV	40	1255	1016	140	92	3.6	1060
22 LR Silhoutte	42	1220	1003	139	94	3.6	1025
22 SSS	60	950	802	120	86	NA	NA
22 LR HV HP	40	1280	1001	146	89	3.5	1085
22 Velocitor GDHP	40	1435	0	0	0	NA	NA
22 LR Hyper HP	32/33/34	1500	1075	165	85	2.8	NA
22 LR Stinger HP	32	1640	1132	191	91	2.6	1395
22 LR Hyper Vel	30	1750	1191	204	93	NA	NA
22 LR Shot #12	31	950	NA	NA	NA	NA	NA
22 WRF LFN	45	1300	1015	169	103	3	NA
22 Win. Mag.	30	2200	1373	322	127	1.4	1610
22 Win. Mag. V-Max BT	33	2000	1495	293	164	0.60	NA
22 Win. Mag. JHP	34	2120	1435	338	155	1.4	NA
22 Win. Mag. JHP	40	1910	1326	324	156	1.7	1480
22 Win. Mag. FMJ	40	1910	1326	324	156	1.7	1480
22 Win. Mag. Dyna Point	45	1550	1147	240	131	2.60	NA
22 Win. Mag. JHP	50	1650	1280	300	180	1.3	NA
22 Win. Mag. Shot #11	52	1000	—	NA	—	—	NA

Above: Author's 12 year-old son likes the 41 Marlin, too. Right: The Marlin 1894FG

The right side of the long M657. The speedloaders are full of Remington 210-grain LSWCs.

AN ACCUMULATION OF 41 MAGNUMS

by Lee Arten

I've always been more interested in the 41 Magnum than in its bigger, older brother. It could be because when the 41 was introduced in 1964, I was buying my first gun magazines. I was also shooting 22 rifles in JROTC, learning to shoot handguns, and looking forward to my first deer season. Maybe I was influenced by gun magazine hype, or oddball guns might have already started to attract me.

I now own six 41 Magnums: five revolvers and a Marlin lever-action. It took me until the 1990s to buy my first, but since then I haven't looked back.

My son, Isaac, and I attended the late, lamented, Second Chance Bowling Pin Shoot. My first pins fell to an old 1911. A few years later, I was whacking them with a customized Para-Ordnance with an integrally compensated Hybrid barrel. The Para was a great pin gun, but I started to get the itch for a big-bore revolver. Since a 41 Magnum was also on my list, I decided a big Smith & Wesson 41 was what I needed.

Just as the 41 itch really began to need scratching, professional shooter Jerry Miculek posted a list of guns for sale at Second Chance. There were several good revolvers on it, but the one that caught my eye was a 6-inch M57. I asked to see it and Miculek dug it out of his trailer and handed it over. He said he'd never shot the gun and couldn't remember which match he'd won it in (I remember wishing I had that problem!). I found a ding in the finish on the recoil shield, and Miculek said he'd send the M57 back to Smith & Wesson and have it taken care of.

A couple months later the M57, completely reblued, arrived at my local dealer. I shot it a few times with the factory wood and then put on Pachmayr "Gripper" grips. Then I bought some speed loaders and started practicing shooting pins.

The next June, Isaac and I shot the M57 at Second Chance. My loads were made with Starline brass, a 210-grain LSWC bullet, Winchester primers, and 8.1 grains of Unique. They were light enough so we could recover from recoil and shoot quickly, but at around 1000 feet per second (fps), the pins left the table pronto, in a shower of splinters. I have photos of Isaac clearing a table with the M57 in the "Five Pin" event. He also used it to win a Ruger M77/22 in a special juniors event at the 1998 match.

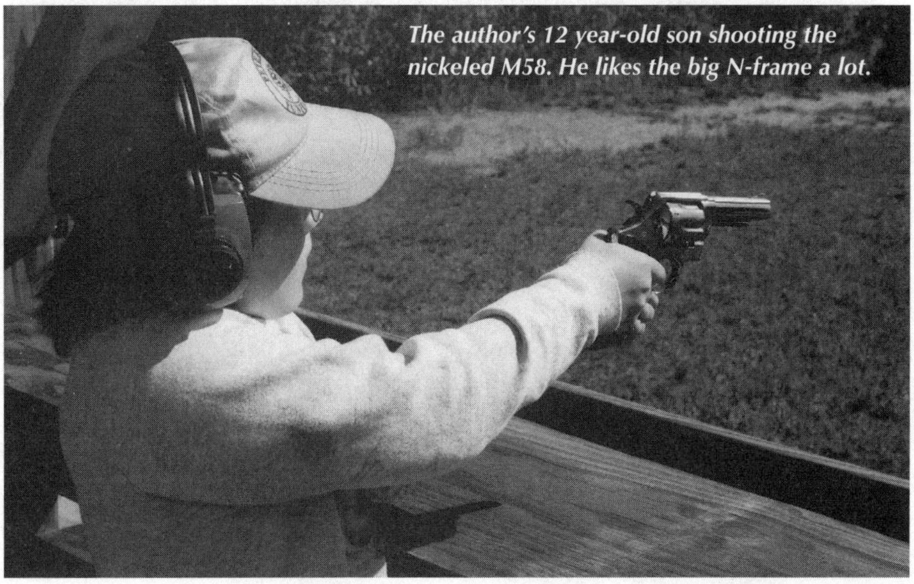

The author's 12 year-old son shooting the nickeled M58. He likes the big N-frame a lot.

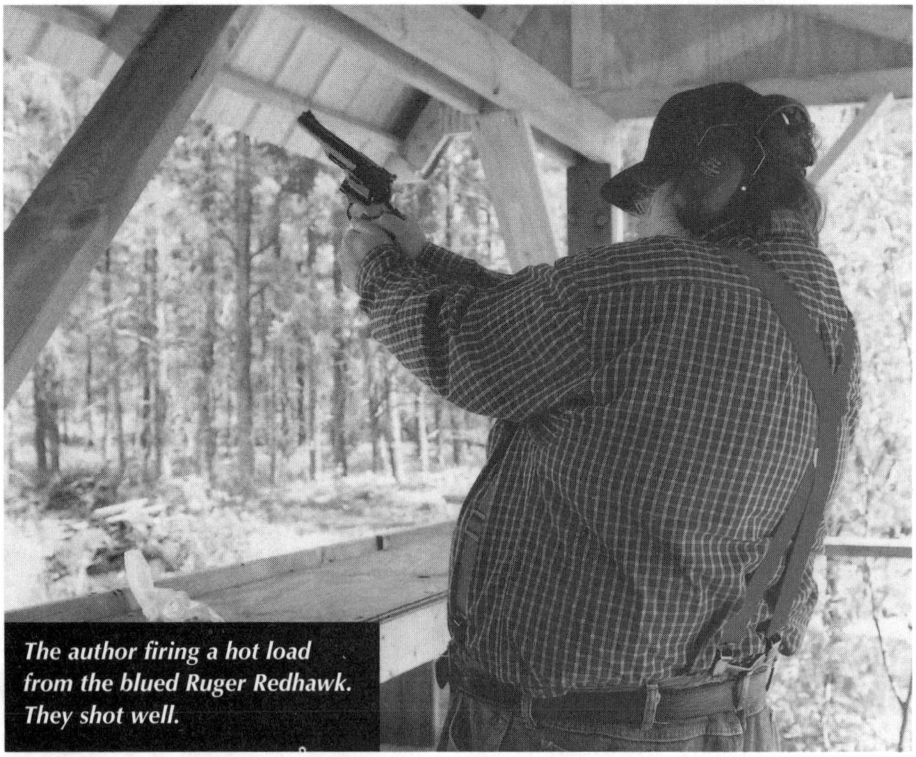

The author firing a hot load from the blued Ruger Redhawk. They shot well.

Cylinder & Slide from Fremont, Nebraska, used to set up a gunsmith's trailer at Second Chance. I took the M57 there one summer and had the trigger grooves smoothed off. I prefer smooth triggers for double-action shooting.

My brother Jon isn't as big a shooter as I am, but he had a 41 before me. Living outside Atlanta at the time, he walked into a gun shop one day and found discontinued stainless Ruger Redhawk 41 Magnums being sold off for $350 each. He pulled his wallet with a smooth, swift motion and bought one. I shot it a few times not long afterward and that ignited my desire for a 41 Magnum. Although I bought the M57 first, a 41 Redhawk stayed on my mind.

Jon moved to Florida and then, a few years later, to Saipan. He couldn't take his 41 with him, due to restrictive gun laws on the island. My Dad had it for a while, and then I got it from him.

The stainless Redhawk has a 7 1/2-inch barrel and is factory stock––a large, beefy revolver. I've thought of changing the grips, but probably won't. The Ruger factory grips are from a nice piece of walnut and are much more comfortable for me than the factory stocks on Smith & Wessons. The difference is especially evident when shooting heavy loads like 250-grain Federal Cast Cores. To me, the Redhawk's double-action trigger seems easier to manage than its single -action pull (I may just be spoiled by my Smith's trigger).

I found my next 41 Magnum when a retired cop I knew from Second Chance posted an ad on an Internet gun board. He wanted to move a 4-inch Smith M57, a 5 1/2-inch Ruger Redhawk 41, and a Marlin 1894S carbine in 41 Magnum. I was too slow with my checkbook and missed the carbine, but did manage to buy the Redhawk. The blued Redhawk is also big revolver. It came with black rubber Pachmayr Presentation grips that are big for my hands. They handle the recoil from heavy loads easily, but I'll probably put Pachmayr Grippers on the shorter Redhawk, eventually.

In the deal I also got hundreds of 41 cases, bullets, a bag of speedloaders and some loaded ammo. Since the guy was also from Michigan, and

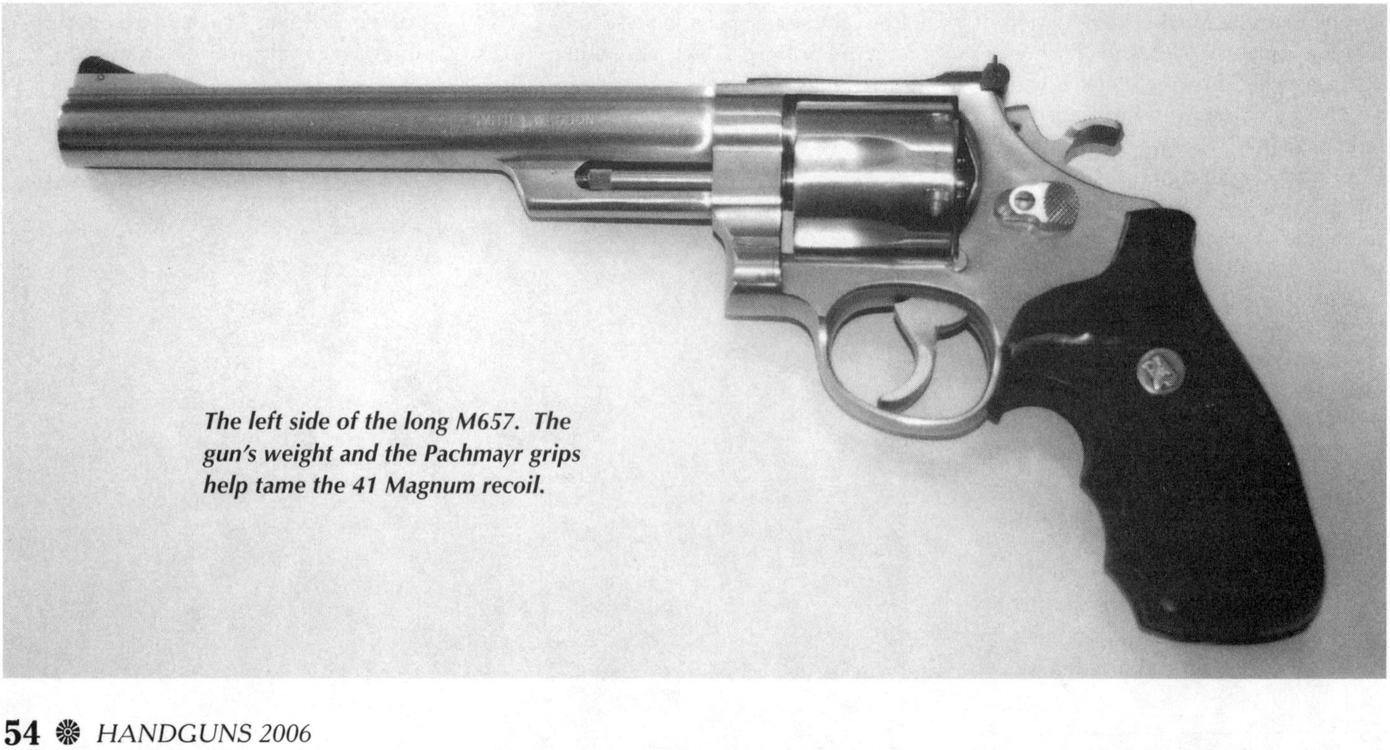

The left side of the long M657. The gun's weight and the Pachmayr grips help tame the 41 Magnum recoil.

felt like taking a ride, I got the stuff delivered too. (It was February and I appreciated not having to interrupt my hibernation and go on the road.)

The ammunition included 210-grain Remington jacketed softpoints and lead bullet "Police" loads. The lead loads shot well in most of my 41s. I wasn't surprised, since they were just a little slower than my bowling pin reloads. The blued Redhawk shoots lighter loads well, but seems to appreciate the hotter loads more.

I've been to two big Cabelas stores; one in Owatonna, Minnesota, and one in Dundee, Michigan. The Minnesota store left distinct memories. The aquariums full of fish from the region were neat, the mounted whitetail bucks were striking, and the African game display––complete with President Theodore Roosevelt's elephant––was spectacular. The same kind of displays must have been in Dundee, but I have only dim memories of mounted antelopes and a few fish. The thing I focused on, while my family roamed the store, was a factory nickel S&W M58. I toured The Gun Library first thing, of course, and spotted an N-frame with 41 Magnum on the tag in a case near the counter.

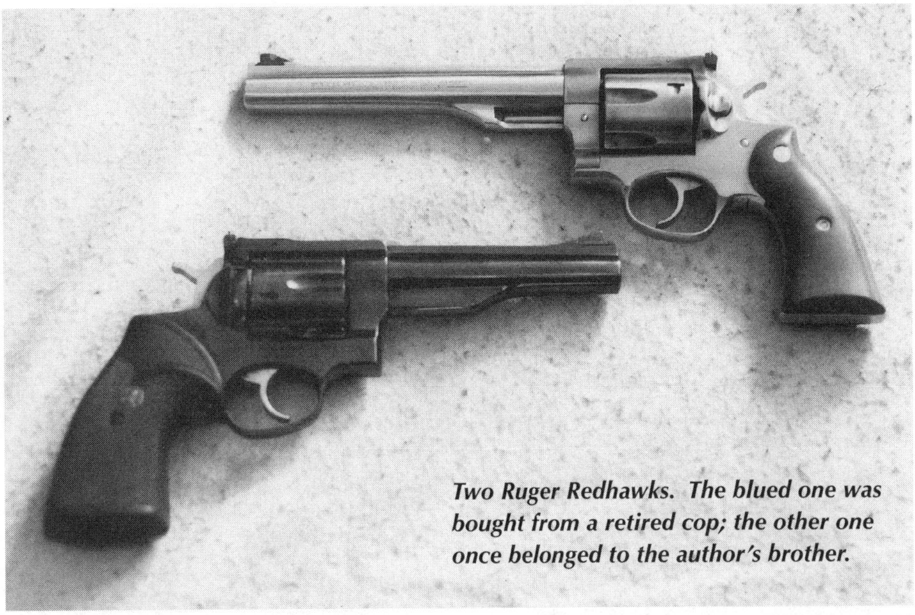

Two Ruger Redhawks. The blued one was bought from a retired cop; the other one once belonged to the author's brother.

"That's expensive for an M57," I thought, "Even nickeled." Right afterward I realized it was an M58!

A guy was concluding a deal on a rifle, so I had to wait to ask about the Smith. The leather wing chair I sat in was comfortable, but I was too intent on the M58 to enjoy it. When my chance came, I talked the salesman down a bit and slapped my credit card on the counter. I paid the same for the nickeled gun with Pachmayr Grippers, as was asked for a blued M58 I'd missed years earlier. I'd have changed the grips anyway, so I was

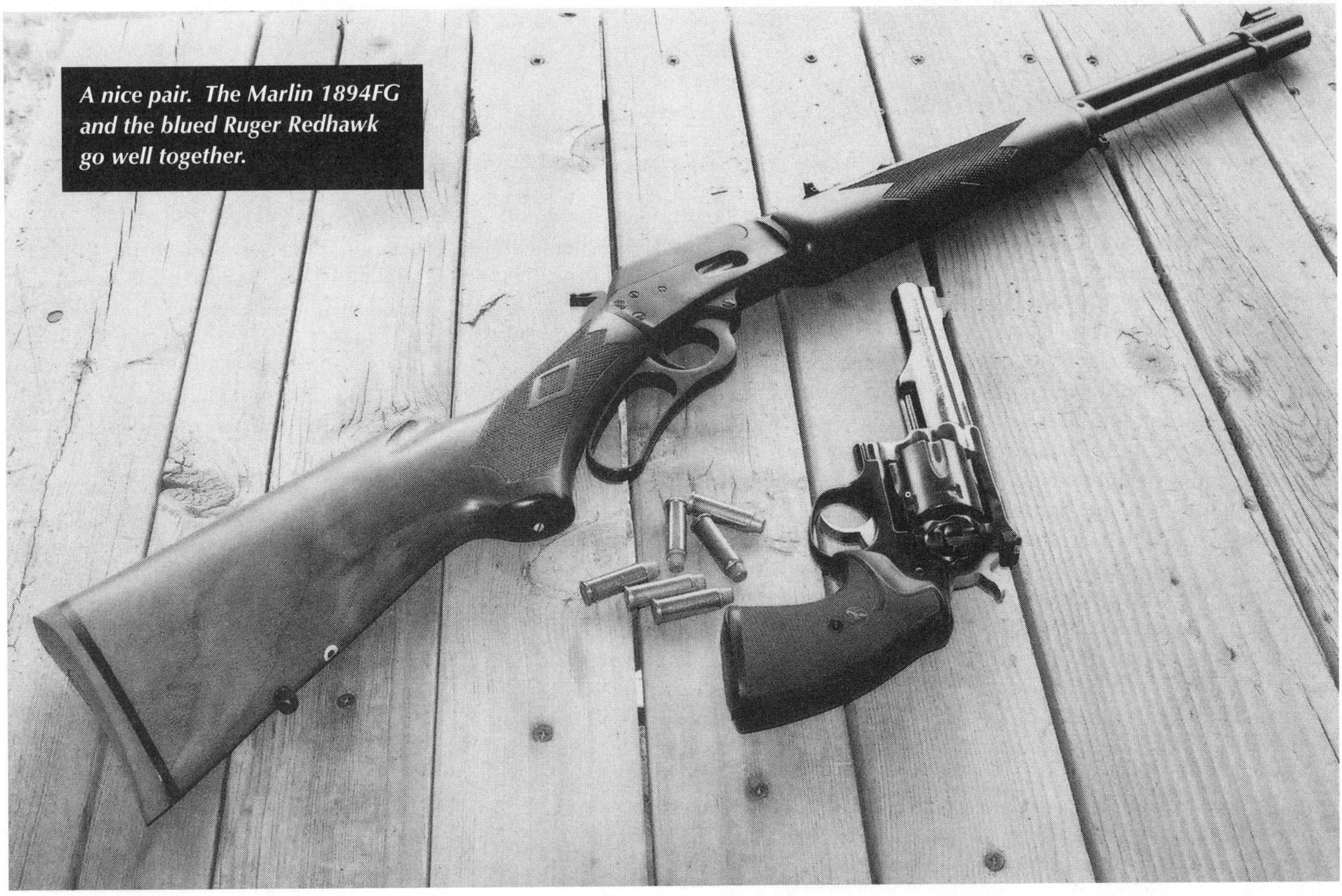

A nice pair. The Marlin 1894FG and the blued Ruger Redhawk go well together.

The author's collection of 41 Magnums (so far): From the top – Marlin 1894FG; S&W nickel M58; Ruger Redhawk, stainless; S&W M57, Ruger Redhawk, blued; and S&W M657 with 8 3/8-inch barrel.

happy. I've seen higher prices on M58s since I bought mine and that gives me another reason to grin.

The nickel on the M58 is bright, but the top strap and the top of the barrel are matted. The front sight has a red plastic insert. The gun had been shot, but I didn't think it had been fired much. The bore is great. The single-action trigger is good; the double-action trigger is heavier but usable.

The 4-inch M58 barks loudly, and bucks more than the M57 or the Rugers. It's quite accurate with LSWC loads, however. Sometimes, I shoot better groups with the M58 than with longer-barreled revolvers.

I intended to shoot the M58 in some IDPA matches and needed a holster. N-frame holsters are scarce here, so I ordered an El Paso Saddlery No. 88 "Street Combat" holster. Allergy flare-ups kept me out of the matches, but I've carried the M58 in the El Paso holster. Another that fits the M58 is a Ted Blocker thumb-break holster I bought to use with an M28. That was another Internet buy, found on the S&W Forum.

In late 2002 I heard rumors that Marlin was going to make a run of 41 Magnum carbines. In early 2003 I saw an announcement to that effect in a magazine. In March, I called Freeman's Firearms in Hancock, Michigan and asked my favorite dealer, Rick, if he'd heard anything about the new 41s.

"They're already back ordered," he said, "If you want one, I'd better order one now."

Production was supposed to take place in May and June but a call from his supplier surprised him in April. A few 41 Magnum carbines were already available. I didn't hesitate,

"Order me one!"

On April 30, Rick called. I'd been napping and said a drowsy "Hello." He said, "Your rifle's here."

That woke me up.

I picked the Marlin up the next day. I was impressed then––and still am. The 1894FG's bluing is dark and even. The pistol grip and forend are checkered. The wood has some figure, and sling swivel studs came installed. A hammer spur, an Allen wrench to install it, and a trigger lock are included. The rifle weighs a little less than six pounds empty, and has a solid feel. I sold a Rossi '92 in 357 to buy the Marlin and don't regret it.

I've been buying used firearms for years, usually getting good guns at bargain prices. Because used Marlin 41 Magnums are scarce, buying new seemed best. I'd run after a used Marlin 1894S for years, and the thrill had gone out of the chase.

My ammo stock included a quantity of 41 Magnum pin loads. They shot fairly well in the Marlin, printing groups in the 1 1/2-inch range at 50 feet. At 50 yards the groups grew to three inches. My eyes and the carbine's open iron sights didn't work together well at 100 yards. There, I made a 10 3/4-inch group on an International Silhouette target. I shot some faster loads with a 170-grain jacketed hollowpoint bullet, too. That load printed groups of 4 and 7 inches at 50 feet and 50 yards. I was cold and tired by then, so the problems may have been mostly with the shooter rather than the shooting iron.

I plan to put a receiver peep, or a tang sight, on the 1894FG. I haven't decided which to get, so I'm continuing to shoot the Marlin with the original buckhorn rear and hooded front post.

My 12 year-old son, Ethan, has been shooting 22s for almost half his life. Recently, he's been getting interested in larger calibers. He fired the M58 a few weeks ago, and put some rounds through the carbine last week. He liked both, and thinks he might like to hunt deer with the Marlin someday.

I went back to the Internet, and the used rack, for my most recent 41 Magnum. A long-barreled stainless Smith began to appeal to me strongly. I checked the gun sale sites on the net and found an M657 in California. I rescued it with my credit card, and had it shipped to my local dealer. The M657 has a couple of small scuffs near the muzzle on the right, and the front sight needs some touch-up paint. It has a split at the front of the Gripper grips, and a small cut in the side. All that was minor, and not a problem.

The long revolver has a target hammer, a smooth trigger, and the best single-action trigger I've found on any revolver. The double-action pull is heavier but also smooth and easy to manage.

Although I'd shot my 10-inch Contender in Hunter's Pistol Silhouette matches, the M657, with its 8 3/8-inch barrel, is the longest revolver I've fired. I'm pleased with the way it feels and shoots; the extra barrel length doesn't get in the way at the range, and the extra weight minimizes recoil.

Deer hunting came to mind when I first handled the M657. I stalked the last deer I killed to within 30 yards. It would have been a perfect shot for the iron-sighted M657. Before I bought the long revolver, I picked up a Bianchi X15 shoulder holster from a local dealer's bargain box. The M657 fits the Bianchi rig perfectly. It may be the only holster I use with the long revolver.

I'm happy with my six 41 Magnums, but still have some more on my list. I have narrowly missed a Ruger Blackhawk in 41 Magnum two or three times. I plan to buy the next one I see, and use it in cowboy action matches. I think it will look good next to the Marlin 41 and a 16-gauge side-by-side. Farther down the road, unless one turns up tomorrow, is a 3- or 4-inch Smith. I'd like a 3-incher in stainless or a nickel M57, in a heartbeat. Way down the road, I may dimly see a 41 Magnum Contender barrel. I don't think they're made any more, but they still pop up now and then.

Although I think of myself as a shooter, rather than a collector, I've been acting something like a collector when it comes to 41s. I started wanting one to use on pins, and an occasional or deer, or rabbit. Then, I decided I "needed" different varieties of the 41. Using that logic, suspect as it might be, I've acquired a nice collection of 41s, without even getting into S&W's dash numbers and special editions. I don't think I'll have to go there, but you never know. ❋

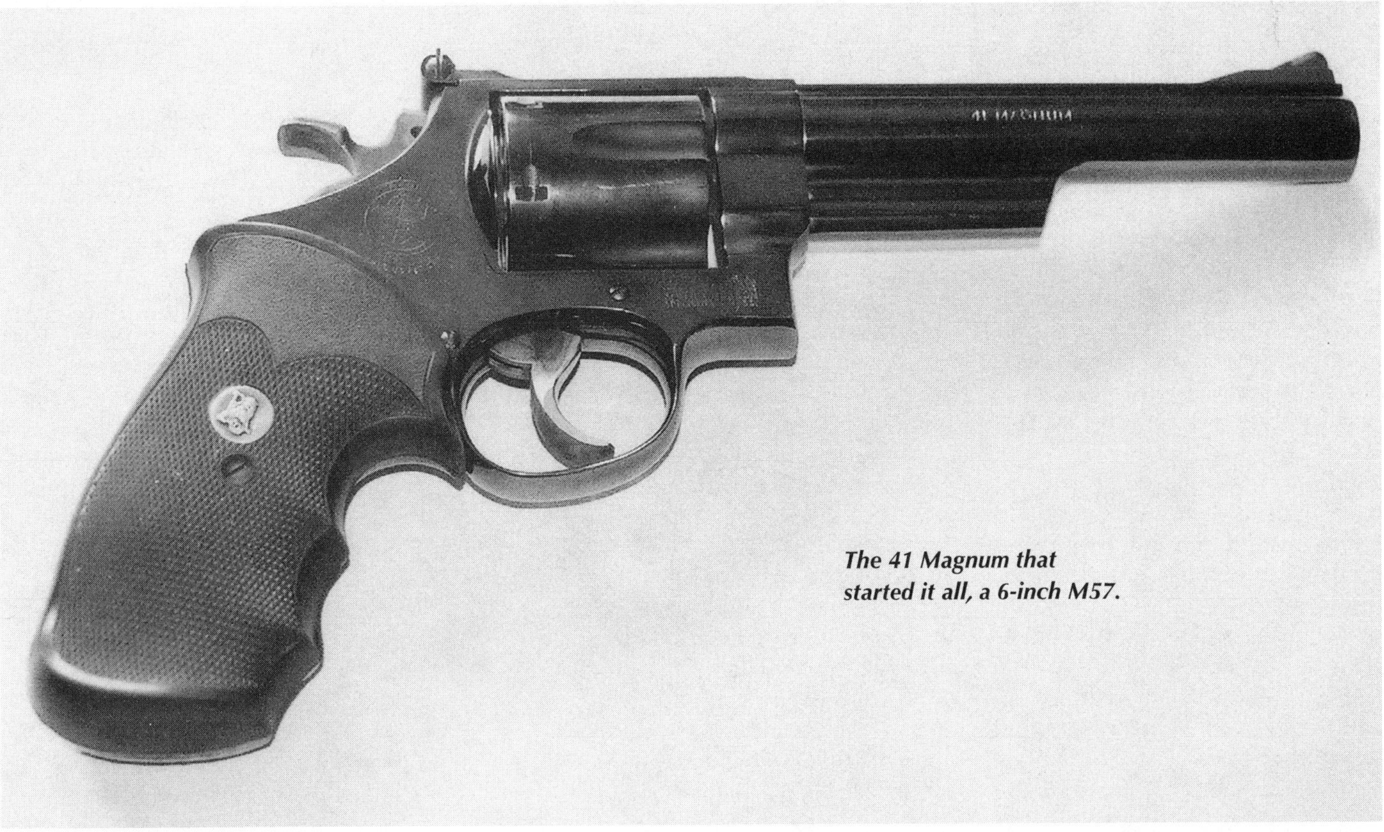

The 41 Magnum that started it all, a 6-inch M57.

Photo courtesy of Barry Lee Hands.

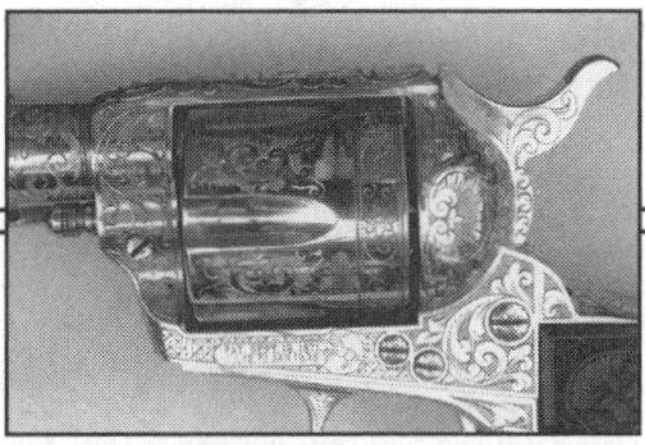

ENGRAVED & CUSTOM HANDGUNS

by Tom Turpin

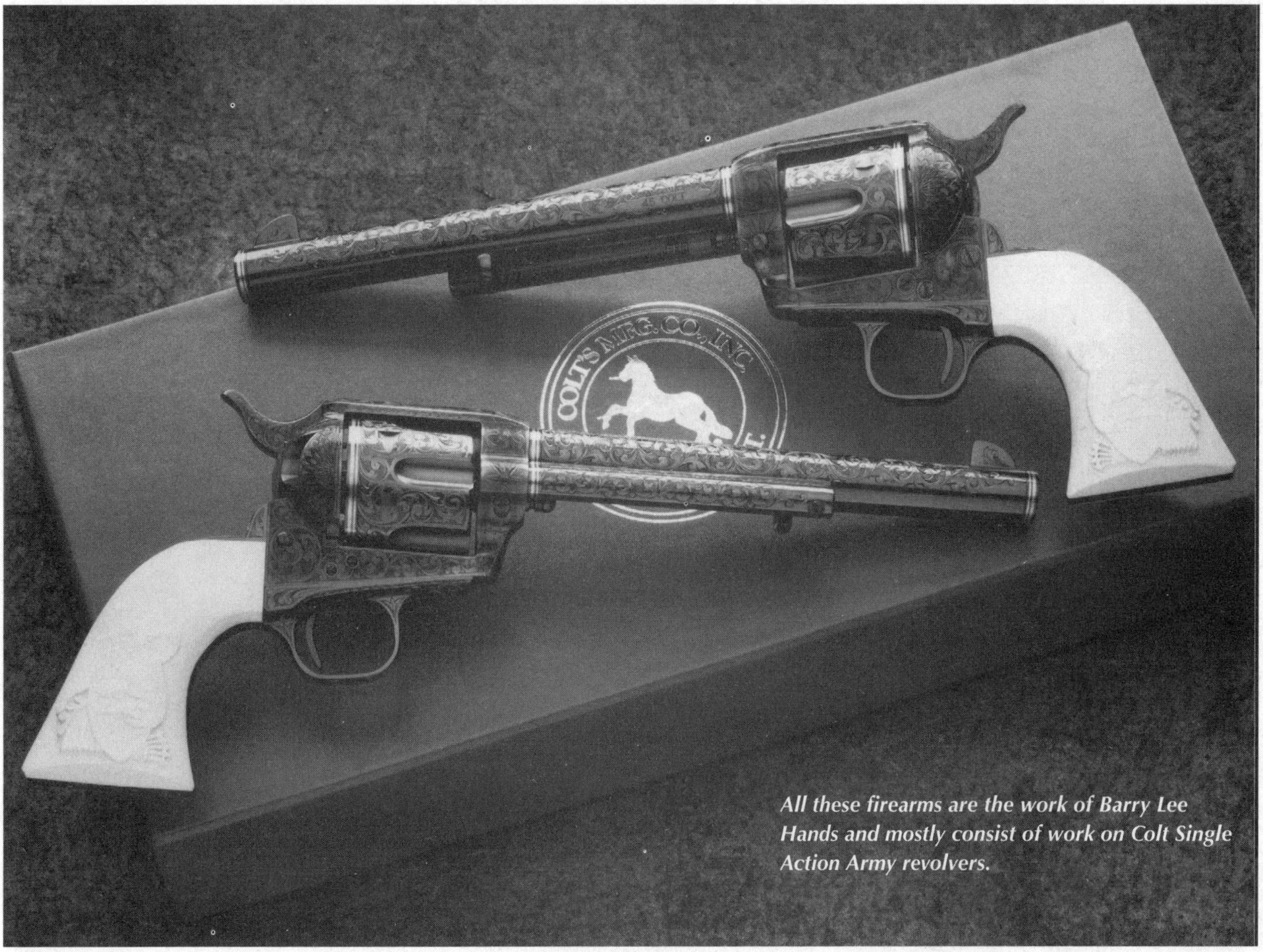

All these firearms are the work of Barry Lee Hands and mostly consist of work on Colt Single Action Army revolvers.

Photo courtesy of Barry Lee Hands.

BARRY LEE HANDS (*CONTINUED*)

Photo courtesy of Barry Lee Hands.

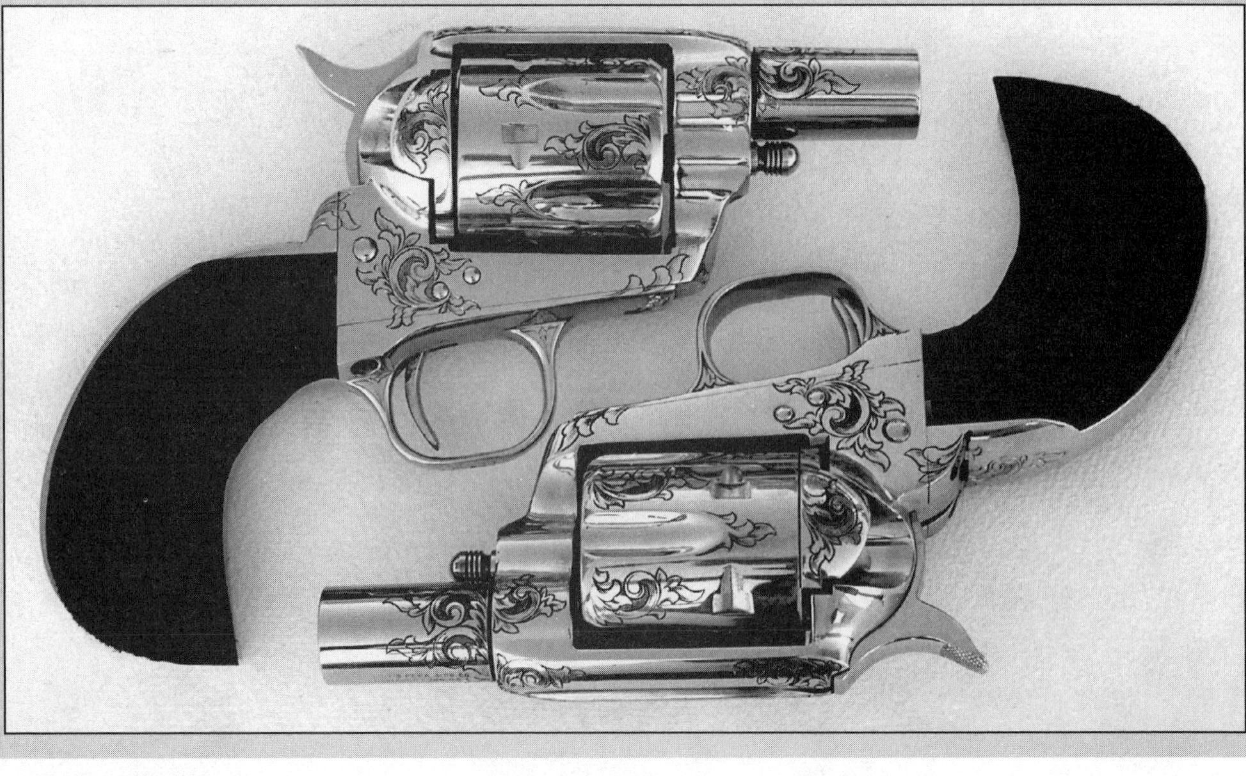

Photo courtesy of Barry Lee Hands.

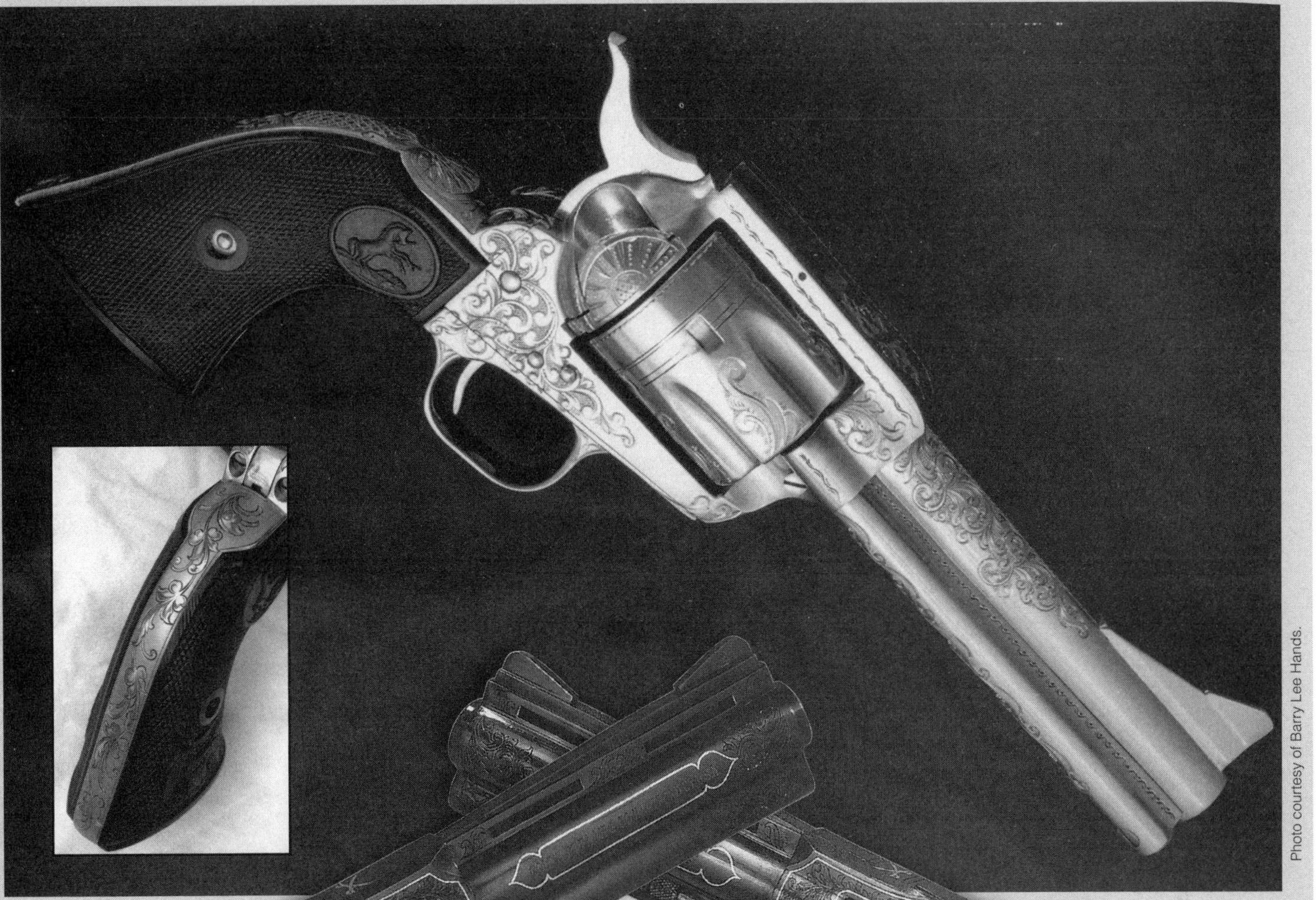

Photo courtesy of Barry Lee Hands.

Two views of a stock out-of-the-box Colt Diamondback revolver engraved in the Montana shop of Bill Rankin. The engraving and the gold line inlay work were executed by Rankin in accordance with the wishes of his client. Photo by Tom Alexander Photography.

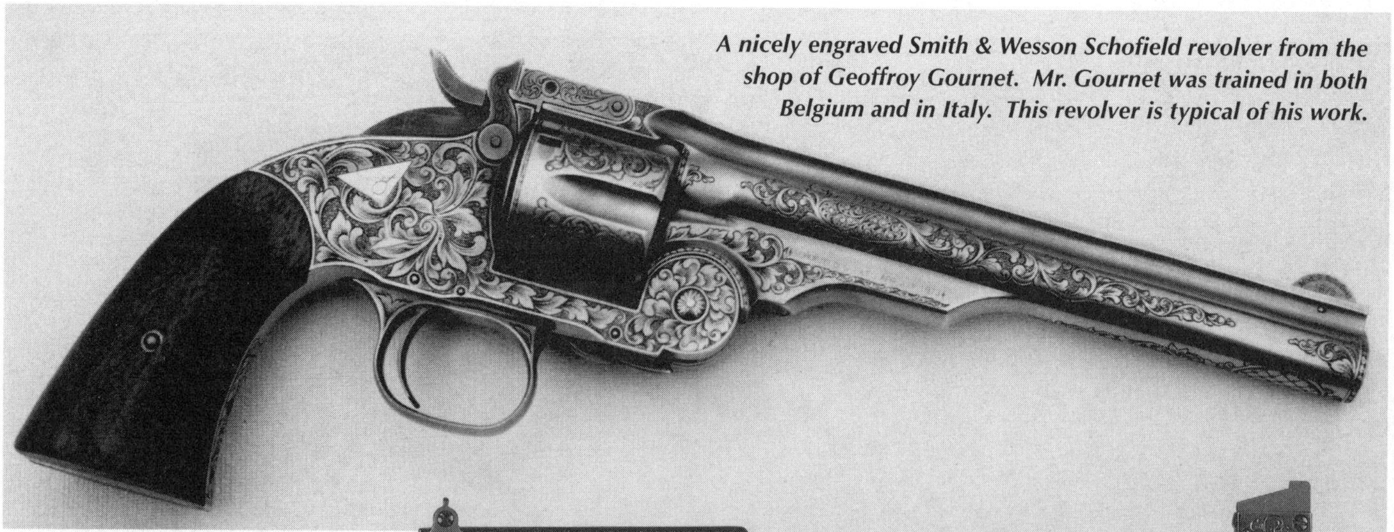

A nicely engraved Smith & Wesson Schofield revolver from the shop of Geoffroy Gournet. Mr. Gournet was trained in both Belgium and in Italy. This revolver is typical of his work.

Photo courtesy of Geoffroy Gournet.

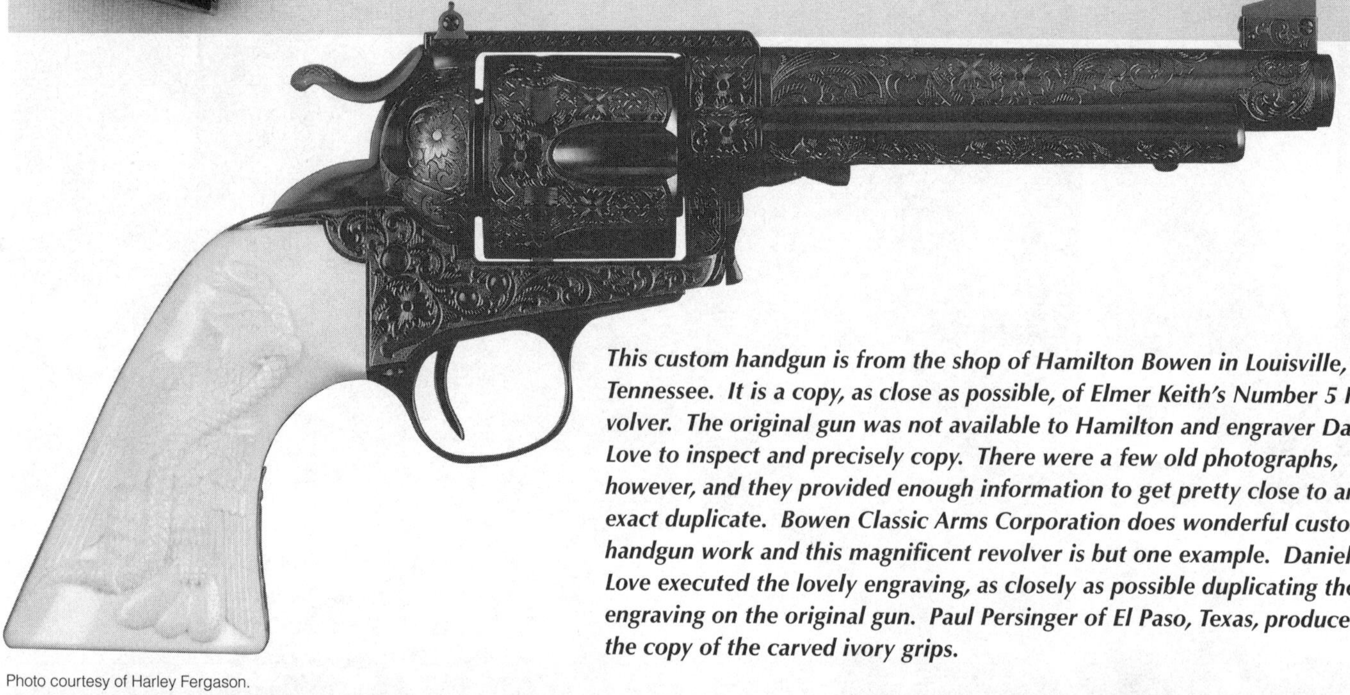

This custom handgun is from the shop of Hamilton Bowen in Louisville, Tennessee. It is a copy, as close as possible, of Elmer Keith's Number 5 Revolver. The original gun was not available to Hamilton and engraver Daniel Love to inspect and precisely copy. There were a few old photographs, however, and they provided enough information to get pretty close to an exact duplicate. Bowen Classic Arms Corporation does wonderful custom handgun work and this magnificent revolver is but one example. Daniel Love executed the lovely engraving, as closely as possible duplicating the engraving on the original gun. Paul Persinger of El Paso, Texas, produced the copy of the carved ivory grips.

Photo courtesy of Harley Fergason.

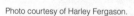

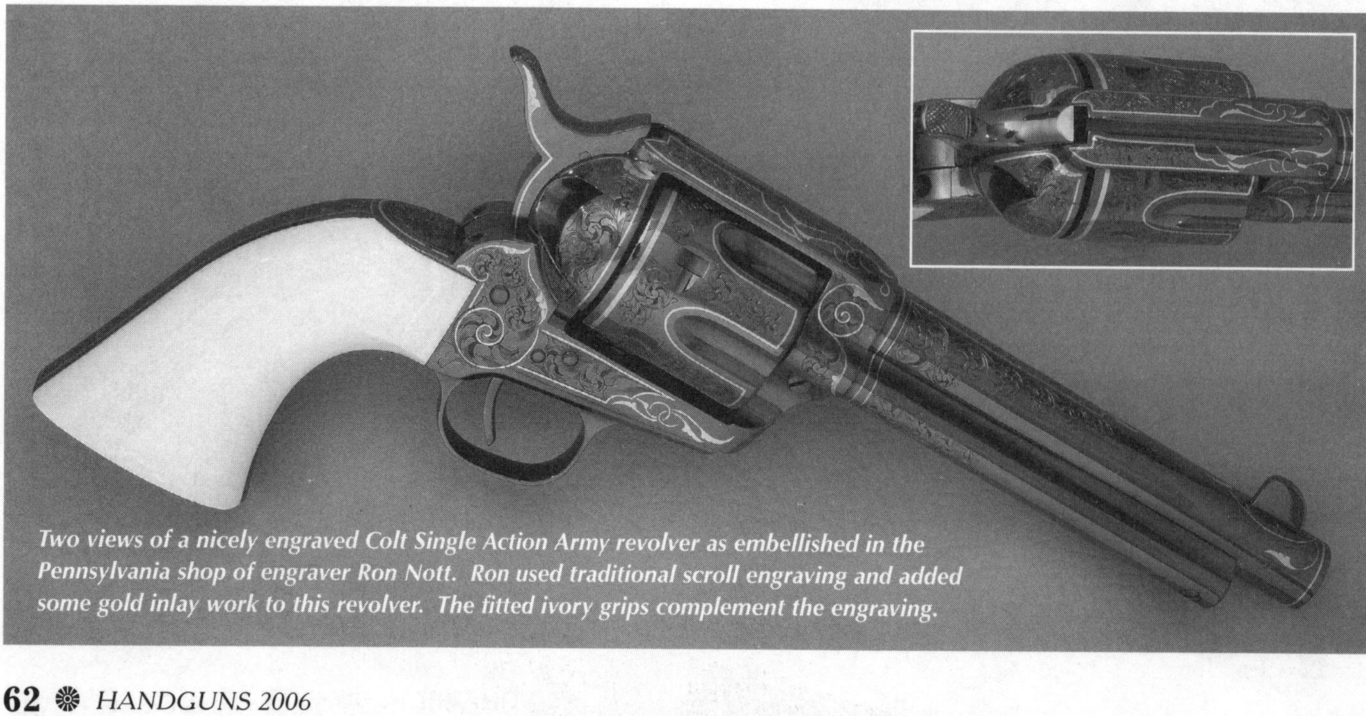

Two views of a nicely engraved Colt Single Action Army revolver as embellished in the Pennsylvania shop of engraver Ron Nott. Ron used traditional scroll engraving and added some gold inlay work to this revolver. The fitted ivory grips complement the engraving.

Photos courtesy of Tom Alexander Photography.

Photos courtesy of Tom Alexander Photography.

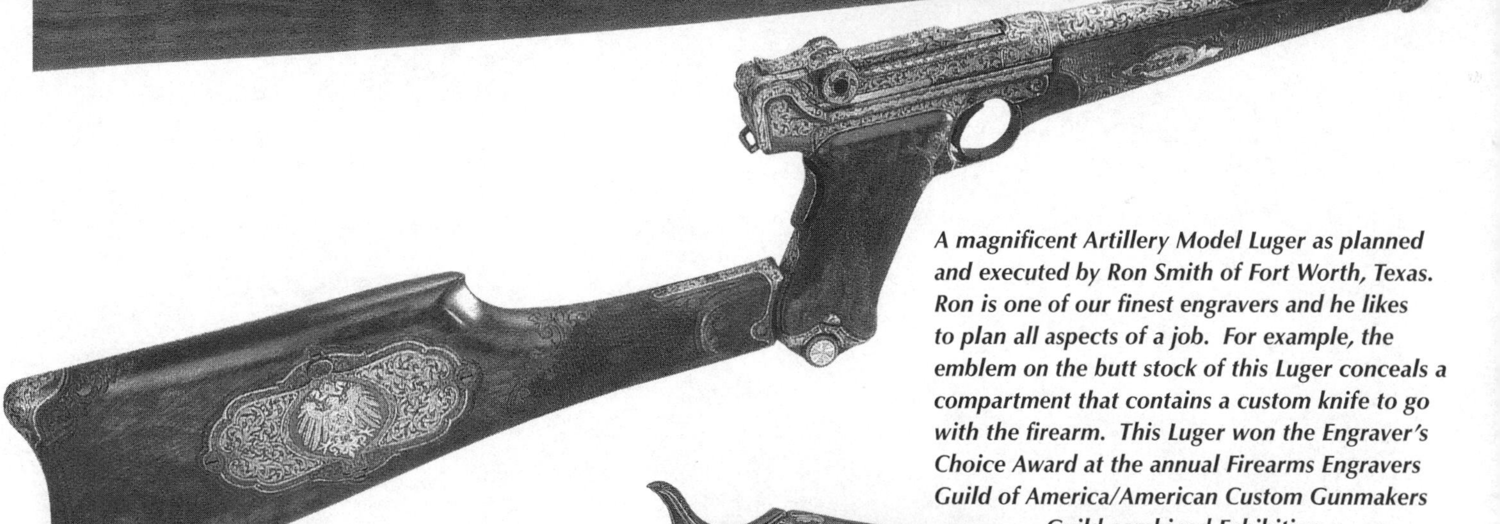

A magnificent Artillery Model Luger as planned and executed by Ron Smith of Fort Worth, Texas. Ron is one of our finest engravers and he likes to plan all aspects of a job. For example, the emblem on the butt stock of this Luger conceals a compartment that contains a custom knife to go with the firearm. This Luger won the Engraver's Choice Award at the annual Firearms Engravers Guild of America/American Custom Gunmakers Guild combined Exhibition.

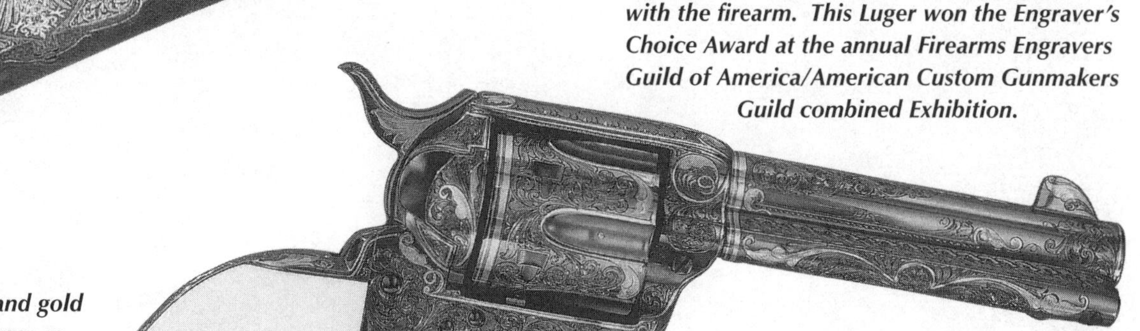

This superlative engraved and gold inlaid Colt Single Action Army revolver and matching belt buckle and accessories are the artistic work of Hoosier Mike Dubber. His shop in Evansville, Indiana is constantly turning out masterpiece examples of the engravers art.

Photo courtesy of Tom Alexander Photography.

Photo Courtesy United States Firearms Mfg. Co., Inc.

USFA: UNITED STATES FIRE ARMS

MANUFACTURING COMPANY

by Thomas D. Schiffer

The United States Fire Arms Manufacturing Company (USFA), located in Hartford, Connecticut, entered the firearms business a little over a decade ago. They manufacture single-action revolvers in many of the historic configurations. They also manufacture a pump-action re-creation of the old Lightning Magazine Rifle. These arms are machined from bar stock and finished in the United States; most of it right there in Hartford. At first, USFA's business involved importing parts for single-action pistols for assembly and finishing in Hartford. They did this under the "Blue Dome," recently vacated by the Colt Firearms Manufacturing Company, which lent a certain distinction to a fledgling company entering a competitive market.

About three years ago, USFA moved to a nearby, more modern facility and tooled up with state-of-the-art machinery. Today, some products are completely finished in-house; others are finished and heat-treated by Doug Turnbull, near Buffalo, New York. Turnbull's firm has made its way into the very center of finishing/heat-treat techniques for both new and refurbished arms. Refinishing classic old Parker shotguns, Winchester lever guns, Colts and a myriad of other arms well-known to collectors and shooters is grist for Turnbull's mill

Much of USFA's competition is from long-established overseas arms manufacturers. Among the products offered by USFA are rather exact reproductions of some of the most sought-after collector and shooter firearms of history. Along with the classic single-action six-shooter are the Flat Top Target, Bisley model and USFA's newly introduced re-creation of the old Lightning Model pump-action magazine rifle, out of production for over a century.

I had the opportunity to tour USFA's manufacturing facility in Hartford. While waiting in their reception area, I had occasion to observe a tiny corner of their production facility. My thinking was that the factory was not yet in production

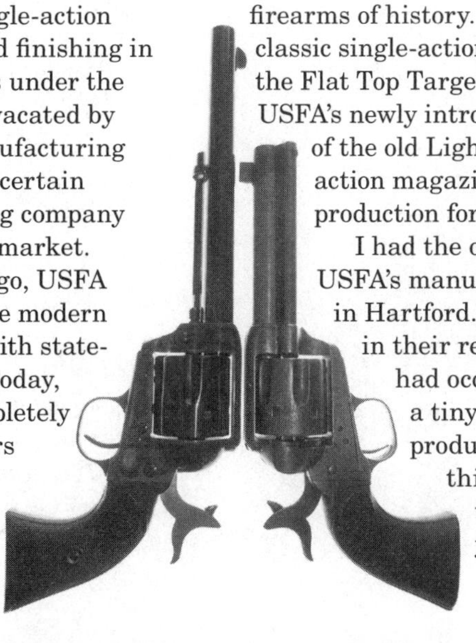

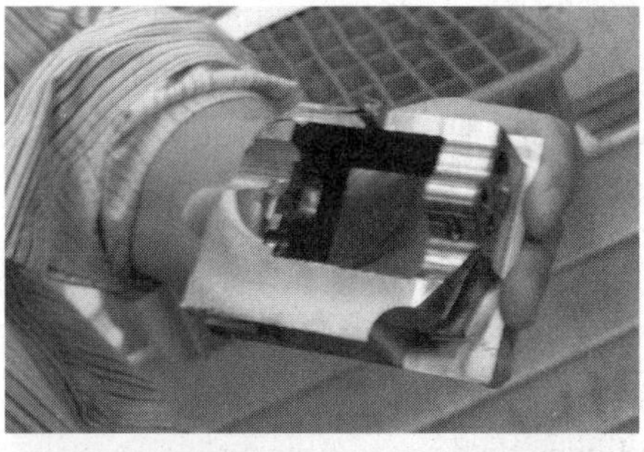

Top: Single-action frame shown here as the right side emerges from the solid block of 4140 steel.
Above: Tote pan with single-action cylinders.
Left: USFA 22 Plinker frame compared to center-fire frame, showing the difference in the firing pin location...the rimfire pin striking over an eighth inch higher in the frame. The centerfire pistol is a Colt made in 1881.

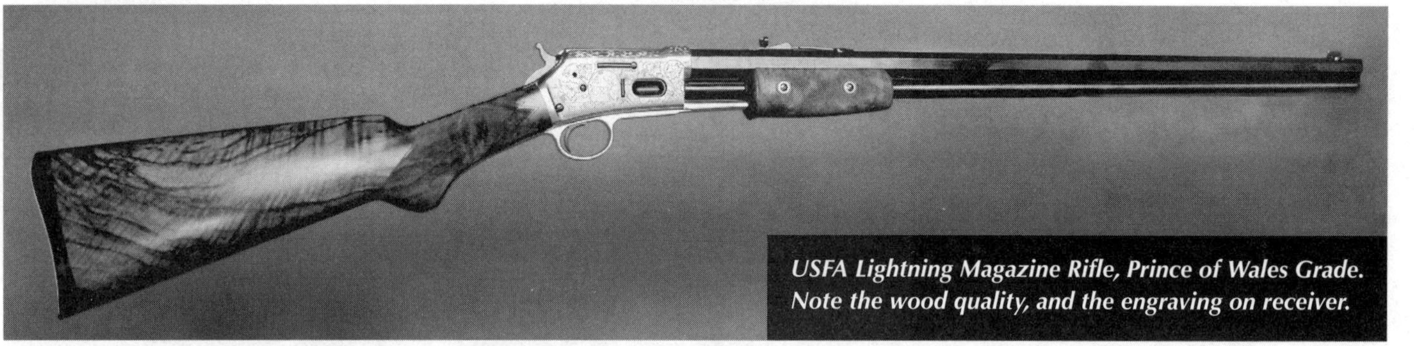

USFA Lightning Magazine Rifle, Prince of Wales Grade. Note the wood quality, and the engraving on receiver.

as the usual cutting oils had not soaked the floor covering or permeated the atmosphere within. Being ushered into their conference room I was able to observe a rick, or more likely, a cord or so of "lumber" that would quicken the pulse of anyone who knows fine gunstock wood.

Entering the production workspaces, however, made it very apparent that there was, indeed, production on-going. I saw single-action hammers, frames, backstraps and trigger guards emerge from simple blocks of 4140 steel. I was told about, but did not see, automatic lathes turning out screws, pins, firing pins and other essentially round-piece finished parts that lend themselves to these machines. They also have in-house electron discharge machines (EDM). These machines, with a shaped, sacrificial probe, can "punch" oddly-shaped holes into, or through, the hardest steel. These latter, I would suspect, are used to "mill" the mortise in the single-action frame for the hand (or pawl) that rotates the cylinder.

The machined parts are gathered and sent to the finishing department, where a great deal of skilled handwork is performed. Parts to be color case-hardened, such as frames and hammers, are sent to Doug Turnbull, then returned for final assembly. The plant appears clean, neat and up-to-date and, before I left, I noted the usual "hum" of activity that tells the practiced ear that all is going forward... periodically punctuated with the sound of shots from the testing/proving department.

The firearms observed in the USFA plant, and later on my range, gave the overall impression that they were the products of a century and more ago, without the patina of age. If there was any difference in general appearance, it was in favor of the current production. Ed McGivern, in his *Fast and Fancy Revolver Shooting,* (1938), after acknowledging some of its weaknesses, said of the single action: *"It is only fair, however, to call attention to the fact that if there were no other revolvers or pistols available, the army, navy and all law enforcement officers could fulfill all of their hand-gun shooting requirements in a very satisfactory and efficient manner with the single action revolvers."* His observation rings true to this day.

But, outside appearance does not address what is inside...what makes them tick. Accordingly, I asked for—and received—a firearm that could be taken apart and examined in detail, and then test-fired on my range. The first sent was their Gunslinger model, which is subjected to an aging process that makes it look like "your great-grandad's pistol." The general visual impression is that it is a run-of-the-mill ordinary pistol. However, cocking the hammer produces an evenly cadenced *...click... click...snick...clack*! , revealing that the timing of the cam, bolt and hammer notches are as they should be. Trigger pull is a very smooth, if a tiny bit creepy, 3-1/2 pounds on my scale. On single actions of this design, this is much better than all but some of the highly-tuned triggers from custom gunsmiths... and this is a production gun.

The empty, cocked pistol was then examined for cylinder end play *(none)*, slop on the bushing/axle *(none)* and tightness of the bolt lockup. This is the tightest such revolver—new, rebuilt, custom or otherwise—that I have handled over the past half-century. I could barely find any side-to-side play of the bolt. It was obvious the bolt snapped up at the correct time to avoid dragging on, and marking, the cylinder. Cocked slowly or rapidly, the bolt never failed to lock the cylinder firmly in position; nor was the action sticky.

Looking down the barrel of the empty pistol, with the hammer cocked and a strong light reflected into the

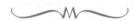

Left: USFA Gunslinger Model with antiqued finish.

Inset: 25-yard Standard American pistol target showing where the Gunslinger pistol, with its fixed sights, shot for me offhand. This group consists of two five-shot groups cut out and superimposed on the target.

Above: USFA 22 caliber Plinker Model Single Action pistol.

Left: USFA 22 Caliber "Plinker" Model. Not shown is the identical-appearing cylinder for the 22 WMRF cylinder that comes with it.

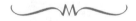

bore through the firing pin hole, did not reveal any misalignment. All screws in the pistol were found firmly set up, but not so much as to cause problems in disassembly. This included the bolt/trigger spring and the mainspring mounting screws, both of which were run up snugly, resulting in a bit stiffer mainspring than I prefer; likely "the way they were."

Shooting the pistol on my range had to be done offhand. As is usual in fixed-sight pistols, the point of impact was not exactly centered for *me*. I shoot in the old one-hand, arm-extended fashion, not the modified Weaver or other two-handed stances that are so favored *(and effective)* today. I took two of my better five-shot groups, cut them out and placed them to advantage *(as if the group was centered on the X-ring)*, and scored 97x100 on the Standard American 25-yard pistol target... about the limit of my ability in recent years. Slight surgery on the front sight would raise the point of impact, and tightening the barrel slightly would move the group into the 10-ring, if not the X-ring. This is work best trusted to a knowledgeable gunsmith.

Looking at the fired primers revealed the firing pin indents were perfectly centered, a strong indication the machining was accurately done, allowing all of the parts to function together within close tolerances. Being a bit off-center will not really affect ignition...most revolver indents are a bit off-center. But seeing the indent centered is a strong indication the barrel and cylinder chambers have their respective centerlines in close coincidence; a critical relationship with respect to the accuracy of the revolver. Cylinder/barrel gap ran about 0.004/0.005-inch on the two pistols that I measured. The rifling pitch was left-hand in the 38 Special and right-hand in the 22 LR .

A 22 LR Plinker model was also sent for evaluation. It has the classic single-action case-hardened frame and blued trim. The "plain Jane" single-action finish appears to be a "foot or so deep;" polishing is excellent. The sides of the frame are almost optically flat, and the backstrap and trigger guard flats blend with the frame sides. Of course, one surface is blued and the other case-colored, which makes for a stunning, yet nearly seamless contrast. A plus, as far as I am concerned, is the lack of recessed cartridge heads in the rimfire cylinder chambers. One glance into each side of the revolver frame *(if you know where and how to look)*, and you can see if there are cartridges in the chambers, or not—all without touching the hammer or loading gate. I hope the day is long past when there are concerns about burst cartridge heads. Rimfire 22 cases were upgraded about 1930, when copper was abandoned as rimfire cartridge case material.

This is but a sampling of the full line of single actions in the current USFA catalog. Some of their current single-action designs *(both standard and Bisley)* have patent protection, and the USFA Custom Shop adds yet another dimension.

The proof of the pudding is in the eating, and the proof of a firearm is in the using. If the experience with the single action is any indication, the "pudding" will likely be tasty indeed. The rifle sent, and all others I saw in the USFA plant, certainly pass visual muster.

The seed for this article was planted by my friend, the late John Bivins. One of John's long rifles, combining his rather unique mix of artistry and history with impeccable craftsmanship, graced the cover of Gun Digest back in 1977, and led to our getting acquainted. As our friendship deepened over the years, we decided we would create two 44-caliber flat-top single-action target pistols—one for each of us.

Unfortunately, John passed away in 2001 and the project languished. Last fall, friend and custom pistolsmith Hamilton Bowen told me that USFA was again producing flat-top single-action pistols. Since, in my opinion, the USFA products fit Bivins' rather stringent ideas of what proper fit, finish and function of firearms should be, I believe I will have USFA bring this dream to fruition. USFA also has a policy of allowing custom serial numbers, and I can have one made with John's touchmark or hallmark, "I B", as part of the serial number. ❋

Beretta's Mini Cougar in 45 ACP, an excellent downrange performer, easily shooting 10-shot "cloverleaf" groups with Hornady's Custom 200-grain JHP/XTP ammunition.

The Beretta Mini Cougar

GONE BUT NOT FORGOTTEN

by Jerry Burke

He was a master barrel-maker; that's "gun" barrel, not the type used to age fine wine. His name was Bartolemeo Beretta, and although a contemporary of Michelangelo and da Vinci, he took his creativity in a different direction. Beretta created the Italian firm of Fabbrica d'Armi P. Beretta in 1526, and every generation of the Beretta family since that time has carried on his tradition of innovation and superb craftsmanship. Of course, the biggest "splash" Beretta's American subsidiary has made thus far was the 1985 selection of the Model 92F as the standard issue sidearm for all U.S. armed forces. In addition, more than 1000 law enforcement agencies in the U.S., not to mention numerous military organizations world-wide, rely on the 9mm 92F and the Model 96 in 40 S&W every day.

In 1995 Beretta followed the success of the 92/96 by introducing compact semi-autos, dubbed the Cougar 8000 Series, which were designed primarily as undercover law enforcement weapons. Then, Beretta took the concept one step further with the introduction of the Mini Cougar series in 1998. Neither the Cougar nor the Mini Cougar pistols are chopped-down versions of the 92/96, but designed-from-the-ground-up pistols using a proven locked-breech system with rotating barrel. This locking system requires a closed-slide design, breaking Beretta's open-slide tradition but producing results well worth the change. The barrel rotates approximately 30 degrees as the slide travels to the rear during the firing sequence; and, rotates back the same distance during forward movement of the slide. Add a central block which helps absorb the recoil shock of barrel and slide before it is transferred to the frame, and the result is unusually

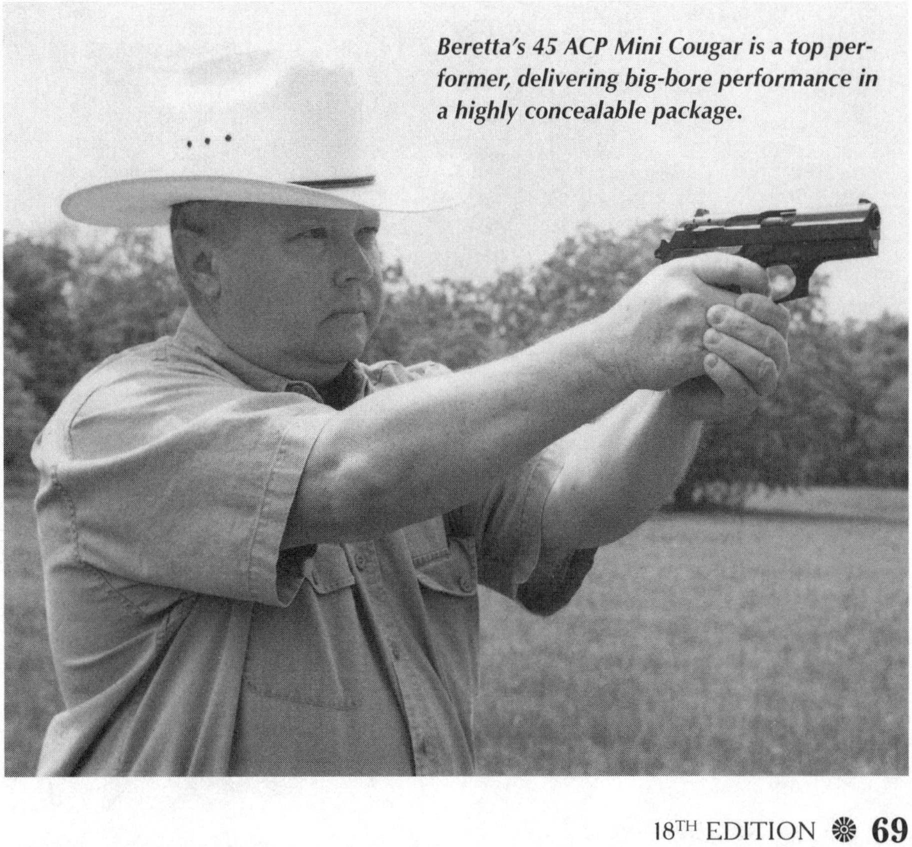

Beretta's 45 ACP Mini Cougar is a top performer, delivering big-bore performance in a highly concealable package.

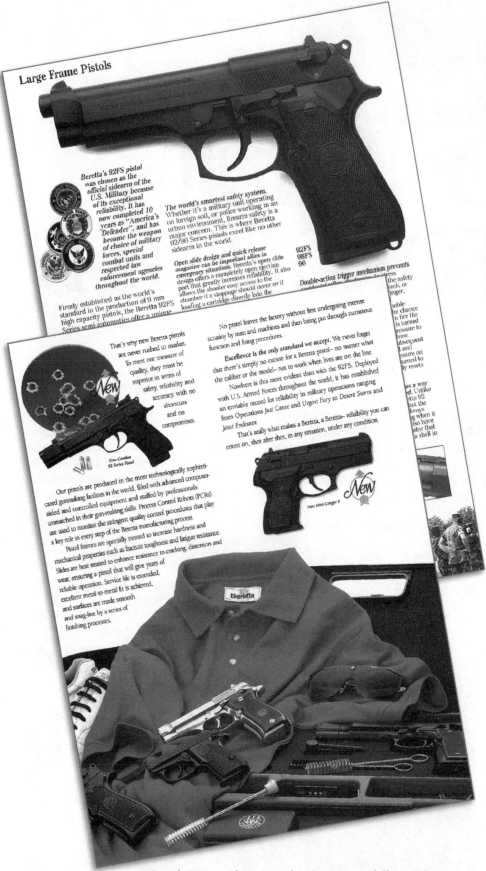

1995 and 1998 catalog pages showing Beretta followed the success of the 92/96 by introducing compact semi-autos in 1995, dubbed the Cougar 8000 Series, which was taken one step further with the introduction of the Mini Cougar series in 1998

limited "felt" recoil. Besides making training easier and practice sessions more enjoyable, reduced recoil allows the shooter to fire accurate follow-up shots with greater speed.

The Cougar/Mini Cougar series' short-recoil action and in-line feeding system between the top round in the magazine and the barrel chamber not only contribute to the accuracy of these handguns but perhaps more importantly, their reliable functioning. The frames, crafted from an aluminum alloy used in high-performance jet aircraft landing gear, are contoured to make the Cougar/Mini Cougar series popular with small-handed shooters, while providing plenty of protection for those with average-to-extra-large paws. A horizontally-serrated trigger guard face accommodates the index finger for those using a 2-hand grip, and the trigger guard itself is large enough to allow operation of the handgun while wearing gloves. Barrels are cold hammer-forged and hard chrome-lined for added strength and exceptional durability. Potentially snagging edges all over these Beretta handguns have been rounded or beveled, solving a number of potential problems before they can occur. Beretta applied their exclusive Bruniton non-reflective matte-black finish to the Cougar/Mini Cougar series pistols, providing superior corrosion resistance.

For safety's sake, both the Cougar and Mini Cougar Berettas have the same system found on their larger 92/96 Model counterparts. Most obvious is the ambidextrous manual safety on "F" Models, which also doubles as a decocking lever. When the hammer is cocked and the safety-decocking lever is pressed downward, the hammer is lowered while the firing pin unit is shielded from the hammer blow; the safety-decocker remains in the lowered or *ON* position and the linkage between trigger and sear is disconnected. There's also an automatic firing pin safety; when the trigger is not pulled completely back, a blocking device secures the firing pin and prevents it from moving forward. There's also a chamber-loaded indicator, providing evidence both visually and by touch if there is a cartridge in the chamber. In addition,

A Kuartet of Kompact Kahrs

THE PM9, PM40, TP9 AND T40

by Paul Scarlata / photos by James Walters

The readers of this fine publication are no doubt familiar with the Kahr Arms Company. Established in Blauvelt, New York in 1993 to produce the revolutionary K9 pistol, they quickly became a major player in the concealed-carry handgun market with a line of compact and subcompact pistols that have proven capable of handling the hottest 9x19 and 40 S&W ammunition with aplomb.

Kahr's pistols are not, as are the compacts offered by many companies, merely cut-down versions of larger handguns. They were designed from the ground up for one purpose—close-range personal protection by plain-clothes officers and licensed civilians—and thus include all the features one might desire from a small, lightweight handgun intended for concealed carry.

Their pistols' biggest claim to fame is, without a doubt, its Double Action Only (DAO) trigger. I am a big fan of this style of trigger on semiauto pistols and am being completely honest when I tell you that Kahr handguns feature some of the smoothest DAO triggers I have ever felt on a semiauto pistol. This is accomplished by means of a cocking cam system in which a trigger stroke of approximately 5/8-inch rotates a cam that unlocks the passive safety, completely cocks and releases the striker.

Kahr pistols have no external safety levers; instead, in the partially-cocked position, a spring-loaded Striker Block immobilizes the striker from any

Below: Kahr's PM40 (top) and PM9 are the smallest pistols available in 40 and 9mm on today's market. They are perfect choices for concealed carry by plainclothes/off-duty police and licensed civilians.

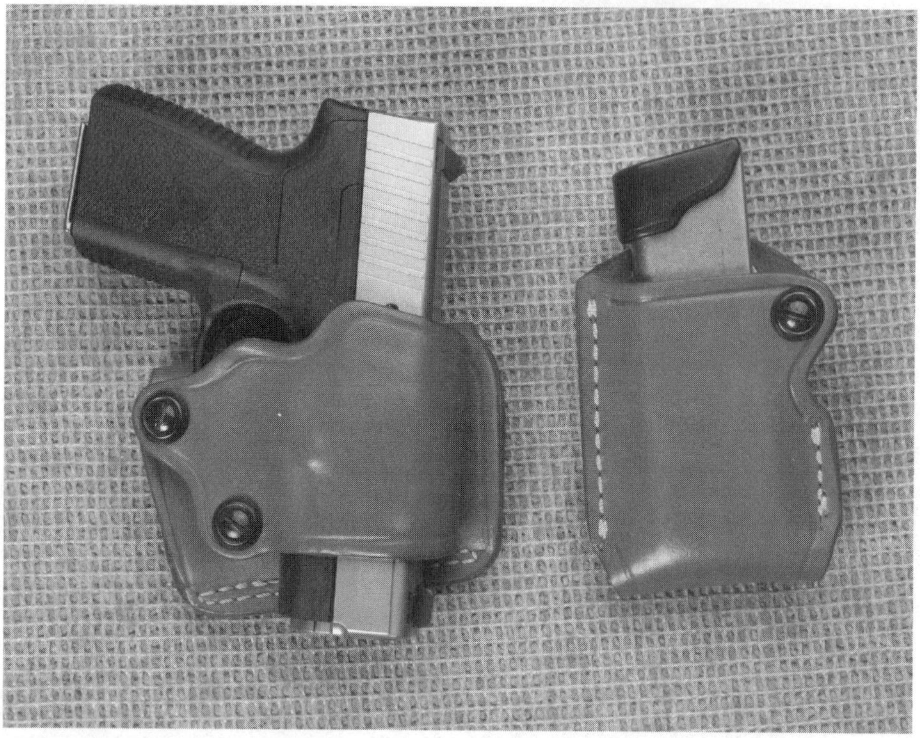

The Gould & Goodrich Yaqui Slide holster's design allows it to be used with all models of Kahr pistols. It provides complete concealment, comfort—and allows a fast, snag-free presentation.

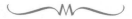

movement whatsoever and which is released only when the trigger is pulled through a full stroke. The absence of external controls give Kahr pistols a snag-free exterior—very important for a pistol meant to be carried concealed; simplicity of operation is an essential trait for any handgun intended for personal protection. In use the drill is simple: draw pistol, aim, pull trigger. When you are done shooting, all one must do to make the pistol "safe" is remove their finger from inside the trigger guard.

Breech locking is achieved by the barrel hood moving up into the ejection port where its front edge bears against the slide, locking both units together. As the two units move rearward under recoil, a cam groove on the barrel lug articulates on the slide stop shaft, pulling the barrel down, unlocking it from the slide. The slide continues to the rear, extracting and ejecting the spent cartridge case, then the recoil spring pulls it forward, stripping the next round out of the magazine and chambering it. As the slide goes into battery, the barrel hood moves up into the ejection port, locking the barrel and slide together while the striker remains in a semi-cocked position, locked in place by the Striker Block.

Despite their small size, all Kahr pistols display excellent ergonomics and with their "larger" pistols, a full three-finger grip is possible. This was accomplished by the use of an "offset barrel" design which places the trigger mechanism beside the barrel lug, instead of under it, permitting the grip frame to be designed so the shooter can get a very high, controllable, grip close to the centerline of the bore. The result being a small, but remarkably controllable, pistol with reduced muzzle flip and felt recoil.

Lastly, reliability is enhanced by a self-cleaning extractor that is designed to force powder residue away from the extractor, preventing fouling buildup. In addition, the extractor is designed so that it employs the slide itself to limit its movement, drastically reducing the possibility of failure to extract. Six U.S. patents were obtaining covering the Kahr's locking, firing and extraction systems.

In 2000, Kahr joined the "plastic revolution" with the introduction of their P9 pistol. The polymer frame contains the normal "innards" but the slide reciprocates on dual metal inserts at the rear of the frame rails. The P9 was soon followed by the 40-caliber P40 and P40 Covert pistols in addition to the PM9, the smallest 9mm Para pistol available on today's market. To say that Kahr pistols have proven popular for concealed carry by law enforcement officers and licensed civilians would be a gross understatement...so I won't say it.

But what about those shooters who

All test firing was performed with Cor-Bon's new DPX ammunition. Performance and accuracy were excellent.

Left: The PM9's seven-round magazine not only provides additional firepower but a full, three-finger grip. The PM40 also comes with a longer magazine that provides an extra round of firepower.

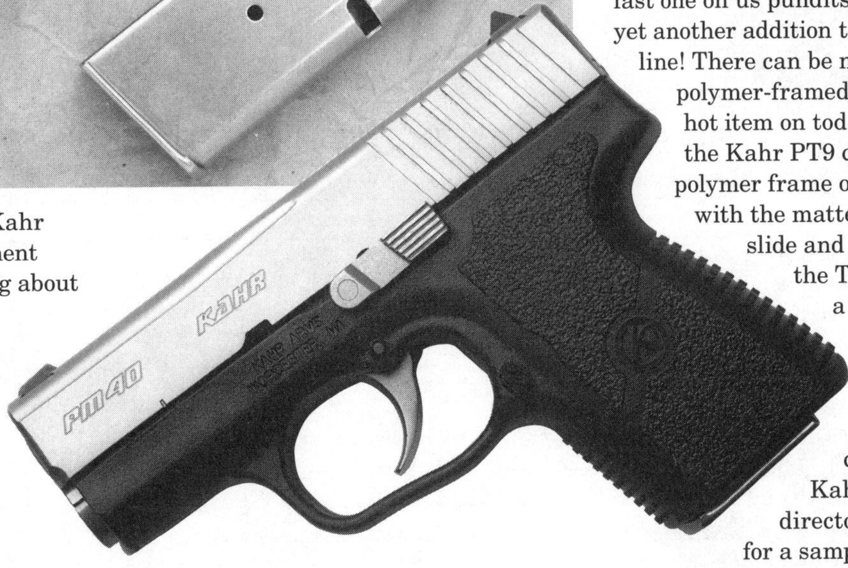

Below: Being dimensionally identical to the PM9, the PM40 is the smallest 40-caliber pistol available today.

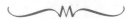

wanted all the benefits of the Kahr system, but for whom concealment was not a necessity? I'm talking about people who wanted a pistol for home defense and those police agencies or security personnel who have not been taken in by the high-capacity myth. Well, as behooves any entrepreneurial organization in our capitalistic system, the marketing boffins at Kahr put this to their designers who came up with the T9 Tactical and T9 Target.

Based upon the tried and true Kahr DAO mechanism, the T9 pistols differed from their predecessors in height, length, weight and magazine capacity. With their 4-inch barrels, these 100-percent stainless steel pistols were 0.5-inch longer, 0.45-inch taller, and weighed 3.1 ounces more than the standard K9. These dimensional changes translated into improved ergonomics, balance, recoil control, higher bullet velocity, larger magazine capacity and—thanks to the longer sight radius, accuracy— all in a package that is still light enough to carry all day in complete comfort and slim enough for people with small hands to shoot comfortably. The only difference between the Tactical and Target models is that the former comes equipped with Novak night sights while the latter features MMC adjustable sights.

While their PM9 and T9 pistols were hot-selling items, the aforementioned marketing types began to ponder whether or not they could sell more pistols if they chambered this pair of proven products for the most popular pistol cartridge on the American market—the 40 S&W. Hmmmmm..........? "Well...," they decided, "...there is only one way to find out."

Thus it came about that at the 2004 SHOT Show, Kahr introduced two (three?) new pistols: the PM40, T40 Tactical, and T40 Target. As the more astute of our readers have already ascertained, the only differences between these and the PM9 and T9 pistols are the cartridges they are chambered for. Other than lower magazine capacities dictated by the fatter 40-caliber cartridge and weighing slightly more, their dimensions are identical. Now that I think about it, the PM40 holds claim to being the smallest 40-caliber pistol available on today's market.

But the folks at Kahr then pulled a fast one on us pundits by announcing yet another addition to their extensive line! There can be no denying that polymer-framed pistols are the hot item on today's market, so the Kahr PT9 combines the polymer frame of the P9 series with the matte stainless steel slide and 4-inch barrel of the T9 pistols. Who'd a thought.....?

With this plethora of pistols before me, I had no choice but to ask Kahr's marketing director Frank Harris for a sampling to put through their paces. Being I was already the proud owner of a PM9, I requested a PM40, a TP9 and a T40 with the MMC sights. When this trio of Kahrs arrived, I found little to be excited about—but I don't mean that as a negative remark. I have owned Kahr pistols since they first hit the market and I have always found them to be made from high-grade materials, exhibit excellent workmanship, above average ergonomics and that trigger pull....well, you just have to try one to understand what I'm talking about.

For the last several months I have been suffering from a severe case of "writer's wrist," better known as carpal tunnel syndrome. This is a nerve condition caused by repetitive motion; the forty years I have spent in front of typewriters and keyboards have apparently caught up with me. On the advice of my surgeon—and considering that I have a strong

TEST FIRING RESULTS

PISTOL	GROUP/IN.
PM9	2.5
TP9	1.5
PM40	2
T40	1.75

SPECIFICATIONS:

T40 TACTICAL & T40 TARGET

Chambering	40 S&W
Capacity	7 + 1
Operation	trigger cocking DAO; lock breech; "Browning – type" recoil lug; passive striker block; no magazine disconnect
Barrel	4.0", polygonal rifling; right-hand twist
Overall Length	6.6"
Height	5"
Slide Width	0.94"
Weight (unloaded)	29.1 oz.
Grip	Checkered Hogue Pau Ferro wood
Sights	front: Tritium night sight (Tactical); MMC blade with white dot (Target) rear: Novak low profile 2-dot Tritium night sight (Tactical); MMC adjustable (Target)
Finish	Matte stainless steel
Special features	two magazines, high-impact carrying box, trigger lock, limited lifetime warranty

PM 9 & PM40

Chamberings	9mm Para/40 S&W
Capacity	6 & 7 + 1 / 5 & 6+1
Operation	trigger cocking DAO; lock breech; "Browning - type" recoil lug; passive striker block; no magazine disconnect
Barrel	3.0", polygonal rifling; right-hand twist
Overall Length	5.3"
Height	3"
Slide Width	0.94"
Weight (unloaded)	15.9 oz./16.9 oz.
Grip	textured polymer
Sights	front: white dot rear: white bar *
Finish	Tungsten DLC / matte stainless steel
Special features	two magazines, high-impact carrying box, trigger lock, limited lifetime warranty. * Tritium night sights available as an option

TP9

Chambering	9mm Para
Capacity	7 & 8 + 1
Operation	trigger cocking DAO; lock breech; "Browning – type" recoil lug; passive striker block; no magazine disconnect
Barrel	4.0", polygonal rifling; right-hand twist
Overall Length	6.6"
Height	4.5"
Slide Width	0.9"
Weight (unloaded)	19.1 oz.
Grip	textured polymer
Sights	front: Tritium night sight; MMC blade with white dot rear: Novak low-profile 2-dot Tritium night sight; MMC adjustable
Finish	Matte stainless steel
Special features	two magazines, high impact carrying box, trigger lock, limited lifetime warranty

For further information:
Cor-Bon Ammunition - 1311 Industry Road, Sturgis, SD 57785. Gould & Goodrich - 709 E. McNeil St., Lillington, NC 27546.
Kahr Arms - P.O. Box 220, Blauvelt, NY 10913.

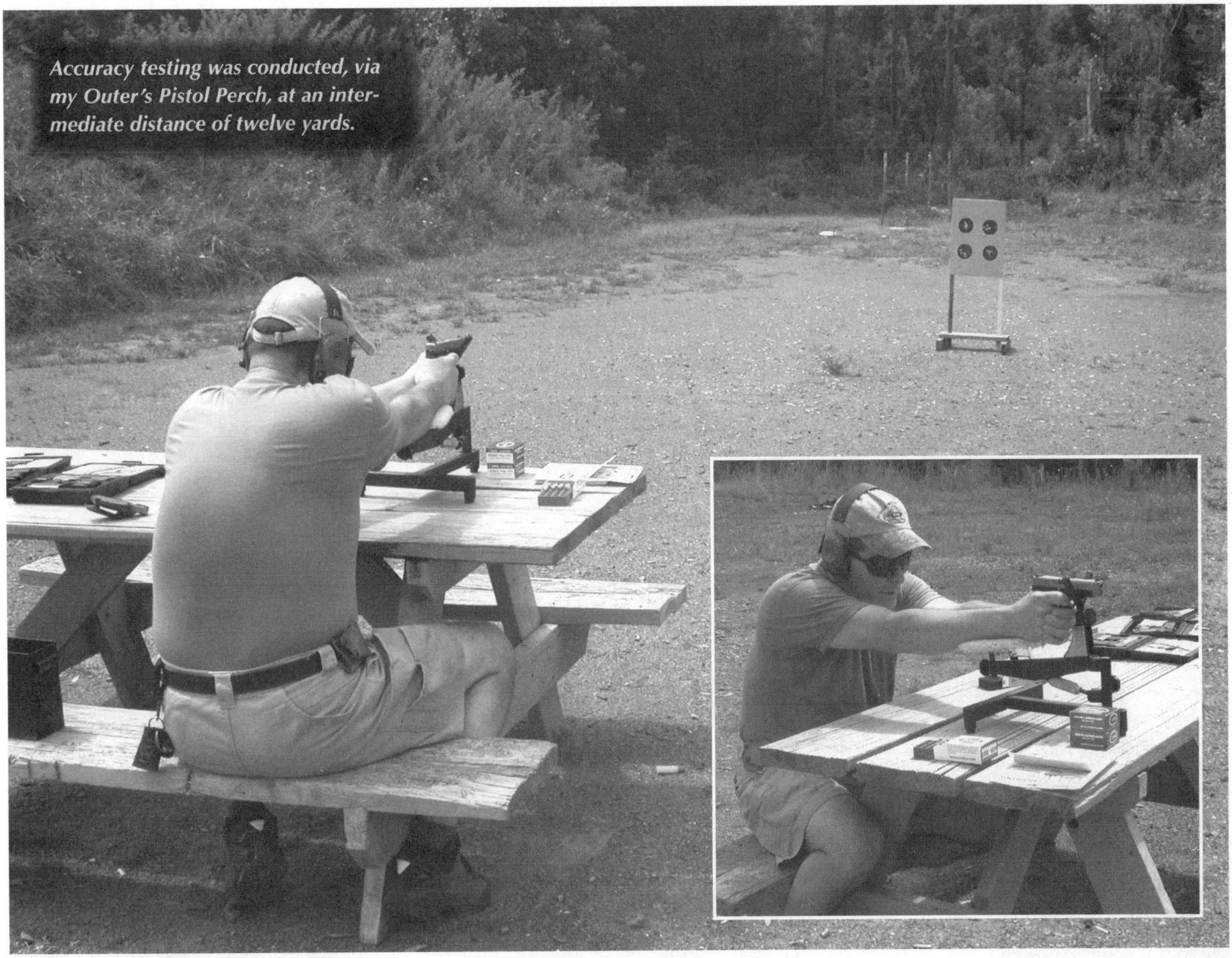

Accuracy testing was conducted, via my Outer's Pistol Perch, at an intermediate distance of twelve yards.

aversion to discomfort in all of its forms—I sought the services of my good friend and respected gunsmith Lin Webb, when it came to test-firing our quartet of Kahrs.

As the practice continues to thrill ammunition manufacturers everywhere, our first task consisted of testing the four pistols for accuracy. Cor-Bon was kind enough to supply me with a quantity of their new DPX ammunition consisting of 9mm Parabellum 115-grain+P and 40 S&W 140-grain JHP loads. Considering their DAO triggers, and intended purpose as close-range defensive handguns, this chore was performed from a rest at a moderate twelve yards. Not being well versed in the mysteries of DAO triggers, I allowed Lin a dozen or so rounds to get the hang of things before he began shooting for score. Shooting across an Outer's Pistol Perch, he proceeded to fire a five-shot group with each pistol, the results of which can be seen in the photos and the chart below. Honorable mention goes to the TP9 which produced a very nice group measuring exactly 1.5 inches.

With this (rather unexciting?) task accomplished, we got down to having some fu...I mean, running each pistol through a complete evaluation to

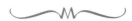

Left: The T40 was the heaviest of our test pistols, and had the largest grips. Result was five rounds in an impressive 1.75 inches.

Right: The TP9 helped him redeem his pride with this very nice 1.5 inch group (bottom right). Pretty good shooting, Mr. Webb!

All Kahr pistols are disassembled the same way, and strip down to six parts.

ascertain its offhand/combat capabilities. For this stage of our evaluation, Ms. Kim Fiedler of Gould & Goodrich supplied us with one of their Yaqui Slide holsters, whose design permitted it to be used with all four pistols, and a spare magazine pouch. Accordingly, several D-1 targets were set up at seven yards and the following series of drills were performed with each of our test guns.

1. Draw pistol and fire six rounds on target, slow aimed fire. [1]

2. Draw pistol and double-tap target. Re-holster and repeat twice.

3. Repeat drill #2 firing the pistol unsupported (one-handed).

4. Draw pistol, fire six rounds on target as fast as a flash sight picture can be acquired. Perform a combat reload and repeat.

First up was the PM9, a pistol which—I'm sorry to say considering my high opinion of it—Lin found wanting as far as offhand shooting went. While he was able to put all of his rounds on the target, he was not able to group them very tightly. I am at a loss to explain this as I have always found the PM9 a very easy-handling and fine-shooting little pistol. Oh well, all guns do not fit all shooters the same. On the positive side, he found the PM9 quite controllable and easy to conceal.

My friend quickly discovered that the 9mm Kahr TP9 was a different story. With its longer barrel, longer sight radius and greater weight it proved "...a regular pussycat to shoot." To Lin's delight—and as a much-needed boost to his self esteem—the next thirty rounds he fired formed a much tighter pattern on the D-1 target.

As it is of the same size and only slightly heavier than its 9mm cousin, Lin looked with a bit of trepidation upon the PM40. But to our joint amazement he proceeded to perforate the target in a most impressive manner with this mini-forty! After firing thirty rounds, he stood there flexing his fingers and commented that "Recoil is sort of 'whippy' with this thing."

The last pistol, the T40, was to give Mr. Webb an entirely new outlook on Kahr products. In fact, even before firing it, he found himself taken with the pistol's nicely-shaped grips, extra weight and excellent balance. As he proceeded with the drills, it quickly became evident that this was the Kahr for him. It seemed no matter in which mode he fired it, the majority of the rounds sent downrange found their way into the target's X-ring. When we walked down to examine the target

1 Because of their varying magazine capacities, all strings of fire were limited to six rounds.

it was obvious that only his strong sense of modesty prevented him from bragging about his prowess—but as I took a photo of him standing next to the target, a big grin spread across his face as he said "Now THIS is my kind of pistol!"

While not wantinging to burst his bubble when it came to his choice of Kahrs, I mentioned I felt the reason he fired the largest groups with my (beloved) PM9 was that it was the first pistol fired in these drills but, as he gained experience with the DAO triggers, his grouping progressively improved. Lin admitted this might be a factor and then pointed out that his sterling performance with the T40 might have been influenced by the fact

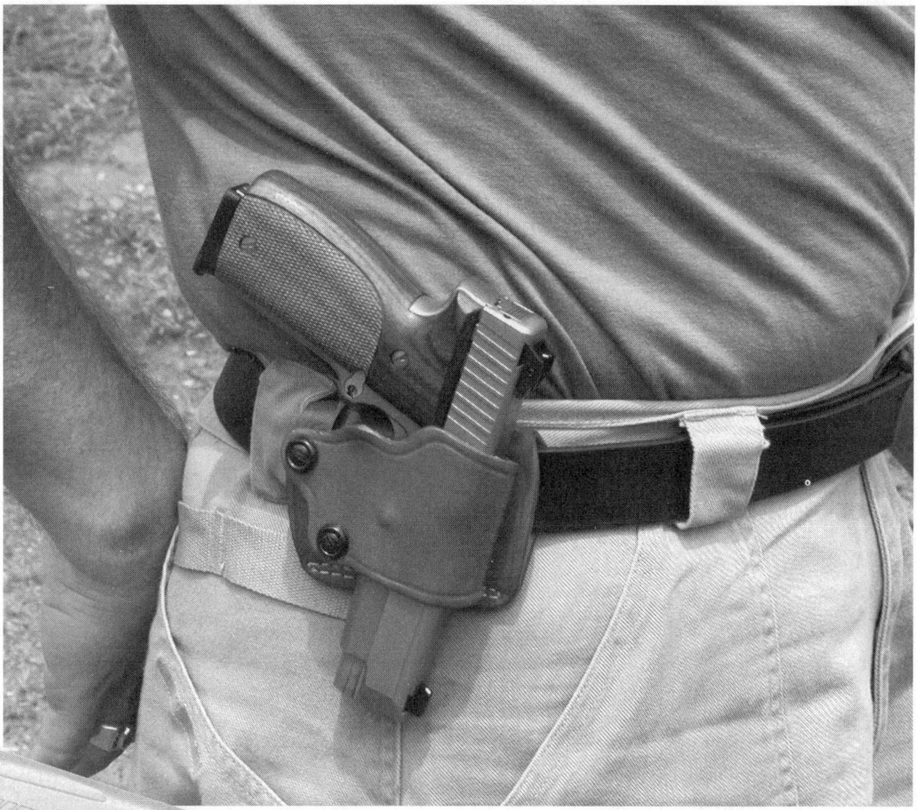

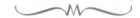

The Gould & Goodrich Yaqui Slide holster's design allows it to be used with all models of Kahr pistols. It provides complete concealment, comfort—and allows a fast, snag-free presentation.

The T40 Tactical and Target are Kahr's newest, full-sized pistols. They only differ in that the former has Novak night sights while the latter is fitted with MMC adjustable sights.

that its MMC sights were "...identical to the ones I have on my two regular competition pistols." Hmmmm.......?

We spent the remainder of the afternoon plinking with the four Kahr pistols at various drink cans placed on the backstop. Despite my physical affliction, I took the opportunity to fire all four pistols and, much to my delight, proceeded to outshoot Lin with my PM9. We were enjoying ourselves so much that it was only lack of ammunition that forced us to pack all the gear in my truck and head for home.

I have been impressed with Kahr pistols from day one, and came away from this shooting session with my opinion of them elevated even further. If you are a police officer, security personnel or civilian who needs a compact, easy-to-use, utterly reliable pistol that fires authoritative cartridges—I'm telling you now—if you can't find what you need in the Kahr line, you're in a lot of trouble!

PARA-ORDNANCE LTC

LIGHTWEIGHT AND STEEL FRAME VERSIONS ARE BOTH GOOD CHOICES FOR PERSONAL PROTECTION

by Dave Workman

Para-Ordnance climbed to prominence by producing large-capacity variations of the Model 1911 platform, including double-action guns built around an innovative trigger system called the LDA (for "Light double Action") that got plenty of attention from not only the gun press, but shooters across the country.

Years ago, a colleague who became rather enthralled with the concept of launching a dozen 45-caliber projectiles downrange without changing magazines got hold of an early Para, and when I sort of smirked and shook my head, he handed me the pistol. I lost the condescending smile and focused my attention on this Canadian-made handgun. The wide grip actually did not strain my average-size hand, and I'll have to admit, the math (a dozen rounds instead of eight in a magazine) appealed to my survival instincts. But one hears all kinds of tales about handguns these days, and among some – certainly not all – of my acquaintances, Para pistols did not have a sterling reputation. A lot of that turned out to be hearsay; one guy telling another guy about something that happened to a friend of a friend.

One learns to take a lot of that sort of thing in stride, and until recently, I'd never had much interest in putting a Para-Ordnance pistol through its paces for evaluation. After all, so many other guys, people I trust, had done that quite admirably, so I figured, why bother? Ignoring the hearsay critics, it has been pretty well established that Para Ordnance pistols are pretty well made guns.

Then Para unveiled the LTC, a Commander-sized single-action, single-stack 1911 pistol that I simply could not ignore. It followed closely after the introduction of a full-size Para Ordnance model called the PXT, the significance of which will be shortly obvious. This full-size model was used to premier the striking duo-tone cosmetics that are putting Para's single-stack pistols not simply on the map, but on covers and full-color pages of major firearms periodicals.

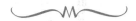

Para-Ordnance LTC pistols come in two versions, one a lightweight with alloy frame and the other an all-steel model. Author ran both through the wringer with a variety of popular 45 ACP ammunition.

Wearing the LTC lightweight model was a delight for the author, who is more used to the weight of an all-steel pistol.

It is pretty widely known that I have this "thing" for Commander-sized pistols. Sure, over the past years I have reviewed—in this book—a couple of very good full-size 1911 pistols, including one I had custom-built by Olympic Arms for a story in the 2001 Handguns annual. They are very good shooters, but for concealed carry, I've found that shaving 3/4-inch off the barrel and slide, while retaining a full-length frame, is a very good idea.

Having never owned a real Commander, I looked around for a used lightweight, one of those guns people seem to purchase and never part with. I have seen some real beaters for sale at gun shows, mind you; pieces that looked as though they had been deliberately abused by their owners, who obviously were proud of their guns because every one of them was for sale at new-in-the-box prices, or better.

A couple of years ago, I bought one of a handful of Commander-sized prototype pistols produced by Auto Ordnance, but never added to the product line. It rattles, but it shoots rather well now that I've added a set of Novak Extreme Duty adjustable tritium sights, a Videcki trigger set at 4.5 pounds, and a beavertail grip safety.

Colt still builds Commanders (their most recent crop is, in my opinion, superb), and other gun makers – notably Kimber – have begun cranking out pistols with 4-inch bushingless barrels that shoot magnificently right out of the box.

All that said, I must give the LTC from Para very high marks and for very good reasons.

First, this pistol retains the 4.25-inch barrel and it has a bushing. That design feature results, in my opinion, in quite possibly the most well-balanced "weight-wise" and visually balanced 1911-style pistols on the planet. This barrel, incidentally, has an integral feed ramp, a feature I neither like nor dislike. I can say, though, that this feature does seem to eliminate feeding problems.

Second, Para designers added low-profile fixed sights dovetailed front and rear into the slide. These are of the three-dot variety, and the only thing I would change with them would be the addition of tritium lamps for low-light shooting. Tritium replacements are available from the factory, and really nowhere else, because Para uses a proprietary dovetail cut. Install someone else's and you'll have to re-cut the dovetails, especially on the front end.

Third, this pistol has a rugged Para Kote Regal finish that is contrasted by the matte stainless controls, hammer and beavertail grip safety. I'm not entirely sold on this approach to the

Do the Para Ordnance LTCs shoot? Absolutely, says Workman, who shows just two examples of groups fired at 15 yards. Top is the all-steel LTC and the tighter group below was fired with the lightweight model. Top group was made with Winchester 230-grain FMJ ball ammo, while the bottom group was fired with Remington/UMC 185-grain FMJ flat points.

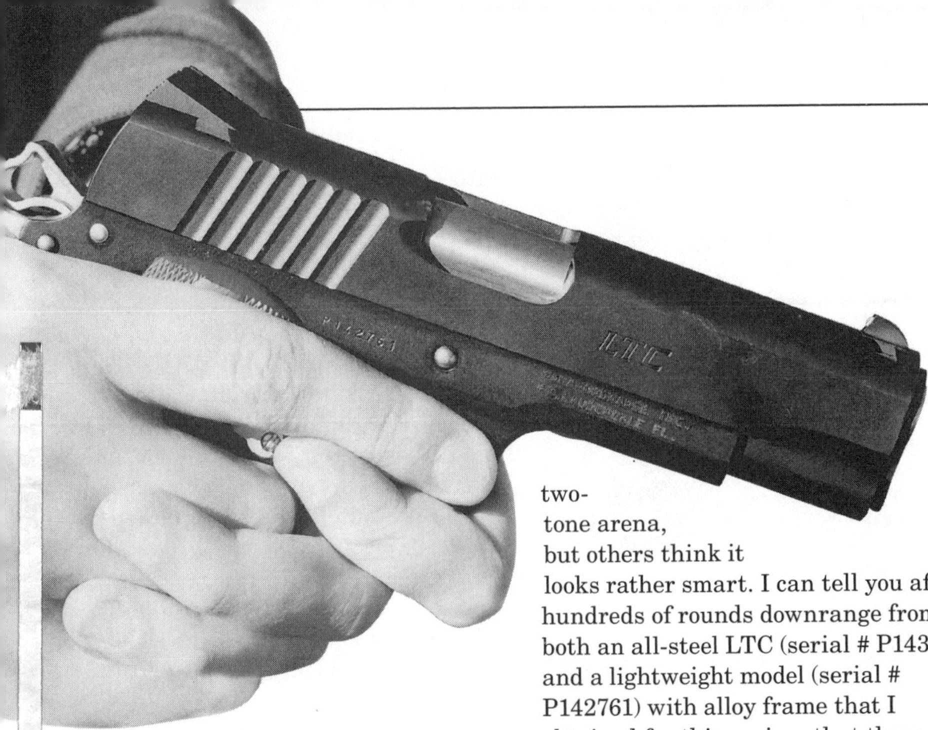

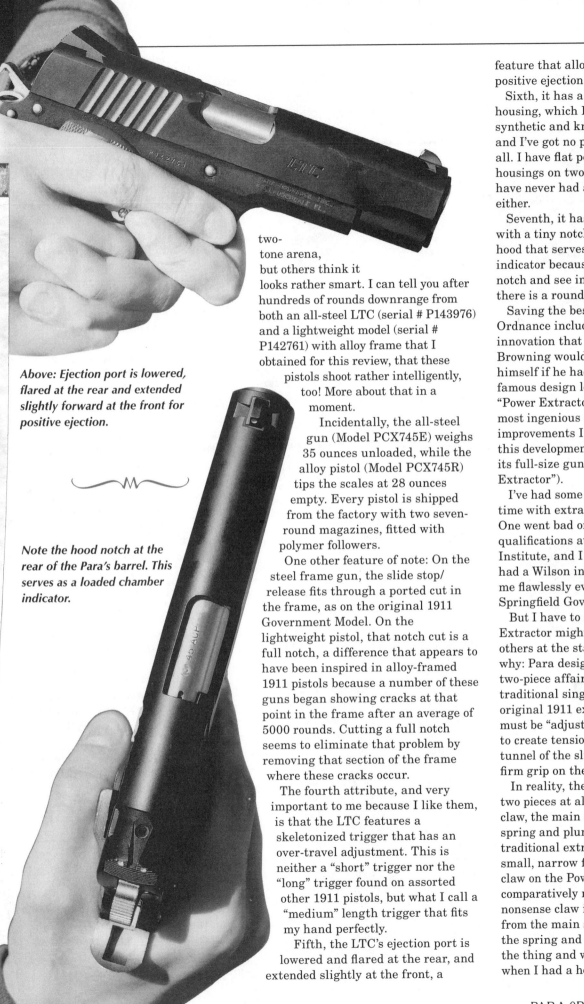

Above: Ejection port is lowered, flared at the rear and extended slightly forward at the front for positive ejection.

Note the hood notch at the rear of the Para's barrel. This serves as a loaded chamber indicator.

two-tone arena, but others think it looks rather smart. I can tell you after hundreds of rounds downrange from both an all-steel LTC (serial # P143976) and a lightweight model (serial # P142761) with alloy frame that I obtained for this review, that these pistols shoot rather intelligently, too! More about that in a moment.

Incidentally, the all-steel gun (Model PCX745E) weighs 35 ounces unloaded, while the alloy pistol (Model PCX745R) tips the scales at 28 ounces empty. Every pistol is shipped from the factory with two seven-round magazines, fitted with polymer followers.

One other feature of note: On the steel frame gun, the slide stop/release fits through a ported cut in the frame, as on the original 1911 Government Model. On the lightweight pistol, that notch cut is a full notch, a difference that appears to have been inspired in alloy-framed 1911 pistols because a number of these guns began showing cracks at that point in the frame after an average of 5000 rounds. Cutting a full notch seems to eliminate that problem by removing that section of the frame where these cracks occur.

The fourth attribute, and very important to me because I like them, is that the LTC features a skeletonized trigger that has an over-travel adjustment. This is neither a "short" trigger nor the "long" trigger found on assorted other 1911 pistols, but what I call a "medium" length trigger that fits my hand perfectly.

Fifth, the LTC's ejection port is lowered and flared at the rear, and extended slightly at the front, a feature that allows for absolutely positive ejection.

Sixth, it has a flat mainspring housing, which I prefer. This part is synthetic and knurled for a firm grip, and I've got no problem with that at all. I have flat polymer mainspring housings on two of my own 1911s and have never had a bit of trouble with either.

Seventh, it has a match-grade barrel with a tiny notch at 12 o'clock on the hood that serves as a loaded chamber indicator because one can peek at this notch and see in an instant whether there is a round in the chamber.

Saving the best for last, Para Ordnance included in the LTC an innovation that I suspect John Moses Browning would have developed himself if he had tinkered with his famous design long enough. It's Para's "Power Extractor," and it is one of the most ingenious engineering improvements I've ever seen. It was this development that led Para to call its full-size gun the "PXT" (for "Power Extractor").

I've had some trouble from time to time with extractors in 1911 pistols. One went bad on me in the middle of qualifications at the Lethal Force Institute, and I trashed it and later had a Wilson installed that has served me flawlessly ever since in a Springfield Government Model.

But I have to say that this Power Extractor might just leave all the others at the starting gate. Here's why: Para designed this extractor as a two-piece affair rather than the traditional single unit that is the original 1911 extractor; a piece that must be "adjusted" by bending slightly to create tension in the extractor tunnel of the slide, thus resulting in a firm grip on the case rim.

In reality, the Power Extractor is not two pieces at all, but four. There is the claw, the main stem, a small internal spring and plunger. While the traditional extractor claw is a rather small, narrow feature, the extractor claw on the Power Extractor is comparatively massive. This no-nonsense claw is pushed via a pivot from the main stem of the extractor by the spring and plunger. I disassembled the thing and was duly impressed when I had a hell of a time pressing it

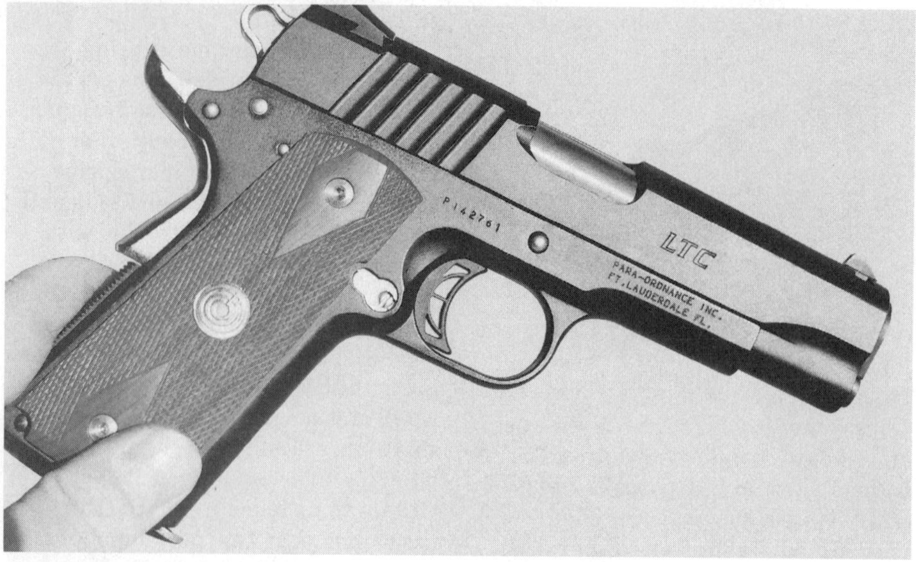

all back together with light finger pressure.

For the record, I suffered not one failure to extract during a variety of shooting exercises, both slow and rapid fire, from either of the two pistols I tested. Not one stovepipe jam, no empties left in the chamber; both Para LTC pistols performed like gangbusters.

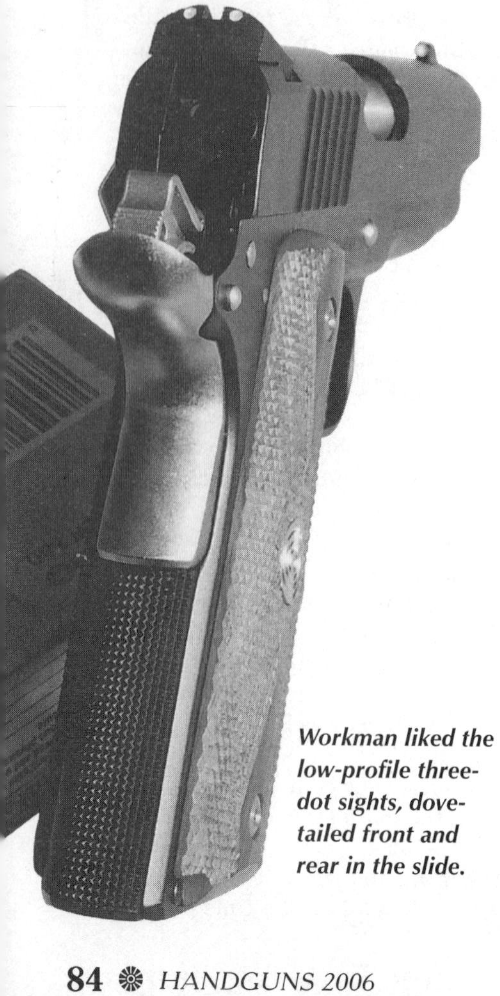

Workman liked the low-profile three-dot sights, dove-tailed front and rear in the slide.

Bottom line: Para's Power Extractor is undoubtedly the single most important design improvement on the basic 1911 platform since the pistol originally debuted nearly a century ago.

Okay, with all of the accolades, is there a down side with the Para LTC? Alas, the one feature I do not care for on this pistol—and would immediately replace—is the full-length recoil spring guide rod. This thing can be a pain in the neck, and the plastic bushing wrench Para included in the box simply had too much flex to really work properly when I disassembled both pistols for cleaning and inspection. I had to use my Brownell's bushing wrench to strip both test pistols down, and reassemble them. This does not happen with a pistol fitted with a simple plug and spring mounted on a traditional short guide.

Granted, many of my contemporaries swear by the full-length guide rod. I see no reason for these things other than aggravation.

Another feature toward which I am more indifferent than critical is the passive firing pin safety. The firing pin may move forward only when the trigger is pressed. I've never quite understood the addition of two more moving parts (that can malfunction) to any semi-auto pistol, but in this day and age of litigious attorneys and people who try to blame their personal carelessness on someone or something else, one presumes we are forever stuck with such design features.

Now, does the LTC perform on the firing line? Absolutely! I gathered an ample variety of ammunition, including standard 230-grain ball, and a selection of 200- and 185-grain JHPs from Winchester, Black Hills, Norma, Remington, Federal and PMC (marketed as the Taurus all-copper Hex bullet) that all fed flawlessly.

Out of the lightweight, I marked my highest velocities over a Chrony Alpha chronograph set 7 feet from the muzzle, using the Remington/UMC 185-grain jacketed flat-point which clocked 1051 fps on average, and 1068 fps at top recorded speed. In the all-steel gun, my highest velocity was produced with the Black Hills 185-grain JHP at 1040 fps, with a high of 1078 fps.

I shot at targets set 10, 15 and 25 yards from the line, and once I determined how both pistols shot, I tossed an empty baked bean can out on the range and peppered it repeatedly using Winchester ball, BEB range ammo and Federal 185-grain Hi Shok JHPs.

I found that the all-steel pistol shot just a bit low, while the lightweight seemed to group its rounds just above the X-ring. Using Birchwood Casey silhouette targets with their terrific Shoot-N-C overlays, I managed to clearly mark bullet hits, and some impressively tight groups.

Off the bench, I found both pistols to group tightly with all bullet weights. The all-steel model especially liked the Winchester 230-grain JHP Personal Defense load, while the lightweight perked along rather well with the Remington/UMC ammo.

My biggest surprise came with loads from Silver Bear, a Russian import that uses a Berdan-primed, zinc-coated aluminum case. Imported by Bear Ammunition, this stuff has a 230-grain FMJ bullet loaded to an advertised 820 fps. Here's a news flash: Out of both pistols, it performed better, clocking at an average of 833.4 fps from the lightweight and 852.6 fps out of the steel-frame gun. The hottest velocity I recorded with this ammunition was 875.3 fps, from the all-steel pistol.

Both handguns fit perfectly in two holsters I utilized for this review. One a belt scabbard from Greg Kramer, which he primarily markets as a women's holster, but which I personally find rather comfortable for outdoors carry. The other was my own D&D Gunleather IWB called the T-Bar II. Both rigs are built for Commander-size pistols, and they fit like gloves, naturally. Kramer's holster is a horsehide number reinforced at the belt loop with what appears to be Kydex. The T-Bar II is cowhide.

What else is there to say? I came away from this project favorably impressed with both the all-steel and alloy versions of the LTC, and with a new assessment of Para Ordnance pistols overall. The two guns I had were well-built, tight but not extremely so, eye-appealing and accurate.

While there were a couple of features I didn't care for, those seem less significant overall when considering how well these pistols functioned.

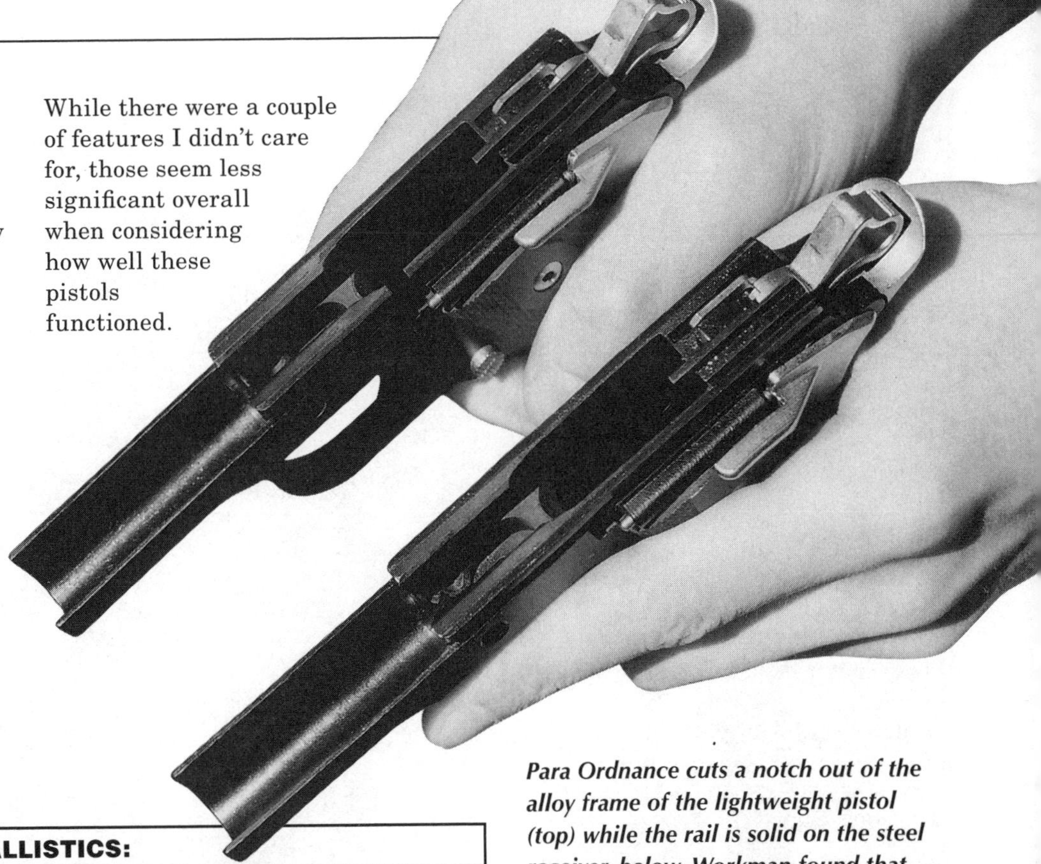

Para Ordnance cuts a notch out of the alloy frame of the lightweight pistol (top) while the rail is solid on the steel receiver, below. Workman found that field-stripping the steel model went more smoothly than with the alloy-frame gun, which was just a hair tighter on the inside of the frame.

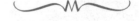

BALLISTICS:

Load	Steel LTC/fps	Alloy LTC/fps
Win. 230-gr. SXT	782.4	798.8
Win. 230-gr. FMJ	764.5	780.4
Win. 230-gr. JHP	819.1	857.7
Taurus 185-gr. HP	944.0	997.6
Federal 185-gr. Hi-Shok	899.6	891.0
Silver Bear 230-gr. FMJ	852.6	833.4
Black Hills 185-gr. JHP	1,040	1,049
Black Hills 185-gr. Gold Dot	944.7	941.0
Rem./UMC 185-gr. FMJ	1,023	1,051
Norma 200-gr. JHP	1,026	1,047

High profile beavertail grip safety and extended thumb safety make the LTC streetworthy. Note the flat, knurled mainspring housing and those handsome checkered double-diamond grips.

From their tough finish to their tough components, I will say that the Para LTC appears to be a handgun entry that is here to stay, and deservedly so. I would not be fearful to carry this pistol into a dangerous place, as I expect a lot from any such handgun, and this one delivers the goods.

Para Ordnance LTC
Para Ordnance
980 Tapscott Road
Toronto, ON Canada M1X 1C3
(416) 297-7855

Chambering: 45 ACP
Capacity: 7+1
Barrel: 4.25 inches, ramped, match-grade with full-length guide rod
Weight: All steel, 35 ounces; alloy, 28 ounces
OAL: 7.75 inches
Height: 5.75 inches
Finish: Black Para Kote
Sights: Low profile fixed,

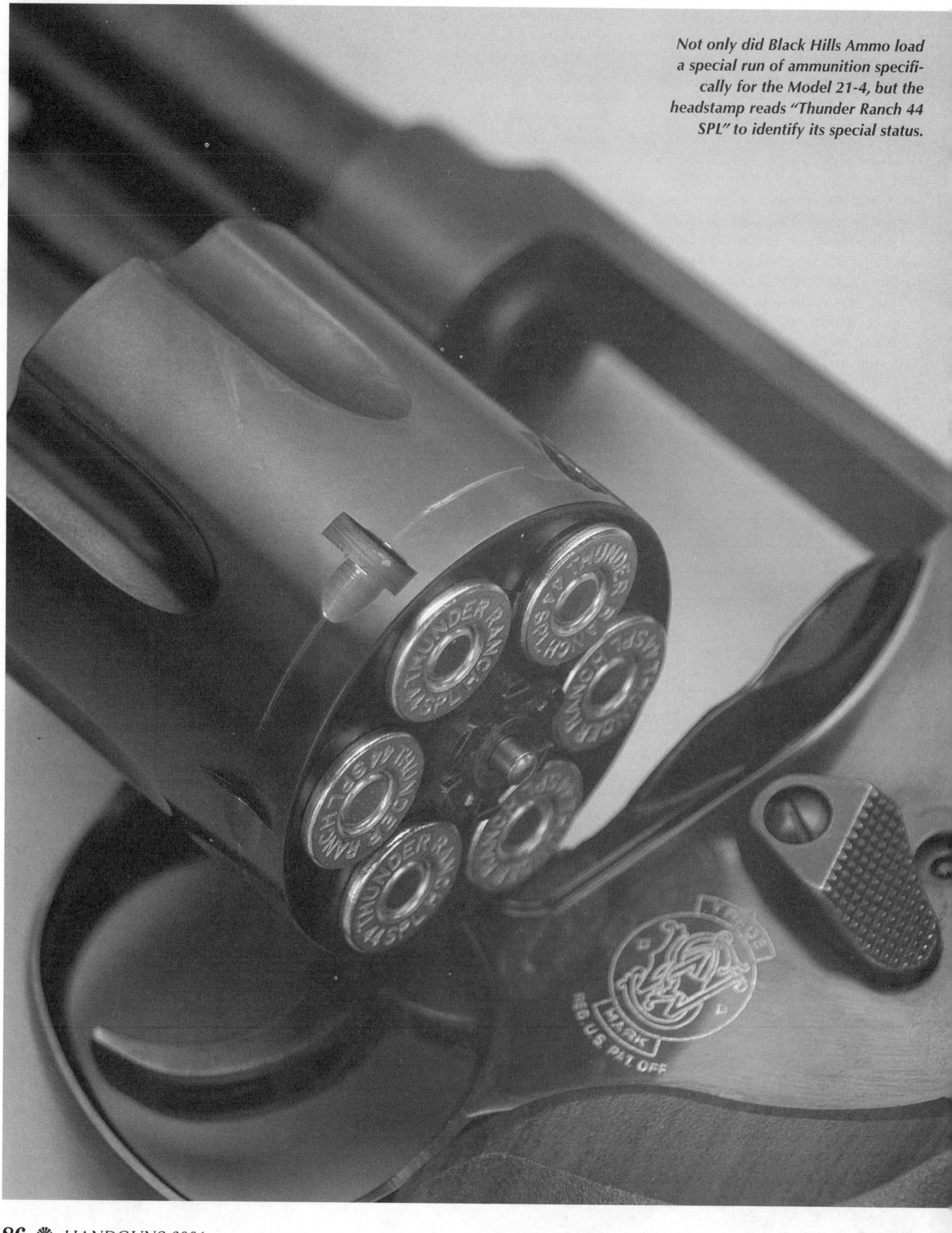

Not only did Black Hills Ammo load a special run of ammunition specifically for the Model 21-4, but the headstamp reads "Thunder Ranch 44 SPL" to identify its special status.

SMITH & WESSON MODEL 21-4:

AN OLD GUY'S GUN & OTHERS

aka: "The Thunder Ranch Special"

by John Taffin

To many new shooters, attempting to discuss a large frame "fighting revolver" in the 21st century is akin to arguing who makes the best steam engine, the pitfalls of home canning––or even the future of the mold board plow.

To most shooters, the idea of a large-frame "fighting revolver" in a big-bore caliber is a dated concept with so little relevance to their present needs and experiences they feel it is merely another one of those 'retro' things––like cowboy action shooting, or a renewed interest in bolt-action World War II rifles. Does that mean a large-frame, double-action, heavy-caliber revolver is a worthless concept?

The answer from more than a few would be a flat "NO!" Leading the pack rejecting this view is a well-known instructor who recently relocated to Oregon from Texas...Clint Smith.

For those who came in late, Clint Smith is the proprietor of Thunder Ranch, formerly located in Mountain Home, Texas and now located in Lakeview, Oregon. Smith has been training people in "...shooting and fighting..." for more years than he cares to remember. For decades he moved from training venue to training venue across the United States, living in a heavy diesel-powered dual-wheel pick-up truck towing a heavily loaded van trailer filled with steel targets. Like he once told me, those were the "old days"...not the "good old days".

Thunder Ranch in Texas was his first permanent facility and it raised the bar for student instruction in terms of the physical plant and the level of instruction. The Thunder Ranch facility in Texas closed in 2004 and he has opened a new facility in Oregon to continue training people in "...shooting and fighting..."

But Smith has never been content to enjoy the status-quo. He is always searching for something new, on both personal and theoretical levels. On the personal level he has established his ability to write firearms and self-defense-oriented articles for national publications. On the theoretical level, he is responsible for the revolver being reviewed here. It is a new production Smith & Wesson Model 21-4 and as such it is in many ways a return to the type of handgun many sought and chose for self-protection during those

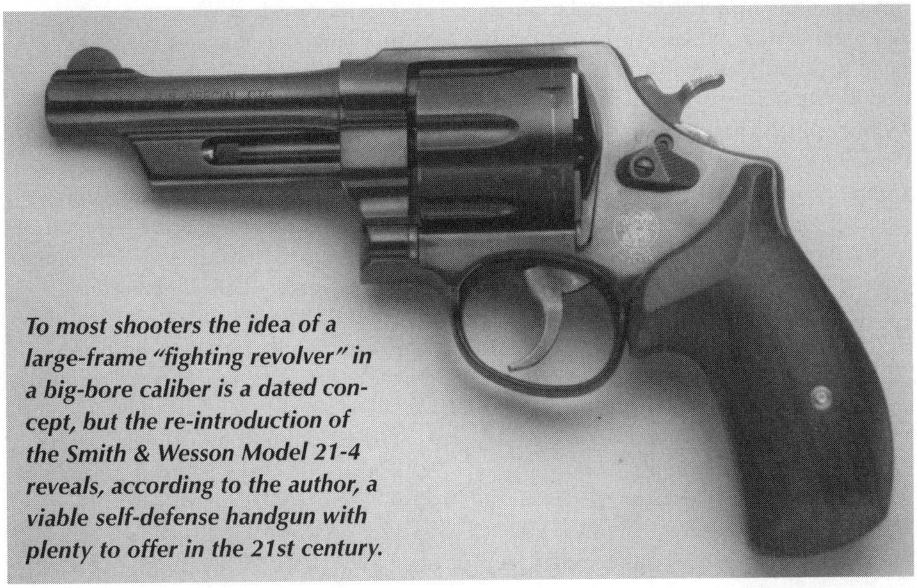

To most shooters the idea of a large-frame "fighting revolver" in a big-bore caliber is a dated concept, but the re-introduction of the Smith & Wesson Model 21-4 reveals, according to the author, a viable self-defense handgun with plenty to offer in the 21st century.

It used to be fixed-sight revolvers dominated the product line for Smith & Wesson, but the big-frame examples disappeared when S&W stopped producing the Model 58 Military & Police revolver in 41 Magnum (top) more than twenty-five years ago. The Model 21-4 (bottom) is shown for comparison purposes to a Model 58 in the author's collection.

years between the two world wars. In fact, it became well known as the revolver of choice for lawmen of that period in the American Southwest.

It is a fixed sight, six-shot, double-action, swing-out cylinder, large frame revolver chambered for the 44 Special cartridge. Of course, this new revolver from Smith & Wesson sports all the 21st century changes, but the idea of the thing dates back to an earlier age when horses were used primarily as draft animals and steam power was generated by burning coal in locomotives. Guns of this type proved decisive in Depression-era gun battles and, for the day and age, they were the best available––but are they relevant today?

The 44 Special...

Smith & Wesson created the 44 Smith & Wesson Special cartridge in 1907 and introduced a completely new revolver to chamber this new round––the "New Century" revolver or the 44 Hand Ejector 1st Model. The New Century became better known as "The Triple Lock" revolver because it features a third lock on the crane, in addition to the locks at the front of the ejector rod and the back of the cylinder at the center pin. The Triple Lock was also the first of what would eventually become known as the N-frame; for the remainder of the 20th century it would represent Smith & Wesson's largest double-action revolver frame.

The 44 Smith & Wesson Special cartridge featured a case that was approximately 0.2-inch longer than the earlier 44 Smith & Wesson Russian round. In 1870 Smith & Wesson designed and manufactured a series of top-break military revolvers for the Imperial Russian Army that chambered this blackpowder cartridge. The 44 Smith & Wesson Russian cartridge earned accolades for its accuracy and proved popular with those settling the American West, as well as Russian military officers.

The introduction of the 44 Smith & Wesson Special cartridge coincided with the introduction of smokeless powder and quickly proved to be one of the more accurate smokeless powder cartridges in a centerfire chambering––both then and even today. The traditional loading for the 44 Smith & Wesson Special has always employed the 246-grain round-nose lead bullet first seen with the 44 Smith & Wesson Russian round. During the period between the two world wars, many shooters discovered the 44 Smith & Wesson Special was "under-loaded" in terms of the power it was capable of delivering safely with the guns being sold and delivered at the time.

This remains true to this day, but it is also important to emphasize that the 44 S&W Special can not be "Magnumized". Even though it was the source of the development of the 44 Smith & Wesson Magnum cartridge, no modern or vintage firearm chambered for the 44 S&W Special cartridge can safely withstand the pressures generated by loads approximating 44 Magnum pressures, or even those approaching 44 Magnum chamber pressures.

However, the combination of this cartridge with well designed double-action revolvers from various manufacturers, the most popular being Smith & Wesson, helped spur the interest in handgun cartridge handloading immediately following World War I up to the present day. If a reasonable increase in terminal power is needed, the 44 S&W Special is capable of delivering it for the practitioner of homebrewed loads, while at the same time upholding the round's reputation for accuracy. This has always made those revolvers chambered for the 44 S&W Special popular with a significant segment of the handgun shooting world, and the Smith & Wesson examples have always been among the better-made examples one could find and experience.

Some Model History Of S&W Revolvers...

The 44 Hand Ejector 1st Model was the first side swing-out cylinder model to chamber the 44 S&W Special cartridge. Smith & Wesson built this elaborate revolver because it wanted to demonstrate the precision and quality of its arms in contrast to the lower quality offerings from its competitors. While the 44 Hand Ejector 1st Model would be manufactured in a wide number of calibers, most especially the 455 Mark II British military caliber for the guns sold to the British military during World War I, it can always be said it was initially designed for the 44 S&W Special round.

Trench warfare soon proved that having a tight, well-fitted, highly finished revolver was not the most appropriate choice in self-defense handguns for the circumstances. The British "Tommies" who were equipped with these revolvers soon learned the protective underlug surrounding all but one side of the ejector rod under the barrel was not an easy area to clean once filled with mud. Keeping the guns sufficiently clean soon proved more difficult than one can imagine and lessened much of the initial enthusiasm for the 44 Hand Ejector 1st Model.

The 44 Hand Ejector 2nd Model reflected the lessons learned in the trenches of the Somme and elsewhere as the 'triple lock' on the crane and the ejector rod shroud were eliminated. *(This also reduced the cost of the gun.)* The 44 Hand Ejector 2nd Model was manufactured from 1915 to 1940, but the odd thing is the vast majority of guns were made with 6 1/2-inch barrels. There were versions made with 4- and 5-inch barrel lengths, but they are rare or scarce *(depending upon your definition of these characterizations)* and a few models were manufactured in the target configuration with adjustable rear sights and a Patridge front sight on a raised base.

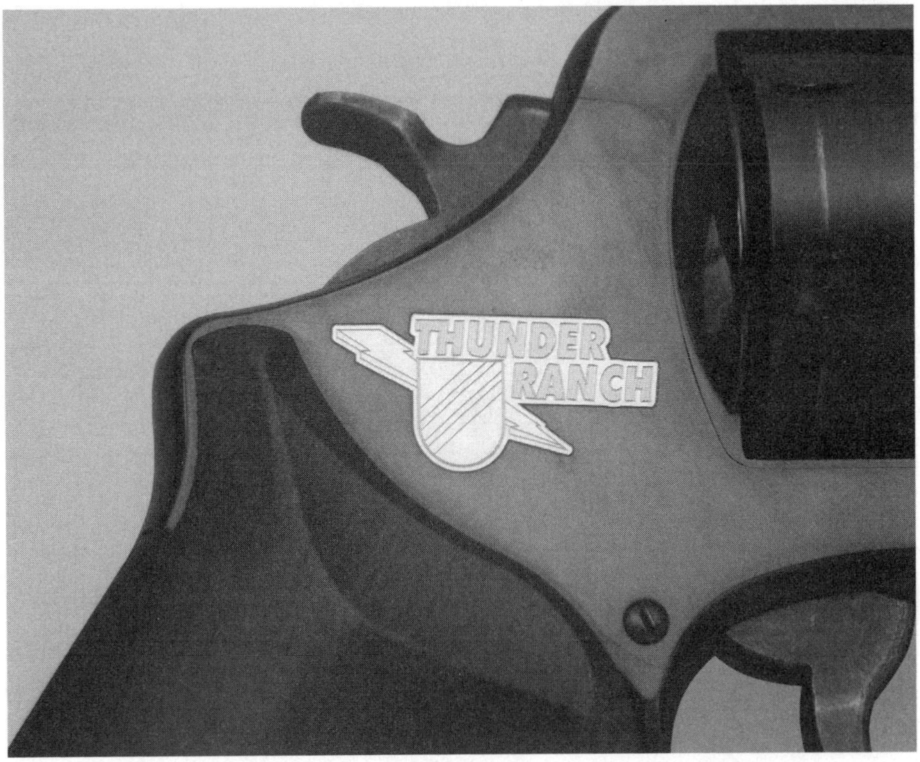

Even though the Model 21-4 is an "...old guy's gun..." many purists object to the laser-engraved gold Thunder Ranch emblem on the sideplate of the revolver. Clint Smith said it wasn't his idea, but that of the marketing department at Smith & Wesson.

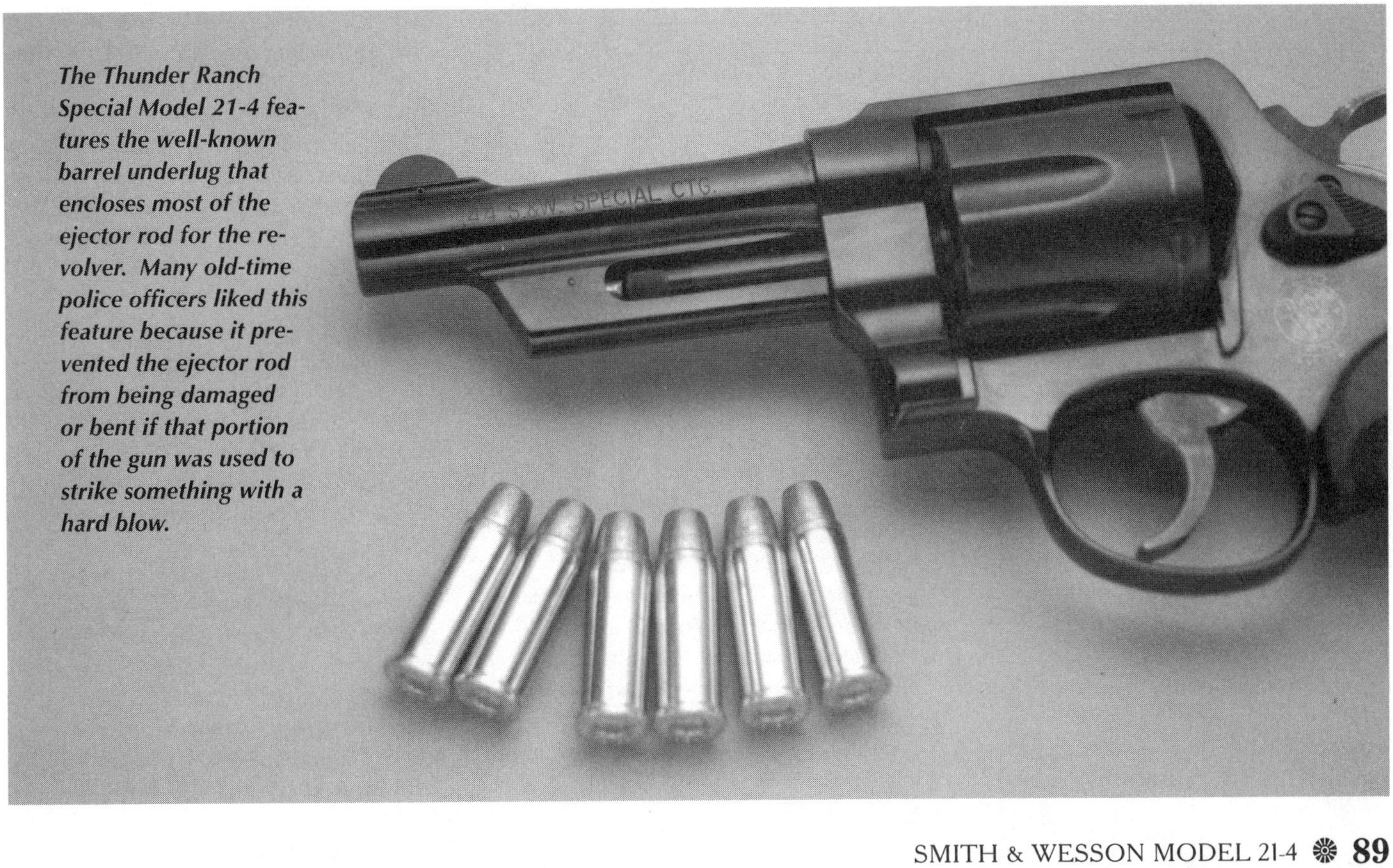

The Thunder Ranch Special Model 21-4 features the well-known barrel underlug that encloses most of the ejector rod for the revolver. Many old-time police officers liked this feature because it prevented the ejector rod from being damaged or bent if that portion of the gun was used to strike something with a hard blow.

Chronograph & Accuracy Test

Cartridge: 44 Special
Firearm: Smith & Wesson
Model: 21-4

Primer	Powder Type	Bullet Wt & Charge	# of Rds. & Type	Ave. tested	Ext. Best Vel. in fps	Spd. Group of 6 in inch @ 25 yd.
FACTORY						
Cor-Bon	–	165-gr. JHP	10	1,154	184	3.25"
NOTE: Point of impact is 3" below point of aim at 25 yards for this load with the test revolver!						
CCI-Blazer	–	200-gr. GD-HP	10	809	41	3.0"
Winchester	–	200-gr. Silvertip HP	10	731	45	5.0"
Winchester "Cowboy Action Loads"	–	240-gr. L-FP-RN	10	688	25	3.25"
Winchester	–	246-gr. LRN	10	661	43	2.75"
Black Hills	–	250 gr. Keith SWC	10	720	49	3.25"
HANDLOADS						
Primer	**Powder Type**	**Bullet Wt & Charge**	**# of Rds. & Type**	**Ave. tested**	**Ext. Best Vel. in fps**	**Spd. Group of 6 in inch @ 25 yd.**
CCI #300 Large Pistol	13.0 grs. Alliant 2400	200-gr. Nosler JHP	10	782	180	3.0"
CCI#300 Large Pistol	7.5 grs. HS-6	245-gr. cast SWC	10	708	65	3.0"
CCI#300 Large Pistol	7.5 grs. Alliant Unique	245-gr. cast SWC	10	990	175	3.0" for 5 rds with 1 called flyer
NOTE: HEAVY LOAD!!						
CCI #300 Large Pistol	6.5 grs. HP38	245-gr. cast SWC	10	1,103	131	3.5"
Chronograph used was an Oehler Model 35P, with the first skyscreen six feet in front of the gun muzzle. Temperature: 40 degrees F. Altitude: 676 feet above sea level.						

The 44 Hand Ejector 3rd Model is the one that established the reputation of the 44 S&W Special through the efforts of lawmen in the American Southwest during the period characterized by Prohibition and the Depression. Wolf and Klar were Smith & Wesson dealers in Fort Worth, Texas and they ordered 3500 of these revolvers, also known as the Model 1926 Hand Ejector, during the depth of the Great Depression. The factory was happy to oblige them and the majority of the 44 Hand Ejector 3rd Model revolvers sported 4-inch barrels. *(Wolf and Klar only received about 1000 of their 3500 order and the reason behind this shortage is hidden in history.)* There were some 5-inch models made and a few with 6 1/2-inch barrels. Very few were made with target features. The big difference between the 2nd and 3rd models, besides the shorter barrel lengths, was the reintroduction of the ejector rod underlug as well as some minor changes in the ejector rod itself. The police department of Houston, Texas purchased three hundred 44 Hand Ejector 3rd Model revolvers with 5-inch barrels in 1931 and they can be identified yet today because the letters "H.P.D," together with an issue number, were inscribed on the backstrap of the revolver's grip frame. The 44 Hand Ejector 3rd Model was manufactured from 1926 through 1941 and it was manufactured simultaneously with the 44 Hand Ejector 2nd Model.

The demand for service pistols during World War II stopped the production of all N-frame revolvers as the company concentrated on arming the American military and its allies. Following the cessation of hostilities, Smith & Wesson restarted the production of the 44 Hand Ejector 3rd Model with the pre-war "long" action. These revolvers are known as the 44 Hand Ejector 3rd Model (Postwar) or 1926 Model 44 Military.

Late in the 1940s, Smith & Wesson developed the "short" action seen on all their double-action revolvers since 1950. The next evolution in the 44 Special revolver from S&W was the 44 Hand Ejector 4th Model Military. When number designations were given to their product line, this revolver became the Model 21.

More or less this brings us up to the present revolver, but it is important to note that over the sixteen years of its production, from 1950 to 1966, only 1200 Model 21s and pre-Model 21s were manufactured and sold by Smith & Wesson. As a result, the Model 21 has always been one of the more sought-after models for anyone interested in post-World War II Smith & Wesson double-action revolvers. Many feel the lack of interest in the Model 21 during these years had more to do with this model's lack of adjustable "target"-style sights than anything else.

Fully adjustable rear sights were proving extremely popular on service-style pistols during this time and the style manufactured by Smith & Wesson soon proved durable and dependable.

About Those Fixed Sights...

Today, fully adjustable rear sights are accepted on just about every self-defense and recreational revolver out there, with the possible exception of the small 5-shot J-frame revolvers. The small J-frame revolvers remain the last redoubt of the fixed-sight double-action revolver and the reason has to be because of their anticipated use at extremely close ranges.

It used to be fixed-sight revolvers dominated the product line for Smith & Wesson, but the big-frame examples disappeared when S&W stopped producing the Model 58 Military & Police revolver in 41

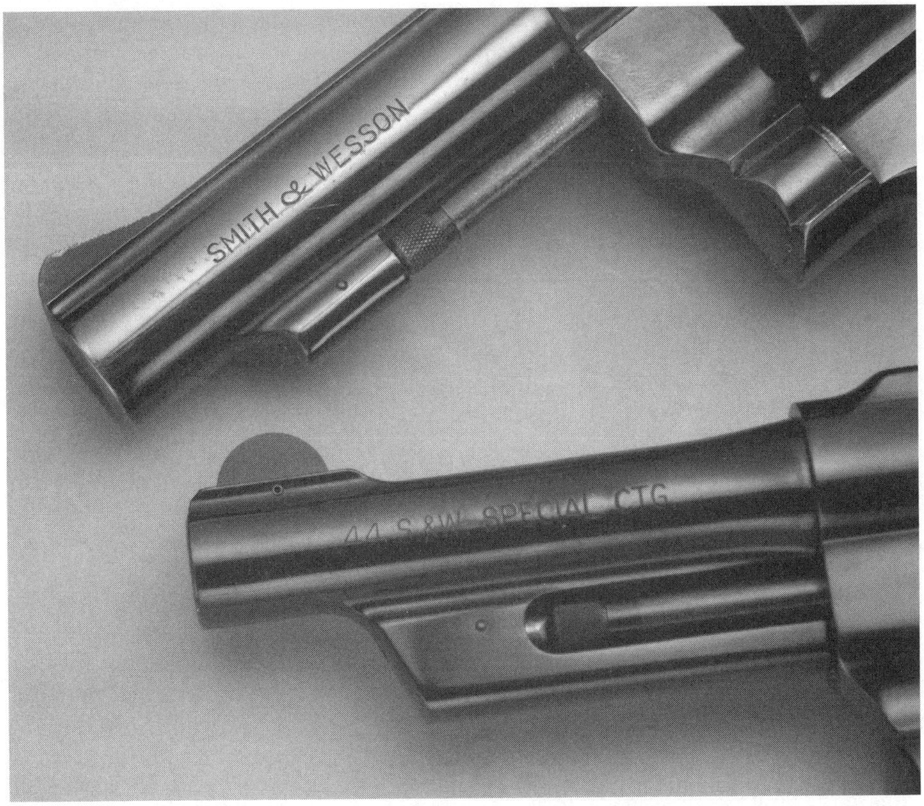

***Above:** The Model 58 (top) had no barrel underlug, while the new Model 21-4 (bottom) does. The re-introduced Model 21-4 breaks from Smith & Wesson tradition by having the caliber designation on the left side of the barrel and the manufacturer's name on the right side.*
***Below:** The width of the rear sight notch milled into the top of the Model 21-4 (left) is wider than that found on the long discontinued Model 58 (right).*

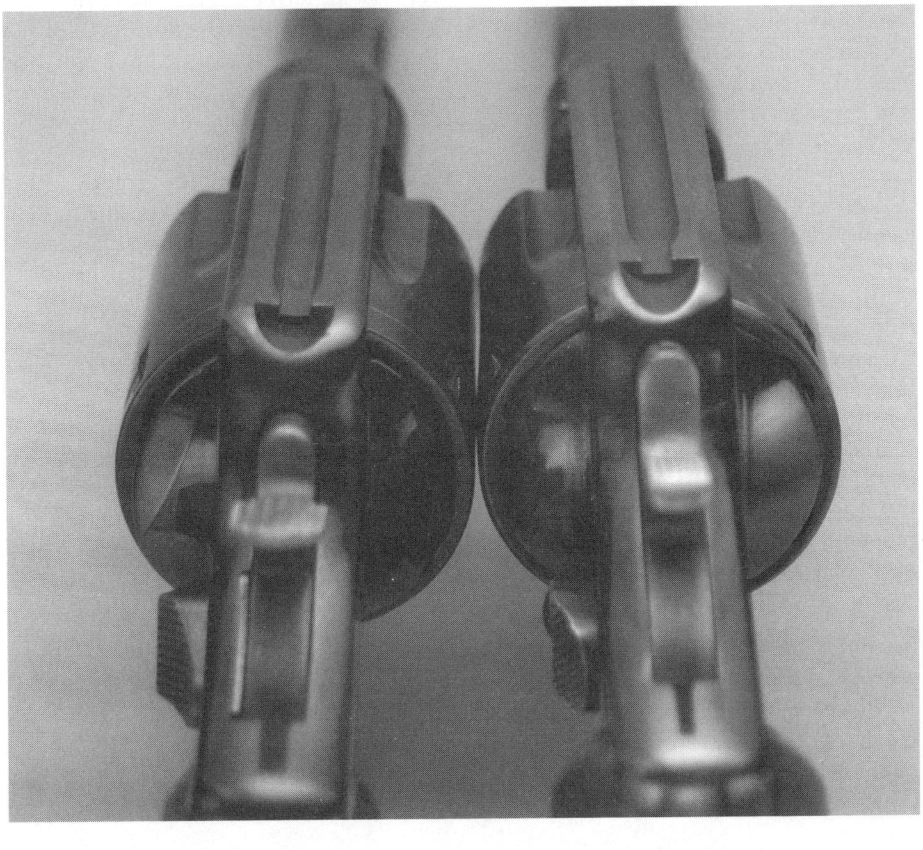

Magnum more than twenty-five years ago. After having spent the majority of my years working with fully adjustable sights on all my revolvers, I can testify to both their advantages and their disadvantages.

The advantage of a fully adjustable rear sight as normally found on a S&W revolver is seen in two distinct ways. The first is enjoyed by those shooters who shoot a wide variety of different bullet weights and widely diverging muzzle velocities as part and parcel of their shooting/reloading hobby. The fully adjustable rear sight makes it an easy task to coordinate point of aim to the changing point of impact when different loads are fired through the gun. Admittedly this is an aspect that most every recreational shooter appreciates and enjoys.

The second advantage to the standard fully adjustable Smith & Wesson rear sight is the actual sight picture presented to the shooter. The rear blade with its square-cut U-notch is crisper and sharper for the eyes of many shooters. Many will testify they shoot these revolvers better than they do the ones with the old fixed sight notches cut in the top of the frame. The width of the rear blade on the adjustable sight makes it easier for the shooter to find quicker than does the narrowness of the fixed sight notch and groove design.

The disadvantages to the Smith & Wesson fully adjustable rear sight lie primarily with the fact they are far more fragile. The internal parts will break. I've broken rear sight blades, sometimes to the point they fall out of the channel holding the blade on the rear of the revolver, but most often the blade is bent and the adjustment, either left or right, is lost. All it takes to achieve this is a sharp blow, either from falling out of the holster *(more a reflection of your holster quality than anything else)* or from hitting a hard object while the gun is in the holster. This was a particular hazard when I worked in an armored delivery truck because the internal space in the back of the truck was confined and every contact surface was hard steel. Not that it takes a hard steel surface to accomplish the same damage because many automotive and home interiors offer sufficient opportunity to damage and bend the rear blade on a fully adjustable S&W rear sight.

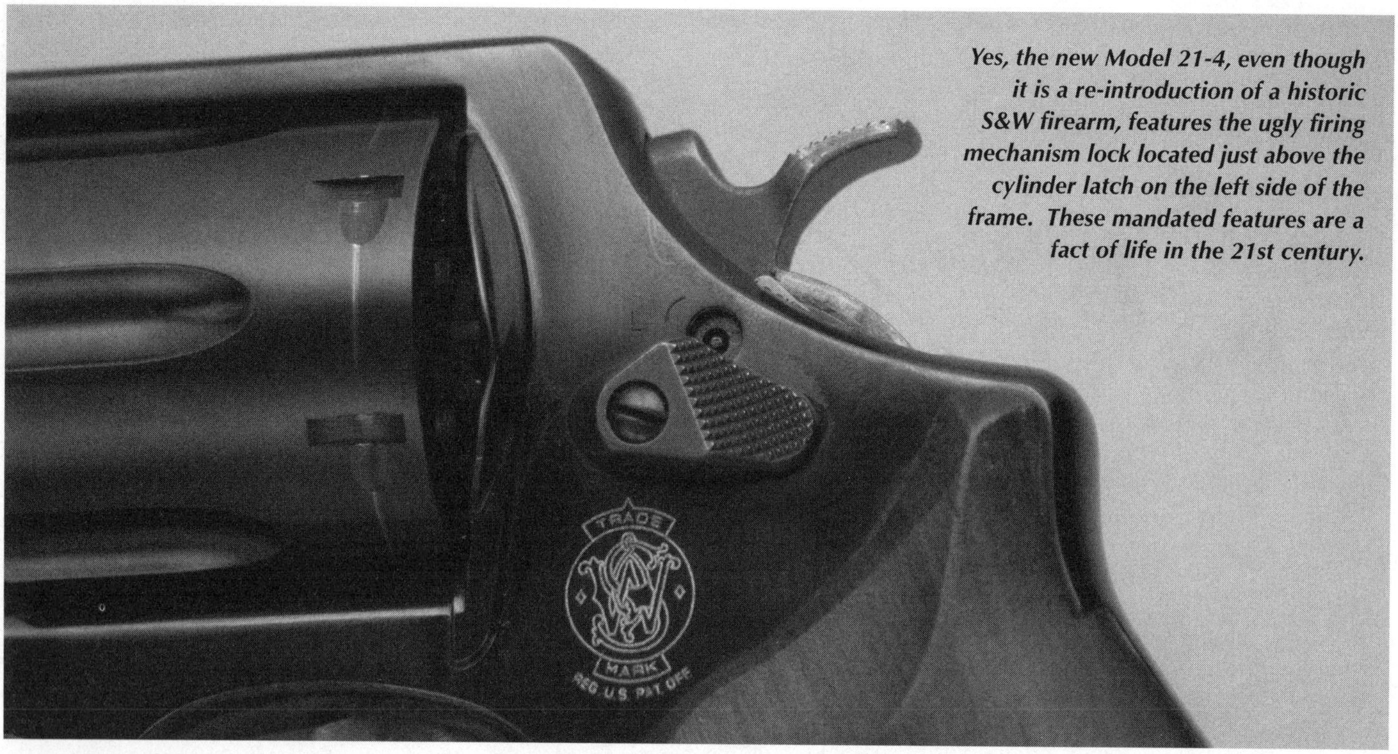

Yes, the new Model 21-4, even though it is a re-introduction of a historic S&W firearm, features the ugly firing mechanism lock located just above the cylinder latch on the left side of the frame. These mandated features are a fact of life in the 21st century.

The Fixed Sight Model 21-4...

Reliability is a prerequisite for a fighting revolver. Forget accuracy, ease of handling––even forget cost––the gun HAS to work, no matter how cheap or expensive it may be. Otherwise, it serves only those who sold it, not those who purchased it for their self-defense. This is the main reason why double-action, swing-out cylinder revolvers lasted so long in American law enforcement when compared to the rest of the world. Until two decades ago they had the better reputation for reliability and most of those revolvers used by police officers were fixed-sight guns, often Smith & Wesson Military & Police models in different calibers.

In front is the Model 21-4 and, as you can see, it uses a longer cylinder than previously seen on Smith & Wesson 44 special revolvers. The back revolver is a Model 24-3 made during the late 1980s; it has a shorter cylinder.

It is extremely difficult to damage the sighting system on a fixed-sight S&W Military & Police revolver. This is its big advantage. It is virtually indestructible and, in the case of the test revolver, there is an added advantage in that the front sight is pinned to the base portion formed as part of the barrel. Yeah, they used a roll-pin versus a solid pin, but at least the entire blade can be replaced without having to machine the whole thing for something new.

The width of the half-moon front sight is substantially thicker than that seen on many of the older M&P N-frame revolvers. The blade thickness on my prewar S&W 38/44 Heavy Duty measures .079-inch, but the blade thickness on the Model 21-4 measures .125-inch with the same Vernier caliper. The corresponding U-notch on the Model 21-4 measures .136-inch while the older gun features a smaller notch that is .090-inch wide. It is interesting to note the front sight blade on my S-prefix Model 58 M&P measures .125-inch with a rear U-notch width of .130-inch, while the front blade width on the Model 21-4 roughly corresponds to that on the early Model 58 M&P revolvers, it also features a far wider rear notch. This is important for those of us with older eyes, because as Clint Smith said, "This is an old guy's gun."

Having said that, there are some specific differences between this new Model 21 and the older versions, this new model features all the recently mandated changes to the Smith & Wesson revolver line-up. Yes, it has the ugly trigger lock located just above the cylinder latch on the left side of the frame. Despite all the protests against these things by those who truly love and appreciate the classic Smith & Wesson double-action revolver, these mandated engineering atrocities are here to stay. You simply can't "wish" them away.

Some of the old guys object to the gold wash Thunder Ranch logo on the sideplate. I don't, but then I also like custom chrome rims on my vehicles, so you can't go by my taste and preferences. It doesn't affect the performance of the gun in the least, and if it was necessary to get this gun re-introduced then I feel it is a small concession to the marketing department of S&W.

An additional modern change is the firing pin is located in the frame and not on the hammer. In the view of those more knowledgeable than myself, this is a good thing because it allows a really skilled pistolsmith the opportunity to "slick up" the action to the point of pure perfection. Many feel the frame-mounted firing pin requires less striking energy to maintain the same level of ignition reliability. Personally, I feel this is a moot point on a self-defense revolver. What is needed and required is a consistent and sufficient striking force to the firing pin and primer to guarantee complete and reliable ignition of the cartridge primer.

Another major difference between the Model 21-4 and previous models is the use of a full-length cylinder versus the shorter cylinder found on revolvers previously made specifically for the 44 Special chambering. The cylinder length on the Model 21-4 Thunder Ranch Special is 1.700 inches, while the cylinder length on my Model 24-3 manufactured during the late 1980s is 1.576 inches. I measured the cylinder on my Model 29-2, with the pinned and recessed cylinder where the rim portion of the cartridge is fully enclosed; its length was 1.746 inches. So, without the recessed feature of the earlier cylinder, the cylinder on the Model 21-4 is the same length as the cylinders used for current production 44 Magnum revolvers. This is an appearance issue more than anything else as I doubt the longer cylinder causes any noticeable difference in accuracy or velocity.

Shooting The Model 21-4...

Testing of the Model 21-4 was a fun-filled experience, but I replaced the Ahrends slim concealed carry-style grips with those that approximated the original diamond center full-size target grips from Eagle Grips. The main reason being I just didn't like the "feel" or balance of the gun with the slim grips, 4-inch barrel and the round butt frame. The Eagle Grips approximated the square butt profile of so many revolvers in my present inventory and felt like those I have used for so many decades. The round-butt frame profile can be appreciated on revolvers with relatively short barrels, but for those guns with longer barrels I prefer the square-butt profile.

After shooting a wide range of both factory and handloaded ammunition through the Model 21-4, the most pleasant and the most accurate load in all my testing proved to be the traditional 246-grain round-nose lead load from Winchester. It put six rounds into a group measuring 2.75 inches at a distance of 25 yards, offhand, and proved to be one of the least objectionable in terms of felt recoil. Stouter loads will make their presence 'felt' by the shooter and the old stand-by, but the seriously heavy handload involving 7.5 grains of Alliant's Unique and a 245-grain SWC bullet proved to be one you didn't want to shoot all afternoon. Still, it put five rounds, offhand, into a group measuring three inches at 25 yards. One flyer opened this group up; the recoil from this lighter steel-frame 44 may have had some influence on the shooter by the time the sixth round came up.

The author found he did not like the balance of the 4-inch barreled Model 21-4 with the supplied Ahrends grips, so he substituted a pair of diamond center target-style grips from Eagle Grips that approximated the square-butt profile found with older examples.

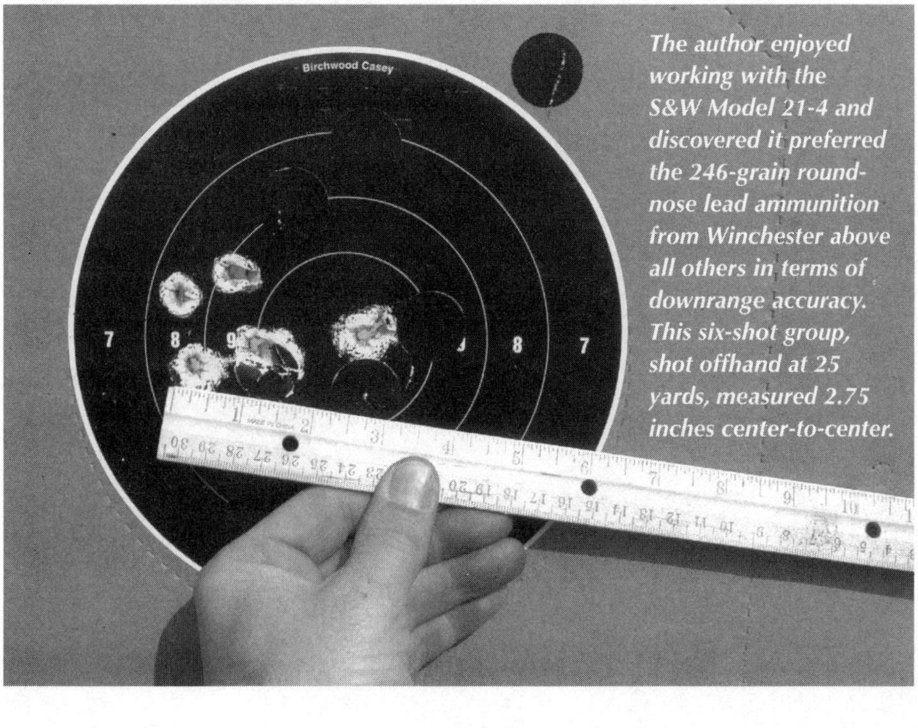

The author enjoyed working with the S&W Model 21-4 and discovered it preferred the 246-grain round-nose lead ammunition from Winchester above all others in terms of downrange accuracy. This six-shot group, shot offhand at 25 yards, measured 2.75 inches center-to-center.

It's hard to argue against a gun and cartridge combination that will throw a modern 200-grain jacketed hollow-point bullet like the Speer Gold Dot design at a muzzle velocity of 800 fps. The Smith & Wesson Model 21-4 is an old idea in a traditional package that utilizes the very latest in modern manufacturing technology.

It's interesting to note that, over sixteen years, Smith & Wesson managed to manufacture and sell only 1200 Model 21 and pre-Model 21 revolvers, but since the Model 21-4 Thunder Ranch Special was introduced they have sold 1700 units in less than a year.

Clearly, this "old guy's gun" is more appreciated now for its many virtues than at any time in its history. Obviously, many feel it is not a "worthless" concept in terms of quality, appearance or defensive firepower. It is still a valid concept for "...shootin' and fightin'..."

HIGH VELOCITY AMMUNITION
COR®BON
PROVEN STOPPING POWER
20 Cartridges
WARNING:
23
AUSTRIA
.40

THE GLOCK 23

The Perfect, All-Around Pistol?

by Paul Scarlata / photos by James Walters & Sal Scarlata

In late autumn I received an assignment from the esteemed editor of this fine publication. Generally, receiving an assignment is a joyful moment for a writer as it means insured income. But when said editor broached the subject of said assignment, your faithful reporter's joy turned to trepidation. In fact, I went so far as to ask him "Are you sure you want *ME* to do this?" When he answered in the affirmative I knew I was doomed. As I hung up the telephone with trembling hands I realized that I had been cursed with the assignment from Hell.

There are certain subjects that gun writers fear more than they do a tax audit, such as those perennial favorites of editors everywhere: *"Is the 270 better than the 30-06?"* and *"Is the 9mm as good as the 45?"* Being we all hold knowledgeable *(?)* opinions on such controversial subjects, these articles are not difficult to produce, but they are fraught with danger. Because, no matter what position we espouse or conclusions we arrive at, they are guaranteed to royally tick off a goodly percentage of the readers and the resulting flood of letters and e-mails runs the gamut from merely amusing to downright threatening!

But my fate was sealed and the outlook was bleak. I would have rather undergone an IRS audit than to have to discuss *"What is the perfect, all-around pistol?"*

For the sake of brevity, I decided to limit my discussion of the "... *perfect, all-around pistol"* to those that I felt were suitable for home defense, civilian concealed carry, and police/security service. My first task was to determine those characteristics that would make it suitable for these diverse duties. After much rumination, I took out a fresh sheet of paper and began my list:

1. It should be of an intermediate size making it suitable for both holster wear and concealed carry.
2. It must be chambered for a cartridge that provides sufficient power for defensive purposes.
3. It must be light enough for comfortable extended carry, without sacrificing recoil control.
4. It must possess

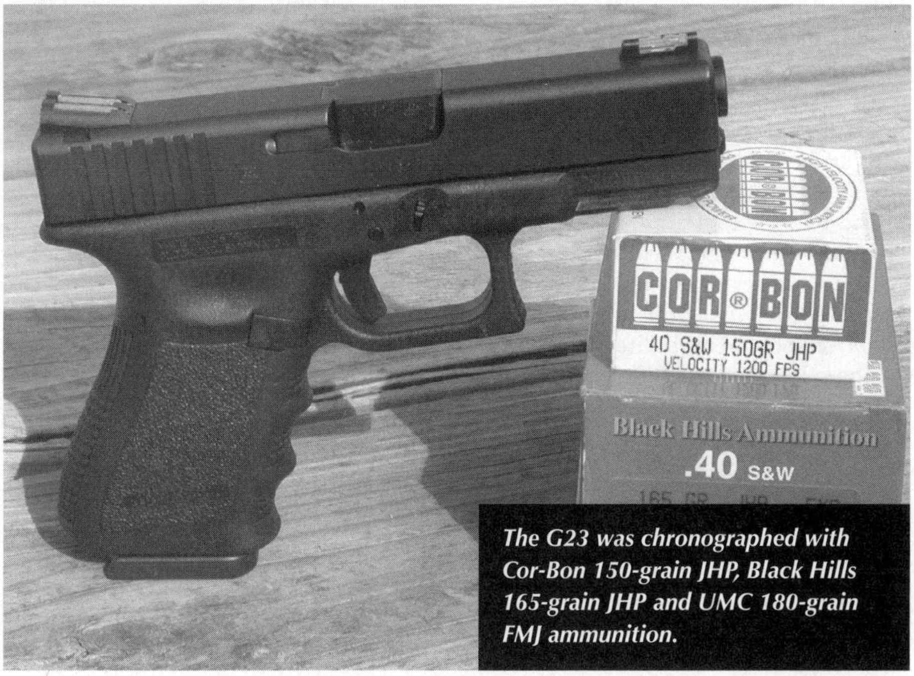

The G23 was chronographed with Cor-Bon 150-grain JHP, Black Hills 165-grain JHP and UMC 180-grain FMJ ammunition.

ergonomics suitable to a wide variety of hand sizes.

5. It must be simple to operate.

6. It must be reliable, resistant to wear, abuse and environmental extremes.

7. It should be capable of accepting aftermarket parts and accessories, making it adaptable to personal preferences and/or special tactical applications.

8. It should have a magazine capacity large enough for special situations.

9. It should be easy to field-strip for cleaning and maintenance.

10. It must be affordable.

I'm sure most of you will agree with me *(it may be the last time?)* that this was a most impressive list and would not be easy to live up to. But now that I knew what I wanted my pistol to do, I had to find one capable of doing it. In fact, the latter part of this process turned out to be fairly easy because I had been carrying it on my belt for the past month and a half—a Glock 23.

I bought my first Glock pistol approximately six months after their G17 first hit the American market. Since that time I have owned—or have used extensively—every model Glock that is available in the U.S. with, I might add, complete satisfaction. In addition to the aforementioned G23, at the present time my gun safe contains two G17s, a G19, G21, G22, G24C, G26, G30, G31, G34, and a G35 *(did I forget any?)*. You are probably safe in assuming that I am a dyed-in-the-wool Glockist!

In 1990 Gaston Glock took the handgun market by surprise *(again!)* when he introduced his G22 and G23, the first production pistols chambered for the 40 S&W cartridge. This new 40-caliber cartridge was developed by Olin/Winchester at the request of police agencies that wanted a service pistol round more authoritative than the 9mm Parabellum. The resulting cartridge used a rimless case 0.850-inch long loaded with a 180-grain JHP bullet moving at approximately 1000 fps and producing 400 ft./lbs. of muzzle energy *(fpe)*. It had the dual advantages of providing 45 ACP-like ballistics and could be used in 9mm-sized pistols. It was an instant hit with police agencies and civilian shooters alike.

The G22 and G23 were built on the same sized *(although reinforced)* frames as the earlier 9mm G17 and G19 pistols and weighed approximately the same. Glock's handguns had proven extremely popular with American shooters and were already well on their way to capturing almost 60 percent of the U.S. police market. The introduction of pistols chambered for the impressive new 40-caliber cartridge just speeded things up.

Glock's popularity with American police and civilian shooters is not hard to fathom. Their Safe Action Trigger *(some refer to it as a "double-action-only")* does away with the need for thumb or grip safeties and greatly eases familiarization and training. All Glock pistols are loaded, operated, fired and field-stripped in the exact same manner. Thus, if you know how to use one Glock, you know how to use them all. I believe that with a handgun intended for defensive or police purposes, such simplicity of operation is of the utmost importance. At the same time, three automatic safety devices (trigger block, firing pin and drop safety) make the Glock one of the safest pistols on today's market.

Glocks are best known for their use of a polymer frame which performs the double—and seemingly contradictory—tasks of reducing weight *AND* recoil at the same time. The polymer frame G23 loaded with 13 rounds of 40-caliber ammunition weighs less than most other pistols in its class. But because the space-age material of the frame actually flexes and absorbs part of the recoil force, despite its lack of mass, a Glock will produce less felt recoil than other pistols of the same size and caliber. Additionally, because the polymer frame does not require grip panels, the Glock has one of the narrowest grip frames of all high-capacity pistols. This makes it suitable to a wide variety of hand sizes and—thanks to its light recoil—for shooters of small stature.

Glock's patented Tenifer finish provides protection from corrosion, abrasion, solvents and wear superior to stainless steel. Field-stripping

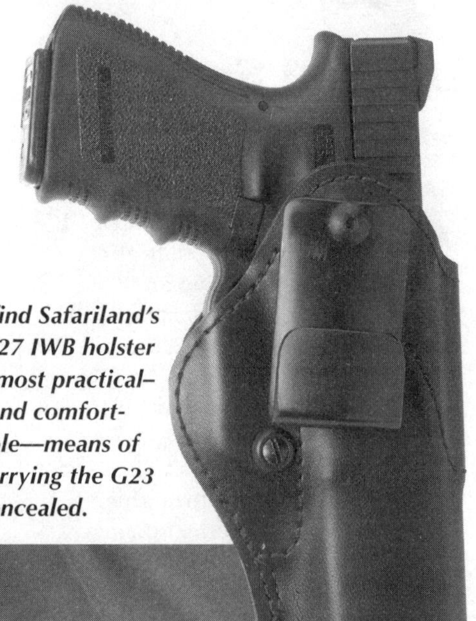

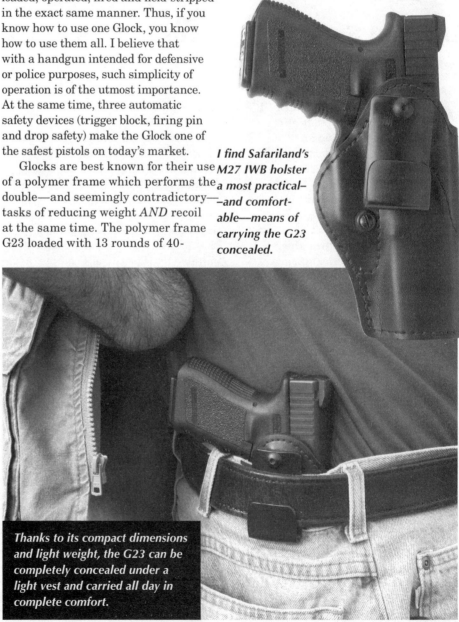

I find Safariland's M27 IWB holster a most practical—and comfortable—means of carrying the G23 concealed.

Thanks to its compact dimensions and light weight, the G23 can be completely concealed under a light vest and carried all day in complete comfort.

RELOADING - IS IT TIME TO START?

by Thomas C. Tabor

Selecting a carry gun is a Many sportsmen have already turned to reloading their own rifle and pistol cartridges as a way of expanding their shooting enjoyment and, at the same time, save a little money in the process. But while reloading is *right* for some shooters—*is this right for you?* If you are one of those shooters asking yourself that question, you need to carefully consider both the benefits and the disadvantages.

Based on the single reason of saving money many shooters have taken up the hobby of reloading. But while the monetary aspects of reloading are important ones, saving money isn't the only reason to consider handloading your own ammunition. By reloading your own cartridges you have the ability to precisely tailor your cartridges to fit each of your firearms and to each of your shooting activities. By doing so, many shooters find that their performance and accuracy is dramatically improved. The available choices in factory loaded ammunition are always limited, but if you handload your own cartridges, the choices are almost endless. These benefits can make you a better and more productive shooter.

***Left:** Reloading manuals are available from many powder and bullet manufacturers. These manuals not only provide you with the necessary loading 'recipes', they often contain valuable tips and instructions.*
***Middle:** The NRA is a great source of information about reloading. Their new book NRA Guide to Reloading would be a great book to add to your library.*
***Right:** There are even videos to help you get started reloading. These often contain good advice from experts in the field.*

But even though there are significant advantages to reloading your own shells, there are some negative aspects to be considered as well. Certainly handloading isn't for every shooter. If you are the type of individual that has a tendency to approach things in a helter-skelter manner, paying little attention to details—maybe you would be better off buying your shells from the factory, already loaded. Careless mistakes made while handloading are dangerous ones. While reloading can save sportsmen money on their shooting costs, it does require a fairly substantial outlay of funds just to produce that first cartridge. In order to save money it usually means you have to, most of all, be a shooter that likes to burn a lot of powder. If you fire only a box or

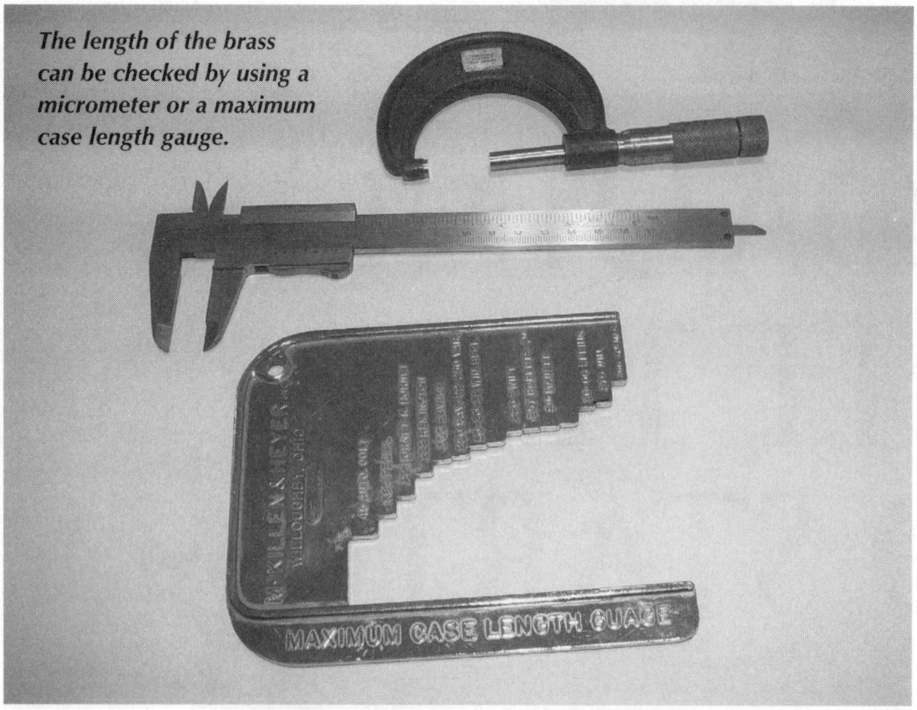

The length of the brass can be checked by using a micrometer or a maximum case length gauge.

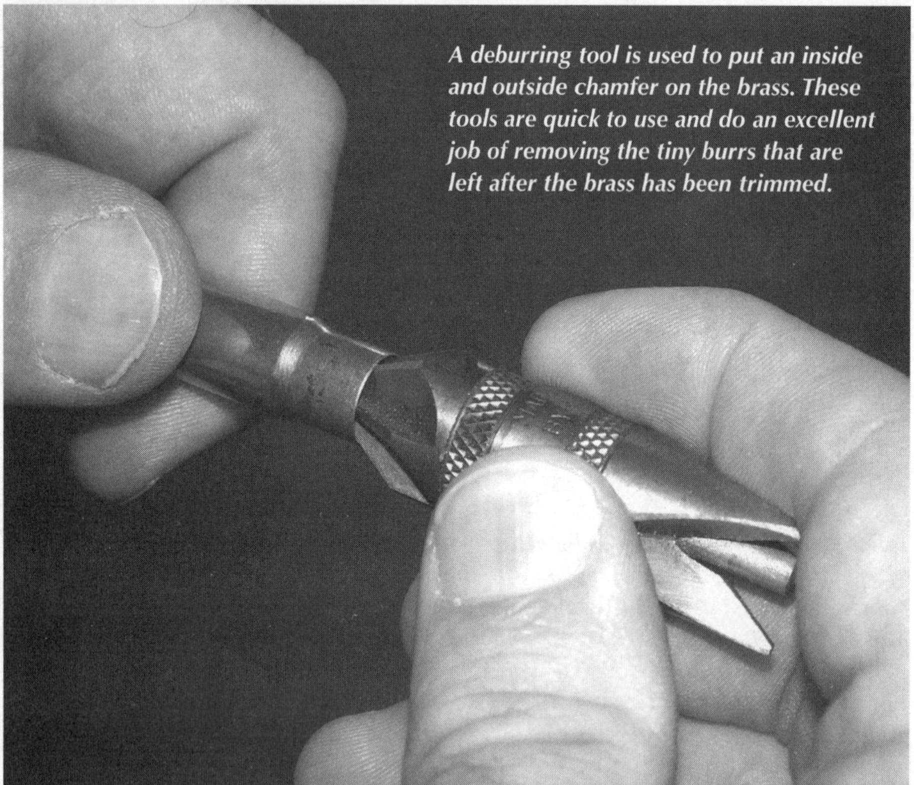

A deburring tool is used to put an inside and outside chamfer on the brass. These tools are quick to use and do an excellent job of removing the tiny burrs that are left after the brass has been trimmed.

two of cartridges a year you can't really expect to see any significant cost savings. If the foregoing doesn't discourage you, give a little thought to the space that reloading takes up. Do you have room for the new hobby?

But that's enough of the negatives. Let's delve deeper into the reasons why so many sportsmen have turned to reloading as a way of furthering their outdoor enjoyment—and take a look at the basic equipment you need to get started.

Unfortunately, making a prediction about how much money you can actually save is difficult. Equipment cost will vary dramatically. The cost of reloading components will also vary, depending upon the quality of the components, where you purchase them, and in what quantity they are purchased. All of these factors are crucially important when you attempt to figure cost saving.

How elaborate *(and costly)* your equipment will be is strictly up to you. At a minimum you will need a reloading press. Most individuals opt to purchase the less expensive single-stage presses over the faster progressive models, at least in the beginning. The single-stage press may be a bit slower, but to do a good job reloading, 'slow and deliberate' is oftentimes best. A progressive-style press is capable of doing multiple operations with each stroke of the handle, but this style of machine is intended more for large-quantity reloading projects. A single-stage press, on the other hand, focuses on a single shell and a single process at a time. The vast majority of shooters find the single-stage reloader best for their shooting needs.

A set of reloading dies will be needed for each cartridge you intend to load. There are a few exceptions to this rule, for example the 38 Special/357 Magnum and 44 Special/44 Magnum cartridges. In these cases a set of dies that would load the 357 or 44 Magnum cartridges could be used for the shorter versions (38 Special or 44 Special) as well. Carbide reloading dies are a good choice, but cost a bit more than the standard steel dies. Unless you intend to do a tremendous amount of reloading, follow the vast majority of the shooters who wind up purchasing the less expensive steel dies. On the other hand, if you're into such activities as pistol competition, or some other activity that requires you to expend a great amount of ammunition, it might pay you to go with carbide.

A shell holder will also be necessary for each caliber you intend to load, but many cartridges possess the same size base dimensions. Consequently, in many cases a shell holder will fit a variety of different cartridges.

Everyone that reloads has to have reloading data, or "recipes" as they are sometimes informally

Top: A piece of equipment that isn't really a requirement to get started reloading, but nice to have, is a brass cleaner like this vibrating RCBS model.

Above: The first step in getting your press started reloading is to mount the resizing die in place.

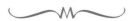

called. There are probably as many reloading manuals on the market as there are rifle calibers. The prices of these will vary, but free manuals are also available from many of the powder and component manufacturers. Sometimes these booklets are available where you purchase reloading equipment, or you can obtain them directly from the manufacturers. The Internet is a great place to find reloading data as well, but you should be a bit cautious that the data is coming from a reputable and reliable source.

Many reloading manuals serve a dual purpose. Not only do they provide you with the 'recipes' to load by, in many cases they are also a great source of basic reloading instructions. Many manuals will contain elaborate chapters on 'How To' reload, plus other interesting and useful information. These manuals are great sources of information for those individuals new to handloading, as well as longtime reloaders. Even if you are only contemplating getting into handloading, one of these manuals can provide you with a great deal of basic information that will help you make informed choices.

The next major piece of equipment that is necessary is a balance, or scale. The primary use for a scale is to accurately and precisely weigh powder charges; a scale also comes in handy to check the weights of bullets and brass. In addition, you will need cartridge case lube, a powder funnel, a case trimmer, a means of checking the length of your brass, and a deburring/chamfering tool.

The case lube is applied to the case prior to resizing in steel dies. It helps reduce the friction associated with this operation. Brass may stretch in length as it is fired and resized, so a case trimmer is needed to keep your brass within the acceptable dimensional limits. There are a couple of different ways to check the length to tell if your brass needs trimming. Some handloaders use a micrometer and others simply rely on a maximum case length gauge. The micrometer will provide an exact measurement of the length and it is useful for other measuring/reloading purposes as well. The maximum case length gauge simply consists of a piece of plastic, or metal that is notched to the length of the various cartridge cases. If the brass case slips cleanly through the area associated with that cartridge—the brass is within acceptable limits. If it does not, the brass is too long and must be trimmed. Once the brass has been trimmed to the acceptable length, a deburring tool should be used to put an inside and outside chamfer on the mouth of the case.

Sometimes reloading activities can take up a sizeable amount of space in your home or shop. There are ways of getting around this, such as designing your setup in a way that permits you to break your equipment down when

Top: A powder measure is a great tool for 'throwing' approximate powder charges, but for both consistency and safety reasons all charges should be weighed on an accurate scale prior to seating the bullet. Above: A powder dribbler makes getting the powder charge exact much easier than simply using a spoon, but a dribber is not absolutely necessary to get started reloading cartridges.

not in use. But no matter how you arrange your reloading equipment, it will be necessary to have a very strong, solid surface to work from since a considerable amount of force is sometimes necessary when resizing the brass. For this reason, the press must be mounted securely to the working surface by heavy bolts or screws. Many handloaders find that an old desk or workbench provides the best working surface, but if working space is at a premium maybe a portable bench is your best option. Several companies currently produce these products.

As mentioned earlier, your initial cost to get started is extremely hard to estimate. There simply are too many choices on the market today to provide a realistic projection. It is usually good advice, though, to buy the best you can afford whenever entering into any new venture—including selecting reloading equipment. That doesn't mean you have to mortgage the family dwelling to purchase a new Ferrari, or to handload your own cartridges. Nevertheless, when you purchase a cheaper, lower end product to begin with, disappointment sometimes follows. While I don't feel there are any bad presses, scales, dies, etc., currently on the market today, some are surely better than others; in most cases, quality comes with a price.

One way you may be able to save on your initial reloading setup is to seek out a package deal, or kit. Some companies offer a kit containing all that is necessary to get started reloading packaged in a single box for a single price. Generally the total price of these package deals is lower than if you purchased each item separately. It should be pointed out, however, that sometimes there are items included that are not absolutely necessary. For example, in some cases these kits may contain a powder measure. While a powder measure is a great accessory and most people find them extremely useful—you could get by without one if your reloading volume was quite small. Consequently, you should consider these purchases carefully by evaluating whether they best fit your overall objectives and your overall spending budget.

The basic stuff to get started reloading may seem like a lot of equipment and tools just to stuff a few pieces of brass. The good news is that once you have purchased the basic equipment, it can be used to load virtually any caliber rifle and pistol cartridge. In many cases all that is necessary to add another caliber is a set of reloading dies and, most likely, a shell holder that will fit the cartridge. Of course different calibers sometimes call for different bullets, powder and primers, but as far as the equipment goes—once you are set up with the 'basics' you are pretty much ready to take on any new cartridge you choose to load.

There is plenty of other equipment and tools that can be added to your reloading bench as time goes on, but these items are not a basic requirement. In many cases they can certainly make the reloading process easier, quicker—and even more fun.

A powder measure certainly falls into that category. These devices allow you to measure the powder charge quickly and easily in volumetric form. It is highly recommended, however, that a powder measure should only be used in conjunction with a powder scale. In most cases, particularly when loading coarse-grain slow-burning rifle powders, the charge can vary a few tenths of a grain when measured by volume. For this reason each charge should be rechecked and adjusted accordingly through the use of an accurate powder scale. By doing so, it will help assure consistency from load to load, the best possible accuracy, and add a degree of safety to your reloading activities.

A powder dribbler is also nice to have, but once again it is not a requirement. When making fine adjustments to the weight of a powder charge, a small spoon can be used, or you can use a powder dribbler. Some people find the dribbler makes the process of precisely achieving the exact weight of powder just a bit easier.

Another great device that you might want to add later on is a cartridge brass tumbler, or polisher. Keeping your brass bright and shiny—much like keeping your car clean and well waxed—gives you a sense of pride in ownership. The tumbler takes the elbow grease out of keeping your brass in a pristine state. If you are looking to save money, however, you can polish the brass by hand, using brass cleaner, or with a piece of fine steel wool.

Other tools that are handy, but not required, are such things as primer pocket cleaners and case neck brushes, primer pocket reamers, bullet pullers, inside and outside neck-turning devices and attachments, brass lubricating devices, cartridge loading blocks,

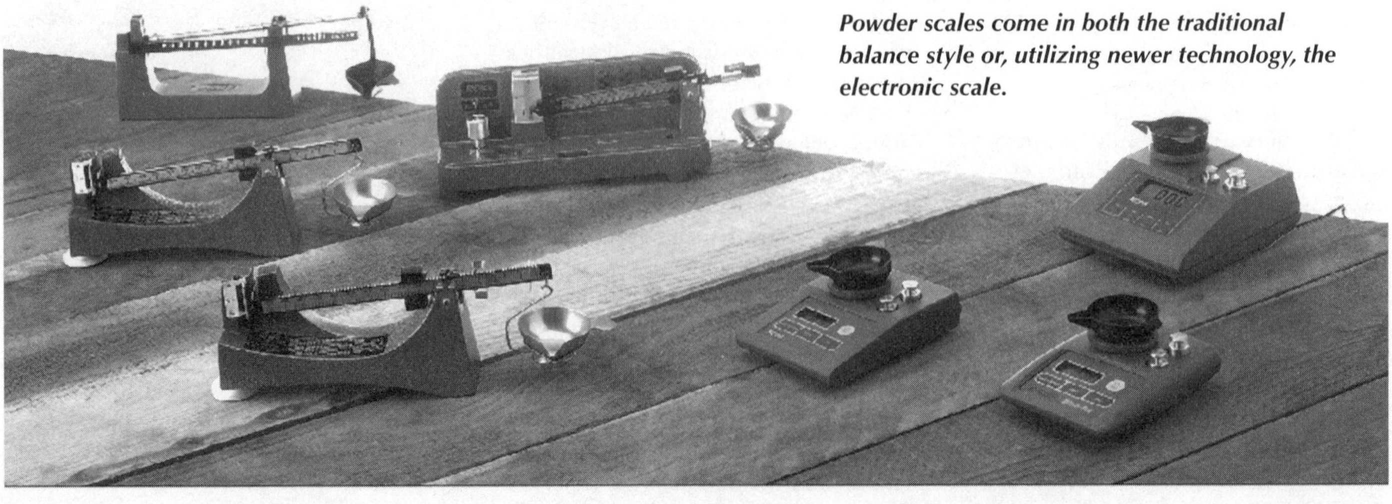

Powder scales come in both the traditional balance style or, utilizing newer technology, the electronic scale.

handheld priming tools—just to name a few of the optional items.

A very big factor in cost savings has to do with the volume of reloading supplies you wind up purchasing. There is often a considerable price break when you buy bullets in quantities of 500 or 1000 versus a box of 50 or 100; primers in quantities of 1000 or more versus a box of 100; powder by the keg rather than by the one-pound can and brass by the 100, 500 or 1000 lot rather than by the box. In addition, you will find a considerable variation in price from one supplier to another, so the key here is to shop around for the best price before buying.

Certainly one of the most beneficial things about reloading your own cartridges is being able to select the best possible bullet to fit your needs. In the case of hunting this particular benefit is a crucially important one. Most manufacturers constantly look for ways to cut production costs, and ammunition manufacturers are no different. As a result, sometimes over-the-counter ammo may contain bullets not designed for a particular hunting or accuracy purpose, simply because the manufacturer wants to sell higher volume through lower prices. This ammunition may be acceptable for use for plinking or practice, but do you really want to cut corners when it comes to your hunting cartridges? By reloading your own ammunition, you have the ability to cut costs and at the same time you can *stuff* your brass with precisely the quality of bullet that best fits your shooting situation.

Factory-loaded ammunition has several other drawbacks that are worth considering. We have already discussed how production considerations may affect the product, but there is another aspect worthy of consideration. While there are many new, strong and safe firearms in use today—there are also some older, not-so-safe guns still being used. The goal for the ammunition industry is to produce a product that will be safe throughout this diverse range of firearm quality. This means that the factory ammo you are shooting may not be delivering your gun's potential. For the shooter who reloads his own ammo, no such sacrifices are required. You can load your cartridges however you see fit, as long as you keep the pressure within acceptable safe limits. Through careful experimentation of different recommended loads, the handloader has the ability of finding and shooting the best possible load for his particular firearm.

Today the computerized generation has even reached into handloading. Several companies, including Hodgdon Powder Co., are now providing their reloading data on computer software.

If you shoot a handgun that generates a lot of recoil, like a magnum, you know just how hard it can be on your hand and wrist. In many cases a handloader can 'load down' their cartridges in order to produce a more acceptable and favorable recoil level. But a word of caution is in order here. No shooter should ever deviate from the standardized reloading data that has been published and distributed by reputable sources. You might think that by simply reducing the powder charge in a cartridge that it will always produce less pressure, *but this is not always the case*!! Experimentation in the area of powder volumes beyond what is recommended is never advisable. Counter to what some may believe, dangerously high chamber pressures can sometimes be generated, particularly in magnum cartridges, if the powder levels are reduced below the recommended starting load levels.

The author has loaded his own ammunition for well over 30 years. Over that time he has fired thousands of custom-constructed rounds. These have been shot for plinking, punching holes in paper targets, knocking silhouettes around, for competition and for hunting purposes. Without a doubt, most of these loads were better than what a commercial production operation is capable of. You, like the author, can produce a better cartridge if you choose to get into reloading. It may take time to work up the perfect load, and it will require some extra shooting, but isn't that what we are all about—*shooting*?

Only you can determine whether handloading is for you, but if you are a sportsman that relishes all facets of the shooting sports— it might be just the activity to extend your enjoyment of the outdoors. Certainly handloading has its drawbacks, but when you load your own ammo it is a bit like the bird hunter that hunts over a dog that he/she has personally trained. The personal satisfaction of seeing your own dog staunchly on point over a covey of birds increases the enjoyment of the hunt at least 100-fold. A similar feeling of contentment and accomplishment is experienced when you know your handload was responsible for putting that trophy animal on the ground, or shooting the winning score in a handgun silhouette match.

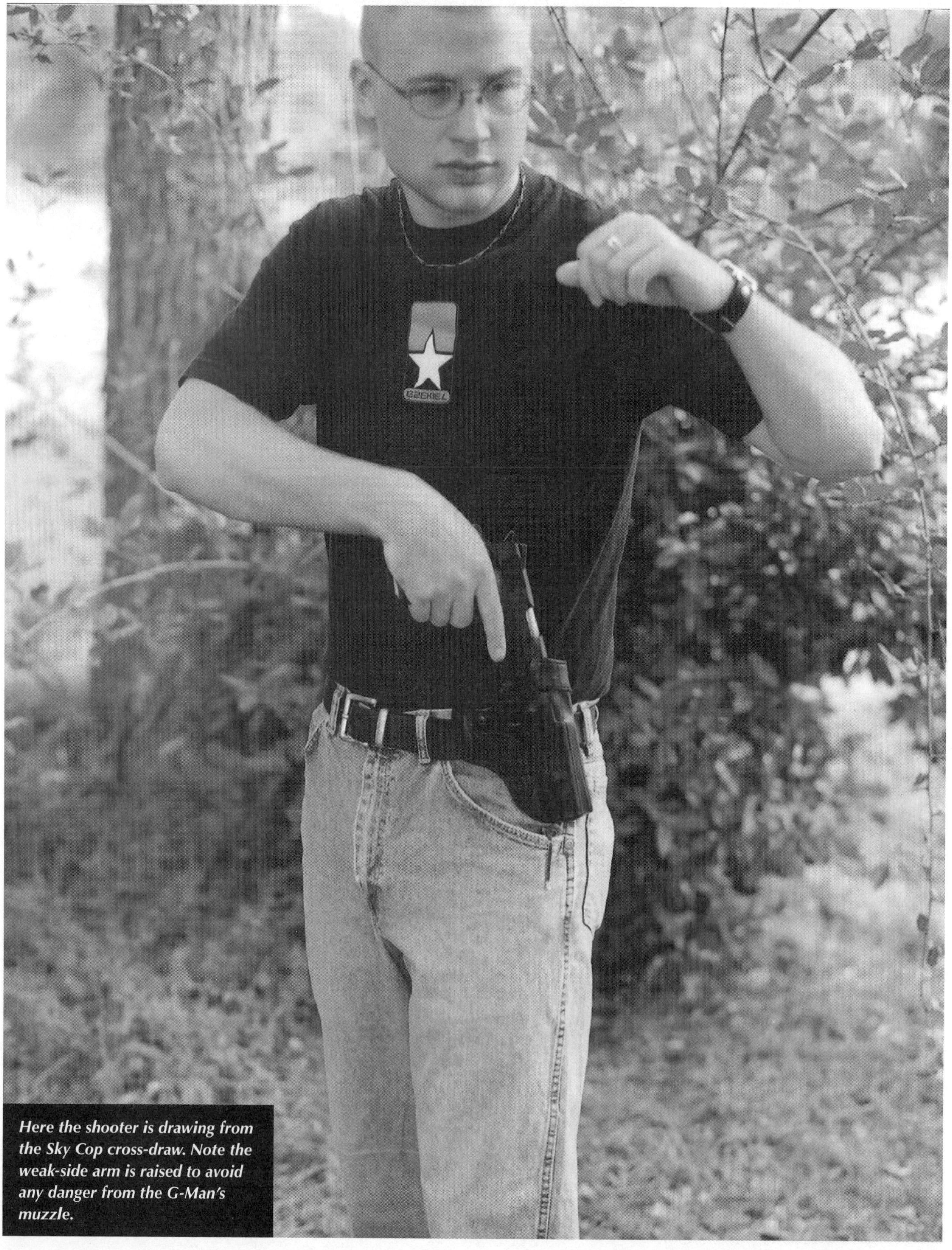

Here the shooter is drawing from the Sky Cop cross-draw. Note the weak-side arm is raised to avoid any danger from the G-Man's muzzle.

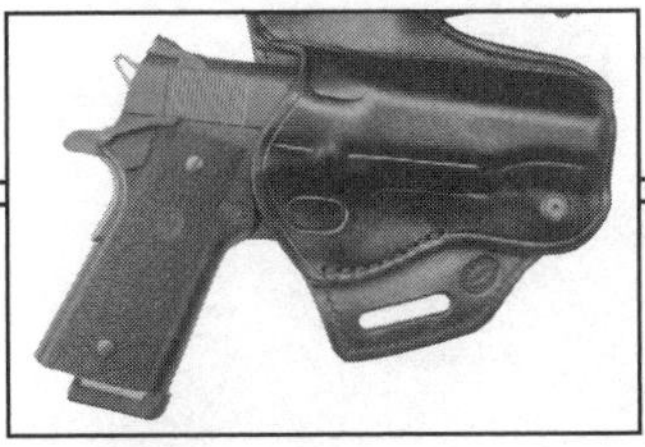

SENSIBLE CUSTOM

MODIFICATIONS FOR DAILY WEAR

by Bob Campbell

I am often surprised at the behavior of normally sensible people when it comes to custom handguns. People who are downright stingy when ordering a vehicle or sundry wares tend to order everything they don't need when a custom handgun is on the agenda. Let's face it, for most folks a custom handgun is a personal statement. I have made it, I can handle it and I deserve it! At least, let's hope this is the case. Custom handguns are not inexpensive, and wealth and good sense by no means go hand in hand. I have seen horrendous mistakes when it comes to custom pistols—and I have seen a number of understated, capable handguns that really do the business. But realize this—the majority of battles won by the good guys and girls are won by ordinary gear. Service-grade handguns deliver outstanding results in the hands of practiced operators.

My ideas concerning custom handguns have been fluid, with each handgun a case unto itself, based on the perceived needs of the day. Still, my observations have coalesced into a consensus as to what is needed in a combat (carry) handgun.

Reliability is a hundred times more important than anything else. If I have significant difficulty during a modest break-in period, I will trade or scrap the handgun rather than trust it. I prefer to begin with a handgun that has proven reliable out of the box. Remedial fixes are fine as far as they go, but a new pistol should work.

Next, I value a good trigger compression. I understand that heavy triggers are designed into certain pistols as a fail-safe and that some shooters cannot handle a lighter trigger. I prefer a pistol with a three- to four-pound trigger action. I wish to be able to strike small objects at close range, and man-sized targets to one hundred yards, and a good trigger is necessary for success.

Finally, good sights are a must. A good trigger compression is of little use if the sights are too small and imprecise to allow proper alignment and sight picture. Today, some of the very best handgun sights are readily available. There are other areas of concern, including the grips, but these are the basics.

A final modification I have demanded in recent years is an all-weather self-lubricating finish. After ruining the finish of a Star PD while carrying

As issued, the High Standard G-Man is an attractive pistol with many good features. Standard features include high visibility self-luminous sights, a match-grade barrel, and attractive checkered grips.

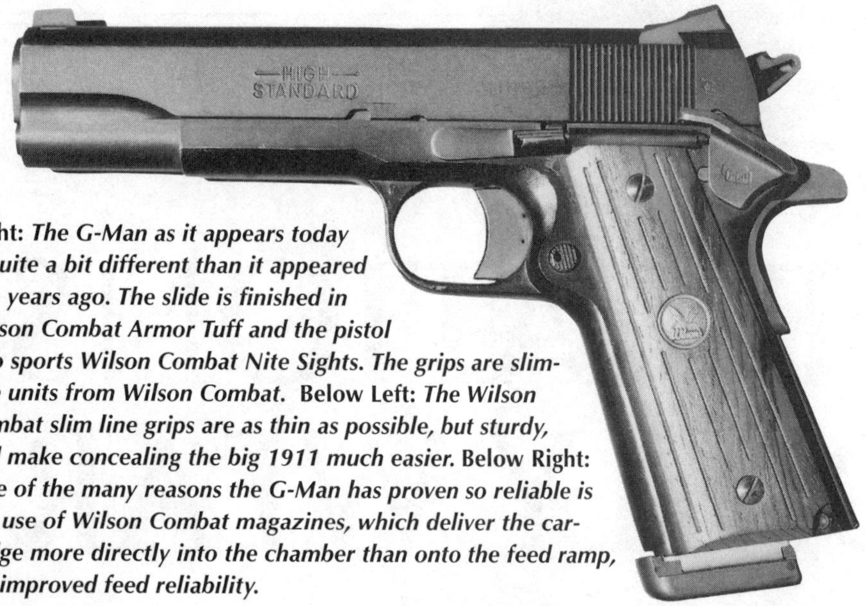

Right: ***The G-Man as it appears today is quite a bit different than it appeared five years ago. The slide is finished in Wilson Combat Armor Tuff and the pistol also sports Wilson Combat Nite Sights. The grips are slimline units from Wilson Combat.*** **Below Left:** ***The Wilson Combat slim line grips are as thin as possible, but sturdy, and make concealing the big 1911 much easier.*** **Below Right:** ***One of the many reasons the G-Man has proven so reliable is the use of Wilson Combat magazines, which deliver the cartridge more directly into the chamber than onto the feed ramp, for improved feed reliability.***

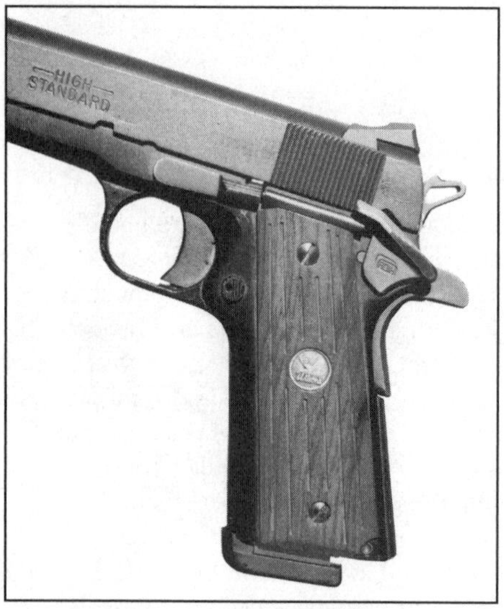

the pistol close to my body on special assignment, I realized that traditional blueing simply didn't make it.

My current concealed-carry pistols are the most suited to my personal style of shooting and defense needs than anything I have deployed in the past. They represent the high point on my learning curve. By the same token, they are not drastically different from anything else I have trusted during my adult life. I have used the 1911 and the Hi-Power for over thirty years, and see no reason to change.

The pistols available today are better than ever, ammunition is much better, and I dare say shooters may be better. I still favor the black 1911 in full-length Government Model form. But a new variation on the Hi-Power has impressed me enough that it is now among my most often carried handguns. My threat profile is no longer what it was when I was on the hit list of neo-Nazi groups but knowing our protein-fed ex-con criminal class as I do, I have no wish to be naked before them. What follows is my choice in personal defense handguns.

The 1911

When we say 1911, we may mean Springfield, Colt, Rock Island Armory or a number of other makers. My personal pistol is a High Standard. Best known for resurrecting the excellent High Standard rimfire pistols, the new company also produces first-rate variations on the 1911 45 auto. The version I chose is the high-end G-Man. The G-Man is designed to give an operator every advantage in a critical incident.

When first examining the handgun, I was most impressed by the fit and finish. The slide glided smoothly on the slide rails. When the slide was racked, the link and locking lugs worked in perfect union. Whoever put this pistol together knows their business, and it was a hands-on affair. Normally, I prefer a 1911 I can fieldstrip with my hands. The fit of the barrel bushing is tight, so tight that a bushing wrench is required to take the pistol down for routine maintenance. Once I fired the pistol and bench-rested it for accuracy, I compromised on this issue and left the match-grade bushing intact. Five-shot groups at 25 yards with premium ammunition have been as small as one inch, as good as it gets for a 1911. A realistic average is two inches with good ammunition. I can live with a tight barrel bushing that produces truly outstanding accuracy.

The High Standard was supplied with night sights and a space-age Teflon-based finish. But the pistol has great appeal to those of us who value traditional appearance. The Teflon finish was black and all business and the G-Man is issued with a very attractive set of rosewood-toned stocks.

The pistol came out of the box ready. As long as the magazine well is properly centered in the frame, the pistol should feed anything well and this one does. I have never experienced a problem of any kind with jacketed hollow-point, lead semi-wadcutter, or +P ammunition. The pistol fed, chambered, fired and ejected every type without fail.

The G-Man was ordered with one option, largely on an experimental basis. The 1911 must be carried cocked and locked: hammer to the rear and the safety on. This gives some folks cold chills and not necessarily the folks carrying the pistol. Why, even my dearly beloved recently asked if I had to carry the hammer back on my Hi-Power!

For those who cannot tolerate cocked and locked carry or who serve under an administrator who will not allow cocked and locked carry, the Safety Fast Shooting system makes a lot of sense. The Safety Fast Shooting system allows the use of the Colt 1911 or Browning H-Power in the ready mode but allows hammer-down carry. Available as a factory option from High Standard, the Safety Fast Shooting system can be fitted to existing handguns by Cylinder and Slide Shop, Inc. I strongly prefer the

1911 system, but I could live with the SFS better than any other alternative.

The SFS works as follows––the pistol is loaded in the normal manner. The pistol is now cocked and the handgun chamber loaded, but the safety cannot be moved to the *on* position. The SFS conversion features an internal ring and two-piece hammer. There is an internal spring in the hammer. When the pistol is cocked, simply press the hammer forward and the outer hammer locks in place and the safety moves to the *on* position. There is also a safety block between the hammer and firing pin.

When you wish to fire, move the safety to the *off* position and the hammer is released and flies to the full-cock position. The only real difference in handling is that the hammer is pressed forward to make the gun safe, instead of placing the safety on. As delivered, with the SFS option, the G-Man trigger broke at just over 3.5 pounds and has settled into a very smooth and crisp 3.5 pounds. The pistol has proven quite accurate; accuracy that has not dimmed after well over 15,000 rounds of ammunition.

I have used the G-Man as the main vehicle in numerous projects, and results have always been good. But what makes it my first choice as a carry gun is reliability and hit probability. I have found I can bring the pistol up and on target quickly, and connect with confidence. Firing at small targets at known and unknown ranges is more a measure of the pistol than firing bench-rest groups. Along the way, I chose the Black Hills 230-grain JHP as the duty load. With hit probability proven, the pistol eventually was modified to the ideal carry gun configuration.

The first change was the sights. The issue sights provide a good sight picture and are more developed than many. At about 10,000 rounds, the tritium dot removed itself from the front sight, above average longevity for these types. Although the sight picture remained great in good light, I elected to replace the existing sights with the best night sight configuration available. I sent the pistol to Wilson Combat for a set of Night Eyes.

Night Eyes are bright sights with an excellent sight picture. The rear sight is a design that offers a pyramid-type configuration that is easily and quickly picked up by the eye. The long tunnel of the rear sight is not prone to trapping shadows. Overall, a superior sight picture for any situation. Since the sight installation required machine work, Wilson Combat offered to finish the slide in Armor Tuff.

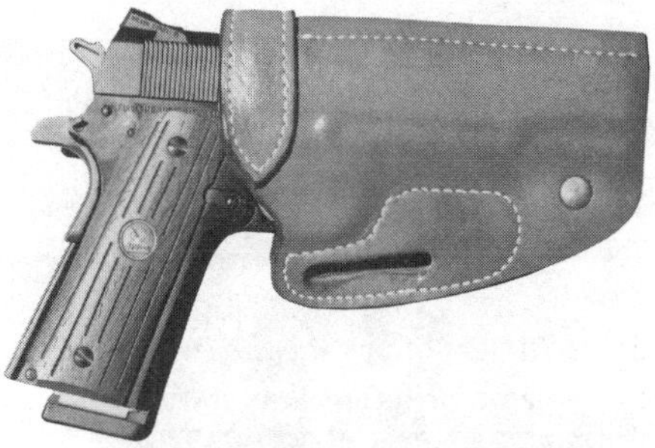

Top: The author found the Blocker ST 17 among the most versatile and effective holsters of all. The ST 17 allows both strong-side and cross-draw carry. Note retention screw and solid reinforcement of the holster mouth. This reinforcement, known as a welt, is part of every high-quality holster.
Middle: The DeSantis Sky Cop features a partially open welt that allows the pistol to be drawn quickly from the correct angle. Strong double-stitched belt loops and a retention screw add up to a well-designed and executed holster.
Bottom: The author likes his DeSantis Sky Cop cross-draw so much, he now owns several. The Sky Cop for the 1911 is great but the version for the snub 38 is also well put together.

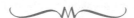

Armor Tuff has certain advantages in the process itself. Corrosion resistance is the number one priority, but the finish has survived literally thousands of presentations from the holster without blemish. The coating is a barrier against acids, oils––and even industrial solvent. But before Armor Tuff is applied, the pistol is thoroughly sand-blasted and carefully dehorned. This means sharp edges are melted away.

The steel is Parkerized before Armor Tuff is applied. Armor Tuff is available in a variety of tones, and I do appreciate a two-tone pistol. Let's face it––a beautiful deep blue is fine, but you will agonize over every nick and scratch. Armor Tuff is ideal for a hard-use pistol.

For most of the first few months, I carried the G-Man in a Kramer Sharkskin holster. The man who fully developed horsehide for holster use has also managed to master sharkskin and other exotics. Sharkskin has numerous advantages, including high scuff resistance. I enjoy this holster very much. Unlike the pistol, the holster is no worse for wear despite over five years of use.

As time went by, I adopted a dedicated cross-draw, and another holster suitable for either the cross-draw or strong-side––no small feat. I own several versions of the DeSantis Sky Cop holster. This holster is a purpose-designed cross-draw that affords good comfort when seated or driving. The advantages of a cross-draw holster are many. When seated, the hands can be practically touching the pistol. A strong-side draw from a seated position would be difficult indeed. So, the Sky Cop has done yeoman service.

To round out the holsters––and we need several holsters for true versatility––I have adopted the Blocker ST 17. I have used Blocker holsters for some twenty years with excellent results. The ST 17 can be worn as a strong-side holster with almost neutral cant. As such it hugs the body and conceals well. The ST 17 is also an excellent cross-draw. I often use the ST 17 in this manner, concealing the G-Man under a light jacket. When carrying two handguns, the ST 17 is a good choice for the backup.

I have also used the Milt Sparks C CAT with good results. While training

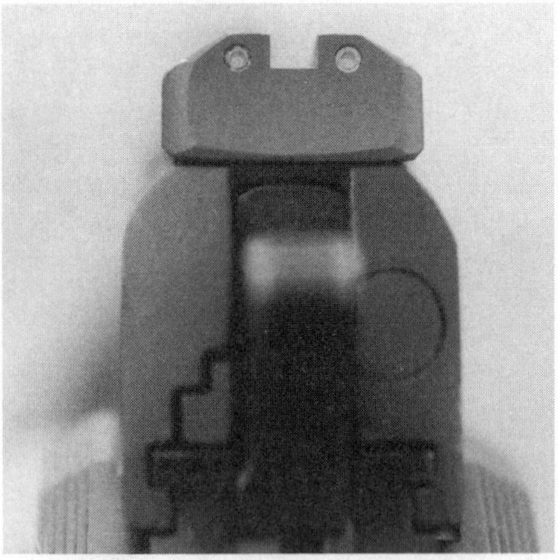

Wilson Combat Nite Eyes are the author's favorite night sight, offering bright, clear "lamps" and an excellent daytime sight picture.

a group to use pistols and gas masks simultaneously, my primary concern was proper airflow and the avoidance of heat stroke. The C Cat offered instant access to the training pistol. Draws are smooth and re-holstering without visual confirmation is not difficult. During this time, I adopted the black tactical look and fitted a set of Falcon grips to the pistol with good results. But still more was to come as my days in law enforcement were coming to an end.

Writing, training and sporting use dictated my modest battery more than purely tactical concerns. The G-Man became a trusted concealed carry handgun. A Summer Special holster from Milt Sparks was one step, and the addition of slim-line grips from Wilson Combat another. The grips require replacing the grip screw bushings with shortened versions. They are noticeably thinner and do not grab clothing as some grips may. The final configuration of this pistol was years in the making and now suits this user to a "T".

The second pistol is a far different proposition. I chose this pistol for a variety of reasons related to my current situation. The job is long on alertness and short on training time. I wished to have a general purpose defensive handgun that would be my 24-hour piece, for those casual strolls in the park with my loved ones, for example. While I prefer a Government Model 1911 45 for all-around defense, a lighter handgun is indicated for discreet carry. The Hi-Power types have always been my favorite 9mm and remain so today. During the past few months I have tested, evaluated and taken apart several FM-produced Hi-Powers. These Argentine Hi-Powers have impressed me with their reliability and accuracy. The pistols have good sights and a much improved ambidextrous safety that makes them truly user-friendly. The level of workmanship is high. The Hi-Power fits my hands well and the controls are well-placed for rapid manipulation. There is no conflict in my muscle memory between this handgun and the 1911.

Even better, FM has a short slide version of the Hi-Power known as the Detective. The Detective required some engineering to properly function in this abbreviated mode. The captive guide rod and spring have been modified to the SIG-type guide rod. The guide rod now extends past the slide when the pistol recoils. Often as not, short-slide pistols are not as reliable as the full-length version, but the short FM pistols have proven fully as reliable, and with a wide spectrum of ammunition.

I proofed my personal Detective and found it capable and effective. I carried the handgun in a Summer Special holster originally molded for the Officers ACP and found it a perfect fit. This is not good business, as a holster should be molded for a specific handgun, but with the IWB type and tension against the body, all has gone well. The Detective is shorter than either the 1911 or a Hi-Power, allowing the pistol's user to sit with far less chance of a pinched buttock. The handgun fairly leaps into the hand and the short sight radius allows the user to get on target quickly. The Hi-Power is the only pistol as fast to an accurate first shot as the 1911, and the FM Detective defines this speed.

Like the G-Man, the Detective sports ambidextrous safety levers, important in a carry gun. The shooting hand may be injured or pinned, and the ambidextrous levers allow the user to access and deploy the pistol with either hand. When using the Milt Sparks Summer Special holster, I can quickly draw the handgun from either side, a great advantage. I admit I retain more control with the light-kicking 9mm than the 45 and that is part of the advantage of the pistol.

A problem with the FM is the finish. A baked-on enamel of the popular

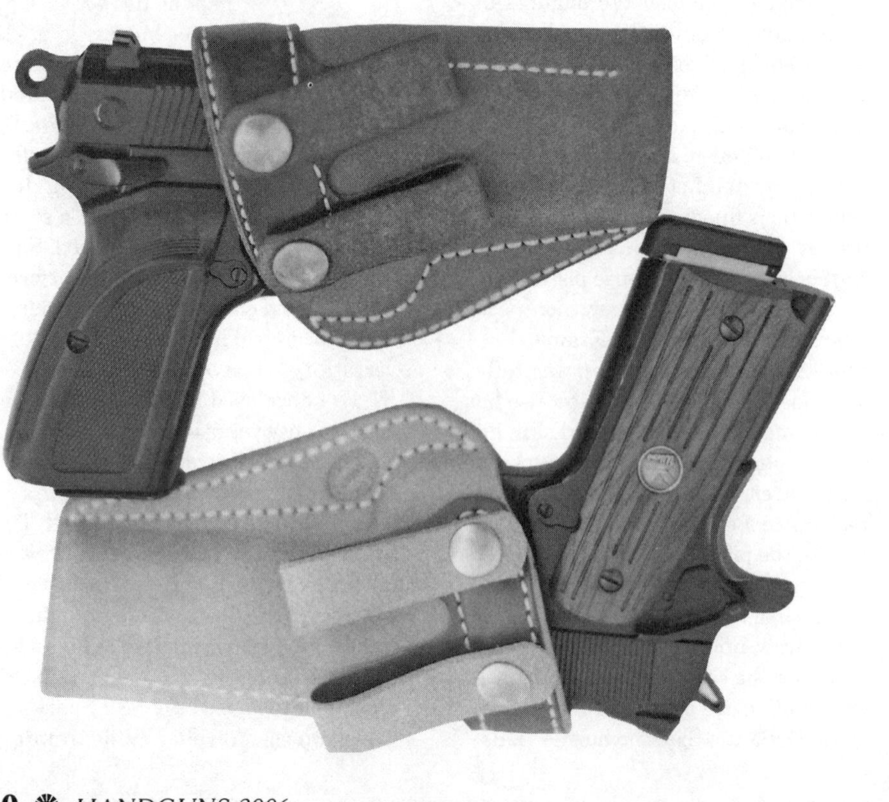

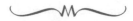

The author has found that the Milt Sparks Summer Special is an outstanding inside-the-waistband holster, well suited to concealed carry needs. The holster that holds the G-Man is new, the other is well worn from a decade of use, but still perfectly viable. Note the holster has turned color from exposure to oil and perspiration.

type, this is not the preferred hard-use finish. I elected to go with a space-age finish and let a little vanity intrude. The pistol was sent to Robar for a two-tone treatment. The slide was treated to Roguard, a dark finish with excellent corrosion-resistant properties. Roguard is soft to the touch, a quality unique among space-age finishes. The frame is finished in NP3, a blend of electroless nickel and Teflon: attractive, and immune to corrosion. Two-tone guns are a Robar specialty that appeal to many of us. A crowning touch was a set of special grips from Ajax grips. If you cannot find a suitable pair of grips at Ajax, you aren't looking hard enough! Ajax carries not only their own brand but many other popular grip styles. I chose rosewood with fleur de lis trim, pleasing on many levels, and the border is tastefully done. Nothing was done mechanically, the piece was delivered with a smooth four-pound trigger I found usable as issued.

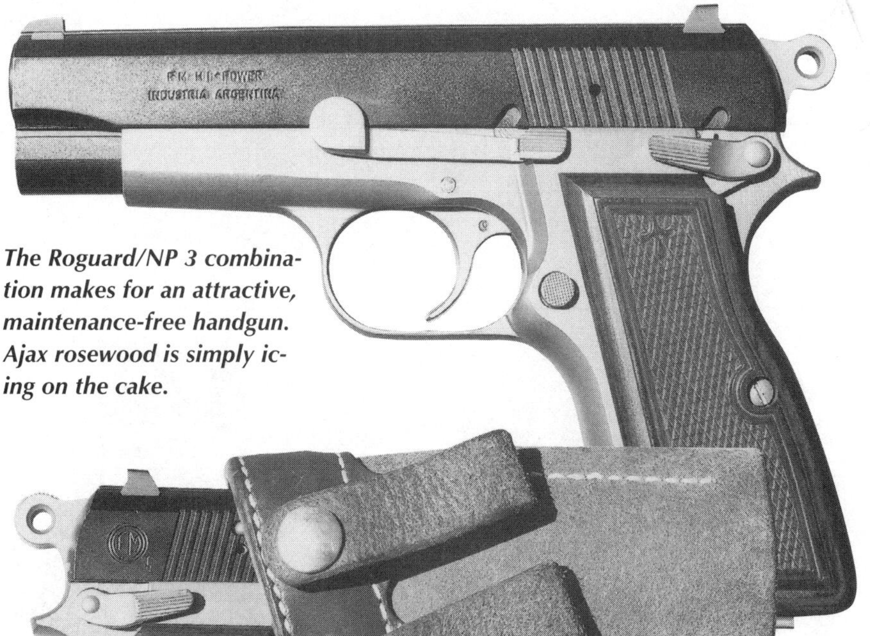

The Roguard/NP 3 combination makes for an attractive, maintenance-free handgun. Ajax rosewood is simply icing on the cake.

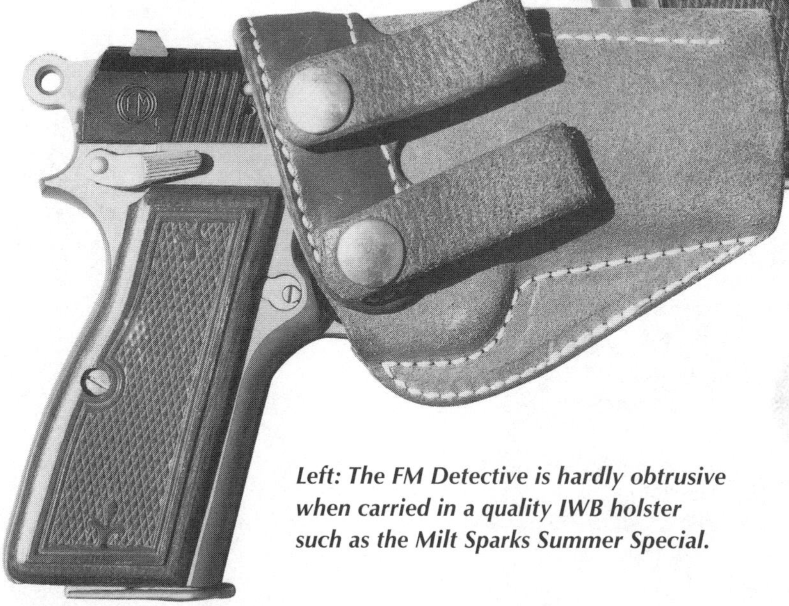

Left: The FM Detective is hardly obtrusive when carried in a quality IWB holster such as the Milt Sparks Summer Special.

I do not stress the piece with +P or +P+ loads on a daily basis, but have proofed my FM with a number of loads of the type. The 9mm demands a +P for effect, and with the abbreviated barrel losing velocity in relation to the longer pistol, we simply have to use an effective cartridge. The search is ongoing, but for the present I have settled on the Black Hills 115-grain JHP +P. This load will group five bullets into three inches at 25 yards, if I do my part. At more realistic ranges, ten yards or so, a full magazine will cut one ragged hole. For practice, I have used prodigious amounts of factory ball ammunition and handloads––and enjoyed every round!

I am very happy with my two most used custom pistols. Each represents choices that fit my lifestyle. As for the reliability of either type, both have been faultless in this regard.

The G-Man has used Wilson Combat magazines from day one and has benefited from these high-end magazines. There have been three minor problems with the G-Man, two the result of hard use. When using Wilson Combat magazines the pistol gave no problem, but I discovered that certain other brands dragged, because of over-tightened or too-long grip screws. This was corrected early on. The front ampule for the tritium sight came out at 10,000 rounds, which often happens with these ampules. They are shock-mounted in rubber in the sight, and the constant pounding of a heavy pistol takes its toll. Ten thousand rounds is not a great deal of shooting for me over a five-year span, but is still a lot of ammunition.

The third problem is more serious, but did not stop the pistol from working. The SFS unit's weak-side safety wing is of synthetic material and recently broke loose. It was a little spongy for a few weeks and hard pressure finished the job. I may replace it or consider other options, but at present I have a pistol that is right handed just as the majority of 1911s.

Comparing the G-Man's record with two other pistols that also reached 15,000 rounds (both custom numbers), I find a cracked barrel bushing, a cracked frame and a sprung plunger tube among the problems encountered. But no 1911 that stopped working. The G-Man in general and my modified pistol in particular get a clean bill of health.

The FM will not be used as heavily in training and practice but common sense tells me it will reach 5000 rounds in a few years, and I will report again at that time. As for now, I am well pleased with my custom pistols.

SOURCES

Ajax Grips
P.O. 560129
Dallas, Texas 75356

Ted Blocker Holsters
9438 S.W. Tigard St.
Tigard, Oregon 97223

DeSantis
432 Bayview Avenue
Amityville, New York 11701

High Standard
5200 Mitchelldale
Suite E 17
Houston, Texas 77092

Kramer
P.O. 112154
Tacoma, Washington 98411

Robar
21438 North 7th Avenue
Phoenix, Arizona 85027

Milt Sparks
605 E. 44th Street
Boise, Idaho 83714

Wilson Combat
2234 CR 719
Berryville, Arkansas 72616

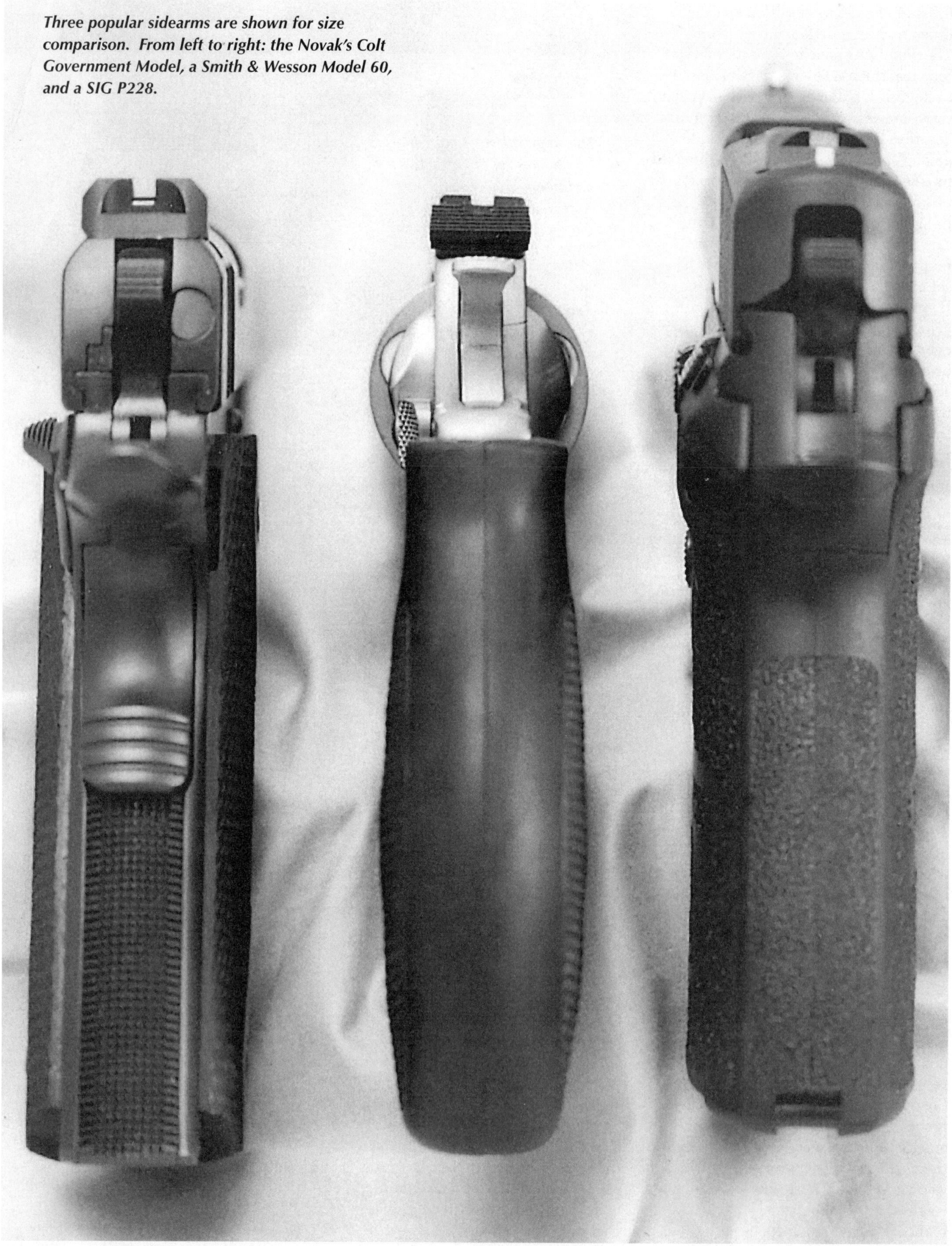

Three popular sidearms are shown for size comparison. From left to right: the Novak's Colt Government Model, a Smith & Wesson Model 60, and a SIG P228.

THE IDEAL CARRY GUN...

THE NOVAK'S COLT

by Jerry Stordahl

Selecting a carry gun is a highly individual matter, and personal preference can often overshadow practicality. The word "practical" means designed for use; utilitarian. Practical stresses "effectiveness, as tested by actual experience or as measured by a completely realistic approach to life or the particular circumstances involved."[1] For shooters it means choosing the best tool for the job, and luckily, in the efficient, industrialized world we live in, we have choices... many choices.

The wide variety of choices means plenty of "new" offerings, but I prefer the old and classic 1911 design, chambered for the 45 ACP. Some shooters will denigrate the 1911, and the comment heard most often is... that design is old! It's older than petrified wood! Why choose that? Usually the questions and statements will come from someone infatuated with the double stack magazine class of pistols, spoken with the appropriate amount of subdued scorn. Like many of today's generation, they think "new means better."

The answer is usually short. The 1911 is chosen because it works. It offers enough power in a controllable and easily handled package to get the job done... that of protecting lives. Plus it has proven itself in a couple of world wars, several minor conflicts, and in everyday use in the holsters of law enforcement and civilians alike. It works. It is dependable. It is 45-caliber. It gets the job done. It is practical and effective. A shooter does not have to agree with the selection, but a pistol design that has worked in the debris of war is an optimum choice for the relatively prosaic environment of everyday life. Practical stresses effectiveness.

This Novak's Colt offers just the right "enhancements" for discreet carry and reliable operation.

The ideal carry pistol should first be reliable. Without reliability, there cannot be confidence in the chosen tool. Reliability is paramount, and without it, the person is courting risk to a much greater

1 Webster's New World Dictionary, second college edition.

There are no real differences in carrying comfort between the Colt Government and the SIG P228. The Colt is somewhat thinner, while the SIG is shorter.

degree than necessary. Not every pistol is reliable... not every 1911 is reliable, but it is essential in ANY firearm chosen for defensive use.

I have owned some stock 1911 Colts for more years than I care to recall. My favorite has become the Series 70, Mark IV rendition of the Colt Government Model, and it has always worked well. It has always fired and cycled without a hitch, using reloads and factory ammunition, but I have heard of plenty of shooters experiencing trouble with their 1911s. Some of the pistols would not eject properly, others had the "spring fingers" of the collet bushing break, and still others had slide stop and feeding malfunctions. This time I asked... why?

I found the answer, I think. The 1911 originated in the Colt factory, assembled by meticulous craftsmen. Each part met specifications according to the original blueprints. Each pistol was the same, and in today's market, with every major gun manufacturer trying to capitalize on the 1911 popularity, the engineers have deviated from the original specifications to enhance production and offer different models. Enough variations can exist in critical dimensions and tolerances to cause a few problems. Even the durability of the parts can vary, when one considers the heat treatment or wear resistance of a particular part. Low quality parts or out of spec frames and slides are to be avoided, if a reliable pistol is desired. Remember, the original 1911 design worked, and it worked very well.

MIM (Metal Injection Molded) parts have replaced tool steel in some cases. Shortened slides, chopped barrels, altered magazines (as in stuffing eight rounds in a container designed to hold seven rounds), plus ill-fitting parts... they all have the potential to contribute to reduced reliability.

Though tool steel parts are preferred, the MIM parts often give no problems whatsoever, if the process has been properly accomplished. Metal injection molding saves the manufacturers money and keeps some products affordable. There is little or no machining after the part is manufactured. If it meets a certain specification, the part is installed in a pistol. If the part breaks, it is the shooter's problem... or life. To be fair, the MIM process has come a long way towards reliability and durability, though machined bar stock is preferred by most users when it comes to firearms parts.

I decided I wanted better sights on my Colt, so after narrowing my choice to Novak Low Mount tritium configuration, I began to study the other options available from this premier company. Attracted by their "Reliability Job" offering, I ultimately decided on the "Carry Package" which included the sights and reliability work, plus there were other "enhancements" included. A conversation with Wayne Novak at Novak's Inc. nailed down the options I wanted to add to the "Carry Package," and the pistol was on its way.

There is no other auto pistol in gun-making history that has significantly

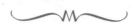

The Novak's Colt is a wise choice for a sidearm, and magazines should be tested to assure reliable functioning.

Cocked and locked is the normal carry mode for a 1911. In order to fire, the hand must depress the beavertail grip safety, and the additional safety on the left side of the frame must be swept down.

surpassed the 1911 platform when it comes to custom parts, features, and gunsmith focus. Part of the appeal of the 1911 may be the wide variety of services and aftermarket parts for the pistol. The parts availability list must number in the hundreds, but I like to think those shooters who have chosen the 1911, do so because they love the feel, the design, the handling qualities... and because it always has been THE 45 auto pistol, reigning over all others for decades.

The aftermarket equipment is there to make improvements, cosmetic and functional. The gunsmiths are there to offer expertise and options not found on the stock pistol, such as checkering, dehorning, better sights, and match-grade barrels, although manufacturers, in the last few years, have added many features to some of their top-of-the-line models to satisfy consumer demand for "enhancements." Colt, Springfield Armory, and Kimber come to mind.

The Colt Series 70 Government Models and many Series 80 guns came from the Colt factory with spring-fingered collet bushings to support and consistently align the barrel muzzle in the slide during barrel lockup. Not only was this less labor intensive than fitting the solid bushings of pre-Series 70 guns, but shooters were demanding more accuracy. The spring-fingered collet bushing must have seemed like a pot of gold to the Colt engineers, and they enthusiastically stuffed these into their auto pistols for several years. It was a great idea... the problem was, they weren't always reliable.

Well, they helped some in the accuracy department, compared to a loosely fitted solid bushing, but sometimes there wasn't quite enough clearance between slide and barrel. When the fingers contacted the slide at the muzzle end of the barrel, the fingers would experience a sort of "squeezing" or reverse leverage, if inadequate clearance was a factor. Eventually the finger would become fatigued and shear off, tying up the gun.

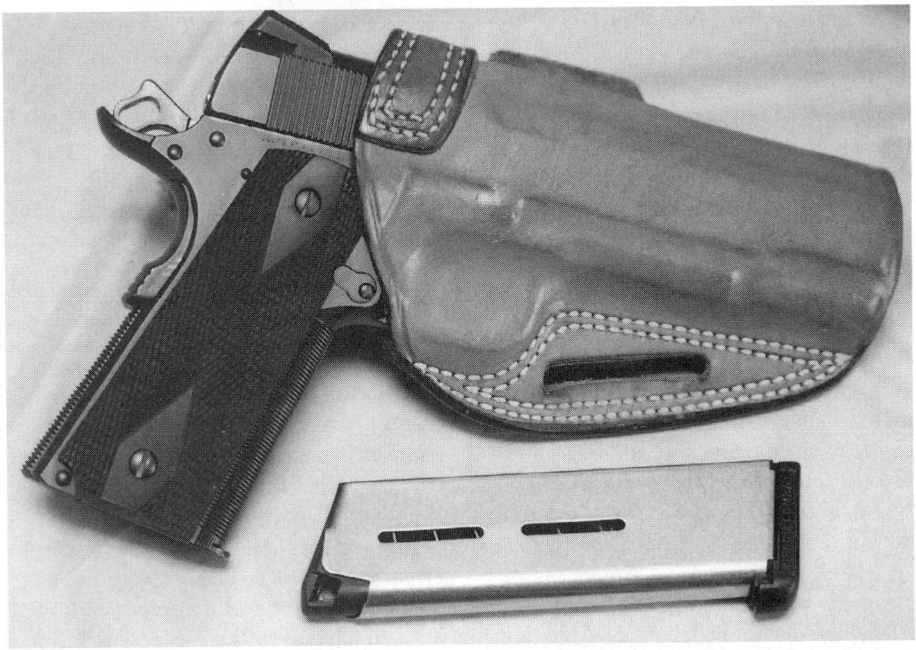

A cocked and locked Colt is shown with an old "Askins Avenger" holster, manufactured by Bianchi. Below is a Wilson magazine.

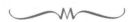

Though my Colt never had problems in this area, reliability work attempts to identify and replace or tune any area that could compromise the dependability of the pistol. Novak's replaced the stock collet bushing with a fitted, solid, National Match stainless steel bushing.

Other reliability work consisted of checking the chamber dimensions and polishing it for reliable chambering and extraction, plus the feed ramp was polished to glassy smoothness. The breech face dimensions were checked and the barrel throated and polished. The firing pin hole was deburred, and the extractor tension was checked, as this part is critical for dependable removal of the fired case. I added optional lowering and contouring of the ejection port to provide unobstructed exit for the fired brass.

If reliability in a carry pistol is number one, then accurate bullet placement is number two, and accurate

Graceful lines and subtle beauty make this finely crafted Novak's Colt a genuine pleasure to use.

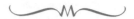

shooting is about controlling the weapon and using the sights. We all want to hit what we aim at, whether at the target range or in a tense defensive situation. To do this, the chosen pistol must have visible and useable sights. Tritium night sights were part of Novak's Carry Package, so I chose the bar/dot configuration in green. Aligning the front dot with the horizontal rear bar is fast and natural. The Low Mount sights required machining dovetails at both front and rear of the slide for installation, providing highly visible sighting equipment with a low profile, to help prevent snagging on clothing. Novak sight systems are top of the line, quality additions to any handgun.

Speaking of accuracy, Novak's offers stainless steel match-grade barrels from Barstow and carbon steel barrels from Kart, but I retained the stock Colt barrel. For defensive use, it is accurate enough to get the job done, it is fitted and finished well, and when it wears out, one of the custom barrels can be purchased. The gunsmiths at Novak's machined a beautiful, concave crown on the stock barrel. Using the stock barrel is called the practical approach... especially since the objective was the ideal carry gun, rather than a match-winning Gold Cup.

The stock Colt trigger was replaced with a Videki trigger as part of the Carry Package, with a trigger job included in the installation. I selected the long, solid trigger versus the perforated style, and the trigger breaks at a clean five pounds. The trigger does not need to be ultra light as long as the release is crisp and clean. Using standard sear engagement and standard springs, the five-pound trigger is about normal for these specifications.

Comfort is important in carrying a pistol unobtrusively, and a bevel job was included in the Novak Carry Package. This was accomplished by removing sharp external edges on the slide and frame, which helps prevent lacerations to skin or wear on the holster. The smoothed edges assist snag-free drawing from the concealed carry position and aid in reholstering the pistol. It is one of those subtle enhancements that pleases the eye, yet offers real utility. Often referred to as dehorning, the beveling gives the Colt a touch of class, by softening the hard line edges. At Novak's the beveling is done by hand, not with buffing wheels. The magazine well opening was also beveled to facilitate mag insertion.

After reliability and accuracy options have been achieved, the shooter should think about modifications to improve handling qualities. These are the parts that make a pistol ergonomically delightful, and they are intertwined with the reliability and useable accuracy of a pistol. A good word to use would be controllability. An extended and lowered thumb safety does not seem like much, but as part of the Carry Package, I found it enhances positive manipulation of the thumb safety upon drawing the pistol. I dislike the ambidextrous safeties seen on many pistols, though some shooters find them desirable. Streamlined simplicity is preferred for the ideal carry gun.

Another enhancement provided with the Novak's Carry Package is the beavertail grip safety. The one fitted to the Colt provides a raised, ribbed pad near the bottom portion to assure pressure is achieved to allow firing the pistol. The grip safety also provides a grooved nest for the optional skeletonized and rounded hammer, when the pistol is cocked.

I chose to have the arched mainspring housing replaced with a 20-lines-per-inch checkered flat housing and, though expensive, the front strap was checkered at 25 lines-per-inch. The front and rear checkering complement each other, to enhance control and grip of the pistol, not only during firing, but also upon initial hand contact with the pistol, prior to the draw.

Under normal shooting circumstances, a shooter can get along without front strap checkering, but if the hands become slippery with sweat, blood, or mud, the checkering aids continued firm control. It is probably one of the most beneficial options available for handling and controlling the carry gun, plus it completes the "finished" look of the ideal carry pistol.

Black micarta double-diamond checkered grips were already installed on the pistol before shipping to Novak's. These were manufactured by Navidrex and are available from Brownell's. Combined with the front strap checkering and the checkered mainspring housing, the grip panels provide as much control as possible, without gluing the pistol to one's hand. Control of the pistol is just as important as reliability and good sights.

The entire frame and slide were bead-blasted and refinished in a pleasing matte black. The Novak logo was stamped on the forward flat of the Colt's right side, adding a special touch to the ideal carry gun. It was returned to me with the Colt nestled in a black, zippered and padded, soft pistol case...made in the U.S.A., by the way. I like that, as it fits with the rest of the picture of the ideal carry gun. Here's a fine old U.S.A. Colt pistol, excellent U.S.A. Novak's gunsmithing craftsmanship, and a U.S.A.-manufactured pistol case. Can it get more ideal than that?

Well, yes, it does get more ideal. The day it arrived home, I loaded up a bunch of Wilson 7-round magazines, number 47s, and proceeded to run over a hundred rounds through the pistol. The sights just lined up perfectly, and a 45 hole would appear on target. It shot like I expected...... slow fire and rapid..... it didn't matter... the Colt provided impeccable feeding, cycling, and firing.

And later as I was field-stripping the pistol for cleaning, I began studying the polished ramp and the finely beveled edges of the frame and slide. Simple and tasteful enhancements, I thought, but what makes a carry gun ideal? Is it the size, the weight, or the caliber? Is it nostalgia or great ergonomics? Perhaps it is all of that and more.

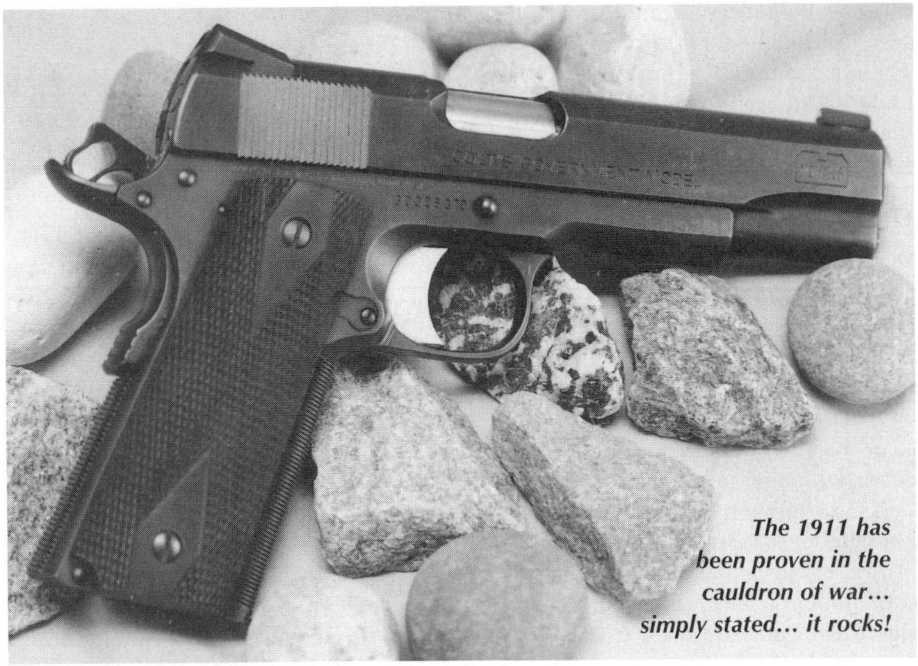
The 1911 has been proven in the cauldron of war... simply stated... it rocks!

But not everybody loves the 1911 Government Model. Weighing in at about 46 ounces loaded, it surely cannot be considered a lightweight, and the size––8.625 inches long by 5.25 inches high––is not considered small. The addition of the beavertail grip safety adds another quarter-inch, making the Novak Colt 8.875 inches. Some shooters choose the Commander Model, which is less than an inch shorter and only 3 ounces lighter, and some go for the Officer's Model at 40 ounces. Not me. I gave up on the abbreviated models long ago. The lighter slide mass, the different spring

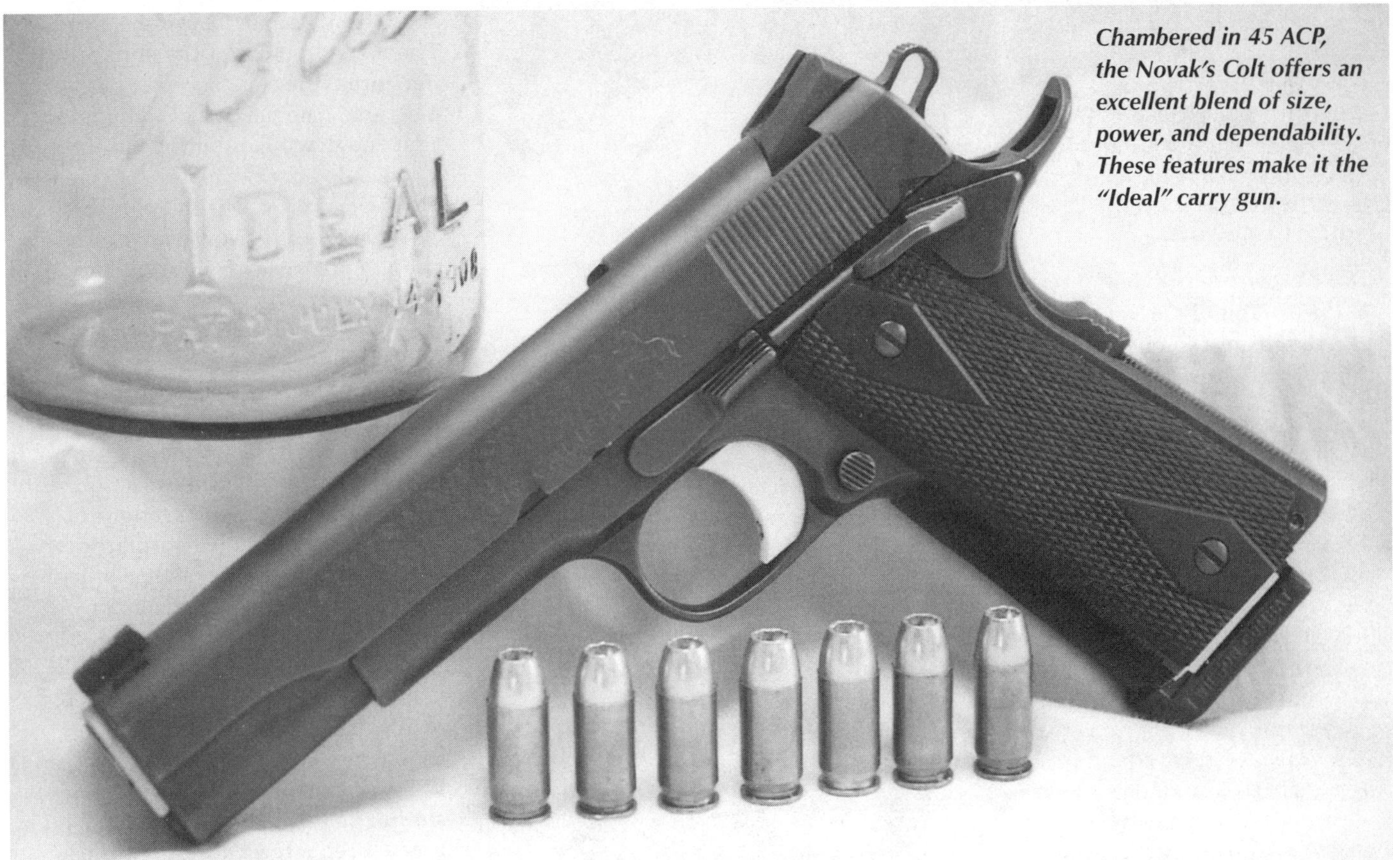

Chambered in 45 ACP, the Novak's Colt offers an excellent blend of size, power, and dependability. These features make it the "Ideal" carry gun.

rates––all deviating from the original specifications––mean "finicky" when it is reliability that counts.

I guess I suffer from what Robert H. Boatman in one of his 1911 articles called, "the terminal deficiency of passion for 'small' 45s." (*The Accurate Rifle* magazine, January 2004) That only means I don't care much for them. I had a Detonics, when dwarves were all the rage. It was beautiful in its midget dimensions, but it liked to hiccup and burp a little. I finally passed it on to someone who could give it the love it deserved, and I've been shooting a Colt Government Model ever since. Aspirin doesn't cure all headaches.

Out of curiosity, I dug out the calipers and a couple of other sidearms. I measured a J-frame Smith & Wesson, Model 60-4 with a 3-inch full underlug barrel and adjustable rear sights. Chambered in 38 Special, the J-frame is often chosen as a carry gun or backup piece, though usually found in the 2-inch models. This revolver was 7.5 inches long by 5 inches tall including sights.... not a lot of reduction over the Colt's 8.875 inch length and 5.25 inch height (5.5 inches with Wilson magazine with base pad). The J-frame measured 1.305 inches thick across the cylinder and 1.142 inches thick at the center of the rubber grips. The Novak Colt tallied 0.913-inch thick just in front of the ejection port. The Colt was 1.252 inches thick through the grip panels. There's not a lot of difference. The Smith J-frame not only appears smaller to the eye, but the loaded weight is lighter.

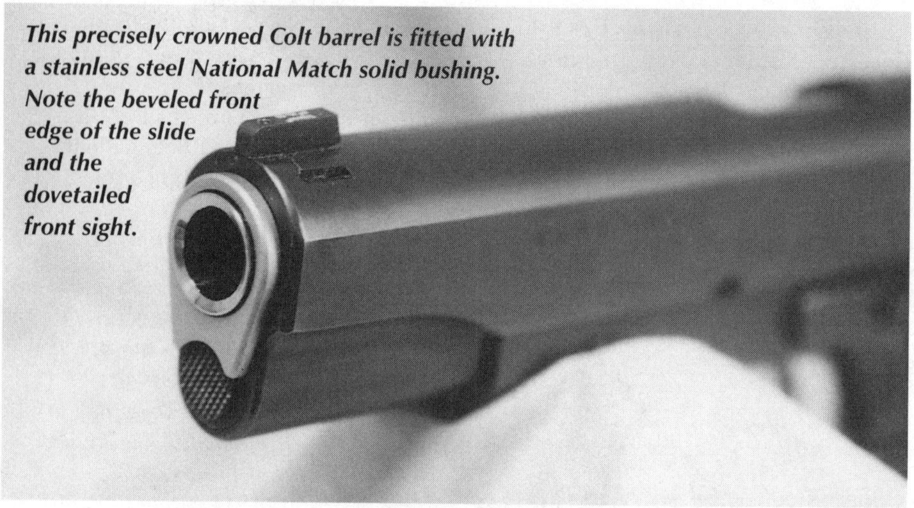

This precisely crowned Colt barrel is fitted with a stainless steel National Match solid bushing. Note the beveled front edge of the slide and the dovetailed front sight.

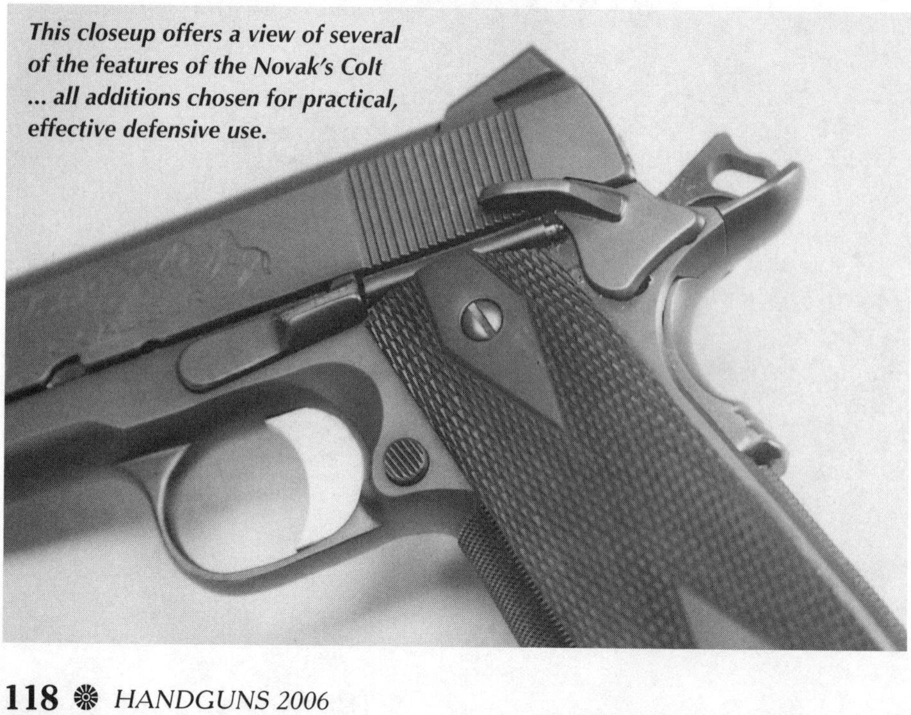

This closeup offers a view of several of the features of the Novak's Colt ... all additions chosen for practical, effective defensive use.

That, of course is its advantage, along with the reliable double-action mechanism. Its disadvantages include the 38 Special chambering, the 5-round cylinder, and the reduced velocity from the abbreviated barrel, especially the 2-inchers.

The Novak Colt was then compared to another popular type of auto pistol, a SIG P228, one of the typical high-capacity, double-action 9mm handguns. It measured 7 inches in length, 5.25 inches in height including sights, and the grip thickness scored 1.258 inches. The slide thickness in front of the ejection port was 1.05 inches at its thickest lower portion. This is nearly identical to the Colt, but the grip configuration is such that it has an entirely different feel. Though I have never been much of a fan of the Parabellum, I've kept the SIG P228, just so I had something capable of firing the 9mm cartridge.

So, why does the Colt rule? Why is the 1911 so popular? I have to say again, because it works. It is practical. It is accurate. It is a 45 ACP. It exudes subtle grace, with a lean, balanced look. It offers a solid, comfortable feel to the hand. The measurement of the slide width indicates it is compact where it matters... the portion of the pistol that fits down behind the belt in a concealed carry holster. This is narrower than a J-frame Smith's cylinder, yet it offers seven of those chunky 45s ready for deployment.

The 1911 or any auto pistol will only be reliable with quality magazines. This is one reason I chose to supply the Novak Colt with a few Wilson Combat number 47 stainless steel mags. These are made from heat-treated 17-7 stainless steel, with self-lubricating polymer followers. They have removable floorplates for easy cleaning and a black polymer base pad to protect the magazine when released from the pistol.

Normal thickness range on a magazine runs from 0.540 to 0.543-inch, with the standard Colt mags measuring 0.538 to 0.540-inch. The Wilson magazines ran 0.535 to 0.539, similar to military mag dimensions. I measured a few generic stainless magazines at 0.540 to 0.544 inch.

Knowing that magazine sizes will vary, it is best to select and test them in a particular firearm to avoid any surprises on the street.

Eight-round mags are available also, but to squeeze eight of the fat 45 rounds in a tube designed for seven required a reduction of spring wire size. This in turn has caused early spring fatigue, resulting in feeding malfunctions with some magazines. Perhaps, it is wise to change the magazine springs more frequently and rotate the loaded ones if 8-round mags are used. I prefer to stick with the 7-rounders, as they have a solid reputation for dependability. Other 1911 users like the Chip McCormick 8-round Power Mags. These have an excellent reputation for quality and durability. Novak's is offering a 1911 magazine, and there are others. The best course of action is to test them. Then test them again.

And a pistol is only as good as the ammunition fired in it. Though, I generally shoot handloaded ammo for informal target shooting, Winchester 230-grain Ranger Talon JHP (RA45T) and CCI Gold Dot 230-grain JHP are two loads recommended by Doctor Gary K. Roberts in testing done in conjunction with the International Wound Ballistics Association. These are two of the loads giving sufficient penetration and expansion capabilities. The CCI Gold Dot loads are the easiest to locate for purchase.

Another option is the Black Hills 230-grain load utilizing the Gold Dot bullets. For general shooting and training, Winchester U.S.A. 230-grain hardball is fine... if it shoots to the same point of aim as the carry ammunition. I have found the Colt shoots into 2 to 3 inches with some loads at 25 yards from sandbags, if I do a good job of holding and sight alignment. Other loads group as much as 4 to 5 inches at the same distance.

The Colt 1911 is a pistol proven in war, and if further commentary is desired, one should latch onto a copy of *A Rifleman Went To War*, by Captain Herbert W. McBride.[2] Though he was a rifleman and machinegunner foremost, he had some interesting comments on pistols in the trenches of World War I.

Made in the U.S.A. in this case means Colt's Manufacturing, Novak's premier gunsmithing, and a genuine U.S.-built pistol case.

McBride writes; "But the main thing in considering any military pistol is the matter of dependability. Will it work in all kinds of weather? In mud, in sand, in water? Well, we all know what tests were applied during the two or three years before our Ordnance officers finally approved the Colt... and then the tests for what you might call 'durability' in which all others fell by the wayside while the old Colt, refusing to quit, finally wore out the time and patience of the members of the Board and had to leave it with an unfinished run of some ten thousand rounds without a stoppage or malfunction. I was present at that last test, and that may have something to do with my attitude towards the ugly brute."

McBride again; "As to the various kinds of pistols used, both by the Allies and the Germans, after all these years during which to think it over, I still believe that the Colt 45 Automatic is king of them all."

Practical stresses effectiveness, and Novak's, Inc., stresses excellence. Providing some of the highest quality sights and pistol work obtainable, the 'smiths at Novak's give true credence to the words "premium craftsmanship." They use only the best quality parts from Wilson Combat, Ed Brown, Kart, Barstow, and King's. They can make your 1911 into the "Ideal Carry Gun," a weapon to rely on... a practical and effective carry pistol. It still is the "King of Them All."

If Herbert W. McBride were reading this, he'd be smiling and nodding his head right now... he'd probably be saying, "Son, you didn't have to spend all that money to make that 45 reliable." And he'd be right.....the stock Colt worked well, but all I can say is...."It sure is nice." ❋

CONTACT INFORMATION:

Novak's, Inc.
P.O. Box 4045
Parkersburg, WV 26104
website: www.novaksights.com
(Sights and pistolsmithing)

Brownell's
200 South Front Street
Montezuma, IA 50171
website: www.brownells.com
(Sights, 1911 parts, etc.)

2 A Rifleman Went To War, by Herbert W. McBride, 1987 Lancer Militaria. Originally published in 1935 by Small Arms Technical Publishing Company.

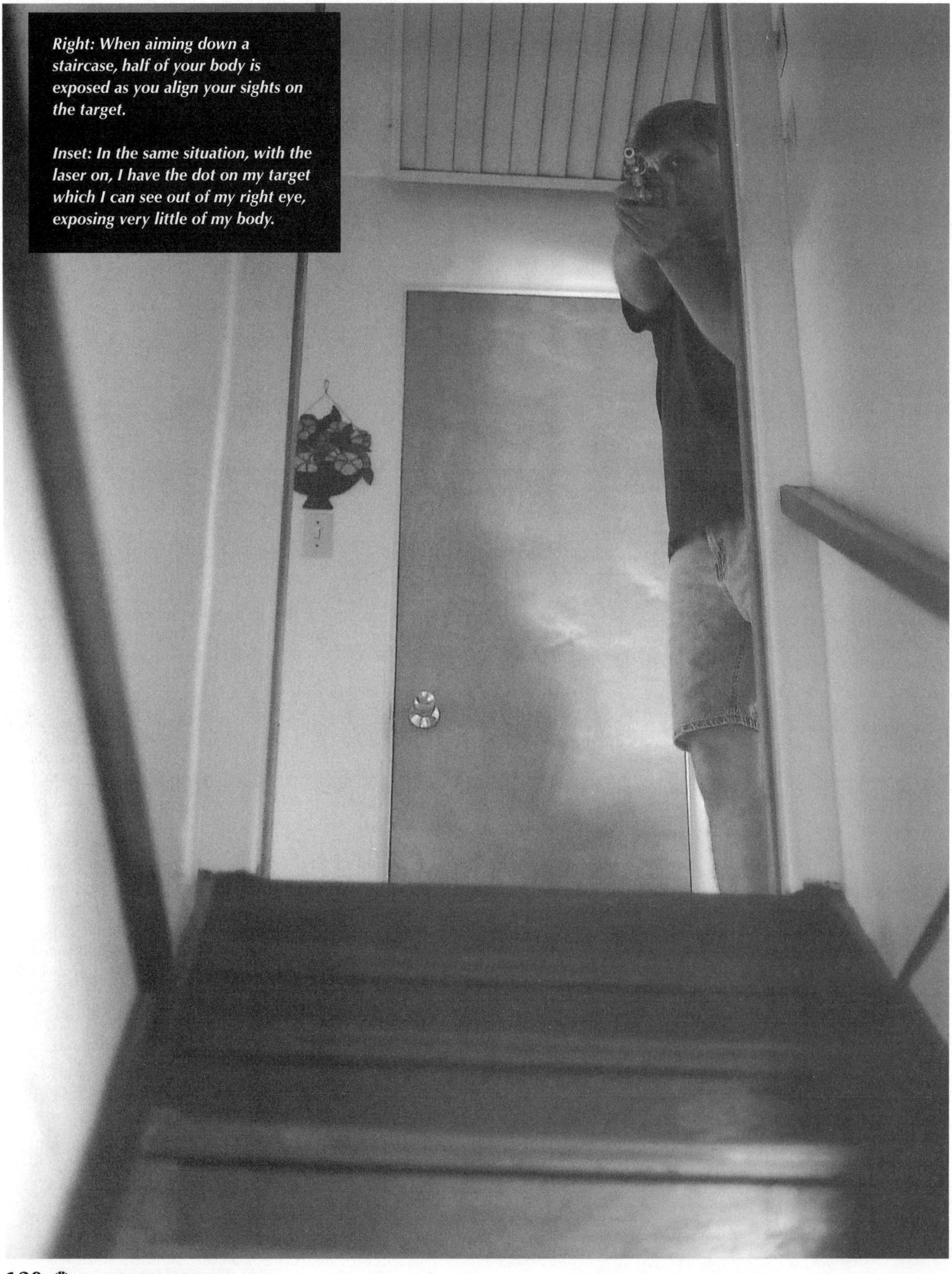

Right: When aiming down a staircase, half of your body is exposed as you align your sights on the target.

Inset: In the same situation, with the laser on, I have the dot on my target which I can see out of my right eye, exposing very little of my body.

Increase Your Defensive Capabilities with Electronic Sight Technology

LASER SIGHTS MAKE SENSE

by George E. Dvorchak

During the war (Desert Storm) in Iraq, and afterwards, we saw soldiers on the nightly news with all kinds of far-out equipment on their small arms; some of this new equipment utilizes laser technology!

Although I have used Crimson Trace laser sights on some of my handguns for years, I recently realized that many folks do not understand how a laser's use not only helps place a projectile but can also act as a deterrent of sorts. I will quote from a letter sent to Crimson Trace from a soldier who used one in Iraq; referring to his laser sight, he wrote "it has saved lives over here. Not only those of U.S. service members but also lives of Iraqis." He then went on to say "Often we are faced with tense situations where the intimidation factor of the "little red dot" makes the difference in the need for deadly force. Even with the language barrier, the little red dot speaks volumes for us."

A laser, by definition, is a device that produces a very narrow but powerful beam of light. In the high-tech world in which we now live, very few have not heard of the laser relating to many applications––use on firearms being only one. As examples, computer users may own or work with a laser

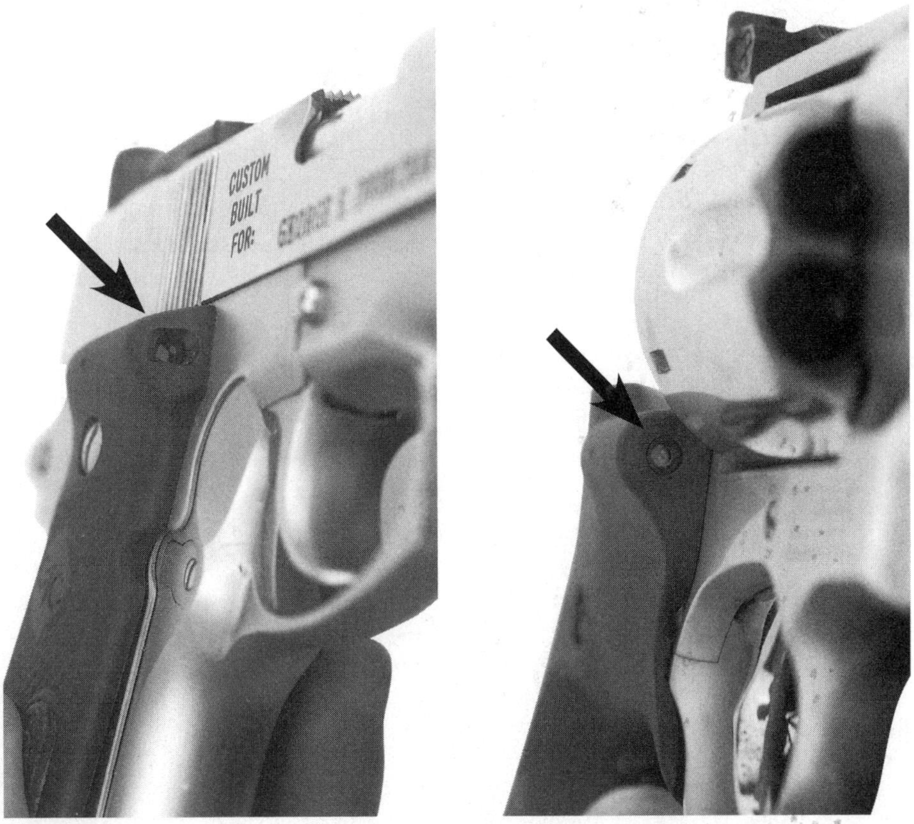

Most laser grips are nearly identical in thickness to the original grip with the exception that with plastic laser grips, the laser beam exits from the upper right side of these grips on both revolvers and autoloaders.

printer, and in the realm of medical treatment, most have heard of laser surgery. Where firearms are involved, laser-sighting technology helps one hit a target, especially when the shooter is not in the best of positions.

It Improves with Time

When this technology was in its infancy, such sights for handguns were quite noticeable since they usually were attached below the slide on a popular defense handgun, the autoloader. Today, with technology improving and prices dropping, these devices are no longer a luxury and are becoming quite popular for use on all types of firearms, including autoloaders and revolvers.

Sighting Concepts

To hit a target, one obviously has to align the front sight with the rear––although, after a lot of practice and gun familiarity, a form of "instinct" shooting develops wherein the shooter ignores the rear sight and "points" that front sight on the target.

When we "aim" the normal way by using alignment of a front and rear sight, there is a tendency to lose some focus of the target. This is only natural since we have trouble focusing on near and far objects at the same time, especially as we get older. When you align the sights and concentrate on the target, you put yourself into a state best described as tunnel vision. Example: When driving through a tunnel, you only see what is immediately ahead, not to the sides. If there are threats there, by the time you see them, it may be too late. The advantage of a laser sight is that with the illuminated dot placed on the target, you are on target instantly––without using the open sights. While your firearm is thus aimed, you see the target clearly *as well as* any peripheral threats.

Now, with only one area to focus on, our field of view has suddenly been made larger. This one factor now helps us better see the full-picture scenario, thanks to having an impressive dot of bright red light placed on the target. This also gives the individual so equipped somewhat of an advantage, both psychological and/or practical. A report I read on laser sights stated "Agencies using Crimson Trace Lasergrips are seeing hit ratios of over 90 percent in officer-involved shootings." Since over 80 percent of armed encounters occur at night, aiming with conventional sights is difficult, but here is where a laser sight shines!

A good laser sight does promote accuracy, but that is only a small part of its benefit. The red dot is a reality check for a sane individual who now sees that red dot on his chest. What I mean is that few individuals will continue the fight or take a situation to the next level when they see a bright dot on their body showing where a bullet will hit if fired. Since over 70 percent of law enforcement shootings occur during low light, the dot becomes even more effective as a deterrent. For the police officer, a simple lighted dot acts to immediately show who is in charge and the darker it is, the more pronounced this "target dot" becomes. Such a sobering experience can serve to put the brakes on an aggressor and stop a situation that could turn deadly. That benefit alone is worth the average per-unit cost of $200 to $300 versus the cost and aggravation of litigation resulting from a shooting by a police officer or licensed individual––even if that individual was clearly in the right.

Mechanics

When laser sights first evolved, they were restricted to special units, such as SWAT teams, and mechanically, were big and bulky. Now they are small, self-contained, reasonably priced and have become an optional add-on for police and those who use a handgun for home defense.

Today's laser sights are also easy to use; the various grip models from Crimson Trace are in the *Ready* mode once the switch is flipped on and the handgun is in the holster. To activate that dot, just squeeze the grip switch and aim without having to worry about turning it on since the unit was activated when the switch was flipped.

A Visual Training Tool

During practice, one gets instant visual feedback from where the shot went, permitting diagnosis of problems with trigger control and flinching. We have all fired that first shot on the range and realized we pulled the shot, possibly off the paper. The first time I did that at a 25-yard target with a laser system, I saw where my shot went by watching the dot move across the target and off to the side as I jerked the trigger. With the second and subsequent shots, I focused and did not jerk the trigger again. Instant feedback sobers the mind real quick!

Not for all Situations

Within 10 yards on a bright sunny day, the dot was usually visible. Out there at 25 yards, at times I would lose it, which brings out another consideration, do not take anything for granted. Yes, get good with the laser, but do not forget to practice using the pistol's open sights since they are your back-up system and, in bright light, your only equipment for aiming. You must become good with both!

Stress and Activation

Some early systems required the device be turned on just before use, which meant the user had to

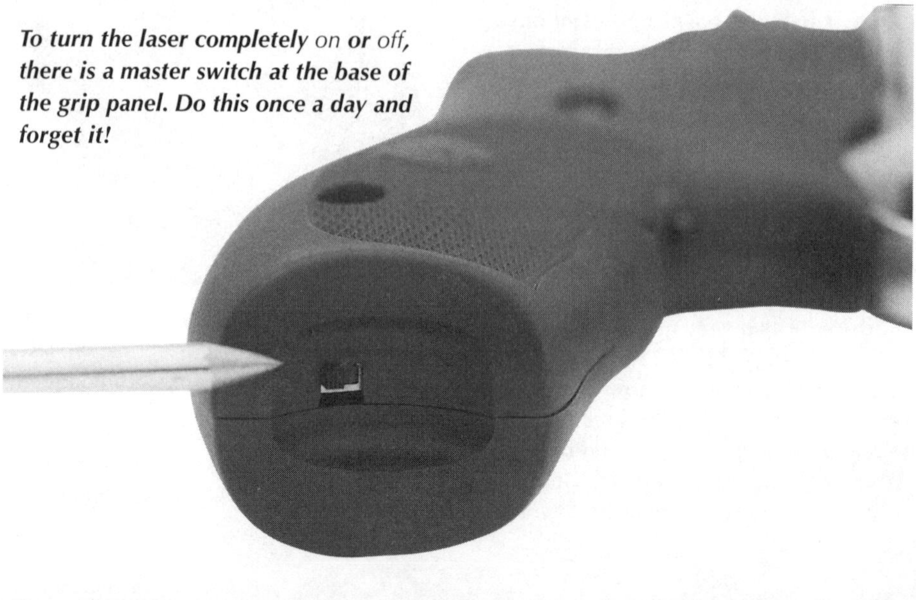

To turn the laser completely* on *or* off*, there is a master switch at the base of the grip panel. Do this once a day and forget it!

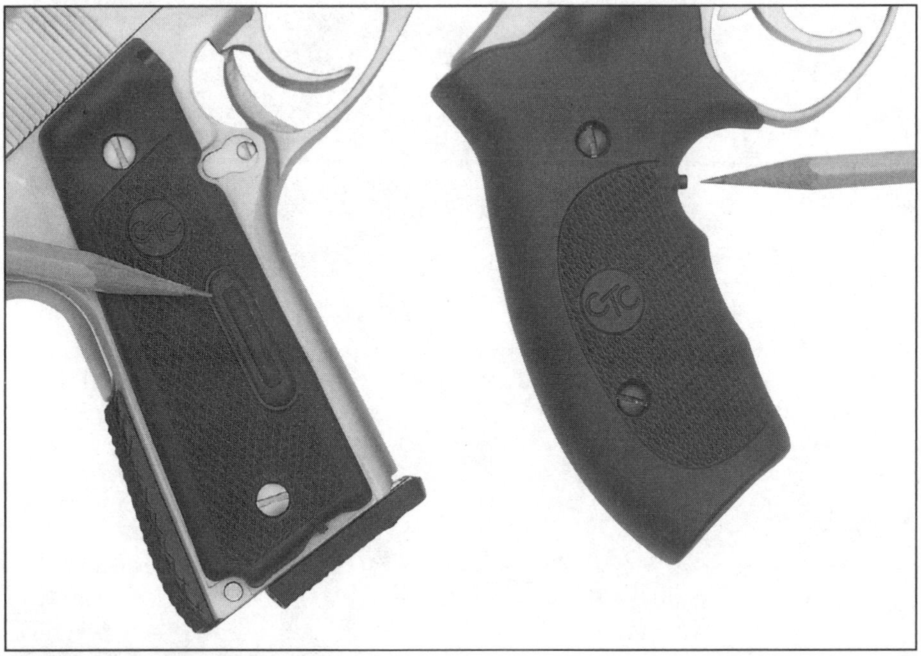

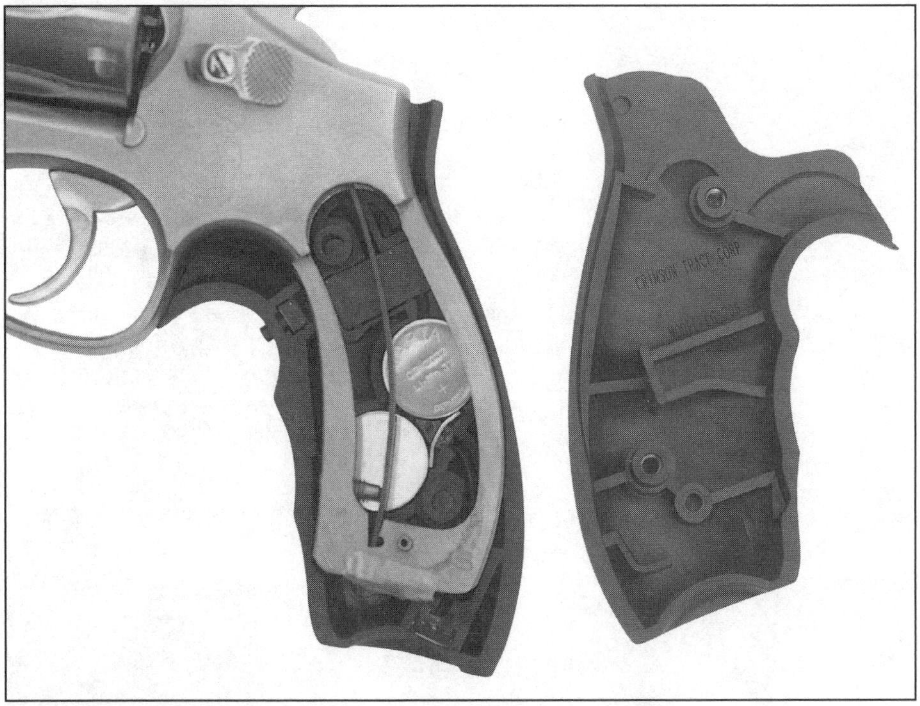

Top: To activate a laser once the switch has been turned on, squeeze the little "button" with your finger on the revolver, or palm with the autoloader to turn the beam from off *to* on. *Simple.*
Above: Almost everything is getting smaller today! Within the grip is the power source: two batteries and the laser components.

think about it, and then do it. Under stress, the thought process is not always rational and therefore, you may not turn on the laser. With the Crimson Trace system, free of wires and contained in a standard-size pistol grip, drawing the handgun (with either hand) and automatically squeezing the activation switch, turns the dot on––ready to go. Then, put the dot on the target and decide whether or not to pull the trigger.

Real Life Police Situations

The worst situation a police officer can find himself in is a shootout where, within seconds, someone can die. Most of these confrontations happen in dim light, the dark of night or indoors where space is usually cramped and lighting can also be bad. Here, individuals are thrown into close proximity, usually within 20 feet of each other. Hopefully, a first round hit will put an end to the assault and additional shots will not be necessary.

New Age in Tactics

The more you use your handgun, the more your motor memory proficiency increases with that firearm. Here are some Crimson Trace Corporation tips, slightly modified, on using laser sights.

1. Lead with your laser, not your face. As we all do when on the range, to hit our target, we first align the sights by raising the handgun in front of our face. This move exposes your head, and turns it and your torso into a huge target. With a laser, all that is required is that the illuminated "dot" be put on the target; the shooter does not have to align anything. Now, expose just enough of the handgun so that the laser is not covered. Thus, only a small part of your anatomy is exposed, just enough so you can pull the trigger while keeping the dot on the target.

2. Point Shooting. Put your dot on the target just by looking at the target, and ignore the standard front and rear sights. The longer you practice this technique, the better you become at drawing, pointing and firing. With enough practice, your hand/eye coordination improves to where point shooting becomes natural, even with the laser turned off, as long as the range is fairly short.

3. Practice real-world combat positions. When practicing at the range, we mostly shoot either standing or kneeling; sometimes prone. Yet, what if you were knocked down and had to draw while on your back, and accurately fire from where you lay. With laser sights, you can practice in this manner ––in your home and without firing a round *(please make sure your handgun is indeed EMPTY)*. I have a friend, a police firearms instructor, who years ago shot a hole in his TV while practicing dry firing with an "empty" revolver. All it takes is one mistake!

Most laser grips are nearly identical in thickness to the original grip with the exception that with plastic laser grips, the laser beam exits from the upper right side of these grips on both revolvers and autoloaders.

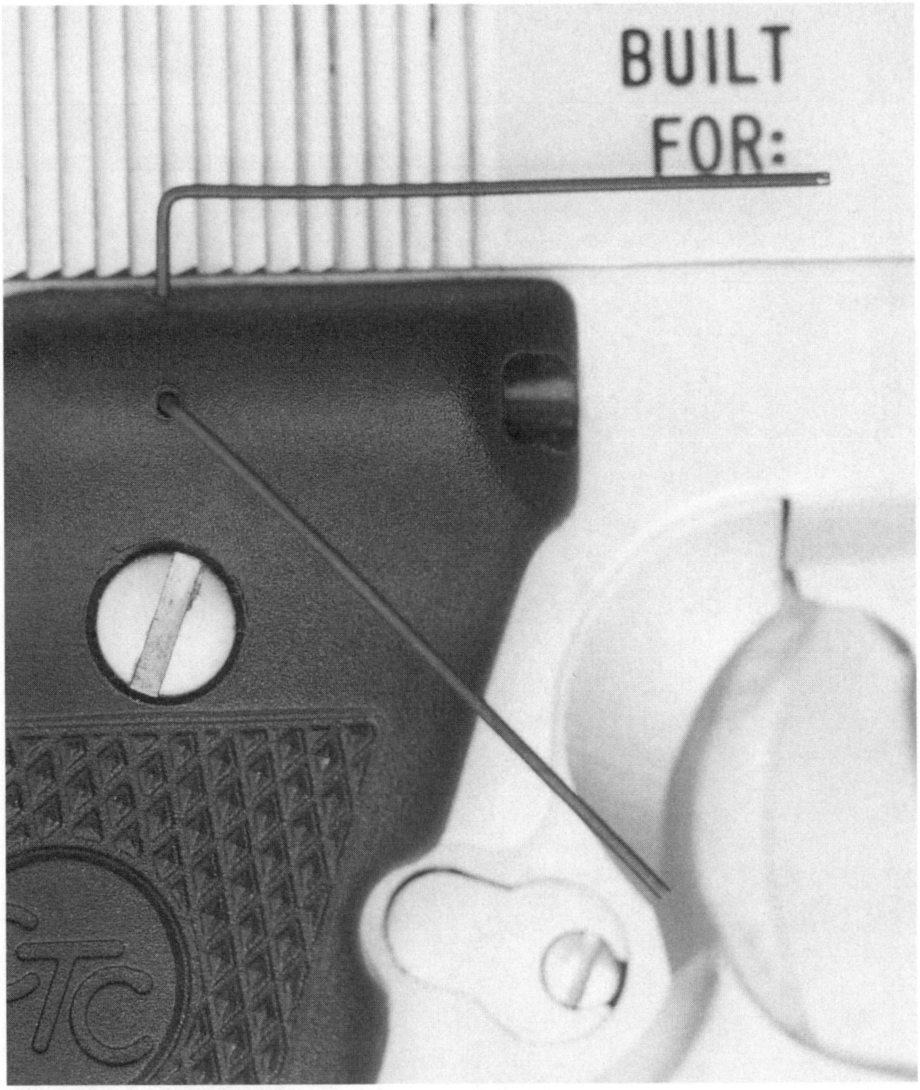

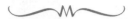

Water, no problem! This system works even if submerged in water. If this happens, just dry out the battery compartment within 8 hours. If you want to adjust your laser sight for elevation and windage, this is easily done by turning two screws with the supplied 0.028-inch Allen wrench, as shown on this autoloader.

4. Survive in low light conditions. This is an important item since over 70 percent of law enforcement shootings take place indoors and/or in the evening. White light from a flashlight can combine with the laser light to augment each other in identifying and, if need be, hitting a target. I find that even in darkness, without a flashlight, the laser light illuminates the silhouette target enough to make a good hit *(if the distance is not excessive)*. On the negative side, the laser light usually does not offer enough lighting to easily identify the target. Play it safe and when possible, use both before you shoot!

5. Training without Firing. Putting a dot on a target at home can supplement actual firing. It helps you become familiar with your handgun, which translates into confidence with the firearm and laser sights.

Litigation is not fun

It has been stated that the cost of any civil litigation, even if the defendant was acquitted, can be so great that the only ones who emerge unscathed and with a financial reward are the lawyers. When this happens, if the shooting involved a police officer, the department defending the officer can become financially strapped over just one such incident. A private citizen, who is forced to shoot protecting his family, can be ruined financially. All involved in a shooting can suffer, so any device that can get the attention of an aggressor and head off a gunfight is quite an asset to police officer and civilian alike.

Available Systems

Crimson Trace Laser grips are just that, a laser device within a handgun grip of standard configuration. These are available for Beretta 92/96; SigSauer P220, 226, 228, 229; Walther PPK/S; Colt 1911 types; Ruger Mark II and SP-101; S&W J-, K-, L- and N-frame revolvers, as well as the small-frame Taurus. For the Glock, a version is available that must be installed at the factory since it is incorporated into the polymer Glock frame. As of 2003, they even have a model available for the AR-15 and M-16.

I have and use these modern laser sights on both autoloaders and revolvers. They are compact, reliable and––what really impressed me––unobtrusive. Of all the laser-sighted handguns I've shot over the years, nothing impressed me like those with that CTC logo.

Specifications

Beam Intensity: 5 mw peak, 633 nm diode. Visible up to 1000 yards at night and between 20 to 50 feet in daylight, which varies on the intensity of light.

Batteries: Two #2032 Duracell lithiums that provide between 4-6 hours of *ON TIME* light.

Warranty: Three years unconditional.

Street Price: Depending on the model, from $200 to $300. The Glock, due to factory-fitting requirement, is more. For law enforcement, there are some special considerations given so give them a call.

Contact Information:
Crimson Trace Corporation
8089 SW Cirrus Drive
Beaverton, Oregon 97209
(800) 442-2406
www.crimsontrace.com

The little Model 160 TK-1 Tether Knife from Benchmade.

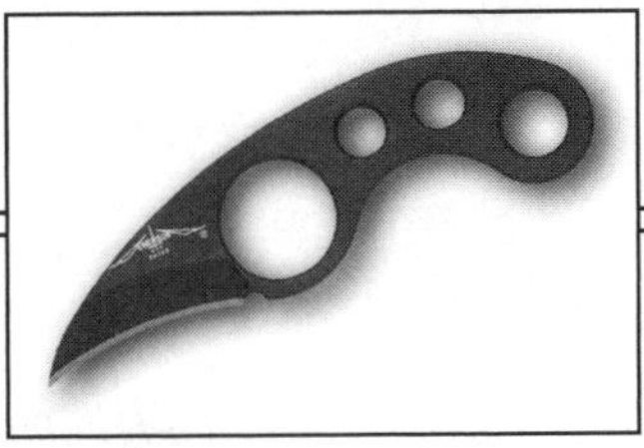

KNIVES IN UNUSUAL PLACES!

by Roger Combs

There was a time when most of us carried knives, either in a pocket, purse or on a belt sheath. OK. There always have been boot knives, sleeve knives, neck knives and rifle bayonets. But lately, these unusual carrying locations are increasingly found on military pack shoulder straps and not elsewhere while in public places.

It should be noted that the purpose of carrying knives in places other than the belt or the pocket, is not necessarily to conceal them, but rather to have the blades handy for use under all situations. We never know when we may have need of a knife. Perhaps we're out jogging, bicycling, driving, shopping, visiting; almost anyplace where knives are not prohibited. A neck knife or backpack strap location might be ideal. A small neck knife, tucked under the T-shirt or sweatshirt, is reassuring to have while running or working out.

Alphabetically, here is a look at some of the available carry options. The listing reflects only a small part of all the factory-made models available. Many custom knifemakers will produce a knife that can be carried in unusual locations. Many companies offer dozens of other similar designs. Prices, where shown, are the manufacturer's suggested retail price (MSRP) and may not reflect the actual retailers' or street price for any knife.

Benchmade

The little Model 160 TK-1 Tether Knife is worn on a cord around the neck. It is made of 440C stainless steel, producing a two-inch blade, with a choice of all plain edge or partly serrated with optional black coating. The knife is 5-3/4 inches long overall. The handle is skeletonized black Thermoplastic-coated for a non-slip grip. The sheath is molded Kydex/Thermoplastic. Knife and sheath weigh 2.5 ounces. $60.

The Benchmade Model 5 Rescue Hook may be carried, in its pouch, on a neck lanyard, on webbing or on a belt. The 440C stainless steel hooked blade is expressly designed for slicing through belts, ropes or lines. The handle design includes an oxygen valve wrench for EMT use. The Rescue Hook weighs slightly more than a half ounce. $35, plus optional-cost pouches, sheaths or lash tabs.

Boker

Boker calls this Robert Voros design, "Neck the Knife." Now carried in the Magnum line and made in Taiwan, the knife features an aluminum frame around a 3 3/8-inch stainless steel blade. The frame acts as a skeletonized handle when the blade swings open. The weight is 2.6 ounces and a neck lanyard is included. The silver frame with matte finish blade is $47.95. The optional black frame and black-coated blade is $49.95.

Buck Knives

The company has recently moved its manufacturing and business operations from California to Idaho. One of the new designs is the Short Revolution, a hybrid knife with a hanging clip to attach to backpacks, shoulder straps or belt loops, much like a climber's carabiner. The design is part of the Buck/Peter Whittaker series with plenty of mountain climbing heritage. Post Falls, Idaho, the new location of Buck Knives, is not that far from the Cascade mountain range with its many high peaks.

The blade pivots out of the handle and is locked open or closed with a push button. The spear point 2 1/2-inch blade is made of 440HC stainless steel, surrounded by an aluminum handle. The knife weighs slightly more than 2.5 ounces. The handle features four color options: platinum and forest green, and color-fade red-to-gold or dark blue-to-blue. $72.

The Cold Steel Spike neck knife; blade and handle is all one piece.

Coast Cutlery

Coast is importing and distributing the line of German Puma knives, including the new Puma Survival model, designed by German army Major Jermer. The 3 1/2-inch D1.4110 steel blade has a tanto-style shape with a screwdriver tip. Overall, the knife measures eight inches long. The skeletonized handle is wrapped with leather and includes a leather lanyard for neck wear. The edge is a combination plain and partially serrated, with a wrench slot to fit several bolt sizes. A bottle opener and wire stripper are included in the design. The nylon sheath with safety strap can be attached to a belt, chest, and backpack straps, or worn in the boot. $199.99.

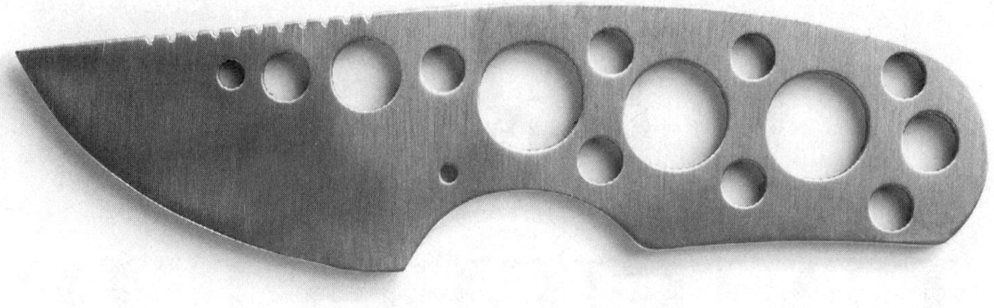

CRKT's Side Hawg was designed by knifemaker Mike Franklin.

Cold Steel

The Kobun (soldier) boot knife features a 5 1/2-inch tanto-style blade made of 420 Sub Zero quench steel, heavy enough to produce a strong tip. The 4 3/8-inch handle is made of deeply checkered Kraton for a firm grip. The sheath is of Concealex plastic for boot or belt wear.

Custom knifemaker Barry Dawson designed the Cold Steel Spike neck knife; blade and handle is all one piece. The 4-inch blade choices are tanto, spike and talon shapes, all of 420 Sub Zero Quench steel. Each weights about 2-1/2 ounces and the four-inch handle portions are wrapped with black cord. Each includes a Secure-Ex sheath and steel bead neck lanyard.

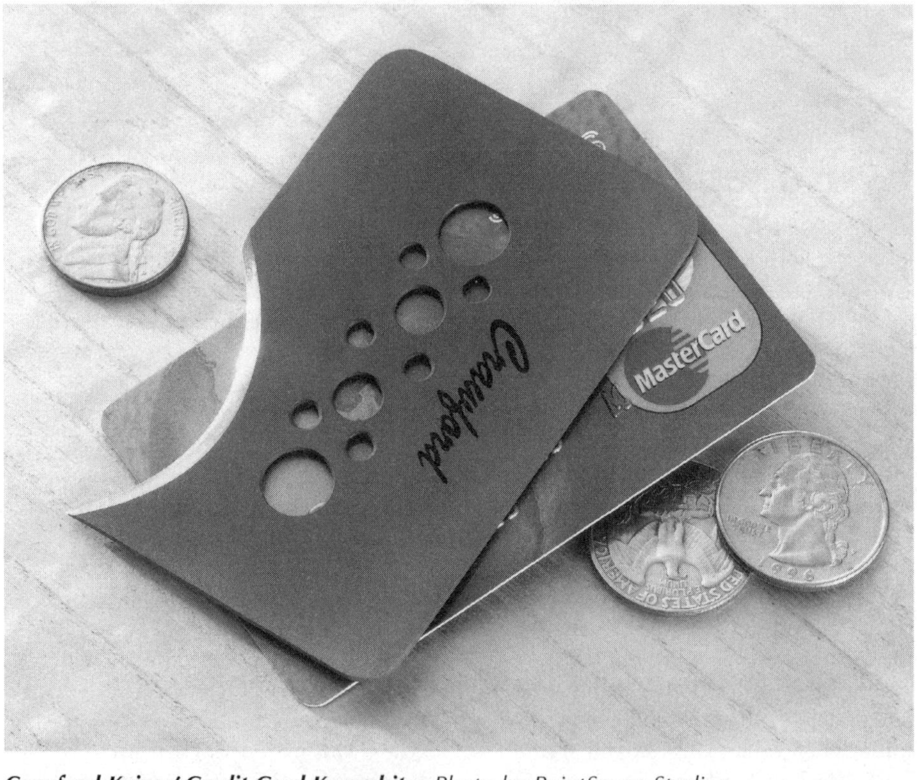

Crawford Knives' Credit Card Karambits. Photo by PointSeven Studios.

Columbia River Knife & Tool

The Side Hawg was designed by longtime custom knifemaker Mike Franklin. The little fixed blade knife is carried flat against a black Zytel sheath plate, pivoting out and off of a locking position for use. Overall, the 420J2 stainless steel knife is less than 4-1/2 inches long, with a 1.6-inch cutting edge. The knife weighs 1.6 ounces. The knife and plate attach to D-rings, loops or lanyards with the included carabiner and nylon strap. $29.95.

Another custom knifemaker, Kit Carson, designed the CRKT F4 fixed blade knife for a neck chain or lashing carry mode. The Zytel sheath is reversible with holes and slots for several carrying positions. The knife is made of 420J2 steel, 2.6 inches long, with an all plain or a partly serrated edge. The handle is made of textured Zytel for a firm grip. The knife measures 5-1/2 inches long overall and weighs 1.3 ounces. $24.99 for either type blade edge.

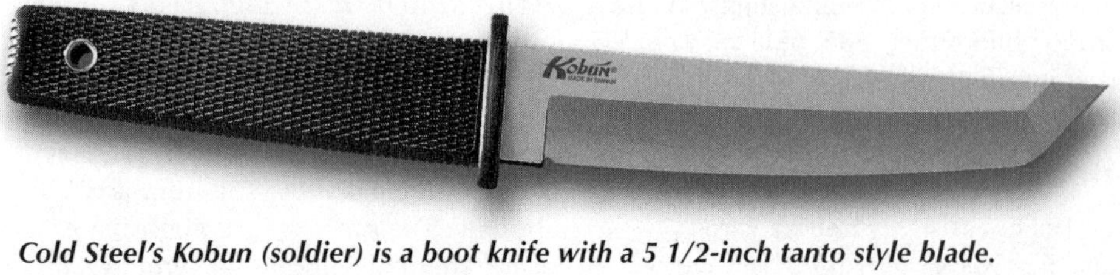

Cold Steel's Kobun (soldier) is a boot knife with a 5 1/2-inch tanto style blade.

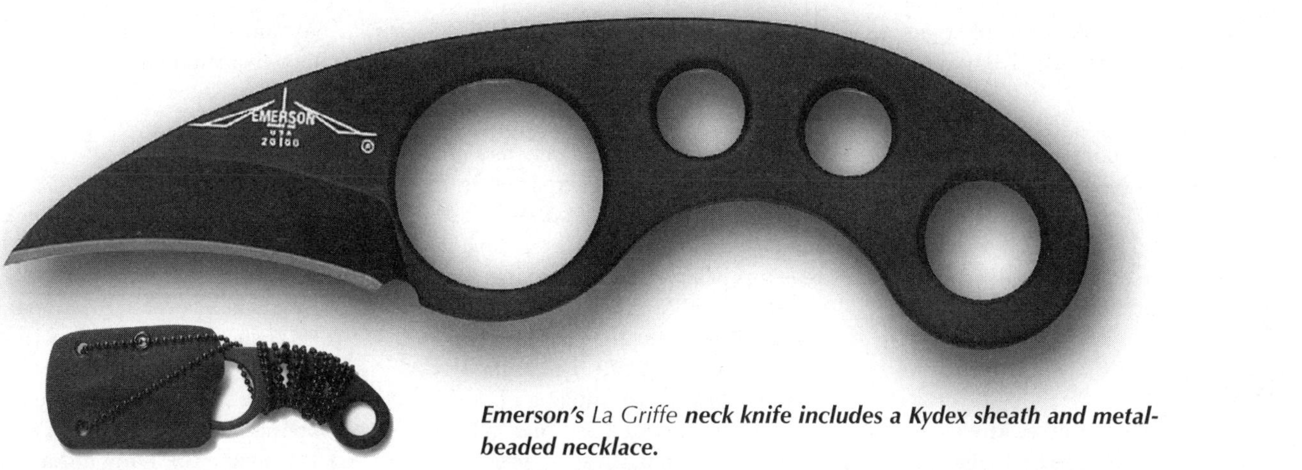

Emerson's** La Griffe **neck knife includes a Kydex sheath and metal-beaded necklace.

Crawford Knives

In the recent past, we might have been able to carry one of the Crawford Knives' Credit Card Karambits almost anywhere. But the little device will no longer be passed through airport or public building security. The little blade is made from titanium, drilled out for even lighter weight. It is designed to be carried in the wallet or purse. The size of a credit card, it is bead-blasted and anodized and has a razor-sharp edge. Pat and Wes Crawford sell them by the dozen whenever shown. $49.95.

Emerson Knives

Well-known custom knifemaker Ernie Emerson had another custom maker, Fred Perrin, designed the La Griffe (The Claw). The little neck knife is made of 154CM steel, finished in black oxide or silver satin. The knife is 4.9 inches long overall, with a 1 3/4-inch concave curved blade. The knife weighs 1.6 ounces and includes a Kydex sheath and metal-beaded necklace. The water rescue version in silver satin features a rounded-off blade tip and full serrations. $99.95.

Ka-Bar

The traditional, famous Ka-Bar is not what one might think of first for anything other than a belt sheath knife. But the Desert Fighting/Utility knife is carried in a hard plastic sheath designed to be lashed to a pack strap or leg strap. The sheath and non-slip Kraton G handle are sand-colored. The seven-inch 1095 cro-van low alloy carbon with chrome and vanadium carbide steel blade is black epoxy powder-coated. The knife is locked into the plastic sheath for safe handle-down carry. For those who already have a Ka-Bar, the desert hard plastic sheath is available by itself for $18.71. Otherwise, the Desert Ka-Bar and sheath lists for $82.03.

Kershaw

The Model 1006L Boot Knife features a 3 3/4-inch blade of 420J2 stainless steel with an open tang handle. A co-polymer insert reduces overall weight. The knife is 7-3/4 inches long overall. A boot sheath is included. $59.95.

Masters of Defense

The MOD Scorpion neck knife was designed by Jim Ray. It is lightweight, small and versatile. Held with the curved edge down, it functions as a skinner with plenty of control and leverage. Reversing the grip with the edge upward, the back serrations and the blade edge act as an effective defense tool. $89.98.

Ontario Knife

This Aircrew Survival Egress Knife is, as the name implies, meant to be used in emergency situations. The knife and accessories are worn strapped to

Kershaw's Model 1006L Boot Knife has a 3 3/4-inch blade and comes with a boot sheath.

the upper thigh of the user and held in a nylon sheath with a Kydex insert. The carbon steel blade is 5 inches long; the knife is 10-1/4 inches long overall with a zinc phosphate finish. The molded handle includes spear mounting holes and the butt cap may be used as a hammer. The included accessory acts as a strap cutter, screwdriver, honing rod and lanyard. $160.

SIGARMS

Here is a new name in knives, but not a new name in firearms. A number of firearms makers have found a market for knives bearing the same brand name; now SIGARMS has jumped in. The SigTac neck knife features a three-inch AUS6 stainless steel blade with black Teflon coating. Overall, the full tang knife is 6-1/2 inches long. The handle is of textured black polymer material for a non-slip grip. A Kydex sheath is included and has a clip that may be carried in the boot or on a belt. A metal beaded chain is included. $49.95.

SOG

The new Topo Contour offers one of the surest non-slip grips you're likely to encounter. The handle is made of molded Zytel material that features SOG's patent pending Topo construction for a tactile outer layer and stepped ergonomics that is very functional. The 2 1/2-inch blade is of AUS8 stainless steel and the knife is just under 6-1/2 inches long overall. It weighs three ounces. Both the sheath and the knife handle are cut out to display the SOG logo. The boot/belt clip on the sheath may be completely removed for neck wear and a lanyard is included. The polished satin blade is $64.00. The black TiAIN-coated blade is $99.

Spyderco

The Self Protection Option Tool (S.P.O.T.) is Spyderco's first neck knife. It features a skeletal handle for lighter weight and a reverse S-pattern blade 1-3/8 inches long. The edge may be all plain or Spyderco's serrated almost to the tip. The little knife weighs 1.3 ounces and is carried in a small Boltaron sheath, lying flat against the chest via a ball chain covered with a black Para-Cord sleeve that is easy on the neck. The AUS6 knife with a dull beaded finish is $69.95. The VG-

A little damascus steel neck knife by custom knifemaker Dave Ellis.

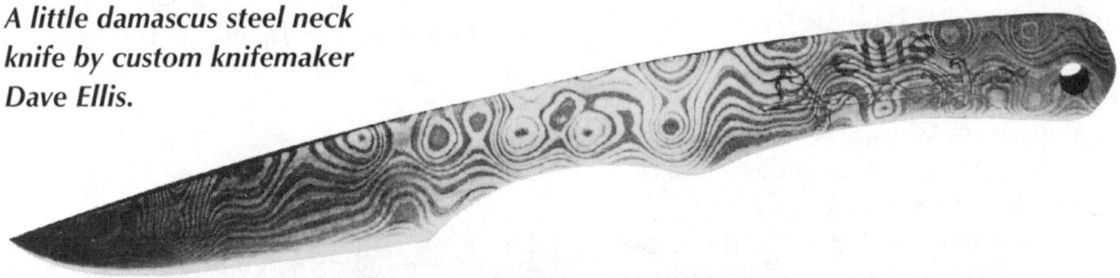

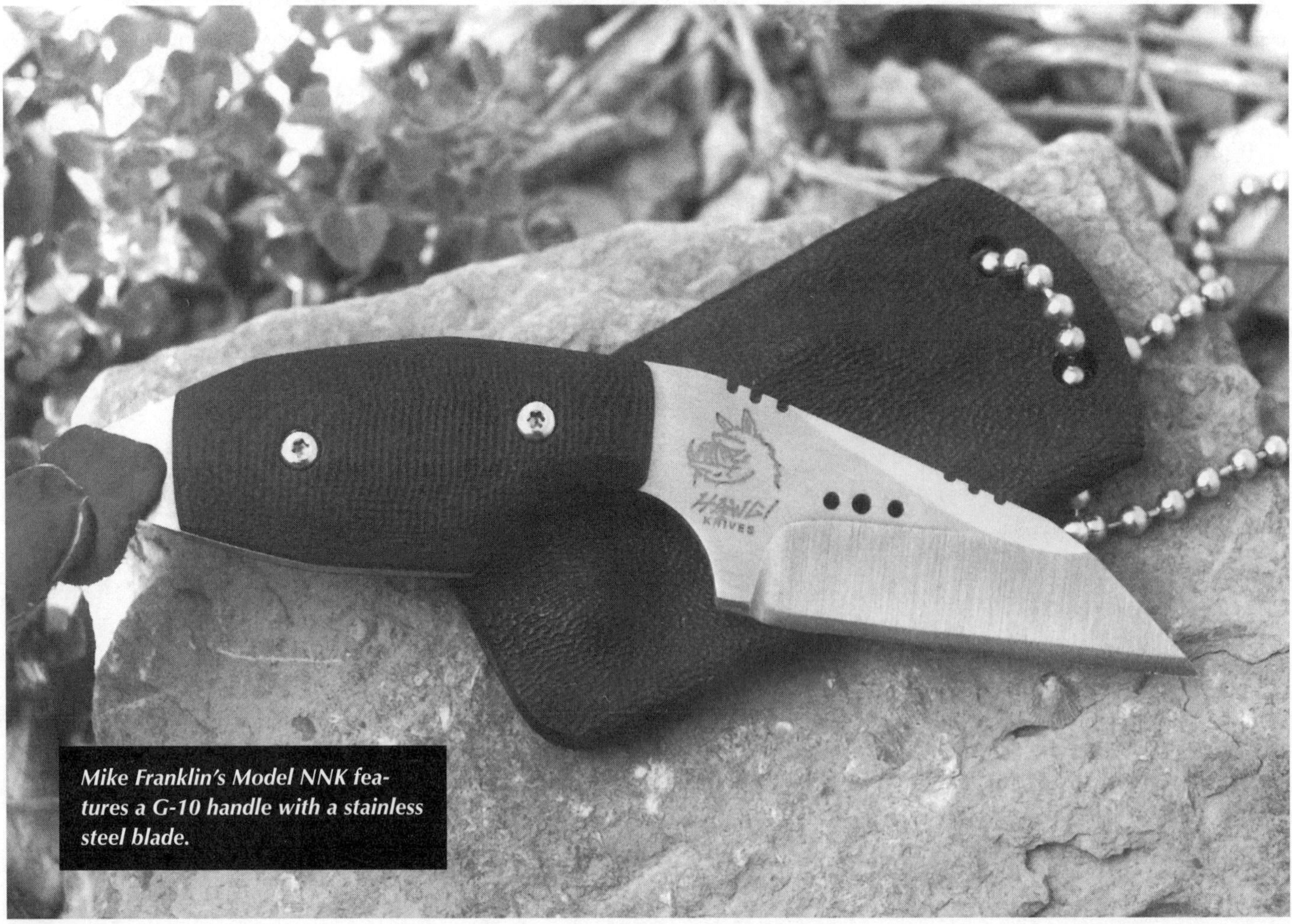

Mike Franklin's Model NNK features a G-10 handle with a stainless steel blade.

10 steel adds a black Micarta edging along the handle's rim for $124.95.

United Cutlery

The Mini Guardian is part of a series of knives designed by custom knifemaker Fred Carter. This little neck knife has a 2 5/16-inch blade of 440 stainless steel. The handle and sheath are made of ABS. The knife is 5-1/8 inches long overall. A black lanyard cord and a belt clip are included. $24.95.

The United T-Handle Knife Combo contains not one, but two little push knives: one plain edge and the other a serrated edge. The blades are made of 420 stainless steel, each 1-5/16 inches long. The fiber-reinforced nylon sheath is designed to be worn on the forearm or leg using the adjustable elastic strap. It can also be fastened to a belt or pack strap.

Custom Knifemakers

In theory, then, any custom knifemaker might be able and willing to make any knife design for the customer. But that is a theory only. Many custom makers specialize in certain types of knives and/or produce only the designs they have found to sell well. And some may have abnormally long waiting times from order to fulfillment, because of their popularity.

That said, the following custom knifemakers are known for their boot or neck knives. There are probably dozens of other knifemakers who can and will turn out a special knife for unusual carry. They range in prices from something less than a hundred dollars, up to and beyond several hundred. Neck knives are not that complicated in design, so that tends to keep the prices down. On the other hand, the type of steel and the reputation of the maker may easily drive the price as high as the traffic will bear. For those reasons, custom makers' prices are negotiated between maker and buyer; we won't quote any here.

Dave Ellis

Custom knifemaker Dave Ellis was the first Californian to be designated as a Mastersmith by the American Bladesmith Society. His little damascus steel neck knife is about 5-1/4 inches long overall, with a 2-inch edge. Because the damascus steel is handmade by Ellis, each knife is different. The weight, including a custom-made leather sheath, is negligible.

Mike Franklin

Custom knifemaker Mike Franklin likes to call his productions, "Knives With An Attitude." His Model NNK features G-10 handle with a stainless steel blade. A short leather thong through the butt is typical Franklin and helps with fast removal of the knife from the neck sheath.

Dolores Hayes

There are not many female custom knifemakers in the world, but Dolores Hayes has been at it for many years. She specializes in unusual designs and handle materials, as well as in small, jewelry knives. Her custom necklace knife has a 1 1/4-inch blade of AEB stainless steel and uses sterling silver fittings.

Chuck Stapel

Custom maker Chuck Stapel has been making movie prop knives and rugged using knives for the past 30 years. His boot knife is not a prop, but is a knife with a 4 1/2-inch AEB stainless steel blade and a handle of ivory Micarta. The buyer may specify almost any handle material desired. A leather booth knife sheath is included.

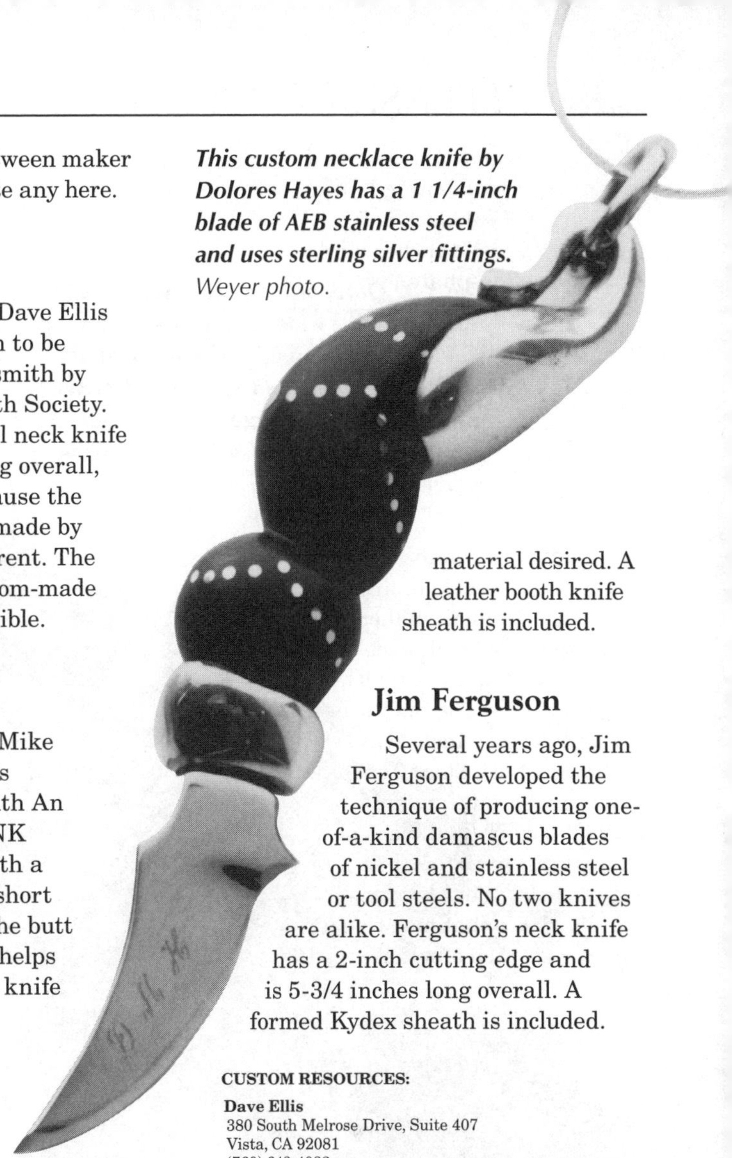

This custom necklace knife by Dolores Hayes has a 1 1/4-inch blade of AEB stainless steel and uses sterling silver fittings. *Weyer photo.*

Jim Ferguson

Several years ago, Jim Ferguson developed the technique of producing one-of-a-kind damascus blades of nickel and stainless steel or tool steels. No two knives are alike. Ferguson's neck knife has a 2-inch cutting edge and is 5-3/4 inches long overall. A formed Kydex sheath is included.

CUSTOM RESOURCES:

Dave Ellis
380 South Melrose Drive, Suite 407
Vista, CA 92081
(760) 643-4032

Mike Franklin
9878 Big Run Road
Aberdeen, OH 45101
(937) 549-2598

Dolores Hayes
P.O. Box 41405
Los Angeles, CA 90041

Chuck Stapel
P.O. Box 1617
Glendale, CA 91209
(213) 705-6433
Jim Ferguson

Twisted Nickel Knives
32131 Via Bande
Temecula, CA 92592
(909) 302-0267

Caution

The world changed on September 11, 2001. Knives are now prohibited aboard any commercial airliner, as well as in most schools, courthouses, public buildings and in many businesses. We probably never will return to the times before that day of terrorist attacks, to be able to carry a knife almost anywhere, any time. Laws and rules keep changing, so the user must first be familiar and comply with current ordinances. ❋

Chuck Stapel's boot knife has a 4 1/2-inch AEB stainless steel blade and a handle of ivory Micarta.

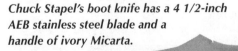

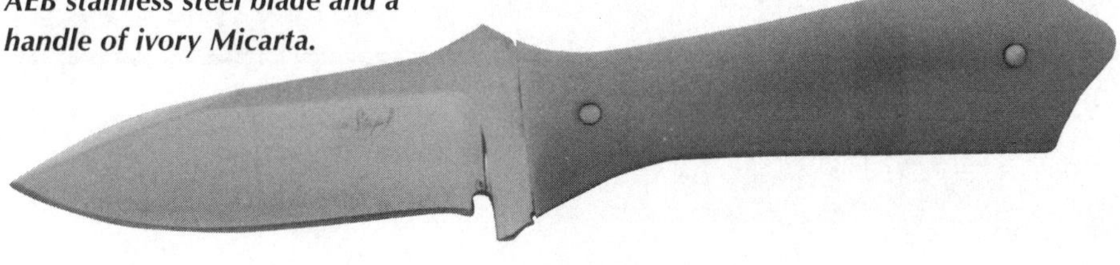

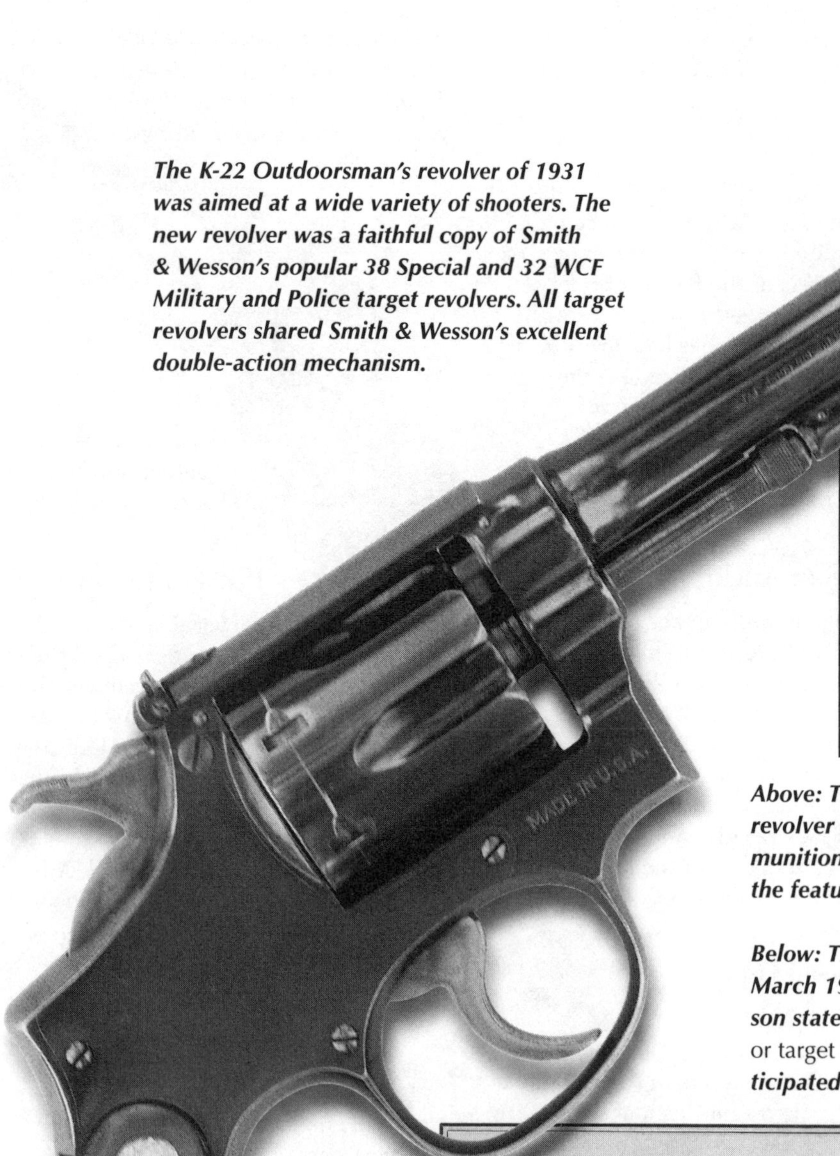

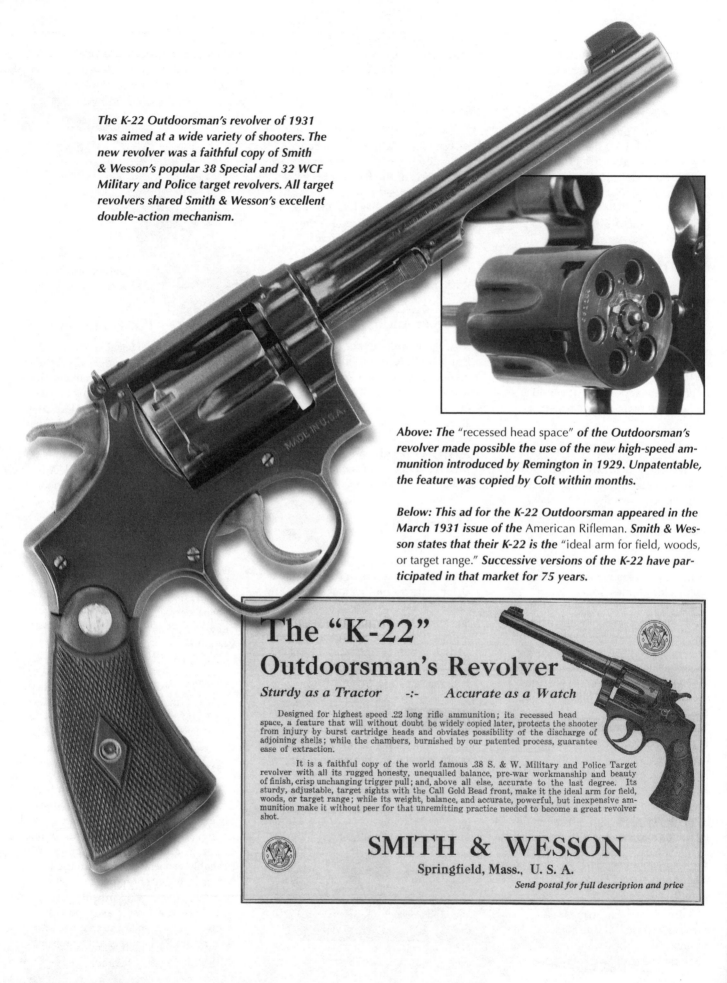

The K-22 Outdoorsman's revolver of 1931 was aimed at a wide variety of shooters. The new revolver was a faithful copy of Smith & Wesson's popular 38 Special and 32 WCF Military and Police target revolvers. All target revolvers shared Smith & Wesson's excellent double-action mechanism.

Above: The "recessed head space" ***of the Outdoorsman's revolver made possible the use of the new high-speed ammunition introduced by Remington in 1929. Unpatentable, the feature was copied by Colt within months.***

Below: This ad for the K-22 Outdoorsman appeared in the March 1931 issue of the American Rifleman. ***Smith & Wesson states that their K-22 is the*** "ideal arm for field, woods, or target range." ***Successive versions of the K-22 have participated in that market for 75 years.***

The "K-22"
Outdoorsman's Revolver
Sturdy as a Tractor -:- Accurate as a Watch
Designed for highest speed .22 long rifle ammunition; its recessed head space, a feature that will without doubt be widely copied later, protects the shooter from injury by burst cartridge heads and obviates possibility of the discharge of adjoining shells; while the chambers, burnished by our patented process, guarantee ease of extraction.
It is a faithful copy of the world famous .38 S. & W. Military and Police Target revolver with all its rugged honesty, unequalled balance, pre-war workmanship and beauty of finish, crisp unchanging trigger pull; and, above all else, accurate to the last degree. Its sturdy, adjustable, target sights with the Call Gold Bead front, make it the ideal arm for field, woods, or target range; while its weight, balance, and accurate, powerful, but inexpensive ammunition make it without peer for that unremitting practice needed to become a great revolver shot.
SMITH & WESSON
Springfield, Mass., U. S. A.
Send postal for full description and price

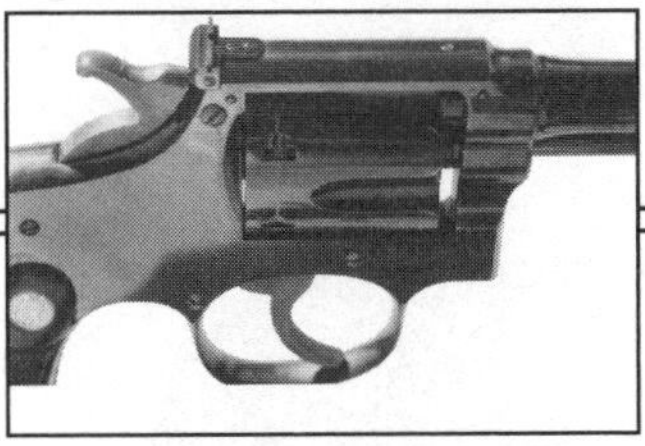

THE SMITH & WESSON K-22 TARGET REVOLVER

by Hollis M. Flint

"For the sportsman, the outdoorsman, the target shot and the plain gun bug, the advent of the K-22 is a most attractive milestone in revolver progress."

Major Julien S. Hatcher, *American Rifleman, March 1931.*

Origins

There are times in history where you find a combination of existing technology and new ideas comprehended by men capable of bringing the possibilities to fruition. Such is the case with Horace Smith (1808-1893) and Daniel Wesson (1825-1906) and their 22-caliber rimfire cartridge and revolver with bored-through cylinder to shoot it.

Smith & Wesson's 22 rimfire Number 1 cartridge, the 22 Short, and the seven-shot spur-trigger Number 1 revolver were introduced in 1857. Variations of the miniscule Number 1 were produced until 1881. Smith & Wesson did not again produce a 22-caliber revolver until the hand-ejector design was perfected at the turn of the century. The first Smith & Wesson hand-ejector revolver was the I-frame Model of 1896, chambered for the 32 Smith & Wesson Long cartridge. The new hand-ejector design was incorporated into the smaller M-frame 22-caliber Ladysmith revolver introduced in 1902. The seven-shot capacity of the Model 1 was retained, but the cylinder was chambered for the 22 Long rimfire cartridge of 1871. Ladysmith revolvers remained in the line until 1921. A few Ladysmith revolvers were produced with target sights and barrel lengths to six inches. However, with a weight of about 10 ounces, these revolvers were too light for competitive shooting. Smith & Wesson saw no imperative to produce a target revolver for 22-rimfire ammunition.

Major W. D. Frazer, in his article "Heavy-Frame .22-Caliber Handguns" published in the May 1932 *American Rifleman*, sheds light on the history of 22-caliber handgun competition. Frazer states *"When one recalls the ridicule to which the pioneers in small-bore shooting were subjected about half a century ago because they believed in the possibilities of the .22 as a target weapon, we are sometimes led to suspect that the revolver makers failed to develop handguns in this caliber for fear of popular disapproval."* At the turn of the century the small-bore revolver was generally made in a light-frame pocket design *"...suitable only for use of the fair sex..."* Target shooting with 22-rimfire cartridges was the domain of the single-shot pistols produced by several manufacturers. Slow fire matches at 50 yards did not require a repeating 22-caliber firearm. None were available in any case. That was about to change. In 1908 Phil Bekeart thought he saw a market for a better 22-caliber target revolver.

Phil Bekeart, a San Francisco gun dealer, envisioned a 22 rimfire target revolver with six-inch barrel based on Smith & Wesson's proven 32 hand-ejector I-frame revolver. Roy Jinks, Smith & Wesson historian, notes in his article "22/32 Bekeart" that *"Mr. Bekeart felt that this combination would make an excellent heavy target revolver."* Bekeart backed up his lobbying with purchase orders. Some 1044 revolvers were produced and sold to Bekeart and other dealers. According to Jinks, the *"Bekeart Model"* 22-target revolver was produced on demand until about 1914, when Smith & Wesson formally cataloged it. The revolver, with modifications, was produced until 1973. It was cataloged initially as the 22/32 Heavy Target, then the 22/32 Target Model, Model of 1953 22/32 Target, and finally as the Model 35. It was, and is, a great little revolver that Smith & Wesson should re-introduce. The shorter barreled versions of this revolver are familiar to readers as the 22/32 Kit gun and the Models 34 and stainless 63. However, at 23 ounces, the 22/32 Heavy Target revolver was still not a competitive target revolver. The K-frame is far more suitable for a heavy target revolver.

Left: The rear sight of the Outdoorsman was the same as that of Smith & Wesson's other K-frame target revolvers of the period. The sight blade is pushed back and forth by opposing screws, and the sight tang is polished to the contour of the top strap. This uncalibrated sight was replaced by the new "Micrometer Click Sight" ***in the K-22 Masterpiece of 1940.***

Right: The Call gold bead sight was standard on the Outdoorsman. The bead is polished flush with the Patridge post and can be blackened for target shooting.

Pre-World War II K-22 Target Revolvers

The first Smith & Wesson K-frame target revolvers for the 22 Long Rifle cartridge were produced about 1910. Walter Roper, a former Smith & Wesson employee, wrote about his experience with one of these revolvers in *The Old and the New* in the May 1944 issue of the *American Rifleman*. Roper relates that a group of army officer's persuaded Smith & Wesson to build a small lot of round-butt K-frame 22-caliber target-sighted revolvers. The revolvers proved to be inaccurate for target shooting. Blame was placed on the long bullet jump to the rifling imposed by the 38 Special-length cylinder. The revolvers were returned to Smith & Wesson and destroyed—except for one, which was retained by Smith & Wesson. About 1920, Roper's boss handed him the surviving K-22 and said, *"Sometime you might like to try this gun. Maybe you can discover why it doesn't shoot as it should."* Roper's tests revealed, *"It threw too many flyers to be a first-class target revolver."* Roper screwed in a re-threaded barrel from a single-shot target pistol: *"I got no more flyers!"* He then found the original K-22 barrels were inexplicably rifled with one turn in 10 inches. Roper concluded *"… certainly Smith & Wesson knew that one turn in about sixteen inches was correct for the .22 Long Rifle bullet, yet the gun was made with one turn in ten inches."* This error *"…caused the abandonment of an otherwise fine gun—the first of the heavy-frame 22's."* (Note: There is a variation of this story in McHenry and Roper's book *Smith & Wesson Hand Guns*. I have taken Roper's first-hand account from the *American Rifleman*.) Thus it was that the world had to wait until 1931 for Smith & Wesson to bring out a K-22 with the correct rifling twist, the K-22 Outdoorsman's revolver.

Roy Jinks, in his book *History of Smith & Wesson*, outlines the genesis of the K-22 Outdoorsman's revolver: *"As early as 1927, Smith & Wesson began receiving suggestions from competitive shooters to develop a 22-caliber revolver with the same balance as the .38 M & P Target model."* And *"…upon investigating various facets of the market, they found that a revolver of this kind was also in heavy demand by sportsmen…."* Summing up: *"Smith & Wesson's advertising proudly referred to this model as the K-22 Outdoorsman, signifying the market appeal for this revolver."* Smith & Wesson initially advertised the K-22 Outdoorsman's revolver as *"…the ideal arm for field, woods, or target range."*

Major Julian S. Hatcher, technical editor of the *American Rifleman*, reviewed the new Smith & Wesson K-22 Outdoorsman's revolver in "A New Revolver of Advanced Design" published in the March 1931 issue. The foremost feature and a *"…radical departure in the manner of handling cartridges in revolvers…* [was] *…counter-boring or recessing each chamber at the rear to give space for the head of the cartridge* [a feature then incorporated into the 22/32 revolver]*."* Furthermore, *"The firing pin of the revolver…is built into the frame of the gun in such a way that gas cannot escape past it."* At the time 22-rimfire cartridge cases were made of copper except for the new high velocity cartridges with brass cases. Ruptured cases occurred even *"…in the best target rifles."* These Smith & Wesson innovations were designed to protect the shooter from escaping gas and metal particles. Hatcher also noted *"The cylinder is made of heat-treated nickel steel with ample strength to withstand… the high pressure of the new Hi-Speed and Super-X cartridges."* The muzzle velocity of the K-22 revolver with high-speed ammunition was approximately 1100 feet per second (fps); a velocity previously obtained only in rifles. The increase from about 850 to 1100 fps in the revolver brought killing power comparable to *"…rifles that have been used successfully for small-game hunting for over 50 years."* Hatcher found the new revolver weighed 35 ounces with its six-inch barrel. Other features noted were Circassian-walnut stocks, grooved trigger and straps and factory-adjusted trigger pull of three to four pounds without creep. The chambers were burnished to final dimension to permit easy extraction. This was the first time Smith & Wesson applied their patented burnishing process to 22-caliber arms. Hatcher states *"The rifling and chambering are such that these revolvers shoot into the 1 1/2-inch circle at 50 yards from machine rests."* Smith & Wesson claimed that the accuracy life of their new K-22 was at least 100,000 rounds. Hatcher was also impressed with the adjustable rear sight. *"The sights are simple, strong and sturdy…."* He found that *"The adjusting screws are so threaded that one turn will change the point of impact 1 inch for each 10 yards of range."* The front sight was the Patridge type with *"Call"* gold bead fitted flush with the face for game shooting. Blackening the face made the sight useful for target shooting. However,

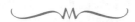

This ad for the K-22 Masterpiece revolver of 1940 appeared in the December 1945 American Rifleman. ***The K-22 Masterpiece improved upon the K-22 Outdoorsman, but World War II halted production in 1941. The K-22 Masterpiece was further revised in post-war production.***

Hatcher found the new revolver *"...is ideally suited for the sport of "plinking."* Hatcher sums up: *"...in fact, the full correct name is the K-22 Outdoorsman's Revolver. It has been intended not only for target practice but for hunting small game or for just shooting around at tin cans, bottles, etc., for fun."*

Elmer Keith, a double-action fun shooter, compared the new 22 heavy-frame Colt, introduced in 1930, and Smith & Wesson Outdoorsman's revolver in the chapter "Double Action Shooting" in *Sixguns by Keith: "We played the old game of trying to hit a gallon can six shots straight when tossed up with the left hand, using the Colt Officer's model .22 and the K-22 Smith & Wesson. The K-22 S. & W. proved the faster of the two. I many times made five hits and sometimes six, but rarely got over three with the tougher Colt D. A. pull."* You can imagine which revolver Keith would take to the field.

The K-22 Outdoorsman's revolver was numbered with other revolvers made with the Military and Police 1905 fourth change K-frame. K-22 Outdoorsman serial numbers are found within the 632132 to 682419 range. Jinks indicates that 17,117 were built.

Was there some reluctance on Smith & Wesson's part to sell the K-22 Outdoorsman as a target revolver dedicated to competition? Handgun competition since about 1920 included slow, timed and rapid fire stages in the National Rifle Association's national match course. However, revolvers were not the handgun of choice for most competitors. E. B. Mann, associate editor of the *American Rifleman*, provides a view of 22-caliber handguns for competition prior to World War II in "Choosing a Handgun" in the 1944 GUN DIGEST: *"...the shooter who uses a revolver in competition against automatics of equal qualifications, handicaps himself. And since 95% of the match shooters in this country use automatics in all 22-caliber matches, the choice is obvious."* Perhaps Smith & Wesson thought they needed a better revolver to compete with autoloaders in handgun competition. They brought their K-22 Masterpiece to market in 1940. The K-22 Masterpiece was finally a full-on target shooter. It is, for collectors, the K-22 second model.

Walter Roper reviewed the second model K-22, the K-22 Masterpiece, in the May 1944 *American Rifleman. "Never before have we been offered a .22 revolver with factory-built, short hammer throw, speed action, anti-slap trigger, and a rear sight that is self-locking and with micrometer adjustments."* Roper found in cocking the hammer of the Masterpiece *"...the thumb need only be bent a natural amount. With such a hammer motion, Rapid and Timed Fire with a revolver is less difficult."* Of the factory-set trigger over-travel: *"When the trigger lets go...the muzzle drops unless the trigger is instantly stopped as it is when a trigger control such as that in the Masterpiece is used."* Roper found each *"click"* of the adjusting screws of the new micrometer sight moved the group one inch at 50 yards. On the new sight: *"I am really enthusiastic over this improvement."* Roper's only lament was *"No club where I can shoot it, no ammunition to shoot in it if there was a range!"*

Only 1067 second model K-22 Masterpiece revolvers were produced before World War II put an end to Smith & Wesson's commercial production in 1941. Serial numbers are in the 682404 to 696952 range of the Military and Police K-frame series.

The Loyal Opposition

You may wonder why it took Smith & Wesson until 1931 to bring out its K-frame Outdoorsman's revolver. In a word: Colt. Colt initiated the 22 target revolver competition about 1910 with their 22 Police Positive Target revolver. This coincided with the special order-only introduction of Smith & Wesson's 22/32 Bekeart Model. The Colt and Smith & Wesson revolvers weighed 26 and 23 ounces, respectively, each with a six-inch barrel. Colt finally realized there was a demand for a truly heavyweight 22 target revolver and brought out their 22 Officer's Model Target in 1930. The new Colt weighed 38 ounces with six-inch barrel. Major Julian Hatcher is quoted in a full page Colt ad in the September 1930 *American Rifleman*: *"It fills a long-felt need for a man-sized .22...."* Furthermore, he said *"...it has a distinct field of its own as a first-class target arm."* Smith & Wesson must have scrambled to get their K-22 Outdoorsman to market in January 1931! Major W.D. Frazer summarized the situation in the May

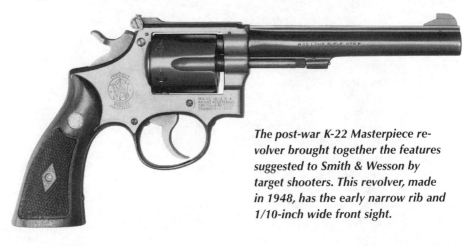

The post-war K-22 Masterpiece revolver brought together the features suggested to Smith & Wesson by target shooters. This revolver, made in 1948, has the early narrow rib and 1/10-inch wide front sight.

1932 *American Rifleman*: *"With the advent of the Colt heavy-frame revolvers, and their popular reception, the Smith & Wesson firm threw their hats in the ring in a challenge to Colt's progressiveness, and brought out their new K-22 target revolver…which is the design they should have originally produced twenty years ago, instead of the .22-32 Bekeart."*

The Colt, however, could not safely use the new high-speed 22 cartridges introduced in 1929. Unfortunately for Smith & Wesson, the *"recessed head space"* of the Outdoorsman was not patentable. Robert Neal and Roy Jinks in *Smith & Wesson 1857-1945* state that the feature was not patentable due to prior use in conversion of cap and ball revolvers to rimfire cartridges. Colt recessed headspace in the 22 Officer's Model Target and Police Positive Target revolvers within months following the introduction of the K-22. In a two-page ad in the December 1931 *American Rifleman,* Colt announced *"The New Colt Embedded Head Cylinder"*. The two new revolvers now differed mainly in weight. The Colt Officer's Model target was built on Colt's *"Heavy .41 caliber frame"* and outweighed the Smith & Wesson by nearly three ounces. Smith & Wesson would not catch up in weight until 1946. Production figures from introduction to 1940 indicate nearly equal sales of heavy-frame 22-caliber target revolvers; 22,000 for Colt compared to 17,000 for Smith & Wesson.

The post-war Smith & Wesson K-22 target revolver matched the 38-ounce weight of the pre-war Colt. However, in 1949 Colt screwed a heavier barrel into their 22-caliber New Colt Officer's Model Special and achieved a weight of 43 ounces. Colt thereby regained the heavyweight title in 22 target revolvers. The 22 Colt Officer's Model was discontinued in 1970, well past the use of 22 revolvers in competition. Rivalry between Colt and Smith & Wesson was a major force in developing 22 target revolvers in the twentieth century.

The Post-War K-22 Target Revolver

Major Julian Hatcher shot the pilot model of the postwar K-22 Masterpiece at the Smith & Wesson testing range. Hatcher then reported on one of the production-run revolvers in New Models of Handgun Favorites in the March 1947 *American Rifleman.* His opinion was *"The new gun is a beautiful example of the gunmaker's art. Surprisingly enough, it is really a great improvement over the prewar K-22."* Hatcher quotes Carl R. Hellstrom, President of Smith & Wesson: *"Regarding the K-22/46, we determined wherever at all possible, to incorporate the requirements found desirable by the target shooters themselves."* Hatcher noted the 38-ounce weight of the new Masterpiece was three ounces greater than the pre-war version. This was due to the new heavy barrel with rib. Other post-war improvements he found were magna stocks, new front sight with an integral ramp base, a slightly shorter action due to changes in stud locations, lighter double-action pull, improved hammer spur, new adjustable stop at the rear of the trigger guard to limit over travel and new hammer block to prevent accidental discharge from a blow to the hammer. The chambers were tighter and the bore was .003-inch smaller, with wider and deeper grooves than the pre-war version. After shooting at 20 yards, Hatcher states *"My conclusion is that in some way the makers must have found a way to give the gun a very high degree of barrel accuracy."* Smith & Wesson had achieved the ultimate 22-caliber target revolver at a time when target shooters had largely abandoned revolvers for autoloaders.

Jack O'Connor received K-22 number K19303 from Smith & Wesson in May 1948. Robert Anderson, in his 2002 book *Jack O'Connor,* lists the gun as one of O'Connor's favorite firearms. O'Connor wrote in his contemporary *Outdoor Life* column that the new K-22 was *"…sleek, handsome and smooth-working."* and *"…one of the easiest-shooting handguns I have ever seen."* However, he found the revolver *"…a shade on the heavy side."* O'Connor used his K-22 for plinking and small game, not for competitive shooting.

The new K-Masterpiece revolvers were given their own serial number series beginning with a K prefix. The first production Masterpiece revolver was K-22 number K101. This is the third model K-22 revolver, also called the Pre-Model 17.

The K-22 Masterpiece, with minor modifications, continued in production until 1989 when a full-lug barrel version was introduced. A full-lug barrel stainless steel K-22 remains in production. There were many improvements over the years.

Wider target hammers and target grips became available for the K-22 Masterpiece in 1950. Target triggers were added to the options in 1957. The five-screw frame was used in the K-22 from 1931 to 1955. In 1955 the upper side-plate screw was deleted leaving a four-screw frame. The K-22 Masterpiece

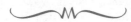

If you have ever dumped a box of these 22 cartridges in your pocket you are probably a senior citizen. I always reached for Super-X hollowpoints when I went hunting woodchucks and crows in the early 1950s in rural New Hampshire.

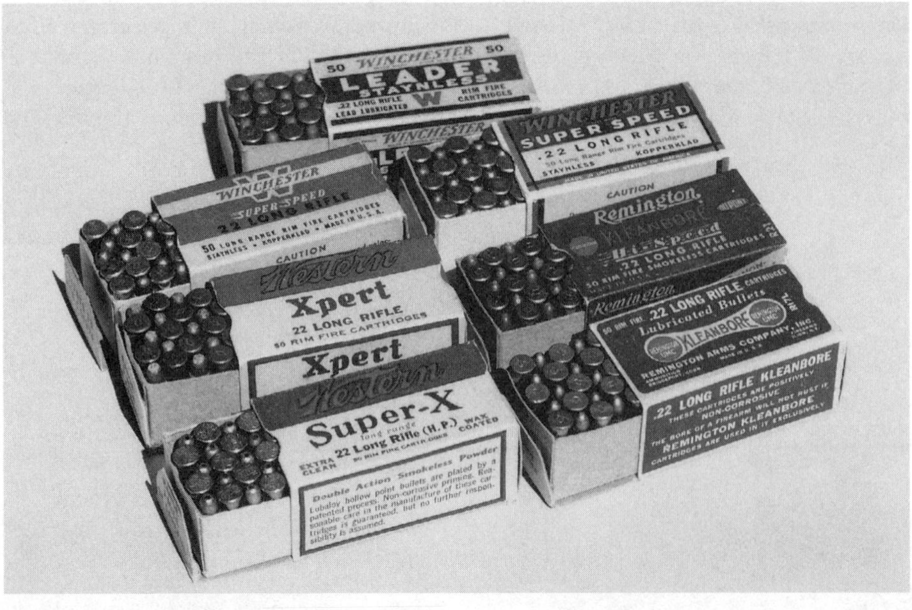

became the Model 17 in 1957. The 8 3/8-inch barrel became available in 1958. In 1961 the cylinder-stop plunger screw in the trigger guard was deleted leaving the current three-screw frame. The standard barrel length was 6 inches until the full-lug barrel series began in 1990. The diamond in the checkering around the grip screw was deleted in 1969. Pinned barrels were eliminated in 1982. Chambers of Smith & Wesson K-22 revolvers remain recessed to support the head of their rimfire ammunition. The Model 17 underwent major changes when the full-lug barrel version of 1990-1994 was introduced. Available lengths of full-lug barrels were 4, 6 and 8-3/8 inches. In 1996 the Model 17 was further changed with a 10-shot alloy cylinder *(briefly)* and round-butt frame. Production of blued steel Model 17 revolvers ended in 1999.

Smith and Wesson introduced a stainless steel version of the K-22, the Model 617, well before the last blue-steel Model 17 revolvers left Springfield. The Model 617 of 1990 came with a six-shot stainless steel cylinder, full-lug barrel and square-butt frame. Later, rubber grips were fitted to the new round-butt frame attached to 4, 6 and 8 3/8-inch full-lug barrels. A 10-shot alloy cylinder version was introduced in 1996, but the unpopular alloy cylinder was replaced with a stainless steel 10-shot cylinder in 1997. Smith & Wesson's late catalog shows the all-stainless steel Model 617 with 6-inch full-lug barrel and either six- or ten-shot cylinder. A 4-inch Model 617 with 10-shot cylinder is also offered. A summary of the various dash-numbered versions of the Model 17 and 617 is shown in Table 1. Not shown in Table 1 are the 617-5 (2001) and 617-6 (2002-today) reflecting further changes in lockwork. The minor variations in these revolvers are too numerous to list. Please refer to Supica and Nahas' book *Standard Catalog of Smith & Wesson* for further details. See the Smith & Wesson website, www.smith-wesson.com, for current production.

Table 1. Features of Smith & Wesson Post-War K-22 Revolvers

Model	Dates of production	Main Features/changes
K-22	1946-1957	Delete upper sideplate screw 1955, 4-screw frame
17	1957-1959	Stamp model number, 8-3/8" barrel in 1958
17-1	1959-1961	Extractor rod to left-hand thread
17-2	1961-1967	Delete trigger guard screw, 3-screw frame
17-3	1967-1977	Rear sight leaf screw relocated, last diamond grips 1968
17-4	1977-1988	Relocate gas ring from yoke to cylinder, last pinned barrel 1982
17-5	1988-1989	New yoke retention system, lock work
17-6	1990-1994	Full-lug barrel 4, 6, 8-3/8", combat grips, 8-3/8" barrel deleted 1993
17-7	1994-1996	Drill and tap for scope
17-8	1996-1998	Round-butt frame, rubber grips, 10-shot alloy cylinder
17-9	1998-1999	Numerous changes to lockwork, Last Model 17 1999
617	1990-1994	Full-lug barrel 4, 6, 8-3/8"
617-1	1994-1996	Drill and tap for scope, rubber grips
617-2	1996-1998	Ten-shot alloy cylinder, round-butt frame, alloy cylinder deleted 1997
617-3	1998-1998	Numerous changes to lockwork, six-shot stainless steel cylinder
617-4	1998-2001	Six or 10-shot stainless steel cylinder, various full-lug barrel lengths

Dates of production are approximate.

The 22 Long Rifle Cartridge

Jim Foral outlines the origin of the 22 Long Rifle cartridge in his 1998 GUN DIGEST article "*UMC Thomas:* A Recognition" "*Early in 1887, J. Stevens Arms and Tool Co. became displeased with the mediocre target accuracy of the 22 Short and 22 Long rimfires, turning to Union Metalic Cartridge for a solution. Thomas* [William M. Thomas, ballistician] *took the existing 22 Long case and powder charge, and added a new outside-lubricated bullet the same diameter as the case. The 40-grain bullet was not crimped into the shell and was propelled by 5 grains of fine blackpowder. The new cartridge was referred to as the 22-5-40...*" The bullets were crimped in place for use in repeating rifles in 1900.

For many years the 22 Long Rifle was available loaded with black, semi-

The K-22 Combat Masterpiece was a worthy companion to the target version of the K-22. The Combat K-22 was produced from 1949 to 1985. I have not found any significant difference in accuracy between the four and six-inch barrels, but I prefer the balance of the six-inch barrel.

Table 2. Specifications of Tested K-22 Target Revolvers

Model	Serial number	Year made	Trigger pull pounds	Barrel/cyl. gap inches	Weight ounces
Outdoorsman	651XXX	1935	2.0	.004	35.8
Masterpiece	K42XXX	1948	3.6	.004	37.6
17-3	8K53XXX	1975	3.1	.005	41.8
17-6	BEJ2XXX	1994	3.8	.007	47.5

smokeless (Lesmok, King's Semi-smokeless), or smokeless powder. Blackpowder velocities were about 950 fps from rifles, with pressures around 10,000 pounds per square inch (psi). With smokeless powder, the velocities increased to 1100 fps at about 15,000 psi. In 1929, the Remington Arms Company brought out their *Kleanbore Palma Hi-Speed* cartridge with pressures around 20,000 psi. Colonel Townsend Whelen, outdoorsman, shooter and author, reviewed the new load in the August 1930 issue of the *American Rifleman*: *"The Remington Arms Company have just succeeded in perfecting a new .22-caliber Long Rifle cartridge having a muzzle velocity of 1,300 f.s., a muzzle energy of 143 foot-pounds and capable of averaging 1 1/2-inch groups at 100 yards in high-grade small-bore target rifles."* The new round used brass instead of copper for its cases. Furthermore, the new cartridge was primed with Remington's *"Kleanbore"* priming, the first non-corrosive primer to appear in America, according to Whelen. A harder bullet alloy was also used to reduce leading. Whelen, ever the experimenter, brought the new cartridges to his friend Al Woodworth at Springfield Armory for testing in their indoor range. Four Springfield Model 1922 M1 rifles in machine rests each sent 100 rounds down-range at 100 yards. The four rifles placed 99, 97, 98 and 96 shots in a 2-inch circle. The largest pattern went 2-1/2 inches. Whelen felt the results *"...indicate a very high order of shooting on the part of both ammunition and rifles."* Remington's new 22 Long Rifle ammunition was perhaps the greatest combination of advances ever with this cartridge.

Western Cartridge Company, seldom second in ammunition development, brought out their high velocity *Super-X* 22 cartridges in 1931. Western managed to improve the brass cases with nickel plating and the bullet with their *"Lubaloy"* plating. Best of all, velocity was increased to 1400 fps by using their *"double-action"* (progressive-burning) powder and new non-corrosive priming. However, Western stated their Super-X ammunition was to be regarded as hunting ammunition. Again, Townsend Whelen was the reviewer, writing in the July 1931 *American Rifleman.* Whelen found the new cartridges chronographed 1375 fps with the 40-grain solid bullet. He also fired the hollowpoint ammunition in his K-22 Outdoorsman and obtained 1100 fps and found *"...splendid accuracy in this revolver."* Summing up: *"It is a very distinct advance ballistically in rim-fire ammunition."* While we have a far greater variety of 22 Long Rifle ammunition today, we have regressed as far as velocity goes for non-specialty 22 cartridges. The 40-grain slug now travels 1255 fps in deference to the millions of older 22 firearms in existence.

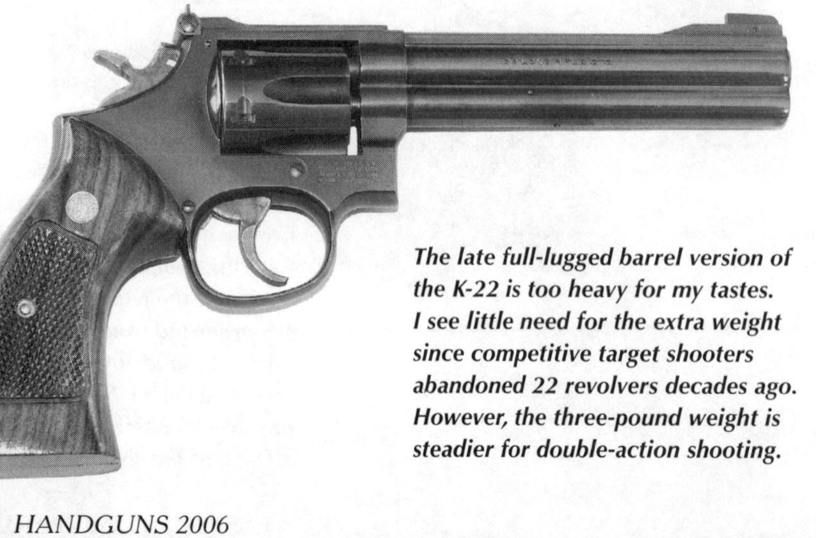

The late full-lugged barrel version of the K-22 is too heavy for my tastes. I see little need for the extra weight since competitive target shooters abandoned 22 revolvers decades ago. However, the three-pound weight is steadier for double-action shooting.

A Look at Some K-22s

Four K-22 revolvers, with specifications shown in Table 2, were tested for grouping ability when held in a Ransom Rest. These revolvers are representative of the K-22 line over a major span of its production. The earliest example, the Outdoorsman, was shipped from Smith & Wesson July 2, 1935, and delivered to Wm. H. Hoegee Co., Los Angeles, California (see Factory Letters in the Bibliography). It is standard production, having the Patridge front sight with Call gold bead, Circassian walnut grips with silver medallions, long action of the K-frame fourth change design, and having the serial number stamped on the barrel, cylinder, extractor star, right grip panel and butt of the grip frame. This revolver shows extremely close fitting of parts and soft dark bluing characteristic of prewar Smith & Wesson handguns.

The K-22 Masterpiece was shipped from Smith & Wesson on September 14, 1948, and delivered to Pritzlaff Hardware Company, Milwaukee, Wisconsin. It is standard early postwar production having micrometer rear sight, 1/10-inch wide Patridge front sight, walnut magna grips with silver medallions, short-action design, narrow barrel rib, and serial number stamped as on the Outdoorsman's revolver. The finish is satin blue. Both Outdoorsman and Masterpiece revolvers have the five-screw frame used from 1905 to 1955.

The Model 17-3 was produced in 1975 and has standard hammer and trigger, wide barrel rib with 1/8-inch wide Patridge front sight, Goncala Alves target grips and three-screw frame introduced in 1961. The serial number is stamped on the butt of the grip frame and in the yoke cut. The finish on this revolver is highly polished bright blue. The Model 17-6 was produced in 1994 and has semi-target hammer and smooth combat trigger, full-lug barrel, 1/8-inch wide Patridge front sight, Goncala Alves target grips *(replaced combat grips?)* and serial number and model number stamped as on the Model 17-3. Finish is bright blue.

All four revolvers have 6-inch barrels, six-shot fluted cylinders with chambers recessed for cartridge heads. The Model 17-6 does not have a pinned barrel. All four revolvers are about 99-percent condition and were cleaned and lightly oiled prior to testing.

Five 22 Long Rifle ammunitions were tested: Remington brass-plated 36-grain hollowpoints (Rem BPHP), Western Super-X 40-grain solids of 1960 vintage (Wes SX), Federal Gold Medal Target 40-grain solids (Fed GMT), CC1 Pistol Match 40-grain solids (CCI PM) and CCI Velocitor 40-grain Gold-Dot hollowpoints (CCI GDHP). The Super-X ammunition came from a brick in my possession, properly stored, since 1960. All the other ammunition was current manufacture and of the same lot number for each ammunition.

Accuracy tests were conducted on a sheltered outdoor range with the test revolvers held in a Ransom Rest. The rest was mounted on a bench designed for machine-rest testing. A reversed B21 silhouette target, 35 by 45 inches, was placed on a target stand 50 yards from the muzzle of the revolver. A reversed target presents a large surface area for collecting the 25 groups required for each revolver. Groups were fired in vertically oriented strings of five groups. Groups within a vertical string were obtained by lowering or raising the elevation adjustment of the Ransom Rest. The target stand was moved approximately five inches between vertical strings of groups rather than adjusting the Ransom Rest. Five initial settling shots were fired after placing the revolver in the rest. Each record group consisted of a cylinder full of six cartridges. The test revolver was cleaned in position between changes of ammunition. Three fouling shots with each ammunition were fired over the target into the backstop before depressing the revolver for record shots. A total of 150 record shots were fired from each revolver. Velocities of the first 18 record shots from each ammunition were recorded on a Beta Chrony chronograph set three feet from the muzzle of the test revolver. Record groups were measured with a micrometer.

Results and Discussion

The K-22 revolvers and ammunitions I tested averaged about 2- to 3-inch six-shot groups at 50 yards. The average group size and standard deviation of each of the four revolvers with the five ammunitions were 3.04± .17, 2.38± .30, 2.81± .35 and 3.01± .52 inches for Outdoorsman, Masterpiece, 17-3 and 17-6, respectively. Ninety-five percent of all shots fired by each revolver should fall within a group described by the revolver's average group and standard deviation. A difference exists between the average groups of two revolvers when there is no overlapping of their standard deviations. Considering the above data, the Masterpiece revolver produced a smaller average group than the Outdoorsman's revolver (group size of 2.08 to 2.68 inches compared to 2.87 to 3.21 inches, respectively). There are no other differences between the grouping of the four revolvers in this test.

Similarly, the average group size and standard deviation for each of the five ammunitions fired in the four revolvers were 2.95± .43, 2.60± .25, 2.79± .35, 3.11± .42 and 2.61± .50 for Remington BPHP, Western SX, CCI PM, Federal GMT and CCI GDHP, respectively. There are no differences in the average grouping of the five ammunitions in this test.

This does not mean that some combinations of revolver and ammunition did not shoot smaller groups than other combinations. Referring to Table 3, the average group produced by the combination of Masterpiece revolver and CCI GDHP ammunition was smaller than the average group produced by the combination of Model 17-6 and Fed GMT ammunition (1.9± .6 compared to 3.8± .5 inches, respectively).

Shooting a lot of groups with revolvers held in a Ransom Rest is instructive. Shots fired with the same revolver and ammunition often appear to distribute horizontally or vertically within individual groups. A round group is an exception. Also, consecutive groups fired under presumably the same conditions will vary considerably in size. For example, the five groups fired by the Masterpiece revolver and Federal GMT ammunition were 2.77, 2.95, 2.47, 1.90 and 3.19 inches. The variation is documented in the standard deviation.

I enjoy the results of "chasing" a tin can along the bottom of a wash. Try double-action shooting and/or tennis balls for a greater challenge.

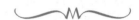

The velocities obtained with CCI GDHP ammunition were impressive, averaging 1101 to 1194 fps, depending on the revolver. Keep in mind this is a 40-grain hollowpoint. These velocities generally exceed the 1100 fps reported by Whelen for his Outdoorsman's revolver in 1931. Whelen used Western Super-X 37-grain hollow-point ammunition. Western advertised their Super-X 40-grain ammunition in 1931 as averaging 1075 fps from a six-inch barrel, likely a revolver. My 1935 Outdoorsman's revolver gave an average velocity of 1073 fps with 1960 Western Super-X ammunition. It appears that CCI GDHP ammunition is the fastest 40-grain ammunition ever available for revolvers with six-inch barrels.

The greater barrel/cylinder gap, .007-inch, of the Model 17-6 produced generally lower average velocities than the other revolvers. Barrel/cylinder gap is a very important factor in the velocities obtained from revolvers.

None of the revolvers, under my test conditions, produced the one and one-half inch groups that Hatcher suggested for the Outdoorsman in 1931. Hatcher does not provide grouping data for the Outdoorsman or the post-war

Masterpiece revolver he reviewed for the *American Rifleman.* I could not find any grouping claims for K-22 revolvers in the limited Smith & Wesson literature I have. There is indirect evidence for the claim. Roy McHenry and Walter Roper state in *Smith & Wesson Hand Guns "However, machine rest tests showed that it* [Outdoorsman] *would group its shots inside an inch and a half circle...."* No distance is given, but 50 yards is a reasonable assumption. Perhaps this data is the source of the 1 1/2-inch groups cited by Hatcher, Keith and others.

Fred Seguin tested seven 22 autoloaders and two revolvers for his article "How Accurate Are They?" in the August 1948 issue of the *American Rifleman.* Seguin included *"A brand new 1947 S. & W. Masterpiece."* He tested eight ammunitions, firing one 10-shot group with each at 50 yards, machine rest. Somewhat unorthodox, Seguin then drew a box around each group providing vertical and horizontal dimensions. I took the average of the widest dimension for each group and came up with an average of 2.42 inches for the Masterpiece revolver. A Colt Officer's Model averaged 1.99 inches in the same test. The best group for both revolvers was 1.56 inches, produced by Western Super-X and Peters Target ammunition, respectively. Seguin concluded the autoloaders, Colt and High Standard, did better: *"Automatic pistols produce tighter groups than revolvers."*

Skeeter Skelton used a Ransom Rest to test a K-22 Masterpiece and reported his results in the May 1978 issue of *Shooting Times.* Shooting Western Mark IV Pistol Match ammunition at 20 yards *"...gave six-shot groups averaging around 0.87-inch, usually with one small hole containing four shots, then a couple of flyers opening the group to as much as an inch."* He found no particular chambers were at fault.

The *American Rifleman* staff report on a 10-shot Model 617 with aluminum cylinder in the January 1997 issue. A Ransom Rest was used in shooting five five-shot groups with each of three ammunitions at 25 yards. Federal Gold Medal Target produced groups averaging 1.43 inches. The overall average group size was 1.99 inches. The staff felt this was *"generally good, though not outstanding."*

I have six additional reports for accuracy tests of Model 17 and 617

Table 3. Grouping of K-22 Target Revolvers Held in a Ransom Rest

	Average velocity and group size for indicated load[a]				
Model	**Rem BPHP**	**Wes SX**	**CCI PM**	**Fed. GMT**	**CCI GDHP**
Outdoorsman	1023±35 3.2±.3	1073±11 2.8±.3	951±19 3.2±.4	971±13 3.1±.5	1152±36 2.9±.4
Masterpiece	983±35 2.3±.5	1043±12 2.7±.3	923±15 2.3±.6	939±15 2.7±.5	1150±45 1.9±.6
17-3	1037±30 3.4±.3	1076±25 2.7±.4	952±17 2.6±.4	977±13 2.9±.5	1194±42 2.4±.3
17-6	947±47 2.9±.3	1005±19 2.2±.4	919±15 3.0±.4	934±14 3.8±.5	1101±39 3.2±.6

[a] Average velocity in feet per second at three feet for 18 shots and average group size in inches for five six-shot groups at 50 yards. See text for description of ammunition tested.

revolvers published in trade magazines since 1990. All the tests were conducted with hand-held revolvers, bench rest. However, I do not feel the results of these tests can be compared to the results of tests using machine rests. Too much depends on who is holding the revolver. I have taken the hand-held data into consideration in drawing the following conclusion.

I think it is fair to say most K-22 revolvers will approach two-inch groups at 50 yards with selected ammunition, and some recent versions may do better. Most of the time, if you miss a soda can or small game animal at 25 yards with your K-22 it will be your fault. However, in my view the K-22 has another laudable use besides plinking and small-game hunting.

The K-22 is one of the best handguns for introducing a new handgunner to the sport. A full-size handgun, safe with its single- or double-action cocking, accurate enough to reward proper technique, free of recoil and muzzle blast, and shooting incredibly cheap ammunition, the K-22 is just right for the beginner. The older I get the more I appreciate these qualities for myself. The K-22 is my favorite Smith & Wesson handgun.

I see the K-22 as Smith and Wesson originally advertised it, an *"Outdoorsman's revolver"* with *"rugged honesty, unequaled balance, beauty of finish, and accurate to the last degree."* That is why the K-22 remains in production after more than 70 years. Smith & Wesson got the market right in 1931.

BIBLIOGRAPHY

Anderson, Robert M. *Jack O'Connor.* Safari Press, Inc. Long Beach, California. 2002.

Anonymous. "Smith & Wesson 617 Plus .22". *American Rifleman* Dope Bag. January 1997.

Factory Letters. Send complete firearm description and a money order for 30 dollars to: Mr. Roy Jinks, Smith & Wesson Historian, P.O. Box 2208, Springfield, Massachusetts, 01102-2208.

Foral, Jim. "UMC Thomas: A Recognition". GUN DIGEST. Krause Publications. Iola, Wisconsin. 1998.

Frazer, Major W. D. "Heavy-Frame .22-Caliber Handguns". *American Rifleman.* May 1932.

Hatcher, Major Julian S. "A New Revolver of Advanced Design". *American Rifleman.* March 1931.

Hatcher, Major-General Julian S. "New Models of Handgun Favorites". *American Rifleman.* March 1947.

Jinks, Roy G. 22/32 Bekeart. *Smith & Wesson Collectors News.* Vol. 7, No. 4. 1975.

Jinks, Roy G. *History of Smith & Wesson.* Beinfeld Publishing, Inc. North Hollywood, California. Tenth Edition. 1992.

Keith, Elmer. *Sixguns by Keith.* Bonanza Books. New York, New York. 1961.

Mann, E. B. "Choosing a Handgun and Learning to Shoot It". GUN DIGEST. Reprint of 1944 first edition. The Gun Digest Company. Chicago, Illinois. 1944.

McHenry, Roy C. and Roper, Walter F. *Smith & Wesson Handguns.* Wolfe Publishing Company. Prescott, Arizona. Reprint edition. 1994.

Neal, Robert J. and Jinks, Roy G. *Smith & Wesson 1857-1945.* R & R Books. Livonia, New York. Revised edition. 1975.

Roper, Walter F. " The Old and the New". *American Rifleman.* May 1944.

Seguin, Fred M. "How Accurate Are They?" *American Rifleman.* August 1948.

Skelton, Skeeter. "S & W's Masterpieces. Over 30 Years and Still Going Strong". *Shooting Times.* May 1978.

Smith & Wesson Collectors Association. Miscellaneous Publications. For association information, contact: Administrative Assistant, P.O. Box 32, Great Bend, Kansas, 67530. On line at swca @ greatbend.com

Supica, Jim and Nahas, Richard. *Standard Catalog of Smith & Wesson.* Krause Publications. Iola, Wisconsin. Second edition. 2001.

Whelen, Townsend. "The Remington Kleanbore Palma Hi-Speed .22-Caliber Long Rifle Cartridge". *American Rifleman.* August 1930.

Whelen, Townsend. "The Super-X .22 Cartridges". *American Rifleman.* July 1931.

SHOOTER'S MARKETPLACE

PRODUCT NEWS FOR THE ACTIVE SHOOTING SPORTSMAN

The companies represented on the following pages will be happy to provide additional information – feel free to contact them.

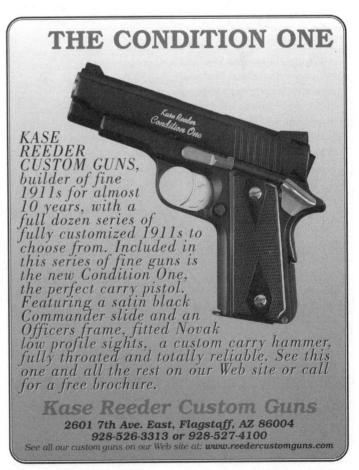

Doug Turnbull Restoration
Big Bore Classics

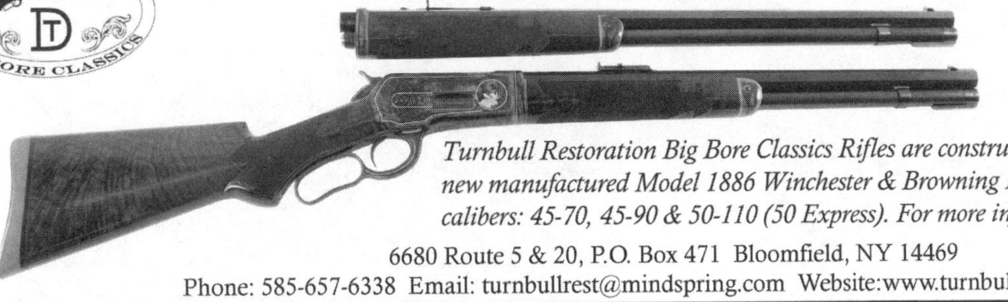

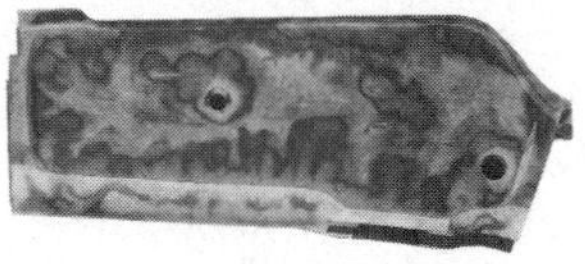

Turnbull Restoration Big Bore Classics Rifles are constructed using original and new manufactured Model 1886 Winchester & Browning Rifles. Available in calibers: 45-70, 45-90 & 50-110 (50 Express). For more information contact us at:

6680 Route 5 & 20, P.O. Box 471 Bloomfield, NY 14469

Phone: 585-657-6338 Email: turnbullrest@mindspring.com Website:www.turnbullrestoration.com

COMBINATION RIFLE AND OPTICS REST

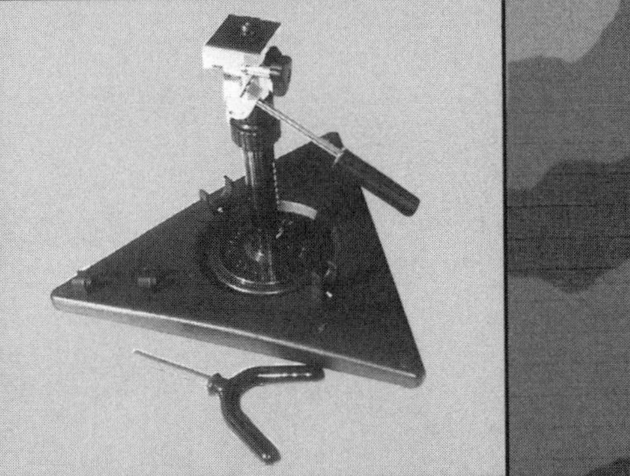

The Magna-Pod weighs less than two pounds, yet firmly supports more than most expensive tripods. It will hold 50 pounds at its low 9-inch height and over 10 pounds extended to 17 inches. It sets up in seconds where there is neither time nor space for a tripod and keeps your expensive equipment safe from knock-overs by kids, pets, pedestrians, or even high winds. It makes a great mono-pod for camcorders, etc., and its carrying box is less than 13" x 13" x 3 1/4" high for easy storage and access.

Attached to its triangle base it becomes an extremely stable table-pod or rifle bench rest. The rifle yoke pictured in photo is included. It's 5 pods in 1: Magna-Pod, Mono-Pod, Table-Pod, Shoulder-Pod and Rifle Rest. Send for free catalog.

SHEPHERD ENTERPRISES, INC.

Box 189, Waterloo, NE 68069

Phone: 402-779-2424 • Fax: 402-779-4010

E-mail: shepherd@shepherdscopes.com • Web: www.shepherdscopes.com

THE CONDITION ONE

KASE REEDER CUSTOM GUNS, builder of fine 1911s for almost 10 years, with a full dozen series of fully customized 1911s to choose from. Included in this series of fine guns is the new Condition One, the perfect carry pistol. Featuring a satin black Commander slide and an Officers frame, fitted Novak low profile sights, a custom carry hammer, fully throated and totally reliable. See this one and all the rest on our Web site or call for a free brochure.

Kase Reeder Custom Guns

2601 7th Ave. East, Flagstaff, AZ 86004

928-526-3313 or 928-527-4100

*See all our custom guns on our Web site at: **www.reedercustomguns.com***

ULTIMATE BLACK WIDOW

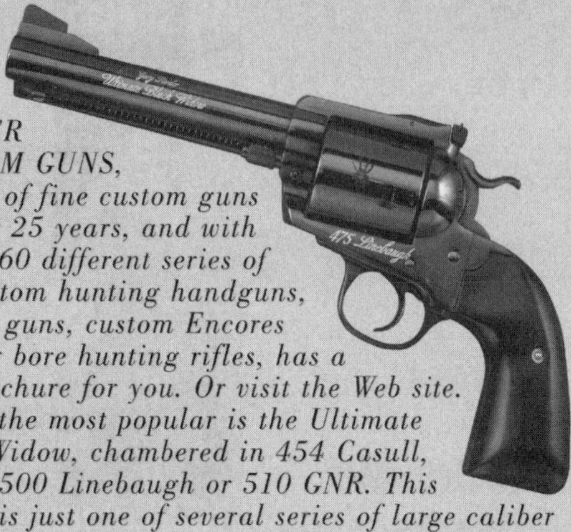

GARY REEDER CUSTOM GUNS, builder of fine custom guns for over 25 years, and with almost 60 different series of full custom hunting handguns, cowboy guns, custom Encores and big bore hunting rifles, has a free brochure for you. Or visit the Web site. One of the most popular is the Ultimate Black Widow, chambered in 454 Casull, 475 or 500 Linebaugh or 510 GNR. This beauty is just one of several series of large caliber 5-shot revolvers for the serious handgunner. For more information contact....

GARY REEDER CUSTOM GUNS
2601 7th AVE. E., Flagstaff, AZ 86004
Phone: 928-527-4100 or 928-526-3313
Web site: www.reedercustomguns.com

FOLDING BIPODS

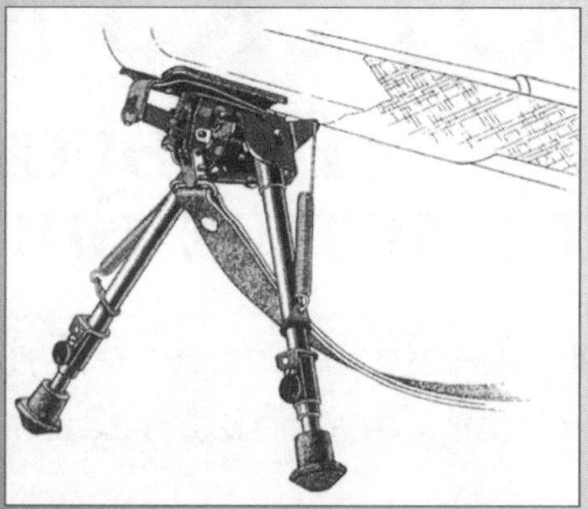

Harris Bipods clamp securely to most stud-equipped bolt-action rifles and are quick-detachable. With adapters, they will fit some other guns. On all models except the Model LM, folding legs have completely adjustable spring-return extensions. The sling swivel attaches to the clamp. This time-proven design is manufactured with heat-treated steel and hard alloys and has a black anodized finish.

Series S Bipods rotate 35° for instant leveling on uneven ground. Hinged base has tension adjustment and buffer springs to eliminate tremor or looseness in crotch area of bipod. They are otherwise similar to non-rotating Series 1A2. Thirteen models are available from Harris Engineering; literature is free.

HARRIS ENGINEERING INC.
Dept: GD54, Barlow, KY 42024
Phone: 270-334-3633 • Fax: 270-334-3000

FINE GUN STOCKS

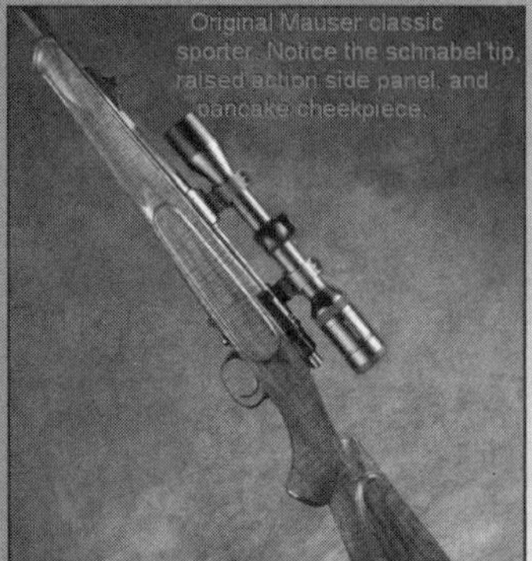

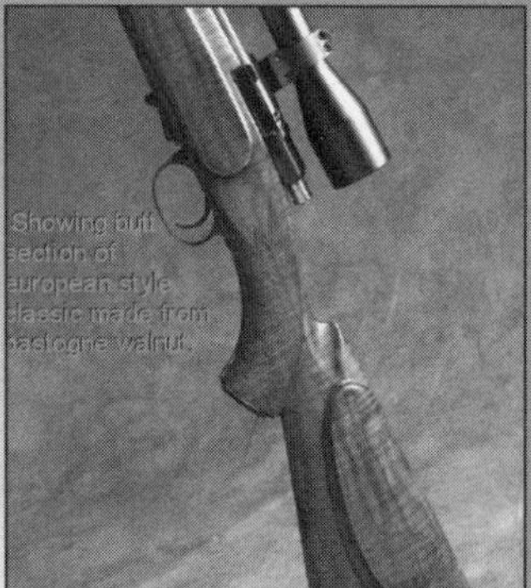

Manufacturing custom and production gunstocks for hundreds of models of rifles and shotguns–made from the finest stock woods and available in all stages of completion.

Visit www.gunstocks.com to view their bargain list of fine custom gunstocks. Each displayed in full color.

GREAT AMERICAN GUNSTOCK COMPANY
3420 Industrial Drive, Yuba City, CA 95993
Phone: 530-671-4570 • Fax: 530-671-3906
Gunstock Hotline: 800-784-GUNS (4867)
Web: www.gunstocks.com
E-mail: gunstox@syix.com

HIGH QUALITY OPTICS

One of the best indicators of quality is a scope's resolution number. The smaller the number, the better. Our scope has a resolution number of 2.8 seconds of angle. This number is about 20% smaller (better) than other well-known scopes costing much more. It means that two .22 caliber bullets can be a hair's breadth apart and edges of each still be clearly seen. With a Shepherd at 800 yards, you will be able to tell a four inch antler from a four inch ear and a burrowing owl from a prairie dog. Bird watchers will be able to distinguish a Tufted Titmouse from a Ticked-Off Field Mouse. Send for free catalog.

SHEPHERD ENTERPRISES, INC.
Box 189, Waterloo, NE 68069
Phone: 402-779-2424 • Fax: 402-779-4010
E-mail: shepherd@shepherdscopes.com
Web: www.shepherdscopes.com

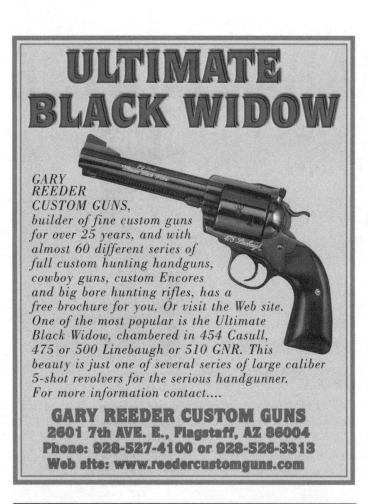

DANGER?
Not since I carry my Bond Arms Defender in .45 Colt & .410 shotshell!
.410 Shotgun Shell
3" Cartridge • 000 Buck
Five .357 Diameter Balls
Manageable Recoil
14 INTERCHANGEABLE BARRELS
25 SEPARATE CARTRIDGES
ALL ON ONE FRAME!
BOND ARMS INC.
The Finest in Double Barrel Protection.
www.bondarms.com
817-573-4445
P.O. Box 1296
Granbury, Texas 76048
OBEY LOCAL LAWS TO CARRY PISTOL LEGALLY.

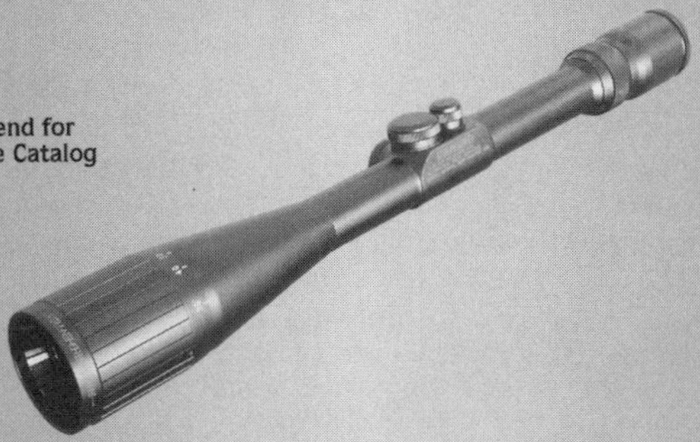

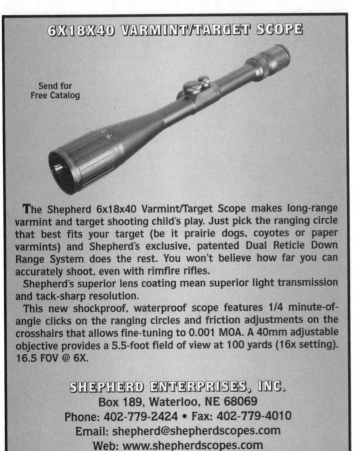

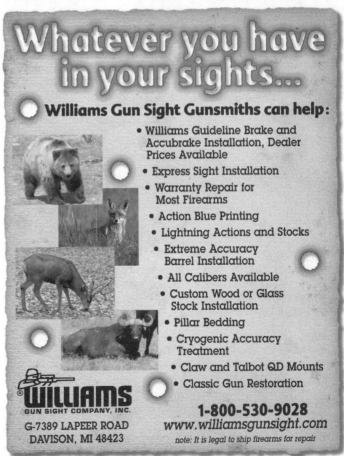

CALI'CO
HARDWOODS, INC.
GUNSTOCK BLANKS
In French Walnut, Claro Walnut, Myrtle & Maple

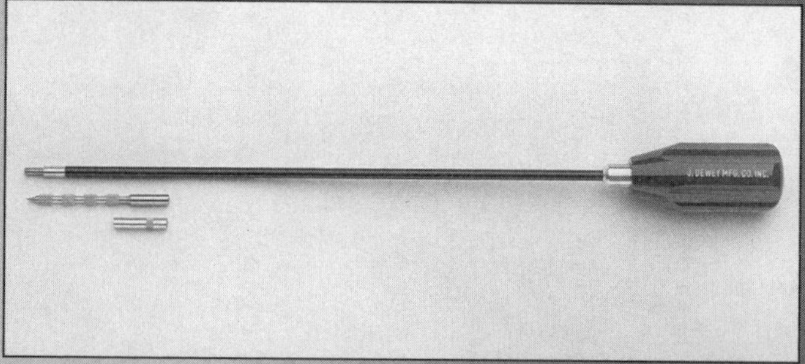

J. DEWEY MFG. CO. INC.

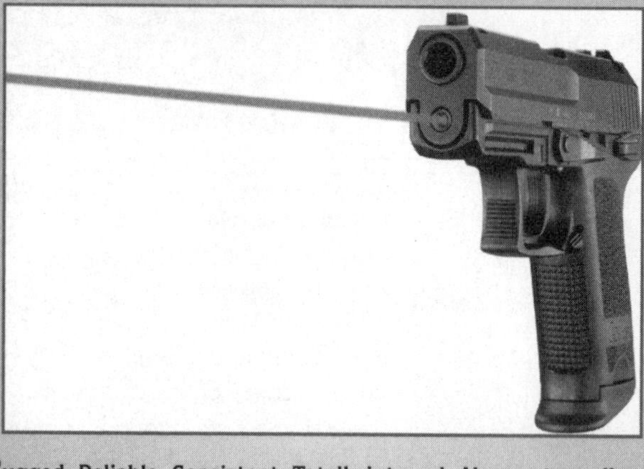

FIREARMS PARTS CATALOG
#27
GUN PARTS
NUMRICH
CORPORATION

RIFLE, PISTOL, AND SHOTGUN MAGAZINES

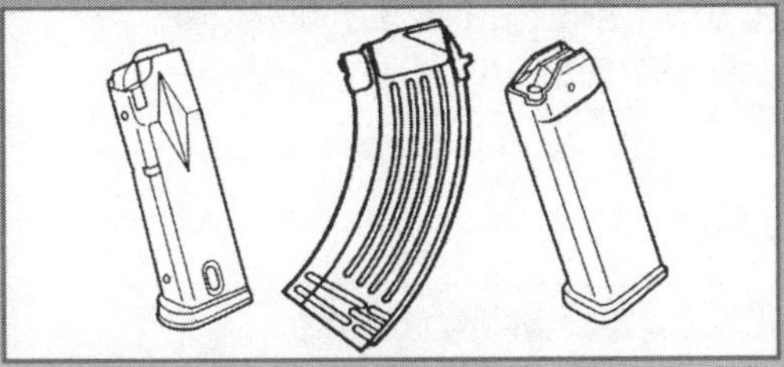

Forrest, Inc. offers shooters one of the largest selections of standard and extended high-capacity magazines in the United States. Whether you're looking for a few spare magazines for that obsolete 22-rifle or pistol, or to purchase some high-capacity factory or top-quality after-market, all are available from this California firm. They offer competitive pricing especially for dealers wanting to buy in quantity. Gun show dealers are our specialty.

Forrest Inc. also stocks parts and accessories for the MIA, Colt AR-15 1911 45 Auto pistol, the SKS and MAK-90 rifles as well as many U.S. military rifles. One of their specialty parts is firing pins for obsolete weapons. They also carry many different magazine loaders.

Call or write Forrest, Inc. for more information and a free brochure. Be sure and mention *Shooter's Marketplace.*

FORREST, INC.

P.O. Box 326, Dept: #100, Lakeside, CA 92040
Phone: 619-561-5800 • Fax: 619-561-0227
E-mail: info@gunmags.com
Web. www.gunmags.com

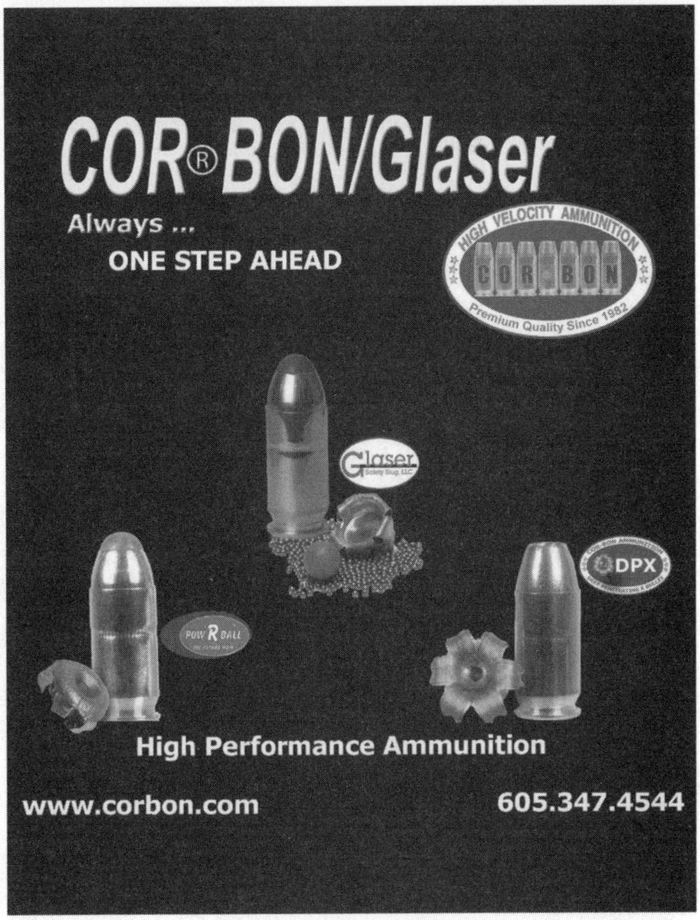

COMPLETE COMPACT CATALOG

HANDGUNS 2006

GUNDEX

A

B

C

D

E

F

GUNDEX

GUNDEX

T

U

V

W

NUMBERS

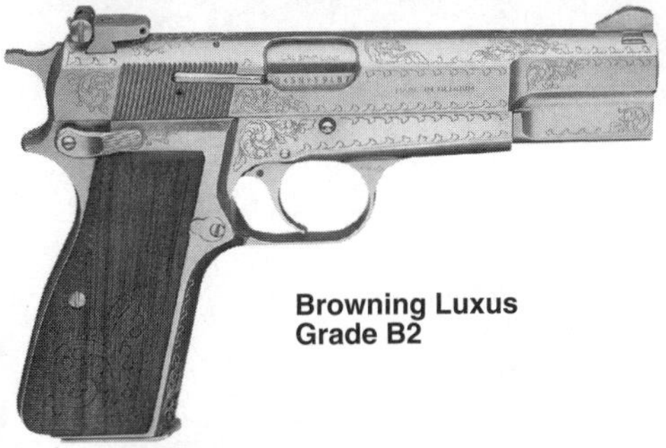

Browning Luxus Grade B2

Browning Luxus Renaissance Argent

Browning Luxus Renaissance OR

Ed Brown Classic Class A

Ed Brown Kobra Carry

Kimber Ultra CDP

Kimber Custom Target II

BRILEY 1911-STYLE AUTO PISTOLS

Caliber: 9mm Para., 38 Super, 40 S&W, 10-shot magazine; 45 ACP, 8-shot magazine. **Barrel:** 3.6" or 5". **Weight:** NA. **Length:** NA. **Grips:** Rosewood or rubber. **Sights:** Bo-Mar adjustable rear, Briley dovetail blade front. **Features:** Modular or Caspian alloy, carbon steel or stainless steel frame; match barrel and trigger group; lowered and flared ejection port; front and rear serrations on slide; beavertail grip safety; hot blue, hard chrome or stainless steel finish. Introduced 2000. Made in U.S. From Briley Manufacturing Inc.

Price: Fantom (3.6" bbl., fixed low-mount rear sight, armor coated lower receiver), from **$1,900.00**

Price: Fantom with two-port compensator, from **$2,245.00**

Price: Advantage (5" bbl., adj. low-mount rear sight, checkered mainspring housing), from **$1,650.00**

Price: Versatility Plus (5" bbl., adj. low-mount rear sight, modular or Caspian frame), from **$1,850.00**

Price: Signature Series (5" bbl., adj. low-mount rear sight, 40 S&W only), from **$2,250.00**

Price: Plate Master (5" bbl. with compensator, lightened slide, Briley scope mount), from **$1,895.00**

Price: El Presidente (5" bbl. with Briley quad compensator, Briley scope mount), from **$2,550.00**

BROWNING HI-POWER LUXUS

The legendary Browning Hi-Power pistol still produced in Belgium is available in four grades in the Luxus series: Grade II, Renaissance Argent, Grade B2 and the gold-finished Renaissance OR. Other specifications NA.

Price: From **$4,391.00**

ED BROWN CLASSIC CUSTOM AND CLASS A LIMITED 1911-STYLE AUTO PISTOLS

Caliber: 45 ACP; 7-shot magazine; 40 S&W, 400 Cor-Bon, 38 Super, 9x23, 9mm Para. **Barrel:** 4.25", 5", 6". **Weight:** NA. **Length:** NA. **Grips:** Hogue exotic checkered wood. **Sights:** Bo-Mar or Novak rear, blade front. **Features:** Blued or stainless steel frame; ambidextrous safety; beavertail grip safety; checkered forestrap and mainspring housing; match-grade barrel; slotted hammer; long lightweight or Videki short steel trigger. Many options offered. Made in U.S. by Ed Brown Products, Inc.

Price: Classic Custom (45 ACP, 5" barrel), from **$2,895.00**

Price: Executive Elite (45 ACP, 5" barrel), from **$2,195.00**

Price: Executive Carry (4.25" bbl., has "bobtail™" modification to reduce overall length), from **$2,295.00**

Price: Kobra (45 ACP only, 5" bbl., completely hand-fitted with heavy dehorning), from **$1,995.00**

Price: Kobra Carry (45 ACP only, 4.25" bbl., has exclusive snakeskin pattern on frame, top portion of mainspring housing and slide), from **$2,195.00**

NEW! Price: Executive Target, (45 ACP, 5" government model, features exclusive 25 lpi checkering and Bo-Mar adjustable sights), from **$2,370.00**

KIMBER CUSTOM II 1911-STYLE AUTO PISTOLS

Caliber: 9mm Para., 38 Super, 9-shot magazines; 40 S&W, 8-shot magazine; 45 ACP, 7-shot magazine. **Barrel:** 5". **Weight:** 38 oz. **Length:** 8.7" overall. **Grips:** Black synthetic, smooth or double-diamond checkered rosewood, or double-diamond checkered walnut. **Sights:** McCormick low profile or Kimber adjustable rear, blade front. **Features:** Machined steel slide, frame and barrel; front and rear beveled slide serrations; cut and button-rifled, match-grade barrel; adjustable aluminum trigger; full-length guide rod; Commander-style hammer; high-ride beavertail safety; beveled magazine well. Other models available. Made in U.S. by Kimber Mfg. Inc.

Price: Custom II (black matte finish) **$730.00**

Price: Custom Royal II (polished blue finish, checkered rosewood grips) **$886.00**

Price: Custom Stainless II (satin-finished stainless steel frame and slide) **$832.00**

Price: Custom Target II (matte black or stainless finish, Kimber adj. sight) **$945.00**

Price: Custom Compact CDP II (4" bbl., alum. frame, tritium three-dot sights, 28 oz.) **$1,141.00**

Price: Custom Pro CDP II (4" bbl., alum. frame, tritium sights, full-length grip, 28 oz.) **$1,141.00**

Price: Ultra CDP II (3" bbl., aluminum frame, tritium sights, 25 oz.) **$1,141.00**

Price: Gold Match II (polished blue finish, hand-fitted barrel, ambid. safety), from **$1,168.00**

Price: Stainless Gold Match II (stainless steel frame and slide, hand-fitted bbl., amb. safety) . . . . . **$1,315.00 to $1,345.00**

SEMI-CUSTOM HANDGUNS — Autoloaders

Les Baer Thunder Ranch Special

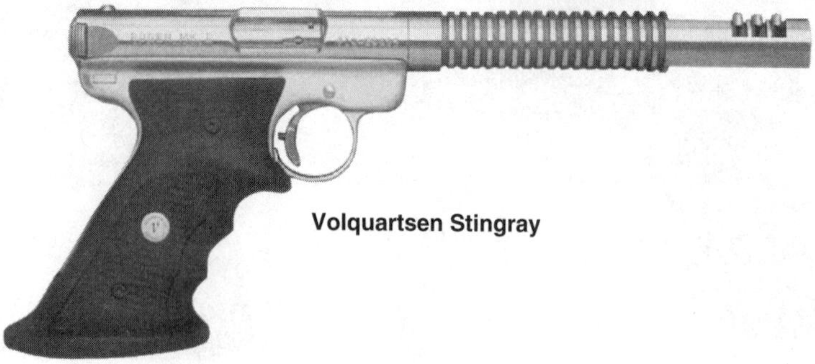

Volquartsen Stingray

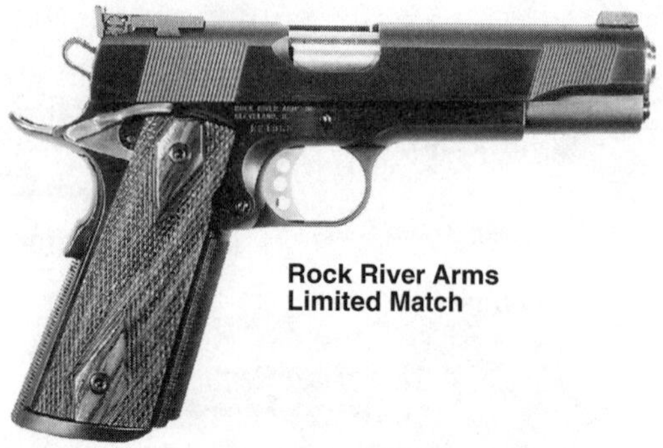

Rock River Arms Limited Match

LES BAER CUSTOM 1911-STYLE AUTO PISTOLS
Caliber: 9mm Para., 38 Super, 40 S&W, 45 ACP, 400 Cor-Bon; 7- or 8-shot magazine. **Barrel:** 4-1/4", 5", 6". **Weight:** 28 to 40 oz. **Length:** NA. **Grips:** Checkered cocobolo. **Sights:** Low-mount combat fixed, combat fixed with tritium inserts or low-mount adjustable rear, dovetail front. **Features:** Forged steel or aluminum frame; slide serrated front and rear; lowered and flared ejection port; beveled magazine well; speed trigger with 4-pound pull; beavertail grip safety; ambidextrous safety. Other models available. Made in U.S. by Les Baer Custom.

Price: Baer 1911 Premier II 5" Model (5" bbl., optional stainless steel frame and slide), from **$1,498.00**
Price: Premier II 6" Model (6" barrel), from **$1,675.00**
Price: Premier II LW1 (forged aluminum frame, steel slide and barrel), from **$1,835.00**
Price: Custom Carry (4" or 5" barrel, steel frame), from **$1,728.00**
Price: Custom Carry (4" barrel, aluminum frame), from **$2,039.00**
Price: Swift Response Pistol (fixed tritium sights, Bear Coat finish), from **$2,339.00**
Price: Monolith (5" barrel and slide with extra-long dust cover), from **$1,660.00**
Price: Stinger (4-1/4" barrel, steel or aluminum frame), from . . . **$1,552.00**
Price: Thunder Ranch Special (tritium fixed combat sight, Thunder Ranch logo), from **$1,685.00**
Price: National Match Hardball (low-mount adj. sight; meets DCM rules), from **$1,425.00**
Price: Bullseye Wadcutter Pistol (Bo-Mar rib w/ adj. sight, guar. 2-1/2" groups), from **$1,560.00**
Price: Ultimate Master Combat (5" or 6" bbl., adj. sights, checkered front strap), from **$2,530.00**
Price: Ultimate Master Combat Compensated (four-port compensator, adj. sights), from **$2,558.00**

ROCK RIVER ARMS 1911-STYLE AUTO PISTOLS
Caliber: 9mm Para., 38 Super, 40 S&W, 45 ACP. **Barrel:** 4" or 5". **Weight:** NA. **Length:** NA. **Grips:** Double-diamond, checkered cocobolo or black synthetic. **Sights:** Bo-Mar low-mount adjustable, Novak fixed with tritium inserts, Heine fixed or Rock River scope mount; dovetail front blade. **Features:** Chrome-moly, machined steel frame and slide; slide serrated front and rear; aluminum speed trigger with 3.5-4 lb. pull; national match KART barrel; lowered and flared ejection port; tuned and polished extractor; beavertail grip safety; beveled mag. well. Other frames offered. Made in U.S. by Rock River Arms Inc.

Price: Elite Commando (4" barrel, Novak tritium sights) **$1,395.00**
Price: Standard Match (5" barrel, Heine fixed sights) **$1,150.00**
Price: National Match Hardball (5" barrel, Bo-Mar adj. sights), from **$1,275.00**
Price: Bullseye Wadcutter (5" barrel, Rock River slide scope mount), from **$1,380.00**
Price: Basic Limited Match (5" barrel, Bo-Mar adj. sights), from . **$1,395.00**
Price: Limited Match (5" barrel, guaranteed 1-1/2" groups at 50 yards), from **$1,795.00**
Price: Hi-Cap Basic Limited (5" barrel, four frame choices), from **$1,895.00**
Price: Ultimate Match Achiever (5" bbl. with compensator, mount and Aimpoint), from **$2,255.00**
Price: Match Master Steel (5" bbl. with compensator, mount and Aimpoint) **$5,000.00**

STI COMPACT AUTO PISTOLS
Caliber: 9mm, 40 S&W. **Barrel:** 3.4". **Weight:** 28 oz. **Length:** 7" overall. **Grips:** Checkered double-diamond rosewood. **Sights:** Heine Low Mount fixed rear, slide integral front. **Features:** Similar to STI 2011 models except has compact frame, 7-shot magazine in 9mm (6-shot in 40 cal.), single-sided thumb safety, linkless barrel lockup system, matte blue finish. From STI International.

Price: (9mm or 40 S&W), from **$746.50**

VOLQUARTSEN CUSTOM 22 CALIBER AUTO PISTOLS
Caliber: 22 LR; 10-shot magazine. **Barrel:** 3.5" to 10"; stainless steel air gauge. **Weight:** 2-1/2 to 3 lbs. 10 oz. **Length:** NA. **Grips:** Finger-grooved plastic or walnut. **Sights:** Adjustable rear and blade front or Weaver-style scope mount. **Features:** Conversions of Ruger Mk. II Auto pistol. Variety of configurations featuring compensators, underlug barrels, etc. Stainless steel finish; black Teflon finish available for additional $85; target hammer, trigger. Made in U.S. by Volquartsen Custom.

Price: 3.5 Compact (3.5" barrel, T/L adjustable rear sight, scope base optional) **$640.00**
Price: Deluxe (barrel to 10", T/L adjustable rear sight) **$675.00**
Price: Deluxe with compensator **$745.00**
Price: Masters (6.5" barrel, finned underlug, T/L adjustable rear sight, compensator) **$950.00**
Price: Olympic (7" barrel, recoil-reducing gas chamber, T/L adjustable rear sight) **$870.00**
Price: Stingray (7.5" ribbed, ported barrel; red-dot sight) **$995.00**
Price: Terminator (7.5" ported barrel, grooved receiver, scope rings) **$730.00**
Price: Ultra-Light Match (6" tensioned barrel, Weaver mount, weighs 2-1/2 lbs.) **$885.00**
Price: V-6 (6", triangular, ventilated barrel with underlug, T/L adj. sight) **$1,030.00**
Price: V-2000 (6" barrel with finned underlug, T/L adj. sight) **$1,095.00**
Price: V-Magic II (7.5" barrel, red-dot sight) **$1,055.00**

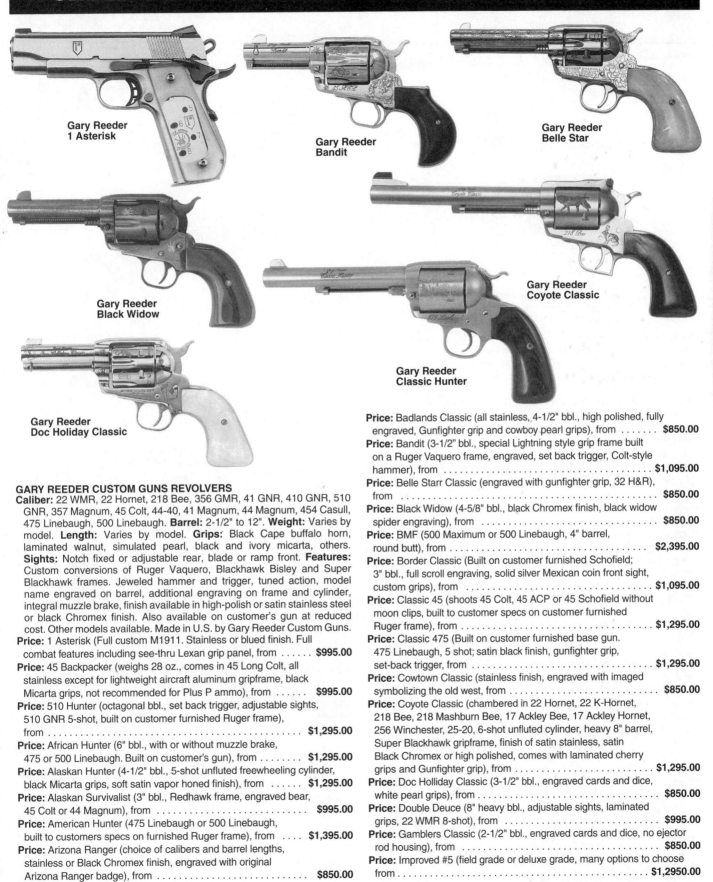

SEMI-CUSTOM HANDGUNS — Revolvers

Gary Reeder
1 Asterisk

Gary Reeder
Bandit

Gary Reeder
Belle Star

Gary Reeder
Black Widow

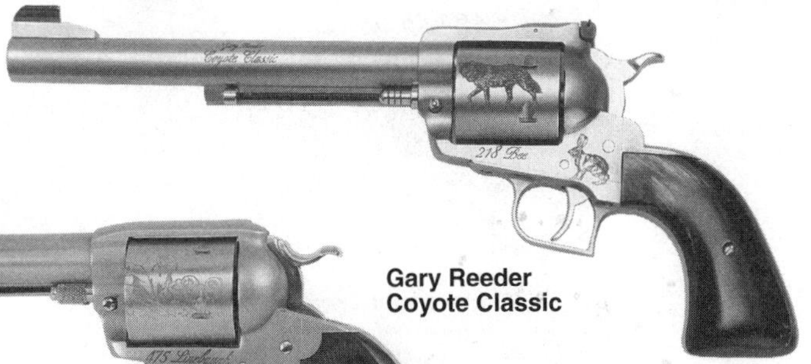

Gary Reeder
Coyote Classic

Gary Reeder
Classic Hunter

Gary Reeder
Doc Holiday Classic

GARY REEDER CUSTOM GUNS REVOLVERS

Caliber: 22 WMR, 22 Hornet, 218 Bee, 356 GMR, 41 GNR, 410 GNR, 510 GNR, 357 Magnum, 45 Colt, 44-40, 41 Magnum, 44 Magnum, 454 Casull, 475 Linebaugh, 500 Linebaugh. **Barrel:** 2-1/2" to 12". **Weight:** Varies by model. **Length:** Varies by model. **Grips:** Black Cape buffalo horn, laminated walnut, simulated pearl, black and ivory micarta, others. **Sights:** Notch fixed or adjustable rear, blade or ramp front. **Features:** Custom conversions of Ruger Vaquero, Blackhawk Bisley and Super Blackhawk frames. Jeweled hammer and trigger, tuned action, model name engraved on barrel, additional engraving on frame and cylinder, integral muzzle brake, finish available in high-polish or satin stainless steel or black Chromex finish. Also available on customer's gun at reduced cost. Other models available. Made in U.S. by Gary Reeder Custom Guns.

Price: 1 Asterisk (Full custom M1911. Stainless or blued finish. Full combat features including see-thru Lexan grip panel, from **$995.00**

Price: 45 Backpacker (weighs 28 oz., comes in 45 Long Colt, all stainless except for lightweight aircraft aluminum gripframe, black Micarta grips, not recommended for Plus P ammo), from **$995.00**

Price: 510 Hunter (octagonal bbl., set back trigger, adjustable sights, 510 GNR 5-shot, built on customer furnished Ruger frame), from **$1,295.00**

Price: African Hunter (6" bbl., with or without muzzle brake, 475 or 500 Linebaugh. Built on customer's gun), from **$1,295.00**

Price: Alaskan Hunter (4-1/2" bbl., 5-shot unfluted freewheeling cylinder, black Micarta grips, soft satin vapor honed finish), from **$1,295.00**

Price: Alaskan Survivalist (3" bbl., Redhawk frame, engraved bear, 45 Colt or 44 Magnum), from **$995.00**

Price: American Hunter (475 Linebaugh or 500 Linebaugh, built to customers specs on furnished Ruger frame), from **$1,395.00**

Price: Arizona Ranger (choice of calibers and barrel lengths, stainless or Black Chromex finish, engraved with original Arizona Ranger badge), from **$850.00**

Price: Badlands Classic (all stainless, 4-1/2" bbl., high polished, fully engraved, Gunfighter grip and cowboy pearl grips), from **$850.00**

Price: Bandit (3-1/2" bbl., special Lightning style grip frame built on a Ruger Vaquero frame, engraved, set back trigger, Colt-style hammer), from **$1,095.00**

Price: Belle Starr Classic (engraved with gunfighter grip, 32 H&R), from **$850.00**

Price: Black Widow (4-5/8" bbl., black Chromex finish, black widow spider engraving), from **$850.00**

Price: BMF (500 Maximum or 500 Linebaugh, 4" barrel, round butt), from **$2,395.00**

Price: Border Classic (Built on customer furnished Schofield; 3" bbl., full scroll engraving, solid silver Mexican coin front sight, custom grips), from **$1,095.00**

Price: Classic 45 (shoots 45 Colt, 45 ACP or 45 Schofield without moon clips, built to customer specs on customer furnished Ruger frame), from **$1,295.00**

Price: Classic 475 (Built on customer furnished base gun. 475 Linebaugh, 5 shot; satin black finish, gunfighter grip, set-back trigger, from **$1,295.00**

Price: Cowtown Classic (stainless finish, engraved with imaged symbolizing the old west, from **$850.00**

Price: Coyote Classic (chambered in 22 Hornet, 22 K-Hornet, 218 Bee, 218 Mashburn Bee, 17 Ackley Bee, 17 Ackley Hornet, 256 Winchester, 25-20, 6-shot unfluted cylinder, heavy 8" barrel, Super Blackhawk gripframe, finish of satin stainless, satin Black Chromex or high polished, comes with laminated cherry grips and Gunfighter grip), from **$1,295.00**

Price: Doc Holliday Classic (3-1/2" bbl., engraved cards and dice, white pearl grips), from **$850.00**

Price: Double Deuce (8" heavy bbl., adjustable sights, laminated grips, 22 WMR 8-shot), from **$995.00**

Price: Gamblers Classic (2-1/2" bbl., engraved cards and dice, no ejector rod housing), from **$850.00**

Price: Improved #5 (field grade or deluxe grade, many options to choose from **$1,2950.00**

SEMI-CUSTOM HANDGUNS — Revolvers

Gary Reeder
Rio Grande

Gary Reeder
Southern Comfort

Gary Reeder
Ultimate Black Widow

500 Linebaugh Long

500 Linebaugh

Price: Kodiak Magnum (heavy 8-1/2" bbl. with deep crown and tight barrel/cylinder gap, satin vapor honed finish), from **$850.00**
Price: Lawman Classic (Full custom Vaquero, two-tone finish, Lawman-style engraving, special Lawman gripframe with lanyard ring), from **$950.00**
Price: Lonestar Classic (7-1/2" bbl., highly polished, to a mirror finish, engraved with items relevant to the state of Texas), from **$850.00**
Price: Long Rider Classic (45 long Colt, choice of barrel lengths, midnight black trigger and hammer, gold rings), from **$950.00**
Price: Montana Hunter Series (45 long Colt, 4-5/8" bbl., all stainless steel, 5-shot, soft satin finish, walnut grips), from **$1,295.00**
NEW! Price: Night Hawk (4" bbl., dual purpose as conceal carry or hunting revolver), from **$1,095.00**
Price: Night Rider (7-1/2" bbl., fully engraved with contrasting light colored stag grips), from **$850.00**
Price: O.K. Corral Classic (12-1/2" bbl., engraved with western trappings, Black Chromex finish), from **$950.00**
Price: Professional Hunter (stretch frame stainless 5-shot available in calibers including 475 Maximum and 500 Maximum), from **$2,395.00**
Price: Rio Grande Classic (built on any caliber Vaquero in barrel length of choice, Gunfighter grip, engraving is old southwest type with a few western features, specially designed base pin, long tapered hammer, from **$1,095.00**
NEW! Price: Sidewinder (3-1/2" bbl., snake scales over entire frame and barrel, black micarta grips), from **$950.00**
Price: Southern Comfort (5-shot cylinder, heavy duty base pin, tear drop hammer, special set back trigger, interchangeable blade system, special gripframe, satin Vapor Honed finish), from **$1,295.00**
Price: Texas Ranger Classic (45 long Colt, 5-1/2" bbl. with other calibers and barrel lengths available, engraved with Texas Ranger badge, gunfighter grip, simulated pearl handles, Black Chromex finish), from **$950.00**
Price: Tombstone Classic (3-1/2" bbl. with gold bands, notch sight, birdshead grips), from **$850.00**
Price: Trail Rider Classic (7-1/2" bbl., more lengths available, fully engraved with western trappings, pearl grips), from **$950.00**
Price: Ultimate 41 (410 GNR 5-shot, built on customer furnished Ruger frame), from **$1,195.00**
Price: Ultimate 44 (ported, special recoil-taming grip frame, sling swivels, 44 Mag. 5-shot, built on customer furnished Ruger Hunter), from **$1,395.00**
Price: Ultimate 50 (choice of barrel lengths in any centerfire caliber, 5-shot stainless steel 50 Action Express, freewheeling cylinder), from **$1,295.00**
Price: Ultimate 410 GNR (5-shot 410 GNR freewheeling cylinder), from **$1,295.00**
Price: Ultimate 480 (choice of barrel lengths in any caliber, full vapor honed stainless steel, satin finish Black Chromex or two-toned finish, 5-shot cylinder, heavy barrel, Gunfighter grip, full action job, custom laminated grips, freewheeling cylinder, Belt Mountain base pin), from **$1,195.00**
Price: Ultimate 500 (built on stretch frame in 500 S&W, 5-shot. Choice of bbl. lengths, gunfigher grip, set-back trigger, from **$2,495.00**
Price: Ultimate Back Up (3-1/2" bbl., fixed sights, choice of animal engraving, 475 Linebaugh, 500 Linebaugh built on customer's gun.), from **$1,395.00**
Price: Ultimate Black Widow (475 Linebaugh or 500 Linebaugh, heavy duty 5 shot cylinder, heavy high grade barrel, Gunfighter Grip with black Micarta grips, Belt Mountain base pin), from .. **$1,395.00**
Price: Ultimate Vaquero (engraved barrel, frame and cylinder, made to customer specs), from **$950.00**
Price: Western Classic (standard fieid grade and deluxe grade, many options to choose from) **$1,295.00**
Price: Wichita Classic (41 Special, stainless steel pins and screws) **$1,095.00**

LINEBAUGH CUSTOM SIXGUNS REVOLVERS

Caliber: 45 Colt, 44 Linebaugh Long, 458 Linebaugh, 475 Linebaugh, 500 Linebaugh, 500 Linebaugh Long, 445 Super Mag. **Barrel:** 4-3/4", 5-1/2", 6", 7- 1/2"; other lengths available. **Weight:** NA. **Length:** NA. **Grips:** Dustin Linebaugh Custom made to customer's specs. **Sights:** Bowen steel rear or factory Ruger; blade front. **Features:** Conversions using customer's Ruger Blackhawk Bisley and Vaquero Bisley frames. Made in U.S. by Linebaugh Custom Sixguns.
Price: Small 45 Colt conversion (rechambered cyl., new barrel), from **$1,200.00**
Price: Large 45 Colt conversion (oversized cyl., new barrel, 5- or 6-shot), from **$1,800.00**
Price: 475 Linebaugh, 500 Linebaugh conversions, from **$1,800.00**
Price: Linebaugh and 445 Super Mag calibers on 357 Maximum frame, from **$3,000.00**

SEMI-CUSTOM HANDGUNS — Single-Shot

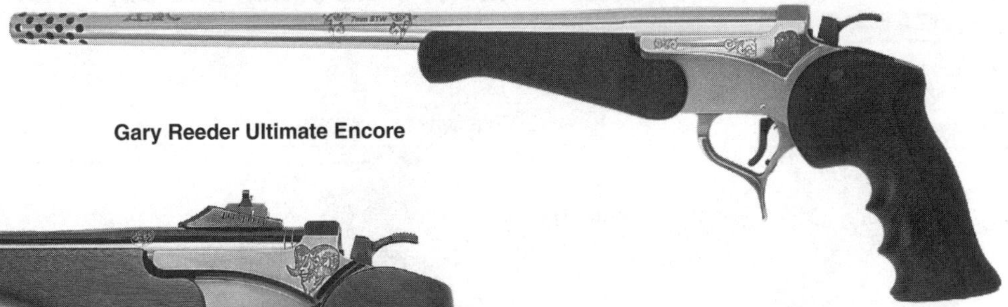

Gary Reeder Ultimate Encore

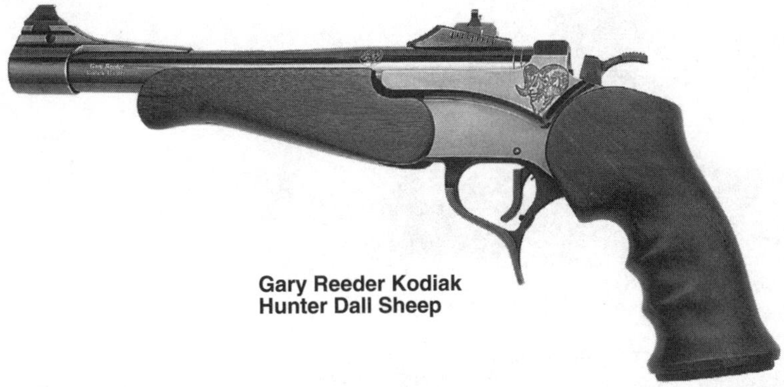

Gary Reeder Kodiak Hunter Dall Sheep

SSK Industries Contender

GARY REEDER CUSTOM GUNS CONTENDER AND ENCORE PISTOLS

Caliber: 22 Cheetah, 218 Bee, 22 K-Hornet, 22 Hornet, 218 Mashburn Bee, 22-250 Improved, 6mm/284, 7mm STW, 7mm GNR, 30 GNR, 338 GNR, 300 Win. Magnum, 338 Win. Magnum, 350 Rem. Magnum, 358 STA, 375 H&H, 378 GNR, 416 Remington, 416 GNR, 450 GNR, 475 Linebaugh, 500 Linebaugh, 50 Alaskan, 50 AE, 454 Casull; others available. **Barrel:** 8" to 15" (others available). **Weight:** NA. **Length:** Varies with barrel length. **Grips:** Walnut fingergroove. **Sights:** Express-style adjustable rear and barrel band front (Kodiak Hunter); none furnished most models. **Features:** Offers complete guns and barrels in the T/C Contender and Encore. Integral muzzle brake, engraved animals and model name, tuned action, high-polish or satin stainless steel or black Chromex finish. Made in U.S. by Gary Reeder Custom Guns.

Price: Kodiak Hunter (50 AE, 475 Linebaugh, 500 Linebaugh, 510 GNR, or 454 Casull, Kodiak bear and Dall sheep engravings), from **$1,195.00**

Price: Ultimate Encore (15" bbl. with muzzle brake, custom engraving), from **$1,095.00**

SSK INDUSTRIES CONTENDER AND ENCORE PISTOLS

Caliber: More than 200, including most standard pistol and rifle calibers, as well as 226 JDJ, 6mm JDJ, 257 JDJ, 6.5mm JDJ, 7mm JDJ, 6.5mm Mini-Dreadnaught, 30-06 JDJ, 280 JDJ, 375 JDJ, 6mm Whisper, 300 Whisper and 338 Whisper. **Barrel:** 10" to 26"; blued or stainless; variety of configurations. **Weight:** Varies with barrel length and features. **Length:** Varies with barrel length. **Grips:** Pachmayr, wood models available. **Features:** Offers frames, barrels and complete guns in the T/C Contender and Encore. Fluted, diamond, octagon and round barrels; flatside Contender frames; chrome-plating; muzzle brakes; trigger jobs; variety of stocks and forends; sights and optics. Made in U.S. by SSK Industries.

Price: Blued Contender frame, from **$390.00**

Price: Stainless Contender frame, from **$390.00**

Price: Blued Encore frame, from **$290.00**

Price: Stainless Encore frame, from **$318.00**

Price: Contender barrels, from **$315.00**

Price: Encore barrels, from **$340.00**

HANDGUNS — Autoloaders, Service & Sport

Includes models suitable for several forms of competition and other sporting purposes.

Accu-Tek HC-380

Accu-Tek XL-9

Auto-Ordnance 1911A1 Standard

Baer Custom Carry

Auto-Ordnance Deluxe

Baer Premium II

ACCU-TEK MODEL HC-380 AUTO PISTOL

Caliber: 380 ACP, 10-shot magazine. **Barrel:** 2.75". **Weight:** 26 oz. **Length:** 6" overall. **Grips:** Checkered black composition. **Sights:** Blade front, rear adjustable for windage. **Features:** External hammer; manual thumb safety with firing pin and trigger disconnect; bottom magazine release. Stainless steel construction. Introduced 1993. Price includes cleaning kit and gun lock. Made in U.S.A. by Accu-Tek.

Price: Satin stainless **$249.00**

ACCU-TEK XL-9 AUTO PISTOL

Caliber: 9mm Para., 5-shot magazine. **Barrel:** 3". **Weight:** 24 oz. **Length:** 5.6" overall. **Grips:** Black pebble composition. **Sights:** 3-dot system; rear adjustable for windage. **Features:** Stainless steel construction; double-action-only mechanism. Introduced 1999. Price includes cleaning kit and gun lock, two magazines. Made in U.S.A. by Accu-Tek.

Price: **$267.00**

AMERICAN DERRINGER LM-5 AUTOMATIC PISTOL

Caliber: 25 ACP, 5-shot magazine. **Barrel:** 2-1/4". **Weight:** 15 oz. **Length:** NA. **Grips:** Wood. **Sights:** Fixed. **Features:** Compact, stainless, semi-auto, single-action hammerless design.

Price: **$425.00**

AUTAUGA 32 AUTO PISTOL

Caliber: 32 ACP, 6-shot magazine. **Barrel:** 2". **Weight:** 11.3 oz. **Length:** 4.3" overall. **Grips:** Black polymer. **Sights:** Fixed. **Features:** Double-action-only mechanism. Stainless steel construction.

Price: .... **NA**

AUTO-ORDNANCE 1911A1 AUTOMATIC PISTOL

Caliber: 45 ACP, 7-shot magazine. **Barrel:** 5". **Weight:** 39 oz. **Length:** 8-1/2" overall. **Grips:** Checkered plastic with medallion. **Sights:** Blade front, rear adjustable for windage. **Features:** Same specs as 1911A1 military guns-parts interchangeable. Frame and slide blued; each radius has non-glare finish. Made in U.S.A. by Auto-Ordnance Corp.

Price: 45 ACP, blue **$511.00**

Price: 45 ACP, Parkerized **$515.00**

Price: 45 ACP Deluxe (3-dot sights, textured rubber wraparound grips) **$525.00**

AUTOBOND 450

Caliber: 450 Autobond (also 45 ACP). Model 1911-style. **Barrel:** 5".

Price: **$1,150.00**

BAER 1911 CUSTOM CARRY AUTO PISTOL

Caliber: 45 ACP, 7- or 10-shot magazine. **Barrel:** 5". **Weight:** 37 oz. **Length:** 8.5" overall. **Grips:** Checkered walnut. **Sights:** Baer improved ramp-style dovetailed front, Novak low-mount rear. **Features:** Baer forged NM frame, slide and barrel with stainless bushing. Baer speed trigger with 4-lb. pull. Partial listing shown. Made in U.S.A. by Les Baer Custom, Inc.

Price: Standard size, blued **$1,640.00**

Price: Standard size, stainless **$1,690.00**

Price: Comanche size, blued **$1,640.00**

Price: Comanche size, stainless **$1,690.00**

Price: Comanche size, aluminum frame, blued slide **$1,923.00**

Price: Comanche size, aluminum frame, stainless slide **$1,995.00**

BAER 1911 PREMIER II AUTO PISTOL

Caliber: 9x23, 38 Super, 400 Cor-Bon, 45 ACP, 7- or 10-shot magazine. **Barrel:** 5". **Weight:** 37 oz. **Length:** 8.5" overall. **Grips:** Checkered rosewood, double diamond pattern. **Sights:** Baer dovetailed front, low-mount Bo-Mar rear with hidden leaf. **Features:** Baer NM forged steel frame and barrel with stainless bushing, deluxe Commander hammer and sear, beavertail grip safety with pad, extended ambidextrous safety; flat mainspring housing; 30 lpi checkered front strap. Made in U.S.A. by Les Baer Custom, Inc.

Price: Blued **$1,428.00**

Price: Stainless **$1,558.00**

Price: 6" model, blued, from **$1,595.00**

BAER 1911 S.R.P. PISTOL

Caliber: 45 ACP. **Barrel:** 5". **Weight:** 37 oz. **Length:** 8.5" overall. **Grips:** Checkered walnut. **Sights:** Trijicon night sights. **Features:** Similar to the F.B.I. contract gun except uses Baer forged steel frame. Has Baer match barrel with supported chamber, Complete tactical action. Has Baer Ultra Coat finish. Introduced 1996. Made in U.S.A. by Les Baer Custom, Inc.

Price: Government or Comanche length **$2,240.00**

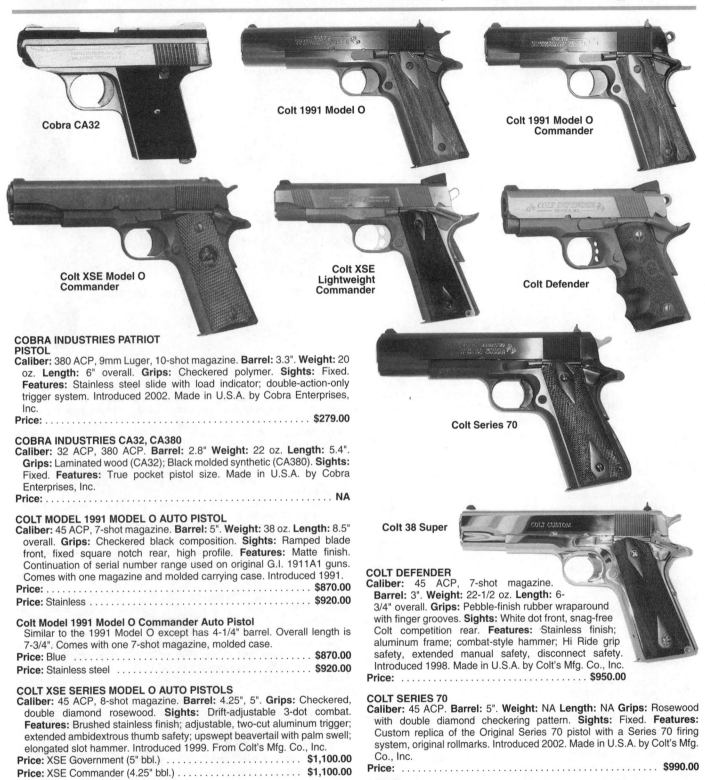

Cobra CA32

Colt 1991 Model O

Colt 1991 Model O Commander

Colt XSE Model O Commander

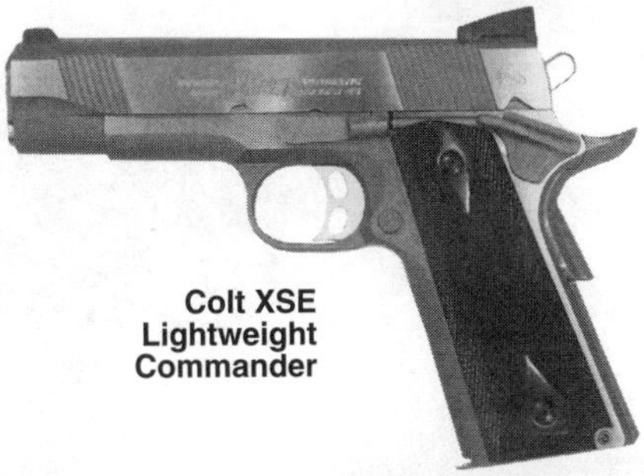

Colt XSE Lightweight Commander

Colt Defender

Colt Series 70

Colt 38 Super

COBRA INDUSTRIES PATRIOT PISTOL

Caliber: 380 ACP, 9mm Luger, 10-shot magazine. **Barrel:** 3.3". **Weight:** 20 oz. **Length:** 6" overall. **Grips:** Checkered polymer. **Sights:** Fixed. **Features:** Stainless steel slide with load indicator; double-action-only trigger system. Introduced 2002. Made in U.S.A. by Cobra Enterprises, Inc.

Price: **$279.00**

COBRA INDUSTRIES CA32, CA380

Caliber: 32 ACP, 380 ACP. **Barrel:** 2.8" **Weight:** 22 oz. **Length:** 5.4". **Grips:** Laminated wood (CA32); Black molded synthetic (CA380). **Sights:** Fixed. **Features:** True pocket pistol size. Made in U.S.A. by Cobra Enterprises, Inc.

Price: . . . . **NA**

COLT MODEL 1991 MODEL O AUTO PISTOL

Caliber: 45 ACP, 7-shot magazine. **Barrel:** 5". **Weight:** 38 oz. **Length:** 8.5" overall. **Grips:** Checkered black composition. **Sights:** Ramped blade front, fixed square notch rear, high profile. **Features:** Matte finish. Continuation of serial number range used on original G.I. 1911A1 guns. Comes with one magazine and molded carrying case. Introduced 1991.

Price: **$870.00**

Price: Stainless **$920.00**

Colt Model 1991 Model O Commander Auto Pistol

Similar to the 1991 Model O except has 4-1/4" barrel. Overall length is 7-3/4". Comes with one 7-shot magazine, molded case.

Price: Blue **$870.00**

Price: Stainless steel **$920.00**

COLT XSE SERIES MODEL O AUTO PISTOLS

Caliber: 45 ACP, 8-shot magazine. **Barrel:** 4.25", 5". **Grips:** Checkered, double diamond rosewood. **Sights:** Drift-adjustable 3-dot combat. **Features:** Brushed stainless finish; adjustable, two-cut aluminum trigger; extended ambidextrous thumb safety; upswept beavertail with palm swell; elongated slot hammer. Introduced 1999. From Colt's Mfg. Co., Inc.

Price: XSE Government (5" bbl.) **$1,100.00**

Price: XSE Commander (4.25" bbl.) **$1,100.00**

COLT XSE LIGHTWEIGHT COMMANDER AUTO PISTOL

Caliber: 45 ACP, 8-shot. **Barrel:** 4-1/4". **Weight:** 26 oz. **Length:** 7-3/4" overall. **Grips:** Double diamond checkered rosewood. **Sights:** Fixed, glare-proofed blade front, square notch rear; 3-dot system. **Features:** Brushed stainless slide, nickeled aluminum frame; McCormick elongated slot enhanced hammer, McCormick two-cut adjustable aluminum hammer. Made in U.S.A. by Colt's Mfg. Co., Inc.

Price: Stainless **$1,100.00**

COLT DEFENDER

Caliber: 45 ACP, 7-shot magazine. **Barrel:** 3". **Weight:** 22-1/2 oz. **Length:** 6-3/4" overall. **Grips:** Pebble-finish rubber wraparound with finger grooves. **Sights:** White dot front, snag-free Colt competition rear. **Features:** Stainless finish; aluminum frame; combat-style hammer; Hi Ride grip safety, extended manual safety, disconnect safety. Introduced 1998. Made in U.S.A. by Colt's Mfg. Co., Inc.

Price: **$950.00**

COLT SERIES 70

Caliber: 45 ACP. **Barrel:** 5". **Weight:** NA **Length:** NA **Grips:** Rosewood with double diamond checkering pattern. **Sights:** Fixed. **Features:** Custom replica of the Original Series 70 pistol with a Series 70 firing system, original rollmarks. Introduced 2002. Made in U.S.A. by Colt's Mfg. Co., Inc.

Price: **$990.00**

COLT 38 SUPER

Caliber: 38 Super. **Barrel:** 5" **Weight:** NA. **Length:** 8-1/2" **Grips:** Checkered rubber (stainless and blue models); wood with double diamond checkering pattern (bright stainless model). **Sights:** 3-dot. **Features:** Beveled magazine well, standard thumb safety and service-style grip safety. Introduced 2003. Made in U.S.A. by Colt's Mfg. Co., Inc.

Price: . . . . (Blue) **$950.00** (Stainless steel) **$980.00**

Price: (Bright stainless steel) **$1,200.00**

HANDGUNS — Autoloaders, Service & Sport

Colt Gunsite

CZ 75B 9mm

CZ 75B Decocker

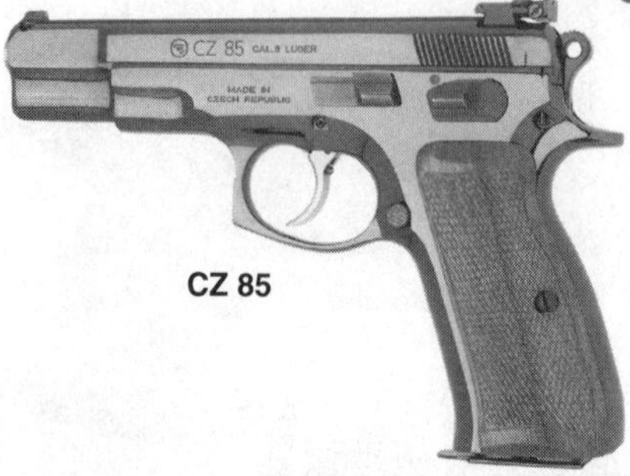

CZ 85

CZ 97B

CZ 75/85 Kadet

COLT GUNSITE PISTOL

Caliber: 45 ACP **Barrel:** 5". **Weight:** NA. **Length:** NA. **Grips:** Rosewood. **Sights:** Heinie front, Novak rear. **Features:** Contains most all of the Gunsite-school recommended features such as Series 70 firing system, Smith & Alexander metal grip safety w/palm swell, serrated flat mainspring housing. Available in blue or stainless steel. Introduced 2003. Made in U.S.A. by Colt's Mfg. Co., Inc.

Price: . . . . **NA**

CZ 75B AUTO PISTOL

Caliber: 9mm Para., 40 S&W, 10-shot magazine. **Barrel:** 4.7". **Weight:** 34.3 oz. **Length:** 8.1" overall. **Grips:** High impact checkered plastic. **Sights:** Square post front, rear adjustable for windage; 3-dot system. **Features:** Single action/double action design; firing pin block safety; choice of black polymer, matte or high-polish blue finishes. All-steel frame. Imported from the Czech Republic by CZ-USA.

Price: Black polymer **$529.00**
Price: Glossy blue **$559.00**
Price: Dual-tone or satin nickel **$559.00**
Price: 22 LR conversion unit **$399.00**

CZ 75B Decocker

Similar to the CZ 75B except has a decocking lever in place of the safety lever. All other specifications are the same. Introduced 1999. Imported from the Czech Republic by CZ-USA.

Price: 9mm, black polymer **$559.00**
Price: 40 S&W **$569.00**

CZ 75B Compact Auto Pistol

Similar to the CZ 75 except has 10-shot magazine, 3.9" barrel and weighs 32 oz. Has removable front sight, non-glare ribbed slide top. Trigger guard is squared and serrated; combat hammer. Introduced 1993. Imported from the Czech Republic by CZ-USA.

Price: 9mm, black polymer **$559.00**
Price: Dual tone or satin nickel **$569.00**
Price: D Compact, black polymer **$569.00**
Price: CZ2075 Sub-compact RAMI **$559.00**

CZ 75M IPSC Auto Pistol

Similar to the CZ 75B except has a longer frame and slide, slightly larger grip to accommodate new heavy-duty magazine. Ambidextrous thumb safety, safety notch on hammer; two-port in-frame compensator; slide racker; frame-mounted Firepoint red dot sight. Introduced 2001. Imported from the Czech Republic by CZ USA.

Price: 40 S&W, 10-shot mag. **$1,551.00**
Price: CZ 75 Standard IPSC (40 S&W, adj. sights) **$1,038.00**

CZ 85B Auto Pistol

Same gun as the CZ 75 except has ambidextrous slide release and safety levers; non-glare, ribbed slide top; squared, serrated trigger guard; trigger stop to prevent overtravel. Introduced 1986. Imported from the Czech Republic by CZ-USA.

Price: Black polymer **$483.00**
Price: Combat, black polymer **$540.00**
Price: Combat, dual-tone **$487.00**
Price: Combat, glossy blue **$499.00**

CZ 85 Combat

Similar to the CZ 85B (9mm only) except has an adjustable rear sight, trigger adjustable for overtravel, free-fall magazine, extended magazine catch. Does not have the firing pin block safety. Introduced 1999. Imported from the Czech Republic by CZ-USA.

Price: 9mm, black polymer **$540.00**
Price: 9mm, glossy blue **$566.00**
Price: 9mm, dual-tone or satin nickel **$586.00**

CZ 83B DOUBLE-ACTION PISTOL

Caliber: 9mm Makarov, 32 ACP, 380 ACP, 10-shot magazine. **Barrel:** 3.8". **Weight:** 26.2 oz. **Length:** 6.8" overall. **Grips:** High impact checkered plastic. **Sights:** Removable square post front, rear adjustable for windage; 3-dot system. **Features:** Single action/double action; ambidextrous magazine release and safety. Blue finish; non-glare ribbed slide top. Imported from the Czech Republic by CZ-USA.

Price: Blue **$378.00**
Price: Nickel **$397.00**

CZ 97B AUTO PISTOL

Caliber: 45 ACP, 10-shot magazine. **Barrel:** 4.85". **Weight:** 40 oz. **Length:** 8.34" overall. **Grips:** Checkered walnut. **Sights:** Fixed. **Features:** Single action/double action; full-length slide rails; screw-in barrel bushing; linkless barrel; all-steel construction; chamber loaded indicator; dual transfer bars. Introduced 1999. Imported from the Czech Republic by CZ-USA.

Price: Black polymer **$625.00**
Price: Glossy blue **$641.00**

CZ 75/85 KADET AUTO PISTOL

Caliber: 22 LR, 10-shot magazine. **Barrel:** 4.88". **Weight:** 36 oz. **Grips:** High impact checkered plastic. **Sights:** Blade front, fully adjustable rear. **Features:** Single action/double action mechanism; all-steel construction. Introduced 1999. Imported from the Czech Republic by CZ-USA.

Price: Black polymer **$486.00**

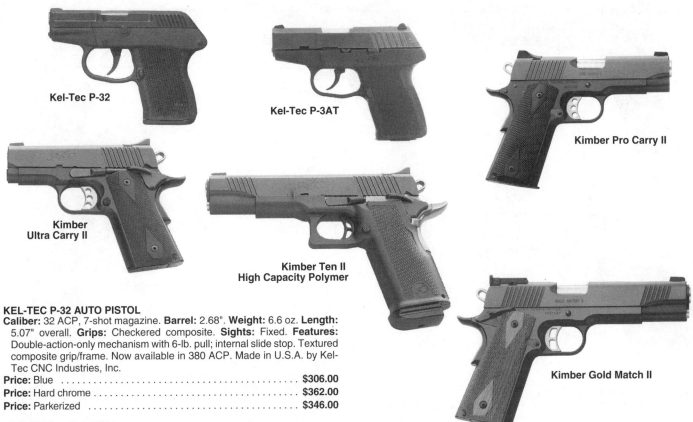

Kel-Tec P-32

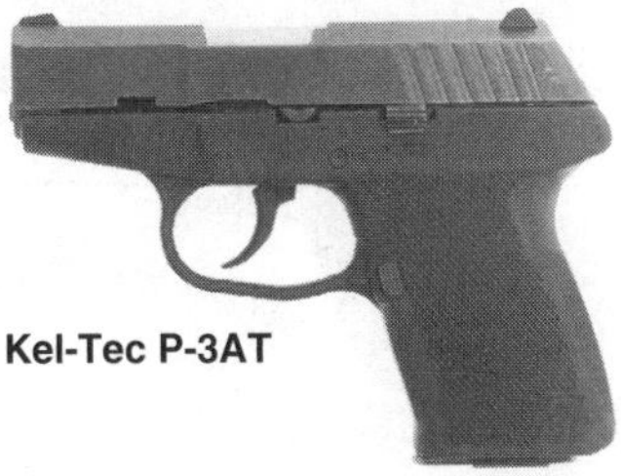

Kel-Tec P-3AT

Kimber Pro Carry II

Kimber
Ultra Carry II

Kimber Ten II
High Capacity Polymer

Kimber Gold Match II

KEL-TEC P-32 AUTO PISTOL

Caliber: 32 ACP, 7-shot magazine. **Barrel:** 2.68". **Weight:** 6.6 oz. **Length:** 5.07" overall. **Grips:** Checkered composite. **Sights:** Fixed. **Features:** Double-action-only mechanism with 6-lb. pull; internal slide stop. Textured composite grip/frame. Now available in 380 ACP. Made in U.S.A. by Kel-Tec CNC Industries, Inc.

Price: Blue **$306.00**
Price: Hard chrome **$362.00**
Price: Parkerized **$346.00**

KEL-TEC P-3AT PISTOL

Caliber: 380 Auto; 7-rounds. **Weight:** 7.2 oz. **Length:** 5.2". **Features:** Lightest 380 auto made; aluminum frame, steel barrel.

Price: Blue **$311.00**
Price: Hard Chrome **$367.00**
Price: Parkerized **$351.00**

KIMBER CUSTOM II AUTO PISTOL

Caliber: 45 ACP, 40 S&W, 38 Super, 9mm, 10mm. **Barrel:** 5", match grade; 9mm, 10mm, 40 S&W, 38 Super barrels ramped. **Weight:** 38 oz. **Length:** 8.7" overall. **Grips:** Checkered black rubber, walnut, rosewood. **Sights:** Dovetailed front and rear, Kimber low profile adj. or fixed sights. **Features:** Slide, frame and barrel machined from steel or stainless steel. Match grade barrel, chamber and trigger group. Extended thumb safety, beveled magazine well, beveled front and rear slide serrations, high ride beavertail grip safety, checkered flat mainspring housing, kidney cut under trigger guard, high cut grip, match grade stainless steel barrel bushing, polished breech face, Commander-style hammer, lowered and flared ejection port, Wolff springs, bead blasted black oxide or matte stainless finish. Introduced in 1996. Made in U.S.A. by Kimber Mfg., Inc.

Price: Custom II **$768.00**
Price: Custom II Walnut (double-diamond walnut grips) **$775.00**
Price: Stainless II **$865.00**
Price: Stainless II 40 S&W **$884.00**
Price: Stainless II Target 45 ACP (stainless, adj. sight) **$983.00**
Price: Stainless II Target 38 Super **$1,014.00**

Kimber Compact Stainless II Auto Pistol

Similar to Pro Carry II except has stainless steel frame, 4-inch bbl., grip is .400" shorter than standard, no front serrations. Weighs 34 oz. 45 ACP only. Introduced in 1998. Made in U.S.A. by Kimber Mfg., Inc.

Price: **$907.00**

Kimber Pro Carry II Auto Pistol

Similar to Custom II, has aluminum frame, 4" bull barrel fitted directly to the slide without bushing. HD with stainless steel frame. Introduced 1998. Made in U.S.A. by Kimber Mfg., Inc.

Price: Pro Carry II **$779.00**
Price: Pro Carry II w/night sights **$902.00**
Price: Pro Carry II Stainless w/night sights **$985.00**
Price: Pro Carry HD II **$906.00**

Kimber Ultra Carry II Auto Pistol

Lightweight aluminum frame, 3" match grade bull barrel fitted to slide without bushing. Grips .4" shorter. Low effort recoil. Weighs 25 oz. Introduced in 1999. Made in U.S.A. by Kimber Mfg., Inc.

Price: **$791.00**
Price: Ultra Carry II Stainless **$875.00**
Price: Ultra Carry II Stainless 40 S&W **$921.00**

Kimber Ten II High Capacity Polymer Pistol

Similar to Custom II, Pro Carry II and Ultra Carry II depending on barrel length. Thirteen-round magazine capacity (double stack and flush fitting). Polymer grip frame molded over stainless steel or aluminum (BP Ten pistols only) frame insert. Checkered front strap and belly of trigger guard. All models have fixed sights except Gold Match Ten II, which has adjustable sight. Frame grip dimensions approximately that of the standard 1911. **Weight:** 24 to 34 oz. Improved version of the Kimber Polymer series. Made in U.S.A. by Kimber Mfg., Inc.

Price: Pro Carry Ten II **$794.00**
Price: Stainless Ten II **$786.00**

Kimber Gold Match II Auto Pistol

Similar to Custom II models. Includes stainless steel barrel with match grade chamber and barrel bushing, ambidextrous thumb safety, adjustable sight, premium aluminum trigger, hand-checkered double diamond rosewood grips. Barrel hand-fitted for target accuracy. Made in U.S.A. by Kimber Mfg., Inc.

Price: Gold Match II **$1,204.00**
Price: Gold Match Stainless II 45 ACP **$1,369.00**
Price: Gold Match Stainless II 40 S&W **$1,400.00**

HANDGUNS — Autoloaders, Service & Sport

Kimber Gold Combat II

Kimber CDP II

Kimber Eclipse II

Kimber Eclipse Pro II

Kimber LTP II

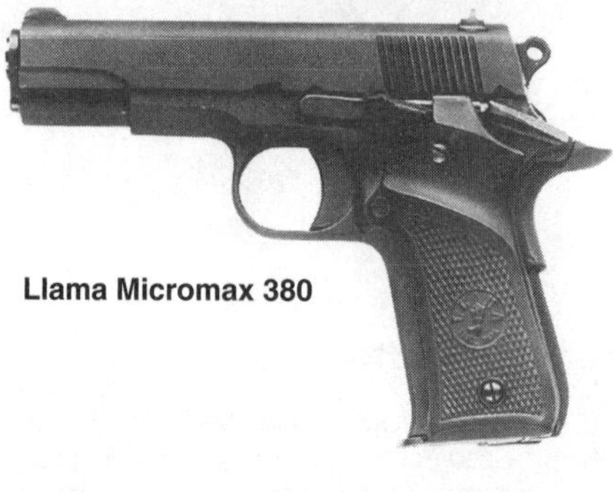

Llama Micromax 380

Kimber Gold Match Ten II Polymer Auto Pistol
Similar to Stainless Gold Match II. High capacity polymer frame with 13-round magazine. Thumb safety. Introduced 1999. Made in U.S.A. by Kimber Mfg., Inc.
Price: $1,072.00

Kimber Gold Combat II Auto Pistol
Similar to Gold Match II except designed for concealed carry. Extended and beveled magazine well, Meprolight Tritium night sights; premium aluminum trigger; 30 lpi front strap checkering; extended magazine well. Introduced 1999. Made in U.S.A. by Kimber Mfg., Inc.
Price: Gold Combat II $1,733.00
Price: Gold Combat Stainless II $1,674.00

Kimber CDP II Series Auto Pistol
Similar to Custom II, but designed for concealed carry. Aluminum frame. Standard features include stainless steel slide, fixed Meprolight tritium 3-dot (green) dovetail-mounted night sights, match grade barrel and chamber, 30 LPI front strap checkering, two-tone finish, ambidextrous thumb safety, hand-checkered double diamond rosewood grips. Introduced in 2000. Made in U.S.A. by Kimber Mfg., Inc.
Price: Ultra CDP II 40 S&W $1,215.00
Price: Ultra CDP II (3" barrel, short grip) $1,177.00
Price: Compact CDP II (4" barrel, short grip) $1,177.00
Price: Pro CDP II (4" barrel, full length grip) $1,177.00
Price: Custom CDP II (5" barrel, full length grip) $1,177.00

Kimber Eclipse II Series Auto Pistol
Similar to Custom II and other stainless Kimber pistols. Stainless slide and frame, black oxide, two-tone finish. Gray/black laminated grips. 30 lpi front strap checkering. All models have night sights; Target versions have Meprolight adjustable Bar/Dot version. Made in U.S.A. by Kimber Mfg., Inc.
Price: Eclipse Ultra II (3" barrel, short grip) $1,085.00
Price: Eclipse Pro II (4" barrel, full length grip) $1,085.00
Price: Eclipse Pro Target II (4" barrel, full length grip, adjustable sight) $1,189.00
Price: Eclipse Custom II (5" barrel, full length grip) $1,105.00
Price: Eclipse Target II (5" barrel, full length grip, adjustable sight) $1,189.00
Price: Eclipse Custom II (10mm) $1,220.00

Kimber LTP II Auto Pistol
Similar to Gold Match II. Built for Limited Ten competition. First Kimber pistol with new, innovative Kimber external extractor. KimPro premium finish. Stainless steel match grade barrel. Extended and beveled magazine well. Checkered front strap and trigger guard belly. Tungsten full length guide rod. Premium aluminum trigger. Ten-round single stack magazine. Wide ambidextrous thumb safety. Made in U.S.A. by Kimber Mfg., Inc.
Price: $2,099.00

Kimber Super Match II Auto Pistol
Similar to Gold Match II. Built for target and action shooting competition. Tested for accuracy, target included. Stainless steel barrel and chamber. KimPro finish on stainless steel slide. Stainless steel frame. 30 lpi checkered front strap, premium aluminum trigger, Kimber adjustable sight. Introduced in 1999.
Price: $1,986.00

KORTH PISTOL
Caliber: 40 S&W, 357 SIG (9-shot); 9mm Para, 9x21 (10-shot). **Barrel:** 4" (standard), 5" (optional). **Weight:** 3.3 lbs. (single action), 11 lbs. (double action). **Sights:** Fully adjustable. **Features:** Recoil-operated action, mechanically-locked via large pivoting bolt block. Accessories include sound suppressor for qualified buyers. Imported by Korth U.S.A.
Price: $7,578.00

LLAMA MICROMAX 380 AUTO PISTOL
Caliber: 32 ACP (9-shot), 380 ACP (8-shot). **Barrel:** 3-11/16". **Weight:** 23 oz. **Length:** 6-1/2" overall. **Grips:** Checkered high impact polymer. **Sights:** 3-dot combat. **Features:** Single-action. Mini custom extended slide release; mini custom extended beavertail grip safety; combat-style hammer. Introduced 1997. Distributed by Import Sports, Inc.
Price: Matte blue $281.95
Price: Satin chrome (380 only) $299.95

LLAMA MINIMAX SERIES
Caliber: 40 S&W (8-shot); 45 ACP (7-shot). **Barrel:** 3-1/2". **Weight:** 35 oz. **Length:** 7-1/3" overall. **Grips:** Checkered rubber. **Sights:** 3-dot combat. **Features:** Single action, skeletonized combat-style hammer, extended slide release, cone-style barrel, flared ejection port. Introduced 1996. Distributed by Import Sports, Inc.
Price: Blue $308.95
Price: Duo-tone finish (45 only) $315.95
Price: Satin chrome $333.95

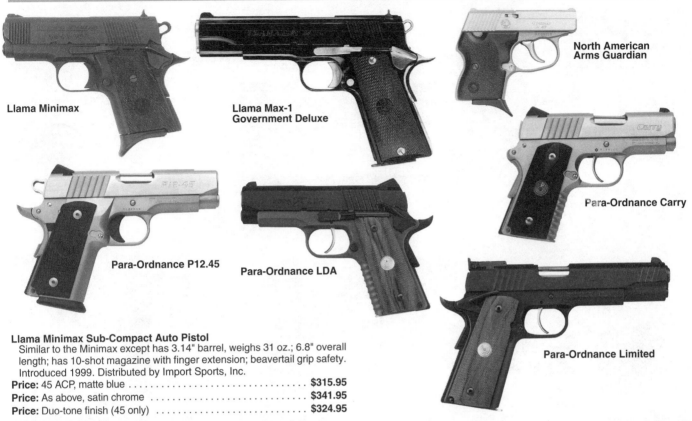

Llama Minimax

Llama Max-1
Government Deluxe

North American
Arms Guardian

Para-Ordnance Carry

Para-Ordnance P12.45

Para-Ordnance LDA

Para-Ordnance Limited

Llama Minimax Sub-Compact Auto Pistol
Similar to the Minimax except has 3.14" barrel, weighs 31 oz.; 6.8" overall length; has 10-shot magazine with finger extension; beavertail grip safety. Introduced 1999. Distributed by Import Sports, Inc.
Price: 45 ACP, matte blue **$315.95**
Price: As above, satin chrome **$341.95**
Price: Duo-tone finish (45 only) **$324.95**

LLAMA MAX-I AUTO PISTOLS
Caliber: 45 ACP, 7-shot. **Barrel:** 5-1/8". **Weight:** 36 oz. **Length:** 8-1/2" overall. **Grips:** Polymer. **Sights:** Blade front; 3-dot system. **Features:** Single-action trigger; skeletonized combat-style hammer; steel frame; extended manual and grip safeties, matte finish. Introduced 1995. Distributed by Import Sports, Inc.
Price: 45 ACP, 7-round, Government model **$358.95**
Price: Maxi II, 17-round model **$324.95**

NORTH AMERICAN ARMS GUARDIAN PISTOL
Caliber: 32 ACP, 380 ACP, 32NAA, 6-shot magazine. **Barrel:** 2.1". **Weight:** 13.5 oz. **Length:** 4.36" overall. **Grips:** Black polymer. **Sights:** Fixed. **Features:** Double-action only mechanism. All stainless steel construction. Introduced 1998. Made in U.S.A. by North American Arms.
Price: . . . . **$402.00 to $479.00**

OLYMPIC ARMS OA-93 AR PISTOL
Caliber: 5.56 NATO. **Barrel:** 6.5", chrome-moly steel. **Weight:** 5.8 lbs. **Length:** 26.5". **Sights:** None. **Features:** Black matte finish; flash suppressor; tubular handguard. Introduced 2005. Made in U.S.A. by Olympic Arms, Inc.
Price: **$1,020.00**

Olympic Arms OA-98 AR Pistol
Similar to the OA-93 except has removable 7-shot magazine, weighs 3 lbs. Introduced 1999. Made in U.S.A. by Olympic Arms, Inc.
Price: **$1,020.00**

PARA-ORDNANCE P-SERIES AUTO PISTOLS
Caliber: 9mm Para., 40 S&W, 45 ACP, 10-shot magazine. **Barrel:** 3", 3-1/2", 4-1/4", 5". **Weight:** From 24 oz. (alloy frame). **Length:** 8.5" overall. **Grips:** Textured composition. **Sights:** Blade front, rear adjustable for windage. High visibility 3-dot system. **Features:** Available with alloy, steel or stainless steel frame with black finish (silver or stainless gun). Steel and stainless steel frame guns weigh 40 oz. (P14.45), 36 oz. (P13.45), 34 oz. (P12.45). Grooved match trigger, rounded combat-style hammer. Beveled magazine well. Manual thumb, grip and firing pin lock safeties. Solid barrel bushing. Contact maker for full details. Introduced 1990. Made in Canada by Para-Ordnance.
Price: Steel frame **$855.00**
Price: Alloy frame **$840.00**
Price: Stainless steel **$988.00**

Para-Ordnance Limited Pistols
Similar to the P-Series pistols except with full-length recoil guide system; fully adjustable rear sight; tuned trigger with over-travel stop; beavertail grip safety; competition hammer; front and rear slide serrations; ambidextrous safety; lowered ejection port; ramped match-grade barrel; dove-tailed front sight. Introduced 1998. Made in Canada by Para-Ordnance.
Price: 9mm, 40 S&W, 45 ACP **$1,105.00**

Para-Ordnance LDA Auto Pistols
Similar to P-series except has double-action trigger mechanism. Steel frame with matte black finish, checkered composition grips. Available in 9mm Para., 40 S&W, 45 ACP. Introduced 1999. Made in Canada by Para-Ordnance.
Price: . . . . **$899.00 to $973.00**

Para-Ordnance LDA Limited Pistols
Similar to LDA, has ambidextrous safety, adjustable rear sight, front slide serrations and full-length recoil guide system. Made in Canada by Para-Ordnance.
Price: Black finish **$1,105.00**
Price: Stainless **$1,049.00**

PARA-ORDNANCE 45 LDA PARA CARRY
Caliber: 45 ACP. **Barrel:** 3", 7-shot. **Weight:** 30 oz. **Length:** 6.5". **Grips:** Double diamond checkered cocobolo. **Features:** Stainless finish and receiver. Para LDA trigger system and safeties.
Price: **$988.00**

PARA-ORDNANCE 45 LDA PARA COMPANION
Caliber: 45 ACP. **Barrel:** 3.5", 8-shot. **Weight:** 32 oz. **Length:** 7". **Grips:** Double diamond checkered cocobolo. **Features:** Para LDA trigger system with Para LDA 3 safeties (slide lock, firing pin block and grip safety). Lightning speed, full size capacity.
Price: **$899.00**

HANDGUNS — Autoloaders, Service & Sport

Peters Stahl High Capacity

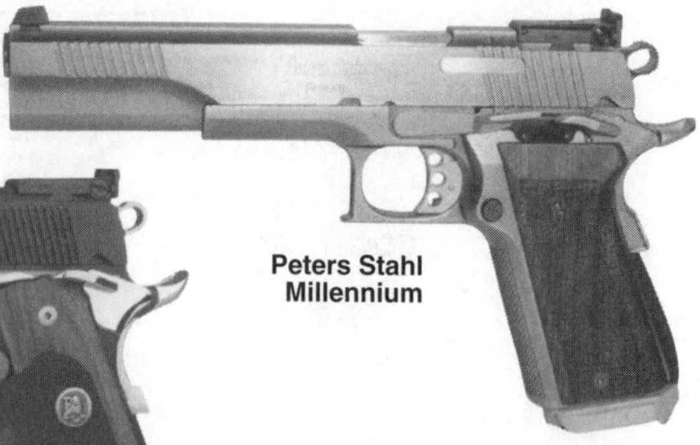

Peters Stahl Millennium

Peters Stahl Trophy Master

Phoenix Arms HP22

Ruger P89

Ruger P90

Rock River Standard Match

PETERS STAHL AUTOLOADING PISTOLS
Caliber: 9mm Para., 45 ACP. **Barrel:** 5" or 6". **Grips:** Walnut or walnut with rubber wrap. **Sights:** Fully adjustable rear, blade front. **Features:** Stainless steel extended slide stop, safety and extended magazine release button; speed trigger with stop, approx. 3-lb. pull; polished ramp. Introduced 2000. Imported from Germany by Phillips & Rogers.
Price: High Capacity (accepts 15-shot magazines in 45 cal.; includes 10-shot magazine) **$1,695.00**
Price: Trophy Master (blued or stainless, 7-shot in 45, 8-shot in 9mm) **$1,995.00**
Price: Millennium Model (titanium coating on receiver and slide) **$2,195.00**

PHOENIX ARMS HP22, HP25 AUTO PISTOLS
Caliber: 22 LR, 10-shot (HP22), 25 ACP, 10-shot (HP25). **Barrel:** 3". **Weight:** 20 oz. **Length:** 5-1/2" overall. **Grips:** Checkered composition. **Sights:** Blade front, adjustable rear. **Features:** Single action, exposed hammer; manual hold-open; button magazine release. Available in satin nickel, polished blue finish. Introduced 1993. Made in U.S.A. by Phoenix Arms.
Price: With gun lock and cable lanyard **$130.00**
Price: HP Rangemaster kit with 5" bbl., locking case and assessories **$171.00**
Price: HP Deluxe Rangemaster kit with 3" and 5" bbls., 2 mags., case **$210.00**

ROCK RIVER ARMS STANDARD MATCH AUTO PISTOL
Caliber: 45 ACP. **Barrel:** NA. **Weight:** NA. **Length:** NA. **Grips:** Cocobolo, checkered. **Sights:** Heine fixed rear, blade front. **Features:** Chrome-moly steel frame and slide; beavertail grip safety with raised pad; checkered slide stop; ambidextrous safety; polished feed ramp and extractor; aluminum speed trigger with 3.5 lb. pull. Made in U.S.A. From Rock River Arms.
Price: **$1,025.00**

ROCKY MOUNTAIN ARMS PATRIOT PISTOL
Caliber: 223, 10-shot magazine. **Barrel:** 7", with muzzle brake. **Weight:** 5 lbs. **Length:** 20.5" overall. **Grips:** Black composition. **Sights:** None furnished. **Features:** Milled upper receiver with enhanced Weaver base; milled lower receiver from billet plate; machined aluminum National Match handguard. Finished in DuPont Teflon-S matte black or NATO green. Comes with black nylon case, one magazine. Introduced 1993. From Rocky Mountain Arms, Inc.
Price: With A-2 handle top . . . . **$2,500.00 to $2,800.00**
Price: Flat top model . . . . **$3,000.00 to $3,500.00**

RUGER P89 AUTOLOADING PISTOL
Caliber: 9mm Para., 15-shot magazine. **Barrel:** 4.50". **Weight:** 32 oz. **Length:** 7.84" overall. **Grips:** Grooved black synthetic composition. **Sights:** Square post front, square notch rear adjustable for windage, both with white dot inserts. **Features:** Double action, ambidextrous slide-mounted safety-levers. Slide 4140 chrome-moly steel or 400-series stainless steel, frame lightweight aluminum alloy. Ambidextrous magazine release. Blue, stainless steel. Introduced 1986; stainless 1990.
Price: P89, blue, extra mag and mag loader, plastic case locks . . . **$475.00**
Price: KP89, stainless, extra mag and mag loader, plastic case locks **$525.00**

Ruger P89D Decocker Autoloading Pistol
Similar to standard P89 except has ambidextrous decocking levers in place of regular slide-mounted safety. Decocking levers move firing pin inside slide where hammer cannot reach. Blue, stainless steel. Introduced 1990.
Price: P89D, blue, extra mag and mag loader, plastic case locks . . **$475.00**
Price: KP89D, stainless, extra mag and mag loader, plastic case locks **$525.00**

RUGER P90 MANUAL SAFETY MODEL AUTOLOADING PISTOL
Caliber: 45 ACP, 8-shot magazine. **Barrel:** 4.50". **Weight:** 33.5 oz. **Length:** 7.75" overall. **Grips:** Grooved black synthetic composition. **Sights:** Square post front, square notch rear adjustable for windage, both with white dot. **Features:** Double action; ambidextrous slide-mounted safety-levers. Stainless steel only. Introduced 1991.
Price: KP90 with extra mag, loader, case and gunlock **$565.00**
Price: P90 (blue) **$525.00**

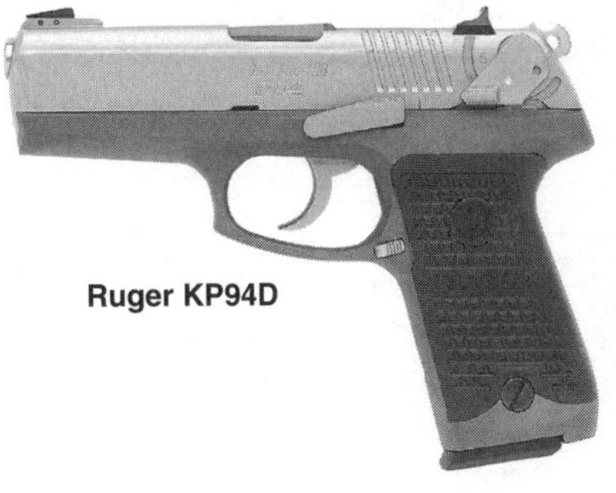

Ruger KP94D

Ruger 22/45-P4

Ruger KP512

Ruger KP90 Decocker Autoloading Pistol

Similar to the P90 except has a manual decocking system. Ambidextrous decocking levers move the firing pin inside the slide where the hammer cannot reach it. Available only in stainless steel. Overall length 7.75", weighs 33.5 oz. Introduced 1991.

Price: KP90D with case, extra mag and mag loading tool **$565.00**

Ruger KP94 Autoloading Pistol

Sized midway between full-size P-Series and compact KP94. 4.25" barrel, 7.5" overall length, weighs about 33 oz. KP94 manual safety model; KP94D is decocker-only in 40-caliber with 10-shot magazine. Slide gripping grooves roll over top of slide. KP94 has ambidextrous safety-levers; KP944D has ambidextrous decocking levers. Matte finish stainless slide, barrel, alloy frame. Also blue. Includes hard case and lock. Introduced 1994. Made in U.S.A. by Sturm, Ruger & Co.

Price: P944, blue (manual safety) **$495.00**

Price:KP944 (40-caliber) (manual safety-stainless) **$575.00**

Price: KP944D (40-caliber)-decocker only **$575.00**

RUGER P95 AUTOLOADING PISTOL

Caliber: 9mm Para., 15-shot magazine. **Barrel:** 3.9". **Weight:** 27 oz. **Length:** 7.25" overall. **Grips:** Grooved; integral with frame. **Sights:** Blade front, rear drift adjustable for windage; 3-dot system. **Features:** Molded polymer grip frame, stainless steel or chrome-moly slide. Suitable for +P+ ammunition. Safety model, decocker or DAO. Introduced 1996. Made in U.S.A. by Sturm, Ruger & Co. Comes with lockable plastic case, spare magazine, loader and lock.

Price: P95D15 decocker only **$425.00**

Price: P9515 stainless steel decocker only **$475.00**

Price: KP9515 safety model, stainless steel **$475.00**

Price: P9515 safety model, blued finish **$425.00**

RUGER MARK II STANDARD AUTOLOADING PISTOL

Caliber: 22 LR, 10-shot magazine. **Barrel:** 4-3/4" or 6". **Weight:** 35 oz. (4-3/4" bbl.). **Length:** 8-5/16" (4-3/4" bbl.). **Grips:** Checkered composition grip panels. **Sights:** Fixed, wide blade front, fixed rear. **Features:** Updated design of original Standard Auto. New bolt hold-open latch. 10-shot magazine, magazine catch, safety and trigger. Introduced 1982.

Price: Blued (MKIII4, MKIII6) **$322.00**

Ruger 22/45 Mark II Pistol

Similar to other 22 Mark II autos except has grip frame of Zytel that matches angle and magazine latch of Model 1911 45 ACP pistol. Available in 4" standard, 4-3/4" and 5-1/2" bull barrels. Comes with extra magazine, plastic case, lock. Introduced 1992.

Price: P4MKIII, 4" standard barrel, adjustable sights **$307.00**

Price: KP512 (5-1/2" bull bbl.), stainless steel, adj. sights **$398.00**

Price: P512 (5-1/2" bull bbl., all blue), adj. sights **$307.00**

SAFARI ARMS ENFORCER PISTOL

Caliber: 45 ACP, 6-shot magazine. **Barrel:** 3.8", stainless. **Weight:** 36 oz. **Length:** 7.3" overall. **Grips:** Smooth walnut with etched black widow spider logo. **Sights:** Ramped blade front, LPA adjustable rear. **Features:** Extended safety, extended slide release; Commander-style hammer; beavertail grip safety; throated, polished, tuned. Parkerized matte black or satin stainless steel finishes. Made in U.S.A. by Safari Arms, Inc.

Price: **$630.00**

SAFARI ARMS GI SAFARI PISTOL

Caliber: 45 ACP, 7-shot magazine. **Barrel:** 5", 416 stainless. **Weight:** 39.9 oz. **Length:** 8.5" overall. **Grips:** Checkered walnut. **Sights:** G.I.-style blade front, drift-adjustable rear. **Features:** Beavertail grip safety; extended thumb safety and slide release; Commander-style hammer. Parkerized finish. Reintroduced 1996.

Price: **$439.00**

SAFARI ARMS CARRIER PISTOL

Caliber: 45 ACP, 7-shot magazine. **Barrel:** 6", 416 stainless steel. **Weight:** 30 oz. **Length:** 9.5" overall. **Grips:** Wood. **Sights:** Ramped blade front, LPA adjustable rear. **Features:** Beavertail grip safety; extended controls; full-length recoil spring guide; Commander-style hammer. Throated, polished and tuned. Satin stainless steel finish. Introduced 1999. Made in U.S.A. by Safari Arms, Inc.

Price: **$714.00**

SAFARI ARMS COHORT PISTOL

Caliber: 45 ACP, 7-shot magazine. **Barrel:** 3.8", 416 stainless. **Weight:** 37 oz. **Length:** 8.5" overall. **Grips:** Smooth walnut with laser-etched black widow logo. **Sights:** Ramped blade front, LPA adjustable rear. **Features:** Combines the Enforcer model, slide and MatchMaster frame. Beavertail grip safety; extended thumb safety and slide release; Commander-style hammer. Satin stainless finish. Introduced 1996. Made in U.S.A. by Safari Arms, Inc.

Price: **$654.00**

SAFARI ARMS MATCHMASTER PISTOL

Caliber: 45 ACP, 7-shot. **Barrel:** 5" or 6", 416 stainless steel. **Weight:** 38 oz. (5" barrel). **Length:** 8.5" overall. **Grips:** Smooth walnut. **Sights:** Ramped blade, LPA adjustable rear. **Features:** Beavertail grip safety; extended controls; Commander-style hammer; throated, polished, tuned. Parkerized matte-black or satin stainless steel. Made in U.S.A. by Olympic Arms, Inc.

Price: 5" barrel **$594.00**

Price: 6" bbl. **$654.00**

Safari Arms Carry Comp Pistol

Similar to the Matchmaster except has Wil Schueman-designed hybrid compensator system. Made in U.S.A. by Olympic Arms, Inc.

Price: **$1,067.00**

SEECAMP LWS 32 STAINLESS DA AUTO

Caliber: 32 ACP Win. Silvertip, 6-shot magazine. **Barrel:** 2", integral with frame. **Weight:** 10.5 oz. **Length:** 4-1/8" overall. **Grips:** Glass-filled nylon. **Sights:** Smooth, no-snag, contoured slide and barrel top. **Features:** Aircraft quality 17-4 PH stainless steel. Inertia-operated firing pin. Hammer fired double-action-only. Hammer automatically follows slide down to safety rest position after each shot, no manual safety needed. Magazine safety disconnector. Polished stainless. Introduced 1985. From L.W. Seecamp.

Price: **$425.00**

HANDGUNS — Autoloaders, Service & Sport

SIG-Sauer P220

SIG-Sauer P245 Compact

SIG-Sauer Pro 2009

SIG-Sauer P229 Sport

SIG-Sauer P232

SEMMERLING LM-4 SLIDE-ACTION PISTOL
Caliber: 45 ACP, 4-shot magazine. **Barrel:** 2". **Weight:** 24 oz. **Length:** NA. **Grips:** NA. **Sights:** NA. **Features:** The Semmerling LM-4 is a super compact pistol employing a thumb activated slide mechanism (the slide is manually retracted between shots). From American Derringer Corp.
Price: **$2,635.00**

SIG-SAUER P220 SERVICE AUTO PISTOL
Caliber: 45 ACP, (7- or 8-shot magazine). **Barrel:** 4-3/8". **Weight:** 27.8 oz. **Length:** 7.8" overall. **Grips:** Checkered black plastic. **Sights:** Blade front, drift adjustable rear for windage. Optional Siglite night sights. **Features:** Double action. Decocking lever permits lowering hammer onto locked firing pin. Squared combat-type trigger guard. Slide stays open after last shot. Imported from Germany by SIGARMS, Inc.
Price: Blue SA/DA or DAO **$790.00**
Price: Blue, Siglite night sights **$880.00**
Price: K-Kote or nickel slide **$830.00**
Price: K-Kote or nickel slide with Siglite night sights **$930.00**

SIG-Sauer P220 Sport Auto Pistol
Similar to the P220 except has 4.9" barrel, ported compensator, stainless steel frame and slide, adjustable sights, extended competition controls. Overall length is 9.9", weighs 43.5 oz. Introduced 1999. From SIGARMS, Inc.
Price: **$1,320.00**

SIG-Sauer P245 Compact Auto Pistol
Similar to the P220 except has 3.9" barrel, shorter grip, 6-shot magazine, 7.28" overall length, and weighs 27.5 oz. Introduced 1999. From SIGARMS, Inc.
Price: Blue **$780.00**
Price: Blue, with Siglite sights **$850.00**
Price: Two-tone **$830.00**
Price: Two-tone with Siglite sights **$930.00**
Price: With K-Kote finish **$830.00**
Price: K-Kote with Siglite sights **$930.00**

SIG-Sauer P229 DA Auto Pistol
Similar to the P228 except chambered for 9mm Para., 40 S&W, 357 SIG. Has 3.86" barrel, 7.08" overall length and 3.35" height. Weight is 30.5 oz. Introduced 1991. Frame made in Germany, stainless steel slide assembly made in U.S.; pistol assembled in U.S. From SIGARMS, Inc.
Price: **$795.00**
Price: With nickel slide **$890.00**
Price: Nickel slide Siglite night sights **$935.00**

SIG PRO AUTO PISTOL
Caliber: 9mm Para., 40 S&W, 10-shot magazine. **Barrel:** 3.86". **Weight:** 27.2 oz. **Length:** 7.36" overall. **Grips:** Composite and rubberized one-piece. **Sights:** Blade front, rear adjustable for windage. Optional Siglite night sights. **Features:** Polymer frame, stainless steel slide; integral frame accessory rail; replaceable steel frame rails; left- or right-handed magazine release. Introduced 1999. From SIGARMS, Inc.
Price: SP2340 (40 S&W) **$596.00**
Price: SP2009 (9mm Para.) **$596.00**
Price: As above with Siglite night sights **$655.00**

SIG-Sauer P226 Service Pistol
Similar to the P220 pistol except has 4.4" barrel, and weighs 28.3 oz. 357 SIG or 40 S&W. Imported from Germany by SIGARMS, Inc.
Price: Blue SA/DA or DAO **$830.00**
Price: With Siglite night sights **$930.00**
Price: Blue, SA/DA or DAO 357 SIG **$830.00**
Price: With Siglite night sights **$930.00**
Price: K-Kote finish, 40 S&W only or nickel slide **$830.00**
Price: K-Kote or nickel slide Siglite night sights **$930.00**
Price: Nickel slide 357 SIG **$875.00**
Price: Nickel slide, Siglite night sights **$930.00**

SIG-Sauer P229 Sport Auto Pistol
Similar to the P229 except in 357 SIG only; 4.8" heavy barrel; 8.6" overall length; weighs 40.6 oz.; vented compensator; adjustable target sights; rubber grips; extended slide latch and magazine release. Stainless steel. Introduced 1998. From SIGARMS, Inc.
Price: **$1,320.00**

SIG-SAUER P232 PERSONAL SIZE PISTOL
Caliber: 380 ACP, 7-shot. **Barrel:** 3-3/4". **Weight:** 16 oz. **Length:** 6-1/2" overall. **Grips:** Checkered black composite. **Sights:** Blade front, rear adjustable for windage. **Features:** Double action/single action or DAO. Blowback operation, stationary barrel. Introduced 1997. Imported from Germany by SIGARMS, Inc.
Price: Blue SA/DA or DAO **$505.00**
Price: In stainless steel **$545.00**
Price: With stainless steel slide, blue frame **$525.00**
Price: Stainless steel, Siglite night sights, Hogue grips **$585.00**

Smith & Wesson 457 TDA

Smith & Wesson 908

Smith & Wesson 4013 TSW

Smith & Wesson 410 DA

Smith & Wesson 910 DA

Smith & Wesson 3913 LadySmith

SIG-SAUER P239 PISTOL

Caliber: 9mm Para., 8-shot, 357 SIG 40 S&W, 7-shot magazine. **Barrel:** 3.6". **Weight:** 25.2 oz. **Length:** 6.6" overall. **Grips:** Checkered black composite. **Sights:** Blade front, rear adjustable for windage. Optional Siglite night sights. **Features:** SA/DA or DAO; blackened stainless steel slide, aluminum alloy frame. Introduced 1996. Made in U.S.A. by SIGARMS, Inc.

Price: SA/DA or DAO **$620.00**
Price: SA/DA or DAO with Siglite night sights **$720.00**
Price: Two-tone finish **$665.00**
Price: Two-tone finish, Siglite sights **$765.00**

SMITH & WESSON MODEL 457 TDA AUTO PISTOL

Caliber: 45 ACP, 7-shot magazine. **Barrel:** 3-3/4". **Weight:** 29 oz. **Length:** 7-1/4" overall. **Grips:** One-piece Xenoy, wraparound with straight backstrap. **Sights:** Post front, fixed rear, 3-dot system. **Features:** Aluminum alloy frame, matte blue carbon steel slide; bobbed hammer; smooth trigger. Introduced 1996. Made in U.S.A. by Smith & Wesson.

Price: Blue finish **$649.00**
Price: Matte finish **$676.00**

SMITH & WESSON MODEL 908 AUTO PISTOL

Caliber: 9mm Para., 8-shot magazine. **Barrel:** 3-1/2". **Weight:** 24 oz. **Length:** 6-13/16". **Grips:** One-piece Xenoy, wraparound with straight backstrap. **Sights:** Post front, fixed rear, 3-dot system. **Features:** Aluminum alloy frame, matte blue carbon steel slide; bobbed hammer; smooth trigger. Introduced 1996. Made in U.S.A. by Smith & Wesson.

Price: Blue finish **$587.00**
Price: Matte finish **$611.00**

SMITH & WESSON MODEL 4013 TSW AUTO

Caliber: 40 S&W, 9-shot magazine. **Barrel:** 3-1/2". **Weight:** 26.8 oz. **Length:** 6 3/4" overall. **Grips:** Xenoy one-piece wraparound. **Sights:** Novak 3-dot system. **Features:** Traditional double-action system; stainless slide, alloy frame; fixed barrel bushing; ambidextrous decocker; reversible magazine catch, equipment rail. Introduced 1997. Made in U.S.A. by Smith & Wesson.

Price: Model 4013 TSW **$973.00**

SMITH & WESSON MODEL 410 DA AUTO PISTOL

Caliber: 40 S&W, 10-shot magazine. **Barrel:** 4". **Weight:** 28.5 oz. **Length:** 7.5". **Grips:** One-piece Xenoy, wraparound with straight backstrap. **Sights:** Post front, fixed rear; 3-dot system. **Features:** Aluminum alloy frame; blued carbon steel slide; traditional double action with left-side slide-mounted decocking lever. Introduced 1996. Made in U.S.A. by Smith & Wesson.

Price: Model 410 .... **$649.00**
Price: Model 410S, matte finish **$669.00**
Price: Crimson trace grips **$993.00**

SMITH & WESSON MODEL 910 DA AUTO PISTOL

Caliber: 9mm Para., 10-shot magazine. **Barrel:** 4". **Weight:** 28 oz. **Length:** 7-3/8" overall. **Grips:** One-piece Xenoy, wraparound with straight backstrap. **Sights:** Post front with white dot, fixed 2-dot rear. **Features:** Alloy frame, blue carbon steel slide. Slide-mounted decocking lever. Introduced 1995.

Price: Model 910 .... **$587.00**
Price: Model 910, matte finish **$602.00**

SMITH & WESSON MODEL 3913 TRADITIONAL DOUBLE ACTION

Caliber: 9mm Para., 8-shot magazine. **Barrel:** 3-1/2". **Weight:** 24.8 oz. **Length:** 6-3/4" overall. **Grips:** One-piece Delrin wraparound, textured surface. **Sights:** Post front with white dot, Novak LoMount Carry with two dots. **Features:** Aluminum alloy frame, stainless slide (M3913). Bobbed hammer with no half-cock notch; smooth .304" trigger with rounded edges. Straight backstrap. Equipment rail. Extra magazine included. Introduced 1989.

Price: **$834.00**

Smith & Wesson Model 3913-LS Ladysmith Auto

Similar to the standard Model 3913 except has frame that is upswept at the front, rounded trigger guard. Comes in frosted stainless steel with matching gray grips. Grips are ergonomically correct for a woman's hand. Novak LoMount Carry rear sight adjustable for windage. Extra magazine included. Introduced 1990.

Price: **$858.00**

SMITH & WESSON MODEL SW1911

Caliber: 45 ACP, 8 rounds. **Barrel:** 5". **Weight:** 39 oz. **Length:** 8.7". **Grips:** Wood/rubber. **Sights:** Novak Lo-Mount Carry, white dot front.

Price: Stainless steel frame **$960.00**
Price: Adjustable sights, stainless **$1,049.00**
Price: Carbon steel frame **$960.00**
Price: Stainless w/Crimson Trace Lasergrip **$1,281.00**
Price: Doug Koenig Pro Series **$1,213.00**

Smith & Wesson 4006

Smith & Wesson 4566 TSW

Smith & Wesson Sigma SW40V

Springfield, Inc. 1911A1 Standard

Springfield, Inc. Full-Size 1911A1

Springfield, Inc. TRP

SMITH & WESSON MODEL SW1911PD

Caliber: 45 ACP, 8 rounds. **Barrel:** 4-1/4" or 5". **Weight:** 28 oz. **Length:** 7-5/8" or 8.7". **Grips:** Wood. **Sights:** Novak Lo-Mount Carry, white dot front.

Price: 4-1/4" bbl. **$1,029.00**
Price: 5" **$1,029.00**
Price: Carbon steel frame **$960.00**
Price: Scandium alloy w/Crimson Trace Lasergrip **$1,330.00**

SMITH & WESSON MODEL 4040PD

Caliber: 40 S&W, 7 rounds. **Barrel:** 3.5". **Weight:** 25.6 oz. **Length:** 6.9". **Grips:** Rubber. **Sights:** Novak Lo-Mount Carry, white dot front.

Price: Scandium alloy frame **$840.00**

SMITH & WESSON MODEL SW990L COMPACT

Caliber: 9mm (10 rounds), 40 S&W (8 rounds). **Barrel:** 3.5". **Weight:** 23 oz. **Length:** 6.6". **Grips:** Polymer. **Sights:** Adj. rear, white dot front.

Price: **$694.00**
Price: Model 5946 DAO (as above, stainless frame and slide) **$863.00**

SMITH & WESSON ENHANCED SIGMA SERIES DAO PISTOLS

Caliber: 9mm Para., 40 S&W, 10-shot magazine. **Barrel:** 4". **Weight:** 24.7 oz. **Length:** 7-1/4" overall. **Grips:** Integral. **Sights:** White dot front, fixed rear; 3-dot system. Tritium night sights available. **Features:** Ergonomic polymer frame; low barrel centerline; internal striker firing system; corrosion-resistant slide; Teflon-filled, electroless-nickel coated magazine, equipment rail. Introduced 1994. Made in U.S.A. by Smith & Wesson.

Price: **$379.00**

SMITH & WESSON MODEL CS9 CHIEF'S SPECIAL AUTO

Caliber: 9mm Para., 7-shot magazine. **Barrel:** 3". **Weight:** 20.8 oz. **Length:** 6-1/4" overall. **Grips:** Hogue wraparound rubber. **Sights:** White dot front, fixed 2-dot rear. **Features:** Traditional double-action trigger mechanism. Alloy frame, stainless slide. Ambidextrous safety. Introduced 1999. Made in U.S.A. by Smith & Wesson.

Price: Stainless **$747.00**

SMITH & WESSON MODEL CS45 CHIEF'S SPECIAL AUTO

Caliber: 45 ACP, 6-shot magazine. **Weight:** 23.9 oz. **Features:** Introduced 1999. Made in U.S.A. by Smith & Wesson.

Price: Stainless **$787.00**

SMITH & WESSON MODEL SW990L

Caliber: 9mm Para. 4" barrel; 40 S&W 4-1/8" barrel; adj. sights. **Features:** Traditional double action satin stainless, black polymer frame, equipment rail, Saf-T-Trigger, interchangeable backstrap.

Price: 9mm, 40 S&W **$694.00**
Price: 45 ACP **$736.00**

SPRINGFIELD ARMORY FULL-SIZE 1911A1 AUTO PISTOL

Caliber: 9mm Para., 9-shot; 38 Super, 9-shot; 40 S&W, 9-shot; 45 ACP, 7-shot. **Barrel:** 5". **Weight:** 35.6 oz. **Length:** 8-5/8" overall. **Grips:** Cocobolo. **Sights:** Fixed 3-dot system. **Features:** Beveled magazine well; lowered and flared ejection port. All forged parts, including frame, barrel, slide. All new production. Introduced 1990. From Springfield Armory.

Price: Mil-Spec 45 ACP, Parkerized **$640.00**
Price: Tactical, 45 ACP, TRP Armory Kote, Novak sights **$1,560.00**
Price: Standard, 45 ACP, stainless, Novak sights **$876.00**
Price: Lightweight 45 ACP (28.6 oz., matte finish, night sights) . . . **$922.00**
Price: 40 S&W, stainless **$1,409.00**
Price: 9mm, stainless **$948.00**

Springfield Armory TRP Pistols

Similar to 1911A1 except 45 ACP only, checkered front strap and mainspring housing, Novak Night Sight combat rear sight and matching dovetailed front sight, tuned, polished extractor, oversize barrel link; lightweight speed trigger and combat action job, match barrel and bushing, extended ambidextrous thumb safety and fitted beavertail grip safety. Checkered cocobolo wood grips, comes with two Wilson 7-shot magazines. Frame is engraved "Tactical," both sides of frame with "TRP." Introduced 1998. From Springfield Armory.

Price: Standard with Armory Kote finish **$1,560.00**
Price: Standard, stainless steel **$1,409.00**
Price: Standard with Operator Light Rail Armory Kote **$1,573.00**

Springfield Armory 1911A1 High Capacity Pistol

Similar to Standard 1911A1, available in 45 ACP with 10-shot magazine. Commander-style hammer, walnut grips, beveled magazine well, plastic carrying case. Can accept higher-capacity Para-Ordnance magazines. Introduced 1993. From Springfield Armory.

Price: Mil-Spec 45 ACP **$559.00**
Price: 45 ACP Ultra Compact (3-1/2" bbl.) **$922.00**

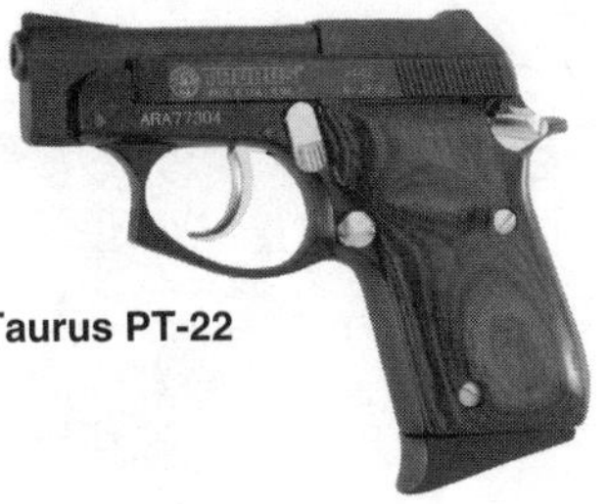

Taurus PT-22

Taurus PT-24

Taurus PT-92

Taurus PT-100

Springfield Armory 1911A1 Champion Pistol
Similar to standard 1911A1, slide is 4". Available in 45 ACP only. Novak Night Sights. Delta hammer and cocobolo grips. Parkerized or stainless. Introduced 1989.
Price: Stainless **$886.00**

Springfield Armory Ultra Compact Pistol
Similar to 1911A1 Compact, shorter slide, 3.5" barrel, beavertail grip safety, beveled magazine well, Novak Low Mount or Novak Night Sights, Videki speed trigger, flared ejection port, stainless steel frame, blued slide, match grade barrel, rubber grips. Introduced 1996. From Springfield Armory.
Price: Stainless 45 ACP, Novak Tritium sights **$922.00**
NEW! Price: Lightweight Bi-Tone stainless **$1,184.00**

Springfield Armory Compact Lightweight Bi-Tone
Mates a Springfield Inc. Champion length slide with the shorter Ultra-Compact forged alloy frame for concealability. In 45 ACP.
Price: **$1,184.00**

Springfield Armory Trophy Match 1911A1 Pistol
Similar to Full Size model, 5" match barrel and slide, fully adjustable sights. From Springfield Armory.
Price: Trophy Match 45 ACP, stainless **$1,049.00**
Price: Trophy Match, 40 S&W, Polymer **$1,409.00**

SPRINGFIELD ARMORY MICRO-COMPACT 1911A1 PISTOL
Caliber: 45 ACP, 40 S&W 6+1 capacity. **Barrel:** 3" 1:16 LH. **Weight:** 24 oz. **Length:** 5.7". **Sights:** Novak LoMount tritium. Dovetail front. **Features:** Forged frame and slide, ambi thumb safety, extreme carry bevel treatment, lockable plastic case, 2 magazines.
Price: . . . . **$922.00 to $1,247.00**

SPRINGFIELD ARMORY DEFENDER
Caliber: 9mm, 40 S&W, 45 GAP. **Barrel:** 3". **Weight:** 23 oz. **Length:** NA **Sights:** Novak low mount. **Features:** Alloy frame, slide and barrel; adjustable trigger; Delta lightweight hammer; loaded chamber indicator.
Price: . . . . **NA**

STEYR M & S SERIES AUTO PISTOLS
Caliber: 9mm Para., 40 S&W, 357 SIG; 10-shot magazine. **Barrel:** 4" (3.58" for Model S). **Weight:** 28 oz. (22.5 oz. for Model S). **Length:** 7.05" overall (6.53" for Model S). **Grips:** Ultra-rigid polymer. **Sights:** Drift-adjustable, white-outline rear; white-triangle blade front. **Features:** Polymer frame; trigger-drop firing pin, manual and key-lock safeties; loaded chamber indicator; 5.5-lb. trigger pull; 111-degree grip. Introduced 2000. Imported from Austria by GSI Inc.
Price: Model M (full-sized frame with 4" barrel) **$609.95**
Price: Model S (compact frame with 3.58" barrel) **$609.95**
Price: Extra 10-shot magazines (Model M or S) **$39.00**

TAURUS MODEL PT-22/PT-25 AUTO PISTOLS
Caliber: 22 LR, 8-shot (PT 22); 25 ACP, 9-shot (PT 25). **Barrel:** 2.75". **Weight:** 12.3 oz. **Length:** 5.25" overall. **Grips:** Smooth rosewood or mother-of-pearl. **Sights:** Fixed. **Features:** Double action. Tip-up barrel for loading, cleaning. Blue, nickel, duo-tone or blue with gold accents. Introduced 1992. Made in U.S.A. by Taurus International.
Price: 22 LR, 25 ACP, blue, nickel or with duo-tone finish with rosewood grips **$219.00**
Price: 22 LR, 25 ACP, blue with gold trim, rosewood grips **$234.00**
Price: 22 LR, 25 ACP, blue, nickel or duo-tone finish with checkered wood grips **$219.00**
Price: 22 LR, 25 ACP, blue with gold trim, mother-of-pearl grips . . **$250.00**

TAURUS MODEL PT-24/7
Caliber: 9mm, 10+1 shot; 40 cal., 10+1 shot. **Barrel:** 4". **Weight:** 27.2 oz. **Length:** 7-18". **Grips:** RIBBER rubber-finned overlay on polymer. **Sights:** Adjustable. **Features:** Accessory rail, four safeties, blue or stainless finish. Introduced 2003. Imported from Brazil by Taurus International.
Price: 9mm **$578.00**
Price: 40 cal. **$594.00**

TAURUS MODEL PT-92 AUTO PISTOL
Caliber: 9mm Para., 10-shot mag. **Barrel:** 5". **Weight:** 34 oz. **Length:** 8.5" overall. **Grips:** Checkered rubber, rosewood, mother-of-pearl. **Sights:** Fixed notch rear. 3-dot sight system. Also offered with micrometer-click adjustable night sights. **Features:** Double action, ambidextrous 3-way hammer drop safety, allows cocked & locked carry. Blue, stainless steel, blue with gold highlights, stainless steel with gold highlights, forged aluminum frame, integral key-lock. .22 LR conversion kit available. Imported from Brazil by Taurus International.
Price: Blue . . . . **$578.00 to $672.00**

Taurus Model PT-99 Auto Pistol
Similar to PT-92, fully adjustable rear sight.
Price: Blue . . . . **$575.00 to $670.00**
Price: 22 Conversion kit for PT 92 and PT99 (includes barrel and slide) **$266.00**

TAURUS MODEL PT-100/101 AUTO PISTOL
Caliber: 40 S&W, 10-shot mag. **Barrel:** 5". **Weight:** 34 oz. **Length:** 8-1/2". **Grips:** Checkered rubber, rosewood, mother-of-pearl. **Sights:** 3-dot fixed or adjustable; night sights available. **Features:** Single/double action with three-position safety/decocker. Reintroduced in 2001. Imported by Taurus International.
Price: PT100 . . . . **$578.00 to $672.00**
Price: PT101 . . . . **$594.00 to $617.00**

TAURUS MODEL PT-111 MILLENNIUM PRO AUTO PISTOL
Caliber: 9mm Para., 10-shot mag. **Barrel:** 3.25". **Weight:** 18.7 oz. **Length:** 6-1/8" overall. **Grips:** Polymer. **Sights:** 3-dot fixed; night sights available. Low profile, 3-dot combat. **Features:** Double action only, polymer frame, matte stainless or blue steel slide, manual safety, integral key-lock. Deluxe models with wood grip inserts.
Price: . . . . **$445.00 to $539.00**

Taurus PT-132 Millennium Pro

Taurus PT-138 Millennium Pro

Taurus PT-140 Millennium Pro

Taurus PT-145 Millennium

Taurus PT-911

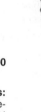

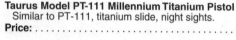

Taurus PT-938

Taurus PT-940

Taurus PT-945

Taurus Model PT-111 Millennium Titanium Pistol
Similar to PT-111, titanium slide, night sights.
Price: **$586.00**

TAURUS PT-132 MILLENNIUM PRO AUTO PISTOL
Caliber: 32 ACP, 10-shot mag. **Barrel:** 3.25". **Weight:** 18.7 oz. **Grips:** Polymer. **Sights:** 3-dot fixed; night sights available. **Features:** Double-action-only, polymer frame, matte stainless or blue steel slide, manual safety, integral key-lock action. Introduced 2001.
Price: . . . . **$445.00 to $461.00**

TAURUS PT-138 MILLENNIUM PRO SERIES
Caliber: 380 ACP, 10-shot mag. **Barrel:** 3.25". **Weight:** 18.7 oz. **Grips:** Polymer. **Sights:** Fixed 3-dot fixed. **Features:** Double-action-only, polymer frame, matte stainless or blue steel slide, manual safety, integral key-lock.
Price: . . . . **$445.00 to $461.00**

TAURUS PT-140 MILLENNIUM PRO AUTO PISTOL
Caliber: 40 S&W, 10-shot mag. **Barrel:** 3.25". **Weight:** 18.7 oz. **Grips:** Checkered polymer. **Sights:** 3-dot fixed; night sights available. **Features:** Double action only; matte stainless or blue steel slide, black polymer frame, manual safety, integral key-lock action. From Taurus International.
Price: . . . . **$484.00 to $578.00**

TAURUS PT-145 MILLENNIUM AUTO PISTOL
Caliber: 45 ACP, 10-shot mag. **Barrel:** 3.27". **Weight:** 23 oz. **Stock:** Checkered polymer. **Sights:** 3-dot fixed; night sights available. **Features:** Double-action only, matte stainless or blue steel slide, black polymer frame, manual safety, integral key-lock. From Taurus International.
Price: . . . . **$484.00 to $578.00**

TAURUS MODEL PT-911 AUTO PISTOL
Caliber: 9mm Para., 10-shot mag. **Barrel:** 4". **Weight:** 28.2 oz. **Length:** 7" overall. **Grips:** Checkered rubber, rosewood, mother-of-pearl. **Sights:** Fixed, 3-dot blue or stainless; night sights optional. **Features:** Double action, semi-auto ambidextrous 3-way hammer drop safety, allows cocked & locked carry. Blue, stainless steel, blue with gold highlights, or stainless steel with gold highlights, forged aluminum frame, integral key-lock.
Price: . . . . **$523.00 to $617.00**

TAURUS MODEL PT-938 AUTO PISTOL
Caliber: 380 ACP, 10-shot mag. **Barrel:** 3.72". **Weight:** 27 oz. **Length:** 6.5" overall. **Grips:** Checkered rubber. **Sights:** Fixed, 3-dot. **Features:** Double action, ambidextrous 3-way hammer drop allows cocked & locked carry. Forged aluminum frame. Integral key-lock. Imported by Taurus International.
Price: Blue **$516.00**
Price: Stainless **$531.00**

TAURUS MODEL PT-940 AUTO PISTOL
Caliber: 40 S&W, 10-shot mag. **Barrel:** 3-5/8". **Weight:** 28.2 oz. **Length:** 7" overall. **Grips:** Checkered rubber, rosewood or mother-of-pearl. **Sights:** Fixed, 3-dot blue or stainless; night sights optional. **Features:** Double action, semi-auto ambidextrous 3-way hammer drop safety, allows cocked & locked carry. Blue, stainless steel, blue with gold highlights, or stainless steel with gold hightlights, forged aluminum frame, integral key-lock.
Price: . . . . **$523.00 to $617.00**

TAURUS MODEL PT-945 SERIES
Caliber: 45 ACP, 8-shot mag. **Barrel:** 4.25". **Weight:** 28.2/29.5 oz. **Length:** 7.48" overall. **Grips:** Checkered rubber, rosewood or mother-of-pearl. **Sights:** Fixed, 3-dot; night sights optional. **Features:** Double-action with ambidextrous 3-way hammer drop safety allows cocked & locked carry. Forged aluminum frame, PT-945C has ported barrel/slide. Blue, stainless, blue with gold highlights, stainless with gold highlights, integral key-lock. Introduced 1995. Imported by Taurus International.
Price: . . . . **$563.00 to $641.00**

Taurus PT-957

Walther PPK

Walther PPK/S

Walther P99

Walther P22

Wilkinson Sherry

TAURUS MODEL PT-957 AUTO PISTOL

Caliber: 357 SIG, 10-shot mag. **Barrel:** 4". **Weight:** 28 oz. **Length:** 7" overall. **Grips:** Checkered rubber, rosewood or mother-of-pearl. **Sights:** Fixed, 3-dot blue or stainless; night sights optional. **Features:** Double-action, blue, stainless steel, blue with gold accents or stainless with gold accents, ported barrel/slide, three-position safety with decocking lever and ambidextrous safety. Forged aluminum frame, integral key-lock. Introduced 1999. Imported by Taurus International.

Price: . . . . **$525.00 to $620.00**

Price: Non-ported . . . . **$525.00 to $535.00**

TAURUS MODEL 922 SPORT PISTOL

Caliber: .22 LR, 10-shot magazine. **Barrel:** 6". **Weight:** 24.8 oz. **Length:** 9-1/8". **Grips:** Polymer. **Sights:** Adjustable. **Features:** Matte blue steel finish, machined target crown, polymer frame, single and double action, easy disassembly for cleaning.

Price: . . . . (blue) **$310.00**

Price: . . . . (stainless) **$328.00**

WALTHER PPK/S AMERICAN AUTO PISTOL

Caliber: 380 ACP, 7-shot magazine. **Barrel:** 3.27". **Weight:** 23-1/2 oz. **Length:** 6.1" overall. **Stocks:** Checkered plastic. **Sights:** Fixed, white markings. **Features:** Double action; manual safety blocks firing pin and drops hammer; chamber loaded indicator on 32 and 380; extra finger rest magazine provided. Made in the United States. Introduced 1980.

Price: 380 ACP only, blue **$563.00**

Price: As above, 32 ACP or 380 ACP, stainless **$543.00**

Walther PPK American Auto Pistol

Similar to Walther PPK/S except weighs 21 oz., has 6-shot capacity. Made in the U.S. Introduced 1986.

Price: Stainless, 32 ACP or 380 ACP **$543.00**

Price: Blue, 380 ACP only **$543.00**

WALTHER P99 AUTO PISTOL

Caliber: 9mm Para., 9x21, 40 S&W,10-shot magazine. **Barrel:** 4". **Weight:** 25 oz. **Length:** 7" overall. **Grips:** Textured polymer. **Sights:** Blade front (comes with three interchangeable blades for elevation adjustment), micrometer rear adjustable for windage. **Features:** Double-action mechanism with trigger safety, decock safety, internal striker safety; chamber loaded indicator; ambidextrous magazine release levers; polymer frame with interchangeable backstrap inserts. Comes with two magazines. Introduced 1997. Imported from Germany by Smith & Wesson U.S.A.

Price: **$665.00**

WALTHER P22 PISTOL

Caliber: 22 LR. **Barrel:** 3.4", 5". **Weight:** 19.6 oz. (3.4"), 20.3 oz. (5"). **Length:** 6.26", 7.83". **Grips:** NA. **Sights:** Interchangeable white dot, front, 2-dot adjustable, rear. **Features:** A rimfire version of the Walther P99 pistol, available in nickel slide with black frame, or green frame with black slide versions. Made in Germany and distributed in the U.S. by Smith & Wesson.

Price: From **$295.00**

WILKINSON SHERRY AUTO PISTOL

Caliber: 22 LR, 8-shot magazine. **Barrel:** 2-1/8". **Weight:** 9-1/4 oz. **Length:** 4-3/8" overall. **Grips:** Checkered black plastic. **Sights:** Fixed, groove. **Features:** Crossbolt safety locks the sear into the hammer. Available in all-blue finish or blue slide and trigger with gold frame. Introduced 1985.

Price: **$280.00**

WILKINSON LINDA AUTO PISTOL

Caliber: 9mm Para. **Barrel:** 8-5/16". **Weight:** 4 lbs., 13 oz. **Length:** 12-1/4" overall. **Grips:** Checkered black plastic pistol grip, walnut forend. **Sights:** Protected blade front, aperture rear. **Features:** Semi-auto only. Straight blowback action. Crossbolt safety. Removable barrel. From Wilkinson Arms.

Price: **$675.00**

CONSULT
SHOOTER'S MARKETPLACE
Page 141, This Issue

HANDGUNS — Competition

Includes models suitable for several forms of competition and other sporting purposes.

Baer 1911 Ultimate Master

Baer 1911 Bullseye Wadcutter

BF Ultimate

Browning Buck Mark Target 5.5

Browning Buck Mark Bullseye

BAER 1911 ULTIMATE MASTER COMBAT PISTOL
Caliber: 9x23, 38 Super, 400 Cor-Bon 45 ACP (others available), 10-shot magazine. **Barrel:** 5", 6"; Baer NM. **Weight:** 37 oz. **Length:** 8.5" overall. **Grips:** Checkered rosewood. **Sights:** Baer dovetail front, low-mount Bo-Mar rear with hidden leaf. **Features:** Full-house competition gun. Baer forged NM blued steel frame and double serrated slide; Baer triple port, tapered cone compensator; fitted slide to frame; lowered, flared ejection port; Baer reverse recoil plug; full-length guide rod; recoil buff; beveled magazine well; Baer Commander hammer, sear; Baer extended ambidextrous safety, extended ejector, checkered slide stop, beavertail grip safety with pad, extended magazine release button; Baer speed trigger. Made in U.S.A. by Les Baer Custom, Inc.
Price: Compensated, open sights **$2,476.00**
Price: 6" Model 400 Cor-Bon **$2,541.00**

BAER 1911 NATIONAL MATCH HARDBALL PISTOL
Caliber: 45 ACP, 7-shot magazine. **Barrel:** 5". **Weight:** 37 oz. **Length:** 8.5" overall. **Grips:** Checkered walnut. **Sights:** Baer dovetail front with under-cut post, low-mount Bo-Mar rear with hidden leaf. **Features:** Baer NM forged steel frame, double serrated slide and barrel with stainless bushing; slide fitted to frame; Baer match trigger with 4-lb. pull; polished feed ramp, throated barrel; checkered front strap, arched mainspring housing; Baer beveled magazine well; lowered, flared ejection port; tuned extractor; Baer extended ejector, checkered slide stop; recoil buff. Made in U.S.A. by Les Baer Custom, Inc.
Price: **$1,335.00**

Baer 1911 Bullseye Wadcutter Pistol
Similar to National Match Hardball except designed for wadcutter loads only. Polished feed ramp and barrel throat; Bo-Mar rib on slide; full length recoil rod; Baer speed trigger with 3-1/2-lb. pull; Baer deluxe hammer and sear; Baer beavertail grip safety with pad; flat mainspring housing checkered 20 lpi. Blue finish; checkered walnut grips. Made in U.S.A. by Les Baer Custom, Inc.
Price: From **$1,495.00**
Price: With 6" barrel, from **$1,690.00**

BF ULTIMATE SILHOUETTE HB SINGLE SHOT PISTOL
Caliber: 7mm U.S., 22 LR Match and 100 other chamberings. **Barrel:** 10.75" Heavy Match Grade with 11-degree target crown. **Weight:** 3 lbs., 15 oz. **Length:** 16" overall. **Grips:** Thumbrest target style. **Sights:** Bo-Mar/Bond ScopeRib I Combo with hooded post front adjustable for height and width, rear notch available in .032", .062", .080" and .100" widths; 1/2-MOA clicks. **Features:** Designed to meet maximum rules for IHMSA Production Gun. Hand fitted and headspaced. Etched receiver; gold-colored trigger. Introduced 1988. Made in U.S.A. by E. Arthur Brown Co. Inc.
Price: **$669.00**

BF Classic Hunting Pistol
Similar to BF Ultimate Silhouette HB Single Shot Pistol, except no sights; drilled and tapped for scope mount. Barrels from 8" to 15". Variety of options offered. Made in U.S.A. by E. Arthur Brown Co. Inc.
Price: **$599.00**

BROWNING BUCK MARK TARGET 5.5
Caliber: 22 LR, 10-shot magazine. **Barrel:** 5-1/2" barrel with .900" diameter. **Weight:** 35-1/2 oz. **Length:** 9-5/8" overall. **Grips:** Contoured walnut grips with thumbrest, or finger-groove walnut. **Sights:** Hooded sights mounted on scope base that accepts optical or reflex sight. Rear sight is Browning fully adjustable Pro Target, front sight is adjustable post that customizes to different widths, can be adjusted for height. **Features:** Matte blue finish. Introduced 1990. From Browning.
Price: **$496.00**

Browning Buck Mark Field 5.5
Same as Target 5.5, hoodless ramp-style front sight and low profile rear sight. Matte blue finish, contoured or finger-groove walnut stocks. Introduced 1991.
Price: **$496.00**

Browning Buck Mark Bullseye
Similar to Buck Mark Silhouette, 7-1/4" heavy barrel with three flutes per side; trigger adjusts from 2-1/2 to 5 lbs.; specially designed rosewood target or three-finger-groove stocks with competition-style heel rest, or with contoured rubber grip. Overall length 11-5/16", weighs 36 oz. Introduced 1996. Made in U.S.A. From Browning.
Price: With ambidextrous moulded composite stocks **$468.00**
Price: With rosewood stocks, or wraparound finger groove **$604.00**

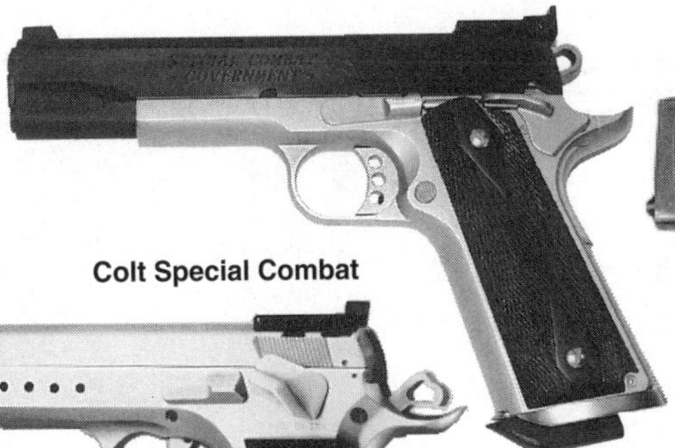

Colt Special Combat

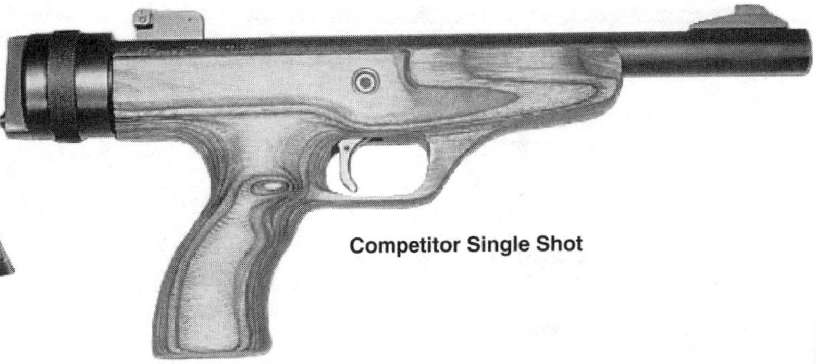

Competitor Single Shot

EAA Witness Gold Team

COLT DEFENDER XSE
Caliber: 45 ACP. **Barrel:** 3", 4.25" and 5". **Weight:** 23-40 oz. **Sights:** Fixed. **Features:** Rubber wraparound or rosewood grips; single-action; carbon or stainless steel; blue or stainless finish, 7- or 8-round magazines.
Price: Blue **$9500.00**
Price: Stainless **$1,100.00**

COLT GOLD CUP
Caliber: 45 ACP. **Barrel:** 5". **Weight:** 39 oz. **Sights:** Dovetail front, BoMar-style rear; or Colt adjustable staked front. **Features:** Stainless or blue finish; adjustable trigger; furnished with 7- and 8-round magazines.
Price: Blued **$1,300.00**
Price: Stainless **$1,400.00**

COLT GUNSITE PISTOL
Caliber: 45 ACP. **Barrel:** 5", 4.5". **Weight:** 38 to 36 oz. **Sights:** Heinie front, Novak rear. **Features:** Brushed stainless or blue finish; short trigger; Wilson safety; grip safety. Furnished with two 6- and 8-round magazines.
Price: **$1,400.00**

COLT COMBAT GOVERNMENT
Caliber: 45 ACP, 38 Super. **Barrel:** 5". **Weight:** 39 oz. **Sights:** Dovetail front, Bo-Mar-style rear. **Features:** Chromed or blued slide; ambidextrous thumb safety; 8-round standard with bumper magazines.
Price: **$2,000.00**

COLT MODEL 1991/2991
Caliber: 45 ACP, 28 Super. **Barrel:** 5". **Weight:** 39 oz. **Sight:** Fixed white dot style. **Features:** Stainless or blue finish; furnished with 7-round magazines.
Price: .... **$870.00 to $980.00**

COLT GOLD CUP MODEL O PISTOL
Caliber: 45 ACP, 8-shot magazine. **Barrel:** 5", with new design bushing. **Weight:** 39 oz. **Length:** 8-1/2". **Grips:** Checkered rubber composite with silver-plated medallion. **Sights:** Patridge-style front, Bo-Mar-style rear adjustable for windage and elevation, sight radius 6-3/4". **Features:** Arched or flat housing; wide, grooved trigger with adjustable stop; ribbed-top slide, hand fitted, with improved ejection port.
Price: Blue **$1,300.00**
Price: Stainless **$1,400.00**

COLT SPECIAL COMBAT GOVERNMENT
Caliber: 45 ACP. **Barrel:** 5". **Weight:** NA. **Length:** 8-1/2". **Grips:** Rosewood w/double diamond checkering pattern. **Sights:** Clark dovetail, front; Bo-Mar adjustable, rear. **Features:** A competition-ready pistol with enhancements such as skeletonized trigger, upswept grip safety, custom tuned action, polished feed ramp. Blue or satin nickel finish. Introduced 2003. Made in U.S.A. by Colt's Mfg. Co.
Price: **$2,000.00**

COMPETITOR SINGLE SHOT PISTOL
Caliber: 22 LR through 50 Action Express, including belted magnums. **Barrel:** 14" standard; 10.5" silhouette; 16" optional. **Weight:** About 59 oz. (14" bbl.). **Length:** 15.12" overall. **Grips:** Ambidextrous; synthetic (standard) or laminated or natural wood. **Sights:** Ramp front, adjustable rear. **Features:** Rotary canon-type action cocks on opening; cammed ejector; interchangeable barrels, ejectors. Adjustable single stage trigger, sliding thumb safety and trigger safety. Matte blue finish. Introduced 1988. From Competitor Corp., Inc.
Price: 14", standard calibers, synthetic grip **$414.95**
Price: Extra barrels .... **From $159.95**

CZ 75 CHAMPION COMPETITION PISTOL
Caliber: 9mm Para., 9x21, 40 S&W, 10-shot mag. **Barrel:** 4.49". **Weight:** 35 oz. **Length:** 9.44" overall. **Grips:** Black rubber. **Sights:** Blade front, fully adjustable rear. **Features:** Single-action trigger mechanism; three-port compensator (40 S&W, 9mm have two port) full-length guide rod; extended magazine release; ambidextrous safety; flared magazine well; fully adjustable match trigger. Introduced 1999. Imported from the Czech Republic by CZ-USA.
Price: 9mm Para., 9x21, 40 S&W, dual-tone finish **$1,551.00**

CZ 75 ST IPSC AUTO PISTOL
Caliber: 40 S&W, 10-shot magazine. **Barrel:** 5.12". **Weight:** 2.9 lbs. **Length:** 8.86" overall. **Grips:** Checkered walnut. **Sights:** Fully adjustable rear. **Features:** Single-action mechanism; extended slide release and ambidextrous safety; full-length slide rail; double slide serrations. Introduced 1999. Imported from the Czech Republic by CZ-USA.
Price: Dual-tone finish **$1,038.00**

EAA/BAIKAL IZH-35 AUTO PISTOL
Caliber: 22 LR, 5-shot mag. **Barrel:** 6". **Grips:** Walnut; fully adjustable right-hand target-style. **Sights:** Fully adjustable rear, blade front; detachable scope mount. **Features:** Hammer-forged target barrel; machined steel receiver; adjustable trigger; manual slide hold back, grip and manual trigger-bar disconnect safeties; cocking indicator. Introduced 2000. Imported from Russia by European American Armory.
Price: Blued finish **$489.00**

EAA WITNESS GOLD TEAM AUTO
Caliber: 9mm Para., 9x21, 38 Super, 40 S&W, 45 ACP. **Barrel:** 5.1". **Weight:** 44 oz. **Length:** 10.5" overall. **Grips:** Checkered walnut, competition-style. **Sights:** Square post front, fully adjustable rear. **Features:** Triple-chamber cone compensator; competition SA trigger; extended safety and magazine release; competition hammer; beveled magazine well; beavertail grip. Hand-fitted major components. Hard chrome finish. Match-grade barrel. From E.A.A. Custom Shop. Introduced 1992. From European American Armory.
Price: **$1,699.00**

EAA Witness Silver Team Auto
Similar to Witness Gold Team with double-chamber compensator, oval magazine release, black rubber grips, double-dip blue finish. Super Sight and drilled and tapped for scope mount. Introduced 1992. From European American Armory Custom Shop.
Price: 9mm Para., 9x21, 38 Super, 40 S&W, 45 ACP **$968.00**

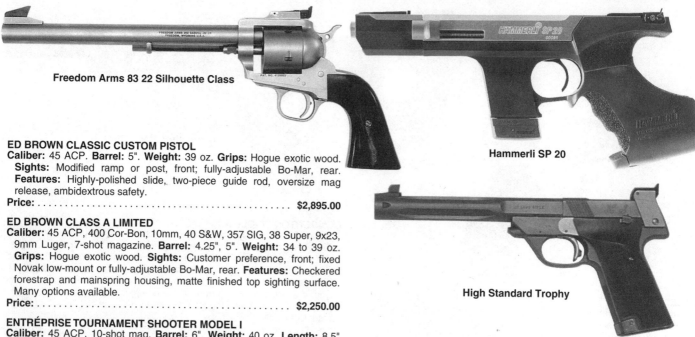

HANDGUNS — Competition

Freedom Arms 83 22 Silhouette Class

Hammerli SP 20

High Standard Trophy

ED BROWN CLASSIC CUSTOM PISTOL
Caliber: 45 ACP. **Barrel:** 5". **Weight:** 39 oz. **Grips:** Hogue exotic wood. **Sights:** Modified ramp or post, front; fully-adjustable Bo-Mar, rear. **Features:** Highly-polished slide, two-piece guide rod, oversize mag release, ambidextrous safety.
Price: **$2,895.00**

ED BROWN CLASS A LIMITED
Caliber: 45 ACP, 400 Cor-Bon, 10mm, 40 S&W, 357 SIG, 38 Super, 9x23, 9mm Luger, 7-shot magazine. **Barrel:** 4.25", 5". **Weight:** 34 to 39 oz. **Grips:** Hogue exotic wood. **Sights:** Customer preference, front; fixed Novak low-mount or fully-adjustable Bo-Mar, rear. **Features:** Checkered forestrap and mainspring housing, matte finished top sighting surface. Many options available.
Price: **$2,250.00**

ENTRÉPRISE TOURNAMENT SHOOTER MODEL I
Caliber: 45 ACP, 10-shot mag. **Barrel:** 6". **Weight:** 40 oz. **Length:** 8.5" overall. **Grips:** Black ultra-slim double diamond checkered synthetic. **Sights:** Dovetailed Patridge front, adjustable rear. **Features:** Oversized magazine release button; flared magazine well; fully machined parallel slide rails; front and rear slide serrations; serrated top of slide; stainless ramped bull barrel with fully supported chamber; full-length guide rod with plug; stainless firing pin; match extractor; polished ramp; tuned match extractor; black oxide. Introduced 1998. Made in U.S.A. by Entréprise Arms.
Price: **$2,300.00**
Price: TSMIII (Satin chrome finish, two-piece guide rod) **$2,700.00**

EXCEL INDUSTRIES CP-45, XP-45 AUTO PISTOL
Caliber: 45 ACP, 6-shot & 10-shot mags. **Barrel:** 3-1/4". **Weight:** 31 oz. & 25 oz. **Length:** 6-3/8" overall. **Grips:** Checkered black nylon. **Sights:** Fully adjustable rear. **Features:** Stainless steel frame and slide; single action with external hammer and firing pin block, manual thumb safety; last-shot hold open. Includes gun lock and cleaning kit. Introduced 2001. Made in U.S.A. by Excel Industries Inc.
Price: CP-45 . . . . **$425.00**
Price: XP-45 . . . . **$465.00**

FEINWERKEBAU AW93 TARGET PISTOL
Caliber: 22. **Barrel:** 6". **Grips:** Fully adjustable orthopaedic. **Sights:** Fully adjustable micrometer. **Features:** Advanced Russian design with German craftmanship. Imported from Germany by Nygord Precision Products.
Price: **$1,495.00**

FREEDOM ARMS MODEL 83 22 FIELD GRADE SILHOUETTE CLASS
Caliber: 22 LR, 5-shot cylinder. **Barrel:** 10". **Weight:** 63 oz. **Length:** 15.5" overall. **Grips:** Black Micarta. **Sights:** Removable Patridge front blade; Iron Sight Gun Works silhouette rear, click adjustable for windage and elevation (optional adj. front sight and hood). **Features:** Stainless steel, matte finish, manual sliding-bar safety system; dual firing pins, lightened hammer for fast lock time, pre-set trigger stop. Introduced 1991. Made in U.S.A. by Freedom Arms.
Price: Silhouette Class **$1,901.75**
Price: Extra fitted 22 WMR cylinder **$264.00**

FREEDOM ARMS MODEL 83 CENTERFIRE SILHOUETTE MODELS
Caliber: 357 Mag., 41 Mag., 44 Mag.; 5-shot cylinder. **Barrel:** 10", 9" (357 Mag. only). **Weight:** 63 oz. (41 Mag.). **Length:** 15.5", 14-1/2" (357 only). **Grips:** Pachmayr Presentation. **Sights:** Iron Sight Gun Works silhouette rear sight, replaceable adjustable front sight blade with hood. **Features:** Stainless steel, matte finish, manual sliding-bar safety system. Made in U.S.A. by Freedom Arms.
Price: Silhouette Models **$1,634.85**

GAUCHER GP SILHOUETTE PISTOL
Caliber: 22 LR, single shot. **Barrel:** 10". **Weight:** 42.3 oz. **Length:** 15.5" overall. **Grips:** Stained hardwood. **Sights:** Hooded post on ramp front, open rear adjustable for windage and elevation. **Features:** Matte chrome barrel, blued bolt and sights. Other barrel lengths available on special order. Introduced 1991. Imported by Mandall Shooting Supplies.
Price: **$425.00**

HAMMERLI SP 20 TARGET PISTOL
Caliber: 22 LR, 32 S&W. **Barrel:** 4.6". **Weight:** 34.6-41.8 oz. **Length:** 11.8" overall. **Grips:** Anatomically shaped synthetic Hi-Grip available in five sizes. **Sights:** Integral front in three widths, adjustable rear with changeable notch widths. **Features:** Extremely low-level sight line; anatomically shaped trigger; adjustable JPS buffer system for different recoil characteristics. Receiver available in red, blue, gold, violet or black. Introduced 1998. Imported from Switzerland by SIGARMS, Inc and Hammerli Pistols USA.
Price: Hammerli 22 LR **$1,668.00**
Price: Hammerli 32 S&W **$1,743.00**

HAMMERLI X-ESSE SPORT PISTOL
An all-steel .22 LR target pistol with a Hi-Grip in a new anatomical shape and an adjustable hand rest. Made in Switzerland. Introduced 2003.
Price: **$710.00**

HARRIS GUNWORKS SIGNATURE JR. LONG RANGE PISTOL
Caliber: Any suitable caliber. **Barrel:** To customer specs. **Weight:** 5 lbs. **Stock:** Gunworks fiberglass. **Sights:** None furnished; comes with scope rings. **Features:** Right- or left-hand benchrest action of titanium or stainless steel; single shot or repeater. Comes with bipod. Introduced 1992. Made in U.S.A. by Harris Gunworks, Inc.
Price: **$2,700.00**

HIGH STANDARD TROPHY TARGET PISTOL
Caliber: 22 LR, 10-shot mag. **Barrel:** 5-1/2" bull or 7-1/4" fluted. **Weight:** 44 oz. **Length:** 9.5" overall. **Stock:** Checkered hardwood with thumbrest. **Sights:** Undercut ramp front, frame-mounted micro-click rear adjustable for windage and elevation; drilled and tapped for scope mounting. **Features:** Gold-plated trigger, slide lock, safety-lever and magazine release; stippled front grip and backstrap; adjustable trigger and sear. Barrel weights optional. From High Standard Manufacturing Co., Inc.
Price: 5-1/2", scope base **$540.00**
Price: 7.25" **$689.00**
Price: 7.25", scope base **$625.00**

HANDGUNS — Competition

High Standard Victor

Kimber Super Match II

HIGH STANDARD VICTOR TARGET PISTOL
Caliber: 22 LR, 10-shot magazine. **Barrel:** 4-1/2" or 5-1/2"; push-button takedown. **Weight:** 46 oz. **Length:** 9.5" overall. **Stock:** Checkered hardwood with thumbrest. **Sights:** Undercut ramp front, micro-click rear adjustable for windage and elevation. Also available with scope mount, rings, no sights. **Features:** Stainless steel construction. Full-length vent rib. Gold-plated trigger, slide lock, safety-lever and magazine release; stippled front grip and backstrap; polished slide; adjustable trigger and sear. Comes with barrel weight. From High Standard Manufacturing Co., Inc.
Price: 4-1/2" scope base **$564.00**
Price: 5-1/2", sights **$625.00**
Price: 5-1/2" scope base **$564.00**

KIMBER SUPER MATCH II
Caliber: 45 ACP, 7-shot magazine. **Barrel:** 5". **Weight:** 38 oz. **Length:** 18.7" overall. **Sights:** Blade front, Kimber fully adjustable rear. **Features:** Guaranteed shoot 1" group at 25 yards. Stainless steel frame, black KimPro slide; two-piece magazine well; premium aluminum match-grade trigger; 30 lpi front strap checkering; stainless match-grade barrel; ambidextrous safety; special Custom Shop markings. Introduced 1999. Made in U.S.A. by Kimber Mfg., Inc.
Price: **$1,986.00**

KORTH MATCH REVOLVER
Caliber: 357 Mag., 38 Special, 32 S&W Long, 9mm Para., 22 WMR, 22 LR. **Barrel:** 5-1/4", 6". **Grips:** Adjustable match of oiled walnut with matte finish. **Sights:** Fully adjustable rear sight leaves (width of sight notch: 3.4mm, 3.5mm, 3.6mm); undercut Patridge, front. Trigger: Equipped with machined trigger shoe. Interchangeable caliber cylinders available as well as a variety of finishes. Made in Germany.
Price: From **$7,619.00**

MORINI MODEL 84E FREE PISTOL
Caliber: 22 LR, single shot. **Barrel:** 11.4". **Weight:** 43.7 oz. **Length:** 19.4" overall. **Grips:** Adjustable match type with stippled surfaces. **Sights:** Interchangeable blade front, match-type fully adjustable rear. **Features:** Fully adjustable electronic trigger. Introduced 1995. Imported from Switzerland by Nygord Precision Products.
Price: **$1,450.00**

PARDINI MODEL SP, HP TARGET PISTOLS
Caliber: 22 LR, 32 S&W, 5-shot magazine. **Barrel:** 4.7". **Weight:** 38.9 oz. **Length:** 11.6" overall. **Grips:** Adjustable; stippled walnut; match type. **Sights:** Interchangeable blade front, interchangeable, fully adjustable rear. **Features:** Fully adjustable match trigger. Introduced 1995. Imported from Italy by Nygord Precision Products.
Price: Model SP (22 LR) **$995.00**
Price: Model HP (32 S&W) **$1,095.00**

PARDINI GP RAPID FIRE MATCH PISTOL
Caliber: 22 Short, 5-shot magazine. **Barrel:** 4.6". **Weight:** 43.3 oz. **Length:** 11.6" overall. **Grips:** Wraparound stippled walnut. **Sights:** Interchangeable post front, fully adjustable match rear. Introduced 1995. Imported from Italy by Nygord Precision Products.
Price: Model GP **$1,095.00**
Price: Model GP-E Electronic, has special parts **$1,595.00**

PARDINI K22 FREE PISTOL
Caliber: 22 LR, single shot. **Barrel:** 9.8". **Weight:** 34.6 oz. **Length:** 18.7" overall. **Grips:** Wrap-around walnut; adjustable match type. **Sights:** Interchangeable post front, fully adjustable match open rear. **Features:** Removable, adjustable match trigger. Barrel weights mount above the barrel. Upgraded model introduced in 2002. Imported from Italy by Nygord Precision Products.
Price: **$1,295.00**

PARDINI GT45 TARGET PISTOL
Caliber: 45, 9mm, 40 S&W. **Barrel:** 5", 6". **Grips:** Checkered forestrap. **Sights:** Interchangeable post front, fully adjustable match open rear. **Features:** Ambi-safeties, trigger pull adjustable. Fits Helweg Glock holsters for defense shooters. Imported from Italy by Nygord Precision Products.
Price: 5" **$1,050.00**
Price: 6" **$1,125.00**
Price: Frame mount available .... **$75.00 extra**
Price: Slide mount available .... **$35.00 extra**

PARDINI/NYGORD "MASTER" TARGET PISTOL
Caliber: 22 cal. **Barrel:** 5-1/2". **Grips:** Semi-wraparound. **Sights:** Micrometer rear and red dot. **Features:** Reciprocating internal weight barrel shroud. Imported from Italy by Nygord Precision Products.
Price: **$1,145.00**

RUGER MARK III TARGET MODEL AUTOLOADING PISTOL
Caliber: 22 LR, 10-shot magazine. **Barrel:** 6-7/8". **Weight:** 42 oz. **Length:** 11-1/8" overall. **Grips:** Checkered composition grip panels. **Sights:** .125" blade front, micro-click rear, adjustable for windage and elevation, loaded chamber indicator; integral lock, magazine disconnect. Sight radius 9-3/8". Plastic case with lock included. **Features:** Introduced 1982.
Price: Blued (MK-678) **$382.00**
Price: Stainless models .... **$483.00 to $567.00**

Ruger Mark III Government Target Model
Same gun as Mark III Target Model except has 6-7/8" barrel, higher sights and is roll marked "Government Target Model" on right side of receiver below rear sight. Identical in all aspects to military model except markings. Comes with factory test target, also lockable plastic case. Introduced 1987.
Price: Blued (MK-678G) **$425.00**
Price: Stainless (KMK-678G) **$509.00**

Ruger Stainless Competition Model Pistol
Similar to Mark III Government Target Model stainless pistol, 6-7/8" slab-sided barrel; receiver top is fitted with Ruger scope base of blued, chrome-moly steel; has Ruger 1" stainless scope rings for mounting variety of optical sights; checkered laminated grip panels with right-hand thumbrest. Blued open sights with 9-1/4" radius. Overall length 11-1/8", weight 45 oz. Case and lock included. Introduced 1991.
Price: KMK III 678 and 678 GC .... **$382.00 to $555.00**

Ruger Mark III Bull Barrel
Same gun as Target Model except has 5-1/2" or 10" heavy barrel. Weight with 5-1/2" barrel is 42 oz. Case with lock included.
Price: Blued (MKIII-512) **$382.00**
Price: Stainless (KMKIII-512) **$483.00**

HANDGUNS — Competition

Smith & Wesson Model 41

Smith & Wesson Model 22A

Smith & Wesson Model 22S

Springfield, Inc. 1911A1
Bullseye Wadcutter

SAFARI ARMS BIG DEUCE PISTOL

Caliber: 45 ACP, 7-shot magazine. **Barrel:** 6", 416 stainless steel. **Weight:** 40.3 oz. **Length:** 9.5" overall. **Grips:** Smooth walnut. **Sights:** Ramped blade front, LPA adjustable rear. **Features:** Beavertail grip safety; extended thumb safety and slide release; Commander-style hammer. Throated, polished and tuned. Parkerized matte black slide with satin stainless steel frame. Introduced 1995. Made in U.S.A. by Safari Arms, Inc.

Price: **$714.00**

SMITH & WESSON MODEL 41 TARGET

Caliber: 22 LR, 10-shot clip. **Barrel:** 5-1/2", 7". **Weight:** 41 oz. (5-1/2" barrel). **Length:** 10-1/2" overall (5-1/2" barrel). **Grips:** Checkered walnut with modified thumbrest, usable with either hand. **Sights:** 1/8" Patridge on ramp base; micro-click rear adjustable for windage and elevation. **Features:** 3/8" wide, grooved trigger; adjustable trigger stop drilled and tapped.

Price: S&W Bright Blue, either barrel **$1,062.00**

SMITH & WESSON MODEL 22A TARGET PISTOL

Caliber: 22 LR, 10-shot magazine. **Barrel:** 5-1/2" bull. **Weight:** 39 oz. **Length:** 9-1/2" overall. **Grips:** Dymondwood® with ambidextrous thumbrests and flared bottom or rubber soft touch with thumbrest. **Sights:** Patridge front, fully adjustable rear. **Features:** Sight bridge with Weaver-style integral optics mount; alloy frame, stainless barrel and slide; blue finish. Introduced 1997. Made in U.S.A. by Smith & Wesson.

Price: **$407.00**
Price: HiViz front sight **$429.00**
Price: Camo model **$367.00**
Price: Two-tone model **$401.00**
Price: Light barrel model **$324.00**
Price: 4" bbl. **$293.00**
Price: 7" bbl. **$367.00**

Smith & Wesson Model 22S Target Pistol

Similar to the Model 22A except has stainless steel frame. Introduced 1997. Made in U.S.A. by Smith & Wesson.

Price: **$434.00**
Price: HiViz front sight **$453.00**

SPRINGFIELD ARMORY 1911A1 BULLSEYE WADCUTTER PISTOL

Caliber: 38 Super, 45 ACP. **Barrel:** 5". **Weight:** 45 oz. **Length:** 8.59" overall (5" barrel). **Grips:** Checkered walnut. **Sights:** Bo-Mar rib with undercut blade front, fully adjustable rear. **Features:** Built for wadcutter loads only. Has full-length recoil spring guide rod, fitted Videki speed trigger with 3.5-lb. pull; match Commander hammer and sear; beavertail grip safety; lowered and flared ejection port; tuned extractor; fitted slide to frame; recoil buffer system; beveled and polished magazine well; checkered front strap and steel mainspring housing (flat housing standard); polished and throated National Match barrel and bushing. Comes with two magazines, plastic carrying case, test target. Introduced 1992. From Springfield Armory.

Price: **$1,499.00**
Price: Adj. Target **$1,049.00**
Price: M1911SC, Commander-style **$1,029.00**

Springfield Armory Basic Competition Pistol

Has low-mounted Bo-Mar adjustable rear sight, undercut blade front; match throated barrel and bushing; polished feed ramp; lowered and flared ejection port; fitted Videki speed trigger with tuned 3.5-lb. pull; fitted slide to frame; recoil buffer system; checkered walnut grips; serrated, arched mainspring housing. Comes with two magazines with slam pads, plastic carrying case. Introduced 1992. From Springfield Armory.

Price: 45 ACP, blue, 5" only **$1,295.00**

CONSULT
SHOOTER'S MARKETPLACE
Page 141, This Issue

Springfield, Inc. Expert

Springfield, Inc. 1911A1 Trophy Match

Springfield, Inc. N.M. Hardball

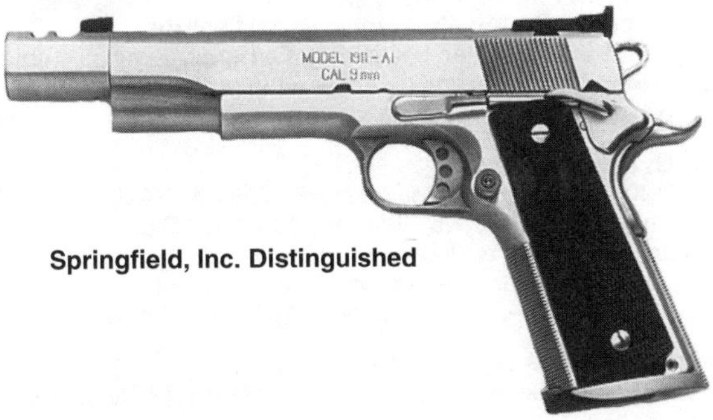

Springfield, Inc. Distinguished

Springfield Armory Expert Pistol
Similar to the Competition Pistol except has triple-chamber tapered cone compensator on match barrel with dovetailed front sight; lowered and flared ejection port; fully tuned for reliability; fitted slide to frame; extended ambidextrous thumb safety, extended magazine release button; beavertail grip safety; Pachmayr wraparound grips. Comes with two magazines, plastic carrying case. Introduced 1992. From Springfield Armory.

Price: 45 ACP, Duo-tone finish **$1,724.00**
Price: Expert Ltd. (non-compensated) **$1,624.00**

Springfield Armory Distinguished Pistol
Has all the features of the 1911A1 Expert except is full-house pistol with deluxe Bo-Mar low-mounted adjustable rear sight; full-length recoil spring guide rod and recoil spring retainer; checkered frontstrap; S&A magazine well; walnut grips. Hard chrome finish. Comes with two magazines, plastic carrying case. From Springfield Armory

Price: 45 ACP **$2,445.00**
Price: Distinguished Limited (non-compensated) **$2,345.00**

Springfield Armory 1911A1 N.M. Hardball Pistol
Has Bo-Mar adjustable rear sight with undercut front blade; fitted match Videki trigger with 4-lb. pull; fitted slide to frame; throated National Match barrel and bushing; recoil buffer system; tuned extractor; Herrett walnut grips. Comes with two magazines, plastic carrying case, test target. Introduced 1992. From Springfield Armory

Price: 45 ACP, blue **$1,336.00**

Springfield Armory Leatham Legend TGO Series Pistols
Three models of 5" barrel, 45 ACP 1911 pistols built for serious competition. TGO 1 has deluxe low mount Bo-Mar rear sight, Dawson fiber optics front sight, 3.5 lb. trigger pull. TGO 2 has Bo-Mar low mount adjustable rear sight, Dawson fiber optic front sight, 4.5 to 5 lb. trigger pull. TGO 3 has Springfield Armory fully adjustable rear sight with low mount BoMar cut Dawson fiber optic front sight, 4.5 to 5 lb. trigger.

Price: TGO 1 . . . . **$2,999.00**
Price: TGO 2 . . . . **$1,899.00**
Price: TGO 3 . . . . **$1,295.00**

Springfield Armory Trophy Match Pistol
Similar to Springfield Armory's Full Size model, but designed for bullseye and action shooting competition. Available with a Service Model 5" frame with matching slide and barrel in 5" and 6" lengths. Fully adjustable sights, checkered frame front strap, match barrel and bushing. In 45 ACP only. From Springfield Inc.

Price: **$1,248.00**

STI EAGLE 5.0, 6.0 PISTOL
Caliber: 9mm, 9x21, 38 & 40 Super, 40 S&W, 10mm, 45 ACP, 10-shot magazine. **Barrel:** 5", 6" bull. **Weight:** 34.5 oz. **Length:** 8.62" overall. **Grips:** Checkered polymer. **Sights:** STI front, Novak or Heine rear. **Features:** Standard frames plus 7 others; adjustable match trigger; skeletonized hammer; extended grip safety with locator pad. Introduced 1994. Made in U.S.A. by STI International.

Price: . . . . (5.0 Eagle) **$1,794.00**, (6.0 Eagle) **$1,894.00**

STI EXECUTIVE PISTOL
Caliber: 40 S&W. **Barrel:** 5" bull. **Weight:** 39 oz. **Length:** 8-5/8". **Grips:** Gray polymer. **Sights:** Dawson fiber optic, front; STI adjustable rear. **Features:** Stainless mag. well, front and rear serrations on slide. Made in U.S.A. by STI.

Price: **$2,389.00**

STI TROJAN
Caliber: 9mm, 38 Super, 40S&W, 45 ACP. **Barrel:** 5", 6". **Weight:** 36 oz. **Length:** 8.5". **Grips:** Rosewood. **Sights:** STI front with STI adjustable rear. **Features:** Stippled front strap, flat top slide, one-piece steel guide rod.

Price: (Trojan 5") **$1,024.00**
Price: (Trojan 6", not available in 38 Super) **$1,232.50**

WALTHER GSP MATCH PISTOL
Caliber: 22 LR, 32 S&W Long (GSP-C), 5-shot magazine. **Barrel:** 4.22". **Weight:** 44.8 oz. (22 LR), 49.4 oz. (32). **Length:** 11.8" overall. **Grips:** Walnut. **Sights:** Post front, match rear adjustable for windage and elevation. **Features:** Available with either 2.2-lb. (1000 gm) or 3-lb. (1360 gm) trigger. Spare magazine, barrel weight, tools supplied. Imported from Germany by Nygord Precision Products.

Price: GSP, with case **$1,495.00**
Price: GSP-C, with case **$1,595.00**

Includes models suitable for hunting and competitive courses of fire, both police and international.

Comanche III

Dan Wesson Firearms Model 445 Supermag

ARMSPORT MODEL 4540 REVOLVER
Caliber: 38 Special. **Barrel:** 4". **Weight:** 32 oz. **Length:** 9" overall. **Sights:** Fixed rear, blade front. **Features:** Ventilated rib; blued finish. Imported from Argentina by Armsport Inc.
Price: **$140.00**

COLT SINGLE-ACTION ARMY
Caliber: 32-20, 38 Special, 357 Magnum, 38-40, 44-4-, 44 Special, 45 Long Colt. **Barrel:** 4.7 5", 5.5", 7.5". **Weight:** 40-44 oz. **Sights:** Blade front, notch rear. **Features:** Available in black powder and sheriff's models; nickel, blued or case-hardened frame; 6-round cylinder.
Price: .... (Blued) **$1,380.00;** (Stainless) **$1,530.00**

COMANCHE I, II, III DA REVOLVERS
Features: Adjustable sights. Blue or stainless finish. Distributed by SGS Importers.
Price: I 22 LR, 6" bbl., 9-shot, blue **$236.95**
Price: I 22LR, 6" bbl., 9-shot, stainless **$258.95**
Price: II 38 Special, 3", 4" bbl., 6-shot, blue **$219.95**
Price: II 38 Special, 4" bbl., 6-shot, stainless **$236.95**
Price: III 357 Mag, 3", 4", 6" bbl., 6-shot, blue **$253.95**
Price: III 357 Mag, 3", 4", 6" bbl., 6-shot, stainless **$274.95**
Price: II 38 Special, 3" bbl., 6-shot, stainless steel **$236.95**

DAN WESSON FIREARMS MODEL 722 SILHOUETTE REVOLVER
Caliber: 22 LR, 6-shot. **Barrel:** 10" vented heavy. **Weight:** 53 oz. **Grips:** Combat style. **Sights:** Patridge-style front, .080" narrow notch rear. **Features:** Single action only. Satin brushed stainless finish. Reintroduced 1997. Made in U.S.A. by Dan Wesson Firearms.
Price: 722 VH10 (vent heavy 10" bbl.) **$888.00**
Price: 722 VH10 SRS1 (Super Ram Silhouette, Bo-Mar sights, front hood, trigger job) **$1,164.00**

DAN WESSON FIREARMS MODEL 3220/73220 TARGET REVOLVER
Caliber: 32-20, 6-shot. **Barrel:** 2.5", 4", 6", 8", 10" standard vent, vent heavy. **Weight:** 47 oz. (6" VH). **Length:** 11.25" overall. **Grips:** Hogue Gripper rubber (walnut, exotic hardwoods optional). **Sights:** Red ramp interchangeable front, fully adjustable rear. **Features:** Bright blue (3220) or stainless (73220). Reintroduced 1997. Made in U.S.A. by Dan Wesson Firearms.
Price: 3220 VH2.5 (blued, 2.5" vent heavy bbl.) **$643.00**
Price: 73220 VH10 (stainless 10" vent heavy bbl.) **$873.00**

DAN WESSON FIREARMS MODEL 40/740 REVOLVERS
Caliber: 357 Maximum, 6-shot. **Barrel:** 4", 6", 8", 10". **Weight:** 72 oz. (8" bbl.). **Length:** 14.3" overall (8" bbl.). **Grips:** Hogue Gripper rubber (walnut or exotic hardwood optional). **Sights:** 1/8" serrated front, fully adjustable rear. **Features:** Blue or stainless steel. Made in U.S.A. by Dan Wesson Firearms.
Price: Blue, 4" **$702.00**
Price: Blue, 6" **$749.00**
Price: Blue, 8" **$795.00**
Price: Blue, 10" **$858.00**
Price: Stainless, 4" **$834.00**
Price: Stainless, 6" **$892.00**
Price: Stainless, 8" slotted **$1,024.00**
Price: Stainless, 10" **$998.00**
Price: 4", 6", 8" Compensated, blue .... **$749.00 to $885.00**
Price: As above, stainless .... **$893.00 to $1,061.00**

Dan Wesson Firearms Model 414/7414 and 445/7445 SuperMag Revolvers
Similar size and weight as Model 40 revolvers. Chambered for 414 SuperMag or 445 SuperMag cartridge. Barrel lengths of 4", 6", 8", 10". Contact maker for complete price list. Reintroduced 1997. Made in the U.S.A. by Dan Wesson Firearms.
Price: 4", vent heavy, blue or stainless **$904.00**
Price: 8", vent heavy, blue or stainless **$1,026.00**
Price: 10", vent heavy, blue or stainless **$1,103.00**
Price: Compensated models .... **$965.00 to $1,149.00**

DAN WESSON FIREARMS MODEL 22/722 REVOLVERS
Caliber: 22 LR, 22 WMR, 6-shot. **Barrel:** 2-1/2", 4", 6", 8" or 10"; interchangeable. **Weight:** 36 oz. (2-1/2"), 44 oz. (6"). **Length:** 9-1/4" overall (4" barrel). **Grips:** Hogue Gripper rubber (walnut, exotic woods optional). **Sights:** 1/8" serrated, interchangeable front, white outline rear adjustable for windage and elevation. **Features:** Built on the same frame as the Wesson 357; wide trigger with over-travel adjustment, wide spur hammer, with short double-action travel. Available in blue or stainless steel. Reintroduced 1997.
Price: 22 VH2.5/722 VH2.5 (blued or stainless 2-1/2" bbl.) **$551.00**
Price: 22VH10/722 VH10 (blued or stainless 10" bbl.) **$750.00**

Dan Wesson 722M Small Frame Revolver
Similar to Model 22/722 except chambered for 22 WMR. Blued or stainless finish, 2-1/2", 4", 6", 8" or 10" barrels.
Price: Blued or stainless finish .... **$643.00 to $873.00**

DAN WESSON FIREARMS MODEL 15/715 and 32/732 REVOLVERS
Caliber: 32-20, 32 H&R Mag. (Model 32), 357 Mag. (Model 15). **Barrel:** 2-1/2", 4", 6", 8" (M32), 2-1/2", 4", 6", 8", 10" (M15); vented heavy. **Weight:** 36 oz. (2-1/2" barrel). **Length:** 9-1/4" overall (4" barrel). **Grips:** Checkered, interchangeable. **Sights:** 1/8" serrated front, fully adjustable rear. **Fea-tures:** New Generation Series. Interchangeable barrels; wide, smooth trigger, wide hammer spur; short double-action travel. Available in blue or stainless. Reintroduced 1997. Made in U.S.A. by Dan Wesson Firearms.
Price: Model 15/715, 2-1/2" (blue or stainless) **$551.00**
Price: Model 15/715, 8" (blue or stainless) **$612.00**
Price: Model 15/715, compensated .... **$704.00 to $827.00**
Price: Model 32/732, 4" (blue or stainless) **$674.00**
Price: Model 32/732, 8" (blue or stainless) **$766.00**

DAN WESSON FIREARMS MODEL 41/741, 44/744 and 45/745 REVOLVERS
Caliber: 41 Mag., 44 Mag., 45 Colt, 6-shot. **Barrel:** 4", 6", 8", 10"; interchangeable; 4", 6", 8" compensated. **Weight:** 48 oz. (4"). **Length:** 12" overall (6" bbl.) **Grips:** Smooth. **Sights:** 1/8" serrated front, white outline rear adjustable for windage and elevation. **Features:** Available in blue or stainless steel. Smooth, wide trigger with adjustable over-travel, wide hammer spur. Available in Pistol Pac set also. Reintroduced 1997. Made in U.S.A. by Dan Wesson Firearms.
Price: 41 Mag., 4", vent heavy (blue or stainless) **$643.00**
Price: 44 Mag., 6", vent heavy (blue or stainless) **$689.00**
Price: 45 Colt, 8", vent heavy (blue or stainless) **$766.00**
Price: Compensated models (all calibers) .... **$812.00 to $934.00**

HANDGUNS — Double-Action Revolvers, Service & Sport

Dan Wesson Firearms
Super Ram Silhouette

Dan Wesson Firearms
Alaskan Guide Special

EAA Windicator

DAN WESSON FIREARMS LARGE FRAME SERIES REVOLVERS
Caliber: 41, 741/41 Magnum; 44, 744/44 Magnum; 45, 745/45 Long Colt; 360, 7360/357; 460, 7460/45. **Barrel:** 2"-10". **Weight:** 49 oz.-69 oz. **Grips:** Standard, Hogue rubber Gripper Grips. **Sights:** Standard front, serrated ramp with color insert. Standard rear, adustable wide notch. Other sight options available. **Features:** Available in blue or stainless steel. Smooth, wide trigger with overtravel, wide hammer spur. Double and single action.
Price: . . . . **$769.00 to $889.00**

DAN WESSON FIREARMS MODEL 360/7360 REVOLVERS
Caliber: 357 Mag. **Barrel:** 4", 6", 8", 10"; vent heavy. **Weight:** 64 oz. (8" barrel). **Grips:** Hogue rubber finger groove. **Sights:** Interchangeable ramp or Patridge front, fully adjustable rear. **Features:** New Generation Large Frame Series. Interchangeable barrels and grips; smooth trigger, wide hammer spur. Blue (360) or stainless (7360). Introduced 1999. Made in U.S.A. by Dan Wesson Firearms.
Price: 4" bbl., blue or stainless **$735.00**
Price: 10" bbl., blue or stainless **$873.00**
Price: Compensated models . . . . **$858.00 to $980.00**

DAN WESSON FIREARMS MODEL 460/7460 REVOLVERS
Caliber: 45 ACP, 45 Auto Rim, 45 Super, 45 Winchester Magnum and 460 Rowland. **Barrel:** 4", 6", 8", 10"; vent heavy. **Weight:** 49 oz. (4" barrel). **Grips:** Hogue rubber finger groove; interchangeable. **Sights:** Interchangeable ramp or Patridge front, fully adjustable rear. **Features:** New Generation Large Frame Series. Shoots five cartridges (45 ACP, 45 Auto Rim, 45 Super, 45 Winchester Magnum and 460 Rowland; six half-moon clips for auto cartridges included). Interchangeable barrels and grips. Available with non-fluted cylinder and slotted lightweight barrel shroud. Introduced 1999. Made in U.S.A. by Dan Wesson Firearms.
Price: 4" bbl., blue or stainless **$735.00**
Price: 10" bbl., blue or stainless **$888.00**
Price: Compensated models . . . . **$919.00 to $1,042.00**

DAN WESSON FIREARMS STANDARD SILHOUETTE REVOLVERS
Caliber: 357 SuperMag/Maxi, 41 Mag., 414 SuperMag, 445 SuperMag. **Barrel:** 8", 10". **Weight:** 64 oz. (8" barrel). **Length:** 14.3" overall (8" barrel). **Grips:** Hogue rubber finger groove; interchangeable. **Sights:** Patridge front, fully adjustable rear. **Features:** Interchangeable barrels and grips, fluted or non-fluted cylinder, satin brushed stainless finish. Introduced 1999. Made in U.S.A. by Dan Wesson Firearms.
Price: 357 SuperMag/Maxi, 8" **$1,057.00**
Price: 41 Mag., 10" **$888.00**
Price: 414 SuperMag., 8" **$1,057.00**
Price: 445 SuperMag., 8" **$1,057.00**

Dan Wesson Firearms Super Ram Silhouette Revolver
Similar to Standard Silhouette except has 10 land and groove Laser Coat barrel, Bo-Mar target sights with hooded front, special laser engraving. Fluted or non-fluted cylinder. Introduced 1999. Made in U.S.A. by Dan Wesson Firearms.
Price: 357 SuperMag/Maxi, 414 SuperMag., 445 SuperMag., 8", blue or stainless **$1,364.00**
Price: 41 Magnum, 44 Magnum, 8", blue or stainless **$1,241.00**
Price: 41 Magnum, 44 Magnum, 10", blue or stainless **$1,333.00**

DAN WESSON FIREARMS ALASKAN GUIDE SPECIAL
Caliber: 445 SuperMag, 44 Magnum. **Barrel:** Compensated 4" vent heavy barrel assembly. **Features:** Stainless steel with baked on, non-glare, matte black coating, special laser engraving.
Price: Model 7445 VH4C AGS **$995.00**
Price: Model 744 VH4C AGS **$855.00**

EAA WINDICATOR REVOLVERS
Caliber: 38 Spec., 6-shot; 357 magnum, 6-shot. **Barrel:** 2", 4". **Weight:** 38 oz. (22 rimfire, 4"). **Length:** 8.5" overall (4" bbl.). **Grips:** Rubber with finger grooves. **Sights:** Blade front, fixed or adjustable on rimfires; fixed only on 32, 38. **Features:** Swing-out cylinder; hammer block safety; blue finish. Introduced 1991. Imported from Germany by European American Armory.
Price: 38 Special 2" **$249.00**
Price: 38 Special, 4" **$259.00**
Price: 357 Magnum, 2" **$259.00**
Price: 357 Magnum, 4" **$279.00**

KORTH COMBAT REVOLVER
Caliber: 357 Mag., 32 S&W Long, 9mm Para., 22 WMR, 22 LR. **Barrel:** 3", 4", 5-1/4", 6", 8". **Sights:** Fully adjustable, rear; Baughman ramp, front. **Grips:** Walnut (checkered or smooth). Also available as a Target model in 22 LR, 38 Spl., 32 S&W Long, 357 Mag. with undercut Patridge front sight; fully adjustable rear. Made in Germany. Imported by Korth USA.
Price: From **$7,203.00**

KORTH TROJA REVOLVER
Caliber: .357 Mag. **Barrel:** 6". **Finish:** Matte blue. **Grips:** Smooth, oversized finger contoured walnut. Introduced 2003. Imported from Germany by Korth USA.
Price: From **$5,593.00**

CONSULT
SHOOTER'S MARKETPLACE
Page 141, This Issue

Medusa Model 47

Rossi Model 971

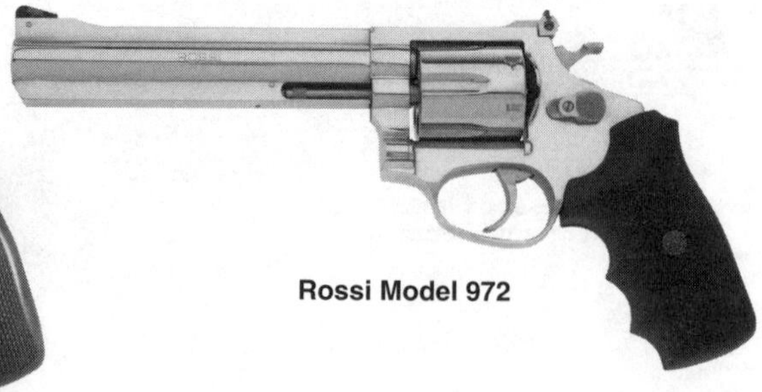

Rossi Model 972

Rossi Model 851

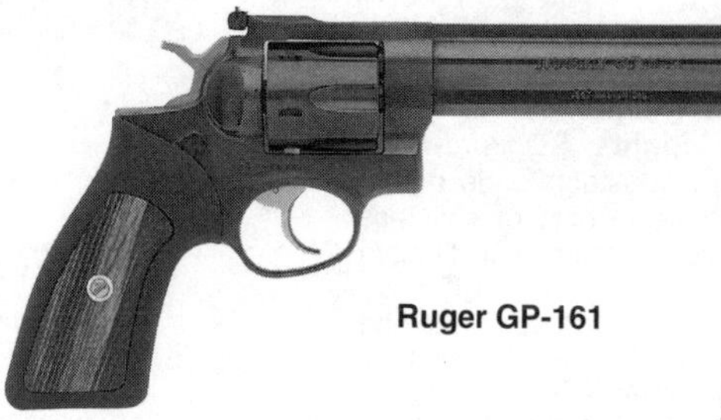

Ruger GP-161

Ruger KGP-141

MEDUSA MODEL 47 REVOLVER

Caliber: Most 9mm, 38 and 357 caliber cartridges; 6-shot cylinder. **Barrel:** 2-1/2", 3", 4", 5", 6"; fluted. **Weight:** 39 oz. **Length:** 10" overall (4" barrel). **Grips:** Gripper-style rubber. **Sights:** Changeable front blades, fully adjustable rear. **Features:** Patented extractor allows gun to chamber, fire and extract over 25 different cartridges in the 355 to 357 range without half-moon clips. Steel frame and cylinder; match quality barrel. Matte blue finish. Introduced 1996. Made in U.S.A. by Phillips & Rogers, Inc.

Price: **$899.00**

ROSSI MODEL 351/352 REVOLVERS

Caliber: 38 Special +P, 5-shot. **Barrel:** 2". **Weight:** 24 oz. **Length:** 6-1/2" overall. **Grips:** Rubber. **Sights:** Blade front, fixed rear. **Features:** Patented key-lock Taurus Security System; forged steel frame. Introduced 2001. Imported by BrazTech/Taurus.

Price: Model 351 (blued finish) **$298.00**

Price: Model 352 (stainless finish) **$345.00**

ROSSI MODEL 461/462 REVOLVERS

Caliber: 357 Magnum +P, 6-shot. **Barrel:** 2". **Weight:** 26 oz. **Length:** 6-1/2" overall. **Grips:** Rubber. **Sights:** Fixed. **Features:** Single/double action. Patented key-lock Taurus Security System; forged steel frame. Introduced 2001. Imported by BrazTech/Taurus.

Price: Model 461 (blued finish) **$298.00**

Price: Model 462 (stainless finish) **$345.00**

ROSSI MODEL 971/972 REVOLVERS

Caliber: 357 Magnum +P, 6-shot. **Barrel:** 4", 6". **Weight:** 40-44 oz. **Length:** 8-1/2" or 10-1/2" overall. **Grips:** Rubber. **Sights:** Fully adjustable. **Features:** Single/double action. Patented key-lock Taurus Security System; forged steel frame. Introduced 2001. Imported by BrazTech/Taurus.

Price: Model 971 (blued finish, 4" bbl.) **$345.00**

Price: Model 972 (stainless steel finish, 6" bbl.) **$391.00**

Rossi Model 851

Similar to Model 971/972, chambered for 38 Special +P. Blued finish, 4" barrel. Introduced 2001. From BrazTech/Taurus.

Price: **$298.00**

RUGER GP-100 REVOLVERS

Caliber: 38 Spec., 357 Mag., 6-shot. **Barrel:** 3", 3" full shroud, 4", 4" full shroud, 6", 6" full shroud. **Weight:** 3" barrel-35 oz., 3" full shroud-36 oz., 4" barrel-37 oz., 4" full shroud-38 oz. **Sights:** Fixed; adjustable on 4" full shroud, all 6" barrels. **Grips:** Ruger Santoprene Cushioned Grip with Goncalo Alves inserts. **Features:** Uses action, frame features of both the Security-Six and Redhawk revolvers. Full length, short ejector shroud. Satin blue and stainless steel.

Price: GP-141 (357, 4" full shroud, adj. sights, blue) **$499.00**

Price: GP-160 (357, 6", adj. sights, blue) **$499.00**

Price: GP-161 (357, 6" full shroud, adj. sights, blue), 46 oz. **$499.00**

Price: GPF-331 (357, 3" full shroud) **$495.00**

Price: GPF-340 (357, 4") **$495.00**

Price: GPF-341 (357, 4" full shroud) **$495.00**

Price: KGP-141 (357, 4" full shroud, adj. sights, stainless) **$555.00**

Price: KGP-160 (357, 6", adj. sights, stainless), 43 oz. **$555.00**

Price: KGP-161 (357, 6" full shroud, adj. sights, stainless) 46 oz. . **$555.00**

Price: KGPF-330 (357, 3", stainless) **$555.00**

Price: KGPF-331 (357, 3" full shroud, stainless) **$555.00**

Price: KGPF-340 (357, 4", stainless), KGPF-840 (38 Special) **$555.00**

Price: KGPF-341 (357, 4" full shroud, stainless) **$555.00**

Price: KGPF-840 (38 Special, 4", stainless) **$555.00**

Ruger SP101 Double-Action-Only Revolver

Similar to standard SP101 except double-action-only with no single-action sear notch. Spurless hammer, floating firing pin and transfer bar safety system. Available with 2-1/4" barrel in 357 Magnum. Weighs 25 oz., overall length 7.06". Natural brushed satin, high-polish stainless steel. Introduced 1993.

Price: KSP321XL (357 Mag.) **$495.00**

RUGER SP101 REVOLVERS

Caliber: 22 LR, 32 H&R Mag., 6-shot; 38 Spec. +P, 357 Mag., 5-shot. **Barrel:** 2-1/4", 3-1/16", 4". **Weight:** (38 & 357 mag models) 2-1/4"-25 oz.; 3-1/16"-27 oz. **Sights:** Adjustable on 22, 32, fixed on others. **Grips:** Ruger Cushioned Grip with inserts. **Features:** Compact, small frame, double-action revolver. Full-length ejector shroud. Stainless steel only. Introduced 1988.

Price: KSP-821X (2-1/4", 38 Spec.) **$495.00**

Price: KSP-831X (3-1/16", 38 Spec.) **$495.00**

Price: KSP-241X (4" heavy bbl., 22 LR), 34 oz. **$495.00**

Price: KSP-3231X (3-1/16", 32 H&R), 30 oz. **$495.00**

Price: KSP-321X (2-1/4", 357 Mag.) **$495.00**

Price: KSP-331X (3-1/16", 357 Mag.) **$495.00**

Price: KSP-3241X (32 Mag., 4" bbl.) **$495.00**

HANDGUNS — Double-Action Revolvers, Service & Sport

Ruger Redhawk

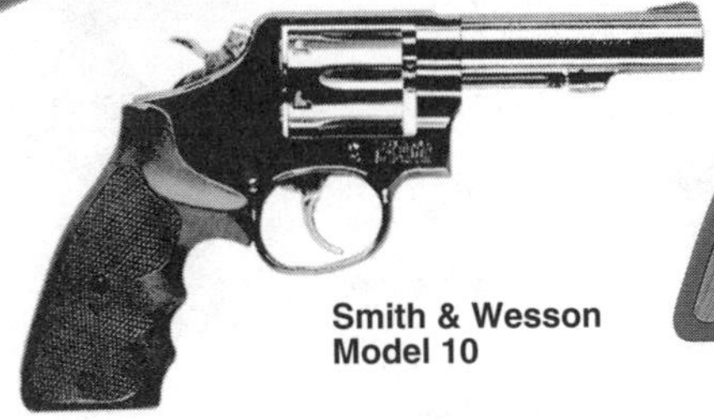

Smith & Wesson Model 10

Ruger Super Redhawk

Smith & Wesson Model 386

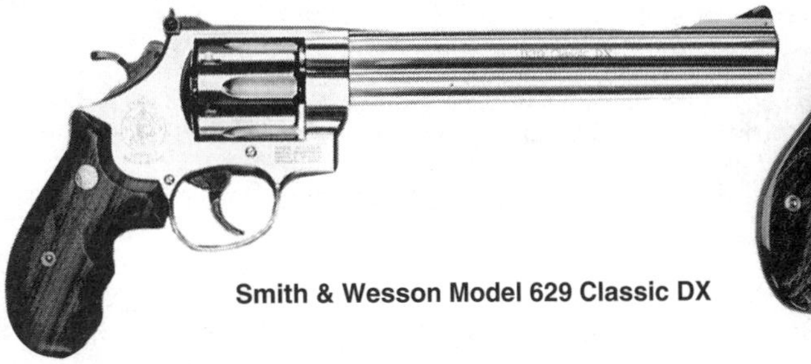

Smith & Wesson Model 629 Classic DX

Smith & Wesson Model 36LS

RUGER REDHAWK

Caliber: 44 Rem. Mag., 45 Colt, 6-shot. **Barrel:** 5-1/2", 7-1/2". **Weight:** About 54 oz. (7-1/2" bbl.). **Length:** 13" overall (7-1/2" barrel). **Grips:** Square butt cushioned grip panels. **Sights:** Interchangeable Patridge-type front, rear adjustable for windage and elevation. **Features:** Stainless steel, brushed satin finish, blued ordnance steel. 9-1/2" sight radius. Introduced 1979.

Price: Blued, 44 Mag., 5-1/2" RH-445, 7-1/2" RH-44 . . . . **$585.00**

Price: Blued, 44 Mag., 7-1/2" RH44R, with scope mount, rings . . . **$625.00**

Price: Stainless, 44 Mag., KRH445, 5-1/2", 7-1/2" KRH-44 . . . . **$645.00**

Price: Stainless, 44 Mag., 7-1/2", with scope mount, rings KRH-44R **$685.00**

Price: Stainless, 45 Colt, KRH455, 5-1/2", 7-1/2" KRH-45 . . . . **$645.00**

Price: Stainless, 45 Colt, 7-1/2", with scope mount and rings KRH-45R **$685.00**

Ruger Super Redhawk Revolver

Similar to standard Redhawk except has heavy extended frame with Ruger Integral Scope Mounting System on wide topstrap. Also available in 454 Casull and 480 Ruger. Wide hammer spur lowered for better scope clearance. Incorporates mechanical design features and improvements of GP-100. Choice of 7-1/2" or 9-1/2" barrel, both ramp front sight base with Redhawk-style Interchangeable Insert sight blades, adjustable rear sight. Target gray stainless steel. Introduced 1987.

Price: KSRH-7 (7-1/2"), KSRH-9 (9-1/2"), 44 Mag **$685.00**

Price: KSRH-7454 (7-1/2") 454 Casull, 9-1/2 KSRH-9454 . . . . **$775.00**

Price: KSRH-7480 (7-1/2") 480 Ruger **$775.00**

Price: KSRH-9480 (9-1/2") 480 Ruger **$775.00**

SMITH & WESSON MODEL 10 M&P HB REVOLVER

Caliber: 38 Spec., 6-shot. **Barrel:** 4". **Weight:** 36 oz. **Length:** 8-7/8" overall. **Grips:** Uncle Mike's Combat soft rubber; square butt. **Sights:** Fixed; ramp front, square notch rear.

Price: Blue **$544.00**

SMITH & WESSON MODEL 325PD

Caliber: 45 ACP, 6-round. **Barrel:** 2-1/2". **Weight:** 21.5 oz. **Length:** 7-1/4". **Grips:** Wood. **Sights:** Adj. rear, HiViz front. **Features:** Alloy large frame, titanium cylinder.

Price: **$939.00**

SMITH & WESSON MODEL 329PD

Caliber: 44 Mag., 44 Spec., 6-round. **Barrel:** 4". **Weight:** 26 oz. **Length:** 9-1/2". **Grips:** Wood. **Sights:** Adj. rear, HiViz front. **Features:** Alloy large frame, titanium cylinder.

Price: **$960.00**

SMITH & WESSON MODEL 386

Caliber: 357 Mag., 38 Spec., 7-round. **Barrel:** 3-1/8". **Weight:** 18.5 oz. **Length:** 8-1/8". **Grips:** Hogue Bantam. **Sights:** Adj. rear, HiViz front. **Features:** Alloy large frame, titanium cylinder.

Price: **$876.00**

SMITH & WESSON MODEL 629 REVOLVERS

Caliber: 44 Magnum, 44 S&W Special, 6-shot. **Barrel:** 4". **Weight:** 45 oz. (6" bbl.). **Length:** 11-5/8" overall (6" bbl.). **Grips:** Soft rubber; wood optional. **Sights:** 1/8" red ramp front, white outline rear, internal lock, adjustable for windage and elevation.

Price: Model 629, 4" **$787.00**

Price: Model 629, 6" **$810.00**

Smith & Wesson Model 629 Classic Revolver

Similar to standard Model 629 with full-lug 5", 6-1/2" or 8-3/8" barrel, chamfered front of cylinder, interchangeable red ramp front sight with adjustable white outline rear, Hogue grips with S&W monogram, drilled and tapped for scope mounting. Factory accurizing and endurance packages. Overall length with 5" barrel is 10-1/2"; weighs 45.5 oz. Introduced 1990.

Price: Model 629 Classic (stainless), 5", 6-1/2" **$843.00**

Price: As above, 8-3/8" **$871.00**

Price: Model 629 Classic with HiViz front sight **$894.00**

SMITH & WESSON MODEL 37 AIRWEIGHT

Caliber: 38 Spec. +P, 5-shot. **Barrel:** 1-7/8". **Weight:** 15.0 oz. **Length:** 6-5/16" (round butt). **Grips:** Round butt soft rubber. **Sights:** Fixed, serrated ramp front, square notch rear. Glass beaded finish.

Price: Model 37 . . . . **$573.00**

Smith & Wesson Model 637 Airweight Revolver

Similar to the Model 37 Airweight except has alloy frame, stainless steel barrel, cylinder and yoke; rated for 38 Spec. +P; Uncle Mike's Boot Grip. Weighs 15 oz. Introduced 1996. Made in U.S.A. by Smith & Wesson.

Price: **$450.00**

SMITH & WESSON MODEL 36LS, 60LS LADYSMITH

Caliber: .38 S&W Special +P (M36), 357 Mag. (M60LS), 5-shot. **Barrel:** 1-7/8, 2-1/8". **Weight:** 20 oz. **Length:** 6-3/16 overall (1-7/8" barrel). **Grips:** Combat Dymondwood® grips with S&W monogram. **Sights:** Serrated ramp front, fixed notch rear. **Features:** Speedloader cutout. Comes in a fitted carry/storage case. Introduced 1989.

Price: Model 36LS **$568.00**

Price: Model 60LS, 2-1/8" bbl. stainless, 357 Magnum **$621.00**

Price: Model 36LS, 38 Spec **$450.00**

HANDGUNS — Double-Action Revolvers, Service & Sport

Smith & Wesson
Model 60 Chief's Special

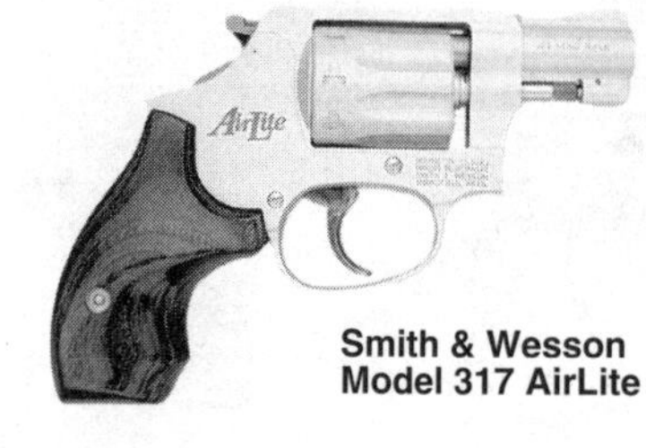

Smith & Wesson
Model 317 AirLite

Smith & Wesson Model 625

SMITH & WESSON MODEL 60 CHIEF'S SPECIAL
Caliber: 357 Magnum, 38 Spec., 5-shot. **Barrel:** 2-1/8", 3" or 5". **Weight:** 24 oz. **Length:** 7-1/2 overall (3" barrel). **Grips:** Rounded butt synthetic grips. **Sights:** Fixed, serrated ramp front, square notch rear. **Features:** Stainless steel construction. 3" full lug barrel, adjustable sights, internal lock. Made in U.S.A. by Smith & Wesson.
Price: 2-1/8" barrel $594.00
Price: 3" bbl. $630.00
Price: 5" bbl. $671.00

SMITH & WESSON MODEL 65
Caliber: 357 Mag. and 38 Spec., 6-shot. **Barrel:** 4". **Weight:** 34 oz. **Length:** 9-5/16" overall (4" bbl.). **Grips:** Uncle Mike's Combat. **Sights:** 1/8" serrated ramp front, fixed square notch rear. **Features:** Heavy barrel. Stainless steel construction. Internal lock.
Price: $531.00

SMITH & WESSON MODEL 317 AIRLITE, 317 KIT GUN REVOLVERS
Caliber: 22 LR, 8-shot. **Barrel:** 1-7/8", 3". **Weight:** 10.05 oz. **Length:** 6-3/16" overall. **Grips:** Dymondwood® Boot or Uncle Mike's Boot. **Sights:** Serrated ramp front, fixed notch rear. **Features:** Aluminum alloy, carbon and stainless steels, and titanium construction. Short spur hammer, smooth combat trigger. Clear Cote finish. Introduced 1997. Made in U.S.A. by Smith & Wesson.
Price: With Uncle Mike's Boot grip $603.00
Price: With Boot grip, 3" barrel, HiViz front sight, internal lock $658.00

SMITH & WESSON MODEL 351PD
Caliber: 22 Mag. **Barrel:** 2". **Features:** Seven-shot, Scandium alloy.
Price: $625.00

SMITH & WESSON MODEL 64 STAINLESS M&P
Caliber: 38 Spec. +P, 6-shot. **Barrel:** 3", 4". **Weight:** 36 oz. **Length:** 8-7/16" overall. **Grips:** Soft rubber. **Sights:** Fixed, 1/8" serrated ramp front, square notch rear. **Features:** Satin finished stainless steel, square butt.
Price: 3", 4" bbl. $583.00

SMITH & WESSON MODEL 648
Caliber: 22 Mag., 6-round. **Barrel:** 6". **Weight:** 45 oz. **Length:** 11-1/8". Grips: Rubber. **Sights:** Adj. rear, Patridge front. **Features:** Stainless steel frame, satin finish.
Price: $703.00

SMITH & WESSON MODEL 619
Caliber: 38 S&W Special; 7 rounds. **Barrel:** 4". **Weight:** 37.5 oz. **Length:** 9-1/2". Grips: Rubber. **Sights:** White outline rear, red ramp front. **Features:** Stainless frame and cylinder.
Price: $615.00

SMITH & WESSON MODEL 620
Caliber: 38 S&W Special; 7 rounds. **Barrel:** 4". **Weight:** 37.5 oz. **Length:** 9-1/2". **Grips:** Rubber. **Sights:** White outline rear, red ramp front. **Features:** Stainles frame and cylinder.
Price: $669.00

SMITH & WESSON MODEL 686
Caliber: 357 Mag., 38 S&W Special; 6 rounds. **Barrel:** 2-1/2", 4", 6". **Weight:** 40 oz. (4"). **Length:** 9-9/16". **Grips:** Rubber. **Sights:** White outline rear, red ramp front. **Features:** Stainless frame and cylinder.
Price: 2-1/2" bbl. $667.00
Price: 4" bbl. $694.00
Price: 6" bbl. $700.00

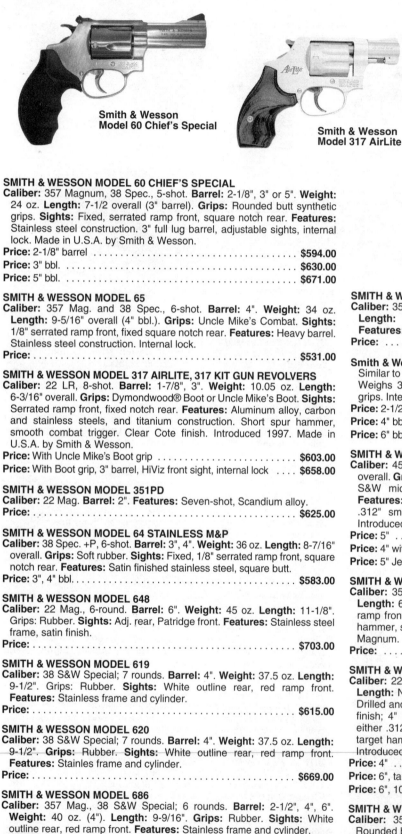

Smith & Wesson
Model 340 PD Airlite Sc

SMITH & WESSON MODEL 686 POWERPORT
Caliber: 357 Mag., 38 S&W Special; 6 rounds. **Barrel:** 6". **Weight:** 44 oz. **Length:** 11-3/8". **Grips:** Rubber. **Sights:** Adj. rear, Patridge front. **Features:** Stainless frame and cylinder.
Price: $747.00

Smith & Wesson Model 686 Magnum PLUS Revolver
Similar to the Model 686 except has 7-shot cylinder, 2-1/2", 4" or 6" barrel. Weighs 34-1/2 oz., overall length 7-1/2" (2-1/2" barrel). Hogue rubber grips. Internal lock. Introduced 1996. Made in U.S.A. by Smith & Wesson.
Price: 2-1/2" bbl. $692.00
Price: 4" bbl. $716.00
Price: 6" bbl. $727.00

SMITH & WESSON MODEL 625 REVOLVER
Caliber: 45 ACP, 6-shot. **Barrel:** 4", 5". **Weight:** 45 oz. **Length:** 10-3/8" overall. **Grips:** Soft rubber; wood optional. **Sights:** Patridge front on ramp, S&W micrometer click rear adjustable for windage and elevation. **Features:** Stainless steel construction with .400" semi-target hammer, .312" smooth combat trigger; full lug barrel. Glass beaded finish. Introduced 1989.
Price: 5" $817.00
Price: 4" with internal lock $817.00
Price: 5" Jerry Miculek Pro series $845.00

SMITH & WESSON MODEL 640 CENTENNIAL DA ONLY
Caliber: 357 Mag., 38 Spec. +P, 5-shot. **Barrel:** 2-1/8". **Weight:** 23 oz. **Length:** 6-3/4" overall. **Grips:** Uncle Mike's Boot grip. **Sights:** Serrated ramp front, fixed notch rear. **Features:** Stainless steel. Fully concealed hammer, snag-proof smooth edges. Internal lock. Introduced 1995 in 357 Magnum.
Price: $658.00

SMITH & WESSON MODEL 617 K-22 MASTERPIECE
Caliber: 22 LR, 6- or 10-shot. **Barrel:** 4", 6". **Weight:** 41 oz. (4" barrel). **Length:** NA. **Grips:** Soft rubber. **Sights:** Patridge front, adjustable rear. Drilled and tapped for scope mount. **Features:** Stainless steel with satin finish; 4" has .312" smooth trigger, .375" semi-target hammer; 6" has either .312" combat or .400" serrated trigger, .375" semi-target or .500" target hammer; 8-3/8" with .400" serrated trigger, .500" target hammer. Introduced 1990.
Price: 4" $707.00
Price: 6", target hammer, target trigger $686.00
Price: 6", 10-shot $734.00

SMITH & WESSON MODEL 340PD AIRLITE Sc CENTENNIAL
Caliber: 357 Magnum, 38 Spec. +P, 5-shot. **Barrel:** 1-7/8". **Grips:** Rounded butt grip. **Sights:** HiViz front. **Features:** Synthetic grip, internal lock. Blue.
Price: HiViz front $877.00
Price: Red ramp front $862.00

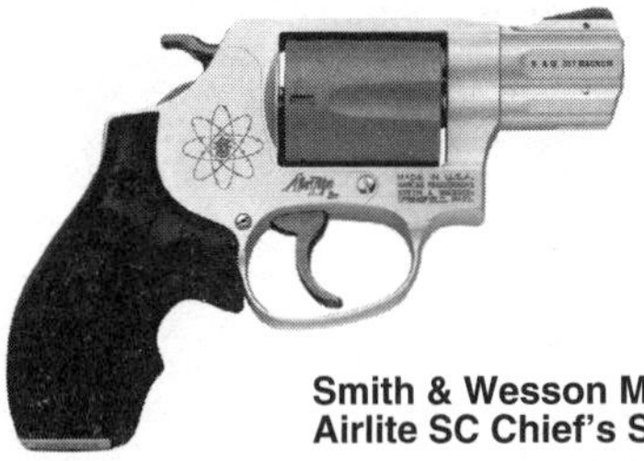

Smith & Wesson Model 360 PD Airlite SC Chief's Special

Smith & Wesson Model 386 PD Airlite SC

Smith & Wesson Model 340

Smith & Wesson Model 360 Kit Gun

Smith & Wesson Model 67

Smith & Wesson Model 442

Smith & Wesson Model 638

SMITH & WESSON MODEL 360PD AIRLITE Sc CHIEF'S SPECIAL
Caliber: 357 Magnum, 38 Spec. +P, 5-shot. **Barrel:** 1-7/8". **Grips:** Rounded butt grip. **Sights:** Fixed. **Features:** Synthetic grip, internal lock. Stainless.
Price: Red ramp front **$834.00**
Price: HiViz front **$858.00**

SMITH & WESSON MODEL 386PD AIRLITE Sc
Caliber: 357 Magnum, 38 Spec. +P, 7-shot. **Barrel:** 2-1/2". **Grips:** Rounded butt grip. **Sights:** Adjustable, HiViz front. **Features:** Synthetic grip, internal lock.
Price: Blue **$873.00**

SMITH & WESSON MODEL 340
Caliber: 357 Mag., 38 Spec., 5-shot. **Barrel:** 1-7/8". **Weight:** 12 oz. **Length:** 6-5/16" overall. **Grips:** Rubber. **Sights:** Black blade ramp front, fixed rear. **Features:** Alloy frame; titanium cylinder; stainless steel barrel liner. Matte finish. Made in U.S.A. by Smith & Wesson.
Price: Model 340 . . . . **$838.00**

Smith & Wesson Model 360 and 260 Kit Gun
Same as Model 340 except with 3" barrel option.
Price: M 360 . . . . **$818.00**
Price: Kit Gun **$865.00**

SMITH & WESSON MODEL 337 CHIEF'S SPECIAL AIRLITE Ti
Caliber: 38 Spec. +P, 5-shot. **Barrel:** 1-7/8". **Weight:** 11.2 oz. (Dymondwood® grips). **Length:** 6-5/16" overall. **Grips:** Uncle Mike's Boot or Dymondwood® Boot. **Sights:** Black serrated front, fixed notch rear. **Features:** Aluminum alloy frame, barrel shroud and yoke; titanium cylinder; stainless steel barrel liner. Matte finish. Introduced 1999. Made in U.S.A. by Smith & Wesson.
Price: **$716.00**

SMITH & WESSON MODEL 431PD/432PD
Caliber: 32 H&R, 6-shot. **Barrel:** 2". **Weight:** 15 oz. **Length:** 6-5/16" overall. **Grips:** Rubber. **Sights:** Black blade front, fixed rear. **Features:** Alloy black frame and cylinder; black finish.
Price: Chief's Special **$450.00**
Price: Centennial frame **$469.00**

SMITH & WESSON MODEL 67
Caliber: 38 S&W Special, 6-shot. **Barrel:** 4". **Weight:** 36 oz. **Length:** 8-7/8". **Grips:** Rubber. **Sights:** Adj. rear, red ramp front. **Features:** Stainless steel frame and cylinder.
Price: **$642.00**

Smith & Wesson Model 442 Centennial Airweight
Similar to Model 640 Centennial, alloy frame, weighs 15 oz. Chambered for 38 Special +P, 1-7/8" carbon steel barrel; carbon steel cylinder; concealed hammer; Uncle Mike's Boot grip. Fixed square notch rear sight, serrated ramp front. DA only, glass beaded finish. Introduced 1993.
Price: Blue **$600.00**

SMITH & WESSON MODEL 638 AIRWEIGHT BODYGUARD
Caliber: 38 Spec. +P, 5-shot. **Barrel:** 1-7/8". **Weight:** 15 oz. **Length:** 6-15/16" overall. **Grips:** Uncle Mike's Boot grip. **Sights:** Serrated ramp front, fixed notch rear. **Features:** Alloy frame, stainless cylinder and barrel; shrouded hammer. Glass beaded finish. Introduced 1997. Made in U.S.A. by Smith & Wesson.
Price: With Uncle Mike's Boot grip **$620.00**

Smith & Wesson Model 642 Airweight Revolver
Similar to Model 442 Centennial Airweight, stainless steel barrel, cylinder and yoke with matte finish; Uncle Mike's Boot grip; DA only; weighs 15 oz. Introduced 1996. Made in U.S.A. by Smith & Wesson.
Price: **$469.00**

Smith & Wesson Model 642LS Ladysmith Revolver
Same as Model 642 except has smooth combat wood grips, comes with deluxe soft case; Dymondwood® grip; aluminum alloy frame, stainless cylinder, barrel and yoke; frosted matte finish. Weighs 14.5 oz. Introduced 1996. Made in U.S.A. by Smith & Wesson.
Price: 1-7/8" **$633.00**

SMITH & WESSON MODEL 649 BODYGUARD REVOLVER
Caliber: 357 Mag., 38 Spec. +P, 5-shot. **Barrel:** 2-1/8". **Weight:** 23 oz. **Length:** 6-5/16" overall. **Grips:** Uncle Mike's Combat. **Sights:** Black pinned ramp front, fixed notch rear. **Features:** Stainless steel construction; shrouded hammer; smooth combat trigger. Internal lock. Made in U.S.A. by Smith & Wesson.
Price: **$651.00**

HANDGUNS — Double-Action Revolvers, Service & Sport

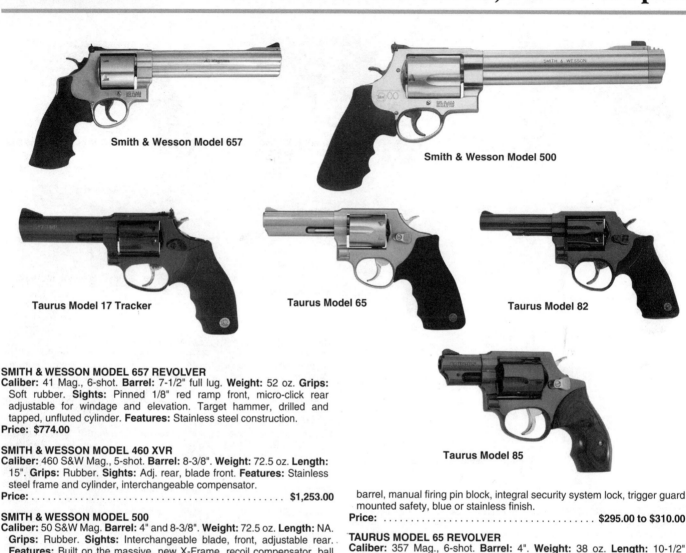

Smith & Wesson Model 657

Smith & Wesson Model 500

Taurus Model 17 Tracker

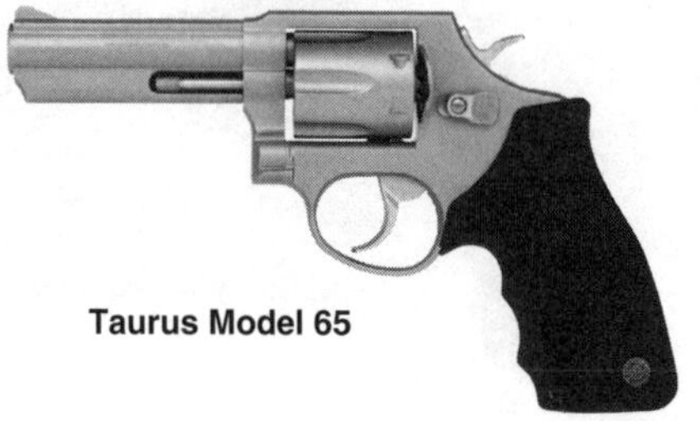

Taurus Model 65

Taurus Model 82

Taurus Model 85

SMITH & WESSON MODEL 657 REVOLVER
Caliber: 41 Mag., 6-shot. **Barrel:** 7-1/2" full lug. **Weight:** 52 oz. **Grips:** Soft rubber. **Sights:** Pinned 1/8" red ramp front, micro-click rear adjustable for windage and elevation. Target hammer, drilled and tapped, unfluted cylinder. **Features:** Stainless steel construction.
Price: $774.00

SMITH & WESSON MODEL 460 XVR
Caliber: 460 S&W Mag., 5-shot. **Barrel:** 8-3/8". **Weight:** 72.5 oz. **Length:** 15". **Grips:** Rubber. **Sights:** Adj. rear, blade front. **Features:** Stainless steel frame and cylinder, interchangeable compensator.
Price: **$1,253.00**

SMITH & WESSON MODEL 500
Caliber: 50 S&W Mag. **Barrel:** 4" and 8-3/8". **Weight:** 72.5 oz. **Length:** NA. **Grips:** Rubber. **Sights:** Interchangeable blade, front, adjustable rear. **Features:** Built on the massive, new X-Frame, recoil compensator, ball detent cylinder latch. Made in U.S.A. by Smith & Wesson.
Price: 4" bbl. **$1,196.00**
Price: 8-3/8" bbl. **$1,130.00**

TAURUS SILHOUETTE REVOLVERS
Available in calibers from 22 LR through 454 Casull, 12" vent rib barrel. An optional arm support that wraps around the forearm is available.
Price: . . . . **$414.00 to $859.00**

TAURUS MODEL 17 "TRACKER"
Caliber: 17 HMR, 7-shot. **Barrel:** 6-1/2". **Weight:** 45.8 oz. **Grips:** Rubber. **Sights:** Adjustable. **Features:** Double action, matte stainless, integral key-lock.
Price: . . . . **$430.00 to $438.00**

TAURUS MODEL 17-12 TARGET "SILHOUETTE"
Caliber: 17 HMR, 7-shot. **Barrel:** 12". **Weight:** 57.8 oz. **Grips:** Rubber. **Sights:** Adjustable. **Features:** Vent rib, double action, adjustable main spring and trigger stop. Matte stainless, integral key-lock.
Price: **$430.00**

Taurus Model 17-C Series
Similar to the Models 17 Tracker and Silhouette series but 8-shot cylinder, 2", 4" or 5" barrel, blue or stainless finish and regular (24 oz.) or UltraLite (18.5 oz.) versions available.
Price: . . . . **$359.00 to $391.00**

TAURUS MODEL 63
Caliber: 22 LR, 10 + 1 shot. **Barrel:** 23". **Weight:** 97.9 oz. **Grips:** Premium hardwood. **Sights:** Adjustable. **Features:** Auto loading action, round barrel, manual firing pin block, integral security system lock, trigger guard mounted safety, blue or stainless finish.
Price: . . . . **$295.00 to $310.00**

TAURUS MODEL 65 REVOLVER
Caliber: 357 Mag., 6-shot. **Barrel:** 4". **Weight:** 38 oz. **Length:** 10-1/2" overall. **Grips:** Soft rubber. **Sights:** Fixed. **Features:** Double action, integral key-lock. Imported by Taurus International.
Price: Blue or matte stainless . . . . **$375.00 to $422.00**

Taurus Model 66 Revolver
Similar to Model 65, 4" or 6" barrel, 7-shot cylinder, adjustable rear sight. Integral key-lock action. Imported by Taurus International.
Price: Blue or matte stainless . . . . **$422.00 to $469.00**

Taurus Model 66 Silhouette Revolver
Similar to Model 66, 12" barrel, 7-shot cylinder, adjustable sight. Integral key-lock action, blue or matte stainless steel finish, rubber grips. Introduced 2001. Imported by Taurus International.
Price: . . . . **$414.00 to $461.00**

TAURUS MODEL 82 HEAVY BARREL REVOLVER
Caliber: 38 Spec., 6-shot. **Barrel:** 4", heavy. **Weight:** 36.5 oz. **Length:** 9-1/4" overall (4" bbl.). **Grips:** Soft black rubber. **Sights:** Serrated ramp front, square notch rear. **Features:** Double action, solid rib, integral key-lock. Imported by Taurus International.
Price: Blue or matte stainless . . . . **$352.00 to $398.00**

TAURUS MODEL 85 REVOLVER
Caliber: 38 Spec., 5-shot. **Barrel:** 2". **Weight:** 17-24.5 oz., titanium 13.5-15.4 oz. **Grips:** Rubber, rosewood or mother-of-pearl. **Sights:** Ramp front, square notch rear. **Features:** Blue, matte stainless, blue with gold accents, stainless with gold accents; rated for +P ammo. Integral keylock. Introduced 1980. Imported by Taurus International.
Price: . . . . **$375.00 to $547.00**
Price: Total Titanium **$531.00**

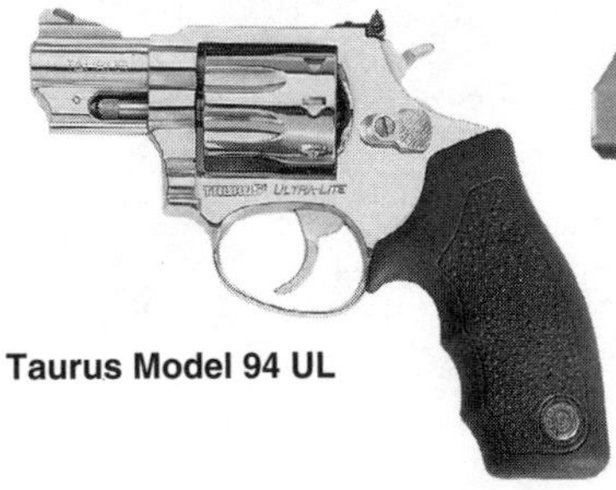

Taurus Model 94 UL

Taurus Model 22H Raging Hornet

Taurus Model 44

Taurus Model 30C Raging Thirty

Taurus Model 218 Raging Bee

Taurus Model 415

Taurus Model 425
Total Titanium

Taurus Model 445

TAURUS MODEL 94 REVOLVER
Caliber: 22 LR, 9-shot cylinder. **Barrel:** 2", 4", 5". **Weight:** 18.5-27.5 oz. **Grips:** Soft black rubber. **Sights:** Serrated ramp front, click-adjustable rear. **Features:** Double action, integral key-lock. Introduced 1989. Imported by Taurus International.
Price: Blue **$325.00**
Price: Matte stainless **$375.00**
Price: Model 94 UL, forged aluminum alloy, 18-18.5 oz. **$365.00**
Price: As above, stainless **$410.00**

TAURUS MODEL 22H RAGING HORNET REVOLVER
Caliber: 22 Hornet, 8-shot. **Barrel:** 10". **Weight:** 50 oz. **Length:** 6.5" overall. **Grips:** Soft black rubber. **Sights:** Fully adjustable, scope mount base included. **Features:** Ventilated rib, stainless steel construction with matte finish. Double-action, integral key-lock. Introduced 1999. Imported by Taurus International.
Price: **$898.00**

TAURUS MODEL 30C RAGING THIRTY
Caliber: 30 Carbine, 8-shot. **Barrel:** 10". **Weight:** 72.3 oz. **Grips:** Soft black rubber. **Sights:** Adjustable. **Features:** Double-action, ventilated rib, matte stainless, comes with five "Stellar" full-moon clips, integral key-lock.
Price: **$898.00**

TAURUS MODEL 44 REVOLVER
Caliber: 44 Mag., 6-shot. **Barrel:** 4", 6-1/2", 8-3/8". **Weight:** 44-3/4 oz. **Grips:** Rubber. **Sights:** Adjustable. **Features:** Double-action. Integral key-lock. Introduced 1994. New Model 44S12 has 12" vent rib barrel. Imported from Brazil by Taurus International Manufacturing, Inc.
Price: Blue or stainless steel . . . . **$445.00 to $602.00**

TAURUS MODEL 217 TARGET "SILHOUETTE"
Caliber: 218 Bee, 8-shot. **Barrel:** 12". **Weight:** 52.3 oz. **Grips:** Rubber. **Sights:** Adjustable. **Features:** Double-action, ventilated rib, adjustable mainspring and trigger stop, matte stainless, integral key-lock.
Price: **$461.00**

TAURUS MODEL 218 RAGING BEE
Caliber: 218 Bee, 7-shot. **Barrel:** 10". **Weight:** 74.9 oz. **Grips:** Rubber. **Sights:** Adjustable rear. **Features:** Ventilated rib, adjustable action, matte stainless, integral key-lock. Also available as Model 218SS6 Tracker with 6-1/2" vent rib barrel.
Price: (Raging Bee) **$898.00**
Price: (Tracker) **$406.00**

TAURUS MODEL 415 REVOLVER
Caliber: 41 Mag., 5-shot. **Barrel:** 2-1/2". **Weight:** 30 oz. **Length:** 7-1/8" overall. **Grips:** Rubber. **Sights:** Fixed. **Features:** Stainless steel construction; matte finish; ported barrel. Double action. Integral key-lock. Introduced 1999. Imported by Taurus International.
Price: **$508.00**
Price: Total Titanium **$602.00**

TAURUS MODEL 425/627 TRACKER REVOLVERS
Caliber: 357 Mag., 7-shot; 41 Mag., 5-shot. **Barrel:** 4" and 6". **Weight:** 28.8-40 oz. (titanium) 24.3-28. (6"). **Grips:** Rubber. **Sights:** Fixed front, adjustable rear. **Features:** Double-action stainless steel, Shadow Gray or Total Titanium; vent rib (steel models only); integral key-lock action. Imported by Taurus International.
Price: . . . . **$508.00 to $516.00**
Price: Total Titanium **$688.00**

TAURUS MODEL 445
Caliber: 44 Special, 5-shot. **Barrel:** 2". **Weight:** 20.3-28.25 oz. **Length:** 6-3/4" overall. **Grips:** Rubber. **Sights:** Ramp front, notch rear. **Features:** Blue or stainless steel. Standard or DAO concealed hammer, optional porting. Introduced 1997. Imported by Taurus International.
Price: . . . . **$345.00 to $500.00**
Price: Total Titanium 19.8 oz. **$600.00**

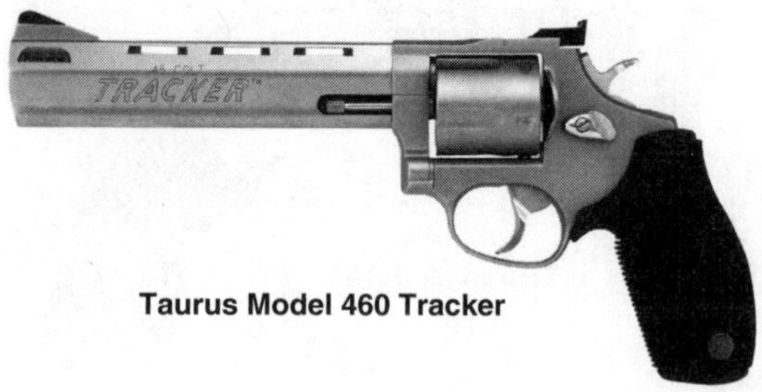

Taurus Model 460 Tracker

Taurus Model 605

Taurus Model 731

Taurus Model 454 Raging Bull

Taurus Model 608

Taurus Model 450

Taurus Raging Bull Model 416

TAURUS MODEL 455 "STELLAR TRACKER"
Caliber: 45 ACP, 5-shot. **Barrel:** 2", 4", 6". **Weight:** 28/33/38.4 oz. **Grips:** Rubber. **Sights:** Adjustable. **Features:** Double-action, matte stainless, includes five "Stellar" full-moon clips, integral key-lock.
Price: **$523.00**

TAURUS MODEL 460 "TRACKER"
Caliber: 45 Colt, 5-shot. **Barrel:** 4" or 6". **Weight:** 33/38.4 oz. **Grips:** Rubber. **Sights:** Adjustable. **Features:** Double-action, ventilated rib, matte stainless steel, comes with five "Stellar" full-moon clips.
Price: **$516.00**
Price: (Shadow Gray, Total Titanium) **$688.00**

TAURUS MODEL 605 REVOLVER
Caliber: 357 Mag., 5-shot. **Barrel:** 2". **Weight:** 24 oz. **Grips:** Rubber. **Sights:** Fixed. **Features:** Double-action, blue or stainless, concealed hammer models DAO, porting optional, integral key-lock. Introduced 1995. Imported by Taurus International.
Price: .... **$375.00 to $438.00**

Taurus Model 731 Revolver
Similar to the Taurus Model 605, except in .32 Magnum.
Price: .... **$438.00 to $531.00**

TAURUS MODEL 608 REVOLVER
Caliber: 357 Mag. 38 Spec., 8-shot. **Barrel:** 4", 6-1/2", 8-3/8". **Weight:** 44-57 oz. **Length:** 9-3/8" overall. **Grips:** Soft black rubber. **Sights:** Adjustable. **Features:** Double-action, integral key-lock action. Available in blue or stainless. Introduced 1995. Imported by Taurus International.
Price: .... **$469.00 to $547.00**

Taurus Model 44 Series Revolver
Similar to Taurus Model 60 series, but in .44 Rem. Mag. With six-shot cylinder, blue and matte stainless finishes.
Price: .... **$500.00 to $578.00**

TAURUS MODEL 650CIA REVOLVER
Caliber: 357 Magnum, 5-shot. **Barrel:** 2". **Weight:** 24.5 oz. **Grips:** Rubber. **Sights:** Ramp front, square notch rear. **Features:** Double-action only, blue or matte stainless steel, integral key-lock, internal hammer. Introduced 2001. From Taurus International.
Price: .... **$406.00 to $453.00**

TAURUS MODEL 651CIA REVOLVER
Caliber: 357 Magnum, 5-shot. **Barrel:** 2". **Weight:** 17-24.5 oz. **Grips:** Rubber. **Sights:** Fixed. **Features:** Concealed single-action/double-action design. Shrouded cockable hammer, blue, matte stainless, Shadow Gray, Total Titanium, integral key-lock. Made in Brazil. Imported by Taurus International Manufacturing, Inc.
Price: .... **$406.00 to $578.00**

TAURUS MODEL 450 REVOLVER
Caliber: 45 Colt, 5-shot. **Barrel:** 2". **Weight:** 21.2-22.3 oz. **Length:** 6-5/8" overall. **Grips:** Rubber. **Sights:** Ramp front, notch rear. **Features:** Double-action, blue or stainless, ported, integral key-lock. Introduced 1999. Imported from Brazil by Taurus International.
Price: **$492.00**
Price: Ultra-Lite (alloy frame) **$523.00**
Price: Total Titanium, 19.2 oz. **$600.00**

TAURUS MODEL 444/454/480 RAGING BULL REVOLVERS
Caliber: 44 Mag., 45 LC, 454 Casull, 480 Ruger, 5-shot. **Barrel:** 5", 6-1/2", 8-3/8". **Weight:** 53-63 oz. **Length:** 12" overall (6-1/2" barrel). **Grips:** Soft black rubber. **Sights:** Patridge front, adjustable rear. **Features:** Double-action, ventilated rib, ported, integral key-lock. Introduced 1997. Imported by Taurus International.
Price: Blue .... **$578.00 to $797.00**
Price: Matte stainless .... **$641.00 to $859.00**

TAURUS RAGING BULL MODEL 416
Caliber: 41 Magnum, 6-shot. **Barrel:** 6-1/2". **Weight:** 61.9 oz. **Grips:** Rubber. **Sights:** Adjustable. **Features:** Double-action, ported, ventilated rib, matte stainless, integral key-lock.
Price: **$641.00**

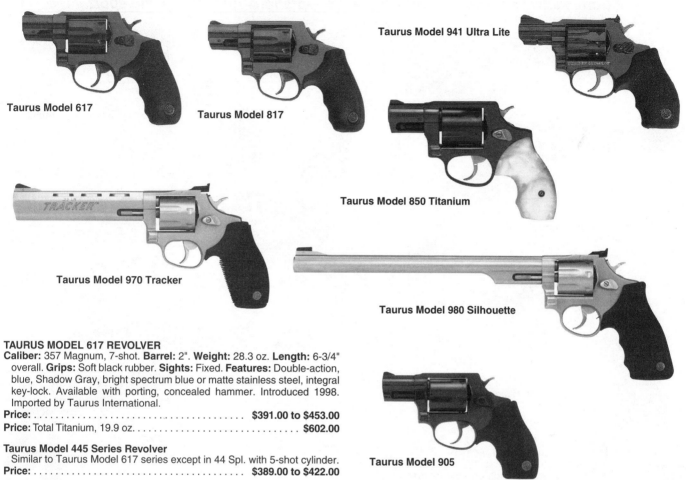

Taurus Model 617

Taurus Model 817

Taurus Model 941 Ultra Lite

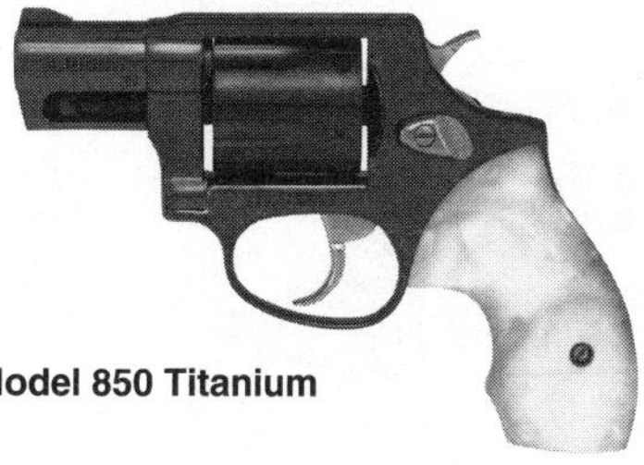

Taurus Model 850 Titanium

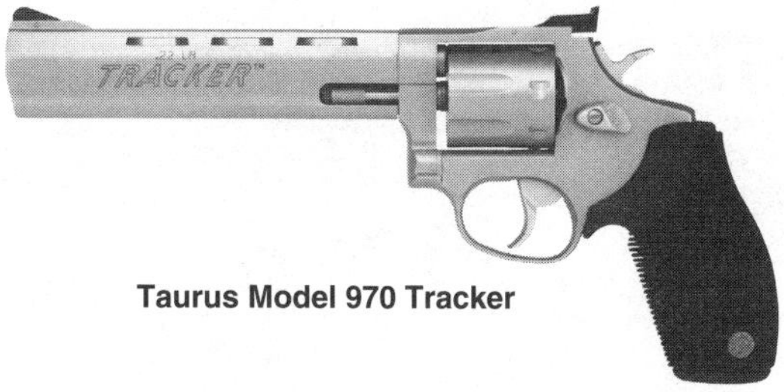

Taurus Model 970 Tracker

Taurus Model 980 Silhouette

Taurus Model 905

TAURUS MODEL 617 REVOLVER
Caliber: 357 Magnum, 7-shot. **Barrel:** 2". **Weight:** 28.3 oz. **Length:** 6-3/4" overall. **Grips:** Soft black rubber. **Sights:** Fixed. **Features:** Double-action, blue, Shadow Gray, bright spectrum blue or matte stainless steel, integral key-lock. Available with porting, concealed hammer. Introduced 1998. Imported by Taurus International.
Price: . . . . **$391.00 to $453.00**
Price: Total Titanium, 19.9 oz. **$602.00**

Taurus Model 445 Series Revolver
Similar to Taurus Model 617 series except in 44 Spl. with 5-shot cylinder.
Price: . . . . **$389.00 to $422.00**

Taurus Model 617ULT Revolver
Similar to Model 617 except aluminum alloy and titanium components, matte stainless finish, integral key-lock action. Weighs 18.5 oz. Available ported or non-ported. Introduced 2001. Imported by Taurus International.
Price: (5-shot cylinder) . . . . **$530.00 to $545.00**

TAURUS MODEL 817 ULTRA-LITE REVOLVER
Caliber: 38 Spec., 7-shot. **Barrel:** 2". **Weight:** 21 oz. **Length:** 6-1/2" overall. **Grips:** Soft rubber. **Sights:** Fixed. **Features:** Double-action, integral key-lock. Rated for +P ammo. Introduced 1999. Imported from Brazil by Taurus International.
Price: Blue **$375.00**
Price: Blue, ported **$395.00**
Price: Matte, stainless **$420.00**
Price: Matte, stainless, ported **$440.00**

TAURUS MODEL 850CIA REVOLVER
Caliber: 38 Special, 5-shot. **Barrel:** 2". **Weight:** 17-24.5 oz. **Grips:** Rubber, mother-of-pearl. **Sights:** Ramp front, square notch rear. **Features:** Double-action only, blue or matte stainless steel, rated for +P ammo, integral key-lock, internal hammer. Introduced 2001. From Taurus International.
Price: . . . . **$406.00 to $453.00**
Price: Total Titanium **$578.00**

TAURUS MODEL 851CIA REVOLVER
Caliber: 38 Spec., 5-shot. **Barrel:** 2". **Weight:** 17-24.5 oz. **Grips:** Rubber. **Sights:** Fixed-UL/ULT adjustable. **Features:** Concealed single-action/double-action design. Shrouded cockable hammer, blue, matte stainless, Total Titanium, blue or stainless UL and ULT, integral key-lock. Rated for +P ammo.
Price: . . . . **$406.00 to $578.00**

TAURUS MODEL 94, 941 REVOLVER
Caliber: 22 LR (Mod. 94), 22 WMR (Mod. 941), 8-shot. **Barrel:** 2", 4", 5". **Weight:** 27.5 oz. (4" barrel). **Grips:** Soft black rubber. **Sights:** Serrated ramp front, rear adjustable. **Features:** Double-action, integral key-lock. Introduced 1992. Imported by Taurus International.
Price: Blue . . . . **$328.00 to $344.00**
Price: Stainless (matte) . . . . **$375.00 to $391.00**
Price: Model 941 Ultra Lite, forged aluminum alloy, 2" . **$359.00 to $375.00**
Price: As above, stainless . . . . **$406.00 to $422.00**

TAURUS MODEL 970/971 TRACKER REVOLVERS
Caliber: 22 LR (Model 970), 22 Magnum (Model 971); 7-shot. **Barrel:** 6". **Weight:** 53.6 oz. **Grips:** Rubber. **Sights:** Adjustable. **Features:** Double barrel, heavy barrel with ventilated rib; matte stainless finish, integral key-lock. Introduced 2001. From Taurus International.
Price: . . . . **$391.00 to $406.00**

TAURUS MODEL 980/981 SILHOUETTE REVOLVERS
Caliber: 22 LR (Model 980), 22 Magnum (Model 981); 7-shot. **Barrel:** 12". **Weight:** 68 oz. **Grips:** Rubber. **Sights:** Adjustable. **Features:** Double-action, heavy barrel with ventilated rib and scope mount, matte stainless finish, integral key-lock. Introduced 2001. From Taurus International.
Price: (Model 980) **$398.00**
Price: (Model 981) **$414.00**

TAURUS MODEL 905, 405, 455 PISTOL CALIBER REVOLVERS
Caliber: 9mm, .40, .45 ACP, 5-shot. **Barrel:** 2", 4", 6-1/2". **Weight:** 21 oz. to 40.8 oz. **Grips:** Rubber. **Sights:** Fixed, adjustable on Model 455SS6 in .45 ACP. **Features:** Produced as a backup gun for law enforcement officers. Introduced 2003. Imported from Brazil by Taurus International.
Price: . . . . **$383.00 to $523.00**

HANDGUNS — Single-Action Revolvers

Both classic six-shooters and modern adaptations for hunting and sport.

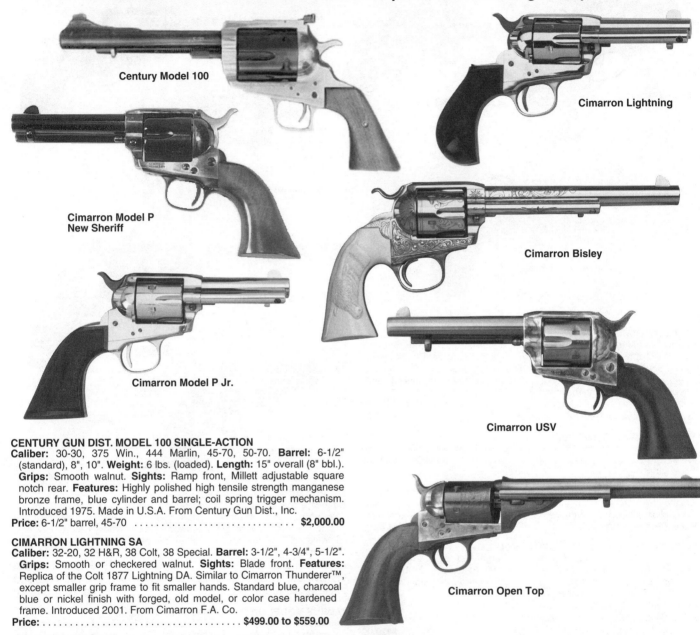

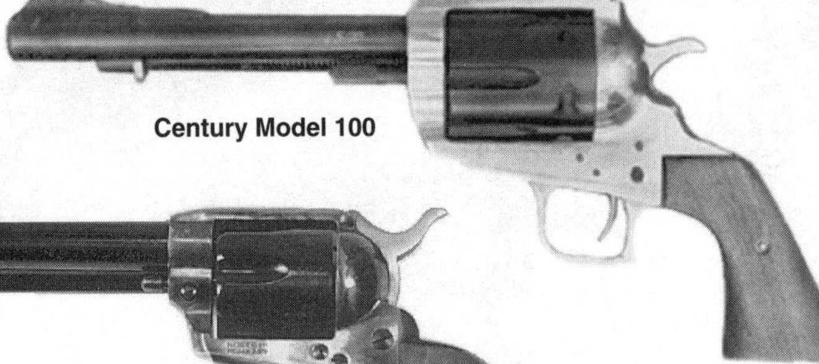

Century Model 100

Cimarron Lightning

Cimarron Model P
New Sheriff

Cimarron Bisley

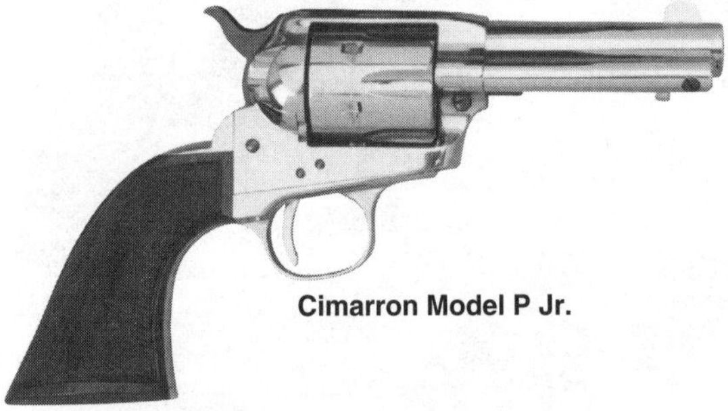

Cimarron Model P Jr.

Cimarron USV

Cimarron Open Top

CENTURY GUN DIST. MODEL 100 SINGLE-ACTION
Caliber: 30-30, 375 Win., 444 Marlin, 45-70, 50-70. **Barrel:** 6-1/2" (standard), 8", 10". **Weight:** 6 lbs. (loaded). **Length:** 15" overall (8" bbl.). **Grips:** Smooth walnut. **Sights:** Ramp front, Millett adjustable square notch rear. **Features:** Highly polished high tensile strength manganese bronze frame, blue cylinder and barrel; coil spring trigger mechanism. Introduced 1975. Made in U.S.A. From Century Gun Dist., Inc.
Price: 6-1/2" barrel, 45-70 .... **$2,000.00**

CIMARRON LIGHTNING SA
Caliber: 32-20, 32 H&R, 38 Colt, 38 Special. **Barrel:** 3-1/2", 4-3/4", 5-1/2". **Grips:** Smooth or checkered walnut. **Sights:** Blade front. **Features:** Replica of the Colt 1877 Lightning DA. Similar to Cimarron Thunderer™, except smaller grip frame to fit smaller hands. Standard blue, charcoal blue or nickel finish with forged, old model, or color case hardened frame. Introduced 2001. From Cimarron F.A. Co.
Price: .... **$499.00 to $559.00**

CIMARRON MODEL P
Caliber: 32 WCF, 38 WCF, 357 Mag., 44 WCF, 44 Spec., 45 Colt, 45LC and 45 ACP. **Barrel:** 4-3/4", 5-1/2", 7-1/2". **Weight:** 39 oz. **Length:** 10" overall (4" barrel). **Grips:** Walnut. **Sights:** Blade front, fixed or adjustable rear. **Features:** Uses "old model" black powder frame with "Bullseye" ejector or New Model frame. Imported by Cimarron F.A. Co.
Price: .... **$499.00 to $559.00**
Price: New Sheriff .... **$499.00 to $559.00**

Cimarron Bisley Model Single-Action Revolvers
Similar to 1873 Model P, special grip frame and trigger guard, knurled wide-spur hammer, curved trigger. Available in 357 Mag., 44 WCF, 44 Spl., 45 Colt. Introduced 1999. Imported by Cimarron F.A. Co.
Price: **$525.00**

CIMARRON MODEL "P" JR.
Caliber: 32-20, 32 H&R, 38 Special. **Barrel:** 3-1/2", 4-3/4", 5-1/2". **Grips:** Checkered walnut. **Sights:** Blade front. **Features:** Styled after 1873 Colt Peacemaker, except 20 percent smaller. Blue finish with color case-hardened frame; Cowboy Comp® action. Introduced 2001. From Cimarron F.A. Co.
Price: .... **$489.00 to $529.00**

CIMARRON U. S. VOLUNTEER ARTILLERY MODEL SINGLE-ACTION
Caliber: 45 Colt. **Barrel:** 5-1/2". **Weight:** 39 oz. **Length:** 11-1/2" overall. **Grips:** Walnut. **Sights:** Fixed. **Features:** U.S. markings and cartouche, case-hardened frame and hammer; 45 Colt only. Imported by Cimarron F.A. Co.
Price: .... **$549.00 to $599.00**

CIMARRON 1872 OPEN TOP REVOLVER
Caliber: 38, 44 Special, 44 Colt, 44 Russian, 45LC, 45 S&W Schofield. **Barrel:** 5-1/2" and 7-1/2". **Grips:** Walnut. **Sights:** Blade front, fixed rear. **Features:** Replica of first cartridge-firing revolver. Blue, charcoal blue, nickel or Original® finish; Navy-style brass or steel Army-style frame. Introduced 2001 by Cimarron F.A. Co.
Price: .... **$529.00 to $599.00**

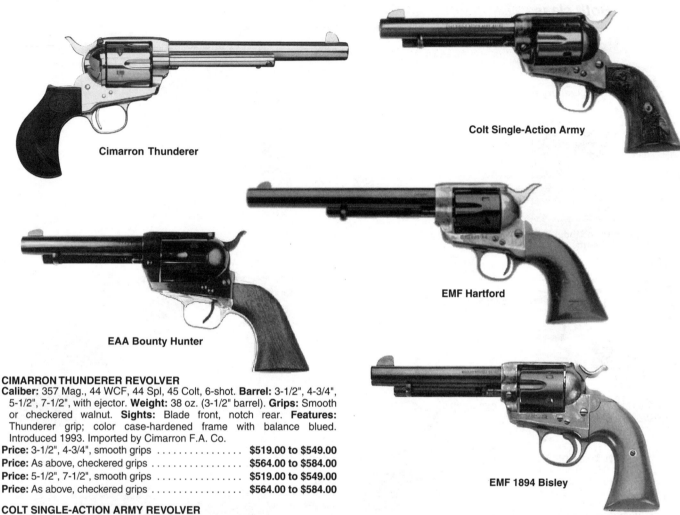

Cimarron Thunderer

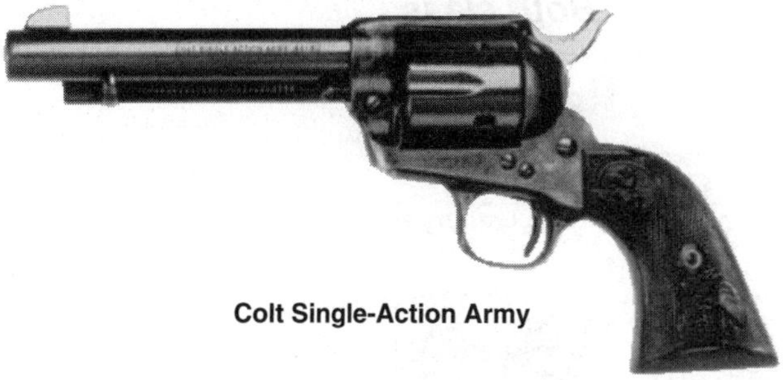
Colt Single-Action Army

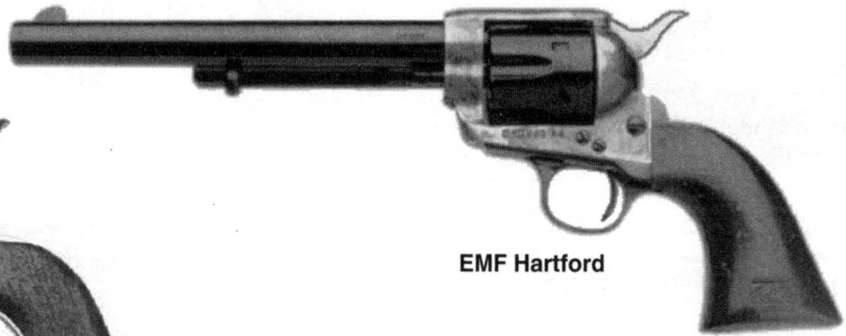
EMF Hartford

EAA Bounty Hunter

EMF 1894 Bisley

CIMARRON THUNDERER REVOLVER

Caliber: 357 Mag., 44 WCF, 44 Spl, 45 Colt, 6-shot. **Barrel:** 3-1/2", 4-3/4", 5-1/2", 7-1/2", with ejector. **Weight:** 38 oz. (3-1/2" barrel). **Grips:** Smooth or checkered walnut. **Sights:** Blade front, notch rear. **Features:** Thunderer grip; color case-hardened frame with balance blued. Introduced 1993. Imported by Cimarron F.A. Co.

Price: 3-1/2", 4-3/4", smooth grips .... **$519.00 to $549.00**
Price: As above, checkered grips .... **$564.00 to $584.00**
Price: 5-1/2", 7-1/2", smooth grips .... **$519.00 to $549.00**
Price: As above, checkered grips .... **$564.00 to $584.00**

COLT SINGLE-ACTION ARMY REVOLVER

Caliber: 357 Mag., 38 Special, .32/20, 44-40, 45 Colt, 6-shot. **Barrel:** 4-3/4", 5-1/2", 7-1/2". **Weight:** 40 oz. (4-3/4" barrel). **Length:** 10-1/4" overall (4-3/4" barrel). **Grips:** Black Eagle composite. **Sights:** Blade front, notch rear. **Features:** Available in full nickel finish with nickel grip medallions, or Royal Blue with color case-hardened frame. Reintroduced 1992.

Price: .... **$1,380.00 to $1,500.00**

EAA BOUNTY HUNTER SA REVOLVERS

Caliber: 22 LR/22 WMR, 357 Mag., 44 Mag., 45 Colt, 6-shot. **Barrel:** 4-1/2", 7-1/2". **Weight:** 2.5 lbs. **Length:** 11" overall (4-5/8" barrel). **Grips:** Smooth walnut. **Sights:** Blade front, grooved topstrap rear. **Features:** Transfer bar safety; 3-position hammer; hammer forged barrel. Introduced 1992. Imported by European American Armory.

Price: Blue or case-hardened **$369.00**
Price: Nickel **$399.00**
Price: 22LR/22WMR, blue **$269.00**
Price: As above, nickel **$299.00**

EMF MODEL 1873 FRONTIER MARSHAL

Caliber: 357 Mag., 45 Colt. **Barrel:** 4-3/4", 5-1/2, 7-1/2". **Weight:** 39 oz. **Length:** 10-1/2" overall. **Grips:** One-piece walnut. **Sights:** Blade front, notch rear. **Features:** Bright brass trigger guard and backstrap, color case-hardened frame, blued barrel and cylinder. Introduced 1998. Imported from Italy by IAR, Inc.

Price: **$395.00**

EMF HARTFORD SINGLE-ACTION REVOLVERS

Caliber: 357 Mag., 32-20, 38-40, 44-40, 44 Spec., 45 Colt. **Barrel:** 4-3/4", 5-1/2", 7-1/2". **Weight:** 45 oz. **Length:** 13" overall (7-1/2" barrel). **Grips:** Smooth walnut. **Sights:** Blade front, fixed rear. **Features:** Identical to the original Colts with inspector cartouche on left grip, original patent dates and U.S. markings. All major parts serial numbered using original Colt-style lettering, numbering. Bullseye ejector head and color case-hardening on frame and hammer. Introduced 1990. From E.M.F.

Price: **$500.00**
Price: Cavalry or Artillery **$390.00**
Price: Nickel plated, add **$125.00**
Price: Case-hardened New Model frame **$365.00**

EMF 1894 Bisley Revolver

Similar to the Hartford single-action revolver except has special grip frame and trigger guard, wide spur hammer; available in 38-40 or 45 Colt, 4-3/4", 5-1/2" or 7-1/2" barrel. Introduced 1995. Imported by E.M.F.

Price: Case-hardened/blue **$400.00**
Price: Nickel **$525.00**

EMF Hartford Pinkerton Single-Action Revolver

Same as the regular Hartford except has 4" barrel with ejector tube and bird's-head grip. Calibers: 357 Mag., 45 Colt. Introduced 1997. Imported by E.M.F.

Price: **$375.00**

EMF Hartford Express Single-Action Revolver

Same as the regular Hartford model except uses grip of the Colt Lightning revolver. Barrel lengths of 4", 4-3/4", 5-1/2". Introduced 1997. Imported by E.M.F.

Price: **$375.00**

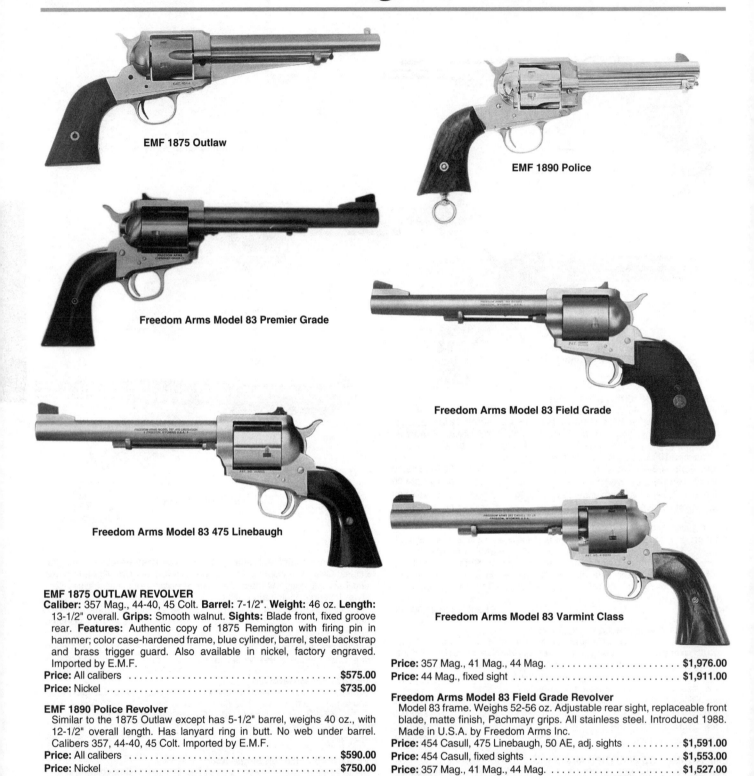

EMF 1875 Outlaw

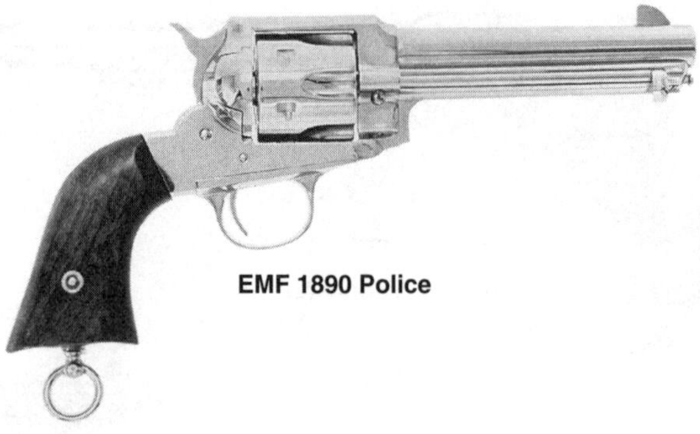

EMF 1890 Police

Freedom Arms Model 83 Premier Grade

Freedom Arms Model 83 Field Grade

Freedom Arms Model 83 475 Linebaugh

Freedom Arms Model 83 Varmint Class

EMF 1875 OUTLAW REVOLVER

Caliber: 357 Mag., 44-40, 45 Colt. **Barrel:** 7-1/2". **Weight:** 46 oz. **Length:** 13-1/2" overall. **Grips:** Smooth walnut. **Sights:** Blade front, fixed groove rear. **Features:** Authentic copy of 1875 Remington with firing pin in hammer; color case-hardened frame, blue cylinder, barrel, steel backstrap and brass trigger guard. Also available in nickel, factory engraved. Imported by E.M.F.

Price: All calibers **$575.00**

Price: Nickel **$735.00**

EMF 1890 Police Revolver

Similar to the 1875 Outlaw except has 5-1/2" barrel, weighs 40 oz., with 12-1/2" overall length. Has lanyard ring in butt. No web under barrel. Calibers 357, 44-40, 45 Colt. Imported by E.M.F.

Price: All calibers **$590.00**

Price: Nickel **$750.00**

FREEDOM ARMS MODEL 83 PREMIER GRADE REVOLVER

Caliber: 357 Mag., 41 Mag., 44 Mag., 454 Casull, 475 Linebaugh, 50 AE, 5-shot. **Barrel:** 4-3/4", 6", 7-1/2", 9" (357 Mag. only), 10". **Weight:** 52.8 oz. **Length:** 13" (7-1/2" bbl.). **Grips:** Impregnated hardwood. **Sights:** Blade front, notch or adjustable rear. **Features:** All stainless steel construction; sliding bar safety system. Lifetime warranty. Made in U.S.A. by Freedom Arms, Inc.

Price: 454 Casull, 475 Linebaugh, 50 AE. **$2,058.00**

Price: 454 Casull, fixed sight **$1,979.00**

Price: 357 Mag., 41 Mag., 44 Mag. **$1,976.00**

Price: 44 Mag., fixed sight **$1,911.00**

Freedom Arms Model 83 Field Grade Revolver

Model 83 frame. Weighs 52-56 oz. Adjustable rear sight, replaceable front blade, matte finish, Pachmayr grips. All stainless steel. Introduced 1988. Made in U.S.A. by Freedom Arms Inc.

Price: 454 Casull, 475 Linebaugh, 50 AE, adj. sights **$1,591.00**

Price: 454 Casull, fixed sights **$1,553.00**

Price: 357 Mag., 41 Mag., 44 Mag. **$1,527.00**

FREEDOM ARMS MODEL 83 VARMINT CLASS REVOLVERS

Caliber: 22 LR, 5-shot. **Barrel:** 5-1/8, 7-1/2". **Weight:** 58 oz. (7-1/2" bbl.). **Length:** 11-1/2" (7-1/2" bbl.). **Grips:** Impregnated hardwood. **Sights:** Steel base adjustable "V" notch rear sight and replaceable brass bead front sight. **Features:** Stainless steel, matte finish, manual sliding bar system, dual firing pins, pre-set trigger stop. Made in U.S.A. by Freedom Arms, Inc.

Price: Varmint Class **$1,828.00**

Price: Extra fitted 22 WMR cylinder **$264.00**

Freedom Arms Model 97 Premier Grade

Heritage Rough Rider

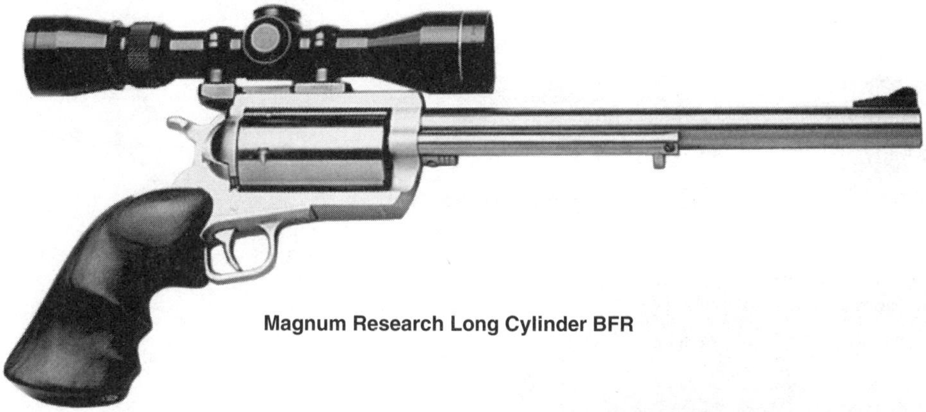
Magnum Research Long Cylinder BFR

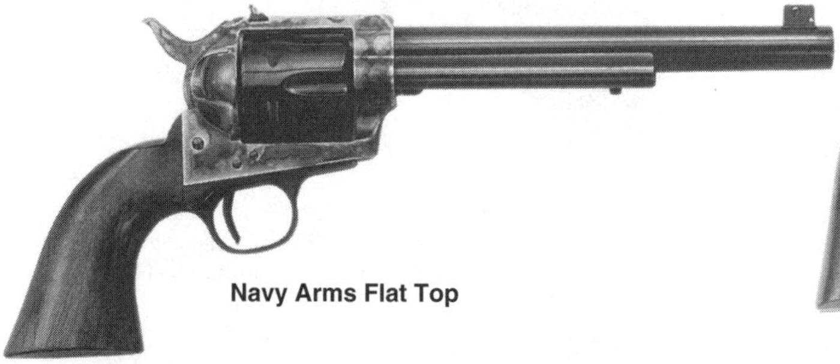
Navy Arms Flat Top

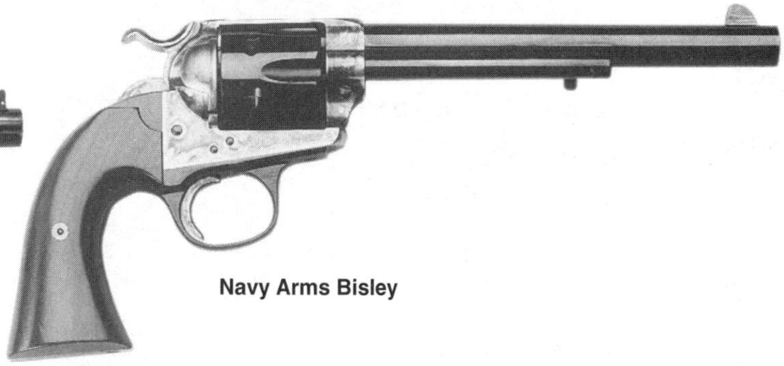
Navy Arms Bisley

FREEDOM ARMS MODEL 97 PREMIER GRADE REVOLVER
Caliber: 22 LR, 357 Mag., 41 Mag., 44 Special, 45 Colt, 5-shot. **Barrel:** 4-1/2", 5-1/2", 7-1/2", 10". **Weight:** 37 oz. (45 Colt 5-1/2"). **Length:** 10-3/4" (5-1/2" bbl.). **Grips:** Impregnated hardwood. **Sights:** Adjustable rear, replaceable blade front. **Features:** Stainless steel, brushed finish, automatic transfer bar safety system. Introduced in 1997. Made in U.S.A. by Freedom Arms.
Price: 357 Mag., 41 Mag., 45 Colt **$1,668.00**
Price: 357 Mag., 45 Colt, fixed sight **$1,576.00**
Price: Extra fitted cylinders 38 Special, 45 ACP **$264.00**
Price: 22 LR with sporting chambers **$1,732.00**
Price: Extra fitted 22 WMR cylinder **$264.00**
Price: Extra fitted 22 LR match grade cylinder **$476.00**
Price: 22 match grade chamber instead of 22 LR sport chamber . . **$214.00**

HERITAGE ROUGH RIDER REVOLVER
Caliber: 17HMR, 17LR, 32 H&R, 32 S&W, 32 S&W Long, .45LC, 22 LR, 22 LR/22 WMR combo, 6-shot. **Barrel:** 2-3/4", 3-1/2", 4-3/4", 6-1/2", 9". **Weight:** 31 to 38 oz. **Length:** NA. **Grips:** Exotic hardwood, laminated wood or mother-of-pearl; bird's-head models offered. **Sights:** Blade front, fixed rear. Adjustable sight on 4", 6" and 9" models. **Features:** Hammer block safety. High polish blue, black satin, silver satin, case-hardened and nickel finish. Introduced 1993. Made in U.S.A. by Heritage Mfg., Inc.
Price: . . . . **$159.95 to $389.95**

MAGNUM RESEARCH BFR SINGLE-ACTION REVOLVER
(Long cylinder) Caliber: 30/30, 45/70 Government, 444 Marlin, 45 LC/410, 450 Marlin, .500 S&W. **Barrel:** 7.5", 10". **Weight:** 4 lbs., 4.36 lbs. **Length:** 15", 17.5".
(Short cylinder) Caliber: 50AE, 454 Casull, 22 Hornet, BFR 480/475. **Barrel:** 6.5", 7.5", 10". **Weight:** 3.2 lbs, 3.5 lbs., 4.36 lbs. (10"). **Length:** 12.75 (6"), 13.75", 16.25".
Sights: All have fully adjustable rear, black blade ramp front. **Features:** Stainless steel construction, rubber grips, all 5-shot capacity. Barrels are stress-relieved and cut rifled. Made in U.S.A. From Magnum Research, Inc.
Price: **$899.00**

NAVY ARMS FLAT TOP TARGET MODEL REVOLVER
Caliber: 45 Colt, 6-shot cylinder. **Barrel:** 7-1/2". **Weight:** 40 oz. **Length:** 13-1/4" overall. **Grips:** Smooth walnut. **Sights:** Spring-loaded German silver front, rear adjustable for windage. **Features:** Replica of Colt's Flat Top Frontier target revolver made from 1888 to 1896. Blue with color case-hardened frame. Introduced 1997. Imported by Navy Arms.
Price: **$450.00**

NAVY ARMS BISLEY MODEL SINGLE-ACTION REVOLVER
Caliber: 44-40 or 45 Colt, 6-shot cylinder. **Barrel:** 4-3/4", 5-1/2", 7-1/2". **Weight:** 40 oz. **Length:** 12-1/2" overall (7-1/2" barrel). **Grips:** Smooth walnut. **Sights:** Blade front, notch rear. **Features:** Replica of Colt's Bisley Model. Polished blue finish, color case-hardened frame. Introduced 1997. Imported by Navy Arms.
Price: . . . . **$425.00 to $460.00**

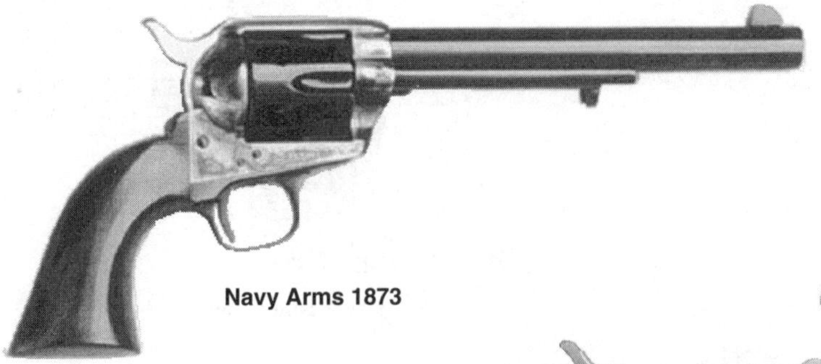

Navy Arms 1873

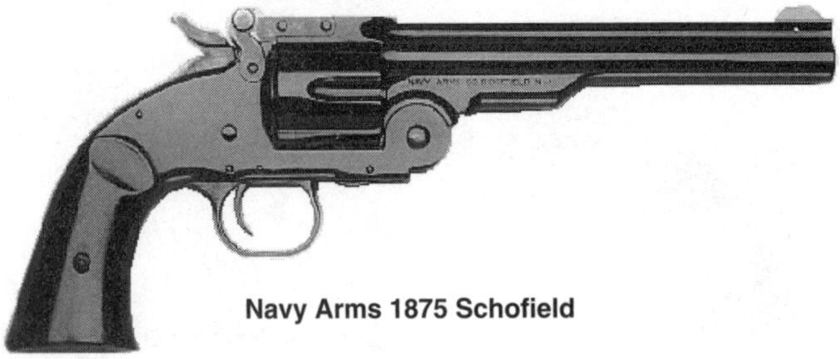

Navy Arms 1875 Schofield

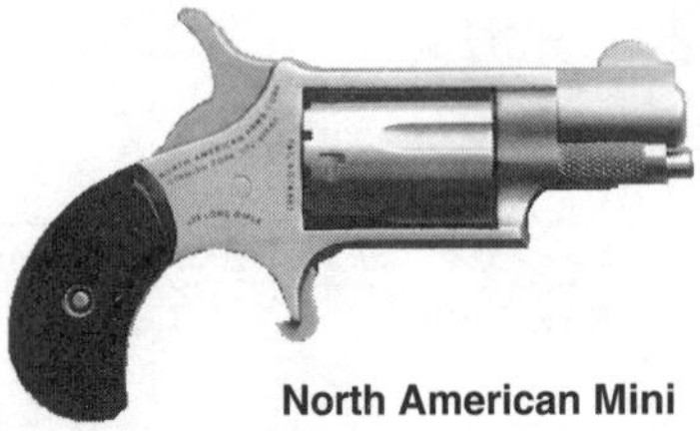

North American Mini

North American Mini-Master

Navy Arms New Model Russian

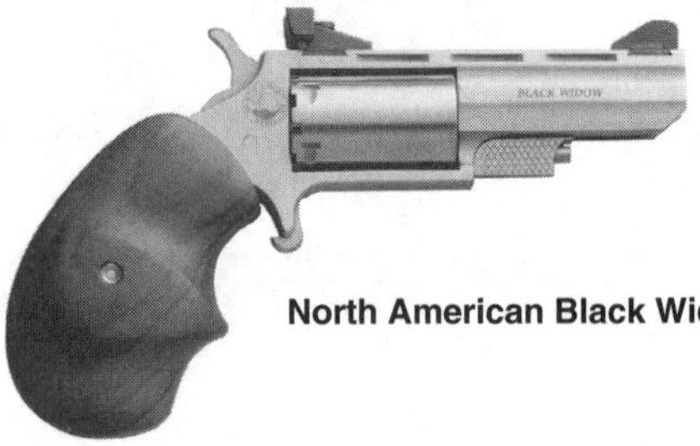

North American Black Widow

NAVY ARMS 1873 SINGLE-ACTION REVOLVER

Caliber: 357 Mag., 44-40, 45 Colt, 6-shot cylinder. **Barrel:** 4-3/4", 5-1/2", 7-1/2". **Weight:** 36 oz. **Length:** 10-3/4" overall (5-1/2" barrel). **Grips:** Smooth walnut. **Sights:** Blade front, notch rear. **Features:** Blue with color case-hardened frame. Introduced 1991. Imported by Navy Arms.

Price: **$405.00**

NAVY ARMS 1875 SCHOFIELD REVOLVER

Caliber: 44-40, 45 Colt, 6-shot cylinder. **Barrel:** 3-1/2", 5", 7". **Weight:** 39 oz. **Length:** 10-3/4" overall (5" barrel). **Grips:** Smooth walnut. **Sights:** Blade front, notch rear. **Features:** Replica of Smith & Wesson Model 3 Schofield. Single-action, top-break with automatic ejection. Polished blue finish. Introduced 1994. Imported by Navy Arms.

Price: Hideout Model, 3-1/2" barrel **$695.00**

Price: Wells Fargo, 5" barrel **$695.00**

Price: U.S. Cavalry model, 7" barrel, military markings **$695.00**

NAVY ARMS NEW MODEL RUSSIAN REVOLVER

Caliber: 44 Russian, 6-shot cylinder. **Barrel:** 6-1/2". **Weight:** 40 oz. **Length:** 12" overall. **Grips:** Smooth walnut. **Sights:** Blade front, notch rear. **Features:** Replica of the S&W Model 3 Russian Third Model revolver. Spur trigger guard, polished blue finish. Introduced 1999. Imported by Navy Arms.

Price: **$769.00**

NAVY ARMS 1851 NAVY CONVERSION REVOLVER

Caliber: 38 Spec., 38 Long Colt. **Barrel:** 5-1/2", 7-1/2". **Weight:** 44 oz. **Length:** 14" overall (7-1/2" barrel). **Grips:** Smooth walnut. **Sights:** Bead front, notch rear. **Features:** Replica of Colt's cartridge conversion revolver. Polished blue finish with color case-hardened frame, silver plated trigger guard and backstrap. Introduced 1999. Imported by Navy Arms.

Price: **$165.00**

NAVY ARMS 1860 ARMY CONVERSION REVOLVER

Caliber: 38 Spec., 38 Long Colt. **Barrel:** 5-1/2", 7-1/2". **Weight:** 44 oz. **Length:** 13-1/2" overall (7-1/2" barrel). **Grips:** Smooth walnut. **Sights:** Blade front, notch rear. **Features:** Replica of Colt's conversion revolver. Polished blue finish with color case-hardened frame, full-size 1860 Army grip with blued steel backstrap. Introduced 1999. Imported by Navy Arms.

Price: **$190.00**

NORTH AMERICAN MINI REVOLVERS

Caliber: 22 Short, 22 LR, 22 WMR, 5-shot. **Barrel:** 1-1/8", 1-5/8". **Weight:** 4 to 6.6 oz. **Length:** 3-5/8" to 6-1/8" overall. **Grips:** Laminated wood. **Sights:** Blade front, notch fixed rear. **Features:** All stainless steel construction. Polished satin and matte finish. Engraved models available. From North American Arms.

Price: 22 Short, 22 LR **$193.00**

Price: 22 WMR, 1-1/8" or 1-5/8" bbl. **$193.00**

Price: 22 WMR, 1-1/8" or 1-5/8" bbl. with extra 22 LR cylinder **$193.00**

NORTH AMERICAN MINI-MASTER

Caliber: 22 LR, 22 WMR, 17 HMR, 5-shot cylinder. **Barrel:** 4". **Weight:** 10.7 oz. **Length:** 7.75" overall. **Grips:** Checkered hard black rubber. **Sights:** Blade front, white outline rear adjustable for elevation, or fixed. **Features:** Heavy vented barrel; full-size grips. Non-fluted cylinder. Introduced 1989.

Price: Adjustable sight, 22 WMR, 17 HMR or 22 LR **$301.00**

Price: As above with extra WMR/LR cylinder **$330.00**

Price: Fixed sight, 22 WMR, 17 HMR or 22 LR **$272.00**

Price: As above with extra WMR/LR cylinder **$330.00**

North American Black Widow Revolver

Similar to Mini-Master, 2" heavy vent barrel. Built on 22 WMR frame. Non-fluted cylinder, black rubber grips. Available with Millett Low Profile fixed sights or Millett sight adjustable for elevation only. Overall length 5-7/8", weighs 8.8 oz. From North American Arms.

Price: Adjustable sight, 22 LR, 17 HMR or 22 WMR **$287.00**

Price: As above with extra WMR/LR cylinder **$316.00**

Price: Fixed sight, 22 LR, 17 HMR or 22 WMR **$287.00**

Price: As above with extra WMR/LR cylinder **$287.00**

HANDGUNS — Single-Action Revolvers

Ruger "Bird's-Head" Single Six

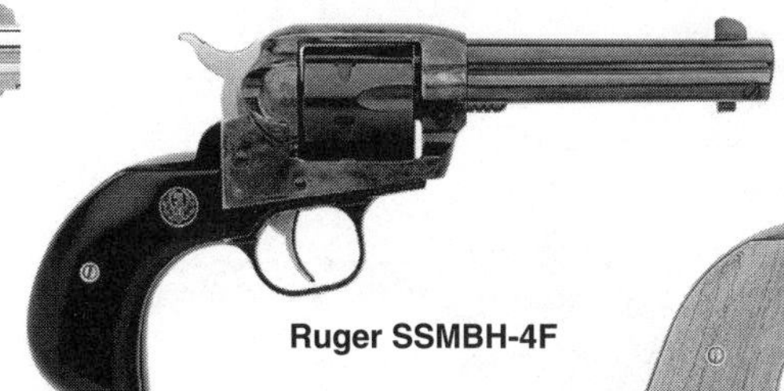
Ruger SSMBH-4F

Ruger Blackhawk

Ruger Bisley Single-Action

Ruger Super Blackhawk Hunter

Ruger Vaquero

RUGER NEW MODEL SINGLE SIX REVOLVER
Caliber: 32 H&R. **Barrel:** 4-5/8", 6-shot. **Grips:** Black Micarta "bird's-head", rosewood with color case. **Sights:** Fixed. **Features:** High impact case, gun lock standard.
Price: Stainless, KSSMBH-4F, bird's-head **$576.00**
Price: Color case, SSMBH-4F, bird's-head **$576.00**
Price: Color case, SSM-4F-S, rosewood **$576.00**

RUGER NEW MODEL BLACKHAWK AND BLACKHAWK CONVERTIBLE
Caliber: 30 Carbine, 357 Mag./38 Spec., 41 Mag., 45 Colt, 6-shot. **Barrel:** 4-5/8" or 5-1/2", either caliber; 7-1/2" (30 carbine and 45 Colt). **Weight:** 42 oz. (6-1/2" bbl.). **Length:** 12-1/4" overall (5-1/2" bbl.). **Grips:** American walnut. **Sights:** 1/8" ramp front, micro-click rear adjustable for windage and elevation. **Features:** Ruger transfer bar safety system, independent firing pin, hardened chrome-moly steel frame, music wire springs throughout. Case and lock included.
Price: Blue 30 Carbine, 7-1/2" (BN31) **$435.00**
Price: Blue, 357 Mag., 4-5/8", 6-1/2" (BN34, BN36) **$435.00**
Price: As above, stainless (KBN34, KBN36) **$530.00**
Price: Blue, 357 Mag./9mm Convertible, 4-5/8", 6-1/2" (BN34X, BN36X) includes extra cylinder **$489.00**
Price: Blue, 41 Mag., 4-5/8", 6-1/2" (BN41, BN42) **$435.00**
Price: Blue, 45 Colt, 4-5/8", 5-1/2", 7-1/2" (BN44, BN455, BN45) . . **$435.00**
Price: Stainless, 45 Colt, 4-5/8", 7-1/2" (KBN44, KBN45) **$530.00**
Price: Blue, 45 Colt/45 ACP Convertible, 4-5/8", 5-1/2" (BN44X, BN455X) includes extra cylinder **$489.00**

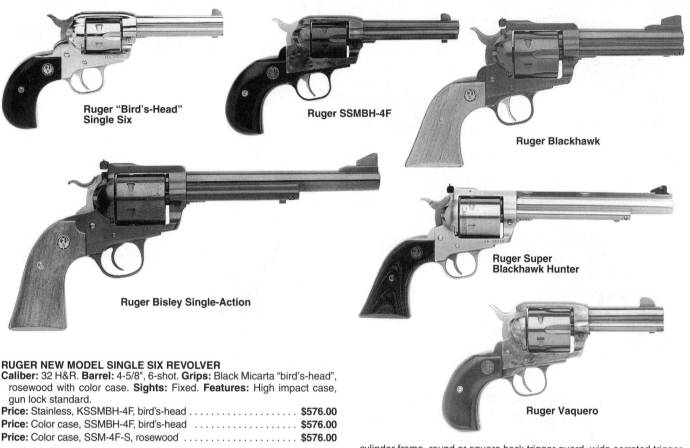

Ruger Bisley Single-Action Revolver
Similar to standard Blackhawk, hammer is lower with smoothly curved, deeply checkered wide spur. The trigger is strongly curved with wide smooth surface. Longer grip frame. Adjustable rear sight, ramp-style front. Unfluted cylinder and roll engraving, adjustable sights. Chambered for 357, 44 Mags. and 45 Colt; 7-1/2" barrel; overall length of 13"; weighs 48 oz. Plastic lockable case. Introduced 1985.
Price: RB-35W, 357Mag, RBD-44W, 44Mag, RB-45W, 45 Colt . . . **$535.00**

RUGER NEW MODEL SUPER BLACKHAWK
Caliber: 44 Mag., 6-shot. Also fires 44 Spec. **Barrel:** 4-5/8", 5-1/2", 7-1/2", 10-1/2" bull. **Weight:** 48 oz. (7-1/2" bbl.), 51 oz. (10-1/2" bbl.). **Length:** 13-3/8" overall (7-1/2" bbl.). **Grips:** American walnut. **Sights:** 1/8" ramp front, micro-click rear adjustable for windage and elevation. **Features:** Ruger transfer bar safety system, fluted or unfluted cylinder, steel grip and cylinder frame, round or square back trigger guard, wide serrated trigger, wide spur hammer. With case and lock.
Price: Blue, 4-5/8", 5-1/2", 7-1/2" (S458N, S45N, S47N) **$519.00**
Price: Blue, 10-1/2" bull barrel (S411N) **$529.00**
Price: Stainless, 4-5/8", 5-1/2", 7-1/2" (KS458N, KS45N, KS47N) . **$535.00**
Price: Stainless, 10-1/2" bull barrel (KS411N) **$545.00**

RUGER NEW MODEL SUPER BLACKHAWK HUNTER
Caliber: 44 Mag., 6-shot. **Barrel:** 7-1/2", full-length solid rib, unfluted cylinder. **Weight:** 52 oz. **Length:** 13-5/8". **Grips:** Black laminated wood. **Sights:** Adjustable rear, replaceable front blade. **Features:** Reintroduced Ultimate SA revolver. Includes instruction manual, high-impact case, set 1" medium scope rings, gun lock, ejector rod as standard.
Price: **$639.00**

RUGER VAQUERO SINGLE-ACTION REVOLVER
Caliber: 357 Mag., 44-40, 44 Mag., 45 LC, 6-shot. **Barrel:** 4-5/8", 5-1/2", 7-1/2". **Weight:** 38-41 oz. **Length:** 13-1/8" overall (7-1/2" barrel). **Grips:** Smooth rosewood with Ruger medallion. **Sights:** Blade front, fixed notch rear. **Features:** Transfer bar safety system and loading gate interlock. Blued model color case-hardened finish on frame, rest polished and blued. Stainless has high-gloss. Introduced 1993. From Sturm, Ruger & Co.
Price: 357 Mag. BNV34, KBNV34 (4-5/8"), BNV35, KBNV35 (5-1/2") **$535.00**
Price: 44-40 BNV40, KBNV40 (4-5/8"). BNV405, KBNV405 (5-1/2"). BNV407, KBNV407 (7-1/2") **$535.00**
Price: 44 Mag., BNV474, KBNV474 (4-5/8"). BNV475, KBNV475 (5-1/2"). BNV477, KBNV477 (7-1/2") **$535.00**
Price: 45 LC, BN444, KBNV44 (4-5/8"). BNV455, KBNV455 (5-1/2"). BNV45, KBNV45 (7-1/2") **$535.00**
Price: 45 LC, BNVBH453, KBNVBH453 3-3/4" with "bird's-head" grip **$576.00**
Price: 357 Mag., RBNV35 (5-1/2") **$535.00**; KRBNV35 (5-1/2") . . . **$555.00**
Price: 45 LC, RBNV44 (4-5/8"), RBNV455 (5-1/2") **$535.00**
Price: 45 LC, KRBNV44 (4-5/8"), KRBNV455 (5-1/2") **$555.00**

HANDGUNS — Single-Action Revolvers

Ruger Bisley-Vaquero

Ruger New Bearcat

Ruger Single-Six

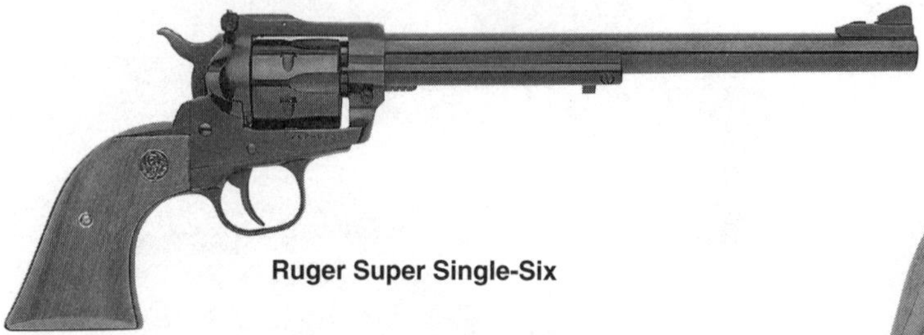

Ruger Super Single-Six

Ruger Bisley

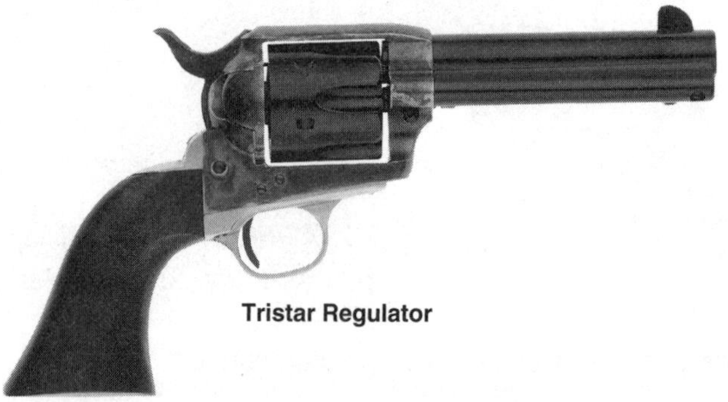

Tristar Regulator

Ruger Bisley-Vaquero Single-Action Revolver
Similar to Vaquero model with Bisley-style hammer, grip and trigger, available in 357 Magnum, 44 Magnum and 45 LC only; 4-5/8" or 5-1/2" barrel. Smooth rosewood grips with Ruger medallion. Roll-engraved, unfluted cylinder. Introduced 1997. From Sturm, Ruger & Co.

Price: Color case-hardened frame, blue grip frame, barrel and cylinder, RBNV-475, RBNV-474, 44 Mag. **$535.00**
Price: High-gloss stainless steel, KRBNV-475, KRBNV-474 . . . . . . **$555.00**
Price: For simulated ivory grips, add . . . . **$41.00 to $44.00**

RUGER NEW BEARCAT SINGLE-ACTION
Caliber: 22 LR, 6-shot. **Barrel:** 4". **Weight:** 24 oz. **Length:** 8-7/8" overall. **Grips:** Smooth rosewood with Ruger medallion. **Sights:** Blade front, fixed notch rear. **Features:** Reintroduction of the Ruger Bearcat with slightly lengthened frame, Ruger patented transfer bar safety system. Available in blue only. Introduced 1993. With case and lock. From Sturm, Ruger & Co.

Price: SBC4, blue **$379.00**
Price: KSBC-4, ss **$429.00**

RUGER MODEL SINGLE-SIX REVOLVER
Caliber: 32 H&R Magnum. **Barrel:** 4-5/8", 6-shot. **Weight:** 33 oz. **Length:** 10-1/8". **Grips:** Blue, rosewood, stainless, simulated ivory. **Sights:** Blade front, notch rear fixed. **Features:** Transfer bar and loading gate interlock safety, instruction manual, high impact case and gun lock.

Price: **$576.00**
Price: Blue, SSM4FS **$576.00**
Price: SS, KSSM4FSI **$576.00**

RUGER SINGLE-SIX AND SUPER SINGLE-SIX CONVERTIBLE
Caliber: 22 LR, 6-shot; 22 WMR in extra cylinder; 17 HMR. **Barrel:** 4-5/8", 5-1/2", 6-1/2", 9-1/2" (6-groove). **Weight:** 35 oz. (6-1/2" bbl.). **Length:** 11-13/16" overall (6-1/2" bbl.). **Grips:** Smooth American walnut. **Sights:** Improved Patridge front on ramp, fully adjustable rear protected by integral frame ribs (super single-six); or fixed sight (single six). **Features:** Transfer bar safety system, loading gate interlock, hardened chrome-moly steel frame, wide trigger, music wire springs throughout, independent firing pin.

Price: 4-5/8", 5-1/2", 6-1/2", 9-1/2" barrel, blue, adjustable sight NR4, NR5, NR6, NR9 . . . . **$399.00**
Price: 5-1/2", 6-1/2" bbl. only, stainless steel, adjustable sight KNR5, KNR6 . . . . **$485.00**
Price: 5-1/2", 6-1/2" barrel, blue fixed sights **$399.00**
Price: 6-1/2" barrel, NR 617, 17 HMR **$399.00**
Price: Ruger 50th Anniversary Single Six with 4-5/8" barrel and a gold-colored rollmark, "50 years of Single Six 1953 to 2003," blued steel finish, cocobolo wood grips with red Ruger medallions and both 22 LR and 22 WMR cylinders **$599.00**
Price: Stainless Hunter **$650.00**

Ruger Bisley Small Frame Revolver
Similar to Single-Six, frame is styled after classic Bisley "flat-top." Hammer is lower and smoothly curved with deeply checkered spur. Trigger is strongly curved with wide smooth surface. Longer grip frame design, and trigger guard is a large oval. Adjustable dovetail rear sight; front sight base accepts interchangeable square blades. Unfluted cylinder and roll engraving. Weighs 41 oz. Chambered for 22 LR, 6-1/2" barrel only. Plastic lockable case. Introduced 1985.

Price: RB-22AW **$422.00**

TRISTAR/UBERTI REGULATOR REVOLVER
Caliber: 45 Colt. **Barrel:** 4-3/4", 5-1/2". **Weight:** 32-38 oz. **Length:** 8-1/4" overall (4-3/4" bbl.) **Grips:** One-piece walnut. **Sights:** Blade front, notch rear. **Features:** Uberti replica of 1873 Colt Model "P" revolver. Color-case hardened steel frame, brass backstrap and trigger guard, hammer-block safety. Imported from Italy by Tristar Sporting Arms.

Price: Regulator **$335.00**
Price: Regulator Deluxe (blued backstrap, trigger guard) **$367.00**

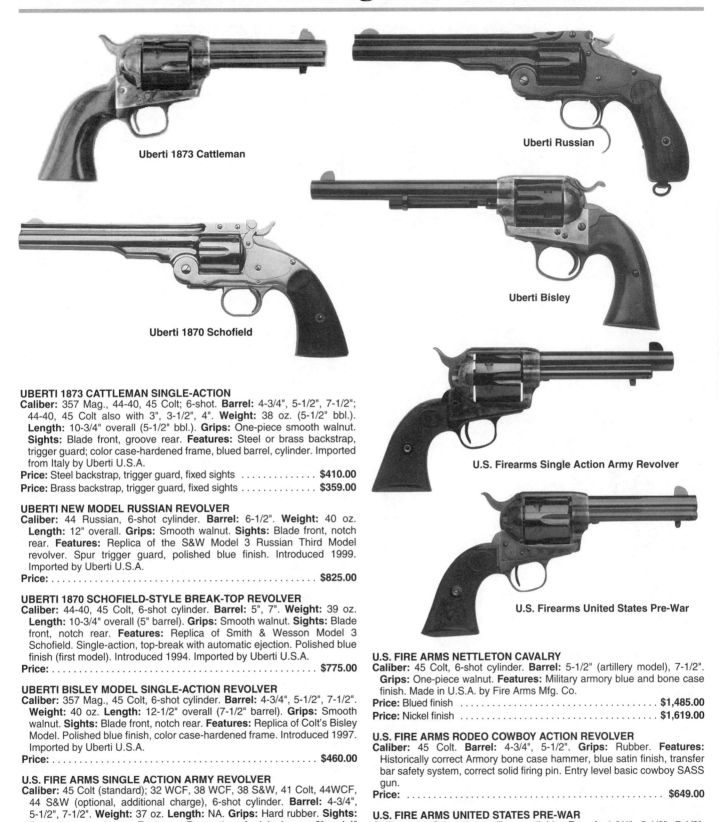

Uberti 1873 Cattleman

Uberti Russian

Uberti Bisley

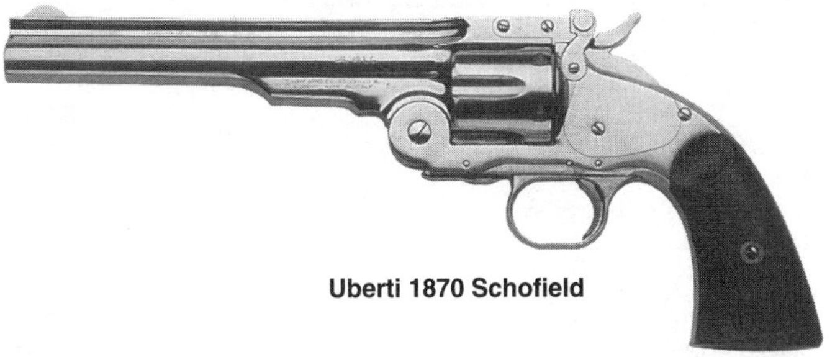

Uberti 1870 Schofield

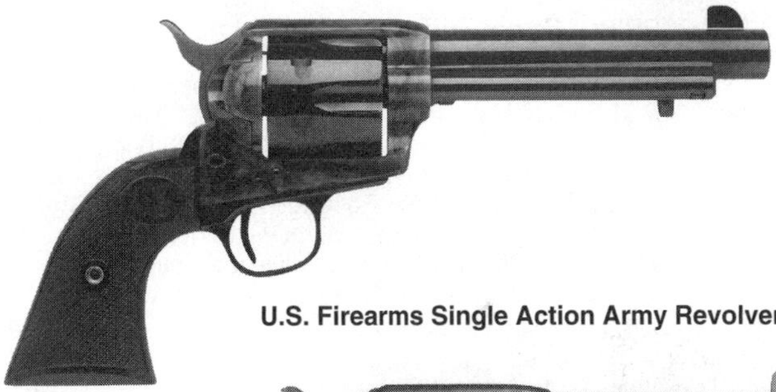

U.S. Firearms Single Action Army Revolver

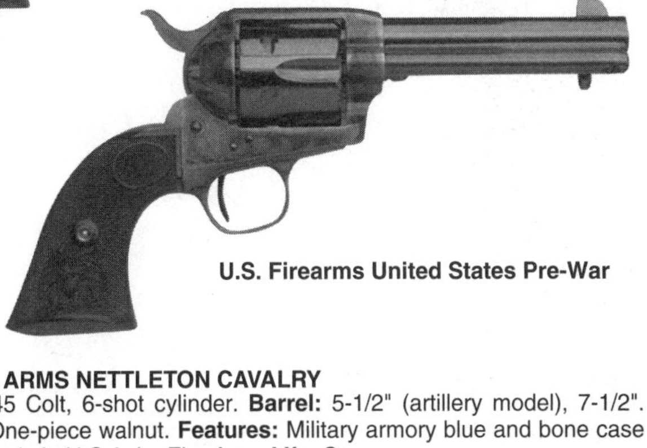

U.S. Firearms United States Pre-War

UBERTI 1873 CATTLEMAN SINGLE-ACTION

Caliber: 357 Mag., 44-40, 45 Colt; 6-shot. **Barrel:** 4-3/4", 5-1/2", 7-1/2"; 44-40, 45 Colt also with 3", 3-1/2", 4". **Weight:** 38 oz. (5-1/2" bbl.). **Length:** 10-3/4" overall (5-1/2" bbl.). **Grips:** One-piece smooth walnut. **Sights:** Blade front, groove rear. **Features:** Steel or brass backstrap, trigger guard; color case-hardened frame, blued barrel, cylinder. Imported from Italy by Uberti U.S.A.

Price: Steel backstrap, trigger guard, fixed sights **$410.00**

Price: Brass backstrap, trigger guard, fixed sights **$359.00**

UBERTI NEW MODEL RUSSIAN REVOLVER

Caliber: 44 Russian, 6-shot cylinder. **Barrel:** 6-1/2". **Weight:** 40 oz. **Length:** 12" overall. **Grips:** Smooth walnut. **Sights:** Blade front, notch rear. **Features:** Replica of the S&W Model 3 Russian Third Model revolver. Spur trigger guard, polished blue finish. Introduced 1999. Imported by Uberti U.S.A.

Price: **$825.00**

UBERTI 1870 SCHOFIELD-STYLE BREAK-TOP REVOLVER

Caliber: 44-40, 45 Colt, 6-shot cylinder. **Barrel:** 5", 7". **Weight:** 39 oz. **Length:** 10-3/4" overall (5" barrel). **Grips:** Smooth walnut. **Sights:** Blade front, notch rear. **Features:** Replica of Smith & Wesson Model 3 Schofield. Single-action, top-break with automatic ejection. Polished blue finish (first model). Introduced 1994. Imported by Uberti U.S.A.

Price: **$775.00**

UBERTI BISLEY MODEL SINGLE-ACTION REVOLVER

Caliber: 357 Mag., 45 Colt, 6-shot cylinder. **Barrel:** 4-3/4", 5-1/2", 7-1/2". **Weight:** 40 oz. **Length:** 12-1/2" overall (7-1/2" barrel). **Grips:** Smooth walnut. **Sights:** Blade front, notch rear. **Features:** Replica of Colt's Bisley Model. Polished blue finish, color case-hardened frame. Introduced 1997. Imported by Uberti U.S.A.

Price: **$460.00**

U.S. FIRE ARMS SINGLE ACTION ARMY REVOLVER

Caliber: 45 Colt (standard); 32 WCF, 38 WCF, 38 S&W, 41 Colt, 44WCF, 44 S&W (optional, additional charge), 6-shot cylinder. **Barrel:** 4-3/4", 5-1/2", 7-1/2". **Weight:** 37 oz. **Length:** NA. **Grips:** Hard rubber. **Sights:** Blade front, notch rear. **Features:** Recreation of original guns; 3" and 4" have no ejector. Available with all-blue, blue with color case-hardening, or full nickel-plate finish. Made in U.S.A. by United States Fire Arms Mfg. Co.

Price: Blue/cased-colors **$949.00**

Price: Nickel **$1,220.00**

U.S. FIRE ARMS NETTLETON CAVALRY

Caliber: 45 Colt, 6-shot cylinder. **Barrel:** 5-1/2" (artillery model), 7-1/2". **Grips:** One-piece walnut. **Features:** Military armory blue and bone case finish. Made in U.S.A. by Fire Arms Mfg. Co.

Price: Blued finish **$1,485.00**

Price: Nickel finish **$1,619.00**

U.S. FIRE ARMS RODEO COWBOY ACTION REVOLVER

Caliber: 45 Colt. **Barrel:** 4-3/4", 5-1/2". **Grips:** Rubber. **Features:** Historically correct Armory bone case hammer, blue satin finish, transfer bar safety system, correct solid firing pin. Entry level basic cowboy SASS gun.

Price: **$649.00**

U.S. FIRE ARMS UNITED STATES PRE-WAR

Caliber: 45 Colt, other caliber available. **Barrel:** 4-3/4", 5-1/2", 7-1/2". **Grips:** Hard rubber. **Features:** Armory bone case/Armory blue finish standard, cross-pin or black powder frame. Introduced 2002. Made in U.S.A. by United States Firearms Mfg. Co.

Price: **$1,345.00**

HANDGUNS — Miscellaneous

Specially adapted single-shot and multi-barrel arms.

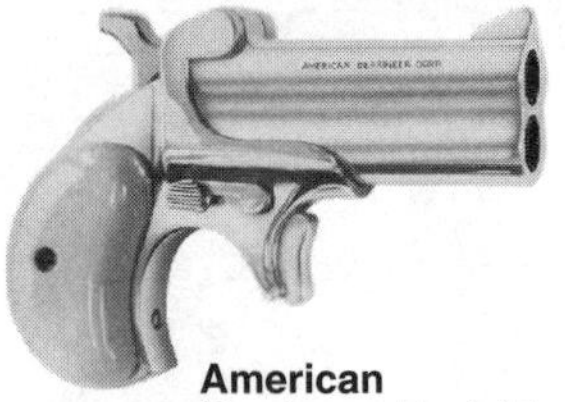
American Derringer Model 1

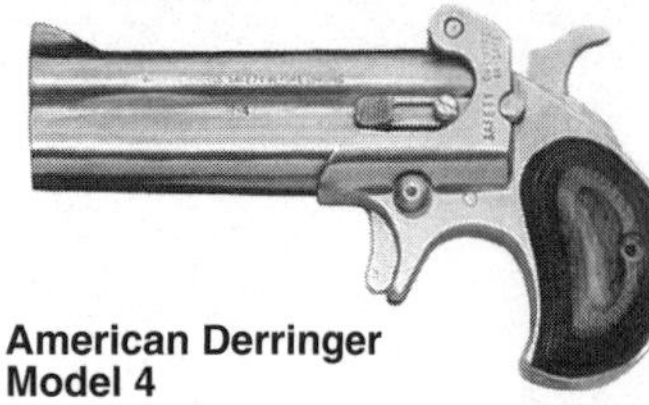
American Derringer Model 4

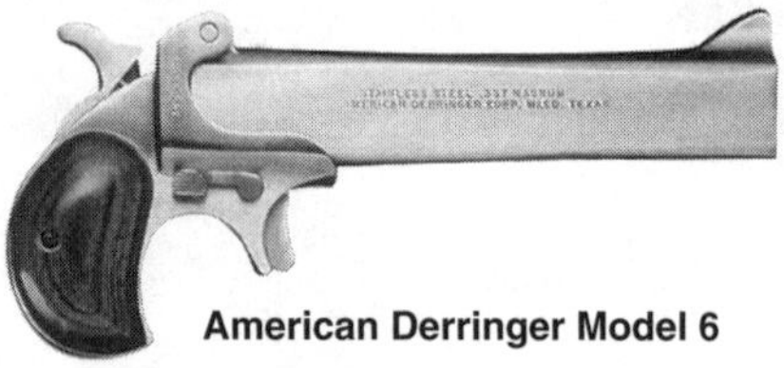
American Derringer Model 6

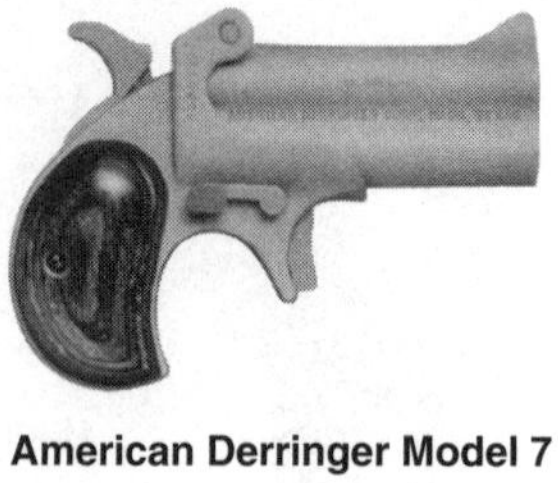
American Derringer Model 7

American Derringer Lady Derringer

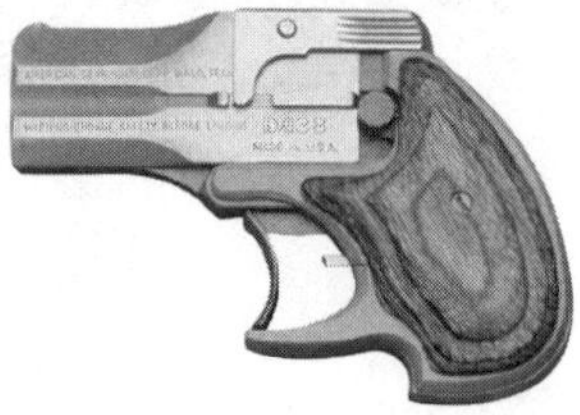
American Derringer DA 38

AMERICAN DERRINGER MODEL 1

Caliber: 22 LR, 22 WMR, 30 Carbine, 30 Luger, 30-30 Win., 32 H&R Mag., 32-20, 380 ACP, 38 Super, 38 Spec., 38 Spec. shotshell, 38 Spec. +P, 9mm Para., 357 Mag., 357 Mag./45/410, 357 Maximum, 10mm, 40 S&W, 41 Mag., 38-40, 44-40 Win., 44 Spec., 44 Mag., 45 Colt, 45 Win. Mag., 45 ACP, 45 Colt/410, 45-70 single shot. **Barrel:** 3". **Weight:** 15-1/2 oz. (38 Spec.). **Length:** 4.82" overall. **Grips:** Rosewood, Zebra wood. **Sights:** Blade front. **Features:** Made of stainless steel with high-polish or satin finish. Two-shot capacity. Manual hammer block safety. Introduced 1980. Available in most pistol calibers. From American Derringer Corp.

Price: 22 LR . . . . . **CALL**
Price: 38 Spec. . . . . . **CALL**
Price: 357 Maximum . . . . . **CALL**
Price: 357 Mag. . . . . . **CALL**
Price: 9mm, 380 . . . . . **CALL**
Price: 40 S&W . . . . . **CALL**
Price: 44 Spec. . . . . . **CALL**
Price: 44-40 Win. . . . . . **CALL**
Price: 45 Colt . . . . . **CALL**
Price: 30-30, 45 Win. Mag. . . . . . **CALL**
Price: 41, 44 Mags. . . . . . **CALL**
Price: 45-70, single shot . . . . . **CALL**
Price: 45 Colt, 410, 2-1/2" . . . . . **CALL**
Price: 45 ACP, 10mm Auto . . . . . **CALL**

American Derringer Model 4

Similar to the Model 1 except has 4.1" barrel, overall length of 6", and weighs 16-1/2 oz.; chambered for 357 Mag., 357 Maximum, 45-70, 3" 410-bore shotshells or 45 Colt or 44 Mag. Made of stainless steel. Manual hammer block safety. Introduced 1980.

Price: 3" 410/45 Colt **$425.00**
Price: 45-70 . . . . . **$560.00**
Price: 44 Mag. with oversize grips **$515.00**
Price: Alaskan Survival model
(45-70 upper barrel, 410 or 45 Colt lower) **$475.00**

American Derringer Model 6

Similar to the Model 1 except has 6" barrel chambered for 3" 410 shotshells or 22 WMR, 357 Mag., 45 ACP, 45 Colt; rosewood stocks; 8.2" o.a.l. and weighs 21 oz. Manual hammer block safety. Introduced 1980.

Price: 22 WMR **$440.00**
Price: 357 Mag. **$440.00**
Price: 45 Colt/410 . . . . . **$450.00**
Price: 45 ACP **$440.00**

American Derringer Model 7 Ultra Lightweight

Similar to Model 1 except made of high strength aircraft aluminum. Weighs 7-1/2 oz., 4.82" o.a.l., rosewood stocks. Available in 22 LR, 22 WMR, 32 H&R Mag., 380 ACP, 38 Spec., 44 Spec. Introduced 1980.

Price: 22 LR, WMR **$325.00**
Price: 38 Spec. **$325.00**
Price: 380 ACP **$325.00**
Price: 32 H&R Mag/32 S&W Long **$325.00**
Price: 44 Spec. **$565.00**

American Derringer Model 10 Ultra Lightweight

Similar to the Model 1 except frame is aluminum, giving weight of 10 oz. Stainless barrels. Available in 38 Spec., 45 Colt or 45 ACP only. Matte gray finish. Introduced 1980.

Price: 45 Colt **$385.00**
Price: 45 ACP **$330.00**
Price: 38 Spec. **$305.00**

American Derringer Lady Derringer

Same as the Model 1 except has tuned action, is fitted with scrimshawed synthetic ivory grips; chambered for 32 H&R Mag. and 38 Spec.; 357 Mag., 45 Colt, 45/410. Deluxe Grade is highly polished; Deluxe Engraved is engraved in a pattern similar to that used on 1880s derringers. All models come in a French-fitted jewelry box. Introduced 1989.

Price: 32 H&R Mag. **$375.00**
Price: 357 Mag. **$405.00**
Price: 38 Spec. **$360.00**
Price: 45 Colt, 45/410 . . . . . **$435.00**

American Derringer Texas Commemorative

Model 1 Derringer with solid brass frame, stainless steel barrel and rosewood grips. Available in 38 Spec., 44-40 Win., or 45 Colt. Introduced 1980.

Price: 38 Spec. **$365.00**
Price: 44-40 . . . . . **$420.00**
Price: Brass frame, 45 Colt **$450.00**

AMERICAN DERRINGER DA 38 MODEL

Caliber: 22 LR, 9mm Para., 38 Spec., 357 Mag., 40 S&W. **Barrel:** 3". **Weight:** 14.5 oz. **Length:** 4.8" overall. **Grips:** Rosewood, walnut or other hardwoods. **Sights:** Fixed. **Features:** Double-action only; two shots. Manual safety. Made of satin-finished stainless steel and aluminum. Introduced 1989. From American Derringer Corp.

Price: 22 LR **$435.00**
Price: 38 Spec. **$460.00**
Price: 9mm Para. **$445.00**
Price: 357 Mag. **$450.00**
Price: 40 S&W **$475.00**

ANSCHUTZ MODEL 64P SPORT/TARGET PISTOL

Caliber: 22 LR, 22 WMR, 5-shot magazine. **Barrel:** 10". **Weight:** 3 lbs. 8 oz. **Length:** 18-1/2" overall. **Stock:** Choate Rynite. **Sights:** None furnished; grooved for scope mounting. **Features:** Right-hand bolt; polished blue finish. Introduced 1998. Imported from Germany by AcuSport.

Price: 22 LR **$455.95**
Price: 22 WMR **$479.95**

HANDGUNS — Miscellaneous

Bond Arms Texas Defender

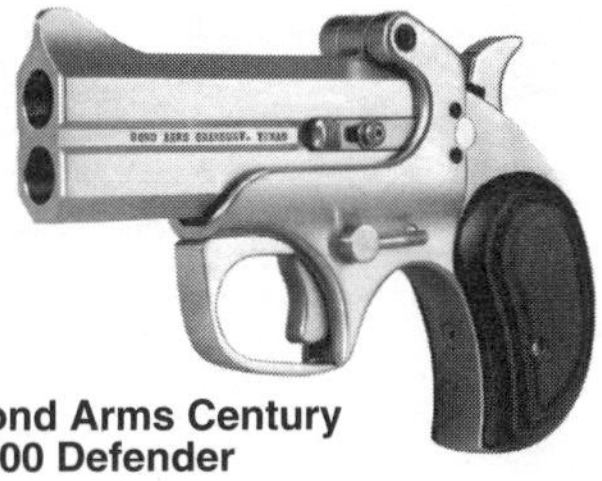
Bond Arms Century 2000 Defender

Cobra Big Bore

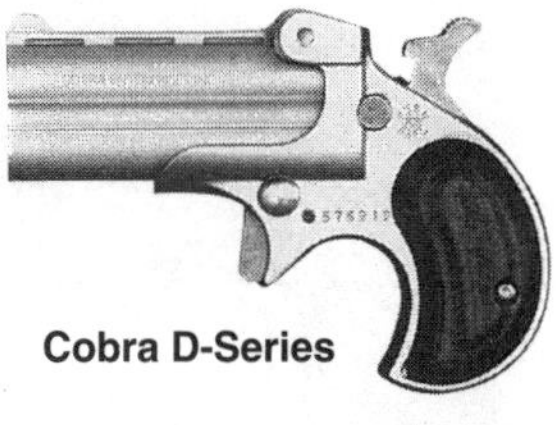
Cobra D-Series

Comanche Super Single Shot

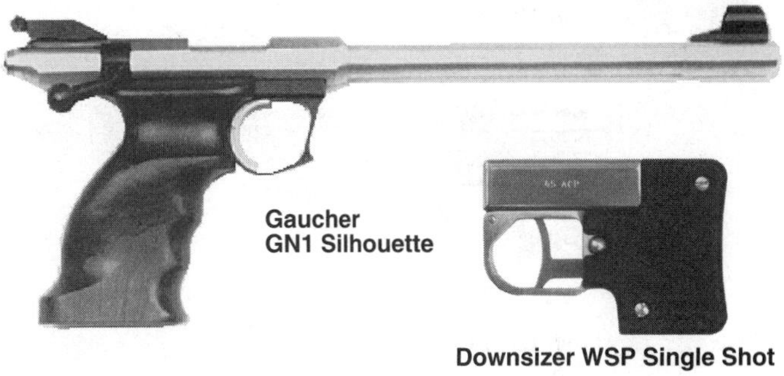
Gaucher GN1 Silhouette

Downsizer WSP Single Shot

BOND ARMS DEFENDER DERRINGER
Caliber: From 22 LR to 45 LC/410 shotshells **Barrel:** 3". **Weight:** 19-20 oz. **Grips:** Rosewood. **Sights:** Blade front, fixed rear. **Features:** Interchangeable barrels, stainless steel firing pins, cross-bolt safety, automatic extractor for rimmed calibers. Stainless steel construction. Right or left hand.
Price: Texas (with removable trigger guard) 3" bbl. **$379.00**

BOND ARMS CENTURY 200
Caliber: 45LC/410 shotshells. **Barrel:** 3.5". **Weight:** 21 oz. **Features:** Similar to Defender series.
Price: **$394.00**

BOND ARMS SNAKE SLAYER
Caliber: 45 LC/410 shotshell (2-1/2" or 3"). **Barrel:** 3.5". **Weight:** 21 oz. Grips: Extended rosewood. **Sights:** Blade front, fixed rear. **Features:** Single-action; interchangeable barrels; stainless steel firing pin. Introduced 2005.
Price: **$445.00**

BROWN CLASSIC SINGLE SHOT PISTOL
Caliber: 17 Ackley Hornet through 375x444. **Barrel:** 15" air-gauged match grade. **Weight:** About 3 lbs. 7 oz. **Grips:** Walnut; thumb rest target-style. **Sights:** None furnished; drilled and tapped for scope mounting. **Features:** Falling block action gives rigid barrel-receiver mating; hand fitted and headspaced. Introduced 1998. Made in U.S.A. by E.A. Brown Mfg.
Price: **$589.00**

COBRA BIG BORE DERRINGERS
Caliber: 22 WMR, 32 H&R Mag., 38 Spec., 9mm Para. **Barrel:** 2.75". **Weight:** 11.5 oz. **Length:** 4.65" overall. **Grips:** Textured black synthetic. **Sights:** Blade front, fixed notch rear. **Features:** Alloy frame, steel-lined barrels, steel breech block. Plunger-type safety with integral hammer block. Chrome or black Teflon finish. Introduced 2002. Made in U.S.A. by Cobra Enterprises.
Price: **$98.00**
Price: 9mm Para **$136.00**

COBRA LONG-BORE DERRINGERS
Caliber: 22 WMR, 38 Spec., 9mm Para. **Barrel:** 3.5". **Weight:** 13 oz. **Length:** 5.65" overall. **Grips:** Textured black synthetic. **Sights:** Fixed. **Features:** Chrome or black Teflon finish. Larger than Davis D-Series models. Introduced 2002. Made in U.S.A. by Cobra Enterprises.
Price: **$136.00**
Price: 9mm Para. **$136.00**
Price: Big-Bore models (same calibers, 3/4" shorter barrels) **$136.00**

COBRA STARBIRD-SERIES DERRINGERS
Caliber: 22 LR, 22 WMR, 25 ACP, 32 ACP. **Barrel:** 2.4". **Weight:** 9.5 oz. **Length:** 4" overall. **Grips:** Laminated wood or pearl. **Sights:** Blade front, fixed notch rear. **Features:** Choice of black powder coat, satin nickel or chrome finish; spur trigger. Introduced 2002. Made in U.S.A. by Cobra Enterprises.
Price: **$112.00**

COMANCHE SUPER SINGLE SHOT PISTOL
Caliber: 45 LC, 410 ga. **Barrel:** 10". **Sights:** Adjustable. **Features:** Blue finish, not available for sale in CA, MA. Distributed by SGS Importers International, Inc.
Price: **$174.95**
Price: Satin nickel **$191.95**
Price: Duo-tone **$185.95**

DOWNSIZER WSP SINGLE SHOT PISTOL
Caliber: 357 Magnum, 45 ACP, 38 Special. **Barrel:** 2.10". **Weight:** 11 oz. **Length:** 3.25" overall. **Grips:** Black polymer. **Sights:** None. **Features:** Single shot, tip-up barrel. Double action only. Stainless steel construction. Measures .900" thick. Introduced 1997. From Downsizer Corp.
Price: **$499.00**

GAUCHER GN1 SILHOUETTE PISTOL
Caliber: 22 LR, single shot. **Barrel:** 10". **Weight:** 2.4 lbs. **Length:** 15.5" overall. **Grips:** European hardwood. **Sights:** Blade front, open adjustable rear. **Features:** Bolt action, adjustable trigger. Introduced 1990. Imported from France by Mandall Shooting Supplies.
Price: About **$525.00**
Price: Model GP Silhouette **$425.00**

CONSULT
SHOOTER'S MARKETPLACE
Page 141, This Issue

HANDGUNS — Miscellaneous

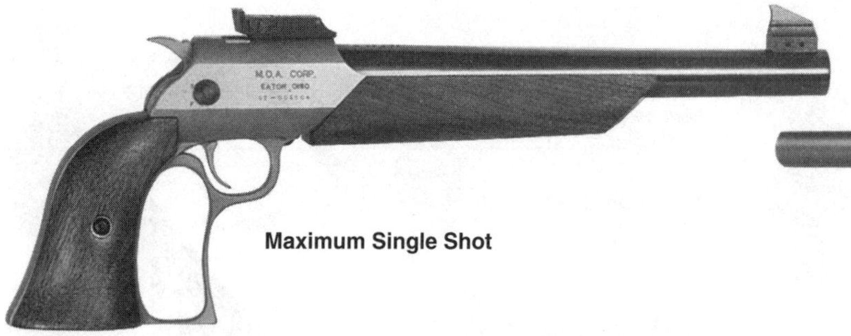

Maximum Single Shot

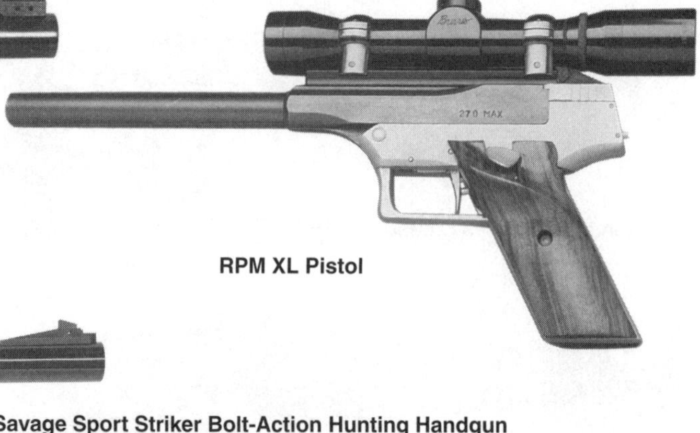

RPM XL Pistol

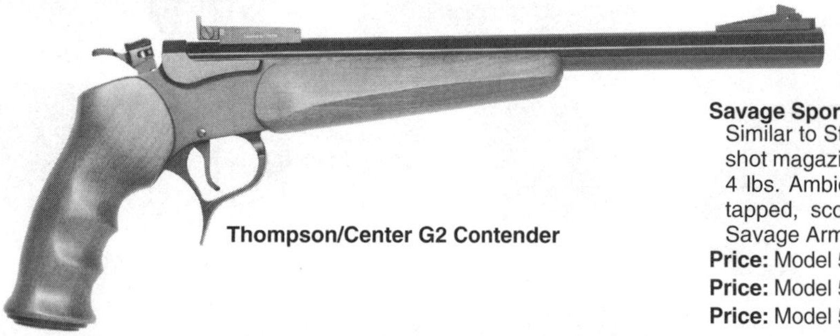

Thompson/Center G2 Contender

MAXIMUM SINGLE SHOT PISTOL

Caliber: 22 LR, 22 Hornet, 22 BR, 22 PPC, 223 Rem., 22-250, 6mm BR, 6mm PPC, 243, 250 Savage, 6.5mm-35M, 270 MAX, 270 Win., 7mm TCU, 7mm BR, 7mm-35, 7mm INT-R, 7mm-08, 7mm Rocket, 7mm Super-Mag., 30 Herrett, 30 Carbine, 30-30, 308 Win., 30x39, 32-20, 350 Rem. Mag., 357 Mag., 357 Maximum, 358 Win., 375 H&H, 44 Mag., 454 Casull. **Barrel:** 8-3/4", 10-1/2", 14". **Weight:** 61 oz. (10-1/2" bbl.); 78 oz. (14" bbl.). **Length:** 15", 18-1/2" overall (with 10-1/2" and 14" bbl., respectively). **Grips:** Smooth walnut stocks and forend. Also available with 17" finger groove grip. **Sights:** Ramp front, fully adjustable open rear. **Features:** Falling block action; drilled and tapped for M.O.A. scope mounts; integral grip frame/receiver; adjustable trigger; Douglas barrel (interchangeable). Introduced 1983. Made in U.S.A. by M.O.A. Corp.

Price: Stainless receiver, blue barrel **$799.00**
Price: Stainless receiver, stainless barrel **$883.00**
Price: Extra blued barrel **$254.00**
Price: Extra stainless barrel **$317.00**
Price: Scope mount **$60.00**

RPM XL SINGLE SHOT PISTOL

Caliber: 22 LR through 45-70. **Barrel:** 8", 10-3/4", 12", 14". **Weight:** About 60 oz. **Grips:** Smooth Goncalo Alves with thumb and heel rests. **Sights:** Hooded front with interchangeable post, or Patridge; ISGW rear adjustable for windage and elevation. **Features:** Barrel drilled and tapped for scope mount. Visible cocking indicator. Spring-loaded barrel lock, positive hammer-block safety. Trigger adjustable for weight of pull and over-travel. Contact maker for complete price list. Made in U.S.A. by RPM.

Price: XL Hunter model (action only) **$1,045.00**
Price: Extra barrel, 8" through 10-3/4" **$407.50**
Price: Extra barrel, 12" through 14" **$547.50**
Price: Muzzle brake **$160.00**
Price: Left-hand action, add **$50.00**

SAVAGE STRIKER BOLT-ACTION HUNTING HANDGUN

Caliber: 223, 243, 7mm-08, 308, 300 WSM 2-shot mag. **Barrel:** 14". **Weight:** About 5 lbs. **Length:** 22-1/2" overall. **Stock:** Black composite ambidextrous mid-grip; grooved forend; "Dual Pillar" bedding. **Sights:** None furnished; drilled and tapped for scope mounting. **Features:** Short left-hand bolt with right-hand ejection; free-floated barrel; uses Savage Model 110 rifle scope rings/bases. Introduced 1998. Made in U.S.A. by Savage Arms, Inc.

Price: Model 503 (blued barrel and action) **$285.00**
Price: Model 503 R17FSS (stainless barrel and action) **$281.00**
Price: Model 516FSAK black stock (ss, aMB, 300 WSM) **$260.00**

Savage Sport Striker Bolt-Action Hunting Handgun

Similar to Striker, but chambered in 22 LR and 22 WMR. Detachable 10-shot magazine (5-shot magazine for 22 WMR). Overall length 19", weighs 4 lbs. Ambidextrous fiberglass/graphite composite rear grip. Drilled and tapped, scope mount installed. Introduced 2000. Made in U.S.A. by Savage Arms Inc.

Price: Model 501F (blue finish, 22 LR) **$236.00**
Price: Model 501FXP with soft case, 1.25-4x28 scope **$258.00**
Price: Model 502F (blue finish, 22 WMR) **$238.00**

SPRINGFIELD M6 SCOUT PISTOL

Caliber: 22 LR/45 LC/410, 22 Hornet, 45 LC/410. **Barrel:** 10". **Weight:** NA. **Length:** NA. **Grips:** NA. **Sights:** NA. **Features:** Adapted from the U.S. Air Force M6 Survival Rifle, also available as a carbine with 16" barrel.

Price: . . . . **$169.00 to $197.00**
Price: Pistol/Carbine . . . . **$183.00 to $209.00**

THOMPSON/CENTER ENCORE PISTOL

Caliber: 22-250, 223, 204 Ruger, 6.8 Rem., 260 Rem., 7mm-08, 243, 308, 270, 30-06, 375 JDJ, 204 Ruger, 44 Mag., 454 Casull, 480 Ruger, 444 Marlin single shot, 450 Marlin with muzzle tamer, no sights. **Barrel:** 12", 15", tapered round. **Weight:** NA. **Length:** 21" overall with 12" barrel. **Grips:** American walnut with finger grooves, walnut forend. **Sights:** Blade on ramp front, adjustable rear, or none. **Features:** Interchangeable barrels; action opens by squeezing the trigger guard; drilled and tapped for scope mounting; blue finish. Announced 1996. Made in U.S.A. by Thompson/Center Arms.

Price: . . . . **$589.00 to $592.00**
Price: Extra 12" barrels **$262.00**
Price: Extra 15" barrels **$270.00**
Price: 45 Colt/410 barrel, 12" **$292.00**
Price: 45 Colt/410 barrel, 15" **$299.00**

Thompson/Center Stainless Encore Pistol

Similar to blued Encore, made of stainless steel, available with 15" barrel in 223, 22-250, 243 Win., 7mm-08, 308, 30/06 Sprgfld., 45/70 Gov't., 45/410 VR. With black rubber grip and forend. Made in U.S.A. by Thompson/Center Arms.

Price: . . . . **$636.00 to $644.00**

Thompson/Center G2 Contender Pistol

A second generation Contender pistol maintaining the same barrel interchangeability with older Contender barrels and their corresponding forends (except Herrett forend). The G2 frame will not accept old-style grips due to the change in grip angle. Incorporates an automatic hammer block safety with built-in interlock. Features include trigger adjustable for overtravel, adjustable rear sight; ramp front sight blade, blued steel finish.

Price: **$570.00**

UBERTI ROLLING BLOCK TARGET PISTOL

Caliber: 22 LR, 22 WMR, 22 Hornet, 357 Mag., 45 Colt, single shot. **Barrel:** 9-7/8", half-round, half-octagon. **Weight:** 44 oz. **Length:** 14" overall. **Stock:** Walnut grip and forend. **Sights:** Blade front, fully adjustable rear. **Features:** Replica of the 1871 rolling block target pistol. Brass trigger guard, color case-hardened frame, blue barrel. Imported by Uberti U.S.A.

Price: **$410.00**

BLACKPOWDER PISTOLS — Single Shot, Flint & Percussion

Dixie Pennsylvania   Harper's Ferry   Kentucky   Le Page   Lyman Plains Pistol

DIXIE PENNSYLVANIA PISTOL
Caliber: 44 (.430" round ball). **Barrel:** 10", (7/8" octagon). **Weight:** 2-1/2 lbs. **Stocks:** Walnut-stained hardwood. **Sights:** Blade front, open rear drift-adjustable for windage; brass. **Features:** Flintlock only. Brass trigger guard, thimbles, instep, wedge plates; high-luster blue barrel. Imported from Italy by Dixie Gun Works.
Price: Finished **$215.00**
Price: Kit **$195.00**

FRENCH-STYLE DUELING PISTOL
Caliber: 44. **Barrel:** 10". **Weight:** 35 oz. **Length:** 15-3/4" overall. **Stocks:** Carved walnut. **Sights:** Fixed. **Features:** Comes with velvet-lined case and accessories. Imported by Mandall Shooting Supplies.
Price: **$295.00**

HARPER'S FERRY 1806 PISTOL
Caliber: 58 (.570" round ball). **Barrel:** 10". **Weight:** 40 oz. **Length:** 16" overall. **Stocks:** Walnut. **Sights:** Fixed. **Features:** Case-hardened lock, brass-mounted browned barrel. Replica of the first U.S. gov't.-made flintlock pistol. Imported by Navy Arms, Dixie Gun Works.
Price: . . . . **$275.00 to $405.00**
Price: Kit (Dixie) **$250.00**

KENTUCKY FLINTLOCK PISTOL
Caliber: 44, 45. **Barrel:** 10-1/8". **Weight:** 32 oz. **Length:** 15-1/2" overall. **Stocks:** Walnut. **Sights:** Fixed. **Features:** Specifications, including caliber, weight and length may vary with importer. Case-hardened lock, blued barrel; available also as brass barrel flintlock Model 1821. Imported by Navy Arms, The Armoury, Dixie Gun Works.
Price: **$300.00**
Price: In kit form. From . . . . **$90.00 to $112.00**
Price: Single cased set (Navy Arms) **$360.00**
Price: Double cased set (Navy Arms) **$590.00**

Kentucky Percussion Pistol
Similar to Flint version but percussion lock. Imported by The Armoury, Navy Arms, CVA (50-cal.).
Price: . . . . **$129.95 to $225.00**
Price: Steel barrel (Armoury) **$179.00**

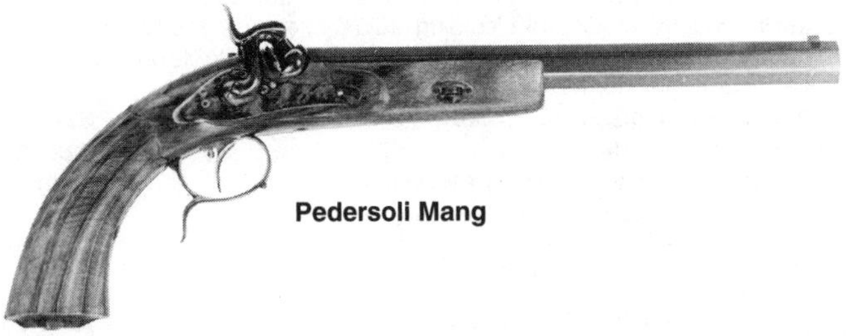

Pedersoli Mang

Price: Single cased set (Navy Arms) **$355.00**
Price: Double cased set (Navy Arms) **$600.00**

LE PAGE PERCUSSION DUELING PISTOL
Caliber: 44. **Barrel:** 10", rifled. **Weight:** 40 oz. **Length:** 16" overall. **Stocks:** Walnut, fluted butt. **Sights:** Blade front, notch rear. **Features:** Double-set triggers. Blued barrel; trigger guard and buttcap are polished silver. Imported by Dixie Gun Works.
Price: **$545.00**

LYMAN PLAINS PISTOL
Caliber: 50 or 54. **Barrel:** 8"; 1:30" twist, both calibers. **Weight:** 50 oz. **Length:** 15" overall. **Stocks:** Walnut half-stock. **Sights:** Blade front, square notch rear adjustable for windage. **Features:** Polished brass trigger guard and ramrod tip, color case-hardened coil spring lock, spring-loaded trigger, stainless steel nipple, blackened iron furniture. Hooked patent breech, detachable belt hook. Introduced 1981. From Lyman Products.
Price: Finished **$244.95**
Price: Kit **$189.95**

PEDERSOLI MANG TARGET PISTOL
Caliber: 38. **Barrel:** 10.5", octagonal; 1:15" twist, **Weight:** 2.5 lbs. **Length:** 17.25" overall. **Stocks:** Walnut with fluted grip. **Sights:** Blade front, open rear adjustable for windage. **Features:** Browned barrel, polished breech plug, remainder color case-hardened. Imported from Italy by Dixie Gun Works.
Price: **$925.00**

BLACKPOWDER PISTOLS — Single Shot, Flint & Percussion

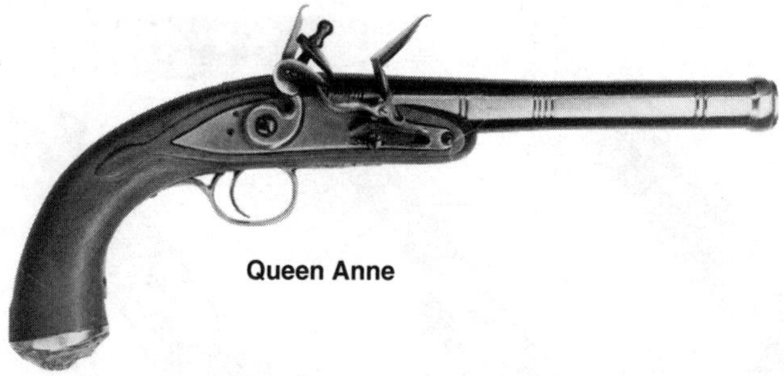

Queen Anne

Traditions Pioneer

Traditions William Parker

Traditions Buckhunter Pro

QUEEN ANNE FLINTLOCK PISTOL
Caliber: 50 (.490" round ball). **Barrel:** 7-1/2", smoothbore. **Stocks:** Walnut. **Sights:** None. **Features:** Browned steel barrel, fluted brass trigger guard, brass mask on butt. Lockplate left in the white. Made by Pedersoli in Italy. Introduced 1983. Imported by Dixie Gun Works.
Price: **$275.00**
Price: Kit **$195.00**

TRADITIONS BUCKHUNTER PRO IN-LINE PISTOL
Caliber: 50. **Barrel:** 9-1/2", round. **Weight:** 48 oz. **Length:** 14" overall. **Stocks:** Smooth walnut or black epoxy-coated hardwood grip and forend. **Sights:** Beaded blade front, folding adjustable rear. **Features:** Thumb safety; removable stainless steel breech plug; adjustable trigger, barrel drilled and tapped for scope mounting. From Traditions.
Price: With walnut grip. **$229.00**
Price: Nickel with black grip **$239.00**
Price: With walnut grip and 12-1/2" barrel **$239.00**
Price: Nickel with black grip, muzzle brake and 14-3/4" fluted barrel **$289.00**
Price: 45 cal. nickel w/bl. grip, muzzle brake and 14-3/4" fluted bbl. **$289.00**

TRADITIONS KENTUCKY PISTOL
Caliber: 50. **Barrel:** 10"; octagon with 7/8" flats; 1:20" twist. **Weight:** 40 oz. **Length:** 15" overall. **Stocks:** Stained beech. **Sights:** Blade front, fixed rear. **Features:** Bird's-head grip; brass thimbles; color case-hardened lock. Percussion only. Introduced 1995. From Traditions.
Price: Finished. **$139.00**
Price: Kit **$109.00**

TRADITIONS PIONEER PISTOL
Caliber: 45. **Barrel:** 9-5/8"; 13/16" flats, 1:16" twist. **Weight:** 31 oz. **Length:** 15" overall. **Stocks:** Beech. **Sights:** Blade front, fixed rear. **Features:** V-type mainspring. Single trigger. German silver furniture, blackened hardware. From Traditions.
Price: **$139.00**
Price: Kit **$119.00**

TRADITIONS TRAPPER PISTOL
Caliber: 50. **Barrel:** 9-3/4"; 7/8" flats; 1:20" twist. **Weight:** 2-3/4 lbs. **Length:** 16" overall. **Stocks:** Beech. **Sights:** Blade front, adjustable rear. **Features:** Double-set triggers; brass buttcap, trigger guard, wedge plate, forend tip, thimble. From Traditions.
Price: Percussion **$189.00**
Price: Flintlock **$209.00**
Price: Kit **$149.00**

TRADITIONS VEST-POCKET DERRINGER
Caliber: 31. **Barrel:** 2-1/4"; brass. **Weight:** 8 oz. **Length:** 4-3/4" overall. **Stocks:** Simulated ivory. **Sights:** Bead front. **Features:** Replica of riverboat gamblers' derringer; authentic spur trigger. From Traditions.
Price: **$109.00**

TRADITIONS WILLIAM PARKER PISTOL
Caliber: 50. **Barrel:** 10-3/8"; 15/16" flats; polished steel. **Weight:** 37 oz. **Length:** 17-1/2" overall. **Stocks:** Walnut with checkered grip. **Sights:** Brass blade front, fixed rear. **Features:** Replica dueling pistol with 1:20" twist, hooked breech. Brass wedge plate, trigger guard, cap guard; separate ramrod. Double-set triggers. Polished steel barrel, lock. Imported by Traditions.
Price:. **$269.00**

CONSULT
SHOOTER'S MARKETPLACE
Page 141, This Issue

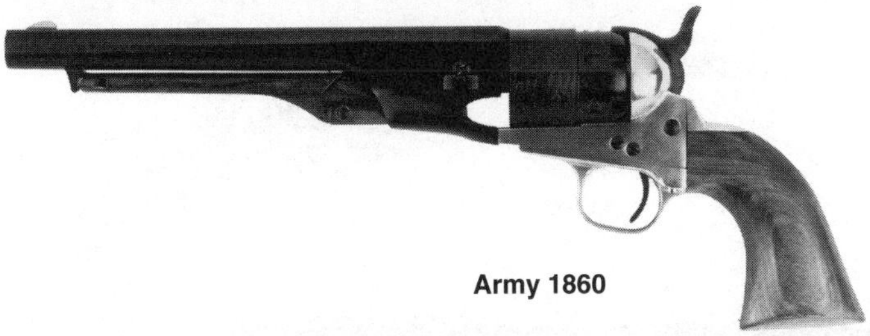

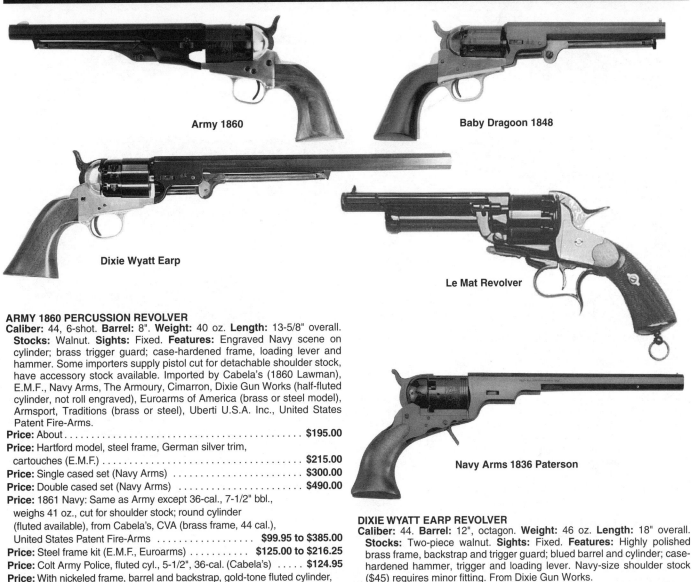

Army 1860

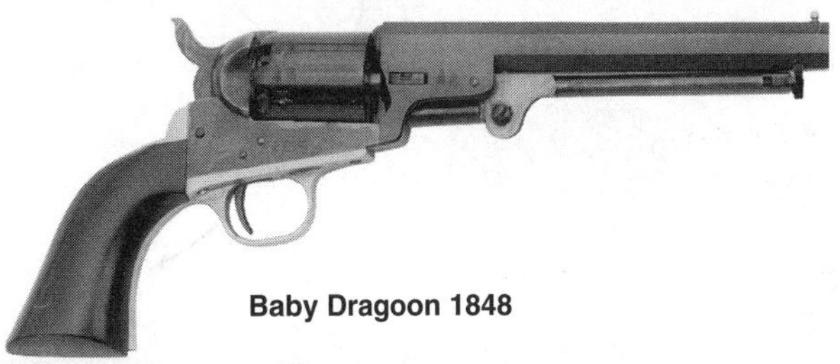

Baby Dragoon 1848

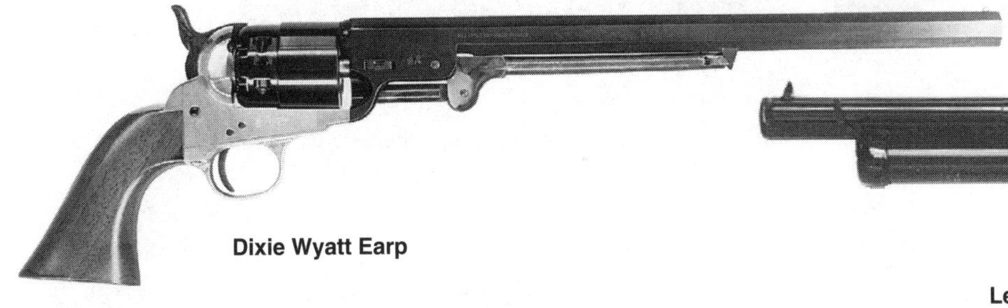

Dixie Wyatt Earp

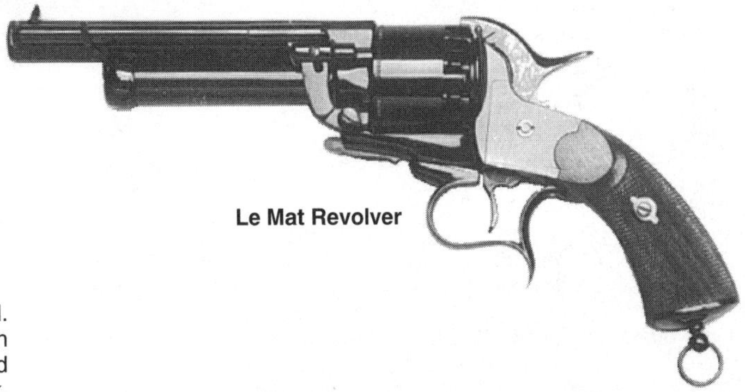

Le Mat Revolver

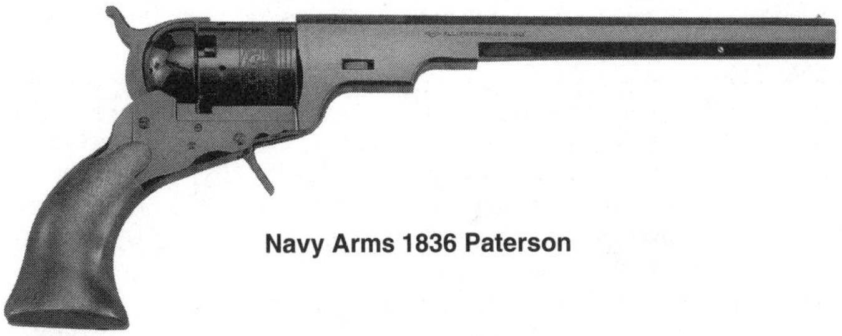

Navy Arms 1836 Paterson

ARMY 1860 PERCUSSION REVOLVER
Caliber: 44, 6-shot. **Barrel:** 8". **Weight:** 40 oz. **Length:** 13-5/8" overall. **Stocks:** Walnut. **Sights:** Fixed. **Features:** Engraved Navy scene on cylinder; brass trigger guard; case-hardened frame, loading lever and hammer. Some importers supply pistol cut for detachable shoulder stock, have accessory stock available. Imported by Cabela's (1860 Lawman), E.M.F., Navy Arms, The Armoury, Cimarron, Dixie Gun Works (half-fluted cylinder, not roll engraved), Euroarms of America (brass or steel model), Armsport, Traditions (brass or steel), Uberti U.S.A. Inc., United States Patent Fire-Arms.
Price: About **$195.00**
Price: Hartford model, steel frame, German silver trim, cartouches (E.M.F.) **$215.00**
Price: Single cased set (Navy Arms) **$300.00**
Price: Double cased set (Navy Arms) **$490.00**
Price: 1861 Navy: Same as Army except 36-cal., 7-1/2" bbl., weighs 41 oz., cut for shoulder stock; round cylinder (fluted available), from Cabela's, CVA (brass frame, 44 cal.), United States Patent Fire-Arms .... **$99.95 to $385.00**
Price: Steel frame kit (E.M.F., Euroarms) .... **$125.00 to $216.25**
Price: Colt Army Police, fluted cyl., 5-1/2", 36-cal. (Cabela's) **$124.95**
Price: With nickeled frame, barrel and backstrap, gold-tone fluted cylinder, trigger and hammer, simulated ivory grips (Traditions) **$199.00**

BABY DRAGOON 1848, 1849 POCKET, WELLS FARGO
Caliber: 31. **Barrel:** 3", 4", 5", 6"; seven-groove; RH twist. **Weight:** About 21 oz. **Stocks:** Varnished walnut. **Sights:** Brass pin front, hammer notch rear. **Features:** No loading lever on Baby Dragoon or Wells Fargo models. Unfluted cylinder with stagecoach holdup scene; cupped cylinder pin; no grease grooves; one safety pin on cylinder and slot in hammer face; straight (flat) mainspring. From Armsport, Cimarron F.A. Co., Dixie Gun Works, Uberti U.S.A. Inc.
Price: 6" barrel, with loading lever (Dixie Gun Works)............ **$275.00**
Price: 4" (Uberti USA Inc.) **$335.00**

CABELA'S 1860 ARMY SNUBNOSE REVOLVER
Caliber: 44. **Barrel:** 3". **Weight:** 2 lbs., 3 oz. **Length:** 9" overall. **Grips:** Hardwood. **Sights:** Blade front, hammer notch near. **Features:** Shortened barrels without loading lever. Brass loading tool included.
Price: Revolver only..................................... **$169.99**
Price: With starter kit **$219.99**

CABELA'S 1862 POLICE SNUBNOSE REVOLVER
Caliber: 36. **Barrel:** 3". **Weight:** 2 lbs., 3 oz. **Length:** 8.5" overall. **Grips:** Hardwood. **Sights:** Blade front, hammer notch rear. **Features:** Shortened barrel, removed loading lever. Separate brass loading tool included.
Price: .... **$159.99** (revolver only); **$209.99** (with starter kit).

DIXIE WYATT EARP REVOLVER
Caliber: 44. **Barrel:** 12", octagon. **Weight:** 46 oz. **Length:** 18" overall. **Stocks:** Two-piece walnut. **Sights:** Fixed. **Features:** Highly polished brass frame, backstrap and trigger guard; blued barrel and cylinder; case-hardened hammer, trigger and loading lever. Navy-size shoulder stock ($45) requires minor fitting. From Dixie Gun Works.
Price: **$160.00**

LE MAT REVOLVER
Caliber: 44/65. **Barrel:** 6-3/4" (revolver); 4-7/8" (single shot). **Weight:** 3 lbs., 7 oz. **Stocks:** Hand-checkered walnut. **Sights:** Post front, hammer notch rear. **Features:** Exact reproduction with all-steel construction; 44-cal. 9-shot cylinder, 65-cal. single barrel; color case-hardened hammer with selector; spur trigger guard; ring at butt; lever-type barrel release. From Navy Arms.
Price: Cavalry model (lanyard ring, spur trigger guard) **$595.00**
Price: Army model (round trigger guard, pin-type barrel release) .. **$595.00**
Price: Naval-style (thumb selector on hammer) **$595.00**

NAVY ARMS NEW MODEL POCKET REVOLVER
Caliber: 31, 5-shot. **Barrel:** 3-1/2", octagon. **Weight:** 15 oz. **Length:** 7-3/4". **Stocks:** Two-piece walnut. **Sights:** Fixed. **Features:** Replica of the Remington New Model Pocket. Available with polished brass frame or nickel-plated finish. Introduced 2000. Imported by Navy Arms.
Price: **$300.00**

NAVY ARMS 1836 PATERSON REVOLVER
Caliber: 36. **Barrel:** 9". **Weight:** 2 lbs., 11 oz. **Length:** NA. **Stocks:** Walnut. **Sights:** NA. **Features:** Hidden trigger, blued barrel, replica of 5-shooter, roll-engraved with stagecoach holdup scene.
Price: .... **$340.00 to $499.00**

BLACKPOWDER REVOLVERS

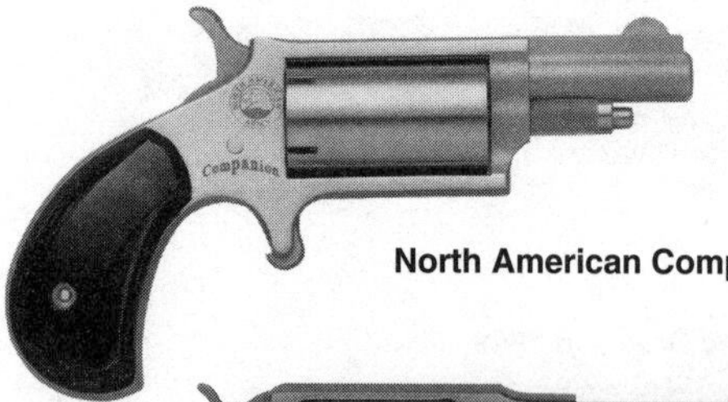

North American Companion

Pocket Police 1862

New Model
1858 Army Percussion

Rogers & Spencer

NAVY MODEL 1851 PERCUSSION REVOLVER
Caliber: 36, 44, 6-shot. **Barrel:** 7-1/2". **Weight:** 44 oz. **Length:** 13" overall. **Stocks:** Walnut finish. **Sights:** Post front, hammer notch rear. **Features:** Brass backstrap and trigger guard; some have 1st Model squareback trigger guard, engraved cylinder with navy battle scene; case-hardened frame, hammer, loading lever. Imported by The Armoury, Cabela's, Cimarron F.A. Co., Navy Arms, E.M.F., Dixie Gun Works, Euroarms of America, Armsport, CVA (44-cal. only), Traditions (44 only), Uberti U.S.A. Inc., United States Patent Fire-Arms.

Price: Brass frame . . . . **$99.95 to $385.00**
Price: Steel frame . . . . **$130.00 to $285.00**
Price: Kit form . . . . **$110.00 to $123.95**
Price: Engraved model (Dixie Gun Works) **$182.50**
Price: Single cased set, steel frame (Navy Arms) **$280.00**
Price: Double cased set, steel frame (Navy Arms) **$455.00**
Price: Confederate Navy (Cabela's) **$89.99**
Price: Hartford model, steel frame, German silver trim, cartouche (E.M.F.) **$190.00**

NEW MODEL 1858 ARMY PERCUSSION REVOLVER
Caliber: 36 or 44, 6-shot. **Barrel:** 6-1/2" or 8". **Weight:** 38 oz. **Length:** 13-1/2" overall. **Stocks:** Walnut. **Sights:** Blade front, groove-in-frame rear. **Features:** Replica of Remington Model 1858. Also available from some importers as Army Model Belt Revolver in 36-cal., a shortened and lightened version of the 44. Target Model (Uberti U.S.A. Inc., Navy Arms) has fully adjustable target rear sight, target front, 36 or 44. Imported by Cabela's, Cimarron F.A. Co., CVA (as 1858 Army, brass frame, 44 only), Dixie Gun Works, Navy Arms, The Armoury, E.M.F., Euroarms of America (engraved, stainless and plain), Armsport, Traditions (44 only), Uberti U.S.A. Inc.

Price: Steel frame, about . . . . **$99.95 to $280.00**
Price: Steel frame kit (Euroarms, Navy Arms) . . . . **$115.95 to $150.00**
Price: Single cased set (Navy Arms) **$290.00**
Price: Double cased set (Navy Arms) **$480.00**
Price: Stainless steel Model 1858 (Euroarms, Uberti U.S.A. Inc., Cabela's, Navy Arms, Armsport, Traditions) . . . . **$169.95 to $380.00**
Price: Target Model, adjustable rear sight (Cabela's, Euroarms, Uberti U.S.A. Inc., Stone Mountain Arms) . . . . **$95.95 to $399.00**
Price: Brass frame (CVA, Cabela's, Traditions, Navy Arms) . . . . **$79.95 to $159.95**
Price: As above, kit (Dixie Gun Works, Navy Arms) . . . **$145.00 to $188.95**
Price: Buffalo model, 44-cal. (Cabela's) **$119.99**
Price: Hartford model, steel frame, German silver trim, cartouche (E.M.F.) **$215.00**

NORTH AMERICAN COMPANION PERCUSSION REVOLVER
Caliber: 22. **Barrel:** 1-1/8". **Weight:** 5.1 oz. **Length:** 4-1/2" overall. **Stocks:** Laminated wood. **Sights:** Blade front, notch fixed rear. **Features:** All stainless steel construction. Uses standard #11 percussion caps. Comes with bullets, powder measure, bullet seater, leather clip holster, gun rag. Long Rifle or Magnum frame size. Introduced 1996. Made in U.S. by North American Arms.

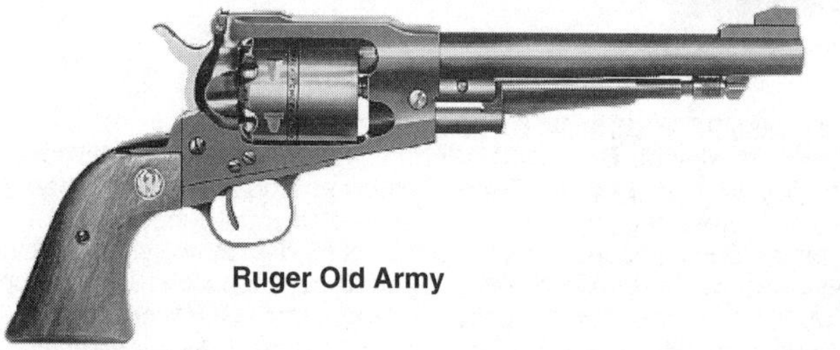

Ruger Old Army

Price: Long Rifle frame **$156.00**

North American Magnum Companion Percussion Revolver
Similar to the Companion except has larger frame. Weighs 7.2 oz., has 1-5/8" barrel, measures 5-7/16" overall. Comes with bullets, powder measure, bullet seater, leather clip holster, gun rag. Introduced 1996. Made in U.S. by North American Arms.

Price: **$215.00**

POCKET POLICE 1862 PERCUSSION REVOLVER
Caliber: 36, 5-shot. **Barrel:** 4-1/2", 5-1/2", 6-1/2", 7-1/2". **Weight:** 26 oz. **Length:** 12" overall (6-1/2" bbl.). **Stocks:** Walnut. **Sights:** Fixed. **Features:** Round tapered barrel; half-fluted and rebated cylinder; case-hardened frame, loading lever and hammer; silver or brass trigger guard and backstrap. Imported by Dixie Gun Works, Navy Arms (5-1/2" only), Uberti U.S.A. Inc. (5-1/2", 6-1/2" only), United States Patent Fire-Arms and Cimarron F.A. Co.

Price: About . . . . **$139.95 to $335.00**
Price: Single cased set with accessories (Navy Arms) **$365.00**
Price: Hartford model, steel frame, German silver trim, cartouche (E.M.F.) **$215.00**

ROGERS & SPENCER PERCUSSION REVOLVER
Caliber: 44. **Barrel:** 7-1/2". **Weight:** 47 oz. **Length:** 13-3/4" overall. **Stocks:** Walnut. **Sights:** Cone front, integral groove in frame for rear. **Features:** Accurate reproduction of a Civil War design. Solid frame; extra large nipple cut-out on rear of cylinder; loading lever and cylinder easily removed for cleaning. From Dixie Gun Works, Euroarms of America (standard blue, engraved, burnished, target models), Navy Arms.

Price: . . . . **$160.00 to $299.95**
Price: Nickel-plated **$215.00**
Price: Engraved (Euroarms) **$287.00**
Price: Kit version . . . . **$245.00 to $252.00**
Price: Target version (Euroarms) . . . . **$239.00 to $270.00**
Price: Burnished London Gray (Euroarms) . . . . **$245.00 to $270.00**

BLACKPOWDER REVOLVERS

Spiller & Burr

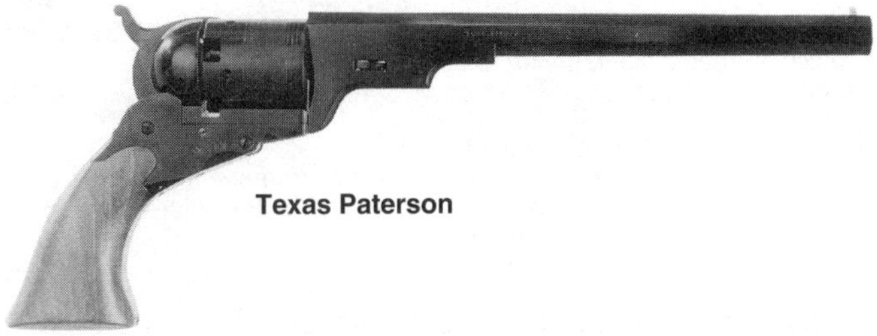

Texas Paterson

3rd U.S. Model Dragoon

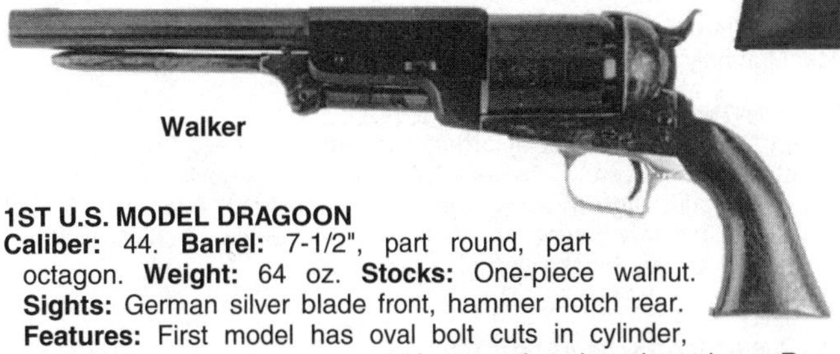

Walker

RUGER OLD ARMY PERCUSSION REVOLVER
Caliber: 45, 6-shot. Uses .457" dia. lead bullets or 454 conical. **Barrel:** 5-1/2", 7-1/2" (6-groove; 1:16" twist). **Weight:** 2-7/8 lbs. **Length:** 11-1/2" and 13-1/2" overall. **Stocks:** Rosewood, simulated ivory. **Sights:** Ramp front, rear adjustable for windage and elevation; or fixed (groove). **Features:** Stainless steel; standard size nipples, chrome-moly steel cylinder and frame, same lockwork as original Super Blackhawk. Also stainless steel. Includes hard case and lock. Made in USA. From Sturm, Ruger & Co.
Price: Blued steel, fixed sight (Model BP-5F) **$541.00**
Price: Stainless steel, fixed sight (Model KBP-5F-I) **$623.00**
Price: Stainless steel (Model KBP-7) **$577.00**
Price: Stainless steel, fixed sight (KBP-7F) **$577.00**

SHERIFF MODEL 1851 PERCUSSION REVOLVER
Caliber: 36, 44, 6-shot. **Barrel:** 5". **Weight:** 40 oz. **Length:** 10-1/2" overall. **Stocks:** Walnut. **Sights:** Fixed. **Features:** Brass backstrap and trigger guard; engraved navy scene; case-hardened frame, hammer, loading lever. Imported by E.M.F.
Price: Steel frame **$169.95**
Price: Brass frame **$140.00**

SPILLER & BURR REVOLVER
Caliber: 36 (.375" round ball). **Barrel:** 7", octagon. **Weight:** 2-1/2 lbs. **Length:** 12-1/2" overall. **Stocks:** Two-piece walnut. **Sights:** Fixed. **Features:** Reproduction of the C.S.A. revolver. Brass frame and trigger guard. Also available as a kit. From Dixie Gun Works, Navy Arms.
Price: **$150.00**
Price: Kit form (Dixie) **$125.00**
Price: Single cased set (Navy Arms) **$270.00**
Price: Double cased set (Navy Arms) **$430.00**

TEXAS PATERSON 1836 REVOLVER
Caliber: 36 (.375" round ball). **Barrel:** 7-1/2". **Weight:** 42 oz. **Stocks:** One-piece walnut. **Sights:** Fixed. **Features:** Copy of Sam Colt's first commercially-made revolving pistol. Comes with loading tool. From Cimarron F.A. Co., Dixie Gun Works, Navy Arms, Uberti U.S.A. Inc.
Price: About **$495.00**
Price: With loading lever (Uberti U.S.A. Inc.) **$450.00**
Price: Engraved (Navy Arms) **$485.00**

UBERTI 1861 NAVY PERCUSSION REVOLVER
Caliber: 36. **Barrel:** 7-1/2", round. **Weight:** 40-1/2 oz. **Stocks:** One-piece oiled American walnut. **Sights:** Brass pin front, hammer notch rear. **Features:** Rounded trigger guard, German silver blade front sight, "creeping" loading lever. Available with fluted or round cylinder. Imported by Uberti U.S.A. Inc.
Price: Steel backstrap, trigger guard, cut for stock **$265.00**

1ST U.S. MODEL DRAGOON
Caliber: 44. **Barrel:** 7-1/2", part round, part octagon. **Weight:** 64 oz. **Stocks:** One-piece walnut. **Sights:** German silver blade front, hammer notch rear. **Features:** First model has oval bolt cuts in cylinder, square-back flared trigger guard, V-type mainspring, short trigger. Ranger and Indian scene roll-engraved on cylinder. Color case-hardened frame, loading lever, plunger and hammer; blue barrel, cylinder, trigger and wedge. Available with old-time charcoal blue or standard blue-black finish. Polished brass backstrap and trigger guard. From Cimarron F.A. Co., Dixie Gun Works, Uberti U.S.A. Inc., Navy Arms.
Price: . . . . **$295.00 to $435.00**

2nd U.S. Model Dragoon Revolver
Similar to the 1st Model except distinguished by rectangular bolt cuts in the cylinder. From Cimarron F.A. Co., Uberti U.S.A. Inc., United States Patent Fire-Arms, Navy Arms, Dixie Gunworks.
Price: . . . . **$295.00 to $435.00**

3rd U.S. Model Dragoon Revolver
Similar to the 2nd Model except for oval trigger guard, long trigger, modifications to the loading lever and latch. Imported by Cimarron F.A. Co., Uberti U.S.A. Inc., United States Patent Fire-Arms, Dixie Gunworks.
Price: Military model (frame cut for shoulder stock, steel backstrap . . . . **$295.00 to $435.00**
Price: Civilian (brass backstrap, trigger guard) . . . . **$295.00 to $325.00**

1861 NAVY PERCUSSION REVOLVER
Caliber: 36, 6-shot. **Barrel:** 7-1/2", 7-groove, round. **Weight:** 2 lbs., 6 oz. **Length:** 13". **Stocks:** One-piece walnut. **Sights:** German silver blade front sight. **Features:** Rounded trigger guard, "creeping" loading lever, fluted or round cylinder, steel backstrap, trigger guard, cut for stock. Imported by Cimarron F.A. Co., Uberti U.S.A. Inc., Dixie Gunworks.
Price: . . . . **$255.00 to $300.00**

1862 POCKET NAVY PERCUSSION REVOLVER
Caliber: 36, 5-shot. **Barrel:** 5-1/2", 6-1/2", octagonal, 7-groove, LH twist. **Weight:** 27 oz. (5-1/2" barrel). **Length:** 10-1/2" overall (5-1/2" bbl.). **Stocks:** One-piece varnished walnut. **Sights:** Brass pin front, hammer notch rear. **Features:** Rebated cylinder, hinged loading lever, brass or silver-plated backstrap and trigger guard, color-cased frame, hammer, loading lever, plunger and latch, rest blued. Has original-type markings. From Cimarron F.A. Co., Uberti U.S.A. Inc., Dixie Gunworks.
Price: With brass backstrap, trigger guard . . . . **$260.00 to $310.00**

WALKER 1847 PERCUSSION REVOLVER
Caliber: 44, 6-shot. **Barrel:** 9". **Weight:** 84 oz. **Length:** 15-1/2" overall. **Stocks:** Walnut. **Sights:** Fixed. **Features:** Case-hardened frame, loading lever and hammer; iron backstrap; brass trigger guard; engraved cylinder. Imported by Cabela's, Cimarron F.A. Co., Navy Arms, Dixie Gun Works, Uberti U.S.A. Inc., E.M.F., Cimarron, Traditions, United States Patent Fire-Arms.
Price: About. . . . . **$225.00 to $445.00**
Price: Single cased set (Navy Arms) **$405.00**
Price: Deluxe Walker with French fitted case (Navy Arms) **$540.00**
Price: Hartford model, steel frame, German silver trim, cartouche (E.M.F.) **$295.00**

AIRFORCE TALON SS AIR PISTOL
Caliber: 177, 22. **Barrel:** 12". **Weight:** 5.25 lbs. **Length:** 32.75" overall. **Power:** NA. **Grips:** NA. **Sights:** None, integral mount supplied. **Features:** 400-1000 fps. Fill pressure: 3000 psi. Air tank volume: 490cc.
Price: 22 w/refill clamp, open sights **$559.95**
Price: 177 w/refill clamp, open sights **$559.95**
Price: Gun only (22 or 177) **$459.95**

AirForce Talon Air Pistol
Same as Talon SS but 32.6" long, weights 5.5 lbs.
Price: 22 w/refill clamp, open sights **$539.95**
Price: 177 w/refill clamp, open sights **$539.95**
Price: Gun only **$439.95**

ARS HUNTING MASTER AR6 AIR PISTOL
Caliber: 22 (177 +20 special order). **Barrel:** 12" rifled. **Weight:** 3 lbs. **Length:** 18.25 overall. **Power:** NA. **Grips:** Indonesian walnut with checkered grip. **Sights:** Adjustable rear, blade front. **Features:** 6 shot repeater with rotary magazine, single or double action, receiver grooved for scope, hammer block and trigger block safeties.
Price: . . . . **NA**

BEEMAN P1 MAGNUM AIR PISTOL
Caliber: 177, 5mm, single shot. **Barrel:** 8.4". **Weight:** 2.5 lbs. **Length:** 11" overall. **Power:** Top lever cocking; spring-piston. **Grips:** Checkered walnut. **Sights:** Blade front, square notch rear with click micrometer adjustments for windage and elevation. Grooved for scope mounting. **Features:** Dual power for 177 and 20 cal.: low setting gives 350-400 fps; high setting 500-600 fps. All Colt 45 auto grips fit gun. Dry-firing feature for practice. Optional wood shoulder stock. Imported by Beeman.
Price: 177, 5mm **$440.00**

BEEMAN P3 AIR PISTOL
Caliber: 177 pellet, single shot. **Barrel:** NA. **Weight:** 1.7 lbs. **Length:** 9.6" overall. **Power:** Single-stroke pneumatic; overlever barrel cocking. **Grips:** Reinforced polymer. **Sights:** Adjustable rear, blade front. **Features:** Velocity 410 fps. Polymer frame; automatic safety; two-stage trigger; built-in muzzle brake.
Price: **$180.00**
Price: Combo **$285.00**

BEEMAN/FEINWERKBAU 103 AIR PISTOL
Caliber: 177, single shot. **Barrel:** 10.1", 12-groove rifling. **Weight:** 2.5 lbs. **Length:** 16.5" overall. **Power:** Single-stroke pneumatic, underlever cocking. **Grips:** Stippled walnut with adjustable palm shelf. **Sights:** Blade front, open rear adjustable for windage and elevation. Notch size adjustable for width. Interchangeable front blades. **Features:** Velocity 510 fps. Fully adjustable trigger. Cocking effort 2 lbs. Imported by Beeman.
Price: Right-hand **$1,236.00**
Price: Left-hand **$1,275.00**

BEEMAN/FWB P34 MATCH AIR PISTOL
Caliber: 177, single shot. **Barrel:** 10-5/16", with muzzle brake. **Weight:** 2.4 lbs. **Length:** 16.5" overall. **Power:** Precharged pneumatic. **Grips:** Stippled walnut; adjustable match type. **Sights:** Undercut blade front, fully adjustable match rear. **Features:** Velocity to 525 fps; up to 200 shots per CO2 cartridge. Fully adjustable trigger; built-in muzzle brake. Imported from Germany by Beeman.
Price: Right-hand **$1,395.00**
Price: Left-hand **$1,440.00**

BEEMAN HW70A AIR PISTOL
Caliber: 177, single shot. **Barrel:** 6-1/4", rifled. **Weight:** 38 oz. **Length:** 12-3/4" overall. **Power:** Spring, barrel cocking. **Grips:** Plastic, with thumbrest. **Sights:** Hooded post front, square notch rear adjustable for windage and elevation. Comes with scope base. **Features:** Adjustable trigger, 31-lb. cocking effort, 440 fps MV; automatic barrel safety. Imported by Beeman.
Price: **$190.00**

BEEMAN/WEBLEY TEMPEST AIR PISTOL
Caliber: 177, 22, single shot. **Barrel:** 6-7/8". **Weight:** 32 oz. **Length:** 8.9" overall. **Power:** Spring-piston, break barrel. **Grips:** Checkered black plastic with thumbrest. **Sights:** Blade front, adjustable rear. **Features:**

Daisy 662X

Velocity to 500 fps (177), 400 fps (22). Aluminum frame; black epoxy finish; manual safety. Imported from England by Beeman.
Price: **$205.00**

Beeman/Webley Hurricane Air Pistol
Similar to the Tempest except has extended frame in the rear for a click-adjustable rear sight; hooded front sight; comes with scope mount. Imported from England by Beeman.
Price: **$255.00**

BENJAMIN SHERIDAN CO2 PELLET PISTOLS
Caliber: 177, 20, 22, single shot. **Barrel:** 6-3/8", rifled brass. **Weight:** 29 oz. **Length:** 9.8" overall. **Power:** 12-gram CO2 cylinder. **Grips:** Walnut. **Sights:** High ramp front, fully adjustable notched rear. **Features:** Velocity to 500 fps. Turnbolt action with cross-bolt safety. Gives about 40 shots per CO2 cylinder. Black or nickel finish. Made in U.S. by Benjamin Sheridan Co.
Price: Black finish, EB17 (177), EB20 (20) **$190.00**

BENJAMIN SHERIDAN PNEUMATIC PELLET PISTOLS
Caliber: 177, 20, 22, single shot. **Barrel:** 9-3/8", rifled brass. **Weight:** 38 oz. **Length:**13-1/8" overall. **Power:** Underlever pnuematic, hand pumped. **Grips:** Walnut stocks and pump handle. **Sights:** High ramp front, fully adjustable notch rear. **Features:** Velocity to 525 fps (variable). Bolt action with cross-bolt safety. Choice of black or nickel finish. Made in U.S. by Benjamin Sheridan Co.
Price: Black finish, HB17 (177), HB20 (20) **$190.00**
Price: HB22 (22) **$199.00**

BRNO TAU-7 CO2 MATCH AIR PISTOL
Caliber: 177. **Barrel:** 10.24". **Weight:** 37 oz. **Length:** 15.75" overall. **Power:** 12.5-gram CO2 cartridge. **Grips:** Stippled hardwood with adjustable palm rest. **Sights:** Blade front, open fully adjustable rear. **Features:** Comes with extra seals and counterweight. Blue finish. Imported by Great Lakes Airguns.
Price: **$299.50**

CROSMAN BLACK VENOM AIR PISTOL
Caliber: 177 pellets, BB, 17-shot magazine; darts, single shot. **Barrel:** 4.75" smooth-bore. **Weight:** 16 oz. **Length:** 10.8" overall. **Power:** Spring. **Grips:** NA. **Sights:** Blade front, adjustable rear. **Features:** Velocity to 270 fps (BBs), 250 fps (pellets). Spring-fed magazine; cross-bolt safety. Made in U.S.A. by Crosman Corp.
Price: **$60.00**

CROSMAN MODEL 1377 AIR PISTOL
Caliber: 177, single shot. **Barrel:** 8", rifled steel. **Weight:** 39 oz. **Length:** 13-5/8". **Power:** Hand pumped. **Grips:** NA. **Sights:** Blade front, rear adjustable for windage and elevation. **Features:** Bolt action, molded plastic grip, hand size pump forearm. Cross-bolt safety. From Crosman.
Price: **$60.00**

CROSMAN AUTO AIR II PISTOLS
Caliber: BB, 17-shot magazine; 177 pellet, single shot. **Barrel:** 8-5/8" steel, smooth-bore. **Weight:** 13 oz. **Length:** 10-3/4" overall. **Power:** CO2 Powerlet. **Grips:** NA. **Sights:** Blade front, adjustable rear; highlighted system. **Features:** Velocity to 480 fps (BBs), 430 fps (pellets). Semi-automatic action with BBs, single shot with pellets. Black. From Crosman.
Price: AAIIB **$38.00**
Price: AAIIBRD . . . . **NA**

AIRGUNS — Handguns

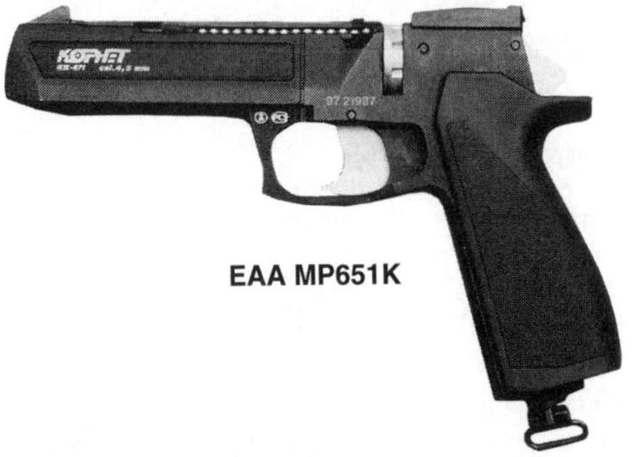

EAA MP651K

Gamo PT-80

CROSMAN MODEL 1008 REPEAT AIR PISTOL
Caliber: 177, 8-shot pellet clip. **Barrel:** 4.25", rifled steel. **Weight:** 17 oz. **Length:** 8.625" overall. **Power:** CO2 Powerlet. **Grips:** Checkered black plastic. **Sights:** Post front, adjustable rear. **Features:** Velocity about 430 fps. Break-open barrel for easy loading; single or double semi-automatic action; two 8-shot clips included. Optional carrying case available. From Crosman.
Price: **$60.00**
Price: Model 1008SB (silver and black finish), about **$60.00**

CROSMAN SEMI AUTO AIR PISTOL
Caliber: 177, pellets. **Barrel:** Rifled steel. **Weight:** 40 oz. **Length:** 8.63". **Power:** CO2. **Grips:** NA. **Sights:** Blade front, rear adjustable. **Features:** Velocity up to 430 fps. Synthetic grips, zinc alloy frame. From Crosman.
Price: C40 . . . . **NA**

CROSMAN MAGNUM AIR PISTOLS
Caliber: 177, pellets. **Barrel:** Rifled steel. **Weight:** 27 oz. **Length:** 9.38". **Power:** CO2. **Grips:** NA. **Sights:** Blade front, rear adjustable. **Features:** Single/double action accepts sights and scopes with standard 3/8" dovetail mount. Model 3576W features 6" barrel for increased accuracy. From Crosman.
Price: 3574W. . . . . **NA**
Price: 3576W . . . . **NA**

DAISY/POWERLINE MODEL 15XT AIR PISTOL
Caliber: 177 BB, 15-shot built-in magazine. **Barrel:** NA. **Weight:** NA. **Length:** 7.21". **Power:** CO2. **Grips:** NA. **Sights:** NA. **Features:** Velocity 425 fps. Made in the U.S.A. by Daisy Mfg. Co.
Price: **$36.95**
New! Price: 15XK Shooting Kit **$59.95**

DAISY/POWERLINE 717 PELLET AIR PISTOL
Caliber: 177, single shot. **Barrel:** 9.61". **Weight:** 2.25 lbs. **Length:** 13-1/2" overall. **Grips:** Molded wood-grain plastic with thumbrest. **Sights:** Blade and ramp front, micro-adjustable notched rear. **Features:** Single pump pneumatic pistol. Rifled steel barrel. Cross-bolt trigger block. Muzzle velocity 385 fps. From Daisy Mfg. Co.
Price: **$71.95**

DAISY/POWERLINE 1270 CO2 AIR PISTOL
Caliber: BB, 60-shot magazine. **Barrel:** Smoothbore steel. **Weight:** 17 oz. **Length:** 11.1" overall. **Power:** CO2 pump action. **Grips:** Molded black polymer. **Sights:** Blade on ramp front, adjustable rear. **Features:** Velocity to 420 fps. Cross-bolt trigger block safety; plated finish. Made in U.S. by Daisy Mfg. Co.
Price: **$39.95**

DAISY/POWERLINE MODEL 93 AIR PISTOL
Caliber: BB, 15-shot magazine. **Barrel:** Smoothbore; steel. **Weight:** 1.1 lbs. **Length:** 7.9" overall. **Power:** CO2 powered semi-auto. **Grips:** Molded brown checkered. **Sights:** Blade on ramp front, fixed open rear. **Features:** Velocity to 400 fps. Manual trigger block. Made in U.S.A. by Daisy Mfg. Co.
Price: **$48.95**

Daisy/Powerline 693 Air Pistol
Similar to Model 93 except has velocity to 235 fps.
Price: **$52.95**

DAISY/POWERLINE 622X PELLET PISTOL
Caliber: 22 (5.5mm), 6-shot. **Barrel:** Rifled steel. **Weight:** 1.3 lbs. **Length:** 8.5". **Power:** CO2. **Grips:** Molded black checkered. **Sights:** Fiber-optic front, fixed open rear. **Features:** Velocity 225 fps. Rotary hammer block. Made by Daisy Mfg. Co.
Price: **$69.95**

DAISY/POWERLINE 45 AIR PISTOL
Caliber: BB, 13-shot magazine. **Barrel:** Rifled steel. **Weight:** 1.25 lbs. **Length:** 8.5" overall. **Power:** CO2 powered semi-auto. **Grips:** Molded black checkered. **Sights:** TruGlo fiber-optic front, fixed open rear. **Features:** Velocity to 224 fps. Manual trigger block. Made in U.S.A. by Daisy Mfg. Co.
Price: **$54.95**

Daisy/Powerline 645 Air Pistol
Similar to Model 93 except has distinctive black and nickel finish.
Price: **$59.95**

EAA/BAIKAL IZH-M46 TARGET AIR PISTOL
Caliber: 177, single shot. **Barrel:** 10". **Weight:** 2.4 lbs. **Length:** 16.8" overall. **Power:** Underlever single-stroke pneumatic. **Grips:** Adjustable wooden target. **Sights:** Micrometer fully adjustable rear, blade front. **Features:** Velocity about 420 fps. Hammer-forged, rifled barrel. Imported from Russia by European American Armory.
Price: **$349.00**

GAMO AUTO 45 AIR PISTOL
Caliber: 177, 12-shot. **Barrel:** 4.25". **Weight:** 1.10 lbs. **Length:** 7.50". **Power:** CO2 cartridge, semi-automatic, 410 fps. **Grips:** Plastic. **Sights:** Rear sights adjusts for windage. **Features:** Glock copy; double-action, manual safety. Imported from Spain by Gamo.
Price: **$99.95**

GAMO COMPACT TARGET PISTOL
Caliber: 177, single shot. **Barrel:** 8.26". **Weight:** 1.95 lbs. **Length:** 12.60". **Power:** Spring-piston, 400 fps. **Grips:** Walnut. **Sights:** Micro-adjustable. **Features:** Rifled steel barrel, adjustable match trigger, recoil and vibration-free. Imported from Spain by Gamo.
Price: **$229.95**

GAMO P-23, P-23 LASER PISTOL
Caliber: 177, 12-shot. **Barrel:** 4.25". **Weight:** 1 lb. **Length:** 7.5". **Power:** CO2 cartridge, semi-automatic, 410 fps. **Grips:** Plastic. **Sights:** NA. **Features:** Walther PPK cartridge pistol copy, optional laser sight. Imported from Spain by Gamo.
Price: . . . . **$89.95**, (with laser) **$129.95**

GAMO PT-80, PT-80 LASER PISTOL
Caliber: 177, 8-shot. **Barrel:** 4.25". **Weight:** 1.2 lbs. **Length:** 7.2". **Power:** CO2 cartridge, semi-automatic, 410 fps. **Grips:** Plastic. **Sights:** 3-dot. **Features:** Optional laser sight and walnut grips available. Imported from Spain by Gamo.
Price: . . . . . **$108.95,** (with laser) **$129.95**, (with walnut grip) **$119.95**

"GAT" AIR PISTOL
Caliber: 177, single shot. **Barrel:** 7-1/2" cocked, 9-1/2" extended. **Weight:** 22 oz. **Length:** NA. **Power:** Spring-piston. **Grips:** Cast checkered metal. **Sights:** Fixed. **Features:** Shoots pellets, corks or darts. Matte black finish. Imported from England by Stone Enterprises, Inc.
Price: **$24.95**

AIRGUNS — Handguns

HAMMERLI AP40 AIR PISTOL
Caliber: 177. **Barrel:** 10". **Length:** NA. **Power:** NA. **Grips:** Adjustable orthopedic. **Sights:** Fully adjustable micrometer. **Features:** Sleek, light, well balanced and accurate. Imported from Switzerland by Nygord Precision Products.
Price: **$1,195.00**

MARKSMAN 2000 REPEATER AIR PISTOL
Caliber: 177, 18-shot BB repeater. **Barrel:** 2-1/2", smoothbore. **Weight:** 24 oz. **Length:** 8-1/4" overall. **Power:** Spring. **Grips:** NA. **Sights:** NA. **Features:** Velocity to 200 fps. Thumb safety. Uses BBs, darts, bolts or pellets. Repeats with BBs only. From Marksman Products.
Price: **$27.00**

MARKSMAN 2005 LASERHAWK™ SPECIAL EDITION AIR PISTOL
Caliber: 177, 24-shot magazine. **Barrel:** 3.8", smoothbore. **Weight:** 22 oz. **Length:** 10.3" overall. **Power:** Spring-air. **Grips:** Checkered. **Sights:** Fixed fiber-optic front sight. **Features:** Velocity to 300 fps with Hyper-Velocity pellets. Square trigger guard with skeletonized trigger; extended barrel. Shoots BBs, pellets, darts or bolts. Made in the U.S. From Marksman Products.
Price: **$32.00**

MORINI 162E MATCH AIR PISTOLS
Caliber: 177, single shot. **Barrel:** 9.4". **Weight:** 32 oz. **Length:** 16.1" overall. **Power:** Scuba air. **Grips:** Adjustable match type. **Sights:** Interchangeable blade front, fully adjustable match-type rear. **Features:** Power mechanism shuts down when pressure drops to a preset level. Adjustable electronic trigger. Imported from Switzerland by Nygord Precision Products.
Price: **$825.00**
Price: 162 EI **$1,075.00**

MORINI SAM K-11 AIR PISTOL
Caliber: 177. **Barrel:** 10". **Weight:** 38 oz. **Length:** NA. **Grips:** Fully adjustable. **Sights:** Fully adjustable. **Features:** Improved trigger, more angle adjustment on grip. Sophisticated counter balance system. Deluxe aluminum case, two cylinders and manometer. Imported from Switzerland by Nygord Precision Products.
Price: **$975.00**

PARDINI K58 MATCH AIR PISTOLS
Caliber: 177, single shot. **Barrel:** 9". **Weight:** 37.7 oz. **Length:** 15.5" overall. **Power:** Precharged compressed air; single-stroke cocking. **Grips:** Adjustable match type; stippled walnut. **Sights:** Interchangeable post front, fully adjustable match rear. **Features:** Fully adjustable trigger. Short version K-2 available. Imported from Italy by Nygord Precision Products.
Price: **$795.00**
Price: K2S model, precharged air pistol, introduced in 1998 ...... **$945.00**

RWS 9B/9N AIR PISTOLS
Caliber: 177, single shot. **Barrel:** NA. **Weight:** NA. **Length:** NA. **Power:** NA. **Grips:** Plastic with thumbrest. **Sights:** Adjustable. **Features:** Spring-piston powered; 550 fps. Black or nickel finish. Imported from Spain by Dynamit Nobel-RWS.
Price: 9B **$169.00**
Price: 9N **$185.00**

STEYR LP 5CP MATCH AIR PISTOL
Caliber: 177, 5-shot magazine. **Weight:** 40.7 oz. **Length:** 15.2" overall. **Power:** Precharged air cylinder. **Grips:** Adjustable match type. **Sights:** Interchangeable blade front, adjustable matched rear. **Features:** Adjustable sight radius; adjustable trigger. Barrel compensator. One-shot magazine available. Imported from Austria by Nygord Precision Products.
Price: **$1,100.00**

STEYR LP10P MATCH AIR PISTOL
Caliber: 177, single shot. **Barrel:** 9". **Weight:** 38.7 oz. **Length:** 15.3" overall. **Power:** Scuba air. **Grips:** Adjustable Morini match, palm shelf, stippled walnut. **Sights:** Interchangeable blade in 4mm, 4.5mm or 5mm widths, adjustable open rear, interchangeable 3.5mm or 4mm leaves. **Features:** Velocity about 500 fps. Adjustable trigger, adjustable sight radius from 12.4" to 13.2". With compensator. Recoil elimination. Imported from Austria by Nygord Precision Products.
Price: **$1,175.00**

TECH FORCE SS2 OLYMPIC COMPETITION AIR PISTOL
Caliber: 177 pellet, single shot. **Barrel:** 7.4". **Weight:** 2.8 lbs. **Length:** 16.5" overall. **Power:** Spring piston, sidelever. **Grips:** Hardwood. **Sights:** Extended adjustable rear, blade front accepts inserts. **Features:** Velocity 520 fps. Recoilless design; adjustments allow duplication of a firearm's feel. Match-grade, adjustable trigger; includes carrying case. Imported from China by Compasseco, Inc.
Price: **$295.00**

TECH FORCE 35 AIR PISTOL
Caliber: 177 pellet, single shot. **Weight:** 2.86 lbs. **Length:** 14.9" overall. **Power:** Spring-piston, underlever. **Grips:** Hardwood. **Sights:** Micrometer adjustable rear, blade front. **Features:** Velocity 400 fps. Grooved for scope mount; trigger safety. Imported from China by Compasseco, Inc.
Price: **$39.95**

Tech Force 8 Air Pistol
Similar to Tech Force 35 but with break-barrel action, ambidextrous polymer grips.
Price: **$59.95**

Tech Force S2-1 Air Pistol
Similar to Tech Force 8 except basic grips and sights for plinking.
Price: **$29.95**

WALTHER LP300 MATCH PISTOL
Caliber: 177. **Barrel:** 236mm. **Weight:** 1.018g. **Length:** NA. **Power:** NA. **Grips:** NA. **Sights:** Integrated front with three different widths, adjustable rear. **Features:** Adjustable grip and trigger. Imported from Germany by Nygord Precision Products.
Price: **$1,095.00**

CONSULT
SHOOTER'S MARKETPLACE
Page 141, This Issue

GRIPS

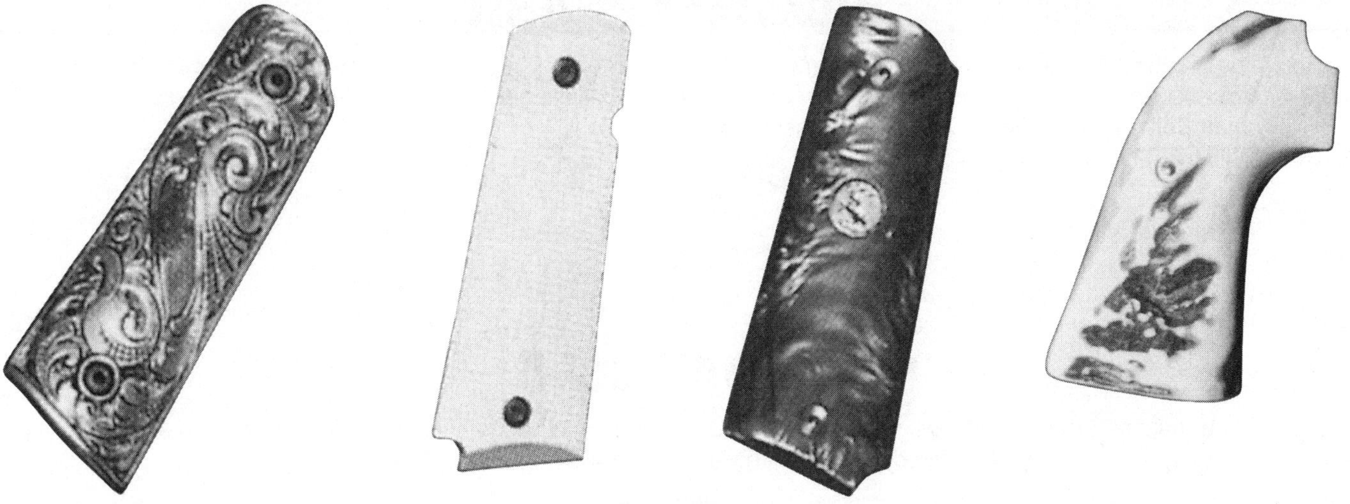

AJAX

Grip materials include genuine stag *(extremely limited supply)*, buffalo horn, colored Pearlite, ivory polymer, white and black Pearlite, exotic woods, buffalo polymer, pewter, genuine ivory and Staglite (imitation stag horn). Available for most single- and double-action revolvers and semi-automatic pistols. Custom fittings are available at extra cost. Some grips may require fitting.

Price: Genuine stag **$250.00**
Price: Genuine buffalo horn .... **$70.00 to $80.00**
Price: Ivory polymer .... **$40.00 to $50.00**
Price: Pearlite .... **$40.00 to $60.00**
Price: Exotic woods (super walnut, cherrywood, black Silverwood) .... **$40.00 to $70.00**
Price: Buffalo polymer .... **$40.00 to 50.00**
Price: Pewter .... **$60.00 to $70.00**
Price: Genuine ivory .... **$325.00 to $350.00**
Price: Staglite .... **$50.00 to $70.00**
Price: Colored Pearlite .... **$40.00 to $70.00**
Price: Aged Ivory Polymer........ **$40.00 to $50.00**

Textured decal grips in various textures also available from Ajax for many semi-automatic pistols.

Price: **$9.95**

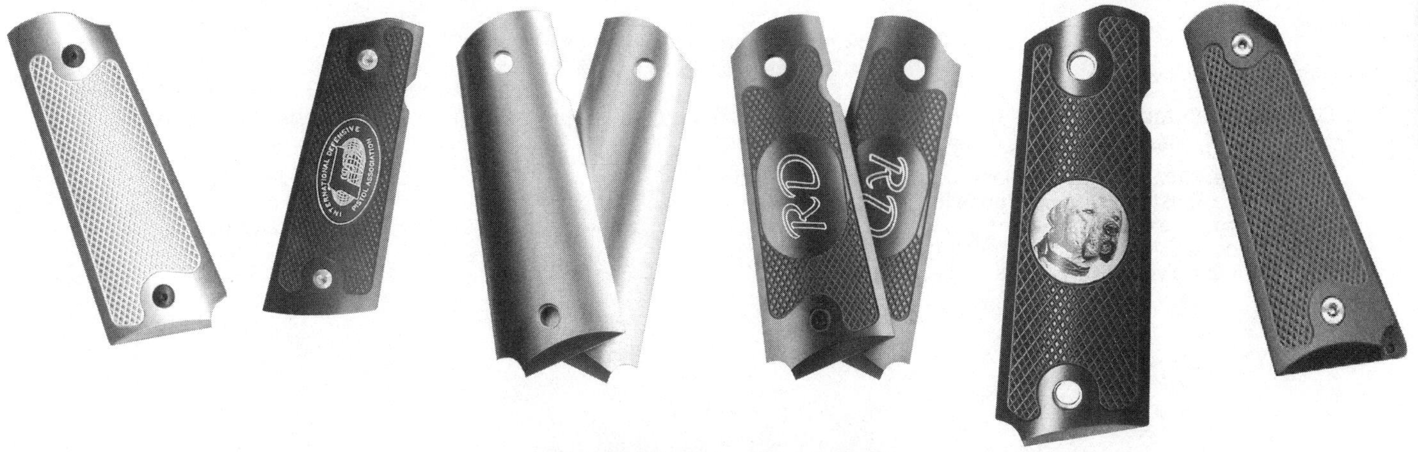

ALUMNA GRIPS

Aluminum handgun grips available in several configurations including checkered, UltraLight, ThinLine, olive gray finish, color choices, laser engraved and Custom Deluxe with up to 3 engraved initials. Anodized aluminum colors also available.

Price: .... **$40.00 and up, depending on options**

GRIPS

BARAMI HIP-GRIP

The Hip-Grip is actually a set of replacement stocks that allows a handgun to be carried without a holster, clipped or hooked inside the waistband or trouser's pocket. Available for certain S&W J-Frame, K-Frame, small Colt, Taurus, Charter Arms and Rossi revolvers.

Price: **$23.95**

BROWNELLS

Not a manufacturer, but an on-line and catalog retailer, supplying gunsmiths and retailers, as well as the shooting public. Many of the products shown here are also available from Brownells.

BUTLER CREEK (UNCLE MIKE'S)

Revolver and pistol grips made of polymer are available for a wide range of handgun models. Revolver grips are made to be hand-filling, but not oversize. Finger grooves are provided on double-action revolver grips for good control. Revolver boot grips are designed not to "print" when used on concealed-carry revolvers, yet allow a controlled rapid draw. Pistol grips are specifically designed to maintain the original stock dimensions. Slip-on grips are offered in three sizes. Medium and large versions have finer grooves.

Price: Slip-on pistol grips **$11.94**

COAST IVORY

Offers handgun grips of elephant ivory, stag, California buckeye burl and other exotic woods, as well as polyester pearl. All ivory is pre-ban material.

Price: Custom-fitted elephant ivory for 1911-style pistols **$450.00**
Price: Custom-fitted ivory grips for Colt single-action revolvers .... **$500.00 and up**
Price: Custom-fitted Derringer ivory grips .... **$200.00 and up**
Price: Custom-fitted stag grips for Colt single-action revolvers **$190.00**
Price: Polyester pearl grips .... **$60.00 to $85.00**

CRIMSON TRACE

Makers of special grip replacements for many popular revolvers and pistols, including Lasergrip sighting systems. Lasergrips are intended for police agencies, military armed citizens.

Price: .... **N/A**

GRIPS

EAGLE GRIPS

Available materials include an extensive variety of rosewood, buffalo horn, ebony, mother-of-pearl, American elk, polymer and Ultra Ivory (imitation elephant ivory). Can produce grips for virtually any handgun. Custom-fittings available.

Price: Rosewood or ebony handgun grips . . . . **$39.95 to $59.95**
Price: Compact revolver Secret Service grips . . . . **$59.95 to $125.95**
Price: Single-action revolver grips . . . . **$59.95 to $125.00**
Price: Stag, buffalo horn, mother-of-pearl, American elk . . . . **$59.95 to $175.00**

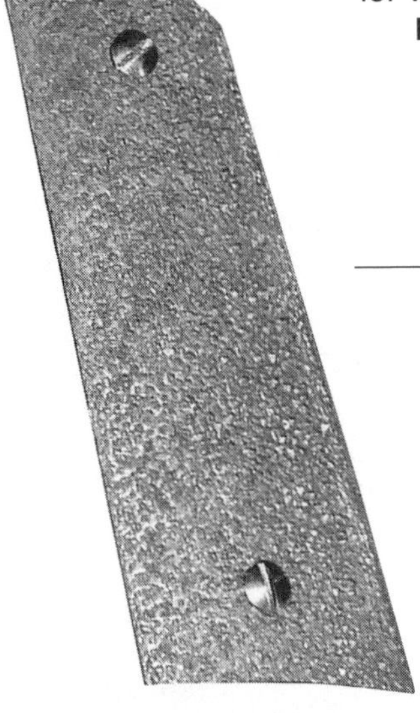

FALCON INDUSTRIES

Producer of the Ergo Grip XT for 1911-type Government and Colt Commander-size frames. Made of textured nylon-based rigid polymer with pebble-grain grip surface. Made in the U.S.A.

Price: **$22.00**

GRIPS

 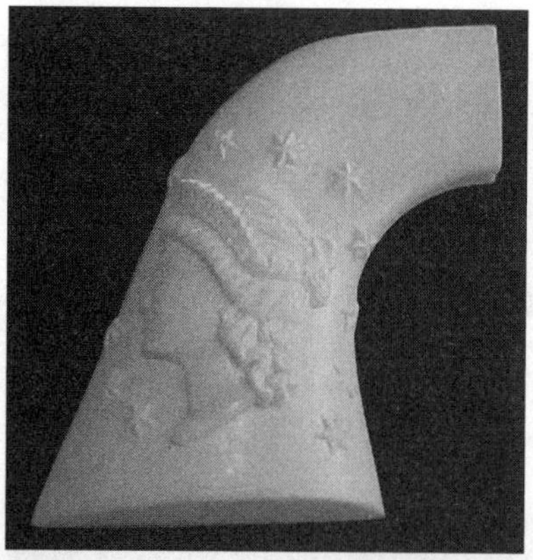 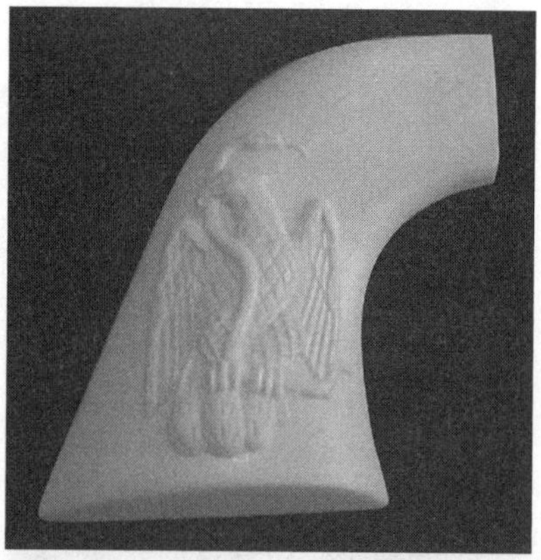

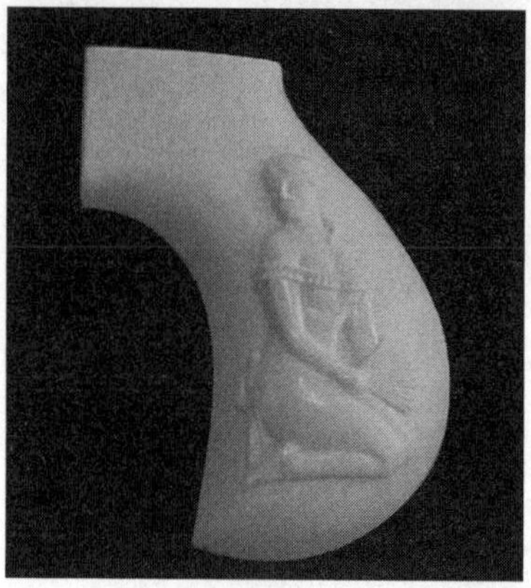 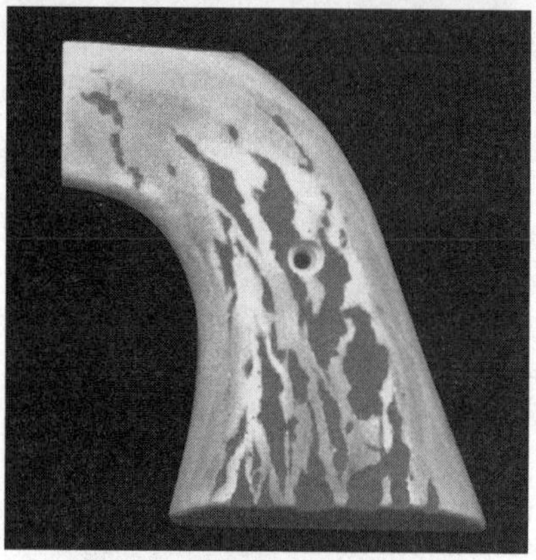 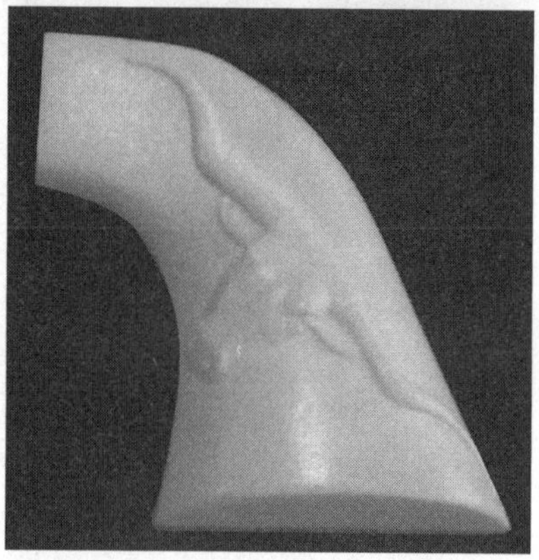

GRIPMAKER

Specializing in the production of original and authentic single-action revolver grip designs from the 1850s to 1890s. Made of white urethane which ages (yellows) like real ivory; also available in stag. Models available to fit Colt Single-Action Army and similar models, blackpowder revolvers (1851 and 1861 Navy, 1860 Army), Ruger single-actions, Smith & Wesson Schofield, #1 & #3 American and Model #3 Russian, and Derringers.

Price: Revolvers (urethane) .... **$40.00 to $50.00**
Price: Revolvers (stag) .... **$60.00 to $75.00**
Price: Derringers (urethane) **$25.00**
Price: Derringers (stag) **$35.00**

GRIPS

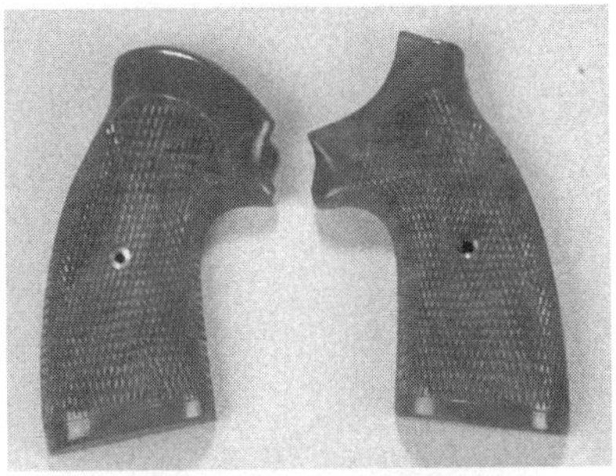
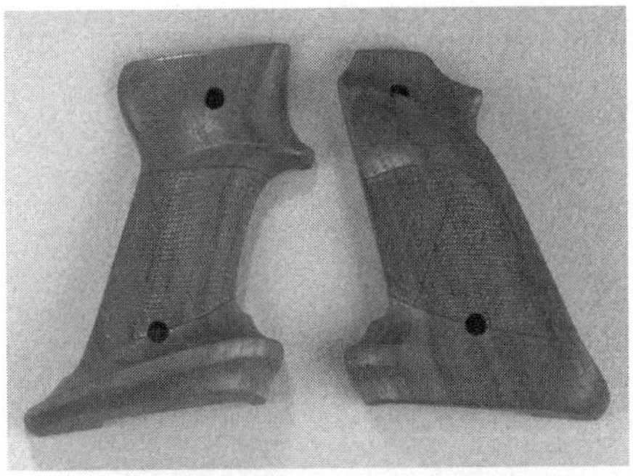
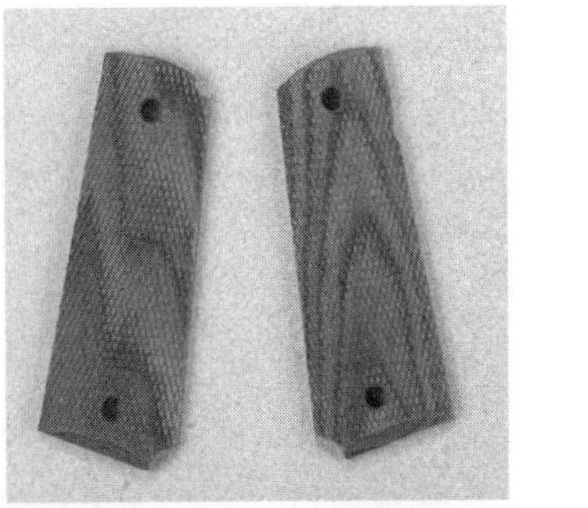

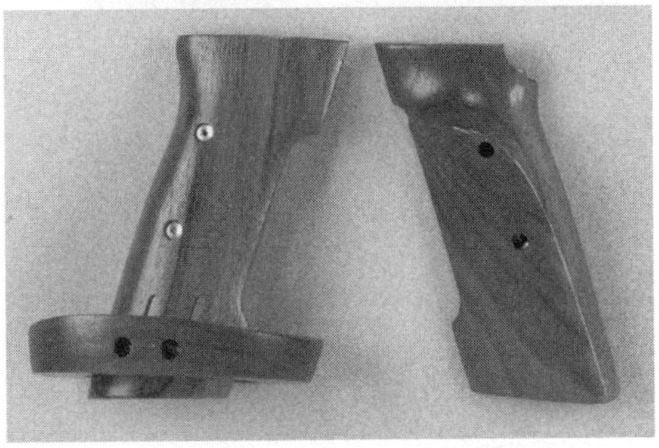
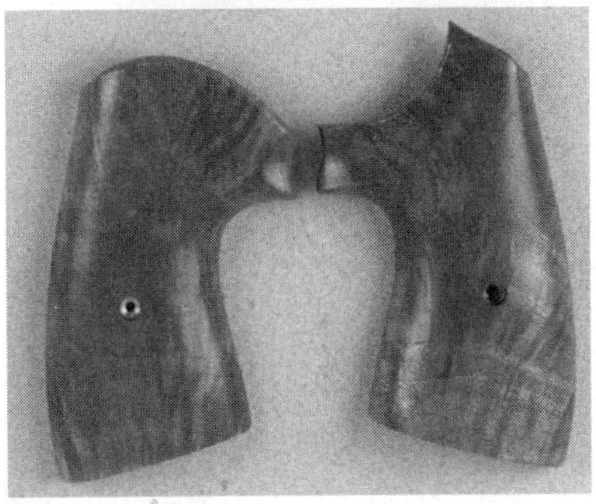

HERRETT'S STOCKS, INC.

Standard and custom hand-fitted grips made of American walnut. Exotic woods such as cocobolo and bubinga are available on request. Grips are available in configurations including target, Camp Perry, combat, field, Jordan trooper, detective, and others. Offered in a variety of checkering patterns, or smooth finish.

Prices:. . . . . **$19.95 to $329.95**

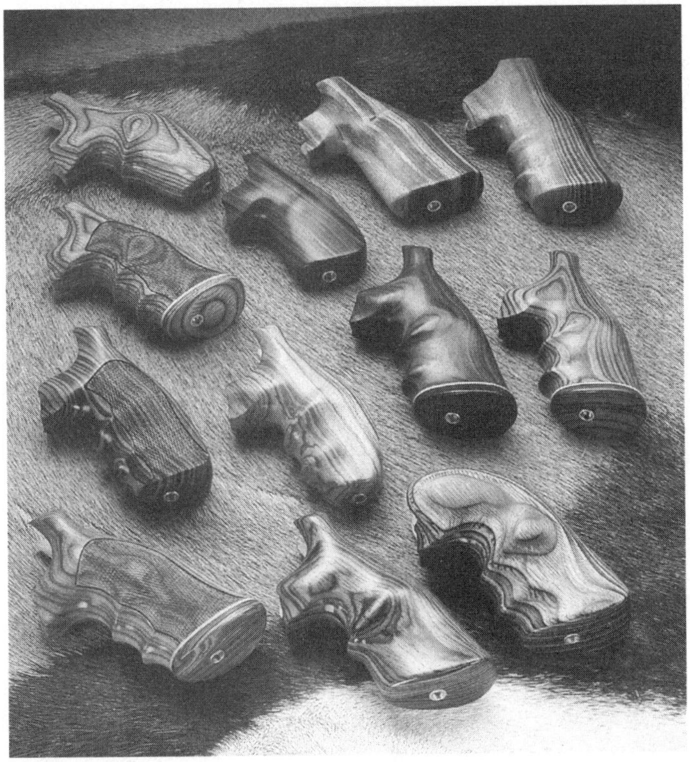

HOGUE, INC.

Producer of a wide range of grips including the Monogrip, a one-piece design that slides on revolver frames from the bottom. Hand-All grip sleeves fit over the original grips of more than 50 handgun models. Grip materials include soft rubber, nylon, laminated hardwoods and fancy hardwoods such as coco bolo, goncalo alves, pau ferro and kingwood. Single-action revolver grips are available in materials such as white and black Micarta, white and black pearlized polymer, ebony, fancy walnut, ivory polymer and exotic hardwoods.

Price: Revolver & pistol grips of rubber or nylon . . . . **$22.95 to $22.95**
Price: Revolver & pistol grips of goncalo alves or pau ferro . . . . **$59.95 to $84.95**
Price: Revolver & pistol grips of laminated or fancy woods . . . . **$69.95 to $109.95**
Price: Revolver & pistol grips of Kingwood, tulipwood or rosewood . . . . **$24.95 to $79.95**
Price: Single-action revolver grips of wood, polymer or Micarta . . . . **$39.95 to $79.95**
Price: HandAll grip sleeves . . . .**$8.95 to $10.95**

GRIPS

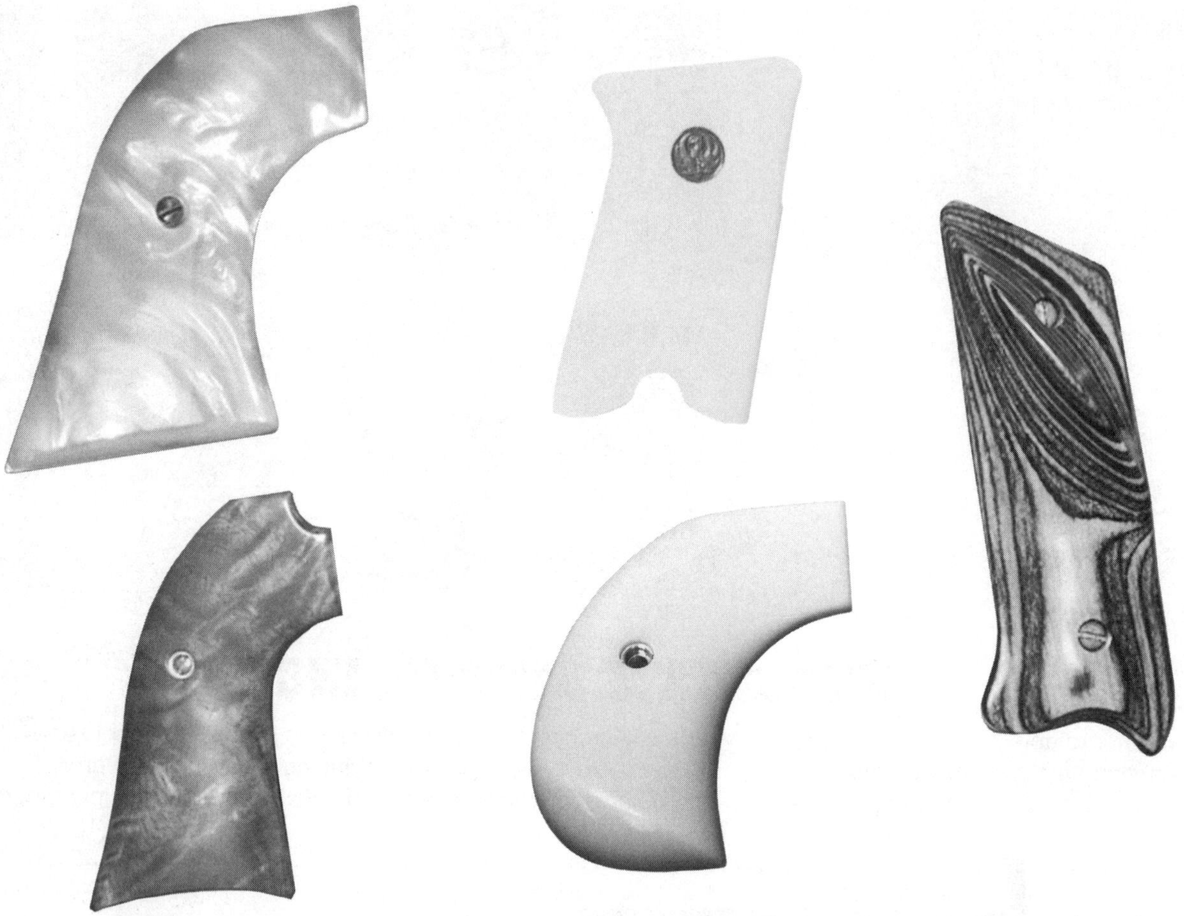

LETT CUSTOM GRIPS

Established in 1940, W. F. Lett Mfg., Inc. has been the principal OEM grip manufacturer for Sturm, Ruger since 1955. Grip materials include fancy hardwoods, such as Bolivian rosewood, zebrawood, bocote, goncalo alves and coco bola. Laminated grips are made of hardwood veneers impregnated with plastic resins. Other materials include black or ivory Micarta, buffalo horn, simulated ivory and pearl-LETT, a synthetic material offering the fiery beauty of genuine mother-of-pearl. Hand-checkering is available on many models.

Price: Available for most Ruger pistols and revolvers .... **$19.95 to $89.95**

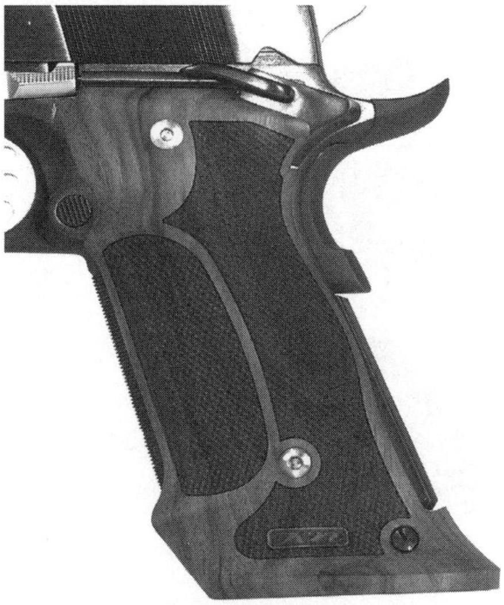
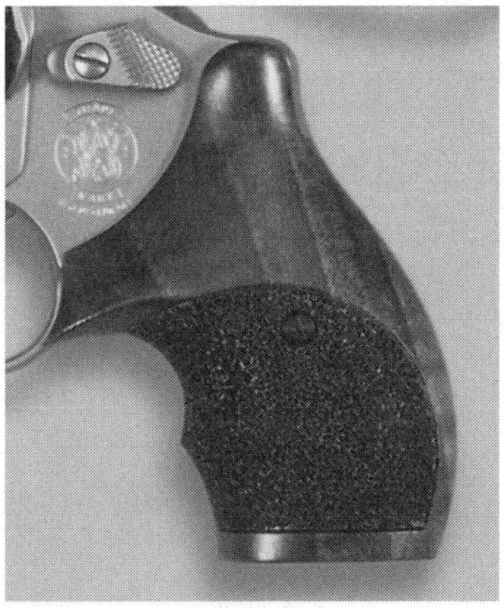
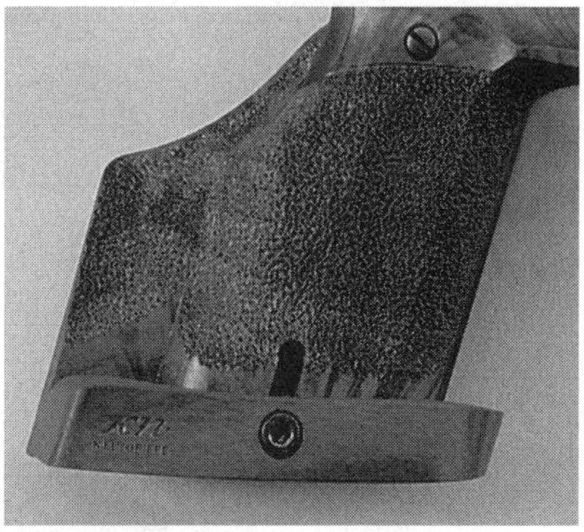
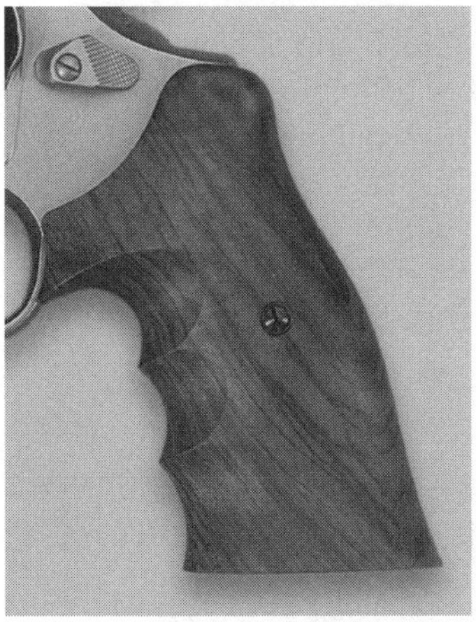
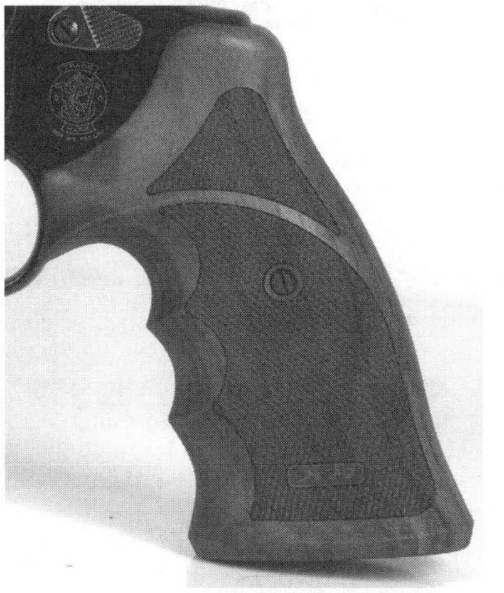
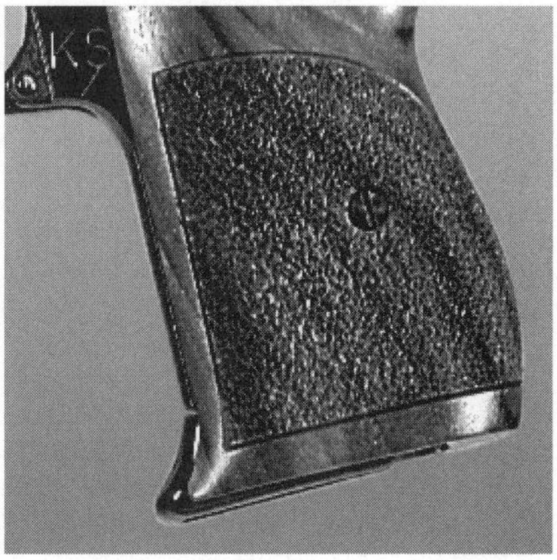

NILL GRIPS

Double-action revolver grips are available with closed or open backstrap area in walnut with smooth, stippled, checkered or Rhomlas finishes, with or without finger grooves in a variety of styles. Anatomical match grips with or without adjustable palm rest are available for standard cartridge handguns and air pistols, as are match grips for Olympic rapid-fire free pistols.
Company no longer has a contact/distributor in U.S.A. Prices subject to international currency fluctuations.

N. C. ORDNANCE

Company manufactures hundreds of grip models for foreign and U.S.-made handguns, pistols and revolvers, old and new. Available materials include black or brown urethane, reproduction Royalwood, ivory-like, stag-like, jigged bone, plain or checkered, including laser-engraved commemoratives.

Price: .... **$20.00 to $95.00**

GRIPS

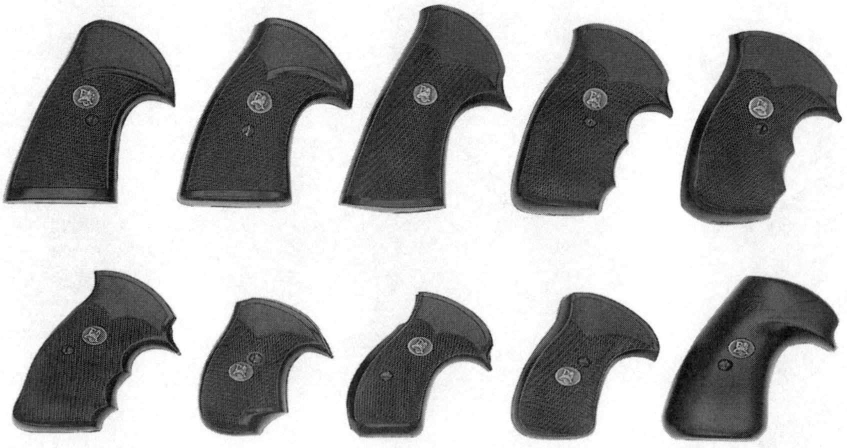

PACHMAYR

Models available in rubber, combination wood and rubber (American Legend Series), and slip-on variations. Some have steel inserts to improve function and finger grooves and/or palm swell available on some models. Decelerator rubber grips are designed to dampen recoil of heavy-recoil handguns. Signature grips are available in full wrap-around or without coverage of the pistol backstrap for use on handguns such as 1911-style pistols with grip safety mechanisms. Slip-on grips come in five sizes to fit virtually any handgun. Compact grips are for small, concealed carry handguns.

Price: . . . . **$9.95 to $45.98**

PEARCE GRIP

Producer of rubber grips for handgun models including those produced by Glock, Beretta, Colt, Makarov, Kahr Arms, Taurus and Para Ordnance. Highly contoured grips with palm swells, finger grooves and ultra-thin grip panels are available, depending on model.

Price: . . . . **$9.95 to $36.00**

WILSON COMBAT

Grips for 1911-A1-style pistols in a variety of woods. Full-checkered models available in coco bolo and Diamondwood. Slim Line grips are laminated from coco bolo or Diamondwood and are 1/3 the thickness of standard 1911-style grips. Exotic wood 1911 grips are offered in cookbook, Kingwood and Diamondwood and have a double-diamond checkering pattern.

Price: . . . . **$49.95 to $59.95**

GRIPS DIRECTORY

Ajax Custom Grips, Inc.
9130 Viscount Row
Dallas, TX 75247
214-630-8893, 800-527-7537
FAX: 214-630-4942
www.ajaxgrips.com

Altamont Co.
901 N. Church St.
Thomasboro, IL 61878
217-643-3125, 800-626-5774
FAX: 217-643-7973
www.altamontco.com

AlumaGrips
2851 N. 34th Place
Mesa, AZ 85213
602-690-5459
FAX: 480-807-3955
www.alumagrips.com

Barami Corp. Hip-Grip
P.O. Box 252224
West Bloomfield, MI 48325-2224
248-738-0462
FAX: 248-738-2542
www.hipgrip.com

Butler Creek Corp.
Michaels of Oregon
P.O. Box 1690
Oregon City, OR 97045
800-948-1356
FAX: 406-388-7204
www.michaels-oregon.com

Coast Ivory
6100 Hans Road
Moss Point, MS 39562
228-475-2877
www.coastivory.com

Crimson Trace/Lasergrips
8089 Southwest Cirrus Drive
Beaverton, OR 97008
503-627-9992, 800-442-2406
FAX: 503-627-0166
www.crimsontrace.com

Eagle Grips, Inc.
460 Randy Road
Carol Stream, IL 60188
630-260-0400, 800-323-6144
FAX: 630-260-0486
www.eaglegrips.com

Falcon Industries
P.O. Box 1060
Edgewood, NM 87015-169
505-281-3783, 877-281-3783
FAX: 505-281-3991
www.ergogrips.net

Herrett's Stocks, Inc.,
P.O. Box 741,
Twin Falls, ID 83303
208-733-1498
www.herrettstocks@msn.com

Hogue Inc.
P.O. Box 1138
Paso Robles, CA 93447
805-239-1440, 800-438-4747
FAX: 805-239-2553
www.getgrip.com

Gripmaker
17401 State Hwy 96
Carthage, MO 64836
417-359-8880
www.gripmaker.com

Lett Custom Grips
672 Currier Rd.
Hopkinton, NH 03229-2652
800-421-5388
FAX: 603-226-4580
www.lettgrips.com

Nill Grips
In Schlattwiesen 3
D-72116 Mossingen
Germany
(+49) 7473/9434-0
FAX: (+49) 7473-9434-30
www.nill-griffe.com

N.C. Ordnance Co.
P.O. Box 3254
Wilson, NC 27895
252-237-2440
FAX: 252-243-9845
www.gungrip.com

Pachmayr Div. Lyman Products
475 Smith St.
Middletown, CT 06457
860-632-2020, 800-225-9626
FAX: 860-632-1699
www.pachmayr.com

Pearce Grip, Inc.
P.O. Box 40367
Fort Worth, TX 76140
817-568-9704, 800-390-9429
FAX: 817-468-9707
www.pearcegrip.com

Wilson Combat
2234 CR 719
Berryville, AR 72616-4573
870-545-3635
FAX: 870-545-3310
www.wilsoncombat.com

WEB DIRECTORY

Ajax Custom Grips, Inc. *www.ajaxgrips.com*
Altamont Co. *www.altamontco.com*
AlumaGrips *www.alumagrips.com*
Barami Corp. *www.hipgrip.com*
Butler Creek Corp. *www.michaels-oregon.com*
Coast Ivory *www.coastivory.com*
Crimson Trace/Lasergrips *www.crimstontrace.com*
Eagle Grips, Inc. *www.aglegrips.com*
Falcon Industries *www.ergogrips.net*
Gripmaker *www.gripmaker.com*
Herrett s Stocks *www.herrettstocks@msn.com*
Hogue Inc. *www.getgrip.com*
Lett Custom Grips *www.lettgrips.com*
Nill-Grips *www.nill-griffe.com*
N.C. Ordnance Co. *www.gungrip.com*
Pachmayr *www.pachmayr.com*
Pearce Grip, Inc. *www.pearcegrip.com*
Wilson Combat *www.wilsoncombat.com*

METALLIC CARTRIDGE PRESSES

CH4D Heavyduty Champion

Frame: Cast iron
Frame Type: O-frame
Die Thread: 7/8-14 or 1-14
Avg. Rounds Per Hour: NA
Ram Stroke: 3-1/4"
Weight: 26 lbs.
Features: 1.185" diameter ram with 16 square inches of bearing surface; ram drilled to allow passage of spent primers; solid steel handle; toggle that slightly breaks over the top dead center. Includes universal primer arm with large and small punches. From CH Tool & Die/4D Custom Die.
Price: **$261.98**

CH4D No. 444 4-Station "H" Press

Frame: Aluminum alloy
Frame Type: H-frame
Die Thread: 7/8-14
Avg. Rounds Per Hour: 200
Ram Stroke: 3-3/4"
Weight: 21 lbs.
Features: Two 7/8" solid steel shaft "H" supports; platen rides on permanently lubed bronze bushings; loads smallest pistol to largest magnum rifle cases and has strength to full-length resize. Includes four rams, large and small primer arm and primer catcher. From CH Tool & Die/4D Custom Die, Co.
Price: **$235.46**

CH4D No. 444-X Pistol Champ

Frame: Aluminum alloy
Frame Type: H-frame
Die Thread: 7/8-14
Avg. Rounds Per Hour: 200
Ram Stroke: 3-3/4"
Weight: 12 lbs.
Features: Tungsten carbide sizing die; Speed Seater seating die with tapered entrance to automatically align bullet on case mouth; automatic primer feed for large or small primers; push-button powder measure with easily changed bushings for 215 powder/load combinations; taper crimp die. Conversion kit for caliber changeover available. From CH Tool & Die/4D Custom Die, Co.
Price: . . . . **$292.00 to $316.50**

CORBIN CSP-2 Mega Mite

Frame: NA
Frame Type: NA
Die Thread: NA
Avg. Rounds Per Hour: NA
Ram Stroke: NA
Weight: 80 lbs.
Features: Handles 50 BMG and 20mm, smaller calibers wtih standard reloading adapter kit included. Die adapters for all threads available. Side-roller handle or extra long power handle, left- or right-hand operation. Ram is bearing guided. Uses standard Corbin-H swaging, drawing and jacket-making dies. Cold-forms lead bullets up to 12 gauge. Optional floor stand available.
Price: **$750.00**

CORBIN CSP-2 Hydro Mite Hyrdraulic Drawing/Swaging Press

Frame: NA
Frame Type: NA
Die Thread: 7/8-14
Avg. Rounds Per Hour: NA
Ram Stroke: NA
Weight: 100 lbs. with power unit
Features: Reloads standard calibers, swages bullets up to 458 caliber, draws jackets and extrudes small diameter lead wire. Optional speed and thrust control unit available. Uses Corbin-S swaging and drawing dies. Comes with T-slot ram adapter for standard shell holders. Make free 22 and 6mm jackets from fired 22 cases using optional Corbin kit.
Price: **$2,995.00**

CORBIN CSP-1 S-Press Benchrest Reloading/Swaging Tool

Frame: NA
Frame Type: NA
Die Thread: NA
Avg. Rounds Per Hour: NA
Ram Stroke: NA
Weight: 22 lbs.
Features: Handles standard calibers and swages bullets up to 458 caliber. Hand built. All moving parts run in bearings. Industrial hard-chromed ram, left- or right-hand operation. Quick stroke change doubles power for bullet swaging. Roller bearing links, expanded neoprene foam grip. Comes with reloading adapter kit for standard T-slot shell holders.
Price: **$329.00**

FORSTER Co-Ax Press B-2

Frame: Cast iron
Frame Type: Modified O-frame
Die Thread: 7/8-14
Avg. Rounds Per Hour: 120
Ram Stroke: 4"
Weight: 18 lbs.
Features: Snap in/snap out die change; spent primer catcher with drop tube threaded into carrier below shellholder; automatic, handle-activated, cammed shellholder with opposing spring-loaded jaws to contact extractor groove; floating guide rods for alignment and reduced friction; no torque on the head due to design of linkage and pivots; shellholder jaws that float with die permitting case to center in the die; right- or left-hand operation; priming device for seating to factory specifications. "S" shellholder jaws included. From Forster Products.
Price: **$336.30**
Price: Extra LS shellholder jaws **$29.00**

CH4D No. 444

CH4D 444-X Pistol Champ

Forster Co-Ax

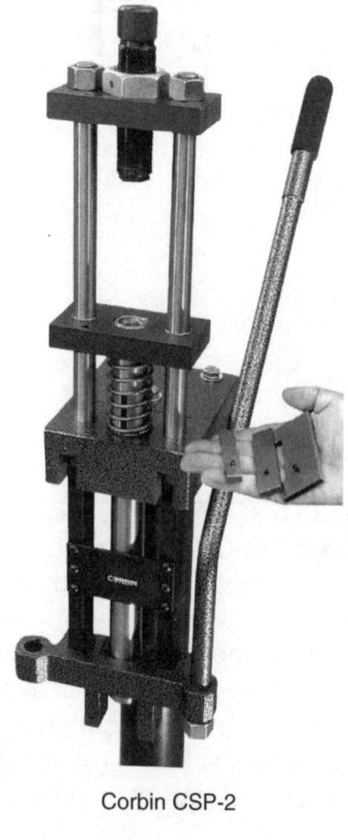

Corbin CSP-2

METALLIC CARTRIDGE PRESSES

Hollywood Senior Turret

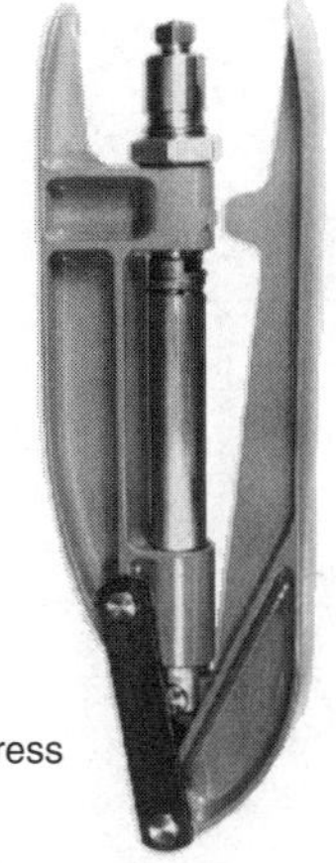

Lee Hand Press

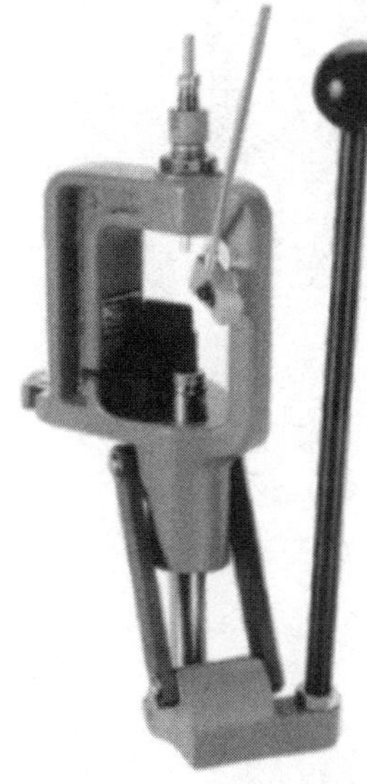

Hornady Lock-N-Load Classic

Lee Reloader

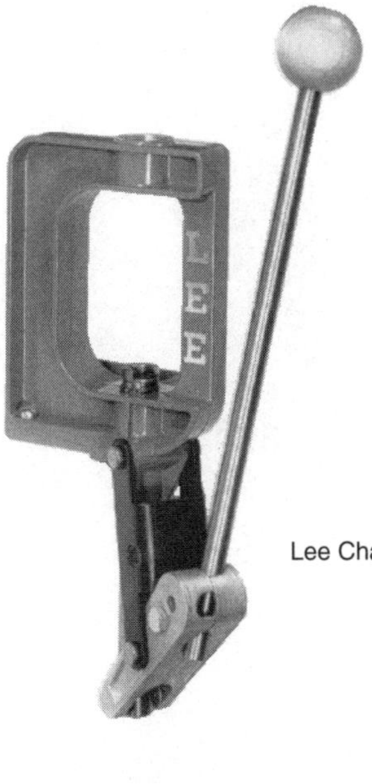

Lee Challenger

HOLLYWOOD Senior Press

Frame: Ductile iron — **Avg. Rounds Per Hour:** 50-100
Frame Type: O-frame — **Ram Stroke:** 6-1/2"
Die Thread: 7/8-14 — **Weight:** 50 lbs.

Features: Leverage and bearing surfaces ample for reloading cartridges or swaging bullets. Precision ground one-piece 2-1/2" pillar with base; operating handle of 3/4" steel and 15" long; 5/8" steel tie-down rod for added strength when swaging; heavy steel toggle and camming arms held by 1/2" steel pins in reamed holes. The 1-1/2" steel die bushing takes standard threaded dies; removed, it allows use of Hollywood shotshell dies. From Hollywood Engineering.

Price: **$600.00**

HOLLYWOOD Senior Turret Press

Frame: Ductile iron — **Avg. Rounds Per Hour:** 50-100
Frame Type: H-frame — **Ram Stroke:** 6-1/2"
Die Thread: 7/8-14 — **Weight:** 50 lbs.

Features: Same features as Senior press except has three-position turret head; holes in turret may be tapped 1-1/2" or 7/8" or four of each. Height 15". Comes complete with one turret indexing handle; one operating handle and three turret indexing handles; one 5/8" tie down bar for swaging. From Hollywood Engineering.

Price: **$700.00**

HORNADY Lock-N-Load Classic

Frame: Die cast heat-treated aluminum alloy — **Avg. Rounds Per Hour:** NA
Frame Type: O-frame — **Ram Stroke:** 3-5/8"
Die Thread: 7/8-14 — **Weight:** 14 lbs.

Features: Features Lock-N-Load bushing system that allows instant die changeovers. Solid steel linkage arms that rotate on steel pins; 30° angled frame design for improved visibility and accessibility; primer arm automatically moves in and out of ram for primer pickup and solid seating; two primer arms for large and small primers; long offset handle for increased leverage and unobstructed reloading; lifetime warranty. Comes as a package with primer catcher, PPS automatic primer feed and three Lock-N-Load die bushings. Dies and shellholder available separately or as a kit with primer catcher, positive priming system, automatic primer feed, three die bushings and reloading accessories. From Hornady Mfg. Co.

Price: Press and Three Die Bushings **$99.95**
Price: Classic Reloading Kit **$259.95**

LEE Hand Press

Frame: ASTM 380 aluminum — **Avg. Rounds Per Hour:** 100
Frame Type: NA — **Ram Stroke:** 3-1/4"
Die Thread: 7/8-14 — **Weight:** 1 lb., 8 oz.

Features: Small and lightweight for portability; compound linkage for handling up to 375 H&H and case forming. Dies and shellholder not included. From Lee Precision, Inc.

Price: **$26.98**

LEE Challenger Press

Frame: ASTM 380 aluminum — **Avg. Rounds Per Hour:** 100
Frame Type: O-frame — **Ram Stroke:** 3-1/2"
Die Thread: 7/8-14 — **Weight:** 4 lbs., 1 oz.

Features: Larger than average opening with 30° offset for maximum hand clearance; steel connecting pins; spent primer catcher; handle adjustable for start and stop positions; handle repositions for left- or right-hand use; shortened handle travel to prevent springing the frame from alignment. Dies and shellholders not included. From Lee Precision, Inc.

Price: **$47.00**

LEE Classic Cast

Features: Cast iron, O-type. Adjustable handle moves from right to left, start and stop position is adjustable. Large 1-1/8" diameter hollow ram catches primers for disposal. Automatic primer arm with bottom of stroke priming. Two assembled primer arms included. From Lee Precision, Inc.

Price: **$99.00**

LEE Reloader Press

Frame: ASTM 380 aluminum — **Avg. Rounds Per Hour:** 100
Frame Type: C-frame — **Ram Stroke:** 3"
Die Thread: 7/8-14 — **Weight:** 1 lb., 12 oz.

Features: Balanced lever to prevent pinching fingers; unlimited hand clearance; left- or right-hand use. Dies and shellholders not included. From Lee Precision, Inc.

Price: **$26.98**

METALLIC CARTRIDGE PRESSES

LEE Turret Press

Frame: ASTM 380 aluminum
Frame Type: O-frame
Die Thread: 7/8-14
Avg. Rounds Per Hour: 300
Ram Stroke: 3"
Weight: 7 lbs., 2 oz.
Features: Replaceable turret lifts out by rotating 30°; T-primer arm reverses for large or small primers; built-in primer catcher; adjustable handle for right- or left-hand use or changing angle of down stroke; accessory mounting hole for Lee Auto-Disk powder measure. Optional Auto-Index rotates die turret to next station for semi-progressive use. Safety override prevents overstressing should turret not turn. From Lee Precision, Inc.
Price: **$69.98**
Price: With Auto-Index **$83.98**
Price: Four-Hole Turret with Auto-Index **$85.98**

LYMAN 310 Tool

Frame: Stainless steel
Frame Type: NA
Die Thread: .609-30
Avg. Rounds Per Hour: NA
Ram Stroke: NA
Weight: 10 oz.
Features: Compact, portable reloading tool for pistol or rifle cartridges. Adapter allows loading rimmed or rimless cases. Die set includes neck resizing/decapping die, primer seating chamber; neck expanding die; bullet seating die; and case head adapter. From Lyman Products Corp.
Price: Dies **$45.00**
Price: Handles **$47.50**
Price: Carrying pouch **$9.95**

LYMAN AccuPress

Frame: Die cast
Frame Type: C-frame
Die Thread: 7/8-14
Avg. Rounds Per Hour: 75
Ram Stroke: 3.4"
Weight: 4 lbs.
Features: Reversible, contoured handle for bench mount or hand-held use; for rifle or pistol; compound leverage; Delta frame design. Accepts all standard powder measures. From Lyman Products Corp.
Price: **$34.95**

LYMAN Crusher II

Frame: Cast iron
Frame Type: O-frame
Die Thread: 7/8-14
Avg. Rounds Per Hour: 75
Ram Stroke: 3-7/8"
Weight: 19 lbs.
Features: Reloads both pistol and rifle cartridges; 1" diameter ram; 4-1/2" press opening for loading magnum cartridges; direct torque design; right- or left-hand use. New base design with 14 square inches of flat mounting surface with three bolt holes. Comes with priming arm and primer catcher. Dies and shellholders not included. From Lyman Products Corp.
Price: **$116.50**

LYMAN T-Mag II

Frame: Cast iron with silver metalflake powder finish
Frame Type: Turret
Die Thread: 7/8-14
Avg. Rounds Per Hour: 125
Ram Stroke: 3-13/16"
Weight: 18 lbs.
Features: Re-engineered and upgraded with new turret system for ease of indexing and tool-free turret removal for caliber changeover; new flat machined base for bench mounting; new nickel-plated non-rust handle and links; and new silver hammertone powder coat finish for durability. Right- or left-hand operation; handles all rifle or pistol dies. Comes with priming arm and primer catcher. Dies and shellholders not included. From Lyman Products Corp.
Price: **$164.95**
Price: Extra turret **$37.50**

MEACHAM Anywhere Portable Reloading Press

Frame: Anodized 6061 T6 aircraft aluminum
Frame Type: Cylindrical
Die Thread: 7/8-14
Avg. Rounds Per Hour: NA
Ram Stroke: 2.7"
Weight: 2 lbs. (hand held); 5 lbs. (with docking kit)
Features: A lightweight portable press that can be used hand-held, or with a docking kit, can be clamped to a table top up to 9.75" thick. Docking kit includes a threaded powder measure mount and holder for the other die. Designed for neck sizing and bullet seating of short action cartridges, it can be used for long action cartridges with the addition of an Easy Seater straight line seating die. Dies not included.
Price: **$99.95**
Price: (with docking kit) **$144.95**
Price: Easy Seater **$114.95**
Price: Re-De-Capper . . . . **NA**

Lyman 310

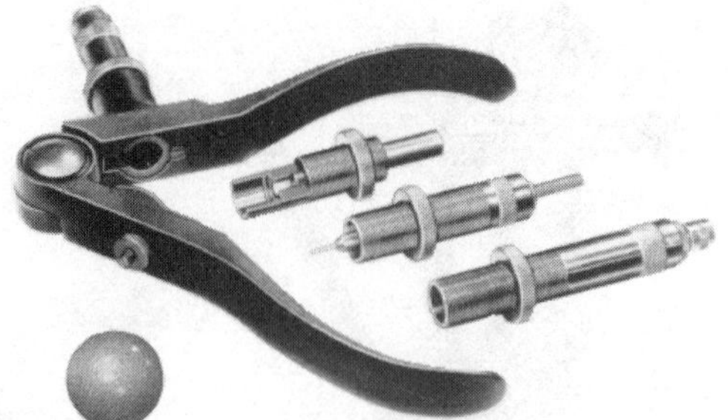

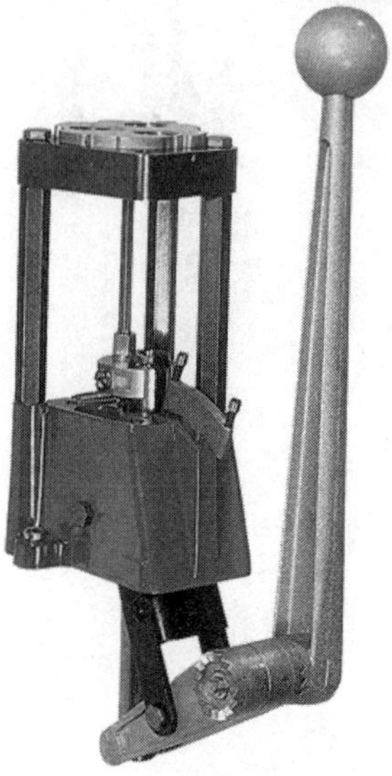

Lee Turret

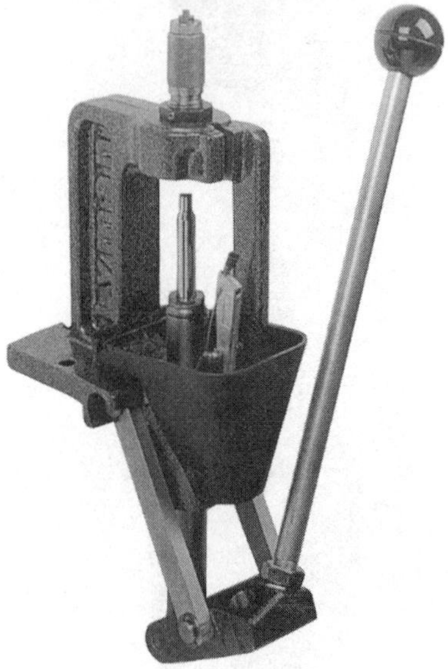

Lyman Crusher II

Turret handle disconnector

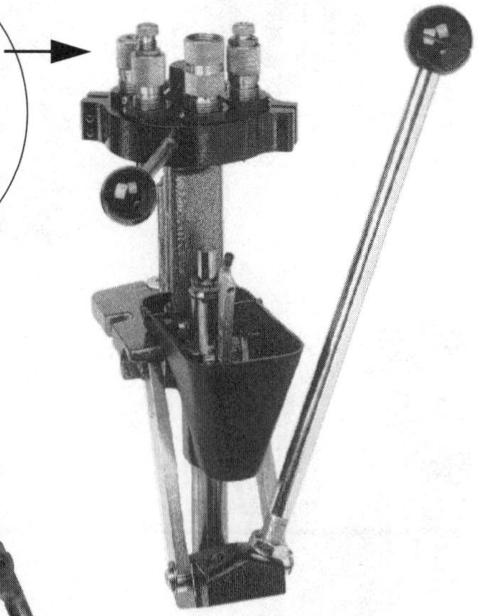

Lyman T-Mag II

Meacham Re-De-Capper

METALLIC CARTRIDGE PRESSES

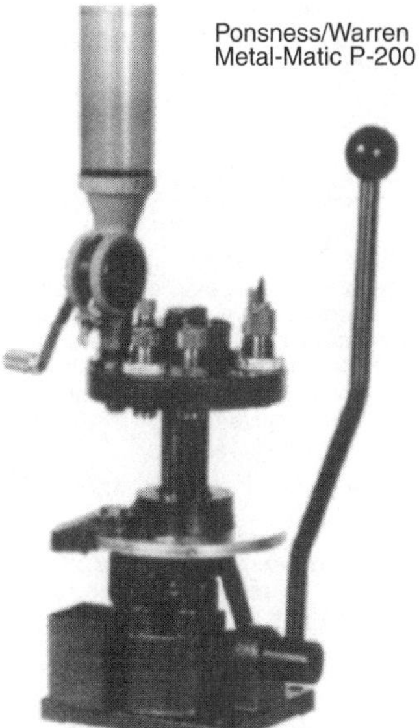

Ponsness/Warren Metal-Matic P-200

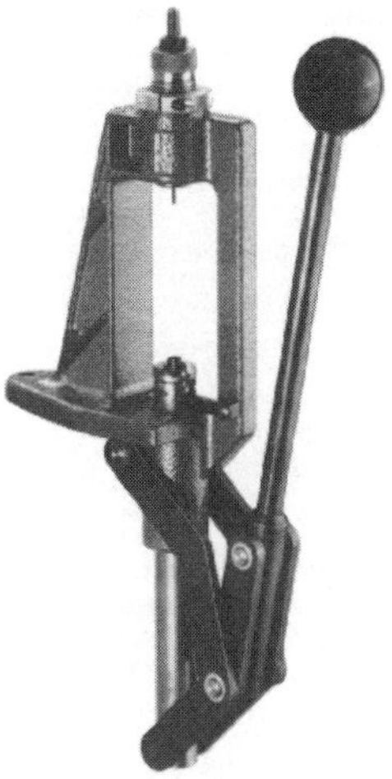

RCBS Partner

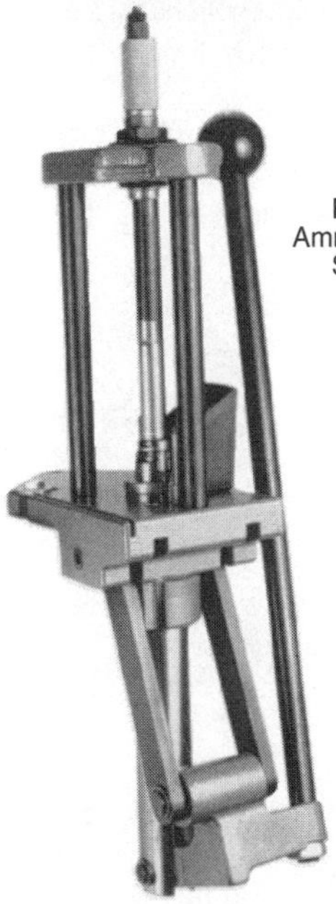

RCBS AmmoMaster Single

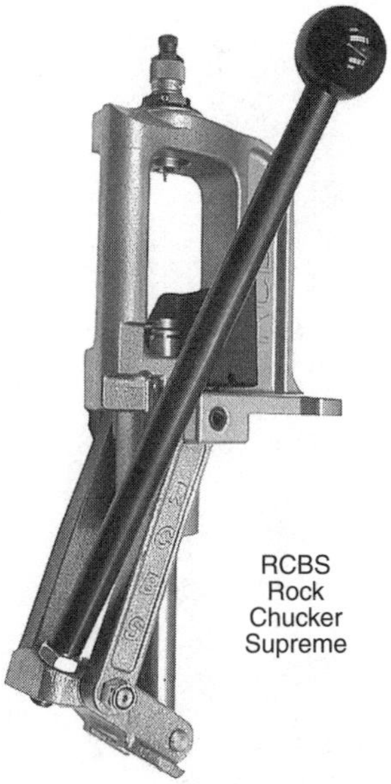

RCBS Rock Chucker Supreme

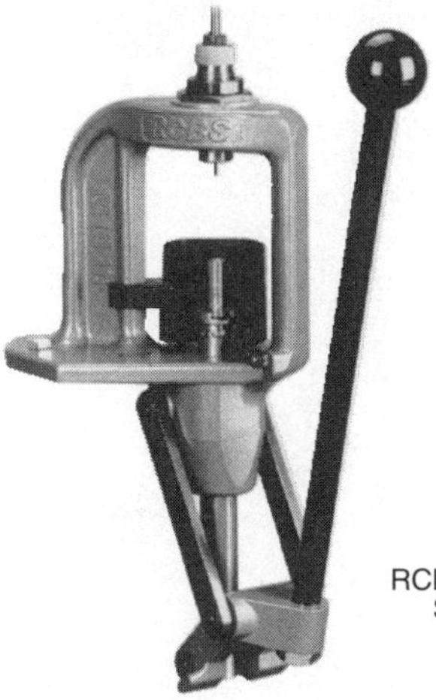

RCBS Reloader Special-5

PONSNESS/WARREN Metal-Matic P-200

Frame: Die cast aluminum
Frame Type: Unconventional
Die Thread: 7/8-14
Avg. Rounds Per Hour: 200+
Weight: 18 lbs.
Features: Designed for straight-wall cartridges; die head with 10 tapped holes for holding dies and accessories for two calibers at one time; removable spent primer box; pivoting arm moves case from station to station. Comes with large and small primer tool. Optional accessories include primer feed, extra die head, primer speed feeder, powder measure extension and dust cover. Dies, powder measure and shellholder not included. From Ponsness/Warren.
Price: **$215.00**
Price: Extra die head **$44.95**
Price: Powder measure extension **$29.95**
Price: Primer feed **$44.95**
Price: Primer speed feed **$14.50**
Price: Dust cover **$21.95**

RCBS Partner

Frame: Aluminum
Frame Type: O-frame
Die Thread: 7/8-14
Avg. Rounds Per Hour: 50-60
Ram Stroke: 3-5/8"
Weight: 5 lbs.
Features: Designed for the beginning reloader. Comes with primer arm equipped with interchangeable primer plugs and sleeves for seating large and small primers. Shellholder and dies not included. Available in kit form (see Metallic Presses-Accessories). From RCBS.
Price: **$69.95**

RCBS AmmoMaster Single

Frame: Aluminum base; cast iron top plate connected by three steel posts.
Frame Type: NA
Die Thread: 1-1/4"-12 bushing; 7/8-14 threads
Avg. Rounds Per Hour: 50-60
Ram Stroke: 5-1/4"
Weight: 19 lbs.
Features: Single-stage press convertible to progressive. Will form cases or swage bullets. Case detection system to disengage powder measure when no case is present in powder charging station; five-station shellplate; Uniflow Powder measure with clear powder measure adaptor to make bridged powders visible and correctable. 50-cal. conversion kit allows reloading 50 BMG. Kit includes top plate to accommodate either 1-3/8" x 12 or 1-1/2" x 12 reloading dies. Piggyback die plate for quick caliber change-overs available. Reloading dies not included. From RCBS.
Price: **$229.95**
Price: 50 conversion kit **$109.95**
Price: Piggyback/AmmoMaster die plate **$23.95**
Price: Piggyback/AmmoMaster shellplate **$31.95**
Price: Press cover **$13.95**

RCBS Reloader Special-5

Frame: Aluminum
Frame Type: 30° offset O-frame
Die Thread: 1-1/4"-12 bushing; 7/8-14 threads
Avg. Rounds Per Hour: 50-60
Ram Stroke: 3-1/16"
Weight: 7.5 lbs.
Features: Single-stage press convertible to progressive with RCBS Piggyback II. Primes cases during resizing operation. Will accept RCBS shotshell dies. From RCBS.
Price: **$123.95**

RCBS Rock Chucker Supreme

Frame: Cast iron
Frame Type: O-frame
Die Thread: 1-1/4"-12 bushing; 7/8-14 threads
Avg. Rounds Per Hour: 50-60
Ram Stroke: 3-1/16"
Weight: 17 lbs.
Features: Redesigned to allow loading of longer cartridge cases. Made for heavy-duty reloading, case forming and bullet swaging. Provides 4" of ram-bearing surface to support 1" ram and ensure alignment; ductile iron toggle blocks; hardened steel pins. Comes standard with Universal Primer Arm and primer catcher. Can be converted from single-stage to progressive with Piggyback II conversion unit. From RCBS.
Price: **$155.95**

METALLIC CARTRIDGE PRESSES

REDDING T-7 Turret Press

Frame: Cast iron
Frame Type: Turret
Die Thread: 7/8-14
Avg. Rounds Per Hour: NA
Ram Stroke: 3.4"
Weight: 23 lbs., 2 oz.
Features: Strength to reload pistol and magnum rifle, case form and bullet swage; linkage pins heat-treated, precision ground and in double shear; hollow ram to collect spent primers; removable turret head for caliber changes; progressive linkage for increased power as ram nears die; rear turret support for stability and precise alignment; 7-station turret head; priming arm for both large and small primers. Also available in kit form with shellholder and one die set. From Redding Reloading Equipment.
Price: **$336.00**
Price: Kit **$382.00**

REDDING Boss

Frame: Cast iron
Frame Type: O-frame
Die Thread: 7/8-14
Avg. Rounds Per Hour: NA
Ram Stroke: 3.4"
Weight: 11 lbs., 8 oz.
Features: 36° frame offset for visibility and accessibility; primer arm positioned at bottom ram travel; positive ram travel stop machined to hit exactly top-dead-center. Also available in kit form with shellholder and set of Redding A dies. From Redding Reloading Equipment.
Price: **$156.00**
Price: Kit **$204.00**
Price: Big Boss Press (heavier frame, longer stroke for mag. cartridges) . . . . . . **$178.50 to $223.50**

REDDING Ultramag

Frame: Cast iron
Frame Type: Non-conventional
Die Thread: 7/8-14
Avg. Rounds Per Hour: NA
Ram Stroke: 4-1/8"
Weight: 23 lbs., 6 oz.
Features: Unique compound leverage system connected to top of press for tons of ram pressure; large 4-3/4" frame opening for loading outsized cartridges; hollow ram for spent primers. Kit available with shellholder and one set Redding A dies. From Redding Reloading Equipment.
Price: **$351.00**
Price: Kit **$396.00**

ROCK CRUSHER Press

Frame: Cast iron
Frame Type: O-frame
Die Thread: 2-3/4"-12 with bushing reduced to 1-1/2"-12
Avg. Rounds Per Hour: 50
Ram Stroke: 6"
Weight: 67 lbs.
Features: Designed to load and form ammunition from 50 BMG up to 23x115 Soviet. Frame opening of 8-1/2" x 3-1/2"; 1-1/2" x 12"; bushing can be removed and bushings of any size substituted; ram pressure can exceed 10,000 lbs. with normal body weight; 40mm diameter ram. Angle block for bench mounting and reduction bushing for RCBS dies available. Accessories for Rock Crusher include powder measure, dies, shellholder, bullet puller, priming tool, case gauge and others. From The Old Western Scrounger.
Price: **$795.00**
Price: Angle block **$57.95**
Price: Reduction bushing **$21.00**
Price: Shellholder **$47.25**
Price: Priming tool, 50 BMG, 20 Lahti **$65.10**

Progressive Presses

CORBIN Benchrest S-Press

Frame: All steel
Frame Type: O-Frame
Die Thread: 7/8-14 and T-slot adapter
Avg. Rounds Per Hour: NA
Ram Stroke: 4"
Weight: 22 lbs.
Features: Roller bearing linkage, removeable head, right- or left-hand mount.
Price: **$298.00**

DILLON RL 550B

Frame: Aluminum alloy
Frame Type: NA
Die Thread: 7/8-14
Avg. Rounds Per Hour: 500-600
Ram Stroke: 3-7/8"
Weight: 25 lbs.
Features: Four stations; removable tool head to hold dies in alignment and allow caliber changes without die adjustment; auto priming system that emits audible warning when primer tube is low; a 100-primer capacity magazine contained in DOM steel tube for protection; new auto powder measure system with simple mechanical connection between measure and loading platform for positive powder bar return; a separate station for crimping with star-indexing system; 220 ejected-round capacity bin; 3/4-lb. capacity powder measure. Height above bench, 35"; requires 3/4" bench overhang. Will reload 120 different rifle and pistol calibers. Comes with one caliber conversion kit. Dies not included. From Dillon Precision Products, Inc.
Price: **$349.95**

DILLON Super 1050

Frame: Ductile iron
Frame Type: Platform type
Die Thread: 7/8-14
Avg. Rounds Per Hour: 1000-1200
Ram Stroke: 2-5/16"
Weight: 62 lbs.
Features: Eight stations; auto case feed; primer pocket swager for military cartridge cases; auto indexing; removable tool head; auto prime system with 100-primer capacity; low primer supply alarm; positive powder bar return; auto powder measure; 515 ejected round bin capacity; 500-600 case feed capacity; 3/4-lb. capacity powder measure. Has lengthened frame and short-stroke crank to accommodate long calibers. Loads all pistol rounds as well as 30 M1 Carbine, 223, and 7.62x39 rifle rounds. Height above the bench, 43". Dies not included. From Dillon Precision Products, Inc.
Price: **$1,449.95**

DILLON Square Deal B

Frame: Zinc alloy
Frame Type: NA
Die Thread: None (unique Dillon design)
Avg. Rounds Per Hour: 400-500
Ram Stroke: 2-5/16"
Weight: 17 lbs.
Features: Four stations; auto indexing; removable tool head; auto prime system with 100-primer capacity; low primer supply alarm; auto powder measure; positive powder bar return; 170 ejected round capacity bin; 3/4-lb. capacity powder measure. Height above the bench, 34". Comes complete with factory adjusted carbide die set. From Dillon Precision Products, Inc.
Price: **$289.95**

Redding Boss

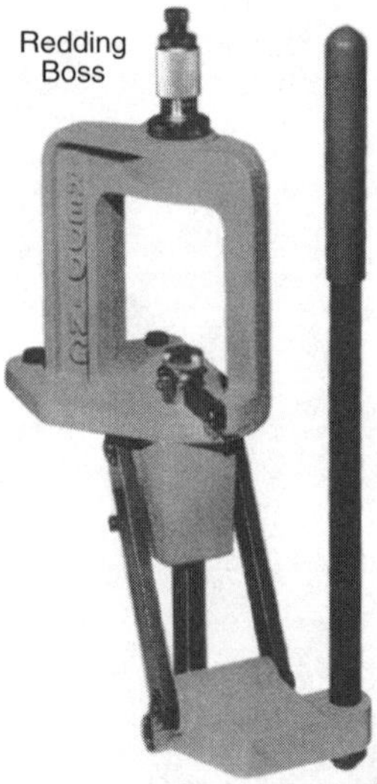

Redding Turret Press

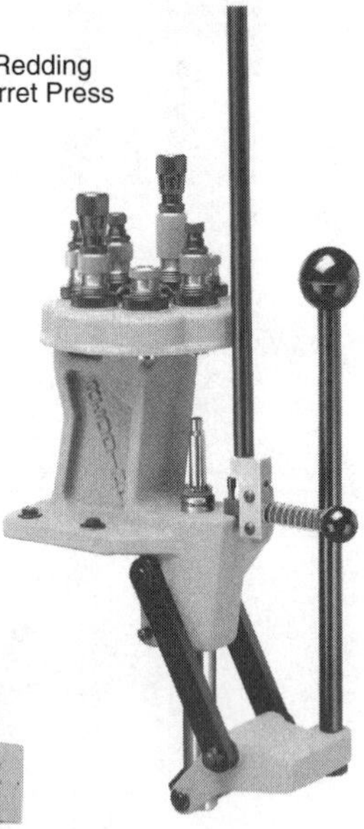

Redding Ultramag

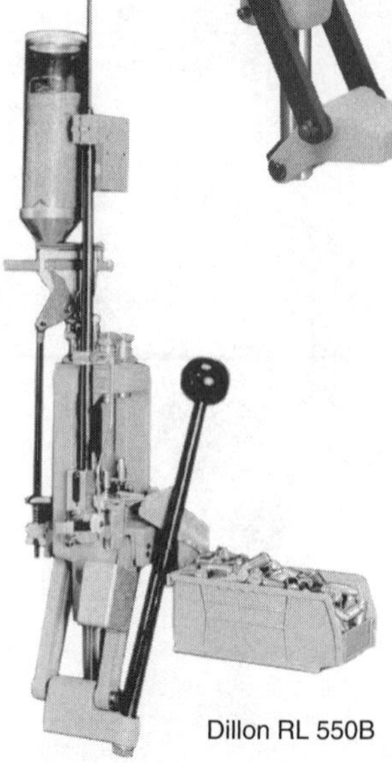

Dillon RL 550B

METALLIC CARTRIDGE PRESSES

DILLON XL 650

Frame: Aluminum alloy
Frame Type: NA
Die Thread: 7/8-14
Avg. Rounds Per Hour: 800-1000
Ram Stroke: 4-9/16"
Weight: 46 lbs.

Features: Five stations; auto indexing; auto case feed; removable tool head; auto prime system with 100-primer capacity; low primer supply alarm; auto powder measure; positive powder bar return; 220 ejected round capacity bin; 3/4-lb. capacity powder measure. 500-600 case feed capacity with optional auto case feed. Loads all pistol/rifle calibers less than 3-1/2" in length. Height above the bench, 44"; 3/4" bench overhang required. From Dillon Precision Products, Inc.

Price: Less dies **$459.95**

HORNADY Lock-N-Load AP

Frame: Die cast heat-treated aluminum alloy
Frame Type: O-frame
Die Thread: 7/8-14
Avg. Rounds Per Hour: NA
Ram Stroke: 3-3/4"
Weight: 26 lbs.

Features: Features Lock-N-Load bushing system that allows instant die changeovers; five-station die platform with option of seating and crimping separately or adding taper-crimp die; auto prime with large and small primer tubes with 100-primer capacity and protective housing; brass kicker to eject loaded rounds into 80-round capacity cartridge catcher; offset operating handle for leverage and unobstructed operation; 2" diameter ram driven by heavy-duty cast linkage arms rotating on steel pins. Comes with five Lock-N-Load die bushings, shellplate, deluxe powder measure, auto powder drop, and auto primer feed and shut-off, brass kicker and primer catcher. Lifetime warranty. From Hornady Mfg. Co.

Price: **$367.65**

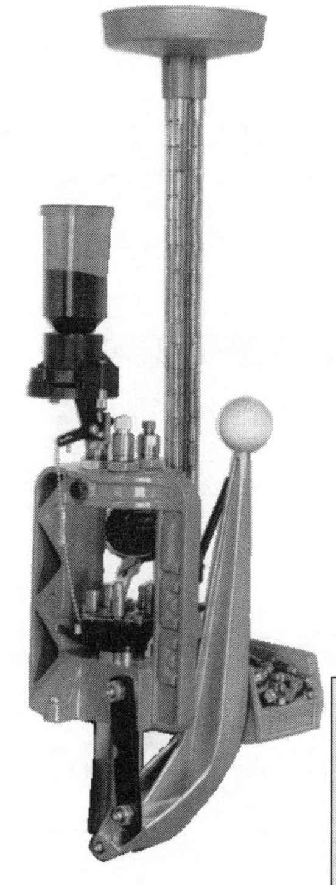
Lee Load-Master

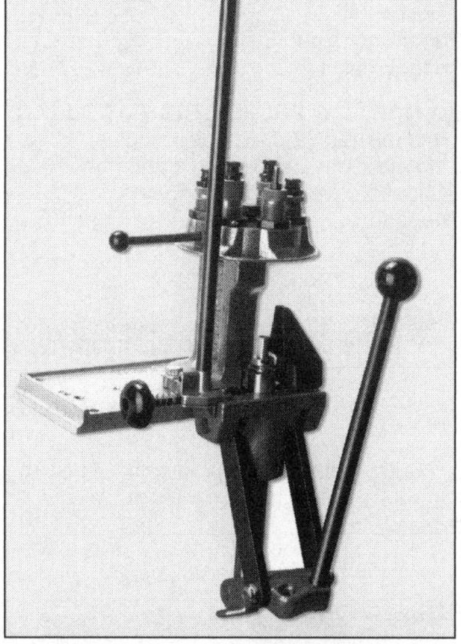
RCBS Turret

Fully-automated Star Universal

LEE Load-Master

Frame: ASTM 380 aluminum
Frame Type: O-frame
Die Thread: 7/8-14
Avg. Rounds Per Hour: 600
Ram Stroke: 3-1/4"
Weight: 8 lbs., 4 oz.

Features: Available in kit form only. A 1-3/4" diameter hard chrome ram for han-dling largest magnum cases; loads rifle or pistol rounds; five station press to fac-tory crimp and post size; auto indexing with wedge lock mechanism to hold one ton; auto priming; removable turrets; four-tube case feeder with optional case collator and bullet feeder (late 1995); loaded round ejector with chute to optional loaded round catcher; quick change shellplate; primer catcher. Dies and shell-holder for one caliber included. From Lee Precision, Inc.

Price: Rifle **$320.00**
Price: Pistol **$330.00**
Price: Extra turret **$14.98**
Price: Adjustable charge bar **$9.98**

LEE Pro 1000

Frame: ASTM 380 aluminum and steel
Frame Type: O-frame
Die Thread: 7/8-14
Avg. Rounds Per Hour: 600
Ram Stroke: 3-1/4"
Weight: 8 lbs., 7 oz.

Features: Optional transparent large/small or rifle case feeder; deluxe auto-disk case-activated powder measure; case sensor for primer feed. Comes complete with carbide die set (steel dies for rifle) for one caliber. Optional accessories include: case feeder for large/small pistol cases or rifle cases; shell plate carrier with auto prime, case ejector, auto-index and spare parts; case collator for case feeder. From Lee Precision, Inc.

Price: **$199.98**

PONSNESS/WARREN Metallic II

Frame: Die cast aluminum
Frame Type: H-frame
Die Thread: 7/8-14
Avg. Rounds Per Hour: 150+
Ram Stroke: NA
Weight: 32 lbs.

Features: Die head with five tapped 7/8-14 holes for dies, powder measure or other accessories; pivoting die arm moves case from station to station; depriming tube for removal of spent primers; auto primer feed; interchangeable die head. Optional accessories include additional die heads, powder measure extension tube to accommodate any standard powder measure, primer speed feeder to feed press primer tube without disassembly. Comes with small and large primer seating tools. Dies, powder measure and shellholder not included. From Ponsness/Warren.

Price: **$375.00**
Price: Extra die head **$56.95**
Price: Primer speed feeder **$14.50**
Price: Powder measure extension **$29.95**
Price: Dust cover **$27.95**

RCBS Pro 2000™

Frame: Cast iron
Frame Type: H-Frame
Die Thread: 7/8-14
Avg. Rounds Per Hour: 500-600
Ram Stroke: NA
Weight: NA

Features: Five-station manual indexing; full-length sizing; removable die plate; fast caliber conversion. Uses APS Priming System. From RCBS.

Price: **$42.95**

RCBS Turret Press

Frame: Cast iron
Frame Type: NA
Die Thread: 7/8-14
Avg. Rounds Per Hour: 50 to 200
Ram Stroke: NA
Weight: NA

Features: Six-station turret head; positive alignment; on-press priming.

Price: **$214.95**

STAR Universal Pistol Press

Frame: Cast iron w/aluminum base
Frame Type: Unconventional
Die Thread: 11/16-24 or 7/8-14
Avg. Rounds Per Hour: 300
Ram Stroke: NA
Weight: 27 lbs.

Features: Four or five-station press depending on need to taper crimp; handles all popular handgun calibers from 32 Long to 45 Colt. Comes completely assembled and adjusted with carbide dies (except 30 Carbine) and shellholder to load one caliber. Prices slightly higher for 9mm and 30 Carbine. From Star Machine Works.

Price: With taper crimp **$1,055.00**
Price: Without taper crimp **$1,025.00**
Price: Extra tool head, taper crimp **$425.00**
Price: Extra tool head, w/o taper crimp **$395.00**

METALLIC SIGHTS

XS Express

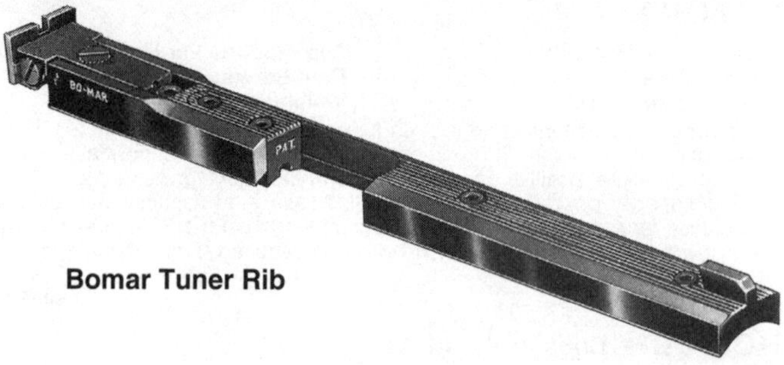

Bomar Tuner Rib

Handgun Sights

XS EXPRESS SIGHTS Low-profile, snag-free express-type sights. Shallow V rear with white vertical line, white dot front. All-steel, matte black finish. Rear is available in different heights. Made for most pistols, many with double set-screws. From XS Sight Systems, Inc.
Price: Standard Set, front and rear **$60.00**
Price: Big Dot Set, front and rear. **$60.00**
Price: Tritium Set, Standard or Big Dot **$90.00**
Price: 24/7 Pro Express, Std. or Big Dot tritium **$120.00**

BO-MAR DELUXE BMCS Gives 3/8" windage and elevation adjustment at 50 yards on Colt Gov't 45; sight radius under 7". For GM and Commander models only. Uses existing dovetail slot. Has shield-type rear blade.
Price: **$65.95**
Price: BMCS-2 (for GM and 9mm) **$68.95**
Price: Flat bottom **$65.95**
Price: BMGC (for Colt Gold Cup), angled serrated blade, rear. **$68.95**
Price: BMGC front sight **$12.95**
Price: BMCZ-75 (for CZ-75,TZ-75, P-9 and most clones). Works with factory front **$68.95**

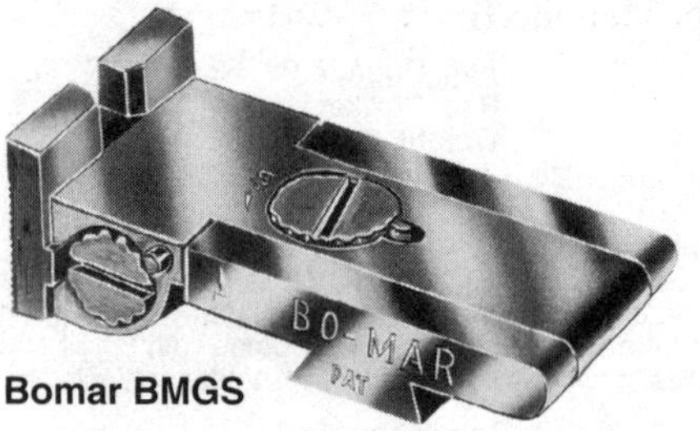

Bomar BMGS

BO-MAR FRONT SIGHTS Dovetail-style for S&W 4506, 4516, 1076; undercut-style (.250", .280", 5/16" high); Fast Draw-style (.210", .250", .230" high).
Price: **$12.95**

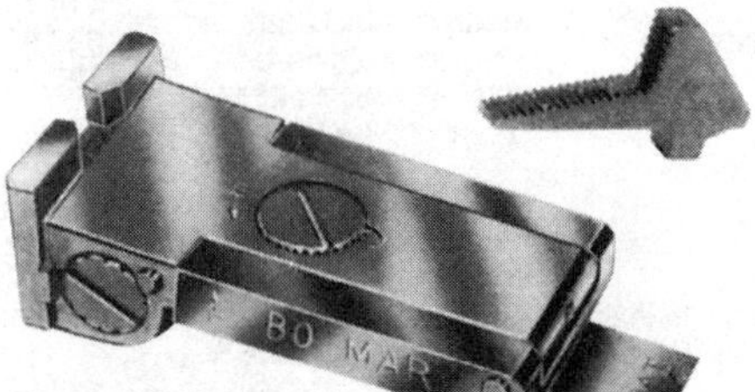

Bomar BMGC

BO-MAR BMU XP-100/T/C CONTENDER No gunsmithing required; has .080" notch.
Price: **$77.00**

Bomar BMU XP-100

Bomar BMML

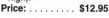

Bomar BMR

BO-MAR BMML For muzzleloaders; has .062" notch, flat bottom.
Price: **$65.95**
Price: With 3/8" dovetail **$65.95**

BO-MAR RUGER "P" ADJUSTABLE SIGHT Replaces factory front and rear sights.
Price: Rear sight **$65.95**
Price: Front sight. **$12.00**

BO-MAR BMR Fully adjustable rear sight for Ruger MKI, MKII Bull barrel autos.
Price: Rear **$65.95**
Price: Undercut front sight. **$12.00**

BO-MAR GLOCK Fully adjustable, all-steel replacement sights. Sight fits factory dovetail. Longer sight radius. Uses Novak Glock .275" high, .135" wide front, or similar.
Price: Rear sight **$68.95**
Price: Front sight. **$20.95**

BO-MAR LOW PROFILE RIB & ACCURACY TUNER Streamlined rib with front and rear sights; 7-1/8" sight radius. Brings sight line closer to the bore than standard or extended sight and ramp. Weight 5 oz. Made for Colt Gov't 45, Super 38, and Gold Cup 45 and 38.
Price: **$140.00**

Bomar Combat Rib

BO-MAR COMBAT RIB For S&W Model 19 revolver with 4" barrel. Sight radius 5-3/4", weight 5-1/2 oz.
Price: **$127.00**

Bomar Winged Rib

BO-MAR WINGED RIB For S&W 4" and 6" length barrels: K-38, M10, HB 14 and 19. Weight for the 6" model is about 7-1/4 oz.
Price: **$140.00**

Bomar Cover-Up Rib

BO-MAR COVER-UP RIB Adjustable rear sight, winged front guards. Fits right over revolver's original front sight. For S&W 4" M-10HB, M-13, M-58, M-64 & 65, Ruger 4" models SDA-34, SDA-84, SS-34, SS-84, GF-34, GF-84.
Price: **$130.00**

Chip McCormick "Drop In"

CHIP MCCORMICK "DROP-IN" A low mount sight that fits any 1911-style slide with a standard military-type dovetail sight cut (60 x .290"). Dovetail front sights also available. From Chip McCormick Corp.
Price: **$47.95**

Chip McCormick Fixed Sight

CHIP MCCORMICK FIXED SIGHTS Same sight picture (.110" rear - .110" front) that's become the standard for pro combat shooters. Low mount design with rounded edges. For 1911-style pistols. May require slide machining for installation. From Chip McCormick Corp.
Price: **$24.95**

C-MORE SIGHTS Replacement front sight blades offered in two types and five styles. Made of DuPont Acetal, they come in a set of five high-contrast colors: blue, green, pink, red and yellow. Easy to install. Patridge-style for Colt Python (all barrels), Ruger Super Blackhawk (7-1/2"), Ruger Blackhawk (4-5/8"); ramp-style for Python (all barrels), Blackhawk (4-5/8"), Super Blackhawk (7-1/2" and 10-1/2"). From C-More Systems.
Price: Per set **$19.95**

G.G. & G. GHOST RINGS Replaces the factory rear sight without gunsmithing. Black phosphate finish. Available for Colt M1911 and Commander, Beretta M92F, Glock, S&W, SIG Sauer.
Price: **$65.00**

Heinie Slant Pro

HEINIE SLANT PRO Made with a slight forward slant, the unique design of these rear sights is snag-free for unimpeded draw from concealment. The combination of the slant and the rear serrations virtually eliminates glare. Made for most popular handguns. From Heinie Specialty Products.
Price: .... **$50.35 to $122.80**

HEINIE STRAIGHT EIGHT SIGHTS Consists of one tritium dot in the front sight and a slightly smaller tritium dot in the rear sight. When aligned correctly, an elongated 'eight' is created. The tritium dots are green in color. Designed with the belief that the human eye can correct vertical alignment faster than horizontal. Available for most popular handguns. From Heinie Specialty Products.
Price: .... **$104.95 to $122.80**

HEINIE CROSS DOVETAIL FRONT SIGHTS Made in a variety of heights, the standard dovetail is 60° x .305" x .062" with a .002 taper. From Heinie Specialty Products.
Price:... **$20.95 to $47.20**

JP GHOST RING Replacement bead front, ghost ring rear for Glock and M1911 pistols. From JP Enterprises.
Price: **$79.95**
Price: Bo-Mar replacement leaf with JP dovetail front bead **$99.95**

LES BAER CUSTOM ADJUSTABLE LOW MOUNT REAR SIGHT Considered one of the top adjustable sights in the world for target shooting with 1911-style pistols. Available with tritium inserts. From Les Baer Custom.
Price: .... **$49.00** (standard); **$99.00** (tritium)

LES BAER DELUXE FIXED COMBAT SIGHT A tactical-style sight with a very low profile. Incorporates a no-snag design and has serrations on sides. For 1911-style pistols. Available with tritium inserts for night shooting. From Les Baer Custom.
Price: .... **$26.00** (standard); **$67.00** (with tritium)

LES BAER DOVETAIL FRONT SIGHT Blank dovetail sight machined from bar stock. Can be contoured to many different configurations to meet user's needs. Available with tritium insert. From Les Baer Custom.
Price: .... **$17.00** (standard);
.... **$47.00** (with tritium insert)

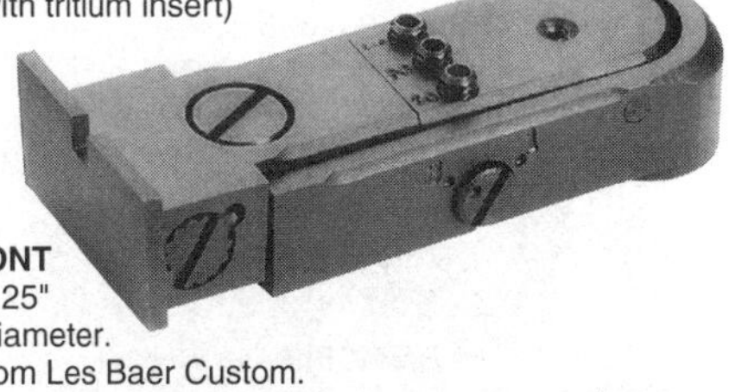

Les Baer PPC-Style Adjustable Rear Sight

LES BAER FIBER-OPTIC FRONT SIGHT Dovetail .330 x 65°, .125" wide post, .185" high, .060" diameter. Red and green fiber-optic. From Les Baer Custom.
Price: **$24.00**

LES BAER PPC-STYLE ADJUSTABLE REAR SIGHT Made for use with custom built 1911-style pistols, allows the user to preset three elevation adjustments for PPC-style shooting. Milling required for installation. Made from 4140 steel. From Les Baer Custom.
Price: $120.00

LES BAER DOVETAIL FRONT SIGHT WITH TRITIUM INSERT This fully contoured and finished front sight comes ready for gunsmith installation. From Les Baer Custom.
Price: **$47.00**

Les Baer Dovetail

MMC TACTICAL ADJUSTABLE SIGHTS Low-profile, snag-free design, 22 click positions for elevation, drift adjustable for windage. Machined from 4140 steel and heat treated to 40 RC. Tritium and non-tritium, 10 different configurations and colors. Three different finishes. For 1911s, all Glock, HK USP, S&W, Browning Hi-Power.
Price: Sight set, tritium **$139.00**
Price: Sight set, white outline or white dot **$124.00**
Price: Sight set, black **$124.00**

MEPROLIGHT TRITIUM NIGHT SIGHTS Replacement sight assemblies for low-light conditions. Available for pistols (fixed and adj.), rifles, shotguns, 12-year warranty for useable illumination, while non-TRU-DOT have a 5-year warranty. Distributed in America by Kimber.

Meprolight Glock

Meprolight Beretta

METALLIC SIGHTS

Meprolight Colt

Meprolight Ruger

Meprolight Smith & Wesson

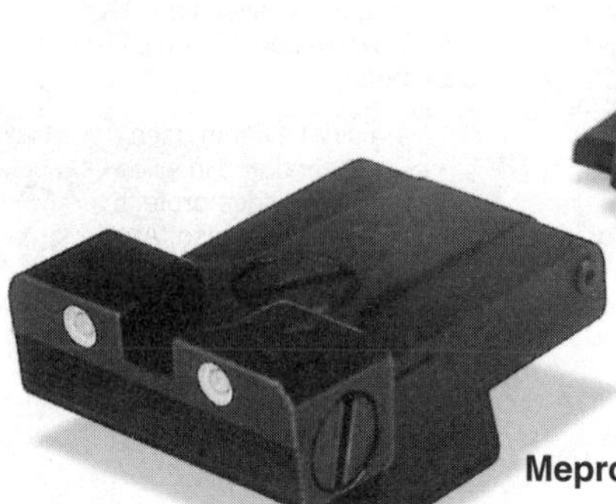

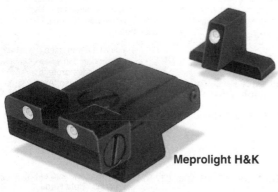

Meprolight H&K

Meprolight Taurus

Price: Kahr K9, K40, fixed, TRU-DOT **$105.00**
Price: Ruger Mini-14R sights (front only). **$55.00**
Price: SIG Sauer P220, P225, P226, P228, TRU-DOT **$105.00**
Price: S&W autos, fixed or adjustable, TRU-DOT **$105.00**
Price: Walther P-99, fixed, TRU-DOT **$105.00**
Price: Shotgun bead **$34.00**
Price: Beretta M92, Cougar, Brigadier, fixed, TRU-DOT **$105.00**
Price: Browning Hi-Power, adjustable, TRU-DOT **$105.00**
Price: Colt M1911 Govt., adjustable, TRU-DOT **$105.00**

MILLETT SERIES 100 REAR SIGHTS All-steel highly visible, click adjustable. Blades in white outline, target black, silhouette, 3-dot. Fit most popular revolvers and autos.
Price: . . . . **$51.77 to $84.00**

Millett Tritium Night Sight

MILLETT BAR-DOT-BAR TRITIUM NIGHT SIGHTS Replacement front and rear combos fit most automatics. Horizontal tritium bars on rear, dot front sight.
Price: **$152.25**

MILLETT BAR/DOT Made with orange or white bar or dot for increased visibility. Available for Beretta 84, 85, 92S, 92SB, Browning, Colt Python & Trooper, Ruger GP 100, P85, Redhawk, Security Six.
Price: . . . . **$14.99 to $24.99**

MILLETT 3-DOT SYSTEM SIGHTS The 3-Dot System sights use a single white dot on the front blade and two dots flanking the rear notch. Fronts available in Dual-Crimp and Wide Stake-On styles, as well as special applications. Adjustable rear sight available for most popular auto pistols and revolvers including Browning Hi-Power, Colt 1911 Government and Ruger P85.
Price: Front, from **$16.80**
Price: Adjustable rear **$55.60**

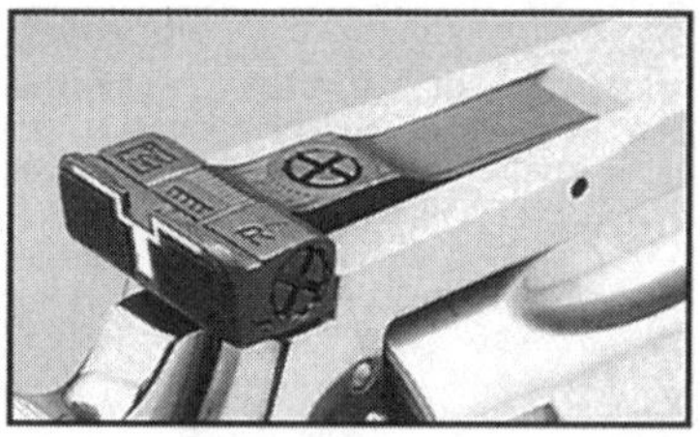

Millett Colt

Millett Ruger

MILLETT REVOLVER FRONT SIGHTS All-steel replacement front sights with either white or orange bar. Easy to install. For Ruger GP-100, Redhawk, Security-Six, Police-Six, Speed-Six, Colt Trooper, Diamondback, King Cobra, Peacemaker, Python, Dan Wesson 22 and 15-2.
Price: . . . . **$13.60 to $16.00**

MILLETT DUAL-CRIMP FRONT SIGHT Replacement front sight for automatic pistols. Dual-Crimp uses an all-steel two-point hollow rivet system. Available in eight heights and four styles. Has a skirted base that covers the front sight pad. Easily installed with the Millett Installation Tool Set. Available in blaze orange bar, white bar, serrated ramp, plain post. Available in heights of .185", .200", .225", .275", .312", .340" and .410".
Price: **$16.80**

MILLETT STAKE-ON FRONT SIGHT Replacement front sight for automatic pistols. Stake-On sights have skirted base that covers the front sight pad. Easily installed with the Millet Installation Tool Set. Available in seven heights and four styles: blaze orange bar, white bar, serrated ramp, plain post. Available for Glock 17L and 24, others.
Price: **$16.80**

METALLIC SIGHTS

MILLETT ADJUSTABLE TARGET Positive light-deflection serration and slant to eliminate glare and sharp edge sight notch. Audible "click" adjustments. For AMT Hardballer, Beretta 84, 85, 92S, 92SB, Browning Hi-Power, Colt 1911 Government and Gold Cup, Colt revolvers, Dan Wesson 15, 41, 44, Ruger revolvers, Glock 17, 17L, 19, 20, 21, 22, 23.
Price: **$44.99**

MILLETT ADJUSTABLE WHITE OUTLINE Similar to the Target sight, except has a white outline on the blade to increase visibility. Available for the same handguns as the Target model, plus BRNO CZ-75/TZ-75/TA-90 without pin on front sight, and Ruger P85.
Price: . . . . **$44.99 to $49.99**

OMEGA OUTLINE SIGHT BLADES Replacement rear sight blades for Colt and Ruger single action guns and the Interarms Virginian Dragoon. Standard Outline available in gold or white notch outline on blue metal. From Omega Sales, Inc.
Price: **$10.00**

OMEGA MAVERICK SIGHT BLADES Replacement "peep-sight" blades for Colt, Ruger SAs, Virginian Dragoon. Three models available: No. 1, plain; No. 2, single bar; No. 3, double bar rangefinder. From Omega Sales, Inc.
Price: Each **$10.00**

ONE RAGGED HOLE Replacement rear sight ghost ring sight for Ruger handguns. Fits Blackhawks, Redhawks, Super Blackhawks, GP series and Mk II target pistols with adjustable sights. From One Ragged Hole, Tallahassee, Florida.
Price: . . . . **NA**

Pachmayr Accu-Set

PACHMAYR ACCU-SET Low-profile, fully adjustable rear sight to be used with existing front sight. Available with target, white outline or 3-dot blade. Blue finish. Uses factory dovetail and locking screw. For Browning, Colt, Glock, SIG Sauer, S&W and Ruger autos. From Pachmayr.
Price: **$59.98**

P-T TRITIUM NIGHT SIGHTS Self-luminous tritium sights for most popular handguns, Colt AR-15, H&K rifles and shotguns. Replacement handgun sight sets available in 3-dot-style (green/green, green/yellow, green/orange) with bold outlines around inserts; Bar-Dot available in green/green with or without white outline rear sight. Functional life exceeds 15 years. From Innovative Weaponry, Inc.
Price: Handgun sight sets **$89.00**
Price: Rifle sight sets **$89.00**
Price: Rifle, front only **$45.00**
Price: Shotgun, front only **$45.00**

T/C Encore Fiber Optic Sight Set

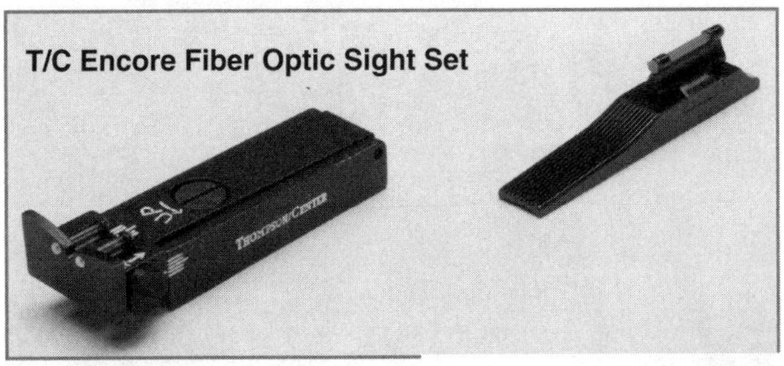

T/C ENCORE FIBER-OPTIC SIGHT SETS Click adjustable, steel rear sight and ramp-style front sight, both fitted with Tru-Glo™ fiber-optics. Specifically-designed for the T/C Encore pistol series. From Thompson/Center Arms.
Price: **$49.35**

T/C Encore Target Rear Sight

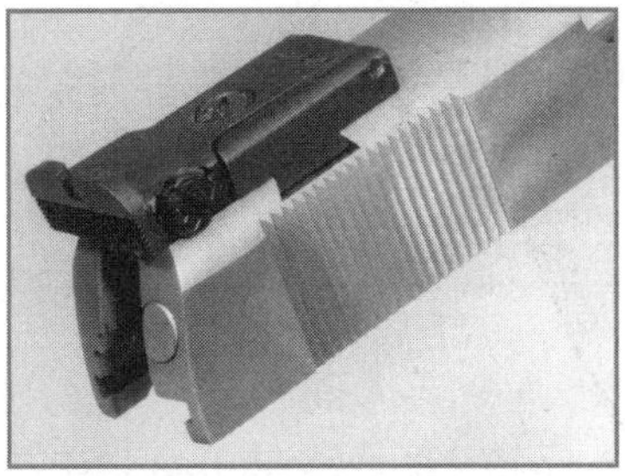

Trijicon Night Sight **Wichita Series 70/80 Sight**

T/C ENCORE TARGET REAR SIGHT Precision, steel construction with click adjustments (via knurled knobs) for windage and elevation. Models available with low, medium and high blades. From Thompson/Center Arms.
Price: **$54.00**

TRIJICON NIGHT SIGHTS Three-dot night sight system uses tritium lamps in the front and rear sights. Tritium "lamps" are mounted in silicone rubber inside a metal cylinder. A polished crystal sapphire provides protection and clarity. Inlaid white outlines provide 3-dot aiming in daylight also. Available for most popular handguns including Glock 17, 19, 20, 21, 23, 24, 25, 26, 29, 30, H&K USP, Ruger P94, SIG P220, P225, 226, Colt 1911. Front and rear sets available. From Trijicon, Inc.
Price: . . . . **$80.00 to $299.00**

TRIJICON 3-DOT Self-luminous front iron night sight for the Ruger SP101.
Price: **$50.00**

WICHITA SERIES 70/80 SIGHT Provides click windage and elevation adjustments with precise repeatability of settings. Sight blade is grooved and angled back at the top to reduce glare. Available in Low Mount Combat or Low Mount Target-styles for Colt 45s and their copies, S&W 645, Hi-Power, CZ 75 and others.
Price: Rear sight, target or combat **$75.00**
Price: Front sight, Patridge or ramp **$18.00**

WICHITA GRAND MASTER DELUXE RIBS Ventilated rib has wings machined into it for better sight acquisition and is relieved for Mag-Na-Porting. Milled to accept Weaver see-through-style rings. Made of stainless; front and rear sights blued. Has Wichita Multi-Range rear sight system, adjustable front sight. Made for revolvers with 6" barrel.
Price: Model 301S, 301B (adj. sight K frames with custom bbl. of 1" to 1.032" dia. L and N frame with 1.062" to 1.100" dia. bbl.) **$225.00**
Price: Model 303S, 303B (adj. sight K, L, N frames with factory barrel) **$225.00**

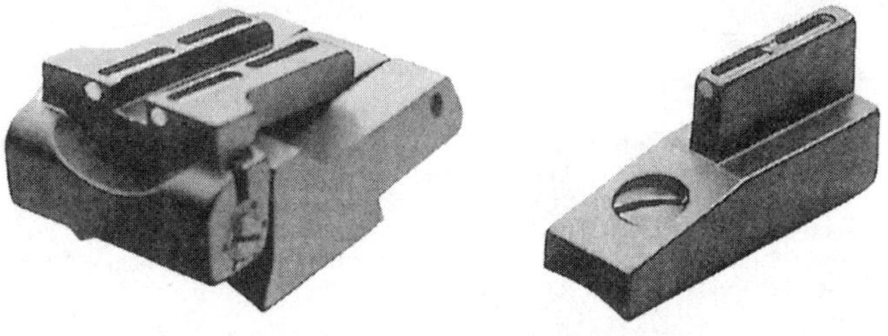

Williams Fire Sight Set

WICHITA MULTI-RANGE QUICK CHANGE SIGHTING SYSTEM Multi-range rear sight can be pre-set to four positive repeatable range settings. Adjustable front sight allows compensation for changing lighting and weather conditions with just one front sight adjustment. Front sight comes with Lyman 17A Globe and set of apertures.
Price: Rear sight **$125.00**
Price: Front, sight **$95.00**

WILLIAMS FIRE SIGHT SETS Red fiber-optic metallic sight replaces the original. Rear sight has two green fiber-optic elements. Made of CNC-machined aluminum. Fits all Glocks, Ruger P-Series (except P-85), S&W 910, Colt Gov't. Model Series 80, Ruger GP 100 and Redhawk, and SIG Sauer (front only).
Price: Front and rear set **$45.95**
Price: SIG Sauer front **$22.95**
Price: Browning BuckMark sight set **$45.95**
Price: Taurus PT111, PT140, PT145, PT1232, PT138 . . . . **$45.95**
Price: Ruger P Series, Glock, S&W 910, Colt Gov't. Series 80, Springfield XD **$44.95**

METALLIC SIGHTS

WILSON ADJUSTABLE REAR SIGHTS Machined from steel, the click adjustment design requires simple cuts and no dovetails for installation. Available in several configurations: matte black standard blade with .128" notch; with .110" notch; with tritium dots and .128" square or "U" shaped notch; and Combat Pyramid. From Wilson Combat.
Price: . . . . **$24.95 to $69.95**

Wilson Nite-Eyes

WILSON NITE-EYES SIGHTS Low-profile, snag-free design with green and yellow tritium inserts. For 1911-style pistols. From Wilson Combat.
Price: **$119.95**

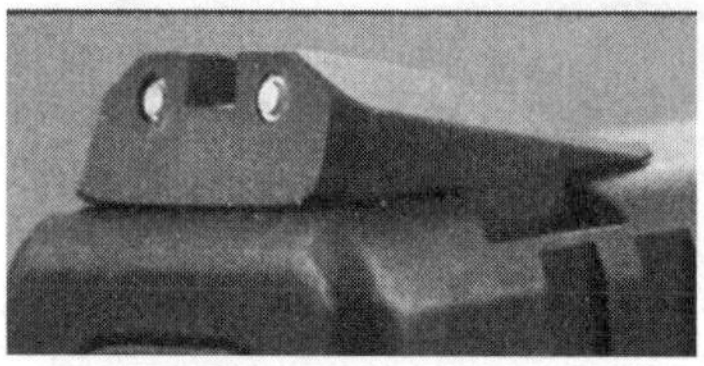

WILSON TACTICAL COMBAT SIGHTS Low-profile and snag-free in design, the sight employs the Combat Pyramid shape. For many 1911-style pistols and some Glock models. From Wilson Combat.
Price: **$139.95**

Sight Attachments

MERIT OPTICAL ATTACHMENT For iron sight shooting with handgun or rifle. Instantly attached by rubber suction cup to prescription or shooting glasses. Swings aside. Aperture adjustable from .020" to .156".
Price: **$65.00**

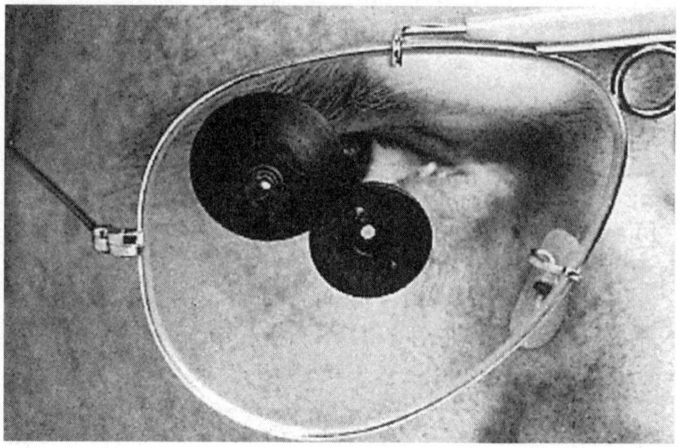

Merit Optical Attachment

MUZZLE BRAKES

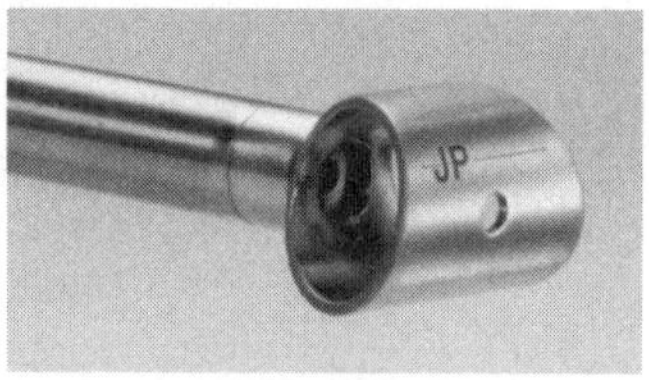

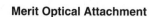

JP Muzzle Brake

JP Muzzle Brake

Designed for single shot handguns, AR-15, Ruger Mini-14, Ruger Mini Thirty and other sporting rifles, the JP Muzzle Brake redirects high pressure gases against a large frontal surface which applies forward thrust to the gun. All gases are directed up, rearward and to the sides. Priced at **$79.95** (AR-15 or sporting rifles), **$89.95** (bull barrel and SKS, AK models), **$89.95** (Ruger Minis), Dual Chamber model **$79.95.** From JP Enterprises, Inc.

Laseraim

Simple, no-gunsmithing compensator reduces felt recoil and muzzle flip by up to 30 percent. Machined from single piece of Stainless Steel (Beretta/Taurus model made of aircraft aluminum). In black and polished finish. For Colt Government/Commander and Beretta/Taurus full-size pistols. Weighs 1 ounce. **$49.00.** From Laseraim Arms Inc.

Mag-Na-Port

Electrical Discharge Machining works on any firearm except those having non-conductive shrouded barrels. EDM is a metal erosion technique using carbon electrodes that control the area to be processed. The Mag-Na-Port venting process utilizes small trapezoidal openings to direct powder gases upward and outward to reduce recoil. No effect is had on bluing or nickeling outside the Mag-Na-Port area so no refinishing is needed. Rifle-style porting on single shot or large caliber handguns with barrels 7 1/2″ or longer is **$115.00**; Dual Trapezoidal porting on most handguns with minimum barrel length of 3″, **$115.00**; standard revolver porting, **$88.50**; porting through the slide and barrel for semi-autos, **$129.50**; traditional rifle porting, **$135.00**. Prices do not include shipping, handling and insurance. From Mag-Na-Port International.

Mag-Na-Brake

A screw-on brake under 2″ long with progressive integrated exhaust chambers to neutralize expanding gases. Gases dissipate with an opposite twist to prevent the brake from unscrewing, and with a 5-degree forward angle to minimize sound pressure level. Available in blue, satin blue, bright or satin stainless. Standard and Light Contour installation cost **$195.00** for bolt-action rifles, many single action and single shot handguns. A knurled thread protector supplied at extra cost. Also available in Varmint style with exhaust chambers covering 220 degrees for prone-position shooters. From Mag-Na-Port International.

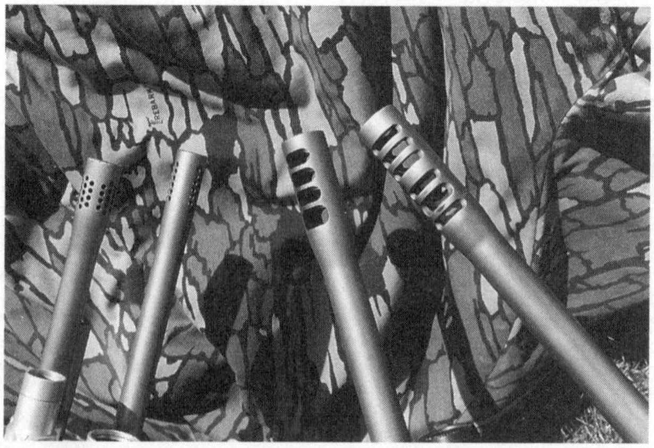

SSK Arrestor Brake

This is a true muzzle brake with an expansion chamber. It takes up about 1″ of barrel and reduces velocity accordingly. Some Arrestors are added to a barrel, increasing its length. Said to reduce the felt recoil of a 458 to that approaching a 30-06. Can be set up to give zero muzzle rise in any caliber, and can be added to most guns. For handgun or rifle. Prices start at **$95.00**. Contact SSK Industries for full data.

Maker and Model	Magn.	Field at 100 Yds. (feet)	Eye Relief (in.)	Length (in.)	Tube Dia. (in.)	W & E Adjustments	Weight (ozs.)	Price	Other Data
ADCO									
Magnum 50 mm[3]	0			4.1	45 mm	Int.	6.8	$269.00	[1]Multi-Color Dot system changes from red to green. [2]Comes with standard dovetail mount. [3]10 MOA dot; black or nickel. [4]Square format; with mount battery. From ADCO Sales.
MIRAGE Ranger 1"	0			5.2	1	Int.	3.9	159.00	
MIRAGE Ranger 30mm	0			5.5	30mm	Int.	5	159.00	
MIRAGE Competitor	0			5.5	30mm	Int.	5.5	229.00	
Square Shooter 2[2]	0			5		Int.	5	99.00	
MIRAGE Eclipse[1]	0			5.5	30mm	Int.	5.5	229.00	
Champ Red Dot	0			4.5		Int.	2	33.95	
Vantage 1"	0			3.9	1	Int.	3.9	129.00	
Vantage 30mm	0			4.2	30mm	Int.	4.9	159.00	
Vision 2000[4]	0	60		4.7		Int.	6.2	79.00	
e-dot ESB[1]	0			4.12	1	Int.	3.7	139.00	
e-dot E1B	0			4.12	1	Int.	3.7	99.00	
e-dot ECB	0			3.8	30mm	Int.	6.4	99.00	
e-dot E30B	0			4.3	30mm	Int.	4.6	99.00	
AIMPOINT									
Comp	0			4.6	30mm	Int.	4.3	331.00	Illuminates red dot in field of view. Noparallax (dot does not need to be centered). Unlimited field of view and eye relief. On/off, adj. intensity. Dot covers 3" @100 yds. [1]Comes with 30mm rings, battery, lens cloth. [2]Requires 1" rings. Black finish. AP Comp avail. in black, blue, SS, camo. [3]Black finish (AP 5000-B); avail. with regular 3-min. or 10-min. Mag Dot as B2 or S2. [4]Band pass reflection coating for compatibility with night vision equipment; U.S. Army contract model; with anti-reflex coated lenses (Comp ML), **$359.00**. From Aimpoint U.S.A.
Comp M[4]	0			5	30mm	Int.	6.1	409.00	
Series 5000[3]	0			6	30mm	Int.	6	297.00	
Series 3000 Universal[2]	0			6.25	1	Int.	6	232.00	
Series 5000/2x[1]	2			7	30mm	Int.	9	388.00	
BEEMAN									
Pistol Scopes									
5021	2	19	10-24	9.1	1	Int.	7.4	85.50	All scopes have 5 point reticle, all glass fully-coated lenses. Imported by Beeman.
5020	1.5	14	11-16	8.3	.75	Int.	3.6	NA	
BSA									
Pistol									
P52x20	2	NA	NA	NA	NA	Int.	NA	89.95	[1]Red dot sights also available in 42mm and 50mm versions. From BSA.
Red Dot									
RD30[1]	0			3.8	30mm	Int.	5	59.95	
PB30[1]	0			3.8	30mm	Int.	4.5	79.95	
BURRIS									
Speeddot 135[7]									Available in Carbon Black, Titanium Gray and Autumn Gold finishes. All scopes avail. with Plex reticle. Steel-on-steel click adjustments. [1]Dot reticle on some models. [2]Matte satin finish. [3]Available with parallax adjustment. [4]Silver matte finish extra. [5]Target knobs extra, standard on silhouette models. LER and XER with P.A., 6x HBR. [6]Available with Posi-Lock. **Speeddot 135:** [7]Waterproof, fogproof, coated lenses, 11 brightness settings; 3-MOA or 11-MOA dot size; includes Weaver-style rings and battery. **Partial listing shown.** Contact Burris for complete details.
Red Dot	1			4.85	35mm	Int.	5	291.00	
Handgun									
1.50-4x LER[1,4,6]	1.6-3	16-11	11-25	10.25	1	Int.	11	411.00	
2-7x LER[2,3,4,6]	2-6.5	21-7	7-27	9.5	1	Int.	12.6	458.00	
2x LER[3,4,5]	1.7	21	10-24	8.75	1	Int.	6.8	286.00	
4x LER[1,3,4,5,6]	3.7	11	10-22	9.625	1	Int.	9	338.00	
3x12x LER[1,3,5]	9.5	4	8-12	13.5	1	Int.	14	558.00	
BUSHNELL									
Elite 3200 Handgun RainGuard									[1]Adj. obj. Circle-X reticle. [2]Only in matte finish. [3]50mm objective. **Partial listings shown. Contact Bushnell Performance Optics for details.**
32-2632M[1]	2-6	10-4	20	9	1	Int.	10	389.95	
32-2636[3]	2-6	10-4	20	9	1	Int.	10	431.95	
Holosight									
.53-0021	1x	Unlimited	Unlimited	6	NA	Int.	12	299.95	
.53-0029	1x	Unlimited	Unlimited	6	NA	Int.	12	299.95	
Trophy									
73-0134	1	68	Unlimited	5.5	1	Int.	6	119.95	
Trophy Handgun									
73-2632[2]	2-6	21-7	9-26	9.1	1	Int.	10.9	251.95	

A reticle is the crosshair or pattern placed in the eyepiece of the scope which establishes the gun's position on the target.

MULTI-X

CIRCLE-X

MIL DOT

3-2-1 LOW-LIGHT

¼ M.O.A.

EUROPEAN

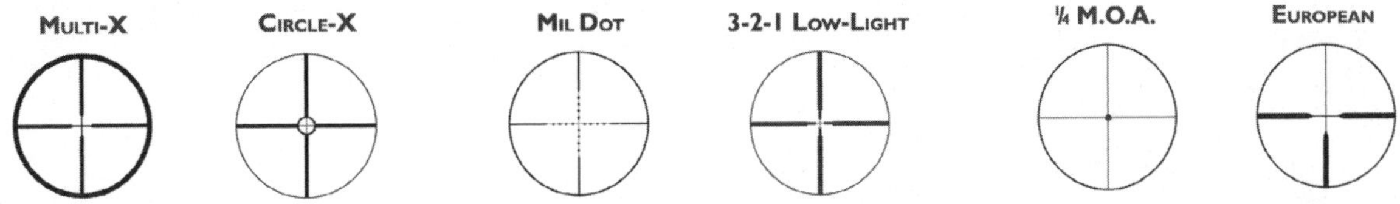

HANDGUN SCOPES

Maker and Model	Magn.	Field at 100 Yds. (feet)	Eye Relief (in.)	Length (in.)	Tube Dia. (in.)	W & E Adjustments	Weight (ozs.)	Price	Other Data
LEUPOLD									
LPS 1.5-6x42	1.5-6	58.7-15.7	4	11.2	30mm	Int.	16	**1,198.99**	Constantly centered reticles, choice of Duplex, tapered CPC, Leupold Dot, Crosshair and Dot. CPC and Dot reticles extra. Partial listing shown. **Contact Leupold for complete details.**
LPS 2.5-10x45	2.6-9.8	37.2	4.5-3.8		1	Int.	17.2	**1,119.99**	
LPS 3.5-14x52	3.5-14	28-7.2	4	13.1	30mm	Int.	22	**1,249.99**	
MILLETT									
SP-1 Compact[1] Red Dot	1	36.65		4.1	1	Int.	3.2	**147.45**	[1]3-MOA dot. [2]5-MOA dot. [3]3- , 5- , 8- , 10-MOA dots. [4]10-MOA dot. All have click adjustments; waterproof, shockproof; 11 dot intensity settings. All avail. in matte/black or silver finish. From Millett Sights.
SP-2 Compact[2] Red Dot	1	58		4.5	30mm	Int.	4.3	**147.45**	
MultiDot SP[3]	1	50		4.8	30mm	Int.	5.3	**179.45**	
30mm Wide View[4]	1	60		5.5	30mm	Int.	5	**179.45**	
NIKON									
2x20 EER	2	22	26.4	8.1	1	Int.	6.3	**169.95**	Super multi-coated lenses and blackening of all internal metal parts for maximum light gathering capability; fogproof; waterproof; shockproof; luster and matte finish. Partial listing shown. From Nikon, Inc.
SIGHTRON									
Pistol									
SII 1x28P[1]	1	30	9-24	9.49	1	Int.	8.46	**314.79**	[1]Satin black; also stainless. Pistol scopes have aluminum tubes, Exac Trak adjustments. Lifetime warranty. From Sightron, Inc.
SII 2x28P[1]	2	16-10	9-24	9.49	1	Int.	8.28	**314.79**	
SIMMONS									
Prohunter Handgun									
7732[1]	2	22	9-17	8.75	1	Int.	7	**109.99**	[1]Matte; also polished finish. [2]Black matte finish; also available in silver. **Only selected models shown.** Contact Simmons Outdoor Corp. for complete details.
7738[2]	4	15	11.8- 17.6	8.5	1	Int.	8	**129.99**	
82200	2-6							**159.99**	
TASCO									
ProPoint									
PDP2	1	40	Un.	5	1	Int.	5.5	**117.95**	
PDP3CMP	1	68	Un.	4.75	1	Int.	5.4	**157.95**	
PDP3	1	52	Un.	5	1	Int.	5.5	**137.95**	
PD3ST1	1	52	Un.	5	1	Int.	5.5	**143.95**	
PDPRGD	1	60	Un.	5.4	1	Int.	5.7	**91.95**	
Red Dot									
BKR30	1	57	Un.	3.75	1	Int.	6	**45.95**	
BKR3022* (22 rimfire)	1	57	Un.	3.75	1	Int.	6	**45.95**	
BKR42	1	62	Un.	3.75	1	Int.	6.7	**57.95**	
THOMPSON/CENTER RECOIL PROOF SERIES									
Pistol Scopes									
8315	2.5-7	15-5	8-21, 8-11	9.25	1	Int.	9.2	**364.00**	
8326	2.5-7	15-5	8-21, 8-11	9.25	1	Int.	10.5	**432.00**	
ULTRA DOT									
Ultra-Dot Sights[1]									[1]Ultra Dot sights include rings, battery, polarized filter, and 5-year warranty. All models available in black or satin finish. [2]Illuminated red dot has eleven brightness settings. Shock-proof aluminum tube. From Ultra Dot Distribution.
Ultra-Dot 25[2]	1			5.1	1	Int.	3.9	**159.00**	
Ultra-Dot 30[2]	1			5.1	30mm	Int.	4	**179.00**	
WEAVER									
Handgun									
H2[1-3]	2	21	4-29	8.5	1	Int.	6.7	**161.43**	[1]Gloss black. [2]Matte black. [3]Silver. One-piece tubes with multi-coated lenses. All scopes are shock-proof, waterproof, and fogproof. Dual-X reticle available in fine X-hair and dots; Qwik-Point red dot scopes which are available in fixed 4 or 12 MOA, or variable 4-8-12 MOA. V16 also available with fine X-hair, dot or Dual-X reticle. T-Series scopes have Micro-Trac® adjustments. From Weaver Products.
H4[1-3]	4	18	11.5-18	8.5	1	Int.	6.7	**175.00**	
VH4[1-3]	1.5-4	13.6-5.8	11-17	8.6	1	Int.	8.1	**215.71**	
VH8[1-3]	2.5-8	8.5-3.7	12.16	9.3	1	Int.	8.3	**228.57**	

LASER SIGHTS

Alpec Mini Shot

Laseraim LA5X

Laseraim LAX

Maker and Model	Wave length (nm)	Beam Color	Lens	Operating Temp. (degrees F.)	Weight (ozs.)	Price	Other Data
ALPEC							[1]Range 1000 yards. [2]Range 300 yards. Mini Shot II range 500 yards, output 650mm, **$129.95.** [3]Range 300 yards; Laser Shot II 500 yards; Super Laser Shot 1000 yards. Black or stainless finish aluminum; removable pressure or push-button switch. Mounts for most handguns, many rifles and shotguns. From Alpec Team, Inc.
Power Shot[1]	635	Red	Glass	NA	2.5	**$199.95**	
Mini Shot[2]	670	Red	Glass	NA	2.5	**99.95**	
Laser Shot[3]	670	Red	Glass	NA	3.0	**99.95**	
BEAMSHOT							[1]Black or silver finish; adj. for windage and elevation; 300-yd. range; also M1000/S (500-yd. range), M1000/u (800-yd.). [2]Black finish; 300-, 500-, 800-yd. models. All come with removable touch pad switch, 5" cable. Mounts to fit virtually any firearm. From Quarton USA Co.
1000[1]	670	Red	Glass	NA	3.8	**NA**	
3000[2]	635/670	Red	Glass	NA	2	**NA**	
1001/u	635	Red	Glass	NA	3.8	**NA**	
780	780	Red	Glass	NA	3.8	**NA**	
BSA							[1]Comes with mounts for 22/air rifle and Weaver-style bases.
LS650[1]	N/A	Red	NA	NA	NA	**49.95**	
LASERAIM							[1]Red dot/laser combo; 300-yd. range: LA3xHD Hotdot has 500-yd. range **$249.00**; [4] MOA dot size, laser gives 2" dot size at 100 yds. 230mm obj. lens: [4]MOA dot at 100 yds: fits Weaver base. 3300-yd range; 2" dot at 100 yds.; rechargeable Nicad battery 41.5-mile range; 1" dot at 100 yds.; 20+ hrs. batt. life. [5]1.5-mile range; 1" dot at 100 yds; rechargeable Nicad battery (comes with in-field charger); [6]Black or satin finish. With mount, **$169.00.** [7]Laser projects 2" dot at 100 yds.: with rotary switch; with Hotdot **$237.00**; with Hotdot touch switch **$357.00.** [8]For Glock 17-27; G1 Hotdot **$299.00**; price installed. 10Fits std. Weaver base, no rings required; 6-MOA dot; seven brightness settings. All have w&e adj.; black or satin silver finish. From Laser aim Technologies, Inc.
LA10 Hotdot[4]				NA	NA	**199.00**	
Lasers							
MA-35RB Mini Aimer[7]				NA	1.0	**129.00**	
G1 Laser[8]				NA	2.0	**229.00**	
LASER DEVICES							[1]For S&W P99 semi-auto pistols; also BA-2, 5 oz., **$339.00.** [2]For revolvers. [3]For HK, Walther P99. [4]For semi-autos. [5]For rifles; also FA-4/ULS, 2.5 oz., **$325.00.** [6]For HK sub guns. [7]For military rifles. [8]For shotguns. [9]For SIG-Pro pistol. [10]Universal, semi-autos. [11]For AR-15 variants. All avail. with Magnum Power Point (650nM) or daytime-visible Super Power Point (632nM) diode. Infrared diodes avail. for law enforcement. From Laser Devices, Inc.
BA-1[1]	632	Red	Glass	NA	2.4	**372.00**	
BA-3[2]	632	Red	Glass	NA	3.3	**332.50**	
BA-5[3]	632	Red	Glass	NA	3.2	**372.00**	
Duty-Grade[4]	632	Red	Glass	NA	3.5	**372.00**	
FA-4[5]	632	Red	Glass	NA	2.6	**358.00**	
LasTac[1]	632	Red	Glass	NA	5.5	**298.00 to 477.00**	

LASER SIGHTS

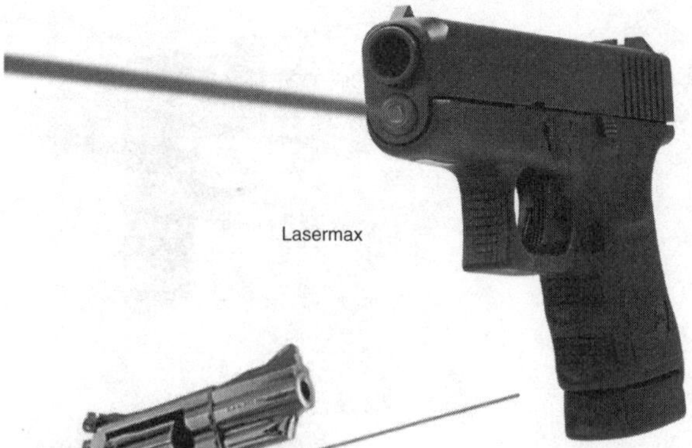

Lasermax

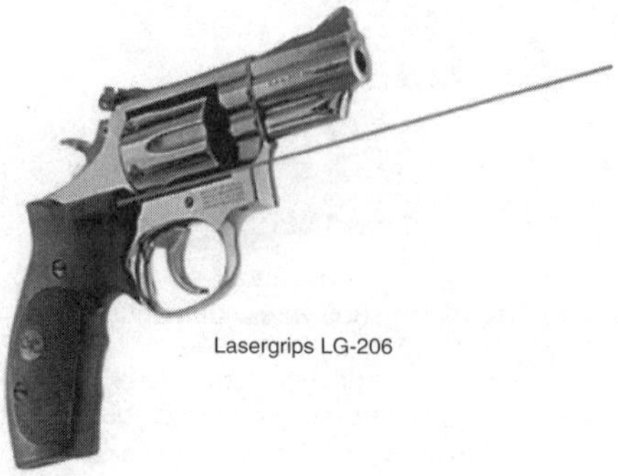

Lasergrips LG-206

Lasermax

Maker and Model	Wave length (nm)	Beam Color	Lens	Operating Temp. (degrees F.)	Weight (ozs.)	Price	Other Data
LASER DEVICES *(cont.)*							
MP-5[6]	632	Red	Glass		2.2	**495.00**	
MR-2[7]	632	Red	Glass		6.3	**485.00**	
SA-2[8]	632	Red	Glass		3.0	**360.00**	
SIG-Pro[9]	632	Red	Glass		2.6	**372.00**	
ULS-2001[10]	632	Red	Glass		4.5	**210.95**	
Universal AR-2A	632	Red	Glass		4.5	**445.00**	
LASERGRIPS							Replaces existing grips with built-in laser high in the right grip panel. Integrated pressure sensitive pad in grip activates the laser. Also has master on/off switch. [1]For Colt 1911/Commander. [2]For all Glock models. Option on/off switch. Requires factory installation. [3]For S&W K, L, N frames, round or square butt (LG-207); [4]For Taurus small-frame revolvers. [5]For Ruger SP-101. [6]For SIG Sauer P226. From Crimson Trace Corp. [7]For Beretta 92/96. [8]For Ruger MK II. [9]For S&W J-frame. [10]For Sig Sauer P228/229. [11]For Colt 1911 full size, wraparound. [12]For Beretta 92/96, wraparound. [13]For Colt 1911 compact, wraparound. [14]For S&W J-frame, rubber.
LG-201[1]	633	Red-Orange	Glass	NA		**299.00**	
LG-206[3]	633	Red-Orange	Glass	NA		**229.00**	
LG-085[4]	633	Red-Orange	Glass	NA		**229.00**	
LG-101[5]	633	Red-Orange	Glass	NA		**229.00**	
LG-226[6]	633	Red-Orange	Glass	NA		**229.00**	
GLS-630[2]	633	Red-Orange	Glass	NA		**595.00**	
LG202[7]	633	Red-Orange	Glass	NA		**299.00**	
LG203[8]	633	Red-Orange	Glass	NA		**299.00**	
LG205[9]	633	Red-Orange	Glass	NA		**299.00**	

LASER SIGHTS

Laser Devices BA-5 on HK USP

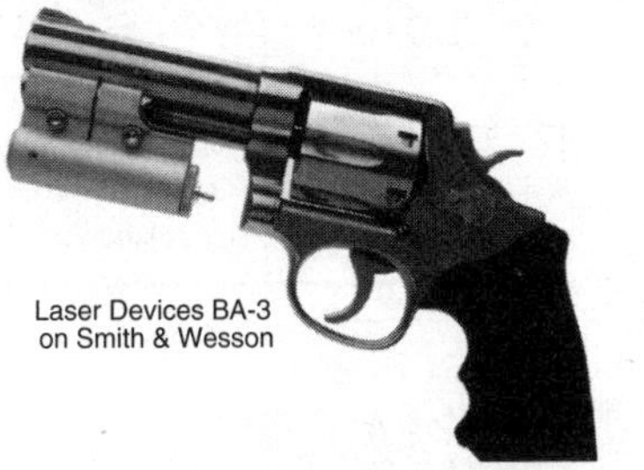

Laser Devices BA-3 on Smith & Wesson

Laser Devices Sig Pro Laser & Tactical Light

Laser Devices ULS 2001 with TLS 8R light

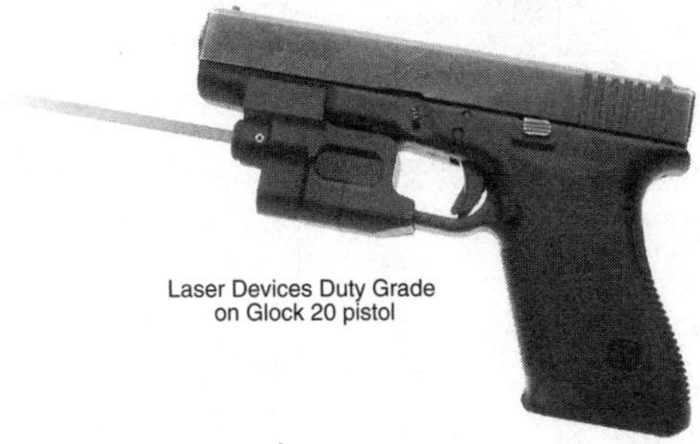

Laser Devices Duty Grade on Glock 20 pistol

Laser Devices Las/Tac on HK USP

Maker and Model	Wave length (nm)	Beam Color	Lens	Operating Temp. (degrees F.)	Weight (ozs.)	Price	Other Data
LASERGRIPS *(cont.)*							
LG229[10]	633	Red-Orange	Glass	NA		**299.00**	
LG301[11]	633	Red-Orange	Glass	NA		**329.00**	
LG302[12]	633	Red-Orange	Glass	NA		**329.00**	
LG304[13]	633	Red-Orange	Glass	NA		**329.00**	
LG305[14]	633	Red-Orange	Glass	NA		**299.00**	
LASERLYTE							[1]Dot/circle or dot/crosshair projection; black or stainless. [2]Also 635/645mm model. From Tac Star Laserlyte. In grip activates the laser. Also has master on/off switch.
LLX-0006-140/090[1]	635/645	Red		NA	1.4	**159.95**	
WPL-0004-140/090[2]	670	Red		NA	1.2	**109.95**	
TPL-0004-140/090[2]	670	Red		NA	1.2	**109.95**	
T7S-0004-140[2]	670	Red		NA	0.8	**109.95**	
LASERMAX							
LMS-1000 Internal Guide Rod	635	Red-Orange	Glass	40-120	.25	**389.00**	Replaces the recoil spring guide rod; includes a customized takedown lever that serves as the laser's insta in grip activates the laser. Also has master on/off switch. Installs in most pistols without gunsmithing. Battery life 1/2 hour to 2 hours in continuous use. From Laser Max.

SCOPE RINGS & BASES

Maker, Model, Type	Adjust.	Scopes	Price
ADCO			
Std. Black or nickel		1"	$13.95
Std. Black or nickel		30mm	$13.95
Rings Black or nickel		30mm with 3/8" grv.	$13.95
Rings Black or nickel		1" raised 3/8" grv.	$13.95
AIMTECH			
AMT Auto Mag II .22 Mag.	No	Weaver rail	$56.99
Astra .44 Mag Revolver	No	Weaver rail	$63.25
Beretta/Taurus 92/99	No	Weaver rail	$63.25
Browning Buckmark/Challenger II	No	Weaver rail	$56.99
Browning Hi-Power	No	Weaver rail	$63.25
Glock 17, 17L, 19, 23, 24 etc. no rail	No	Weaver rail	$63.25
Glock 20, 21 no rail	No	Weaver rail	$63.25
Glock 9mm and .40 with access. rail	No	Weaver rail	$74.95
Govt. 45 Auto/.38 Super	No	Weaver rail	$63.25
Hi-Standard (Mitchell version) 107	No	Weaver rail	$63.25
H&K USP 9mm/40 rail mount	No	Weaver rail	$74.95
Rossi 85/851/951 Revolvers	No	Weaver rail	$63.25
Ruger Mk I, Mk II	No	Weaver rail	$49.95
Ruger P85/P89	No	Weaver rail	$63.25
S&W K, L, N frames	No	Weaver rail	$63.25
S&W K, L, N with tapped top strap*	No	Weaver rail	$69.95
S&W Model 41 Target 22	No	Weaver rail	$63.25
S&W Model 52 Target 38	No	Weaver rail	$63.25
S&W Model 99 Walther frame rail mount	No	Weaver rail	$74.95
S&W 2nd Gen. 59/459/659 etc.	No	Weaver rail	$56.99
S&W 3rd Gen. full size 5906 etc.	No	Weaver rail	$69.95
S&W 422, 622, 2206	No	Weaver rail	$56.99
S&W 645/745	No	Weaver rail	$56.99
S&W Sigma	No	Weaver rail	$64.95
Taurus PT908	No	Weaver rail	$63.25
Taurus 44 6.5" bbl.	No	Weaver rail	$69.95
Walther 99	No	Weaver rail	$74.95

All mounts no-gunsmithing, iron sight usable. All mounts accommodate standard Weaver-style rings of all makers. From Aimtech division, L&S Technologies, Inc. *3-blade sight mount combination.

B-SQUARE

Pistols (centerfire)

Beretta 92, 96/Taurus 99	No	Weaver rail	$69.95
Colt M1911	E only	Weaver rail	$69.95
Desert Eagle	No	Weaver rail	$69.95
Glock	No	Weaver rail	$69.95
H&K USP, 9mm and 40 S&W	No	Weaver rail	$69.95
Ruger P85/89	E only	Weaver rail	$69.95
SIG Sauer P226	E only	Weaver rail	$69.95

Pistols (rimfire)

Browning Buck Mark	No	Weaver rail	$32.95
Colt 22	No	Weaver rail	$49.95
Ruger Mk I/II, bull or taper	No	Weaver rail	$32.95-49.95
Smith & Wesson 41, 2206	No	Weaver rail	$36.95-49.95

Revolvers

Colt Anaconda/Python	No	Weaver rail	$35.95-74.95
Ruger Single-Six	No	Weaver rail	$64.95

Maker, Model, Type	Adjust.	Scopes	Price
B-SQUARE (cont.)			
Ruger GP-100	No	Weaver rail	$64.95
Ruger Blackhawk, Super	No	Weaver rail	$64.95
Ruger Redhawk, Super	No	Weaver rail	$64.95
Smith & Wesson K, L, N	No	Weaver rail	$36.95-74.95
Taurus 66, 669, 607, 608	No	Weaver rail	$64.95

Prices shown for anodized black finish; add $10 for stainless finish. Partial listing of mounts shown here. Contact B-Square for complete listing and details.

BURRIS

Supreme (SU) One-Piece (T)[1]	W only	1" split rings, 3 heights	1-piece base - $23.00-27.00
Trumount (TU) Two-Piece (T)	W only	1" split rings, 3 heights	2-piece base - $21.00-30.00
Trumount (TU) Two-Piece Ext.	W only	1" split rings	$26.00
L.E.R. (LU) Mount Bases[2]	W only	1" split rings	$24.00-52.00
L.E.R. No Drill-No Tap Bases[2,3,4]	W only	1" split rings	$48.00-52.00
Std. 1" Rings[5]		Low, medium, high heights	$29.00-43.00
Signature Rings	No	30mm split rings	$68.00
Double Dovetail (DD) Bases	No	30mm Signature	$23.00-26.00

[1]Universal rings, mounts fit Burris, Universal, Redfield, Leupold and Browning bases. Comparable prices. [2]Universal dovetail; accepts Burris, Universal, Redfield, Leupold rings. For Dan Wesson, S&W, Virginian, Ruger Blackhawk, Win. 94. [3]Selected rings and bases available with matte Safari or silver finish. [4]For S&W K, L, N frames, Colt Python, Dan Wesson with 6" or longer barrels. [5]Also in 30mm.

CATCO

Enfield Drop-In	No	1"	$39.95

Uses Weaver-style rings (not incl.). No gunsmithing required. See-Thru design. From CATCO.

CLEAR VIEW

Universal Rings, Mod. 101[1]	No	1" split rings	$21.95
Standard Model[2]	No	1" split rings	$21.95
Broad View[3]	No	1"	$21.95
22 Model[4]	No	3/4", 7/8", 1"	$13.95
SM-94 Winchester[5]	No	1" split rings	$23.95
94 EJ[6]	No	1" split rings	$21.95

[1]Most rifles by using Weaver-type base; allows use of iron sights. [2]Most popular rifles; allows use of iron sights. [3]Most popular rifles; low profile, wide field of view. [4]22 rifles with grooved receiver. [5]Side mount. [6]For Win. A.E. From Clear View Mfg.

CONETROL

Pistol Bases, 2- or 3-ring[1]	W only		
Metric Rings[2]	W only	26mm, 26.5mm, 30mm	$99.96-149.88

[1]For XP-100, T/C Contender, Colt SAA, Ruger Blackhawk, S&W and others. [2]26mm, 26.5mm, and 30mm rings made in projectionless style, in three heights. Three-ring mount for T/C Contender and other pistols in Conetrol's three grades. Any Conetrol mount available in stainless steel add 50 percent.

EXCEL INDUSTRIES, INC.

Titanium Weaver-Style Rings	No	1" and 30mm, low and high	$179.00
Steel Weaver-Style Rings	No	1" and 30mm, low and high	$149.00
Flashlight Mounts - Titanium and Steel	No	1" and 30mm, low and high	$89.50/75.00

KRIS MOUNTS

One Piece (T)[1]	No	1", 26mm split rings	$12.98

[1]Blackhawk revolver. Mounts have oval hole to permit use of iron sights.

SCOPE RINGS & BASES

Maker, Model, Type	Adjust.	Scopes	Price
LASER AIM	No	Laser Aim	**$19.99-69.00**

Mounts Laser Aim above or below barrel. Available for most popular hand guns, rifles, shotguns, including militaries. From Laser Aim Technologies, Inc.

Maker, Model, Type	Adjust.	Scopes	Price
LEUPOLD			
STD Bases[1]	W only	One- or two-piece bases	**$25.40**
DD RBH Handgun Mounts	No		**$34.00**

[1]Base and two rings; Casull, Ruger, S&W, T/C; add $5.00 for silver finish.

Maker, Model, Type	Adjust.	Scopes	Price
MARLIN			
One-Piece QD (T)	No	1" split rings	**$10.10**

Most Marlin lever actions.

Maker, Model, Type	Adjust.	Scopes	Price
MILLETT			
Black Onyx Smooth		1", low, medium, high	**$32.71**
Chaparral Engraved		engraved	**$50.87**
One-Piece Bases[2]	Yes	1"	**$26.41**
Universal Two-Piece Bases			
700 Series	W only	Two-piece bases	**$26.41**
FN Series	W only	Two-piece bases	**$26.41**
Handgun Bases, Rings[1]		1"	**$36.07-80.38**
30mm Rings		30mm	**$20.95-41.63**
Extension Rings		1"	**$40.43-56.44**
See-Thru Mounts	No	1"	**$29.35-31.45**
Shotgun Mounts	No	1"	**$52.45**
Timber Mount	No	1"	**$81.90**

[1]Two- and three-ring sets for Colt Python, Trooper, Diamondback, Peacekeeper, Dan Wesson, Ruger Redhawk, Super Redhawk. [2]Turn-in bases and Weaver-style for most popular rifles and T/C Contender, XP-100 pistols. From Millett Sights.

Maker, Model, Type	Adjust.	Scopes	Price
THOMPSON/CENTER			
Duo-Ring Mount[1]	No	1"	**$78.00**
Weaver-Style Bases	No		**$14.00–28.50**
Weaver-Style Rings[2]	No	1"	**$36.00**

[1]Attaches directly to T/C Contender bbl., no drilling/tapping; also for T/C M/L rifles, needs base adapter; blue or stainless. [2]Medium and high; blue or silver finish. From Thompson/Center.

Maker, Model, Type	Adjust.	Scopes	Price
WARNE			
Premier Series (all steel)			
T.P.A. (Permanently Attached)	No	1", 4 heights 30mm, 2 heights	**$87.75-98.55**
Premier Series Rings fit Premier Series Bases			
Premier Series (all-steel Q.D. rings)			
Premier Series (all steel) Quick detachable lever	No	1", 4 heights 26mm, 2 heights 30mm, 3 heights	**$129.95-131.25** **$142.00**
All-Steel One-Piece Base, ea.			**$38.50**
All-Steel Two-Piece Base, ea.			**$14.00**
WARNE *(cont.)*			
Maxima Series (fits all Weaver-style bases)			
Permanently Attached[1]	No	1", 3 heights 30mm, 3 heights	**$25.50** **$36.00**
Adjustable Double Lever[2]	No	1", 3 heights 30mm, 3 heights	**$72.60** **$80.75**
Stainless-Steel Two-Piece Base, ea.			**$15.25**

Vertically split rings with dovetail clamp, precise return to zero. Fit most popular rifles, handguns. Regular blue, matte blue, silver finish. [1]All-Steel, non-Q.D. rings. [2]All-steel, Q.D. rings. From Warne Mfg. Co.

Maker, Model, Type	Adjust.	Scopes	Price
WEAVER			
Top Mount	No	7/8", 1", 30mm, 33mm	**$24.95-38.95**
Side Mount	No	1", 1" long	**$14.95-34.95**
Tip-Off Rings	No	7/8", 1"	**$24.95-32.95**
Pivot Mounts	No	1"	**$38.95**
Complete Mount Systems			
Pistol	No	1"	**$75.00-105.00**
See-Thru Mounts			
Detachable	No	1"	**$27.00-32.00**
System (no base required)	No	1"	**$15.00-35.00**
Tip-Off	No	1"	**$15.00**

Nearly all modern rifles, pistols, and shotguns. Detachable rings in standard, See-Thru, and extension styles, in Low, Medium, High or X-High heights; gloss (blued), silver and matte finishes to match scopes. Extension rings are only available in 1" High style and See-Thru X-tensions only in gloss finish. Tip-Off rings only for 3/8" grooved receivers or 3/8" grooved adaptor bases; no base required. No Drill & Tap Pistol systems in gloss or silver for Colt Python, Trooper, 357, Officer's Model, Ruger Single-Six, Security-Six (gloss finish only), Blackhawk, Super Blackhawk, Blackhawk SRM 357, Redhawk, Mini-14 Series (not Ranch), Ruger 22 Auto Pistols, Mark II, Smith & Wesson I- and current K-frames with adj. rear sights. From Weaver.

Maker, Model, Type	Adjust.	Scopes	Price
WEIGAND			
Browning Buck Mark[1]	No		**$29.95**
Integra Mounts[2]	No		**$39.95-69.00**
S&W Revolver[3]	No		**$29.95**
Ruger 10/22[4]	No		**$14.95-39.95**
Ruger Revolver[5]	No		**$29.95**
Taurus Revolver[4]	No		**$29.95-65.00**
Lightweight Rings	No	1", 30mm	**$29.95-39.95**
1911			
SM3[6]	No	Weaver rail	**$99.95**
APCMNT[7]	No		**$69.95**

[1]No gunsmithing. [2]S&W K, L, N frames, Taurus vent rib models, Colt Anaconda/Python, Ruger Redhawk, Ruger 10/22. [3]K, L, N frames. [4]Three models. [5]Redhawk, Blackhawk, GP-100. [6]3rd Gen., drill and tap, without slots **$59.95**. [7]For Aimpoint Comp. Red Dot scope, silver only. From Weigand Combat Handguns, Inc.

SPOTTING SCOPES

Bushnell Collapsible Spotting Scope

ALPEN MODEL 711 20x50 mini-scope, 20x, 50mm eyepiece, field of view at 1,000 yds. 147 ft., multi-coated lens, weighs 10 oz., waterproof.
Price: $60.97

ALPEN MODEL 722 12-36x compact, 50mm eyepiece, field of view at 115/59, multi-coated lens, weighs 27 oz., waterproof.
Price: $124.20

ALPEN MODEL 725 and 728 Compact 15-45x60, 60mm obj., center focus, multi-coated lens, field of view at 115/59, weighs 27 oz., waterproof.
Price: .... $151.62 and $154.85

ALPEN MODEL 730 15-30x50, 60mm obs., field of view at 136-99, multi-coated lens, weighs 28 oz., waterproof.
Price: $116.14

ALPEN MODEL 788 20-60x80, 80mm obj., field of view at 93/47, multi-coated lens, weighs 64 oz., waterproof.
Price: $385.51

BROWNING 15-45x zoom, 65mm objective lens. Weighs 48 oz. Waterproof, fogproof. Tripod, soft and hard cases included.
Price: $559.95

BUSHNELL DISCOVERER, 15x to 60x zoom, 60mm objective. Constant focus throughout range. Field of view at 1,000 yds. 38 ft. (60x), 150 ft. (15x). Comes with lens caps. Length: 17-1/2"; weighs 48.5 oz.
Price: $342.95

BUSHNELL ELITE 15x to 45x zoom, 60mm objective. Field of view at 1,000 yds., 125-65 ft. Length: 12.2"; weighs 26.5 oz. Waterproof, armored. Tripod mount. Comes with black case.
Price: $586.95

BUSHNELL ELITE ZOOM 20x-60x, 70mm objective. Roof prism. Field of view at 1,000 yds. 90-50 ft. Length: 16"; weighs 40 oz. Waterproof, armored. Tripod mount. Comes with black case.
Price: $806.95

BUSHNELL 80MM ELITE 20x-60x zoom, 80mm objective. Field of view at 1,000 yds. 98-50 ft. (zoom). Weighs 51 oz. (20x, 30x), 54 oz. (zoom); length: 17". Interchangeable bayonet-style eyepieces. Built-in peep sight.
Price: With EDPrime Glass $1,173.95

BUSHNELL TROPHY 65mm objective, 20x-60x zoom. Field of view at 1,000 yds. 90 ft. (20x), 45 ft. (60x). Length: 12.7"; weighs 20 oz. Black rubber armored, waterproof. Case included.
Price: $297.95

BUSHNELL COMPACT TROPHY 50mm objective, 20x-50x zoom. Field of view at 1,000 yds. 92 ft. (20x), 52 ft. (50x). Length: 12.2"; weighs 17 oz. Black rubber armored, waterproof. Case included.
Price: $257.95

BUSHNELL COMPACT SENTRY 12-36 zoom, 50mm objective. Field of view at 1,000 yds. 140-46 ft. Length: 8.7", weighs 21.5 oz. Black rubber armored. Comes with hard-side and soft-side carry cases. Waterproof.
Price: $199.95

BUSHNELL SPACEMASTER 20x-45x zoom. Long eye relief. Rubber armored, prismatic. 60mm objective. Field of view at 1,000 yds. 90-58 ft. Minimum focus 20 ft. Length: 12.7"; weighs 43 oz.
Price: With tripod, carrying case and 20x-45x LER eyepiece $491.95

BUSHNELL SPACEMASTER COLLAPSIBLE 15-45x zoom, 50mm objective lens. Field of view at 1,000 yds., 113 ft. (15x), 52 ft. (45x). Length: 8". Weighs 22.8 oz. Comes with tripod, window mount and case.
Price: $209.95

BUSHNELL SPORTVIEW 15x-45x zoom, 50mm objective. Field of view at 1,000 yds. 103 ft. (15x), 35 ft. (45x). Length: 17.4"; weighs 34.4 oz.
Price: With tripod and carrying case $91.95

CELESTRON MINI 50MM ZOOM Offset 45° or straight body. Comes wtih 12x36x eyepiece. 50mm obj. Field of view at 1,000 yds. 160 (or 82), waterproof. Length: 8.5", weighs 1.4 lbs.
Price: .... NA

CELESTRON ULTIMA SERIES Offset 45° or straight body. 18x55, 20-60 zoom or 22-60 zoom. Aperture: 65mm, 80mm or 100mm, field of view at 1,000 yds., 89' at 18x, 38' at 55x, 105' at 20x, 95' at 22x, 53' at 66x. Length: 13", 16" or 19". Weighs 2.3 to 4.5 lbs.
Price: Body .... NA

HERMES 1 70mm objective, 16x, 25x, 40x. Field of view at 1,000 meters 160 ft. (16x), 75 ft. (40x). Length: 12.2"; weighs 33 oz. From CZ-USA.
Price: Body $359.00
Price: 25x eyepiece $86.00
Price: 40x eyepiece $128.00

KOWA TS-500 SERIES Offset 45° or straight body. Comes with 20-40x zoom eyepiece or 20x fixed eyepiece. 50mm obj. Field of view at 1,000 yds.: 171 ft. (20x fixed), 132-74 ft. (20-40x zoom). Length: 8.9-10.4", weighs 13.4-14.8 oz.
Price: TS-501 (offset 45° body w/20x fixed eyepiece) $258.00
Price: TS-502 (straight body w/20x fixed eyepiece) $231.00
Price: TS-501Z (offset 45° body w/20-40x zoom eyepiece) $321.00
Price: TS-502Z (straight body w/20-40x zoom eyepiece) $290.00

KOWA TS-660 SERIES Offset 45° or straight body. Fully waterproof. Available with ED lens.Sunshade and rotating tripod mount. 66mm obj. Field of view at 1,000 yds.: 177 ft. (20xW), 154 ft. (27xW), 131 ft. (30xW), 102 ft. (25x), 92 ft. (25xLER), 108-79 ft. (20-40x multi-coated zoom), 98-62 ft. (20-60x high grade zoom). Length: 12.3"; weighs 34.9-36.7 oz.
Price: TSN-662 body (straight) $610.00
Price: TSN-663 body (45 offset, ED lens) $1,070.00
Price: TSN-664 body (straight, ED lens) $1,010.00
Price: TSE-Z6 (20-40x multi-coatedzoom eyepiece) $378.00
Price: TSE-17HB (25x long eye relief eyepiece) $240.00
Price: TSE-14W (30x wide angle high-grade eyepiece) $288.00
Price: TSE-21WB (20x wide-angle eyepiece) $230.00
Price: TSE-15 WM (27x wide-angle eyepiece) $182.00
Price: TSE-16 PM (25x eyepiece) $108.00
Price: TSN-DA1 digital photo adapter $105.00
Price: DA1 adapter rings $43.00
Price: TSN-PA2 (800mm photo adapter) $269.00
Price: TSN-PA4 (1200mm photo adapter) $330.00
Price: Camera mounts (for use with photo adapter) $30.00
Price Eyepieces for TSN 77mm series, TSN-660 series, 661 body (45° offset) $660.00

KOWA TSN-660 SERIES Offset 45° or straight body. Fully waterproof. Available with fluorite lens. Sunshade and rotating tripod mount. 66mm obj., field of view at 1,000 yds: 177 ft. (20x), 154 ft. (27xW), 131 ft. (30xW), 102 ft. (25x), 92 ft. (25xLER), 62 ft. (40x), 108-79 ft. (20-40x Multi-Coated Zoom), 102-56 ft. (20-60x zoom), 98-62 ft. (20-60x High Grade Zoom). Length: 12.3"; weighs 34.9-36.7 oz. Note: Eyepieces for TSN 77mm Series, TSN-660 Series, and TSN610 Series are interchangeable.
Price: TSN-661 body (45° offset) $660.00
Price: TSN-662 body (straight) $610.00
Price: TSN-663 body (45° offset, fluorite lens) $1,070.00
Price: TSN-664 body (straight, fluorite lens) $1,010.00
Price: TSE-Z4 (20-60x high-grade zoom eyepiece) $378.00
Price: TSE-Z6 (20-40x multi-coated zoom eyepiece) $250.00
Price: TSE-17HB (25x long eye relief eyepiece) $240.00
Price: TSE-14W (30x wide angle eyepiece) $288.00
Price: TSE-21WB (20x wide angle eyepiece) $230.00
Price: TSE-15PM (27x wide angle eyepiece) $182.00
Price: TSE-10PM (40x eyepiece) $108.00
Price: TSE-16PM (25x eyepiece) $105.00
Price: TSN-DA1 (digital photo adapter) $105.00
Price: Adapter rings for DA1 .... $43.00
Price: TSN-PA2 (800mm photo adapter) $269.00
Price: TSN-PA4 (1200mm photo adapter) $330.00
Price: Camera mounts (for use with photo adapter) $30.00

KOWA TSN-820M SERIES Offset 45° or straight body. Fully waterproof. Available with fluorite lens. Sunshade and rotating tripod mount. 82mm obj., field of view at 1,000 yds: 75 ft. (27xLER, 50xW), 126 ft. (32xW), 115-58 ft. (20-60xZoom). Length: 15"; weighs 49.4-52.2 oz.
Price: TSN-821M body (45° offset) $850.00
Price: TSN-822M body (straight) $770.00
Price: TSN-823M body (45° offset, fluorite lens) $1,850.00
Price: TSN-824M body (straight, fluorite lens) $1,730.00
Price: TSE-Z7 (20-60x zoom eyepiece) $433.00
Price: TSE-9W (50x wide angle eyepiece) $345.00
Price: TSE-14WB (32x wide angle eyepiece) $366.00
Price: TSE-17HC (27x long eye relief eyepiece) $248.00
Price: TSN-DA1 (digital photo adapter) $105.00
Price: Adapter rings for DA1 .... $43.00
Price: TSN-PA2C (850mm photo adapter) $300.00
Price: Camera mounts (for use with photo adapter) $30.00

LEUPOLD 10-20x40mm COMPACT 40mm objective, 10-20x. Field of view at 100 yds. 19.9-13.6 ft.; eye relief 18.5mm (10x). Overall length: 7.5", weighs 15.8 oz. Rubber armored.
Price: $439.95

LEUPOLD 55-30x50 COMPACT 50mm objective, 15-30x. Field of view at 100 yds. 13.6 ft.; eye relief 17.5mm; Overall length: 11"; weighs 1.5 oz.
Price: $564.99

LEUPOLD Wind River Sequoia 15-30x60mm, 60mm objective, 15-30x. Field of view at 100 yds.: 13.1 ft.; eye relief: 16.5mm. Overall length: 13". Weighs 35.1 oz.
Price: $294.99

SPOTTING SCOPES

LEUPOLD Wind River Sequoia 15-45x60mm Angled. Armored, 15-45x. Field of view at 100 yds.: 13.1-6.3 ft.; eye relief: 16.5-13.0. Overall length: 12.5". Weighs 35.1 oz.
Price: **$309.99**

LEUPOLD Golden Ring 12-40x60mm; 12.7x38.1x. Field of view at 100 yds.: 16.8-5.2 ft.; eye relief: 30.0; Overall length: 12.4". Weighs 37.0 oz.
Price: **$1,124.99**

LEUPOLD Golden Ring 15-30x50mm Compact Armored; 15.2-30.4x; field of view at 100 yds.: 13.6-8.9 ft.; eye relief: 17.5-17.1; overall length: 11.0". Weighs 21.5 oz.
Price: **$564.99**

MIRADOR TTB SERIES Draw tube armored spotting scopes. Available with 75mm or 80mm objective. Zoom model (28x-62x, 80mm) is 11-7/8" (closed), weighs 50 oz. Field of view at 1,000 yds. 70-42 ft. Comes with lens covers.
Price: 28-62x80mm **$1,133.95**
Price: 32x80mm **$971.95**
Price: 26-58x75mm **$989.95**
Price: 30x75mm **$827.95**

MIRADOR SSD SPOTTING SCOPES 60mm objective, 15x, 20x, 22x, 25x, 40x, 60x, 20-60x; field of view at 1,000 yds. 37 ft.; length: 10 1/4"; weighs 33 oz.
Price: 25x **$575.95**
Price: 22x Wide Angle **$593.95**
Price: 20-60x Zoom **$746.95**
Price: As above, with tripod, case **$944.95**

MIRADOR SIA SPOTTING SCOPES Similar to the SSD scopes except with 45° eyepiece. Length: 12-1/4"; weighs 39 oz.
Price: 25x **$809.95**
Price: 22x Wide Angle **$827.95**
Price: 20-60x Zoom **$980.95**

MIRADOR SSR SPOTTING SCOPES 50mm or 60mm objective. Similar to SSD except rubber armored in black or camouflage. Length: 11-1/8"; weighs 31 oz.
Price: Black, 20x **$521.95**
Price: Black, 18x Wide Angle **$539.95**
Price: Black, 16-48x Zoom **$692.95**
Price: Black, 20x, 60mm, EER **$692.95**
Price: Black, 22x Wide Angle, 60mm **$701.95**
Price: Black, 20-60x Zoom **$854.95**

MIRADOR SSF FIELD SCOPES Fixed or variable power, choice of 50mm, 60mm, 75mm objective lens. Length: 9-3/4"; weighs 20 oz. (15-32x50).
Price: 20x50mm **$359.95**
Price: 25x60mm **$440.95**
Price: 30x75mm **$584.95**
Price: 15-32x50mm Zoom **$548.95**
Price: 18-40x60mm Zoom **$629.95**
Price: 22-47x75mm Zoom **$773.95**

MIRADOR SRA MULTI ANGLE SCOPES Similar to SSF Series except eyepiece head rotates for viewing from any angle.
Price: 20x50mm **$503.95**
Price: 25x60mm **$647.95**
Price: 30x75mm **$764.95**
Price: 15-32x50mm Zoom **$692.95**
Price: 18-40x60mm Zoom **$836.95**
Price: 22-47x75mm Zoom **$953.95**

MIRADOR SIB FIELD SCOPES Short-tube, 45° scopes with porro prism design. 50mm and 60mm objective. Length: 10 1/4"; weighs 18.5 oz. (15-32x50mm); field of view at 1,000 yds. 129-81 ft.
Price: 20x50mm **$386.95**
Price: 25x60mm **$449.95**
Price: 15-32x50mm Zoom **$575.95**
Price: 18-40x60mm Zoom **$638.95**

NIKON FIELDSCOPES 60mm and 78mm lens. Field of view at 1,000 yds. 105 ft. (60mm, 20x), 126 ft. (78mm, 25x). Length: 12.8" (straight 60mm), 12.6" (straight 78mm); weighs 34.5 to 47.5 oz. Eyepieces available separately.
Price: 60mm straight body **$499.99**
Price: 60mm angled body **$519.99**
Price: 60mm straight ED body **$779.99**
Price: 60mm angled ED body **$849.99**
Price: 78mm straight ED body **$899.99**
Price: 78mm angled ED body **$999.99**
Price: Eyepieces (15x to 60x) .... **$146.95 to $324.95**
Price: 20-45x eyepiece (25-56x for 78mm) **$320.55**

NIKON 60mm objective, 20x fixed power or 15-45x zoom. Field of view at 1,000 yds. 145 ft. (20x). Gray rubber armored. Straight or angled eyepiece. Weighs 44.2 oz., length: 12.1" (20x).
Price: 20x60 fixed (with eyepiece) **$290.95**
Price: 15-45x zoom (with case, tripod, eyepiece) **$578.95**

PENTAX PF-80ED 80mm objective lens available in 18x, 24x, 36x, 48x, 72x and 20-60x. Length: 15.6", weighs 11.9 to 19.2 oz.
Price: **$1,320.00**

SIGHTRON SII 2050X63 63mm objective lens, 20x-50x zoom. Field of view at 1,000 yds 91.9 ft. (20x), 52.5 ft. (50x). Length: 14"; weighs 30.8 oz. Black rubber finish. Also available with 80mm objective lens.
Price: 63mm or 80mm **$339.95**

SIMMONS 1280 50mm objective, 15-45x zoom. Black matte finish. Ocular focus. Peep finder sight. Waterproof. Field of view at 95-51 ft. 1,000 yds. Weights 33.5 oz., length: 12".
Price: With tripod **$189.99**

SIMMONS 1281 60mm objective, 20-60x zoom. Black matte finish. Ocular focus. Peep finder sight. Waterproof. Field of view at 78-43 ft. 1,000 yds. Weights 34.5 oz. Length: 12".
Price: With tripod **$209.99**

SIMMONS 77206 PROHUNTER 50mm objectives, 25x fixed power. Field of view at 1,000 yds. 113 ft.; length: 10.25"; weighs 33.25 oz. Black rubber armored.
Price: With tripod case **$160.60**

SIMMONS 41200 REDLINE 50mm objective, 15x-45x zoom. Field of view at 1,000 yds. 104-41 ft.; length: 16.75"; weighs 32.75 oz.
Price: With hard case and tripod **$74.99**
Price: 20-60x, 60mm objective **$99.99**

SWAROVSKI ATS-STS 65mm or 80mm objective, 20-60x zoom, or fixed 20x, 30x 45x eyepieces. Field of view at 1,000 yds. 180 ft. (20xSW), 126 ft. (30xSW), 84 ft. (45xSW), 108-60 ft. (20-60xS) for zoom. Length: 13.98" (ATS/STS 80), 12.8" (ATS/STS 65); weighs 45.93 oz. (ATS 80), 47.70 oz. (ATS 80HD), 45.23 oz. (STS 80), 46.9 oz. (STS 80 HD), 38.3 oz. (ATS 65), 39.9 oz. (ATS 65HD) 38.1 oz. (STS 65), 39.2 oz. (STS 65 HD).
Price: ATS 65 (angled eyepiece) **$1,154.44**
Price: STS 65 (straight eyepiece) **$1,154.44**
Price: ATS-80 .... **$1,410.00**
Price: ATS-80 (HD) **$1,898.89**
Price: 20xSW **$332.00**
Price: 30xSW **$332.00**
Price: 45xSW **$398.89**

SWIFT LYNX M836 15x-45x zoom, 60mm objective. Weighs 7 lbs., length: 14". Has 45° eyepiece, sunshade.
Price: **$315.00**

SWIFT NIGHTHAWK M849U 80mm objective, 20x-60x zoom, or fixed 19, 25x, 31x, 50x, 75x eyepieces. Has rubber armored body, 1.8x optical finder, retractable lens hood, 45° eyepiece. Field of view at 1,000 yds. 60 ft. (28x), 41 ft. (75x). Length: 13.4 oz.; weighs 39 oz.
Price: Body only **$870.00**
Price: 20-68x eyepiece **$370.00**
Price: Fixed eyepieces .... **$130.00 to $240.00**
Price: Model 849 (straight) body **$795.00**

SWIFT LYNX 60mm objective, 15-45x zoom, 45° inclined roof prism, magenta coated on all air-to-glass surfaces, rubber armored body, length: 14", weighs 30 oz. Equipped with sun shade, threaded dust covers and low level tripod.
Price: complete **$330.00**

SWIFT TELEMASTER M841 60mm objective. 15x to 60x variable power. Field of view at 1,000 yds. 160 feet (15x) to 40 feet (60x). Weighs 3.25 lbs.; length: 18" overall.
Price: **$399.50**

SWIFT PANTHER M844 15x-45x zoom or 22x WA, 15x, 20x, 40x. 60mm objective. Field of view at 1,000 yds. 141 ft. (15x), 68 ft. (40x), 95-58 ft. (20x-45x).
Price: Body only **$380.00**
Price: 15x-45x zoom eyepiece **$120.00**
Price: 20x-45x zoom (long eye relief) eyepiece **$140.00**
Price: 15x, 40x eyepiece **$65.00**
Price: 22x WA eyepiece **$80.00**

SWIFT M700T 12x-36x, 50mm objective. Field of view at 100 yds. 16 ft. (12x), 9 ft. (36x). Length: 14"; weighs 3.22 lbs. (with tripod).
Price: **$30.00**

TASCO 15-45x zoom, 50mm objective lens, 20x-60x zoom. Field of view at 100 yds. 19 ft. (15x) Length: 16". Weighs 19 oz. Matte black finish.
Price: **$67.95**

TASCO 20-60x zoom, 60mm objective, 12-36x zoom. Field of view at 100 yds. 12 ft. (20x). Length: 20". Weighs 50 oz. Black finish.
Price: **$95.95**

TASCO 18-36x zoom 50mm objective. Field of view at 100 yds. 12 ft. (18x). Length: 14.5". Weighs 31 oz. Camo or black rubber armor. Includes carrying case.
Price: **$131.95**

UNERTL "FORTY-FIVE" 54mm objective. 20x (single fixed power). Field of view at 100 yds. 10',10"; eye relief 1"; focusing range infinity to 33 ft. Weighs about 32 oz.; overall length: 15-3/4". With lens covers.
Price: With mono-layer magnesium coating **$810.00**

UNERTL STRAIGHT PRISMATIC 24x63. 63.5mm objective, 24x. Field of view at 100 yds., 7 ft. Relative brightness, 6.96. Eye relief 1/2". Weighs 40 oz.; length: closed 19". Push-pull and screw-focus eyepiece. 16x and 32x eyepieces **$125.00 each.**
Price: **$786.00**

UNERTL 20x STRAIGHT PRISMATIC 54mm objective, 20x. Field of view at 100 yds. 8.5 ft. Relative brightness 6.1. Eye relief 1/2". Weighs 36 oz.; length: closed 13-1/2". Complete with lens covers.
Price: **$695.00**

UNERTL TEAM SCOPE 100mm objective. 15x, 24x, 32x eyepieces. Field of view at 100 yds. 13 to 7.5 ft. Relative brightness, 39.06 to 9.79. Eye relief 2" to 1-1/2". Weighs 13 lbs.; length: 29-7/8" overall. Metal tripod, yoke and wood carrying case furnished (total weighs 80 lbs.).
Price: **$3,624.50**

WEAVER 20x50 50mm objective. Field of view 124 ft. at 100 yds. Eye relief .85"; weighs 21 oz.; overall length: 10". Waterproof, armored.
Price: **$249.99**

WEAVER 15-40x60 ZOOM 60mm objective. 15x-40x zoom. Field of view at 100 yds. 119 ft. (15x), 66 ft. (60x). Overall length: 12.5", weighs 26 oz. Waterproof, armored.
Price: **$399.99**

COMPENDIUM OF STATE LAWS GOVERNING FIREARMS

The following chart lists the main provisions of state firearms laws as of the date of publication. In addition to the state provisions, the purchase, sale, and, in certain circumstances, the possession and interstate transportation of firearms are regulated by the Federal Gun Control Act of 1968 as amended by the Firearms Owners' Protection Act of 1986. Also, cities and localities may have their own gun ordinances in addition to federal and state restrictions. Details may be obtained by contacting local law enforcement authorities or by consulting your state's firearms law digest compiled by the NRA Institute for Legislative Action.

STATE	GUN BAN	EXEMPTIONS TO NICS[2]	STATE WAITING PERIOD - NUMBER OF DAYS		LICENSE OR PERMIT TO PURCHASE or other prerequesite		REGISTRATION		RECORD OF SALE REPORTED TO STATE OR LOCAL GOVT.
			HANDGUNS	LONG GUNS	HANDGUNS	LONG GUNS	HANDGUNS	LONG GUNS	
Alabama	—	—	—	—	—	—	—	—	—
Alaska	—	RTC	—	—	—	—	—	—	—
Arizona	—	RTC	—	—	—	—	—	—	—
Arkansas	—	RTC[3]	—	—	—	—	—	—	—
California	X[20]	—	10[14]	10[14,15]	8, 23	—	X	24	X
Colorado	—	—	—	—	—	—	—	—	—
Connecticut	X[20]	—	14[14,15]	14[14,15]	X[16, 23]	—	—	24	X
Delaware	—	—	—	—	—	—	—	—	—
Florida	—	GRTC	3[14,15]	—	—	—	—	—	—
Georgia	—	RTC	—	—	—	—	—	—	—
Hawaii	X[20]	L, RTC	—	—	X[16, 23]	X[16]	X[12]	X[12]	X
Idaho	—	RTC	—	—	—	—	—	—	—
Illinois	20	—	3	2	X[16]	X[16]	4	4	X
Indiana	—	RTC, O[3]	—	—	—	—	—	—	X
Iowa	—	L, RTC	—	—	X[16]	—	—	—	—
Kansas	—	—	1	—	1	—	1	—	1
Kentucky	—	RTC[3]	—	—	—	—	—	—	—
Louisiana	—	GRTC	—	—	—	—	—	—	—
Maine	—	—	—	—	—	—	—	—	—
Maryland	X[20]	O[3]	7[14]	7[9,14]	8, 23	—	—	—	X
Massachusetts	X[20]	GRTC	—	—	X[16]	X[16]	—	—	X
Michigan	—	O[3]	—	—	X[16, 23]	—	X	—	X
Minnesota	—	—	7[16]	16	X[16]	X[16]	—	—	—
Mississippi	—	RTC[3]	—	—	—	—	—	—	—
Missouri	—	—	—	—	X[16]	—	—	—	X
Montana	—	RTC	—	—	—	—	—	—	—
Nebraska	—	L	—	—	X	—	—	—	—
Nevada	—	RTC	1	—	—	—	1	—	—
New Hampshire	—	—	—	—	—	—	—	—	—
New Jersey	X[20]	—	—	—	X[16]	X[16]	—	24	X
New Mexico	—	—	—	—	—	—	—	—	—
New York	X[20]	L, RTC	—	—	X[16, 23]	16	X	7	X
North Carolina	—	L, RTC	—	—	X[16]	—	—	—	X
North Dakota	—	RTC	—	—	—	—	—	—	—
Ohio	20	—	1	—	16	—	1	—	1
Oklahoma	—	—	—	—	—	—	—	—	—
Oregon	—	GRTC	—	—	—	—	—	—	X
Pennsylvania	—	—	—	—	—	—	—	—	X
Rhode Island	—	—	7	7	23	—	—	—	X
South Carolina	—	RTC	8	—	8	—	—	—	X
South Dakota	—	GRTC	2	—	—	—	—	—	X
Tennessee	—	—	—	—	—	—	—	—	—
Texas	—	RTC[3]	—	—	—	—	—	—	—
Utah	—	RTC	—	—	—	—	—	—	—
Vermont	—	—	—	—	—	—	—	—	—
Virginia	X[20]	—	1,8	—	1,8	—	—	—	1
Washington	—	O[3]	5[10]	—	—	—	—	—	X
West Virginia	—	—	—	—	—	—	—	—	—
Wisconsin	—	—	2	—	—	—	—	—	—
Wyoming	—	RTC	—	—	—	—	—	—	—
District of Columbia	X[20]	L	—	—	X[16]	X[16]	X[16]	X	X

COMPENDIUM OF STATE LAWS GOVERNING FIREARMS

Since state laws are subject to frequent change, this chart is not to be considered legal advice or a restatement of the law.

All fifty states have sportsmen's protections laws to halt harrassment.

STATE	STATE PROVISION FOR RIGHT-TO-CARRY CONCEALED	CARRYING OPENLY PROHIBITED	OWNER ID CARDS OR LICENSING	FIREARM RIGHTS CONSTITU-TIONAL PROVISION	STATE FIREARMS PREEMPTION LAWS	RANGE PROTECTION LAW
Alabama	R	X_{11}	—	X	X	X
Alaska	R_{19}	—	—	X	—	X
Arizona	R	—	—	X	X	X
Arkansas	R	X_{5}	—	X	X	X
California	L	X_{6}	—	—	X	X
Colorado	R	25	—	X	X_{25}	X
Connecticut	R	X	—	X	X_{17}	X
Delaware	L	—	—	X	X	—
Florida	R	X	—	X	X	X
Georgia	R	X	—	X	X	X
Hawaii	L	X	X	X	—	—
Idaho	R	—	—	X	X	X
Illinois	D	X	X	X	—	X
Indiana	R	X	—	X	X_{18}	X
Iowa	L	X	—	—	X	X
Kansas	D	1	—	X	—	X
Kentucky	R	—	—	X	X	X
Louisiana	R	—	—	X	X	X
Maine	R	—	—	X	X	X
Maryland	L	X	—	—	X	X
Massachusetts	L	X	X	X	X_{17}	X
Michigan	R	X_{11}	—	X	X	X
Minnesota	R	X	—	—	X	—
Mississippi	R	—	—	X	X	X
Missouri	R	—	—	X	X	X
Montana	R	—	—	X	X	X
Nebraska	D	—	—	X	—	—
Nevada	R	—	—	X	X	X
New Hampshire	R	—	—	X	X	X
New Jersey	L	X	X	—	X_{17}	X
New Mexico	R	—	—	X	X	X
New York	L	X	X	—	X_{22}	X
North Carolina	R	—	—	X	X	X
North Dakota	R	X_{6}	—	X	X	X
Ohio	D	1	16	X	—	X
Oklahoma	R	X_{6}	—	X	X	X
Oregon	R	—	—	X	X	X
Pennsylvania	R	X_{11}	—	X	X	X
Rhode Island	L	X	—	X	X	X
South Carolina	R	X	—	X	X	X
South Dakota	R	—	—	X	X	X
Tennessee	R	X_{5}	—	X	X	X
Texas	R	X	—	X	X	X
Utah	R	X_{6}	—	X	X	X
Vermont	R_{19}	X_{5}	—	X	X	X
Virginia	R	—	—	X	X	X
Washington	R	X_{21}	—	X	X	—
West Virginia	R	—	—	X	X	X
Wisconsin	D	—	—	X	X	X
Wyoming	R	—	—	X	X	X
District of Columbia	D	X	X	NA	—	—

COMPENDIUM OF STATE LAWS GOVERNING FIREARMS

With over 20,000 "gun control" laws on the books in America, there are two challenges facing every gun owner. First, you owe it to yourself to become familiar with the federal laws on gun ownership. Only by knowing the laws can you avoid innocently breaking one.

Second, while federal legislation receives much more media attention, state legislatures and city councils make many more decisions regarding your right to own and carry firearms. NRA members and all gun owners must take extra care to be aware of anti-gun laws and ordinances at the state and local levels.

Notes:

1. In certain cities or counties.

2. **National Instant Check System (NICS) exemption codes:**
RTC-Carry Permit Holders Exempt From NICS
GRTC-Holders of RTC Permits issued before November 30, 1998 exempt from NICS. Holders of more recent permits are not exempt.
L-Holders of state licenses to possess or purchase or firearms ID cards exempt from NICS.
O-Other, See Note 3.

3. **NICS exemption notes**: **Arkansas**: RTC permits issued prior to 11/30/98 and those issued on and after 4/1/99 qualify. Those issued between 11/1/98 and 3/31/99 do not qualify. **Indiana**: Personal protection, hunting and target permits all qualify for exemptions. **Kentucky**: RTC permits issued after July 15, 1998 and prior to November 30, 1998 are exempt. **Maryland:** There are no exemptions for handgun purchases. For long gun purchases, those holding RTC permits issued before November 30, 1998 are exempt. **Michigan:** No exemptions for handguns, license for long guns. **Mississippi**: Permits issued to security guards do not qualify. **Texas**: Texas Peace Officer License, TCLEOSE Card, is valid only if issued prior to November 30, 1998. **Washington**: RTC permits issued after July 1, 1996 and prior to November 30, 1998 are exempt.

4. Chicago only. No handgun not already registered may be possessed.

5. **Arkansas** prohibits carrying a firearm "with a purpose to employ it as a weapon against a person." **Tennessee** prohibits carrying "with the intent to go armed." **Vermont** prohibits carrying a firearm "with the intent or purpose of injuring another."

6. Loaded.

7. New York City only.

8. A permit is required to acquire another handgun before 30 days have elapsed following the acquisition of a handgun.

9. **Maryland** subjects purchases of "assault weapons" to a 7-day waiting period.

10. May be extended by police to 30 days in some circumstances. An individual not holding a driver's license must wait 90 days.

11. Carrying a handgun openly in a motor vehicle requires a license.

12. Every person arriving in **Hawaii** is required to register any firearm(s) brought into the State within 3 days of arrival of the person or firearm(s), whichever occurs later. Handguns purchased from licensed dealers must be registered within 5 days.

13. Concealed carry laws vary significantly between the states. Ratings reflect the real effect a state's particular laws have on the ability of citizens to carry firearms for self-defense.

14. Purchases from dealers only. **Maryland**: 7 business days. Purchasers of regulated firearms must undergo background checks performed by the State Police, either through a dealer or directly through the State Police.

15. The waiting period does not apply to a person holding a valid permit or license to carry a firearm. In **Connecticut**, a hunting license also exempts the holder for long gun purchasers. **California**: transfers of a long gun to a person's parent, child or grandparent are exempt from the waiting period.

16. **Connecticut:** A certificate of eligibility or a carry permit is required to obtain a handgun and a carry permit is required to transport a handgun outside your home. **District of Columbia:** No handgun may be possessed unless it was registered prior to Sept. 23, 1976 and re-registered by Feb. 5, 1977. A permit to purchase is required for a rifle or shotgun. **Hawaii:** Purchase permits, required for all firearms, may not be issued until 14 days after application. A handgun purchase permit is valid for 10 days, for one handgun; a long gun permit is valid for one year, for multiple long guns. **Illinois:** A Firearm Owner's Identification Card (FOI) is required to possess or purchase a firearm, must be issued to qualified applicants within 30 days, and is valid for 5 years. **Iowa:** A purchase permit is required for handguns, and is valid for one year, beginning three days after issuance. **Massachusetts:** Firearms and feeding devices for firearms are divided into classes. Depending on the class, a firearm identification card (FID) or class A license or class B license is required to possess, purchase, or carry a firearm, ammunition thereof, or firearm feeding device, or "large capacity feeding device." **Michigan:** A handgun purchaser must obtain a license to purchase from local law enforcement, and within 10 days present the license and handgun to obtain a certificate of inspection. **Minnesota:** A handgun transfer or carrying permit, or a 7-day waiting period and handgun transfer report, is required to purchase handguns or "assault weapons" from a dealer. A permit or transfer report must be issued to qualified applicants within 7 days. A permit is valid for one year, a transfer report for 30 days. **Missouri:** A purchase permit is required for a handgun, must be issued to qualified applicants within 7 days, and is valid for 30 days. **New Jersey:** Firearm owners must possess a FID, which must be issued to qualified applicants within 30 days. To purchase a handgun, a purchase permit, which must be issued within 30 days to qualified applicants and is valid for 90 days, is required. An FID is required to purchase long guns. **New York:** Purchase, possession and/or carrying of a handgun require a single license, which includes any restrictions made upon the bearer. New York City also requires a license for long guns. **North Carolina:** To purchase a handgun, a license or permit is required, which must be issued to qualified applicants within 30 days. **Ohio:** Some cities require a permit-to-purchase or firearm owner ID card.

17. Preemption through judicial ruling. Local regulation may be instituted in **Massachusetts** if ratified by the legislature.

18. Except Gary and East Chicago and local laws enacted before January, 1994.

19. **Vermont and Alaska** law respect your right to carry without a permit. Alaska also has a permit to carry system to establish reciprocity with other states.

20. "Assault weapons" are prohibited in **California, Connecticut, New Jersey** and **New York**. Some local jurisdictions in **Ohio** also ban "assault weapons." **Hawaii** prohibits "assault pistols." **California** bans "unsafe handguns." **Illinois:** Chicago, Evanston, Oak Park, Morton Grove, Winnetka, Wilmette, and Highland Park prohibit handguns; some cities prohibit other kinds of firearms. **Maryland** prohibits "assault pistols" and the sale or manufacture of any handgun manufactured after Jan. 1, 1985, that appears on the Handgun Roster. **Massachusetts:** It is unlawful to sell, transfer or possess "any assault weapon or large capacity feeding device" [more than 10 rounds] that was not legally possessed on September 13, 1994. **Ohio:** some cities prohibit handguns of certain magazine capacities." **Virginia** prohibits "Street Sweeper" shotguns. The **District of Columbia** prohibits new acquisition of handguns and any semi-automatic firearm capable of using a detachable ammunition magazine of more than 12 rounds capacity. (With respect to some of these laws and ordinances, individuals may retain prohibited firearms owned previously, with certain restrictions.)

21. Local jurisdictions may opt out of prohibition.

22. Preemption only applies to handguns.

23. Requires proof of safety training for purchase. **California**: Must have Handgun Safety Certificate receipt which is valid for five years. **Connecticut:** To receive certificate of eligibility, must complete a handgun safety course approved by the Commissioner of Public Safety. **Hawaii:** Must have completed an approved handgun safety course. **Maryland:** Must complete an approved handgun safety course. **Michigan**: A person must correctly answer 70% of the questions on a basic safety review questionnaire in order to obtain a license to purchase. **New York:** Some counties require a handgun safety training course to receive a license. **Rhode Island**: Must receive a state-issued handgun safety card.

24. "Assault weapon" registration. **California** had two dates by which assault weapons had to be registered or possession after such date would be considered a felony: March 31, 1992 for the named make and model firearms banned in the 1989 legislation and December 31, 2000 for the firearms meeting the definition of the "assault weapons in the 1999 legislation. In **Connecticut**, those firearms banned by specific make and model in the 1993 law had to be registered by October 1, 1994 or possession would be considered a felony. A recent law requires registration of additional guns by October 1, 2003. In **New Jersey**, any "assault weapon" not registered, licensed, or rendered inoperable pursuant to a state police certificate by May 1, 1991, is considered contraband.

25. Local governments cannot enact ordinances that prohibit the sale, purchase, or possession of a firearm. Municipalities cannot restrict a person's ability to travel into, through, or within their jurisdiction for hunting or personal protection. Local governments, including law enforcement agencies, cannot maintain a database of guns or gun owners. Municipalities may prohibit open carry in government buildings if such prohibition is clearly posted.

Concealed carry codes:

R: Right-to-Carry "Shall issue" or less restrictive discretionary permit system (Ala., Conn.) (See also note #21.)
L: Right-to-Carry Limited by local authority's discretion over permit issuance.
D: Right-to-Carry Denied, no permit system exists; concealed carry is prohibited.

NL 00930

Rev. 9/2003 10m

Guide to Right-to-Carry Reciprocity and Recognition

- **The right to self-defense neither begins nor ends at a state border.**
- **A law-abiding citizen does not suffer a character change by crossing a state line.**
- **An "unalienable right" is not determined by geographical boundaries.**
- **A patchwork of state laws regarding the carrying of firearms can make criminals out of honest folks, especially those who frequently must travel the states to earn a living.**
- **Using data for all 3,054 U.S. counties from 1977 to 1994, University of Chicago Prof. John Lott finds that for each additional year a concealed handgun law is in effect the murder rate declines by 3%, robberies by over 2%, and the rape rate by 2%.**

In spite of the truth of these statements and the fact that nearly half of all Americans live in states that allow a law-abiding citizen to carry a firearm concealed for personal protection, it has not been commonplace that these same citizens could carry their firearm across states lines. NRA-ILA is working to pass right-to-carry reciprocity laws granting permit holders the ability to carry their firearms legally while visiting or traveling beyond their home state.

In order to assist NRA Members in determining which states recognize their permits, NRA-ILA has created this guide. This guide is not to be considered as legal advice or a restatement of the law. It is important to remember that state carry laws vary considerably. Be sure to check with state and local authorities outside your home state for a complete listing of restrictions on carrying concealed in that state. Many states restrict carrying in bars, restaurants (where alcohol is served), establishments where packaged alcohol is sold, schools, colleges, universities, churches, parks, sporting events, correctional facilities, courthouses, federal and state government offices/buildings, banks, airport terminals, police stations, polling places, any posted private property restricting the carrying of concealed firearms, etc. In addition to state restrictions, federal law prohibits carrying on military bases, in national parks and the sterile area of airports. National Forests usually follow laws of the state wherein the forest is located.

NOTE: Alaska and Vermont allow the concealed carry of firearms without a permit. Vermont residents traveling to other states must first obtain a non-resident permit from that state—if available—prior to carrying concealed. Alaska still issues permits to those who want them, allowing them to benefit by recognition and reciprocity laws.

NOTE TO READERS: Right To Carry reciprocity and recognition between the various states is subject to frequent change through legislative action and regulatory interpretation. This information is the best available at the time of publication. This summary is not intended as legal advice or restatement of law.

Rev. 3/2004

Alabama

Right-To-Carry Law Type: Reasonable May Issue

Issuing Authority:	County Sheriff
Contact agency for out of state permits:	Permits not granted.
These states recognize your permit:	Alaska, Colorado, Florida, Georgia, Idaho, Indiana, Kentucky, Michigan, Mississippi, Missouri, New Hampshire, North Carolina, North Dakota, Oklahoma, Utah, Tennessee, Vermont, Wyoming
This state recognizes permits from the following states:	Alaska, Colorado, Florida, Georgia, Idaho, Indiana, Kentucky, Michigan, Mississippi, New Hampshire, North Carolina, North Dakota, Oklahoma, Utah, Tennessee, Wyoming
Cost & Term of Permit:	$10 — 1 year
Key Government Offices:	Alabama Dept. of Public Safety 500 Dexter Ave. Montgomery, Alabama 36130 Phone: (334)242-4392 Email: info@dps.state.al.us Attorney General Alabama State House 11 South Union Street, 3rd Floor Montgomery, Alabama 36130 Phone: 334-242-7300 http://www.dps.state.al.us

Alaska

Right-To-Carry Law Type: Shall Issue

Issuing Authority:	State Trooper
Contact agency for out of state permits:	Permits not granted.
These states recognize your permit:	Alabama, Arizona, Colorado, Delaware, Florida, Idaho, Indiana, Kentucky, Michigan, Missouri, Montana, New Hampshire, North Carolina, North Dakota, Oklahoma, South Dakota, Utah, Vermont, Virginia, Wyoming
This state recognizes permits from the following states:	No permit required to carry concealed in Alaska.
Cost & Term of Permit:	$99 — 5 years
Key Government Offices:	Alaska Concealed Handgun Permit Program 5700 East Tudor Road Anchorage, Alaska 99507 Phone: (907) 269-0392 http://www.dps.state.ak.us/ast/achp/

Arizona

Right-To-Carry Law Type: Shall Issue

Issuing Authority:	Arizona Department of Public Safety
Contact agency for out of state permits:	Arizona Department of Public Safety
These states recognize your permit:	Alaska, Arkansas, Colorado, Delaware, Florida, Idaho, Indiana, Kentucky, Michigan, Missouri, Montana, North Carolina, North Dakota, Oklahoma, Tennessee, Texas, Utah, Vermont, Virginia
This state recognizes permits from the following states:	Alaska, Arkansas, California, Colorado ,Connecticut, Deleware, Florida, Iowa, Kentucky, Louisiana, Maryland, Massachusetts, Michigan, Minnesota, Missouri, Montana, Nevada, New Mexico, North Carolina, North Dakota, Oklahoma, Oregon, South Carolina, Tennessee, Texas, Utah, West Virginia, Wyoming
Cost & Term of Permit:	$50 — 4 years
Key Government Offices:	Arizona Department of Public Safety Attn: Concealed Weapons Permit Unit P.O. Box 6488 Phoenix, Arizona 85005 Phone: (602) 256-6280 and (800) 256-6280 Fax: (602) 223-2928 Email: ccw@dps.state.az.us Arizona Attorney General 1275 W. Washington Street Phoenix, Arizona 85007 Phone: (602) 542-4266 and (888) 377-6108 http://www.dps.state.az.us/ccw/default.asp

Connecticut

Right-To-Carry Law Type: Reasonable May Issue

Issuing Authority:	Department of Public Safety, Special Licenses & Firearms Unit	
Contact agency for out of state permits:	Department of Public Safety, Special Licenses & Firearms Unit	
These states recognize your permit:	Alaska, Arizona, Idaho, Indiana, Kentucky, Michigan, Missouri, Montana, Oklahoma, Tennessee, Utah, Vermont	
This state recognizes permits from the following states:	none	
Cost & Term of Permit:	$35.00 plus $24.00 fingerprint processing fee	5 years
Key Government Offices:	Department of Public Safety 1111 Country Club Road Middletown, Connecticut 06450-9294 Phone: (860) 685-8000 Fax: (860) 685-8354 Email: DPS.Feedback@po.state.ct.us	Attorney General 55 Elm Street Hartford, Connecticut 06106 Phone: 860-808-5318 Fax: 860 808-5387 Email: Attorney.General@po.state.ct.us
	http://www.state.ct.us/dps/slfu/index.html	

Delaware

Right-To-Carry Law Type: Restrictive May Issue

Issuing Authority:	Prothonotary of Superior Court	
Contact agency for out of state permits:	Permits not granted.	
These states recognize your permit:	Alaska, Arizona, Florida, Idaho, Indiana, Kentucky, Michigan, Missouri, Montana, North Carolina, Oklahoma, Tennessee, Utah, Vermont	
This state recognizes permits from the following states:	Alaska, Arizona, Colorado, Florida, Michigan, North Carolina, North Dakota, Oklahoma, Tennessee, Utah	
Cost & Term of Permit:	$34.50 plus other fees	Initially 2 years, renewal for 3 years.
Key Government Offices:	Delaware State Police P.O. Box 430 Dover, Delaware 9903-0430 Phone: (302) 739-5900	Attorney General Carvel State Office Building 820 N. French Street Wilmington, Delaware 19801 Email: Attorney.General@State.DE.US
	http://www.state.de.us/dsp/	

Florida

Right-To-Carry Law Type: Shall Issue

Issuing Authority:	Department of Agriculture and Consumer Services, Division of Licensing	
Contact agency for out of state permits:	Department of Agriculture and Consumer Services, Division of Licensing	
These states recognize your permit:	Alabama, Alaska, Arizona, Arkansas, Colorado, Delaware, Georgia, Idaho, Indiana, Kentucky, Louisiana, Michigan, Mississippi, Missouri, Montana, New Hampshire, North Carolina, North Dakota, Oklahoma, Pennsylvania, South Dakota, Tennessee, Texas, Utah, Vermont, Wyoming	
This state recognizes permits from the following states:	Alabama, Alaska, Arizona, Arkansas, Colorado, Delaware, Georgia, Idaho, Indiana, Kentucky, Louisiana, Michigan, Mississippi, Montana, New Hampshire, North Carolina, North Dakota*, Oklahoma, Pennsylvania, South Dakota*, Tennessee, Texas, Utah, Wyoming *must be 21	
Cost & Term of Permit:	Residents: $75 plus fingerprinting fee, Renewal: $65	5 years
Key Government Offices:	Florida Dept. of Agriculture and Consumer Services, Division of Licensing P.O. Box 6687 Tallahassee, Florida 32314-6687 Phone: (850) 488-5381 email: springb@doacs.state.fl.us	Office of Attorney General State of Florida The Capital Tallahasse, Florida 32399-1050 Phone: 850-414-3300 Fax: 850-410-1630 email: ag@oag.state.fl.us
	http://licgweb.doacs.state.fl.us/	

Right-to-Carry Reciprocity and Recognition, cont.

Arkansas

Right-To-Carry Law Type: Shall Issue

Issuing Authority:	State Police	
Contact agency for out of state permits:	Permits not granted.	
These states recognize your permit:	Alaska, Arizona, Florida, Idaho, Indiana, Kentucky, Michigan, Missouri, Montana, North Carolina, Oklahoma, South Carolina, South Dakota, Tennessee, Texas, Utah, Vermont	
This state recognizes permits from the following states:	Arizona, Florida, Kentucky, North Carolina, Oklahoma, South Carolina, Tennessee, Texas, Utah	
Cost & Term of Permit:	$115	4 Years
Key Government Offices:	Regulatory Services Division Attn: Arkansas State Police #1 State Police Plaza Drive Little Rock, Arkansas 72209-2971 Phone: 501-618-8627 Fax: 501-618-8647	Office of the Attorney General 200 Catlett-Prien Tower 323 Center Street Little Rock, Arkansas 72201 Phone: 501-682-1323 (1-800-448-3014) Email: oag@ag.state.ar.us
	www.state.ar.us/chl/chl.html	

California

Right-To-Carry Law Type: Restrictive May Issue

Issuing Authority:	County Sheriff	
Contact agency for out of state permits:	Permits not granted.	
These states recognize your permit:	Alaska, Arizona, Idaho, Indiana, Kentucky, Michigan, Missouri, Montana, Oklahoma, Tennessee, Utah, Vermont	
This state recognizes permits from the following states:	none	
Cost & Term of Permit:	varies	2 years maximum
Key Government Offices:	California Attorney General Attn: Department of Justice P.O. Box 944255 Sacramento, California 94244-2550 Phone: (916) 445-9555	
	http://caag.state.ca.us/	

Colorado

Right-To-Carry Law Type: Shall Issue

Issuing Authority:	County Sheriff	
Contact agency for out of state permits:	Permits not granted.	
These states recognize your permit:	Alabama, Alaska, Arizona, Florida, Georgia, Idaho, Indiana, Kentucky, Michigan, Missouri, Montana, New Hampshire, North Carolina, Oklahoma, South Dakota, Tennessee, Utah, Vermont, Wyoming	
This state recognizes permits from the following states:	Alabama, Alaska, Arizona, Florida, Georgia, Idaho, Iowa, Indiana, Kentucky, Michigan, Montana, New Hampshire, North Carolina, Oklahoma, South Dakota, Tennessee, Utah, Wyoming	
Cost & Term of Permit:	No more than $100	5 years
Key Government Offices:	Attorney General 1525 Sherman 5th Floor Denver, Colorado 80203 Phone: (303) 866-4500 Fax: (303) 866-5691 Email: attorney.general@state.co.us	Colorado Bureau of Investigation 690 Kipling St. Suite 3000 Denver, Colorado 80215 Phone: (303) 239-5850 Email: james.spoden@cdps.state.co.us
	http://cbi.state.co.us/ccw/reciprocity.asp	

Georgia

Right-To-Carry Law Type: Shall Issue

Issuing Authority:	County Probate Judge	
Contact agency for out of state permits:	Permits not granted.	
These states recognize your permit:	Alabama, Alaska, Arizona, Colorado, Florida, Idaho, Indiana, Kentucky, Michigan, Missouri, Montana, New Hampshire, North Caolina, Oklahoma, Pennsylvania, South Dakota, Tennessee, Utah, Vermont, Wyoming	
This state recognizes permits from the following states:	Alabama, Colorado, Florida, Idaho, Indiana, Kentucky, Michigan, Montana, New Hampshire, North Carolina, Pennsylvania, South Dakota, Tennessee, Wyoming	
Cost & Term of Permit:	$24 to GBI and additional fee set by County.	5 years
Key Government Offices:	Georgia Bureau of Investigation P.O. Box 370748 Decatur, Georgia 30037-0748 Phone: (404) 244-2501	Georgia Attorney General 40 Capitol Square, SW Atlanta, Georgia 30334-1300 Phone: 404-656-3300
	http://www.ganet.org/ago/	

Hawaii

Right-To-Carry Law Type: Restrictive May Issue

Issuing Authority:	Chief of Police	
Contact agency for out of state permits:	Permits not granted.	
These states recognize your permit:	Alaska, Idaho, Indiana, Kentucky, Michigan, Missouri, Montana, Oklahoma, Tennessee, Utah, Vermont	
This state recognizes permits from the following states:	none	
Cost & Term of Permit:	varies	varies
Key Government Offices:	Honolulu Police Department Attn: Firearms Division 801 S. Beretania Honolulu, Hawaii Phone: 808-529-3371, Fax: 808-529-3525 hpd@honolulupd.org http://www.honolulupd.org/service/gunlaw/htm	Attorney General Department of the Attorney General 425 Queen Street Honolulu, Hawaii 96813
	http://www.hawaii.gov/ag/index.html	

Idaho

Right-To-Carry Law Type: Shall Issue

Issuing Authority:	County Sheriff	
Contact agency for out of state permits:	Any Sheriffs' Department	
These states recognize your permit:	Alabama, Alaska, Colorado, Florida, Georgia, Indiana, Kentucky, Michigan, Missouri, Montana, New Hampshire, North Carolina, North Dakota, Oklahoma, Tennessee, Utah, Vermont, Virginia, Wyoming	
This state recognizes permits from the following states:	All state permits	
Cost & Term of Permit:	$20 plus fingerprinting fee	4 years
Key Government Offices:	Idaho Department of Law Enforcement 700 S. Stratford Dr P.O. Box 700 Meridian, Idaho 83680-0700 Phone: (208)884-7000	Idaho Attorney General 700 W. Jefferson Street P.O. Box 83720 Boise, Idaho 83720-0010 Phone: (208) 334-2400 Fax: (208) 334-2530
	http://www.state.id.us/dle/dle.htm	

Right-to-Carry Reciprocity and Recognition, cont.

Illinois

Right-To-Carry Law Type: Non-Issue

Issuing Authority:	Permits Not Available	
Contact agency for out of state permits:	Permits not granted.	
These states recognize your permit:	none	
This state recognizes permits from the following states:	none	
Cost & Term of Permit:	n/a	n/a
Key Government Offices:	Illinois State Police P.O. Box 19461 Springfield, Illinois 62794-9461 Phone: 217-782-7263 Fax: 217-785-2821	Attorney General 500 South Second St. Springfield, Illinois 62706 Phone: (217) 782-1090 Email: attorney_general@state.il.us
	http://www.state.il.us/isp/isphpage.htm	

Indiana

Right-To-Carry Law Type: Shall Issue

Issuing Authority:	State Police through Chief Law Enforcement Officer of Municipality	
Contact agency for out of state permits:	Permits not granted.	
These states recognize your permit:	Alabama, Alaska, Colorado, Florida, Georgia, Idaho, Kentucky, Michigan, Missouri, Montana, New Hampshire, North Carolina, North Dakota, Oklahoma, South Dakota, Tennessee, Utah, Vermont, Wyoming	
This state recognizes permits from the following states:	All state permits recognized for non-Indiana residents.	
Cost & Term of Permit:	$30	4 years
Key Government Offices:	State Police 100 North Senate Avenue Indiana Government Center North, 3rd Floor Indianapolis, Indiana 46204-2259 Phone: (317) 232-8200	Indiana Attorney General State House, Room 219 Indianapolis, Indiana 46204 Phone: (317) 232 - 6201
	http://www.state.in.us/isp/	

Iowa

Right-To-Carry Law Type: Reasonable May Issue

Issuing Authority:	Sheriff for residents, Commissioner of Public Safety for non residents	
Contact agency for out of state permits:	Commissioner of Public Safety	
These states recognize your permit:	Alaska, Arizona, Idaho, Indiana, Kentucky, Michigan, Missouri, Montana, Oklahoma, Tennessee, Utah, Vermont	
This state recognizes permits from the following states:	none	
Cost & Term of Permit:	$10 for permit	1 year
Key Government Offices:	Iowa Department of Public Safety Wallace State Office Building Des Moines, Iowa 50319 Phone: (515) 281-3211 Email: webteam@dps.state.ia.us	Attorney General 1305 E. Walnut Street Des Moines, Iowa 50319 Phone: 515-281-5164 Fax: 515-281-4209 Email: webteam@ag.state.ia.us
	http://www.state.ia.us/government/dps/index.html	

Right-to-Carry Reciprocity and Recognition, cont.

Kansas

Right-To-Carry Law Type: Non-Issue

Issuing Authority:	Permits Not Available	
Contact agency for out of state permits:	Permits Not Granted.	
These states recognize your permit:	none	
This state recognizes permits from the following states:	none	
Cost & Term of Permit:	n/a	n/a
Key Government Offices:	Attorney General 301 S.W. 10th Avenue Topeka, Kansas 66612-1597 Phone: (785) 296-2215 Fax: (785) 296-6296 Email: GENERAL@at01po.wpo.state.ks.us	Highway Patrol General Headquarters 122 SW 7th Street Topeka, Kansas 66603-3847 Phone: 785-296-6800 Fax: 785-296-3049
	http://www.ink.org/public/ksag/	

Kentucky

Right-To-Carry Law Type: Shall Issue

Issuing Authority:	State Police	
Contact agency for out of state permits:	Permits not granted.	
These states recognize your permit:	Alabama, Alaska, Arizona, Arkansas, Colorado, Florida, Georgia, Idaho, Indiana, Louisiana, Michigan, Mississippi, Missouri, Montana, New Hampshire, North Carolina, North Dakota, Oklahoma, South Dakota, Pennsylvania, Tennessee, Texas, Utah, West Virginia, Vermont, Wyoming	
This state recognizes permits from the following states:	All state permits recognized.	
Cost & Term of Permit:	$60	5 years
Key Government Offices:	Kentucky State Police 919 Versailles Road Frankfort, Kentucky 40601 Phone: (502) 227-8725	Office of the Kentucky Attorney General Frankfort, Kentucky 40601 Phone: (502) 696-5300
	http://www.kentuckystatepolice.org/conceal.htm#recip	

Louisiana

Right-To-Carry Law Type: Shall Issue

Issuing Authority:	Department of Public Safety & Corrections	
Contact agency for out of state permits:	Permits not granted.	
These states recognize your permit:	Alaska, Arizona, Florida, Idaho, Indiana, Kentucky, Michigan, Minnesota, Missouri, Montana, Oklahoma, Tennessee, Texas, Utah, Vermont, Virginia, Wyoming	
This state recognizes permits from the following states:	Florida, Kentucky, Tennessee, Texas, Wyoming	
Cost & Term of Permit:	$50 for 2 year permit, $100 for 4 year permit.	2 years or 4 years
Key Government Offices:	Louisiana State Police/Department of Public Safety P.O. Box 66614 Baton Rouge, Louisiana 70896-6614 Phone: 225-925-4239 Fax: 225-925-3717 Email: concealed-handguns@dps.state.la.us	Louisiana Attorney General State Capitol, 22nd Floor P.O. Bos 940005 Baton Rouge, Louisiana 70804-9005 Phone: (225) 342-7013 Fax: (225) 342-7335 http://www.ag.state.la.us
	http://www.lsp.org/handguns	

Right-to-Carry Reciprocity and Recognition, cont.

Maine

Right-To-Carry Law Type: Shall Issue

Issuing Authority:	Dept of Public Safety, Maine State Police, Licensing Division	
Contact agency for out of state permits:	Chief of State Police	
These states recognize your permit:	Alaska, Idaho, Indiana, Kentucky, Michigan, Missouri, Oklahoma, Tennessee, Utah, Vermont	
This state recognizes permits from the following states:	none	
Cost & Term of Permit:	Residents: new $35. renewal $20. Non residents: new & renewal $60.	4 years
Key Government Offices:	Department of Public Safety Maine State Police, Licensing Division 164 State House Station Augusta, Maine 043333-0164 Phone: (207) 624-8775	Attorney General 6 State House Station Augusta, Maine 04333 Phone: (207) 626-8800 http://www.me.state.us.ag/homepage.htm
	http://www.state.me.us.dps/msp	

Maryland

Right-To-Carry Law Type: Restrictive May Issue

Issuing Authority:	Superintendent of State Police	
Contact agency for out of state permits:	Superintendent of State Police	
These states recognize your permit:	Alaska, Arizona, Idaho, Indiana, Kentucky, Michigan, Missouri, Montana, Oklahoma, Tennessee, Utah, Vermont	
This state recognizes permits from the following states:	none	
Cost & Term of Permit:	New $117 Renewal $74	2 years
Key Government Offices:	Maryland State Police Attn: Handgun Permit Section 7751 Washington Blvd Jessup, Maryland 20794 Phone: (410) 79-0191, (800) 525-5555	Attorney General 200 St. Paul Place Baltimore, Maryland 21202 Phone: (410) 576-6300 Fax: (410) 576-6447
	http://www.mdsp.maryland.gov/mdsp/downloads/licensingapplications	

Massachusetts

Right-To-Carry Law Type: Restrictive May Issue

Issuing Authority:	Department of State Police, Firearms Record Bureau	
Contact agency for out of state permits:	Permits are technically available for non-residents, but are rarely granted.	
These states recognize your permit:	Alaska, Arizona, Idaho, Indiana, Kentucky, Michigan, Missouri, Montana, Oklahoma, Tennessee, Utah, Vermont	
This state recognizes permits from the following states:	none	
Cost & Term of Permit:	Residents and Non-Residents: $100.	Residents: 4 years. Non res.: 1 year.
Key Government Offices:	Firearms Records Bureau Attn: Firearms License 200 Arlington Street Suite 2200 Chelsea, Massachusetts 02150 Phone: (617) 660-4780	Massachusetts State Police 470 Worcester Road Framingham, Massachusetts 01702 Phone: (508) 820-2300 Email: msp.webmaster@pol.state.ma.us
	http://www.state.ma.us/msp/firearms/index.htm	

Right-to-Carry Reciprocity and Recognition, cont.

Michigan

Right-To-Carry Law Type: Shall Issue

Issuing Authority:	County Gun Board/Sheriff	
Contact agency for out of state permits:	Permits not granted.	
These states recognize your permit:	Alabama, Alaska, Arizona, Colorado, Delaware, Florida, Georgia, Idaho, Indiana, Kentucky, Minnesota, Montana, Missouri, New Hampshire, North Carolina, North Dakota, Oklahoma, Pennsylvania, South Dakota, Tennessee, Utah, Vermont, Virginia, Wyoming	
This state recognizes permits from the following states:	All state permits recognized, as long as permit holder is resident of issuing state.	
Cost & Term of Permit:	$105 New and renewal.	5 years
Key Government Offices:	Michigan Department of State Police 714 S. Harrison Road East Lansing, Michigan 48823 Phone: (517) 332-2521	Michigan Attorney General P.O. Box 30212 Lansing, Michigan 48909 Phone: (517) 373-1110 Fax: (517) 241-1850 http://www.ag.state.mi.us
	http://www.michigan.gov/msp	

Minnesota

Right-To-Carry Law Type: Shall Issue

Issuing Authority:	Chief of Police/County Sheriff	
Contact agency for out of state permits:	Any Minnesota County Sheriff	
These states recognize your permit:	Alaska, Arizona, Idaho, Indiana, Kentucky, Michigan, Missouri, Montana, Oklahoma, Tennessee, Utah, Vermont	
This state recognizes permits from the following states:	Michigan, Louisiana, Wyoming	
Cost & Term of Permit:	Not to exceed $100.	5 years
Key Government Offices:	Minnesota Department of Public Safety 444 Cedar Street Saint Paul, Minnesota 55101 Phone: (651) 282-6565 bca.permitstocarry@state.mn.us	Minnesota Attorney General 102 State Capitol St. Paul, Minnesota 55155 Phone: (651) 296-6196 Fax: (651) 297-4193 http://www.ag.state.mn.us
	http://www.dps.state.mn.us/bca/CJIS/documents/carrypermits/states.html	

Mississippi

Right-To-Carry Law Type: Shall Issue

Issuing Authority:	Department of Public Safety/Highway Patrol	
Contact agency for out of state permits:	Permits not granted.	
These states recognize your permit:	Alabama, Alaska, Florida, Idaho, Indiana, Kentucky, Michigan, Missouri, Montana, Oklahoma, Tennessee, Utah, Vermont, Wyoming	
This state recognizes permits from the following states:	Alabama, Florida, Kentucky, Tennessee, Wyoming	
Cost & Term of Permit:	New: $100. Renewal: $50.	4 years
Key Government Offices:	Mississippi State Police P. O. Box 958 Jackson, Mississippi 39205-0958 Phone: (601) 987-1586 Email: jtucker@dps.state.ms.us	Attorney General P.O. Box 220 Jackson, Mississippi 39205-0220 Phone: (601) 359-3680 http://www.ago.state.ms.us
	http://www.dps.state.ms.us/dps/dps.nsf	

Missouri

Right-To-Carry Law Type: Shall Issue

Issuing Authority:	County Sheriff	
Contact agency for out of state permits:	Permits not granted.	
These states recognize your permit:	Alaska, Arizona, Idaho, Indiana, Kentucky, Michigan, New Hampshire, Oklahoma, Tennessee, Utah, Vermont	
This state recognizes permits from the following states:	All state permits are recognized.	
Cost & Term of Permit:	$100	3 years
Key Government Offices:	Deparment of Public Safety P.O. Box 749 Jefferson City, Missouri 65102-0749 Phone: (573) 751-4905 Fax: (573) 751-5399	Attorney General Supreme Court Building 207 W. High St. P.O. Box 899 Jefferson City, Missouri 65102 Phone: (573) 751-3321 Fax: (573) 751-0774
	http://www.dps.state.mo.us	

Montana

Right-To-Carry Law Type: Shall Issue

Issuing Authority:	County Sheriff	
Contact agency for out of state permits:	Permits not granted.	
These states recognize your permit:	Alaska, Arizona, Colorado, Florida, Idaho, Indiana, Kentucky, Michigan, Missouri, North Carolina, North Dakota, Oklahoma, South Carolina, Tennessee, Utah, Vermont, Wyoming	
This state recognizes permits from the following states:	Alaska, Arizona, Arkansas, California, Colorado, Connecticut, Florida, Georgia, Idaho, Indiana, Iowa, Kentucky, Louisiana, Maryland, Massachusetts, Michigan, Minnesota, Mississippi, Nevada, New Jersey, New Mexico, New York, North Carolina, North Dakota, Oklahoma, Oregon, Pennsylvania, South Carolina, South Dakota, Tennessee, Texas, Utah, Virginia, Washington, West Virginia, Wyoming	
Cost & Term of Permit:	New: $50. Renewal: $25.	4 years
Key Government Offices:	Montana Highway Patrol 2550 Prospect Ave. P.O. Box 201419 Helena, Montana 59620-1419 Phone: (406) 444-3780 Fax: (406) 444-4169	Montana Attorney General P.O. Box 201401 Helena, Montana 59620-1401 Phone: 406-444-2026 Fax: 406-444-3549 contact:doj@state.mt.us
	http://www.doj.state.mt.us/enforcement/concealedweapons.asp	

Nebraska

Right-To-Carry Law Type: Non-Issue

Issuing Authority:	Permits not available	
Contact agency for out of state permits:	Permits not granted.	
These states recognize your permit:	none	
This state recognizes permits from the following states:	none	
Cost & Term of Permit:	n.a	n.a
Key Government Offices:	Nebraska State Patrol P.O. Box 94907 Lincoln, Nebraska 68509 Phone: 402-471-4545	Attorney General 2115 State Capitol P.O. Box 98920 Lincoln, Nebraska 68509-8920 Phone: 402-471-2682 Fax: 402-471-3297
	http://www.nsp.state.ne.us	

Right-to-Carry Reciprocity and Recognition, cont.

Nevada

Right-To-Carry Law Type: Shall Issue

Issuing Authority:	County Sheriff	
Contact agency for out of state permits:	In person with any County Sheriff	
These states recognize your permit:	Alaska, Arizona, Idaho, Indiana, Kentucky, Michigan, Missouri, Montana, Oklahoma, Tennessee, Utah, Vermont	
This state recognizes permits from the following states:	none	
Cost & Term of Permit:	New $60. Renewal $25	5 years; 3 years non-resident
Key Government Offices:		Office of the Attorney General 100 N. Carson Street Carson City, Nevada 89701-4717 Phone: (775)684-1100 Fax: (775) 684-1108 Email: aginfo@ag.state.nv.us
	http://www.ag.state.nv.us	

New Hampshire

Right-To-Carry Law Type: Shall Issue

Issuing Authority:	Selectman/Mayor or Chief of Police	
Contact agency for out of state permits:	Director of State Police	
These states recognize your permit:	Alabama, Alaska, Colorado, Florida, Georgia, Idaho, Indiana, Kentucky, Michigan, Missouri, North Carolina, North Dakota, Oklahoma, Tennessee, Utah, Vermont, Wyoming	
This state recognizes permits from the following states:	Alabama, Alaska, Colorado, Florida, Georgia, Idaho, Indiana, Kentucky, Michigan, North Carolina, North Dakota, Oklahoma, Tennesse, Wyoming	
Cost & Term of Permit:	Residents: $10. Non Residents: $20.	4 years
Key Government Offices:	Director of State Police Permits and Licensing Unit 10 Hazen Drive Concord, New Hampshire 03301 Phone: (603) 271-3575 Fax: (603) 271-1153	
	http://www.state.nh.us/safety/nhsp/plupr.html	

New Jersey

Right-To-Carry Law Type: Restrictive May Issue

Issuing Authority:	Chief of Police/Superintendent of State Police	
Contact agency for out of state permits:	Superintendent of State Police--Permits are technically available for non-residents, but are rarely granted.	
These states recognize your permit:	Alaska, Idaho, Indiana, Kentucky, Michigan, Missouri, Montana, Oklahoma, Tennessee, Utah, Vermont	
This state recognizes permits from the following states:	none	
Cost & Term of Permit:	$20	2 years
Key Government Offices:	New Jersey State Police Firearms Investigation Unit PO Box 7068 West Trenton, NJ 08628-0068 609-882-2000 ext. 2664	Office of the Attorney General Dept. of Law & Public Safety P.O. Box 080 Trenton, New Jersey 08625-0080 Phone: (609) 292-4925, Fax: (609) 292-3508 http://www.njpublicsafety.com
	http://www.njsp.org/faq.html#firearms	

Right-to-Carry Reciprocity and Recognition, cont.

New Mexico

Right-To-Carry Law Type: Shall Issue

Issuing Authority:	Department of Public Safety	
Contact agency for out of state permits:	Permits not granted.	
These states recognize your permit:	Alaska, Arizona, Colorado, Idaho, Indiana, Kentucky, Michigan, Missouri, Oklahoma, Tennessee, Utah, Vermont	
This state recognizes permits from the following states:	A list of reciprocal states is not available at this time, since New Mexico's new law was implemented 1/1/2004.	
Cost & Term of Permit:	$100 for initial permit plus fingerprint fee. $50 for renewal.	2 years
Key Government Offices:	Department of Public Safety P.O. Box 1628 Santa Fe, New Mexico 87504 Phone: (505) 827-3370 or (505) 827-9000	Attorney General 407 Galisteo Street Bataan Memorial Building, Rm 260 Santa Fe, New Mexico 87501 Phone: (505) 827-6000, Fax: (505) 827-5826 http://www.ago.state.nm.us
	http://www.dps.nm.org/	

New York

Right-To-Carry Law Type: Restrictive May Issue

Issuing Authority:	Varies by county	
Contact agency for out of state permits:	Permits not granted.	
These states recognize your permit:	Alaska, Idaho, Indiana, Kentucky, Michigan, Missouri, Montana, Oklahoma, Tennessee, Utah, Vermont	
This state recognizes permits from the following states:	none	
Cost & Term of Permit:	Varies by county	Varies, 2 years to lifetime
Key Government Offices:	State Police Counsel's Office Bldg. 22, 1220 Washington Ave. Albany, New York 12226 Phone: (518) 457-6811	Attorney General 120 Broadway New York, New York 10271-0332 Phone: (212)416-8050 http://www.oag.state.ny.us
	http://www.troopers.state.ny.us/firearms/firearmsindex.html	

North Carolina

Right-To-Carry Law Type: Shall Issue

Issuing Authority:	County Sheriff	
Contact agency for out of state permits:	Permits not granted.	
These states recognize your permit:	Alabama, Alaska, Arizona, Colorado, Delaware, Florida, Georgia, Idaho, Indiana, Kentucky, Michigan, Missouri, Montana, New Hampshire, Oklahoma, Pennsylvania, South Carolina, South Dakota, Tennessee, Utah, Vermont, Virginia	
This state recognizes permits from the following states:	Alabama, Alaska, Arkansas, Arizona, Colorado, Delaware, Florida, Georgia, Idaho, Indiana, Kentucky, Michigan, Montana, New Hampshire, Oklahoma, Pennsylvania, South Carolina, South Dakota, Tennessee, Utah, Virginia, Wyoming	
Cost & Term of Permit:	$80 permit fee	5 years
Key Government Offices:	North Carolina Highway Partol 512 N. Salisbury Street 4702 Mail Service Center Raleigh, North Carolina 27699-4702 Phone: (919) 733-7952 Email: Webmaster@ncshp.org	Attorney General North Carolina Department of Justice P.O. Box 629 Raleigh, North Carolina 27602-0629 Phone: 919-716-6400 Fax: 919-716-6750 Email: agjus@mail.jus.state.nc.us
	http://www.jus.state.nc.us/	

Right-to-Carry Reciprocity and Recognition, cont.

North Dakota

Right-To-Carry Law Type: Shall Issue

Issuing Authority:	Chief of the Bureau of Criminal Investigation	
Contact agency for out of state permits:	Chief of the Bureau of Criminal Investigation	
These states recognize your permit:	Alabama, Alaska*, Arizona, Delaware, Florida*, Idaho, Indiana, Kentucky, Michigan, Missouri, Montana, New Hampshire, Oklahoma, South Dakota, Tennessee, Utah, Vermont, Wyoming *Must be 21 years old	
This state recognizes permits from the following states:	Alabama, Alaska*, Arizona, Florida*, Indiana, Kentucky, Michigan, Montana, New Hampshire, Oklahoma, South Dakota, Tennessee**, Utah, Wyoming *Must be 21 years old **Handguns only	
Cost & Term of Permit:	$25	3 years
Key Government Offices:	North Dakota Office of Attorney General Bureau of Criminal Investigation Bismarck, North Dakota 58502-1054 Phone: (701) 328-5500 Fax: (701) 328-5510 Email: bciinfo@state.nd.us	Office of Attorney General State Capitol 600 E Boulevard Ave. Dept 125 Bismarck, North Dakota 58505-0040 Phone: (701) 328-2210 Fax: (701) 328-2226 Email: ndag@state.nd.us
	http://www.ag.state.nd.us/BCI/reciprocity.htm	

Ohio

Right-To-Carry Law Type: Shall Issue

Issuing Authority:	County Sheriff	
Contact agency for out of state permits:	Permits not granted.	
These states recognize your permit:	Many states will recognize Ohio permits, once Ohio begins issuing them and the Attorney General has reciprocal agreements in place.	
This state recognizes permits from the following states:	HB 12, which gave Ohio citizens the right to carry a firearm concealed, become law in January, 2004. The Attorney General must now negotiate reciprocal agreements with other states.	
Cost & Term of Permit:	$45 new and renewal	4 years
Key Government Offices:	Ohio Highway Patrol P O Box 182074 Columbus, Ohio 43232 http://www.state.oh.us/ohiostatepatrol	Attorney General 30 E. Broad Street 17th Floor Columbus, Ohio 43215-3420 Phone: (614) 466-4320 Fax: (614) 466-5057
	http://www.ag.state.oh.us/	

Oklahoma

Right-To-Carry Law Type: Shall Issue

Issuing Authority:	State Bureau of Investigation	
Contact agency for out of state permits:	Permits not granted.	
These states recognize your permit:	Alabama, Alaska, Arkansas, Arizona, Colorado, Delaware, Florida. Idaho, Indiana, Kentucky, Michigan, Missouri, Montana, New Hampshire, North Carolina, North Dakota, Tennessee, Texas, Utah, Virginia, Vermont, Wyoming	
This state recognizes permits from the following states:	All state permits recognized.	
Cost & Term of Permit:	New $100, Renewal $85.	5 years
Key Government Offices:	Oklahoma State Bureau of Investigation 6600 N. Harvey Suite 300 Oklahoma City, Oklahoma 73116 Phone: (405) 848-6724 or (800)207-6724 outside OK City sda@osbi.state.ok.us	Attorney General 112 State Capitol 2300 N. Lincoln Blvd. Oklahoma City, Oklahoma 73105 Phone: (405) 521-3921, Fax: (405) 521-6246 http://www.oag.state.of.us
	http://www.osbi.state.ok.us/sda.htm	

Right-to-Carry Reciprocity and Recognition, cont.

Oregon

Right-To-Carry Law Type: Shall Issue

Issuing Authority:	County Sheriff	
Contact agency for out of state permits:	Discretionary to residents of contiguous states only	
These states recognize your permit:	Alaska, Arizona, Idaho, Indiana, Kentucky, Michigan, Missouri, Montana, Oklahoma, Tennessee, Utah, Vermont	
This state recognizes permits from the following states:	none	
Cost & Term of Permit:	New: $65. Renewal $50.	4 years
Key Government Offices:	State Police 400 Public Service Bldg. 255 Capitol St. N.E. Salem, Oregon 97310 Phone: (503) 378-3720 Fax: (503) 378-8282 http://www.osp.state.or.us	Attorney General Justice Department 1162 Court St. NE Salem Oregon, 97310 Phone: (503) 378-4400, Fax: (503) 378-5938 http://www.doj.state.or.us
	http://www.osp.state.or.us	

Pennsylvania

Right-To-Carry Law Type: Shall Issue

Issuing Authority:	County Sheriff or Chief of Police	
Contact agency for out of state permits:	Any Sheriff's Department	
These states recognize your permit:	Alaska, Florida, Georgia, Idaho, Indiana, Kentucky, Michigan, Missouri, Montana, North Carolina, Oklahoma, Tennessee, Utah, Vermont, Wyoming	
This state recognizes permits from the following states:	Florida, Georgia, Kentucky, Michigan, North Carolina, Wyoming	
Cost & Term of Permit:	$19	5 years
Key Government Offices:	State Police 1800 Elmerton Avenue Harrisburg, Pennsylvania 17110-9758 Phone: (717) 783-5599 Fax: (717) 787-2948	Attorney General 16th Floor, Strawberry Square Harrisburg, Pennsylvania 17120 Phone: 717-787-3391 Fax: (717) 787-8242 http://www.attorneygeneral.gov
	http://www.psp.state.pa.us	

Rhode Island

Right-To-Carry Law Type: Restrictive May Issue

Issuing Authority:	Attorney General	
Contact agency for out of state permits:	Attorney General by mail only. Permits are technically available for non-residents, but are rarely granted.	
These states recognize your permit:	Alaska, Idaho, Indiana, Kentucky, Michigan, Missouri, Oklahoma, Tennessee, Utah, Vermont	
This state recognizes permits from the following states:	none	
Cost & Term of Permit:	$40	4 years
Key Government Offices:	State Police 311 Danielson Pike North Scituate, Rhode Island 02857 Phone: (401) 444-1000 Fax: (401) 444-1105 http://www.risp.state.ri.us	Attorney General 150 South Main Street Providence, Rhode Island 02903 Phone: (401) 274-4400 Fax: (401) 222-1331 http://www.riag.state.ri.us
	http://www.riag.state.ri.us/	

Right-to-Carry Reciprocity and Recognition, cont.

South Carolina

Right-To-Carry Law Type: Shall Issue

Issuing Authority:	S.C. Law Enforcement Division	
Contact agency for out of state permits:	Permits not granted.	
These states recognize your permit:	Alaska, Arizona, Arkansas, Idaho, Indiana, Kentucky, Michigan, Missouri, Montana, North Carolina, Oklahoma, Tennessee, Utah, Vermont, Virginia, Wyoming	
This state recognizes permits from the following states:	Arkansas, North Carolina, Tennessee, Wyoming	
Cost & Term of Permit:	$50	4 years
Key Government Offices:	South Carolina Law Enforcement Division Attn: Regulatory Services Unit P.O. Box 21398 Columbia, South Carolina 29221 Phone: 803-896-7014	Attorney General Box 11549 Columbia, South Carolina 29211 Phone: (803) 734-3970 Fax: (803) 253-6283 http://www.scattorneygeneral.org
	http://www.sled.state.sc.us	

South Dakota

Right-To-Carry Law Type: Shall Issue

Issuing Authority:	Chief of Police/County Sheriff	
Contact agency for out of state permits:	Permits not granted.	
These states recognize your permit:	Alaska, Colorado, Florida*, Georgia, Idaho, Indiana, Kentucky, Michigan, Missouri, Montana, North Carolina, North Dakota, Oklahoma, Tennessee, Utah, Vermont, Wyoming *must be 21	
This state recognizes permits from the following states:	Alaska, Colorado*, Florida, Georgia, Indiana, Kentucky, Michigan, Montana, North Carolina, North Dakota, Tennessee, Utah, Wyoming *must be 21	
Cost & Term of Permit:	$10	4 years
Key Government Offices:	Highway Patrol 118 West Capitol Pierre, South Dakota 57501 Phone: (605) 773-3105 Fax: (605) 773-6046 http://hp.state.sd.us/information.htm	Attorney General 500 East Capitol Ave. Pierre, South Dakota 57501-5070 Phone: (605)-773-3215 Fax: 605)773-4106 http://www.state.sd.attorney/office/news/concealed.asp
	http://sdsos.gov/firearms	

Tennessee

Right-To-Carry Law Type: Shall Issue

Issuing Authority:	Department of Public Safety	
Contact agency for out of state permits:	Permits not granted.	
These states recognize your permit:	Alaska, Arizona, Arkansas, Colorado, Delaware, Florida, Georgia, Idaho, Indiana, Kentucky, Louisiana, Michigan, Mississippi, Missouri, Montana, New Hampshire, North Carolina, North Dakota, Oklahoma, South Carolina, South Dakota, Texas, Utah, Virginia, Vermont, Wyoming	
This state recognizes permits from the following states:	All state permits recognized.	
Cost & Term of Permit:	New: $115; Renewal: $50	4 years
Key Government Offices:	Tennessee Department of Safety Attn: Handgun Carry Permit Office 1150 Foster Ave Nashville, Tennessee 37249-1000 Phone: (615) 251-8590	Attorney General P.O. Box 20207 Nashville, Tennessee 37202 Phone: (615) 741-3491 Fax: (615) 741-2009 http://www.attorneygeneral.state.tn.us
	http://www.state.tn.us/safety/	

Right-to-Carry Reciprocity and Recognition, cont.

Texas

Right-To-Carry Law Type: Shall Issue

Issuing Authority:	Department of Public Safety	
Contact agency for out of state permits:	Department of Public Safety	
These states recognize your permit:	Alaska, Arizona, Arkansas, Florida, Idaho, Indiana, Kentucky, Louisiana, Michigan, Missouri, Montana, Oklahoma, Tennessee, Utah, Virginia, Vermont, Wyoming	
This state recognizes permits from the following states:	Arizona, Arkansas, Florida, Kentucky, Louisiana, Oklahoma, Tennessee. Wyoming	
Cost & Term of Permit:	$140 ($70 for seniors)	4 years
Key Government Offices:	Texas Department of Public Safety Concealed Handgun Licensing Section P O Box 4143 Austin, Texas 78791-4143 Phone: (512) 424-7293 or (800) 224-5744 http://www.txdps.state.tx.us	Attorney General P. O. Box 12548 Austin, Texas 78711-2548 Phone: (512) 463-2100 Fax: (512) 463-2063 http://www.oag.state.tx.us
	http://www.txdps.state.tx.us/administration/crime_records/chl/reciprocity.htm	

Utah

Right-To-Carry Law Type: Shall Issue

Issuing Authority:	Department of Public Safety	
Contact agency for out of state permits:	Department of Public Safety	
These states recognize your permit:	Alabama, Alaska, Arizona, Arkansas, Delaware, Florida, Idaho, Indiana, Kentucky, Michigan, Missouri, Montana, North Carolina, North Dakota, Oklahoma, South Dakota, Vermont, Wyoming	
This state recognizes permits from the following states:	All state permits recognized.	
Cost & Term of Permit:	New $35, $10 Renewal	5 years
Key Government Offices:	Utah Department of Public Safety Bureau of Criminal Identification 3888 W. 5400 S. P.O. Box 148280 Salt Lake City, Utah 84114-8280 Phone: (801) 965-4445	Utah Attorney General 236 State Capitol Salt Lake City, Utah 84114 Phone: (801) 366-0260 Fax: (801) 538-1121 http://www.attorneygeneral.utah.gov
	http://bci.utah.gov/cfp/cfphome.html	

Vermont

Right-To-Carry Law Type: Permits Not Required

Issuing Authority:	Permits Not Required	
Contact agency for out of state permits:	Permits Not Required	
These states recognize your permit:	none	
This state recognizes permits from the following states:	Permits Not Required	
Cost & Term of Permit:	n/a	n/a
Key Government Offices:		Attorney General 109 State Street Montpelier, Vermont 05609-1001 Phone: (802) 828 3171 Fax: (802) 828 2154
	http://www.state.vt.us/atg/	

Right-to-Carry Reciprocity and Recognition, cont.

Virginia

Right-To-Carry Law Type: Shall Issue

Issuing Authority:	State Circuit Court of residence	
Contact agency for out of state permits:	Permits not granted.	
These states recognize your permit:	Alaska, Idaho, Indiana, Kentucky, Michigan, Missouri, Montana, North Carolina, Oklahoma, Tennessee, Utah, West Virginia, Vermont	
This state recognizes permits from the following states:	Alaska, Arizona, Arkansas, Idaho, Louisiana, Michigan, North Carolina, Oklahoma, South Carolina, Tennessee, Texas, Utah, Washington, West Virginia	
Cost & Term of Permit:	no more than $50	5 years
Key Government Offices:	Virginia State Police P.O. Box 27472 Richmond, Virginia 23261 Phone: (804) 674-2000	Attorney General 900 East Main Street Richmond, Virginia 23219 Phone: (804) 786-2071 Fax: (804) 786-1991 http://www.oag.state.va.us
	http://www.vsp.state.va.us/vsp.html	

Washington

Right-To-Carry Law Type: Shall Issue

Issuing Authority:	Chief of Police/Sheriff	
Contact agency for out of state permits:	Permits not granted.	
These states recognize your permit:	Alaska, Idaho, Indiana, Kentucky, Michigan, Missouri, Montana, Oklahoma, Tennessee, Utah, Vermont, Virginia	
This state recognizes permits from the following states:	none	
Cost & Term of Permit:	New: $36; Renewal: $32	5 years
Key Government Offices:	Washington State Patrol General Administration Building PO Box 42600 Olympia, Washington 98504-2600 Phone: (360) 753-6540 Fax: (360) 753-2492	Attorney General 1125 Washington St. SE Olympia, Washington 98504-0100 Phone: (360) 753-6200 Fax: (360) 664-0988 http://www.atg.wa.gov
	http://www.wsp.wa.gov/newsfaqs/answers.htm#weapons	

West Virginia

Right-To-Carry Law Type: Shall Issue

Issuing Authority:	County Sheriff	
Contact agency for out of state permits:	Permits not granted.	
These states recognize your permit:	Alaska, Arizona, Idaho, Indiana, Kentucky, Michigan, Missouri, Montana, Oklahoma, Tennessee, Utah, Vermont, Virginia	
This state recognizes permits from the following states:	Kentucky, Virginia	
Cost & Term of Permit:	$60	5 years
Key Government Offices:	West Virginia State Police 725 Jefferson Road South Charleston, West Virginia 25309 Phone: (304) 746-2100 Fax: (304) 746-2246	Attorney General State Capitol, Room 26-E 1900 Kanawha Blvd. East Charleston, West Virginia 25305-0220 Phone: (304) 558-2021 Fax: (304) 558-0140
	http://www.wvstatepolice.com/legal/legal.shtml	

Right-to-Carry Reciprocity and Recognition, cont.

Wisconsin	Right-To-Carry Law Type: Non-Issue	
Issuing Authority:	Permits not available	
Contact agency for out of state permits:	Permits not granted.	
These states recognize your permit:	none	
This state recognizes permits from the following states:	none	
Cost & Term of Permit:	n/a	n/a
Key Government Offices:		Attorney General 123 West Washington Ave. PO Box 7857 Madison, Wisconsin 53707-7857 Phone: 608-266-1221 Fax: 608-267-2779
	http://www.doj.state.wi.us/	

Wyoming	Right-To-Carry Law Type: Shall Issue	
Issuing Authority:	Attorney General	
Contact agency for out of state permits:	Permits not granted.	
These states recognize your permit:	Alabama, Alaska, Arizona, Colorado, Florida, Georgia, Idaho, Indiana, Kentucky, Louisiana, Michigan, Minnesota, Mississippi, Missouri, Montana, New Hampshire, North Carolina, North Dakota, Oklahoma, Pennsylvania, South Carolina, South Dakota, Tennessee, Texas, Utah, Vermont	
This state recognizes permits from the following states:	Alabama, Alaska, Colorado, Florida, Georgia, Idaho, Indiana, Kentucky, Louisiana, Michigan, Mississippi, Montana, New Hampshire, North Carolina, North Dakota, Oklahoma, Pennsylvania, South Carolina, South Dakota, Tennessee, Texas, Utah	
Cost & Term of Permit:	$74	5 years
Key Government Offices:		Wyoming Attorney General's Office 123 Capitol Building 200 W. 24th Street Cheyenne, Wyoming 82002 Phone: (307) 777-7841 Fax: (307) 777-6869
	http://attorneygeneral.state.dci.cwp.html	

ARMS ASSOCIATIONS

UNITED STATES

ALABAMA

Alabama Gun Collectors Assn.
Secretary, P.O. Box 70965, Tuscaloosa, AL 35407

ALASKA

Alaska Gun Collectors Assn., Inc.
C.W. Floyd, Pres., 5240 Little Tree, Anchorage, AK 99507

ARIZONA

Arizona Arms Assn.
Don DeBusk, President, 4837 Bryce Ave., Glendale, AZ 85301

CALIFORNIA

California Cartridge Collectors Assn.
Rick Montgomery, 1729 Christina, Stockton, CA 95204
209-463-7216 eves.

California Waterfowl Assn.
4630 Northgate Blvd., #150, Sacramento, CA 95834

Greater Calif. Arms & Collectors Assn.
Donald L. Bullock, 8291 Carburton St., Long Beach, CA 90808-3302

Los Angeles Gun Ctg. Collectors Assn.
F.H. Ruffra, 20810 Amie Ave., Apt. #9, Torrance, CA 90503

Stock Gun Players Assn.
6038 Appian Way, Long Beach, CA, 90803

COLORADO

Colorado Gun Collectors Assn.
L.E.(Bud) Greenwald, 2553 S. Quitman St., Denver, CO 80219/303-935-3850

Rocky Mountain Cartridge Collectors Assn.
John Roth, P.O. Box 757, Conifer, CO 80433

CONNECTICUT

Ye Connecticut Gun Guild, Inc.
Dick Fraser, P.O. Box 425, Windsor, CT 06095

FLORIDA

Unified Sportsmen of Florida
P.O. Box 6565, Tallahassee, FL 32314

GEORGIA

Georgia Arms Collectors Assn., Inc.
Michael Kindberg, President, P.O. Box 277, Alpharetta, GA 30239-0277

ILLINOIS

Illinois State Rifle Assn.
P.O. Box 637, Chatsworth, IL 60921

Mississippi Valley Gun & Cartridge Coll. Assn.
Bob Filbert, P.O. Box 61, Port Byron, IL 61275/309-523-2593

Sauk Trail Gun Collectors
Gordell M. Matson, P.O. Box 1113, Milan, IL 61264

Wabash Valley Gun Collectors Assn., Inc.
Roger L. Dorsett, 2601 Willow Rd., Urbana, IL 61801
217-384-7302

INDIANA

Indiana State Rifle & Pistol Assn.
Thos. Glancy, P.O. Box 552, Chesterton, IN 46304

Southern Indiana Gun Collectors Assn., Inc.
Sheila McClary, 309 W. Monroe St., Boonville, IN 47601/812-897-3742

IOWA

Beaver Creek Plainsmen Inc.
Steve Murphy, Secy., P.O. Box 298, Bondurant, IA 50035

Central States Gun Collectors Assn.
Dennis Greischar, Box 841, Mason City, IA 50402-0841

KANSAS

Kansas Cartridge Collectors Assn.
Bob Linder, Box 84, Plainville, KS 67663

KENTUCKY

Kentuckiana Arms Collectors Assn.
Charles Billips, President, Box 1776, Louisville, KY 40201

Kentucky Gun Collectors Assn., Inc.
Ruth Johnson, Box 64, Owensboro, KY 42302/502-729-4197

LOUISIANA

Washitaw River Renegades
Sandra Rushing, P.O. Box 256, Main St., Grayson, LA 71435

MARYLAND

Baltimore Antique Arms Assn.
Mr. Cillo, 1034 Main St., Darlington, MD 21304

MASSACHUSETTS

Bay Colony Weapons Collectors, Inc.
John Brandt, Box 111, Hingham, MA 02043

Massachusetts Arms Collectors
Bruce E. Skinner, P.O. Box 31, No. Carver, MA 02355/508-866-5259

MICHIGAN

Association for the Study and Research of .22 Caliber Rimfire Cartridges
George Kass, 4512 Nakoma Dr., Okemos, MI 48864

MINNESOTA

Sioux Empire Cartridge Collectors Assn.
Bob Cameron, 14597 Glendale Ave. SE, Prior Lake, MN 55372

MISSISSIPPI

Mississippi Gun Collectors Assn.
Jack E. Swinney, P.O. Box 16323, Hattiesburg, MS 39402

MISSOURI

Greater St. Louis Cartridge Collectors Assn.
Don MacChesney, 634 Scottsdale Rd., Kirkwood, MO 63122-1109

Mineral Belt Gun Collectors Assn.
D.F. Saunders, 1110 Cleveland Ave., Monett, MO 65708

Missouri Valley Arms Collectors Assn., Inc.
L.P Brammer II, Membership Secy., P.O. Box 33033, Kansas City, MO 64114

MONTANA

Montana Arms Collectors Assn.
Dean E. Yearout, Sr., Exec. Secy., 1516 21st Ave. S., Great Falls, MT 59405

Weapons Collectors Society of Montana
R.G. Schipf, Ex. Secy., 3100 Bancroft St., Missoula, MT 59801
406-728-2995

NEBRASKA

Nebraska Cartridge Collectors Club
Gary Muckel, P.O. Box 84442, Lincoln, NE 68501

NEW HAMPSHIRE

New Hampshire Arms Collectors, Inc.
James Stamatelos, Secy., P.O. Box 5, Cambridge, MA 02139

NEW JERSEY

Englishtown Benchrest Shooters Assn.
Michael Toth, 64 Cooke Ave., Carteret, NJ 07008

Jersey Shore Antique Arms Collectors
Joe Sisia, P.O. Box 100, Bayville, NJ 08721-0100

New Jersey Arms Collectors Club, Inc.
Angus Laidlaw, Vice President, 230 Valley Rd., Montclair, NJ 07042/201-746-0939; e-mail: acclaidlaw@juno.com

NEW YORK

Iroquois Arms Collectors Assn.
Bonnie Robinson, Show Secy., P.O. Box 142, Ransomville, NY 14131/716-791-4096

Mid-State Arms Coll. & Shooters Club
Jack Ackerman, 24 S. Mountain Terr., Binghamton, NY 13903

NORTH CAROLINA

North Carolina Gun Collectors Assn.
Jerry Ledford, 3231-7th St. Dr. NE, Hickory, NC 28601

OHIO

Ohio Gun Collectors Assn.
P.O. Box 9007, Maumee, OH 43537-9007/419-897-0861;
Fax: 419-897-0860

Shotshell Historical and Collectors Society
Madeline Bruemmer, 3886 Dawley Rd., Ravenna, OH 44266

The Stark Gun Collectors, Inc.
William I. Gann, 5666 Waynesburg Dr., Waynesburg, OH 44688

OREGON

Oregon Arms Collectors Assn., Inc.
Phil Bailey, P.O. Box 13000-A, Portland, OR 97213-0017
503-281-6864; off.: 503-281-0918

Oregon Cartridge Collectors Assn.
Boyd Northrup, P.O. Box 285, Rhododendron, OR 97049

PENNSYLVANIA

Presque Isle Gun Collectors Assn.
James Welch, 156 E. 37 St., Erie, PA 16504

SOUTH CAROLINA

Belton Gun Club, Inc.
Attn. Secretary, P.O. Box 126, Belton, SC 29627/864-369-6767

Gun Owners of South Carolina
Membership Div.: William Strozier, Secretary, P.O. Box 70, Johns Island, SC 29457-0070/803-762-3240;
Fax: 803-795-0711; e-mail: 76053.222@compuserve. com

SOUTH DAKOTA

Dakota Territory Gun Coll. Assn., Inc.
Curt Carter, Castlewood, SD 57223

TENNESSEE

Smoky Mountain Gun Coll. Assn., Inc.
Hugh W. Yabro, President, P.O. Box 23225, Knoxville, TN 37933

Tennessee Gun Collectors Assn., Inc.
M.H. Parks, 3556 Pleasant Valley Rd., Nashville, TN 37204-3419

TEXAS

Houston Gun Collectors Assn., Inc.
P.O. Box 741429, Houston, TX 77274-1429

Texas Gun Collectors Assn.
Bob Eder, Pres., P.O. Box 12067, El Paso, TX 79913/915-584-8183

Texas State Rifle Assn.
1131 Rockingham Dr., Suite 101, Richardson, TX 75080-4326

VIRGINIA

Virginia Gun Collectors Assn., Inc.
Addison Hurst, Secy., 38802 Charlestown Height, Waterford, VA 20197/540-882-3543

WASHINGTON

Association of Cartridge Collectors on the Pacific Northwest
Robert Jardin, 14214 Meadowlark Drive KPN, Gig Harbor, WA 98329

Washington Arms Collectors, Inc.
Joyce Boss, P.O. Box 389, Renton, WA, 98057-0389/206-255-8410

WISCONSIN

Great Lakes Arms Collectors Assn., Inc.
Edward C. Warnke, 2913 Woodridge Lane, Waukesha, WI 53188

Wisconsin Gun Collectors Assn., Inc.
Lulita Zellmer, P.O. Box 181, Sussex, WI 53089

WYOMING

Wyoming Weapons Collectors
P.O. Box 284, Laramie, WY 82073/307-745-4652 or 745-9530

NATIONAL ORGANIZATIONS

Amateur Trapshooting Assn.
David D. Bopp, Exec. Director, 601 W. National Rd., Vandalia, OH 45377/937-898-4638;
Fax: 937-898-5472

American Airgun Field Target Assn.
5911 Cherokee Ave., Tampa, FL 33604

American Coon Hunters Assn.
Opal Johnston, P.O. Cadet, Route 1, Box 492, Old Mines, MO 63630

American Custom Gunmakers Guild
Jan Billeb, Exec. Director, 22 Vista View Drive, Cody, WY 82414-9606
(307) 587-4297 (phone/fax)
Email: acgg@acgg.org
Website: www.acgg.org

American Defense Preparedness Assn.
Two Colonial Place, 2101 Wilson Blvd., Suite 400, Arlington, VA 22201-3061

American Paintball League
P.O. Box 3561, Johnson City, TN 37602/800-541-9169

American Pistolsmiths Guild
Alex B. Hamilton, Pres., 1449 Blue Crest Lane, San Antonio, TX 78232/210-494-3063

American Police Pistol & Rifle Assn.
3801 Biscayne Blvd., Miami, FL 33137

American Single Shot Rifle Assn.
Gary Staup, Secy., 709 Carolyn Dr., Delphos, OH 45833
419-692-3866.
Website: www.assra.com

American Society of Arms Collectors
George E. Weatherly, P.O. Box 2567, Waxahachie, TX 75165

American Tactical Shooting Assn.(A.T.S.A.)
c/o Skip Gochenour, 2600 N. Third St., Harrisburg, PA 17110
717-233-0402;
Fax: 717-233-5340

Association of Firearm and Tool Mark Examiners
Lannie G. Emanuel, Secy., Southwest Institute of Forensic Sciences, P.O. Box 35728, Dallas, TX 75235/214-920-5979;
Fax: 214-920-5928;
Membership Secy., Ann D. Jones, VA Div. of Forensic Science, P.O. Box 999, Richmond, VA 23208
804-786-4706; Fax: 804-371-8328

Boone & Crockett Club
250 Station Dr., Missoula, MT 59801-2753

Browning Collectors Assn.
Secretary:Scherrie L. Brennac, 2749 Keith Dr., Villa Ridge, MO 63089/314-742-0571

The Cast Bullet Assn., Inc.
Ralland J. Fortier, Editor, 4103 Foxcraft Dr., Traverse City, MI 49684

Citizens Committee for the Right to Keep and Bear Arms
Natl. Hq., Liberty Park, 12500 NE Tenth Pl., Bellevue, WA 98005

Colt Collectors Assn.
25000 Highland Way, Los Gatos, CA 95030/408-353-2658

Contemporary Longrifle Association
P.O. Box 2097, Staunton, VA 24402/540-886-6189
Website: www.CLA@longrifle.ws

Ducks Unlimited, Inc.
Natl. Headquarters, One Waterfowl Way, Memphis, TN 38120
901-758-3937

Fifty Caliber Shooters Assn.
PO Box 111, Monroe UT 84754-0111

Firearms Coalition/Neal Knox Associates
Box 6537, Silver Spring, MD 20906
301-871-3006

Firearms Engravers Guild of America
Rex C. Pedersen, Secy., 511 N. Rath Ave., Lundington, MI 49431
616-845-7695 (Phone/Fax)

Foundation for North American Wild Sheep
720 Allen Ave., Cody, WY 82414-3402; web site: iigi.com/os/non/fnaws/fnaws.htm;
e-mail: fnaws@wyoming.com

Freedom Arms Collectors Assn.
P.O. Box 160302, Miami, FL 33116-0302

Garand Collectors Assn.
P.O. Box 181, Richmond, KY 40475

Glock Collectors Association
P.O. Box 1063, Maryland Heights, MO 63043
314-878-2061 Phone/Fax

Glock Shooting Sports Foundation
BO Box 309, Smyrna GA 30081
770-432-1202
Website: www.gssfonline.com

Golden Eagle Collectors Assn. (G.E.C.A.)
Chris Showler, 11144 Slate Creek Rd., Grass Valley, CA 95945

ARMS ASSOCIATIONS

Gun Owners of America
8001 Forbes Place, Suite 102, Springfield, VA 22151/703-321-8585

Handgun Hunters International
J.D. Jones, Director, P.O. Box 357 MAG, Bloomingdale, OH 43910

Harrington & Richardson Gun Coll. Assn.
George L. Cardet, 330 S.W. 27th Ave., Suite 603, Miami, FL 33135

High Standard Collectors' Assn.
John J. Stimson, Jr., Pres., 540 W. 92nd St., Indianapolis, IN 46260
Website: www.highstandard.org

Hopkins & Allen Arms & Memorabilia Society (HAAMS)
P.O. Box 187, 1309 Pamela Circle, Delphos, OH 45833

International Ammunition Association, Inc.
C.R. Punnett, Secy., 8 Hillock Lane, Chadds Ford, PA 19317
610-358-1285; Fax: 610-358-1560

International Benchrest Shooters
Joan Borden, RR1, Box 250BB, Springville, PA 18844
717-965-2366

International Blackpowder Hunting Assn.
P.O. Box 1180, Glenrock, WY 82637/307-436-9817

IHMSA (Intl. Handgun Metallic Silhouette Assn.)
PO Box 368, Burlington, IA 52601
Website: www.ihmsa.org

International Society of Mauser Arms Collectors
Michael Kindberg, Pres., P.O. Box 277, Alpharetta, GA 30239-0277

Jews for the Preservation of Firearms Ownership (JPFO) 501(c)(3)
2872 S. Wentworth Ave., Milwaukee, WI 53207
414-769-0760; Fax: 414-483-8435

The Mannlicher Collectors Assn.
Membership Office: P.O. Box 1249, The Dalles, Oregon 97058

Marlin Firearms Collectors Assn., Ltd.
Dick Paterson, Secy., 407 Lincoln Bldg., 44 Main St., Champaign, IL 61820

Merwin Hulbert Association,
2503 Kentwood Ct., High Point, NC 27265

Miniature Arms Collectors/Makers Society, Ltd.
Ralph Koebbeman, Pres., 4910 Kilburn Ave., Rockford, IL 61101
815-964-2569

M1 Carbine Collectors Assn. (M1-CCA)
623 Apaloosa Ln., Gardnerville, NV 89410-7840

National Association of Buckskinners (NAB)
Territorial Dispatch—1800s Historical Publication, 4701 Marion St., Suite 324, Livestock Exchange Bldg., Denver, CO 80216
303-297-9671

The National Association of Derringer Collectors
P.O. Box 20572, San Jose, CA 95160

National Assn. of Federally Licensed Firearms Dealers
Andrew Molchan, 2455 E. Sunrise, Ft. Lauderdale, FL 33304

National Association to Keep and Bear Arms
P.O. Box 78336, Seattle, WA 98178

National Automatic Pistol Collectors Assn.
Tom Knox, P.O. Box 15738, Tower Grove Station, St. Louis, MO 63163

National Bench Rest Shooters Assn., Inc.
Pat Ferrell, 2835 Guilford Lane, Oklahoma City, OK 73120-4404
405-842-9585; Fax: 405-842-9575

National Muzzle Loading Rifle Assn.
Box 67, Friendship, IN 47021
812-667-5131
Website: www.nmlra@nmlra.org

National Professional Paintball League (NPPL)
540 Main St., Mount Kisco, NY 10549/914-241-7400

National Reloading Manufacturers Assn.
One Centerpointe Dr., Suite 300, Lake Oswego, OR 97035

National Rifle Assn. of America
11250 Waples Mill Rd., Fairfax, VA 22030/703-267-1000
Website: www.nra.org

National Shooting Sports Foundation, Inc.
Doug Painter, President, Flintlock Ridge Office Center, 11 Mile Hill Rd., Newtown, CT 06470-2359
203-426-1320; Fax: 203-426-1087

National Skeet Shooting Assn.
Dan Snyuder, Director, 5931 Roft Road, San Antonio, TX 78253-9261/800-877-5338
Website: nssa-nsca.com

National Sporting Clays Association
Ann Myers, Director, 5931 Roft Road, San Antonio, TX 78253-9261/800-877-5338
Website: nssa-nsca.com

National Wild Turkey Federation, Inc.
P.O. Box 530, 770 Augusta Rd., Edgefield, SC 29824

North American Hunting Club
P.O. Box 3401, Minnetonka, MN 55343/612-936-9333;
Fax: 612-936-9755

North American Paintball Referees Association (NAPRA)
584 Cestaric Dr., Milpitas, CA 95035

North-South Skirmish Assn., Inc.
Stevan F. Meserve, Exec. Secretary, 507 N. Brighton Court, Sterling, VA 20164-3919

Old West Shooter's Association
712 James Street, Hazel TX 76020
817-444-2049

Remington Society of America
Gordon Fosburg, Secretary, 11900 North Brinton Road, Lake, MI 48623

Rocky Mountain Elk Foundation
P.O. Box 8249, Missoula, MT 59807-8249/406-523-4500;
Fax: 406-523-4581
Website: www.rmef.org

Ruger Collector's Assn., Inc.
P.O. Box 240, Greens Farms, CT 06436

Safari Club International
4800 W. Gates Pass Rd., Tucson, AZ 85745/520-620-1220

Sako Collectors Assn., Inc.
Jim Lutes, 202 N. Locust, Whitewater, KS 67154

Second Amendment Foundation
James Madison Building, 12500 NE 10th Pl., Bellevue, WA 98005

Single Action Shooting Society (SASS)
23255-A La Palma Avenue, Yorba Linda, CA 92887/714-694-1800;
Fax: 714-694-1815
email: sasseot@aol.com
Website: www.sassnet.com

Smith & Wesson Collectors Assn.
Cally Pletl, Admin. Asst.,PO Box 444, Afton, NY 13730

The Society of American Bayonet Collectors
P.O. Box 234, East Islip, NY 11730-0234

Southern California Schuetzen Society
Dean Lillard, 34657 Ave. E., Yucaipa, CA 92399

Sporting Arms and Ammunition Manufacturers' Institute (SAAMI)
Flintlock Ridge Office Center, 11 Mile Hill Rd., Newtown, CT 06470-2359/203-426-4358;
Fax: 203-426-1087

Sporting Clays of America (SCA)
Ron L. Blosser, Pres., 9257 Buckeye Rd., Sugar Grove, OH 43155-9632/614-746-8334;
Fax: 614-746-8605

Steel Challenge
23234 Via Barra, Valencia CA 91355
Website: www.steelchallenge.com

The Thompson/Center Assn.
Joe Wright, President, Box 792, Northboro, MA 01532/508-845-6960

U.S. Practical Shooting Association/IPSC
Dave Thomas, P.O. Box 811, Sedro Woolley, WA 98284/360-855-2245
Website: www.uspsa.org

U.S. Revolver Assn.
Brian J. Barer, 40 Larchmont Ave., Taunton, MA 02780/508-824-4836

U.S.A. Shooting
U.S. Olympic Shooting Center, One Olympic Plaza, Colorado Springs, CO 80909/719-578-4670
Website: wwwusashooting.org

The Varmint Hunters Assn., Inc.
Box 759, Pierre, SD 57501
Member Services 800-528-4868

Weatherby Collectors Assn., Inc.
P.O. Box 478, Pacific, MO 63069
Website: www.weatherbycollectors.com
Email: WCAsecretary@aol.com

The Wildcatters
P.O. Box 170, Greenville, WI 54942

Winchester Arms Collectors Assn.
P.O. Box 230, Brownsboro, TX 75756/903-852-4027

The Women's Shooting Sports Foundation (WSSF)
4620 Edison Avenue, Ste. C, Colorado Springs, CO 80915
719-638-1299; Fax: 719-638-1271
email: wssf@worldnet.att.net

ARGENTINA

Asociacion Argentina de Coleccionistas de Armes y Municiones
Castilla de Correos No. 28, Succursal I B, 1401 Buenos Aires, Republica Argentina

AUSTRALIA

Antique & Historical Arms Collectors of Australia
P.O. Box 5654, GCMC Queensland 9726, Australia

The Arms Collector's Guild of Queensland, Inc.
Ian Skennerton, P.O. Box 433, Ashmore City 4214, Queensland, Australia

Australian Cartridge Collectors Assn., Inc.
Bob Bennett, 126 Landscape Dr., E. Doncaster 3109, Victoria, Australia

Sporting Shooters Assn. of Australia, Inc.
P.O. Box 2066, Kent Town, SA 5071, Australia

BRAZIL

Associaçao de Armaria Coleçao e Tiro (ACOLTI)
Rua do Senado, 258 - 2 andar, Centro, Rio de Janeiro - RJ - 20231-002 Brazil / tel: 0055-21-31817989

CANADA

ALBERTA

Canadian Historical Arms Society
P.O. Box 901, Edmonton, Alb., Canada T5J 2L8

National Firearms Assn.
Natl. Hq: P.O. Box 1779, Edmonton, Alb., Canada T5J 2P1

BRITISH COLUMBIA

The Historical Arms Collectors of B.C. (Canada)
Harry Moon, Pres., P.O. Box 50117, South Slope RPO, Burnaby, BC V5J 5G3, Canada
604-438-0950; Fax: 604-277-3646

ONTARIO

Association of Canadian Cartridge Collectors
Monica Wright, RR 1, Millgrove, ON, LOR IVO, Canada

Tri-County Antique Arms Fair
P.O. Box 122, RR #1, North Lancaster, Ont., Canada KOC 1Z0

EUROPE

BELGIUM

European Cartridge Research Association
Graham Irving, 21 Rue Schaltin, 4900 Spa, Belgium
32.87.77.43.40;
Fax: 32.87.77.27.51

CZECHOSLOVAKIA

Spolecnost Pro Studium Naboju (Czech Cartridge Research Association)
JUDr. Jaroslav Bubak, Pod Homolko 1439, 26601 Beroun 2, Czech Republic

DENMARK

Aquila Dansk Jagtpatron Historic Forening (Danish Historical Cartridge Collectors Club)
Steen Elgaard Møller, Ulriksdalsvej 7, 4840 Nr. Alslev, Denmark 10045-53846218;
Fax: 00455384 6209

ENGLAND

Arms and Armour Society
Hon. Secretary A. Dove, P.O. Box 10232, London, 5W19 2ZD, England

Dutch Paintball Federation
Aceville Publ., Castle House 97 High Street, Colchester, Essex C01 1TH, England/011-44-206-564840

European Paintball Sports Foundation
c/o Aceville Publ., Castle House 97 High St., Colchester, Essex, C01 1TH, England

Historical Breechloading Smallarms Assn.
D.J. Penn M.A., Secy., P.O. Box 12778, London SE1 6BX, England

National Rifle Assn.
(Great Britain) Bisley Camp, Brookwood, Woking Surrey GU24 OPB, England/01483.797777;
Fax: 014730686275

United Kingdom Cartridge Club
Ian Southgate, 20 Millfield, Elmley Castle, Nr. Pershore, Worcestershire, WR10 3HR, England

FRANCE

STAC-Western Co.
3 Ave. Paul Doumer (N.311); 78360 Montesson, France
01.30.53-43-65;
Fax: 01.30.53.19.10

GERMANY

Bund Deutscher Sportschützen e.v. (BDS)
Borsigallee 10, 53125 Bonn 1, Germany

Deutscher Schützenbund
Lahnstrasse 120, 65195 Wiesbaden, Germany

NORWAY

Scandinavian Ammunition Research Association
c/o Morten Stoen, Annerudstubben 3, N-1383 Asker, Norway

NEW ZEALAND

New Zealand Cartridge Collectors Club
Terry Castle, 70 Tiraumea Dr., Pakuranga, Auckland, New Zealand

New Zealand Deerstalkers Association
P.O. Box 6514 TE ARO, Wellington, New Zealand

SOUTH AFRICA

Historical Firearms Soc. of South Africa
P.O. Box 145, 7725 Newlands, Republic of South Africa

Republic of South Africa Cartridge Collectors Assn.
Arno Klee, 20 Eugene St., Malanshof Randburg, Gauteng 2194, Republic of South Africa

S.A.A.C.A. (Southern Africa Arms and Ammunition Assn.)
Gauteng office:
P.O. Box 7597, Weltevreden Park, 1715, Republic of South Africa/ 011-679-1151; Fax: 011-679-1131;
e-mail: saaaca@iafrica.com
Kwa-Zulu Natal office:
P.O. Box 4065, Northway, Kwazulu-Natal 4065, Republic of South Africa

SAGA (S.A. Gunowners' Assn.)
P.O. Box 35203, Northway, Kwazulu-Natal 4065, Republic of South Africa

SPAIN

Asociacion Espanola de Coleccionistas de Cartuchos (A.E.C.C.)
Secretary: Apdo. Correos No. 1086, 2880-Alcala de Henares (Madrid), Spain. President: Apdo. Correos No. 682, 50080 Zaragoza, Spain

PERIODICAL PUBLICATIONS

AAFTA News (M)
5911 Cherokee Ave., Tampa, FL 33604. Official newsletter of the American Airgun Field Target Assn.

The Accurate Rifle
Precisions Shooting, Inc., 222 Mckee Street, Manchester CT 06040. $37 yr. Dedicated to the rifle accuracy enthusiast.

Action Pursuit Games Magazine (M)
CFW Enterprises, Inc., 4201 W. Vanowen Pl., Burbank, CA 91505 818-845-2656. $4.99 single copy U.S., $5.50 Canada. Editor: Dan Reeves. World's leading magazine of paintball sports.

Air Gunner Magazine
4 The Courtyard, Denmark St., Wokingham, Berkshire RG11 2AZ, England/011-44-734-771677. $U.S. $44 for 1 yr. Leading monthly airgun magazine in U.K.

Airgun Ads
Box 33, Hamilton, MT 59840/406-363-3805; Fax: 406-363-4117. $35 1 yr. (for first mailing; $20 for second mailing; $35 for Canada and foreign orders.) Monthly tabloid with extensive For Sale and Wanted airgun listings.

The Airgun Letter
Gapp, Inc., 4614 Woodland Rd., Ellicott City, MD 21042-6329/410-730-5496; Fax: 410-730-9544; e-mail: staff@airgnltr.net; http://www.airgunletter.com. $21 U.S., $24 Canada, $27 Mexico and $33 other foreign orders, 1 yr. Monthly newsletter for airgun users and collectors.

Airgun World
4 The Courtyard, Denmark St., Wokingham, Berkshire RG40 2AZ, England/011-44-734-771677. Call for subscription rates. Oldest monthly airgun magazine in the U.K., now a sister publication to *Air Gunner.*

Alaska Magazine
Morris Communications, 735 Broad Street, Augusta, GA 30901/706-722-6060. Hunting, Fishing and Life on the Last Frontier articles of Alaska and western Canada.

American Firearms Industry
Nat'l. Assn. of Federally Licensed Firearms Dealers, 2455 E. Sunrise Blvd., Suite 916, Ft. Lauderdale, FL 33304. $35.00 yr. For firearms retailers, distributors and manufacturers.

American Guardian
NRA, 11250 Waples Mill Rd., Fairfax, VA 22030. Publications division. $15.00 1 yr. Magazine features personal protection; home-self-defense; family recreation shooting; women's issues; etc.

American Gunsmith
Belvoir Publications, Inc., 75 Holly Hill Lane, Greenwich, CT 06836-2626/203-661-6111. $49.00 (12 issues). Technical journal of firearms repair and maintenance.

American Handgunner*
Publisher's Development Corp., 591 Camino de la Reina, Suite 200, San Diego, CA 92108/800-537-3006 $16.95 yr. Articles for handgun enthusiasts, competitors, police and hunters.

American Hunter (M)
National Rifle Assn., 11250 Waples Mill Rd., Fairfax, VA 22030 (Same address for both.) Publications Div. $35.00 yr. Wide scope of hunting articles.

American Rifleman (M)
National Rifle Assn., 11250 Waples Mill Rd., Fairfax, VA 22030 (Same address for both). Publications Div. $35.00 yr. Firearms articles of all kinds.

American Survival Guide
McMullen Angus Publishing, Inc., 774 S. Placentia Ave., Placentia, CA 92670-6846. 12 issues $19.95/714-572-2255; FAX: 714-572-1864.

Armes & Tir*
c/o FABECO, 38, rue de Trévise 75009 Paris, France. Articles for hunters, collectors, and shooters. French text.

Arms Collecting (Q)
Museum Restoration Service, P.O. Box 70, Alexandria Bay, NY 13607-0070. $22.00 yr.; $62.00 3 yrs.; $112.00 5 yrs.
Australian Shooter *(formerly Australian Shooters Journal)*
Sporting Shooters' Assn. of Australia, Inc., P.O. Box 2066, Kent Town SA 5071, Australia. $60.00 yr. locally; $65.00 yr. overseas surface mail. Hunting and shooting articles.

The Backwoodsman Magazine
P.O. Box 627, Westcliffe, CO 81252. $16.00 for 6 issues per yr.; $30.00 for 2 yrs.; sample copy $2.75. Subjects include muzzle-loading, woodslore, primitive survival, trapping, homesteading, blackpowder cartridge guns, 19th century how-to.

Black Powder Cartridge News (Q)
SPG, Inc., P.O. Box 761, Livingston, MT 59047/Phone/Fax: 406-222-8416. $17 yr. (4 issues) ($6 extra 1st class mailing). For the blackpowder cartridge enthusiast.

Blackpowder Hunting (M)
Intl. Blackpowder Hunting Assn., P.O. Box 1180Z, Glenrock, WY 82637/307-436-9817. $20.00 1 yr., $36.00 2 yrs. How-to and where-to features by experts on hunting; shooting; ballistics; traditional and modern blackpowder rifles, shotguns, pistols and cartridges.

Black Powder Times
P.O. Box 234, Lake Stevens, WA 98258. $20.00 yr.; add $5 per year for Canada, $10 per year other foreign. Tabloid newspaper for blackpowder activities; test reports.

Blade Magazine
Krause Publications, 700 East State St., Iola, WI 54990-0001. $25.98 for 12 issues. Foreign price (including Canada-Mexico) $50.00. A magazine for all enthusiasts of handmade, factory and antique knives.

Caliber
GFI-Verlag, Theodor-Heuss Ring 62, 50668 Koln, Germany. For hunters, target shooters and reloaders.

The Caller (Q) (M)
National Wild Turkey Federation, P.O. Box 530, Edgefield, SC 29824. Tabloid newspaper for members; 4 issues per yr. (membership fee $25.00)

Cartridge Journal (M)
Robert Mellichamp, 907 Shirkmere, Houston, TX 77008/713-869-0558. Dues $12 for U.S. and Canadian members (includes the newsletter); 6 issues.

The Cast Bullet*(M)
Official journal of The Cast Bullet Assn. Director of Membership, 203 E. 2nd St., Muscatine, IA 52761. Annual membership dues $14, includes 6 issues.

Cibles
14, rue du Patronage-Laique, BP 2057, 52902 Chaumont, cedex 9, France. French-language arms magazine also carries a small amount of arms-related and historical content. 12 issues per year. Tel/03-25-03-87-47/Email cibeles@graphycom.com; Website: www.graphycom.com

COLTELLI, che Passione (Q)
Casella postale N.519, 20101 Milano, Italy/Fax:02-48402857. $15 1 yr., $27 2 yrs. Covers all types of knives—collecting, combat, historical. Italian text.

Combat Handguns*
Harris Publications, Inc., 1115 Broadway, New York, NY 10010.

Deer & Deer Hunting Magazine
Krause Publications, 700 E. State St., Iola, WI 54990-0001. $19.95 yr. (9 issues). For the serious deer hunter. Website: www.krause.com

The Derringer Peanut (M)
The National Association of Derringer Collectors, P.O. Box 20572, San Jose, CA 95160. A newsletter dedicated to developing the best derringer information. Write for details.

Deutsches Waffen Journal
Journal-Verlag Schwend GmbH, Postfach 100340, D-74503 Schwäbisch Hall, Germany/0791-404-500; FAX:0791-404-505 and 404-424. DM102 p. yr. (interior); DM125.30 (abroad), postage included. Antique and modern arms and equipment. German text.

Double Gun Journal
P.O. Box 550, East Jordan, MI 49727/800-447-1658. $35 for 4 issues.

Ducks Unlimited, Inc. (M)
1 Waterfowl Way, Memphis, TN 38120

The Engraver (M) (Q)
P.O. Box 4365, Estes Park, CO 80517/970-586-2388; Fax: 970-586-0394. Mike Dubber, editor. The journal of firearms engraving.

The Field
King's Reach Tower, Stamford St., London SE1 9LS England. £36.40 U.K. 1 yr.; 49.90 (overseas, surface mail) yr.; £82.00 (overseas, air mail) yr. Hunting and shooting articles, and all country sports.

Field & Stream
Time4 Media, Two Park Ave., New York, NY 10016/212-779-5000. 12 issues/$19.97. Monthly shooting column. Articles on hunting and fishing.

Field Tests
Belvoir Publications, Inc., 75 Holly Hill Lane; P.O. Box 2626, Greenwich, CT 06836-2626/203-661-6111; 800-829-3361 (subscription line). U.S. & Canada $29 1 yr., $58 2 yrs.; all other countries $45 1 yr., $90 2 yrs. (air).

Fur-Fish-Game
A.R. Harding Pub. Co., 2878 E. Main St., Columbus, OH 43209. $15.95 yr. Practical guidance regarding trapping, fishing and hunting.

The Gottlieb-Tartaro Report
Second Amendment Foundation, James Madison Bldg., 12500 NE 10th Pl., Bellevue, WA 98005/206-454-7012;Fax:206-451-3959. $30 for 12 issues. An insiders guide for gun owners.

Gray's Sporting Journal
Gray's Sporting Journal, P.O. Box 1207, Augusta, GA 30903. $36.95 per yr. for 6 issues. Hunting and fishing journals. Expeditions and Guides Book (Annual Travel Guide).

Gun List†
700 E. State St., Iola, WI 54990. $37.98 yr. (26 issues); $66.98 2 yrs. (52 issues). Indexed market publication for firearms collectors and active shooters; guns, supplies and services. Website: www.krause.com

Gun News Digest (Q)
Second Amendment Fdn., P.O. Box 488, Station C, Buffalo, NY 14209/716-885-6408; Fax:716-884-4471. $10 U.S.; $20 foreign.

The Gun Report
World Wide Gun Report, Inc., Box 38, Aledo, IL 61231-0038. $33.00 yr. For the antique and collectable gun dealer and collector.

Gunmaker (M) (Q)
ACGG, P.O. Box 812, Burlington, IA 52601-0812. The journal of custom gunmaking.

The Gunrunner
Div. of Kexco Publ. Co. Ltd., Box 565G, Lethbridge, Alb., Canada T1J 3Z4. $23.00 yr., sample $2.00. Monthly newspaper, listing everything from antiques to artillery.

Gun Show Calendar (Q)
700 E. State St., Iola, WI 54990. $14.95 yr. (4 issues). Gun shows listed; chronologically and by state. Website: www.krause.com

Gun Tests
11 Commerce Blvd., Palm Coast, FL 32142. The consumer resource for the serious shooter. Write for information.

Gun Trade News
Bruce Publishing Ltd., P.O. Box 82, Wantage, Ozon OX12 7A8, England/44-1-235-771770; Fax: 44-1-235-771848. Britain's only "trade only" magazine exclusive to the gun trade.

Gun Week†
Second Amendment Foundation, P.O. Box 488, Station C, Buffalo, NY 14209. $35.00 yr. U.S. and possessions; $45.00 yr. other countries. Tabloid paper on guns, hunting, shooting and collecting (36 issues).

Gun World
Y-Visionary Publishing, LP 265 South Anita Drive, Ste. 120, Orange, CA 92868. $21.97 yr.; $34.97 2 yrs. For the hunting, reloading and shooting enthusiast.

Guns & Ammo
Primedia, 6420 Wilshire Blvd., Los Angeles, CA 90048/213-782-2780. $23.94 yr. Guns, shooting, and technical articles.

Guns
Publishers Development Corporation, P.O. Box 85201, San Diego, CA 92138/800-537-3006. $19.95 yr. In-depth articles on a wide range of guns, shooting equipment and related accessories for gun collectors, hunters and shooters.

Guns Review
Ravenhill Publishing Co. Ltd., Box 35, Standard House, Bonhill St., London EC 2A 4DA, England. £20.00 sterling (approx. U.S. $38 USA & Canada) yr. For collectors and shooters.

H.A.C.S. Newsletter (M)
Harry Moon, Pres., P.O. Box 50117, South Slope RPO, Burnaby BC, V5J 5G3, Canada/604-438-0950; Fax:604-277-3646. $25 p. yr. U.S. and Canada. Official newsletter of The Historical Arms Collectors of B.C. (Canada).

Handgunner*
Richard A.J. Munday, Seychelles house, Brightlingsen, Essex CO7 ONN, England/012063-305201. £18.00 (sterling).

Handguns*
Primedia, 6420 Wilshire Blvd., Los Angeles, CA 90048/323-782-2868. For the handgunning and shooting enthusiast.

Handloader*
Wolfe Publishing Co., 2626 Stearman Road, Ste. A, Prescott, AZ 86301/520-445-7810;Fax:520-778-5124. $22.00 yr. The journal of ammunition reloading.

INSIGHTS*
NRA, 11250 Waples Mill Rd., Fairfax, VA 22030. Editor, John E. Robbins. $15.00 yr., which includes NRA junior membership; $10.00 for adult subscriptions (12 issues). Plenty of details for the young hunter and target shooter; emphasizes gun safety, marksmanship training, hunting skills.

International Arms & Militaria Collector (Q)
Arms & Militaria Press, P.O. Box 80, Labrador, Qld. 4215, Australia. A$39.50 yr. (U.S. & Canada), 2 yrs. A$77.50; A$37.50 (others), 1 yr., 2 yrs. $73.50 all air express mail; surface mail is less. Editor: Ian D. Skennerton.

International Shooting Sport*/UIT Journal
International Shooting Union (UIT), Bavariaring 21, D-80336 Munich, Germany. Europe: (Deutsche Mark) DM44.00 yr., 2 yrs. DM83.00; outside Europe: DM50.00 yr., 2 yrs. DM95.00 (air mail postage included.) For international sport shooting.

Internationales Waffen-Magazin
Habegger-Verlag Zürich, Postfach 9230, CH-8036 Zürich, Switzerland. SF 105.00 (approx. U.S. $73.00) surface mail for 10 issues. Modern and antique arms, self-defense. German text; English summary of contents.

The Journal of the Arms & Armour Society (M)
A. Dove, P.O. Box 10232, London, SW19 2ZD England. £15.00 surface mail; £20.00 airmail sterling only yr. Articles for the historian and collector.

Journal of the Historical Breechloading Smallarms Assn.
Published annually. P.O. Box 12778, London, SE1 6XB, England. $21.00 yr. Articles for the collector plus mailings of short articles on specific arms, reprints, newsletters, etc.

Knife World
Knife World Publications, P.O. Box 3395, Knoxville, TN 37927. $15.00 yr.; $25.00 2 yrs. Published monthly for knife enthusiasts and collectors. Articles on custom and factory knives; other knife-related interests, monthly column on knife identification, military knives.

Man At Arms*
P.O. Box 460, Lincoln, RI 02865. $27.00 yr., $52.00 2 yrs. plus $8.00 for foreign subscribers. The N.R.A. magazine of arms collecting-investing, with excellent articles for the collector of antique arms and militaria.

The Mannlicher Collector (Q)(M)
Mannlicher Collectors Assn., Inc., P.O. Box 7144, Salem Oregon 97303. $20/ yr. subscription included in membership.

MAGNUM
Rua Madre Rita Amada de Jesus, 182 , Granja Julieta, Sao Paulo – SP – 04721-050 Brazil. No details.

---

*Published bi-monthly
† Published weekly
‡Published three times per month. All others are published monthly.

M=Membership requirements; write for details.
Q=Published Quarterly.

PERIODICAL PUBLICATIONS

MAN/MAGNUM
S.A. Man (Pty) Ltd., P.O. Box 35204, Northway, Durban 4065, Republic of South Africa. SA Rand 200.00 for 12 issues. Africa's only publication on hunting, shooting, firearms, bushcraft, knives, etc.

The Marlin Collector (M)
R.W. Paterson, 407 Lincoln Bldg., 44 Main St., Champaign, IL 61820.

Muzzle Blasts (M)
National Muzzle Loading Rifle Assn., P.O. Box 67, Friendship, IN 47021/812-667-5131. $35.00 yr. annual membership. For the blackpowder shooter.

Muzzleloader Magazine*
Scurlock Publishing Co., Inc., Dept. Gun, Route 5, Box 347-M, Texarkana, TX 75501. $18.00 U.S.; $22.50 U.S./yr. for foreign subscribers. The publication for blackpowder shooters.

National Defense (M)*
American Defense Preparedness Assn., Two Colonial Place, Suite 400, 2101 Wilson Blvd., Arlington, VA 22201-3061/703-522-1820; FAX: 703-522-1885. $35.00 yr. Articles on both military and civil defense field, including weapons, materials technology, management.

National Knife Magazine (M)
Natl. Knife Coll. Assn., 7201 Shallowford Rd., P.O. Box 21070, Chattanooga, TN 37424-0070. Membership $35 yr.; $65.00 International yr.

National Rifle Assn. Journal (British) (Q)
Natl. Rifle Assn. (BR.), Bisley Camp, Brookwood, Woking, Surrey, England. GU24, OPB. £24.00 Sterling including postage.

National Wildlife*
Natl. Wildlife Fed., 1400 16th St. NW, Washington, DC 20036, $16.00 yr. (6 issues); *International Wildlife*, 6 issues, $16.00 yr. Both, $22.00 yr., includes all membership benefits. Write attn.: Membership Services Dept., for more information.

New Zealand GUNS*
Waitekauri Publishing, P.O. 45, Waikino 3060, New Zealand. $NZ90.00 (6 issues) yr. Covers the hunting and firearms scene in New Zealand.

New Zealand Wildlife (Q)
New Zealand Deerstalkers Assoc., Inc., P.O. Box 6514, Wellington, N.Z. $30.00 (N.Z.). Hunting, shooting and firearms/game research articles.

North American Hunter* (M)
P.O. Box 3401, Minnetonka, MN 55343/612-936-9333; e-mail: huntingclub@pclink.com. $18.00 yr. (7 issues). Articles on all types of North American hunting.

Outdoor Life
Time4 Media, Two Park Ave., New York, NY 10016. $14.97/10 issues. Extensive coverage of hunting and shooting. Shooting column by Jim Carmichel.

La Passion des Courteaux (Q)
Phenix Editions, 25 rue Mademoiselle, 75015 Paris, France. French text.

Paintball Games International Magazine
Aceville Publications, Castle House, 97 High St., Colchester, Essex, England CO1 1TH/011-44-206-564840. Write for subscription rates. Leading magazine in the U.K. covering competitive paintball activities.

Paintball News
PBN Publishing, P.O. Box 1608, 24 Henniker St., Hillsboro, NH 03244/603-464-6080. $35 U.S. 1 yr. Bi-weekly. Newspaper covering the sport of paintball, new product reviews and industry features.

Paintball Sports (Q)
Paintball Publications, Inc., 540 Main St., Mount Kisco, NY 10549/941-241-7400. $24.75 U.S. 1 yr., $32.75 foreign. Covering the competitive paintball scene.

Performance Shooter
Belvoir Publications, Inc., 75 Holly Hill Lane, Greenwich, CT 06836-2626/203-661-6111. $45.00 yr. (12 issues). Techniques and technology for improved rifle and pistol accuracy.

Petersen's HUNTING Magazine
Primedia, 6420 Wilshire Blvd., Los Angeles, CA 90048. $19.94 yr.; Canada $29.34 yr.; foreign countries $29.94 yr. Hunting articles for all game; test reports.

P.I. Magazine
America's Private Investigation Journal, 755 Bronx Dr., Toledo, OH 43609. Chuck Klein, firearms editor with column about handguns.

Pirsch
BLV Verlagsgesellschaft GmbH, Postfach 400320, 80703 Munich, Germany/089-12704-0;Fax:089-12705-354. German text.

Point Blank
Citizens Committee for the Right to Keep and Bear Arms (sent to contributors), Liberty Park, 12500 NE 10th Pl., Bellevue, WA 98005

POINTBLANK (M)
Natl. Firearms Assn., Box 4384 Stn. C, Calgary, AB T2T 5N2, Canada. Official publication of the NFA.

The Police Marksman*
6000 E. Shirley Lane, Montgomery, AL 36117. $17.95 yr. For law enforcement personnel.

Police Times (M)
3801 Biscayne Blvd., Miami, FL 33137/305-573-0070.

Popular Mechanics
Hearst Corp., 224 W. 57th St., New York, NY 10019. Firearms, camping, outdoor oriented articles.

Precision Shooting
Precision Shooting, Inc., 222 McKee St., Manchester, CT 06040. $37.00 yr. U.S. Journal of the International Benchrest Shooters, and target shooting in general. Also considerable coverage of varmint shooting, as well as big bore, small bore, schuetzen, lead bullet, wildcats and precision reloading.

Rifle*
Wolfe Publishing Co., 2626 Stearman Road, Ste. A, Prescott, AZ 86301/520-445-7810; Fax: 520-778-5124. $19.00 yr. The sporting firearms journal.

Rifle's Hunting Annual
Wolfe Publishing Co., 2626 Stearman Road, Ste. A, Prescott, AZ 86301/520-445-7810; Fax: 520-778-5124. $4.99 Annual. Dedicated to the finest pursuit of the hunt.

Rod & Rifle Magazine
Lithographic Serv. Ltd., P.O. Box 38-138, Wellington, New Zealand. $50.00 yr. (6 issues). Hunting, shooting and fishing articles.

Safari* (M)
Safari Magazine, 4800 W. Gates Pass Rd., Tucson, AZ 85745/602-620-1220. $55.00 (6 times). The journal of big game hunting, published by Safari Club International. Also publish *Safari Times*, a monthly newspaper, included in price of $55.00 national membership.

Second Amendment Reporter
Second Amendment Foundation, James Madison Bldg., 12500 NE 10th Pl., Bellevue, WA 98005. $15.00 yr. (non-contributors).

Shoot! Magazine*
Shoot! Magazine Corp., 1770 West State Stret PMB 340, Boise ID 83702/208-368-9920; Fax: 208-338-8428. Website: www.shootmagazine.com; $32.95 (6 times/yr.). Articles of interest to the cowboy action shooter, or others interested the Western-era firearms and ammunition.

Shooter's News
23146 Lorain Rd., Box 349, North Olmsted, OH 44070/216-979-5258;Fax:216-979-5259. $29 U.S. 1 yr., $54 2 yrs.; $52 foreign surface. A journal dedicated to precision riflery.

Shooting Industry
Publisher's Dev. Corp., 591 Camino de la Reina, Suite 200, San Diego, CA 92108. $50.00 yr. To the trade. $25.00.

Shooting Sports USA
National Rifle Assn. of America, 11250 Waples Mill Road, Fairfax, VA 22030. Annual subscriptions for NRA members are $5 for classified shooters and $10 for non-classified shooters. Non-NRA member subscriptions are $15. Covering events, techniques and personalities in competitive shooting.

Shooting Sportsman*
P.O. Box 11282, Des Moines, IA 50340/800-666-4955 (for subscriptions). Editorial: P.O. Box 1357, Camden, ME 04843. $19.95 for six issues. The magazine of wingshooting and fine guns.

The Shooting Times & Country Magazine (England)†
IPC Magazines Ltd., King's Reach Tower, Stamford St, 1 London SE1 9LS, England/0171-261-6180;Fax:0171-261-7179. £65 (approx. $98.00) yr.; £79 yr. overseas (52 issues). Game shooting, wild fowling, hunting, game fishing and firearms articles. Britain's best selling field sports magazine.

Shooting Times
Primedia, 2 News Plaza, P.O. Box 1790, Peoria, IL 61656/309-682-6626. $16.97 yr. Guns, shooting, reloading; articles on every gun activity.

The Shotgun News‡
Primedia, 2 News Plaza, P.O. Box 1790, Peoria, IL 61656/800-495-8362. 36 issues/ yr. @ $28.95; 12 issues/yr. @ $19.95. foreign subscription call for rates. Sample copy $4.00. Gun ads of all kinds.

SHOT Business
National Shooting Sports Foundation, Flintlock Ridge Office Center, 11 Mile Hill Rd., Newtown, CT 06470-2359/203-426-1320; FAX: 203-426-1087. For the shooting, hunting and outdoor trade retailer.

Shotgun Sports
P.O. Box 6810, Auburn, CA 95604/916-889-2220; FAX:916-889-9106. $31.00 yr. Trapshooting how-to's, shotshell reloading, shotgun patterning, shotgun tests and evaluations, Sporting Clays action, waterfowl/upland hunting. Call 1-800-676-8920 for a free sample copy.

The Single Shot Exchange Magazine
PO box 1055, York SC 29745/803-628-5326 phone/fax. $31.50/yr., monthly. Articles of interest to the blackpowder cartridge shooter and antique arms collector.

Single Shot Rifle Journal* (M)
Editor John Campbell, PO Box 595, Bloomfield Hills, MI 48303/248-458-8415. Email: jcampbel@dmbb.com Annual dues $35 for 6 issues. Journal of the American Single Shot Rifle Assn.

The Sixgunner (M)
Handgun Hunters International, P.O. Box 357, MAG, Bloomingdale, OH 43910

The Skeet Shooting Review
National Skeet Shooting Assn., 5931 Roft Rd., San Antonio, TX 78253. $20.00 yr. (Assn. membership includes mag.) Competition results, personality profiles of top Skeet shooters, how-to articles, technical, reloading information.

Soldier of Fortune
Subscription Dept., P.O. Box 348, Mt. Morris, IL 61054. $29.95 yr.; $39.95 Canada; $50.95 foreign.
Sporting Classics

Sporting Classics, Inc.
PO Box 23707, Columbia, SC 29223/1-800-849-1004. 1 yr./6 issues/$23.95; 2 yrs./12 issues/$38.95; 3 yrs./18 issues/$47.95. Firearms & outdoor articles and columns.

Sporting Clays Magazine
Patch Communications, 5211 South Washington Ave., Titusville, FL 32780/407-268-5010; FAX: 407-267-7216. $29.95 yr. (12 issues). Official publication of the National Sporting Clays Association.

Sporting Goods Business
Miller Freeman, Inc., One Penn Plaza, 10th Fl., New York, NY 10119-0004. Trade journal.

Sporting Goods Dealer
Two Park Ave., New York, NY 10016. $100.00 yr. Sporting goods trade journal.

Sporting Gun
Bretton Court, Bretton, Peterborough PE3 8DZ, England. £27.00 (approx. U.S. $36.00), airmail £35.50 yr. For the game and clay enthusiasts.

Sports Afield
15621 Chemical Lane, Huntington Beach CA 92648. U.S./800-234-3537. International/714-894-9080. Nine issues for $29.97. Website: www.sportsafield.com. America's oldest outdoor publication is now devoted to high-end sporting pursuits, especially in North America and Africa.

The Squirrel Hunter
P.O. Box 368, Chireno, TX 75937. $14.00 yr. Articles about squirrel hunting.

Stott's Creek Calendar
Stott's Creek Printers, 2526 S 475 W, Morgantown, IN 46160/317-878-5489. 1 yr (3 issues) $11.50; 2 yrs. (6 issues) $20.00. Lists all gun shows everywhere in convenient calendar form; call for information.

Super Outdoors
2695 Aiken Road, Shelbyville, KY 40065/502-722-9463; 800-404-6064; Fax: 502-722-8093. Mark Edwards, publisher. Contact for details.

TACARMI
Via E. De Amicis, 25; 20123 Milano, Italy. $100.00 yr. approx. Antique and modern guns. (Italian text.)

Territorial Dispatch—1800s Historical Publication (M)
National Assn. of Buckskinners, 4701 Marion St., Suite 324, Livestock Exchange Bldg., Denver, CO 80216. Michael A. Nester & Barbara Wyckoff, editors. 303-297-9671.

Trap & Field
1000 Waterway Blvd., Indianapolis, IN 46202. $25.00 yr. Official publ. Amateur Trapshooting Assn. Scores, averages, trapshooting articles.

Turkey Call* (M)
Natl. Wild Turkey Federation, Inc., P.O. Box 530, Edgefield, SC 29824. $25.00 with membership (6 issues per yr.)

Turkey & Turkey Hunting*
Krause Publications, 700 E. State St., Iola, WI 54990-0001. $13.95 (6 issue p. yr.). Magazine with leading-edge articles on all aspects of wild turkey behavior, biology and the successful ways to hunt better with that info. Learn the proper techniques to calling, the right equipment, and more.

The U.S. Handgunner* (M)
U.S. Revolver Assn., 40 Larchmont Ave., Taunton, MA 02780. $10.00 yr. General handgun and competition articles. Bi-monthly sent to members.

U.S. Airgun Magazine
P.O. Box 2021, Benton, AR 72018/800-247-4867; Fax: 501-316-8549. 10 issues a yr. Cover the sport from hunting, 10-meter, field target and collecting. Write for details.

The Varmint Hunter Magazine (Q)
The Varmint Hunters Assn., Box 759, Pierre, SD 57501/800-528-4868. $24.00 yr.

Waffenmarkt-Intern
GFI-Verlag, Theodor-Heuss Ring 62, 50668 Köln, Germany. Only for gunsmiths, licensed firearms dealers and their suppliers in Germany, Austria and Switzerland.

Wild Sheep (M) (Q)
Foundation for North American Wild Sheep, 720 Allen Ave., Cody, WY 82414. Website: http://iigi.com/os/non/fnaws/fnaws.htm; e-mail: fnaws@wyoming.com. Official journal of the foundation.

Wisconsin Outdoor Journal
Krause Publications, 700 E. State St., Iola, WI 54990-0001. $17.97 yr. (8 issues). For Wisconsin's avid hunters and fishermen, with features from all over that state with regional reports, legislative updates, etc. Website: www.krause.com

Women & Guns
P.O. Box 488, Sta. C, Buffalo, NY 14209. $24.00 yr. U.S.; $72.00 foreign (12 issues). Only magazine edited by and for women gun owners.

World War II*
Cowles History Group, 741 Miller Dr. SE, Suite D-2, Leesburg, VA 20175-8920. Annual subscriptions $19.95 U.S.; $25.95 Canada; 43.95 foreign. The title says it—WWII; good articles, ads, etc.

---

*Published bi-monthly
† Published weekly
‡Published three times per month. All others are published monthly.

M=Membership requirements; write for details.
Q=Published Quarterly.

THE HANDGUNNER'S LIBRARY

FOR COLLECTOR ◆ HUNTER ◆ SHOOTER ◆ OUTDOORSMAN

IMPORTANT NOTICE TO BOOK BUYERS

Books listed here may be bought from **Ray Riling Arms Books Co.,** 6844 Gorsten St., Philadelphia, PA 19119, Phone 215-438-2456; FAX: 215-438-5395. E-mail: sales@rayrilingarmsbooks.com. Larry Riling is the researcher and compiler of "The Arms Library" and a seller of gun books for over 32 years. The Riling stock includes books classic and modern, many hard-to-find items, and many not obtainable elsewhere. These pages list a portion of the current stock. They offer prompt, complete service, with delayed shipments occurring only on out-of-print or out-of-stock books.

Visit our Web site at **www.rayrilingarmsbooks.com** and order all of your favorite titles online from our secure site.

NOTICE FOR ALL CUSTOMERS: Remittance in U.S. funds must accompany all orders. For your convenience we accept VISA, MasterCard, Discover & American Express. For shipments in the U.S., add $7.00 for the 1st book and $2.00 for each additional book for postage and insurance. Minimum order $10.00. International Orders add $13.00 for the 1st book and $5.00 for each additional book. All International orders are shipped at the buyer's risk unless an additional $5 for insurance is included. USPS does not offer insurance to all countries unless shipped Air-Mail. Please e-mail or call for pricing.

Payments in excess of order or for "Backorders" are credited or fully refunded at request. Books "As-Ordered" are not returnable except by permission and a handling charge on these of 10% or $2.00 per book, whichever is greater, is deducted from refund or credit. Only Pennsylvania customers must include current sales tax.

A full variety of arms books also available from **Rutgers Book Center**, 127 Raritan Ave., Highland Park, NJ 08904/908-545-4344; FAX: 908-545-6686 or **I.D.S.A. Books**, 1324 Stratford Drive, Piqua, OH 45356/937-773-4203; FAX: 937-778-1922.

BALLISTICS AND HANDLOADING

ABC's of Reloading, 7th Edition, by Bill Chevalier, Iola, WI, Krause Publications, 2005. 288 pp., illustrated with 550 b&w photos. Softcover. NEW. $21.95

Accurate Arms Loading Guide Number 2, by Accurate Arms, McEwen, TN, Accurate Arms Company, Inc., 2000. Paper covers. $22.95

Includes new data on smokeless powders XMR4064 and XMP5744 as well as a special section on cowboy action shooting. The new manual includes 50 new pages of data. An appendix includes nominal rotor charge weights, bullet diameters.

The American Cartridge, by Charles Suydam, Borden Publishing Co. Alhambra, CA, 1986. 184 pp., illus. Softcover $24.95

An illustrated study of the rimfire cartridge in the United States.

Ammo and Ballistics II, by Robert W. Forker, Safari Press, Inc., Huntington Beach, CA, 2002. 298 pp., illus. Paper covers. $19.95

Ballistic data on 125 calibers and 1,400 loads out to 500 yards.

Barnes Bullets Reloading Manual Number 3, Orem, Barnes, 2001. 786 pp. Hardcover. NEW. $29.95

Barnes Reloading Manual #3, Barnes Bullets, American Fork, UT, 2003. 668 pp., illus. $29.95

Features data and trajectories on the new weight X, XBT and Solids in calibers from .22 to .50 BMG.

Blackpowder Loading Manual, 3rd Edition, by Sam Fadala, DBI Books, a division of Krause Publications, Iola, WI, 1995. 368 pp., illus. Paper covers. $20.95

Revised and expanded edition of this landmark blackpowder loading book. Covers hundreds of loads for most of the popular blackpowder rifles, handguns and shotguns.

Black Powder, Pig Lead and Steel Silhouettes, by Paul A. Matthews, Prescott, AZ, Wolfe Publishing, 2002. 132 pp., illustrated with b&w photographs and detailed drawings and diagrams. Softcover. NEW. $16.95

Cartridges of the World, 10th Edition; Revised and Expanded by Frank C. Barnes, Iola, WI, Krause Publications, 2003. 526 pp., 450 b&w photos. Softcover. NEW. $24.95

Cartridge Reloading Tools of the Past, by R.H. Chamberlain, and Tom Quigley, Castle Rock, WA, 1998. 167 pp., illus. Paper covers. $25.00

A detailed treatment of the extensive Winchester and Ideal line of handloading tools and bullet molds, plus Remington, Marlin, Ballard, Browning, Maynard, and many others.

Cast Bullets for the Black Powder Rifle, by Paul A. Matthews, Wolfe Publishing Co., Prescott, AZ, 1996. 133 pp., illus. Paper covers. $22.50

The tools and techniques used to make your cast bullet shooting a success.

Complete Blackpowder Handbook, 4th Edition, by Sam Fadala, DBI Books, a division of Krause Publications, Iola, WI, 2001. 400 pp., illus. Paper covers. $22.95

Expanded and completely rewritten edition of the definitive book on the subject of blackpowder.

Complete Reloading Manual, One Book / One Caliber, CA, Load Books USA, 2000. $7.95 each

Contains unabridged information from U.S. bullet and powder makers. With thousands of proven and tested loads, plus dozens of various bullet designs and different powders. Spiral bound. Available in all calibers.

Designing and Forming Custom Cartridges for Rifles and Handguns, by Ken Howell. Precision Shooting, Manchester, CT. 2002. 600 pp., illus. $59.95

The classic work in its field, out of print for the last few years and virtually unobtainable on the used book market, now returns in an exact reprint of the original. Full size (8-1/2" x 11"), hardcovers. Dozens of cartridge drawings never published anywhere before–dozens you've never heard of (guaranteed!). Precisely drawn to the dimensions specified by the men who designed them, the factories that made them, and the authorities that set the standards. All drawn to the same format and scale (1.5x) for most, how to form them from brass. Other practical information included.

Early Gunpowder Artillery 1300-1600 by John Norris, London, The Crowood Press, 2003. 1st edition. 141 pp., with 160 b&w photos. Hardcover. New in new dust jacket. $34.95

Early Loading Tools & Bullet Molds, Pioneer Press, 1988. 88 pp., illus. Softcover. $7.50

German 7.9mm Military Ammunition 1888-1945, by Daniel Kent, Ann Arbor, MI, Kent, 1990. 153 pp., plus appendix. illus., b&w photos. $35.00

Handbook for Shooters and Reloaders, by P.O. Ackley, Salt Lake City, UT, 1998, (Vol. I), 567 pp., illus. Includes a separate exterior ballistics chart. $24.95; (Vol. II), a new printing with specific new material. 495 pp., illus. $20.95

Handgun Stopping Power; The Definitive Study, by Marshall & Sandow. Boulder, CO, Paladin Press, 1992. 240 pp. $45.00

Offers accurate predictions of the stopping power of specific loads in calibers from 380 Auto to 45 ACP, as well as such specialty rounds as the Glaser Safety Slug, Federal Hydra-Shok, MagSafe, etc. This is the definitive methodology for predicting the stopping power of handgun loads, the first to take into account what really happens when a bullet meets a man.

Handloader's Digest: 18th Edition edited by Ken Ramage, Iola, WI, Krause Publications, 2003. 300 b&w photos, 256 pp. Softcover. NEW. $19.95

Handloader's Manual of Cartridge Conversions, 2nd Revised Edition by John J., Donnelly, Stoeger Publishing Co., So. Hackensack, NJ, 2002. Unpaginated. $39.95

From 14 Jones to 70-150 Winchester in English and American cartridges, and from 4.85 U.K. to 15.2x28R Gevelot in metric cartridges. Over 900 cartridges described in detail.

Hatcher's Notebook, by S. Julian Hatcher, Stackpole Books, Harrisburg, PA, 1992. 488 pp., illus. $39.95

A reference work for shooters, gunsmiths, ballisticians, historians, hunters and collectors.

Headstamped Cartridges and Their Variations; Volume 2 by Daniel L. Shuey, W.R.A. Co., Rockford, IL, WCF Publications, 2003. 351 pp. illustrated with b&w photos. Hardcover. NEW. $55.00

History & Development of Small Arms Ammunition, Volume 1, Second Edition–With A Value Guide, Martial Long Arms, Flintlock through Rimfire, by George A. Hoyem, Missoula, MI, Armory Publications, 2005. Hardcover. New in new dust jacket. $60.00

Hornady Handbook of Cartridge Reloading, 6th Edition, Vol. I and II, edited by Larry Steadman, Hornady Mfg. Co., Grand Island, NE, 2003., illus. $49.95

Two volumes; Volume 1, 773 pp.; Volume 2, 717 pp. New edition of this famous reloading handbook covers rifle and handgun reloading data and ballistic tables. Latest loads, ballistic information, etc.

How-To's for the Black Powder Cartridge Rifle Shooter, by Paul A. Matthews, Wolfe Publishing Co., Prescott, AZ, 1995. 45 pp. Paper covers. $22.50

Covers lube recipes, good bore cleaners and over-powder wads. Tips include compressing powder charges, combating wind resistance, improving ignition and much more.

The Hunter's Guide to Accurate Shooting, by Wayne van Zwoll, Guilford, CT, Lyons Press, 2002. 1st edition. 288 pp. Hardcover. New in new dust jacket. $29.95

The Illustrated Reference of Cartridge Dimensions, edited by Dave Scovill, Wolfe Publishing Co., Prescott, AZ, 1994. 343 pp., illus. Paper covers. $19.00

A comprehensive volume with over 300 cartridges. Standard and metric dimensions have been taken from SAAMI drawings and/or fired cartridges.

Loading the Black Powder Rifle Cartridge, by Paul A. Matthews, Wolfe Publishing Co., Prescott, AZ, 1993. 121 pp., illus. Paper covers. $22.50

Author Matthews brings the blackpowder cartridge shooter valuable information on the basics, including cartridge care, lubes and moulds, powder charges and developing and testing loads in his usual authoritative style.

Lyman 48th Reloading Handbook, No. 48. Connecticut, Lan Publishing Corporation, 2003. 48th edition. 480 pp. Softcover. NEW. $26.95

Lyman Cast Bullet Handbook, 3rd Edition, edited by C. Kenneth Ramage, Lyman Publications, Middlefield, CT, 1980. 416 pp., illus. Paper covers. $19.95

Information on more than 5000 tested cast bullet loads and 19 pages of trajectory and wind drift tables for cast bullets.

Lyman Black Powder Handbook, 2nd Edition, edited by Sam Fadala, Lyman Products for Shooters, Middlefield, CT, 2000. 239 pp., illus. Paper covers. $19.95

Comprehensive load information for the modern blackpowder shooter.

THE HANDGUNNER'S LIBRARY

Lyman Shotshell Handbook, 4th Edition, edited by Edward A. Matunas, Lyman Products Co., Middlefield, CT, 1996. 330 pp., illus. Paper covers. $24.95
Has 9,000 loads, including slugs and buckshot, plus feature articles and a full color I.D. section. Superb reference text.

Make It Accurate - Get the Maximum Performance from Your Hunting Rifle, by Craig Boddington, Long Beach, CA, Safari Press, 1999. Hardcover. New in new dust jacket. $24.95

Metallic Cartridge Conversions: The History of the Guns and Modern Reproductions, by Dennis Adler, Foreword by R. L. Wilson, Iola, WI, Krause Publications, 2003. 1st edition. 208 pp. 250 color photos. Hardcover. New in new dust jacket. $39.95

Modern Exterior Ballistics, by Robert L. McCoy, Schiffer Publishing Co., Atglen, PA, 1999. 128 pp. $95.00
Advanced students of exterior ballistics and flight dynamics will find this comprehensive textbook on the subject a useful addition to their libraries.

Modern Reloading 2nd Edition, by Richard Lee, Inland Press, 2003. 623 pp., illus. $29.95
The how-to's of rifle, pistol and shotgun reloading plus load data for rifle and pistol calibers.

Modern Reloading Manual, 2nd Edition by Richard Lee, privately printed, 2003. 510 pp., illus. Hardcover. NEW. $24.95

Mr. Single Shot's Cartridge Handbook, by Frank de Haas, Mark de Haas, Orange City, IA, 1996. 116 pp., illus. Paper covers. $21.50
This book covers most of the cartridges, both commercial and wildcat, that the author has known and used.

Nosler Reloading Manual #5, edited by Gail Root, Nosler Bullets, Inc., Bend, OR, 2002. 516 pp., illus. $29.99
Combines information on their ballistic tip, partition and handgun bullets with traditional powders and new powders never before used, plus trajectory information from 100 to 500 yards.

The Paper Jacket, by Paul Matthews, Wolfe Publishing Co., Prescott, AZ, 1991. Paper covers. $14.50
Up-to-date and accurate information about paper-patched bullets.

Reloading for Shotgunners, 4th Edition, by Kurt D. Fackler, and M.L. McPherson, DBI Books, a division of Krause Publications, Iola, WI, 1997. 320 pp., illus. Paper covers. $19.95
Expanded reloading tables with over 11,000 loads. Bushing charts for every major press and component maker. All new presentation on all aspects of shotshell reloading by two of the top experts in the field.

Reloading Tools, Sights and Telescopes for S/S Rifles, by Gerald O. Kelver, Brighton, CO, 1982. 163 pp., illus. Softcover. $15.00
A listing of most of the famous makers of reloading tools, sights and telescopes with a brief description of the products they manufactured.

The Rimfire Cartridge in the United States and Canada, Illustrated History of Rimfire Cartridges, Manufacturers, and the Products Made from 1857-1984, by John L. Barber, Thomas Publications, Gettysburg, PA 2000. 1st edition. Profusely illus. 221 pp. $50.00
The author has written an encyclopedia of rimfire cartridges from the 22 to the massive 1.00 in. Gatling. Fourteen chapters, six appendices and an excellent bibliography.

Round Ball to Rimfire: A History of Civil War Small Arms Ammunition, Vol. 3, by Dean S. Thomas, Gettysburg, PA, Thomas Publications, 2003. 488 pp. Hardcover. NEW. $49.95
Federal pistols, revolvers and miscellaneous essays.

Shotshells & Ballistics, Safari Press, 2002. 275 pp., photos. Softcover, $19.95
Accentuated with photos from the field and the range, this is a reference book unlike any other.

Sierra Reloading Manual, 5th Edition: Rifle and Handgun Manual of Reloading Data. Sedalia, MO, Sierra Bullets, 2003. Hardcover. NEW. $39.95

Sixgun Cartridges and Loads, by Elmer Keith, The Gun Room Press, Highland Park, NJ, 1986. 151 pp., illus. $24.95
A manual covering the selection, uses and loading of the most suitable and popular revolver cartridges. Originally published in 1936. Reprint.

Speer Reloading Manual No. 13, edited by members of the Speer research staff, Omark Industries, Lewiston, ID, 1999. 621 pp., illus. $24.95
With 13 new sections containing the latest technical information and reloading trends for both novice and expert in this latest edition. More than 9,300 loads are listed, including new propellant powders from Accurate Arms, Alliant, Hodgdon and Vihtavuori.

Stopping Power: A Practical Analysis of the Latest Handgun Ammunition, by Marshall & Sanow, Boulder, CO, Paladin Press, 2002. 1st edition. 600+ photos, 360 pp. Softcover. $49.95
If you want to know how handgun ammunition will work against human targets in the future, you must look at how similar ammo has worked against human targets in the past. Stopping Power bases its conclusions on real-world facts from real-world gunfights. It provides the latest street results of actual police and civilian shootings in all of the major handgun calibers, from 22 LR to 45 ACP, plus more than 30 chapters of vital interest to all gun owners. The only thing worse than being involved in a gunfight is losing one. The info in this book will help you choose the right bullets for your gun so you don't lose.

Street Stoppers, The Latest Handgun Stopping Power Street Results, by Marshall & Lanow, Boulder, CO, Paladin Press, 1996. 374 pp., illus. Softcover. $42.95
Street Stoppers is the long-awaited sequel to Handgun Stopping Power. It provides the latest results of real-life shootings in all of the major handgun calibers, plus more than 25 thought-provoking chapters that are vital to anyone interested in firearms, wound ballistics, and combat shooting. This book also covers the street results of the hottest new caliber to hit the shooting world in years, the 40 Smith & Wesson. Updated street results of the latest exotic ammunition including Remington Golden Saber and CCI-Speer Gold Dot, plus the venerable offerings from MagSafe, Glaser, Cor-Bon and others. A fascinating look at the development of Hydra-Shok ammunition is included.

Understanding Ballistics, Revised 2nd Edition by Robert A. Rinker, Mulberry House Publishing Co., Corydon, IN, 2000. 430 pp., illus. Paper covers. New, revised and expanded. $24.95
Explains basic to advanced firearm ballistics in understandable terms.

Why Not Load Your Own?, by Col. T. Whelen, Gun Room Press, Highland Park, NJ 1996, 4th ed., rev. 237 pp., illus. $20.00
A basic reference on handloading, describing each step, materials and equipment. Includes loads for popular cartridges.

Wildcat Cartridges Volumes 1 & 2 Combination, by the editors of *Handloaders* magazine, Wolfe Publishing Co., Prescott, AZ, 1997. 350 pp., illus. Paper covers. $39.95
A profile of the most popular information on wildcat cartridges that appeared in the *Handloaders* magazine.

COLLECTORS

The 1 October 1934 SS Dienstalterliste, by the Ulric of England Research Unit San Jose, CA, R. James Bender Publishing, 1994. Reprint softcover. NEW. $29.95

The 10. Panzer Division: In Action in the East, West and North Africa 1939-1943, by Jean Resta and N. Moller, Canada, J.J. Fedorowicz Publishing Inc., 2003. 1st edition. Hardcover. NEW. $89.95

18th Century Weapons of the Royal Welsh Fuziliers from Flixton Hall, by Erik Goldstein, Thomas Publications, Gettysburg, PA, 2002. 1st edition. 126 pp., illustrated with b&w photos. Softcover. $19.95

The .45-70 Springfield Book I, by Albert Frasca and Robert Hill, Frasca Publishing, 2000. Memorial edition. Hardback with gold embossed cover and spine. $95.00
The Memorial edition reprint of the 45-70 Springfield was done to honor Robert H. Hill who was an outstanding Springfield collector, historian, researcher, and gunsmith. Only 1,000 of these highly regarded books were printed, using the same binding and cover material as the original 1980 edition. The book is considered the bible for 45-70 Springfield Trapdoor collectors.

The .45-70 Springfield Book II 1865-1893, by Albert Frasca, Frasca Publishing, Springfield, Ohio 1997 Hardback with gold embossed cover and spine. 400+ pp. and 400+ photographs which cover ALL the trapdoor Springfield models. Hardback with gold embossed cover and spine. $85.00
A MUST for the trapdoor collector!

The .45-70 Springfield, by Joe Poyer and Craig Riesch, North Cape Publications, Tustin, CA, 1996. 150 pp., illus. Paper covers. $16.95
A revised and expanded second edition of a best-selling reference work organized by serial number and date of production to aid the collector in identifying popular "Trapdoor" rifles and carbines.

'51 Colt Navies, by Nathan L. Swayze, The Gun Room Press, Highland Park, NJ, 1993. 243 pp., illus. $59.95
The Model 1851 Colt Navy, its variations and markings.

The 1862 U.S. Cavalry Tactics, by Philip St. George Cooke, Mechanicsburg, PA, Stackpole Books, 2004. 416 pp. Hardcover. New in new dust jacket. $19.89

A Collector's Guide to the '03 Springfield, by Bruce N. Canfield, Andrew Mowbray Inc., Lincoln, RI, 1989. 160 pp., illus. Paper covers. $24.00
A comprehensive guide follows the '03 through its unparalleled tenure of service. Covers all of the interesting variations, modifications and accessories of this highly collectible military rifle.

A Collector's Guide to United States Combat Shotguns, by Bruce N. Canfield, Andrew Mowbray Inc., Lincoln, RI, 1992. 184 pp., illus. Paper covers. $24.00
This book provides full coverage of combat shotguns, from the earliest examples right up to the Gulf War and beyond.

A Collector's Guide to Winchester in the Service, by Bruce N. Canfield, Andrew Mowbray, Inc., Lincoln, RI, 1991. 192 pp., illus. Paper covers. $24.00
The firearms produced by Winchester for the national defense. From Hotchkiss to the M14, each firearm is examined and illustrated.

A Concise Guide to the Artillery at Gettysburg, by Gregory Coco, Thomas Publications, Gettysburg, PA, 1998. 96 pp., illus. Paper covers. $10.00
Coco's 10 book on Gettysburg is a beginner's guide to artillery and its use at the battle. It covers the artillery batteries describing the types of cannons, shells, fuses, etc. using interesting narrative and human interest stories.

A Glossary of the Construction, Decoration and Use of Arms and Armor in All Countries and in All Times, by George Cameron Stone, Dover Publishing, New York 1999. Softcover. $39.95
An exhaustive study of arms and armor in all countries through recorded history - from the Stone Age up to WWII. With over 4,500 b&w illustrations, this Dover edition is an unabridged republication of the work originally published in 1934 by the Southworth Press, Portland, MA. A new Introduction has been specially prepared for this edition.

A Guide to American Trade Catalogs 1744-1900, by Lawrence B. Romaine, Dover Publications, New York, NY. 422 pp., illus. Paper covers. $12.95

A Guide to Ballard Breechloaders, by George J. Layman, Pioneer Press, Union City, TN, 1997. 261 pp., illus. Paper covers. $19.95
Documents the saga of this fine rifle from the first models made by Ball & Williams of Worchester, to its production by the Marlin Firearms Co., to the cessation of 19th century manufacture in 1891, and finally to the modern reproductions made in the 1990s.

A Guide to the Maynard Breechloader, by George J. Layman, George J. Layman, Ayer, MA, 1993. 125 pp., illus. Paper covers. $11.95
The first book dedicated entirely to the Maynard family of breech-loading firearms. Coverage of the arms is given from the 1850s through the 1880s.

A Guide to U. S. Army Dress Helmets 1872-1904, by Kasal and Moore, North Cape Publications, 2000. 88 pp., illus. Paper covers. $15.95
This thorough study provides a complete description of the Model 1872 and 1881 dress helmets worn by the U.S. Army.

A Study of Remington's Smoot Patent and Number Four Revolvers, by Parker Harry, Parker Ora Lee, and Joan Reisch, Foreword by Roy M. Marcot, Santa Ana, CA, Armslore Press, Graphic Publishers, 2003. 1st edition. 120 pp., profusely illus., plus 8-page color section. Softcover. $17.95
A detailed, pictorial essay on Remington's early metallic cartridge-era pocket revolvers: their design, development, patents, models, identification and variations. Includes the biography of arms inventor Wm. S. Smoot, for the first time ever!, as well as a mini-history of the Remington Arms Company.

THE HANDGUNNER'S LIBRARY

Accoutrements of the United States Infantry, Riflemen, and Dragoons 1834-1839, by R.T. Huntington, Historical Arms Series No. 20. Canada, Museum Restoration. 58 pp. illus. Softcover. $8.95

Although the 1841 edition of the U.S. Ordnance Manual provides ample information on the equipment that was in use during the 1840s, it is evident that the patterns of equipment that it describes were not introduced until 1838 or 1839. This guide is intended to fill this gap in our knowledge by providing an overview of what we now know about the accoutrements that were issued to the regular infantryman, rifleman, and dragoon, in the 1830s with excursions into earlier and later years.

Ackermann Military Prints: Uniforms of the British and Indian Armies 1840-1855, by William Y. Carman with Robert W. Kenny Jr., Schiffer Publications, Atglen, PA, 2002. 1st edition. 176 pp., with over 160 color images. $69.95

Afrikakorps: Rommel's Tropical Army in Original Color, by Bernd Peitz, Gary Wilkins. Atglen, PA, Schiffer Publications, 2004. 1st edition. 192 pp., with over 200 color and b&w photographs. Hardcover. New in new dust jacket. $59.95

Air Guns, by Eldon G. Wolff, Duckett's Publishing Co., Tempe, AZ, 1997. 204 pp., illus. Paper covers. $35.00

Historical reference covering many makers, European and American guns, canes and more.

All About Southerners, including a detailed look at the characteristics and design of the "Best Little Pistol in the World," by Lionel J. Bogut, Sun City, CA, White Star, Inc., 2002. A limited edition of 1,000 copies. Signed and numbered. 114 pp., including bibliography, and plenty of b&w photographs and detailed drawings. Hardcover. $29.95

Allgemeine-SS The Commands, Units and Leaders of the General SS, by Mark C. Yerger, Atglen, PA, Schiffer Publications, 1997. 1st edition. Hardcover. New in new dust jacket. $49.95

Allied and Enemy Aircraft: May 1918; Not to be Taken from the Front Lines, Historical Arms Series No. 27. Canada, Museum Restoration. Softcover. $8.95

The basis for this title is a very rare identification manual published by the French government in 1918 that illustrated 60 aircraft with three or more views: French, English American, German, Italian, and Belgian, which might have been seen over the trenches of France. Each is described in a text translated from the original French. This is probably the most complete collection of illustrations of WWI aircraft that has survived.

American Beauty; The Prewar Colt National Match Government Model Pistol, by Timothy J. Mullin, Collector Grade Publications, Cobourg, Ontario, Canada. 72 pp., illus. $34.95

Includes over 150 serial numbers, and 20 spectacular color photos of factory engraved guns and other authenticated upgrades, including rare "double-carved" ivory grips.

American Civil War Artillery 1861-65: Field Artillery, by Philip Oxford Katcher, United Kingdom, Osprey Publishing, 2001. 1st edition. 48 pp. Softcover. $14.95

Perhaps the most influential arm of either army in the prosecution of the American Civil War, the artillery of both sides grew to be highly professional organizations. This book covers all the major artillery pieces employed, including the Napoleon, Parrott Rifle and Mountain Howitzer.

American Military and Naval Belts, 1812-1902, by R. Stephen Dorsey, Eugene, OR, Collectors Library, 2002. 1st edition. Hardcover. $80.00

With introduction by Norm Flayderman, this massive work is the NEW key reference on sword belts, waist belts, sabre belts, shoulder belts and cartridge belts (looped and non-looped). At over 460 pp., this 8-1/2" x 11" book offers over 840 photos (primarily in color) and original period drawings. In addition, this work offers the first, comprehensive research on the Anson Mills woven cartridge belts: the man, the company and its personalities, the belt-related patents and the government contracts from 1880 through 1902. This book is a "must" for all accoutrements collectors, military historians and museums.

American Military Belt Plates, by Michael J. O'Donnell and J. Duncan Campbell. Alexandria, VA, O'Donnell Publishing, 2000. 2nd edition. 614 pp., illus. Hardcover $49.00

At last available and well worth the wait! This massive study encompasses all the known plates from the Revolutionary War through the Spanish-American conflict. A sweeping, handsomely presented study that covers 1776 through 1910. Over 1,025 specimens are illustrated front and back along with many images of soldiers wearing various plates.

American Military Headgear Insignia, by Michael J. O'Donnell and J. Duncan, Campbell, Alexandria, VA, O'Donnell Publishing, 2004. 1st edition. 311 pp., 703 photo figures, 4 sketches. Hardcover. New in new dust jacket. $89.95

The American Military Saddle, 1776-1945, by R. Stephen Dorsey and Kenneth L. McPheeters, Collector's Library, Eugene, OR, 1999. 400 pp., illus. $67.00

The most complete coverage of the subject ever written on the American Military Saddle. Nearly 1,000 actual photos and official drawings, from the major public and private collections in the U.S. and Great Britain.

American Police Collectibles; Dark Lanterns and Other Curious Devices, by Matthew G. Forte, Turn of the Century Publishers, Upper Montclair, NJ, 1999. 248 pp., illus. $24.95

For collectors of police memorabilia (handcuffs, police dark lanterns, mechanical and chain nippers, rattles, billy clubs and nightsticks) and police historians.

An Introduction to the Civil War Small Arms, by Earl J. Coates and Dean S. Thomas, Thomas Publishing Co., Gettysburg, PA, 1990. 96 pp., illus. Paper covers. $10.00

The small arms carried by the individual soldier during the Civil War.

Arming the Glorious Cause; Weapons of the Second War for Independence, by James B. Whisker, Daniel D. Hartzler and Larry W. Tantz, Old Bedford Village Press, Bedford, PA., 1998. 175 pp., illus. $45.00

A photographic study of Confederate weapons.

Arms & Accoutrements of the Mounted Police 1873-1973, by Roger F. Phillips, and Donald J. Klancher, Museum Restoration Service, Ont., Canada, 1982. 224 pp., illus. $49.95

A definitive history of the revolvers, rifles, machine guns, cannons, ammunition, swords, etc. used by the NWMP, the RNWMP and the RCMP during the first 100 years of the Force.

Arms and Armor in Colonial America 1526-1783, by Harold Peterson, Dover Publishing, New York, 2000. 350 pp. with over 300 illustrations, index, bibliography and appendix. Softcover. $34.95

Over 200 years of firearms, ammunition, equipment and edged weapons.

Arms and Armor in the Art Institute of Chicago, by Waltler J. Karcheski, Bulfinch, New York 1999. 128 pp., 103 color photos, 12 b&w illustrations. $50.00

The George F. Harding Collection of arms and armor is the most visited installation at the Art Institute of Chicago–a testament to the enduring appeal of swords, muskets and the other paraphernalia of medieval and early modern war. Organized both chronologically and by type of weapon, this book captures the best of this astonishing collection in 115 striking photographs - most in color–accompanied by illuminating text. Here are intricately filigreed breastplates and ivory-handled crossbows, samurai katana and Toledo-steel scimitars, elaborately decorated maces and beautifully carved flintlocks–a treat for anyone who has ever been beguiled by arms, armor and the age of chivalry.

Arms Makers of Maryland, by Daniel D. Hartzler, George Shumway, York, PA, 1975. 200 pp., illus. $50.00

A thorough study of the gunsmiths of Maryland who worked during the late 18th and early 19th centuries.

Arms Makers of Western Pennsylvania, by James B. Whisker, Old Bedford Village Press. 1st edition. Deluxe hardbound edition, 176 pp., $50.00

Printed on fine coated paper with many large photographs and detailed text describing the period, lives, tools, and artistry of the Arms Makers of Western Pennsylvania.

Arsenal of Freedom: The Springfield Armory 1890-1948, by Lt. Col. William Brophy, Andrew Mowbray, Inc., Lincoln, RI,1997. 20 pgs. of photos. 400 pp. As new, Softcover. $29.95

A year-by-year account drawn from offical records. Packed with reports, charts, tables and line drawings.

The Art of Gun Engraving, by Claude Gaier and Pietro Sabatti, Knickerbocker Press, N.Y., 1999. 160 pp., illus. $34.95

The richness and detail lavished on early firearms represents a craftmanship nearly vanished. Beginning with crossbows, hunting scenes, portraits, or mythological themes are intricately depicted within a few square inches of etched metal. The full-color photos contained herein recaptures this lost art with exquisite detail.

Astra Automatic Pistols, by Leonardo M. Antaris, FIRAC Publishing Co., Sterling, CO, 1989. 248 pp., illus. $55.00

Charts, tables, serial ranges, etc. The definitive work on Astra pistols.

Austrian & German Guns and Rifles (Fucili Da Caccia Austriaci E Tedeschi), by Marco E. Nobili, Italy, Il Volo Srl, 2000. 1st printing. 304 pp., illustrated with b&w photographs, plus 16 full color plates. Text in Italian and English. Hardcover. New in very good dust jacket. $189.95

Ballard: The Great American Single Shot Rifle, by John T. Dutcher. Denver, CO, privately printed, 2002. 1st edition. 380 pp., illustrated with b&w photos, with 8-page color insert. Hardcover. New in new dust jacket. $79.95

Basic Documents on U.S. Martial Arms, commentary by Col. B.R. Lewis, reissue by Ray Riling, Phila., PA, 1956 and 1960. Rifle Musket Model 1855. Each $10.00

The first issue rifle of musket caliber, a muzzleloader equipped with the Maynard Primer, 32 pp. Rifle Musket Model 1863. The typical Union muzzleloader of the Civil War, 26 pp. Breech-Loading Rifle Musket Model 1866. The first of our 50-caliber breechloading rifles, 12 pp. Remington Navy Rifle Model 1870. A commercial type breech-loader made at Springfield, 16 pp. Lee Straight Pull Navy Rifle Model 1895. A magazine cartridge arm of 6mm caliber, 23 pp. Breech-Loading Arms (five models) 27 pp. Ward-Burton Rifle Musket 1871, 16 pp.

Battle Colors: Insignia and Aircraft Markings of the Eighth Air Force in World War II, by Robert A. Watkins, Atglen, PA, Schiffer Publications, 2004. 1st edition. Softcover. $45.00

Battle Weapons of the American Revolution, by George C. Neuman, Scurlock Publishing Co., Texarkana, TX, 2001. 400 pp. Illus. Softcovers. $44.95

The most extensive photographic collection of Revolutionary War weapons ever in one volume. More than 1,600 photos of over 500 muskets, rifles, swords, bayonets, knives and other arms used by both sides in America's War for Independence.

The Bedford County Rifle and Its Makers, by Calvin Hetrick, Introduction by George Shumway, George Shumway Pub., 1975. 40 pp. illus. Softcover. $10.00

The author's study of the graceful and distinctive muzzle-loading rifles made in Bedford County, Pennsylvania, stands as a milestone on the long path to the understanding of America's longrifles.

The Belgian Rattlesnake; The Lewis Automatic Machine Gun, by William M. Easterly, Collector Grade Publications, Cobourg, Ontario, Canada, 1998. 584 pp., illus. $79.95

The most complete account ever published on the life and times of Colonel Isaac Newton Lewis and his crowning invention, the Lewis Automatic machine gun.

Beretta Automatic Pistols, by J.B. Wood, Stackpole Books, Harrisburg, PA, 1985. 192 pp., illus. $26.95

Only English-language book devoted to the Beretta line. Includes all important models.

Best of Holland & Holland, England's Premier Gunmaker, by Michael McIntosh and Jan G. Roosenburg. Safari Press, Inc., Long Beach, CA, 2002. 1st edition. 298 pp. Profuse color illustrations. $69.95

Holland & Holland has had a long history of not only building London's "best" guns but also providing superior guns–the ultimate gun in finish, engraving, and embellishment. From the days of old in which a maharaja would order 100 fancifully engraved H&H shotguns for his guests to use at his duck shoot, to the recent elaborately decorated sets depicting the Apollo 11 moon landing or the history of the British Empire, all of these guns represent the zenith in the art and craft of gunmaking and engraving. These and other H&H guns in the series named "Products of Excellence" are a cut above the ordinary H&H gun and hark back to a time when the British Empire ruled over one-third of the globe–a time when rulers, royalty, and the rich worldwide came to H&H for a gun that would elevate them above the crowd. In this book, master gunwriter and acknowledged English gun expert Michael McIntosh and former H&H director Jan Roosenburg show us in words and pictures the finest products ever produced by H&H and, many would argue, by any gun company on earth. From a dainty and elegant 410 shotgun with gold relief engraving of scenes from Greek and Roman antiquity, to the massive 700 Nitro Express double rifle, some of the most expensive and opulent guns ever produced on earth parade through these pages. An overview of the Products of Excellence series is given as well as a description and history of these special H&H guns. Never before have so many superlative guns from H&H–or any other maker for that manner–been displayed in one book. Many photos shown are firearms from private collections which cannot be seen publicly anywhere except in this book. In addition, many interesting details and a general history of H&H are provided.

The Big Guns, Civil War Siege, Seacoast, and Naval Cannon, by Edwin Olmstead, Wayne E. Stark, and Spencer C. Tucker, Museum Restoration Service, Bloomfield, Ontario, Canada, 1997. 360 pp., illus. $80.00

This book is designed to identify and record the heavy guns available to both sides by the end of the Civil War.

Blue Book of Air Guns, 4th Edition, edited by S.P. Fjestad, Blue Book Publications, Inc. Minneapolis, MN 2005. $24.95

This new edition simply contains more airgun values and information than any other single publication.

Blue Book of Gun Values, 26th Edition, edited by S.P. Fjestad, Blue Book Publications, Inc. Minneapolis, MN 2005. $39.95

This new edition simply contains more firearm values and information than any other single publication. Expanded to over 1,600 pages featuring over 100,000 firearms prices, the new Blue Book of Gun Values also contains over 3/4-million words of text–no other book is even close! Most of the information contained in this publication is simply not available anywhere else, for any price!

Blue Book of Modern Black Powder Values, 4th Edtion by Dennis Adler, Blue Book Publications, Inc. Minneapolis, MN 2005. 271 pp., illus. 41 color photos. Softcover. $24.95

This new title contains more up-to-date blackpowder values and related information than any other single publication. This new book will keep you up-to-date on modern blackpowder models and prices, including most makes and models introduced this year!

The Blunderbuss 1500-1900, by James D. Forman, Historical Arms Series No. 32. Canada, Museum Restoration, 1994. 40 pp., illus. Softcover. $8.95

An excellent and authoritative booklet giving tons of information on the Blunderbuss, a very neglected subject.

Boarders Away Volume I: With Steel-Edged Weapons & Polearms, by William Gilkerson, Andrew Mowbray, Inc. Publishers, Lincoln, RI, 1993. 331 pp. $48.00

Contains the essential 24-page chapter "War at Sea" which sets the historical and practical context for the arms discussed. Includes chapters on Early Naval Weapons, Boarding Axes, Cutlasses, Officers Fighting Swords and Dirks, and weapons at hand of Random Mayhem.

Boarders Away, Volume II: Firearms of the Age of Fighting Sail, by William Gilkerson, Andrew Mowbray, Inc. Publishers, Lincoln, RI, 1993. 331 pp., illus. $65.00

Covers the pistols, muskets, combustibles and small cannons used aboard American and European fighting ships, 1626-1826.

Boston's Gun Bible, by Boston T. Party, Ignacio, CO, Javelin Press, August 2000. Expanded edition. Softcover. $28.00

This mammoth guide for gun owners everywhere is a completely updated and expanded edition (more than 500 new pages!) of Boston T. Party's classic Boston on Guns and Courage. Boston gives new advice on which shoulder weapons and handguns to buy and why, before exploring such topics as why you should consider not getting a concealed carry permit, what guns and gear will likely be outlawed next, how to spend within your budget, why you should go to a quality defensive shooting academy now, which guns and gadgets are inferior and why, how to stay off illegal government gun registration lists, how to spot an undercover agent trying to entrap law-abiding gun owners and much more.

The Bren Gun Saga, by Thomas B. Dugelby, Collector Grade Publications, Cobourg, Ontario, Canada, 1999, revised and expanded edition. 406 pp., illus. $65.95

A modern, definitive book on the Bren in this revised expanded edition, which in terms of numbers of pages and illustrations is nearly twice the size of the original.

British Board of Ordnance Small Arms Contractors 1689-1840, by De Witt Bailey, Rhyl, England, W. S. Curtis, 2000. 150 pp. $18.00

Thirty years of research in the Archives of the Ordnance Board in London has identified more than 600 of these suppliers. The names of many can be found marking the regulation firearms of the period. In the study, the contractors are identified both alphabetically and under a combination of their date period together with their specialist trade.

The British Enfield Rifles, Volume 1, The SMLE MK I and MK III Rifles, by Charles R. Stratton, North Cape Pub., Tustin, CA, 1997. 150 pp., illus. Paper covers. $16.95

A systematic and thorough examination on a part-by-part basis of the famous British battle rifle that endured for nearly 70 years as the British Army's number one battle rifle.

The British Enfield Rifles, Volume 2, No. 4 and No. 5 Rifles, by Charles R. Stratton, North Cape Publications, Tustin, CA, 1999. 150 pp., illus. Paper covers. $16.95

The historical background for the development of both rifles describing each variation and an explanation of all the marks, numbers and codes found on most parts.

The British Enfield Rifles, Volume 4, The Pattern 1914 and U. S. Model 1917 Rifles, by Charles R. Stratton, North Cape Publications, Tustin, CA, 2000. Paper covers. $16.95

One of the least known American and British collectible military rifles is analyzed on a part by part basis. All markings and codes, refurbishment procedures and WWII upgrade are included as are the various sniper rifle versions.

The British Falling Block Breechloading Rifle from 1865, by Jonathan Kirton, Tom Rowe Books, Maynardsville, TN, 2nd edition, 1997. 380 pp., illus. $70.00

Expanded edition of a comprehensive work on the British falling block rifle.

British Gun Engraving, by Douglas Tate, Safari Press, Inc., Huntington Beach, CA, 1999. 240 pp., illus. Limited, signed and numbered edition, in a slipcase. $80.00

A historic and photographic record of the last two centuries.

British Gunmakers: Volume One – London, by Nigel Brown, London, Quiller, 2004. 1st edition 280 pp., 33 colour, 43 b&w photographs, line drawings. Hardcover. NEW. $99.95

British Military Flintlock Rifles 1740-1840, With a Remarkable Wealth of Data about the Riflemen and Regiments that Carried These Weapons, by De Witt Bailey, Andrew Mowbray, Inc. Lincoln, RI, 2002. 1st edition. 264 pp. with over 320 photographs. Hardcover. $47.95

Pattern 1776 Rifles, the Ferguson Breechloader, the famous Baker Rifle, rifles of the Hessians and other German Mercenaries, American Loyalist rifles, rifles given to Indians, Cavalry rifles and rifled carbines, bayonets, accoutrements, ammunition and more.

British Service Rifles and Carbines 1888-1900, by Alan M. Petrillo, Excaliber Publications, Latham, NY, 1994. 72 pp., illus, Paper covers. $11.95

A complete review of the Lee-Metford and Lee-Enfield rifles and carbines.

British Single Shot Rifles, Volume 1, Alexander Henry, by Wal Winfer, Tom Rowe, Maynardsville, TN, 1998, 200 pp., illus. $50.00

Detailed study of the single shot rifles made by Henry. Illustrated with hundreds of photographs and drawings.

British Single Shot Rifles Volume 2, George Gibbs, by Wal Winfer, Tom Rowe, Maynardsville, TN, 1998. 177 pp., illus. $50.00

Detailed study of the Farquharson as made by Gibbs. Hundreds of photos.

British Single Shot Rifles, Volume 3, Jeffery, by Wal Winfer, Rowe Publications, Rochester, N.Y., 1999. 260 pp., illus. $60.00

The Farquharsen as made by Jeffery and his competitors, Holland & Holland, Bland, Westley, Manton. Large section on the development of nitro cartridges including the 600.

British Single Shot Rifles, Vol. 4; Westley Richards, by Wal Winfer, Rowe Publications, Rochester, N.Y., 2000. 265 pp., illus., photos. $60.00

In this 4th volume, Winfer covers a detailed study of the Westley Richards single shot rifles, including Monkey Tails, Improved Martini, 1872,1873, 1878,1881, 1897 Falling Blocks. He also covers Westley Richards cartridges, history and reloading information.

British Sporting Guns & Rifles, compiled by George Hoyem, Armory Publications, Coeur d'Alene, ID, 1997. 1024 pp., illus. Two volumes. $250.00

Eighteen old sporting firearms trade catalogs and a rare book reproduced with their color covers in a limited, signed and numbered edition.

Broad Arrow: British & Empire Factory Production, Proof, Inspection, Armourers, Unit & Issue Markings, by Ian Skennerton. Australia, Arms & Militaria Press, 2001. 140 pp., circa 80 illus. Stiff paper covers. $29.95

Thousands of service markings are illustrated and their applications described. Invaluable reference on units, also ideal for medal collectors.

Browning Dates of Manufacture, compiled by George Madis, Art and Reference House, Brownsboro, TX, 1989. 48 pp. $7.50

Gives the date codes and product codes for all models from 1824 to the present.

Browning–Sporting Arms of Distinction 1903-1992, by Matt Eastman, Long Beach, CA, Safari Press, 2004. 428 pp., profuse illus. Hardcover. New in new dust jacket. $50.00

Browning Sporting Firearms: Dates of Manufacture, by D. R. Morse. Phoenix, AZ, Firing Pin Enterprizes, 2003. 37 pp. Softcover. New. $6.95

Covers their pistols, revolvers, rifles, shotguns and commemoratives, plus, models and serial numbers.

Bullard Firearms, by G. Scott Jamieson, Schiffer Publications, Atglen, PA 2002. 1st edition. 400 pp., with over 1100 color and b&w photographs, charts, diagrams. Hardcover. $100.00

Bullard Firearms is the story of a mechanical genius whose rifles and cartridges were the equal of any made in America in the 1880s, yet little of substance had been written about James H. Bullard or his arms prior to 1988 when the first edition, called Bullard Arms, was published. This greatly expanded volume, with over 1,000 b&w and 150 color plates, most not previously published, answers many of the questions posed in the first edition. The final chapter outlines, in chart form, almost 500 Bullard rifles by serial number, caliber and type. Quick and easy to use, this book is a real benefit for collectors and dealers alike.

Burning Powder, compiled by Major D.B. Wesson, Wolfe Publishing Company, Prescott, AZ, 1992. 110 pp. Soft cover. $10.95

A rare booklet from 1932 for Smith & Wesson collectors.

The Burnside Breech Loading Carbines, by Edward A. Hull, Andrew Mowbray, Inc., Lincoln, RI, 1986. 95 pp., illus. $16.00

No. 1 in the "Man at Arms Monograph Series." A model-by-model historical/technical examination of one of the most widely used cavalry weapons of the American Civil War based upon important and previously unpublished research.

C.S. Armory Richmond: History of the Confederate States Armory, Richmond, VA and the Stock Shop at the C.S. Armory, Macon, GA., by Paul Davies, privately printed, 2000. 368 pp., illustrated with b&w photos. Hardcover. $75.00

The American Society of Arms Collectors is pleased to recommend C.S. Armory Richmond as a useful and valuable reference for collectors and scholars in the field of antique firearms. Gives fantastic explanations of machinery, stocks, barrels, and every facet of the production process during the timeframe covered in this book.

Cacciare A Palla: Uso E Tecnologia Dell'arma Rigata, by Marco E. Nobili, Italy, Il Volo Srl, 1994. 4th Edition - 1st printing. 397 pp., illustrated with b&w photographs. Hardcover. New in new dust jacket. $75.00

The Call of Duty; Military Awards and Decorations of the United States of America, by John E. Strandberg, LTC and Roger James Bender, San Jose, CA, R. James Bender Publishing, 2005. (New expanded edition). 559 pp. illustrated with 1,293 photos (most in color). Hardcover. NEW. $67.95

Camouflage Uniforms of European and NATO Armies; 1945 to the Present, by J. F. Borsarello, Atglen, PA, Schiffer Publications. Over 290 color and b&w photographs, 120 pp. Softcover. $29.95

This full-color book covers nearly all of the NATO, and other European armies' camouflaged uniforms, and not only shows and explains the many patterns, but also their efficacy of design. Described and illustrated are the variety of materials tested in over 40 different armies, and includes the history of obsolete trial tests from 1945 to the present time. This book provides a superb reference for the historian, reenactor, designer, and modeler.

Camouflage Uniforms of the Waffen-SS A Photographic Reference, by Michael Beaver, Schiffer Publishing, Atglen, PA. Over 1,000 color and b&w photographs and illustrations, 296 pp. $69.95

Finally a book that unveils the shroud of mystery surrounding Waffen-SS camouflage clothing. Illustrated here, both in full color and in contemporary b&w photographs, this unparalleled look at Waffen-SS combat troops and their camouflage clothing will benefit both the historian and collector.

THE HANDGUNNER'S LIBRARY

Canadian Colts for the Boer War, by Col. Robert D. Whittington III. Hooks, TX, Brownlee Books, 2003. A limited edition of 1,000 copies. Numbered. 5 pp. Paper covers. New. $15.00

A study of Colt Revolvers issued to the First and Second Canadian Contingents Special Service Force.

Canadian Colts for the Boer War, Part 2, Col. Robert D. by Whittington III, Hooks, TX, Brownlee Books, 2005. A limited edition of 1,000 copies. Numbered. 5 pp. Paper covers, NEW. $5.00

Canadian Gunsmiths from 1608: A Checklist of Tradesmen, by John Belton, Historical Arms Series No. 29. Canada, Museum Restoration, 1992. 40 pp., 17 illustrations. Softcover. $8.95

This checklist is a greatly expanded version of HAS No. 14, listing the names, occupation, location, and dates of more than 1,500 men and women who worked as gunmakers, gunsmiths, armorers, gun merchants, gun patent holders, and a few other gun related trades. A collection of contemporary gunsmiths' letterhead have been provided to add color and depth to the study.

Canadian Miliitaria Directory & Sourcebook Second Edition, by Clive M. Law, Ont. Canada, Service Publications, 1998. pp. 90. Softcover. NEW. $14.95

Cap Guns, by James Dundas, Schiffer Publishing, Atglen, PA, 1996. 160 pp., illus. Paper covers. $29.95

Over 600 full-color photos of cap guns and gun accessories with a current value guide.

Carbines of the Civil War, by John D. McAulay, Pioneer Press, Union City, TN, 1981. 123 pp., illus. Paper covers. $12.95

A guide for the student and collector of the colorful arms used by the Federal cavalry.

Carbines of the U.S. Cavalry 1861-1905, by John D. McAulay, Andrew Mowbray Publishers, Lincoln, RI, 1996. $35.00

Covers the crucial use of carbines from the beginning of the Civil War to the end of the cavalry carbine era in 1905.

Cartridge Carbines of the British Army, by Alan M. Petrillo, Excalibur Publications, Latham, NY, 1998. 72 pp., illus. Paper covers. $11.95

Begins with the Snider-Enfield which was the first regulation cartridge carbine introduced in 1866 and ends with the 303 caliber No.5, Mark 1 Enfield.

Cartridge Reloading Tools of the Past, by R.H. Chamberlain and Tom Quigley, Castle Rock, WA, 1998. 167 pp., illus. Paper covers. $25.00

A detailed treatment of the extensive Winchester and Ideal lines of handloading tools and bulletmolds plus Remington, Marlin, Ballard, Browning and many others.

Cartridges for Collectors, by Fred Datig, Pioneer Press, Union City, TN, 1999. Three volumes of 176 pp. each. Vol. 1 (Centerfire); Vol. 2 (Rimfire and Misc.) types. Volume 1, softcover only, $19.95. Volumes 2 and 3, hardcover. $19.95

Vol. 3 (Additional Rimfire, Centerfire, and Plastic.). All illustrations are shown in full-scale drawings.

Civil War Arms Makers and Their Contracts, edited by Stuart C. Mowbray and Jennifer Heroux, Andrew Mowbray Publishing, Lincoln, RI, 1998. 595 pp. $39.50

A facsimile reprint of the Report by the Commissioner of Ordnance and Ordnance Stores, 1862.

Civil War Arms Purchases and Deliveries, edited by Stuart C. Mowbray, Andrew Mowbray Publishing, Lincoln, RI, 1998. 300pp., illus. $39.50

A facsimile reprint of the master list of Civil War weapons purchases and deliveries including Small Arms, Cannon, Ordnance and Projectiles.

Civil War Battles of the Western Theatre, by Walter Crutcher (Foreword), Bryan S. Bush. Paducah, KY, Turner Publishing, 2000. 204 pp. Hardcover. New in new dust jacket. $39.89

Civil War Breech Loading Rifles, by John D. McAulay, Andrew Mowbray, Inc., Lincoln, RI, 1991. 144 pp., illus. Paper covers. $15.00

All the major breech-loading rifles of the Civil War and most, if not all, of the obscure types are detailed, illustrated and set in their historical context.

Civil War Cartridge Boxes of the Union Infantryman, by Paul Johnson, Andrew Mowbray, Inc., Lincoln, RI, 1998. 352 pp., illus. $45.00

There were four patterns of infantry cartridge boxes used by Union forces during the Civil War. The author describes the development and subsequent pattern changes to these cartridge boxes.

Civil War Collector's Price Guide; Expanded Millennium Edition, by North South Trader, Orange, VA, Publisher's Press, 2000. 9th edition. 260 pps., illus. Softcover. $29.95

All updated prices, scores of new listings, and hundreds of new pictures! It's the one reference work no collector should be without. An absolute must.

Civil War Collector's Price Guide; 30th Anniversary 10th Edition, Orange, VA, Publisher's Press, 2003. All 260 pps., illus. Softcover. NEW. $34.95

Civil War Commanders, by Dean Thomas, Thomas Publications, Gettysburg, PA. 1998. 72 pp., illus., photos. Paper covers. $9.95

138 photographs and capsule biographies of Union and Confederate officers. A convenient personalities reference guide.

Civil War Guns, by William B. Edwards, Thomas Publications, Gettysburg, PA, 1997. 444 pp., illus. $40.00

The complete story of Federal and Confederate small arms; design, manufacture, identifications, procurement issue, employment, effectiveness, and postwar disposal by the recognized expert.

Civil War Heavy Explosive Ordnance: A Guide to Large Artillery Projectiles, Torpedoes, and Mines, by Jack Bell, Denton, TX, University of North Texas Press, 2003. 1,016 b&w photos. 537 pp. Hardcover. New in new dust jacket. $50.00

Civil War Infantryman: In Camp, on the March, and in Battle, by Dean Thomas, Thomas Publications, Gettysburg, PA. 1998. 72 pp., illus. Softcovers. $12.95

Uses first-hand accounts to shed some light on the "common soldier" of the Civil War from enlistment to muster-out, including camp, marching, rations, equipment, fighting, and more.

Civil War Pistols, by John D. McAulay, Andrew Mowbray Inc., Lincoln, RI, 1992. 166 pp., illus. $38.50

A survey of the handguns used during the American Civil War.

Civil War Relic Hunting A to Z, by Robert Buttafuso, Sheridan Books, 2000. 1st edition. illus., 91 pp., b&w illustrations. Softcover. NEW. $21.95

Civil War Sharps Carbines and Rifles, by Earl J. Coates and John D. McAulay, Thomas Publications, Gettysburg, PA, 1996. 108 pp., illus. Paper covers. $12.95

Traces the history and development of the firearms including short histories of specific serial numbers and the soldiers who received them.

Civil War Small Arms of the U.S. Navy and Marine Corps, by John D. McAulay, Mowbray Publishing, Lincoln, RI, 1999. 186 pp., illus. $39.00

The first reliable and comprehensive guide to the firearms and edged weapons of the Civil War Navy and Marine Corps.

Col. Burton's Spiller & Burr Revolver, by Matthew W. Norman, Mercer University Press, Macon, GA, 1997. 152 pp., illus. $22.95

A remarkable archival research project on the arm together with a comprehensive story of the establishment and running of the factory.

Collecting Military Headgear; A Guide to 5000 Years of Helmet History, by Robert Atglen Attard, PA, Schiffer Publications, 2004. 1st edition. Hardcover. New in new dust jacket. $69.95

Collecting Third Reich Recordings, by Stuart McKenzie, San Jose, CA, R. James Bender Publishing, 2001. 1st edition. Softcover. NEW. $29.95

Collector's Illustrated Encyclopedia of the American Revolution, by George C. Neumann and Frank J. Kravic, Rebel Publishing Co., Inc., Texarkana, TX, 1989. 286 pp., illus. $42.95

A showcase of more than 2,300 artifacts made, worn, and used by those who fought in the War for Independence.

Colonel Thomas Claiborne Jr. and the Colt Whitneyville-Walker Pistol, by Col. Robert D. Whittington III, Hooks, TX, Brownlee Books, 2005. A limited edition of 1,000 copies. Numbered. 8 pp. Paper covers, NEW. $7.50

Colonels in Blue: Union Army Colonels of the Civil War, by Roger Hunt, New York, Atglen, PA, Schiffer Publications, 2003. 1st edition. 288 pp., with over 640 b&w photographs. Hardcover. New in new dust jacket. $59.95

Colonial Frontier Guns, by T.M. Hamilton, Pioneer Press, Union City, TN, 1988. 176 pp., illus. Paper covers. $17.50

A complete study of early flint muskets of this country.

The Colt 1909 Military Revolvers; The 1904 Thompson-Lagarde Report, and General John J. Pershing, by Col. Robert D. Whittington III, Hooks, TX, Brownlee Books, 2005. A limited edition of 1,000 copies. Numbered. 10 pp. Paper covers. NEW. $10.00

Colt and Its Collectors Exhibition Catalog for Colt: The Legacy of A Legend, Buffalo Bill Historical Center, Cody, Wyoming. Colt Collectors Association, 2003. 1st edition. Hardcover. New in new dust jacket. $125.00

Colt and Its Collectors accompanies the upcoming special exhibition, Colt: The Legacy of a Legend, opening at the Buffalo Bill Historical Center in May 2003. Numerous essays, over 750 color photographs by Paul Goodwin.

The Colt Armory, by Ellsworth Grant, Man-at-Arms Bookshelf, Lincoln, RI, 1996. 232 pp., illus. $35.00

A history of Colt's Manufacturing Company.

The Colt Engraving Book, Volumes I & II, by R. L. Wilson. Privately printed, 2001. Each volume is appx. 500 pp., with 650 illustrations, most in color. $390.00

This third edition from the original texts of 1974 and 1982 has been fine-tuned and dramatically expanded, and is by far the most illuminating and complete. With over 1,200 illustrations, more than 2/3 of which are in color, this book joins the author's The Book of Colt Firearms, and Fine Colts as companion volumes. Approximately 1,000 pages in two volumes, each signed by the author, serial numbered, and strictly limited to 3000 copies. Volume I covers from the Paterson and pre-Paterson period through c.1921 (end of the Helfricht period). Volume II commences with Kornbrath, and Glahn, and covers Colt embellished arms from c.1919 through 2000.

The Colt Model 1905 Automatic Pistol, by John Potocki, Andrew Mowbray Publishing, Lincoln, RI, 1998. 191 pp., illus. $28.00

Covers all aspects of the Colt Model 1905 Automatic Pistol, from its invention by the legendary John Browning to its numerous production variations.

Colt Peacemaker British Model, by Keith Cochran, Cochran Publishing Co., Rapid City, SD, 1989. 160 pp., illus. $35.00

Covers those revolvers Colt squeezed in while completing a large order of revolvers for the U.S. Cavalry in early 1874, to those magnificent cased target revolvers used in the pistol competitions at Bisley Commons in the 1890s.

Colt Peacemaker Encyclopedia, by Keith Cochran, Cochran Publishing Co., Rapid City, SD, 1986. 434 pp., illus. $60.00

A must-have book for the Peacemaker collector.

Colt Peacemaker Encyclopedia, Volume 2, by Keith Cochran, Cochran Publishing Co., SD, 1992. 416 pp., illus. $60.00

Included in this volume are extensive notes on engraved, inscribed, historical and noted revolvers, as well as those revolvers used by outlaws, lawmen, movie and television stars.

Colt Pistols, Texas, and the U.S. Army 1847-1861, by Col. Robert D. Whittington III, Hooks, TX, Brownlee Books, 2005. A limited edition of 1,000 copies. Numbered. 8 pp. Paper covers, NEW. $7.50

Colt Presentations: From the Factory Ledgers 1856-1869, by Herbert G. Houze. Lincoln, RI, Andrew Mowbray, Inc., 2003. 112 pp., 45 b&w photos. Softcover. $21.95

Samuel Colt was a generous man. He also used gifts to influence government decision makers. But after Congress investigated him in 1854, Colt needed to hide the gifts from prying eyes, which makes it very difficult for today's collectors to document the many revolvers presented by Colt and the factory. Using the original account journals of the Colt's Patent Fire Arms Manufacturing Co., renowned arms authority Herbert G. Houze finally gives us the full details behind hundreds of the most exciting Colts ever made.

Colt Revolvers and the Tower of London, by Joseph G. Rosa, Royal Armouries of the Tower of London, London, England, 1988. 72 pp., illus. Softcover. $15.00

Details the story of Colt in London through the early cartridge period.

Colt Single Action Army Revolver Study: New Discoveries, by Kenneth Moore, Lincoln, RI, Andrew Mowbray, Inc., 2003. 1st edition. 200 pp., with 77 photos and illustrations. Hardcover. New. $49.95

25 years after co-authoring the classic Study of the Colt Single Action Army Revolver, Ken fills in the gaps and sets the record straight. Decades in the making, this impressive new study brings us entirely up to date, including all the new research that the author has painstakingly

gathered over the years. The serial number data alone will astound you. Includes, ejector models, special section on low serial numbers, U.S. Army testing data, new details about militia S.A.A.'s plus a true wealth of cartridge info.

Colt Single Action Army Revolvers: The Legend, the Romance and the Rivals, by "Doc" O'Meara, Krause Publications, Iola, WI, 2000. 160 pp., illustrated with 250 photos in b&w and a 16-page color section. $22.95

Production figures, serial numbers by year, and rarities.

Colt Single Action Army Revolvers and Alterations, by C. Kenneth Moore, Mowbray Publishers, Lincoln, RI, 1999. 112 pp., illus. $35.00

A comprehensive history of the revolvers that collectors call "Artillery Models." These are the most historical of all S.A.A. Colts, and this new book covers all the details.

Colt Single Action Army Revolvers and the London Agency, by C. Kenneth Moore, Andrew Mowbray Publishers, Lincoln, RI, 1990. 144 pp., illus. $35.00

Drawing on vast documentary sources, this work chronicles the relationship between the London Agency and the Hartford home office.

Colt Sporting Firearms: Dates of Manufacture, by D.R. Morse, Phoenix, AZ, Firing Pin Enterprizes, 2003. 82 pp. Softcover. New. $6.95

Covers their pistols, revolvers, rifles, shotguns and commemoratives, plus models and serial numbers.

The Colt U.S. General Officers' Pistols, by Horace Greeley IV, Andrew Mowbray Inc., Lincoln, RI, 1990. 199 pp., illus. $38.00

These unique weapons, issued as a badge of rank to General Officers in the U.S. Army from WWII onward, remain highly personal artifacts of the military leaders who carried them. Includes serial numbers and dates of issue.

Colts from the William M. Locke Collection, by Frank Sellers, Andrew Mowbray Publishers, Lincoln, RI, 1996. 192 pp., illus. $55.00

This important book illustrates all of the famous Locke Colts, with captions by arms authority Frank Sellers.

Colt's Dates of Manufacture 1837-1978, by R.L. Wilson, published by Maurie Albert, Coburg, Australia; N.A. distributor Madis Books, TX, 1997. 61 pp. $7.50

An invaluable pocket guide to the dates of manufacture of Colt firearms up to 1978.

Colt's Pocket '49: Its Evolution Including the Baby Dragoon and Wells Fargo, by Robert Jordan and Darrow Watt, privately printed, Loma Mar, CA 2000. 304 pp., with 984 color photos, illus. Beautifully bound in a deep blue leather-like case. $125.00

Detailed information on all models and covers engaving, cases, accoutrements, holsters, fakes, and much more. Included is a summary booklet containing information such as serial numbers, production ranges and identifing photos. This book is a masterpiece on its subject.

Colt's SAA Post War Models, by George Garton, The Gun Room Press, Highland Park, NJ, 1995. 166 pp., illus. $39.95

Complete facts on the post-war Single Action Army revolvers. Information on calibers, production numbers and variations taken from factory records.

Combat Helmets of the Third Reich: A Study in Photographs, by Thomas Kibler, Pottsboro, TX, Reddick Enterprises, 2003. 1st edition. 96 pp., illustrated in full color. Pictorial softcover. NEW. $19.95

The Combat Perspective The Thinking Man's Guide to Self-Defense, by Gabriel Suarez, Boulder, CO, Paladin Press, 2003. 1st edition. 112 pp. Softcover. NEW. $15.00

Complete Guide to all United States Military Medals 1939 to Present, by Colonel Frank C. Foster, Medals of America Press, Fountain Inn, SC, 2000. 121 pp., illus., photos. $29.95

Complete criteria for every Army, Navy, Marine, Air Force, Coast Guard, and Merchant Marine award since 1939. All decorations, service medals, and ribbons shown in full color and accompanied by dates and campaigns, as well as detailed descriptions on proper wear and display.

Complete Guide to the M1 Garand and the M1 Carbine, by Bruce N. Canfield, 2nd printing, Andrew Mowbray Inc., Lincoln, RI, 1999. 296 pp., illus. $39.50

Expanded and updated coverage of both the M1 Garand and the M1 Carbine, with more than twice as much information as the author's previous book on this topic.

The Complete Guide to U.S. Infantry Weapons of the First War, by Bruce Canfield, Andrew Mowbray, Publisher, Lincoln, RI, 2000. 304 pp., illus. $39.95

The definitive study of the U.S. Infantry weapons used in WWI.

The Complete Guide to U.S. Infantry Weapons of World War Two, by Bruce Canfield, Andrew Mowbray, Publisher, Lincoln, RI, 1995. 303 pp., illus. $39.95

A definitive work on the weapons used by the United States Armed Forces in WWII.

Confederate Belt Buckles & Plates by Steve E. Mullinax, O'Donnell Publishing, Alexandria, VA, 1999. Expanded edition. 247 pp., illus. Hardcover. $34.00

Hundreds of crisp photographs augment this classic study of Confederate accoutrement plates.

Confederate Carbines & Musketoons Cavalry Small Arms Manufactured in and for the Southern Confederacy 1861-1865. by John M. Murphy, Santa Ana, CA, privately printed, 2002. Reprint. Hardcover. New in new dust jacket. $79.95

Confederate Rifles & Muskets: Infantry Small Arms Manufactured in the Southern Confederacy 1861-1865, by John M. Murphy. Santa Ana, CA, privately printed, 1996. Reprint. 768 pp., 8 pp. color plates, profusely illustrated. Hardcover. $119.95

The first in-depth and academic analysis and discussion of the "long" longarms produced in the South by and for the Confederacy during the American Civil War. The collection of Dr. Murphy is doubtless the largest and finest grouping of Confederate longarms in private hands today.

Confederate Saddles & Horse Equipment, by Ken R. Knopp, Orange, VA, Publisher's Press, 2002. 194 pps., illus. Hardcover. $39.95

Confederate Saddles & Horse Equipment is a pioneer work on the subject. After 10 years of research Ken Knopp has compiled a thorough and fascinating study of the little-known field of Confederate saddlery and equipment. His analysis of ordnance operations coupled with his visual presentation of surviving examples offers an indispensable source for collectors and historians.

Cooey Firearms, Made in Canada 1919-1979, by John A. Belton, Museum Restoration, Canada, 1998. 36pp., with 46 illus. Paper covers. $8.95

More than 6 million rifles and at least 67 models were made by this small Canadian riflemaker. They have been identified from the first 'Cooey Canuck' through the last variations made by the 'Winchester-Cooey'. Each is descibed and most are illustrated in this first book on the Cooey.

Cougar Attacks: Encounters of the Worst Kind, by Kathy Etling, New York, Lyons Press, 2004. 1st edition. Softcover. NEW. $14.95

Cowboy and Gunfighter Collectible, by Bill Mackin, Mountain Press Publishing Co., Missoula, MT, 1995. 178 pp., illus. Paper covers. $25.00

A photographic encyclopedia with price guide and makers' index.

Cowboy Collectibles and Western Memorabilia, by Bob Bell and Edward Vebell, Schiffer Publishing, Atglen, PA, 1992. 160 pp., illus. Paper covers. $29.95

The exciting era of the cowboy and the wild west collectibles including rifles, pistols, gun rigs, etc.

Cowboy Culture: The Last Frontier of American Antiques, by Michael Friedman, Schiffer Publishing, Ltd., West Chester, PA, 2002. 300 pp., illus. $89.95

Covers the artful aspects of the old west, the antiques and collectibles. Illustrated with clear color plates of over 1,000 items such as spurs, boots, guns, saddles, etc.

Cowboys and the Trappings of the Old West, by William Manns and Elizabeth Clair Flood, Zon International Publishing Co., Santa Fe, NM, 1997, 1st edition. 224 pp., illus. $45.00

A pictorial celebration of the cowboy dress and trappings.

Custer & His Wolverines: The Michigan Cavalry Brigade, 1861-1865, by Edward G. Longacre, Cambridge, MA, Da Capo Press, 2004. 2nd edition, 24 b&w photos, 5 maps; 6" x 9", 352 pp. Softcover. NEW. $18.00

Custom Firearms Engraving, by Tom Turpin, Krause Publications, Iola, WI, 1999. 208 pp., illus. $49.95

Over 200 four-color photos with more than 75 master engravers profiled. Engravers directory with addresses in the U.S. and abroad.

Daisy Air Rifles & BB Guns: The First 100 Years, by Neal Punchard. St. Paul, MN, Motorbooks, 2002. 1st edition. 10" x 10", 156 pp., 300 color. Hardcover. $29.95

Flash back to the days of your youth and recall fond memories of your Daisy. Daisy Air Rifles and BB Guns looks back fondly on the first 100 years of Daisy BB rifles and pistols, toy and cork guns, accessories, packaging, period advertising and literature.

The Decorations, Medals, Ribbons, Badges and Insignia of the United States Army; World War II to Present, by Col. Frank C. Foster, Medals of America Press, Fountain Inn, SC. 2001. 145 pp., illus. $29.95

The most complete guide to United States Army medals, ribbons, rank, insignia and patches from WWII to the present day. Each medal and insignia shown in full color. Includes listing of respective criteria and campaigns.

The Decorations, Medals, Ribbons, Badges and Insignia of the United States Navy; World War II to Present, by James G. Thompson, Medals of America Press, Fountain Inn, SC. 2000. 123 pp., illus. $29.95

The most complete guide to United States Army medals, ribbons, rank, insignia and patches from WWII to the present day. Each medal and insignia shown in full color. Includes listing of respective criteria and campaigns.

Defending the Dominion, Canadian Military Rifles, 1855-1955, by David Edgecombe. Service Publications, Ont., Canada, 2003. 168 pp., with 60+ illustrations. Hardcover. $39.95

This book contains much new information on the Canadian acquisition, use and disposal of military rifles during the most significant century in the development of small arms. In addition to the venerable Martini-Henry, there are chapters on the Winchester, Snider, Starr, Spencer, Peabody, Enfield rifles and others.

The Derringer in America, Volume 1, The Percussion Period, by R.L. Wilson and L.D. Eberhart, Andrew Mowbray Inc., Lincoln, RI, 1985. 271 pp., illus. $48.00

A long awaited book on the American percussion derringer.

The Derringer in America, Volume 2, the Cartridge Period, by L.D. Eberhart and R.L. Wilson, Andrew Mowbray Inc., Publishers, Lincoln, RI, 1993. 284 pp., illus. $65.00

Comprehensive coverage of cartridge derringers organized alphabetically by maker. Includes all types of derringers known by the authors to have been offered in the American market.

The Devil's Paintbrush: Sir Hiram Maxim's Gun, by Dolf Goldsmith, 3rd Edition, expanded and revised, Collector Grade Publications, Toronto, Canada, 2002. 384 pp., illus. $79.95

The classic work on the world's first true automatic machine gun.

Die Wehrmacht, Volume One, by Uwe Feist, Ryton Publications, Bellingham, WA, 2000. Large format (8-3/4" x 11-1/2") hardbound book with over 250 b&w photos and 240 color prints, all on high quality coated paper. Hardcover. $65.00

This is a great reference book, the first in a new series dedicated to the weapons, uniforms and equipment of the German Wehrmacht in WWII. Includes color photos of each weapon, plus hundreds of wartime photos.

Dr. Josephus Requa Civil War Dentist and the Billinghurst-Requa Volley Gun, by John M. Hyson Jr., and Margaret Requa DeFrancisco, Museum Restoration Service, Bloomfield, Ont., Canada, 1999. 36 pp., illus. Paper covers. $8.95

The story of the inventor of the first practical rapid-fire gun to be used during the American Civil War.

The Dutch Luger (Parabellum) A Complete History, by Bas J. Martens and Guus de Vries, Ironside International Publishers, Inc., Alexandria, VA, 1995. 268 pp., illus. $49.95

The history of the Luger in the Netherlands. An extensive description of the Dutch pistol and trials and the different models of the Luger in the Dutch service.

E. F.Lli Piotti Italian Fine Gun Maker, by Marco Nobili, Italy, Il Volo Srl, 2000. 1st printing. 221 pp., illustrated with b&w photographs, plus 22 full color plates. Text in Italian and English. Hardcover. New in new dust jacket. $189.95

E.C. Prudhomme's Gun Engraving Review, by E. C. Prudhomme, R&R Books, Livonia, NY, 1994. 164 pp., illus. $60.00

As a source for engravers and collectors, this book is an indispensable guide to styles and techniques of the world's foremost engravers.

THE HANDGUNNER'S LIBRARY

The Eagle on U.S. Firearms, by John W. Jordan, Pioneer Press, Union City, TN, 1992. 140 pp., illus. Paper covers. $17.50

Stylized eagles have been stamped on government owned or manufactured firearms in the U.S. since the beginning of our country. This book lists and illustrates these various eagles in an informative and refreshing manner.

Early Gunpowder Artillery 1300-1600, by John Norris, London, The Crowood Press, 2003. 1st edition. 141 pp., with 160 b&w photos. Hardcover. $34.95

In the 300-year time span covered by this book, gunpowder artillery was developed from a novelty to a serious weapon of war. By 1600 the cannon was to be found in large numbers on the battlefield, on board ship and on defensive positions on buildings and city walls. Illustrated with contemporary and modern photographs of surviving and recreated weapons, Early Gunpowder Artillery 1300-1600 sheds light on these earliest ancestors of the modern cannon and field gun.

Emblems of Honor; Patches and Insignia of the U.S. Army from the Great War to the Early Cold War Vol. Iv Armor - Cavalry - Tank Destroyer, by Kurt Keller, Constabulary, PA, privately printed, 2005. 1st edition, signed. 232 pp., with over 600 color photos. Hardcover. New in new dust jacket. $59.95

The Emma Gees, by Capt. Herbert W. McBride, Mt. Ida, AR, Lancer Publishing, 2003. 224 pp., b&w photos. Softcover. NEW. $19.95

Encyclopedia of Rifles & Handguns; A Comprehensive Guide to Firearms, edited by Sean Connolly, Chartwell Books, Inc., Edison, NJ., 1996. 160 pp., illus. $26.00

Encyclopedia of United States Army Insignia and Uniforms, by William Emerson, OK, University of Oklahoma Press, 1996. Hardcover. NEW. $134.95

Enemies Foreign and Domestic, by Matthew Bracken, San Diego, CA, Steelcutter Publishing, 2003. Softcover. NEW. $19.89

Eprouvettes: A Comprehensive Study of Early Devices for the Testing of Gunpowder, by R.T.W. Kempers, Royal Armouries Museum, Leeds, England, 1999. 352 pp., illustrated with 240 b&w and 28 color plates. $125.00

Equipment of the WWII Tommy, by David Gordon, Missoula, MT, Pictorial Histories Publishing, 2004. 1st edition. Softcover. NEW. $24.95

Fifteen Years in the Hawken Lode, by John D. Baird, The Gun Room Press, Highland Park, NJ, 1976. 120 pp., illus. $24.95

A collection of thoughts and observations gained from many years of intensive study of the guns from the shop of the Hawken brothers.

Fighting Colors: The Creation of Military Aircraft Nose Art, by Gary Velasco, Paducah, KY, Turner Publishing, 2005. 1st edition. Hardcover. New in new dust jacket. $57.95

Fighting Iron, by Art Gogan, Andrew Mowbray, Inc., Lincoln, R.I., 2002. 176 pp., illus. $28.00

It doesn't matter whether you collect guns, swords, bayonets or accoutrement–sooner or later you realize that it all comes down to the metal. If you don't understand the metal, you don't understand your collection.

Fine Colts, The Dr. Joseph A. Murphy Collection, by R.L. Wilson, Sheffield Marketing Associates, Inc., Doylestown, PA, 1999. 258 pp., illus. Limited edition signed and numbered. $99.00

This lavish work covers exquisite, deluxe and rare Colt arms from Paterson and other percussion revolvers to the cartridge period and up through modern times.

Firearm Suppressor Patents; Volume 1: United States Patents, by N.R. Parker, Foreword by Alan C. Paulson, Boulder, CO, Paladin Press, 2004. 392 pp., illus. Softcover. NEW. $45.00

Firearms, by Derek Avery, Desert Publications, El Dorado, AR, 1999. 95 pp., illus. $9.95

The firearms included in this book are by necessity only a selection, but nevertheless one that represents the best and most famous weapons seen since the WWII.

Firearms and Tackle Memorabilia, by John Delph, Schiffer Publishing, Ltd., West Chester, PA, 1991. 124 pp., illus. $39.95

A collector's guide to signs and posters, calendars, trade cards, boxes, envelopes, and other highly sought after memorabilia. With a value guide.

Firearms from Europe, 2nd Edition, by David Noe, Larry W. Yantz, Dr. James B. Whisker, Rowe Publications, Rochester, N.Y., 2002. 192 pp., illus. $45.00

A history and description of firearms imported during the American Civil War by the United States of America and the Confederate States of America.

Firearms of the American West 1803-1865, Volume 1, by Louis A. Garavaglia and Charles Worman, University of Colorado Press, Niwot, CO, 1998. 402 pp., illus. $79.95

Traces the development and uses of firearms on the frontier during this period.

Firearms of the American West 1866-1894, Volume 2, by Louis A. Garavaglia and Charles G. Worman, University of Colorado Press, Niwot, CO, 1998. 416 pp., illus. $79.95

A monumental work that offers both technical information on all of the important firearms used in the West during this period and a highly entertaining history of how they were used, who used them, and why.

Firepower from Abroad, by Wiley Sword, Andrew Mowbray Publishing, Lincoln, R.I., 2000. 120 pp., illus. $23.00

The Confederate Enfield and the LeMat revolver and how they reached the Confederate market.

Flayderman's Guide to Antique American Firearms and Their Values, 8th Edition, edited by Norm Flayderman, Krause Publications, Iola, WI, 2001. 692 pp., illus. Paper covers. $34.95

A completely updated and new edition with more than 3,600 models and variants extensively described with all marks and specifications necessary for quick identification.

The FN-FAL Rifle, et al, by Duncan Long, Paladin Press, Boulder, CO, 1999. 144 pp., illus. Paper covers. $18.95

Detailed descriptions of the basic models produced by Fabrique Nationale and the myriad variants that evolved as a result of the firearms' universal acceptance.

Freund & Bro. Pioneer Gunmakers to the West, by F.J. Pablo Balentine, Graphic Publishers, Newport Beach, CA, 1997. 380 pp., illus. $69.95

The story of Frank W. and George Freund, skilled German gunsmiths who plied their trade on the Western American frontier during the final three decades of the nineteenth century.

The Fusil de Tulole in New France, 1691-1741, by Russel Bouchard, Museum Restorations Service, Bloomfield, Ontario, Canada, 1997. 36 pp., illus. Paper covers. $8.95

The development of the company and the identification of their arms.

The Gas Trap Garand, by Billy Pyle, Collector Grade Publications, Cobourg, Ontario, Canada, 1999 316 pp., illus. $59.95

The in-depth story of the rarest Garands of them all, the initial 80 Model Shop rifles made under the personal supervision of John Garand himself in 1934 and 1935, and the first 50,000 plus production "gas trap" M1's manufactured at Springfield Armory between August, 1937 and August, 1940.

George Schreyer, Sr. and Jr., Gunmakers of Hanover, Pennsylvania, by George Shumway, George Shumway Publishers, York, PA, 1990. 160pp., illus. $50.00

This monograph is a detailed photographic study of almost all known surviving longrifles and smoothbore guns made by highly regarded gunsmiths George Schreyer, Sr. and George Schreyer Jr.

The German Assault Rifle 1935-1945, by Peter R. Senich, Paladin Press, Boulder, CO, 1987. 328 pp., illus. $60.00

A complete review of machine carbines, machine pistols and assault rifles employed by Hitler's Wehrmacht during WWII.

German Belt Buckles 1845-1945: Buckles of the Enlisted Soldiers, by Peter Nash Atglen, PA, Schiffer Publications, 2003. 1st edition. Hardcover. New in new dust jacket. $59.95

German Camouflaged Helmets of the Second World War; Volume 1: Painted and Textured Camouflage, by Branislav Atglen Radovic, PA, Schiffer Publications, 2004. 1st edition. Hardcover. New in new dust jacket. $79.95

German Camouflaged Helmets of the Second World War; Volume 2: Wire, Netting, Covers, Straps, Interiors, Miscellaneous, by Branislav Atglen Radovic, PA, Schiffer Publications, 2004. 1st edition. Hardcover. New in new dust jacket. $79.95

German Cross in Gold - Holders of the SS and Police, by Mark Yerger, San Jose, CA, Bender Publishing, 2004. 1st edition. 432 pp., 295 photos and illustrations, deluxe binding. Hardcover. NEW. $44.95

The German K98k Rifle, 1934-1945: The Backbone of the Wehrmacht, by Richard D. Law, Collector Grade Publications, Toronto, Canada, 1993. 336 pp., illus. $69.95

The most comprehensive study ever published on the 14,000,000 bolt-action K98k rifles produced in Germany between 1934 and 1945.

German Machine Guns, by Daniel D. Musgrave, revised edition, Ironside International Publishers, Inc. Alexandria, VA, 1992. 586 pp., 650 illus. $49.95

The most definitive book ever written on German machine guns. Covers the introduction and development of machine guns in Germany from 1899 to the rearmament period after WWII.

German Military Abbreviations, by Military Intelligence Service, Canada, Service Publications. 268 pp. Stiff paper covers. NEW. $16.95

German Military Rifles and Machine Pistols, 1871-1945, by Hans Dieter Gotz, Schiffer Publishing Co., West Chester, PA, 1990. 245 pp., illus. $35.00

This book portrays, in words and pictures, the development of the modern German weapons and their ammunition, including the scarcely known experimental types.

German Paratroops: Uniforms, Insignia & Equipment of the Fallschirmjager in World War II, by Robert Atglen Kurtz, PA, Schiffer Publications, 2003. 1st edition. Hardcover. New in new dust jacket. $59.95

German Print Advertising 1933-1945, by Ray and Josephine Cowdery, self published, 2004. 1st Am. edition. Hardcover. 176 pp. NEW. $45.00

German Tanks of World War II in Color, by Michael Green; Thomas Anderson; Frank Schultz, St. Paul, MN, MBI Publishing Company, 2000. 1st edition. Softcover. NEW. $14.95

Gods and Generals Photographic Companion, by Rob Gibson and Dennis Frye. Gettysburg, PA, Thomas Publications, 2003. 1st edition. 88 pp. Softcover. NEW. $19.95

Gold Dust & Gunsmoke, by John Boessenecker, New York, John Wiley & Sons, 2000. 370 pp. Softcover. NEW. $10.00

Government Issue: U.S. Army European Theater of Operations Collector Guide, by Henry-Paul Enjames, Philippe Charbonnier, France, Histoire & Collections, 2004. Hardcover, NEW. $49.89

The Government Models, by William H.D. Goddard, Andrew Mowbray Publishing, Lincoln, RI, 1998. 296 pp., illus. $58.50

The most authoritative source on the development of the Colt model of 1911.

Grasshoppers and Butterflies, by Adrian B. Caruana, Museum Restoration Service, Alexandria Bay, N.Y., 1999. 32 pp., illus. Paper covers. $8.95

No.39 in the Historical Arms Series. The light 3 pounders of Pattison and Townsend.

The Greener Story, by Graham Greener, Quiller Press, London, England, 2000. 256 pp., illustrated with 32 pp. of color photos. $69.95

W.W. Greener, his family history, inventions, guns, patents, and more.

The Greenhill Dictionary of Guns and Gunmakers: From Colt's First Patent to the Present Day, 1836-2001, by John Walter, Greenhill Publishing, 2001, 1st edition, 576 pp., illustrated with 200 photos, 190 trademarks and 40 line drawings, Hardcover. $59.95

Covers military small arms, sporting guns and rifles, air and gas guns, designers, inventors, patentees, trademarks, brand names and monograms.

Grenade - British and Commonwealth Hand and Rifle Grenades, by Rick Landers, Norman Bonney and Gary Oakley. Australia, privately printed, 2001. 1st edition. 294 pp., illustrated with b&w photos drawings. Hardcover. New in new dust jacket. $69.95

Covers from Type No.1 to No. 95 includes dischargers, fuzes, markings, equipment.

The Gun and Its Development, by W.W. Greener, New York, Lyons Press, 2002. 9th Edition. Rewritten, and with many additional illustrations. 804 pp. plus advertising section. Contains over 700 illustrations plus many tables. Softcover. $19.95

A famed book of great value, truly encyclopedic in scope and sought after by firearms collectors.

THE HANDGUNNER'S LIBRARY

Gun Powder Cans & Kegs, by Ted and David Bacyk and Tom Rowe, Rowe Publications, Rochester, NY, 1999. 150 pp., illus. $65.00

The first book devoted to powder tins and kegs. All cans and kegs in full color. With a price guide and rarity scale.

Gun Tools, Their History and Identification by James B. Shaffer, Lee A. Rutledge and R. Stephen Dorsey, Collector's Library, Eugene, OR, 1992. 375 pp., illus. $30.00

Written history of foreign and domestic gun tools from the flintlock period to WWII.

Gun Tools, Their History and Identifications, Volume 2, by Stephen Dorsey and James B. Shaffer, Collectors' Library, Eugene, OR, 1997. 396 pp., illus. Paper covers. $30.00

Gun tools from the Royal Armouries Museum in England, Pattern Room, Royal Ordnance Reference Collection in Nottingham and from major private collections.

Gunmakers of London 1350-1850 with Supplement, by Howard L. Blackmore, Museum Restoration Service, Alexandria Bay, NY, 1999. 222 pp., illus. Two volumes. Slipcased. $135.00

A listing of all the known workmen of gun making in the first 500 years, plus a history of the guilds, cutlers, armourers, founders, blacksmiths, etc. 260 gunmarks are illustrated. Supplement is 156 pages, and begins with an introductory chapter on "foreign" gunmakers followed by records of all the new information found about previously unidentified armourers, gunmakers and gunsmiths.

The Guns of Dagenham: Lanchester, Patchett, Sterling, by Peter Laidler and David Howroyd, Collector Grade Publications, Inc., Cobourg, Ont., Canada, 1995. 310 pp., illus. $39.95

An in-depth history of the small arms made by the Sterling Company of Dagenham, Essex, England, from 1940 until Sterling was purchased by British Aerospace in 1989 and closed.

The Guns of Remington: Historic Firearms Spanning Two Centuries, compiled by Howard M. Madaus, Biplane Productions, Publisher, in cooperation with Buffalo Bill Historical Center, Cody, WY, 1998. 352 pp., illustrated with over 800 color photos. $79.95

A complete catalog of the firearms in the exhibition, "It Never Failed Me: The Arms & Art of Remington Arms Company" at the Buffalo Bill Historical Center, Cody, Wyoming.

Guns of the Western Indian War, by R. Stephen Dorsey, Collector's Library, Eugene, OR, 1997. 220 pp., illus. Paper covers. $30.00

The full story of the guns and ammunition that made western history in the turbulent period of 1865-1890.

The Guns that Won the West: Firearms of the American Frontier, 1865-1898, by John Walter, Stackpole Books, Inc., Mechanicsburg, PA., 1999. 256 pp., illus. $34.95

Here is the story of the wide range of firearms from pistols to rifles used by plainsmen and settlers, gamblers, native Americans and the U.S. Army.

Gunsmiths of Illinois, by Curtis L. Johnson, George Shumway Publishers, York, PA, 1995. 160 pp., illus. $50.00

Genealogical information is provided for nearly 1,000 gunsmiths. Contains hundreds of illustrations of rifles and other guns, of handmade origin, from Illinois.

The Gunsmiths of Manhattan, 1625-1900: A Checklist of Tradesmen, by Michael H. Lewis, Museum Restoration Service, Bloomfield, Ont., Canada, 1991. 40 pp., illus. Paper covers. $8.95

This listing of more than 700 men in the arms trade in New York City prior to about the end of the 19th century will provide a guide for identification and further research.

Gunsmiths of Maryland, by Daniel D. Hartzler and James B. Whisker, Old Bedford Village Press, Bedford, PA, 1998. 208 pp., illus. $45.00

Covers firelock Colonial period through the breech-loading patent models. Featuring longrifles.

Gunsmiths of the Carolinas 1660-1870, by Daniel D. Hartzler and James B. Whisker, Old Bedford Village Press, Bedford, PA, 1998. 176 pp., illus. $40.00

This deluxe hard bound edition is printed on fine coated paper, with about 90 pages of large photographs of fine longrifles from the Carolinas, and about 90 pages of detailed research on the gunsmiths who created the highly prized and highly collectable longrifles.

Gunsmiths of Virginia, by Daniel D. Hartzler and James B. Whisker, Old Bedford Village Press, Bedford, PA, 1992. 206 pp., illus. $40.00

A photographic study of American longrifles.

Gunsmiths of West Virginia, by Daniel D. Hartzler and James B. Whisker, Old Bedford Village Press, Bedford, PA, 1998. 176 pp., illus. $40.00

A photographic study of American longrifles.

Gunsmiths of York County, Pennsylvania, by Daniel D. Hartzler and James B. Whisker, Old Bedford Village Press, Bedford, PA, 1998. 160 pp., illus. $40.00

Photographs and research notes on the longrifles and gunsmiths of York County, Pennsylvania.

Harrington & Richardson Sporting Firearms: Dates of Manufacture 1871-1991, by D.R. Morse. Phoenix, AZ, Firing Pin Enterprizes, 2003. 14 pp. Softcover. NEW. $6.95

Covers their pistols, revolvers, rifles, shotguns and commemoratives, plus models.

The Hawken Rifle: Its Place in History, by Charles E. Hanson Jr., The Fur Press, Chadron, NE, 1979. 104 pp., illus. Paper covers. $15.00

A definitive work on this famous rifle.

Hi-Standard Sporting Firearms: Dates of Manufacture, by D.R. Morse. 1926-1992. Phoenix, AZ, Firing Pin Enterprizes, 2003. 22 pp. Softcover. New. $6.95

Covers their pistols, revolvers, rifles, shotguns and commemoratives, plus models and serial numbers.

High Standard: A Collector's Guide to the Hamden & Hartford Target Pistols, by Tom Dance, Andrew Mowbray, Inc., Lincoln, RI, 1991. 192 pp., illus. Paper covers. $24.00

From Citation to Supermatic, all of the production models and specials made from 1951 to 1984 are covered according to model number or series.

Historical Hartford Hardware, by William W. Dalrymple, Colt Collector Press, Rapid City, SD, 1976. 42 pp., illus. Paper covers. $10.00

Historically associated Colt revolvers.

The History of Colt Firearms, by Dean Boorman, Lyons Press, New York, NY, 2001. 144 pp., illus. $29.95

Discover the fascinating story of the world's most famous revolver, complete with more than 150 stunning full-color photographs.

History of Modern U.S. Military Small Arms Ammunition, Volume 1, 1880-1939, revised by F.W. Hackley, W.H. Woodin and E.L. Scranton, Thomas Publications, Gettysburg, PA, 1998. 328 pp., illus. $49.95

This revised edition incorporates all publicly available information concerning military small arms ammunition for the period 1880 through 1939 in a single volume.

History of Modern U.S. Military Small Arms Ammunition, Volume 2, 1940-1945, by F.W. Hackley, W.H. Woodin and E.L. Scranton, Gun Room Press, Highland Park, NJ. 300+ pp., illus. $39.95

Based on decades of original research conducted at the National Archives, numerous military, public and private museums and libraries, as well as individual collections, this edition incorporates all publicly available information concerning military small arms ammunition for the period 1940 through 1945.

The History of Smith & Wesson Firearms, by Dean Boorman, Lyons Press, New York, NY, 2002. 44 pp., illustrated in full color. Hardcover. New in new dust jacket. $29.95

The definitive guide to one of the world's best-known firearms makers. Takes the story through the years of the Military and Police 38 and of the Magnum cartridge, to today's wide range of products for law-enforcement customers.

The History of Winchester Rifles, by Dean Boorman, Lyons Press, New York, NY, 2001. 144 pp., illus. 150 full-color photos. $29.95

A captivating and wonderfully photographed history of one of the most legendary names in gun lore.

Honour Bound: The Chauchat Machine Rifle, by Gerard Demaison and Yves Buffetaut, Collector Grade Publications, Inc., Cobourg, Ont., Canada, 1995. $39.95

The story of the CSRG (Chauchat) machine rifle, the most manufactured automatic weapon of WWI.

Hunting Weapons from the Middle Ages to the Twentieth Century, by Howard L. Blackmore, Dover Publications, Meneola, NY, 2000. 480 pp., illus. Paper covers. $16.95

Dealing mainly with the different classes of weapons used in sport–swords, spears, crossbows, guns, and rifles–from the Middle Ages until the present day.

Identification Handbook of British Grenades 1900-1960 (Numerical Series), by Rick Landers, Norman Bonney and Gary Oakley. Australia. Privately printed, 2001. 1st edition. 48 pp., illustrated with b&w photos and drawings. Softcover. New. $10.95

Description, illustration and identification details of all British grenades in the numerical series.

Illustrations of United States Military Arms 1776-1903 and Their Inspector's Marks, compiled by Turner Kirkland, Pioneer Press, Union City, TN, 1988. 37 pp., illus. Paper covers. $7.00

Reprinted from the 1949 Bannerman catalog. Valuable information for both the advanced and beginning collector.

Imperial German Military Officers' Helmets and Headdress 1871-1918, by Thomas N.G. Stubbs, Atglen, PA, Schiffer Publications, 2003. 1st edition. Hardcover. New in new dust jacket. $79.95

Imperial Japanese Grenade Rifles and Launchers, by Gregory A. Babich and Thomas A. Keep Lemont, PA, Dutch Harlow Publishing, 2004. 1st edition. Hardcover. New in new dust jacket. $75.00

Indian War Cartridge Pouches, Boxes and Carbine Boots, by R. Stephen Dorsey, Collector's Library, Eugene, OR, 1993. 156 pp., illus. Paper covers. $20.00

The key reference work to the cartridge pouches, boxes, carbine sockets and boots of the Indian War period 1865-1890.

International Armament, with History, Data, Technical Information and Photographs of Over 800 Weapons, 2nd edition, new printing, by George B. Johnson, Alexandria, VA, Ironside International, 2002. Hardcover. New in new dust jacket. $59.95

The development and progression of modern military small arms. All significant weapons have been included and examined in depth. Over 800 photographs and illustrations with both historical and technical data. Two volumes are now bound into one book.

Islamic Weapons Maghrib to Mohul, by Anthony C. Tirri, Canada, John Denner, 2003. 1st edition. 483 pp. Hardcover. New in new dust jacket. $149.95

Ithaca Iver Johnson Sporting Firearms: Dates of Manufacture, by D.R. Morse, Phoenix, AZ, Firing Pin Enterprizes, 2003. Softcover. NEW. $6.95

J. P. Sauer & Sohn, Sauer "Dein Waffenkamerad" Volume 2, by Cate & Krause, Walsworth Publishing, Chattanooga, TN, 2000. 440 pp., illus. $69.95

A historical study of Sauer automatic pistols. This new volume includes a great deal of new knowledge that has surfaced about the J.P. Sauer firm. You will find new photos, documentation, serial number ranges and historial facts which will expand the knowledge and interest in the oldest and best of the German firearms companies.

Jaeger Rifles, Collected Articles Published in Muzzle Blasts, by George Shumway, York PA, 2003. Reprint. 108 pp., illus. Stiff paper covers. New. $30.00

Thirty-six articles previously published in Muzzle Blasts are reproduced here.

Japanese Rifles of World War Two, by Duncan O. McCollum, Excalibur Publications, Latham, NY, 1996. 64 pp., illus. Paper covers. $18.95

A sweeping view of the rifles and carbines that made up Japan's arsenal during the conflict.

Kalashnikov "Machine Pistols, Assault Rifles, and Machine Guns, 1945 to the Present", by John Walter, Stackpole Books, Mechanicsburg, PA 1999, hardcover, photos, illus., 146 pp. $22.95

This exhaustive work published by Greenhill Military Manuals features a gun-by-gun directory of Kalashnikov variants. Technical specifications and illustrations are provided throughout, along with details of sights, bayonets, markings and ammunition. A must for the serious collector and historian.

The Kentucky Pistol, by Roy Chandler and James Whisker, Old Bedford Village Press, Bedford, PA, 1997. 225 pp., illus. $60.00

A photographic study of Kentucky pistols from famous collections.

THE HANDGUNNER'S LIBRARY

The Kentucky Rifle, by Captain John G.W. Dillin, George Shumway Publisher, York, PA, 1993. 221 pp., illus. $50.00

This well-known book was the first attempt to tell the story of the American longrifle. This edition retains the original text and illustrations with supplemental footnotes provided by Dr. George Shumway.

Know Your Broomhandle Mausers, by R.J. Berger, Blacksmith Corp., Southport, CT, 1996. 96 pp., illus. Paper covers. $14.95

An interesting story on the big Mauser pistol and its variations.

Law Enforcement Memorabilia Price and Identification Guide, by Monty McCord, DBI Books, a division of Krause Publications, Inc. Iola, WI, 1999. 208 pp., illus. Paper covers. $19.95

Lebeau and Courally Guns & Rifles Maker Since 1865, by Marco E. Nobili, Italy, Il Volo Srl, 1997. 1st printing. 176 pp., illustrated with b&w photographs, plus 16 full-color plates. Text in Italian and English. Hardcover. New in new dust jacket. $189.95

Legendary Sporting Guns, by Eric Joly, Abbeville Press, New York, N.Y., 1999. 228 pp., illus. $65.00

A survey of hunting through the ages and relates how many different types of firearms were created and refined for use afield.

Legends and Reality of the AK, by Val Shilin and Charlie Cutshaw, Paladen Press, Boulder, CO, 2000. 192 pp., illus. Paper covers. $35.00

A behind-the-scenes look at history, design and impact of the Kalashnikov family of weapons.

The Light 6-Pounder Battalion Gun of 1776, by Adrian Caruana, Museum Restoration Service, Bloomfield, Ontario, Canada, 2001. 76 pp., illus. Paper covers. $8.95

The London Gun Trade, 1850-1920, by Joyce E. Gooding, Museum Restoration Service, Bloomfield, Ontario, Canada, 2001. 48 pp., illus. Paper covers. $8.95

Names, dates and locations of London gunmakers working between 1850 and 1920 are listed. Compiled from the original Kelly's post office directories of the City of London.

The London Gunmakers and the English Duelling Pistol, 1770-1830, by Keith R. Dill, Museum Restoration Service, Bloomfield, Ontario, Canada, 1997. 36 pp., illus. Paper covers. $8.95

Ten gunmakers made London one of the major gunmaking centers of the world. This book examines how the design and construction of their pistols contributed to that reputation and how these characteristics may be used to date flintlock arms.

Longrifles of Pennsylvania, Volume 1, Jefferson, Clarion & Elk Counties, by Russel H. Harringer, George Shumway Publisher, York, PA, 1984. 200 pp., illus. $50.00

First in series that will treat in great detail the longrifles and gunsmiths of Pennsylvania.

The Luger Handbook, by Aarron Davis, Krause Publications, Iola, WI, 1997. 112 pp., illus. Paper covers. $9.95

Quick reference to classify Luger models and variations with complete details including proofmarks.

The Luger Story, by John Walter, Stackpole Books, Mechanicsburg, PA, 2001. 256 pp., illus. Paper covers $19.95

The standard history of the world's most famous handgun.

Lugers at Random, by Charles Kenyon Jr., Handgun Press, Glenview, IL, 1990. 420 pp., illus. $59.95

A new printing of this classic, comprehensive reference for all Luger collectors.

The M-1 Carbine: A Revolution in Gun-Stocking, by Grafton H. Cook II and Barbara W. Cook, Lincoln, RI, Andrew Mowbray, Inc., 2002. 1st edition. 208 pp., heavily illustrated with 157 rare photographs of the guns and the men and women who made them. Softcover. $29.95

Shows you, step by step, how M1 carbine stocks were made, right through to assembly with the hardware. Learn about M1 Carbine development, and how the contracting and production process actually worked. Also contains lots of detailed information about other military weapons, like the M1A1, the M1 Garand, the M14 and much, much more.

M1 Carbine: Design, Development, and Production, by Larry Ruth, Gun Room Press, Highland Park, NJ, 1987. 291 pp., illus. Paper $19.95

The origin, development, manufacture and use of this famous carbine of WWII.

The M1 Carbine Owner's Guide, by Larry Ruth and Scott A. Duff, Scott A. Duff Publications, Export, PA, 1997. 126 pp., illus. Paper covers. $21.95

This book answers the questions M1 owners most often ask concerning maintenance activities not encounted by military users.

The M1 Garand: Owner's Guide, by Scott A. Duff, Scott A. Duff Publications, Export, PA, 1998. 132 pp., illus. Paper covers. $21.95

This book answers the questions M1 owners most often ask concerning maintenance activities not encounted by military users.

The M1 Garand: Post World War, by Scott A. Duff, Scott A. Duff Publications, Export, PA, 1990. 139 pp., illus. Softcover. $21.95

A detailed account of the activities at Springfield Armory through this period. International Harvester, H&R, Korean War production and quantities delivered. Serial numbers.

The M1 Garand: World War II, by Scott A. Duff, Scott A. Duff Publications, Export, PA, 2001. 210 pp., illus. Paper covers. $34.95

The most comprehensive study available to the collector and historian on the M1 Garand of WWII.

The M1 Garand 1936 to 1957, by Joe Poyer and Craig Riesch, North Cape Publications, Tustin, CA, 1996. 216 pp., illus. Paper covers. $19.95

Describes the entire range of M1 Garand production in text and quick-scan charts.

The M1 Garand Serial Numbers and Data Sheets, by Scott A. Duff, Scott A. Duff Publications, Export, PA, 1995. 101 pp., illus. Paper covers. $11.95

Provides the reader with serial numbers related to dates of manufacture and a large sampling of data sheets to aid in identification or restoration.

Machine Guns, by Ian V. Hogg, Iola, WI, Krause Publications, 2002. 1st edition. 336 pp., illustrated with b&w photos with a 16-page color section. Softcover. $29.95

A detailed history of the rapid-fire gun, 14th Century to present. Covers the development, history and specifications.

Made in the C.S.A.: Saddle Makers of the Confederacy, by Ken R. Knopp, Hattiesburg, MS, privately printed, 2003. 1st edition signed. 205 pp., illus., signed by the author. Softcover. NEW. $30.00

Maine Made Guns and Their Makers, by Dwight B. Demeritt Jr., Maine State Museum, Augusta, ME, 1998. 209 pp., illus. $55.00

An authoritative, biographical study of Maine gunsmiths.

Marlin Firearms: A History of the Guns and the Company That Made Them, by Lt. Col. William S. Brophy, USAR, Ret., Stackpole Books, Harrisburg, PA, 1989. 672 pp., illus. $80.00

The definitive book on the Marlin Firearms Co. and their products.

Martini-Henry .450 Rifles & Carbines, by Dennis Lewis, Excalibur Publications, Latham, NY, 1996. 72 pp., illus. Paper covers. $11.95

The stories of the rifles and carbines that were the mainstay of the British soldier through the Victorian wars.

Mauser Bolt Rifles, by Ludwig Olson, F. Brownell & Son, Inc., Montezuma, IA, 1999. 364 pp., illus. $64.95

The most complete, detailed, authoritative and comprehensive work ever done on Mauser bolt rifles. Completely revised deluxe 3rd edition.

Mauser Military Rifle Markings, by Terence W. Lapin, Arlington, VA, Hyrax Publishers, LLC, 2001. 167 pp., illus. 2nd edition. Revised and expanded. Softcover. $22.95

A general guide to reading and understanding the often mystifying markings found on military Mauser rifles. Includes German Regimental markings as well as German police markings and WWII German Mauser subcontractor codes. A handy reference to take to gun shows.

Mauser Military Rifles of the World, 3rd Edition, by Robert Ball, Krause Publications, Iola, WI, 2003. 304 pp., illustrated with 1,000 b&w photos and a 48-page color section. $44.95

This 3rd edition brings more than 100 new photos of these historic rifles and the wars in which they were carried.

Mauser Smallbores Sporting, Target and Training Rifles, by Jon Speed, Collector Grade Publications, Cobourg, Ontario, Canada 1998. 349 pp., illus. $67.50

A history of all the smallbore sporting, target and training rifles produced by the legendary Mauser-Werke of Obendorf Am Neckar.

Metallic Cartridge Conversions: The History of the Guns and Modern Reproductions, by Dennis Adler, Foreword by R. L. Wilson. Krause Publications, 2003. 208 pp., 250 color photos. Hardcover. $39.95

Collectors and enthusiasts will track the history of the original conversions of the 1800s through historic text and both new and archival photographs. All current modern reproductions are represented with photos, technical details, and performance test results. In-depth coverage of the original revolvers includes models from Colt, Remington, Smith & Wesson, Rollin White, Richards, and Richards-Mason. Modern guns from American Western Arms, Navy Arms, and Cimarron F.A. Co. are highlighted. Color section highlights engraved and presentation models.

Military Holsters of World War II, by Eugene J. Bender, Rowe Publications, Rochester, NY, 1998. 200 pp., illus. $45.00

A revised edition with a new price guide of the most definitive book on this subject.

The Military Remington Rolling Block Rifle, by George Layman, Pioneer Press, TN, 1998. 146 pp., illus. Paper covers. $24.95

A standard reference for those with an interest in the Remington rolling block family of firearms.

Military Rifles of Japan, 5th Edition, by F.L. Honeycutt, Julin Books, Lake Park, FL, 1999. 208 pp., illus. $42.95

A new revised and updated edition. Includes the early Murata-period markings, etc.

Military Small Arms Data Book, by Ian V. Hogg, Stackpole Books, Mechanicsburg, PA, 1999. 336 pp., illus. $44.95

Data on more than 1,500 weapons. Covers a vast range of weapons from pistols to anti-tank rifles. Essential data, 1870-2000, in one volume.

Modern Gun Identification & Value Guide, 13th Edition, by Russell and Steve Quertermous, Collector Books, Paducah, KY, 1998. 504 pp., illus. Paper covers. $14.95

Features current values for over 2,500 models of rifles, shotguns and handguns, with over 1,800 illustrations.

More Single Shot Rifles, by James C. Grant, Gun Room Press, Highland Park, NJ, 1976. 324 pp., illus. $35.00

Details the guns made by Frank Wesson, Milt Farrow, Holden, Borchardt, Stevens, Remington, Winchester, Ballard and Peabody-Martini.

Mortimer, the Gunmakers, 1753-1923, by H. Lee Munson, Andrew Mowbray Inc., Lincoln, RI, 1992. 320 pp., illus. $65.00

Seen through a single, dominant, English gunmaking dynasty, this fascinating study provides a window into the classical era of firearms artistry.

The Mosin-Nagant Rifle, by Terence W. Lapin, North Cape Publications, Tustin, CA, 1998. 30 pp., illus. Paper covers. $19.95

The first ever complete book on the Mosin-Nagant rifle written in English. Covers every variation.

Mossberg Sporting Firearms: Dates of Manufacture, by D.R. Morse, Phoenix, AZ, Firing Pin Enterprizes, 2003. Softcover. NEW. $6.95

Covers their pistols, revolvers, rifles, shotguns and commemoratives, plus models and serial numbers.

The MP38, 40, 40/1 & 41 Submachine Gun, by de Vries & Martens. Propaganda Photo Series, Volume II. Alexandria, VA, Ironside International, 2001. 1st edition. 150 pp., illustrated with 200 high quality b&w photos. Hardcover. $34.95

Covers all essential information on history and development, ammunition and accessories, codes and markings, and contains photos of nearly every model and accessory. Includes a unique selection of original German WWII propaganda photos, most never published before.

The Navy Luger, by Joachim Gortz and John Walter, Handgun Press, Glenview, IL, 1988. 128 pp., illus. $24.95

The 9mm Pistole 1904 and the Imperial German Navy. A concise illustrated history.

The New World of Russian Small Arms and Ammunition, by Charlie Cutshaw, Paladin Press, Boulder, CO, 1998. 160 pp., illus. $42.95

Detailed descriptions, specifications and first-class illustrations of the AN-94, PSS silent pistol, Bizon SMG, Saifa-12 tactical shotgun, the GP-25 grenade launcher and more cutting edge Russian weapons.

THE HANDGUNNER'S LIBRARY

The Number 5 Jungle Carbine, by Alan M. Petrillo, Excalibur Publications, Latham, NY, 1994. 32 pp., illus. Paper covers. $7.95

A comprehensive treatment of the rifle that collectors have come to call the "Jungle Carbine"–the Lee-Enfield Number 5, Mark 1.

Observations on Colt's Second Contract, November 2, 1847, by G. Maxwell Longfield and David T. Basnett, Museum Restoration Service, Bloomfield, Ontario, Canada, 1997. 36 pp., illus. Paper covers. $6.95

This study traces the history and the construction of the Second Model Colt Dragoon supplied in 1848 to the U.S. Cavalry.

The Official Soviet SVD Manual, by Major James F. Gebhardt (Ret.), Paladin Press, Boulder, CO, 1999. 112 pp., illus. Paper covers. $22.00

Operating instructions for the 7.62mm Dragunov, the first Russian rifle developed from scratch specifically for sniping.

Old Gunsights: A Collector's Guide, 1850 to 2000, by Nicholas Stroebel, Krause Publications, Iola, WI, 1998. 320 pp., illus. Paper covers. $29.95

An in-depth and comprehensive examination of old gunsights and the rifles on which they were used to get accurate feel for prices in this expanding market.

Orders, Decorations and Badges of the Socialist Republic of Vietnam and the National Front for the Liberation of South Vietnam, by Edward J. Emering, Schiffer Publications, Atglen, PA. 2000. 96 pages, 190 color and b&w photographs, line drawings. $24.95

The Orders and Decorations of the "enemy" during the Vietnam War have remained shrouded in mystery for many years. References to them are scarce and interrogations of captives during the war often led to the proliferation of misinformation concerning them. Includes value guide.

Ordnance Tools, Accessories & Appendages of the M1 Rifle, by Billy Pyle. Houston, TX, privately printed, 2002. 2nd edition. 206 pp., illustrated with b&w photos. Softcover $40.00

The P-08 Parabellum Luger Automatic Pistol, edited by J. David McFarland, Desert Publications, Cornville, AZ, 1982. 20 pp., illus. Paper covers. $11.95

Covers every facet of the Luger, plus a listing of all known Luger models.

Packing Iron, by Richard C. Rattenbury, Zon International Publishing, Millwood, NY, 1993. 216 pp., illus. $45.00

The best book yet produced on pistol holsters and rifle scabbards. Over 300 variations of holster and scabbards are illustrated in large, clear plates.

Painted Steel, Steel Pots Volume 2, by Chris Armold, Bender Publishing, San Jose, CA, 2001. 384 pp. - 1,053 photos, hundreds in color. $57.95

From the author of "Steel Pots: The History of America's Steel Combat Helmets" comes "Painted Steel: Steel Pots, Vol. II." This companion volume features detailed chapters on painted and unit marked helmets of WWI and WWII, plus a variety of divisional, regimental and subordinate markings. Special full-color plates detail subordinate unit markings such as the tactical markings used by the U.S. 2nd Division in WWI.

Pattern Dates for British Ordnance Small Arms, 1718-1783, by DeWitt Bailey, Thomas Publications, Gettysburg, PA, 1997. 116 pp., illus. Paper covers. $20.00

The weapons discussed in this work are those carried by troops sent to North America between 1737 and 1783, or shipped to them as replacement arms while in America.

Percussion Ammunition Packets 1845-1888 Union, Confederate & European, by John J. Malloy, Dean S. Thomas and Terry A. White with Foreward by Norm Flayderman. Gettysburg, PA, Thomas Publications, 2003. 1st edition. 134 pp., illustrated with color photos. Hardcover. New. $75.00

Finally a means to recognize the untold variety of labeled types of ammunition box labels.

Peters & King, by Thomas D. Schiffer. Krause Publications, Iola, WI 2002. 1st edition. 256 pp., 200+ b&w photos with a 32-page color section. Hardcover. $44.95

Discover the history behind Peters Cartridge and King Powder and see how they shaped the arms industry into what it is today and why their products fetch hundreds, even thousands of dollars at auctions. Current values are provided for their highly collectible product packaging and promotional advertising premiums such as powder kegs, tins, cartridge boxes, and calendars.

The Pitman Notes on U.S. Martial Small Arms and Ammunition, 1776-1933, Volume 2, Revolvers and Automatic Pistols, by Brig. Gen. John Pitman, Thomas Publications, Gettysburg, PA, 1990. 192 pp., illus. $29.95

A most important primary source of information on United States military small arms and ammunition.

Plates and Buckles of the American Military 1795-1874, by Sydney C. Kerksis, Orange, VA, Publisher's Press, 1998. 5th edition. 568 pp., illustrated with hundreds of b&w photos. Hardcover. $39.00

The single most comprehensive reference for U.S. and Confederate plates.

The Presentation and Commercial Colt Walker Pistols, by Col. Robert D. Whittington III, Hooks, TX, Brownlee Books, 2003. A limited edition of 1,000 copies. Numbered. 21 pp. Paper covers. New. $15.00

A study of events at the Whitneyville Armoury and Samuel Colt's Hartford Factory from 1 June 1847 to 29 November 1848.

Production Statistics U.S. Arms Makers From Armalite to Winchester, by Phoenix, AZ, Firing Pin Enterprizes, 1997. 262 pp. Softcover. NEW. $19.95

Proud Promise: French Autoloading Rifles, 1898-1979, by Jean Huon, Collector Grade Publications, Inc., Cobourg, Ont., Canada, 1995. 216 pp., illus. $39.95

The author has finally set the record straight about the importance of French contributions to modern arms design.

Purdey Gun and Rifle Makers: The Definitive History, by Donald Dallas, Quiller Press, London, 2000. 245 pp., illus. Color throughout. A limited edition of 3,000 copies. Signed and numbered. With a PURDEY book plate. $99.95

The Queen Anne Pistol, 1660-1780: A History of the Turn-Off Pistol, by John W. Burgoyne, Bloomfield, Ont., Canada, Museum Restoration Service, 2002. 1st edition - Historical Arms New Series No. 1. 120 pp., a detailed, fast moving, thoroughly researched text and almost 200 cross-referenced illustrations. Pictorial hardcover. $35.00

This distinctive breech-loading arm was developed in the middle years of the 17th century but found popularity during the reign of the monarch (1702-1714), by whose name it is known.

Red Shines The Sun: A Pictorial History of the Fallschirm-Infantrie, by Eric Queen. San Jose, CA, R. James Bender Publishing, 2003. 1st edition. Hardcover. $69.95

A culmination of 12 years of research, this reference work traces the history of the Army paratroopers of the Fallschirm-Infanterie from their origins in 1937, to the expansion to battalion strength in 1938, then on through operations at Wola Gulowska (Poland), and Moerdijk (Holland). This 240-page comprehensive look at their history is supported by 600 images, many of which are in full color, and nearly 90% are previously unpublished.

Reloading Tools, Sights and Telescopes for Single Shot Rifles, by Gerald O. Kelver, Brighton, CO, 1982. 163 pp., illus. Paper covers. $13.95

A listing of most of the famous makers of reloading tools, sights and telescopes with a brief description of the products they manufactured.

The Remington-Lee Rifle, by Eugene F. Myszkowski, Excalibur Publications, Latham, NY, 1995. 100 pp., illus. Paper covers. $22.50

Features detailed descriptions, including serial number ranges, of each model from the first Lee magazine rifle produced for the U.S. Navy to the last Remington-Lee small bore shipped to the Cuban Rural Guard.

Remington 'America's Oldest Gunmaker', The Official Authorized History of the Remington Arms Company, by Roy Marcot. Madison, NC, Remington Arms Company, 1999. 1st edition. 312 pp., with 167 b&w illustrations, plus 291 color plates. $79.95

This is without a doubt the finest history of that firm ever to have been compiled. Based on firsthand research in the Remington company archives, it is extremely well written.

Remington Sporting Firearms: Dates of Manufacture, by D.R. Morse, Phoenix, AZ, Firing Pin Enterprizes, 2003. 43 pp. Softcover. New. $6.95

Covers their pistols, revolvers, rifles, shotguns and commemoratives, plus models and serial numbers.

Remington's Vest Pocket Pistols, by Robert E. Hatfield, Lincoln, RI, Andrew Mowbray, Inc., 2002. 117 pp. Hardcover. $29.95

While Remington Vest Pocket pistols have always been popular with collectors, very little solid information has been available about them. Inside you will find 100+ photographs, serial number data, exploded views of all four Remington Vest Pocket pistol sizes, component parts lists and a guide to disassembly and reassembly. Also includes a discussion of Vest Pocket Wire-Stocked Buggy/Bicycle rifles, plus the documented serial number story.

Revolvers of the British Services 1854-1954, by W.H.J. Chamberlain and A.W.F. Taylerson, Museum Restoration Service, Ottawa, Canada, 1989. 80 pp., illus. $27.50

Covers the types issued among many of the United Kingdom's naval, land or air services.

Rifles of the U.S. Army 1861-1906, by John D. McAulay, Andrew Mowbray, Inc., Lincoln, RI, 2003. 1st edition. Over 40 rifles covered, 278 pp., illus. Hardcover. New. $47.95

There have been several excellent books written about the manufacture of rifles for the U.S. Army from the time of the Civil War to the early 20th century. However, few of these books have focused upon what happened to these rifles after they were issued. This exciting new book by renowned authority John McAulay fills this gap. It gives the reader detailed coverage of the issue and actual field service of America's fighting rifles, both in peacetime and in war, including their military service with the infantry, artillery, cavalry and engineers.

One feature that all readers will value is the impressive number of historical photos, taken during the Civil War, the Mexican War, the Indian Wars, the Spanish-American War, the Philippine Insurrection and more, showing these rifles in the hands of the men who fought with them. Procurement information, issue details and historical background.

Rifles of the World, by Oliver Achard, Chartwell Books, Inc., Edison, NJ, 141 pp., illus. $24.95

A unique insight into the world of long guns, not just rifles, but also shotguns, carbines and all the usual multi-barreled guns that once were so popular with European hunters, especially in Germany and Austria.

Round Ball to Rimfire: A History of Civil War Small Arms Ammunition, Vol. 1, by Dean Thomas, Thomas Publications, Gettysburg, PA, 1997. 144 pp., illus. $40.00

The first of a two-volume set of the most complete history and guide for all small arms ammunition used in the Civil War. The information includes data from research and development to the arsenals that created it.

Round Ball to Rimfire: A History of Civil War Small Arms Ammunition, Vol. 2, by Dean Thomas, Thomas Publications, Gettysburg, PA 2002. 528 pp. Hardcover. $49.95

Completely discusses the ammunition for Federal breechloading carbines and rifles. The seven chapters with 18 appendices detailing the story of the 27 or so different kinds of breechloaders actually purchased or ordered by the Ordnance Department during the Civil War. The book is conveniently divided by the type of priming–external or internal–and then alphabetically by maker or supplier. A wealth of new information and research has proven that these weapons either functioned properly or were inadequate relative to the design and ingenuity of the proprietary cartridges.

Round Ball to Rimfire: A History of Civil War Small Arms Ammunition, Vol. 3, by Dean Thomas, Thomas Publications, Gettysburg, PA, 2003. 488 pp., illus. $49.95

Completely discusses the ammunition for Federal pistols and revolvers. The seven chapters with 18 appendices detailing the story of the 27 or so different kinds of breechloaders actually purchased or ordered by the Ordnance Department during the Civil War. A wealth of new information and research has proven that these weapons either functioned properly or were inadequate relative to the design and ingenuity of the proprietary cartridges.

Ruger and his Guns, by R.L. Wilson, Simon & Schuster, New York, NY, 1996. 358 pp., illus. $65.00

A history of the man, the company and their firearms.

Russell M. Catron and His Pistols, by Warren H. Buxton, Ucross Books, Los Alamos, NM, 1998. 224 pp., illus. Paper covers. $49.50

An unknown American firearms inventor and manufacturer of the mid-twentieth century. Military, commerical, ammunition.

The SAFN-49 and the FAL, by Joe Poyer and Dr. Richard Feirman, North Cape Publications, Tustin, CA, 1998. 160 pp., illus. Paper covers. $14.95

The first complete overview of the SAFN-49 battle rifle, from its pre-WWII beginnings to its military service in countries as diverse as the Belgian Congo and Argentina. The FAL was a "light" version of the SAFN-49 and it became the Free World's most adopted battle rifle.

THE HANDGUNNER'S LIBRARY

Savage Sporting Firearms: Dates of Manufacture 1907-1997, by D.R. Morse. Phoenix, AZ, Firing Pin Enterprizes, 2003. 22 pp. Softcover. New. $6.95

Covers their pistols, revolvers, rifles, shotguns and commemoratives, plus models and serial numbers.

Scale Model Firearms, by Joseph D. Kramer. Pittsburgh, PA, privately printed, 1999. 1st edition. 136 pp., oversize, many color photos, index. Softcover. New. $35.00

Each of the models, which are nearly all in one-half scale, require a year or more to complete and in most cases only one example was made. Mr. R. E. Hutchen's uncompromising devotion to the production of these models, is a tribute to a man who is known internationally to be the finest maker of model firearms in the world.

Scottish Firearms, by Claude Blair and Robert Woosnam-Savage, Museum Restoration Service, Bloomfield, Ont., Canada, 1995. 52 pp., illus. Paper covers. $8.95

This revision of the first book devoted entirely to Scottish firearms is supplemented by a register of surviving Scottish long guns.

Sharps Firearms, by Frank Seller, Denver, CO, 1998. 358 pp., illus. $59.95

Traces the development of Sharps firearms with full range of guns made including all martial variations.

Silk and Steel: Women at Arms, by R. L. Wilson, New York, Random House, 2003. 1st edition. 300+ Striking four-color images; 8-1/2" x 11", 320 pgs. Hardcover. New in new dust jacket. (9775). $65.00

Beginning with Artemis and Diana, goddesses of hunting, evolving through modern times, here is the first comprehensive presentation on the subject of women and firearms. No object has had a greater impact on world history over the past 650 years than the firearm, and a surprising number of women have been keen on the subject, as shooters, hunters, collectors, engravers, and even gunmakers.

The SKS Carbine, by Steve Kehaya and Joe Poyer, North Cape Publications, Tustin, CA, 1997. 150 pp., illus. Paper covers. $16.95

The first comprehensive examination of a major historical firearm used through the Vietnam conflict to the diamond fields of Angola.

The SKS Type 45 Carbines, by Duncan Long, Desert Publications, El Dorado, AZ, 1992. 110 pp., illus. Paper covers. $19.95

Covers the history and practical aspects of operating, maintaining and modifying this abundantly available rifle.

Slave Badges and the Slave-Hire System in Charleston, South Carolina, 1783-1865, by Harlan Greene, Harry S. Hutchins Jr., Brian E. Hutchins. Jefferson, NC, McFarland & Company, 2004. 152 pp. Hardcover, NEW. $35.00

Smith & Wesson 1857-1945, by Robert J. Neal and Roy G. Jinks, R&R Books, Livonia, NY, 1996. 434 pp., illus. $50.00

The bible for all existing and aspiring Smith & Wesson collectors.

Smith & Wesson Sporting Firearms: Dates of Manufacture, by D.R. Morse, Phoenix, AZ, Firing Pin Enterprizes, 2003. 76 pp. Softcover. NEW. $6.95

Covers their pistols, revolvers, rifles, shotguns and commemoratives, plus models and serial numbers.

Sniper Variations of the German K98k Rifle, by Richard D. Law, Collector Grade Publications, Ontario, Canada, 1997. 240 pp., illus. $47.50

Volume 2 of "Backbone of the Wehrmacht" the author's in-depth study of the German K98k rifle. This volume concentrates on the telescopic-sighted rifle of choice for most German snipers during WWII.

Southern Derringers of the Mississippi Valley, by Turner Kirkland, Pioneer Press, Tenn., 1971. 80 pp., illus., paper covers. $4.00

A guide for the collector and a much-needed study.

Soviet Russian Postwar Military Pistols and Cartridges, by Fred A. Datig, Handgun Press, Glenview, IL, 1988. 152 pp., illus. $29.95

Thoroughly researched, this definitive sourcebook covers the development and adoption of the Makarov, Stechkin and the new PSM pistols. Also included in this source book is coverage on Russian clandestine weapons and pistol cartridges.

Soviet Russian Tokarev "TT" Pistols and Cartridges 1929-1953, by Fred Datig, Graphic Publishers, Santa Ana, CA, 1993. 168 pp., illus. $39.95

Details of rare arms and their accessories are shown in hundreds of photos. It also contains a complete bibliography and index.

Spencer Repeating Firearms, by Roy M. Marcot, New York, Rowe Publications, 2002. 316 pp.; numerous b&w photos and illustrations. Hardcover. $65.00

Sporting Collectibles, by Jim and Vivian Karsnitz, Schiffer Publishing Ltd., West Chester, PA, 1992. 160 pp., illus. Paper covers. $29.95

The fascinating world of hunting related collectibles presented in an informative text.

The Springfield 1903 Rifles, by Lt. Col. William S. Brophy, USAR, Ret., Stackpole Books Inc., Harrisburg, PA, 1985. 608 pp., illus. $75.00

The illustrated, documented story of the design, development, and production of all the models, appendages, and accessories.

Springfield Model 1903 Service Rifle Production and Alteration, 1905-1910, by C.S. Ferris and John Beard, Arvada, CO, 1995. 66 pp., illus. Paper covers. $12.50

A highly recommended work for any serious student of the Springfield Model 1903 rifle.

Springfield Shoulder Arms 1795-1865, by Claud E. Fuller, S. & S. Firearms, Glendale, NY, 1996. 76 pp., illus. Paper covers. $14.95

Exact reprint of the scarce 1930 edition of one of the most definitive works on Springfield flintlock and percussion muskets ever published.

SS Headgear, by Kit Wilson. Johnson Reference Books, Fredericksburg, VA. 72 pp., 15 full-color plates and over 70 b&w photos. $16.50

An excellent source of information concerning all types of SS headgear, to include Allgemeine-SS, Waffen-SS, visor caps, helmets, overseas caps, M-43's and miscellaneous headgear. Also includes a guide on the availability and current values of SS headgear. This guide was compiled from auction catalogs, dealer price lists, and input from advanced collectors in the field.

SS Helmets: A Collector's Guide, Vol 1, by Kelly Hicks, Johnson Reference Books, Fredericksburg, VA. 96 pp., illus. $17.50

Deals only with SS helmets and features some very nice color close-up shots of the different SS decals used. Over 85 photographs, 27 in color. The author has documented most of the known types of SS helmets, and describes in detail all of the vital things to look for in determining the originality, style type, and finish.

SS Helmets: A Collector's Guide, Vol 2, by Kelly Hicks. Johnson Reference Books, Fredericksburg, VA. 2000. 128 pp. 107 full-color photos, 14 period photos. $25.00

Volume II contains dozen of highly detailed, full-color photos of rare and original SS and Field Police helmets, featuring both sides as well as interior view. The outstanding decal section offers detailed close-ups of original SS and Police decals, and in conjunction with Volume I, completes the documentation of virtually all types of original decal variations used between 1934 and 1945.

SS Steel; Parade and Combat Helmets of Germany's Third Reich Elite, by Kelly Hicks, San Jose, CA, Bender Publishing, 2004. 1st edition. 241 pp., 400 photos and illustrations in color, deluxe binding. Hardcover. NEW. $44.95

SS Uniforms, Insignia and Accoutrements, by A. Hayes. Schiffer Publications, Atglen, PA. 1996. 248 pp., with over 800 color and b&w photographs. $69.95

This new work explores in detailed color the complex subject of Allgemeine and Waffen-SS uniforms, insignia, and accoutrements. Hundreds of authentic items are extensively photographed in close-up to enable the reader to examine and study.

Standard Catalog of Firearms, 15th Edition, by Ned Schwing, Krause Publications, Iola, WI, 2005. 1504 pp., illus. 7,000 b&w photos plus a 16-page color section. Paper covers. $34.95

This is the largest, most comprehensive and best-selling firearm book of all time! And this year's edition is a blockbuster for both shooters and firearm collectors. More than 14,000 firearms are listed and priced in up to six grades of condition. That's almost 100,000 prices! Gun enthusiasts will love the new full-color section of photos highlighting the finest firearms sold at auction this past year.

Steel Pots: The History of America's Steel Combat Helmets, by Chris Armold. Bender Publishing, San Jose, CA, 2000. $47.95

Packed with hundreds of color photographs, detailed specification diagrams and supported with meticulously researched data, this book takes the reader on a fascinating visual journey covering 80 years of American helmet design and development.

Sturm Ruger Sporting Firearms: Dates of Manufacture, by D.R. Morse, Phoenix, AZ, Firing Pin Enterprizes, 2003. 22 pp. Softcover, NEW. $6.95

Covers their pistols, revolvers, rifles, shotguns and commemoratives, plus models and serial numbers.

The Sumptuous Flaske, by Herbert G. Houze, Andrew Mowbray, Inc., Lincoln, RI, 1989. 158 pp., illus. Softcover. $35.00

Catalog of a recent show at the Buffalo Bill Historical Center bringing together some of the finest European and American powder flasks of the 16th to 19th centuries.

The Swedish Mauser Rifles, by Steve Kehaya and Joe Poyer, North Cape Publications, Tustin, CA, 1999. 267 pp., illus. Paper covers. $19.95

Every known variation of the Swedish Mauser carbine and rifle is described, all match and target rifles and all sniper versions. Includes serial number and production data.

System Lefaucheaux: Continuing the Study of Pinfire Cartridge Arms Including Their Role in the American Civil War, by Chris C. Curtis, Foreword by Norm Flayderman, Armslore Press, 2002. 1st edition. 312 pp., heavily illustrated with b&w photos. Hardcover. New in new dust jacket. $44.95

Thompson: The American Legend, by Tracie L. Hill, Collector Grade Publications, Ontario, Canada, 1996. 584 pp., illus. $85.00

The story of the first American submachine gun. All models are featured and discussed.

Thoughts on the Kentucky Rifle in its Golden Age, by Joe K. Kindig, III. York, PA, George Shumway Publisher, 2002. Annotated second edition. 561 pp.; Illustrated. This scarce title, long out of print, is once again available. Hardcover. $85.00

The definitive book on the Kentucky Rifle, illustrating 266 of these guns in 856 detailed photographs.

Tin Lids–Canadian Combat Helmets, #2 in "Up Close" Series, by Roger V. Lucy, Ottawa, Ontario, Service Publications, 2000. 2nd edition. 48 pp. Softcover. NEW. $17.95

Toys That Shoot and Other Neat Stuff, by James Dundas, Schiffer Books, Atglen, PA, 1999. 112 pp., illus. Paper covers. $24.95

Shooting toys from the twentieth century, especially 1920s to 1960s, in over 420 color photographs of BB guns, cap shooters, marble shooters, squirt guns and more. Complete with a price guide.

Trade Guns of the Hudson's Bay Company 1670-1970, Historical Arms New Series No. 2. by S. James Gooding, Bloomfield, Ont. Canada, Museum Restoration Service, 2003. 1st edition. 158 pp., thoroughly researched text. Includes bibliographical references. Pictorial hardcover. NEW. $35.00

The Trapdoor Springfield, by M.D. Waite and B.D. Ernst, The Gun Room Press, Highland Park, NJ, 1983. 250 pp., illus. $39.95

The first comprehensive book on the famous standard military rifle of the 1873-92 period.

Treasures of the Moscow Kremlin: Arsenal of the Russian Tsars, A Royal Armories and the Moscow Kremlin exhibition, HM Tower of London 13, June 1998 to 11 September, 1998. BAS Printers, Over Wallop, Hampshire, England. xxii plus 192 pp. over 180 color illustrations. Text in English and Russian. $65.00

For this exhibition catalog, each of the 94 objects on display are photographed and described in detail to provide the most informative record of this important exhibition.

U.S. Army Headgear 1812-1872, by John P. Langellier and C. Paul Loane. Atglen, PA, Schiffer Publications, 2002. 167 pp., with over 350 color and b&w photos. Hardcover. $69.95

This profusely illustrated volume represents more than three decades of research in public and private collections by military historian John P. Langellier and Civil War authority C. Paul Loane.

U.S. Army Rangers & Special Forces of World War II Their War in Photographs, by Robert Todd Ross, Atglen, PA, Schiffer Publications, 2002. 216 pp., over 250 b&w and color photographs. Hardcover. $59.95

Never before has such an expansive view of WWII elite forces been offered in one volume. An extensive search of public and private archives unearthed an astonishing number of rare and never before seen images, including color. Most notable are the nearly 20 exemplary photographs of Lieutenant Colonel William O. Darby's Ranger Force in Italy, taken by Robert Capa, considered by many to be the greatest combat photographer of all time.

THE HANDGUNNER'S LIBRARY

U.S. Handguns of World War II: The Secondary Pistols and Revolvers, by Charles W. Pate, Andrew Mowbray, Inc., Lincoln, RI, 1998. 515 pp., illus. $39.00

This indispensable new book covers all of the American military handguns of WWII except for the M1911A1 Colt automatic.

U.S. Martial Single Shot Pistols, by Daniel D. Hartzler and James B. Whisker, Old Bedford Village Press, Bedford, PA, 1998. 128 pp., illus. $45.00

A photographic chronicle of military and semi-martial pistols supplied to the U.S. Government and the several States.

U.S. Military Arms Dates of Manufacture from 1795, by George Madis, Dallas, TX, 1995. 64 pp. Softcover. $9.95

Lists all U.S. military arms of collector interest alphabetically, covering about 250 models.

U.S. M1 Carbines: Wartime Production, by Craig Riesch, North Cape Publications, Tustin, CA, 1994. 72 pp., illus. Paper covers. $16.95

Presents only verifiable and accurate information. Each part of the M1 Carbine is discussed fully in its own section; including markings and finishes.

U.S. Naval Handguns, 1808-1911, by Fredrick R. Winter, Andrew Mowbray Publishers, Lincoln, RI, 1990. 128 pp., illus. $26.00

The story of U.S. Naval handguns spans an entire century–included are sections on each of the important naval handguns within the period.

U.S. Silent Service - Dolphins & Combat Insignia 1924-1945, by David Jones. Bender Publishing, San Jose, CA, 2001. 224 pp., 532 photos (most in full color). $39.95

After eight years of extensive research, the publication of this book is a submarine buff and collector's dream come true. This beautiful full-color book chronicles, with period letters and sketches, the developmental history of U.S. submarine insignia prior to 1945. It also contains many rare and never before published photographs, plus interviews with WWII submarine veterans, from enlisted men to famous skippers. All known contractors are covered plus embroidered versions, mess dress variations, the Roll of Honor, submarine combat insignia, battleflags, launch memorabilia and related submarine collectibles (postal covers, match book covers, jewelry, posters, advertising art, postcards, etc.).

Uniform and Dress Army and Navy of the Confederate States of America (Official Regulations), by Confederate States of America., Ray Riling Arms Books, Philadelphia, PA, 1960. $20.00

A portfolio containing a complete set of nine color plates especially prepared for framing, reproduced in exactly 200 sets from the very rare Richmond, VA., 1861 regulations.

Uniforms & Equipment of the Austro-Hungarian Army in World War One, by Spencer A. Coil, Atglen, PA, Schiffer Publications, 2003. 1st edition. 352 pp., with over 550 b&w and color photographs. Hardcover. New in new dust jacket. $69.95

Uniforms and Insignia of the Cossacks in the German Wehrmacht in World War II, by Peter Schuster and Harald Tiede, Atglen, PA, Schiffer Publications, 2003. 1st edition. 160 pp., illustrated with over 420 b&w and color photographs. Hardcover. New in new dust jacket. $49.95

Uniforms & Equipment of the Imperial German Army 1900-1918: A Study in Period Photographs, by Charles Woolley, Schiffer Publications, Atglen, PA, 2000. 375 pp., over 500 b&w photographs and 50 color drawings. Fully illustrated. $69.95

Features formal studio portraits of pre-war dress and wartime uniforms of all arms. Also contains photo postal cards taken in the field of Infantry, Pionier, Telegraph-Signal, Landsturm, and Mountain Troops, vehicles, artillery, musicians, the Bavarian Leib Regiment, specialized uniforms and insignia, small arms close-ups, unmotorized transport, group shots and Balloon troops and includes a 60-page full-color uniform section reproduced from rare 1914 plates.

Uniforms of the Third Reich: A Study in Photographs, by Maguire Hayes, Schiffer Publications, Atglen, PA, 1997. 200 pp., with over 400 color photographs. $69.95

This new book takes a close look at a variety of authentic WWII era German uniforms including examples from the Army, Luftwaffe, Kriegsmarine, Waffen-SS, Allgemeine-SS, Hitler youth and political leaders. The pieces are shown in large full frame front and rear shots, and in painstaking detail to show tailors' tags, buttons, insignia detail etc. and allow the reader to see what the genuine article looks like. Various accoutrements worn with the uniforms are also included to aid the collector.

Uniforms of the United States Army, 1774-1889, by Henry Alexander Ogden, Dover Publishing, Mineola, NY. 1998. 48 pp. of text plus 44 color plates. Softcover. $9.95

A republication of the work published by the quarter-master general, United States army in 1890. A striking collection of lithographs and a marvelous archive of military, social, and costume history portraying the gamut of U.S. Army uniforms from fatigues to full dress, between 1774 and 1889.

Uniforms of the Waffen-SS; Black Service Uniform - LAH Guard Uniform - SS Earth-Grey Service Uniform - Model 1936 Field Service Uniform - 1939-1940 - 1941 Volume 1, by Michael D. Beaver, Schiffer Publications, Atglen, PA, 2002. 272 pp., with 500 color, and b&w photos. $79.95

This spectacular work is a heavily documented record of all major clothing articles of the Waffen-SS. Hundreds of unpublished photographs were used in production. Original and extremely rare SS uniforms of various types are carefully photographed and presented here. Among the subjects covered in this multi volume series are field-service uniforms, sports, drill, dress, armored personnel, tropical, and much more. This book is indispensable and an absolute must-have for any serious historian of WWII German uniforms.

Uniforms of the Waffen-SS; Sports and Drill Uniforms - Black Panzer Uniform - Camouflage - Concentration Camp Personnel-SD-SS Female Auxiliaries, Volume 3, by Michael D. Beaver, Schiffer Publications, Atglen, PA, 2002. 272 pp., with 500 color, and b&w photos. $79.95

Uniforms of the Waffen-SS; 1942-1943 - 1944-1945 - Ski Uniforms - Overcoats - White Service Uniforms - Tropical Clothing, Volume 2, by Michael D. Beaver, Schiffer Publications, Atglen, PA, 2002. 272 pp., with 500 color, and b&w photos. $79.95

Uniforms, Organization, and History of the German Police, Volume I, by John R. Angolia and Hugh Page Taylor, San Jose, CA, R. James Bender Publishing, 2004. 704 pp. illustrated with b&w and color photos. Hardcover. NEW. $59.95

Uniforms, Organization, and History of the NSKK/NSFK, by John R. Angolia and David Littlejohn, Bender Publishing, San Jose, CA, 2000. $44.95

This work is part of the on-going study of political organizations that formed the structure of the Hitler hierarchy, and is authored by two of the most prominent authorities on the subject of uniforms and insignia of the Third Reich. This comprehensive book covers details on the NSKK and NSFK such as history, organization, uniforms, insignia, special insignia, flags and standards, gorgets, daggers, awards, "day badges," and much more!

United States Martial Flintlocks, by Robert M. Reilly, Mowbray Publishing Co., Lincoln, RI, 1997. 264 pp., illus. $40.00

A comprehensive history of American flintlock longarms and handguns (mostly military) c. 1775 to c. 1840.

Variations of Colt's New Model Police and Pocket Breech Loading Pistols, by John D. Breslin, William Q. Pirie and David E. Price, Lincoln, RI, Andrew Mowbray Publishers, 2002. 1st edition. 158 pp., heavily illustrated with over 160 photographs and superb technical detailed drawings and diagrams. Pictorial hardcover. $37.95

A type-by-type guide to what collectors call small frame conversions.

Vietnam Order of Battle, by Shelby L. Stanton, William C. Westmoreland. Mechanicsburg, PA, Stackpole Books, 2003. 1st edition. 416 pp., 32 in full color, 101 pp. halftones. Hardcover. New in new dust jacket. $69.95

Visor Hats of the United States Armed Forces 1930-1950, by Joe Tonelli, Atglen, PA, Schiffer Publications, 2003. 1st edition. Hardcover. New in new dust jacket. $79.95

The W.F. Cody Buffalo Bill Collector's Guide with Values, by James W. Wojtowicz, Collector Books, Paducah, KY, 1998. 271 pp., illus. $24.95

A profusion of colorful collectibles including lithographs, programs, photographs, books, medals, sheet music, guns, etc. and today's values.

The Walker's Walkers Controversy is Solved, by Col. Robert D. Whittington III, Hooks, TX, Brownlee Books, 2003. A limited edition of 1,000 copies. Numbered. 17 pp. Paper covers. New. $15.00

The truth about serial numbers on the Colt Whitneyville-Walker pistols presented to Captain Samuel Hamilton Walker by Sam Colt and J. B. Colt on July 28th, 1847.

Walther: A German Legend, by Manfred Kersten, Safari Press, Inc., Huntington Beach, CA, 2000. 400 pp., illus. $85.00

This comprehensive book covers, in rich detail, all aspects of the company and its guns, including an illustrious and rich history, the WWII years, all the pistols (models 1 through 9), the P-38, P-88, the long guns, 22 rifles, centerfires, Wehrmacht guns, and even a gun that could shoot around a corner.

The Walther Handgun Story: A Collector's and Shooter's Guide, by Gene Gangarosa, Steiger Publications, 1999. 300 pp., illus. Paper covers. $21.95

Covers the entire history of the Walther empire. Illustrated with over 250 photos.

Walther Models PP & PPK, 1929-1945 – Volume 1, by James L. Rankin, Coral Gables, FL, 1974. 142 pp., illus. $40.00

Complete coverage on the subject as to finish, proofmarks and Nazi Party inscriptions.

Walther P-38 Pistol, by Maj. George Nonte, Desert Publications, Cornville, AZ, 1982. 100 pp., illus. Paper covers. $12.95

Complete volume on one of the most famous handguns to come out of WWII. All models covered.

Walther Pistols: Models 1 Through P99, Factory Variations and Copies, by Dieter H. Marschall, Ucross Books, Los Alamos, NM. 2000. 140 pp., with 140 b&w illustrations, index. Paper covers. $19.95

This is the English translation, revised and updated, of the highly successful and widely acclaimed German language edition. This book provides the collector with a reference guide and overview of the entire line of the Walther military, police, and self-defense pistols from the very first to the very latest. Models 1-9, PP, PPK, MP, AP, HP, P.38, P1, P4, P38K, P5, P88, P99 and the Manurhin models. Variations, where issued, serial ranges, calibers, marks, proofs, logos, and design aspects in an astonishing quantity and variety are crammed into this very well researched and highly regarded work.

Walther Volume II, Engraved, Presentation and Standard Models, by James L. Rankin, J.L. Rankin, Coral Gables, FL, 1977. 112 pp., illus. $40.00

The new Walther book on embellished versions and standard models. Has 88 photographs, including many color plates.

Walther, Volume III, 1908-1980, by James L. Rankin, Coral Gables, FL, 1981. 226 pp., illus. $40.00

Covers all models of Walther handguns from 1908 to date, includes holsters, grips and magazines.

Warman's Civil War Collectibles (Encyclopedia of Antiques and Collectibles), Iola, WI, Krause Publications, 2003. 1st edition. This new volume is a huge 518 pp. full of information on Civil War memorabilia that you'll thrill to, as there are more than 1,000 images plus over 3,000 price listings! Softcover. NEW. $16.95

Winchester an American Legend, by R.L. Wilson, New York, Book Sales, 2004. Reprint. Hardcover. New in new dust jacket. $39.95

Winchester Bolt Action Military & Sporting Rifles 1877 to 1937, by Herbert G. Houze, Andrew Mowbray Publishing, Lincoln, RI, 1998. 295 pp., illus. $45.00

Winchester was the first American arms maker to commercially manufacture a bolt action repeating rifle, and this book tells the exciting story of these Winchester bolt actions.

The Winchester Book, by George Madis, David Madis Gun Book Distributor, Dallas, TX, 2000. 650 pp., illus. $54.50

A new, revised 25th anniversary edition of this classic book on Winchester firearms. Complete serial ranges have been added.

Winchester Commemoratives, by Tom Trolard, Coos Bay, OR, Commemorative Investments Press Library, 2003. 2nd printing - Limited to 1,500 copies. Signed by the author. Hardcover. New in new dust jacket. $109.95

Winchester Dates of Manufacture 1849-1984, by George Madis, Art & Reference House, Brownsboro, TX, 1984. 59 pp. $9.50

A most useful work, compiled from records of the Winchester factory.

Winchester Engraving, by R.L. Wilson, Beinfeld Books, Springs, CA, 1989. 500 pp., illus. $135.00

A classic reference work of value to all arms collectors.

The Winchester Handbook, by George Madis, Art & Reference House, Lancaster, TX, 1982. 287 pp., illus. $26.95

The complete line of Winchester guns, with dates of manufacture, serial numbers, etc.

THE HANDGUNNER'S LIBRARY

Winchester Lever Action Repeating Firearms, Vol. 1, The Models of 1866, 1873 and 1876, by Arthur Pirkle, North Cape Publications, Tustin, CA, 1995. 112 pp., illus. Paper covers. $19.95

Complete, part-by-part description, including dimensions, finishes, markings and variations throughout the production run of these fine, collectible guns.

Winchester Lever Action Repeating Rifles, Vol. 2, The Models of 1886 and 1892, by Arthur Pirkle, North Cape Publications, Tustin, CA, 1996. 150 pp., illus. Paper covers. $19.95

Describes each model on a part-by-part basis by serial number range complete with finishes, markings and changes.

Winchester Lever Action Repeating Rifles, Vol. 3, The Model of 1894, by Arthur Pirkle, North Cape Publications, Tustin, CA, 1998. 150 pp., illus. Paper covers. $19.95

The first book ever to provide a detailed description of the Model 1894 rifle and carbine.

The Winchester Lever Legacy, by Clyde "Snooky" Williamson, Buffalo Press, Zachary, LA, 1988. 664 pp., illus. $75.00

A book on reloading for the different calibers of the Winchester lever action rifle.

The Winchester Model 1876 "Centennial" Rifle, by Herbert G. Houze. Lincoln, RI, Andrew Mowbray, Inc., 2001. Illustrated with over 180 b&w photographs. 192 pp. Hardcover. $45.00

The first authoritative study of the Winchester Model 1876 written using the company's own records. This book dispels the myth that the Model 1876 was merely a larger version of the Winchester company's famous Model 1873 and instead traces its true origins to designs developed immediately after the American Civil War. The specifics of the model–such as the numbers made in its standard calibers, barrel lengths, finishes and special order features–are fully listed here for the first time. For Winchester collectors, and those interested in the mechanics of the 19th-century arms industry, this book provides a wealth of previously unpublished information.

Winchester Pocket Guide: Identification & Pricing for 50 Collectible Rifles and Shotguns, by Ned Schwing, lola, WI, Krause Publications, 2004. 1st edition. 224 pp., illus. Softcover. NEW. $12.95

Winchester Repeating Arms Company Its History & Development from 1865 to 1981, by Herbert G. Houze, lola, WI, Krause Publications, 2004. 1st edition. Softcover. NEW. $34.98

The Winchester Single-Shot, Volume 1; A History and Analysis, by John Campbell, Andrew Mowbray, Inc., Lincoln, RI, 1995. 272 pp., illus. $55.00

Covers every important aspect of this highly-collectible firearm.

The Winchester Single-Shot, Volume 2; Old Secrets and New Discoveries, by John Campbell, Andrew Mowbray, Inc., Lincoln, RI, 2000. 280 pp., illus. $55.00

An exciting follow-up to the classic first volume.

Winchester Sporting Firearms: Dates of Manufacture, by D.R. Morse, Phoenix, AZ, Firing Pin Enterprizes, 2003. 45 pp. Softcover. NEW. $6.95

Covers their pistols, revolvers, rifles, shotguns and commemoratives, plus models and serial numbers.

The Winchester-Lee Rifle, by Eugene Myszkowski, Excalibur Publications, Tucson, AZ 2000. 96 pp., illus. Paper covers. $22.95

The development of the Lee Straight Pull, the cartridge and the approval for military use. Covers details of the inventor and memorabilia of Winchester-Lee related material.

World War One Collectors Handbook Volumes 1 and 2, by Paul Schulz, Hayes Otoupalik and Dennis Gordon, Missoula, MT, privately printed, 2002. Two volumes in one edition. 110 pp., loaded with b&w photos. Softcover. NEW. $21.95

Covers, uniforms, insignia, equipment, weapons, souvenirs and miscellaneous. Includes price guide. For all of you Doughboy collectors, this is a must.

World War II German War Booty, A Study in Photographs, by Thomas M. Johnson, Atglen, PA, Schiffer Publications, 2003. 1st edition. 368 pp. Hardcover. New in new dust jacket. $79.95

Worldwide Webley and the Harrington and Richardson Connection, by Stephen Cuthbertson, Ballista Publishing and Distributing Ltd., Gabriola Island, Canada, 1999. 259 pp., illus. $50.00

A masterpiece of scholarship. Over 350 photographs plus 75 original documents, patent drawings, and advertisements accompany the text.

The World's Great Handguns: From 1450 to the Present Day, by Roger Ford, Secaucus, NJ, Chartwell Books, Inc., 1997. 1st edition. 176 pp. Hardcover. New in new dust jacket. $19.95

GENERAL

Action Shooting: Cowboy Style, by John Taffin, Krause Publications, Iola, WI, 1999. 320 pp., illus. $39.95

Details on the guns and ammunition. Explanations of the rules used for many events.

Advanced Muzzleloader's Guide, by Toby Bridges, Stoeger Publishing Co., So. Hackensack, NJ, 1985. 256 pp., illus. Paper covers. $14.95

The complete guide to muzzle-loading rifles, pistols and shotguns–flintlock and percussion.

Aids to Musketry for Officers & NCOs, by Capt. B.J. Friend, Excalibur Publications, Latham, NY, 1996. 40 pp., illus. Paper covers. $7.95

A facsimile edition of a pre-WWI British manual filled with useful information for training the common soldier.

Airgun Odyssey, by Steve Hanson, Manchester, CT, Precision Shooting, Inc., 2004. 1st edition. 175 pp. Pictorial softcover. $27.95

America's Great Gunmakers, by Wayne van Zwoll, Stoeger Publishing Co., So. Hackensack, NJ, 1992. 288 pp., illus. Paper covers. $16.95

This book traces in great detail the evolution of guns and ammunition in America and the men who formed the companies that produced them.

American Air Rifles, by James E. House. Krause Publications, Iola, WI, 2002. 1st edition. 208 pp., with 198 b&w photos. Softcover. $22.95

Air rifle ballistics, sights, pellets, games, and hunting caliber recommendations are thoroughly explained to help shooters get the most out of their American air rifles. Evaluation of more than a dozen American-made and American-imported air rifle models.

American and Imported Arms, Ammunition and Shooting Accessories, Catalog No. 18 of the Shooter's Bible, Stoeger, Inc., reprinted by Fayette Arsenal, Fayetteville, NC, 1988. 142 pp., illus. Paper covers. $10.95

A facsimile reprint of the 1932 Stoeger's Shooter's Bible.

The American B.B. Gun: A Collector's Guide, by Arni T. Dunathan. A.S. Barnes and Co., Inc., South Brunswick, 2001. 154 pp., illustrated with nearly 200 photographs, drawings and detailed diagrams. Hardcover. $35.00

Annie Oakley of the Wild West, by Walter Havighurst, New York, Castle Books, 2000. 246 pp. Hardcover. New in new dust jacket. $10.00

Armed and Female, by Paxton Quigley, E.P. Dutton, New York, NY, 2001. 237 pp., illus. Softcover $9.95

The first complete book on one of the hottest subjects in the media today, the arming of the American woman.

Arming the Glorious Cause: Weapons of the Second War for Independence, by James B. Whisker, Daniel D. Hartzler and Larry W. Yantz, R & R Books, Livonia, NY, 1998. 175 pp., illus. $45.00

A photographic study of Confederate weapons.

Armor Battles of the Waffen SS:1943-45, by Will Fey, translated by Henri Henschler Mechanicsburg, PA, Greenhill Books, 2003. 1st edition. 384 pp., 32 b&w photos in a 16-page section, 15 drawings & 4 maps. Softcover. NEW. $19.95

Arms & Armor in the Art Institute of Chicago, by Walter J. Karcheski Jr., Bulfinch Press, Boston, MA, 1995. 128 pp., illus. $35.00

Now, for the first time, the Art Institute of Chicago's arms and armor collection is presented in the visual delight of 103 color illustrations.

Arms for the Nation: Springfield Longarms, edited by David C. Clark, Scott A. Duff, Export, PA, 1994. 73 pp., illus. Paper covers. $9.95

A brief history of the Springfield Armory and the arms made there.

Arrowmaker Frontier Series Volume 1, by Roy Chandler, Jacksonville, NC, Ron Brigade Armory, 2000. 390 pp. Hardcover. New in new dust jacket. $38.95

Arsenal of Freedom, The Springfield Armory, 1890-1948: A Year-by-Year Account Drawn from Official Records, compiled and edited by Lt. Col. William S. Brophy, USAR Ret., Andrew Mowbray, Inc., Lincoln, RI, 1991. 400 pp., illus. Softcover. $29.95

A "must buy" for all students of American military weapons, equipment and accoutrements.

The Art of American Arms Makers Marketing Guns, Ammunition, and Western Adventure During the Golden Age of Illustration, by Richard C., Rattenbury, Oklahoma City, OK, National Cowboy Museum, 2004. 132 pp. of color photos. Softcover. NEW. $29.95

The Art of American Game Calls, by Russell E. Lewis, Paducah, KY, Collector Books, 2005. 1st edition. 176 pp. Pictorial hardcover. NEW. $24.95

The Art of Blacksmithing, by Alex W. Bealer, New York, Book Sales, 1996. Revised edition. 440 pp. Hardcover. New in new dust jacket. $10.00

The Art of Remington Arms, Sporting Classics, 2004, by Tom Davis. 1st edition. Hardcover. NEW. $60.00

Battle of the Bulge: Hitler's Alternate Scenarios, by Peter Tsouras, Mechanicsburg, PA, Stackpole Books, 2004. 1st edition. 256 pp., 24 b&w photos, 10 maps. Hardcover. NEW. $34.95

The Belgian Rattlesnake: The Lewis Automatic Machine Gun, by William M. Easterly, Collector Grade Publications, Inc., Cobourg, Ont. Canada, 1998. 542 pp., illus. $79.95

A social and technical biography of the Lewis automatic machine gun and its inventors.

The Benchrest Shooting Primer, edited by Dave Brennan, Precision Shooting, Inc., Manchester, CT, 2000. 2nd edition. 420 pp., illustrated with b&w photographs, drawings and detailed diagrams. Pictorial softcover. $24.95

The very best articles on shooting and reloading for the most challenging of all the rifle accuracy disciplines…benchrest shooting.

The Big Guns: Civil War Siege, Seacoast, and Naval Cannon, by Edwin Olmstead, Wayne E. Stark and Spencer C. Tucker, Museum Restoration Service, Bloomfield, Ontario, Canada, 1997. 360 pp., illus. $80.00

This book is designed to identify and record the heavy guns available to both sides during the Civil War.

Black Powder, Pig Lead And Steel Silhouettes, by Paul A. Matthews, Wolfe Publishing, Prescott, AZ, 2002. 132 pp., illustrated with b&w photographs and detailed drawings and diagrams. Softcover. $16.95

The Black Rifle Frontier Series Volume 2, by Roy Chandler, Jacksonville, NC, Iron Brigade Armory, 2002. 226 pp. Hardcover. New in new dust jacket. $42.95

In 1760, inexperienced Jack Elan settles in Sherman's Valley, suffers tragedy, is captured by hostiles, escapes, and fights on. This is the "2nd" book in the Frontier Series.

Blue Book of Airguns 4th Edition, by Robert Beeman and John Allen, Minneapolis, MN, Blue Book Publications, Inc., 2004. Softcover. NEW. $17.39

Blue Book of Gun Values, 25th Edition (2004 Edition), by S.P. Fjestad, Minneapolis, MN, Blue Book Publications, Inc., 628 pp., illus. Paper covers. $27.95

Blue Book of Modern Black Powder Values, 4th Edition, by Dennis Adler, John Allen, Minneapolis, MN, Blue Book Publications, Inc., 2004. Softcover. NEW. $18.95

British Small Arms of World War II, by Ian D. Skennerton, Arms & Militaria Press, Australia, 1988. 110 pp., 37 illus. $25.00

Carbine and Shotgun Speed Shooting: How to Hit Hard and Fast in Combat, by Steve Moses. Paladin Press, Boulder, CO. 2002. 96 pp., illus. Softcover $18.00

In this groundbreaking book, he breaks down the mechanics of speed shooting these weapons, from stance and grip to sighting, trigger control and more, presenting them in a concise and easily understood manner.

Cavalry Raids of the Civil War, by Col. Robert W. Black, Mechanicsburg, PA, Stackpole Books, 2004. 1st edition. 288 pp., 30 b&w drawings. Softcover. NEW. $17.95

CO2 Pistols and Rifles, by James E. House, lola, WI, Krause Publications, 2004. 1st edition 240 pp., with 198 b&w photos. Softcover. NEW. $24.95

THE HANDGUNNER'S LIBRARY

The Complete .50-caliber Sniper Course, by Dean Michaelis, Paladin Press, Boulder, CO, 2000. 576 pp., illus., $60.00
The history from German Mauser T-Gewehr of WWI to the Soviet PTRD and beyond. Includes the author's Program of Instruction for Special Operations Hard-Target Interdiction Course.

The Complete Blackpowder Handbook, 4th Edition, by Sam Fadala, DBI Books, a division of Krause Publications, Iola, WI, 2002. 400 pp., illus. Paper covers. $21.95
Expanded and completely rewritten edition of the definitive book on the subject of blackpowder.

The Complete Guide to Game Care and Cookery, 4th Edition, by Sam Fadala, Krause Publications, Iola, WI, 2003. 320 pp., illus. Paper covers. $21.95
Over 500 photos illustrating the care of wild game in the field and at home with a separate recipe section providing over 400 tested recipes.

The Concealed Handgun Manual, 4th Edition, by Chris Bird, San Antonio, TX, Privateer Publications, 2004. 332 pp., illus. Softcover, NEW. $21.95

Cowboys & the Trappings of the Old West, by William Manns & Elizabeth Clair Flood, Santa Fe, NM, ZON International Publishing Company, 1997. 224 pp., 550 colorful photos. Foreword by Roy Rogers. Hardcover. $45.00
Big & beautiful book covering: Hats, boots, spurs, chaps, guns, holsters, saddles and more. It's really a pictorial cele bration of the old time buckaroo. This exceptional book presents all the accoutrements of the cowboy life in a comprehensive tribute to the makers. The history of the craftsmen and the evolution of the gear are lavishly illustrated.

Cowgirls: Women of the Wild West, by Elizabeth Clair Flood and William Maims, edited by Helene Helene, Santa Fe, NM, ZON International Publishing Company, 2000. 1st edition. Hardcover. New in new dust jacket. $45.00

Custom Firearms Engraving, by Tom Turpin, Krause Publications, Iola, WI, 1999. 208 pp., illus. $49.95
Provides a broad and comprehensive look at the world of firearms engraving. The exquisite styles of more than 75 master engravers are shown on beautiful examples of handguns, rifles, shotguns, and other firearms, as well as knives.

Daisy Air Rifles & BB Guns: The First 100 Years, by Neal Punchard, St. Paul, MN, Motorbooks, 2002. 1st edition. Hardcover, 10" x 10", 156 pp., 300 color. Hardcover. NEW. $29.95

Dead On, by Tony Noblitt and Warren Gabrilska, Paladin Press, Boulder, CO, 1998. 176 pp., illus. Paper covers. $22.00
The long-range marksman's guide to extreme accuracy.

Do or Die A Supplementary Manual on Individual Combat, by Lieut. Col. A.J. Drexel Biddle, U.S.M.C.R., Boulder, CO, Paladin Press, 2004. 80 pp., illus. Softcover, NEW. $15.00

Down to Earth: The 507th Parachute Infantry Regiment in Normandy: June 6-july 11 1944, by Martin Morgan ICA, Atglen, PA, Schiffer Publishing, 2004. 1st edition. 304 pp., color and b&w photos. Hardcover. New in new dust jacket. $69.95

Early American Flintlocks, by Daniel D. Hartzler and James B. Whisker, Bedford Valley Press, Bedford, PA 2000. 192 pp., Illustrated. $45.00
Covers early Colonial guns, New England guns, Pennsylvania Guns and Southern guns.

Effective Defense: The Woman, the Plan, the Gun, by Gila Hayes, Onalaska, WA, Police Bookshelf, 2000. 2nd edition. Photos, 264 pp. Softcover. NEW. $16.95

Elmer Keith: The Other Side of a Western Legend, by Gene Brown., Precision Shooting, Inc., Manchester, CT 2002. 1st edition. 168 pp., illustrated with b&w photos. Softcover. $19.95
An updated and expanded edition of his original work, incorporating new tales and information that have come to light in the past six years. Gene Brown was a long time friend of Keith, and today is unquestionably the leading authority on Keith's books.

Encyclopedia of Native American Bows, Arrows and Quivers, by Steve Allely and Jim Hamm, The Lyons Press, N.Y., 1999. 160 pp., illus. $29.95
A landmark book for anyone interested in archery history, or Native Americans.

The Exercise of Armes, by Jacob de Gheyn, Dover Publications, Inc., Mineola, NY, 1999. 144 pp., illus. Paper covers. $14.95
Republications of all 117 engravings from the 1607 classic military manual. A meticulously accurate portrait of uniforms and weapons of the 17th century Netherlands.

Fighting Iron: A Metals Handbook for Arms Collectors, by Art Gogan, Mowbray Publishers, Inc., Lincoln, RI, 2002. 176 pp., illus. $28.00
A guide that is easy to use, explains things in simple English and covers all of the different historical periods that we are interested in.

Fine Art of the West, by Byron B. Price and Christopher Lyon, New York, Abbeville Press, 2004. Hardcover. NEW. $75.00

Firearms Assembly Disassembly; Part 4: Centerfire Rifles (2nd Edition), by J. B. Wood, lola, WI, Krause Publications, 2004. 2nd edition. 576 pp., 1,750 b&w photos. Softcover. NEW. $24.95

Fireworks: A Gunsight Anthology, by Jeff Cooper, Paladin Press, Boulder, CO, 1998. 192 pp., illus. Paper cover. $27.00
A collection of wild, hilarious, shocking and always meaningful tales from the remarkable life of an American firearms legend.

Fort Robinson, Frontier Series, Volume 4, by Roy Chandler, Jacksonville, NC, Ron Brigade Armory, 2003. 1st edition. 560 pp. Hardcover. New in new dust jacket. $39.95

Frederic Remington: The Color of Night, by Nancy Anderson, Princeton University Press, 2003. 1st edition. 136 color illus, 24 halftones; 10" x 11", 208 pgs. Hardcover, New in new dust jacket. $49.95; UK $52.49

From a Stranger's Doorstep to the Kremlin Gate, by Mikhail Kalashnikov, Ironside International Publishers, Inc., Alexandria, VA, 1999. 460 pp., illus. $34.95
A biography of the most influential rifle designer of the 20th century. His AK-47 assault rifle has become the most widely used (and copied) assault rifle of this century.

The Frontier Rifleman, by H.B. LaCrosse Jr., Pioneer Press, Union City, TN, 1989. 183 pp., illus. Softcover. $17.50
The Frontier rifleman's clothing and equipment during the era of the American Revolution, 1760-1800.

Galloping Thunder: The Stuart Horse Artillery Battalion, by Robert Trout, Mechanicsburg, PA, Stackpole Books, 2002. 1st edition. Hardcover, NEW. $39.95

The Gatling Gun: 19th Century Machine Gun to 21st Century Vulcan, by Joseph Berk, Paladin Press, Boulder, CO, 1991. 136 pp., illus. $34.95
Here is the fascinating on-going story of a truly timeless weapon, from its beginnings during the Civil War to its current role as a state-of-the-art modern combat system.

German Artillery of World War Two, by Ian V. Hogg, Stackpole Books, Mechanicsburg, PA, 1997. 304 pp., illus. $44.95
Complete details of German artillery use in WWII.

Gone Diggin: Memoirs of a Civil War Relic Hunter, by Toby Law, Orange, VA, Publisher's Press, 2002. 1st edition signed. 151 pp., illustrated with b&w photos. $24.95
The true story of one relic hunter's life - The author kept exacting records of every relic hunt and every relic hunter he was with working with.

Grand Old Lady of No Man's Land: The Vickers Machine Gun, by Dolf L. Goldsmith, Collector Grade Publications, Cobourg, Canada, 1994. 600 pp., illus. $79.95
Goldsmith brings his years of experience as a U.S. Army armourer, machine gun collector and shooter to bear on the Vickers, in a book sure to become a classic in its field.

Greenhill Military Manuals; Small Arms: Pistols and Rifles, by Ian Hogg; London, Greenhill Press, 2003. Revised. 160 pp., illus. Hardcover. $24.00
This handy reference guide, by the leading small arms author, provides descriptions, technical specifications and illustrations of 75 of the most important pistols and rifles, including the Heckler & Koch USP/SOCOM pistols, the FN Five-seven 5.7mm pistol, the Heckler & Koch G36 rifle and much more.

Gun Digest 2005, 59th Annual Edition, edited by Ken Ramage, lola, WI, Krause Publications, 2004. Softcover. NEW. $24.95
This all new 59th edition continues the editorial excellence, quality, content and comprehensive cataloguing that firearms enthusiasts have come to know and expect. The most read gun book in the world for the last half century.

Gun Digest Blackpowder Loading Manual New 4th Edition, by Sam Fadala, lola, WI, Krause Publications, 2004. 352 pp., illus. Softcover. NEW. $27.95

The Gun Digest Book of Deer Guns, edited by Dan Shideler, lola, WI, Krause Publications, 2004. 1st edition Softcover, NEW. $14.99

The Gun Digest Book of Guns for Personal Defense Arms & Accessories for Self-Defense, edited by Kevin Michalowski, lola, WI, Krause Publications, 2004. 1st edition Softcover. NEW. $14.99

Gun Engraving, by C. Austyn, Safari Press Publication, Huntington Beach, CA, 1998. 128 pp., plus 24 pp. of color photos. $50.00
A well-illustrated book on fine English and European gun engravers. Includes a fantastic pictorial section that lists types of engravings and prices.

Gun Notes, Volume 1, by Elmer Keith, Safari Press, Huntington Beach, CA, 2002. 219 pp., illus. Softcover. $24.95
A collection of Elmer Keith's most interesting columns and feature stories that appeared in "Guns & Ammo" magazine from 1961 to the late 1970's.

Gun Notes, Volume 2, by Elmer Keith, Safari Press, Huntington Beach, CA, 2002. 292 pp., illus. Softcover. $24.95
Covers articles from Keith's monthly column in "Guns & Ammo" magazine during the period from 1971 through Keith's passing in 1982.

The Gun That Made the Twenties Roar, by Wm. J. Helmer, The Gun Room Press, Highland Park, NJ, 1977. Over 300 pp., illus. $24.95
Historical account of John T. Thompson and his invention, the infamous "Tommy Gun."

Guns & Shooting: A Selected Bibliography, by Ray Riling, Ray Riling Arms Books Co., Phila., PA, 1982. 434 pp., illus. Limited, numbered edition. $75.00
A limited edition of this superb bibliographical work, the only modern listing of books devoted to guns and shooting.

Guns Illustrated 2005: 37th Edition, edited by Ken Ramage, lola, WI, Krause Publications, 2004. Softcover. NEW. $21.95
Highly informative, technical articles on a wide range of shooting topics by some of the top writers in the industry. A catalog section lists more than 3,000 firearms currently manufactured in or imported to the U.S.

The Guns of the Gunfighters: Lawmen, Outlaws & TV Cowboys, by Doc O'Meara, Iola, WI, Krause Publications, 2003. 1st edition. 16-page color section, 225 b&w photos. Hardcover. $34.95
Explores the romance of the Old West, focusing on the guns that the good guys & bad guys, real & fictional characters, carried with them. Profiles of more than 50 gunslingers, half from the Old West and half from Hollywood, include a brief biography of each gunfighter, along with the guns they carried. Fascinating stories about the TV and movie celebrities of the 1950s and 1960s detail their guns and the skill–or lack thereof–they displayed.

Guns, Bullets, and Gunfighters, by Jim Cirillo, Paladin Press, Boulder, CO, 1996. 119 pp., illus. Paper covers. $16.00
Lessons and tales from a modern-day gunfighter.

Gunstock Carving: A Step-by-Step Guide to Engraving Rifles and Shotguns, by Bill Janney, East Pertsburg, PA, Fox Chapel Publishing, October 2002. 89 pp., illustrated in color. Softcover. $19.95
Learn gunstock carving from an expert. Includes step-by-step projects and instructions, patterns, tips and techniques.

Hand-To-Hand Combat: United States Naval Institute, by U.S. Navy Boulder, CO, Paladin Press, 2003. 1st edition. 240 pp. Softcover. $25.00
Now you can own one of the classic publications in the history of U.S. military close-quarters combat training. In 11 photo-heavy chapters, Hand-to-Hand Combat covers training tips; vulnerable targets; the brutal fundamentals of close-in fighting; frontal and rear attacks; prisoner search and control techniques; disarming pistols, rifles, clubs and knives; offensive means of "liquidating an enemy"; and much more. After reading this book (originally published by the United States Naval Institute in 1943), you will see why it has long been sought by collectors and historians of hand-to-hand combat.

Hidden in Plain Sight, "A Practical Guide to Concealed Handgun Carry" (Revised 2nd Edition), by Trey Bloodworth and Mike Raley, Paladin Press, Boulder, CO, 1997, softcover, photos, 176 pp. $20.00
Concerned with how to comfortably, discreetly and safely exercise the privileges granted by a CCW permit? This invaluable guide offers the latest advice on what to look for when choosing a CCW, how to dress for comfortable, effective concealed carry, traditional and more

THE HANDGUNNER'S LIBRARY

unconventional carry modes, accessory holsters, customized clothing and accessories, accessibility data based on draw-time comparisons and new holsters on the market. Includes 40 new manufacturer listings.

HK Assault Rifle Systems, by Duncan Long, Paladin Press, Boulder, CO, 1995. 110 pp., illus. Paper covers. $27.95

The little known history behind this fascinating family of weapons tracing its beginnings from the ashes of WWII to the present time.

Holsters for Combat and Concealed Carry, by R.K. Campbell, Boulder, CO, Paladin Press, 2004. 1st edition. 144 pp. Softcover. NEW. $22.00

The Hunter's Guide to Accurate Shooting, by Wayne van Zwoll, Guilford, CT, Lyons Press, 2002. 1st edition. 288 pp. Hardcover. $29.95

Firearms expert van Zwoll explains exactly how to shoot the big-game rifle accurately. Taking into consideration every pertinent factor, he shows a step-by-step analysis of shooting and hunting with the big-game rifle.

The Hunting Time: Adventures in Pursuit of North American Big Game: A Forty-Year Chronicle, by John E. Howard, Deforest, WI, Saint Huberts Press, 2002. 1st edition. 537 pp., illustrated with drawings. Hardcover. $29.95

From a novice's first hunt for whitetailed deer in his native Wisconsin, to a seasoned hunter's pursuit of a Boone and Crockett Club record book caribou in the northwest territories, the author carries the reader along on his forty year journey through the big game fields of North America.

Indian Tomahawks and Frontiersmen Belt Axes, by Daniel Hartzler & James Knowles, New Windsor, MD, privately printed, 2002. 4th revised edition. 279 pp., illustrated with photos and drawings. Hardcover. $65.00

This fourth revised edition has over 160 new tomahawks and trade axes added since the first edition, also a list of 205 makers names. There are 15 chapters from the earliest known tomahawks to the present day. Some of the finest tomahawks in the country are shown in this book with 31 color plates. This comprehensive study is invaluable to any collector.

Jack O'Connor Catalogue of Letters, by Ellen Enzler Herring, Agoura, CA, Trophy Room Books, 2002. 1st edition. Hardcover. NEW. $55.00

Jack O'Connor - The Legendary Life of America's Greatest Gunwriter, by R. Anderson, Long Beach, CA, Safari Press, 2002. 1st edition. 240 pp., profuse photos. Hardcover. $29.95

This is the book all hunters in North America have been waiting for–the long-awaited biography on Jack O'Connor! Jack O'Connor was the preeminent North American big-game hunter and gunwriter of the twentieth century, and Robert Anderson's masterfully written new work is a blockbuster filled with fascinating facts and stories about this controversial character. O'Connor's lifelong friend Buck Buckner has contributed two chapters on his experiences with the master of North American hunting.

Joe Rychertinik Reflects on Guns, Hunting, and Days Gone By, by Joe Rychertinik, Precision Shooting, Inc., Manchester, CT, 1999. 281 pp., illus. Thirty articles by a master story-teller. Paper covers. $16.95

Kill or Get Killed, by Col. Rex Applegate, Paladin Press, Boulder, CO, 1996. 400 pp., illus. $49.95

The best and longest-selling book on close combat in history.

The Lost Classics of Jack O'Connor, edited by Jim Casada, Columbia, SC, Live Oak Press, 2004. 1st edition. Hardcover. New in new dust jacket. $35.00

Manual for H&R Reising Submachine Gun and Semi-Auto Rifle, edited by George P. Dillman, Desert Publications, El Dorado, AZ, 1994. 81 pp., illus. Paper covers. $14.95

A reprint of the Harrington & Richardson 1943 factory manual and the rare military manual on the H&R submachine gun and semi-auto rifle.

The Manufacture of Gunflints, by Sydney B.J. Skertchly, facsimile reprint with new introduction by Seymour de Lotbiniere, Museum Restoration Service, Ontario, Canada, 1984. 90 pp., illus. $24.50

Limited edition reprinting of the very scarce London edition of 1879.

Master Tips, by J. Winokur, Potshot Press, Pacific Palisades, CA, 1985. 96 pp., illus. Paper covers. $11.95

Basics of practical shooting.

The Military and Police Sniper, by Mike R. Lau, Precision Shooting, Inc., Manchester, CT, 1998. 352 pp., illus. Paper covers. $44.95

Advanced precision shooting for combat and law enforcement.

Military Rifle & Machine Gun Cartridges, by Jean Huon, Paladin Press, Boulder, CO, 1990. 392 pp., illus. $34.95

Describes the primary types of military cartridges and their principal loadings, as well as their characteristics, origin and use.

Military Small Arms of the 20th Century, 7th Edition, by Ian V. Hogg and John Weeks, DBI Books, a division of Krause Publications, Iola, WI, 2000. 416 pp., illus. Paper covers. Over 800 photographs and illustrations. $24.95

Covers small arms of 46 countries.

Modern Custom Guns, Walnut, Steel, and Uncommon Artistry, by Tom Turpin, Krause Publications, Iola, WI, 1997. 206 pp., illus. $49.95

From exquisite engraving to breathtaking exotic woods, the mystique of today's custom guns is expertly detailed in word and awe-inspiring color photos of rifles, shotguns and handguns.

Modern Gun Values: 12th Edition, edited by Ken Ramage, Krause Publications, Iola, WI, 2003. Softcover. NEW. $21.95

Modern Machine Guns, by John Walter, Stackpole Books, Inc., Mechanicsburg, PA, 2000. 144 pp., with 146 illustrations. $22.95

A compact and authoritative guide to post-war machine-guns. A gun-by-gun directory identifying individual variants and types including detailed evaluations and technical data.

Modern Sporting Guns, by Christopher Austyn, Safari Press, Huntington Beach, CA, 1994. 128 pp., illus. $40.00

A discussion of the "best" English guns; round action, over-and-under, boxlocks, hammer guns, bolt action and double rifles as well as accessories.

The More Complete Cannoneer, by M.C. Switlik, Museum & Collectors Specialties Co., Monroe, MI, 1990. 199 pp., illus. $19.95

Compiled agreeably to the regulations for the U.S. War Department, 1861, and containing current observations on the use of antique cannons.

More Tactical Reality; Why There's No Such Thing as an Advanced Gunfight, by Louis Awerbuck, Boulder, CO, Paladin Press, 2004. 144 pp. Softcover. NEW. $25.00

The MP-40 Machine Gun, Desert Publications, El Dorado, AZ, 1995. 32 pp., illus. Paper covers. $11.95

A reprint of the hard-to-find operating and maintenance manual for one of the most famous machine guns of WWII.

Naval Percussion Locks and Primers, by Lt. J. A. Dahlgren, Museum Restoration Service, Bloomfield, Canada, 1996. 140 pp., illus. $35.00

First published as an Ordnance Memoranda in 1853, this is the finest existing study of percussion locks and primers origin and development.

The Official Soviet AKM Manual, translated by Maj. James F. Gebhardt (Ret.), Paladin Press, Boulder, CO, 1999. 120 pp., illus. Paper covers. $18.00

This official military manual, available in English for the first time, was originally published by the Soviet Ministry of Defence. Covers the history, function, maintenance, assembly and disassembly, etc. of the 7.62mm AKM assault rifle.

The One-Round War: U.S.M.C. Scout-Snipers in Vietnam, by Peter Senich, Paladin Press, Boulder, CO, 1996. 384 pp., illus. Paper covers $59.95

Sniping in Vietnam focusing specifically on the Marine Corps program.

Optics Digest: Scopes, Binoculars, Rangefinders, and Spotting Scopes, by Clair Rees, Long Beach, CA, Safari Press, 2005. 1st edition. 189 pp. Softcover. NEW. $24.95

OSS Special Operations in China, by Col. F. Mills and John W. Brunner, Williamstown, NJ, Phillips Publications, 2003. 1st edition. 550 pp., illustrated with photos. Hardcover. New in new dust jacket. $34.95

Paintball Digest The Complete Guide to Games, Gear, and Tactics, by Richard Sapp, lola, WI, Krause Publications, 2004. 1st edition. 272 pp. Softcover. NEW. $19.99

Paleo-Indian Artifacts: Identification & Value Guide, by Lar Hothem, Paducah, KY, Collector Books, 2005. 1st edition. 379 pp. Pictorial hardcover. NEW. $29.95

Panzer Aces German Tank Commanders of WWII, by Franz Kurowski, translated by David Johnston, Mechanicsburg, PA, Stackpole Books, 2004. 1st edition. 448 pp., 50 b&w photos Softcover. NEW. $19.95

Parker Brothers: Knight of the Trigger, by Ed Muderlak, Davis, IL, Old Reliable Publishing, 2002. 223 pp. $25.00

Knight of the Trigger tells the story of the Old West when Parker's most famous gun saleman traveled the country by rail, competing in the pigeon ring, hunting with the rich and famous, and selling the "Old Reliable" Parker shotgun. The life and times of Captain Arthur William du Bray, Parker Brothers' on-the-road sales agent from 1884 to 1926, is described in a novelized version of his interesting life.

Peril in the Powder Mills: Gunpowder & Its Men, by David McMahon & Anne Kelly Lane, West Conshohocken, PA, privately printed, 2004. 1st edition. 118 pp. Softcover. NEW. $18.95

Powder Horns and their Architecture; And Decoration as Used by the Soldier, Indian, Sailor and Traders of the Era, by Madison Grant, York, PA, privately printed, 1987. 165 pp., profusely illustrated. Hardcover. $45.00

Covers homemade pieces from the late eighteenth and early nineteenth centuries.

Practically Speaking: An Illustrated Guide - The Game, Guns and Gear of the International Defensive Pistol Association, by Walt Rauch, Lafayette Hills, PA, privately printed, 2002. 1st edition. 79 pp., illustrated with drawings and color photos. Softcover. $24.95

The game, guns and gear of the International Defensive Pistol Association with real-world applications.

Present Sabers: A Popular History of the U.S. Horse Cavalry, by Allan T. Heninger, Tucson, AZ, Excalibur Publications, 2002. 1st edition. 160 pp., with 148 photographs, 45 illustrations and 4 charts. Softcover. $24.95

An illustrated history of America's involvement with the horse cavalry, from its earliest beginnings during the Revolutionary War through its demise in WWII. The book also contains several appendices, as well as depictions of the regular insignia of all the U.S. Cavalry units.

Principles of Personal Defense, by Jeff Cooper, Paladin Press, Boulder, CO, 1999. 56 pp., illus. Paper covers. $14.00

This revised edition of Jeff Cooper's classic on personal defense offers great new illustrations and a new preface while retaining the theory of individual defense behavior presented in the original book.

The Quotable Hunter, edited by Jay Cassell and Peter Fiduccia, The Lyons Press, N.Y., 1999. 224 pp., illus. $20.00

This collection of more than three hundred memorable quotes from hunters through the ages captures the essence of the sport, with all its joys idiosyncrasies, and challenges.

Renaissance Drill Book, by Jacob de Gheyn, edited by David J. Blackmore, Mechanicsburg, PA, Greenhill Books, 2003. 1st edition. 248 pp., 117 illustrations. Hardcover. $24.95

Jacob de Gheyn's Exercise of Armes was an immense success when first published in 1607. It is a fascinating 17th-century military manual, designed to instruct contemporary soldiers how to handle arms effectively, and correctly, and it makes for a unique glimpse into warfare as waged in the Thirty Years War and the English Civil War. In addition, detailed illustrations show the various movements and postures to be adopted during use of the pike.

A Rifleman Went to War, by H. W. McBride, Lancer Militaria, Mt. Ida, AR, 1987. 398 pp., illus. $29.95

The classic account of practical marksmanship on the battlefields of WWI.

Running Recon, A Photo Journey with SOG Special Ops Along the Ho Chi Minh Trail, by Frank Greco, Boulder, CO, Paladin Press, 2004. 1st edition. Hardcover. $79.95

Running Recon is a combination of military memoir and combat photography book. It reflects both the author's experience in Kontum, Vietnam, from April 1969 to April 1970 as part of the top-secret Studies and Observation Group (SOG) and the collective experience of SOG veterans in general. What sets it apart from other Vietnam books is its wealth of more than 700 photographs, many never before published, from the author's personal collection and those of his fellow SOG veterans.

THE HANDGUNNER'S LIBRARY

Sharpshooting for Sport and War, by W.W. Greener, Wolfe Publishing Co., Prescott, AZ, 1995. 192 pp., illus. $30.00

This classic reprint explores the *first* expanding bullet; service rifles; shooting positions; trajectories; recoil; external ballistics; and other valuable information.

Shooting Buffalo Rifles of the Old West, by Mike Venturino, MLV Enterprises, Livingston, MT, 2002. 278 pp., illustrated with b&w photos. Softcover. $30.00

This tome will take you through the history, the usage, the many models, and the actual shooting (and how to's) of the many guns that saw service on the Frontier and are lovingly called "Buffalo Rifles" today. If you love to shoot your Sharps, Ballards, Remingtons, or Springfield "Trapdoors" for hunting or competition, or simply love Old West history, your library WILL NOT be complete without this latest book from Mike Venturino!

Shooting Colt Single Actions, by Mike Venturino, MLV Enterprises, Livingston, MT, 1997. 205 pp., illus. Softcover. $25.00

A complete examination of the Colt Single Action including styles, calibers and generations, b&w photos throughout.

Shooting Lever Guns of the Old West, by Mike Venturino, MLV Enterprises, Livingston, MT, 1999. 300 pp., illus. Softcover. $27.95

Shooting the lever action type repeating rifles of our American West.

Shooting Sixguns of the Old West, by Mike Venturino, MLV Enterprises, Livingston, MT, 1997. 221 pp., illus. Paper covers. $26.50

A comprehensive look at the guns of the early West: Colts, Smith & Wesson and Remingtons, plus blackpowder and reloading specs.

Shooting to Live, by Capt. W.E. Fairbairn and Capt. E.A. Sykes, Paladin Press, Boulder, CO, 1997, 4-1/2" x 7", soft cover, illus., 112 pp. $14.00

Shooting to Live is the product of Fairbairn's and Sykes' practical experience with the handgun. Hundreds of incidents provided the basis for the first true book on life-or-death shootouts with the pistol. Shooting to Live teaches all concepts, considerations and applications of combat pistol craft.

Small Arms of World War II, by Chris Chant, St. Paul, MN, MBI Publishing Company, 2001. 1st edition. 96 pp., single page on each weapon with photograph, description, and a specifications table. Hardcover. New. $13.95

Detailing the design and development of each weapon, this book covers the most important infantry weapons used by both Allied and Axis soldiers between 1939 and 1945. These include both standard infantry bolt-action rifles, such as the German Kar 98 and the British Lee-Enfield, plus the automatic rifles that entered service toward the end of the war, such as the Stg 43. As well as rifles, this book also features submachine guns, machine guns and handguns and a specifications table for each weapon.

Sniper Training, FM 23-10, Reprint of the U.S. Army field manual of August, 1994, Paladin Press, Boulder, CO, 1995. 352 pp., illus. Paper covers. $30.00

The most up-to-date U.S. military sniping information and doctrine.

Song of Blue Moccasin, by Roy Chandler, Jacksonville, NC, Ron Brigade Armory, 2004. 231 pp. Hardcover. New in new dust jacket. $45.00

Special Operations: Weapons and Tactics, by Timothy Mullin, London, Greenhill Press, 2003. 1st edition. 176 pp., with 189 illustrations. $39.95

The tactics and equipment of Special Forces explained in full, Contains 200 images of weaponry and training. This highly illustrated guide covers the full experience of special operations training from every possible angle. There is also considerable information on nonfirearm usage, such as specialized armor and ammunition.

Standard Catalog of Firearms, 15th Edition, by Ned Schwing, Iola, WI, Krause Publications, 2005. 1504 pp., illus. 7,000 b&w photos plus a 16-page color section. Paper covers. $34.95

This is the largest, most comprehensive and best-selling firearm book of all time! And this year's edition is a blockbuster for both shooters and firearm collectors. More than 14,000 firearms are listed and priced in up to six grades of condition. That's almost 100,000 prices! Gun enthusiasts will love the new full-color section of photos highlighting the finest firearms sold at auction this past year.

Standard Catalog of Military Firearms 2nd Edition: The Collector's Price & Reference Guide, by Ned Schwing, Iola, WI, Krause Publications, 2003. 448 pp. Softcover. $22.99

A companion volume to Standard Catalog of Firearms, this revised and expanded second edition comes complete with all the detailed information readers found useful and more. Listings beginning with the early cartridge models of the 1870s to the latest high-tech sniper rifles have been expanded to include more models, variations, historical information, and data, offering more detail for the military firearms collector, shooter, and history buff. Identification of specific firearms is easier with nearly 250 additional photographs. Plus, readers will enjoy "snap shots," small personal articles from experts relating real-life experiences with exclusive models. Revised to include every known military firearm available to the U.S. collector. Special feature articles on focused aspects of collecting and shooting.

Stress Fire, Vol. 1: Stress Fighting for Police, by Massad Ayoob, Police Bookshelf, Concord, NH, 1984. 149 pp., illus. Paper covers. $11.95

Gunfighting for police, advanced tactics and techniques.

Survival Guns, by Mel Tappan, Desert Publications, El Dorado, AZ, 1993. 456 pp., illus. Paper covers. $25.00

Discusses in a frank and forthright manner which handguns, rifles and shotguns to buy for personal defense and securing food, and the ones to avoid.

The Tactical Advantage, by Gabriel Suarez, Paladin Press, Boulder, CO, 1998. 216 pp., illus. Paper covers. $22.00

Learn combat tactics that have been tested in the world's toughest schools.

Tactical Marksman, by Dave M. Lauch, Paladin Press, Boulder, CO, 1996. 165 pp., illus. Paper covers. $35.00

A complete training manual for police and practical shooters.

Tim Murphy Rifleman Frontier Series Volume 3, by Roy Chandler, Jacksonville, NC, Iron Brigade Armory, 2003. 1st edition. 396 pp. Hardcover. $39.95

Tim Murphy may be our young nation's earliest recognized hero. Murphy was seized by Seneca Tribesmen during his infancy. Traded to the Huron, he was renamed and educated by Sir William Johnson, a British colonial officer. Freed during the prisoner exchange of 1764, Murphy discovered his superior ability with a Pennsylvania longrifle. An early volunteer in the Pennsylvania militia, Tim Murphy served valiantly in rifle companies including the justly famed Daniel Morgan's Riflemen. This is Murphy's story.

To Ride, Shoot Straight, and Speak the Truth, by Jeff Cooper, Paladin Press, Boulder, CO, 1997, 5-1/2" x 8-1/2", soft-cover, illus., 384 pp. $32.00

Combat mind-set, proper sighting, tactical residential architecture, nuclear war - these are some of the many subjects explored by Jeff Cooper in this illustrated anthology. The author discusses various arms, fighting skills and the importance of knowing how to defend oneself, and one's honor, in our rapidly changing world.

Trailriders Guide to Cowboy Action Shooting, by James W. Barnard, Pioneer Press, Union City, TN, 1998. 134 pp., plus 91 photos, drawings and charts. Paper covers. $24.95

Covers the complete spectrum of this shooting discipline, from how to dress to authentic leather goods, which guns are legal, calibers, loads and ballistics.

U.S. Marine Corp Rifle and Pistol Marksmanship, 1935, reprinting of a government publication, Lancer Militaria, Mt. Ida, AR, 1991. 99 pp., illus. Paper covers. $11.95

The old corps method of precision shooting.

U.S. Marine Corps Scout/Sniper Training Manual, Lancer Militaria, Mt. Ida, AR, 1989. Softcover. $27.95

Reprint of the original sniper training manual used by the Marksmanship Training Unit of the Marine Corps Development and Education Command in Quantico, Virginia.

U.S. Marine Corps Scout-Sniper, World War II and Korea, by Peter R. Senich, Paladin Press, Boulder, CO, 1994. 236 pp., illus. $44.95

The most thorough and accurate account ever printed on the training, equipment and combat experiences of the U.S. Marine Corps Scout-Snipers.

U.S. Marine Corps Sniping, Lancer Militaria, Mt. Ida, AR, 1989. Irregular pagination. Softcover. $18.95

A reprint of the official Marine Corps FMFM1-3B.

U.S. Marine Uniforms-1912-1940, by Jim Moran, Williamstown, NJ, Phillips Publications, 2001. 174 pp., illustrated with b&w photographs. Hardcover. $49.95

The Ultimate Sniper, by Major John L. Plaster, Paladin Press, Boulder, CO, 1994. 464 pp., illus. Paper covers. $49.95

An advanced training manual for military and police snipers.

Uniforms And Equipment of the Imperial Japanese Army in World War II, by Mike Hewitt, Atglen, PA, Schiffer Publications, 2002. 176 pp., with over 520 color and b&w photos. Hardcover. $59.95

Unrepentant Sinner, by Col. Charles Askins, Paladin Press, Boulder, CO, 2000. 322 pp., illus. $29.95

The autobiography of Colonel Charles Askins.

Vietnam Order of Battle, by Shelby L. Stanton, William C. Westmoreland, Mechanicsburg, PA, Stackpole Books, 2003. 1st edition. 416 pp., 32 in full color, 101 halftones. Hardcover. $69.95

A monumental, encyclopedic work of immense detail concerning U.S. Army and allied forces that fought in the Vietnam War from 1962 through 1973. Extensive lists of units providing a record of every Army unit that served in Vietnam, down to and including separate companies, and also including U.S. Army aviation and riverine units. Shoulder patches and distinctive unit insignia of all divisions and battalions. Extensive maps portraying unit locations at each six-month interval. Photographs and descriptions of all major types of equipment employed in the conflict. Plus much more!

Weapons of Delta Force, by Fred Pushies, St. Paul, MN, MBI Publishing Company, 2002. 1st edition. 128 pgs., 100 b&w and 100 color illustrated. Hardcover. $24.95

America's elite counter-terrorist organization, Delta Force, is a handpicked group of the U.S. Army's finest soldiers. Delta uses some of the most sophisticated weapons in the field today, and all are detailed in this book. Pistols, sniper rifles, special mission aircraft, fast attack vehicles, SCUBA and paratrooper gear, and more are presented in this fully illustrated account of our country's heroes and their tools of the trade.

Weapons of the Waffen-SS, by Bruce Quarrie, Sterling Publishing Co., Inc., 1991. 168 pp., illus. $24.95

An in-depth look at the weapons that made Hitler's Waffen-SS the fearsome fighting machine it was.

Weatherby: The Man, The Gun, The Legend, by Grits and Tom Gresham, Cane River Publishing Co., Natchitoches, LA, 1992. 290 pp., illus. $24.95

A fascinating look at the life of the man who changed the course of firearms development in America.

The Winchester Era, by David Madis, Art & Reference House, Brownsville, TX, 1984. 100 pp., illus. $19.95

Story of the Winchester company, management, employees, etc.

With British Snipers to the Reich, by Capt. C. Shore, Lander Militaria, Mt. Ida, AR, 1988. 420 pp., illus. $29.95

One of the greatest books ever written on the art of combat sniping.

The World's Machine Pistols and Submachine Guns - Vol. 2a 1964 to 1980, by Nelson & Musgrave, Ironside International, Alexandria, VA, 2000. 673 pp. $59.95

Containing data, history and photographs of over 200 weapons. With a special section covering shoulder stocked automatic pistols, 100 additional photos.

The World's Sniping Rifles, by Ian V. Hogg, Stackpole Books, Mechanicsburg, 1998. 144 pp., illus. $24.00

A detailed manual with descriptions and illustrations of more than 50 high-precision rifles from 14 countries and a complete analysis of sights and systems.

Wyatt Earp: A Biography of the Legend: Volume 1: The Cowtown Years, by Lee A. Silva, Santa Ana, CA, privately printed, 2002. 1st edition signed. Hardcover. New in new dust jacket. $86.95

GUNSMITHING

Accurizing the Factory Rifle, by M.L. McPhereson, Precision Shooting, Inc., Manchester, CT, 1999. 335 pp., illus. Paper covers. $44.95

A long-awaiting book, which bridges the gap between the rudimentary (mounting sling swivels, scope blocks and that general level of accomplishment) and the advanced (precision chambering, barrel fluting, and that general level of accomplishment) books that are currently available today.

THE HANDGUNNER'S LIBRARY

The Art of Engraving, by James B. Meek, F. Brownell & Son, Montezuma, IA, 1973. 196 pp., illus. $42.95

A complete, authoritative, imaginative and detailed study in training for gun engraving. The first book of its kind–and a great one.

Checkering and Carving of Gun Stocks, by Monte Kennedy, Stackpole Books, Harrisburg, PA, 1962. 175 pp., illus. $39.95

Revised, enlarged cloth-bound edition of a much sought-after, dependable work.

Firearms Assembly/Disassembly, Part I: Automatic Pistols, 2nd Revised Edition, The Gun Digest Book of, by J.B. Wood, DBI Books, a division of Krause Publications, Iola, WI, 1999. 480 pp., illus. Paper covers. $24.95

Covers 58 popular autoloading pistols plus nearly 200 variants of those models integrated into the text and completely cross-referenced in the index.

Firearms Assembly/Disassembly Part II: Revolvers, Revised Edition, The Gun Digest Book of, by J.B. Wood, DBI Books, a division of Krause Publications, Iola, WI, 1997. 480 pp., illus. Paper covers. $27.95

Covers 49 popular revolvers plus 130 variants. The most comprehensive and professional presentation available to either hobbyist or gunsmith.

Firearms Assembly/Disassembly Part III: Rimfire Rifles, Revised Edition, The Gun Digest Book of, by J. B. Wood, DBI Books, a division of Krause Publications, Iola, WI, 1994. 480 pp., illus. Paper covers. $19.95

Greatly expanded edition covering 65 popular rimfire rifles plus over 100 variants all completely cross-referenced in the index.

Firearms Assembly/Disassembly Part IV: Centerfire Rifles, 3rd Revised Edition, The Gun Digest Book of, by J.B. Wood, Krause Publications, Iola, WI, 2004. 480 pp., illus. Paper covers. $24.95

Covers 54 popular centerfire rifles plus 300 variants. The most comprehensive and professional presentation available to either hobbyist or gunsmith.

Firearms Assembly/Disassembly, Part V: Shotguns, Revised Edition, The Gun Digest Book of, by J.B. Wood, Krause Publications, Iola, WI, 2002. 480 pp., illus. Paper covers. $24.95

Covers 46 popular shotguns plus over 250 variants with step-by-step instructions on how to dismantle and reassemble each. The most comprehensive and professional presentation available to either hobbyist or gunsmith.

Firearms Assembly 3: The NRA Guide to Rifle and Shotguns, NRA Books, Wash., DC, 1980. 264 pp., illus. Paper covers. $14.95

Text and illustrations explaining the takedown of 125 rifles and shotguns, domestic and foreign.

Firearms Assembly 4: The NRA Guide to Pistols and Revolvers, NRA Books, Wash., DC, 1980. 253 pp., illus. Paper covers. $14.95

Text and illustrations explaining the takedown of 124 pistol and revolver models, domestic and foreign.

Firearms Bluing and Browning, by R.H. Angier, Stackpole Books, Harrisburg, PA. 151 pp., illus. $19.95

A world master gunsmith reveals his secrets of building, repairing and renewing a gun, quite literally, lock, stock and barrel. A useful, concise text on chemical coloring methods for the gunsmith and mechanic.

Guns and Gunmaking Tools of Southern Appalachia, by John Rice Irwin, Schiffer Publishing Ltd., 1983. 118 pp., illus. Paper covers. $9.95

The story of the Kentucky rifle.

Gunsmith Kinks, by F.R. (Bob) Brownell, F. Brownell & Son, Montezuma, IA, 1st ed., 1969. 496 pp., well illus. $22.98

A widely useful accumulation of shop kinks, short cuts, techniques and pertinent comments by practicing gunsmiths from all over the world.

Gunsmith Kinks 2, by Bob Brownell, F. Brownell & Son, Publishers, Montezuma, IA, 1983. 496 pp., illus. $22.95

A collection of gunsmithing knowledge, shop kinks, new and old techniques, shortcuts and general know-how straight from those who do them best–the gunsmiths.

Gunsmith Kinks 3, edited by Frank Brownell, Brownells Inc., Montezuma, IA, 1993. 504 pp., illus. $24.95

Tricks, knacks and "kinks" by professional gunsmiths and gun tinkerers. Hundreds of valuable ideas are given in this volume.

Gunsmith Kinks 4, edited by Frank Brownell, Brownells Inc., Montezuma, IA, 2001. 564 pp., illus. $27.75

332 detailed illustrations. 560+ pages with 706 separate subject headings and over 5000 cross-indexed entries. An incredible gold mine of information.

The Gunsmith of Grenville County: Building the American Longrifle, by Peter Alexander, Texarkana, TX, Scurlock Publishing Co., 2002. 400 pp.in, with hundreds of illustrations, and six color photos of original rifles. Stiff paper covers. $45.00

The most extensive how-to book on building longrifles ever published. Takes you through every step of building your own longrifle, from shop set up and tools to engraving, carving and finishing.

Gunsmithing, by Roy F. Dunlap, Stackpole Books, Harrisburg, PA, 1990. 742 pp., illus. $34.95

A manual of firearm design, construction, alteration and remodeling. For amateur and professional gunsmiths and users of modern firearms.

Gunsmithing at Home: Lock, Stock and Barrel, by John Traister, Stoeger Publishing Co., Wayne, NJ, 1997. 320 pp., illus. Paper covers. $19.95

A complete step-by-step fully illustrated guide to the art of gunsmithing.

Gunsmithing Shotguns: The Complete Guide to Care & Repair, by David Henderson, New York, Globe Pequot, 2003. 1st edition. Hardcover. NEW. $24.95

Gunsmithing Tips and Projects, a collection of the best articles from the *Handloader* and *Rifle* magazines, by various authors, Wolfe Publishing Co., Prescott, AZ, 1992. 443 pp., illus. Paper covers. $25.00

Includes such subjects as shop, stocks, actions, tuning, triggers, barrels, customizing, etc.

Gunsmithing: Guns of the Old West: Expanded 2nd Edition, by David Chicoine, lola, WI, Krause Publications, 2004. 446 pp.in, illus. Softcover. NEW. $29.95

Gunsmithing: Pistols & Revolvers: Expanded 2nd Edition, by Patrick Sweeney, lola, WI, Krause Publications, 2004. Softcover, NEW. $19.99

Gunsmithing: Rifles, by Patrick Sweeney, Krause Publications, Iola, WI, 1999. 352 pp., illus. Paper covers. $24.95

Tips for lever-action rifles. Building a custom Ruger 10/22. Building a better hunting rifle.

Home Gunsmithing the Colt Single Action Revolvers, by Loren W. Smith, Ray Riling Arms Books, Co., Phila., PA, 2001. 119 pp., illus. $29.95

Affords the Colt Single Action owner detailed, pertinent information on the operating and servicing of this famous and historic handgun.

How to Convert Military Rifles, Williams Gun Sight Co., Davision, MI, new and enlarged seventh edition, 1997. 76 pp., illus. Paper covers. $13.95

This latest edition updated the changes that have occured over the past thirty years. Tips, instructions and illustratons on how to convert popular military rifles as the Enfield, Mauser 96 and SKS just to name a few are presented.

Mauser M98 & M96, by R.A. Walsh, Wolfe Publishing Co., Prescott, AR, 1998. 123 pp., illus. Paper covers. $32.50

How to build your own favorite custom Mauser rifle from two of the best bolt action rifle designs ever produced–the military Mauser Model 1898 and Model 1896 bolt rifles.

Mr. Single Shot's Gunsmithing-Idea-Book, by Frank de Haas, Mark de Haas, Orange City, IA, 1996. 168 pp., illus. Paper covers. $22.50

Offers easy to follow, step-by-step instructions for a wide variety of gunsmithing procedures all reinforced by plenty of photos.

Professional Stockmaking, by D. Wesbrook, Wolfe Publishing Co., Prescott, AZ, 1995. 308 pp., illus. $54.00

A step-by-step how-to with complete photographic support for every detail of the art of working wood into riflestocks.

Recreating the American Longrifle, by William Buchele, et al, George Shumway Publisher, York, Pa, 5th edition, 1999. 175 pp., illus. $40.00

Includes full size plans for building a Kentucky rifle.

The Story of Pope's Barrels, by Ray M. Smith, R&R Books, Livonia, NY, 1993. 203 pp., illus. $39.00

A reissue of a 1960 book whose author knew Pope personally. It will be of special interest to Schuetzen rifle fans, since Pope's greatest days were at the height of the Schuetzen-era before WWI.

Survival Gunsmithing, by J.B. Wood, Desert Publications, Cornville, AZ, 1986. 92 pp., illus. Paper covers. $11.95

A guide to repair and maintenance of the most popular rifles, shotguns and handguns.

The Tactical 1911, by Dave Lauck, Paladin Press, Boulder, CO, 1998. 137 pp., illus. Paper covers. $20.00

Here is the only book you will ever need to teach you how to select, modify, employ and maintain your Colt.

HANDGUNS

.22 Caliber Handguns; A Shooter's Guide, by D.F. Geiger, Lincoln, RI, Andrew Mowbray, Inc., 2003. 1st edition. Softcover. $21.95

The .380 Enfield No. 2 Revolver, by Mark Stamps and Ian Skennerton, I.D.S.A. Books, Piqua, OH, 1993. 124 pp., 80 illus. Paper covers. $19.95

9mm Parabellum; The History & Development of the World's 9mm Pistols & Ammunition, by Klaus-Peter Konig and Martin Hugo, Schiffer Publishing Ltd., Atglen, PA, 1993. 304 pp., illus. $39.95

Detailed history of 9mm weapons from Belguim, Italy, Germany, Israel, France, U.S.A., Czechoslovakia, Hungary, Poland, Brazil, Finland and Spain.

Advanced Master Handgunning, by Charles Stephens, Paladin Press, Boulder, CO, 1994. 72 pp., illus. Paper covers. $14.00

Secrets and surefire techniques for winning handgun competitions.

Advanced Tactical Marksman More High Performance Techniques for Police, Military, and Practical Shooters, by Dave M. Lauck. Paladin Press, Boulder, CO, 2002. 1st edition. 232 pp., photos, illus. Softcover $35.00

Lauck, one of the most respected names in high-performance shooting and gunsmithing, refines and updates his 1st book. Dispensing with overcomplicated mil-dot formulas and minute-of-angle calculations, Lauck shows you how to achieve superior accuracy and figure out angle shots, train for real-world scenarios, choose optics and accessories.

American Beauty: The Prewar Colt National Match Government Model Pistol, by Timothy Mullin, Collector Grade Publications, Canada, 1999. 72 pp., 69 illus. $34.95

69 illustrations, 20 in full color photos of factory engraved guns and other authenticated upgrades, including rare 'double-carved' ivory grips.

The Automatic Pistol, by J.B.L. Noel, Foreword by Timothy J. Mullin, Boulder, CO, Paladin Press, 2004. 128 pp., illus. Softcover. NEW. $14.00

The Ayoob Files: The Book, by Massad Ayoob, Police Bookshelf, Concord, NH, 1995. 223 pp., illus. Paper covers. $14.95

The best of Massad Ayoob's acclaimed series in *American Handgunner* magazine.

The Belgian Browning Pistols 1889-1949, by Anthony Vanderlinden, Wet Dog Publications, Geensboro, NC 2001. Limited edition of 2000 copies, signed by the author. 243 pp. plus index. Illustrated with b&w photos. Hardcover. $65.00

Includes the 1899 Compact, 1899 Large, 1900, 1903, Grand Browning, 1910, 1922 Grand Rendement and high power pistols. Also includes a chapter on holsters.

Big Bore Handguns, by John Taffin, Krause Publications, Iola, WI, 2002. 1st edition. 352 pp., 320 b&w photos with a 16-page color section. Hardcover. $39.95

Gives honest reviews and an inside look at shooting, hunting, and competing with the biggest handguns around. Covers handguns from major gunmakers, as well as handgun customizing, accessories, reloading, and cowboy activities. Significant coverage is also given to handgun customizing, accessories, reloading, and popular shooting hobbies including hunting and cowboy activities.

Big Bore Sixguns, by John Taffin, Krause Publications, Iola, WI, 1997. 336 pp., illus. $39.95

The author takes aim on the entire range of big bores from .357 Magnums to .500 Maximums, single actions and cap-and-ball sixguns to custom touches for big bores.

THE HANDGUNNER'S LIBRARY

Bill Ruger's .22 Pistol: A Photographic Essay of the Ruger Rimfire Pistol, by Don Findlay, New York, Simon & Schuster, 2000. 2nd printing. Hardcover, NEW. $100.00

The Browning High Power Automatic Pistol (Expanded Edition), by Blake R. Stevens, Collector Grade Publications, Canada, 1996. 310 pp., with 313 illus. $49.95

An in-depth chronicle of seventy years of High Power history, from John M. Browning's original 16-shot prototypes to the present. Profusely illustrated with rare original photos and drawings from the FN Archive to describe virtually every sporting and military version of the High Power. The Expanded Edition contains 30 new pages on the interesting Argentine full-auto High Power, the latest FN 'MK3' and BDA9 pistols, plus FN's revolutionary P90 5.7x28mm Personal Defense Weapon, and more!

Browning Hi-Power Pistols, Desert Publications, Cornville, AZ, 1982. 20 pp., illus. Paper covers. $11.95

Covers all facets of the various military and civilian models of the Browning Hi-Power pistol.

Canadian Military Handguns 1855-1985, by Clive M. Law, Museum Restoration Service, Bloomfield, Ont., Canada, 1994. 130pp., illus. $40.00

A long-awaited and important history for arms historians and pistol collectors.

Collecting U. S. Pistols & Revolvers, 1909-1945, by J. C. Harrison. The Arms Chest, Oklahoma City, OK, 1999. 2nd edition (revised). 185 pp., illus. Spiral bound. $35.00

Valuable and detailed reference book for the collector of U.S. pistols & revolvers. Identifies standard issue original military models of the M1911, M1911A1 and M1917 Cal .45 pistols and revolvers as produced by all manufacturers from 1911 through 1945. Plus .22 Ace models, National Match models, and similar foreign military models produced by Colt or manufactured under Colt license, plus arsenal repair, refinish and lend-lease models.

The Colt .45 Auto Pistol, compiled from U.S. War Dept. Technical Manuals, and reprinted by Desert Publications, Cornville, AZ, 1978. 80 pp., illus. Paper covers. $12.95

Covers every facet of this famous pistol from mechanical training, manual of arms, disassembly, repair and replacement of parts.

Colt Single Action Army Revolver Study: New Discoveries, by Kenneth Moore, Lincoln, RI, Andrew Mowbray, Inc., 2003. 1st edition. Hardcover. NEW. $47.95

The Combat Perspective; The Thinking Man's Guide to Self-Defense, by Gabriel Suarez, Boulder, CO, Paladin Press, 2003. 1st edition. 112 pp. Softcover. $15.00

In The Combat Perspective, Suarez keys in on developing your knowledge about and properly organizing your mental attitude toward combat to improve your odds of winning – not just surviving – such a fight. The principles are as applicable to the bladesman as they are to the rifleman, to the unarmed fighter as they are to the sniper. In this book he examines each in a logical and scientific manner, demonstrating why, when it comes to defending your life, the mental edge is at least as critical to victory as the tactical advantage.

Complete Encyclopedia of Pistols & Revolvers, by A.E. Hartnik, Knickerbocker Press, New York, NY, 2003. 272 pp., illus. $19.95

A comprehensive encyclopedia specially written for collectors and owners of pistols and revolvers.

Concealable Pocket Pistols: How to Choose and Use Small-Caliber Handguns, by Terence McLeod, Paladin Press, 2001. 1st edition. 80 pp. Softcover. $14.00

Small-caliber handguns are often maligned as too puny for serious self-defense, but millions of Americans own and carry these guns and have used them successfully to stop violent assaults. This is the first book ever devoted to eliminating the many misconceptions about the usefulness of these popular guns. Find out what millions of Americans already know about these practical self-defense tools.

The Custom Government Model Pistol, by Layne Simpson, Wolfe Publishing Co., Prescott, AZ, 1994. 639 pp., illus. Paper covers. $26.95

The book about one of the world's greatest firearms and the things pistolsmiths do to make it even greater.

The Custom Revolver, by Hamilton S. Bowen, Foreword by Ross Seyfried. Louisville, TN, privately printed, 2001. 1st edition. New in new dust jacket. $49.95

The Darling Pepperbox: The Story of Samuel Colt's Forgotten Competitors in Bellingham, Mass. and Woonsocket, RI, by Stuart C. Mowbray, Lincoln, RI, Andrew Mowbray, Inc., 2004. 1st edition. 104 pp. Softcover. NEW. $19.95

Developmental Cartridge Handguns of .22 Calibre, as Produced in the United States & Abroad from 1855 to 1875, by John S. Laidacker, Atglen, PA, Schiffer Publications, 2003. Reprint. 597 pp., with over 860 b&w photos, drawings, and charts. Hardcover. $100.00

This book is a reprint edition of the late John Laidacker's personal study of early .22 Cartridge Handguns from 1855-1875. Laidacker's primary aim was to offer a quick reference to the collector, and his commentary on the wide variety of types, variations and makers, as well as detailed photography, make this a superb addition to any firearm library.

Engraved Handguns of .22 Calibre, by John S. Laidacker, Atglen, PA, Schiffer Publications, 2003. 1st edition. 192 pp., with over 400 color and b&w photos. $69.95

The Farnam Method of Defensive Handgunning, by John S. Farnam, Police Bookshelf, 1999. 191 pp., illus. Paper covers. $24.00

A book intended to not only educate the new shooter, but also to serve as a guide and textbook for his and his instructor's training courses.

Fast and Fancy Revolver Shooting, by Ed McGivern, Anniversary Edition, Winchester Press, Piscataway, NJ, 1984. 484 pp., illus. $19.95

A fascinating volume, packed with handgun lore and solid information by the acknowledged dean of revolver shooters.

German Handguns: The Complete Book of the Pistols and Revolvers of Germany, 1869 to the Present, by Ian Hogg, Greenhill Publishing, 2001. 320 pp., 270 illustrations. Hardcover. $49.95

Ian Hogg examines the full range of handguns produced in Germany from such classics as the Luger M1908, Mauser HsC and Walther PPK, to more unusual types such as the Reichsrevolver M1879 and the Dreyse 9mm. He presents the key data (length, weight, muzzle velocity, and range) for each weapon discussed and also gives its date of introduction and service record, evaluates and discusses peculiarities, and examines in detail particular strengths and weaknesses.

Glock: The New Wave in Combat Handguns, by Peter Alan Kasler, Paladin Press, Boulder, CO, 1993. 304 pp., illus. $27.00

Kasler debunks the myths that surround what is the most innovative handgun to be introduced in some time.

Glock's Handguns, by Duncan Long, Desert Publications, El Dorado, AR, 1996. 180 pp., illus. Paper covers. $19.95

An outstanding volume on one of the world's newest and most successful firearms of the century.

Greenhill Military Manual: Combat Handguns, by Leroy Thompson, London, Greenhill Publishing, 2004. 1st edition Hardcover. NEW. $24.00

Gun Digest Book of Combat Handgunnery 5th Edition, Complete Guide to Combat Shooting, by Massad Ayoob, lola, WI, Krause Publications, 2002. Softcover. NEW. $19.95

The Gun Digest Book of the 1911, by Patrick Sweeney, Krause Publications, Iola, WI, 2002. 336 pp., with 700 b&w photos. Softcover. $27.95

Complete guide of all models and variations of the Model 1911. The author also includes repair tips and information on buying a used 1911.

Gun Digest Book of the Glock; A Comprehensive Review, Design, History and Use, Iola, WI, Krause Publications, 2003. 1st edition. 303 pp., with 500 b&w photos. Softcover. 24.95

Examine the rich history and unique elements of the most important and influential firearms design of the past 50 years, the Glock autoloading pistol. This comprehensive review of the revolutionary pistol analyzes the performance of the various models and chamberings and features a complete guide to available accessories and little-known factory options. You'll see why it's the preferred pistol for law enforcement use and personal protection.

Hand Cannons: The World's Most Powerful Handguns, by Duncan Long, Paladin Press, Boulder, CO, 1995. 208 pp., illus. Paper covers. $22.00

Long describes and evaluates each powerful gun according to their features.

Handgun Stopping Power "The Definitive Study," by Evan P. Marshall & Edwin J. Sanow, Paladin Press, Boulder, CO, 1997. 240 pp. photos. Softcover. $45.00

Dramatic first-hand accounts of the results of handgun rounds fired into criminals by cops, storeowners, cabbies and others are the heart and soul of this long-awaited book. This is the definitive methodology for predicting the stopping power of handgun loads, the first to take into account what really happens when a bullet meets a man.

Handguns 2005: 17th Edition, edited by Ken Ramage, lola, WI, Krause Publications, 2004. Softcover. NEW. $24.99

Target shooters, handgun hunters, collectors and those who rely upon handguns for self-defense will want to pack this value-loaded and entertaining volume in their home libraries. Shooters will find the latest pistol and revolver designs and accessories, plus test reports on several models. The handgun becomes an artist's canvas in a showcase of engraving talents. The catalog section–with comprehensive specs on every known handgun in production–includes a new display of semi-custom handguns, plus an expanded, illustrated section on the latest grips, sights, scopes and other aiming devices. Offer easy access to products, services and manufacturers.

Handguns of the Armed Organizations of the Soviet Occupation Zone and German Democratic Republic, by Dieter H. Marschall, Los Alamos, NM, Ucross Books, 2000. Softcover. NEW. $29.95

Translated from German this groundbreaking treatise covers the period from May 1945 through 1996. The organizations that used these pistols are described along with the guns and holsters. Included are the P08, P38, PP, PPK, P1001, PSM, Tokarev, Makarov, (including .22 LR, cutaway, silenced, Suhl marked), Stechlin, plus Hungarian, Romanian and Czech pistols.

Heckler & Koch's Handguns, by Duncan Long, Desert Publications, El Dorado, AR, 1996. 142 pp., illus. Paper covers. $19.95

Traces the history and the evolution of H&K's pistols from the company's beginning at the end of WWII to the present.

Hidden in Plain Sight, by Trey Bloodworth & Mike Raley, Professional Press, Chapel Hill, NC, 1995. Paper covers. $19.95

A practical guide to concealed handgun carry.

High Standard: A Collectors Guide to the Hamden & Hartford Target Pistols, by Tom Dance, Andrew Mowbray, Inc., Lincoln, RI, 1999. 192 pp., heavily illustrated with b&w photographs and technical drawings. $24.00

From Citation to Supermatic, all of the production models and specials made from 1951 to 1984 are covered according to model number or series, making it easy to understand the evolution to this favorite of shooters and collectors.

High Standard Automatic Pistols 1932-1950, by Charles E. Petty, The Gun Room Press, Highland Park, NJ, 1989. 124 pp., illus. $14.95

A definitive source of information for the collector of High Standard arms.

Hi-Standard Pistols and Revolvers, 1951-1984, by James Spacek, Chesire, CT, 1998. 128 pp., illus. Paper covers. $4.95

Technical details, marketing features and instruction/parts manual of every model High Standard pistol and revolver made between 1951 and 1984. Most accurate serial number information available.

History of Smith & Wesson Firearms, by Dean Boorman, New York, Lyons Press, 2002. 1st edition. 144 pp., illustrated in full color. Hardcover. $29.95

The definitive guide to one of the world's best-known firearms makers. Takes the story through the years of the Military & Police .38 & of the Magnum cartridge, to today's wide range of products for law-enforcement customers.

How to Become a Master Handgunner: The Mechanics of X-Count Shooting, by Charles Stephens, Paladin Press, Boulder, CO, 1993. 64 pp., illus. Paper covers. $14.00

Offers a simple formula for success to the handgunner who strives to master the technique of shooting accurately.

The Inglis Diamond: The Canadian High Power Pistol, by Clive M. Law, Collector Grade Publications, Canada, 2001. 312 pp., illus. $49.95

This definitive work on Canada's first and indeed only mass produced handgun, in production for a very brief span of time and consequently made in relatively few numbers, the venerable Inglis-made Browning High Power covers the pistol's initial history, the story of Chinese and British adoption, use post-war by Holland, Australia, Greece, Belgium, New Zealand, Peru, Brasil and other countries. All new information on the famous light-weights and the Inglis

Diamond variations. Completely researched through official archives in a dozen countries. Many of the bewildering variety of markings have never been satisfactorily explained until now

Japanese Military Cartridge Handguns 1893-1945, A Revised and Expanded Edition of Hand Cannons of Imperial Japan, by Harry L. Derby III and James D. Brown, Atglen, PA, Schiffer Publications, 2003. 1st edition. Hardcover. New in new dust jacket. $79.95

When originally published in 1981, The Hand Cannons of Imperial Japan was heralded as one of the most readable works on firearms ever produced. To arms collectors and scholars, it remains a prized source of information on Japanese handguns, their development, and their history. In this new Revised and Expanded edition, original author Harry Derby has teamed with Jim Brown to provide a thorough update reflecting twenty years of additional research. An appendix on valuation has also been added, using a relative scale that should remain relevant despite inflationary pressures. For the firearms collector, enthusiast, historian or dealer, this is the most complete and up-to-date work on Japanese military handguns ever written.

Know Your 45 Auto Pistols–Models 1911 & A1, by E.J. Hoffschmidt, Blacksmith Corp., Southport, CT, 1974. 58 pp., illus. Paper covers. $14.95

A concise history of the gun with a wide variety of types and copies.

Know Your Ruger Single Actions: The Second Decade 1963-1973, by John C. Dougan, Blacksmith Corp., North Hampton, OH, 1994. 143 pp., illus. Paper covers. $19.95

Know Your Ruger S/A Revolvers 1953-1963 (revised edition), by John C. Dougan. Blacksmith Corp., North Hampton, OH, 2002. 191 pp., illus. Paper covers. $19.95

Know Your Walther P38 Pistols, by E.J. Hoffschmidt, Blacksmith Corp., Southport, CT, 1974. 77 pp., illus. Paper covers. $14.95

Covers the Walther models Armee, M.P., H.P., P.38–history and variations.

Know Your Walther PP & PPK Pistols, by E.J. Hoffschmidt, Blacksmith Corp., Southport, CT, 1975. 87 pp., illus. Paper covers. $14.95

A concise history of the guns with a guide to the variety and types.

La Connaissance du Luger, Tome 1, (The Knowledge of Luger, Volume 1, translated), by Gerard Henrotin, H & L Publishing, Belguim, 1996. b&w and color photos. French text. 144 pp., illus. $45.00

Living with Glocks: The Complete Guide to the New Standard in Combat Handguns, by Robert H. Boatman, Boulder, CO, Paladin Press, 2002. 1st edition. 184 pp., illus. Hardcover. $29.95

In addition to demystifying the enigmatic Glock trigger, Boatman describes and critiques each Glock model in production. Separate chapters on the G36, the enhanced G20 and the full-auto G18 emphasize the job-specific talents of these standout models for those seeking insight on which Glock pistol might best meet their needs. And for those interested in optimizing their Glock's capabilities, this book addresses all the peripherals–holsters, ammo, accessories, silencers, modifications and conversions, training programs and more.

Luger Artiglieria: (The Luger Artillery: From the Prototypes up to the Mauser Commemorative, the History and the Accessories), by Mauro Baudino, Italy, Editoriale Olimpia, 2003. 1st edition. Softcover. NEW. $31.95

The Luger Handbook, by Aarron Davis, Krause Publications, Iola, WI, 1997. 112 pp., illus. Paper covers. $9.95

Now you can identify any of the legendary Luger variations using a simple decision tree. Each model and variation includes pricing information, proof marks and detailed attributes in a handy, user-friendly format. Plus, it's fully indexed. Instantly identify that Luger!

The Luger Story, by John Walter, Stackpole Books, Mechanicsburg, PA, 2001. 256 pp., illus. Paper covers. $19.95

The standard history of the world's most famous handgun.

Lugers at Random (Revised Format Edition), by Charles Kenyon Jr., Handgun Press, Glenview, IL, 2000. 420 pp., illus. $59.95

A new printing of this classic, comprehensive reference for all Luger collectors.

The Mauser Self-Loading Pistol, by Belford & Dunlap, Borden Publishing Co., Alhambra, CA. Over 200 pp., 300 illus., large format. $29.95

The long-awaited book on the "Broom Handles," covering their inception in 1894 to the end of production. Complete and in detail: pocket pistols, Chinese and Spanish copies.

Mental Mechanics of Shooting: How to Stay Calm at the Center, by Vishnu Karmakar and Thomas Whitney, Littleton, CO, Center Vision, Inc., 2001. 144 pp. Softcover. $19.95

Not only will this book help you stay free of trigger jerk, it will help you in all areas of your shooting.

Model 1911 Automatic Pistol, by Robert Campbell, Accokeek, Maryland, Stoeger Publications, 2004. Hardcover. NEW. $24.95

Modern Law Enforcement Weapons & Tactics, 3rd Edition, by Patrick Sweeney, Iola, WI, Krause Publications, 2004. 256 pp. Softcover. NEW. $22.99

The Official 9mm Markarov Pistol Manual, translated into English by Major James Gebhardt, U.S. Army (Ret.), Desert Publications, El Dorado, AR, 1996. 84 pp., illus. Paper covers. $14.95

The information found in this book will be of enormous benefit and interest to the owner or a prospective owner of one of these pistols.

The Operator's Tactical Pistol Shooting Manual; A Practical Guide to Combat Marksmanship, by Erik Lawrence, Linesville, PA, Blackheart Publishing, 2003. 1st edition. 233 pp. Softcover. $24.50

This manual-type book begins with the basics of safety with a pistol and progresses into advanced pistol handling. A self-help guide for improving your capabilities with a pistol at your own pace.

The P08 Luger Pistol, by de Vries & Martens, Alexandria, VA, Ironside International, 2002. 152 pp., illustrated with 200 high quality b&w photos. Hardcover. $34.95

Covers all essential information on history and development, ammunition and accessories, codes and markings, and contains photos of nearly every model and accessory. Includes a unique selection of original German WWII propoganda photos, most never published before.

The P-08 Parabellum Luger Automatic Pistol, edited by J. David McFarland, Desert Publications, Cornville, AZ, 1982. 20 pp., illus. Paper covers. $14.95

Covers every facet of the Luger, plus a listing of all known Luger models.

The P-38 Pistol: Postwar Distributions, 1945-1990. Volume 3, by Warren Buxton, Ucross Books, Los Alamos, MN 1999, plus an addendum to Volumes 1 & 2. 272 pp. with 342 illustrations. $68.50

The P-38 Pistol: The Contract Pistols, 1940-1945. Volume 2., by Warren Buxton, Ucross Books, Los Alamos, MN 1999. 256 pp. with 237 illustrations. $68.50

The P-38 Pistol: The Walther Pistols, 1930-1945. Volume 1, by Warren Buxton, Ucross Books, Los Alamos, MN 1999. $68.50

A limited run reprint of this scarce and sought-after work on the P-38 Pistol. 328 pp. with 160 illustrations.

Pistols of World War I, by Robert J. Adamek, Pittsburgh, Pentagon Press, 2001. 1st edition signed and numbered. Over 90 pistols illustrated, technical data, designers, history, proof marks. 296 pp. with illustrations and photos. Softcover. $45.00

Over 25 pistol magazines illustrated with dimensions, serial number ranges. Over 35 cartridges illustrated with dimensions, manufactures, year of introduction. Weapons from 16 countries involved in WWI, statistics, quantities made, identification.

The Ruger .22 Automatic Pistol, Standard/Mark I/Mark II Series, by Duncan Long, Paladin Press, Boulder, CO, 1989. 168 pp., illus. Paper covers. $16.00

The definitive book about the pistol that has served more than 1 million owners so well.

Ruger .22 Automatic Pistols: The Complete Guide for all Models from 1947 to 2003, Grand Rapids, MI, The Ruger Store, 2004. 74 pp., 66 high-resolution grayscale images. Printed in the U.S.A. with card stock cover and bright white paper. Softcover. NEW. $12.95

Includes 'rare' complete serial numbers and manufacturing dates from 1949-2004.

The Ruger "P" Family of Handguns, by Duncan Long, Desert Publications, El Dorado, AZ, 1993. 128 pp., illus. Paper covers. $14.95

A full-fledged documentary on a remarkable series of Sturm Ruger handguns.

The Semiautomatic Pistols in Police Service and Self Defense, by Massad Ayoob, Police Bookshelf, Concord, NH, 1990. 25 pp., illus. Softcover. $11.95

First quantitative, documented look at actual police experience with 9mm and 45 police service automatics.

Shooting Colt Single Actions, by Mike Venturino, Livingston, MT, 1997. 205 pp., illus. Paper covers. $25.00

A definitive work on the famous Colt SAA and the ammunition it shoots.

Sig Handguns, by Duncan Long, Desert Publications, El Dorado, AZ, 1995. 150 pp., illus. Paper covers. $19.95

The history of Sig/Sauer handguns, including Sig, Sig-Hammerli and Sig/Sauer variants.

Sixgun Cartridges and Loads, by Elmer Keith, reprint edition by The Gun Room Press, Highland Park, NJ, 1984. 151 pp., illus. $24.95

A manual covering the selection, use and loading of the most suitable and popular revolver cartridges.

Sixguns, by Elmer Keith, Wolfe Publishing Company, Prescott, AZ, 1992. 336 pp. Paper covers. $29.95. Hardcover $35.00

The history, selection, repair, care, loading, and use of this historic frontiersman's friend–the one-hand firearm.

Smith & Wesson's Automatics, by Larry Combs, Desert Publications, El Dorado, AZ, 1994. 143 pp., illus. Paper covers. $19.95

A must for every S&W auto owner or prospective owner.

Spanish Handguns: The History of Spanish Pistols and Revolvers, by Gene Gangarosa Jr., Stoeger Publishing Co., Accokeek, MD, 2001. 320 pp., illustrated, b&w photos. Paper covers. $21.95

Standard Catalog of Smith & Wesson, 2nd Edition, by Jim Supica and Richard Nahas, Krause Publications, Iola, WI, 2001. 272 pp., 350 b&w photos, with 16-page color section. Pictorial hardcover. $34.95

Clearly details 775 Smith & Wesson models, knives, holsters, ammunition and police items with complete pricing information, illustrated glossary and index.

Star Firearms, by Leonardo M. Antaris, Davenport, TA, Firac Publications Co., 2002. 1st edition. Hardcover. New in new dust jacket. $119.95

Street Stoppers: The Latest Handgun Stopping Power Street Results, by Evan P. Marshall and Edwin J. Sandow, Paladin Press, Boulder, CO, 1997. 392 pp., illus. Paper covers. $42.95

Compilation of the results of real-life shooting incidents involving every major handgun caliber.

The Tactical 1911, by Dave Lauck, Paladin Press, Boulder, CO, 1999. 152 pp., illus. Paper covers. $22.00

The cop's and SWAT operator's guide to employment and maintenance.

The Tactical Pistol, by Gabriel Suarez, Foreword by Jeff Cooper, Paladin Press, Boulder, CO, 1996. 216 pp., illus. Paper covers. $25.00

Advanced gunfighting concepts and techniques.

The Thompson/Center Contender Pistol, by Charles Tephens, Paladin Press, Boulder, CO, 1997. 58 pp., illus. Paper covers. $14.00

How to tune and time, load and shoot accurately with the Contender pistol.

The Truth About Handguns, by Duane Thomas, Paladin Press, Boulder, CO, 1997. 136 pp., illus. Paper covers. $18.00

Exploding the myths, hype, and misinformation about handguns.

U.S. Handguns of World War II, The Secondary Pistols and Revolvers, by Charles W. Pate, Mowbray Publishers, Lincoln, RI, 1997. 368 pp., illus. $39.00

This indispensable new book covers all of the American military handguns of WWII except for the M1911A1.

Walther Pistols: Models 1 Through P99, Factory Variations and Copies, by Dieter H. Marschall, Ucross Books, Los Alamos, NM. 2000. 140 pp., with 140 b&w illustrations, index. Paper covers. $19.95

This is the English translation, revised and updated, of the highly successful and widely acclaimed German language edition. This book provides the collector with a reference guide and overview of the entire line of the Walther military, police, and self-defense pistols from the very first to the very latest Variations, where issued, serial ranges, calibers, marks, proofs, logos, and design aspects in an astonishing quantity and variety are crammed into this very well researched and highly regarded work.

DIRECTORY OF THE HANDGUNNING TRADE

HANDGUNS 2006

PRODUCT & SERVICE DIRECTORY

AMMUNITION COMPONENTS, SHOTSHELL

A.W. Peterson Gun Shop, Inc., The
Ballistic Products, Inc.
Blount, Inc., Sporting Equipment Div.
CCI/Speer Div of ATK
Cheddite, France S.A.
Claybuster Wads & Harvester Bullets
Garcia National Gun Traders, Inc.
Gentner Bullets
Guncrafter Industries
Magtech Ammunition Co. Inc.
Precision Reloading, Inc.
Ravell Ltd.
Tar-Hunt Custom Rifles, Inc.
Vitt/Boos

AMMUNITION COMPONENTS– BULLETS, POWDER, PRIMERS, CASES

A.W. Peterson Gun Shop, Inc., The
Acadian Ballistic Specialties
Accuracy Unlimited
Accurate Arms Co., Inc.
Action Bullets & Alloy Inc.
ADCO Sales, Inc.
Alaska Bullet Works, Inc.
Alex, Inc.
Alliant Techsystems, Smokeless Powder Group
Allred Bullet Co.
Alpha LaFranck Enterprises
American Products, Inc.
Ammo Load Worldwide, Inc.
Arizona Ammunition, Inc.
Armfield Custom Bullets
A-Square Co.
Baer's Hollows
Ballard Rifle & Cartridge Co., LLC
Barnes
Barnes Bullets, Inc.
Beartooth Bullets
Bell Reloading, Inc.
Berger Bullets Ltd.
Berry's Mfg., Inc.
Big Bore Bullets of Alaska
Big Bore Express
Bitterroot Bullet Co.
Black Belt Bullets (See Big Bore Express)
Black Hills Shooters Supply
Black Powder Products
Blount, Inc., Sporting Equipment Div.
Blue Mountain Bullets
Brenneke GmbH
Briese Bullet Co., Inc.
Brown Dog Ent.
BRP, Inc. High Performance Cast Bullets
Buck Stix-SOS Products Co.
Buckeye Custom Bullets
Buckskin Bullet Co.
Buffalo Arms Co.
Buffalo Bullet Co., Inc.
Buffalo Rock Shooters Supply
Bull-X, Inc.
Butler Enterprises
Cain's Outdoors, Inc.
Calhoon Mfg.
Cambos Outdoorsman
Canyon Cartridge Corp.
Cascade Bullet Co., Inc.
Cast Performance Bullet Company
Casull Arms Corp.
CCI/Speer Div of ATK
Champion's Choice, Inc.
Cheddite, France S.A.
CheVron Bullets
Chuck's Gun Shop
Clean Shot Technologies
Competitor Corp., Inc.
Cook Engineering Service
Corbin Mfg. & Supply, Inc.
Cummings Bullets
Curtis Cast Bullets
Curtis Gun Shop (See Curtis Cast Bullets)
Custom Bullets by Hoffman
D.L. Unmussig Bullets
Dakota Arms, Inc.
Davide Pedersoli and Co.
DKT, Inc.
Dohring Bullets
Eichelberger Bullets, Wm.
Federal Cartridge Co.
Fiocchi of America, Inc.
Firearm Brokers
Forkin Custom Classics
Fowler Bullets
Fowler, Bob (See Black Powder Products)
Freedom Arms, Inc.
Garcia National Gun Traders, Inc.
Gehmann, Walter (See Huntington Die Specialties)
GOEX, Inc.
Golden Bear Bullets
Gotz Bullets
Grayback Wildcats
Grier's Hard Cast Bullets
GTB-Custom Bullets
Gun City
Gun Works, The
Harris Enterprises
Harrison Bullets
Hart & Son, Inc.
Hawk Laboratories, Inc. (See Hawk, Inc.)
Hawk, Inc.
Heidenstrom Bullets
Hercules, Inc. (See Alliant Techsystems Smokeless Powder Group)
Hi-Performance Ammunition Company
Hirtenberger AG
Hobson Precision Mfg. Co.
Hodgdon Powder Co.
Hornady Mfg. Co.
HT Bullets
Hunters Supply, Inc.
Huntington Die Specialties
Impact Case & Container, Inc.
Imperial Magnum Corp.
IMR Powder Co.
Intercontinental Distributors, Ltd.
J&D Components
J&L Superior Bullets (See Huntington Die Specialties)
J.R. Williams Bullet Co.
Jamison International
Jensen Bullets
Jensen's Firearms Academy
Jericho Tool & Die Co., Inc.
Jester Bullets
JLK Bullets
JRP Custom Bullets
Ka Pu Kapili
Kaswer Custom, Inc.
Keith's Bullets
Keng's Firearms Specialty, Inc./US Tactical Systems
Ken's Kustom Kartridges
Knight Rifles
Knight Rifles (See Modern Muzzleloading, Inc.)
Lawrence Brand Shot (See Precision Reloading, Inc.)
Liberty Shooting Supplies
Lightning Performance Innovations, Inc.
Lindsley Arms Cartridge Co.
Littleton, J. F.
Lomont Precision Bullets
Lyman Products Corp.
Magnus Bullets
Magtech Ammunition Co. Inc.
Marchmon Bullets
Markesbery Muzzle Loaders, Inc.
Marshall Fish Mfg. Gunsmith Sptg. Co.
MAST Technology, Inc.
McMurdo, Lynn
Meister Bullets (See Gander Mountain)
Men-Metallwerk Elisenhuette GmbH
Midway Arms, Inc.
Mitchell Bullets, R.F.
MI-TE Bullets
Montana Precision Swaging
Mulhern, Rick
Murmur Corp.
Nagel's Custom Bullets
Nammo Lapua Oy
National Bullet Co.
Naval Ordnance Works
North American Shooting Systems
North Devon Firearms Services
Northern Precision
Northwest Custom Projectile
Nosler, Inc.
OK Weber, Inc.
Oklahoma Ammunition Co.
Old Wagon Bullets
Old Western Scrounger Ammunition Inc.
Ordnance Works, The
Oregon Trail Bullet Company
Pacific Rifle Co.
Page Custom Bullets
Penn Bullets
Petro-Explo Inc.
Phillippi Custom Bullets, Justin
Pinetree Bullets
PMC/Eldorado Cartridge Corp.
Polywad, Inc.
Pony Express Reloaders
Power Plus Enterprises, Inc.
Precision Delta Corp.
Prescott Projectile Co.
Price Bullets, Patrick W.
PRL Bullets, c/o Blackburn Enterprises
Professional Hunter Supplies
Proofmark Corp.
PWM Sales Ltd.
Quality Cartridge
Quarton Beamshot
Rainier Ballistics
Ramon B. Gonzalez Guns
Ravell Ltd.
Redwood Bullet Works
Reloading Specialties, Inc.
Remington Arms Co., Inc.
Rhino
Robinson H.V. Bullets
Rubright Bullets
Russ Haydon's Shooters' Supply
SAECO (See Redding Reloading Equipment)
Scharch Mfg., Inc.-Top Brass
Schneider Bullets
Schroeder Bullets
Schumakers Gun Shop
Scot Powder
Seebeck Assoc., R.E.
Shappy Bullets
Sharps Arms Co., Inc., C.
Shilen, Inc.
Sierra Bullets
SOS Products Co. (See Buck Stix-SOS Products Co.)
Southern Ammunition Co., Inc.
Specialty Gunsmithing
Speer Bullets
Spencer's Rifle Barrels, Inc.
SSK Industries
Stanley Bullets
Star Ammunition, Inc.
Star Custom Bullets
Starke Bullet Company
Starline, Inc.
Stewart's Gunsmithing
Swift Bullet Co.
T.F.C. S.p.A.
Taracorp Industries, Inc.
Tar-Hunt Custom Rifles, Inc.
TCCI
TCSR
Thompson Bullet Lube Co.
Thompson Precision
Traditions Performance Firearms
Trico Plastics
True Flight Bullet Co.
Tucson Mold, Inc.
USAC
Vann Custom Bullets
Vihtavuori Oy/Kaltron-Pettibone
Vincent's Shop
Viper Bullet and Brass Works
Walters Wads
Warren Muzzleloading Co., Inc.
Watson Bullets
Western Nevada West Coast Bullets
Widener's Reloading & Shooting Supply, Inc.
Wildey F. A., Inc.
Winchester Div. Olin Corp.
Woodleigh (See Huntington Die Specialties)
Worthy Products, Inc.
Wyant Bullets
Wyoming Custom Bullets
Zero Ammunition Co., Inc.

AMMUNITION, COMMERCIAL

3-Ten Corp.
A.W. Peterson Gun Shop, Inc., The
Ad Hominem
Air Arms
American Ammunition
Arizona Ammunition, Inc.
Arms Corporation of the Philippines
Arundel Arms & Ammunition, Inc., A.
A-Square Co.
Ballistic Products, Inc.
Benjamin/Sheridan Co., Crosman
Big Bear Arms & Sporting Goods, Inc.
Black Hills Ammunition, Inc.
Blammo Ammo
Blount, Inc., Sporting Equipment Div.
Brenneke GmbH
Buchsenmachermeister
Buffalo Arms Co.
Buffalo Bullet Co., Inc.
Bull-X, Inc.
Cabela's
Cambos Outdoorsman
Casull Arms Corp.
CBC
CCI/Speer Div of ATK
Champion's Choice, Inc.
Cor-Bon Inc./Glaser LLC
Crosman Airguns
Cubic Shot Shell Co., Inc.
Daisy Outdoor Products
Dead Eye's Sport Center
Delta Arms Ltd.
Delta Frangible Ammunition LLC
Dynamit Nobel-RWS, Inc.
Effebi SNC-Dr. Franco Beretta
Eley Ltd.
Elite Ammunition
Ellett Bros.
Estate Cartridge, Inc.
Federal Cartridge Co.
Fiocchi of America, Inc.
Firearm Brokers
Garcia National Gun Traders, Inc.
Garrett Cartridges, Inc.
Garthwaite Pistolsmith, Inc., Jim
Gibbs Rifle Co., Inc.
Gil Hebard Guns, Inc.
Glaser LLC
Glaser Safety Slug, Inc.
GOEX, Inc.
Goodwin's Guns
Gun City
Gun Room Press, The
Gun Works, The
Guncrafter Industries
Hansen & Co.
Hart & Son, Inc.
Hastings
Hi-Performance Ammunition Company
Hirtenberger AG
Hofer Jagdwaffen, P.
Hornady Mfg. Co.
Hunters Supply, Inc.
Intercontinental Distributors, Ltd.
Ion Industries, Inc.
Keng's Firearms Specialty, Inc./US Tactical Systems
Kent Cartridge America, Inc.
Knight Rifles
Lethal Force Institute (See Police Bookshelf)
Lock's Philadelphia Gun Exchange
Lomont Precision Bullets
Magnum Research, Inc.
MagSafe Ammo Co.
Magtech Ammunition Co. Inc.
Mandall Shooting Supply Inc.
Markell, Inc.
Marshall Fish Mfg. Gunsmith Sptg. Co.
Men-Metallwerk Elisenhuette GmbH
Mullins Ammunition
Nammo Lapua Oy
New England Ammunition Co.
Oklahoma Ammunition Co.
Old Western Scrounger Ammunition Inc.
Outdoor Sports Headquarters, Inc.
P.S.M.G. Gun Co.
Paragon Sales & Services, Inc.
Parker & Sons Shooting Supply
Peterson Gun Shop, Inc., A.W.
PMC/Eldorado Cartridge Corp.
Police Bookshelf
Polywad, Inc.
Pony Express Reloaders
Precision Delta Corp.
Pro Load Ammunition, Inc.
Quality Cartridge
R.E.I.
Ravell Ltd.
Remington Arms Co., Inc.
Rucker Dist. Inc.
RWS (See U.S. Importer-Dynamit Nobel-RWS, Inc.)
Sellier & Bellot, USA, Inc.
Southern Ammunition Co., Inc.
Speer Bullets
TCCI
Thompson Bullet Lube Co.
USAC
VAM Distribution Co. LLC
Victory USA
Vihtavuori Oy/Kaltron-Pettibone
Visible Impact Targets
Voere-KGH GmbH
Weatherby, Inc.
Westley Richards & Co. Ltd.
Whitestone Lumber Corp.
Widener's Reloading & Shooting Supply, Inc.
Wildey F. A., Inc.
William E. Phillips Firearms
Winchester Div. Olin Corp.
Zero Ammunition Co., Inc.

AMMUNITION, CUSTOM

3-Ten Corp.
A.W. Peterson Gun Shop, Inc., The
Accuracy Unlimited
AFSCO Ammunition
Allred Bullet Co.
American Derringer Corp.
American Products, Inc.
Arizona Ammunition, Inc.
Arms Corporation of the Philippines
Ballard Rifle & Cartridge Co., LLC

PRODUCT & SERVICE DIRECTORY

Bear Arms
Belding's Custom Gun Shop
Berger Bullets Ltd.
Big Bore Bullets of Alaska
Black Hills Ammunition, Inc.
Blue Mountain Bullets
Brynin, Milton
Buckskin Bullet Co.
Buffalo Arms Co.
CBC
CFVentures
Champlin Firearms, Inc.
Country Armourer, The
Cubic Shot Shell Co., Inc.
Custom Tackle and Ammo
D.L. Unmussig Bullets
Dakota Arms, Inc.
Dead Eye's Sport Center
Delta Frangible Ammunition LLC
DKT, Inc.
Elite Ammunition
Estate Cartridge, Inc.
GDL Enterprises
Gentner Bullets
GOEX, Inc.
Grayback Wildcats
Hawk, Inc.
Hirtenberger AG
Hobson Precision Mfg. Co.
Horizons Unlimited
Hornady Mfg. Co.
Hunters Supply, Inc.
Jensen Bullets
Jensen's Custom Ammunition
Jensen's Firearms Academy
Kaswer Custom, Inc.
L. E. Jurras & Assoc.
L.A.R. Mfg., Inc.
Lethal Force Institute (See Police Bookshelf)
Lindsley Arms Cartridge Co.
Linebaugh Custom Sixguns
MagSafe Ammo Co.
Magtech Ammunition Co. Inc.
MAST Technology, Inc.
McMurdo, Lynn
Men-Metallwerk Elisenhuette GmbH
Milstor Corp.
Mullins Ammunition
Oklahoma Ammunition Co.
P.S.M.G. Gun Co.
Peterson Gun Shop, Inc., A.W.
Phillippi Custom Bullets, Justin
Police Bookshelf
Power Plus Enterprises, Inc.
Precision Delta Corp.
Professional Hunter Supplies
Quality Cartridge
R.E.I.
Ramon B. Gonzalez Guns
Sandia Die & Cartridge Co.
SOS Products Co. (See Buck Stix-SOS Products Co.)
Specialty Gunsmithing
Spencer's Rifle Barrels, Inc.
SSK Industries
Star Custom Bullets
Stewart's Gunsmithing
TCCI
Vitt/Boos
Vulpes Ventures, Inc., Fox Cartridge Division
Warren Muzzleloading Co., Inc.
Watson Bullets
Worthy Products, Inc.
Zero Ammunition Co., Inc.

AMMUNITION, FOREIGN

A.W. Peterson Gun Shop, Inc., The
Ad Hominem
AFSCO Ammunition
Air Arms
Armscorp USA, Inc.
B&P America
Cape Outfitters
CBC
Cheddite, France S.A.
Cubic Shot Shell Co., Inc.
Dead Eye's Sport Center
DKT, Inc.
Dynamit Nobel-RWS, Inc.
E. Arthur Brown Co. Inc.
Fiocchi of America, Inc.
Gamebore Division, Polywad, Inc.
Gibbs Rifle Co., Inc.
GOEX, Inc.
Gunsmithing, Inc.
Hansen & Co.
Heidenstrom Bullets
Hirtenberger AG
Hornady Mfg. Co.
International Shooters Service
Intrac Arms International
Jack First, Inc.
K.B.I. Inc.
MagSafe Ammo Co.
Magtech Ammunition Co. Inc.
Mandall Shooting Supply Inc.
Marksman Products
MAST Technology, Inc.
Mullins Ammunition
Navy Arms Company
Oklahoma Ammunition Co.
P.S.M.G. Gun Co.
Paragon Sales & Services, Inc.
Paul Co., The
Peterson Gun Shop, Inc., A.W.
Petro-Explo Inc.
Precision Delta Corp.
R.E.T. Enterprises
Ramon B. Gonzalez Guns
RWS (See U.S. Importer-Dynamit Nobel-RWS, Inc.)
Samco Global Arms, Inc.
Sentinel Arms
Southern Ammunition Co., Inc.
Speer Bullets
Stratco, Inc.
T.F.C. S.p.A.
Vector Arms, Inc.
Victory Ammunition
Vihtavuori Oy/Kaltron-Pettibone
Wolf Performance Ammunition

ANTIQUE ARMS DEALER

Ackerman & Co.
Ad Hominem
Antique American Firearms
Antique Arms Co.
Aplan Antiques & Art
Armoury, Inc., The
Arundel Arms & Ammunition, Inc., A.
Ballard Rifle & Cartridge Co., LLC
Bear Mountain Gun & Tool
Bob's Tactical Indoor Shooting Range & Gun Shop
Buffalo Arms Co.
Cape Outfitters
CBC-BRAZIL
Chadick's Ltd.
Chambers Flintlocks Ltd., Jim
Champlin Firearms, Inc.
Chuck's Gun Shop
Cleland's Outdoor World, Inc.
Clements' Custom Leathercraft, Chas
Cole's Gun Works
Cousin Bob's Mountain Products
D&D Gunsmiths, Ltd.
David R. Chicoine
Dixie Gun Works
Dixon Muzzleloading Shop, Inc.
Duffy, Charles E. (See Guns Antique & Modern DBA)
Ed's Gun House
Enguix Import-Export
Fagan Arms
Flayderman & Co., Inc.
Getz Barrel Company
Glass, Herb
Goergen's Gun Shop, Inc.
Golden Age Arms Co.
Goodwin's Guns
Gun Hunter Books (See Gun Hunter Trading Co.)
Gun Hunter Trading Co.
Gun Room Press, The
Gun Room, The
Gun Works, The
Guns Antique & Modern DBA / Charles E. Duffy
Hallowell & Co.
Hammans, Charles E.
HandCrafts Unltd. (See Clements' Custom Leathercraft)
Handgun Press
Hansen & Co.
Hunkeler, A. (See Buckskin Machine Works)
Imperial Miniature Armory
James Wayne Firearms for Collectors and Investors
Kelley's
Knight's Manufacturing Co.
Ledbetter Airguns, Riley
LeFever Arms Co., Inc.
Lever Arms Service Ltd.
Lock's Philadelphia Gun Exchange
Log Cabin Sport Shop
Logdewood Mfg.
Mandall Shooting Supply Inc.
Marshall Fish Mfg. Gunsmith Sptg. Co.
Martin B. Retting Inc.
Martin's Gun Shop
Michael's Antiques
Mid-America Recreation, Inc.
Montana Outfitters, Lewis E. Yearout
Muzzleloaders Etcetera, Inc.
Navy Arms Company
New England Arms Co.
Olathe Gun Shop
P.S.M.G. Gun Co.
Peter Dyson & Son Ltd.
Pony Express Sport Shop
Powder Horn Ltd.
Ravell Ltd.
Reno, Wayne
Retting, Inc., Martin B.
Robert Valade Engraving
Rutgers Book Center
Samco Global Arms, Inc.
Sarco, Inc.
Scott Fine Guns Inc., Thad
Shootin' Shack
Sportsmen's Exchange & Western Gun Traders, Inc.
Steves House of Guns
Stott's Creek Armory, Inc.
Turnbull Restoration, Doug
Vic's Gun Refinishing
Wallace, Terry
Westley Richards & Co. Ltd.
Wild West Guns
Winchester Consultants
Winchester Sutler, Inc., The
Yearout, Lewis E. (See Montana Outfitters)

APPRAISER - GUNS, ETC.

A.W. Peterson Gun Shop, Inc., The
Ackerman & Co.
Antique Arms Co.
Armoury, Inc., The
Arundel Arms & Ammunition, Inc., A.
Barta's Gunsmithing
Beitzinger, George
Blue Book Publications, Inc.
Bob's Tactical Indoor Shooting Range & Gun Shop
Bonham's & Butterfields
Bullet N Press
Cape Outfitters
Chadick's Ltd.
Champlin Firearms, Inc.
Christie's East
Clark Firearms Engraving
Cleland's Outdoor World, Inc.
Clements' Custom Leathercraft, Chas
Cole's Gun Works
Colonial Arms, Inc.
Colonial Repair
Corry, John
Custom Tackle and Ammo
D&D Gunsmiths, Ltd.
David R. Chicoine
DGR Custom Rifles
Dietz Gun Shop & Range, Inc.
Dixie Gun Works
Dixon Muzzleloading Shop, Inc.
Duane's Gun Repair (See DGR Custom Rifles)
Ed's Gun House
Eversull Co., Inc.
Fagan Arms
Ferris Firearms
Firearm Brokers
Flayderman & Co., Inc.
Forty-Five Ranch Enterprises
Frontier Arms Co., Inc.
Gene's Custom Guns
Getz Barrel Company
Gillmann, Edwin
Goergen's Gun Shop, Inc.
Golden Age Arms Co.
Griffin & Howe, Inc.
Griffin & Howe, Inc.
Gun City
Gun Hunter Books (See Gun Hunter Trading Co.)
Gun Hunter Trading Co.
Gun Room Press, The
Gun Shop, The
Gun Works, The
Guncraft Books (See Guncraft Sports, Inc.)
Guncraft Sports, Inc.
Guncraft Sports, Inc.
Gunsmithing, Inc.
Hallowell & Co.
Hammans, Charles E.
HandCrafts Unltd. (See Clements' Custom Leathercraft)
Handgun Press
Hank's Gun Shop
Hansen & Co.
Irwin, Campbell H.
Ithaca Classic Doubles
Jackalope Gun Shop
James Wayne Firearms for Collectors and Investors
Jensen's Custom Ammunition
JG Airguns, LLC
Kelley's
Ken Eyster Heritage Gunsmiths, Inc.
L.L. Bean, Inc.
Lampert, Ron
LaRocca Gun Works
Ledbetter Airguns, Riley
LeFever Arms Co., Inc.
Lock's Philadelphia Gun Exchange
Log Cabin Sport Shop
Logdewood Mfg.
Long, George F.
Mahony, Philip Bruce
Mandall Shooting Supply Inc.
Marshall Fish Mfg. Gunsmith Sptg. Co.
Martin B. Retting Inc.
Martin's Gun Shop
Mathews Gun Shop & Gunsmithing, Inc.
McCann Industries
Mercer Custom Guns
Montana Outfitters, Lewis E. Yearout
Muzzleloaders Etcetera, Inc.
Navy Arms Company
New England Arms Co.
Olathe Gun Shop
Orvis Co., The
P&M Sales & Services, LLC
P.S.M.G. Gun Co.
Pasadena Gun Center
Pentheny de Pentheny
Perazone-Gunsmith, Brian
Peterson Gun Shop, Inc., A.W.
Pettinger Books, Gerald
Pony Express Sport Shop
Powder Horn Ltd.
R.A. Wells Custom Gunsmith
R.E.T. Enterprises
Ramon B. Gonzalez Guns
Retting, Inc., Martin B.
Robert Valade Engraving
Russ Haydon's Shooters' Supply
Rutgers Book Center
Scott Fine Guns Inc., Thad
Shootin' Shack
Spencer Reblue Service
Sportsmen's Exchange & Western Gun Traders, Inc.
Steven Dodd Hughes
Stott's Creek Armory, Inc.
Stratco, Inc.
Swampfire Shop, The (See Peterson Gun Shop, Inc., A.W.)
Ten-Ring Precision, Inc.
Vic's Gun Refinishing
Walker Arms Co., Inc.
Wallace, Terry
Wasmundt, Jim
Weber & Markin Custom Gunsmiths
Werth, T. W.
Whildin & Sons Ltd., E.H.
Whitestone Lumber Corp.
Wild West Guns
Williams Shootin' Iron Service, The Lynx-Line
Winchester Consultants
Winchester Sutler, Inc., The
Yearout, Lewis E. (See Montana Outfitters)

AUCTIONEER - GUNS, ETC.

"Little John's" Antique Arms
Bonham's & Butterfields
Buck Stix-SOS Products Co.
Christie's East
Fagan Arms
Pete de Coux Auction House
Sotheby's

BOOKS & MANUALS (PUBLISHERS & DEALERS)

"Su-Press-On", Inc.
A.W. Peterson Gun Shop, Inc., The
Alpha 1 Drop Zone
American Gunsmithing Institute
American Handgunner Magazine
Armory Publications
Arms & Armour Press
Ballistic Products, Inc.
Ballistic Products, Inc.
Barnes Bullets, Inc.
Bauska Barrels
Beartooth Bullets
Beeman Precision Airguns
Blacksmith Corp.
Blacktail Mountain Books
Blue Book Publications, Inc.
Blue Ridge Machinery & Tools, Inc.
Boone's Custom Ivory Grips, Inc.
Brownells, Inc.
Buchsenmachermeister
Bullet N Press
C. Sharps Arms Co. Inc./Montana Armory
Cain's Outdoors, Inc.
Cape Outfitters
Cheyenne Pioneer Products
Collector's Armoury, Ltd.
Colonial Repair
Corbin Mfg. & Supply, Inc.
David R. Chicoine
deHaas Barrels

PRODUCT & SERVICE DIRECTORY

Dixon Muzzleloading Shop, Inc.
Excalibur Publications
Executive Protection Institute
F&W Publications, Inc.
Fulton Armory
Galati International
GAR
Golden Age Arms Co.
Gun City
Gun Hunter Books (See Gun Hunter Trading Co.)
Gun Hunter Trading Co.
Gun List (See F&W Publications)
Gun Room Press, The
Gun Works, The
Guncraft Books (See Guncraft Sports, Inc.)
Guncraft Sports, Inc.
Gunnerman Books
GUNS Magazine
Gunsmithing, Inc.
H&P Publishing
Handgun Press
Harris Publications
Hawk Laboratories, Inc. (See Hawk, Inc.)
Hawk, Inc.
Heritage/VSP Gun Books
Hodgdon Powder Co.
Hofer Jagdwaffen, P.
Hornady Mfg. Co.
Huntington Die Specialties
I.D.S.A. Books
Info-Arm
Ironside International Publishers, Inc.
Jantz Supply
Kelley's
King & Co.
Koval Knives
KP Books Division of F&W Publications
L.B.T.
Lebeau-Courally
Lethal Force Institute (See Police Bookshelf)
Lyman Products Corp.
Machinist's Workshop-Village Press
Madis Books
Magma Engineering Co.
Mandall Shooting Supply Inc.
Marshall Fish Mfg. Gunsmith Sptg. Co.
Montana Armory, Inc.
Montana Precision Swaging
Mulberry House Publishing
Nammo Lapua Oy
Navy Arms Company
NgraveR Co., The
Numrich Gun Parts Corporation
OK Weber, Inc.
Outdoor Sports Headquarters, Inc.
Paintball Games International Magazine Aceville
Pansch, Robert F
Pejsa Ballistics
Pettinger Books, Gerald
PFRB Co.
Police Bookshelf
Precision Reloading, Inc.
Precision Shooting, Inc.
Primedia Publishing Co.
Professional Hunter Supplies
Ravell Ltd.
Ray Riling Arms Books Co.
Remington Double Shotguns
Rocky Mountain Wildlife Products
Russ Haydon's Shooters' Supply
Rutgers Book Center
S&S Firearms
Safari Press, Inc.
Saunders Gun & Machine Shop
Scharch Mfg., Inc.-Top Brass
Scharch Mfg., Inc.-Top Brass
Semmer, Charles (See Remington Double Shotguns)
Sharps Arms Co., Inc., C.
Shotgun Sports Magazine, dba Shootin' Accessories Ltd.
Sierra Bullets
Speer Bullets
SPG LLC
Stackpole Books
Star Custom Bullets
Stewart Game Calls, Inc., Johnny
Stoeger Industries
Stoeger Publishing Co. (See Stoeger Industries)
Swift Bullet Co.
Thomas, Charles C.
Track of the Wolf, Inc.
Trafalgar Square
Trotman, Ken
Tru-Balance Knife Co.
Vega Tool Co.
VSP Publishers (See Heritage/VSP Gun Books)
W.E. Brownell Checkering Tools
WAMCO-New Mexico
Wells Creek Knife & Gun Works
Wilderness Sound Products Ltd.
Williams Gun Sight Co.
Winchester Consultants
Winfield Galleries LLC
Wolfe Publishing Co.

BULLET CASTING, ACCESSORIES

A.W. Peterson Gun Shop, Inc., The
Ballisti-Cast, Inc.
Buffalo Arms Co.
Bullet Metals
Cast Performance Bullet Company
CFVentures
Cooper-Woodward Perfect Lube
Davide Pedersoli and Co.
Ferguson, Bill
Hanned Line, The
Huntington Die Specialties
Lee Precision, Inc.
Lithi Bee Bullet Lube
Lyman Products Corp.
MA Systems, Inc.
Magma Engineering Co.
Ox-Yoke Originals, Inc.
Rapine Bullet Mould Mfg. Co.
Redding Reloading Equipment
SPG LLC

BULLET CASTING, FURNACES & POTS

A.W. Peterson Gun Shop, Inc., The
Ballisti-Cast, Inc.
Buffalo Arms Co.
Bullet Metals
Ferguson, Bill
GAR
Gun Works, The
Lee Precision, Inc.
Lyman Products Corp.
Magma Engineering Co.
Rapine Bullet Mould Mfg. Co.
RCBS/ATK
Redding Reloading Equipment
Thompson Bullet Lube Co.

BULLET CASTING, LEAD

A.W. Peterson Gun Shop, Inc., The
Action Bullets & Alloy Inc.
Ames Metal Products
Buckskin Bullet Co.
Buffalo Arms Co.
Bullet Metals
Gun Works, The
Hunters Supply, Inc.
Jericho Tool & Die Co., Inc.
Lee Precision, Inc.
Lithi Bee Bullet Lube
Magma Engineering Co.
Montana Precision Swaging
Ox-Yoke Originals, Inc.
Penn Bullets
Proofmark Corp.
SPG LLC
Splitfire Sporting Goods, L.L.C.
Walters Wads

BULLET PULLERS

A.W. Peterson Gun Shop, Inc., The
Battenfeld Technologies, Inc.
Davide Pedersoli and Co.
Gun Works, The
Hollywood Engineering
Howell Machine, Inc.
Huntington Die Specialties
Royal Arms Gunstocks

BULLET TOOLS

A.W. Peterson Gun Shop, Inc., The
Brynin, Milton
Camdex, Inc.
Corbin Mfg. & Supply, Inc.
Cumberland Arms
Eagan, Donald V.
Hanned Line, The
Holland's Gunsmithing
Hollywood Engineering
Lee Precision, Inc.
Niemi Engineering, W. B.
North Devon Firearms Services
Rorschach Precision Products
Sport Flite Manufacturing Co.
WTA Manufacturing

BULLET, CASE & DIE LUBRICANTS

Beartooth Bullets
Bonanza (See Forster Products)
Buckskin Bullet Co.
Buffalo Arms Co.
Camp-Cap Products
CFVentures
Cooper-Woodward Perfect Lube
CVA
E-Z-Way Systems
Ferguson, Bill
Forster Products, Inc.
GAR
Guardsman Products
Hanned Line, The
Heidenstrom Bullets
Hollywood Engineering
Hornady Mfg. Co.
Imperial (See E-Z-Way Systems)
Knoell, Doug
L.B.T.
Le Clear Industries (See E-Z-Way Systems)
Lee Precision, Inc.
Lithi Bee Bullet Lube
MI-TE Bullets
RCBS Operations/ATK
Reardon Products
Rooster Laboratories
Shay's Gunsmithing
Tamarack Products, Inc.
Uncle Mike's (See Michaels of Oregon, Co.)
Warren Muzzleloading Co., Inc.
Widener's Reloading & Shooting Supply, Inc.
Young Country Arms

CARTRIDGES FOR COLLECTORS

Ackerman & Co.
Ad Hominem
Armory Publications
Cameron's
Campbell, Dick
Cherry Creek State Park Shooting Center
Cole's Gun Works
Colonial Repair
Country Armourer, The
Cubic Shot Shell Co., Inc.
Duane's Gun Repair (See DGR Custom Rifles)
Ed's Gun House
Ed's Gun House
Enguix Import-Export
Forty-Five Ranch Enterprises
Goergen's Gun Shop, Inc.
Grayback Wildcats
Gun City
Gun Hunter Books (See Gun Hunter Trading Co.)
Gun Hunter Trading Co.
Gun Room Press, The
Jack First, Inc.
Kelley's
Liberty Shooting Supplies
Mandall Shooting Supply Inc.
MAST Technology, Inc.
Michael's Antiques
Montana Outfitters, Lewis E. Yearout
Numrich Gun Parts Corporation
Pasadena Gun Center
Pete de Coux Auction House
Samco Global Arms, Inc.
SOS Products Co. (See Buck Stix-SOS Products Co.)
Stone Enterprises Ltd.
Ward & Van Valkenburg
Winchester Consultants
Yearout, Lewis E. (See Montana Outfitters)

CASE & AMMUNITION PROCESSORS, INSPECTORS, BOXERS

A.W. Peterson Gun Shop, Inc., The
Ammo Load, Inc.
Hafner World Wide, Inc.
Scharch Mfg., Inc.-Top Brass

CASE CLEANERS & POLISHING MEDIA

A.W. Peterson Gun Shop, Inc., The
Battenfeld Technologies, Inc.
Buffalo Arms Co.
G96 Products Co., Inc.
Gun Works, The
Huntington Die Specialties
Lee Precision, Inc.
Penn Bullets
Tru-Square Metal Products, Inc.
VibraShine, Inc.

CASE PREPARATION TOOLS

A.W. Peterson Gun Shop, Inc., The
Battenfeld Technologies, Inc.
Forster Products, Inc.
High Precision
Hoehn Sales, Inc.
Huntington Die Specialties
J. Dewey Mfg. Co., Inc.
K&M Services
Lee Precision, Inc.
Match Prep-Doyle Gracey
Plum City Ballistic Range
PWM Sales Ltd.
RCBS Operations/ATK
Redding Reloading Equipment
Russ Haydon's Shooters' Supply
Sinclair International, Inc.
Stoney Point Products, Inc.

CASE TRIMMERS, TRIM DIES & ACCESSORIES

A.W. Peterson Gun Shop, Inc., The
Buffalo Arms Co.
Creedmoor Sports, Inc.
Forster Products, Inc.
Fremont Tool Works
Hollywood Engineering
K&M Services
Lyman Products Corp.
Match Prep-Doyle Gracey
OK Weber, Inc.
PWM Sales Ltd.
RCBS/ATK
Redding Reloading Equipment

CASE TUMBLERS, VIBRATORS, MEDIA & ACCESSORIES

4-D Custom Die Co.
A.W. Peterson Gun Shop, Inc., The
Battenfeld Technologies, Inc.
Berry's Mfg., Inc.
Dillon Precision Products, Inc.
Penn Bullets
Raytech Div. of Lyman Products Corp.
Tru-Square Metal Products, Inc.
VibraShine, Inc.

CASES, CABINETS, RACKS & SAFES - GUN

All Rite Products, Inc.
Allen Co., Inc.
Alumna Sport by Dee Zee
American Display Co.
American Security Products Co.
Americase
Art Jewel Enterprises Ltd.
Bagmaster Mfg., Inc.
Barramundi Corp.
Berry's Mfg., Inc.
Big Spring Enterprises "Bore Stores"
Bison Studios
Black Sheep Brand
Brauer Bros.
Browning Arms Co.
Bushmaster Hunting & Fishing
Cannon Safe, Inc.
Chipmunk (See Oregon Arms, Inc.)
Connecticut Shotgun Mfg. Co.
D&L Industries (See D.J. Marketing)
D.J. Marketing
Dara-Nes, Inc. (See Nesci Enterprises, Inc.)
Deepeeka Exports Pvt. Ltd.
Doskocil Mfg. Co., Inc.
DTM International, Inc.
EMF Co. Inc.
English, Inc., A.G.
Enhanced Presentations, Inc.
Eversull Co., Inc.
Flambeau, Inc.
Fort Knox Security Products
Freedom Arms, Inc.
Frontier Safe Co.
Galati International
GALCO International Ltd.
Gun-Ho Sports Cases
Hall Plastics, Inc., John
Homak
Hoppe's Div. Penguin Industries, Inc.
Hunter Co., Inc.
Hydrosorbent Products
Impact Case & Container, Inc.
Johanssons Vapentillbehor, Bert
Kalispel Case Line
KK Air International (See Impact Case & Container Co., Inc.)
Knock on Wood Antiques
Kolpin Outdoors, Inc.
Lakewood Products LLC
Liberty Safe
Mandall Shooting Supply Inc.
Marsh, Mike
McWelco Products
Morton Booth Co.

PRODUCT & SERVICE DIRECTORY

MPC
MTM Molded Products Co., Inc.
Nalpak
Necessary Concepts, Inc.
Nesci Enterprises Inc.
Oregon Arms, Inc. (See Rogue Rifle Co., Inc.)
Outa-Site Gun Carriers
Outdoor Connection, Inc., The
Pflumm Mfg. Co.
Poburka, Philip (See Bison Studios)
Powell & Son (Gunmakers) Ltd., William
Prototech Industries, Inc.
Rogue Rifle Co., Inc.
S.A.R.L. G. Granger
Schulz Industries
Silhouette Leathers
Southern Security
Sportsman's Communicators
Sun Welding Safe Co.
Surecase Co., The
Sweet Home, Inc.
Tinks & Ben Lee Hunting Products (See Wellington Outdoors)
Trulock Tool
Universal Sports
W. Waller & Son, Inc.
Whitestone Lumber Corp.
Wilson Case, Inc.
Woodstream
Zanotti Armor, Inc.
Ziegel Engineering

CHRONOGRAPHS & PRESSURE TOOLS

Air Rifle Specialists
C.W. Erickson's L.L.C.
Clearview Products
Competition Electronics, Inc.
D&H Precision Tooling
Hege Jagd-u. Sporthandels GmbH
Hutton Rifle Ranch
Mac-1 Airgun Distributors
Oehler Research, Inc.
PACT, Inc.
Romain's Custom Guns, Inc.
Savage Arms, Inc.
Stratco, Inc.
Tepeco

CLEANERS & DEGREASERS

A.W. Peterson Gun Shop, Inc., The
Barnes Bullets, Inc.
Camp-Cap Products
Cubic Shot Shell Co., Inc.
G96 Products Co., Inc.
Gun Works, The
Hafner World Wide, Inc.
Half Moon Rifle Shop
Kleen-Bore, Inc.
Modern Muzzleloading, Inc.
Northern Precision
Parker & Sons Shooting Supply
Parker Gun Finishes
PrOlixr Lubricants
R&S Industries Corp.
Rusteprufe Laboratories
Sheffield Knifemakers Supply, Inc.
Shooter's Choice Gun Care
Sierra Specialty Prod. Co.
Spencer's Rifle Barrels, Inc.
United States Products Co.

CLEANING & REFINISHING SUPPLIES

A.W. Peterson Gun Shop, Inc., The
AC Dyna-tite Corp.
Alpha 1 Drop Zone
American Gas & Chemical Co., Ltd.,
Answer Products Co.
Armite Laboratories
Atlantic Mills, Inc.
Atsko/Sno-Seal, Inc.
Barnes Bullets, Inc.
Battenfeld Technologies, Inc.
Beeman Precision Airguns
Bill's Gun Repair
Birchwood Casey
Blount, Inc., Sporting Equipment Div.
Blount/Outers ATK
Blue and Gray Products Inc. (See Ox-Yoke Originals)
Break-Free, Inc.
Bridgers Best
Brownells, Inc.
C.S. Van Gorden & Son, Inc.
Cain's Outdoors, Inc.
Cambos Outdoorsman
Cambos Outdoorsman
Camp-Cap Products
CCI/Speer Div of ATK
Connecticut Shotgun Mfg. Co.
Creedmoor Sports, Inc.
CRR, Inc./Marble's Inc.
Custom Products (See Jones Custom Products)
Cylinder & Slide, Inc., William R. Laughridge
Dara-Nes, Inc. (See Nesci Enterprises, Inc.)
Deepeeka Exports Pvt. Ltd.
Dem-Bart Checkering Tools, Inc.
Desert Mountain Mfg.
Du-Lite Corp.
Dykstra, Doug
E&L Mfg., Inc.
Effebi SNC-Dr. Franco Beretta
Ekol Leather Care
Faith Associates
Flitz International Ltd.
Fluoramics, Inc.
Frontier Products Co.
G96 Products Co., Inc.
Golden Age Arms Co.
Guardsman Products
Gunsmithing, Inc.
Hafner World Wide, Inc.
Half Moon Rifle Shop
Hammans, Charles E.
Hoppe's Div. Penguin Industries, Inc.
Hornady Mfg. Co.
Hydrosorbent Products
Iosso Products
J. Dewey Mfg. Co., Inc.
Jantz Supply
Jantz Supply
Jonad Corp.
K&M Industries, Inc.
Kellogg's Professional Products
Kesselring Gun Shop
Kleen-Bore, Inc.
Knight Rifles
Laurel Mountain Forge
Lee Supplies, Mark
Lewis Lead Remover, The (See Brownells, Inc.)
List Precision Engineering
LPS Laboratories, Inc.
Lyman Products Corp.
Mac-1 Airgun Distributors
Mandall Shooting Supply Inc.
Marble Arms (See CRR, Inc./Marble's Inc.)
Mark Lee Supplies
Micro Sight Co.
Minute Man High Tech Industries
MTM Molded Products Co., Inc.
Muscle Products Corp.
Nesci Enterprises Inc.
Northern Precision
October Country Muzzleloading
Otis Technology, Inc.
Outers Laboratories Div. of ATK
Ox-Yoke Originals, Inc.
Parker & Sons Shooting Supply
Parker Gun Finishes
Paul Co., The
Pendleton Royal, c/o Swingler Buckland Ltd.
Pete Rickard, Inc.
Precision Airgun Sales, Inc.
Precision Reloading, Inc.
PrOlixr Lubricants
Pro-Shot Products, Inc.
R&S Industries Corp.
Radiator Specialty Co.
Richards MicroFit Stocks, Inc.
Rooster Laboratories
Rusteprufe Laboratories
Rusty Duck Premium Gun Care Products
Saunders Gun & Machine Shop
Schumakers Gun Shop
Shooter's Choice Gun Care
Shotgun Sports Magazine, dba Shootin' Accessories Ltd.
Silencio/Safety Direct
Sinclair International, Inc.
Sno-Seal, Inc. (See Atsko/Sno-Seal, Inc.)
Southern Bloomer Mfg. Co.
Splitfire Sporting Goods, L.L.C.
Starr Trading Co., Jedediah
Stoney Point Products, Inc.
Svon Corp.
T.F.C. S.p.A.
TDP Industries, Inc.
Tennessee Valley Mfg.
Tetra Gun Care
Texas Platers Supply Co.
Track of the Wolf, Inc.
Tru-Square Metal Products, Inc.
United States Products Co.
Van Gorden & Son Inc., C. S.
Venco Industries, Inc. (See Shooter's Choice Gun Care)
VibraShine, Inc.
Volquartsen Custom Ltd.
Warren Muzzleloading Co., Inc.
Watson Bullets
WD-40 Co.
Wick, David E.
Willow Bend
Young Country Arms

COMPUTER SOFTWARE - BALLISTICS

Action Target, Inc.
AmBr Software Group Ltd.
Arms Software
Arms, Programming Solutions (See Arms Software)
Ballistic Program Co., Inc., The
Barnes Bullets, Inc.
Corbin Mfg. & Supply, Inc.
Country Armourer, The
Data Tech Software Systems
Gun Works, The
Hodgdon Powder Co.
J.I.T. Ltd.
Jensen Bullets
Oehler Research, Inc.
Outdoor Sports Headquarters, Inc.
PACT, Inc.
Pejsa Ballistics
Powley Computer (See Hutton Rifle Ranch)
RCBS Operations/ATK
Sierra Bullets
Tioga Engineering Co., Inc.
W. Square Enterprises

CUSTOM GUNSMITH

A&W Repair
A.A. Arms, Inc.
A.W. Peterson Gun Shop, Inc., The
Acadian Ballistic Specialties
Accuracy Unlimited
Acra-Bond Laminates
Adair Custom Shop, Bill
Ahlman Guns
Aldis Gunsmithing & Shooting Supply
Alpha Precision, Inc.
Alpine Indoor Shooting Range
Amrine's Gun Shop
Answer Products Co.
Antique Arms Co.
Armament Gunsmithing Co., Inc.
Arms Craft Gunsmithing
Armscorp USA, Inc.
Artistry in Wood
Art's Gun & Sport Shop, Inc.
Arundel Arms & Ammunition, Inc., A.
Autauga Arms, Inc.
Baelder, Harry
Bain & Davis, Inc.
Bansner's Ultimate Rifles, LLC
Barnes Bullets, Inc.
Baron Technology
Barrel & Gunworks
Barta's Gunsmithing
Bear Arms
Bear Mountain Gun & Tool
Behlert Precision, Inc.
Beitzinger, George
Belding's Custom Gun Shop
Bengtson Arms Co., L.
Bill Adair Custom Shop
Billings Gunsmiths
BlackStar AccuMax Barrels
BlackStar Barrel Accurizing (See BlackStar AccuMax)
Bob Rogers Gunsmithing
Bond Custom Firearms
Borden Ridges Rimrock Stocks
Borovnik K.G., Ludwig
Bowen Classic Arms Corp.
Brace, Larry D.
Briese Bullet Co., Inc.
Briganti Custom Gunsmith
Briley Mfg. Inc.
Broad Creek Rifle Works, Ltd.
Brockman's Custom Gunsmithing
Broken Gun Ranch
Brown Precision, Inc.
Brown Products, Inc., Ed
Buchsenmachermeister
Buckhorn Gun Works
Budin, Dave
Bull Mountain Rifle Co.
Bullberry Barrel Works, Ltd.
Burkhart Gunsmithing, Don
Calhoon Mfg.
Cambos Outdoorsman
Cambos Outdoorsman
Campbell, Dick
Carolina Precision Rifles
Carter's Gun Shop
Caywood, Shane J.
CBC-BRAZIL
Chambers Flintlocks Ltd., Jim
Champlin Firearms, Inc.
Chicasaw Gun Works
Chuck's Gun Shop
Clark Custom Guns, Inc.
Clark Firearms Engraving
Classic Arms Company
Classic Arms Corp.
Clearview Products
Cleland's Outdoor World, Inc.
Coffin, Charles H.
Cogar's Gunsmithing
Cole's Gun Works
Colonial Arms, Inc.
Colonial Repair
Colorado Gunsmithing Academy
Colorado School of Trades
Colt's Mfg. Co., Inc.
Competitive Pistol Shop, The
Conrad, C. A.
Corkys Gun Clinic
Cullity Restoration
Custom Shop, The
Custom Single Shot Rifles
D&D Gunsmiths, Ltd.
D.L. Unmussig Bullets
Dangler, Homer L.
D'Arcy Echols & Co.
Darlington Gun Works, Inc.
Dave's Gun Shop
David Miller Co.
David R. Chicoine
David W. Schwartz Custom Guns
Davis, Don
Delorge, Ed
Del-Sports, Inc.
DGR Custom Rifles
DGS, Inc., Dale A. Storey
Dietz Gun Shop & Range, Inc.
Dilliott Gunsmithing, Inc.
Don Klein Custom Guns
Donnelly, C. P.
Duane A. Hobbie Gunsmithing
Duane's Gun Repair (See DGR Custom Rifles)
Duffy, Charles E. (See Guns Antique & Modern DBA)
Duncan's Gun Works, Inc.
E. Arthur Brown Co. Inc.
Eckelman Gunsmithing
Ed Brown Products, Inc.
Eggleston, Jere D.
Entreprise Arms, Inc.
Erhardt, Dennis
Eversull Co., Inc.
Evolution Gun Works, Inc.
FERLIB
Ferris Firearms
Fisher, Jerry A.
Fisher Custom Firearms
Fleming Firearms
Flynn's Custom Guns
Forkin Custom Classics
Forster, Kathy (See Custom Checkering)
Forster, Larry L.
Forthofer's Gunsmithing & Knifemaking
Fred F. Wells/Wells Sport Store
Frontier Arms Co., Inc.
Fullmer, Geo. M.
Fulton Armory
G.G. & G.
Galaxy Imports Ltd., Inc.
Garthwaite Pistolsmith, Inc., Jim
Gary Reeder Custom Guns
Gator Guns & Repair
Genecco Gun Works
Gene's Custom Guns
Gentry Custom LLC
George Hoenig, Inc.
Gillmann, Edwin
Gilmore Sports Concepts, Inc.
Goens, Dale W.
Gonic Arms North American Arms, Inc.
Goodling's Gunsmithing
Grace, Charles E.
Grayback Wildcats
Graybill's Gun Shop
Green, Roger M.
Greg Gunsmithing Repair
Gre-Tan Rifles
Griffin & Howe, Inc.
Griffin & Howe, Inc.
Gruning Precision, Inc.
Gun Doc, Inc.
Gun Shop, The
Gun Works, The
Guncraft Books (See Guncraft Sports, Inc.)
Guncraft Sports, Inc.
Guncraft Sports, Inc.
Guns Antique & Modern DBA / Charles E. Duffy
Gunsite Training Center
Gunsmithing Ltd.
Hamilton, Alex B. (See Ten-Ring Precision, Inc.)
Hammans, Charles E.
Hammerli Service-Precision Mac
Hammond Custom Guns Ltd.
Hank's Gun Shop
Hanson's Gun Center, Dick
Harry Lawson Co.

Hart & Son, Inc.
Hart Rifle Barrels, Inc.
Hartmann & Weiss GmbH
Hawken Shop, The (See Dayton Traister)
Hecht, Hubert J., Waffen-Hecht
Heilmann, Stephen
Heinie Specialty Products
Hensley, Gunmaker, Darwin
High Bridge Arms, Inc.
High Performance International
High Precision
High Standard Mfg. Co./F.I., Inc.
Highline Machine Co.
Hill, Loring F.
Hiptmayer, Armurier
Hiptmayer, Klaus
Hoag, James W.
Hodgson, Richard
Hoehn Sales, Inc.
Hofer Jagdwaffen, P.
Holland's Gunsmithing
Huebner, Corey O.
Hunkeler, A. (See Buckskin Machine Works)
Imperial Magnum Corp.
Irwin, Campbell H.
Israel Arms Inc.
Ivanoff, Thomas G. (See Tom's Gun Repair)
J&S Heat Treat
J.J. Roberts / Engraver
Jack Dever Co.
Jackalope Gun Shop
Jamison's Forge Works
Jarrett Rifles, Inc.
Jarvis, Inc.
Jay McCament Custom Gunmaker
Jeffredo Gunsight
Jensen's Custom Ammunition
Jim Norman Custom Gunstocks
Jim's Precision, Jim Ketchum
John Rigby & Co.
John's Custom Leather
Jones Custom Products, Neil A.
Juenke, Vern
K. Eversull Co., Inc.
KDF, Inc.
Keith's Custom Gunstocks
Ken Eyster Heritage Gunsmiths, Inc.
Ken Starnes Gunmaker
Ketchum, Jim (See Jim's Precision)
Kilham & Co.
King's Gun Works
Kleinendorst, K. W.
KOGOT
Korzinek Riflesmith, J.
L. E. Jurras & Assoc.
LaFrance Specialties
Lampert, Ron
LaRocca Gun Works
Larry Lyons Gunworks
Lathrop's, Inc.
Laughridge, William R. (See Cylinder & Slide, Inc.)
Lawson Co., Harry
Lazzeroni Arms Co.
LeFever Arms Co., Inc.
Les Baer Custom, Inc.
Linebaugh Custom Sixguns
List Precision Engineering
Lock's Philadelphia Gun Exchange
Lone Star Rifle Company
Long, George F.
Mag-Na-Port International, Inc.
Mahony, Philip Bruce
Mahony, Philip Bruce
Mahovsky's Metalife
Makinson, Nicholas
Mandall Shooting Supply Inc.
Marshall Fish Mfg. Gunsmith Sptg. Co.
Martin's Gun Shop
Martz, John V.
Mathews Gun Shop & Gunsmithing, Inc.
Mazur Restoration, Pete
McCann, Tom
McCluskey Precision Rifles
McGowen Rifle Barrels
McMillan Rifle Barrels
MCS, Inc.
Mercer Custom Guns
Michael's Antiques
Mid-America Recreation, Inc.
Middlebrooks Custom Shop
Miller Arms, Inc.
Miller Custom
Mills Jr., Hugh B.
Moeller, Steve
Monell Custom Guns
Morrison Custom Rifles, J. W.
Morrow, Bud
Mo's Competitor Supplies (See MCS, Inc.)
Mowrey's Guns & Gunsmithing
Mullis Guncraft
Muzzleloaders Etcetera, Inc.
NCP Products, Inc.
Neil A. Jones Custom Products
Nelson's Custom Guns, Inc.
Nettestad Gun Works
New England Arms Co.
New England Custom Gun Service
Newman Gunshop
Nicholson Custom
Nickels, Paul R.
North American Shooting Systems
Nu Line Guns
Old World Gunsmithing
Olson, Vic
Orvis Co., The
Ottmar, Maurice
Ox-Yoke Originals, Inc.
Ozark Gun Works
P&M Sales & Services, LLC
P.S.M.G. Gun Co.
PAC-NOR Barreling
Pagel Gun Works, Inc.
Parker & Sons Shooting Supply
Parker Gun Finishes
Pasadena Gun Center
Paterson Gunsmithing
Paulsen Gunstocks
Peacemaker Specialists
PEM's Mfg. Co.
Pence Precision Barrels
Pennsylvania Gunsmith School
Penrod Precision
Pentheny de Pentheny
Perazone-Gunsmith, Brian
Performance Specialists
Pete Mazur Restoration
Peterson Gun Shop, Inc., A.W.
Piquette's Custom Engraving
Plum City Ballistic Range
Powell & Son (Gunmakers) Ltd., William
Power Custom, Inc.
Professional Hunter Supplies
Quality Custom Firearms
R&J Gun Shop
R.A. Wells Custom Gunsmith
Ramon B. Gonzalez Guns
Ray's Gunsmith Shop
Renfrew Guns & Supplies
Ridgetop Sporting Goods
Ries, Chuck
RMS Custom Gunsmithing
Robar Co., Inc., The
Robert Valade Engraving
Robinson, Don
Rocky Mountain Arms, Inc.
Romain's Custom Guns, Inc.
Ron Frank Custom Classic Arms
Ruger's Custom Guns
Rupert's Gun Shop
Savage Arms, Inc.
Schiffman, Mike
Schumakers Gun Shop
Score High Gunsmithing
Sharp Shooter Supply
Shaw, Inc., E. R. (See Small Arms Mfg. Co.)
Shay's Gunsmithing
Shockley, Harold H.
Shooters Supply
Shootin' Shack
Shotguns Unlimited
Silver Ridge Gun Shop (See Goodwin Guns)
Simmons Gun Repair, Inc.
Singletary, Kent
Siskiyou Gun Works (See Donnelly, C. P.)
Skeoch, Brian R.
Sklany's Machine Shop
Small Arms Mfg. Co.
Small Arms Specialists
Smith, Art
Snapp's Gunshop
Speiser, Fred D.
Spencer Reblue Service
Spencer's Rifle Barrels, Inc.
Splitfire Sporting Goods, L.L.C.
Sportsmen's Exchange & Western Gun Traders, Inc.
Springfield Armory
Springfield, Inc.
SSK Industries
Star Custom Bullets
Steelman's Gun Shop
Steffens, Ron
Steven Dodd Hughes
Stiles Custom Guns
Stott's Creek Armory, Inc.
Sturgeon Valley Sporters
Sullivan, David S. (See Westwind Rifles, Inc.)
Swampfire Shop, The (See Peterson Gun Shop, Inc., A.W.)
Swann, D. J.
Swenson's 45 Shop, A. D.
Swift River Gunworks
Szweda, Robert (See RMS Custom Gunsmithing)
Taconic Firearms Ltd., Perry Lane
Tank's Rifle Shop
Tar-Hunt Custom Rifles, Inc.
Tarnhelm Supply Co., Inc.
Taylor & Robbins
Tennessee Valley Mfg.
Ten-Ring Precision, Inc.
Terry K. Kopp Professional Gunsmithing
Theis, Terry
Time Precision
Tom's Gun Repair, Thomas G. Ivanoff
Tom's Gunshop
Trevallion Gunstocks
Trulock Tool
Tucker, James C.
Turnbull Restoration, Doug
Upper Missouri Trading Co.
Van Horn, Gil
Van Patten, J. W.
Van's Gunsmith Service
Vest, John
Vic's Gun Refinishing
Virgin Valley Custom Guns
Volquartsen Custom Ltd.
Walker Arms Co., Inc.
Wallace, Terry
Wasmundt, Jim
Weatherby, Inc.
Weber & Markin Custom Gunsmiths
Weems, Cecil
Werth, T. W.
Wessinger Custom Guns & Engraving
Westley Richards & Co. Ltd.
Westwind Rifles, Inc., David S. Sullivan
White Barn Wor
White Rifles, Inc.
Wichita Arms, Inc.
Wiebe, Duane
Wild West Guns
William E. Phillips Firearms
Williams Gun Sight Co.
Williams Shootin' Iron Service, The Lynx-Line
Williamson Precision Gunsmithing
Wilsom Combat
Winter, Robert M.
Wise Guns, Dale
Wiseman and Co., Bill
Wright's Gunstock Blanks
Zeeryp, Russ

CUSTOM METALSMITH

A&W Repair
A.W. Peterson Gun Shop, Inc., The
Ackerman & Co.
Ahlman Guns
Alaskan Silversmith, The
Aldis Gunsmithing & Shooting Supply
Alpha Precision, Inc.
Amrine's Gun Shop
Answer Products Co.
Antique Arms Co.
Artistry in Wood
Baron Technology
Barrel & Gunworks
Bear Mountain Gun & Tool
Behlert Precision, Inc.
Beitzinger, George
Bengtson Arms Co., L.
Bill Adair Custom Shop
Billings Gunsmiths
Billingsley & Brownell
Bob Rogers Gunsmithing
Bowen Classic Arms Corp.
Brace, Larry D.
Briganti Custom Gunsmith
Broad Creek Rifle Works, Ltd.
Brown Precision, Inc.
Buckhorn Gun Works
Bull Mountain Rifle Co.
Bullberry Barrel Works, Ltd.
Campbell, Dick
Carter's Gun Shop
Caywood, Shane J.
Checkmate Refinishing
Colonial Repair
Colorado Gunsmithing Academy
Craftguard
Crandall Tool & Machine Co.
Cullity Restoration
Custom Shop, The
Custom Single Shot Rifles
D&D Gunsmiths, Ltd.
D&H Precision Tooling
D'Arcy Echols & Co.
Dave's Gun Shop
Delorge, Ed
DGS, Inc., Dale A. Storey
Dietz Gun Shop & Range, Inc.
Dilliott Gunsmithing, Inc.
Don Klein Custom Guns
Duane's Gun Repair (See DGR Custom Rifles)
Duncan's Gun Works, Inc.
Erhardt, Dennis
Eversull Co., Inc.
Ferris Firearms
Fisher, Jerry A.
Forster, Larry L.
Forthofer's Gunsmithing & Knifemaking
Fred F. Wells/Wells Sport Store
Fullmer, Geo. M.
Genecco Gun Works
Gentry Custom LLC
Grace, Charles E.
Grayback Wildcats
Graybill's Gun Shop
Green, Roger M.
Gun Shop, The
Gunsmithing Ltd.
Hamilton, Alex B. (See Ten-Ring Precision, Inc.)
Harry Lawson Co.
Hartmann & Weiss GmbH
Hecht, Hubert J., Waffen-Hecht
Heilmann, Stephen
High Precision
Highline Machine Co.
Hiptmayer, Armurier
Hiptmayer, Klaus
Hoag, James W.
Holland's Gunsmithing
Ivanoff, Thomas G. (See Tom's Gun Repair)
J J Roberts Firearm Engraver
J&S Heat Treat
J.J. Roberts / Engraver
Jamison's Forge Works
Jay McCament Custom Gunmaker
Jeffredo Gunsight
KDF, Inc.
Ken Eyster Heritage Gunsmiths, Inc.
Ken Starnes Gunmaker
Kilham & Co.
Kleinendorst, K. W.
Lampert, Ron
LaRocca Gun Works
Larry Lyons Gunworks
Lawson Co., Harry
Les Baer Custom, Inc.
List Precision Engineering
Lock's Philadelphia Gun Exchange
Mahovsky's Metalife
Makinson, Nicholas
Mandall Shooting Supply Inc.
Mazur Restoration, Pete
McCann Industries
Mid-America Recreation, Inc.
Miller Arms, Inc.
Morrison Custom Rifles, J. W.
Morrow, Bud
Mullis Guncraft
Nelson's Custom Guns, Inc.
Nettestad Gun Works
New England Custom Gun Service
Nicholson Custom
Noreen, Peter H.
Nu Line Guns
Olson, Vic
Ozark Gun Works
P.S.M.G. Gun Co.
Pagel Gun Works, Inc.
Parker & Sons Shooting Supply
Parker Gun Finishes
Pasadena Gun Center
Penrod Precision
Pete Mazur Restoration
Precision Specialties
Quality Custom Firearms
R.A. Wells Custom Gunsmith
Rice, Keith (See White Rock Tool & Die)
Robar Co., Inc., The
Robinson, Don
Rocky Mountain Arms, Inc.
Romain's Custom Guns, Inc.
Ron Frank Custom Classic Arms
Score High Gunsmithing
Simmons Gun Repair, Inc.
Singletary, Kent
Skeoch, Brian R.
Sklany's Machine Shop
Small Arms Specialists
Smith, Art
Smith, Sharmon
Snapp's Gunshop
Spencer Reblue Service
Spencer's Rifle Barrels, Inc.
Sportsmen's Exchange & Western Gun Traders, Inc.
SSK Industries
Steffens, Ron
Stiles Custom Guns
Taylor & Robbins
Ten-Ring Precision, Inc.
Tom's Gun Repair, Thomas G. Ivanoff
Turnbull Restoration, Doug
Van Horn, Gil
Van Patten, J. W.
Vic's Gun Refinishing
Waldron, Herman
Wallace, Terry
Weber & Markin Custom Gunsmiths
Werth, T. W.
Wessinger Custom Guns & Engraving

PRODUCT & SERVICE DIRECTORY

White Rock Tool & Die
Wiebe, Duane
Wild West Guns
Williams Shootin' Iron Service, The Lynx-Line
Williamson Precision Gunsmithing
Winter, Robert M.
Wise Guns, Dale
Wright's Gunstock Blanks

DIE ACCESSORIES, METALLIC

A.W. Peterson Gun Shop, Inc., The
Ammo Load Worldwide, Inc.
High Precision
Howell Machine, Inc.
King & Co.
Rapine Bullet Mould Mfg. Co.
Redding Reloading Equipment
Royal Arms Gunstocks
Sinclair International, Inc.
Sport Flite Manufacturing Co.

DIES, METALLIC

4-D Custom Die Co.
A.W. Peterson Gun Shop, Inc., The
Bald Eagle Precision Machine Co.
Buffalo Arms Co.
Competitor Corp., Inc.
Dakota Arms, Inc.
Dillon Precision Products, Inc.
Dixie Gun Works
Fremont Tool Works
Gruning Precision, Inc.
Jones Custom Products, Neil A.
King & Co.
Lee Precision, Inc.
Montana Precision Swaging
Neil A. Jones Custom Products
Ozark Gun Works
PWM Sales Ltd.
Rapine Bullet Mould Mfg. Co.
RCBS Operations/ATK
RCBS/ATK
Romain's Custom Guns, Inc.
Sinclair International, Inc.
Spencer's Rifle Barrels, Inc.
Sport Flite Manufacturing Co.
SSK Industries
Vega Tool Co.

DIES, SWAGE

4-D Custom Die Co.
A.W. Peterson Gun Shop, Inc., The
Ammo Load Worldwide, Inc.
Bullet Swaging Supply, Inc.
Competitor Corp., Inc.
Corbin Mfg. & Supply, Inc.
D.L. Unmussig Bullets
Howell Machine, Inc.
Montana Precision Swaging
Sport Flite Manufacturing Co.

ENGRAVER, ENGRAVING TOOLS

Ackerman & Co.
Adair Custom Shop, Bill
Ahlman Guns
Alaskan Silversmith, The
Alfano, Sam
Allard, Gary/Creek Side Metal & Woodcrafters
Allen Firearm Engraving
Altamont Co.
American Pioneer Video
Baron Technology
Barraclough, John K.
Bates Engraving, Billy
Bill Adair Custom Shop
Billy Bates Engraving
Boessler, Erich
Brooker, Dennis
Buchsenmachermeister
Churchill, Winston G.
Clark Firearms Engraving
Collings, Ronald
Creek Side Metal & Woodcrafters
Cullity Restoration
Cupp, Alana, Custom Engraver
Dayton Traister
Delorge, Ed
Dolbare, Elizabeth
Drain, Mark
Dremel Mfg. Co.
Dubber, Michael W.
Engraving Artistry
Eversull Co., Inc.
Firearms Engraver's Guild of America
Forty-Five Ranch Enterprises
Fountain Products
Frank Knives
Fred F. Wells/Wells Sport Store
Gary Reeder Custom Guns
Gene's Custom Guns
Glimm's Custom Gun Engraving
Golden Age Arms Co.
Gournet Artistic Engraving
Grant, Howard V.
GRS/Glendo Corp.
Gun Room, The
Gurney, F. R.
Half Moon Rifle Shop
Harris Hand Engraving, Paul A.
Hawken Shop, The (See Dayton Traister)
Hiptmayer, Armurier
Hiptmayer, Heidemarie
Hofer Jagdwaffen, P.
J J Roberts Firearm Engraver
J.J. Roberts / Engraver
Jantz Supply
Jeff Flannery Engraving
Jim Blair Engraving
John J. Adams & Son Engravers
Kane, Edward
Kehr, Roger
Kelly, Lance
Ken Eyster Heritage Gunsmiths, Inc.
Kenneth W. Warren Engraver
Klingler Woodcarving
Koevenig's Engraving Service
Larry Lyons Gunworks
LeFever Arms Co., Inc.
Lindsay Engraving & Tools
McCombs, Leo
McDonald, Dennis
McKenzie, Lynton
Mele, Frank
Mid-America Recreation, Inc.
Nelson, Gary K.
New Orleans Jewelers Supply Co.
NgraveR Co., The
Pedersen, C. R.
Pedersen, Rex C.
Peter Hale/Engraver
Piquette's Custom Engraving
Potts, Wayne E.
Quality Custom Firearms
Rabeno, Martin
Ralph Bone Engraving
Reed, Dave
Reno, Wayne
Riggs, Jim
Robert Evans Engraving
Robert Valade Engraving
Robinson, Don
Rohner, Hans
Rohner, John
Rosser, Bob
Rundell's Gun Shop
Sam Welch Gun Engraving
Sampson, Roger
Schiffman, Mike
Sheffield Knifemakers Supply, Inc.
Sherwood, George
Singletary, Kent
Smith, Mark A.
Smith, Ron
Smokey Valley Rifles
SSK Industries
Steve Kamyk Engraver
Swanson, Mark
Theis, Terry
Thiewes, George W.
Thirion Gun Engraving, Denise
Viramontez Engraving
Vorhes, David
W.E. Brownell Checkering Tools
Wagoner, Vernon G.
Wallace, Terry
Warenski Engraving
Weber & Markin Custom Gunsmiths
Wells, Rachel
Wessinger Custom Guns & Engraving
Winchester Consultants

GAUGES, CALIPERS & MICROMETERS

Blue Ridge Machinery & Tools, Inc.
Gruning Precision, Inc.
Huntington Die Specialties
JGS Precision Tool Mfg., LLC
K&M Services
King & Co.
Spencer's Rifle Barrels, Inc.
Starrett Co., L. S.
Stoney Point Products, Inc.

GUN PARTS, U.S. & FOREIGN

"Su-Press-On", Inc.
A.A. Arms, Inc.
A.W. Peterson Gun Shop, Inc., The
Ahlman Guns
Amherst Arms
Antique Arms Co.
Armscorp USA, Inc.
Auto-Ordnance Corp.
B.A.C.
Ballard Rifle & Cartridge Co., LLC
Bar-Sto Precision Machine
Bear Mountain Gun & Tool
Billings Gunsmiths
Bill's Gun Repair
Bob's Gun Shop
Briese Bullet Co., Inc.
Brown Products, Inc., Ed
Brownells, Inc.
Bryan & Assoc.
Buffer Technologies
Cambos Outdoorsman
Cambos Outdoorsman
Cape Outfitters
Caspian Arms, Ltd.
CBC-BRAZIL
Century International Arms, Inc.
Chicasaw Gun Works
Chip McCormick Corp.
Cleland's Outdoor World, Inc.
Cole's Gun Works
Colonial Arms, Inc.
Colonial Repair
Colt's Mfg. Co., Inc.
Cylinder & Slide, Inc., William R. Laughridge
Dan Wesson Firearms
David R. Chicoine
Delta Arms Ltd.
DGR Custom Rifles
Dibble, Derek A.
Dixie Gun Works
Duane's Gun Repair (See DGR Custom Rifles)
Duffy, Charles E. (See Guns Antique & Modern DBA)
E.A.A. Corp.
EMF Co. Inc.
Enguix Import-Export
Entreprise Arms, Inc.
European American Armory Corp. (See E.A.A. Corp.)
Evolution Gun Works, Inc.
Falcon Industries, Inc.
Felk Pistols, Inc.
Fleming Firearms
Fulton Armory
Gentry Custom LLC
Glimm's Custom Gun Engraving
Granite Mountain Arms, Inc.
Greider Precision
Gre-Tan Rifles
Gun Doc, Inc.
Gun Hunter Books (See Gun Hunter Trading Co.)
Gun Hunter Trading Co.
Gun Room Press, The
Gun Shop, The
Gun Works, The
Guns Antique & Modern DBA / Charles E. Duffy
Gunsmithing, Inc.
Hawken Shop, The (See Dayton Traister)
High Performance International
High Standard Mfg. Co./F.I., Inc.
Irwin, Campbell H.
Jack First, Inc.
Jamison's Forge Works
JG Airguns, LLC
Jonathan Arthur Ciener, Inc.
Kimber of America, Inc.
Knight's Manufacturing Co.
Krico Deutschland GmbH
LaFrance Specialties
Lampert, Ron
LaPrade
Laughridge, William R. (See Cylinder & Slide, Inc.)
Leapers, Inc.
List Precision Engineering
Lodewick, Walter H.
Logdewood Mfg.
Lomont Precision Bullets
Long, George F.
Mandall Shooting Supply Inc.
Markell, Inc.
Martin's Gun Shop
MCS, Inc.
Mid-America Recreation, Inc.
Mobile Area Networks, Inc.
Morrow, Bud
Mo's Competitor Supplies (See MCS, Inc.)
North Star West
Northwest Arms
Nu Line Guns
Numrich Gun Parts Corporation
Nygord Precision Products, Inc.
Olathe Gun Shop
Olympic Arms Inc.
P.S.M.G. Gun Co.
Pacific Armament Corp
Perazone-Gunsmith, Brian
Performance Specialists
Peter Dyson & Son Ltd.
Peterson Gun Shop, Inc., A.W.
Ranch Products
Randco UK
Ravell Ltd.
Retting, Inc., Martin B.
Romain's Custom Guns, Inc.
Ruger (See Sturm Ruger & Co., Inc.)
Rutgers Book Center
S&S Firearms
Sabatti SPA
Samco Global Arms, Inc.
Sarco, Inc.
Scherer Supplies
Shockley, Harold H.
Shootin' Shack
Silver Ridge Gun Shop (See Goodwin Guns)
Simmons Gun Repair, Inc.
Smires, C. L.
Smith & Wesson
Southern Ammunition Co., Inc.
Southern Armory, The
Sportsmen's Exchange & Western Gun Traders, Inc.
Springfield Sporters, Inc.
Springfield, Inc.
Steyr Mannlicher GmbH & Co. KG
STI International
Strayer-Voigt, Inc.
Sturm Ruger & Co. Inc.
Sunny Hill Enterprises, Inc.
Swampfire Shop, The (See Peterson Gun Shop, Inc., A.W.)
T&S Industries, Inc.
Tank's Rifle Shop
Tarnhelm Supply Co., Inc.
Taylor's & Co., Inc.
Terry K. Kopp Professional Gunsmithing
Tom Forrest, Inc.
VAM Distribution Co. LLC
W. Waller & Son, Inc.
W.C. Wolff Co.
Walker Arms Co., Inc.
Wescombe, Bill (See North Star West)
Wild West Guns
Williams Mfg. of Oregon
Winchester Sutler, Inc., The
Wise Guns, Dale
Wisners, Inc.

GUNS & GUN PARTS, REPLICA & ANTIQUE

A.W. Peterson Gun Shop, Inc., The
Ackerman & Co.
Ahlman Guns
Armi San Paolo
Auto-Ordnance Corp.
Ballard Rifle & Cartridge Co., LLC
Bear Mountain Gun & Tool
Billings Gunsmiths
Bob's Gun Shop
Buffalo Arms Co.
Cache La Poudre Rifleworks
Cash Mfg. Co., Inc.
CBC-BRAZIL
CCL Security Products
Chambers Flintlocks Ltd., Jim
Chicasaw Gun Works
Cimarron F.A. Co.
Cogar's Gunsmithing
Cole's Gun Works
Colonial Repair
Colt Blackpowder Arms Co.
Colt's Mfg. Co., Inc.
Custom Single Shot Rifles
Delhi Gun House
Delta Arms Ltd.
Dilliott Gunsmithing, Inc.
Dixie Gun Works
Dixon Muzzleloading Shop, Inc.
Ed's Gun House
Euroarms of America, Inc.
Flintlocks, Etc.
Getz Barrel Company
Golden Age Arms Co.
Gun Doc, Inc.
Gun Hunter Books (See Gun Hunter Trading Co.)
Gun Hunter Trading Co.
Gun Room Press, The
Gun Works, The
Hastings
Heidenstrom Bullets
Hunkeler, A. (See Buckskin Machine Works)
IAR Inc.
Imperial Miniature Armory
Ithaca Classic Doubles
Jack First, Inc.
JG Airguns, LLC
Ken Starnes Gunmaker
L&R Lock Co.
Leonard Day
List Precision Engineering
Lock's Philadelphia Gun Exchange
Logdewood Mfg.
Lone Star Rifle Company
Lucas, Edward E
Mandall Shooting Supply Inc.

Martin's Gun Shop
Mathews Gun Shop & Gunsmithing, Inc.
Mid-America Recreation, Inc.
Mowrey Gun Works
Navy Arms Company
Neumann GmbH
North Star West
Nu Line Guns
Numrich Gun Parts Corporation
Olathe Gun Shop
Parker & Sons Shooting Supply
Pasadena Gun Center
Pecatonica River Longrifle
PEM's Mfg. Co.
Peter Dyson & Son Ltd.
Pony Express Sport Shop
R.A. Wells Custom Gunsmith
Randco UK
Ravell Ltd.
Retting, Inc., Martin B.
Rutgers Book Center
S&S Firearms
Samco Global Arms, Inc.
Sarco, Inc.
Shootin' Shack
Silver Ridge Gun Shop (See Goodwin Guns)
Simmons Gun Repair, Inc.
Sklany's Machine Shop
Southern Ammunition Co., Inc.
Starr Trading Co., Jedediah
Stott's Creek Armory, Inc.
Taylor's & Co., Inc.
Tennessee Valley Mfg.
Tiger-Hunt Longrifle Gunstocks
Turnbull Restoration, Doug
Upper Missouri Trading Co.
VTI Gun Parts
Weber & Markin Custom Gunsmiths
Wescombe, Bill (See North Star West)
Whitestone Lumber Corp.
Winchester Sutler, Inc., The

GUNS, AIR

A.W. Peterson Gun Shop, Inc., The
Air Arms
Air Rifle Specialists
Air Venture Airguns
AirForce Airguns
Airrow
Allred Bullet Co.
Arms Corporation of the Philippines
BEC, Inc.
Beeman Precision Airguns
Benjamin/Sheridan Co., Crosman
Bryan & Assoc.
BSA Guns Ltd.
Compasseco, Ltd.
Component Concepts, Inc.
Conetrol Scope Mounts
Crosman Airguns
Daisy Outdoor Products
Daystate Ltd.
Domino
Dynamit Nobel-RWS, Inc.
Effebi SNC-Dr. Franco Beretta
European American Armory Corp. (See E.A.A. Corp.)
Feinwerkbau Westinger & Altenburger
Gamo USA, Inc.
Gaucher Armes, S.A.
Great Lakes Airguns
Gun Room Press, The
Hammerli Service-Precision Mac
IAR Inc.
International Shooters Service
J.G. Anschutz GmbH & Co. KG
JG Airguns, LLC
Labanu Inc.
Leapers, Inc.
List Precision Engineering
Mac-1 Airgun Distributors
Marksman Products
Maryland Paintball Supply
Nationwide Airgun Repair
Nygord Precision Products, Inc.
Olympic Arms Inc.
Pardini Armi Srl
Park Rifle Co., Ltd., The
Precision Airgun Sales, Inc.
Ripley Rifles
Robinson, Don
RWS (See U.S. Importer-Dynamit Nobel-RWS, Inc.)
Safari Arms/Schuetzen Pistol Works
Savage Arms, Inc.
Smith & Wesson
Steyr Mannlicher GmbH & Co. KG
Stone Enterprises Ltd.
Tippman Pneumatics, Inc.
Tristar Sporting Arms, Ltd.
Trooper Walsh
UltraSport Arms, Inc.
Visible Impact Targets
Walther GmbH, Carl
Webley and Scott Ltd.
Weihrauch KG, Hermann

GUNS, FOREIGN MANUFACTURER U.S. IMPORTER

A.W. Peterson Gun Shop, Inc., The
Accuracy Internationl Precision Rifles (See U.S.)
Accuracy Int'l. North America, Inc.
Ad Hominem
Air Arms
Armas Garbi, S.A.
Armas Kemen S. A. (See U.S. Importers)
Armi Perazzi S.P.A.
Armi San Marco (See Taylor's & Co.)
Armi Sport (See Cape Outfitters)
Arms Corporation of the Philippines
Armscorp USA, Inc.
Arrieta S.L.
Astra Sport, S.A.
Atamec-Bretton
AYA (See U.S. Importer-New England Custom Gun Serv
B.A.C.
B.C. Outdoors
BEC, Inc.
Benelli Armi S.P.A.
Benelli USA Corp.
Beretta S.P.A., Pietro
Beretta U.S.A. Corp.
Bernardelli, Vincenzo
Bersa S.A.
Bertuzzi (See U.S. Importer-New England Arms Co.)
Bill Hanus Birdguns, LLC
Blaser Jagdwaffen GmbH
Borovnik K.G., Ludwig
Bosis (See U.S. Importer-New England Arms Co.)
Brenneke GmbH
Browning Arms Co.
Bryan & Assoc.
BSA Guns Ltd.
Buchsenmachermeister
Cabanas (See U.S. Importer-Mandall Shooting Supply
Cabela's
Cache La Poudre Rifleworks
Cape Outfitters
CBC
Champlin Firearms, Inc.
Chapuis Armes
Churchill (See U.S. Importer-Ellett Bros.)
Collector's Armoury, Ltd.
Conetrol Scope Mounts
Cosmi Americo & Figlio S.N.C.
Crucelegui, Hermanos (See U.S. Importer-Mandall)
Cubic Shot Shell Co., Inc.
Dakota (See U.S. Importer-EMF Co., Inc.)
Dakota Arms, Inc.
Daly, Charles/KBI
Davide Pedersoli and Co.
Domino
Dumoulin, Ernest
Eagle Imports, Inc.
EAW (See U.S. Importer-New England Custom Gun Serv
Ed's Gun House
Effebi SNC-Dr. Franco Beretta
EMF Co. Inc.
Eversull Co., Inc.
F.A.I.R.
Fabarm S.p.A.
FEG
Feinwerkbau Westinger & Altenburger
Felk Pistols, Inc.
FERLIB
Fiocchi Munizioni S.A. (See U.S. Importer-Fiocch
Firearms Co. Ltd. / Alpine (See U.S. Importer-Mandall
Flintlocks, Etc.
Galaxy Imports Ltd., Inc.
Gamba S.p.A. Societa Armi Bresciane Srl
Gamo (See U.S. Importers-Arms United Corp., Daisy M
Gaucher Armes, S.A.
Gibbs Rifle Co., Inc.
Glock GmbH
Goergen's Gun Shop, Inc.
Griffin & Howe, Inc.
Griffin & Howe, Inc.
Grulla Armes
Hammerli AG
Hammerli USA
Hartford (See U.S. Importer-EMF Co. Inc.)
Hartmann & Weiss GmbH
Heckler & Koch, Inc.
Hege Jagd-u. Sporthandels GmbH
Helwan (See U.S. Importer-Interarms)
Hofer Jagdwaffen, P.
Holland & Holland Ltd.
Howa Machinery, Ltd.
I.A.B. (See U.S. Importer-Taylor's & Co., Inc.)
IAR Inc.
IGA (See U.S. Importer-Stoeger Industries)
Imperial Magnum Corp.
Imperial Miniature Armory
Import Sports Inc.
Inter Ordnance of America LP
International Shooters Service
Intrac Arms International
J.G. Anschutz GmbH & Co. KG
JSL Ltd. (See U.S. Importer-Specialty Shooters Supply)
K. Eversull Co., Inc.
Kimar (See U.S. Importer-IAR, Inc.)
Korth Germany GmbH
Krico Deutschland GmbH
Krieghoff Gun Co., H.
Lakefield Arms Ltd. (See Savage Arms, Inc.)
Laurona Armas Eibar, S.A.L.
Lebeau-Courally
Lever Arms Service Ltd.
Llama Gabilondo Y Cia
Lomont Precision Bullets
London Guns Ltd.
Mandall Shooting Supply Inc.
Marocchi F.lli S.p.A
Mauser Werke Oberndorf Waffensysteme GmbH
McCann Industries
MEC-Gar S.R.L.
Merkel
Mitchell's Mauser
Morini (See U.S. Importers-Mandall Shooting Supplies, Inc.)
Nammo Lapua Oy
New England Custom Gun Service
New SKB Arms Co.
Norica, Avnda Otaola
Norinco
Norma Precision AB (See U.S. Importers-Dynamit)
Northwest Arms
Nygord Precision Products, Inc.
OK Weber, Inc.
Para-Ordnance Mfg., Inc.
Pardini Armi Srl
Perugini Visini & Co. S.r.l.
Peters Stahl GmbH
Pietta (See U.S. Importers-Navy Arms Co, Taylor's
Piotti (See U.S. Importer-Moore & Co., Wm. Larkin)
PMC/Eldorado Cartridge Corp.
Powell & Son (Gunmakers) Ltd., William
Prairie Gun Works
Rizzini F.lli (See U.S. Importers-Wm. Larkin Moore & Co., N.E. Arms Corp.)
Rizzini SNC
Robinson Armament Co.
Rossi Firearms
Rottweil Compe
Rutten (See U.S. Importer-Labanu Inc.)
RWS (See U.S. Importer-Dynamit Nobel-RWS, Inc.)
S.A.R.L. G. Granger
S.I.A.C.E. (See U.S. Importer-IAR Inc.)
Sabatti SPA
Sako Ltd. (See U.S. Importer-Stoeger Industries)
San Marco (See U.S. Importers-Cape Outfitters-EMF Co., Inc.
Sarsilmaz Shotguns-Turkey (see B.C. Outdoors)
Sauer (See U.S. Importers-Paul Co., The Sigarms Inc.)
Savage Arms (Canada), Inc.
SIG
Sigarms Inc.
SIG-Sauer (See U.S. Importer-Sigarms, Inc.)
SKB Shotguns
Small Arms Specialists
Societa Armi Bresciane Srl (See U.S. Importer-Cape Outfitters)
Sphinx Systems Ltd.
Springfield Armory
Springfield, Inc.
Starr Trading Co., Jedediah
Steyr Mannlicher GmbH & Co. KG
T.F.C. S.p.A.
Tanfoglio Fratelli S.r.l.
Tanner (See U.S. Importer-Mandall Shooting Supplies, Inc.)
Taurus International Firearms (See U.S. Importer Taurus Firearms, Inc.)
Taurus S.A. Forjas
Techno Arms (See U.S. Importer-Auto-Ordnance Corp.)
Tikka (See U.S. Importer-Stoeger Industries)
TOZ (See U.S. Importer-Nygord Precision Products, Inc.)
Ugartechea S. A., Ignacio
Ultralux (See U.S. Importer-Keng's Firearms Specialty, Inc.)
Valtro USA, Inc.
Verney-Carron
Voere-KGH GmbH
Walther GmbH, Carl
Webley and Scott Ltd.
Weihrauch KG, Hermann
Westley Richards & Co. Ltd.
Yankee Gunsmith "Just Glocks"
Zabala Hermanos S.A.

GUNS, FOREIGN-IMPORTER

A.W. Peterson Gun Shop, Inc., The
Accuracy International
AcuSport Corporation
Air Rifle Specialists
Auto-Ordnance Corp.
B.A.C.
B.C. Outdoors
Bell's Legendary Country Wear
Benelli USA Corp.
Big Bear Arms & Sporting Goods, Inc.
Bill Hanus Birdguns, LLC
Bridgeman Products
British Sporting Arms
Browning Arms Co.
Cape Outfitters
Century International Arms, Inc.
Champion Shooters' Supply
Champion's Choice, Inc.
Cimarron F.A. Co.
CVA
CZ USA
Dixie Gun Works
Dynamit Nobel-RWS, Inc.
E&L Mfg., Inc.
E.A.A. Corp.
Eagle Imports, Inc.
Ellett Bros.
EMF Co. Inc.
Euroarms of America, Inc.
Eversull Co., Inc.
Fiocchi of America, Inc.
Flintlocks, Etc.
Franzen International, Inc. (See U.S. Importer-Importer Co.)
G.U., Inc. (See U.S. Importer-New SKB Arms Co.)
Galaxy Imports Ltd., Inc.
Gamba, USA
Gamo USA, Inc.
Giacomo Sporting USA
Glock, Inc.
GSI, Inc.
Gun Shop, The
Guncraft Books (See Guncraft Sports, Inc.)
Guncraft Sports, Inc.
Gunsite Training Center
Hammerli USA
IAR Inc.
Imperial Magnum Corp.
Imperial Miniature Armory
Import Sports Inc.
Intrac Arms International
K. Eversull Co., Inc.
K.B.I. Inc.
Kemen America
Keng's Firearms Specialty, Inc./US Tactical Systems
Krieghoff International,Inc.
Labanu Inc.
Legacy Sports International
Lion Country Supply
London Guns Ltd.
Magnum Research, Inc.
Marlin Firearms Co.
Marx, Harry (See U.S. Importer for FERLIB)
MCS, Inc.
MEC-Gar U.S.A., Inc.
Mitchell Mfg. Corp.
Navy Arms Company
New England Arms Co.
Nu Line Guns
Nygord Precision Products, Inc.
OK Weber, Inc.
Orvis Co., The
P.S.M.G. Gun Co.
Para-Ordnance, Inc.
Paul Co., The
Perazone-Gunsmith, Brian
Perazzi U.S.A. Inc.
Powell Agency, William
Quality Arms, Inc.

PRODUCT & SERVICE DIRECTORY

Rocky Mountain Armoury
S.D. Meacham
Safari Arms/Schuetzen Pistol Works
Samco Global Arms, Inc.
Savage Arms, Inc.
Scott Fine Guns Inc., Thad
Sigarms Inc.
SKB Shotguns
Small Arms Specialists
Southern Ammunition Co., Inc.
Specialty Shooters Supply, Inc.
Springfield, Inc.
Stoeger Industries
Stone Enterprises Ltd.
Swarovski Optik North America Ltd.
Taurus Firearms, Inc.
Taylor's & Co., Inc.
Track of the Wolf, Inc.
Traditions Performance Firearms
Tristar Sporting Arms, Ltd.
Trooper Walsh
U.S. Importer-Wm. Larkin Moore
VAM Distribution Co. LLC
Vector Arms, Inc.
VTI Gun Parts
Westley Richards Agency USA (See U.S. Importer
Wingshooting Adventures
Yankee Gunsmith "Just Glocks"

GUNS, SURPLUS, PARTS & AMMUNITION

A.W. Peterson Gun Shop, Inc., The
Ahlman Guns
Alpha 1 Drop Zone
Armscorp USA, Inc.
Arundel Arms & Ammunition, Inc., A.
B.A.C.
Bob's Gun Shop
Cambos Outdoorsman
Century International Arms, Inc.
Cole's Gun Works
Conetrol Scope Mounts
Delta Arms Ltd.
Ed's Gun House
Firearm Brokers
Fleming Firearms
Fulton Armory
Garcia National Gun Traders, Inc.
Gun City
Gun Hunter Books (See Gun Hunter Trading Co.)
Gun Hunter Trading Co.
Gun Room Press, The
Hank's Gun Shop
Hege Jagd-u. Sporthandels GmbH
Jackalope Gun Shop
Ken Starnes Gunmaker
LaRocca Gun Works
Lever Arms Service Ltd.
Log Cabin Sport Shop
Martin B. Retting Inc.
Martin's Gun Shop
Navy Arms Company
Northwest Arms
Numrich Gun Parts Corporation
Oil Rod and Gun Shop
Olathe Gun Shop
Paragon Sales & Services, Inc.
Pasadena Gun Center
Power Plus Enterprises, Inc.
Ravell Ltd.
Retting, Inc., Martin B.
Rutgers Book Center
Samco Global Arms, Inc.
Sarco, Inc.
Shootin' Shack
Silver Ridge Gun Shop (See Goodwin Guns)
Simmons Gun Repair, Inc.
Sportsmen's Exchange & Western Gun Traders, Inc.
Springfield Sporters, Inc.
T.F.C. S.p.A.
Tarnhelm Supply Co., Inc.
Taylor's & Co., Inc.
Whitestone Lumber Corp.
Williams Shootin' Iron Service, The Lynx-Line

GUNS, U.S. MADE

3-Ten Corp.
A.A. Arms, Inc.
A.W. Peterson Gun Shop, Inc., The
Accu-Tek
Acra-Bond Laminates
Ad Hominem
Airrow
Allred Bullet Co.
American Derringer Corp.
AR-7 Industries, LLC
ArmaLite, Inc.
Armscorp USA, Inc.
Arundel Arms & Ammunition, Inc., A.
A-Square Co.
Austin & Halleck, Inc.
Autauga Arms, Inc.
Auto-Ordnance Corp.
Ballard Rifle & Cartridge Co., LLC
Barrett Firearms Manufacturer, Inc.
Bar-Sto Precision Machine
Benjamin/Sheridan Co., Crosman
Beretta S.P.A., Pietro
Beretta U.S.A. Corp.
Big Bear Arms & Sporting Goods, Inc.
Bill Hanus Birdguns, LLC
Bill Russ Trading Post
Bond Arms, Inc.
Borden Ridges Rimrock Stocks
Borden Rifles Inc.
Brockman's Custom Gunsmithing
Brown Products, Inc., Ed
Browning Arms Co.
Bryan & Assoc.
Bushmaster Firearms, Inc.
C. Sharps Arms Co. Inc./Montana Armory
Cabela's
Cache La Poudre Rifleworks
Calico Light Weapon Systems
Cambos Outdoorsman
Cape Outfitters
Casull Arms Corp.
CCL Security Products
Century Gun Dist. Inc.
Champlin Firearms, Inc.
Charter 2000
Cobra Enterprises, Inc.
Colt's Mfg. Co., Inc.
Competitor Corp., Inc.
Competitor Corp., Inc.
Conetrol Scope Mounts
Connecticut Shotgun Mfg. Co.
Connecticut Valley Classics (See CVC, BPI)
Cooper Arms
Crosman Airguns
Cumberland Arms
Cumberland Mountain Arms
CVA
Daisy Outdoor Products
Dakota Arms, Inc.
Dan Wesson Firearms
Dayton Traister
Detonics USA
Dixie Gun Works
Downsizer Corp.
DS Arms, Inc.
DunLyon R&D, Inc.
E&L Mfg., Inc.
E. Arthur Brown Co. Inc.
Eagle Arms, Inc. (See ArmaLite, Inc.)
Ed Brown Products, Inc.
Ellett Bros.
Emerging Technologies, Inc. (See Laseraim Technologies, Inc.)
Empire Rifles
Entreprise Arms, Inc.
Essex Arms
Excel Industries, Inc.
Firearm Brokers
Fletcher-Bidwell, LLC
FN Manufacturing
Freedom Arms, Inc.
Fulton Armory
Galena Industries AMT
Garcia National Gun Traders, Inc.
Gary Reeder Custom Guns
Genecco Gun Works
Gentry Custom LLC
George Hoenig, Inc.
Gibbs Rifle Co., Inc.
Gil Hebard Guns, Inc.
Gilbert Equipment Co., Inc.
Goergen's Gun Shop, Inc.
Granite Mountain Arms, Inc.
Grayback Wildcats
Gun Room Press, The
Gun Works, The
Guncrafter Industries
H&R 1871.LLC
Hammans, Charles E.
Hammerli USA
Harrington & Richardson (See H&R 1871, Inc.)
Hart & Son, Inc.
Hatfield Gun
Hawken Shop, The (See Dayton Traister)
Heritage Firearms (See Heritage Mfg., Inc.)
Heritage Manufacturing, Inc.
Hesco-Meprolight
High Precision
High Standard Mfg. Co./F.I., Inc.
Hi-Point Firearms/MKS Supply
HJS Arms, Inc.
H-S Precision, Inc.
Hutton Rifle Ranch
IAR Inc.
Imperial Miniature Armory
Israel Arms Inc.
Ithaca Classic Doubles
Ithaca Gun Company LLC
Jim Norman Custom Gunstocks
John Rigby & Co.
John's Custom Leather
JP Enterprises, Inc.
K.B.I. Inc.
Kahr Arms
Kehr, Roger
Kelbly, Inc.
Kel-Tec CNC Industries, Inc.
Keystone Sporting Arms, Inc. (Crickett Rifles)
Kimber of America, Inc.
Knight Rifles
Knight's Manufacturing Co.
Kolar
L.A.R. Mfg., Inc.
LaFrance Specialties
Lakefield Arms Ltd. (See Savage Arms, Inc.)
Laseraim Technologies, Inc.
Les Baer Custom, Inc.
Lever Arms Service Ltd.
Ljutic Industries, Inc.
Lock's Philadelphia Gun Exchange
Lomont Precision Bullets
Lone Star Rifle Company
Mag-Na-Port International, Inc.
Magnum Research, Inc.
Mandall Shooting Supply Inc.
Marlin Firearms Co.
Marshall Fish Mfg. Gunsmith Sptg. Co.
Mathews Gun Shop & Gunsmithing, Inc.
Maverick Arms, Inc.
McCann Industries
Meacham Tool & Hardware Co., Inc.
Mid-America Recreation, Inc.
Miller Arms, Inc.
MKS Supply, Inc. (See Hi-Point Firearms)
MOA Corporation
Montana Armory, Inc.
MPI Stocks
Navy Arms Company
NCP Products, Inc.
New Ultra Light Arms, LLC
Noreen, Peter H.
North American Arms, Inc.
North Star West
Northwest Arms
Nowlin Mfg. Co.
Olympic Arms Inc.
Oregon Arms, Inc. (See Rogue Rifle Co., Inc.)
P&M Sales & Services, LLC
Parker & Sons Shooting Supply
Parker Gun Finishes
Phillips & Rogers, Inc.
Phoenix Arms
Precision Small Arms Inc.
ProWare, Inc.
Rapine Bullet Mould Mfg. Co.
Remington Arms Co., Inc.
Rifles, Inc.
Robinson Armament Co.
Rock River Arms
Rocky Mountain Arms, Inc.
Rogue Rifle Co., Inc.
Rogue River Rifleworks
Rohrbaugh
Romain's Custom Guns, Inc.
RPM
Ruger (See Sturm Ruger & Co., Inc.)
Safari Arms/Schuetzen Pistol Works
Savage Arms (Canada), Inc.
Schumakers Gun Shop
Searcy Enterprises
Sharps Arms Co., Inc., C.
Sigarms Inc.
Sklany's Machine Shop
Small Arms Specialists
Smith & Wesson
Sound Tech Silencers
Spencer's Rifle Barrels, Inc.
Springfield Armory
Springfield, Inc.
SSK Industries
STI International
Stoeger Industries
Strayer-Voigt, Inc.
Sturm Ruger & Co. Inc.
Sunny Hill Enterprises, Inc.
T&S Industries, Inc.
Taconic Firearms Ltd., Perry Lane
Tank's Rifle Shop
Tar-Hunt Custom Rifles, Inc.
Taurus Firearms, Inc.
Taylor's & Co., Inc.
Texas Armory (See Bond Arms, Inc.)
Thompson/Center Arms
Time Precision
Tristar Sporting Arms, Ltd.
U.S. Repeating Arms Co., Inc.
Uselton/Arms, Inc.
Vector Arms, Inc.
Visible Impact Targets
Volquartsen Custom Ltd.
Wallace, Terry
Weatherby, Inc.
Wescombe, Bill (See North Star West)
Wessinger Custom Guns & Engraving
Whildin & Sons Ltd., E.H.
Whitestone Lumber Corp.
Wichita Arms, Inc.
Wildey F. A., Inc.
Wilsom Combat
Winchester Consultants
Z-M Weapons

GUNSMITH SCHOOL

American Gunsmithing Institute
Colorado Gunsmithing Academy
Colorado School of Trades
Cylinder & Slide, Inc., William R. Laughridge
Gun Doc, Inc.
Lassen Community College, Gunsmithing Dept.
Laughridge, William R. (See Cylinder & Slide, Inc.)
Log Cabin Sport Shop
Modern Gun Repair School
Murray State College
North American Correspondence Schools, The Gun Pro
Nowlin Mfg. Co.
NRI Gunsmith School
Pennsylvania Gunsmith School
Piedmont Community College
Pine Technical College
Professional Gunsmiths of America
Smith & Wesson
Southeastern Community College
Spencer's Rifle Barrels, Inc.
Trinidad St. Jr. Col. Gunsmith Dept.
Wright's Gunstock Blanks
Yavapai College

GUNSMITH SUPPLIES, TOOLS & SERVICES

A.W. Peterson Gun Shop, Inc., The
Actions by "T" Teddy Jacobson
Alaskan Silversmith, The
Aldis Gunsmithing & Shooting Supply
Alley Supply Co.
Allred Bullet Co.
Alpec Team, Inc.
American Gunsmithing Institute
Ballard Rifle & Cartridge Co., LLC
Bar-Sto Precision Machine
Battenfeld Technologies, Inc.
Bauska Barrels
Bear Mountain Gun & Tool
Bengtson Arms Co., L.
Bill's Gun Repair
Blue Ridge Machinery & Tools, Inc.
Boyds' Gunstock Industries, Inc.
Briley Mfg. Inc.
Brockman's Custom Gunsmithing
Brown Products, Inc., Ed
Brownells, Inc.
Bryan & Assoc.
B-Square Company, Inc.
Buffer Technologies
Bushmaster Firearms, Inc.
C.S. Van Gorden & Son, Inc.
Cain's Outdoors, Inc.
Carbide Checkering Tools (See J&R Engineering)
Caywood, Shane J.
CBC-BRAZIL
Chapman Manufacturing Co.
Chicasaw Gun Works
Chip McCormick Corp.
Choate Machine & Tool Co., Inc.
Colonial Arms, Inc.
Colorado School of Trades
Colt's Mfg. Co., Inc.
Conetrol Scope Mounts
Corbin Mfg. & Supply, Inc.
Cousin Bob's Mountain Products
CRR, Inc./Marble's Inc.
Cumberland Arms
Cumberland Mountain Arms
Custom Checkering Service, Kathy Forster
Dan's Whetstone Co., Inc.
D'Arcy Echols & Co.
Dem-Bart Checkering Tools, Inc.
Dem-Bart Checkering Tools, Inc.
Dixie Gun Works
Dixie Gun Works
Dremel Mfg. Co.
Du-Lite Corp.
Entreprise Arms, Inc.
Erhardt, Dennis
Evolution Gun Works, Inc.
Faith Associates
FERLIB
Fisher, Jerry A.
Forgreens Tool & Mfg., Inc.
Forster, Kathy (See Custom Checkering)

PRODUCT & SERVICE DIRECTORY

Forster Products, Inc.
Gentry Custom LLC
Gilmore Sports Concepts, Inc.
Grace Metal Products
Gre-Tan Rifles
Gruning Precision, Inc.
Gun Works, The
Gunline Tools
Half Moon Rifle Shop
Hammond Custom Guns Ltd.
Hastings
Henriksen Tool Co., Inc.
High Performance International
High Precision
Holland's Gunsmithing
Import Sports Inc.
Ironsighter Co.
Israel Arms Inc.
Ivanoff, Thomas G. (See Tom's Gun Repair)
J&R Engineering
J&S Heat Treat
J. Dewey Mfg. Co., Inc.
Jantz Supply
Jenkins Recoil Pads
JGS Precision Tool Mfg., LLC
Jonathan Arthur Ciener, Inc.
Jones Custom Products, Neil A.
Kailua Custom Guns Inc.
Kasenit Co., Inc.
Kleinendorst, K. W.
Korzinek Riflesmith, J.
L. E. Jurras & Assoc.
LaBounty Precision Reboring, Inc
LaFrance Specialties
Laurel Mountain Forge
Lee Supplies, Mark
List Precision Engineering
Lock's Philadelphia Gun Exchange
London Guns Ltd.
Mahovsky's Metalife
Marble Arms (See CRR, Inc./Marble's Inc.)
Mark Lee Supplies
Marsh, Mike
Martin's Gun Shop
McFarland, Stan
Menck, Gunsmith Inc., T.W.
Metalife Industries (See Mahovsky's Metalife)
Micro Sight Co.
Midway Arms, Inc.
MMC
Mo's Competitor Supplies (See MCS, Inc.)
Mowrey's Guns & Gunsmithing
Neil A. Jones Custom Products
New England Custom Gun Service
NgraveR Co., The
Ole Frontier Gunsmith Shop
Olympic Arms Inc.
Parker & Sons Shooting Supply
Parker Gun Finishes
Parker Gun Finishes
Paulsen Gunstocks
PEM's Mfg. Co.
Perazone-Gunsmith, Brian
Peter Dyson & Son Ltd.
Power Custom, Inc.
Practical Tools, Inc.
Precision Specialties
R.A. Wells Custom Gunsmith
Ranch Products
Ransom International Corp.
Reardon Products
Rice, Keith (See White Rock Tool & Die)
Richards MicroFit Stocks, Inc.
Robar Co., Inc., The
Rocky Mountain Arms, Inc.
Romain's Custom Guns, Inc.
Royal Arms Gunstocks
Rusteprufe Laboratories
Score High Gunsmithing
Sharp Shooter Supply
Shooter's Choice Gun Care
Simmons Gun Repair, Inc.
Smith Abrasives, Inc.
Southern Bloomer Mfg. Co.
Spencer Reblue Service
Spencer's Rifle Barrels, Inc.
Spradlin's
Starr Trading Co., Jedediah
Starrett Co., L. S.
Stiles Custom Guns
Stoney Point Products, Inc.
Sullivan, David S. (See Westwind Rifles, Inc.)
Sunny Hill Enterprises, Inc.
T&S Industries, Inc.
T.W. Menck Gunsmith, Inc.
Tank's Rifle Shop
Tar-Hunt Custom Rifles, Inc.
Texas Platers Supply Co.
Theis, Terry
Tom's Gun Repair, Thomas G. Ivanoff
Track of the Wolf, Inc.
Trinidad St. Jr. Col. Gunsmith Dept.
Trulock Tool
Turnbull Restoration, Doug
United States Products Co.
Van Gorden & Son Inc., C. S.
Venco Industries, Inc. (See Shooter's Choice Gun Care)
W.C. Wolff Co.
Warne Manufacturing Co.
Washita Mountain Whetstone Co.
Weigand Combat Handguns, Inc.
Wessinger Custom Guns & Engraving
White Rock Tool & Die
Wilcox All-Pro Tools & Supply
Wild West Guns
Will-Burt Co.
Williams Gun Sight Co.
Williams Shootin' Iron Service, The Lynx-Line
Willow Bend
Windish, Jim
Wise Guns, Dale
Wright's Gunstock Blanks
Yavapai College
Ziegel Engineering

HANDGUN ACCESSORIES

"Su-Press-On", Inc.
A.A. Arms, Inc.
A.W. Peterson Gun Shop, Inc., The
Action Direct, Inc.
ADCO Sales, Inc.
Advantage Arms, Inc.
Aimtech Mount Systems
Ajax Custom Grips, Inc.
Alpha 1 Drop Zone
American Derringer Corp.
Arms Corporation of the Philippines
Astra Sport, S.A.
Autauga Arms, Inc.
Bagmaster Mfg., Inc.
Bar-Sto Precision Machine
Behlert Precision, Inc.
Berry's Mfg., Inc.
Blue and Gray Products Inc. (See Ox-Yoke Originals)
Bond Custom Firearms
Bowen Classic Arms Corp.
Bridgeman Products
Broken Gun Ranch
Brooks Tactical Systems-Agrip
Brown Products, Inc., Ed
Bushmaster Hunting & Fishing
Butler Creek Corp.
Cannon Safe, Inc.
Centaur Systems, Inc.
Central Specialties Ltd. (See Trigger Lock Division)
Charter 2000
Cheyenne Pioneer Products
Chicasaw Gun Works
Clark Custom Guns, Inc.
Classic Arms Company
Concealment Shop, Inc., The
Conetrol Scope Mounts
Crimson Trace Lasers
CRR, Inc./Marble's Inc.
Cylinder & Slide, Inc., William R. Laughridge
D&L Industries (See D.J. Marketing)
D.J. Marketing
Dade Screw Machine Products
Dan Wesson Firearms
Delhi Gun House
DeSantis Holster & Leather Goods, Inc.
Dixie Gun Works
Doskocil Mfg. Co., Inc.
E&L Mfg., Inc.
E. Arthur Brown Co. Inc.
E.A.A. Corp.
Eagle Imports, Inc.
Ed Brown Products, Inc.
Essex Arms
European American Armory Corp. (See E.A.A. Corp.)
Evolution Gun Works, Inc.
Falcon Industries, Inc.
Feinwerkbau Westinger & Altenburger
Fisher Custom Firearms
Fleming Firearms
Freedom Arms, Inc.
G.G. & G.
Galati International
GALCO International Ltd.
Garcia National Gun Traders, Inc.
Garthwaite Pistolsmith, Inc., Jim
Gil Hebard Guns, Inc.
Gilmore Sports Concepts, Inc.
Glock, Inc.
Gould & Goodrich Leather, Inc.
Gun Works, The
Gun-Alert
Gun-Ho Sports Cases
H.K.S. Products
Hafner World Wide, Inc.
Hammerli USA
Heinie Specialty Products
Henigson & Associates, Steve
High Standard Mfg. Co./F.I., Inc.
Hill Speed Leather, Ernie
HIP-GRIP Barami Corp.
Hi-Point Firearms/MKS Supply
Hobson Precision Mfg. Co.
Hoppe's Div. Penguin Industries, Inc.
H-S Precision, Inc.
Hume, Don
Hunter Co., Inc.
Impact Case & Container, Inc.
Import Sports Inc.
Jarvis, Inc.
JB Custom
Jeffredo Gunsight
Jim Noble Co.
John's Custom Leather
Jonathan Arthur Ciener, Inc.
JP Enterprises, Inc.
Kalispel Case Line
KeeCo Impressions, Inc.
Keller Co., The
King's Gun Works
KK Air International (See Impact Case & Container Co., Inc.)
Kolpin Outdoors, Inc.
L&S Technologies Inc. (See Aimtech Mount Systems)
Lakewood Products LLC
LaserMax, Inc.
Les Baer Custom, Inc.
Lock's Philadelphia Gun Exchange
Lohman Mfg. Co., Inc.
Mag-Na-Port International, Inc.
Mag-Pack Corp.
Mahony, Philip Bruce
Mandall Shooting Supply Inc.
Marble Arms (See CRR, Inc./Marble's Inc.)
Markell, Inc.
MEC-Gar S.R.L.
Menck, Gunsmith Inc., T.W.
Middlebrooks Custom Shop
Millett Sights
Mobile Area Networks, Inc.
Mogul Co./Life Jacket
MTM Molded Products Co., Inc.
No-Sho Mfg. Co.
Numrich Gun Parts Corporation
Omega Sales
Outdoor Sports Headquarters, Inc.
Ox-Yoke Originals, Inc.
Pachmayr Div. Lyman Products
Pager Pal
Parker & Sons Shooting Supply
Pearce Grip, Inc.
Phoenix Arms
Practical Tools, Inc.
Precision Small Arms Inc.
Protector Mfg. Co., Inc., The
Ram-Line ATK
Ranch Products
Ransom International Corp.
RPM
Simmons Gun Repair, Inc.
Southern Bloomer Mfg. Co.
Springfield Armory
Springfield, Inc.
SSK Industries
Sturm Ruger & Co. Inc.
T.F.C. S.p.A.
Tactical Defense Institute
Tanfoglio Fratelli S.r.l.
Thompson/Center Arms
Trigger Lock Division / Central Specialties Ltd.
Trijicon, Inc.
Triple-K Mfg. Co., Inc.
Truglo, Inc.
United States Products Co.
Universal Sports
Volquartsen Custom Ltd.
W. Waller & Son, Inc.
W.C. Wolff Co.
Warne Manufacturing Co.
Weigand Combat Handguns, Inc.
Wessinger Custom Guns & Engraving
Whitestone Lumber Corp.
Wichita Arms, Inc.
Wild West Guns
Williams Gun Sight Co.
Wilsom Combat
Yankee Gunsmith "Just Glocks"
Ziegel Engineering

HANDGUN GRIPS

A.A. Arms, Inc.
A.W. Peterson Gun Shop, Inc., The
African Import Co.
Ahrends Grips
Ahrends, Kim
Ajax Custom Grips, Inc.
Altamont Co.
American Derringer Corp.
Arms Corporation of the Philippines
Art Jewel Enterprises Ltd.
Baelder, Harry
Big Bear Arms & Sporting Goods, Inc.
Bob's Gun Shop
Boone Trading Co., Inc.
Boone's Custom Ivory Grips, Inc.
Boyds' Gunstock Industries, Inc.
Brooks Tactical Systems-Agrip
Brown Products, Inc., Ed
Clark Custom Guns, Inc.
Claro Walnut Gunstock Co.
Cole-Grip
Colonial Repair
Crimson Trace Lasers
Custom Firearms (See Ahrends, Kim)
Cylinder & Slide, Inc., William R. Laughridge
Dixie Gun Works
Dolbare, Elizabeth
E.A.A. Corp.
Eagle Imports, Inc.
EMF Co. Inc.
Essex Arms
European American Armory Corp. (See E.A.A. Corp.)
Falcon Industries, Inc.
Feinwerkbau Westinger & Altenburger
Fibron Products, Inc.
Fisher Custom Firearms
Garthwaite Pistolsmith, Inc., Jim
Goodwin's Guns
Herrett's Stocks, Inc.
High Standard Mfg. Co./F.I., Inc.
HIP-GRIP Barami Corp.
Hogue Grips
H-S Precision, Inc.
Huebner, Corey O.
International Shooters Service
Israel Arms Inc.
John Masen Co. Inc.
KeeCo Impressions, Inc.
Korth Germany GmbH
Les Baer Custom, Inc.
Lett Custom Grips
Linebaugh Custom Sixguns
Lyman Products Corp.
Mandall Shooting Supply Inc.
Michaels of Oregon Co.
Millett Sights
Mobile Area Networks, Inc.
N.C. Ordnance Co.
Newell, Robert H.
Northern Precision
Pachmayr Div. Lyman Products
Pardini Armi Srl
Parker & Sons Shooting Supply
Pearce Grip, Inc.
Precision Small Arms Inc.
Radical Concepts
Robinson, Don
Rosenberg & Son, Jack A.
Roy's Custom Grips
Spegel, Craig
Stoeger Industries
Sturm Ruger & Co. Inc.
Sunny Hill Enterprises, Inc.
Tactical Defense Institute
Taurus Firearms, Inc.
Tirelli
Tom Forrest, Inc.
Triple-K Mfg. Co., Inc.
Uncle Mike's (See Michaels of Oregon, Co.)
Volquartsen Custom Ltd.
Western Mfg. Co.
Whitestone Lumber Corp.
Wright's Gunstock Blanks

HEARING PROTECTORS

A.W. Peterson Gun Shop, Inc., The
Aero Peltor
Ajax Custom Grips, Inc.
Browning Arms Co.
Creedmoor Sports, Inc.
David Clark Co., Inc.
Dillon Precision Products, Inc.
Dixie Gun Works
E-A-R, Inc.
Electronic Shooters Protection, Inc.
Gentex Corp.
Gun Room Press, The
Gunsmithing, Inc.
Hoppe's Div. Penguin Industries, Inc.
Kesselring Gun Shop
Mandall Shooting Supply Inc.
Mobile Area Networks, Inc.
Parker & Sons Shooting Supply
Paterson Gunsmithing
Peltor, Inc. (See Aero Peltor)
R.E.T. Enterprises
Ridgeline, Inc.
Rucker Dist. Inc.
Silencio/Safety Direct
Tactical Defense Institute
Triple-K Mfg. Co., Inc.
Watson Bullets
Whitestone Lumber Corp.

PRODUCT & SERVICE DIRECTORY

HOLSTERS & LEATHER GOODS

A.A. Arms, Inc.
A.W. Peterson Gun Shop, Inc., The
Action Direct, Inc.
Action Products, Inc.
Aker International, Inc.
AKJ Concealco
Alessi Holsters, Inc.
Arratoonian, Andy (See Horseshoe Leather Products)
Autauga Arms, Inc.
Bagmaster Mfg., Inc.
Baker's Leather Goods, Roy
Bandcor Industries, Div. of Man-Sew Corp.
Bang-Bang Boutique (See Holster Shop, The)
Beretta S.P.A., Pietro
Bianchi International, Inc.
Bond Arms, Inc.
Brooks Tactical Systems-Agrip
Browning Arms Co.
Bull-X, Inc.
Cape Outfitters
Cathey Enterprises, Inc.
Chace Leather Products
Churchill Glove Co., James
Cimarron F.A. Co.
Classic Old West Styles
Clements' Custom Leathercraft, Chas
Cobra Sport S.R.I.
Collector's Armoury, Ltd.
Colonial Repair
Counter Assault
Delhi Gun House
DeSantis Holster & Leather Goods, Inc.
Dillon Precision Products, Inc.
Dixie Gun Works
Eagle Imports, Inc.
Ekol Leather Care
El Paso Saddlery Co.
Ellett Bros.
EMF Co. Inc.
Faust Inc., T. G.
Freedom Arms, Inc.
Gage Manufacturing
GALCO International Ltd.
Garcia National Gun Traders, Inc.
Gil Hebard Guns, Inc.
Gilmore Sports Concepts, Inc.
GML Products, Inc.
Gould & Goodrich Leather, Inc.
Gun Leather Limited
Gun Works, The
Hafner World Wide, Inc.
HandCrafts Unltd. (See Clements' Custom Leathercraft)
Hank's Gun Shop
Heinie Specialty Products
Henigson & Associates, Steve
Hill Speed Leather, Ernie
HIP-GRIP Barami Corp.
Hobson Precision Mfg. Co.
Hogue Grips
Horseshoe Leather Products
Hume, Don
Hunter Co., Inc.
Import Sports Inc.
Jim Noble Co.
John's Custom Leather
Keller Co., The
Kirkpatrick Leather Co.
Kolpin Outdoors, Inc.
Korth Germany GmbH
Kramer Handgun Leather
L.A.R. Mfg., Inc.
Lawrence Leather Co.
Lock's Philadelphia Gun Exchange
Lone Star Gunleather
Mandall Shooting Supply Inc.
Markell, Inc.
Marksman Products
Michaels of Oregon Co.
Minute Man High Tech Industries
Navy Arms Company
No-Sho Mfg. Co.
Null Holsters Ltd. K.L.
October Country Muzzleloading
Oklahoma Leather Products, Inc.
Old West Reproductions, Inc. R.M. Bachman
Outdoor Connection, Inc., The
Pager Pal
Parker & Sons Shooting Supply
Pathfinder Sports Leather
Protektor Model
PWL Gunleather
Ramon B. Gonzalez Guns
Renegade
Ringler Custom Leather Co.
Rogue Rifle Co., Inc.
S&S Firearms
Safariland Ltd., Inc.
Scharch Mfg., Inc.-Top Brass
Schulz Industries
Second Chance Body Armor
Silhouette Leathers
Smith Saddlery, Jesse W.
Sparks, Milt
Stalker, Inc.
Starr Trading Co., Jedediah
Strong Holster Co.
Stuart, V. Pat
Tabler Marketing
Tactical Defense Institute
Ted Blocker Holsters, Inc.
Tex Shoemaker & Sons, Inc.
Thad Rybka Custom Leather Equipment
Torel, Inc./Tandy Brands Outdoors/AA & E
Triple-K Mfg. Co., Inc.
Tristar Sporting Arms, Ltd.
Uncle Mike's (See Michaels of Oregon, Co.)
Venus Industries
W. Waller & Son, Inc.
Walt's Custom Leather, Walt Whinnery
Watson Bullets
Westley Richards & Co. Ltd.
Whinnery, Walt (See Walt's Custom Leather)
Wild Bill's Originals
Wilsom Combat

KNIVES & KNIFEMAKER'S SUPPLIES

A.G. Russell Knives, Inc.
A.W. Peterson Gun Shop, Inc., The
Action Direct, Inc.
Adventure 16, Inc.
African Import Co.
Aitor-Cuchilleria Del Norte S.A.
American Target Knives
Art Jewel Enterprises Ltd.
Atlanta Cutlery Corp.
B&D Trading Co., Inc.
Barteaux Machete
Benchmark Knives (See Gerber Legendary Blades)
Beretta S.P.A., Pietro
Beretta U.S.A. Corp.
Big Bear Arms & Sporting Goods, Inc.
Bill Russ Trading Post
Boker USA, Inc.
Boone Trading Co., Inc.
Boone's Custom Ivory Grips, Inc.
Bowen Knife Co., Inc.
Brooks Tactical Systems-Agrip
Browning Arms Co.
Buck Knives, Inc.
Buster's Custom Knives
Cain's Outdoors, Inc.
Camillus Cutlery Co.
Campbell, Dick
Case & Sons Cutlery Co., W R
Chicago Cutlery Co.
Claro Walnut Gunstock Co.
Clements' Custom Leathercraft, Chas
Cold Steel Inc.
Coleman Co., Inc.
Collector's Armoury, Ltd.
Compass Industries, Inc.
Creative Craftsman, Inc., The
Crosman Blades (See Coleman Co., Inc.)
CRR, Inc./Marble's Inc.
Cutco Cutlery
damascususa@inteliport.com
Dan's Whetstone Co., Inc.
Deepeeka Exports Pvt. Ltd.
Delhi Gun House
DeSantis Holster & Leather Goods, Inc.
Diamond Machining Technology Inc. (See DMT)
Dixie Gun Works
Dolbare, Elizabeth
EdgeCraft Corp., S. Weiner
Empire Cutlery Corp.
Eze-Lap Diamond Prods.
Flitz International Ltd.
Forrest Tool Co.
Forthofer's Gunsmithing & Knifemaking
Fortune Products, Inc.
Frank Knives
Frost Cutlery Co.
Galati International
George Ibberson (Sheffield) Ltd.
Gerber Legendary Blades
Glock, Inc.
Golden Age Arms Co.
Gun Room, The
Gun Works, The
H&B Forge Co.
Hafner World Wide, Inc.
Hammans, Charles E.
HandCrafts Unltd. (See Clements' Custom Leathercraft)
Harris Publications
High North Products, Inc.
Hoppe's Div. Penguin Industries, Inc.
Hunter Co., Inc.
Imperial Schrade Corp.
J.A. Blades, Inc. (See Christopher Firearms Co.)
J.A. Henckels Zwillingswerk Inc.
Jackalope Gun Shop
Jantz Supply
Jenco Sales, Inc.
Jim Blair Engraving
Johnson Wood Products
KA-BAR Knives
Kasenit Co., Inc.
Kershaw Knives
Knifeware, Inc.
Koval Knives
Lamson & Goodnow Mfg. Co.
Lansky Sharpeners
Leapers, Inc.
Leatherman Tool Group, Inc.
Lethal Force Institute (See Police Bookshelf)
Linder Solingen Knives
Mandall Shooting Supply Inc.
Marble Arms (See CRR, Inc./Marble's Inc.)
Marshall Fish Mfg. Gunsmith Sptg. Co.
Matthews Cutlery
McCann Industries
Normark Corp.
October Country Muzzleloading
Outdoor Edge Cutlery Corp.
Plaza Cutlery, Inc.
Police Bookshelf
Queen Cutlery Co.
R&C Knives & Such
R. Murphy Co., Inc.
Randall-Made Knives
Ringler Custom Leather Co.
Robert Valade Engraving
Scansport, Inc.
Schiffman, Mike
Sheffield Knifemakers Supply, Inc.
Smith Saddlery, Jesse W.
Springfield Armory
Spyderco, Inc.
T.F.C. S.p.A.
Theis, Terry
Traditions Performance Firearms
Traditions Performance Firearms
Tru-Balance Knife Co.
Tru-Nord Compass
United Cutlery Corp.
Utica Cutlery Co.
Venus Industries
W.R. Case & Sons Cutlery Co.
Washita Mountain Whetstone Co.
Wells Creek Knife & Gun Works
Wenger North America/Precise Int'l.
Western Cutlery (See Camillus Cutlery Co.)
Whinnery, Walt (See Walt's Custom Leather)
Wideview Scope Mount Corp.
Wyoming Knife Corp.

LABELS, BOXES & CARTRIDGE HOLDERS

Ballistic Products, Inc.
Berry's Mfg., Inc.
Cabinet Mtn. Outfitters Scents & Lures
Cheyenne Pioneer Products
Del Rey Products
DeSantis Holster & Leather Goods, Inc.
Flambeau, Inc.
Hafner World Wide, Inc.
J&J Products, Inc.
Kolpin Outdoors, Inc.
Liberty Shooting Supplies
Midway Arms, Inc.
MTM Molded Products Co., Inc.
Outdoor Connection, Inc., The
Pendleton Royal, c/o Swingler Buckland Ltd.
Ringler Custom Leather Co.
Walt's Custom Leather, Walt Whinnery
Ziegel Engineering

LEAD WIRES & WIRE CUTTERS

Ames Metal Products
Big Bore Express
Bullet Swaging Supply, Inc.
D.L. Unmussig Bullets
Liberty Metals
Lightning Performance Innovations, Inc.
Montana Precision Swaging
Northern Precision
Sport Flite Manufacturing Co.
Star Ammunition, Inc.

LOAD TESTING & PRODUCT TESTING

Ballistic Research
Bridgeman Products
Briese Bullet Co., Inc.
Buckskin Bullet Co.
Bull Mountain Rifle Co.
CFVentures
Claybuster Wads & Harvester Bullets
Clearview Products
D&H Precision Tooling
Dead Eye's Sport Center
Defense Training International, Inc.
Duane's Gun Repair (See DGR Custom Rifles)
Gruning Precision, Inc.
H.P. White Laboratory, Inc.
Hank's Gun Shop
Henigson & Associates, Steve
Hutton Rifle Ranch
J&J Sales
Jackalope Gun Shop
Jensen Bullets
Jonathan Arthur Ciener, Inc.
L. E. Jurras & Assoc.
Liberty Shooting Supplies
Linebaugh Custom Sixguns
Lomont Precision Bullets
MAST Technology, Inc.
McMurdo, Lynn
Middlebrooks Custom Shop
Modern Gun Repair School
Multiplex International
Northwest Arms
Oil Rod and Gun Shop
Plum City Ballistic Range
R.A. Wells Custom Gunsmith
Rupert's Gun Shop
SOS Products Co. (See Buck Stix-SOS Products Co.)
Spencer's Rifle Barrels, Inc.
Tar-Hunt Custom Rifles, Inc.
Trinidad St. Jr. Col. Gunsmith Dept.
Vulpes Ventures, Inc., Fox Cartridge Division
W. Square Enterprises
X-Spand Target Systems

LOADING BLOCKS, METALLIC & SHOTSHELL

A.W. Peterson Gun Shop, Inc., The
Battenfeld Technologies, Inc.
Buffalo Arms Co.
Huntington Die Specialties
Jericho Tool & Die Co., Inc.
Sinclair International, Inc.

LUBRISIZERS, DIES & ACCESSORIES

A.W. Peterson Gun Shop, Inc., The
Ballisti-Cast, Inc.
Buffalo Arms Co.
Cast Performance Bullet Company
Cooper-Woodward Perfect Lube
Corbin Mfg. & Supply, Inc.
GAR
Hart & Son, Inc.
Javelina Lube Products
Lee Precision, Inc.
Lithi Bee Bullet Lube
Lyman Products Corp.
Magma Engineering Co.
PWM Sales Ltd.
RCBS Operations/ATK
S&S Firearms
SPG LLC
Thompson Bullet Lube Co.
United States Products Co.
WTA Manufacturing

MOULDS & MOULD ACCESSORIES

A.W. Peterson Gun Shop, Inc., The
Ad Hominem
American Products, Inc.
Ballisti-Cast, Inc.
Buffalo Arms Co.
Bullet Swaging Supply, Inc.
Cast Performance Bullet Company
Corbin Mfg. & Supply, Inc.
Davide Pedersoli and Co.
GAR
Gun Works, The
Huntington Die Specialties
Lee Precision, Inc.
Lyman Products Corp.
Magma Engineering Co.
Mobile Area Networks, Inc.

PRODUCT & SERVICE DIRECTORY

Old West Bullet Moulds
Pacific Rifle Co.
Penn Bullets
Peter Dyson & Son Ltd.
Rapine Bullet Mould Mfg. Co.
RCBS Operations/ATK
S&S Firearms

MUZZLE-LOADING GUNS, BARRELS & EQUIPMENT

A.W. Peterson Gun Shop, Inc., The
Accuracy Unlimited
Ackerman & Co.
Adkins, Luther
Allen Mfg.
Armi San Paolo
Armoury, Inc., The
Austin & Halleck, Inc.
Bauska Barrels
Bentley, John
Big Bore Express
Birdsong & Assoc., W. E.
Black Powder Products
Blount/Outers ATK
Blue and Gray Products Inc. (See Ox-Yoke Originals)
Bridgers Best
Buckskin Bullet Co.
Bullberry Barrel Works, Ltd.
Butler Creek Corp.
Cabela's
Cache La Poudre Rifleworks
Cain's Outdoors, Inc.
California Sights (See Fautheree, Andy)
Cash Mfg. Co., Inc.
Caywood Gunmakers
CBC-BRAZIL
Chambers Flintlocks Ltd., Jim
Chicasaw Gun Works
Cimarron F.A. Co.
Claybuster Wads & Harvester Bullets
Cogar's Gunsmithing
Colonial Repair
Colt Blackpowder Arms Co.
Conetrol Scope Mounts
Cousin Bob's Mountain Products
Cumberland Arms
Cumberland Mountain Arms
Curly Maple Stock Blanks (See Tiger-Hunt)
CVA
Dangler, Homer L.
Davide Pedersoli and Co.
Dayton Traister
deHaas Barrels
Delhi Gun House
Dixie Gun Works
Dixie Gun Works
Dixon Muzzleloading Shop, Inc.
Dolbare, Elizabeth
Ellett Bros.
EMF Co. Inc.
Euroarms of America, Inc.
Flintlocks, Etc.
Fort Hill Gunstocks
Fowler, Bob (See Black Powder Products)
Frontier
Getz Barrel Company
Goergen's Gun Shop, Inc.
Golden Age Arms Co.
Gonic Arms North American Arms, Inc.
Green Mountain Rifle Barrel Co., Inc.
Gun Works, The
H&R 1871.LLC
Hastings
Hawken Shop, The
Hawken Shop, The (See Dayton Traister)
Hege Jagd-u. Sporthandels GmbH
Hodgdon Powder Co.
Hoppe's Div. Penguin Industries, Inc.
Hornady Mfg. Co.
House of Muskets, Inc., The
Hunkeler, A. (See Buckskin Machine Works)
IAR Inc.
Impact Case & Container, Inc.
Ironsighter Co.
J. Dewey Mfg. Co., Inc.
Jamison's Forge Works
Jones Co., Dale
K&M Industries, Inc.
Kalispel Case Line
Kennedy Firearms
Knight Rifles
Knight Rifles (See Modern Muzzleloading, Inc.)
Kolar
L&R Lock Co.
L&S Technologies Inc. (See Aimtech Mount Systems)
Lakewood Products LLC
Lodgewood Mfg.
Log Cabin Sport Shop
Lothar Walther Precision Tool Inc.
Lyman Products Corp.
Markesbery Muzzle Loaders, Inc.
Mathews Gun Shop & Gunsmithing, Inc.
McCann, Tom
Michaels of Oregon Co.
Millennium Designed Muzzleloaders
Modern Muzzleloading, Inc.
Mowrey Gun Works
Navy Arms Company
Newman Gunshop
North Star West
October Country Muzzleloading
Oklahoma Leather Products, Inc.
Olson, Myron
Orion Rifle Barrel Co.
Ox-Yoke Originals, Inc.
Pacific Rifle Co.
Parker & Sons Shooting Supply
Parker Gun Finishes
Pecatonica River Longrifle
Peter Dyson & Son Ltd.
Pioneer Arms Co.
Prairie River Arms
Rossi Firearms
Rusty Duck Premium Gun Care Products
S&S Firearms
Selsi Co., Inc.
Simmons Gun Repair, Inc.
Sklany's Machine Shop
Smokey Valley Rifles
South Bend Replicas, Inc.
Southern Bloomer Mfg. Co.
Splitfire Sporting Goods, L.L.C.
Starr Trading Co., Jedediah
Stone Mountain Arms
Sturm Ruger & Co. Inc.
Taylor's & Co., Inc.
Tennessee Valley Mfg.
Thompson Bullet Lube Co.
Thompson/Center Arms
Track of the Wolf, Inc.
Traditions Performance Firearms
Truglo, Inc.
Uncle Mike's (See Michaels of Oregon, Co.)
Universal Sports
Upper Missouri Trading Co.
Venco Industries, Inc. (See Shooter's Choice Gun Care)
Village Restorations & Consulting, Inc.
Virgin Valley Custom Guns
Voere-KGH GmbH
W.E. Birdsong & Assoc.
Warne Manufacturing Co.
Warren Muzzleloading Co., Inc.
Wescombe, Bill (See North Star West)
White Rifles, Inc.
William E. Phillips Firearms
Woodworker's Supply
Wright's Gunstock Blanks
Young Country Arms
Ziegel Engineering

PISTOLSMITH

A.W. Peterson Gun Shop, Inc.
A.W. Peterson Gun Shop, Inc., The
Acadian Ballistic Specialties
Accuracy Unlimited
Actions by "T" Teddy Jacobson
Adair Custom Shop, Bill
Ahlman Guns
Ahrends, Kim
Aldis Gunsmithing & Shooting Supply
Alpha Precision, Inc.
Alpine Indoor Shooting Range
Armament Gunsmithing Co., Inc.
Arundel Arms & Ammunition, Inc., A.
Bain & Davis, Inc.
Bar-Sto Precision Machine
Behlert Precision, Inc.
Bengtson Arms Co., L.
Bill Adair Custom Shop
Billings Gunsmiths
Bob Rogers Gunsmithing
Bowen Classic Arms Corp.
Broken Gun Ranch
Caraville Manufacturing
Chicasaw Gun Works
Chip McCormick Corp.
Clark Custom Guns, Inc.
Colonial Repair
Colorado School of Trades
Colt's Mfg. Co., Inc.
Corkys Gun Clinic
Custom Firearms (See Ahrends, Kim)
Cylinder & Slide, Inc., William R. Laughridge
D&D Gunsmiths, Ltd.
D&L Sports
David R. Chicoine
Dayton Traister
Dilliott Gunsmithing, Inc.
Ellicott Arms, Inc. / Woods Pistolsmithing
Evolution Gun Works, Inc.
Ferris Firearms
Firearm Brokers
Fisher Custom Firearms
Forkin Custom Classics
G.G. & G.
Garthwaite Pistolsmith, Inc., Jim
Gary Reeder Custom Guns
Genecco Gun Works
Gentry Custom LLC
Greider Precision
Gun Doc, Inc.
Gun Works, The
Guncraft Sports, Inc.
Guncraft Sports, Inc.
Gunsite Training Center
Hamilton, Alex B. (See Ten-Ring Precision, Inc.)
Hammerli Service-Precision Mac
Hammond Custom Guns Ltd.
Hank's Gun Shop
Hanson's Gun Center, Dick
Hawken Shop, The (See Dayton Traister)
Heinie Specialty Products
High Bridge Arms, Inc.
High Standard Mfg. Co./F.I., Inc.
Highline Machine Co.
Hoag, James W.
Irwin, Campbell H.
Ivanoff, Thomas G. (See Tom's Gun Repair)
J&S Heat Treat
Jarvis, Inc.
Jeffredo Gunsight
Jensen's Custom Ammunition
Jungkind, Reeves C.
Kaswer Custom, Inc.
Ken Starnes Gunmaker
Kilham & Co.
King's Gun Works
La Clinique du .45
LaFrance Specialties
LaRocca Gun Works
Lathrop's, Inc.
Lawson, John G. (See Sight Shop, The)
Leckie Professional Gunsmithing
Les Baer Custom, Inc.
Linebaugh Custom Sixguns
List Precision Engineering
Long, George F.
Mag-Na-Port International, Inc.
Mahony, Philip Bruce
Mahovsky's Metalife
Mandall Shooting Supply Inc.
Marvel, Alan
Mathews Gun Shop & Gunsmithing, Inc.
MCS, Inc.
Middlebrooks Custom Shop
Miller Custom
Mitchell's Accuracy Shop
MJK Gunsmithing, Inc.
Modern Gun Repair School
Mo's Competitor Supplies (See MCS, Inc.)
Mowrey's Guns & Gunsmithing
Mullis Guncraft
NCP Products, Inc.
Novak's, Inc.
Nowlin Mfg. Co.
Olathe Gun Shop
Paris, Frank J.
Pasadena Gun Center
Peacemaker Specialists
PEM's Mfg. Co.
Performance Specialists
Peterson Gun Shop, Inc., A.W.
Piquette's Custom Engraving
Power Custom, Inc.
Precision Specialties
Ramon B. Gonzalez Guns
Randco UK
Ries, Chuck
Rim Pac Sports, Inc.
Robar Co., Inc., The
Rocky Mountain Arms, Inc.
RPM
Ruger's Custom Guns
Score High Gunsmithing
Shooters Supply
Shootin' Shack
Sight Shop, The
Singletary, Kent
Springfield, Inc.
SSK Industries
Swenson's 45 Shop, A. D.
Swift River Gunworks
Ten-Ring Precision, Inc.
Terry K. Kopp Professional Gunsmithing
Time Precision
Tom's Gun Repair, Thomas G. Ivanoff
Turnbull Restoration, Doug
Vic's Gun Refinishing
Volquartsen Custom Ltd.
Walker Arms Co., Inc.
Walters Industries
Wardell Precision Handguns Ltd.
Wessinger Custom Guns & Engraving
White Barn Wor
Wichita Arms, Inc.
Wild West Guns
Williams Gun Sight Co.
Williamson Precision Gunsmithing
Wilson Combat
Wright's Gunstock Blanks

POWDER MEASURES, SCALES, FUNNELS & ACCESSORIES

4-D Custom Die Co.
A.W. Peterson Gun Shop, Inc., The
Battenfeld Technologies, Inc.
Buffalo Arms Co.
Cain's Outdoors, Inc.
Davide Pedersoli and Co.
Dillon Precision Products, Inc.
Fremont Tool Works
Frontier
GAR
High Precision
Hoehn Sales, Inc.
Jones Custom Products, Neil A.
Modern Muzzleloading, Inc.
Neil A. Jones Custom Products
Pacific Rifle Co.
Precision Reloading, Inc.
Ramon B. Gonzalez Guns
RCBS Operations/ATK
RCBS/ATK
Redding Reloading Equipment
Saunders Gun & Machine Shop
Schumakers Gun Shop
Spencer's Rifle Barrels, Inc.
Vega Tool Co.
VibraShine, Inc.
VTI Gun Parts

PRESS ACCESSORIES, METALLIC

A.W. Peterson Gun Shop, Inc., The
Buffalo Arms Co.
Corbin Mfg. & Supply, Inc.
Hollywood Engineering
Huntington Die Specialties
MA Systems, Inc.
R.E.I.
Redding Reloading Equipment
Royal Arms Gunstocks
Thompson Tool Mount
Vega Tool Co.

PRESS ACCESSORIES, SHOTSHELL

A.W. Peterson Gun Shop, Inc., The
Hollywood Engineering
Lee Precision, Inc.
MEC, Inc.
Precision Reloading, Inc.
R.E.I.

PRESSES, METALLIC

4-D Custom Die Co.
A.W. Peterson Gun Shop, Inc., The
Battenfeld Technologies, Inc.
Dillon Precision Products, Inc.
Fremont Tool Works
Hornady Mfg. Co.
Huntington Die Specialties
Lee Precision, Inc.
Meacham Tool & Hardware Co., Inc.
Midway Arms, Inc.
R.E.I.
Ramon B. Gonzalez Guns
RCBS Operations/ATK
RCBS/ATK
Spencer's Rifle Barrels, Inc.

PRESSES, SWAGE

A.W. Peterson Gun Shop, Inc., The
Ammo Load Worldwide, Inc.
Bullet Swaging Supply, Inc.
Howell Machine, Inc.

PRIMING TOOLS & ACCESSORIES

A.W. Peterson Gun Shop, Inc., The
Bald Eagle Precision Machine Co.
GAR
Hart & Son, Inc.
Huntington Die Specialties
K&M Services
RCBS Operations/ATK
Simmons, Jerry
Sinclair International, Inc.

PRODUCT & SERVICE DIRECTORY

REBORING & RERIFLING

Ahlman Guns
Barrel & Gunworks
Bauska Barrels
BlackStar AccuMax Barrels
BlackStar Barrel Accurizing (See BlackStar AccuMax)
Buffalo Arms Co.
Champlin Firearms, Inc.
Ed's Gun House
Fred F. Wells/Wells Sport Store
Gun Works, The
Ivanoff, Thomas G. (See Tom's Gun Repair)
Jackalope Gun Shop
Jonathan Arthur Ciener, Inc.
LaBounty Precision Reboring, Inc
NCP Products, Inc.
Pence Precision Barrels
Redman's Rifling & Reboring
Rice, Keith (See White Rock Tool & Die)
Ridgetop Sporting Goods
Savage Arms, Inc.
Shaw, Inc., E. R. (See Small Arms Mfg. Co.)
Siegrist Gun Shop
Simmons Gun Repair, Inc.
Stratco, Inc.
Terry K. Kopp Professional Gunsmithing
Time Precision
Tom's Gun Repair, Thomas G. Ivanoff
Turnbull Restoration, Doug
Van Patten, J. W.
White Rock Tool & Die

RELOADING TOOLS AND ACCESSORIES

4-D Custom Die Co.
Advance Car Mover Co., Rowell Div.
American Products, Inc.
Ammo Load, Inc.
Armfield Custom Bullets
Armite Laboratories
Arms Corporation of the Philippines
Atsko/Sno-Seal, Inc.
Bald Eagle Precision Machine Co.
Ballistic Products, Inc.
Berger Bullets Ltd.
Berry's Mfg., Inc.
Blount, Inc., Sporting Equipment Div.
Blue Mountain Bullets
Blue Ridge Machinery & Tools, Inc.
Bonanza (See Forster Products)
BRP, Inc. High Performance Cast Bullets
Brynin, Milton
B-Square Company, Inc.
Buck Stix-SOS Products Co.
Buffalo Arms Co.
Bull Mountain Rifle Co.
C&D Special Products (See Claybuster Wads & Harvester Bullets)
Camdex, Inc.
Canyon Cartridge Corp.
Case Sorting System
CCI/Speer Div of ATK
CH Tool & Die Co. (See 4-D Custom Die Co.)
CheVron Bullets
Claybuster Wads & Harvester Bullets
Cook Engineering Service
Crouse's Country Cover
Cumberland Arms
Curtis Cast Bullets
Custom Products (See Jones Custom Products)
CVA
D.C.C. Enterprises
Davide Pedersoli and Co.
Davis, Don
Davis Products, Mike
Denver Instrument Co.
Dillon Precision Products, Inc.
Dropkick
E&L Mfg., Inc.
Eagan, Donald V.
Eichelberger Bullets, Wm.
Enguix Import-Export
Euroarms of America, Inc.
E-Z-Way Systems
Federated-Fry (See Fry Metals)
Ferguson, Bill
Fisher Custom Firearms
Flambeau, Inc.
Flitz International Ltd.
Forster Products, Inc.
Fremont Tool Works
Fry Metals
Gehmann, Walter (See Huntington Die Specialties)
Graf & Sons
Graphics Direct
Graves Co.
Green, Arthur S.
Greenwood Precision
GTB-Custom Bullets
Gun City
Hanned Line, The
Hanned Precision (See The Hanned Line)
Harrell's Precision
Harris Enterprises
Harrison Bullets
Heidenstrom Bullets
High Precision
Hirtenberger AG
Hodgdon Powder Co.
Hoehn Sales, Inc.
Holland's Gunsmithing
Hornady Mfg. Co.
Howell Machine, Inc.
Hunters Supply, Inc.
Hutton Rifle Ranch
Image Ind. Inc.
Imperial Magnum Corp.
INTEC International, Inc.
Iosso Products
J&L Superior Bullets (See Huntington Die Specialties)
Jack First, Inc.
Javelina Lube Products
JLK Bullets
Jonad Corp.
Jones Custom Products, Neil A.
Jones Moulds, Paul
K&M Services
Kapro Mfg. Co. Inc. (See R.E.I.)
Knoell, Doug
Korzinek Riflesmith, J.
L.A.R. Mfg., Inc.
L.E. Wilson, Inc.
Le Clear Industries (See E-Z-Way Systems)
Lee Precision, Inc.
Liberty Metals
Liberty Shooting Supplies
Lightning Performance Innovations, Inc.
Lithi Bee Bullet Lube
Littleton, J. F.
Lock's Philadelphia Gun Exchange
Lortone Inc.
Lyman Instant Targets, Inc. (See Lyman Products Corp.)
Lyman Products Corp.
MA Systems, Inc.
Magma Engineering Co.
Match Prep-Doyle Gracey
Mayville Engineering Co. (See MEC, Inc.)
MCS, Inc.
MEC, Inc.
Midway Arms, Inc.
MI-TE Bullets
Montana Armory, Inc.
Mo's Competitor Supplies (See MCS, Inc.)
MTM Molded Products Co., Inc.
MWG Co.
Nammo Lapua Oy
Navy Arms Company
Newman Gunshop
North Devon Firearms Services
Old West Bullet Moulds
Original Box, Inc.
Outdoor Sports Headquarters, Inc.
Paragon Sales & Services, Inc.
Pinetree Bullets
Ponsness, Warren
Prairie River Arms
Prime Reloading
Professional Hunter Supplies
Pro-Shot Products, Inc.
Protector Mfg. Co., Inc., The
R.A. Wells Custom Gunsmith
R.E.I.
Rapine Bullet Mould Mfg. Co.
Redding Reloading Equipment
Reloading Specialties, Inc.
Rice, Keith (See White Rock Tool & Die)
Rochester Lead Works
Rooster Laboratories
Rorschach Precision Products
SAECO (See Redding Reloading Equipment)
Sandia Die & Cartridge Co.
Saunders Gun & Machine Shop
Saville Iron Co. (See Greenwood Precision)
Seebeck Assoc., R.E.
Sharp Shooter Supply
Sharps Arms Co., Inc., C.
Sierra Specialty Prod. Co.
Silver Eagle Machining
Skip's Machine
Sno-Seal, Inc. (See Atsko/Sno-Seal, Inc.)
SOS Products Co. (See Buck Stix-SOS Products Co.)
Spencer's Rifle Barrels, Inc.
SPG LLC
SSK Industries
Stalwart Corporation
Star Custom Bullets
Starr Trading Co., Jedediah
Stillwell, Robert
Stoney Point Products, Inc.
Stratco, Inc.
Tamarack Products, Inc.
Taracorp Industries, Inc.
TCCI
TCSR
TDP Industries, Inc.
Tetra Gun Care
Thompson/Center Arms
Vega Tool Co.
Venco Industries, Inc. (See Shooter's Choice Gun Care)
VibraShine, Inc.
Vibra-Tek Co.
Vihtavuori Oy/Kaltron-Pettibone
Vitt/Boos
W.B. Niemi Engineering
W.J. Riebe Co.
WD-40 Co.
Webster Scale Mfg. Co.
White Rock Tool & Die
Widener's Reloading & Shooting Supply, Inc.
Wise Custom Guns
Woodleigh (See Huntington Die Specialties)
Yesteryear Armory & Supply
Young Country Arms

RESTS BENCH, PORTABLE AND ACCESSORIES

A.W. Peterson Gun Shop, Inc., The
Adventure 16, Inc.
Armor Metal Products
B.M.F. Activator, Inc.
Bald Eagle Precision Machine Co.
Bald Eagle Precision Machine Co.
Bartlett Engineering
Battenfeld Technologies, Inc.
Blount/Outers ATK
Browning Arms Co.
B-Square Company, Inc.
Clift Mfg., L. R.
Desert Mountain Mfg.
Greenwood Precision
Harris Engineering Inc.
Hart & Son, Inc.
Hidalgo, Tony
Hoehn Sales, Inc.
Hoppe's Div. Penguin Industries, Inc.
J&J Sales
Keng's Firearms Specialty, Inc./US Tactical Systems
Kolpin Outdoors, Inc.
Kramer Designs
Midway Arms, Inc.
Millett Sights
Outdoor Connection, Inc., The
Protektor Model
Ransom International Corp.
Russ Haydon's Shooters' Supply
Saville Iron Co. (See Greenwood Precision)
Sinclair International, Inc.
Stoney Point Products, Inc.
Thompson Target Technology
Tonoloway Tack Drives
Torel, Inc./Tandy Brands Outdoors/AA & E
Varmint Masters, LLC
Wichita Arms, Inc.
York M-1 Conversion
Zanotti Armor, Inc.
Ziegel Engineering

SCOPES, MOUNTS, ACCESSORIES, OPTICAL EQUIPMENT

A.R.M.S., Inc.
A.W. Peterson Gun Shop, Inc., The
Accu-Tek
Ackerman, Bill (See Optical Services Co.)
Action Direct, Inc.
ADCO Sales, Inc.
Aimtech Mount Systems
Air Rifle Specialists
Air Venture Airguns
All Rite Products, Inc.
Alpec Team, Inc.
Apel GmbH, Ernst
ArmaLite, Inc.
Arundel Arms & Ammunition, Inc., A.
B.A.C.
B.M.F. Activator, Inc.
Bansner's Ultimate Rifles, LLC
Barrett Firearms Manufacturer, Inc.
Beaver Park Product, Inc.
BEC, Inc.
Beeman Precision Airguns
Benjamin/Sheridan Co., Crosman
Bill Russ Trading Post
BKL Technologies
Blount, Inc., Sporting Equipment Div.
Blount/Outers ATK
Borden Rifles Inc.
Broad Creek Rifle Works, Ltd.
Brockman's Custom Gunsmithing
Brownells, Inc.
Brunton U.S.A.
BSA Optics
B-Square Company, Inc.
Bull Mountain Rifle Co.
Burris Co., Inc.
Bushmaster Firearms, Inc.
Bushnell Sports Optics Worldwide
Butler Creek Corp.
Cabela's
Carl Zeiss Inc.
Center Lock Scope Rings
Chuck's Gun Shop
Clark Custom Guns, Inc.
Clearview Mfg. Co., Inc.
Compass Industries, Inc.
Compasseco, Ltd.
Concept Development Corp.
Conetrol Scope Mounts
Creedmoor Sports, Inc.
Crimson Trace Lasers
Crosman Airguns
D.C.C. Enterprises
D.L. Unmussig Bullets
Daisy Outdoor Products
Del-Sports, Inc.
DHB Products
Dolbare, Elizabeth
E. Arthur Brown Co. Inc.
Eagle Imports, Inc.
Edmund Scientific Co.
Eggleston, Jere D.
Ellett Bros.
Emerging Technologies, Inc. (See Laseraim Technologies, Inc.)
Entreprise Arms, Inc.
Euro-Imports
Evolution Gun Works, Inc.
Excalibur Electro Optics, Inc.
Excel Industries, Inc.
Falcon Industries, Inc.
Farr Studio, Inc.
Freedom Arms, Inc.
Fujinon, Inc.
G.G. & G.
Galati International
Gentry Custom LLC
Gil Hebard Guns, Inc.
Gilmore Sports Concepts, Inc.
Goodwin's Guns
GSI, Inc.
Gun South, Inc. (See GSI, Inc.)
Guns Div. of D.C. Engineering, Inc.
Gunsmithing, Inc.
Hakko Co. Ltd.
Hammerli USA
Hart & Son, Inc.
Harvey, Frank
Highwood Special Products
Hiptmayer, Armurier
Hiptmayer, Klaus
Holland's Gunsmithing
Hunter Co., Inc.
Impact Case & Container, Inc.
Ironsighter Co.
Jeffredo Gunsight
Jena Eur
Jerry Phillips Optics
Jewell Triggers, Inc.
John Masen Co. Inc.
John's Custom Leather
Kahles A. Swarovski Company
Kalispel Case Line
KDF, Inc.
Keng's Firearms Specialty, Inc./US Tactical Systems
Kesselring Gun Shop
Kimber of America, Inc.
Knight's Manufacturing Co.
Kowa Optimed, Inc.
KVH Industries, Inc.
Kwik-Site Co.
L&S Technologies Inc. (See Aimtech Mount Systems)
L.A.R. Mfg., Inc.
Laser Devices, Inc.
Laseraim Technologies, Inc.
LaserMax, Inc.
Leapers, Inc.
Leica USA, Inc.
Les Baer Custom, Inc.
Leupold & Stevens, Inc.
List Precision Engineering
Lohman Mfg. Co., Inc.
Lomont Precision Bullets
London Guns Ltd.
Mac-1 Airgun Distributors
Mag-Na-Port International, Inc.
Mandall Shooting Supply Inc.

Marksman Products
Maxi-Mount Inc.
McMillan Optical Gunsight Co.
MCS, Inc.
MDS
Merit Corp.
Military Armament Corp.
Millett Sights
Mirador Optical Corp.
Mitchell Optics, Inc.
MMC
Mo's Competitor Supplies (See MCS, Inc.)
MWG Co.
Navy Arms Company
New England Custom Gun Service
Nikon, Inc.
Norincoptics (See BEC, Inc.)
Olympic Optical Co.
Op-Tec
Optical Services Co.
Orchard Park Enterprise
Oregon Arms, Inc. (See Rogue Rifle Co., Inc.)
Outdoor Connection, Inc., The
Parker & Sons Shooting Supply
Parsons Optical Mfg. Co.
PECAR Herbert Schwarz GmbH
PEM's Mfg. Co.
Pentax U.S.A., Inc.
PMC/Eldorado Cartridge Corp.
Precision Sport Optics
Premier Reticles
Quarton Beamshot
R.A. Wells Custom Gunsmith
Ram-Line ATK
Ramon B. Gonzalez Guns
Ranch Products
Randolph Engineering, Inc.
Rice, Keith (See White Rock Tool & Die)
Robinson Armament Co.
Rogue Rifle Co., Inc.
Romain's Custom Guns, Inc.
RPM
S&K Scope Mounts
Saunders Gun & Machine Shop
Schmidt & Bender, Inc.
Schumakers Gun Shop
Scope Control, Inc.
Score High Gunsmithing
Segway Industries
Selsi Co., Inc.
Sharp Shooter Supply
Shepherd Enterprises, Inc.
Sightron, Inc.
Simmons Outdoor Corp.
Six Enterprises
Southern Bloomer Mfg. Co.
Spencer's Rifle Barrels, Inc.
Splitfire Sporting Goods, L.L.C.
Sportsmatch U.K. Ltd.
Springfield Armory
Springfield, Inc.
SSK Industries
Stiles Custom Guns
Stoeger Industries
Stoney Point Products, Inc.
Sturm Ruger & Co. Inc.
Sunny Hill Enterprises, Inc.
Swarovski Optik North America Ltd.
Swift Instruments, Inc.
T.K. Lee Co.
Talley, Dave
Tasco Sales, Inc.
Tele-Optics
Thompson/Center Arms
Traditions Performance Firearms
Trijicon, Inc.
Truglo, Inc.
U.S. Optics, A Division of Zeitz Optics U.S.A.
Ultra Dot Distribution
Uncle Mike's (See Michaels of Oregon, Co.)
Unertl Optical Co., Inc.
United Binocular Co.
Virgin Valley Custom Guns
Visible Impact Targets
Voere-KGH GmbH
Warne Manufacturing Co.
Warren Muzzleloading Co., Inc.
Watson Bullets
Weaver Products ATK
Weaver Scope Repair Service
Webley and Scott Ltd.
Weigand Combat Handguns, Inc.
Wessinger Custom Guns & Engraving
Westley Richards & Co. Ltd.
White Rifles, Inc.
White Rock Tool & Die
Whitestone Lumber Corp.
Wideview Scope Mount Corp.
Wilcox Industries Corp.
Wild West Guns
Williams Gun Sight Co.
York M-1 Conversion
Zanotti Armor, Inc.

SHELLHOLDERS

A.W. Peterson Gun Shop, Inc., The
Corbin Mfg. & Supply, Inc.
Fremont Tool Works
GAR
Hart & Son, Inc.
Hollywood Engineering
Huntington Die Specialties
K&M Services
King & Co.
Protektor Model
PWM Sales Ltd.
RCBS Operations/ATK
Redding Reloading Equipment
Vega Tool Co.

SHOOTING/TRAINING SCHOOL

Alpine Indoor Shooting Range
American Gunsmithing Institute
American Small Arms Academy
Auto Arms
Beretta U.S.A. Corp.
Bob's Tactical Indoor Shooting Range & Gun Shop
Bridgeman Products
Chapman Academy of Practical Shooting
Chelsea Gun Club of New York City Inc.
Cherry Creek State Park Shooting Center
Cleland's Outdoor World, Inc.
CQB Training
Defense Training International, Inc.
Executive Protection Institute
Ferris Firearms
Firearm Training Center, The
Front Sight Firearms Training Institute
G.H. Enterprises Ltd.
Gene's Custom Guns
Gentner Bullets
Gilmore Sports Concepts, Inc.
Griffin & Howe, Inc.
Griffin & Howe, Inc.
Gun Doc, Inc.
Guncraft Books (See Guncraft Sports, Inc.)
Guncraft Sports, Inc.
Guncraft Sports, Inc.
Gunsite Training Center
Henigson & Associates, Steve
High North Products, Inc.
Jensen's Custom Ammunition
Jensen's Firearms Academy
Kemen America
L.L. Bean, Inc.
Lethal Force Institute (See Police Bookshelf)
Long, George F.
McMurdo, Lynn
Mendez, John A.
Midwest Shooting School, The
NCP Products, Inc.
North American Shooting Systems
North Mountain Pine Training Center (See Executive Protection Institute)
Nowlin Mfg. Co.
Paxton Quigley's Personal Protection Strategies
Pentheny de Pentheny
Performance Specialists
Police Bookshelf
Protektor Model
SAFE
Shoot Where You Look
Shooter's World
Shooters, Inc.
Shooting Gallery, The
Sigarms Inc.
Smith & Wesson
Specialty Gunsmithing
Starlight Training Center, Inc.
Tactical Defense Institute
Thunden Ranch
Western Missouri Shooters Alliance
Yankee Gunsmith "Just Glocks"
Yavapai Firearms Academy Ltd.

SIGHTS, METALLIC

100 Straight Products, Inc.
A.W. Peterson Gun Shop, Inc., The
Accura-Site (See All's, The Jim Tembelis Co., Inc.)
Ad Hominem
Alley Supply Co.
All's, The Jim J. Tembelis Co., Inc.
Alpec Team, Inc.
Andela Tool & Machine, Inc.
AO Sight Systems
ArmaLite, Inc.
Aspen Outfitting Co.
Axtell Rifle Co.
B.A.C.
Ballard Rifle & Cartridge Co., LLC
BEC, Inc.
Bob's Gun Shop
Bo-Mar Tool & Mfg. Co.
Bond Custom Firearms
Bowen Classic Arms Corp.
Brockman's Custom Gunsmithing
Brooks Tactical Systems-Agrip
Brown Dog Ent.
Brownells, Inc.
Buffalo Arms Co.
Bushmaster Firearms, Inc.
C. Sharps Arms Co. Inc./Montana Armory
California Sights (See Fautheree, Andy)
Campbell, Dick
Cape Outfitters
Cape Outfitters
Cash Mfg. Co., Inc.
Center Lock Scope Rings
Champion's Choice, Inc.
Chip McCormick Corp.
C-More Systems
Colonial Repair
CRR, Inc./Marble's Inc.
Davide Pedersoli and Co.
DHB Products
Dixie Gun Works
DPMS (Defense Procurement Manufacturing Services, Inc.)
E. Arthur Brown Co. Inc.
Effebi SNC-Dr. Franco Beretta
Evolution Gun Works, Inc.
Farr Studio, Inc.
G.G. & G.
Garthwaite Pistolsmith, Inc., Jim
Goergen's Gun Shop, Inc.
Gun Doctor, The
Guns Div. of D.C. Engineering, Inc.
Gunsmithing, Inc.
Hank's Gun Shop
Heidenstrom Bullets
Heinie Specialty Products
Hesco-Meprolight
Hiptmayer, Armurier
Hiptmayer, Klaus
Innovative Weaponry Inc.
International Shooters Service
J.G. Anschutz GmbH & Co. KG
JP Enterprises, Inc.
Keng's Firearms Specialty, Inc./US Tactical Systems
Knight Rifles
Knight's Manufacturing Co.
L.P.A. Inc.
Leapers, Inc.
Les Baer Custom, Inc.
List Precision Engineering
London Guns Ltd.
Lyman Instant Targets, Inc. (See Lyman Products Corp.)
Mandall Shooting Supply Inc.
Marble Arms (See CRR, Inc./Marble's Inc.)
MCS, Inc.
MEC-Gar S.R.L.
Meprolight (See Hesco-Meprolight)
Merit Corp.
Mid-America Recreation, Inc.
Middlebrooks Custom Shop
Millett Sights
MMC
Modern Muzzleloading, Inc.
Montana Armory, Inc.
Montana Vintage Arms
Mo's Competitor Supplies (See MCS, Inc.)
Navy Arms Company
New England Custom Gun Service
Newman Gunshop
Novak's, Inc.
OK Weber, Inc.
One Ragged Hole
Parker & Sons Shooting Supply
PEM's Mfg. Co.
Perazone-Gunsmith, Brian
RPM
Sharps Arms Co., Inc., C.
Slug Site
STI International
T.F.C. S.p.A.
Talley, Dave
Tank's Rifle Shop
Trijicon, Inc.
Truglo, Inc.
U.S. Optics, A Division of Zeitz Optics U.S.A.
Warne Manufacturing Co.
Weigand Combat Handguns, Inc.
Wichita Arms, Inc.
Wild West Guns
Williams Gun Sight Co.
Wilsom Combat
Wilsom Combat
XS Sight Systems

STUCK CASE REMOVERS

A.W. Peterson Gun Shop, Inc., The
GAR
Huntington Die Specialties
Redding Reloading Equipment
Tom's Gun Repair, Thomas G. Ivanoff

TARGETS, BULLET & CLAYBIRD TRAPS

A.W. Peterson Gun Shop, Inc., The
Action Target, Inc.
Air Arms
American Target
Autauga Arms, Inc.
Beeman Precision Airguns
Benjamin/Sheridan Co., Crosman
Birchwood Casey
Blount, Inc., Sporting Equipment Div.
Blount/Outers ATK
Blue and Gray Products Inc. (See Ox-Yoke Originals)
Brown Precision, Inc.
Bull-X, Inc.
Caswell International
Champion Target Co.
Creedmoor Sports, Inc.
Crosman Airguns
D.C.C. Enterprises
Daisy Outdoor Products
Diamond Mfg. Co.
Federal Champion Target Co.
G.H. Enterprises Ltd.
H-S Precision, Inc.
Hunterjohn
J.G. Dapkus Co., Inc.
Kennebec Journal
Kleen-Bore, Inc.
Lakefield Arms Ltd. (See Savage Arms, Inc.)
Leapers, Inc.
Littler Sales Co.
Lyman Instant Targets, Inc. (See Lyman Products Corp.)
Marksman Products
Mendez, John A.
Mountain Plains Industries
MSR Targets
N.B.B., Inc.
National Target Co.
North American Shooting Systems
Outers Laboratories Div. of ATK
Ox-Yoke Originals, Inc.
Palsa Outdoor Products
Passive Bullet Traps, Inc. (See Savage Range Systems, Inc.)
PlumFire Press, Inc.
Precision Airgun Sales, Inc.
Protektor Model
Quack Decoy & Sporting Clays
Remington Arms Co., Inc.
Rockwood Corp.
Rocky Mountain Target Co.
Savage Range Systems, Inc.
Schaefer Shooting Sports
Seligman Shooting Products
Shooters Supply
Shoot-N-C Targets (See Birchwood Casey)
Target Shooting, Inc.
Thompson Target Technology
Trius Traps, Inc.
Universal Sports
Visible Impact Targets
Watson Bullets
Woods Wise Products
World of Targets (See Birchwood Casey)
X-Spand Target Systems

TAXIDERMY

African Import Co.
Bill Russ Trading Post
Kulis Freeze Dry Taxidermy
World Trek, Inc.

MANUFACTURER'S DIRECTORY

A

A Zone Bullets, 2039 Walter Rd., Billings, MT 59105 / 800-252-3111; FAX: 406-248-1961
A&W Repair, 2930 Schneider Dr., Arnold, MO 63010 / 617-287-3725
A.A. Arms, Inc., 4811 Persimmont Ct., Monroe, NC 28110 / 704-289-5356; or 800-935-1119; FAX: 704-289-5859
A.B.S. III, 9238 St. Morritz Dr., Fern Creek, KY 40291
A.G. Russell Knives, Inc., 1920 North 26th Street, Lowell, AR 72745-8489 / 800-255-9034; FAX: 479-636-8493 ag@agrussell.com agrussell.com
A.R.M.S., Inc., 230 W. Center St., West Bridgewater, MA 02379-1620 / 508-584-7816; FAX: 508-588-8045
A.W. Peterson Gun Shop, Inc., 4255 W. Old U.S. 441, Mt. Dora, FL 32757-3299 / 352-383-4258; FAX: 352-735-1001
A.W. Peterson Gun Shop, Inc., The, 4255 West Old U.S. 441, Mount Dora, FL 32757-3299 / 352-383-4258
AC Dyna-tite Corp., 155 Kelly St., P.O. Box 0984, Elk Grove Village, IL 60007 / 847-593-5566; FAX: 847-593-1304
Acadian Ballistic Specialties, P.O. Box 787, Folsom, LA 70437 / 504-796-0078 gunsmith@neasolft.com
Accuracy Den, The, 25 Bitterbrush Rd., Reno, NV 89523 / 702-345-0225
Accuracy International, Foster, P.O. Box 111, Wilsall, MT 59086 / 406-587-7922; FAX: 406-585-9434
Accuracy Internationl Precision Rifles (See U.S.)
Accuracy Int'l. North America, Inc., P.O. Box 5267, Oak Ridge, TN 37831 / 423-482-0330; FAX: 423-482-0336
Accuracy Unlimited, 7479 S. DePew St., Littleton, CO 80123
Accuracy Unlimited, 16036 N. 49 Ave., Glendale, AZ 85306 / 602-978-9089; FAX: 602-978-9089 fglenn@cox.net www.glenncustom.com
Accura-Site (See All's, The Jim Tembelis Co., Inc.)
Accurate Arms Co., Inc., 5891 Hwy. 230 West, McEwen, TN 37101 / 931-729-4207; FAX: 931-729-4211 burrensburg@aac-ca.com www.accuratepowder.com
Accu-Tek, 4510 Carter Ct., Chino, CA 91710
Ackerman & Co., Box 133 U.S. Highway Rt. 7, Pownal, VT 05261 / 802-823-9874 muskets@togsther.net
Ackerman, Bill (See Optical Services Co.)
Acra-Bond Laminates, 134 Zimmerman Rd., Kalispell, MT 59901 / 406-257-9003; FAX: 406-257-9003 merlins@digisys.net www.acrabondlaminates.com
Action Bullets & Alloy Inc., RR 1, P.O. Box 189, Quinter, KS 67752 / 785-754-3609; FAX: 785-754-3629 bullets@ruraltel.net
Action Direct, Inc., P.O. Box 770400, Miami, FL 33177 / 305-969-0056; FAX: 305-256-3541 www.action-direct.com
Action Products, Inc., 22 N. Mulberry St., Hagerstown, MD 21740 / 301-797-1414; FAX: 301-733-2073
Action Target, Inc., P.O. Box 636, Provo, UT 84603 / 801-377-8033; FAX: 801-377-8096 www.actiontarget.com
Actions by "T" Teddy Jacobson, 16315 Redwood Forest Ct., Sugar Land, TX 77478 / 281-277-4008; FAX: 281-277-9112 tjacobson@houston.rr.com www.actionsbyt.us
AcuSport Corporation, 1 Hunter Place, Bellefontaine, OH 43311-3001 / 513-593-7010; FAX: 513-592-5625
Ad Hominem, 3130 Gun Club Lane, RR #3, Orillia, ON L3V 6H3 CANADA / 705-689-5303; FAX: 705-689-5303
Adair Custom Shop, Bill, 2886 Westridge, Carrollton, TX 75006
ADCO Sales, Inc., 4 Draper St. #A, Woburn, MA 01801 / 781-935-1799; FAX: 781-935-1011
Adkins, Luther, 1292 E. McKay Rd., Shelbyville, IN 46176-8706 / 317-392-3795
Advance Car Mover Co., Rowell Div., P.O. Box 1, 240 N. Depot St., Juneau, WI 53039 / 414-386-4464; FAX: 414-386-4416
Advantage Arms, Inc., 25163 W. Ave. Stanford, Valencia, CA 91355 / 661-257-2290
Adventure 16, Inc., 4620 Alvarado Canyon Rd., San Diego, CA 92120 / 619-283-6314
Aero Peltor, 90 Mechanic St., Southbridge, MA 01550 / 508-764-5500; FAX: 508-764-0188
African Import Co., 22 Goodwin Rd., Plymouth, MA 02360 / 508-746-8552; FAX: 508-746-0404 africanimport@aol.com
AFSCO Ammunition, 731 W. Third St., P.O. Box L, Owen, WI 54460 / 715-229-2516 sailers@webtv.net
Ahlman Guns, 9525 W. 230th St., Morristown, MN 55052 / 507-685-4243; FAX: 507-685-4280 www.ahlmans.com
Ahrends Grips, Box 203, Clarion, IA 50525 / 515-532-3449; FAX: 515-532-3926 ahrends@goldfieldaccess.net
Ahrends, Kim, Box 203, Clarion, IA 50525 / 515-532-3449; FAX: 515-532-3926
Aimtech Mount Systems, P.O. Box 223, Thomasville, GA 31799 / 229-226-4313; FAX: 229-227-0222 mail@aimtech-mounts.com www.aimtech-mounts.com
Air Arms, Hailsham Industrial Park, Diplocks Way, Hailsham, E. Sussex, BN27 3JF ENGLAND / 011-0323-845853; FAX: 1323 440573 general.air-arms.co.uk. www.air-arms.co.uk.
Air Rifle Specialists, P.O. Box 138, 130 Holden Rd., Pine City, NY 14871-0138 / 607-734-7340; FAX: 607-733-3261 ars@stny.rr.com www.air-rifles.com
Air Venture Airguns, 9752 E. Flower St., Bellflower, CA 90706 / 562-867-6355
AirForce Airguns, P.O. Box 2478, Fort Worth, TX 76113 / 817-451-8966; FAX: 817-451-1613 www.airforceairguns.com
Airrow, 11 Monitor Hill Rd., Newtown, CT 06470 / 203-270-6343
Aitor-Cuchilleria Del Norte S.A., Izelaieta, 17, 48260, Ermua, SPAIN / 43-17-08-50 info@aitor.com www.ailor.com
Ajax Custom Grips, Inc., 9130 Viscount Row, Dallas, TX 75247 / 214-630-8893; FAX: 214-630-4942
Aker International, Inc., 2248 Main St., Suite 6, Chula Vista, CA 91911 / 619-423-5182; FAX: 619-423-1363 aker@akerleather.com www.akerleather.com
AKJ Concealco, P.O. Box 871596, Vancouver, WA 98687-1596 / 360-891-8222; FAX: 360-891-8221 Concealco@aol.com www.greatholsters.com
Alana Cupp Custom Engraver, P.O. Box 207, Annabella, UT 84711 / 801-896-4834
Alaska Bullet Works, Inc., 9978 Crazy Horse Drive, Juneau, AK 99801 / 907-789-3834; FAX: 907-789-3433
Alaskan Silversmith, The, 2145 Wagner Hollow Rd., Fort Plain, NY 13339 / 518-993-3983 sidbell@capital.net www.sidbell.cizland.com
Aldis Gunsmithing & Shooting Supply, 502 S. Montezuma St., Prescott, AZ 86303 / 602-445-6723; FAX: 602-445-6763
Alessi Holsters, Inc., 2465 Niagara Falls Blvd., Amherst, NY 14228-3527 / 716-691-5615
Alex, Inc., 3420 Cameron Bridge Rd., Manhattan, MT 59741-8523 / 406-282-7396; FAX: 406-282-7396
Alfano, Sam, 36180 Henry Gaines Rd., Pearl River, LA 70452 / 504-863-3364; FAX: 504-863-7715
All American Lead Shot Corp., P.O. Box 224566, Dallas, TX 75062
All Rite Products, Inc., 9554 Wells Circle, Suite D, West Jordan, UT 84088-6226 / 800-771-8471; FAX: 801-280-8302 info@allriteproducts.com www.allriteproducts.com
Allard, Gary/Creek Side Metal & Woodcrafters, Fishers Hill, VA 22626 / 540-465-3903
Allen Co., Inc., 525 Burbank St., Broomfield, CO 80020 / 303-469-1857; or 800-876-8600; FAX: 303-466-7437
Allen Firearm Engraving, P.O. Box 155, Camp Verde, AZ 86322 / 928-567-6711 rosebudmulgco@netzero.com rosebudmulgco@netzero.com
Allen Mfg., 6449 Hodgson Rd., Circle Pines, MN 55014 / 612-429-8231
Alley Supply Co., P.O. Box 848, Gardnerville, NV 89410 / 775-782-3800; FAX: 775-782-3827 jetalley@aol.com www.alleysupplyco.com
Alliant Techsystems, Smokeless Powder Group, P.O. Box 6, Rt. 114, Bldg. 229, Radford, VA 24141-0096 www.alliantpowder.com
Allred Bullet Co., 932 Evergreen Drive, Logan, UT 84321 / 435-752-6983; FAX: 435-752-6983
All's, The Jim J. Tembelis Co., Inc., 216 Loper Ct., Neenah, WI 54956 / 920-725-5251; FAX: 920-725-5251
Alpec Team, Inc., 201 Ricken Backer Cir., Livermore, CA 94550 / 510-606-8245; FAX: 510-606-4279
Alpha 1 Drop Zone, 2121 N. Tyler, Wichita, KS 67212 / 316-729-0800; FAX: 316-729-4262 www.alpha1dropzone.com
Alpha LaFranck Enterprises, P.O. Box 81072, Lincoln, NE 68501 / 402-466-3193
Alpha Precision, Inc., 3238 Della Slaton Rd., Comer, GA 30629-2212 / 706-783-2131 jim@alphaprecisioninc.com www.alphaprecisioninc.com
Alpine Indoor Shooting Range, 2401 Government Way, Coeur d'Alene, ID 83814 / 208-676-8824; FAX: 208-676-8824
Altamont Co., 901 N. Church St., P.O. Box 309, Thomasboro, IL 61878 / 217-643-3125; or 800-626-5774; FAX: 217-643-7973
Alumna Sport by Dee Zee, 1572 NE 58th Ave., P.O. Box 3090, Des Moines, IA 50316 / 800-798-9899
Amadeo Rossi S.A., Rua: Amadeo Rossi, 143, Sao Leopoldo, RS 93030-220 BRAZIL / 051-592-5566 rossi.firearms@pnet.com.br
Amato, Jeff. See: J&M PRECISION MACHINING
AmBr Software Group Ltd., P.O. Box 301, Reistertown, MD 21136-0301 / 800-888-1917; FAX: 410-526-7212
American Ammunition, 3545 NW 71st St., Miami, FL 33147 / 305-835-7400; FAX: 305-694-0037
American Derringer Corp., 127 N. Lacy Dr., Waco, TX 76705 / 800-642-7817; or 254-799-9111; FAX: 254-799-7935
American Display Co., 55 Cromwell St., Providence, RI 02907 / 401-331-2464; FAX: 401-421-1264
American Gas & Chemical Co., Ltd.,, 220 Pegasus Ave., Northvale, NJ 07647 / 201-767-7300
American Gunsmithing Institute, 1325 Imola Ave. #504, Napa, CA 94559 / 707-253-0462; FAX: 707-253-7149 www.americangunsmith.com
American Handgunner Magazine, 12345 World Trade Dr., San Diego, CA 92128 / 800-537-3006; FAX: 858-605-0204 www.americanhandgunner.com
American Pioneer Video, P.O. Box 50049, Bowling Green, KY 42102-2649 / 800-743-4675
American Products, Inc., 14729 Spring Valley Road, Morrison, IL 61270 / 815-772-3336; FAX: 815-772-8046
American Safe Arms, Inc., 1240 Riverview Dr., Garland, UT 84312 / 801-257-7472; FAX: 801-785-8156
American Security Products Co., 11925 Pacific Ave., Fontana, CA 92337 / 909-685-9680; or 800-421-6142; FAX: 909-685-9685
American Small Arms Academy, P.O. Box 12111, Prescott, AZ 86304 / 602-778-5623
American Target, 1328 S. Jason St., Denver, CO 80223 / 303-733-0433; FAX: 303-777-0311
American Target Knives, 1030 Brownwood NW, Grand Rapids, MI 49504 / 616-453-1998
Americase, P.O. Box 271, 1610 E. Main, Waxahachie, TX 75165 / 800-880-3629; FAX: 214-937-8373
Ames Metal Products, 4323 S. Western Blvd., Chicago, IL 60609 / 773-523-3230; or 800-255-6937; FAX: 773-523-3854
Amherst Arms, P.O. Box 1457, Englewood, FL 34295 / 941-475-2020; FAX: 941-473-1212
Ammo Load Worldwide, Inc., 815 D St., Lewiston, ID 83501 / 208-743-7418; FAX: 208-746-1703 ammoload@microwavedsl.com
Ammo Load, Inc., 1560 E. Edinger, Suite G, Santa Ana, CA 92705 / 714-558-8858; FAX: 714-569-0319
Amrine's Gun Shop, 937 La Luna, Ojai, CA 93023 / 805-646-2376
Amsec, 11925 Pacific Ave., Fontana, CA 92337
Analog Devices, Box 9106, Norwood, MA 02062
Andela Tool & Machine, Inc., RD3, Box 246, Richfield Springs, NY 13439
Anderson Manufacturing Co., Inc., 22602 53rd Ave. SE, Bothell, WA 98021 / 206-481-1858; FAX: 206-481-7839
Andres & Dworsky KG, Bergstrasse 18, A-3822 Karlstein, Thaya, AUSTRIA / 0 28 44-285; FAX: 0 28 44-28619 andres.dnorsky@wvnet.as
Angelo & Little Custom Gun Stock Blanks, P.O. Box 240046, Dell, MT 59724-0046
Answer Products Co., 1519 Westbury Drive, Davison, MI 48423 / 810-653-2911
Antique American Firearms, P.O. Box 71035, Dept. GD, Des Moines, IA 50325 / 515-224-6552
Antique Arms Co., 1110 Cleveland Ave., Monett, MO 65708 / 417-235-6501
AO Sight Systems, 2401 Ludelle St., Fort Worth, TX 76105 / 888-744-4880; or 817-536-0136; FAX: 817-536-3517
Apel GmbH, Ernst, Am Kirschberg 3, D-97218, Gerbrunn, GERMANY / 0 (931) 707192 info@eaw.de www.eaw.de
Aplan Antiques & Art, James O., HC 80, Box 793-25, Piedmont, SD 57769 / 605-347-5016
AR-7 Industries, LLC, 998 N. Colony Rd., Meriden, CT 06450 / 203-630-3536; FAX: 203-630-3637
Arizona Ammunition, Inc., 21421 No. 14th Ave., Suite E, Phoenix, AZ 85027 / 623-516-9004; FAX: 623-516-9012 www.azammo.com
ArmaLite, Inc., P.O. Box 299, Geneseo, IL 61254 / 800-336-0184; or 309-944-6939; FAX: 309-944-6949
Armament Gunsmithing Co., Inc., 525 Rt. 22, Hillside, NJ 07205 / 908-686-0960; FAX: 718-738-5019 armamentgunsmithing@worldnet.att.net
Armas Garbi, S.A., 12-14 20.600 Urki, 12, Eibar (Guipuzcoa), SPAIN / 943 20 3873; FAX: 943 20 3873 armosgarbi@euskalnet.n
Armas Kemen S. A. (See U.S. Importers)

MANUFACTURER'S DIRECTORY

Armfield Custom Bullets, 10584 County Road 100, Carthage, MO 64836 / 417-359-8480; FAX: 417-359-8497
Armi Perazzi S.P.A., Via Fontanelle 1/3, 1-25080, Botticino Mattina, ITALY / 030-2692591; FAX: 030-2692594
Armi San Marco (See Taylor's & Co.)
Armi San Paolo, 172-A, I-25062, via Europa, ITALY / 030-2751725
Armi Sport (See Cape Outfitters)
Armite Laboratories, 1560 Superior Ave., Costa Mesa, CA 92627 / 213-587-7768; FAX: 213-587-5075
Armoloy Co. of Ft. Worth, 204 E. Daggett St., Fort Worth, TX 76104 / 817-332-5604; FAX: 817-335-6517
Armor (See Buck Stop Lure Co., Inc.)
Armor Metal Products, P.O. Box 4609, Helena, MT 59604 / 406-442-5560; FAX: 406-442-5650
Armory Publications, 2120 S. Reserve St., PMB 253, Missoula, MT 59801 / 406-549-7670; FAX: 406-728-0597 armorypub@aol.com www.armorypub.com
Armoury, Inc., The, Rt. 202, Box 2340, New Preston, CT 06777 / 860-868-0001; FAX: 860-868-2919
Arms & Armour Press, Wellington House, 125 Strand, London, WC2R 0BB ENGLAND / 0171-420-5555; FAX: 0171-240-7265
Arms Corporation of the Philippines, Bo. Parang Marikina, Metro Manila, PHILIPPINES / 632-941-6243; or 632-941-6244; FAX: 632-942-0682
Arms Craft Gunsmithing, 1106 Linda Dr., Arroyo Grande, CA 93420 / 805-481-2830
Arms Software, 4851 SW Madrona St., Lake Oswego, OR 97035 / 800-366-5559; or 503-697-0533; FAX: 503-697-3337
Arms, Programming Solutions (See Arms Software)
Armscor Precision, 5740 S. Arville St. #219, Las Vegas, NV 89118 / 702-362-7750
Armscorp USA, Inc., 4424 John Ave., Baltimore, MD 21227 / 410-247-6200; FAX: 410-247-6205 info@armscorpusa.com www.armscorpusa.com
Arratoonian, Andy (See Horseshoe Leather Products)
Arrieta S.L., Morkaiko 5, 20870, Elgoibar, SPAIN / 34-43-743150; FAX: 34-43-743154
Art Jewel Enterprises Ltd., Eagle Business Ctr., 460 Randy Rd., Carol Stream, IL 60188 / 708-260-0400
Artistry in Wood, 134 Zimmerman Rd., Kalispell, MT 59901 / 406-257-9003; FAX: 406-257-9167 merlins@digisys.net www.acrabondlaminates.com
Art's Gun & Sport Shop, Inc., 6008 Hwy. Y, Hillsboro, MO 63050
Arundel Arms & Ammunition, Inc., A., 24A Defense St., Annapolis, MD 21401 / 410-224-8683
Aspen Outfitting Co., Jon Hollinger, 9 Dean St., Aspen, CO 81611 / 970-925-3406
A-Square Co., 205 Fairfield Ave., Jeffersonville, IN 47130 / 812-283-0577; FAX: 812-283-0375
Astra Sport, S.A., Apartado 3, 48300 Guernica, Espagne, SPAIN / 34-4-6250100; FAX: 34-4-6255186
Atamec-Bretton, 19 rue Victor Grignard, F-42026, St.-Etienne (Cedex 1, FRANCE / 33-77-93-54-69; FAX: 33-77-93-57-98
Atlanta Cutlery Corp., 2143 Gees Mill Rd., Box 839 CIS, Conyers, GA 30207 / 800-883-0300; FAX: 404-388-0246
Atlantic Mills, Inc., 1295 Towbin Ave., Lakewood, NJ 08701-5934 / 800-242-7374
Atsko/Sno-Seal, Inc., 2664 Russell St., Orangeburg, SC 29115 / 803-531-1820; FAX: 803-531-2139 info@atsko.com www.atsko.com
Auguste Francotte & Cie S.A., rue du Trois Juin 109, 4400 Herstal-Liege, BELGIUM / 32-4-248-13-18; FAX: 32-4-948-11-79
Austin & Halleck, Inc., 2150 South 950 East, Provo, UT 84606-6285 / 877-543-3256; or 801-374-9990; FAX: 801-374-9998 www.austinhallek.com
Austin Sheridan USA, Inc., P.O. Box 577, 36 Haddam Quarter Rd., Durham, CT 06422 / 860-349-1772; FAX: 860-349-1771 swalzer@palm.net
Autauga Arms, Inc., Pratt Plaza Mall No. 13, Prattville, AL 36067 / 800-262-9563; FAX: 334-361-2961
Auto Arms, 738 Clearview, San Antonio, TX 78228 / 512-434-5450
Auto-Ordnance Corp., P.O. Box 220, Blauvelt, NY 10913 / 914-353-7770
Autumn Sales, Inc. (Blaser), 1320 Lake St., Fort Worth, TX 76102 / 817-335-1634; FAX: 817-338-0119
Avnda Otaola Norica, 16 Apartado 68, 20600, Eibar, SPAIN
AWC Systems Technology, P.O. Box 41938, Phoenix, AZ 85080-1938 / 623-780-1050; FAX: 623-780-2967 awc@awcsystech.com www.awcsystech.com
Axtell Rifle Co., 353 Mill Creek Road, Sheridan, MT 59749 / 406-842-5814
AYA (See U.S. Importer-New England Custom Gun Serv

B

B&D Trading Co., Inc., 3935 Fair Hill Rd., Fair Oaks, CA 95628 / 800-334-3790; or 916-967-9366; FAX: 916-967-4873
B&P America, 12321 Brittany Cir., Dallas, TX 75230 / 972-726-9069
B.A.C., 17101 Los Modelos St., Fountain Valley, CA 92708 / 435-586-3286
B.B. Walker Co., P.O. Box 1167, 414 E Dixie Dr., Asheboro, NC 27204 / 910-625-1380; FAX: 910-625-8125
B.C. Outdoors, Larry McGhee, PO Box 61497, Boulder City, NV 89006 / 702-294-3056; FAX: 702-294-0413 jdalton@pmcammo.com www.pmcammo.com
B.M.F. Activator, Inc., 12145 Mill Creek Run, Plantersville, TX 77363 / 936-894-2397; FAX: 936-894-2397 bmf25years@aol.com
Baelder, Harry, Alte Goennebeker Strasse 5, 24635, Rickling, GERMANY / 04328-722732; FAX: 04328-722733
Baer's Hollows, P.O. Box 603, Taft, CA 93268 / 719-438-5718
Bagmaster Mfg., Inc., 2731 Sutton Ave., St. Louis, MO 63143 / 314-781-8002; FAX: 314-781-3363 sales@bagmaster.com www.bagmaster.com
Bain & Davis, Inc., 307 E. Valley Blvd., San Gabriel, CA 91776-3522 / 626-573-4241; FAX: 323-283-7449 baindavis@aol.com
Baker, Stan. See: STAN BAKER SPORTS
Baker's Leather Goods, Roy, P.O. Box 893, Magnolia, AR 71754 / 870-234-0344 pholsters@ipa.net
Bald Eagle Precision Machine Co., 101-A Allison St., Lock Haven, PA 17745 / 570-748-6772; FAX: 570-748-4443 bepmachine@aol.com baldeaglemachine.com
Balickie, Joe, 408 Trelawney Lane, Apex, NC 27502 / 919-362-5185
Ballard, Donald. See: BALLARD INDUSTRIES
Ballard Industries, Donald Ballard Sr., P.O. Box 2035, Arnold, CA 95223 / 408-996-0957; FAX: 408-257-6828
Ballard Rifle & Cartridge Co., LLC, 113 W. Yellowstone Ave., Cody, WY 82414 / 307-587-4914; FAX: 307-527-6097 ballard@wyoming.com www.ballardrifles.com
Ballistic Products, Inc., 20015 75th Ave. North, Corcoran, MN 55340-9456 / 763-494-9237; FAX: 763-494-9236 info@ballisticproducts.com www.ballisticproducts.com
Ballistic Program Co., Inc., The, 2417 N. Patterson St., Thomasville, GA 31792 / 912-228-5739 or 800-368-0835
Ballistic Research, 1108 W. May Ave., McHenry, IL 60050 / 815-385-0037
Ballisti-Cast, Inc., P.O. Box 1057, Minot, ND 58702-1057 / 701-497-3333; FAX: 701-497-3335
Bandcor Industries, Div. of Man-Sew Corp., 6108 Sherwin Dr., Port Richey, FL 34668 / 813-848-0432
Bang-Bang Boutique (See Holster Shop, The)
Bansner's Ultimate Rifles, LLC, P.O. Box 839, 261 E. Main St., Adamstown, PA 19501 / 717-484-2370; FAX: 717-484-0523 bansner@aol.com www.bansnersrifle.com
Barbour, Inc., 55 Meadowbrook Dr., Milford, NH 03055 / 603-673-1313; FAX: 603-673-6510
Barnes, 4347 Tweed Dr., Eau Claire, WI 54703-6302
Barnes Bullets, Inc., P.O. Box 215, American Fork, UT 84003 / 801-756-4222; or 800-574-9200; FAX: 801-756-2465 email@barnesbullets.com www.barnesbullets.com
Baron Technology, 62 Spring Hill Rd., Trumbull, CT 06611 / 203-452-0515; FAX: 203-452-0663 dbaron@baronengraving.com www.baronengraving.com
Barraclough, John K., 55 Merit Park Dr., Gardena, CA 90247 / 310-324-2574 johnbar120@aol.com
Barramundi Corp., P.O. Drawer 4259, Homosassa Springs, FL 32687 / 904-628-0200
Barrel & Gunworks, 2601 Lake Valley Rd., Prescott Valley, AZ 86314 / 928-772-4060 www.cutrifle.com
Barrett Firearms Manufacturer, Inc., P.O. Box 1077, Murfreesboro, TN 37133 / 615-896-2938; FAX: 615-896-7313
Bar-Sto Precision Machine, 73377 Sullivan Rd., P.O. Box 1838, Twentynine Palms, CA 92277 / 760-367-2747; FAX: 760-367-2407 barsto@eee.org www.barsto.com
Barta's Gunsmithing, 10231 U.S. Hwy. 10, Cato, WI 54230 / 920-732-4472
Barteaux Machete, 1916 SE 50th Ave., Portland, OR 97215-3238 / 503-233-5880
Bartlett Engineering, 40 South 200 East, Smithfield, UT 84335-1645 / 801-563-5910
Bates Engraving, Billy, 2302 Winthrop Dr. SW, Decatur, AL 35603 / 256-355-3690 bbrn@aol.com www.angelfire.com/al/billybates
Battenfeld Technologies, Inc., 5885 W. Van Horn Tavern Rd., Columbia, MO 65203 / 573-445-9200; FAX: 573-447-4158 battenfeldtechnologies.com
Bauer, Eddie, 15010 NE 36th St., Redmond, WA 98052
Baumgartner Bullets, 3011 S. Alane St., W. Valley City, UT 84120
Bauska Barrels, 105 9th Ave. W., Kalispell, MT 59901 / 406-752-7706
Bear Archery, RR 4, 4600 Southwest 41st Blvd., Gainesville, FL 32601 / 904-376-2327
Bear Arms, 374-A Carson Rd., St. Mathews, SC 29135
Bear Mountain Gun & Tool, 120 N. Plymouth, New Plymouth, ID 83655 / 208-278-5221; FAX: 208-278-5221
Beartooth Bullets, P.O. Box 491, Dept. HLD, Dover, ID 83825-0491 / 208-448-1865 bullets@beartoothbullets.com beartoothbullets.com
Beaver Park Product, Inc., 840 J St., Penrose, CO 81240 / 719-372-6744
BEC, Inc., 1227 W. Valley Blvd., Suite 204, Alhambra, CA 91803 / 626-281-5751; FAX: 626-293-7073
Beeks, Mike. See: GRAYBACK WILDCATS
Beeman Precision Airguns, 5454 Argosy Dr., Huntington Beach, CA 92649 / 714-890-4808; FAX: 714-890-4808
Behlert Precision, Inc., P.O. Box 288, 7067 Easton Rd., Pipersville, PA 18947 / 215-766-8681; or 215-766-7301; FAX: 215-766-8681
Beitzinger, George, 116-20 Atlantic Ave., Richmond Hill, NY 11419 / 718-847-7661
Belding's Custom Gun Shop, 10691 Sayers Rd., Munith, MI 49259 / 517-596-2388
Bell & Carlson, Inc., Dodge City Industrial Park, 101 Allen Rd., Dodge City, KS 67801 / 800-634-8586; or 620-225-6688; FAX: 620-225-6688 email@bellandcarlson.com www.bellandcarlson.com
Bell Reloading, Inc., 1725 Harlin Lane Rd., Villa Rica, GA 30180
Bell's Gun & Sport Shop, 3309-19 Mannheim Rd., Franklin Park, IL 60131
Bell's Legendary Country Wear, 22 Circle Dr., Bellmore, NY 11710 / 516-679-1158
Benchmark Knives (See Gerber Legendary Blades)
Benelli Armi S.P.A., Via della Stazione, 61029, Urbino, ITALY / 39-722-307-1; FAX: 39-722-327427
Benelli USA Corp., 17603 Indian Head Hwy., Accokeek, MD 20607 / 301-283-6981; FAX: 301-283-6988 benelliusa.com
Bengtson Arms Co., L., 6345-B E. Akron St., Mesa, AZ 85205 / 602-981-6375
Benjamin/Sheridan Co., Crosman, Rts. 5 and 20, E. Bloomfield, NY 14443 / 716-657-6161; FAX: 716-657-5405 www.crosman.com
Bentley, John, 128-D Watson Dr., Turtle Creek, PA 15145
Beretta S.P.A., Pietro, Via Beretta, 18, 25063, Gardone Vae Trompia, ITALY / 39-30-8341-1 info@benetta.com www.benetta.com
Beretta U.S.A. Corp., 17601 Beretta Dr., Accokeek, MD 20607 / 301-283-2191; FAX: 301-283-0435
Berger Bullets Ltd., 5443 W. Westwind Dr., Glendale, AZ 85310 / 602-842-4001; FAX: 602-934-9083
Bernardelli, Vincenzo, P.O. Box 460243, Houston, TX 77056-8243 www.bernardelli.com
Bernardelli, Vincenzo, Via Grande, 10, Sede Legale Torbole Casaglia, Brescia, ITALY / 39-30-8912851-2-3; FAX: 39-030-2150963 bernardelli@bernardelli.com www.bernardelli.com
Berry's Mfg., Inc., 401 North 3050 East St., St. George, UT 84770 / 435-634-1682; FAX: 435-634-1683 sales@berrysmfg.com www.berrysmfg.com
Bersa S.A., Benso Bonadimani, Magallanes 775 B1704 FLC, Ramos Mejia, ARGENTINA / 011-4656-2377; FAX: 011-4656-2093+ info@bersa-sa.com.dr www.bersa-sa.com.ar
Bert Johanssons Vapentillbehor, S-430 20 Veddige, SWEDEN,
Bertuzzi (See U.S. Importer-New England Arms Co.)
Better Concepts Co., 663 New Castle Rd., Butler, PA 16001 / 412-285-9000

MANUFACTURER'S DIRECTORY

Beverly, Mary, 3201 Horseshoe Trail, Tallahassee, FL 32312
Bianchi International, Inc., 100 Calle Cortez, Temecula, CA 92590 / 909-676-5621; FAX: 909-676-6777
Big Bear Arms & Sporting Goods, Inc., 1112 Milam Way, Carrollton, TX 75006 / 972-416-8051; or 800-400-BEAR; FAX: 972-416-0771
Big Bore Bullets of Alaska, P.O. Box 521455, Big Lake, AK 99652 / 907-373-2673; FAX: 907-373-2673 doug@mtaonline.net ww.awloo.com/bbb/index.
Big Bore Express, 2316 E. Railroad St., Nampa, ID 83651 / 800-376-4010 FAX: 208-466-6927 info@powerbeltbullets.com bigbore.com
Big Spring Enterprises "Bore Stores", P.O. Box 1115, Big Spring Rd., Yellville, AR 72687 / 870-449-5297; FAX: 870-449-4446
Bilal, Mustafa. See: TURK'S HEAD PRODUCTIONS
Bilinski, Bryan. See: FIELDSPORT LTD.
Bill Adair Custom Shop, 2886 Westridge, Carrollton, TX 75006 / 972-418-0950
Bill Austin's Calls, Box 284, Kaycee, WY 82639 / 307-738-2552
Bill Hanus Birdguns, LLC, P.O. Box 533, Newport, OR 97365 / 541-265-7433; FAX: 541-265-7400 www.billhanusbirdguns.com
Bill Russ Trading Post, William A. Russ, 25 William St., Addison, NY 14801-1326 / 607-359-3896
Bill Wiseman and Co., P.O. Box 3427, Bryan, TX 77805 / 409-690-3456; FAX: 409-690-0156
Billeb, Stephen. See: QUALITY CUSTOM FIREARMS
Billings Gunsmiths, 1841 Grand Ave., Billings, MT 59102 / 406-256-8390; FAX: 406-256-6530 blgsgunsmiths@msn.com www.billingsgunsmiths.net
Billingsley & Brownell, P.O. Box 25, Dayton, WY 82836 / 307-655-9344
Bill's Gun Repair, 1007 Burlington St., Mendota, IL 61342 / 815-539-5786
Billy Bates Engraving, 2302 Winthrop Dr. SW, Decatur, AL 35603 / 256-355-3690 bbrn@aol.com www.angelfire.com/al/billybates
Birchwood Casey, 7900 Fuller Rd., Eden Prairie, MN 55344 / 800-328-6156; or 612-937-7933; FAX: 612-937-7979
Birdsong & Assoc., W. E., 1435 Monterey Rd., Florence, MS 39073-9748 / 601-366-8270
Bismuth Cartridge Co., 3500 Maple Ave., Suite 1650, Dallas, TX 75219 / 214-521-5880; FAX: 214-521-9035
Bison Studios, 1409 South Commerce St., Las Vegas, NV 89102 / 702-388-2891; FAX: 702-383-9967
Bitterroot Bullet Co., 2001 Cedar Ave., Lewiston, ID 83501-0412 / 208-743-5635 brootbil@lewiston.com
BKL Technologies, P.O. Box 5237, Brownsville, TX 78523
Black Belt Bullets (See Big Bore Express)
Black Hills Ammunition, Inc., P.O. Box 3090, Rapid City, SD 57709-3090 / 605-348-5150; FAX: 605-348-9827
Black Hills Shooters Supply, P.O. Box 4220, Rapid City, SD 57709 / 800-289-2506
Black Powder Products, 67 Township Rd. 1411, Chesapeake, OH 45619 / 614-867-8047
Black Sheep Brand, 3220 W. Gentry Pkwy., Tyler, TX 75702 / 903-592-3853; FAX: 903-592-0527
Blacksmith Corp., P.O. Box 280, North Hampton, OH 45349 / 937-969-8389; FAX: 937-969-8399 sales@blacksmithcorp.com www.blacksmithcorp.com
BlackStar AccuMax Barrels, 11501 Brittmoore Park Drive, Houston, TX 77041 / 281-721-6040; FAX: 281-721-6041
BlackStar Barrel Accurizing (See BlackStar AccuMax)
Blacktail Mountain Books, 42 First Ave. W., Kalispell, MT 59901 / 406-257-5573
Blammo Ammo, P.O. Box 1677, Seneca, SC 29679 / 803-882-1768
Blaser Jagdwaffen GmbH, D-88316, Isny Im Allgau, GERMANY
Blount, Inc., Sporting Equipment Div., 2299 Snake River Ave., P.O. Box 856, Lewiston, ID 83501 / 800-627-3640; or 208-746-2351; FAX: 208-799-3904
Blount/Outers ATK, P.O. Box 39, Onalaska, WI 54650 / 608-781-5800; FAX: 608-781-0368
Blue and Gray Products Inc. (See Ox-Yoke Originals)
Blue Book Publications, Inc., 8009 34th Ave. S., Ste. 175, Minneapolis, MN 55425 / 952-854-5229; FAX: 952-853-1486 bluebook@bluebookinc.com www.bluebookinc.com
Blue Mountain Bullets, 64146 Quail Ln., Box 231, John Day, OR 97845 / 541-820-4594; FAX: 541-820-4594
Blue Ridge Machinery & Tools, Inc., P.O. Box 536-GD, Hurricane, WV 25526 / 800-872-6500; FAX: 304-562-5311 blueridgemachine@worldnet.att.net www.blueridgemachinery.com
BMC Supply, Inc., 26051 - 179th Ave. SE, Kent, WA 98042
Bob Allen Co., P.O. Box 477, 214 SW Jackson, Des Moines, IA 50315 / 800-685-7020; FAX: 515-283-0779
Bob Allen Sportswear, 220 S. Main St., Osceola, IA 50213 / 210-344-8531; FAX: 210-342-2703 sales@bob-allen.com www.bob-allen.com
Bob Rogers Gunsmithing, P.O. Box 305, 344 S. Walnut St., Franklin Grove, IL 61031 / 815-456-2685; FAX: 815-456-2685
Bob's Gun Shop, P.O. Box 200, Royal, AR 71968 / 501-767-1970; FAX: 501-767-1970 gunparts@hsnp.com www.gun-parts.com
Bob's Tactical Indoor Shooting Range & Gun Shop, 90 Lafayette Rd., Salisbury, MA 01952 / 508-465-5561
Boessler, Erich, Am Vogeltal 3, 97702, Munnerstadt, GERMANY
Boker USA, Inc., 1550 Balsam Street, Lakewood, CO 80214 / 303-462-0662; FAX: 303-462-0668 sales@bokerusa.com bokerusa.com
Boltin, John M., P.O. Box 644, Estill, SC 29918 / 803-625-2185
Bo-Mar Tool & Mfg. Co., 6136 State Hwy. 300, Longview, TX 75604 / 903-759-4784; FAX: 903-759-9141 marykor@earthlink.net bo-mar.com
Bonadimani, Benso. See: BERSA S.A.
Bonanza (See Forster Products), 310 E. Lanark Ave., Lanark, IL 61046 / 815-493-6360; FAX: 815-493-2371
Bond Arms, Inc., P.O. Box 1296, Granbury, TX 76048 / 817-573-4445; FAX: 817-573-5636
Bond Custom Firearms, 8954 N. Lewis Ln., Bloomington, IN 47408 / 812-332-4519
Bonham's & Butterfields, 220 San Bruno Ave., San Francisco, CA 94103 / 415-861-7500; FAX: 415-861-0183 arms@butterfields.com www.butterfields.com
Boone Trading Co., Inc., P.O. Box 669, Brinnon, WA 98320 / 800-423-1945; or 360-796-4330; FAX: 360-796-4511 sales@boonetrading.com boonetrading.com
Boone's Custom Ivory Grips, Inc., 562 Coyote Rd., Brinnon, WA 98320 / 206-796-4330
Boonie Packer Products, P.O. Box 12517, Salem, OR 97309-0517 / 800-477-3244; or 503-581-3244; FAX: 503-581-3191 customerservice@booniepacker.com www.booniepacker.com
Borden Ridges Rimrock Stocks, RR 1 Box 250 BC, Springville, PA 18844 / 570-965-2505; FAX: 570-965-2328
Borden Rifles Inc., RD 1, Box 250 #BC, Springville, PA 18844 / 717-965-2505; FAX: 717-965-2328
Border Barrels Ltd., Riccarton Farm, Newcastleton, SCOTLAND UK
Borovnik K.G., Ludwig, 9170 Ferlach, Bahnhofstrasse 7, AUSTRIA / 042 27 24 42; FAX: 042 26 43 49
Bosis (See U.S. Importer-New England Arms Co.)
Boss Manufacturing Co., 221 W. First St., Kewanee, IL 61443 / 309-852-2131; or 800-447-4581; FAX: 309-852-0848
Bostick Wildlife Calls, Inc., P.O. Box 728, Estill, SC 29918 / 803-625-2210; or 803-625-4512
Bowen Classic Arms Corp., P.O. Box 67, Louisville, TN 37777 / 865-984-3583 www.bowenclassicarms.com
Bowen Knife Co., Inc., P.O. Box 590, Blackshear, GA 31516 / 912-449-4794
Bowerly, Kent, 710 Golden Pheasant Dr., Redmond, OR 97756 / 541-923-3501 jkbowerly@aol.com
Boyds' Gunstock Industries, Inc., 25376 403 Rd. Ave., Mitchell, SD 57301 / 605-996-5011; FAX: 605-996-9878 www.boydsgunstocks.com
Brace, Larry D., 771 Blackfoot Ave., Eugene, OR 97404 / 541-688-1278; FAX: 541-607-5833
Brauer Bros., 1520 Washington Ave., St. Louis, MO 63103 / 314-231-2864; FAX: 314-249-4952 www.brauerbros.com
Break-Free, Inc., 13386 International Pkwy., Jacksonville, FL 32218 / 800-428-0588; FAX: 904-741-5407 contactus@armorholdings.com www.break-free.com
Brenneke GmbH, P.O. Box 1646, 30837, Langenhagen, GERMANY / +49-511-97262-0; FAX: +49-511-97262-62 info@brenneke.de brenneke.com
Bridgeman Products, Harry Jaffin, 153 B Cross Slope Ct., Englishtown, NJ 07726 / 732-536-3604; FAX: 732-972-1004
Bridgers Best, P.O. Box 1410, Berthoud, CO 80513
Briese Bullet Co., Inc., 3442 42nd Ave. SE, Tappen, ND 58487 / 701-327-4578; FAX: 701-327-4579
Brigade Quartermasters, 1025 Cobb International Blvd., Dept. VH, Kennesaw, GA 30144-4300 / 404-428-1248; or 800-241-3125; FAX: 404-426-7726
Briganti, A.J. See: BRIGANTI CUSTOM GUNSMITH
Briganti Custom Gunsmith, A.J. Briganti, 512 Rt. 32, Highland Mills, NY 10930 / 845-928-9573
Briley Mfg. Inc., 1230 Lumpkin, Houston, TX 77043 / 800-331-5718; or 713-932-6995; FAX: 713-932-1043
Brill, R. See: ROYAL ARMS INTERNATIONAL
British Sporting Arms, RR 1, Box 130, Millbrook, NY 12545 / 914-677-8303
Broad Creek Rifle Works, Ltd., 120 Horsey Ave., Laurel, DE 19956 / 302-875-5446; FAX: 302-875-1448 bcrw4guns@aol.com
Brockman's Custom Gunsmithing, P.O. Box 357, Gooding, ID 83330 / 208-934-5050
Broken Gun Ranch, 10739 126 Rd., Spearville, KS 67876 / 316-385-2587; FAX: 316-385-2597 nbowlin@ucom.net www.brokengunranch
Brooker, Dennis, Rt. 1, Box 12A, Derby, IA 50068 / 515-533-2103
Brooks Tactical Systems-Agrip, 279-C Shorewood Ct., Fox Island, WA 98333 / 253-549-2866 FAX: 253-549-2703 brooks@brookstactical.com www.brookstactical.com
Brown Dog Ent., 2200 Calle Camelia, 1000 Oaks, CA 91360 / 805-497-2318; FAX: 805-497-1618
Brown Precision, Inc., 7786 Molinos Ave., Los Molinos, CA 96055 / 530-384-2506; FAX: 916-384-1638 www.brownprecision.com
Brown Products, Inc., Ed, 43825 Muldrow Trl., Perry, MO 63462 / 573-565-3261; FAX: 573-565-2791 edbrown@edbrown.com www.edbrown.com
Brownells, Inc., 200 S. Front St., Montezuma, IA 50171 / 800-741-0015; FAX: 800-264-3068 orderdesk@brownells.com www.brownells.com
Browning Arms Co., One Browning Place, Morgan, UT 84050 / 801-876-2711; FAX: 801-876-3331 www.browning.com
Browning Arms Co. (Parts & Service), 3005 Arnold Tenbrook Rd., Arnold, MO 63010 / 617-287-6800; FAX: 617-287-9751
BRP, Inc. High Performance Cast Bullets, 1210 Alexander Rd., Colorado Springs, CO 80909 / 719-633-0658
Brunton U.S.A., 620 E. Monroe Ave., Riverton, WY 82501 / 307-856-6559; FAX: 307-857-4702 info@brunton.com www.brunton.com
Bryan & Assoc., R. D. Sauls, P.O. Box 5772, Anderson, SC 29623-5772 / 864-261-6810 bryanandac@aol.com www.huntersweb.com/bryanandac
Brynin, Milton, P.O. Box 383, Yonkers, NY 10710 / 914-779-4333
BSA Guns Ltd., Armoury Rd. Small Heath, Birmingham B11 2PP, ENGLAND / 011-021-772-8543; FAX: 011-021-773-0845 sales@bsagun.com www.bsagun.com
BSA Optics, 3911 SW 47th Ave., Ste. 914, Ft. Lauderdale, FL 33314 / 954-581-2144; FAX: 954-581-3165 4info@basaoptics.com www.bsaoptics.com
B-Square Company, Inc., P.O. Box 11281, 2708 St. Louis Ave., Ft. Worth, TX 76110 / 817-923-0964 or 800-433-2909; FAX: 817-926-7012
Buchsenmachermeister, Peter Hofer Jagdwaffen, A-9170 Ferlach, Kirchgasse 24, Kirchgasse, AUSTRIA / 43 4227 3683; or 43 664 3200216; FAX: 43 4227 368330 peterhofer@hoferwaffen.com www.hoferwaffen.com
Buck Knives, Inc., 1900 Weld Blvd., P.O. Box 1267, El Cajon, CA 92020 / 619-449-1100; or 800-326-2825; FAX: 619-562-5774
Buck Stix-SOS Products Co., Box 3, Neenah, WI 54956
Buck Stop Lure Co., Inc., 3600 Grow Rd. NW, P.O. Box 636, Stanton, MI 48888 / 989-762-5091; FAX: 989-762-5124 buckstop@nethawk.com www.buckstopscents.com
Buckeye Custom Bullets, 6490 Stewart Rd., Elida, OH 45807 / 419-641-4463
Buckhorn Gun Works, 8109 Woodland Dr., Black Hawk, SD 57718 / 605-787-6472
Buckskin Bullet Co., P.O. Box 1893, Cedar City, UT 84721 / 435-586-3286
Budin, Dave, 817 Main St., P.O. Box 685, Margaretville, NY 12455 / 914-568-4103; FAX: 914-586-4105
Budin, Dave. See: DEL-SPORTS, INC.
Buenger Enterprises/Goldenrod Dehumidifier, 3600 S. Harbor Blvd., Oxnard, CA 93035 / 800-451-6797; or 805-985-5828; FAX: 805-985-1534
Buffalo Arms Co., 660 Vermeer Ct., Ponderay, ID 83852 / 208-263-6953; FAX: 208-265-2096 www.buffaloarms.com
Buffalo Bullet Co., Inc., 12637 Los Nietos Rd., Unit A, Santa Fe Springs, CA 90670 / 800-423-8069; FAX: 562-944-5054
Buffalo Gun Center, 3385 Harlem Rd., Buffalo, NY 14225 / 716-833-2581; FAX: 716-833-2265 www.buffaloguncenter.com

MANUFACTURER'S DIRECTORY

Buffalo Rock Shooters Supply, R.R. 1, Ottawa, IL 61350 / 815-433-2471
Buffer Technologies, P.O. Box 104930, Jefferson City, MO 65110 / 573-634-8529; FAX: 573-634-8522
Bull Mountain Rifle Co., 6327 Golden West Terrace, Billings, MT 59106 / 406-656-0778
Bullberry Barrel Works, Ltd., 2430 W. Bullberry Ln., Hurricane, UT 84737 / 435-635-9866; FAX: 435-635-0348 fred@bullberry.com www.bullberry.com
Bullet Metals, Bill Ferguson, P.O. Box 1238, Sierra Vista, AZ 85636 / 520-458-5321; FAX: 520-458-1421 info@theantimonyman.com www.bullet-metals.com
Bullet N Press, 1210 Jones St., Gastonia, NC 28052 / 704-853-0265 bnpress@quik.com www.oldwestgunsmith.com
Bullet Swaging Supply, Inc., P.O. Box 1056, 303 McMillan Rd., West Monroe, LA 71291 / 318-387-3266; FAX: 318-387-7779 leblackmon@colla.com
Bull-X, Inc., 411 E. Water St., Farmer City, IL 61842-1556 / 309-928-2574 or 800-248-3845; FAX: 309-928-2130
Burkhart Gunsmithing, Don, P.O. Box 852, Rawlins, WY 82301 / 307-324-6007
Burnham Bros., P.O. Box 1148, Menard, TX 78659 / 915-396-4572; FAX: 915-396-4574
Burris Co., Inc., P.O. Box 1747, 331 E. 8th St., Greeley, CO 80631 / 970-356-1670; FAX: 970-356-8702
Bushmaster Firearms, Inc., 999 Roosevelt Trail, Windham, ME 04062 / 800-998-7928; FAX: 207-892-8068 info@bushmaster.com www.bushmaster.com
Bushmaster Hunting & Fishing, 451 Alliance Ave., Toronto, ON M6N 2J1 CANADA / 416-763-4040; FAX: 416-763-0623
Bushnell Sports Optics Worldwide, 9200 Cody, Overland Park, KS 66214 / 913-752-3400 or 800-423-3537; FAX: 913-752-3550
Buster's Custom Knives, P.O. Box 214, Richfield, UT 84701 / 435-896-5319; FAX: 435-896-8333 www.warenskiknives.com
Butler Creek Corp., 2100 S. Silverstone Way, Meridian, ID 83642-8151 / 800-423-8327 or 406-388-1356; FAX: 406-388-7204
Butler Enterprises, 834 Oberting Rd., Lawrenceburg, IN 47025 / 812-537-3584
Buzz Fletcher Custom Stockmaker, 117 Silver Road, P.O. Box 189, Taos, NM 87571 / 505-758-3486

C

C&D Special Products (See Claybuster Wads & Harvester Bullets)
C&H Research, 115 Sunnyside Dr., Box 351, Lewis, KS 67552 / 316-324-5445; or 888-324-5445; FAX: 620-324-5984 info@mercuryrecoil.com www.mercuryrecoil.com
C. Palmer Manufacturing Co., Inc., P.O. Box 220, West Newton, PA 15089 / 412-872-8200; FAX: 412-872-8302
C. Sharps Arms Co. Inc./Montana Armory, 100 Centennial Dr., P.O. Box 885, Big Timber, MT 59011 / 406-932-4353; FAX: 406-932-4443
C.S. Van Gorden & Son, Inc., 1815 Main St., Bloomer, WI 54724 / 715-568-2612 vangorden@bloomer.net
C.W. Erickson's L.L.C., 530 Garrison Ave. NE, P.O. Box 522, Buffalo, MN 55313 / 763-682-3665; FAX: 763-682-4328 www.archerhunter.com
Cabanas (See U.S. Importer-Mandall Shooting Supply
Cabela's, One Cabela Drive, Sidney, NE 69160 / 308-254-5505; FAX: 308-254-8420
Cabinet Mtn. Outfitters Scents & Lures, P.O. Box 766, Plains, MT 59859 / 406-826-3970
Cache La Poudre Rifleworks, 140 N. College, Ft. Collins, CO 80524 / 920-482-6913
Cain's Outdoors, Inc., 1832 Williams Hwy., Williamstown, WV 26187 / 304-375-7842; FAX: 304-375-7842 muzzleloading@cainsoutdoor.com www.cainsoutdoor.com
Calhoon Mfg., 4343 U.S. Highway 87, Havre, MT 59501 / 406-395-4079 www.jamescalhoon.com
Cali'co Hardwoods, Inc., 3580 Westwind Blvd., Santa Rosa, CA 95403 / 707-546-4045; FAX: 707-546-4027 calicohardwoods@msn.com
Calico Light Weapon Systems, 1489 Greg St., Sparks, NV 89431
California Sights (See Fautheree, Andy)
Cambos Outdoorsman, 532 E. Idaho Ave., Ontario, OR 97914 / 541-889-3135; FAX: 541-889-2633
Cambos Outdoorsman, Fritz Hallberg, 532 E. Idaho Ave., Ontario, OR 97914 / 541-889-3135; FAX: 541-889-2633
Camdex, Inc., 2330 Alger, Troy, MI 48083 / 810-528-2300; FAX: 810-528-0989
Cameron's, 16690 W. 11th Ave., Golden, CO 80401 / 303-279-7365; FAX: 303-568-1009 ncnoremac@aol.com
Camillus Cutlery Co., 54 Main St., Camillus, NY 13031 / 315-672-8111; FAX: 315-672-8832
Campbell, Dick, 196 Garden Homes Dr., Colville, WA 99114 / 509-684-6080; FAX: 509-684-6080 dicksknives@aol.com
Camp-Cap Products, P.O. Box 3805, Chesterfield, MO 63006 / 866-212-4639; FAX: 636-536-6320 www.langenberghats.com
Cannon Safe, Inc., 216 S. 2nd Ave. #BLD-932, San Bernardino, CA 92400 / 310-692-0636; or 800-242-1055; FAX: 310-692-7252
Canyon Cartridge Corp., P.O. Box 152, Albertson, NY 11507 FAX: 516-294-8946
Cape Outfitters, 599 County Rd. 206, Cape Girardeau, MO 63701 / 573-335-4103; FAX: 573-335-1555
Caraville Manufacturing, P.O. Box 4545, Thousand Oaks, CA 91359 / 805-499-1234
Carbide Checkering Tools (See J&R Engineering)
Carhartt, Inc., P.O. Box 600, 3 Parklane Blvd., Dearborn, MI 48121 / 800-358-3825; or 313-271-8460; FAX: 313-271-3455
Carl Walther GmbH, B.P. 4325, D-89033, Ulm, GERMANY
Carl Zeiss Inc., 13005 N. Kingston Ave., Chester, VA 23836 / 800-441-3005; FAX: 804-530-8481
Carolina Precision Rifles, 1200 Old Jackson Hwy., Jackson, SC 29831 / 803-827-2069
Carrell, William. See: CARRELL'S PRECISION FIREARMS
Carrell's Precision Firearms, William Carrell, 1952 W.Silver Falls Ct., Meridian, ID 83642-3837
Carry-Lite, Inc., P.O. Box 1587, Fort Smith, AR 72902 / 479-782-8971; FAX: 479-783-0234
Carter's Gun Shop, 225 G St., Penrose, CO 81240 / 719-372-6240 rlewiscarter@msn.com
Cascade Bullet Co., Inc., 2355 South 6th St., Klamath Falls, OR 97601 / 503-884-9316
Cascade Shooters, 2155 N.W. 12th St., Redwood, OR 97756
Case & Sons Cutlery Co., W R, Owens Way, Bradford, PA 16701 / 814-368-4123; or 800-523-6350; FAX: 814-768-5369
Case Sorting System, 12695 Cobblestone Creek Rd., Poway, CA 92064 / 619-486-9340
Cash Mfg. Co., Inc., P.O. Box 130, 201 S. Klein Dr., Waunakee, WI 53597-0130 / 608-849-5664; FAX: 608-849-5664
Caspian Arms, Ltd., 14 North Main St., Hardwick, VT 05843 / 802-472-6454; FAX: 802-472-6709
Cast Bullet Association, The, 12857 S. Road, Hoyt, KS 66440-9116 cbamemdir@castbulletassoc.org www.castbulletassoc.org
Cast Performance Bullet Company, P.O. Box 153, Riverton, WY 82501 / 307-857-2940; FAX: 307-857-3132 castperform@wyoming.com castperformance.com
Casull Arms Corp., P.O. Box 1629, Afton, WY 83110 / 307-886-0200
Caswell International, 720 Industrial Dr. No. 112, Cary, IL 60013 / 847-639-7666; FAX: 847-639-7694 www.caswellintl.com
Cathey Enterprises, Inc., P.O. Box 2202, Brownwood, TX 76804 / 915-643-2553; FAX: 915-643-3653
Cation, 2341 Alger St., Troy, MI 48083 / 810-689-0658; FAX: 810-689-7558
Caywood, Shane J., P.O. Box 321, Minocqua, WI 54548 / 715-277-3866
Caywood Gunmakers, 18 Kings Hill Estates, Berryville, AR 72616 / 870-423-4741 www.caywoodguns.com
CBC, Avenida Humberto de Campos 3220, 09400-000, Ribeirao Pires, SP, BRAZIL / 55 11 4822 8378; FAX: 55 11 4822 8323 export@cbc.com.bc www.cbc.com.bc
CBC-BRAZIL, 3 Cuckoo Lane, Honley, Yorkshire HD7 2BR, ENGLAND / 44-1484-661062; FAX: 44-1484-663709
CCG Enterprises, 5217 E. Belknap St., Halton City, TX 76117 / 800-819-7464
CCI/Speer Div of ATK, P.O. Box 856, 2299 Snake River Ave., Lewiston, ID 83501 / 800-627-3640 or 208-746-2351
CCL Security Products, 199 Whiting St., New Britain, CT 06051 / 800-733-8588
Cedar Hill Game Calls, LLC, 238 Vic Allen Rd., Downsville, LA 71234 / 318-982-5632; FAX: 318-982-2031
Centaur Systems, Inc., 1602 Foothill Rd., Kalispell, MT 59901 / 406-755-8609; FAX: 406-755-8609
Center Lock Scope Rings, 9901 France Ct., Lakeville, MN 55044 / 952-461-2114; FAX: 952-461-2194 marklee55044@usfamily.net
Central Specialties Ltd. (See Trigger Lock Division)
Century Gun Dist. Inc., 1467 Jason Rd., Greenfield, IN 46140 / 317-462-4524
Century International Arms, Inc., 430 S. Congress Ave. Ste. 1, Delray Beach, FL 33445-4701 / 800-527-1252; FAX: 561-998-1993 support@centuryarms.com www.centuryarms.com
CFVentures, 509 Harvey Dr., Bloomington, IN 47403-1715 paladinwilltravel@yahoo.com www.caversam16.freeserve.co.uk
CH Tool & Die Co. (See 4-D Custom Die Co.), 711 N Sandusky St., P.O. Box 889, Mt. Vernon, OH 43050-0889 / 740-397-7214; FAX: 740-397-6600
Chace Leather Products, 507 Alden St., Fall River, MA 02722 / 508-678-7556; FAX: 508-675-9666 chacelea@aol.com www.chaceleather.com
Chadick's Ltd., P.O. Box 100, Terrell, TX 75160 / 214-563-7577
Chambers Flintlocks Ltd., Jim, 116 Sams Branch Rd., Candler, NC 28715 / 828-667-8361; FAX: 828-665-0852 www.flintlocks.com
Champion Shooters' Supply, P.O. Box 303, New Albany, OH 43054 / 614-855-1603; FAX: 614-855-1209
Champion Target Co., 232 Industrial Parkway, Richmond, IN 47374 / 800-441-4971
Champion's Choice, Inc., 201 International Blvd., LaVergne, TN 37086 / 615-793-4066; FAX: 615-793-4070 champ.choice@earthlink.net www.champchoice.com
Champlin Firearms, Inc., P.O. Box 3191, Woodring Airport, Enid, OK 73701 / 580-237-7388; FAX: 580-242-6922 info@champlinarms.com www.champlinarms.com
Chapman Academy of Practical Shooting, 4350 Academy Rd., Hallsville, MO 65255 / 573-696-5544; FAX: 573-696-2266 hq@chapmanacademy.com chapmanacademy.com
Chapman, J. Ken. See: OLD WEST BULLET MOULDS
Chapman Manufacturing Co., 471 New Haven Rd., P.O. Box 250, Durham, CT 06422 / 860-349-9228; FAX: 860-349-0084 sales@chapmanmfg.com www.chapmanmfg.com
Chapuis Armes, Z1 La Gravoux, BP15, 42380 P.O. Box 15, St. Bonnet-le-Chatea, FRANCE / (33)477.50.06.96; FAX: (33)477 50 10 70 info@chapuis.armes.com www.chapuis-armes.com
Charter 2000, 273 Canal St., Shelton, CT 06484 / 203-922-1652
Checkmate Refinishing, 370 Champion Dr., Brooksville, FL 34601 / 352-799-5774; FAX: 352-799-2986 checkmatecustom.com
Cheddite, France S.A., 99 Route de Lyon, F-26501, Bourg-les-Valence, FRANCE / 33-75-56-4545; FAX: 33-75-56-3587 export@cheddite.com
Chelsea Gun Club of New York City Inc., 237 Ovington Ave., Apt. D53, Brooklyn, NY 11209 / 718-836-9422; or 718-833-2704
Cherry Creek State Park Shooting Center, 12500 E. Belleview Ave., Englewood, CO 80111 / 303-693-1765
CheVron Bullets, RR1, Ottawa, IL 61350 / 815-433-2471
Cheyenne Pioneer Products, P.O. Box 28425, Kansas City, MO 64188 / 816-413-9196; FAX: 816-455-2859 cheyennepp@aol.com www.cartridgeboxes.com
Chicago Cutlery Co., 1536 Beech St., Terre Haute, IN 47804 / 800-457-2665
Chicasaw Gun Works, 4 Mi. Mkr., Pluto Rd., Box 868, Shady Spring, WV 25918-0868 / 304-763-2848; FAX: 304-763-3725
Chip McCormick Corp., P.O. Box 1560, Manchaca, TX 78652 / 800-328-2447; FAX: 512-280-4282 www.chipmccormick.com
Chipmunk (See Oregon Arms, Inc.)
Choate Machine & Tool Co., Inc., P.O. Box 218, 116 Lovers Ln., Bald Knob, AR 72010 / 501-724-6193; or 800-972-6390; FAX: 501-724-5873
Christensen Arms, 192 East 100 North, Fayette, UT 84630 / 435-528-7999; FAX: 435-528-7494 www.christensenarms.com
Christie's East, 20 Rockefeller Plz., New York, NY 10020-1902 / 212-606-0406 christics.com
Chu Tani Ind., Inc., P.O. Box 2064, Cody, WY 82414-2064
Chuck's Gun Shop, P.O. Box 597, Waldo, FL 32694 / 904-468-2264

MANUFACTURER'S DIRECTORY

Churchill (See U.S. Importer-Ellett Bros.)
Churchill, Winston G., 2838 20 Mile Stream Rd., Proctorville, VT 05153 / 802-226-7772
Churchill Glove Co., James, P.O. Box 298, Centralia, WA 98531 / 360-736-2816; FAX: 360-330-0151
CIDCO, 21480 Pacific Blvd., Sterling, VA 22170 / 703-444-5353
Cimarron F.A. Co., P.O. Box 906, Fredericksburg, TX 78624-0906 / 830-997-9090; FAX: 830-997-0802 cimgraph@koc.com www.cimarron-firearms.com
Cincinnati Swaging, 2605 Marlington Ave., Cincinnati, OH 45208
Clark Custom Guns, Inc., 336 Shootout Lane, Princeton, LA 71067 / 318-949-9884; FAX: 318-949-9829
Clark Firearms Engraving, 6347 Avon Ave., San Gabriel, CA 91775-1801 / 818-287-1652
Clarkfield Enterprises, Inc., 1032 10th Ave., Clarkfield, MN 56223 / 612-669-7140
Claro Walnut Gunstock Co., 1235 Stanley Ave., Chico, CA 95928 / 530-342-5188; FAX: 530-342-5199 wally@clarowalnutgunstocks.com www.clarowalnutgunstocks.com
Classic Arms Company, Rt 1 Box 120F, Burnet, TX 78611 / 512-756-4001
Classic Arms Corp., P.O. Box 106, Dunsmuir, CA 96025-0106 / 530-235-2000
Classic Old West Styles, 1060 Doniphan Park Circle C, El Paso, TX 79936 / 915-587-0684
Claybuster Wads & Harvester Bullets, 309 Sequoya Dr., Hopkinsville, KY 42240 / 800-922-6287; or 800-284-1746; FAX: 502-885-8088
Clean Shot Technologies, 21218 St. Andrews Blvd. Ste 504, Boca Raton, FL 33433 / 888-866-2532
Clearview Mfg. Co., Inc., 413 S. Oakley St., Fordyce, AR 71742 / 501-352-8557; FAX: 501-352-7120
Clearview Products, 3021 N. Portland, Oklahoma City, OK 73107
Cleland's Outdoor World, Inc., 10306 Airport Hwy., Swanton, OH 43558 / 419-865-4713; FAX: 419-865-5865 mail@clelands.com www.clelands.com
Clements' Custom Leathercraft, Chas, 1741 Dallas St., Aurora, CO 80010-2018 / 303-364-0403; FAX: 303-739-9824 gryphons@home.com kuntaoslcat.com
Clenzoil Worldwide Corp., Jack Fitzgerald, 25670 1st St., Westlake, OH 44145-1430 / 440-899-0482; FAX: 440-899-0483
Clift Mfg., L. R., 3821 Hammonton Rd., Marysville, CA 95901 / 916-755-3390; FAX: 916-755-3393
Clymer Mfg. Co., 1645 W. Hamlin Rd., Rochester Hills, MI 48309-3312 / 248-853-5555; FAX: 248-853-1530
C-More Systems, P.O. Box 1750, 7553 Gary Rd., Manassas, VA 20108 / 703-361-2663; FAX: 703-361-5881
Cobra Enterprises, Inc., 1960 S. Milestone Drive, Suite F, Salt Lake City, UT 84104 FAX: 801-908-8301 www.cobrapistols@networld.com
Cobra Sport S.R.I., Via Caduti Nei Lager No. 1, 56020 San Romano, Montopoli v/Arno Pi, ITALY / 0039-571-450490; FAX: 0039-571-450492
Coffin, Charles H., 3719 Scarlet Ave., Odessa, TX 79762 / 915-366-4729; FAX: 915-366-4729
Cogar's Gunsmithing, 206 Redwine Dr., Houghton Lake, MI 48629 / 517-422-4591
Coghlan's Ltd., 121 Irene St., Winnipeg, MB R3T 4C7 CANADA / 204-284-9550; FAX: 204-475-4127
Cold Steel Inc., 3036 Seaborg Ave. Ste. A, Ventura, CA 93003 / 800-255-4716; or 800-624-2363; FAX: 805-642-9727
Cole-Grip, 16135 Cohasset St., Van Nuys, CA 91406 / 818-782-4424
Coleman Co., Inc., 3600 N. Hydraulic, Wichita, KS 67219 / 800-835-3278; www.coleman.com
Cole's Gun Works, Old Bank Building, Rt. 4 Box 250, Moyock, NC 27958 / 919-435-2345
Collector's Armoury, Ltd., Tom Nelson, 9404 Gunston Cove Rd., Lorton, VA 22079 / 703-493-9120; FAX: 703-493-9424 www.collectorsarmoury.com
Collings, Ronald, 1006 Cielta Linda, Vista, CA 92083
Colonial Arms, Inc., P.O. Box 636, Selma, AL 36702-0636 / 334-872-9455; FAX: 334-872-9540 colonialarms@mindspring.com www.colonialarms.com
Colonial Repair, 47 Navarre St., Roslindale, MA 02131-4725 / 617-469-4951
Colorado Gunsmithing Academy, RR 3 Box 79B, El Campo, TX 77437 / 719-336-4099; or 800-754-2046; FAX: 719-336-9642
Colorado School of Trades, 1575 Hoyt St., Lakewood, CO 80215 / 800-234-4594; FAX: 303-233-4723
Colt Blackpowder Arms Co., 110 8th Street, Brooklyn, NY 11215 / 718-499-4678; FAX: 718-768-8056
Colt's Mfg. Co., Inc., P.O. Box 1868, Hartford, CT 06144-1868 / 800-962-COLT; or 860-236-6311; FAX: 860-244-1449
Compass Industries, Inc., 104 East 25th St., New York, NY 10010 / 212-473-2614 or 800-221-9904; FAX: 212-353-0826
Compasseco, Ltd., 151 Atkinson Hill Ave., Bardtown, KY 40004 / 502-349-0910
Competition Electronics, Inc., 3469 Precision Dr., Rockford, IL 61109 / 815-874-8001; FAX: 815-874-8181
Competitive Pistol Shop, The, 5233 Palmer Dr., Fort Worth, TX 76117-2433 / 817-834-8479
Competitor Corp., Inc., 26 Knight St. Unit 3, P.O. Box 352, Jaffrey, NH 03452 / 603-532-9483; FAX: 603-532-8209 competitorcorp@aol.com competitor-pistol.com
Component Concepts, Inc., 530 S. Springbrook Road, Newberg, OR 97132 / 503-554-8095; FAX: 503-554-9370 cci@cybcon.com www.phantomonline.com
Concealment Shop, Inc., The, 3550 E. Hwy. 80, Mesquite, TX 75149 / 972-289-8997; or 800-444-7090; FAX: 972-289-4410 info@theconcealmentshop.com www.theconcealmentshop.com
Concept Development Corp., 16610 E. Laser Drive, Suite 5, Fountain Hills, AZ 85268-6644
Conetrol Scope Mounts, 10225 Hwy. 123 S., Seguin, TX 78155 / 830-379-3030; or 800-CONETROL; FAX: 830-379-3030 email@conetrol.com www.conetrol.com
Connecticut Shotgun Mfg. Co., P.O. Box 1692, 35 Woodland St., New Britain, CT 06051 / 860-225-6581; FAX: 860-832-8707
Connecticut Valley Classics (See CVC, BPI)
Conrad, C. A., 3964 Ebert St., Winston-Salem, NC 27127 / 919-788-5469
Cook Engineering Service, 891 Highbury Rd., Vict 3133, 3133 AUSTRALIA
Cooper Arms, P.O. Box 114, Stevensville, MT 59870 / 406-777-0373; FAX: 406-777-5228
Cooper-Woodward Perfect Lube, 4120 Oesterle Rd., Helena, MT 59602 / 406-459-2287 cwperfectlube@mt.net cwperfectlube.com
Corbin Mfg. & Supply, Inc., 600 Industrial Circle, P.O. Box 2659, White City, OR 97503 / 541-826-5211; FAX: 541-826-8669 sales@corbins.com www.corbins.com
Cor-Bon Inc./Glaser LLC, P.O. Box 173, 1311 Industry Rd., Sturgis, SD 57785 / 605-347-4544; or 800-221-3489; FAX: 605-347-5055 email@corbon.com www.corbon.com
Corkys Gun Clinic, 4401 Hot Springs Dr., Greeley, CO 80634-9226 / 970-330-0516
Corry, John, 861 Princeton Ct., Neshanic Station, NJ 08853 / 908-369-8019
Cosmi Americo & Figlio S.N.C., Via Flaminia 307, Ancona, ITALY / 071-888208; FAX: 39-071-887008
Coulston Products, Inc., P.O. Box 30, 201 Ferry St. Suite 212, Easton, PA 18044-0030 / 215-253-0167; or 800-445-9927; FAX: 215-252-1511
Counter Assault, 120 Industrial Court, Kalispell, MT 59901 / 406-257-4740; FAX: 406-257-6674
Country Armourer, The, P.O. Box 308, Ashby, MA 01431-0308 / 508-827-6797; FAX: 508-827-4845
Cousin Bob's Mountain Products, 7119 Ohio River Blvd., Ben Avon, PA 15202 / 412-766-5114; FAX: 412-766-9354
CP Bullets, 1310 Industrial Hwy #5-6, South Hampton, PA 18966 / 215-953-7264; FAX: 215-953-7275
CQB Training, P.O. Box 1739, Manchester, MO 63011
Craftguard, 3624 Logan Ave., Waterloo, IA 50703 / 319-232-2959; FAX: 319-234-0804
Crandall Tool & Machine Co., 19163 21 Mile Rd., Tustin, MI 49688 / 616-829-4430
Creative Craftsman, Inc., The, 95 Highway 29 N., P.O. Box 331, Lawrenceville, GA 30246 / 404-963-2112; FAX: 404-513-9488
Creedmoor Sports, Inc., 3052 Industry St. #103, Oceanside, CA 92054 / 767-757-5529; FAX: 760-757-5558 shoot@creedmoorsports.com www.creedmoorsports.com
Creek Side Metal & Woodcrafters, Fishers Hill, VA 22626 / 703-465-3903
Creighton Audette, 19 Highland Circle, Springfield, VT 05156 / 802-885-2331
Crimson Trace Lasers, 8090 S.W. Cirrus Dr., Beverton, OR 97008 / 800-442-2406; FAX: 503-627-0166 www.crimsontrace.com
Crit'R Call (See Rocky Mountain Wildlife Products)
Crosman Airguns, Rts. 5 and 20, E. Bloomfield, NY 14443 / 716-657-6161; FAX: 716-657-5405
Crosman Blades (See Coleman Co., Inc.)
Crouse's Country Cover, P.O. Box 160, Storrs, CT 06268 / 860-423-8736
CRR, Inc./Marble's Inc., 420 Industrial Park, P.O. Box 111, Gladstone, MI 49837 / 906-428-3710; FAX: 906-428-3711
Crucelegui, Hermanos (See U.S. Importer-Mandall)
Cubic Shot Shell Co., Inc., 98 Fatima Dr., Campbell, OH 44405 / 330-755-0349
Cullity Restoration, 209 Old Country Rd., East Sandwich, MA 02537 / 508-888-1147
Cumberland Arms, 514 Shafer Road, Manchester, TN 37355 / 800-797-8414
Cumberland Mountain Arms, P.O. Box 710, Winchester, TN 37398 / 615-967-8414; FAX: 615-967-9199
Cummings Bullets, 1417 Esperanza Way, Escondido, CA 92027
Cupp, Alana, Custom Engraver, P.O. Box 207, Annabella, UT 84711 / 801-896-4834
Curly Maple Stock Blanks (See Tiger-Hunt)
Curtis Cast Bullets, 527 W. Babcock St., Bozeman, MT 59715 / 406-587-8117; FAX: 406-587-8117
Curtis Gun Shop (See Curtis Cast Bullets)
Custom Bullets by Hoffman, 2604 Peconic Ave., Seaford, NY 11783
Custom Calls, 607 N. 5th St., Burlington, IA 52601 / 319-752-4465
Custom Checkering Service, Kathy Forster, 2124 S.E. Yamhill St., Portland, OR 97214 / 503-236-5874
Custom Firearms (See Ahrends, Kim)
Custom Products (See Jones Custom Products)
Custom Shop, The, 890 Cochrane Crescent, Peterborough, ON K9H 5N3 CANADA / 705-742-6693
Custom Single Shot Rifles, 9651 Meadows Lane, Guthrie, OK 73044 / 405-282-3634
Custom Tackle and Ammo, P.O. Box 1886, Farmington, NM 87499 / 505-632-3539
Cutco Cutlery, P.O. Box 810, Olean, NY 14760 / 716-372-3111
CVA, 5988 Peachtree Corners East, Norcross, GA 30071 / 770-449-4687; FAX: 770-242-8546 info@cva.com www.cva.com
Cylinder & Slide, Inc., William R. Laughridge, 245 E. 4th St., Fremont, NE 68025 / 402-721-4277; FAX: 402-721-0263 bill@cylinder-slide.com www.clinder-slide.com
CZ USA, P.O. Box 171073, Kansas City, KS 66117 / 913-321-1811; FAX: 913-321-4901

D

D&D Gunsmiths, Ltd., 363 E. Elmwood, Troy, MI 48083 / 248-583-1512; FAX: 248-583-1524
D&G Precision Duplicators (See Greenwood Precision)
D&H Precision Tooling, 7522 Barnard Mill Rd., Ringwood, IL 60072 / 815-653-4011
D&L Industries (See D.J. Marketing)
D&L Sports, P.O. Box 651, Gillette, WY 82717 / 307-686-4008
D.C.C. Enterprises, 259 Wynburn Ave., Athens, GA 30601
D.J. Marketing, 10602 Horton Ave., Downey, CA 90241 / 310-806-0891; FAX: 310-806-6231
D.L. Unmussig Bullets, 7862 Brentford Dr., Richmond, VA 23225 / 804-320-1165; FAX: 804-320-4587
Dade Screw Machine Products, 2319 N.W. 7th Ave., Miami, FL 33127 / 305-573-5050
Daisy Outdoor Products, P.O. Box 220, Rogers, AR 72757 / 479-636-1200; FAX: 479-636-0573 www.daisy.com
Dakota (See U.S. Importer-EMF Co., Inc.)
Dakota Arms, Inc., 130 Industry Road, Sturgis, SD 57785 / 605-347-4686; FAX: 605-347-4459 info@dakotaarms.com www.dakotaarms.com
Dakota Corp., 77 Wales St., P.O. Box 543, Rutland, VT 05701 / 802-775-6062; or 800-451-4167; FAX: 802-773-3919
Daly, Charles/KBI, P.O. Box 6625, Harrisburg, PA 17112 / 866-DALY GUN
Da-Mar Gunsmith's, Inc., 102 1st St., Solvay, NY 13209
damascususa@inteliport.com, 149 Deans Farm Rd., Tyner, NC 27980 / 252-221-2010; FAX: 252-221-2010 damascususa@inteliport.com www.damascususa.com
Dan Wesson Firearms, 5169 Rt. 12 South, Norwich, NY 13815 / 607-336-1174; FAX: 607-336-2730 danwessonfirearms@citlink.net danwessonfirearms.com
Dangler, Homer L., 2870 Lee Marie Dr., Adrian, MI 49221 / 517-266-1997
Danner Shoe Mfg. Co., 12722 N.E. Airport Way, Portland, OR 97230 / 503-251-1100; or 800-345-0430; FAX: 503-251-1119

MANUFACTURER'S DIRECTORY

Dan's Whetstone Co., Inc., 418 Hilltop Rd., Pearcy, AR 71964 / 501-767-1616; FAX: 501-767-9598 questions@danswhetstone.com www.danswhetstone.com
Danuser Machine Co., 550 E. Third St., P.O. Box 368, Fulton, MO 65251 / 573-642-2246; FAX: 573-642-2240 sales@danuser.com www.danuser.com
Dara-Nes, Inc. (See Nesci Enterprises, Inc.)
D'Arcy Echols & Co., P.O. Box 421, Millville, UT 84326 / 435-755-6842
Darlington Gun Works, Inc., P.O. Box 698, 516 S. 52 Bypass, Darlington, SC 29532 / 803-393-3931
Dart Bell/Brass (See MAST Technology Inc.)
Darwin Hensley Gunmaker, P.O. Box 329, Brightwood, OR 97011 / 503-622-5411
Data Tech Software Systems, 19312 East Eldorado Drive, Aurora, CO 80013
Dave Norin Schrank's Smoke & Gun, 2010 Washington St., Waukegan, IL 60085 / 708-662-4034
Dave's Gun Shop, P.O. Box 2824, Casper, WY 82602-2824 / 307-754-9724
David Clark Co., Inc., P.O. Box 15054, Worcester, MA 01615 / 508-756-6216; FAX: 508-753-5827 sales@davidclark.com www.davidclark.com
David Condon, Inc., 109 E. Washington St., Middleburg, VA 22117 / 703-687-5642
David Miller Co., 3131 E. Greenlee Rd., Tucson, AZ 85716 / 520-326-3117
David R. Chicoine, 1210 Jones Street, Gastonia, NC 28052 / 704-853-0265 bnpress@quik.com www.oldwestgunsmith.com
David W. Schwartz Custom Guns, 2505 Waller St., Eau Claire, WI 54703 / 715-832-1735
Davide Pedersoli and Co., Via Artigiani 57, Gardone VT, Brescia 25063, ITALY / 030-8915000; FAX: 030-8911019 info@davidepedersoli.com www.davide_pedersoli.com
Davis, Don, 1619 Heights, Katy, TX 77493 / 713-391-3090
Davis Industries (See Cobra Enterprises, Inc.)
Davis Products, Mike, 643 Loop Dr., Moses Lake, WA 98837 / 509-765-6178; or 509-766-7281
Daystate Ltd., Birch House Lanee, Cotes Heath Staffs, ST15.022, ENGLAND / 01782-791755; FAX: 01782-791617
Dayton Traister, 4778 N. Monkey Hill Rd., P.O. Box 593, Oak Harbor, WA 98277 / 360-679-4657; FAX: 360-675-1114
D-Boone Ent., Inc., 5900 Colwyn Dr., Harrisburg, PA 17109
Dead Eye's Sport Center, 76 Baer Rd., Shickshinny, PA 18655 / 570-256-7432 deadeyeprizz@aol.com
Deepeeka Exports Pvt. Ltd., D-78, Saket, Meerut-250-006, INDIA / 011-91-121-640363 or ; FAX: 011-91-121-640988 deepeeka@poboxes.com www.deepeeka.com
Defense Training International, Inc., 749 S. Lemay, Ste. A3-337, Ft. Collins, CO 80524 / 303-482-2520; FAX: 303-482-0548
deHaas Barrels, 20049 W. State Hwy. Z, Ridgeway, MO 64481 / 660-872-6308
Del Rey Products, P.O. Box 5134, Playa Del Rey, CA 90296-5134 / 213-823-0494
Delhi Gun House, 1374 Kashmere Gate, New Delhi 110 006, INDIA / 2940974; or 394-0974; FAX: 2917344 dgh@vsnl.com
Delorge, Ed, 6734 W. Main, Houma, LA 70360 / 985-223-0206 delorge@triparish.net www.eddelorge.com
Del-Sports, Inc., Dave Budin, P.O. Box 685, 817 Main St., Margaretville, NY 12455 / 845-586-4103; FAX: 845-586-4105
Delta Arms Ltd., P.O. Box 1000, Delta, VT 84624-1000
Delta Enterprises, 284 Hagemann Drive, Livermore, CA 94550
Delta Frangible Ammunition LLC, P.O. Box 2350, Stafford, VA 22555-2350 / 540-720-5778; or 800-339-1933; FAX: 540-720-5667 dfa@dfanet.com www.dfanet.com
Dem-Bart Checkering Tools, Inc., 1825 Bickford Ave., Snohomish, WA 98290 / 360-568-7356 walt@dembartco.com www.dembartco.com
Denver Instrument Co., 6542 Fig St., Arvada, CO 80004 / 800-321-1135; or 303-431-7255; FAX: 303-423-4831
DeSantis Holster & Leather Goods, Inc., 431 Bayview Ave., Amityville, NY 11701 / 631-841-6300; FAX: 631-841-6320 www.desantisholster.com
Desert Mountain Mfg., P.O. Box 130184, Coram, MT 59913 / 800-477-0762; or 406-387-5361; FAX: 406-387-5361
Detonics USA, 53 Perimeter Center East #200, Atlanta, GA 30346 / 866-759-1169
DGR Custom Rifles, 4191 37th Ave. SE, Tappen, ND 58487 / 701-327-8135
DGS, Inc., Dale A. Storey, 1117 E. 12th, Casper, WY 82601 / 307-237-2414; FAX: 307-237-2414 dalest@trib.com www.dgsrifle.com
DHB Products, 336 River View Dr., Verona, VA 24482-2547 / 703-836-2648
Diamond Machining Technology Inc. (See DMT)
Diamond Mfg. Co., P.O. Box 174, Wyoming, PA 18644 / 800-233-9601
Dibble, Derek A., 555 John Downey Dr., New Britain, CT 06051 / 203-224-2630
Dietz Gun Shop & Range, Inc., 421 Range Rd., New Braunfels, TX 78132 / 210-885-4662
Dilliott Gunsmithing, Inc., 657 Scarlett Rd., Dandridge, TN 37725 / 865-397-9204 gunsmithd@aol.com dilliottgunsmithing.com
Dillon Precision Products, Inc., 8009 East Dillon's Way, Scottsdale, AZ 85260 / 480-948-8009; or 800-762-3845; FAX: 480-998-2786 sales@dillonprecision.com www.dillonprecision.com
Dina Arms Corporation, P.O. Box 46, Royersford, PA 19468 / 610-287-0266; FAX: 610-287-0266
Dixie Gun Works, P.O. Box 130, Union City, TN 38281 / 731-885-0700; FAX: 731-885-0440 info@dixiegunworks.com www.dixiegunworks.com
Dixon Muzzleloading Shop, Inc., 9952 Kunkels Mill Rd., Kempton, PA 19529 / 610-756-6271 dixonmuzzleloading.com
DKT, Inc., 14623 Vera Dr., Union, MI 49130-9744 / 800-741-7083 orders; FAX: 616-641-2015
DLO Mfg., 10807 SE Foster Ave., Arcadia, FL 33821-7304
DMT-Diamond Machining Technology, Inc., 85 Hayes Memorial Dr., Marlborough, MA 01752 FAX: 508-485-3924
Dohring Bullets, 100 W. 8 Mile Rd., Ferndale, MI 48220
Dolbare, Elizabeth, P.O. Box 502, Dubois, WY 82513-0502 / 307-450-7500 edolbare@hotmail.com www.scrimshaw-engraving.com
Domino, P.O. Box 108, 20019 Settimo Milanese, Milano, ITALY / 1-39-2-33512040; FAX: 1-39-2-33511587
Don Klein Custom Guns, 433 Murray Park Dr., Ripon, WI 54971 / 920-748-2931 daklein@charter.net www.donkleincustomguns.com
Donnelly, C. P., 405 Kubli Rd., Grants Pass, OR 97527 / 541-846-6604
Doskocil Mfg. Co., Inc., P.O. Box 1246, 4209 Barnett, Arlington, TX 76017 / 817-467-5116; FAX: 817-472-9810
Douglas Barrels, Inc., 5504 Big Tyler Rd., Charleston, WV 25313-1398 / 304-776-1341; FAX: 304-776-8560 www.benchrest.com/douglas
Downsizer Corp., P.O. Box 710316, Santee, CA 92072-0316 / 619-448-5510 www.downsizer.com
DPMS (Defense Procurement Manufacturing Services, Inc.), 13983 Industry Ave., Becker, MN 55308 / 800-578-DPMS; or 763-261-5600; FAX: 763-261-5599
Dr. O's Products Ltd., P.O. Box 111, Niverville, NY 12130 / 518-784-3333; FAX: 518-784-2800
Drain, Mark, SE 3211 Kamilche Point Rd., Shelton, WA 98584 / 206-426-5452
Dremel Mfg. Co., 4915-21st St., Racine, WI 53406
Dri-Slide, Inc., 411 N. Darling, Fremont, MI 49412 / 616-924-3950
Dropkick, 1460 Washington Blvd., Williamsport, PA 17701 / 717-326-6561; FAX: 717-326-4950
DS Arms, Inc., P.O. Box 370, 27 West 990 Industrial Ave., Barrington, IL 60010 / 847-277-7258; FAX: 847-277-7259 www.dsarms.com
DTM International, Inc., 40 Joslyn Rd., P.O. Box 5, Lake Orion, MI 48362 / 313-693-6670
Duane A. Hobbie Gunsmithing, 2412 Pattie Ave., Wichita, KS 67216 / 316-264-8266
Duane's Gun Repair (See DGR Custom Rifles)
Dubber, Michael W., P.O. Box 312, Evansville, IN 47702 / 812-424-9000; FAX: 812-424-6551
Duffy, Charles E. (See Guns Antique & Modern DBA), Williams Ln., P.O. Box 2, West Hurley, NY 12491 / 914-679-2997
Du-Lite Corp., 171 River Rd., Middletown, CT 06457 / 203-347-2505; FAX: 203-347-9404
Dumoulin, Ernest, Rue Florent Boclinville 8-10, 13-4041, Votten, BELGIUM / 41 27 78 92
Duncan's Gun Works, Inc., 1619 Grand Ave., San Marcos, CA 92069 / 760-727-0515
DunLyon R&D, Inc., 52151 E. U.S. Hwy. 60, Miami, AZ 85539 / 928-473-9027
Duofold, Inc., RD 3 Rt. 309, Valley Square Mall, Tamaqua, PA 18252 / 717-386-2666; FAX: 717-386-3652
Dybala Gun Shop, P.O. Box 1024, FM 3156, Bay City, TX 77414 / 409-245-0866
Dykstra, Doug, 411 N. Darling, Fremont, MI 49412 / 616-924-3950
Dynalite Products, Inc., 215 S. Washington St., Greenfield, OH 45123 / 513-981-2124
Dynamit Nobel-RWS, Inc., 81 Ruckman Rd., Closter, NJ 07624 / 201-767-7971; FAX: 201-767-1589

E

E&L Mfg., Inc., 4177 Riddle Bypass Rd., Riddle, OR 97469 / 541-874-2137; FAX: 541-874-3107
E. Arthur Brown Co. Inc., 4353 Hwy. 27 E., Alexandria, MN 56308 / 320-762-8847; FAX: 320-763-4310 www.eabco.com
E.A.A. Corp., P.O. Box 1299, Sharpes, FL 32959 / 407-639-4842; or 800-536-4442; FAX: 407-639-7006
Eagan, Donald V., P.O. Box 196, Benton, PA 17814 / 717-925-6134
Eagle Arms, Inc. (See ArmaLite, Inc.)
Eagle Grips, Eagle Business Center, 460 Randy Rd., Carol Stream, IL 60188 / 800-323-6144; or 708-260-0400; FAX: 708-260-0486
Eagle Imports, Inc., 1750 Brielle Ave., Unit B1, Wanamassa, NJ 07712 / 732-493-0333; FAX: 732-493-0301 gsodini@aol.com www.bersa-llama.com
E-A-R, Inc., Div. of Cabot Safety Corp., 5457 W. 79th St., Indianapolis, IN 46268 / 800-327-3431; FAX: 800-488-8007
EAW (See U.S. Importer-New England Custom Gun Serv
Eckelman Gunsmithing, 3125 133rd St. SW, Fort Ripley, MN 56449 / 218-829-3176
Ed Brown Products, Inc., P.O. Box 492, Perry, MO 63462 / 573-565-3261; FAX: 573-565-2791 edbrown@edbrown.com www.edbrown.com
Edenpine, Inc. c/o Six Enterprises, Inc., 320 D Turtle Creek Ct., San Jose, CA 95125 / 408-999-0201; FAX: 408-999-0216
EdgeCraft Corp., S. Weiner, 825 Southwood Rd., Avondale, PA 19311 / 610-268-0500; or 800-342-3255; FAX: 610-268-3545 www.edgecraft.com
Edmisten Co., P.O. Box 1293, Boone, NC 28607
Edmund Scientific Co., 101 E. Gloucester Pike, Barrington, NJ 08033 / 609-543-6250
Ed's Gun House, Ed Kukowski, P.O. Box 62, Minnesota City, MN 55959 / 507-689-2925
Effebi SNC-Dr. Franco Beretta, via Rossa, 4, 25062, ITALY / 030-2751955; FAX: 030-2180414
Eggleston, Jere D., 400 Saluda Ave., Columbia, SC 29205 / 803-799-3402
Eichelberger Bullets, Wm., 158 Crossfield Rd., King Of Prussia, PA 19406
Ekol Leather Care, P.O. Box 2652, West Lafayette, IN 47906 / 317-463-2250; FAX: 317-463-7004
El Paso Saddlery Co., P.O. Box 27194, El Paso, TX 79926 / 915-544-2233; FAX: 915-544-2535 info@epsaddlery.com www.epsaddlery.com
Electro Prismatic Collimators, Inc., 1441 Manatt St., Lincoln, NE 68521
Electronic Shooters Protection, Inc., 15290 Gadsden Ct., Brighton, CO 80603 / 800-797-7791; FAX: 303-659-8668 esp@usa.net espamerican.com
Eley Ltd., Selco Way Minworth Industrial Estate, Minworth Sutton Coldfield, West Midlands, B76 1BA ENGLAND / 44 0 121-313-4567; FAX: 44 0 121-313-4568 www.eley.co.uk
Elite Ammunition, P.O. Box 3251, Oakbrook, IL 60522 / 708-366-9006
Ellett Bros., 267 Columbia Ave., P.O. Box 128, Chapin, SC 29036 / 803-345-3751; or 800-845-3711; FAX: 803-345-1820 www.ellettbrothers.com
Ellicott Arms, Inc. / Woods Pistolsmithing, 8390 Sunset Dr., Ellicott City, MD 21043 / 410-465-7979
EMAP USA, 6420 Wilshire Blvd., Los Angeles, CA 90048 / 213-782-2000; FAX: 213-782-2867
Emerging Technologies, Inc. (See Laseraim Technologies, Inc.)
EMF Co. Inc., 1900 E. Warner Ave., Suite 1-D, Santa Ana, CA 92705 / 949-261-6611; FAX: 949-756-0133

MANUFACTURER'S DIRECTORY

Empire Cutlery Corp., 12 Kruger Ct., Clifton, NJ 07013 / 201-472-5155; FAX: 201-779-0759
Empire Rifles, P.O. Box 406, Meriden, NH 03770 info@empirerifles.com www.empirerifles.com
English, Inc., A.G., 708 S. 12th St., Broken Arrow, OK 74012 / 918-251-3399 www.agenglish.com
Engraving Artistry, 36 Alto Rd., Burlington, CT 06013 / 860-673-6837 bobburt44@hotmail.com
Enguix Import-Export, Alpujarras 58, Alzira, Valencia, SPAIN / (96) 241 43 95; FAX: (96) 241 43 95
Enhanced Presentations, Inc., 5929 Market St., Wilmington, NC 28405 / 910-799-1622; FAX: 910-799-5004
Enlow, Charles, Box 895, Beaver, OK 73932 / 405-625-4487
Ensign-Bickford Co., The, 660 Hopmeadow St., Simsbury, CT 06070
Entreprise Arms, Inc., 5321 Irwindale Ave., Irwindale, CA 91706-2025 / 626-962-8712; FAX: 626-962-4692 www.entreprise.com
EPC, 1441 Manatt St., Lincoln, NE 68521 / 402-476-3946
Erhardt, Dennis, 4508 N. Montana Ave., Helena, MT 59602 / 406-442-4533
Essex Arms, P.O. Box 363, Island Pond, VT 05846 / 802-723-6203; FAX: 802-723-6203
Estate Cartridge, Inc., 900 Bob Ehlen Dr., Anoka, MN 55303-7502 / 409-856-7277; FAX: 409-856-5486
Euber Bullets, No. Orwell Rd., Orwell, VT 05760 / 802-948-2621
Euroarms of America, Inc., P.O. Box 3277, Winchester, VA 22604 / 540-662-1863; FAX: 540-662-4464 www.euroarms.net
Euro-Imports, 2221 Upland Ave. S., Pahrump, NV 89048 / 775-751-6671; FAX: 775-751-6671
European American Armory Corp. (See E.A.A. Corp.)
Eversull Co., Inc., 1 Tracemont, Boyce, LA 71409 / 318-793-8728; FAX: 318-793-5483 bestguns@aol.com
Evolution Gun Works, Inc., 48 Belmont Ave., Quakertown, PA 18951-1347 www.egw-guns.com
Excalibur Electro Optics, Inc., P.O. Box 400, Fogelsville, PA 18051-0400 / 610-391-9105; FAX: 610-391-9220
Excalibur Publications, P.O. Box 89667, Tucson, AZ 85752 / 520-575-9057 excalibureditor@earthlink.net
Excel Industries, Inc., 4510 Carter Ct., Chino, CA 91710 / 909-627-2404; FAX: 909-627-7817
Executive Protection Institute, P.O. Box 802, Berryville, VA 22611 / 540-554-2540; FAX: 540-554-2558 ruk@crosslink.net www.personalprotecion.com
Eze-Lap Diamond Prods., P.O. Box 2229, 15164 W. State St., Westminster, CA 92683 / 714-847-1555; FAX: 714-897-0280
E-Z-Way Systems, P.O. Box 4310, Newark, OH 43058-4310 / 614-345-6645; or 800-848-2072; FAX: 614-345-6600

F

F&W Publications, Inc., 700 E. State St., Iola, WI 54990 / 715-445-2214; FAX: 715-445-4087
F.A.I.R., Via Gitti, 41, 25060 Marcheno Bresc, ITALY / 030 861162-8610344; FAX: 030 8610179 info@fair.it www.fair.it
Fabarm S.p.A., Via Averolda 31, 25039 Travagliato, Brescia, ITALY / 030-6863629; FAX: 030-6863684 info@fabarm.com www.fabarm.com
Fagan Arms, 22952 15 Mile Rd., Clinton Township, MI 48035 / 810-465-4637; FAX: 810-792-6996
Faith Associates, P.O. Box 549, Flat Rock, NC 28731-0549 FAX: 828-697-6827
Falcon Industries, Inc., P.O. Box 1690, Edgewood, NM 87015 / 505-281-3783; FAX: 505-281-3991 shines@ergogrips.net www.ergogrips.net
Far North Outfitters, Box 1252, Bethel, AK 99559
Farm Form Decoys, Inc., 1602 Biovu, P.O. Box 748, Galveston, TX 77553 / 409-744-0762; or 409-765-6361; FAX: 409-765-8513
Farr Studio, Inc., 17149 Bournbrook Ln., Jeffersonton, VA 22724-1796 / 615-638-8825
Farrar Tool Co., Inc., 11855 Cog Hill Dr., Whittier, CA 90601-1902 / 310-863-4367; FAX: 310-863-5123
Faulhaber Wildlocker, Dipl.-Ing. Norbert Wittasek, Seilergasse 2, A-1010 Wien, AUSTRIA / 43-1-5137001; FAX: 43-1-5137001 faulhaber1@utanet.at
Faulk's Game Call Co., Inc., 616 18th St., Lake Charles, LA 70601 / 337-436-9726; FAX: 337-494-7205
Faust Inc., T. G., 544 Minor St., Reading, PA 19602 / 610-375-8549; FAX: 610-375-4488
Fautheree, Andy, P.O. Box 4607, Pagosa Springs, CO 81157 / 970-731-5003; FAX: 970-731-5009
Feather, Flex Decoys, 4500 Doniphan Dr., Neosho, MO 64850 / 318-746-8596; FAX: 318-742-4815
Federal Cartridge Co., 900 Ehlen Dr., Anoka, MN 55303 / 612-323-2300; FAX: 612-323-2506
Federal Champion Target Co., 232 Industrial Pkwy., Richmond, IN 47374 / 800-441-4971; FAX: 317-966-7747
Federated-Fry (See Fry Metals)
FEG, Budapest, Soroksariut 158, H-1095, HUNGARY
Feinwerkbau Westinger & Altenburger, Neckarstrasse 43, 78727, Oberndorf a. N., GERMANY / 07423-814-0; FAX: 07423-814-200 info@feinwerkbau.de www.feinwerkbau.de
Felk Pistols, Inc., P.O. Box 33, Bracey, VA 23919 / 434-636-2537; FAX: 208-988-4834
Ferguson, Bill, P.O. Box 1238, Sierra Vista, AZ 85636 / 520-458-5321; FAX: 520-458-9125
Ferguson, Bill. See: BULLET METALS
FERLIB, Via Parte 33 Marcheno/BS, Marcheno/BS, ITALY / 00390308610191; FAX: 00390308966882 info@ferlib.com www.ferlib.com
Ferris Firearms, 7110 F.M. 1863, Bulverde, TX 78163 / 210-980-4424
Fibron Products, Inc., P.O. Box 430, Buffalo, NY 14209-0430 / 716-886-2378; FAX: 716-886-2394
Fieldsport Ltd., Bryan Bilinski, 3313 W. South Airport Rd., Traverse City, MI 49684 / 616-933-0767
Fiocchi Munizioni S.A. (See U.S. Importer-Fiocch
Fiocchi of America, Inc., 5030 Fremont Rd., Ozark, MO 65721 / 417-725-4118; or 800-721-2666; FAX: 417-725-1039
Firearm Brokers, 4143 Taylor Blvd., Louisville, KY 40215 / 502-366-0555 firearmbrokers@aol.com www.firearmbrokers.com
Firearm Training Center, The, 9555 Blandville Rd., West Paducah, KY 42086 / 502-554-5886
Firearms Co. Ltd. / Alpine (See U.S. Importer-Mandall
Firearms Engraver's Guild of America, 3011 E. Pine Dr., Flagstaff, AZ 86004 / 928-527-8427 fegainfo@fega.com
Fisher, Jerry A., 631 Crane Mt. Rd., Big Fork, MT 59911 / 406-837-2722
Fisher Custom Firearms, 2199 S. Kittredge Way, Aurora, CO 80013 / 303-755-3710
Fitzgerald, Jack. See: CLENZOIL WORLDWIDE CORP.
Flambeau, Inc., 15981 Valplast Rd., Middlefield, OH 44062 / 216-632-1631; FAX: 216-632-1581 www.flambeau.com
Flayderman & Co., Inc., P.O. Box 2446, Fort Lauderdale, FL 33303 / 954-761-8855 www.flayderman.com
Fleming Firearms, 7720 E. 126th St. N., Collinsville, OK 74021-7016 / 918-665-3624
Fletcher-Bidwell, LLC, 305 E. Terhune St., Viroqua, WI 54665-1631 / 866-637-1860 fbguns@netscape.net
Flintlocks, Etc., 160 Rossiter Rd., P.O. Box 181, Richmond, MA 01254 / 413-698-3822; FAX: 413-698-3866 flintetc@berkshire.rr.com
Flitz International Ltd., 821 Mohr Ave., Waterford, WI 53185 / 414-534-5898; FAX: 414-534-2991
Fluoramics, Inc., 18 Industrial Ave., Mahwah, NJ 07430 / 800-922-0075; FAX: 201-825-7035
Flynn's Custom Guns, P.O. Box 7461, Alexandria, LA 71306 / 318-455-7130
FN Manufacturing, P.O. Box 24257, Columbia, SC 29224 / 803-736-0522
Folks, Donald E., 205 W. Lincoln St., Pontiac, IL 61764 / 815-844-7901
Foothills Video Productions, Inc., P.O. Box 651, Spartanburg, SC 29304 / 803-573-7023; or 800-782-5358
Foredom Electric Co., Rt. 6, 16 Stony Hill Rd., Bethel, CT 06801 / 203-792-8622
Forgett, Valmore. See: NAVY ARMS COMPANY
Forgreens Tool & Mfg., Inc., P.O. Box 955, Robert Lee, TX 76945 / 915-453-2800; FAX: 915-453-2460
Forkin Custom Classics, 205 10th Ave. S.W., White Sulphur Spring, MT 59645 / 406-547-2344
Forrest Tool Co., P.O. Box 768, 44380 Gordon Ln., Mendocino, CA 95460 / 707-937-2141; FAX: 717-937-1817
Forster, Kathy (See Custom Checkering)
Forster, Larry L., Box 212, 216 Hwy. 13 E., Gwinner, ND 58040-0212 / 701-678-2475
Forster Products, Inc., 310 E. Lanark Ave., Lanark, IL 61046 / 815-493-6360; FAX: 815-493-2371 info@forsterproducts.com www.forsterproductscom
Fort Hill Gunstocks, 12807 Fort Hill Rd., Hillsboro, OH 45133 / 513-466-2763
Fort Knox Security Products, 1051 N. Industrial Park Rd., Orem, UT 84057 / 801-224-7233; or 800-821-5216; FAX: 801-226-5493
Forthofer's Gunsmithing & Knifemaking, 5535 U.S. Hwy. 93S, Whitefish, MT 59937-8411 / 406-862-2674
Fortune Products, Inc., 205 Hickory Creek Rd., Marble Falls, TX 78654 / 210-693-6111; FAX: 210-693-6394 randy@accusharp.com
Forty-Five Ranch Enterprises, Box 1080, Miami, OK 74355-1080 / 918-542-5875
Foster, . See: ACCURACY INTERNATIONAL
Fountain Products, 492 Prospect Ave., West Springfield, MA 01089 / 413-781-4651; FAX: 413-733-8217
Fowler Bullets, 806 Dogwood Dr., Gastonia, NC 28054 / 704-867-3259
Fowler, Bob (See Black Powder Products)
Fox River Mills, Inc., P.O. Box 298, 227 Poplar St., Osage, IA 50461 / 515-732-3798; FAX: 515-732-5128
Frank Knives, 13868 NW Keleka Pl., Seal Rock, OR 97376 / 541-563-3041; FAX: 541-563-3041
Frank Mittermeier, Inc., P.O. Box 1, Bronx, NY 10465
Franzen International, Inc. (See U.S. Importer-Importer Co.)
Fred F. Wells/Wells Sport Store, 110 N. Summit St., Prescott, AZ 86301 / 928-445-3655 www.wellssportstore@cableone.net
Freedom Arms, Inc., P.O. Box 150, Freedom, WY 83120 / 307-883-2468; FAX: 307-883-2005
Fremont Tool Works, 1214 Prairie, Ford, KS 67842 / 316-369-2327
Front Sight Firearms Training Institute, P.O. Box 2619, Aptos, CA 95001 / 800-987-7719; FAX: 408-684-2137
Frontier, 2910 San Bernardo, Laredo, TX 78040 / 956-723-5409; FAX: 956-723-1774
Frontier Arms Co., Inc., 401 W. Rio Santa Cruz, Green Valley, AZ 85614-3932
Frontier Products Co., 2401 Walker Rd., Roswell, NM 88201-8950 / 614-262-9357
Frontier Safe Co., 3201 S. Clinton St., Fort Wayne, IN 46806 / 219-744-7233; FAX: 219-744-6678
Frost Cutlery Co., P.O. Box 22636, Chattanooga, TN 37422 / 615-894-6079; FAX: 615-894-9576
Fry Metals, 4100 6th Ave., Altoona, PA 16602 / 814-946-1611
Fujinon, Inc., 10 High Point Dr., Wayne, NJ 07470 / 201-633-5600; FAX: 201-633-5216
Fullmer, Geo. M., 2499 Mavis St., Oakland, CA 94601 / 510-533-4193
Fulton Armory, 8725 Bollman Place No. 1, Savage, MD 20763 / 301-490-9485; FAX: 301-490-9547 www.fulton.armory.com
Furr Arms, 91 N. 970 West, Orem, UT 84057 / 801-226-3877; FAX: 801-226-3877

G

G&H Decoys, Inc., P.O. Box 1208, Hwy. 75 North, Henryetta, OK 74437 / 918-652-3314; FAX: 918-652-3400
G.C. Bullet Co., Inc., 40 Mokelumne River Dr., Lodi, CA 95240
G.G. & G., 3602 E. 42nd Stravenue, Tucson, AZ 85713 / 520-748-7167; FAX: 520-748-7583 ggg&3@aol.com www.ggg&3.com
G.H. Enterprises Ltd., Bag 10, Okotoks, AB T0L 1T0 CANADA / 403-938-6070
G.U., Inc. (See U.S. Importer-New SKB Arms Co.)
G96 Products Co., Inc., 85 5th Ave., Bldg. #6, Paterson, NJ 07544 / 973-684-4050; FAX: 973-684-3848 g96prod@aol
Gage Manufacturing, 663 W. 7th St., A, San Pedro, CA 90731 / 310-832-3546
Gaillard Barrels, Box 68, St. Brieux, SK S0K 3V0 CANADA / 306-752-3769; FAX: 306-752-5969
Galati International, P.O. Box 10, 616 Burley Ridge Rd., Wesco, MO 65586 / 636-584-0785; FAX: 573-775-4308 support@galatiinternational.com www.galatiinternational.com
Galaxy Imports Ltd., Inc., P.O. Box 3361, Victoria, TX 77903 / 361-573-4867; FAX: 361-576-9622 galaxy@cox-internet.com
GALCO International Ltd., 2019 W. Quail Ave., Phoenix, AZ 85027 / 623-474-7070; FAX: 623-582-6854 customerservice@usgalco.com www.usgalco.com
Galena Industries AMT, 5463 Diaz St., Irwindale, CA 91706 / 626-856-8883; FAX: 626-856-8878
Gamba S.p.A. Societa Armi Bresciane Srl, Renato, Via Artigiani 93, ITALY / 30-8911640; FAX: 30-8911648
Gamba, USA, P.O. Box 60452, Colorado Springs, CO 80960 / 719-578-1145; FAX: 719-444-0731
Game Haven Gunstocks, 13750 Shire Rd., Wolverine, MI 49799 / 616-525-8257

MANUFACTURER'S DIRECTORY

Gamebore Division, Polywad, Inc., P.O. Box 7916, Macon, GA 31209 / 478-477-0669; or 800-998-0669
Gamo (See U.S. Importers-Arms United Corp., Daisy M
Gamo USA, Inc., 3911 SW 47th Ave., Suite 914, Fort Lauderdale, FL 33314 / 954-581-5822; FAX: 954-581-3165 gamousa@gate.net www.gamo.com
Gander Mountain, Inc., 12400 Fox River Rd., Wilmont, WI 53192 / 414-862-6848
GAR, 590 McBride Ave., West Paterson, NJ 07424 / 973-754-1114; FAX: 973-754-1114 garreloading@aol.com www.garreloading.com
Garcia National Gun Traders, Inc., 225 SW 22nd Ave., Miami, FL 33135 / 305-642-2355
Garrett Cartridges, Inc., P.O. Box 178, Chehalis, WA 98532 / 360-736-0702 www.garrettcartridges.com
Garthwaite Pistolsmith, Inc., Jim, 12130 State Route 405, Watsontown, PA 17777 / 570-538-1566; FAX: 570-538-2965 www.garthwaite.com
Gary Goudy Classic Stocks, 1512 S. 5th St., Dayton, WA 99328 / 509-382-2726 goudy@innw.net
Gary Reeder Custom Guns, 2601 7th Ave. E., Flagstaff, AZ 86004 / 928-526-3313; FAX: 928-527-0840 gary@reedercustomguns.com www.reedercustomguns.com
Gator Guns & Repair, 7952 Kenai Spur Hwy., Kenai, AK 99611-8311
Gaucher Armes, S.A., 46 rue Desjoyaux, 42000, Saint-Etienne, FRANCE / 04-77-33-38-92; FAX: 04-77-61-95-72
GDL Enterprises, 409 Le Gardeur, Slidell, LA 70460 / 504-649-0693
Gehmann, Walter (See Huntington Die Specialties)
Genco, P.O. Box 5704, Asheville, NC 28803
Genecco Gun Works, 10512 Lower Sacramento Rd., Stockton, CA 95210 / 209-951-0706; FAX: 209-931-3872
Gene's Custom Guns, P.O. Box 10534, White Bear Lake, MN 55110 / 651-429-5105; FAX: 651-429-7365
Gentex Corp., 5 Tinkham Ave., Derry, NH 03038 / 603-434-0311; FAX: 603-434-3002 sales@derry.gentexcorp.com www.derry.gentexcorp.com
Gentner Bullets, 109 Woodlawn Ave., Upper Darby, PA 19082 / 610-352-9396 dongentner@rcn.com www.gentnerbullets.com
Gentry Custom LLC, 314 N. Hoffman, Belgrade, MT 59714 / 406-388-GUNS gentryshop@earthlink.net www.gentrycustom.com
George & Roy's, P.O. Box 2125, Sisters, OR 97759-2125 / 503-228-5424; or 800-553-3022; FAX: 503-225-9409
George Hoenig, Inc., 6521 Morton Dr., Boise, ID 83704 / 208-375-1116; FAX: 208-375-1116
George Ibberson (Sheffield) Ltd., 25-31 Allen St., Sheffield, S3 7AW ENGLAND / 0114-2766123; FAX: 0114-2738465 sales@eggintongroupco.uk www.eggintongroup.co.uk
Gerber Legendary Blades, 14200 SW 72nd Ave., Portland, OR 97223 / 503-639-6161; or 800-950-6161; FAX: 503-684-7008
Gervais, Mike, 3804 S. Cruise Dr., Salt Lake City, UT 84109 / 801-277-7729
Getz Barrel Company, P.O. Box 88, 426 E. Market St., Beavertown, PA 17813 / 570-658-7263; FAX: 570-658-4110 www.getzbrl.com
Giacomo Sporting USA, 6234 Stokes Lee Center Rd., Lee Center, NY 13363
Gibbs Rifle Co., Inc., 219 Lawn St., Martinsburg, WV 25401 / 304-262-1651; FAX: 304-262-1658 support@gibbsrifle.com www.gibbsrifle.com
Gil Hebard Guns, Inc., 125 Public Square, Knoxville, IL 61448 / 309-289-2700; FAX: 309-289-2233
Gilbert Equipment Co., Inc., 960 Downtowner Rd., Mobile, AL 36609 / 205-344-3322
Gillmann, Edwin, 33 Valley View Dr., Hanover, PA 17331 / 717-632-1662 gillmaned@superpa.net
Gilmore Sports Concepts, Inc., 5949 S. Garnett Rd., Tulsa, OK 74146 / 918-250-3810; FAX: 918-250-3845 info@gilmoresports.com www.gilmoresports.com
Glacier Glove, 4890 Aircenter Circle, Suite 210, Reno, NV 89502 / 702-825-8225; FAX: 702-825-6544
Glaser LLC, P.O. Box 173, Sturgis, SD 57785 / 605-347-4544; or 800-221-3489; FAX: 605-347-5055 email@corbon.com www.safetyslug.com
Glaser Safety Slug, Inc., P.O. Box 8223, Foster City, CA 94404 / 800-221-3489; FAX: 510-785-6685 safetyslug.com
Glass, Herb, P.O. Box 25, Bullville, NY 10915 / 914-361-3021
Glimm, Jerome. See: GLIMM'S CUSTOM GUN ENGRAVING
Glimm's Custom Gun Engraving, Jerome C. Glimm, 19 S. Maryland, Conrad, MT 59425 / 406-278-3574 jandlglimm@mcn.net www.gunengraver.biz
Glock GmbH, P.O. Box 50, A-2232, Deutsch, Wagram, AUSTRIA
Glock, Inc., P.O. Box 369, Smyrna, GA 30081 / 770-432-1202; FAX: 770-433-8719
Glynn Scobey Duck & Goose Calls, Rt. 3, Box 37, Newbern, TN 38059 / 731-643-6128
GML Products, Inc., 394 Laredo Dr., Birmingham, AL 35226 / 205-979-4867
Goens, Dale W., P.O. Box 224, Cedar Crest, NM 87008 / 505-281-5419
Goergen's Gun Shop, Inc., 17985 538th Ave., Austin, MN 55912 / 507-433-9280
GOEX, Inc., P.O. Box 659, Doyline, LA 71023-0659 / 318-382-9300; FAX: 318-382-9303 mfahringer@goexpowder.com www.goexpowder.com
Golden Age Arms Co., 115 E. High St., Ashley, OH 43003 / 614-747-2488
Golden Bear Bullets, 3065 Fairfax Ave., San Jose, CA 95148 / 408-238-9515
Gonic Arms North American Arms, Inc., 134 Flagg Rd., Gonic, NH 03839 / 603-332-8456; or 603-332-8457
Goodling's Gunsmithing, 1950 Stoverstown Rd., Spring Grove, PA 17362 / 717-225-3350
Goodwin, Fred. See: GOODWIN'S GUNS
Goodwin's Guns, Fred Goodwin, Silver Ridge, ME 04776 / 207-365-4451
Gotz Bullets, 11426 Edgemere Ter., Roscoe, IL 61073-8232
Gould & Goodrich Leather, Inc., 709 E. McNeil St., Lillington, NC 27546 / 910-893-2071; FAX: 910-893-4742 info@gouldusa.com www.gouldusa.com
Gournet Artistic Engraving, Geoffroy Gournet, 820 Paxinosa Ave., Easton, PA 18042 / 610-559-0710 www.geoffroygournet.com
Gournet, Geoffroy. See: GOURNET ARTISTIC ENGRAVING
Grace, Charles E., 718 E. 2nd, Trinidad, CO 81082 / 719-846-9435 chuckgrace@sensonics.org
Grace Metal Products, P.O. Box 67, Elk Rapids, MI 49629 / 616-264-8133
Graf & Sons, 4050 S. Clark St., Mexico, MO 65265 / 573-581-2266; FAX: 573-581-2875 customerservice@grafs.com www.grafs.com
Grand Slam Hunting Products, Box 121, 25454 Military Rd., Cascade, MD 21719 / 301-241-4900; FAX: 301-241-4900 rlj6call@aol.com
Granite Mountain Arms, Inc., 3145 W. Hidden Acres Trail, Prescott, AZ 86305 / 520-541-9758; FAX: 520-445-6826
Grant, Howard V., Hiawatha 15, Woodruff, WI 54568 / 715-356-7146
Graphics Direct, P.O. Box 372421, Reseda, CA 91337-2421 / 818-344-9002
Graves Co., 1800 Andrews Ave., Pompano Beach, FL 33069 / 800-327-9103; FAX: 305-960-0301
Grayback Wildcats, Mike Beeks, 5306 Bryant Ave., Klamath Falls, OR 97603 / 541-884-1072; FAX: 541-884-1072 graybackwildcats@aol.com
Graybill's Gun Shop, 1035 Ironville Pike, Columbia, PA 17512 / 717-684-2739
Great American Gunstock Co., 3420 Industrial Drive, Yuba City, CA 95993 / 800-784-4867; FAX: 530-671-3906 gunstox@hotmail.com www.gunstocks.com
Great Lakes Airguns, 6175 S. Park Ave., Hamburg, NY 14075 / 716-648-6666; FAX: 716-648-6666 www.greatlakesairguns.com
Green, Arthur S., 485 S. Robertson Blvd., Beverly Hills, CA 90211 / 310-274-1283
Green, Roger M., P.O. Box 984, 435 E. Birch, Glenrock, WY 82637 / 307-436-9804
Green Head Game Call Co., RR 1, Box 33, Lacon, IL 61540 / 309-246-2155
Green Mountain Rifle Barrel Co., Inc., P.O. Box 2670, 153 W. Main St., Conway, NH 03818 / 603-447-1095; FAX: 603-447-1099 info@gmriflebarrel.com www.gmriflebarrel.com
Greenwood Precision, P.O. Box 407, Rogersville, MO 65742 / 417-725-2330
Greg Gunsmithing Repair, 3732 26th Ave. N., Robbinsdale, MN 55422 / 612-529-8103
Greg's Superior Products, P.O. Box 46219, Seattle, WA 98146
Greider Precision, 431 Santa Marina Ct., Escondido, CA 92029 / 760-480-8892; FAX: 760-480-9800 greider@msn.com
Gre-Tan Rifles, 29742 W.C.R. 50, Kersey, CO 80644 / 970-353-6176; FAX: 970-356-5940 www.gtrtooling.com
Grier Hard Cast Bullets, P.O. Box 41, Tillamook, OR 97141-0041 / 503-963-8796
Grier's Hard Cast Bullets, 1107 11th St., LaGrande, OR 97850 / 503-963-8796
Griffin & Howe, Inc., 340 W. Putnam Ave., Greenwich, CT 06830 / 203-618-0270 info@griffinhowe.com www.griffinhowe.com
Griffin & Howe, Inc., 33 Claremont Rd., Bernardsville, NJ 07924 / 908-766-2287; FAX: 908-766-1068 info@griffinhowe.com www.griffinhowe.com
Grifon, Inc., 58 Guinam St., Waltham, MS 02154
Groenewold, John. See: JG AIRGUNS, LLC
GRS/Glendo Corp., P.O. Box 1153, 900 Overlander St., Emporia, KS 66801 / 620-343-1084; or 800-836-3519; FAX: 620-343-9640 glendo@glendo.com www.glendo.com
Grulla Armes, Apartado 453, Avda Otaloa 12, Eiber, SPAIN
Gruning Precision, Inc., 7101 Jurupa Ave., No. 12, Riverside, CA 92504 / 909-289-4371; FAX: 909-689-7791 gruningprecision@earthlink.net www.gruningprecision.com
GSI, Inc., 7661 Commerce Ln., Trussville, AL 35173 / 205-655-8299
GTB-Custom Bullets, 482 Comerwood Court, S. San Francisco, CA 94080 / 650-583-1550
Guarasi, Robert. See: WILCOX INDUSTRIES CORP.
Guardsman Products, 411 N. Darling, Fremont, MI 49412 / 616-924-3950
Gun City, 212 W. Main Ave., Bismarck, ND 58501 / 701-223-2304
Gun Doc, Inc., 5405 NW 82nd Ave., Miami, FL 33166 / 305-477-2777; FAX: 305-477-2778 www.gundoc.com
Gun Doctor, The, 435 E. Maple, Roselle, IL 60172 / 708-894-0668
Gun Hunter Books (See Gun Hunter Trading Co.), 5075 Heisig St., Beaumont, TX 77705 / 409-835-3006; FAX: 409-838-2266 gunhuntertrading@hotmail.com
Gun Hunter Trading Co., 5075 Heisig St., Beaumont, TX 77705 / 409-835-3006; FAX: 409-838-2266 gunhuntertrading@hotmail.com
Gun Leather Limited, 116 Lipscomb, Fort Worth, TX 76104 / 817-334-0225; FAX: 800-247-0609
Gun List (See F&W Publications), 700 E. State St., Iola, WI 54990 / 715-445-2214; FAX: 715-445-4087
Gun Room Press, The, 127 Raritan Ave., Highland Park, NJ 08904 / 732-545-4344; FAX: 732-545-6686 gunbooks@rutgersgunbooks.com www.rutgersgunbooks.com
Gun Room, The, 1121 Burlington, Muncie, IN 47302 / 765-282-9073; FAX: 765-282-5270 bshstleguns@aol.com
Gun Shop, The, 62778 Spring Creek Rd., Montrose, CO 81401
Gun Shop, The, 5550 S. 900 East, Salt Lake City, UT 84117 / 801-263-3633
Gun South, Inc. (See GSI, Inc.)
Gun Vault, 7339 E. Acoma Dr., Ste. 7, Scottsdale, AZ 85260 / 602-951-6855
Gun Works, The, 247 S. 2nd St., Springfield, OR 97477 / 541-741-4118; FAX: 541-988-1097 gunworks@worldnet.att.net www.thegunworks.com
Gun-Alert, 1010 N. Maclay Ave., San Fernando, CA 91340 / 818-365-0864; FAX: 818-365-1308
Guncraft Books (See Guncraft Sports, Inc.), 10737 Dutchtown Rd., Knoxville, TN 37932 / 865-966-4545; FAX: 865-966-4500 findit@guncraft.com www.guncraft.com
Guncraft Sports, Inc., 10737 Dutchtown Rd., Knoxville, TN 37932 / 865-966-4545; FAX: 865-966-4500 findit@guncraft.com www.usit.net/guncraft
Guncraft Sports, Inc., Marie C. Wiest, 10737 Dutchtown Rd., Knoxville, TN 37932 / 865-966-4545; FAX: 865-966-4500 findit@guncraft.com www.guncraft.com
Guncrafter Industries, 171 Madison 1510, Huntsville, AR 72740 / 479-665-2466 www.guncrafterindustries.com
Gun-Ho Sports Cases, 110 E. 10th St., St. Paul, MN 55101 / 612-224-9491
Gunline Tools, 2950 Saturn St., "O", Brea, CA 92821 / 714-993-5100; FAX: 714-572-4128
Gunnerman Books, P.O. Box 81697, Rochester Hills, MI 48308 / 248-608-2856 gunnermanbks@att.net

MANUFACTURER'S DIRECTORY

Guns Antique & Modern DBA / Charles E. Duffy, Williams Lane, West Hurley, NY 12491 / 914-679-2997
Guns Div. of D.C. Engineering, Inc., 8633 Southfield Fwy., Detroit, MI 48228 / 313-271-7111; or 800-886-7623; FAX: 313-271-7112 guns@rifletech.com www.rifletech.com
GUNS Magazine, 12345 World Trade Dr., San Diego, CA 92128-3743 / 619-297-5350; FAX: 619-297-5353
Gunsight, The, 1712 N. Placentia Ave., Fullerton, CA 92631
Gunsite Training Center, P.O. Box 700, Paulden, AZ 86334 / 520-636-4565; FAX: 520-636-1236
Gunsmithing Ltd., 57 Unquowa Rd., Fairfield, CT 06824 / 203-254-0436; FAX: 203-254-1535
Gunsmithing, Inc., 30 W. Buchanan St., Colorado Springs, CO 80907 / 719-632-3795; FAX: 719-632-3493 www.nealsguns.com
Gurney, F. R., Box 13, Sooke, BC V0S 1N0 CANADA / 604-642-5282; FAX: 604-642-7859

H

H&B Forge Co., Rt. 2, Geisinger Rd., Shiloh, OH 44878 / 419-895-1856
H&P Publishing, 7174 Hoffman Rd., San Angelo, TX 76905 / 915-655-5953
H&R 1871.LLC, 60 Industrial Rowe, Gardner, MA 01440 / 508-632-9393; FAX: 508-632-2300 hr1871@hr1871.com www.hr1871.com
H. Krieghoff Gun Co., Boschstrasse 22, D-89079, Ulm, GERMANY / 731-401820; FAX: 731-4018270
H.K.S. Products, 7841 Founion Dr., Florence, KY 41042 / 606-342-7841; or 800-354-9814; FAX: 606-342-5865
H.P. White Laboratory, Inc., 3114 Scarboro Rd., Street, MD 21154 / 410-838-6550; FAX: 410-838-2802 info@hpwhite.com www.hpwhite.com
Hafner World Wide, Inc., P.O. Box 1987, Lake City, FL 32055 / 904-755-6481; FAX: 904-755-6595 hafner@isgroupe.net
Hakko Co. Ltd., 1-13-12, Narimasu, Itabashiku Tokyo, JAPAN / 03-5997-7870/2; FAX: 81-3-5997-7840
Half Moon Rifle Shop, 490 Halfmoon Rd., Columbia Falls, MT 59912 / 406-892-4409 halfmoonrs@centurytel.net
Hall Manufacturing, 142 CR 406, Clanton, AL 35045 / 205-755-4094
Hall Plastics, Inc., John, P.O. Box 1526, Alvin, TX 77512 / 713-489-8709
Hallberg, Fritz. See: CAMBOS OUTDOORSMAN
Hallowell & Co., P.O. Box 1445, Livingston, MT 59047 / 406-222-4770; FAX: 406-222-4792 morris@hallowellco.com www.hallowellco.com
Hally Caller, 443 Wells Rd., Doylestown, PA 18901 / 215-345-6354; FAX: 215-345-6354 info@hallycaller.com www.hallycaller.com
Hamilton, Alex B. (See Ten-Ring Precision, Inc.)
Hammans, Charles E., P.O. Box 788, 2022 McCracken, Stuttgart, AR 72160-0788 / 870-673-1388
Hammerli AG, Industrieplaz, a/Rheinpall, CH-8212 Neuhausen, SWITZERLAND info@hammerli.com www.haemmerliich.com
Hammerli Service-Precision Mac, Rudolf Marent, 9711 Tiltree St., Houston, TX 77075 / 713-946-7028 rmarent@webtv.net
Hammerli USA, 19296 Oak Grove Circle, Groveland, CA 95321 FAX: 209-962-5311
Hammond Custom Guns Ltd., 619 S. Pandora, Gilbert, AZ 85234 / 602-892-3437
HandCrafts Unltd. (See Clements' Custom Leathercraft), 1741 Dallas St., Aurora, CO 80010-2018 / 303-364-0403; FAX: 303-739-9824 gryphons@home.com kuntaoslcat.com
Handgun Press, P.O. Box 406, Glenview, IL 60025 / 847-657-6500; FAX: 847-724-8831 handgunpress@comcast.net
Hank's Gun Shop, Box 370, 50 W. 100 South, Monroe, UT 84754 / 435-527-4456 hanksgs@compuvision.com
Hanned Line, The, 4463 Madoc Way, San Jose, CA 95130 smith@hanned.com www.hanned.com
Hanned Precision (See The Hanned Line)
Hansen & Co., 244-246 Old Post Rd., Southport, CT 06490 / 203-259-6222; FAX: 203-254-3832
Hanson's Gun Center, Dick, 233 Everett Dr., Colorado Springs, CO 80911
Harford (See U.S. Importer-EMF Co., Inc.)
Harper's Custom Stocks, 928 Lombrano St., San Antonio, TX 78207 / 210-732-7174
Harrell's Precision, 5756 Hickory Dr., Salem, VA 24153 / 540-380-2683
Harrington & Richardson (See H&R 1871, Inc.)
Harris Engineering Inc., Dept. GD54, 999 Broadway, Barlow, KY 42024 / 270-334-3633; FAX: 270-334-3000
Harris Enterprises, P.O. Box 105, Bly, OR 97622 / 503-353-2625
Harris Hand Engraving, Paul A., 113 Rusty Ln., Boerne, TX 78006-5746 / 512-391-5121
Harris Publications, 1115 Broadway, New York, NY 10010 / 212-807-7100; FAX: 212-627-4678
Harrison Bullets, 6437 E. Hobart St., Mesa, AZ 85205
Harry Lawson Co., 3328 N. Richey Blvd., Tucson, AZ 85716 / 520-326-1117; FAX: 520-326-1117
Hart & Son, Inc., Robert W., 401 Montgomery St., Nescopeck, PA 18635 / 717-752-3655; FAX: 717-752-1088
Hart Rifle Barrels, Inc., P.O. Box 182, 1690 Apulia Rd., Lafayette, NY 13084 / 315-677-9841; FAX: 315-677-9610 hartrb@aol.com hartbarrels.com
Hartford (See U.S. Importer-EMF Co. Inc.)
Hartmann & Weiss GmbH, Rahlstedter Bahnhofstr. 47, 22143, Hamburg, GERMANY / (40) 677 55 85; FAX: (40) 677 55 92 hartmannundweiss@t-online.de
Harvey, Frank, 218 Nightfall, Terrace, NV 89015 / 702-558-6998
Hastings, P.O. Box 135, Clay Center, KS 67432 / 785-632-3169; FAX: 785-632-6554
Hatfield Gun, 224 N. 4th St., St. Joseph, MO 64501
Hawk Laboratories, Inc. (See Hawk, Inc.), 849 Hawks Bridge Rd., Salem, NJ 08079 / 609-299-2700; FAX: 609-299-2800
Hawk, Inc., 849 Hawks Bridge Rd., Salem, NJ 08079 / 609-299-2700; FAX: 609-299-2800 info@hawkbullets.com www.hawkbullets.com
Hawken Shop, The, P.O. Box 593, Oak Harbor, WA 98277 / 206-679-4657; FAX: 206-675-1114
Hawken Shop, The (See Dayton Traister)
Haydel's Game Calls, Inc., 5018 Hazel Jones Rd., Bossier City, LA 71111 / 318-746-3586; FAX: 318-746-3711 www.haydels.com
Hecht, Hubert J., Waffen-Hecht, P.O. Box 2635, Fair Oaks, CA 95628 / 916-966-1020
Heckler & Koch GmbH, P.O. Box 1329, 78722 Oberndorf, Neckar, GERMANY / 49-7423179-0; FAX: 49-7423179-2406
Heckler & Koch, Inc., 21480 Pacific Blvd., Sterling, VA 20166-8900 / 703-450-1900; FAX: 703-450-8160 www.hecklerkoch-usa.com
Hege Jagd-u. Sporthandels GmbH, P.O. Box 101461, W-7770, Ueberlingen a. Boden, GERMANY
Heidenstrom Bullets, Dalghte 86-3660 Rjukan, 35091818, NORWAY, olau.joh@online.tuo
Heilmann, Stephen, P.O. Box 657, Grass Valley, CA 95945 / 530-272-8758; FAX: 530-274-0285 sheilmann@jps.net www.metalwood.com
Heinie Specialty Products, 301 Oak St., Quincy, IL 62301-2500 / 217-228-9500; FAX: 217-228-9502 rheinie@heinie.com www.heinie.com
Helwan (See U.S. Importer-Interarms)
Henigson & Associates, Steve, P.O. Box 2726, Culver City, CA 90231 / 310-305-8288; FAX: 310-305-1905
Henriksen Tool Co., Inc., 8515 Wagner Creek Rd., Talent, OR 97540 / 541-535-2309; FAX: 541-535-2309
Henry Repeating Arms Co., 110 8th St., Brooklyn, NY 11215 / 718-499-5600; FAX: 718-768-8056 info@henryrepeating.com www.henryrepeating.com
Hensley, Gunmaker, Darwin, P.O. Box 329, Brightwood, OR 97011 / 503-622-5411
Heppler, Keith. See: KEITH'S CUSTOM GUNSTOCKS
Hercules, Inc. (See Alliant Techsystems Smokeless Powder Group)
Heritage Firearms (See Heritage Mfg., Inc.)
Heritage Manufacturing, Inc., 4600 NW 135th St., Opa Locka, FL 33054 / 305-685-5966; FAX: 305-687-6721 infohmi@heritagemfg.com www.heritagemfg.com
Heritage/VSP Gun Books, P.O. Box 887, McCall, ID 83638 / 208-634-4104; FAX: 208-634-3101 heritage@gunbooks.com www.gunbooks.com
Herrett's Stocks, Inc., P.O. Box 741, Twin Falls, ID 83303 / 208-733-1498
Herter's Manufacturing Inc., 111 E. Burnett St., P.O. Box 518, Beaver Dam, WI 53916-1811 / 414-887-1765; FAX: 414-887-8444
Hesco-Meprolight, 2139 Greenville Rd., LaGrange, GA 30241 / 706-884-7967; FAX: 706-882-4683
Hesse Arms, Robert Hesse, 1126 70th St. E., Inver Grove Heights, MN 55077-2416 / 651-455-5760; FAX: 612-455-5760
Hesse, Robert. See: HESSE ARMS
Heydenberk, Warren R., 1059 W. Sawmill Rd., Quakertown, PA 18951 / 215-538-2682
Hickman, Jaclyn, Box 1900, Glenrock, WY 82637
Hidalgo, Tony, 12701 SW 9th Pl., Davie, FL 33325 / 954-476-7645
High Bridge Arms, Inc., 3185 Mission St., San Francisco, CA 94110 / 415-282-8358
High North Products, Inc., P.O. Box 2, Antigo, WI 54409 / 715-627-2331; FAX: 715-623-5451
High Performance International, 5734 W. Florist Ave., Milwaukee, WI 53218 / 414-466-9040; FAX: 414-466-7050 mike@hpirifles.com hpirifles.com
High Precision, Bud Welsh, 80 New Road, E. Amherst, NY 14051 / 716-688-6344; FAX: 716-688-0425 welsh5168@aol.com www.high-precision.com
High Standard Mfg. Co./F.I., Inc., 5200 Mitchelldale St., Ste. E17, Houston, TX 77092-7222 / 713-462-4200; or 800-272-7816; FAX: 713-681-5665 info@highstandard.com www.highstandard.com
High Tech Specialties, Inc., P.O. Box 839, 293 E Main St., Rear, Adamstown, PA 19501 / 717-484-0405; FAX: 717-484-0523 bansner@aol.com www.bansmersrifle.com/hightech
Highline Machine Co., Randall Thompson, Randall Thompson, 654 Lela Place, Grand Junction, CO 81504 / 970-434-4971
Highwood Special Products, 1531 E. Highwood, Pontiac, MI 48340
Hill, Loring F., 304 Cedar Rd., Elkins Park, PA 19027
Hill Speed Leather, Ernie, 4507 N 195th Ave., Litchfield Park, AZ 85340 / 602-853-9222; FAX: 602-853-9235
Hinman Outfitters, Bob, 107 N Sanderson Ave., Bartonville, IL 61607-1839 / 309-691-8132
Hi-Performance Ammunition Company, 484 State Route 366, Apollo, PA 15613 / 304-674-9000; FAX: 304-675-6700
HIP-GRIP Barami Corp., P.O. Box 252224, West Bloomfield, MI 48325-2224 / 248-738-0462; FAX: 248-738-2542 hipgripja@aol.com www.hipgrip.com
Hi-Point Firearms/MKS Supply, 8611-A North Dixie Dr., Dayton, OH 45414 / 877-425-4867; FAX: 937-454-0503 www.hi-pointfirearms.com
Hiptmayer, Armurier, RR 112 750, P.O. Box 136, Eastman, PQ J0E 1P0 CANADA / 514-297-2492
Hiptmayer, Heidemarie, RR 112 750, P.O. Box 136, Eastman, PQ J0E 1P0 CANADA / 514-297-2492
Hiptmayer, Klaus, RR 112 750, P.O. Box 136, Eastman, PQ J0E 1P0 CANADA / 514-297-2492
Hirtenberger AG, Leobersdorferstrasse 31, A-2552, Hirtenberg, AUSTRIA / 43(0)2256 81184; FAX: 43(0)2256 81808 www.hirtenberger.ot
HJS Arms, Inc., P.O. Box 3711, Brownsville, TX 78523-3711 / 956-542-2767; FAX: 956-542-2767
Hoag, James W., 8523 Canoga Ave., Suite C, Canoga Park, CA 91304 / 818-998-1510
Hobson Precision Mfg. Co., 210 Big Oak Ln., Brent, AL 35034 / 205-926-4662; FAX: 205-926-3193 cahobbob@dbtech.net
Hodgdon Powder Co., 6231 Robinson, Shawnee Mission, KS 66202 / 913-362-9455; FAX: 913-362-1307
Hodgman, Inc., 1750 Orchard Rd., Montgomery, IL 60538 / 708-897-7555; FAX: 708-897-7558
Hodgson, Richard, 9081 Tahoe Lane, Boulder, CO 80301
Hoehn Sales, Inc., 2045 Kohn Road, Wright City, MO 63390 / 636-745-8144; FAX: 636-745-7868 hoehnsal@usmo.com
Hofer Jagdwaffen, P., A9170 Ferlach, Kirchgasse 24, Kirchgasse, AUSTRIA / 43 4227 3683; or 43 664 3200216; FAX: 43 4227 368330 peterhofer@hoferwaffen.com www.hoferwaffen.com
Hoffman New Ideas, 821 Northmoor Rd., Lake Forest, IL 60045 / 312-234-4075
Hogue Grips, P.O. Box 1138, Paso Robles, CA 93447 / 800-438-4747 or 805-239-1440; FAX: 805-239-2553
Holland & Holland Ltd., 33 Bruton St., London, ENGLAND / 44-171-499-4411; FAX: 44-171-408-7962
Holland's Gunsmithing, P.O. Box 69, Powers, OR 97466 / 541-439-5155; FAX: 541-439-5155
Hollinger, Jon. See: ASPEN OUTFITTING CO.
Hollywood Engineering, 10642 Arminta St., Sun Valley, CA 91352 / 818-842-8376; FAX: 818-504-4168 cadqueenel1@aol.com
Homak, 350 N. La Salle Dr. Ste. 1100, Chicago, IL 60610-4731 / 312-523-3100; FAX: 312-523-9455
Hoppe's Div. Penguin Industries, Inc., P.O. Box 1690, Oregon City, OR 97045-0690 / 610-384-6000
Horizons Unlimited, P.O. Box 426, Warm Springs, GA 31830 / 706-655-3603; FAX: 706-655-3603

MANUFACTURER'S DIRECTORY

Hornady Mfg. Co., P.O. Box 1848, Grand Island, NE 68802 / 800-338-3220 or 308-382-1390; FAX: 308-382-5761
Horseshoe Leather Products, Andy Arratoonian, The Cottage Sharow, Ripon, ENGLAND U.K. / 44-1765-605858 andy@horseshoe.co.uk www.holsters.org
House of Muskets, Inc., The, PO Box 4640, Pagosa Springs, CO 81157 / 970-731-2295
Houtz & Barwick, P.O. Box 435, W. Church St., Elizabeth City, NC 27909 / 800-775-0337; or 919-335-4191; FAX: 919-335-1152
Howa Machinery, Ltd., Sukaguchi, Shinkawa-cho Nishikasugai-gun, Aichi 452-8601, JAPAN / 81-52-408-1231; FAX: 81-52-401-4999 howa@howa.co.jp http://www.howa.cojpl
Howell Machine, Inc., 815 D St., Lewiston, ID 83501 / 208-743-7418; FAX: 208-746-1703
H-S Precision, Inc., 1301 Turbine Dr., Rapid City, SD 57701 / 605-341-3006; FAX: 605-342-8964
HT Bullets, 244 Belleville Rd., New Bedford, MA 02745 / 508-999-3338
Hubert J. Hecht Waffen-Hecht, P.O. Box 2635, Fair Oaks, CA 95628 / 916-966-1020
Huebner, Corey O., P.O. Box 564, Frenchtown, MT 59834 / 406-721-7168 bugsboys@hotmail.com
Huey Gun Cases, 820 Indiana St., Lawrence, KS 66044-2645 / 785-842-0062; FAX: 785-842-0062 hueycases@aol.com www.hueycases.com
Hume, Don, P.O. Box 351, Miami, OK 74355 / 800-331-2686; FAX: 918-542-4340 info@donhume.com www.donhume.com
Hunkeler, A. (See Buckskin Machine Works), 3235 S 358th St., Auburn, WA 98001 / 206-927-5412
Hunter Co., Inc., 3300 W. 71st Ave., Westminster, CO 80030 / 303-427-4626; FAX: 303-428-3980 debbiet@huntercompany.com www.huntercompany.com
Hunterjohn, P.O. Box 771457, St. Louis, MO 63177 / 314-531-7250 www.hunterjohn.com
Hunter's Specialties Inc., 6000 Huntington Ct. NE, Cedar Rapids, IA 52402-1268 / 319-395-0321; FAX: 319-395-0326
Hunters Supply, Inc., P.O. Box 313, Tioga, TX 76271 / 940-437-2458; FAX: 940-437-2228 hunterssupply@hotmail.com www.hunterssupply.net
Huntington Die Specialties, 601 Oro Dam Blvd., Oroville, CA 95965 / 530-534-1210; FAX: 530-534-1212 buy@huntingtons.com www.huntingtons.com
Hutton Rifle Ranch, P.O. Box 170317, Boise, ID 83717 / 208-345-8781 www.martinbrevik@aol.com
Hydrosorbent Products, P.O. Box 437, Ashley Falls, MA 01222 / 800-448-7903; FAX: 413-229-8743 orders@dehumidify.com www.dehumidify.com

I

I.A.B. (See U.S. Importer-Taylor's & Co., Inc.)
I.D.S.A. Books, 1324 Stratford Drive, Piqua, OH 45356 / 937-773-4203; FAX: 937-778-1922
I.N.C. Inc. (See Kickeez I.N.C., Inc.)
I.S.W., 106 E. Cairo Dr., Tempe, AZ 85282
IAR Inc., 33171 Camino Capistrano, San Juan Capistrano, CA 92675 / 949-443-3642; FAX: 949-443-3647 sales@iar-arms.com iar-arms.com
Ide, Ken. See: STURGEON VALLEY SPORTERS
IGA (See U.S. Importer-Stoeger Industries)
Image Ind. Inc., 11220 E. Main St., Huntley, IL 60142-7369 / 630-766-2402; FAX: 630-766-7373
Impact Case & Container, Inc., P.O. Box 1129, Rathdrum, ID 83858 / 877-687-2452; FAX: 208-687-0632 bradk@icc-case.com www.icc-case.com
Imperial (See E-Z-Way Systems), P.O. Box 4310, Newark, OH 43058-4310 / 614-345-6645; FAX: 614-345-6600 ezway@infinet.com www.jcunald.com
Imperial Magnum Corp., P.O. Box 249, Oroville, WA 98844 / 604-495-3131; FAX: 604-495-2816
Imperial Miniature Armory, 1115 FM 359, Houston, TX 77035-3305 / 800-646-4288; FAX: 832-595-8787 miniguns@houston.rr.com www.1800miniature.com
Imperial Schrade Corp., 7 Schrade Ct., Box 7000, Ellenville, NY 12428 / 914-647-7601; FAX: 914-647-8701 csc@schradeknives.com www.schradeknives.com
Import Sports Inc., 1750 Brielle Ave., Unit B1, Wanamassa, NJ 07712 / 732-493-0302; FAX: 732-493-0301 gsodini@aol.com www.bersa-llama.com
IMR Powder Co., 1080 Military Turnpike, Suite 2, Plattsburgh, NY 12901 / 518-563-2253; FAX: 518-563-6916
Info-Arm, P.O. Box 1262, Champlain, NY 12919 / 514-955-0355; FAX: 514-955-0357 infoarm@qc.aira.com
Innovative Weaponry Inc., 2513 E. Loop 820 N., Fort Worth, TX 76118 / 817-284-0099 or 800-334-3573
INTEC International, Inc., P.O. Box 5708, Scottsdale, AZ 85261 / 602-483-1708
Inter Ordnance of America LP, 3305 Westwood Industrial Dr., Monroe, NC 28110-5204 / 704-821-8337; FAX: 704-821-8523
Intercontinental Distributors, Ltd., P.O. Box 815, Beulah, ND 58523
International Shooters Service, P.O. Box 185234, Ft. Worth, TX 76181 / 817-595-2090; FAX: 817-595-2090 is_s_@sbcglobal.net
Intrac Arms International, 5005 Chapman Hwy., Knoxville, TN 37920
Ion Industries, Inc., 3508 E Allerton Ave., Cudahy, WI 53110 / 414-486-2007; FAX: 414-486-2017
Iosso Products, 1485 Lively Blvd., Elk Grove Village, IL 60007 / 847-437-8400; FAX: 847-437-8478
Iron Bench, 12619 Bailey Rd., Redding, CA 96003 / 916-241-4623
Ironside International Publishers, Inc., P.O. Box 1050, Lorton, VA 22199
Ironsighter Co., P.O. Box 85070, Westland, MI 48185 / 734-326-8731; FAX: 734-326-3378 www.ironsighter.com
Irwin, Campbell H., 140 Hartland Blvd., East Hartland, CT 06027 / 203-653-3901
Israel Arms Inc., 5625 Star Ln. #B, Houston, TX 77057 / 713-789-0745; FAX: 713-914-9515 www.israelarms.com
Ithaca Classic Doubles, Stephen Lamboy, No. 5 Railroad St., Victor, NY 14564 / 716-924-2710; FAX: 716-924-2737 ithacadoubles.com
Ithaca Gun Company LLC, 901 Rt. 34 B, King Ferry, NY 13081 / 315-364-7171; FAX: 315-364-5134 info@ithacagun.com
Ivanoff, Thomas G. (See Tom's Gun Repair)

J

J J Roberts Firearm Engraver, 7808 Lake Dr., Manassas, VA 20111 / 703-330-0448; FAX: 703-264-8600 james.roberts@angelfire.com www.angelfire.com/va2/engraver
J&D Components, 75 East 350 North, Orem, UT 84057-4719 / 801-225-7007 www.jdcomponents.com
J&J Products, Inc., 9240 Whitmore, El Monte, CA 91731 / 818-571-5228; FAX: 800-927-8361
J&J Sales, 1501 21st Ave. S., Great Falls, MT 59405 / 406-727-9789 mtshootingbench@yahoo.com www.j&jsales.us
J&L Superior Bullets (See Huntington Die Specialties)
J&M Precision Machining, Jeff Amato, RR 1 Box 91, Bloomfield, IN 47424
J&R Engineering, P.O. Box 77, 200 Lyons Hill Rd., Athol, MA 01331 / 508-249-9241
J&R Enterprises, 4550 Scotts Valley Rd., Lakeport, CA 95453
J&S Heat Treat, 803 S. 16th St., Blue Springs, MO 64015 / 816-229-2149; FAX: 816-228-1135
J. Dewey Mfg. Co., Inc., P.O. Box 2014, Southbury, CT 06488 / 203-264-3064; FAX: 203-262-6907 deweyrods@worldnet.att.net www.deweyrods.com
J. Korzinek Riflesmith, RD 2, Box 73D, Canton, PA 17724 / 717-673-8512
J.A. Blades, Inc. (See Christopher Firearms Co.)
J.A. Henckels Zwillingswerk Inc., 9 Skyline Dr., Hawthorne, NY 10532 / 914-592-7370
J.G. Anschutz GmbH & Co. KG, Daimlerstr. 12, D-89079 Ulm, Ulm, GERMANY / 49 731 40120; FAX: 49 731 4012700 JGA-info@anschuetz-sport.com www.anschuetz-sport.com
J.G. Dapkus Co., Inc., Commerce Circle, P.O. Box 293, Durham, CT 06422 www.explodingtargets.com
J.I.T. Ltd., P.O. Box 230, Freedom, WY 83120 / 708-494-0937
J.J. Roberts / Engraver, 7808 Lake Dr., Manassas, VA 20111 / 703-330-0448 jjrengraver@aol.com www.angelfire.com/va2/engraver
J.R. Williams Bullet Co., 2008 Tucker Rd., Perry, GA 31069 / 912-987-0274
J.W. Morrison Custom Rifles, 4015 W. Sharon, Phoenix, AZ 85029 / 602-978-3754
Jack A. Rosenberg & Sons, 12229 Cox Ln., Dallas, TX 75234 / 214-241-6302
Jack Dever Co., 8520 NW 90th St., Oklahoma City, OK 73132 / 405-721-6393 jbdever1@home.com
Jack First, Inc., 1201 Turbine Dr., Rapid City, SD 57703 / 605-343-8481; FAX: 605-343-9420
Jack Jonas Appraisals & Taki, 13952 E. Marina Dr., #604, Aurora, CO 80014
Jackalope Gun Shop, 1048 S. 5th St., Douglas, WY 82633 / 307-358-3441
Jaffin, Harry. See: BRIDGEMAN PRODUCTS
Jagdwaffen, Peter. See: BUCHSENMACHERMEISTER
James Churchill Glove Co., PO Box 298, Centralia, WA 98531 / 360-736-2816; FAX: 360-330-0151 churchillglove@localaccess.com
James Wayne Firearms for Collectors and Investors, 2608 N. Laurent, Victoria, TX 77901 / 361-578-1258; FAX: 361-578-3559
Jamison International, Marc Jamison, 3551 Mayer Ave., Sturgis, SD 57785 / 605-347-5090; FAX: 605-347-4704 jbell2@masttechnology.com
Jamison, Marc. See: JAMISON INTERNATIONAL
Jamison's Forge Works, 4527 Rd. 6.5 NE, Moses Lake, WA 98837 / 509-762-2659
Jantz Supply, 309 West Main Dept HD, Davis, OK 73030-0584 / 580-369-2316; FAX: 580-369-3082 jantz@brightok.net www.knifemaking.com
Jarrett Rifles, Inc., 383 Brown Rd., Jackson, SC 29831 / 803-471-3616 www.jarrettrifles.com
Jarvis, Inc., 1123 Cherry Orchard Lane, Hamilton, MT 59840 / 406-961-4392
Javelina Lube Products, P.O. Box 337, San Bernardino, CA 92402 / 909-350-9556; FAX: 909-429-1211
Jay McCament Custom Gunmaker, Jay McCament, 1730-134th St. Ct. S., Tacoma, WA 98444 / 253-531-8832
JB Custom, P.O. Box 6912, Leawood, KS 66206 / 913-381-2329
Jeff Flannery Engraving, 11034 Riddles Run Rd., Union, KY 41091 / 859-384-3127; FAX: 859-384-2222 engraving@fuse.net http://home.fuse.net/engraving/
Jeffredo Gunsight, P.O. Box 669, San Marcos, CA 92079 / 760-728-2695
Jena Eur, P.O. Box 319, Dunmore, PA 18512
Jenco Sales, Inc., P.O. Box 1000, Manchaca, TX 78652 / 800-531-5301; FAX: 800-266-2373 jencosales@sbcglobal.net
Jenkins Recoil Pads, 5438 E. Frontage Ln., Olney, IL 62450 / 618-395-3416
Jensen Bullets, RR 1 Box 187, Arco, ID 83213 / 208-785-5590
Jensen's Custom Ammunition, 5146 E. Pima, Tucson, AZ 85712 / 602-325-3346; FAX: 602-322-5704
Jensen's Firearms Academy, 1280 W. Prince, Tucson, AZ 85705 / 602-293-8516
Jericho Tool & Die Co., Inc., 121 W. Keech Rd., Bainbridge, NY 13733-3248 / 607-563-8222; FAX: 607-563-8560 jerichotool.com www.jerichotool.com
Jerry Phillips Optics, P.O. Box L632, Langhorne, PA 19047 / 215-757-5037; FAX: 215-757-7097
Jesse W. Smith Saddlery, 0499 County Road J, Pritchett, CO 81064 / 509-325-0622
Jester Bullets, Rt. 1 Box 27, Orienta, OK 73737
Jewell Triggers, Inc., 3620 Hwy. 123, San Marcos, TX 78666 / 512-353-2999; FAX: 512-392-0543
JG Airguns, LLC, John Groenewold, P.O. Box 830, Mundelein, IL 60060 / 847-566-2365; FAX: 847-566-4065 jgairguns@jgairguns www.jgairguns.com
JGS Precision Tool Mfg., LLC, 60819 Selander Rd., Coos Bay, OR 97420 / 541-267-4331; FAX: 541-267-5996 jgstools@harborside.com www.jgstools.com
Jim Blair Engraving, P.O. Box 64, Glenrock, WY 82637 / 307-436-8115 jblairengrav@msn.com
Jim Noble Co., 204 W. 5th St., Vancouver, WA 98660 / 360-695-1309; FAX: 360-695-6835 jnobleco@aol.com
Jim Norman Custom Gunstocks, 14281 Cane Rd., Valley Center, CA 92082 / 619-749-6252
Jim's Precision, Jim Ketchum, 1725 Moclips Dr., Petaluma, CA 94952 / 707-762-3014
JLK Bullets, 414 Turner Rd., Dover, AR 72837 / 501-331-4194
Johanssons Vapentillbehor, Bert, S-430 20, Veddige, SWEDEN

MANUFACTURER'S DIRECTORY

John Hall Plastics, Inc., P.O. Box 1526, Alvin, TX 77512 / 713-489-8709
John J. Adams & Son Engravers, 7040 VT Rt 113, Vershire, VT 05079 / 802-685-0019
John Masen Co. Inc., 1305 Jelmak, Grand Prairie, TX 75050 / 817-430-8732; FAX: 817-430-1715
John Partridge Sales Ltd., Trent Meadows Rugeley, Staffordshire, WS15 2HS ENGLAND
John Rigby & Co., 500 Linne Rd. Ste. D, Paso Robles, CA 93446 / 805-227-4236; FAX: 805-227-4723 jrigby@calinet www.johnrigbyandco.com
John's Custom Leather, 523 S. Liberty St., Blairsville, PA 15717 / 724-459-6802; FAX: 724-459-5996
Johnson Wood Products, 34897 Crystal Road, Strawberry Point, IA 52076 / 563-933-6504 johnsonwoodproducts@yahoo.com
Jonad Corp., 2091 Lakeland Ave., Lakewood, OH 44107 / 216-226-3161
Jonathan Arthur Ciener, Inc., 8700 Commerce St., Cape Canaveral, FL 32920 / 321-868-2200; FAX: 321-868-2201 www.22lrconversions.com
Jones Co., Dale, 680 Hoffman Draw, Kila, MT 59920 / 406-755-4684
Jones Custom Products, Neil A., 17217 Brookhouser Rd., Saegertown, PA 16433 / 814-763-2769; FAX: 814-763-4228 njones@mdul.net neiljones.com
Jones, J. See: SSK INDUSTRIES
Jones Moulds, Paul, 4901 Telegraph Rd., Los Angeles, CA 90022 / 213-262-1510
JP Enterprises, Inc., P.O. Box 378, Hugo, MN 55038 / 651-426-9196; FAX: 651-426-2472 www.jprifles.com
JP Sales, Box 307, Anderson, TX 77830
JRP Custom Bullets, RR2 2233 Carlton Rd., Whitehall, NY 12887 / 518-282-0084 or 802-438-5548
JSL Ltd. (See U.S. Importer-Specialty Shooters Supply)
Juenke, Vern, 25 Bitterbush Rd., Reno, NV 89523 / 702-345-0225
Jungkind, Reeves C., 509 E. Granite St., Llano, TX 78643-3055 / 325-247-1151
Jurras, L. See: L. E. JURRAS & ASSOC.
Justin Phillippi Custom Bullets, P.O. Box 773, Ligonier, PA 15658 / 412-238-9671

K

K&M Industries, Inc., Box 66, 510 S. Main, Troy, ID 83871 / 208-835-2281; FAX: 208-835-5211
K&M Services, 5430 Salmon Run Rd., Dover, PA 17315 / 717-292-3175; FAX: 717-292-3175
K. Eversull Co., Inc., 1 Tracemont, Boyce, LA 71409 / 318-793-8728; FAX: 318-793-5483 bestguns@aol.com
K.B.I. Inc., P.O. Box 6625, Harrisburg, PA 17112 / 717-540-8518; FAX: 717-540-8567
Ka Pu Kapili, P.O. Box 745, Honokaa, HI 96727 / 808-776-1644; FAX: 808-776-1731
KA-BAR Knives, 200 Homer St., Olean, NY 14760 / 800-282-0130; FAX: 716-790-7188 info@ka-bar.com www.ka-bar.com
Kahles A. Swarovski Company, 2 Slater Rd., Cranston, RI 02920 / 401-946-2220; FAX: 401-946-2587
Kahr Arms, P.O. Box 220, 630 Route 303, Blauvelt, NY 10913 / 845-353-7770; FAX: 845-353-7833 www.kahr.com
Kailua Custom Guns Inc., 51 N. Dean Street, Coquille, OR 97423 / 541-396-5413 kailuacustom@aol.com www.kailuacustom.com
Kalispel Case Line, P.O. Box 267, Cusick, WA 99119 / 509-445-1121
Kamik Outdoor Footwear, 554 Montee de Liesse, Montreal, PQ H4T 1P1 CANADA / 514-341-3950; FAX: 514-341-1861
Kane, Edward, P.O. Box 385, Ukiah, CA 95482 / 707-462-2937
Kapro Mfg. Co. Inc. (See R.E.I.)
Kasenit Co., Inc., 39 Park Ave., Highland Mills, NY 10930 / 845-928-9595; FAX: 845-986-8038
Kaswer Custom, Inc., 13 Surrey Drive, Brookfield, CT 06804 / 203-775-0564; FAX: 203-775-6872
KDF, Inc., 2485 Hwy. 46 N., Seguin, TX 78155 / 830-379-8141; FAX: 830-379-5420
KeeCo Impressions, Inc., 346 Wood Ave., North Brunswick, NJ 08902 / 800-468-0546
Kehr, Roger, 2131 Agate Ct. SE, Lacy, WA 98503 / 360-491-0691
Keith's Bullets, 942 Twisted Oak, Algonquin, IL 60102 / 708-658-3520
Keith's Custom Gunstocks, Keith M. Heppler, 540 Banyan Circle, Walnut Creek, CA 94598 / 925-934-3509; FAX: 925-934-3143 kmheppler@hotmail.com
Kelbly, Inc., 7222 Dalton Fox Lake Rd., North Lawrence, OH 44666 / 216-683-4674; FAX: 216-683-7349
Keller Co., The, P.O. Box 4057, Port Angeles, WA 98363-0997 / 214-770-8585
Kelley's, P.O. Box 125, Woburn, MA 01801-0125 / 800-879-7273; FAX: 781-272-7077 kels@star.net www.kelsmilitary.com
Kellogg's Professional Products, 325 Pearl St., Sandusky, OH 44870 / 419-625-6551; FAX: 419-625-6167 skwigton@aol.com
Kelly, Lance, 1723 Willow Oak Dr., Edgewater, FL 32132 / 904-423-4933
Kel-Tec CNC Industries, Inc., P.O. Box 236009, Cocoa, FL 32923 / 407-631-0068; FAX: 407-631-1169
Kemen America, 2550 Hwy. 23, Wrenshall, MN 55797 / 218-384-3670 patrickl@midwestshootingschool.com midwestshootingschool.com
Ken Eyster Heritage Gunsmiths, Inc., 6441 Bisop Rd., Centerburg, OH 43011 / 740-625-6131; FAX: 740-625-7811
Ken Starnes Gunmaker, 15940 SW Holly Hill Rd., Hillsboro, OR 97123-9033 / 503-628-0705; FAX: 503-443-2096 kstarnes@kdsa.com
Keng's Firearms Specialty, Inc./US Tactical Systems, 875 Wharton Dr., P.O. Box 44405, Atlanta, GA 30336-1405 / 404-691-7611; FAX: 404-505-8445
Kennebec Journal, 274 Western Ave., Augusta, ME 04330 / 207-622-6288
Kennedy Firearms, 10 N. Market St., Muncy, PA 17756 / 717-546-6695
Kenneth W. Warren Engraver, P.O. Box 2842, Wenatchee, WA 98807 / 509-663-6123; FAX: 509-665-6123
Ken's Kustom Kartridges, 331 Jacobs Rd., Hubbard, OH 44425 / 216-534-4595
Kent Cartridge America, Inc., P.O. Box 849, 1000 Zigor Rd., Kearneysville, WV 25430
Keowee Game Calls, 608 Hwy. 25 North, Travelers Rest, SC 29690 / 864-834-7204; FAX: 864-834-7831
Kershaw Knives, 18600 SW Teton Ave., Tualatin, OR 97062 / 503-682-1966; or 800-325-2891; FAX: 503-682-7168
Kesselring Gun Shop, 4024 Old Hwy. 99N, Burlington, WA 98233 / 360-724-3113; FAX: 360-724-7003 info@kesselrings.com www.kesselrings.com
Ketchum, Jim (See Jim's Precision)
Keystone Sporting Arms, Inc. (Crickett Rifles), 8920 State Route 405, Milton, PA 17847 / 800-742-2777; FAX: 570-742-1455
Kickeez I.N.C., Inc., 301 Industrial Dr., Carl Junction, MO 64834-8806 / 419-649-2100; FAX: 417-649-2200 kickeez@gbronline.com www.kickeez.net
Kilham & Co., Main St., P.O. Box 37, Lyme, NH 03768 / 603-795-4112
Kimar (See U.S. Importer-IAR, Inc.)
Kimber of America, Inc., 1 Lawton St., Yonkers, NY 10705 / 800-880-2418; FAX: 914-964-9340
King & Co., P.O. Box 1242, Bloomington, IL 61702 / 309-473-3964; or 800-914-5464; FAX: 309-473-2161
King's Gun Works, 1837 W. Glenoaks Blvd., Glendale, CA 91201 / 818-956-6010; FAX: 818-548-8606
Kirkpatrick Leather Co., P.O. Box 677, Laredo, TX 78040 / 956-723-6631; FAX: 956-725-0672 mike@kirkpatrickleather.com www.kirkpatrickleather.com
KK Air International (See Impact Case & Container Co., Inc.)
Kleen-Bore, Inc., 16 Industrial Pkwy., Easthampton, MA 01027 / 413-527-0300; FAX: 413-527-2522 info@kleen-bore.com www.kleen-bore.com
Kleinendorst, K. W., RR 1, Box 1500, Hop Bottom, PA 18824 / 717-289-4687
Klingler Woodcarving, P.O. Box 141, Thistle Hill, Cabot, VT 05647 / 802-426-3811 www.vermartcrafts.com
Knifeware, Inc., P.O. Box 3, Greenville, WV 24945 / 304-832-6878
Knight Rifles, 21852 Hwy. J46, P.O. Box 130, Centerville, IA 52544 / 515-856-2626; FAX: 515-856-2628 www.knightrifles.com
Knight Rifles (See Modern Muzzleloading, Inc.)
Knight's Manufacturing Co., 701 Columbia Blvd., Titusville, FL 32780 / 321-607-9900; FAX: 321-268-1498 civiliansales@knightarmco.com www.knightarmco.com
Knock on Wood Antiques, 355 Post Rd., Darien, CT 06820 / 203-655-9031
Knoell, Doug, 9737 McCardle Way, Santee, CA 92071 / 619-449-5189
Knopp, Gary. See: SUPER 6 LLC
Koevenig's Engraving Service, Box 55 Rabbit Gulch, Hill City, SD 57745 / 605-574-2239 ekoevenig@msn.com
KOGOT, 410 College, Trinidad, CO 81082 / 719-846-9406; FAX: 719-846-9406
Kolar, 1925 Roosevelt Ave., Racine, WI 53406 / 414-554-0800; FAX: 414-554-9093
Kolpin Outdoors, Inc., P.O. Box 107, 205 Depot St., Fox Lake, WI 53933 / 414-928-3118; FAX: 414-928-3687 cdutton@kolpin.com www.kolpin.com
Korth Germany GmbH, Robert Bosch Strasse, 11, D-23909, 23909 Ratzeburg, GERMANY / 4541-840363; FAX: 4541-84 05 35 info@korthwaffen.de www.korthwaffen.com
Korth USA, 437R Chandler St., Tewksbury, MA 01876 / 978-851-8656; FAX: 978-851-9462 info@kortusa.com www.korthusa.com
Korzinek Riflesmith, J., RD 2 Box 73D, Canton, PA 17724 / 717-673-8512
Koval Knives, 5819 Zarley St., Suite A, New Albany, OH 43054 / 614-855-0777; FAX: 614-855-0945 koval@kovalknives.com www.kovalknives.com
Kowa Optimed, Inc., 20001 S. Vermont Ave., Torrance, CA 90502 / 310-327-1913; FAX: 310-327-4177 scopekowa@kowa.com www.kowascope.com
KP Books Division of F&W Publications, 700 E. State St., Iola, WI 54990-0001 / 715-445-2214
Kramer Designs, P.O. Box 129, Clancy, MT 59634 / 406-933-8658; FAX: 406-933-8658
Kramer Handgun Leather, P.O. Box 112154, Tacoma, WA 98411 / 800-510-2666; FAX: 253-564-1214 www.kramerleather.com
Krico Deutschland GmbH, Nurnbergerstrasse 6, D-90602, Pyrbaum, GERMANY / 09180-2780; FAX: 09180-2661
Krieger Barrels, Inc., 2024 Mayfield Rd, Richfield, WI 53076 / 262-628-8558; FAX: 262-628-8748
Krieghoff Gun Co., H., Boschstrasse 22, D-89079 Elm, GERMANY / 731-4018270
Krieghoff International,Inc., 7528 Easton Rd., Ottsville, PA 18942 / 610-847-5173; FAX: 610-847-8691
Kukowski, Ed. See: ED'S GUN HOUSE
Kulis Freeze Dry Taxidermy, 725 Broadway Ave., Bedford, OH 44146 / 216-232-8352; FAX: 216-232-7305 jkulis@kastaway.com kastaway.com
KVH Industries, Inc., 110 Enterprise Center, Middletown, RI 02842 / 401-847-3327; FAX: 401-849-0045
Kwik-Site Co., 5555 Treadwell St., Wayne, MI 48184 / 734-326-1500; FAX: 734-326-4120 kwiksiteco@aol.com

L

L&R Lock Co., 2328 Cains Mill Rd., Sumter, SC 29154 / 803-481-5790; FAX: 803-481-5795
L&S Technologies Inc. (See Aimtech Mount Systems)
L. Bengtson Arms Co., 6345-B E. Akron St., Mesa, AZ 85205 / 602-981-6375
L. E. Jurras & Assoc., L. E. Jurras, P.O. Box 680, Washington, IN 47501 / 812-254-6170; FAX: 812-254-6170 jurras@sbcglobal.net www.leejurras.com
L.A.R. Mfg., Inc., 4133 W. Farm Rd., West Jordan, UT 84088 / 801-280-3505; FAX: 801-280-1972
L.B.T., Judy Smith, HCR 62, Box 145, Moyie Springs, ID 83845 / 208-267-3588
L.E. Wilson, Inc., Box 324, 404 Pioneer Ave., Cashmere, WA 98815 / 509-782-1328; FAX: 509-782-7200
L.L. Bean, Inc., Freeport, ME 04032 / 207-865-4761; FAX: 207-552-2802
L.P.A. Inc., Via Alfieri 26, Gardone V.T., Brescia, ITALY / 30-891-14-81; FAX: 30-891-09-51
L.R. Clift Mfg., 3821 Hammonton Rd., Marysville, CA 95901 / 916-755-3390; FAX: 916-755-3393
La Clinique du .45, 1432 Rougemont, Chambly, PQ J3L 2L8 CANADA / 514-658-1144
Labanu Inc., 2201-F Fifth Ave., Ronkonkoma, NY 11779 / 516-467-6197; FAX: 516-981-4112
LaBoone, Pat. See: MIDWEST SHOOTING SCHOOL, THE
LaBounty Precision Reboring, Inc, 7968 Silver Lake Rd., PO Box 186, Maple Falls, WA 98266 / 360-599-2047; FAX: 360-599-3018
LaCrosse Footwear, Inc., 18550 NE Riverside Parkway, Portland, OR 97230 / 503-766-1010; or 800-323-2668; FAX: 503-766-1015
LaFrance Specialties, P.O. Box 87933, San Diego, CA 92138 / 619-293-3373; FAX: 619-293-0819 timlafrance@att.net lafrancespecialties.com
Lake Center Marina, P.O. Box 670, St. Charles, MO 63302 / 314-946-7500
Lakefield Arms Ltd. (See Savage Arms, Inc.)

MANUFACTURER'S DIRECTORY

Lakewood Products LLC, 275 June St., Berlin, WI 54923 / 800-872-8458; FAX: 920-361-7719 lakewood@centurytel.net www.lakewoodproducts.com
Lamboy, Stephen. See: ITHACA CLASSIC DOUBLES
Lampert, Ron, Rt. 1, 44857 Schoolcraft Trl., Guthrie, MN 56461 / 218-854-7345
Lamson & Goodnow Mfg. Co., 45 Conway St., Shelburne Falls, MA 03170 / 413-625-6564; or 800-872-6564; FAX: 413-625-9816 www.lamsonsharp.com
Lansky Levine, Arthur. See: LANSKY SHARPENERS
Lansky Sharpeners, Arthur Lansky Levine, P.O. Box 50830, Las Vegas, NV 89016 / 702-361-7511; FAX: 702-896-9511
LaPrade, P.O. Box 250, Ewing, VA 24248 / 423-733-2615
LaRocca Gun Works, 51 Union Place, Worcester, MA 01608 / 508-754-2887; FAX: 508-754-2887 www.laroccagunworks.com
Larry Lyons Gunworks, 110 Hamilton St., Dowagiac, MI 49047 / 616-782-9478
Laser Devices, Inc., 2 Harris Ct. A-4, Monterey, CA 93940 / 831-373-0701; FAX: 831-373-0903 sales@laserdevices.com www.laserdevices.com
Laseraim Technologies, Inc., P.O. Box 3548, Little Rock, AR 72203 / 501-375-2227
Laserlyte, 2201 Amapola Ct., Torrance, CA 90501
LaserMax, Inc., 3495 Winton Place, Bldg. B, Rochester, NY 14623-2807 / 800-527-3703; FAX: 716-272-5427 customerservice@lasermax-inc.com www.lasermax.com
Lassen Community College, Gunsmithing Dept., P.O. Box 3000, Hwy. 139, Susanville, CA 96130 / 916-251-8800; FAX: 916-251-8838 staylor@lassencollege.edu www.lassencommunitycollege.edu
Lathrop's, Inc., 5146 E. Pima, Tucson, AZ 85712 / 520-881-0266; or 800-875-4867; FAX: 520-322-5704
Laughridge, William R. (See Cylinder & Slide, Inc.)
Laurel Mountain Forge, P.O. Box 52, Crown Point, IN 46308 / 219-548-2950; FAX: 219-548-2950
Laurona Armas Eibar, S.A.L., Avenida de Otaola 25, P.O. Box 260, Eibar 20600, SPAIN / 34-43-700600; FAX: 34-43-700616
Lawrence Brand Shot (See Precision Reloading, Inc.)
Lawrence Leather Co., P.O. Box 1479, Lillington, NC 27546 / 910-893-2071; FAX: 910-893-4742
Lawson Co., Harry, 3328 N Richey Blvd., Tucson, AZ 85716 / 520-326-1117; FAX: 520-326-1117
Lawson, John. See: SIGHT SHOP, THE
Lawson, John G. (See Sight Shop, The)
Lazzeroni Arms Co., P.O. Box 26696, Tucson, AZ 85726 / 888-492-7247; FAX: 520-624-4250
Le Clear Industries (See E-Z-Way Systems)
Leapers, Inc., 7675 Five Mile Rd., Northville, MI 48167 / 248-486-1231; FAX: 248-486-1430
Leatherman Tool Group, Inc., 12106 NE Ainsworth Cir., P.O. Box 20595, Portland, OR 97294 / 503-253-7826; FAX: 503-253-7830
Lebeau-Courally, Rue St. Gilles, 386 4000, Liege, BELGIUM / 042-52-48-43; FAX: 32-4-252-2008 info@lebeau-courally.com www.lebeau-courally.com
Leckie Professional Gunsmithing, 546 Quarry Rd., Ottsville, PA 18942 / 215-847-8594
Ledbetter Airguns, Riley, 1804 E Sprague St., Winston Salem, NC 27107-3521 / 919-784-0676
Lee Precision, Inc., 4275 Hwy. U, Hartford, WI 53027 / 262-673-3075; FAX: 262-673-9273 info@leeprecision.com www.leeprecision.com
Lee Supplies, Mark, 9901 France Ct., Lakeville, MN 55044 / 612-461-2114
LeFever Arms Co., Inc., 6234 Stokes, Lee Center Rd., Lee Center, NY 13363 / 315-337-6722; FAX: 315-337-1543
Legacy Sports International, 206 S. Union St., Alexandria, VA 22314 / 703-548-4837 www.legacysports.com
Leica USA, Inc., 156 Ludlow Ave., Northvale, NJ 07647 / 201-767-7500; FAX: 201-767-8666
Leonard Day, 3 Kings Hwy., West Hatfield, MA 01027-9506 / 413-337-8369
Les Baer Custom, Inc., 29601 34th Ave., Hillsdale, IL 61257 / 309-658-2716; FAX: 309-658-2610 www.lesbaer.com
LesMerises, Felix. See: ROCKY MOUNTAIN ARMOURY
Lethal Force Institute (See Police Bookshelf), P.O. Box 122, Concord, NH 03301 / 603-224-6814; FAX: 603-226-3554
Lett Custom Grips, 672 Currier Rd., Hopkinton, NH 03229-2652 / 800-421-5388; FAX: 603-226-4580 info@lettgrips.com www.lettgrips.com
Leupold & Stevens, Inc., 14400 NW Greenbrier Pky., Beaverton, OR 97006 / 503-646-9171; FAX: 503-526-1455
Lever Arms Service Ltd., 2131 Burrard St., Vancouver, BC V6J 3H7 CANADA / 604-736-2711; FAX: 604-738-3503 leverarms@leverarms.com www.leverarms.com
Lew Horton Dist. Co., Inc., 15 Walkup Dr., Westboro, MA 01581 / 508-366-7400; FAX: 508-366-5332
Lewis Lead Remover, The (See Brownells, Inc.)
Liberty Metals, 2233 East 16th St., Los Angeles, CA 90021 / 213-581-9171; FAX: 213-581-9351 libertymfgsolder@hotmail.com
Liberty Safe, 999 W. Utah Ave., Payson, UT 84651-1744 / 800-247-5625; FAX: 801-489-6409
Liberty Shooting Supplies, P.O. Box 357, Hillsboro, OR 97123 / 503-640-5518; FAX: 503-640-5518 info@libertyshootingsupplies.com www.libertyshootingsupplies.com
Lightning Performance Innovations, Inc., RD1 Box 555, Mohawk, NY 13407 / 315-866-8819; FAX: 315-867-5701
Lilja Precision Rifle Barrels, P.O. Box 372, Plains, MT 59859 / 406-826-3084; FAX: 406-826-3083 lilja@riflebarrels.com www.riflebarrels.com
Lincoln, Dean, Box 1886, Farmington, NM 87401
Linder Solingen Knives, 4401 Sentry Dr. #B, Tucker, GA 30084 / 770-939-6915; FAX: 770-939-6738
Lindsay Engraving & Tools, Steve Lindsay, 3714 W. Cedar Hills, Kearney, NE 68845 / 308-236-7885 steve@lindsayengraving.com www.handgravers.com
Lindsay, Steve. See: LINDSAY ENGRAVING & TOOLS
Lindsley Arms Cartridge Co., P.O. Box 757, 20 College Hill Rd., Henniker, NH 03242 / 603-428-3127
Linebaugh Custom Sixguns, P.O. Box 455, Cody, WY 82414 / 307-645-3332 www.sixgunner.com
Lion Country Supply, P.O. Box 480, Port Matilda, PA 16870
List Precision Engineering, Unit 1 Ingley Works, 13 River Road, Barking, ENGLAND / 011-081-594-1686
Lithi Bee Bullet Lube, 1728 Carr Rd., Muskegon, MI 49442 / 616-788-4479 lithibee@att.net
"Little John's" Antique Arms, 1740 W. Laveta, Orange, CA 92668
Littler Sales Co., 20815 W. Chicago, Detroit, MI 48228 / 313-273-6889; FAX: 313-273-1099 littlersales@aol.com
Littleton, J. F., 275 Pinedale Ave., Oroville, CA 95966 / 916-533-6084
Ljutic Industries, Inc., 732 N. 16th Ave., Suite 22, Yakima, WA 98902 / 509-248-0476; FAX: 509-576-8233 ljuticgun@earthlink.net www.ljuticgun.com
Llama Gabilondo Y Cia, Apartado 290, E-01080, Victoria, SPAIN
Lock's Philadelphia Gun Exchange, 6700 Rowland Ave., Philadelphia, PA 19149 / 215-332-6225; FAX: 215-332-4800 locks.gunshop@verizon.net
Lodewick, Walter H., 2816 NE Halsey St., Portland, OR 97232 / 503-284-2554 wlodewick@aol.com
Lodgewood Mfg., P.O. Box 611, Whitewater, WI 53190 / 262-473-5444; FAX: 262-473-6448 lodgewd@idcnet.com lodgewood.com
Log Cabin Sport Shop, 8010 Lafayette Rd., Lodi, OH 44254 / 330-948-1082; FAX: 330-948-4307 logcabin@logcabinshop.com www.logcabinshop.com
Logan, Harry M., Box 745, Honokaa, HI 96727 / 808-776-1644
Logdewood Mfg., P.O. Box 611, Whitewater, WI 53190 / 262-473-5444; FAX: 262-473-6448 lodgewd@idcnet.com www.lodgewood.com
Lohman Mfg. Co., Inc., 4500 Doniphan Dr., P.O. Box 220, Neosho, MO 64850 / 417-451-4438; FAX: 417-451-2576
Lomont Precision Bullets, 278 Sandy Creek Rd., Salmon, ID 83467 / 208-756-6819; FAX: 208-756-6824 www.klomont.com
London Guns Ltd., Box 3750, Santa Barbara, CA 93130 / 805-683-4141; FAX: 805-683-1712
Lone Star Gunleather, 1301 Brushy Bend Dr., Round Rock, TX 78681 / 512-255-1805
Lone Star Rifle Company, 11231 Rose Road, Conroe, TX 77303 / 936-856-3363; FAX: 936-856-3363 dave@lonestar.com
Long, George F., 1402 Kokanee Ln., Grants Pass, OR 97527 / 541-476-0836
Lortone Inc., 2856 NW Market St., Seattle, WA 98107
Lothar Walther Precision Tool Inc., 3425 Hutchinson Rd., Cumming, GA 30040 / 770-889-9998; FAX: 770-889-4919 lotharwalther@mindspring.com www.lothar-walther.com
LPS Laboratories, Inc., 4647 Hugh Howell Rd., P.O. Box 3050, Tucker, GA 30084 / 404-934-7800
Lucas, Edward E, 32 Garfield Ave., East Brunswick, NJ 08816 / 201-251-5526
Lupton, Keith. See: PAWLING MOUNTAIN CLUB
Lyman Instant Targets, Inc. (See Lyman Products Corp.)
Lyman Products Corp., 475 Smith St., Middletown, CT 06457-1541 / 800-423-9704; FAX: 860-632-1699 lymansales@cshore.com www.lymanproducts.com

M

M.H. Canjar Co., 6510 Raleigh St., Arvada, CO 80003 / 303-295-2638; FAX: 303-295-2638
MA Systems, Inc., P.O. Box 894, Pryor, OK 74362-0894 / 918-824-3705; FAX: 918-824-3710
Mac-1 Airgun Distributors, 13974 Van Ness Ave., Gardena, CA 90249-2900 / 310-327-3581; FAX: 310-327-0238 mac1@maclairgun.com www.mac1airgun.com
Machinist's Workshop-Village Press, P.O. Box 1810, Traverse City, MI 49685 / 800-447-7367; FAX: 616-946-3289
Madis Books, 2453 West Five Mile Pkwy., Dallas, TX 75233 / 214-330-7168
Madis, George. See: WINCHESTER CONSULTANTS
MAG Instrument, Inc., 1635 S. Sacramento Ave., Ontario, CA 91761 / 909-947-1006; FAX: 909-947-3116
Magma Engineering Co., P.O. Box 161, 20955 E. Ocotillo Rd., Queen Creek, AZ 85242 / 602-987-9008; FAX: 602-987-0148
Mag-Na-Port International, Inc., 41302 Executive Dr., Harrison Twp., MI 48045-1306 / 586-469-6727; FAX: 586-469-0425 email@magnaport.com www.magnaport.com
Magnum Power Products, Inc., P.O. Box 17768, Fountain Hills, AZ 85268
Magnum Research, Inc., 7110 University Ave. NE, Minneapolis, MN 55432 / 800-772-6168 or 763-574-1868; FAX: 763-574-0109 info@magnumresearch.com
Magnus Bullets, P.O. Box 239, Toney, AL 35773 / 256-420-8359; FAX: 256-420-8360 bulletman@mchsi.com www.magnusbullets.com
Mag-Pack Corp., P.O. Box 846, Chesterland, OH 44026 / 440-285-9480 magpack@hotmail.com
MagSafe Ammo Co., 4700 S US Highway 17/92, Casselberry, FL 32707-3814 / 407-834-9966; FAX: 407-834-8185 www.magsafeonline.com
Magtech Ammunition Co. Inc., 6845 20th Ave. S., Ste. 120, Centerville, MN 55038 / 651-762-8500; FAX: 651-429-9485 www.magtechammunition.com
Mahony, Philip Bruce, 67 White Hollow Rd., Lime Rock, CT 06039-2418 / 860-435-9341 filbalony-redbeard@snet.net
Mahovsky's Metalife, R.D. 1, Box 149a Eureka Road, Grand Valley, PA 16420 / 814-436-7747
Makinson, Nicholas, RR 3, Komoka, ON N0L 1R0 CANADA / 519-471-5462
Mallardtone Game Calls, 10406 96th St., Court West, Taylor Ridge, IL 61284 / 309-798-2481; FAX: 309-798-2501
Mandall Shooting Supply Inc., 5442 E. Cambridge Ave., Phoenix, AZ 85008-1721 / 602-952-0097; FAX: 480-949-0734
Marble Arms (See CRR, Inc./Marble's Inc.)
Marchmon Bullets, 6502 Riverdale Rd., Whitmore Lake, MI 48189
Marent, Rudolf. See: HAMMERLI SERVICE-PRECISION MAC
Mark Lee Supplies, 9901 France Ct., Lakeville, MN 55044 / 952-461-2114; FAX: 952-461-2194 marklee55044@usfamily.net
Markell, Inc., 422 Larkfield Center 235, Santa Rosa, CA 95403 / 707-573-0792; FAX: 707-573-9867
Markesbery Muzzle Loaders, Inc., 7785 Foundation Dr., Ste. 6, Florence, KY 41042 / 606-342-5553 or 606-342-2380
Marksman Products, 5482 Argosy Dr., Huntington Beach, CA 92649 / 714-898-7535; or 800-822-8005; FAX: 714-891-0782
Marlin Firearms Co., 100 Kenna Dr., North Haven, CT 06473 / 203-239-5621; FAX: 203-234-7991 www.marlinfirearms.com
Marocchi F.lli S.p.A, Via Galileo Galilei 8, I-25068 Zanano, ITALY
Marsh, Mike, Croft Cottage, Main St., Derbyshire, DE4 2BY ENGLAND / 01629 650 669
Marshall Enterprises, 792 Canyon Rd., Redwood City, CA 94062

MANUFACTURER'S DIRECTORY

Marshall Fish Mfg. Gunsmith Sptg. Co., 87 Champlain Ave., Westport, NY 12993 / 518-962-4897; FAX: 518-962-4897
Martin B. Retting Inc., 11029 Washington, Culver City, CA 90232 / 213-837-2412 retting@retting.com
Martini & Hagn, 1264 Jimsmith Lake Rd., Cranbrook, BC V1C 6V6 CANADA / 250-417-2926; FAX: 250-417-2928
Martin's Gun Shop, 937 S. Sheridan Blvd., Lakewood, CO 80226 / 303-922-2184
Martz, John V., 8060 Lakeview Lane, Lincoln, CA 95648 FAX: 916-645-3815
Marvel, Alan, 3922 Madonna Rd., Jarretsville, MD 21084 / 301-557-6545
Marx, Harry (See U.S. Importer for FERLIB)
Maryland Paintball Supply, 8507 Harford Rd., Parkville, MD 21234 / 410-882-5607
MAST Technology, Inc., 14555 US Hwy. 95 S., P.O. Box 60969, Boulder City, NV 89006 / 702-293-6969; FAX: 702-293-7255 info@masttechnology.com www.bellammo.com
Master Lock Co., 2600 N. 32nd St., Milwaukee, WI 53245 / 414-444-2800
Match Prep-Doyle Gracey, P.O. Box 155, Tehachapi, CA 93581 / 661-822-5383; FAX: 661-823-8680 gracenotes@csurpers.net www.matchprep.com
Mathews Gun Shop & Gunsmithing, Inc., 10224 S. Paramount Blvd., Downey, CA 90241 / 562-928-2129; FAX: 562-928-8629
Matthews Cutlery, 4401 Sentry Dr. #B, Tucker, GA 30084 / 770-939-6915
Mauser Werke Oberndorf Waffensysteme GmbH, Postfach 1349, 78722, Oberndorf/N., GERMANY
Maverick Arms, Inc., 7 Grasso Ave., P.O. Box 497, North Haven, CT 06473 / 203-230-5300; FAX: 203-230-5420
Maxi-Mount Inc., P.O. Box 291, Willoughby Hills, OH 44096-0291 / 440-944-9456; FAX: 440-944-9456 maximount454@yahoo.com
Mayville Engineering Co. (See MEC, Inc.)
Mazur Restoration, Pete, 13083 Drummer Way, Grass Valley, CA 95949 / 530-268-2412
McCament, Jay. See: JAY MCCAMENT CUSTOM GUNMAKER
McCann, Tom, 14 Walton Dr., New Hope, PA 18938 / 215-862-2728
McCann Industries, P.O. Box 641, Spanaway, WA 98387 / 253-537-6919; FAX: 253-537-6919 mccann.machine@worldnet.att.net www.mccannindustries.com
McCluskey Precision Rifles, 10502 14th Ave. NW, Seattle, WA 98177 / 206-781-2776
McCombs, Leo, 1862 White Cemetery Rd., Patriot, OH 45658 / 740-256-1714
McDonald, Dennis, 8359 Brady St., Peosta, IA 52068 / 319-556-7940
McFarland, Stan, 2221 Idella Ct., Grand Junction, CO 81505 / 970-243-4704
McGhee, Larry. See: B.C. OUTDOORS
McGowen Rifle Barrels, 5961 Spruce Lane, St. Anne, IL 60964 / 815-937-9816; FAX: 815-937-4024
Mchalik, Gary. See: ROSSI FIREARMS
McKenzie, Lynton, 6940 N. Alvernon Way, Tucson, AZ 85718 / 520-299-5090
McMillan Fiberglass Stocks, Inc., 1638 W. Knudsen Dr. #102, Phoenix, AZ 85027 / 623-582-9635; FAX: 623-581-3825 mfsinc@mcmfamily.com www.mcmfamily.com
McMillan Optical Gunsight Co., 28638 N. 42nd St., Cave Creek, AZ 85331 / 602-585-7868; FAX: 602-585-7872
McMillan Rifle Barrels, P.O. Box 3427, Bryan, TX 77805 / 409-690-3456; FAX: 409-690-0156
McMurdo, Lynn, P.O. Box 404, Afton, WY 83110 / 307-886-5535
MCS, Inc., 166 Pocono Rd., Brookfield, CT 06804-2023 / 203-775-1013; FAX: 203-775-9462
McWelco Products, 6730 Santa Fe Ave., Hesperia, CA 92345 / 619-244-8876; FAX: 619-244-9398 products@mcwelco.com www.mcwelco.com
MDS, P.O. Box 1441, Brandon, FL 33509-1441 / 813-653-1180; FAX: 813-684-5953
Meacham Tool & Hardware Co., Inc., 37052 Eberhardt Rd., Peck, ID 83545 / 208-486-7171 smeacham@clearwater.net www.meachamrifles.com
Measurement Group Inc., Box 27777, Raleigh, NC 27611
Measures, Leon. See: SHOOT WHERE YOU LOOK
MEC, Inc., 715 South St., Mayville, WI 53050 reloaders@mayvl.com www.mecreloaders.com
MEC-Gar S.R.L., Via Madonnina 64, Gardone V.T. Brescia, ITALY / 39-030-3733668; FAX: 39-030-3733687 info@mec-gar.it www.mec-gar.it
MEC-Gar U.S.A., Inc., Hurley Farms Industr. Park, 115, Hurley Road 6G, Oxford, CT 06478 / 203-262-1525; FAX: 203-262-1719 mecgar@aol.com www.mec-gar.com
Mech-Tech Systems, Inc., 1602 Foothill Rd., Kalispell, MT 59901 / 406-755-8055
Meister Bullets (See Gander Mountain)
Mele, Frank, 201 S. Wellow Ave., Cookeville, TN 38501 / 615-526-4860
Menck, Gunsmith Inc., T.W., 5703 S 77th St., Ralston, NE 68127
Mendez, John A., 1309 Continental Dr., Daytona Beach, FL 32117-3807 / 407-344-2791
Men-Metallwerk Elisenhuette GmbH, P.O. Box 1263, Nassau/Lahn, D-56372 GERMANY / 2604-7819
Meprolight (See Hesco-Meprolight)
Mercer Custom Guns, 216 S. Whitewater Ave., Jefferson, WI 53549 / 920-674-3839
Merit Corp., P.O. Box 9044, Schenectady, NY 12309 / 518-346-1420 sales@meritcorporation.com www.meritcorporation.com
Merkel, Schutzenstrasse 26, D-98527 Suhl, Suhl, GERMANY FAX: 011-49-3681-854-203 www.merkel-waffen.de
Metal Merchants, P.O. Box 186, Walled Lake, MI 48390-0186
Metalife Industries (See Mahovsky's Metalife)
Michael's Antiques, Box 591, Waldoboro, ME 04572
Michaels of Oregon Co., P.O. Box 1690, Oregon City, OR 97045 www.michaels-oregon.com
Micro Sight Co., 242 Harbor Blvd., Belmont, CA 94002 / 415-591-0769; FAX: 415-591-7531
Microfusion Alfa S.A., Paseo San Andres N8, P.O. Box 271, Eibar 20600, 20600 SPAIN / 34-43-11-89-16; FAX: 34-43-11-40-38
Mid-America Recreation, Inc., 1328 5th Ave., Moline, IL 61265 / 309-764-5089; FAX: 309-764-5089 fmilcusguns@aol.com www.midamericarecreation.com
Middlebrooks Custom Shop, 7366 Colonial Trail East, Surry, VA 23883 / 757-357-0881; FAX: 757-365-0442
Midway Arms, Inc., 5875 W. Van Horn Tavern Rd., Columbia, MO 65203 / 800-243-3220; FAX: 800-992-8312 www.midwayusa.com
Midwest Gun Sport, 1108 Herbert Dr., Zebulon, NC 27597 / 919-269-5570
Midwest Shooting School, The, Pat LaBoone, 2550 Hwy. 23, Wrenshall, MN 55797 / 218-384-3670 shootingschool@starband.net
Midwest Sport Distributors, Box 129, Fayette, MO 65248
Mike Davis Products, 643 Loop Dr., Moses Lake, WA 98837 / 509-765-6178; or 509-766-7281
Mike Yee Custom Stocking, 29927 56 Pl. S., Auburn, WA 98001 / 253-839-3991
Military Armament Corp., P.O. Box 120, Mt. Zion Rd., Lingleville, TX 76461 / 817-965-3253
Millennium Designed Muzzleloaders, P.O. Box 536, Routes 11 & 25, Limington, ME 04049 / 207-637-2316
Miller Arms, Inc., P.O. Box 260 Purl St., St. Onge, SD 57779 / 605-642-5160; FAX: 605-642-5160
Miller Custom, 210 E. Julia, Clinton, IL 61727 / 217-935-9362
Miller Single Trigger Mfg. Co., 6680 Rt. 5-20, P.O. Box 471, Bloomfield, NY 14469 / 585-657-6338
Millett Sights, 7275 Murdy Circle, Adm. Office, Huntington Beach, CA 92647 / 714-842-5575 or 800-645-5388; FAX: 714-843-5707
Mills Jr., Hugh B., 3615 Canterbury Rd., New Bern, NC 28560 / 919-637-4631
Milstor Corp., 80-975 Indio Blvd. C-7, Indio, CA 92201 / 760-775-9998; FAX: 760-775-5229 milstor@webtv.net
Minute Man High Tech Industries, 10611 Canyon Rd. E., Suite 151, Puyallup, WA 98373 / 800-233-2734
Mirador Optical Corp., P.O. Box 11614, Marina Del Rey, CA 90295-7614 / 310-821-5587; FAX: 310-305-0386
Mitchell, Jack, c/o Geoff Gaebe, Addieville East Farm, 200 Pheasant Dr., Mapleville, RI 02839 / 401-568-3185
Mitchell Bullets, R.F., 430 Walnut St., Westernport, MD 21562
Mitchell Mfg. Corp., P.O. Box 9295, Fountain Valley, CA 92728 / 714-444-2220
Mitchell Optics, Inc., 2072 CR 1100 N, Sidney, IL 61877 / 217-688-2219; or 217-621-3018; FAX: 217-688-2505 mitchell@attglobal.net
Mitchell's Accuracy Shop, 68 Greenridge Dr., Stafford, VA 22554 / 703-659-0165
Mitchell's Mauser, P.O. Box 9295, Fountain Valley, CA 92728 / 714-979-7663; FAX: 714-899-3660
MI-TE Bullets, 1396 Ave. K, Ellsworth, KS 67439 / 785-472-4575; FAX: 785-472-5579
Mittleman, William, P.O. Box 65, Etna, CA 96027
Mixson Corp., 7635 W. 28th Ave., Hialeah, FL 33016 / 305-821-5190; or 800-327-0078; FAX: 305-558-9318
MJK Gunsmithing, Inc., 417 N. Huber Ct., E. Wenatchee, WA 98802 / 509-884-7683
MKS Supply, Inc. (See Hi-Point Firearms)
MMC, 2700 W. Sahara Ave. Ste. 440, Las Vegas, NV 89102-1703 / 817-831-9557; FAX: 817-834-5508
MOA Corporation, 2451 Old Camden Pike, Eaton, OH 45320 / 937-456-3669 www.moaguns.com
Mobile Area Networks, Inc., 2772 Depot St., Sanford, FL 32773 / 407-333-2350; FAX: 407-333-9903 georgew@mobilan.com
Modern Gun Repair School, P.O. Box 846, Saint Albans, VT 05478 / 802-524-2223; FAX: 802-524-2053 jfwp@dlilearn.com www.mgsinfoadlifearn.com
Modern Muzzleloading, Inc., P.O. Box 130, Centerville, IA 52544 / 515-856-2626
Moeller, Steve, 1213 4th St., Fulton, IL 61252 / 815-589-2300
Mogul Co./Life Jacket, 500 N. Kimball Rd., Ste. 109, South Lake, TX 76092
Monell Custom Guns, 228 Red Mills Rd., Pine Bush, NY 12566 / 914-744-3021
Moneymaker Guncraft Corp., 1420 Military Ave., Omaha, NE 68131 / 402-556-0226
Montana Armory, Inc., 100 Centennial Dr., P.O. Box 885, Big Timber, MT 59011 / 406-932-4353; FAX: 406-932-4443
Montana Outfitters, Lewis E. Yearout, 308 Riverview Dr. E., Great Falls, MT 59404 / 406-761-0859; or 406-727-4560
Montana Precision Swaging, P.O. Box 4746, Butte, MT 59702 / 406-494-0600; FAX: 406-494-0600
Montana Rifleman, Inc., 2593A Hwy. 2 East, Kalispell, MT 59901 / 406-755-4867
Montana Vintage Arms, 2354 Bear Canyon Rd., Bozeman, MT 59715
Morini (See U.S. Importers-Mandall Shooting Supplies, Inc.)
Morrison Custom Rifles, J. W., 4015 W Sharon, Phoenix, AZ 85029 / 602-978-3754
Morrison Precision, 6719 Calle Mango, Hereford, AZ 85615 / 520-378-6207 morprec@c2i2.com
Morrow, Bud, 11 Hillside Lane, Sheridan, WY 82801-9729 / 307-674-8360
Morton Booth Co., P.O. Box 123, Joplin, MO 64802 / 417-673-1962; FAX: 417-673-3642
Mo's Competitor Supplies (See MCS, Inc.)
Moss Double Tone, Inc., P.O. Box 1112, 2101 S. Kentucky, Sedalia, MO 65301 / 816-827-0827
Mountain Plains Industries, 3720 Otter Place, Lynchburg, VA 24503 / 800-687-3000; FAX: 434-845-6594 MPItargets@verizon.com
Mowrey Gun Works, P.O. Box 246, Waldron, IN 46182 / 317-525-6181; FAX: 317-525-9595
Mowrey's Guns & Gunsmithing, 119 Fredericks St., Canajoharie, NY 13317 / 518-673-3483
MPC, P.O. Box 450, McMinnville, TN 37110-0450 / 615-473-5513; FAX: 615-473-5516 thebox@blomand.net www.mpc-thebox.com
MPI Stocks, P.O. Box 83266, Portland, OR 97283 / 503-226-1215; FAX: 503-226-2661
MSR Targets, P.O. Box 1042, West Covina, CA 91793 / 818-331-7840
MTM Molded Products Co., Inc., 3370 Obco Ct., Dayton, OH 45414 / 937-890-7461; FAX: 937-890-1747
Mulberry House Publishing, P.O. Box 2180, Apache Junction, AZ 85217 / 888-738-1567; FAX: 480-671-1015
Mulhern, Rick, Rt. 5, Box 152, Rayville, LA 71269 / 318-728-2688
Mullins Ammunition, Rt. 2 Box 304N, Clintwood, VA 24228 / 276-926-6772; FAX: 276-926-6092 mammo@extremeshockusa.com www.extremeshockusa.com
Mullis Guncraft, 3523 Lawyers Road E., Monroe, NC 28110 / 704-283-6683
Multiplex International, 26 S. Main St., Concord, NH 03301 FAX: 603-796-2223
Multipropulseurs, La Bertrandiere, 42580, FRANCE / 77 74 01 30; FAX: 77 93 19 34
Mundy, Thomas A., 69 Robbins Road, Somerville, NJ 08876 / 201-722-2199
Murmur Corp., 2823 N. Westmoreland Ave., Dallas, TX 75222 / 214-630-5400
Murphy, R.R. Murphy Co., Inc. See: MURPHY, R.R. CO., INC.
Murphy, R.R. Co., Inc., R.R. Murphy Co., Inc. Murphy, P.O. Box 102, Ripley, TN 38063 / 901-635-4003; FAX: 901-635-2320
Murray State College, 1 Murray Campus St., Tishomingo, OK 73460 / 508-371-2371 darnold@mscol.edu

MANUFACTURER'S DIRECTORY

Muscle Products Corp., 112 Fennell Dr., Butler, PA 16002 / 800-227-7049; or 724-283-0567; FAX: 724-283-8310 mpc@mpc_home.com www.mpc_home.com
Muzzleloaders Etcetera, Inc., 9901 Lyndale Ave. S., Bloomington, MN 55420 / 952-884-1161 www.muzzleloaders-etcetera.com
MWG Co., P.O. Box 971202, Miami, FL 33197 / 800-428-9394; or 305-253-8393; FAX: 305-232-1247

N

N.B.B., Inc., 24 Elliot Rd., Sterling, MA 01564 / 508-422-7538; or 800-942-9444
N.C. Ordnance Co., P.O. Box 3254, Wilson, NC 27895 / 919-237-2440; FAX: 919-243-9845
Nagel's Custom Bullets, 100 Scott St., Baytown, TX 77520-2849
Nalpak, 1937-C Friendship Drive, El Cajon, CA 92020 / 619-258-1200
Nammo Lapua Oy, P.O. Box 5, Lapua, FINLAND / 358-6-4310111; FAX: 358-6-4310317 info@nammo.ti www.lapua.com
Nastoff, Steve. See: NASTOFFS 45 SHOP, INC.
Nastoffs 45 Shop, Inc., Steve Nastoff, 1057 Laverne Dr., Youngstown, OH 44511
National Bullet Co., 1585 E. 361 St., Eastlake, OH 44095 / 216-951-1854; FAX: 216-951-7761
National Target Co., 3958-D Dartmouth Ct., Frederick, MD 21703 / 800-827-7060; FAX: 301-874-4764
Nationwide Airgun Repair, 2310 Windsor Forest Dr., Louisville, KY 40272 / 502-937-2614; FAX: 812-637-1463 shortshoestring@insightbb.com
Naval Ordnance Works, 467 Knott Rd., Sheperdstown, WV 25443 / 304-876-0998; FAX: 304-876-0998 nvordfdy@earthlink.net
Navy Arms Co., 219 Lawn St., Martinsburg, WV 25401 / 304-262-9870; FAX: 304-262-1658
Navy Arms Company, Valmore J. Forgett Jr., 815 22nd Street, Union City, NJ 07087 / 201-863-7100; FAX: 201-863-8770 info@navyarms.com www.navyarms.com
NCP Products, Inc., 3500 12th St. N.W., Canton, OH 44708 / 330-456-5130; FAX: 330-456-5234
Necessary Concepts, Inc., P.O. Box 571, Deer Park, NY 11729 / 516-667-8509; FAX: 516-667-8588
NEI Handtools, Inc., 10960 Gary Player Dr., El Paso, TX 79935
Neil A. Jones Custom Products, 17217 Brookhouser Road, Saegertown, PA 16433 / 814-763-2769; FAX: 814-763-4228
Nelson, Gary K., 975 Terrace Dr., Oakdale, CA 95361 / 209-847-4590
Nelson, Stephen. See: NELSON'S CUSTOM GUNS, INC.
Nelson's Custom Guns, Inc., Stephen Nelson, 7430 Valley View Dr. N.W., Corvallis, OR 97330 / 541-745-5232 nelsons-custom@attbi.com
Nesci Enterprises Inc., P.O. Box 119, Summit St., East Hampton, CT 06424 / 203-267-2588
Nesika Bay Precision, 22239 Big Valley Rd., Poulsbo, WA 98370 / 206-697-3830
Nettestad Gun Works, 38962 160th Avenue, Pelican Rapids, MN 56572 / 218-863-1338
Neumann GmbH, Am Galgenberg 6, 90575, GERMANY / 09101/8258; FAX: 09101/6356
New England Ammunition Co., 1771 Post Rd. East, Suite 223, Westport, CT 06880 / 203-254-8048
New England Arms Co., Box 278, Lawrence Lane, Kittery Point, ME 03905 / 207-439-0593; FAX: 207-439-0525 info@newenglandarms.com www.newenglandarms.com
New England Custom Gun Service, 438 Willow Brook Rd., Plainfield, NH 03781 / 603-469-3450; FAX: 603-469-3471 bestguns@adelphia.net www.newenglandcustom.com
New Orleans Jewelers Supply Co., 206 Charters St., New Orleans, LA 70130 / 504-523-3839; FAX: 504-523-3836
New SKB Arms Co., C.P.O. Box 1401, Tokyo, JAPAN / 81-3-3943-9550; FAX: 81-3-3943-0695
New Ultra Light Arms, LLC, P.O. Box 340, Granville, WV 26534
Newark Electronics, 4801 N. Ravenswood Ave., Chicago, IL 60640
Newell, Robert H., 55 Coyote, Los Alamos, NM 87544 / 505-662-7135
Newman Gunshop, 2035 Chester Ave. #411, Ottumwa, IA 52501-3715 / 515-937-5775
NgraveR Co., The, 67 Wawecus Hill Rd., Bozrah, CT 06334 / 860-823-1533; FAX: 860-887-6252 ngraver98@aol.com www.ngraver.com
Nicholson Custom, 17285 Thornlay Road, Hughesville, MO 65334 / 816-826-8746
Nickels, Paul R., 4328 Seville St., Las Vegas, NV 89121 / 702-435-5318
Niemi Engineering, W. B., Box 126 Center Rd., Greensboro, VT 05841 / 802-533-7180; FAX: 802-533-7141
Nikon, Inc., 1300 Walt Whitman Rd., Melville, NY 11747 / 516-547-8623; FAX: 516-547-0309
Noreen, Peter H., 5075 Buena Vista Dr., Belgrade, MT 59714 / 406-586-7383
Norica, Avnda Otaola, 16 Apartado 68, Eibar, SPAIN
Norinco, 7A Yun Tan N, Beijing, CHINA
Norincoptics (See BEC, Inc.)
Norma Precision AB (See U.S. Importers-Dynamit)
Normark Corp., 10395 Yellow Circle Dr., Minnetonka, MN 55343-9101 / 612-933-7060; FAX: 612-933-0046
North American Arms, Inc., 2150 South 950 East, Provo, UT 84606-6285 / 800-821-5783; or 801-374-9990; FAX: 801-374-9998
North American Correspondence Schools, The Gun Pro, Oak & Pawney St., Scranton, PA 18515 / 717-342-7701
North American Shooting Systems, P.O. Box 306, Osoyoos, BC V0H 1V0 CANADA / 250-495-3131; FAX: 250-495-3131 rifle@cablerocket.com
North Devon Firearms Services, 3 North St., Braunton, EX33 1AJ ENGLAND / 01271 813624; FAX: 01271 813624
North Mountain Pine Training Center (See Executive Protection Institute)
North Star West, P.O. Box 488, Glencoe, CA 95232 / 209-293-7010 northstarwest.com
Northern Precision, 329 S. James St., Carthage, NY 13619 / 315-493-1711
Northside Gun Shop, 2725 NW 109th, Oklahoma City, OK 73120 / 405-840-2353
Northwest Arms, 26884 Pearl Rd., Parma, ID 83660 / 208-722-6771; FAX: 208-722-1062
Northwest Custom Projectile, P.O. Box 127, Butte, MT 59703-0127 www.customprojectile.com
No-Sho Mfg. Co., 10727 Glenfield Ct., Houston, TX 77096 / 713-723-5332
Nosler, Inc., P.O. Box 671, Bend, OR 97709 / 800-285-3701; or 541-382-3921; FAX: 541-388-4667 www.nosler.com
Novak's, Inc., 1206 1/2 30th St., P.O. Box 4045, Parkersburg, WV 26101 / 304-485-9295; FAX: 304-428-6722 www.novaksights.com
Nowlin Mfg. Co., 20622 S 4092 Rd., Claremore, OK 74017 / 918-342-0689; FAX: 918-342-0624 nowlinguns@msn.com nowlinguns.com
NRI Gunsmith School, P.O. Box 182968, Columbus, OH 43218-2968
Nu Line Guns, 8150 CR 4055, Rhineland, MO 65069 / 573-676-5500; FAX: 314-447-5018 nlg@ktis.net
Null Holsters Ltd. K.L., 161 School St. N.W., Resaca, GA 30735 / 706-625-5643; FAX: 706-625-9392 ken@klnullholsters.com www.klnullholsters.com
Numrich Gun Parts Corporation, 226 Williams Lane, P.O. Box 299, West Hurley, NY 12491 / 866-686-7424; FAX: 877-GUNPART info@gunpartscorp.com www.@-gunparts.com
Nygord Precision Products, Inc., P.O. Box 12578, Prescott, AZ 86304 / 928-717-2315; FAX: 928-717-2198 nygords@northlink.com www.nygordprecision.com

O

O.F. Mossberg & Sons, Inc., 7 Grasso Ave., North Haven, CT 06473 / 203-230-5300; FAX: 203-230-5420
Oakman Turkey Calls, RD 1, Box 825, Harrisonville, PA 17228 / 717-485-4620
Obermeyer Rifled Barrels, 23122 60th St., Bristol, WI 53104 / 262-843-3537; FAX: 262-843-2129 www.obermeyerbarrels.com
October Country Muzzleloading, P.O. Box 969, Dept. GD, Hayden, ID 83835 / 208-772-2068; FAX: 208-772-9230 ocinfo@octobercountry.com www.octobercountry.com
Oehler Research, Inc., P.O. Box 9135, Austin, TX 78766 / 512-327-6900; or 800-531-5125; FAX: 512-327-6903 www.oehler-research.com
Oil Rod and Gun Shop, 69 Oak St., East Douglas, MA 01516 / 508-476-3687
OK Weber, Inc., P.O. Box 7485, Eugene, OR 97401 / 541-747-0458; FAX: 541-747-5927 okweber@pacinfo www.okweber.com
Oker's Engraving, P.O. Box 126, Shawnee, CO 80475 / 303-838-6042
Oklahoma Ammunition Co., 3701A S. Harvard Ave., No. 367, Tulsa, OK 74135-2265 / 918-396-3187; FAX: 918-396-4270
Oklahoma Leather Products, Inc., 500 26th NW, Miami, OK 74354 / 918-542-6651; FAX: 918-542-6653
Olathe Gun Shop, 716-A South Rogers Road, Olathe, KS 66062 / 913-782-6900; FAX: 913-782-6902 info@olathegunshop.com www.olathegunshop.com
Old Wagon Bullets, 32 Old Wagon Rd., Wilton, CT 06897
Old West Bullet Moulds, J. Ken Chapman, P.O. Box 519, Flora Vista, NM 87415 / 505-334-6970
Old West Reproductions, Inc. R.M. Bachman, 446 Florence S. Loop, Florence, MT 59833 / 406-273-2615; FAX: 406-273-2615 rick@oldwestreproductions.com www.oldwestreproductions.com
Old Western Scrounger Ammunition Inc., 50 Industrial Parkway, Carson City, NV 89706 / 775-246-2091; FAX: 775-246-2095 www.ows-ammunition.com
Old World Gunsmithing, 2901 SE 122nd St., Portland, OR 97236 / 503-760-7681
Ole Frontier Gunsmith Shop, 2617 Hwy. 29 S., Cantonment, FL 32533 / 904-477-8074
Olson, Myron, 989 W. Kemp, Watertown, SD 57201 / 605-886-9787
Olson, Vic, 5002 Countryside Dr., Imperial, MO 63052 / 314-296-8086
Olympic Arms Inc., 620-626 Old Pacific Hwy. SE, Olympia, WA 98513 / 360-456-3471; FAX: 360-491-3447 info@olyarms.com www.olyarms.com
Olympic Optical Co., P.O. Box 752377, Memphis, TN 38175-2377 / 901-794-3890; or 800-238-7120; FAX: 901-794-0676
Omega Sales, P.O. Box 1066, Mt. Clemens, MI 48043 / 810-469-7323; FAX: 810-469-0425
One Of A Kind, 15610 Purple Sage, San Antonio, TX 78255 / 512-695-3364
One Ragged Hole, P.O. Box 13624, Tallahassee, FL 32317-3624
Op-Tec, P.O. Box L632, Langhorn, PA 19047 / 215-757-5037; FAX: 215-757-7097
Optical Services Co., P.O. Box 1174, Santa Teresa, NM 88008-1174 / 505-589-3833
Orchard Park Enterprise, P.O. Box 563, Orchard Park, NY 14127 / 616-656-0356
Ordnance Works, The, 2969 Pigeon Point Rd., Eureka, CA 95501 / 707-443-3252
Oregon Arms, Inc. (See Rogue Rifle Co., Inc.)
Oregon Trail Bullet Company, P.O. Box 529, Dept. P, Baker City, OR 97814 / 800-811-0548; FAX: 514-523-1803
Original Box, Inc., 700 Linden Ave., York, PA 17404 / 717-854-2897; FAX: 717-845-4276
Original Deer Formula Co., The, P.O. Box 1705, Dickson, TN 37056 / 800-874-6965; FAX: 615-446-0646 deerformula1@aol.com www.deerformula.com
Orion Rifle Barrel Co., RR2, 137 Cobler Village, Kalispell, MT 59901 / 406-257-5649
Orvis Co., The, Rt. 7, Manchester, VT 05254 / 802-362-3622; FAX: 802-362-3525
Otis Technology, Inc., RR 1 Box 84, Boonville, NY 13309 / 315-942-3320
Ottmar, Maurice, Box 657, 113 E. Fir, Coulee City, WA 99115 / 509-632-5717
Outa-Site Gun Carriers, 219 Market St., Laredo, TX 78040 / 210-722-4678; or 800-880-9715; FAX: 210-726-4858
Outdoor Connection, Inc., The, 7901 Panther Way, Waco, TX 76712-6556 / 800-533-6076; FAX: 254-776-3553 info@outdoorconnection.com www.outdoorconnection.com
Outdoor Edge Cutlery Corp., 4699 Nautilus Ct. S. Ste. 503, Boulder, CO 80301-5310 / 303-530-7667; FAX: 303-530-7020 www.outdooredge.com
Outdoor Enthusiast, 3784 W. Woodland, Springfield, MO 65807 / 417-883-9841
Outdoor Sports Headquarters, Inc., 967 Watertower Ln., West Carrollton, OH 45449 / 513-865-5855; FAX: 513-865-5962
Outers Laboratories Div. of ATK, Route 2, P.O. Box 39, Onalaska, WI 54650 / 608-781-5800; FAX: 608-781-0368
Ox-Yoke Originals, Inc., 34 Main St., Milo, ME 04463 / 800-231-8313; or 207-943-7351; FAX: 207-943-2416
Ozark Gun Works, 11830 Cemetery Rd., Rogers, AR 72756 / 479-631-1024; FAX: 479-631-1024 ozarkgunworks@cox.net www.geocities.com

MANUFACTURER'S DIRECTORY

P

P&M Sales & Services, LLC, 4697 Tote Rd. Bldg. H-B, Comins, MI 48619 / 989-848-8364; FAX: 989-848-8364 info@pmsales-online.com
P.S.M.G. Gun Co., 10 Park Ave., Arlington, MA 02174 / 781-646-1699; FAX: 781-643-7212 psmg2@aol.com
Pachmayr Div. Lyman Products, 475 Smith St., Middletown, CT 06457 / 860-632-2020; or 800-225-9626; FAX: 860-632-1699 lymansales@cshore.com www.pachmayr.com
Pacific Armament Corp, 4813 Enterprise Way, Unit K, Modesto, CA 95356 / 209-545-2800 gunsparts@att.net
Pacific Rifle Co., P.O. Box 841, Carlton, OR 97111 / 503-852-6276 pacificrifle@aol.com
PAC-NOR Barreling, 99299 Overlook Rd., P.O. Box 6188, Brookings, OR 97415 / 503-469-7330; FAX: 503-469-7331 info@pac-nor.com www.pac-nor.com
PACT, Inc., P.O. Box 535025, Grand Prairie, TX 75053 / 972-641-0049; FAX: 972-641-2641
Page Custom Bullets, P.O. Box 25, Port Moresby, NEW GUINEA
Pagel Gun Works, Inc., 2 SE 1st St., Grand Rapids, MN 55744
Pager Pal, 200 W Pleasantview, Hurst, TX 76054 / 800-561-1603; FAX: 817-285-8769 www.pagerpal.com
Paintball Games International Magazine Aceville, Castle House 97 High St., Essex, ENGLAND / 011-44-206-564840
Palsa Outdoor Products, P.O. Box 81336, Lincoln, NE 68501 / 402-488-5288; FAX: 402-488-2321
Pansch, Robert F, 1004 Main St. #10, Neenah, WI 54956 / 920-725-8175
Paragon Sales & Services, Inc., 2501 Theodore St., Crest Hill, IL 60435-1613 / 815-725-9212; FAX: 815-725-8974
Para-Ordnance Mfg., Inc., 980 Tapscott Rd., Scarborough, ON M1X 1E7 CANADA / 416-297-7855; FAX: 416-297-1289
Para-Ordnance, Inc., 1919 NE 45th St., Ste 215, Ft. Lauderdale, FL 33308 info@paraord.com www.paraord.com
Pardini Armi Srl, Via Italica 154, 55043, Lido Di Camaiore Lu, ITALY / 584-90121; FAX: 584-90122
Paris, Frank J., 17417 Pershing St., Livonia, MI 48152-3822
Park Rifle Co., Ltd., The, Unit 6a Dartford Trade Park, Power Mill Lane, Dartford DA7 7NX, ENGLAND / 011-0322-222512
Parker & Sons Shooting Supply, 9337 Smoky Row Road, Strawberry Plains, TN 37871 / 865-933-3286; FAX: 865-932-8586
Parker Gun Finishes, 9337 Smokey Row Rd., Strawberry Plains, TN 37871 / 865-933-3286; FAX: 865-932-8586 parcraft7838@netzero.com
Parsons Optical Mfg. Co., PO Box 192, Ross, OH 45061 / 513-867-0820; FAX: 513-867-8380 psscopes@concentric.net
Partridge Sales Ltd., John, Trent Meadows, Rugeley, ENGLAND
Pasadena Gun Center, 206 E. Shaw, Pasadena, TX 77506 / 713-472-0417; FAX: 713-472-1322
Passive Bullet Traps, Inc. (See Savage Range Systems, Inc.)
Paterson Gunsmithing, 438 Main St., Paterson, NJ 07502 / 201-345-4100
Pathfinder Sports Leather, 2920 E. Chambers St., Phoenix, AZ 85040 / 602-276-0016
Patrick W. Price Bullets, 16520 Worthley Drive, San Lorenzo, CA 94580 / 510-278-1547
Pattern Control, 114 N. Third St., P.O. Box 462105, Garland, TX 75046 / 214-494-3551; FAX: 214-272-8447
Paul A. Harris Hand Engraving, 113 Rusty Lane, Boerne, TX 78006-5746 / 512-391-5121
Paul and Sharon Dressel, 209 N. 92nd Ave., Yakima, WA 98908 / 509-966-9233; FAX: 509-966-3365 dressels@nwinfo.net www.dressels.com
Paul Co., The, 27385 Pressonville Rd., Wellsville, KS 66092 / 785-883-4444; FAX: 785-883-2525
Paul D. Hillmer Custom Gunstocks, 7251 Hudson Heights, Hudson, IA 50643 / 319-988-3941
Paul Jones Moulds, 4901 Telegraph Rd., Los Angeles, CA 90022 / 213-262-1510
Paulsen Gunstocks, Rt. 71, Box 11, Chinook, MT 59523 / 406-357-3403
Pawling Mountain Club, Keith Lupton, P.O. Box 573, Pawling, NY 12564 / 914-855-3825
Paxton Quigley's Personal Protection Strategies, 9903 Santa Monica Blvd., 300, Beverly Hills, CA 90212 / 310-281-1762 www.defend-net.com/paxton
Payne Photography, Robert, Robert, P.O. Box 141471, Austin, TX 78714 / 512-272-4554
Peacemaker Specialists, P.O. Box 157, Whitmore, CA 96096 / 530-472-3438 www.peacemakerspecialists.com
Pearce Grip, Inc., P.O. Box 40367, Fort Worth, TX 76140 / 817-568-9704; FAX: 817-568-9707 info@pearcegrip.com www.pearcegrip.com
PECAR Herbert Schwarz GmbH, Kreuzbergstrasse 6, 10965, Berlin, GERMANY / 004930-785-7383; FAX: 004930-785-1934 michael.schwart@pecar-berlin.de www.pecar-berlin.de
Pecatonica River Longrifle, 5205 Nottingham Dr., Rockford, IL 61111 / 815-968-1995; FAX: 815-968-1996
Pedersen, C. R., 2717 S. Pere Marquette Hwy., Ludington, MI 49431 / 231-843-2061; FAX: 231-845-7695 fega@fega.com
Pedersen, Rex C., 2717 S. Pere Marquette Hwy., Ludington, MI 49431 / 231-843-2061; FAX: 231-845-7695 fega@fega.com
Peifer Rifle Co., P.O. Box 220, Nokomis, IL 62075
Pejsa Ballistics, 1314 Marquette Ave., Apt 906, Minneapolis, MN 55403 / 612-332-5073; FAX: 612-332-5204 pejsa@sprintmail.com pejsa.com
Peltor, Inc. (See Aero Peltor)
PEM's Mfg. Co., 5063 Waterloo Rd., Atwater, OH 44201 / 216-947-3721
Pence Precision Barrels, 7567 E. 900 S., S. Whitley, IN 46787 / 219-839-4745
Pendleton Royal, c/o Swingler Buckland Ltd., 4/7 Highgate St., Birmingham, ENGLAND / 44 121 440 3060; or 44 121 446 5898; FAX: 44 121 446 4165
Pendleton Woolen Mills, P.O. Box 3030, 220 N.W. Broadway, Portland, OR 97208 / 503-226-4801
Penn Bullets, P.O. Box 756, Indianola, PA 15051
Pennsylvania Gun Parts Inc., RR 7 Box 150, Mount Pleasant, PA 15666
Pennsylvania Gunsmith School, 812 Ohio River Blvd., Avalon, Pittsburgh, PA 15202 / 412-766-1812; FAX: 412-766-0855 pgs@pagunsmith.com www.pagunsmith.com
Penrod, Mark. See: PENROD PRECISION
Penrod Precision, Mark Penrod, 312 College Ave., P.O. Box 307, N. Manchester, IN 46962 / 260-982-8385; FAX: 260-982-1819 markpenrod@kconline.com
Pentax U.S.A., Inc., 600 12th St. Ste. 300, Golden, CO 80401 / 303-799-8000; FAX: 303-460-1628 www.pentaxlightseeker.com
Pentheny de Pentheny, c/o H.P. Okelly, 321 S. Main St., Sebastopol, CA 95472 / 707-824-1637; FAX: 707-824-1637
Perazone-Gunsmith, Brian, Cold Spring Rd., Roxbury, NY 12474 / 607-326-4088; FAX: 607-326-3140 bpgunsmith@catskill.net www.bpgunsmith@catskill.net
Perazzi U.S.A. Inc., 1010 West Tenth, Azusa, CA 91702 / 626-334-1234; FAX: 626-334-0344 perazziusa@aol.com
Performance Specialists, 308 Eanes School Rd., Austin, TX 78746 / 512-327-0119
Perugini Visini & Co. S.r.l., Via Camprelle, 126, 25080 Nuvolera, ITALY / 30-6897535; FAX: 30-6897821 peruvisi@virgilia.it
Pete de Coux Auction House, 14940 Brenda Dr., Prescott, AZ 86305-7447 / 928-776-8285; FAX: 928-776-8276 pdbullets@commspeed.net
Pete Mazur Restoration, 13083 Drummer Way, Grass Valley, CA 95949 / 530-268-2412; FAX: 530-268-2412
Pete Rickard, Inc., 115 Roy Walsh Rd, Cobleskill, NY 12043 / 518-234-2731: FAX: 518-234-2454 rickard@telenet.net www.peterickard.com
Peter Dyson & Son Ltd., 3 Cuckoo Lane, Honley, Holmfirth, West Yorkshire, HD9 6AS ENGLAND / 44-1484-661062; FAX: 44-1484-663709 peter@peterdyson.co.uk www.peterdyson.co.uk
Peter Hale/Engraver, 997 Maple Dr., Spanish Fork, UT 84660-2524 / 801-798-8215
Peters Stahl GmbH, Stettiner Strasse 42, D-33106, Paderborn, GERMANY / 05251-750025; FAX: 05251-75611
Peterson Gun Shop, Inc., A.W., 4255 W. Old U.S. 441, Mt. Dora, FL 32757-3299 / 352-383-4258; FAX: 352-735-1001
Petro-Explo Inc., 7650 U.S. Hwy. 287, Suite 100, Arlington, TX 76017 / 817-478-8888
Pettinger Books, Gerald, 47827 300th Ave., Russell, IA 50238 / 641-535-2239 gpettinger@lisco.com
Pflumm Mfg. Co., 10662 Widmer Rd., Lenexa, KS 66215 / 800-888-4867; FAX: 913-451-7857
PFRB Co., P.O. Box 1242, Bloomington, IL 61702 / 309-473-3964; or 800-914-5464; FAX: 309-473-2161
Philip S. Olt Co., P.O. Box 550, 12662 Fifth St., Pekin, IL 61554 / 309-348-3633; FAX: 309-348-3300
Phillippi Custom Bullets, Justin, P.O. Box 773, Ligonier, PA 15658 / 724-238-2962; FAX: 724-238-9671 jrp@wpa.net http://www.wpa.net~jrphil
Phillips & Rogers, Inc., 852 FM 980 Rd., Conroe, TX 77320 / 409-435-0011
Phoenix Arms, 4231 Brickell St., Ontario, CA 91761 / 909-937-6900; FAX: 909-937-0060
Piedmont Community College, P.O. Box 1197, Roxboro, NC 27573 / 336-599-1181; FAX: 336-597-3817 www.piedmont.cc.nc.us
Pietta (See U.S. Importers-Navy Arms Co, Taylor's
Pine Technical College, 1100 4th St., Pine City, MN 55063 / 800-521-7463; FAX: 612-629-6766
Pinetree Bullets, 133 Skeena St., Kitimat, BC V8C 1Z1 CANADA / 604-632-3768; FAX: 604-632-3768
Pioneer Arms Co., 355 Lawrence Rd., Broomall, PA 19008 / 215-356-5203
Piotti (See U.S. Importer-Moore & Co., Wm. Larkin)
Piquette, Paul. See: PIQUETTE'S CUSTOM ENGRAVING
Piquette's Custom Engraving, Paul R. Piquette, 511 Southwick St., Feeding Hills, MA 01030 / 413-789-4582 ppiquette@comcast.net www.pistoldynamics.com
Plaza Cutlery, Inc., 3333 Bristol, 161 South Coast Plaza, Costa Mesa, CA 92626 / 714-549-3932
Plum City Ballistic Range, N2162 80th St., Plum City, WI 54761 / 715-647-2539
PlumFire Press, Inc., 30-A Grove Ave., Patchogue, NY 11772-4112 / 800-695-7246; FAX: 516-758-4071
PMC/Eldorado Cartridge Corp., P.O. Box 62508, 12801 U.S. Hwy. 95 S., Boulder City, NV 89005 / 702-294-0025; FAX: 702-294-0121 kbauer@pmcammo.com www.pmcammo.com
Poburka, Philip (See Bison Studios)
Pointing Dog Journal, Village Press Publications, P.O. Box 968, Dept. PGD, Traverse City, MI 49685 / 800-272-3246; FAX: 616-946-3289
Police Bookshelf, P.O. Box 122, Concord, NH 03301 / 603-224-6814; FAX: 603-226-3554
Polywad, Inc., P.O. Box 7916, Macon, GA 31209 / 478-477-0669; or 800-998-0669 FAX: 478-477-0666 polywadmpb@aol.com www.polywad.com
Ponsness, Warren, 7634 W. Ohio St., Rathdrum, ID 83858 / 800-732-0706; FAX: 208-687-2233 www.reloaders.com
Pony Express Reloaders, 608 E. Co. Rd. D, Suite 3, St. Paul, MN 55117 / 612-483-9406; FAX: 612-483-9884
Pony Express Sport Shop, 23404 Lyons Ave., PMB 448, Newhall, CA 91321-2511 / 818-895-1231
Potts, Wayne E., 1580 Meade St. Apt. A, Denver, CO 80204-5930 / 303-355-5462
Powder Horn Ltd., P.O. Box 565, Glenview, IL 60025 / 305-565-6060
Powell & Son (Gunmakers) Ltd., William, 35-37 Carrs Lane, Birmingham, B4 7SX ENGLAND / 121-643-0689; FAX: 121-631-3504 sales@william-powell.co.uk www.william-powell.co.uk
Powell Agency, William, 22 Circle Dr., Bellmore, NY 11710 / 516-679-1158
Power Custom, Inc., 29739 Hwy. J, Gravois Mills, MO 65037 / 573-372-5684; FAX: 573-372-5799 rwpowers@laurie.net www.powercustom.com
Power Plus Enterprises, Inc., P.O. Box 38, Warm Springs, GA 31830 / 706-655-2132
Powley Computer (See Hutton Rifle Ranch)
Practical Tools, Inc., 7067 Easton Rd., P.O. Box 133, Pipersville, PA 18947 / 215-766-7301; FAX: 215-766-8681
Prairie Gun Works, 1-761 Marion St., Winnipeg, MB R2J 0K6 CANADA / 204-231-2976; FAX: 204-231-8566
Prairie River Arms, 1220 N. Sixth St., Princeton, IL 61356 / 815-875-1616; or 800-445-1541; FAX: 815-875-1402
Pranger, Ed G., 1414 7th St., Anacortes, WA 98221 / 206-293-3488
Precision Airgun Sales, Inc., 5247 Warrensville Ctr Rd., Maple Hts., OH 44137 / 216-587-5005; FAX: 216-587-5005
Precision Cast Bullets, 101 Mud Creek Lane, Ronan, MT 59864 / 406-676-5135
Precision Delta Corp., P.O. Box 128, Ruleville, MS 38771 / 662-756-2810; FAX: 662-756-2590
Precision Firearm Finishing, 25 N.W. 44th Avenue, Des Moines, IA 50313 / 515-288-8680; FAX: 515-244-3925
Precision Gun Works, 104 Sierra Rd., Dept. GD, Kerrville, TX 78028 / 830-367-4587
Precision Reloading, Inc., P.O. Box 122, Stafford Springs, CT 06076 / 860-684-7979; FAX: 860-684-6788 info@precisionreloading.com www.precisionreloading.com

MANUFACTURER'S DIRECTORY

Precision Shooting, Inc., 222 McKee St., Manchester, CT 06040 / 860-645-8776; FAX: 860-643-8215 www.theaccuraterifle.com or precisionshooting.com
Precision Small Arms Inc., 9272 Jeronimo Rd., Ste. 121, Irvine, CA 92618 / 800-554-5515; or 949-768-3530; FAX: 949-768-4808 www.tcbebe.com
Precision Specialties, 131 Hendom Dr., Feeding Hills, MA 01030 / 413-786-3365; FAX: 413-786-3365
Precision Sport Optics, 15571 Producer Lane, Unit G, Huntington Beach, CA 92649 / 714-891-1309; FAX: 714-892-6920
Premier Reticles, 920 Breckinridge Lane, Winchester, VA 22601-6707 / 540-722-0601; FAX: 540-722-3522
Prescott Projectile Co., 1808 Meadowbrook Road, Prescott, AZ 86303
Preslik's Gunstocks, 4245 Keith Ln., Chico, CA 95926 / 916-891-8236
Price Bullets, Patrick W., 16520 Worthley Dr., San Lorenzo, CA 94580 / 510-278-1547
Prime Reloading, 30 Chiswick End, Meldreth, ROYSTON UK / 0763-260636
Primedia Publishing Co., 6420 Wilshire Blvd., Los Angeles, CA 90048 / 213-782-2000; FAX: 213-782-2867
Primos Hunting Calls, 604 First St., Flora, MS 39071 / 601-879-9323; FAX: 601-879-9324 www.primos.com
PRL Bullets, c/o Blackburn Enterprises, 114 Stuart Rd., Ste. 110, Cleveland, TN 37312 / 423-559-0340
Pro Load Ammunition, Inc., 5180 E. Seltice Way, Post Falls, ID 83854 / 208-773-9444; FAX: 208-773-9441
Professional Gunsmiths of America, Rt 1 Box 224, Lexington, MO 64067 / 660-259-2636
Professional Hunter Supplies, P.O. Box 608, 468 Main St., Ferndale, CA 95536 / 707-786-9140; FAX: 707-786-9117 wmebride@humboldt.com
PrOlixr Lubricants, P.O. Box 1348, Victorville, CA 92393 / 760-243-3129; FAX: 760-241-0148 prolix@accex.net www.prolixlubricant.com
Pro-Mark Div. of Wells Lamont, 6640 W. Touhy, Chicago, IL 60648 / 312-647-8200
Proofmark Corp., P.O. Box 357, Burgess, VA 22432 / 804-453-4337; FAX: 804-453-4337 proofmark@direzway.com www.proofmarkbullets.com
Pro-Port Ltd., 41302 Executive Dr., Harrison Twp., MI 48045-1306 / 586-469-6727; FAX: 586-469-0425 e-mail@magnaport.com www.magnaport.com
Pro-Shot Products, Inc., P.O. Box 763, Taylorville, IL 62568 / 217-824-9133; FAX: 217-824-8861 www.proshotproducts.com
Protector Mfg. Co., Inc., The, 443 Ashwood Pl., Boca Raton, FL 33431 / 407-394-6011
Protektor Model, 1-11 Bridge St., Galeton, PA 16922 / 814-435-2442 mail@protektormodel.com www.protektormodel.com
Prototech Industries, Inc., 10532 E Road, Delia, KS 66418 / 785-771-3571 prototec@grapevine.net
ProWare, Inc., 15847 NE Hancock St., Portland, OR 97230 / 503-239-0159
PWL Gunleather, P.O. Box 450432, Atlanta, GA 31145 / 800-960-4072; FAX: 770-822-1704 covert@pwlusa.com www.pwlusa.com
PWM Sales Ltd., N.D.F.S., Gowdall Lane, Pollington DN14 0AU, ENGLAND / 01405862688; FAX: 01405862622 Paulwelburn9@aol.com
Pyramyd Stone Inter. Corp., 2447 Suffolk Lane, Pepper Pike, OH 44124-4540

Q

Quack Decoy & Sporting Clays, 4 Ann & Hope Way, P.O. Box 98, Cumberland, RI 02864 / 401-723-8202; FAX: 401-722-5910
Quaker Boy, Inc., 5455 Webster Rd., Orchard Parks, NY 14127 / 716-662-3979; FAX: 716-662-9426
Quality Arms, Inc., Box 19477, Dept. GD, Houston, TX 77224 / 281-870-8377 arrieta2@excite.com www.arrieta.com
Quality Cartridge, P.O. Box 445, Hollywood, MD 20636 / 301-373-3719 www.qual-cart.com
Quality Custom Firearms, Stephen Billeb, 22 Vista View Dr., Cody, WY 82414 / 307-587-4278; FAX: 307-587-4297 stevebilleb@wyoming.com
Quarton Beamshot, 4538 Centerview Dr., Ste. 149, San Antonio, TX 78228 / 800-520-8435; FAX: 210-735-1326 www.beamshot.com
Que Industries, Inc., P.O. Box 2471, Everett, WA 98203 / 425-303-9088; FAX: 206-514-3266 queinfo@queindustries.com
Queen Cutlery Co., P.O. Box 500, Franklinville, NY 14737 / 800-222-5233; FAX: 800-299-2618

R

R&C Knives & Such, 2136 CANDY CANE WALK, Manteca, CA 95336-9501 / 209-239-3722; FAX: 209-825-6947
R&D Gun Repair, Kenny Howell, RR1 Box 283, Beloit, WI 53511
R&J Gun Shop, 337 S. Humbolt St., Canyon City, OR 97820 / 541-575-2130 rjgunshop@highdesertnet.com
R&S Industries Corp., 8255 Brentwood Industrial Dr., St. Louis, MO 63144 / 314-781-5169 ron@miraclepolishingcloth.com www.miraclepolishingcloth.com
R. Murphy Co., Inc., 13 Groton-Harvard Rd., P.O. Box 376, Ayer, MA 01432 / 617-772-3481 www.r.murphyknives.com
R.A. Wells Custom Gunsmith, 3452 1st Ave., Racine, WI 53402 / 414-639-5223
R.E. Seebeck Assoc., P.O. Box 59752, Dallas, TX 75229
R.E.I., P.O. Box 88, Tallevast, FL 34270 / 813-755-0085
R.E.T. Enterprises, 2608 S. Chestnut, Broken Arrow, OK 74012 / 918-251-GUNS; FAX: 918-251-0587
R.F. Mitchell Bullets, 430 Walnut St., Westernport, MD 21562
R.T. Eastman Products, P.O. Box 1531, Jackson, WY 83001 / 307-733-3217; or 800-624-4311
Rabeno, Martin, 530 The Eagle Pass, Durango, CO 81301 / 970-382-0353 fancygun@aol.com
Radack Photography, Lauren, 21140 Jib Court L-12, Aventura, FL 33180 / 305-931-3110
Radiator Specialty Co., 1900 Wilkinson Blvd., P.O. Box 34689, Charlotte, NC 28234 / 800-438-6947; FAX: 800-421-9525 tkrossell@gunk.com www.gunk.com
Radical Concepts, P.O. Box 1473, Lake Grove, OR 97035 / 503-538-7437
Rainier Ballistics, 4500 15th St. East, Tacoma, WA 98424 / 800-638-8722; FAX: 253-922-7854 sales@rainierballistics.com www.rainierballistics.com
Ralph Bone Engraving, 718 N. Atlanta St., Owasso, OK 74055 / 918-272-9745
Ram-Line ATK, P.O. Box 39, Onalaska, WI 54650
Ramon B. Gonzalez Guns, P.O. Box 370, Monticello, NY 12701 / 914-794-4515; FAX: 914-794-4515
Rampart International, 2781 W. MacArthur Blvd., B-283, Santa Ana, CA 92704 / 800-976-7240 or 714-557-6405
Ranch Products, P.O. Box 145, Malinta, OH 43535 / 313-277-3118; FAX: 313-565-8536
Randall-Made Knives, P.O. Box 1988, Orlando, FL 32802 / 407-855-8075
Randco UK, 286 Gipsy Rd., Welling, DA16 1JJ ENGLAND / 44 81 303 4118
Randolph Engineering, Inc., Ranger Shooting Glasses, 26 Thomas Patten Dr., Randolph, MA 02368 / 800-541-1405; FAX: 781-986-0337 sales@randolphusa.com www.randolphusa.com
Randy Duane Custom Stocks, 7822 Church St., Middletown, VA 22645-9521
Range Brass Products Company, P.O. Box 218, Rockport, TX 78381
Ransom International Corp., 1027 Spire Dr., Prescott, AZ 86305 / 928-778-7899; FAX: 928-778-7993 ransom@cableone.net www.ransomrest.com
Rapine Bullet Mould Mfg. Co., 9503 Landis Lane, East Greenville, PA 18041 / 215-679-5413; FAX: 215-679-9795
Ravell Ltd., 289 Diputacion St., 08009, Barcelona, SPAIN / 34(3) 4874486; FAX: 34(3) 4881394
Ray Riling Arms Books Co., 6844 Gorsten St., Philadelphia, PA 19119 / 215-438-2456; FAX: 215-438-5395 sales@rayrilingarmsbooks.com www.rayrilingarmsbooks.com
Ray's Gunsmith Shop, 3199 Elm Ave., Grand Junction, CO 81504 / 970-434-6162; FAX: 970-434-6162
Raytech Div. of Lyman Products Corp., 475 Smith Street, Middletown, CT 06457-1541 / 860-632-2020 or 800-225-9626; FAX: 860-632-1699 raysales@cshore.com www.raytech-ind.com
RCBS Operations/ATK, 605 Oro Dam Blvd., Oroville, CA 95965 / 530-533-5191 or 800-533-5000; FAX: 530-533-1647 www.rcbs.com
RCBS/ATK, 605 Oro Dam Blvd., Oroville, CA 95965 / 800-533-5000; FAX: 916-533-1647
Reardon Products, P.O. Box 126, Morrison, IL 61270 / 815-772-3155
Red Diamond Dist. Co., 1304 Snowdon Dr., Knoxville, TN 37912
Redding Reloading Equipment, 1089 Starr Rd., Cortland, NY 13045 / 607-753-3331; FAX: 607-756-8445 techline@redding-reloading.com www.redding-reloading.com
Redfield Media Resource Center, 4607 N.E. Cedar Creek Rd., Woodland, WA 98674 / 360-225-5000; FAX: 360-225-7616
Redman's Rifling & Reboring, 189 Nichols Rd., Omak, WA 98841 / 509-826-5512
Redwood Bullet Works, 3559 Bay Rd., Redwood City, CA 94063 / 415-367-6741
Reed, Dave, Rt. 1, Box 374, Minnesota City, MN 55959 / 507-689-2944
Reimer Johannsen, Inc., 438 Willow Brook Rd., Plainfield, NH 03781 / 603-469-3450; FAX: 603-469-3471
Reloaders Equipment Co., 4680 High St., Ecorse, MI 48229
Reloading Specialties, Inc., Box 1130, Pine Island, MN 55463 / 507-356-8500; FAX: 507-356-8800
Remington Arms Co., Inc., 870 Remington Drive, P.O. Box 700, Madison, NC 27025-0700 / 800-243-9700; FAX: 910-548-8700
Remington Double Shotguns, 7885 Cyd Dr., Denver, CO 80221 / 303-429-6947
Renato Gamba S.p.A.-Societa Armi Bresciane Srl., Via Artigiani 93, 25063 Gardone, Val Trompia (BS), ITALY / 30-8911640; FAX: 30-8911648
Renegade, P.O. Box 31546, Phoenix, AZ 85046 / 602-482-6777; FAX: 602-482-1952
Renfrew Guns & Supplies, R.R. 4, Renfrew, ON K7V 3Z7 CANADA / 613-432-7080
Reno, Wayne, 2808 Stagestop Road, Jefferson, CO 80456
Republic Arms, Inc. (See Cobra Enterprises, Inc.)
Retting, Inc., Martin B., 11029 Washington, Culver City, CA 90232 / 213-837-2412
RG-G, Inc., P.O. Box 935, Trinidad, CO 81082 / 719-845-1436
RH Machine & Consulting Inc., P.O. Box 394, Pacific, MO 63069 / 314-271-8465
Rhino, P.O. Box 787, Locust, NC 28097 / 704-753-2198
Rhodeside, Inc., 1704 Commerce Dr., Piqua, OH 45356 / 513-773-5781
Rice, Keith (See White Rock Tool & Die)
Richards MicroFit Stocks, Inc., P.O. Box 1066, Sun Valley, CA 91352 / 800-895-7420; FAX: 818-771-1242 sales@rifle-stocks.com www.rifle-stocks.com
Ridgeline, Inc., Bruce Sheldon, P.O. Box 930, Dewey, AZ 86327-0930 / 800-632-5900; FAX: 520-632-5900
Ridgetop Sporting Goods, P.O. Box 306, 42907 Hilligoss Ln. East, Eatonville, WA 98328 / 360-832-6422; FAX: 360-832-6422
Ries, Chuck, 415 Ridgecrest Dr., Grants Pass, OR 97527 / 503-476-5623
Rifles, Inc., 3580 Leal Rd., Pleasanton, TX 78064 / 830-569-2055; FAX: 830-569-2297
Riggs, Jim, 206 Azalea, Boerne, TX 78006 / 210-249-8567
Riley Ledbetter Airguns, 1804 E. Sprague St., Winston Salem, NC 27107-3521 / 919-784-0676
Rim Pac Sports, Inc., 1034 N. Soldano Ave., Azusa, CA 91702-2135
Ringler Custom Leather Co., 31 Shining Mtn. Rd., Powell, WY 82435 / 307-645-3255
Ripley Rifles, 42 Fletcher Street, Ripley, Derbyshire, DE5 3LP ENGLAND / 011-0773-748353
Rizzini F.lli (See U.S. Importers-Wm. Larkin Moore & Co., N.E. Arms Corp.)
Rizzini SNC, Via 2 Giugno, 7/7Bis-25060, Marcheno (Brescia), ITALY
RLCM Enterprises, 110 Hill Crest Drive, Burleson, TX 76028
RMS Custom Gunsmithing, 4120 N. Bitterwell, Prescott Valley, AZ 86314 / 520-772-7626 www.customstockmaker.com
Robar Co., Inc., The, 21438 N. 7th Ave., Suite B, Phoenix, AZ 85027 / 623-581-2648; FAX: 623-582-0059 info@robarguns.com www.robarguns.com
Robert Evans Engraving, 332 Vine St., Oregon City, OR 97045 / 503-656-5693
Robert Valade Engraving, 931 3rd Ave., Seaside, OR 97138 / 503-738-7672
Robinett, R. G., P.O. Box 72, Madrid, IA 50156 / 515-795-2906
Robinson, Don, Pennsylvania Hse, 36 Fairfax Crescent, W Yorkshire, ENGLAND / 0422-364458 donrobinsonuk@yahoo.co.uk www.guns4u2.co.uk

MANUFACTURER'S DIRECTORY

Robinson Armament Co., P.O. Box 16776, Salt Lake City, UT 84116 / 801-355-0401; FAX: 801-355-0402 zdf@robarm.com www.robarm.com
Robinson Firearms Mfg. Ltd., 1699 Blondeaux Crescent, Kelowna, BC V1Y 4J8 CANADA / 604-868-9596
Robinson H.V. Bullets, 3145 Church St., Zachary, LA 70791 / 504-654-4029
Rochester Lead Works, 76 Anderson Ave., Rochester, NY 14607 / 716-442-8500; FAX: 716-442-4712
Rock River Arms, 101 Noble St., Cleveland, IL 61241
Rockwood Corp., Speedwell Division, 136 Lincoln Blvd., Middlesex, NJ 08846 / 800-243-8274; FAX: 980-560-7475
Rocky Mountain Armoury, Mr. Felix LesMerises, 610 Main Street, P.O. Box 691, Frisco, CO 80443-0691 / 970-668-0136; FAX: 970-668-4484 felix@rockymountainarmoury.com
Rocky Mountain Arms, Inc., 1813 Sunset Pl., Unit D, Longmont, CO 80501 / 800-375-0846; FAX: 303-678-8766
Rocky Mountain Target Co., 3 Aloe Way, Leesburg, FL 34788 / 352-365-9598
Rocky Mountain Wildlife Products, P.O. Box 999, La Porte, CO 80535 / 970-484-2768; FAX: 970-484-0807 critrcall@larinet.net www.critrcall.com
Rocky Shoes & Boots, 294 Harper St., Nelsonville, OH 45764 / 800-848-9452; or 614-753-1951; FAX: 614-753-4024
Rogue Rifle Co., Inc., 1140 36th St. N., Ste. B, Lewiston, ID 83501 / 208-743-4355; FAX: 208-743-4163
Rogue River Rifleworks, 500 Linne Road #D, Paso Robles, CA 93446 / 805-227-4706; FAX: 805-227-4723 rrrifles@calinet.com
Rohner, Hans, 1148 Twin Sisters Ranch Rd., Nederland, CO 80466-9600
Rohner, John, 186 Virginia Ave., Asheville, NC 28806 / 828-281-3704
Rohrbaugh, P.O. Box 785, Bayport, NY 11705 / 631-363-2843; FAX: 631-363-2681 API380@aol.com
Romain's Custom Guns, Inc., RD 1, Whetstone Rd., Brockport, PA 15823 / 814-265-1948 romwhetstone@penn.com
Ron Frank Custom Classic Arms, 7131 Richland Rd., Ft. Worth, TX 76118 / 817-284-9300; FAX: 817-284-9300 rfrank3974@aol.com
Rooster Laboratories, P.O. Box 414605, Kansas City, MO 64141 / 816-474-1622; FAX: 816-474-7622
Rorschach Precision Products, 417 Keats Cir., Irving, TX 75061 / 214-790-3487
Rosenberg & Son, Jack A., 12229 Cox Ln., Dallas, TX 75234 / 214-241-6302
Ross, Don, 12813 West 83 Terrace, Lenexa, KS 66215 / 913-492-6982
Rosser, Bob, 2809 Crescent Ave., Suite 20, Homewood, AL 35209 / 205-870-4422; FAX: 205-870-4421 www.hand-engravers.com
Rossi Firearms, Gary Mchalik, 16175 NW 49th Ave., Miami, FL 33014-6314 / 305-474-0401; FAX: 305-623-7506
Rottweil Compe, 1330 Glassell, Orange, CA 92667
Roy Baker's Leather Goods, P.O. Box 893, Magnolia, AR 71754 / 870-234-0344
Royal Arms Gunstocks, 919 8th Ave. NW, Great Falls, MT 59404 / 406-453-1149 royalarms@lmt.net www.lmt.net/~royalarms
Royal Arms International, R J Brill, P.O. Box 6083, Woodland Hills, CA 91365 / 818-704-5110; FAX: 818-887-2059 royalarms.com
Roy's Custom Grips, 793 Mt. Olivet Church Rd., Lynchburg, VA 24504 / 434-993-3470
RPM, 15481 N. Twin Lakes Dr., Tucson, AZ 85739 / 520-825-1233; FAX: 520-825-3333
Rubright Bullets, 1008 S. Quince Rd., Walnutport, PA 18088 / 215-767-1339
Rucker Dist. Inc., P.O. Box 479, Terrell, TX 75160 / 214-563-2094
Ruger (See Sturm Ruger & Co., Inc.)
Ruger, Chris. See: RUGER'S CUSTOM GUNS
Ruger's Custom Guns, Chris Ruger, 1050 Morton Blvd., Kingston, NY 12401 / 845-336-7106; FAX: 845-336-7106 rugerscustom@outdrs.net rugergunsmith.com
Rundell's Gun Shop, 6198 Frances Rd., Clio, MI 48420 / 313-687-0559
Rupert's Gun Shop, 2202 Dick Rd., Suite B, Fenwick, MI 48834 / 517-248-3252 17rupert@pathwaynet.com
Russ Haydon's Shooters' Supply, 15018 Goodrich Dr. NW, Gig Harbor, WA 98329 / 877-663-6249; FAX: 253-857-7884 info@shooters-supply.com www.shooters-supply.com
Russ, William. See: BILL RUSS TRADING POST
Rusteprufe Laboratories, 1319 Jefferson Ave., Sparta, WI 54656 / 608-269-4144; FAX: 608-366-1972 rusteprufe@centurytel.net www.rusteprufe.com
Rusty Duck Premium Gun Care Products, 7785 Foundation Dr., Suite 6, Florence, KY 41042 / 606-342-5553; FAX: 606-342-5556
Rutgers Book Center, 127 Raritan Ave., Highland Park, NJ 08904 / 732-545-4344; FAX: 732-545-6686 gunbooks@rutgersgunbooks.com www.rutgersgunbooks.com
Rutten (See U.S. Importer-Labanu Inc.)
RWS (See U.S. Importer-Dynamit Nobel-RWS, Inc.), 81 Ruckman Rd., Closter, NJ 07624 / 201-767-7971; FAX: 201-767-1589

S

S&K Scope Mounts, RD 2 Box 21C, Sugar Grove, PA 16350 / 814-489-3091; or 800-578-9862; FAX: 814-489-5466 comments@scopemounts.com www.scopemounts.com
S&S Firearms, 74-11 Myrtle Ave., Glendale, NY 11385 / 718-497-1100; FAX: 718-497-1105 info@ssfirearms.com ssfirearms.com
S.A.R.L. G. Granger, 66 cours Fauriel, 42100, Saint Etienne, FRANCE / 04 77 25 14 73; FAX: 04 77 38 66 99
S.C.R.C., P.O. Box 660, Katy, TX 77492-0660 FAX: 281-492-6332
S.D. Meacham, 1070 Angel Ridge, Peck, ID 83545
S.I.A.C.E. (See U.S. Importer-IAR Inc.)
Sabatti SPA, Via A Volta 90, 25063 Gandome V.T.(BS), Brescia, ITALY / 030-8912207-831312; FAX: 030-8912059 info@sabatti.it www.sabatti.com
SAECO (See Redding Reloading Equipment)
Safari Arms/Schuetzen Pistol Works, 620-626 Old Pacific Hwy. SE, Olympia, WA 98513 / 360-459-3471; FAX: 360-491-3447 info@olyarms.com www.olyarms.com
Safari Press, Inc., 15621 Chemical Lane B, Huntington Beach, CA 92649 / 714-894-9080; FAX: 714-894-4949 info@safaripress.com www.safaripress.com
Safariland Ltd., Inc., 3120 E. Mission Blvd., P.O. Box 51478, Ontario, CA 91761 / 909-923-7300; FAX: 909-923-7400
SAFE, P.O. Box 864, Post Falls, ID 83877 / 208-773-3624; FAX: 208-773-6819 staysafe@safe-llc.com www.safe-llc.com
Sako Ltd. (See U.S. Importer-Stoeger Industries)
Sam Welch Gun Engraving, Sam Welch, HC 64 Box 2110, Moab, UT 84532 / 435-259-8131
Samco Global Arms, Inc., 6995 NW 43rd St., Miami, FL 33166 / 305-593-9782; FAX: 305-593-1014 samco@samcoglobal.com www.samcoglobal.com
Sampson, Roger, 2316 Mahogany St., Mora, MN 55051 / 612-679-4868
San Marco (See U.S. Importers-Cape Outfitters-EMF Co., Inc.
Sandia Die & Cartridge Co., 37 Atancacio Rd. NE, Albuquerque, NM 87123 / 505-298-5729
Sarco, Inc., 323 Union St., Stirling, NJ 07980 / 908-647-3800; FAX: 908-647-9413
Sarsilmaz Shotguns-Turkey (see B.C. Outdoors)
Sauer (See U.S. Importers-Paul Co., The Sigarms Inc.)
Sauls, R. See: BRYAN & ASSOC.
Saunders Gun & Machine Shop, 145 Delhi Rd., Manchester, IA 52057 / 563-927-4026
Savage Arms (Canada), Inc., 248 Water St., P.O. Box 1240, Lakefield, ON K0L 2H0 CANADA / 705-652-8000; FAX: 705-652-8431 www.savagearms.com
Savage Arms, Inc., 100 Springdale Rd., Westfield, MA 01085 / 413-568-7001; FAX: 413-562-7764
Savage Range Systems, Inc., 100 Springdale Rd., Westfield, MA 01085 / 413-568-7001; FAX: 413-562-1152 snailtraps@savagearms.com www.snailtraps.com
Saville Iron Co. (See Greenwood Precision)
Scansport, Inc., P.O. Box 700, Enfield, NH 03748 / 603-632-7654
Sceery Game Calls, P.O. Box 6520, Sante Fe, NM 87502 / 505-471-9110; FAX: 505-471-3476
Schaefer Shooting Sports, P.O. Box 1515, Melville, NY 11747-0515 / 516-643-5466; FAX: 516-643-2426 robert@robertschaefer.com www.schaefershooting.com
Scharch Mfg., Inc.-Top Brass, 10325 Co. Rd. 120, Salida, CO 81201 / 800-836-4683; FAX: 719-539-3021 topbrass@scharch.com www.handgun-brass.com
Scherer, Liz. See: SCHERER SUPPLIES
Scherer Supplies, Liz Scherer, Box 250, Ewing, VA 24248 FAX: 423-733-2073
Schiffman, Mike, 8233 S. Crystal Springs, McCammon, ID 83250 / 208-254-9114
Schmidt & Bender, Inc., P.O. Box 134, Meriden, NH 03770 / 603-469-3565; FAX: 603-469-3471 scopes@adelphia.net www.schmidtbender.com
Schmidtke Group, 17050 W. Salentine Dr., New Berlin, WI 53151-7349
Schneider Bullets, 3655 West 214th St., Fairview Park, OH 44126
Schneider Rifle Barrels, Inc., 1403 W. Red Baron Rd., Payson, AZ 85541 / 602-948-2525
School of Gunsmithing, The, 6065 Roswell Rd., Atlanta, GA 30328 / 800-223-4542
Schroeder Bullets, 1421 Thermal Ave., San Diego, CA 92154 / 619-423-3523; FAX: 619-423-8124
Schulz Industries, 16247 Minnesota Ave., Paramount, CA 90723 / 213-439-5903
Schumakers Gun Shop, 512 Prouty Corner Lp. A, Colville, WA 99114 / 509-684-4848
Scope Control, Inc., 5775 Co. Rd. 23 SE, Alexandria, MN 56308 / 612-762-7295
Score High Gunsmithing, 9812-A, Cochiti SE, Albuquerque, NM 87123 / 800-326-5632; or 505-292-5532; FAX: 505-292-2592 scorehi@scorehi.com www.probed2000.com
Scot Powder, Rt. 1 Box 167, McEwen, TN 37101 / 800-416-3006; FAX: 615-729-4211
Scott Fine Guns Inc., Thad, P.O. Box 412, Indianola, MS 38751 / 601-887-5929
Searcy Enterprises, P.O. Box 584, Boron, CA 93596 / 760-762-6771; FAX: 760-762-0191
Second Chance Body Armor, P.O. Box 578, Central Lake, MI 49622 / 616-544-5721; FAX: 616-544-9824
Seebeck Assoc., R.E., P.O. Box 59752, Dallas, TX 75229
Segway Industries, P.O. Box 783, Suffern, NY 10901-0783 / 914-357-5510
Seligman Shooting Products, Box 133, Seligman, AZ 86337 / 602-422-3607 shootssp@yahoo.com
Sellier & Bellot, USA, Inc., P.O. Box 27006, Shawnee Mission, KS 66225 / 913-685-0916; FAX: 913-685-0917
Selsi Co., Inc., P.O. Box 10, Midland Park, NJ 07432-0010 / 201-935-0388; FAX: 201-935-5851
Semmer, Charles (See Remington Double Shotguns), 7885 Cyd Dr., Denver, CO 80221 / 303-429-6947
Sentinel Arms, P.O. Box 57, Detroit, MI 48231 / 313-331-1951; FAX: 313-331-1456
Servus Footwear Co., 1136 2nd St., Rock Island, IL 61204 / 309-786-7741; FAX: 309-786-9808
Shappy Bullets, 76 Milldale Ave., Plantsville, CT 06479 / 203-621-3704
Sharp Shooter Supply, 4970 Lehman Road, Delphos, OH 45833 / 419-695-3179
Sharps Arms Co., Inc., C., 100 Centennial, Box 885, Big Timber, MT 59011 / 406-932-4353
Shaw, Inc., E. R. (See Small Arms Mfg. Co.)
Shay's Gunsmithing, 931 Marvin Ave., Lebanon, PA 17042
Sheffield Knifemakers Supply, Inc., P.O. Box 741107, Orange City, FL 32774-1107 / 386-775-6453; FAX: 386-774-5754
Sheldon, Bruce. See: RIDGELINE, INC.
Shepherd Enterprises, Inc., Box 189, Waterloo, NE 68069 / 402-779-2424; FAX: 402-779-4010 sshepherd@shepherdscopes.com www.shepherdscopes.com
Sherwood, George, 46 N. River Dr., Roseburg, OR 97470 / 541-672-3159
Shilen, Inc., 205 Metro Park Blvd., Ennis, TX 75119 / 972-875-5318; FAX: 972-875-5402
Shiloh Rifle Mfg., P.O. Box 279, Big Timber, MT 59011
Shockley, Harold H., 204 E. Farmington Rd., Hanna City, IL 61536 / 309-565-4524
Shoot Where You Look, Leon Measures, Dept GD, 408 Fair, Livingston, TX 77351
Shooters Arms Manufacturing, Inc., Rivergate Mall, Gen. Maxilom Ave., Cebu City 6000, PHILIPPINES / 6332-254-8478 www.shootersarms.com.ph
Shooter's Choice Gun Care, 15050 Berkshire Ind. Pkwy., Middlefield, OH 44062 / 440-834-8888; FAX: 440-834-3388 www.shooterschoice.com
Shooter's Edge Inc., 3313 Creekstone Dr., Fort Collins, CO 80525
Shooters Supply, 1120 Tieton Dr., Yakima, WA 98902 / 509-452-1181
Shooter's World, 3828 N. 28th Ave., Phoenix, AZ 85017 / 602-266-0170
Shooters, Inc., 5139 Stanart St., Norfolk, VA 23502 / 757-461-9152; FAX: 757-461-9155 gflocker@aol.com
Shootin' Shack, 357 Cypress Drive, No. 10, Tequesta, FL 33469 / 561-842-0990; FAX: 561-545-4861

MANUFACTURER'S DIRECTORY

Shooting Gallery, The, 8070 Southern Blvd., Boardman, OH 44512 / 216-726-7788
Shoot-N-C Targets (See Birchwood Casey)
Shotgun Sports, P.O. Box 6810, Auburn, CA 95604 / 530-889-2220; FAX: 530-889-9106 custsrv@shotgunsportsmagazine.com shotgunsportsmagazine.com
Shotgun Sports Magazine, dba Shootin' Accessories Ltd., P.O. Box 6810, Auburn, CA 95604 / 916-889-2220 custsrv@shotgunsportsmagazine.com shotgunspotsmagazine.com
Shotguns Unlimited, 2307 Fon Du Lac Rd., Richmond, VA 23229 / 804-752-7115
Siegrist Gun Shop, 8752 Turtle Road, Whittemore, MI 48770 / 989-873-3929
Sierra Bullets, 1400 W. Henry St., Sedalia, MO 65301 / 816-827-6300; FAX: 816-827-6300
Sierra Specialty Prod. Co., 1344 Oakhurst Ave., Los Altos, CA 94024 FAX: 415-965-1536
SIG, CH-8212 Neuhausen, SWITZERLAND
Sigarms Inc., 18 Industrial Dr., Exeter, NH 03833 / 603-772-2302; FAX: 603-772-9082 www.sigarms.com
Sight Shop, The, John G. Lawson, 1802 E. Columbia Ave., Tacoma, WA 98404 / 253-474-5465 parahellum9@aol.com www.thesightshop.org
Sightron, Inc., 1672B Hwy. 96, Franklinton, NC 27525 / 919-528-8783; FAX: 919-528-0995 info@sightron.com www.sightron.com
SIG-Sauer (See U.S. Importer-Sigarms, Inc.)
Silencio/Safety Direct, 56 Coney Island Dr., Sparks, NV 89431 / 800-648-1812; or 702-354-4451; FAX: 702-359-1074
Silent Hunter, 1100 Newton Ave., W. Collingswood, NJ 08107 / 609-854-3276
Silhouette Leathers, 8598 Hwy. 51 N. #4, Millington, TN 38053 silhouetteleathers@yahoo.com silhouetteleathers.com
Silver Eagle Machining, 18007 N. 69th Ave., Glendale, AZ 85308
Silver Ridge Gun Shop (See Goodwin Guns)
Simmons, Jerry, 715 Middlebury St., Goshen, IN 46528-2717 / 574-533-8546
Simmons Gun Repair, Inc., 700 S. Rogers Rd., Olathe, KS 66062 / 913-782-3131; FAX: 913-782-4189
Simmons Outdoor Corp., 6001 Oak Canyon, Irvine, CA 92618 / 949-451-1450; FAX: 949-451-1460 www.meade.com
Sinclair International, Inc., 2330 Wayne Haven St., Fort Wayne, IN 46803 / 260-493-1858; or 800-717-8211; FAX: 260-493-2530 sales@sinclairintl.com www.sinclairintl.com
Singletary, Kent, 4538 W. Carol Ave., Glendale, AZ 85302 / 602-526-6836 kent@kscustom www.kscustom.com
Siskiyou Gun Works (See Donnelly, C. P.)
Six Enterprises, 320-D Turtle Creek Ct., San Jose, CA 95125 / 408-999-0201; FAX: 408-999-0216
SKB Shotguns, 4325 S. 120th St., Omaha, NE 68137 / 800-752-2767; FAX: 402-330-8040 skb@skbshotguns.com www.skbshotguns.com
Skeoch, Brian R., P.O. Box 279, Glenrock, WY 82637 / 307-436-9655 skeochbrian@netzero.com
Skip's Machine, 364 29 Road, Grand Junction, CO 81501 / 303-245-5417
Sklany's Machine Shop, 566 Birch Grove Dr., Kalispell, MT 59901 / 406-755-4257
Slug Site, Ozark Wilds, 21300 Hwy. 5, Versailles, MO 65084 / 573-378-6430 john@ebeling.com john.ebeling.com
Small Arms Mfg. Co., 5312 Thoms Run Rd., Bridgeville, PA 15017 / 412-221-4343; FAX: 412-221-4303
Small Arms Specialists, 443 Firchburg Rd., Mason, NH 03048 / 603-878-0427; FAX: 603-878-3905 miniguns@empire.net miniguns.com
Smires, C. L., 5222 Windmill Lane, Columbia, MD 21044-1328
Smith & Wesson, 2100 Roosevelt Ave., Springfield, MA 01104 / 413-781-8300; FAX: 413-731-8980
Smith, Art, P.O. Box 645, Park Rapids, MN 56470 / 218-732-5333
Smith, Mark A., P.O. Box 182, Sinclair, WY 82334 / 307-324-7929
Smith, Michael, 2612 Ashmore Ave., Red Bank, TN 37415 / 615-267-8341
Smith, Ron, 5869 Straley, Fort Worth, TX 76114 / 817-732-6768
Smith, Sharmon, 4545 Speas Rd., Fruitland, ID 83619 / 208-452-6329 sharmon@fmtc.com
Smith Abrasives, Inc., 1700 Sleepy Valley Rd., Hot Springs, AR 71902-5095 / 501-321-2244; FAX: 501-321-9232 www.smithabrasives.com
Smith, Judy. See: L.B.T.
Smith Saddlery, Jesse W., 0499 County Road J, Pritchett, CO 81064 / 509-325-0622
Smokey Valley Rifles, E1976 Smokey Valley Rd., Scandinavia, WI 54977 / 715-467-2674
Snapp's Gunshop, 6911 E. Washington Rd., Clare, MI 48617 / 989-386-9226 snapp@glccomputers.com
Sno-Seal, Inc. (See Atsko/Sno-Seal, Inc.)
Societa Armi Bresciane Srl (See U.S. Importer-Cape Outfitters)
SOS Products Co. (See Buck Stix-SOS Products Co.), Box 3, Neenah, WI 54956
Sotheby's, 1334 York Ave. at 72nd St., New York, NY 10021 / 212-606-7260
Sound Tech Silencers, Box 391, Pelham, AL 35124 / 205-664-5860 silenceio@wmconnect.com www.soundtechsilencers.com
South Bend Replicas, Inc., 61650 Oak Rd., South Bend, IN 46614 / 219-289-4500
Southeastern Community College, 1015 S. Gear Ave., West Burlington, IA 52655 / 319-752-2731
Southern Ammunition Co., Inc., 4232 Meadow St., Loris, SC 29569-3124 / 803-756-3262; FAX: 803-756-3583
Southern Armory, The, 25 Millstone Rd., Woodlawn, VA 24381 / 703-238-1343; FAX: 703-238-1453
Southern Bloomer Mfg. Co., P.O. Box 1621, Bristol, TN 37620 / 615-878-6660; FAX: 615-878-8761
Southern Security, 1700 Oak Hills Dr., Kingston, TN 37763 / 423-376-6297; FAX: 800-251-9992
Sparks, Milt, 605 E. 44th St. No. 2, Boise, ID 83714-4800
Spartan-Realtree Products, Inc., 1390 Box Circle, Columbus, GA 31907 / 706-569-9101; FAX: 706-569-0042
Specialty Gunsmithing, Lynn McMurdo, P.O. Box 404, Afton, WY 83110 / 307-886-5535
Specialty Shooters Supply, Inc., 3325 Griffin Rd., Suite 9mm, Fort Lauderdale, FL 33317
Speer Bullets, P.O. Box 856, Lewiston, ID 83501 / 208-746-2351 www.speer-bullets.com
Spegel, Craig, P.O. Box 387, Nehalem, OR 97131 / 503-368-5653
Speiser, Fred D., 2229 Dearborn, Missoula, MT 59801 / 406-549-8133
Spencer Reblue Service, 1820 Tupelo Trail, Holt, MI 48842 / 517-694-7474
Spencer's Rifle Barrels, Inc., 4107 Jacobs Creek Dr., Scottsville, VA 24590 / 804-293-6836; FAX: 804-293-6836 www.spencersriflebarrels.com
SPG LLC, P.O. Box 1625, Cody, WY 82414 / 307-587-7621; FAX: 307-587-7695 spg@cody.wtp.net www.blackpowderspg.com
Sphinx Systems Ltd., Gesteigtstrasse 12, CH-3800, Matten, BRNE, SWITZERLAND
Splitfire Sporting Goods, L.L.C., P.O. Box 1044, Orem, UT 84059-1044 / 801-932-7950; FAX: 801-932-7959 www.splitfireguns.com
Spolar Power Load, Inc., 17376 Filbert, Fontana, CA 92335 / 800-227-9667
Sport Flite Manufacturing Co., 637 Kingsley Trl., Bloomfield Hills, MI 48304-2320 / 248-647-3747
Sporting Clays Of America, 9257 Bluckeye Rd., Sugar Grove, OH 43155-9632 / 740-746-8334; FAX: 740-746-8605
Sports Afield Magazine, 15621 Chemical Lane B, Huntington Beach, CA 92649 / 714-894-9080; FAX: 714-894-4949 info@sportsafield.com www.sportsafield.com
Sports Innovations, Inc., P.O. Box 5181, 8505 Jacksboro Hwy., Wichita Falls, TX 76307 / 817-723-6015
Sportsman Safe Mfg. Co., 6309-6311 Paramount Blvd., Long Beach, CA 90805 / 800-266-7150; or 310-984-5445
Sportsman's Communicators, 588 Radcliffe Ave., Pacific Palisades, CA 90272 / 800-538-3752
Sportsmatch U.K. Ltd., 16 Summer St. Leighton, Buzzard Beds, Bedfordshire, LU7 1HT ENGLAND / 4401525-381638; FAX: 4401525-851236 info@sportsmatch-uk.com www.sportsmatch-uk.com
Sportsmen's Exchange & Western Gun Traders, Inc., 813 Doris Ave., Oxnard, CA 93030 / 805-483-1917
Spradlin's, 457 Shannon Rd., Texas Creek Cotopaxi, CO 81223 / 719-275-7105; FAX: 719-275-3852 spradlins@prodigy.net www.spradlins.net
Springfield Armory, 420 W. Main St., Geneseo, IL 61254 / 309-944-5631; FAX: 309-944-3676 sales@springfield-armory.com www.springfieldarmory.com
Springfield Sporters, Inc., RD 1, Penn Run, PA 15765 / 412-254-2626; FAX: 412-254-9173
Springfield, Inc., 420 W. Main St., Geneseo, IL 61254 / 309-944-5631; FAX: 309-944-3676
Spyderco, Inc., 820 Spyderco Way, Golden, CO 80403 / 800-525-7770; or 800-525-7770; FAX: 303-278-2229 sales@spyderco.com www.spyderco.com
SSK Industries, J. D. Jones, 590 Woodvue Lane, Wintersville, OH 43953 / 740-264-0176; FAX: 740-264-2257 www.sskindustries.com
Stackpole Books, 5067 Ritter Rd., Mechanicsburg, PA 17055-6921 / 717-796-0411; or 800-732-3669; FAX: 717-796-0412 tmanney@stackpolebooks.com www.stackpolebooks.com
Stalker, Inc., P.O. Box 21, Fishermans Wharf Rd., Malakoff, TX 75148 / 903-489-1010
Stalwart Corporation, P.O. Box 46, Evanston, WY 82931 / 307-789-7687; FAX: 307-789-7688
Stan Baker Sports, Stan Baker, 10000 Lake City Way, Seattle, WA 98125 / 206-522-4575
Stan De Treville & Co., 4129 Normal St., San Diego, CA 92103 / 619-298-3393
Stanley Bullets, 2085 Heatheridge Ln., Reno, NV 89509
Star Ammunition, Inc., 5520 Rock Hampton Ct., Indianapolis, IN 46268 / 800-221-5927; FAX: 317-872-5847
Star Custom Bullets, P.O. Box 608, 468 Main St., Ferndale, CA 95536 / 707-786-9140; FAX: 707-786-9117 wmebridge@humboldt.com
Star Machine Works, P.O. Box 1872, Pioneer, CA 95666 / 209-295-5000
Starke Bullet Company, P.O. Box 400, 605 6th St. NW, Cooperstown, ND 58425 / 888-797-3431
Starkey Labs, 6700 Washington Ave. S., Eden Prairie, MN 55344
Starkey's Gun Shop, 9430 McCombs, El Paso, TX 79924 / 915-751-3030
Starlight Training Center, Inc., Rt. 1, P.O. Box 88, Bronaugh, MO 64728 / 417-843-3555
Starline, Inc., 1300 W. Henry St., Sedalia, MO 65301 / 660-827-6640; FAX: 660-827-6650 info@starlinebrass.com http://www.starlinebrass.com
Starr Trading Co., Jedediah, P.O. Box 2007, Farmington Hills, MI 48333 / 810-683-4343; FAX: 810-683-3282
Starrett Co., L. S., 121 Crescent St., Athol, MA 01331 / 978-249-3551; FAX: 978-249-8495
Steelman's Gun Shop, 10465 Beers Rd., Swartz Creek, MI 48473 / 810-735-4884
Steffens, Ron, 18396 Mariposa Creek Rd., Willits, CA 95490 / 707-485-0873
Stegall, James B., 26 Forest Rd., Wallkill, NY 12589
Steve Henigson & Associates, P.O. Box 2726, Culver City, CA 90231 / 310-305-8288; FAX: 310-305-1905
Steve Kamyk Engraver, 9 Grandview Dr., Westfield, MA 01085-1810 / 413-568-0457 stevek201@comcast.net
Steven Dodd Hughes, P.O. Box 545, Livingston, MT 59047 / 406-222-9377; FAX: 406-222-9377
Steves House of Guns, Rt. 1, Minnesota City, MN 55959 / 507-689-2573
Stewart Game Calls, Inc., Johnny, P.O. Box 7954, 5100 Fort Ave., Waco, TX 76714 / 817-772-3261; FAX: 817-772-3670
Stewart's Gunsmithing, P.O. Box 5854, Pietersburg North 0750, Transvaal, SOUTH AFRICA / 01521-89401
Steyr Mannlicher GmbH & Co. KG, Mannlicherstrasse 1, 4400 Steyr, Steyr, AUSTRIA / 0043-7252-896-0; FAX: 0043-7252-78620 office@steyr-mannlicher.com www.steyr-mannlicher.com
STI International, 114 Halmar Cove, Georgetown, TX 78628 / 800-959-8201; FAX: 512-819-0465 www.stiguns.com
Stiles Custom Guns, 76 Cherry Run Rd., Box 1605, Homer City, PA 15748 / 712-479-9945 glstiles@yourinter.net www.yourinter.net/glstiles
Stillwell, Robert, 421 Judith Ann Dr., Schertz, TX 78154
Stoeger Industries, 17603 Indian Head Hwy., Suite 200, Accokeek, MD 20607-2501 / 301-283-6300; FAX: 301-283-6986 www.stoegerindustries.com
Stoeger Publishing Co. (See Stoeger Industries)
Stone Enterprises Ltd., 426 Harveys Neck Rd., P.O. Box 335, Wicomico Church, VA 22579 / 804-580-5114; FAX: 804-580-8421
Stone Mountain Arms, 5988 Peachtree Corners E., Norcross, GA 30071 / 800-251-9412
Stoney Point Products, Inc., P.O. Box 234, 1822 N. Minnesota St., New Ulm, MN 56073-0234 / 507-354-3360; FAX: 507-354-7236 stoney@newulmtel.net www.stoneypoint.com

MANUFACTURER'S DIRECTORY

Storm, Gary, P.O. Box 5211, Richardson, TX 75083 / 214-385-0862
Stott's Creek Armory, Inc., 2526 S. 475W, Morgantown, IN 46160 / 317-878-5489; FAX: 317-878-9489 sccalendar@aol.com www.Sccalendar.aol.com
Stratco, Inc., P.O. Box 2270, Kalispell, MT 59901 / 406-755-1221; FAX: 406-755-1226
Strayer, Sandy. See: STRAYER-VOIGT, INC.
Strayer-Voigt, Inc., Sandy Strayer, 3435 Ray Orr Blvd., Grand Prairie, TX 75050 / 972-513-0575
Strong Holster Co., 39 Grove St., Gloucester, MA 01930 / 508-281-3300; FAX: 508-281-6321
Strutz Rifle Barrels, Inc., W. C., P.O. Box 611, Eagle River, WI 54521 / 715-479-4766
Stuart, V. Pat, Rt. 1, Box 447-S, Greenville, VA 24440 / 804-556-3845
Sturgeon Valley Sporters, Ken Ide, P.O. Box 283, Vanderbilt, MI 49795 / 989-983-4338 k.ide@mail.com
Sturm Ruger & Co. Inc., 200 Ruger Rd., Prescott, AZ 86301 / 928-541-8820; FAX: 520-541-8850 www.ruger.com
Sullivan, David S. (See Westwind Rifles, Inc.)
"Su-Press-On", Inc., P.O. Box 09161, Detroit, MI 48209 / 313-842-4222
Sun Welding Safe Co., 290 Easy St. No. 3, Simi Valley, CA 93065 / 805-584-6678; or 800-729-SAFE; FAX: 805-584-6169 sunwelding.com
Sunny Hill Enterprises, Inc., W1790 Cty. HHH, Malone, WI 53049 / 920-795-4722; FAX: 920-795-4822
Super 6 LLC, Gary Knopp, 3806 W. Lisbon Ave., Milwaukee, WI 53208 / 414-344-3343; FAX: 414-344-0304
Surecase Co., The, 233 Wilshire Blvd., Ste. 900, Santa Monica, CA 90401 / 800-92ARMLOC
Sure-Shot Game Calls, Inc., P.O. Box 816, 6835 Capitol, Groves, TX 77619 / 409-962-1636; FAX: 409-962-5465
Svon Corp., 2107 W. Blue Heron Blvd., Riviera Beach, FL 33404 / 508-881-8852
Swampfire Shop, The (See Peterson Gun Shop, Inc., A.W.)
Swann, D. J., 5 Orsova Close, Eltham North Vic., 3095 AUSTRALIA / 03-431-0323
Swanndri New Zealand, 152 Elm Ave., Burlingame, CA 94010 / 415-347-6158
Swanson, Mark, 975 Heap Avenue, Prescott, AZ 86301 / 928-778-4423
Swarovski Optik North America Ltd., 2 Slater Rd., Cranston, RI 02920 / 401-946-2220; or 800-426-3089; FAX: 401-946-2587
Sweet Home, Inc., P.O. Box 900, Orrville, OH 44667-0900
Swenson's 45 Shop, A. D., 3839 Ladera Vista Rd., Fallbrook, CA 92028-9431
Swift Bullet Co., P.O. Box 27, 201 Main St., Quinter, KS 67752 / 913-754-3959; FAX: 913-754-2359
Swift Instruments, Inc., 952 Dorchester Ave., Boston, MA 02125 / 617-436-2960; FAX: 617-436-3232
Swift River Gunworks, 450 State St., Belchertown, MA 01007 / 413-323-4052
Szweda, Robert (See RMS Custom Gunsmithing)

T

T&S Industries, Inc., 1027 Skyview Dr., W. Carrollton, OH 45449 / 513-859-8414; FAX: 937-859-8404 keith.tomlinson@tandsshellcatcher.com www.tandsshellcatcher.com
T.F.C. S.p.A., Via G. Marconi 118, B, Villa Carcina 25069, ITALY / 030-881271; FAX: 030-881826
T.G. Faust, Inc., 544 Minor St., Reading, PA 19602 / 610-375-8549; FAX: 610-375-4488
T.K. Lee Co., 1282 Branchwater Ln., Birmingham, AL 35216 / 205-913-5222 odonmich@aol.com www.scopedot.com
T.W. Menck Gunsmith, Inc., 5703 S. 77th St., Ralston, NE 68127 guntools@cox.net http://llwww.members.cox.net/guntools
Tabler Marketing, 2554 Lincoln Blvd., Suite 555, Marina Del Rey, CA 90291 / 818-386-0373; FAX: 818-386-0373
Taconic Firearms Ltd., Perry Lane, P.O. Box 553, Cambridge, NY 12816 / 518-677-2704; FAX: 518-677-5974
Tactical Defense Institute, 2174 Bethany Ridges, West Union, OH 45693 / 937-544-7228; FAX: 937-544-2887 tdiohio@dragonbbs.com www.tdiohio.com
Talley, Dave, P.O. Box 369, Santee, SC 29142 / 803-854-5700; or 307-436-9315; FAX: 803-854-9315 talley@diretway www.talleyrings.com
Talon Industries Inc. (See Cobra Enterprises, Inc.)
Tamarack Products, Inc., P.O. Box 625, Wauconda, IL 60084 / 708-526-9333; FAX: 708-526-9353
Tanfoglio Fratelli S.r.l., via Valtrompia 39, 41, Brescia, ITALY / 011-39-030-8910361; FAX: 011-39-030-8910183 info@tanfoglio.it www.tanfoglio.it
Tanglefree Industries, 1261 Heavenly Dr., Martinez, CA 94553 / 800-982-4868; FAX: 510-825-3874
Tank's Rifle Shop, P.O. Box 474, Fremont, NE 68026-0474 / 402-727-1317 jtank@tanksrifleshop.com www.tanksrifleshop.com
Tanner (See U.S. Importer-Mandall Shooting Supplies, Inc.)
Taracorp Industries, Inc., 1200 Sixteenth St., Granite City, IL 62040 / 618-451-4400
Target Shooting, Inc., P.O. Box 773, Watertown, SD 57201 / 605-882-6955; FAX: 605-882-8840
Tar-Hunt Custom Rifles, Inc., 101 Dogtown Rd., Bloomsburg, PA 17815 / 570-784-6368; FAX: 570-389-9150 www.tar-hunt.com
Tarnhelm Supply Co., Inc., 431 High St., Boscawen, NH 03303 / 603-796-2551; FAX: 603-796-2918 info@tarnhelm.com www.tarnhelm.com
Tasco Sales, Inc., 2889 Commerce Pkwy., Miramar, FL 33025
Taurus Firearms, Inc., 16175 NW 49th Ave., Miami, FL 33014 / 305-624-1115; FAX: 305-623-7506
Taurus International Firearms (See U.S. Importer Taurus Firearms, Inc.)
Taurus S.A. Forjas, Avenida Do Forte 511, Porto Alegre, RS BRAZIL 91360 / 55-51-347-4050; FAX: 55-51-347-3065
Taylor & Robbins, P.O. Box 164, Rixford, PA 16745 / 814-966-3233
Taylor's & Co., Inc., 304 Lenoir Dr., Winchester, VA 22603 / 540-722-2017; FAX: 540-722-2018 info@taylorsfirearms.com www.taylorsfirearms.com
TCCI, P.O. Box 302, Phoenix, AZ 85001 / 602-237-3823; FAX: 602-237-3858
TCSR, 3998 Hoffman Rd., White Bear Lake, MN 55110-4626 / 800-328-5323; FAX: 612-429-0526
TDP Industries, Inc., P.O. Box 249, Ottsville, PA 18942-0249 / 215-345-8687; FAX: 215-345-6057
Techno Arms (See U.S. Importer- Auto-Ordnance Corp.)
Tecnolegno S.p.A., Via A. Locatelli, 6 10, 24019 Zogno, ITALY / 0345-55111; FAX: 0345-55155
Ted Blocker Holsters, Inc., 9396 S.W. Tigard St., Tigard, OR 97223 / 800-650-9742; FAX: 503-670-9692 www.tedblocker.com
Tele-Optics, 630 E. Rockland Rd., P.O. Box 6313, Libertyville, IL 60048 / 847-362-7757; FAX: 847-362-7757
Tennessee Valley Mfg., 14 County Road 521, Corinth, MS 38834 / 601-286-5014 tvm@avsia.com www.avsia.com/tvm
Ten-Ring Precision, Inc., Alex B. Hamilton, 1449 Blue Crest Lane, San Antonio, TX 78232 / 210-494-3063; FAX: 210-494-3066
TEN-X Products Group, 1905 N. Main St., Suite 133, Cleburne, TX 76031-1305 / 972-243-4016; or 800-433-2225; FAX: 972-243-4112
Tepeco, P.O. Box 342, Friendswood, TX 77546 / 713-482-2702
Terry K. Kopp Professional Gunsmithing, Rt 1 Box 224, Lexington, MO 64067 / 816-259-2636
Testing Systems, Inc., 220 Pegasus Ave., Northvale, NJ 07647
Tetra Gun Care, 8 Vreeland Rd., Florham Park, NJ 07932 / 973-443-0004; FAX: 973-443-0263
Tex Shoemaker & Sons, Inc., 714 W. Cienega Ave., San Dimas, CA 91773 / 909-592-2071; FAX: 909-592-2378 texshoemaker@texshoemaker.com www.texshoemaker.com
Texas Armory (See Bond Arms, Inc.)
Texas Platers Supply Co., 2453 W. Five Mile Parkway, Dallas, TX 75233 / 214-330-7168
Thad Rybka Custom Leather Equipment, 2050 Canoe Creek Rd., Springvale, AL 35146-6709
Thad Scott Fine Guns, Inc., P.O. Box 412, Indianola, MS 38751 / 601-887-5929
Theis, Terry, 21452 FM 2093, Harper, TX 78631 / 830-864-4438
Thiewes, George W., 14329 W. Parada Dr., Sun City West, AZ 85375
Things Unlimited, 235 N. Kimbau, Casper, WY 82601 / 307-234-5277
Thirion Gun Engraving, Denise, P.O. Box 408, Graton, CA 95444 / 707-829-1876
Thomas, Charles C., 2600 S. First St., Springfield, IL 62704 / 217-789-8980; FAX: 217-789-9130 books@ccthomas.com ccthomas.com
Thompson Bullet Lube Co., P.O. Box 409, Wills Point, TX 75169 / 866-476-1500; FAX: 866-476-1500 thompsonbulletlube.com www.thompsonbulletlube.com
Thompson Precision, 110 Mary St., P.O. Box 251, Warren, IL 61087 / 815-745-3625
Thompson, Randall. See: HIGHLINE MACHINE CO.
Thompson Target Technology, 4804 Sherman Church Ave. S.W., Canton, OH 44710 / 330-484-6480; FAX: 330-491-1087 www.thompsontarget.com
Thompson Tool Mount, 1550 Solomon Rd., Santa Maria, CA 93455 / 805-934-1281 ttm@pronet.net www.thompsontoolmount.com
Thompson/Center Arms, P.O. Box 5002, Rochester, NH 03866 / 603-332-2394; FAX: 603-332-5133 tech@tcarms.com www.tcarms.com
Thunden Ranch, HCR 1, Box 53, Mountain Home, TX 78058 / 830-640-3138
Tiger-Hunt Longrifle Gunstocks, Box 379, Beaverdale, PA 15921 / 814-472-5161 tigerhunt4@aol.com www.gunstockwood.com
Tikka (See U.S. Importer-Stoeger Industries)
Time Precision, 4 Nicholas Sq., New Milford, CT 06776-3506 / 860-350-8343; FAX: 860-350-6343 timeprecision@aol.com
Tinks & Ben Lee Hunting Products (See Wellington Outdoors)
Tink's Safariland Hunting Corp., P.O. Box 244, 1140 Monticello Rd., Madison, GA 30650 / 706-342-4915; FAX: 706-342-7568
Tioga Engineering Co., Inc., P.O. Box 913, 13 Cone St., Wellsboro, PA 16901 / 570-724-3533; FAX: 570-724-3895 tiogaeng@epix.net
Tippman Pneumatics, Inc., 2955 Adams Center Rd., Fort Wayne, IN 46803
Tirelli, Snc Di Tirelli Primo E.C., Via Matteotti No. 359, Gardone V.T. Brescia, ITALY / 0039-030-8912819; FAX: 0039-030-832240 tirelli@tirelli.it www.tirelli.it
TM Stockworks, 6355 Maplecrest Rd., Fort Wayne, IN 46835 / 219-485-5389
Tom Forrest, Inc., P.O. Box 326, Lakeside, CA 92040 / 619-561-5800; FAX: 888-GUN-CLIP info@gunmag.com www.gunmags.com
Tombstone Smoke`n' Deals, PO Box 31298, Phoenix, AZ 85046 / 602-905-7013; FAX: 602-443-1998
Tom's Gun Repair, Thomas G. Ivanoff, 76-6 Rt. Southfork Rd., Cody, WY 82414 / 307-587-6949
Tom's Gunshop, 3601 Central Ave., Hot Springs, AR 71913 / 501-624-3856
Tonoloway Tack Drives, HCR 81, Box 100, Needmore, PA 17238
Torel, Inc./Tandy Brands Outdoors/AA & E, 208 Industrial Loop, Yoakum, TX 77995 / 361-293-6366; FAX: 361-293-9127
TOZ (See U.S. Importer-Nygord Precision Products, Inc.)
Track of the Wolf, Inc., 18308 Joplin St. NW, Elk River, MN 55330-1773 / 763-633-2500; FAX: 763-633-2550
Traditions Performance Firearms, P.O. Box 776, 1375 Boston Post Rd., Old Saybrook, CT 06475 / 860-388-4656; FAX: 860-388-4657 info@traditionsfirearms.com www.traditionsfirearms.com
Trafalgar Square, P.O. Box 257, N. Pomfret, VT 05053 / 802-457-1911
Trail Visions, 5800 N. Ames Terrace, Glendale, WI 53209 / 414-228-1328
Trax America, Inc., P.O. Box 898, 1150 Eldridge, Forrest City, AR 72335 / 870-633-0410; or 800-232-2327; FAX: 870-633-4788 trax@ipa.net www.traxamerica.com
Treadlok Gun Safe, Inc., 1764 Granby St. NE, Roanoke, VA 24012 / 800-729-8732; or 703-982-6881; FAX: 703-982-1059
Treebone Carving, P.O. Box 551, Cimarron, NJ 87714 / 505-376-2145 treebonecarving.com
Treemaster, P.O. Box 247, Guntersville, AL 35976 / 205-878-3597
Trevallion Gunstocks, 9 Old Mountain Rd., Cape Neddick, ME 03902 / 207-361-1130
Trico Plastics, 28061 Diaz Rd., Temecula, CA 92590 / 909-676-7714; FAX: 909-676-0267 ustinfo@ustplastics.com www.tricoplastics.com
Trigger Lock Division / Central Specialties Ltd., 220-D Exchange Dr., Crystal Lake, IL 60014 / 847-639-3900; FAX: 847-639-3972
Trijicon, Inc., 49385 Shafer Ave., P.O. Box 930059, Wixom, MI 48393-0059 / 248-960-7700; or 800-338-0563
Trilby Sport Shop, 1623 Hagley Rd., Toledo, OH 43612-2024 / 419-472-6222
Trilux, Inc., P.O. Box 24608, Winston-Salem, NC 27114 / 910-659-9438; FAX: 910-768-7720
Trinidad St. Jr. Col. Gunsmith Dept., 600 Prospect St., Trinidad, CO 81082 / 719-846-5631; FAX: 719-846-5667

MANUFACTURER'S DIRECTORY

Triple-K Mfg. Co., Inc., 2222 Commercial St., San Diego, CA 92113 / 619-232-2066; FAX: 619-232-7675 sales@triplek.com www.triplek.com
Tristar Sporting Arms, Ltd., 1814 Linn St. #16, N. Kansas City, MO 64116-3627 / 816-421-1400; FAX: 816-421-4182 tristar@blitz-it.net www.tristarsportingarms
Trius Traps, Inc., P.O. Box 25, 221 S. Miami Ave., Cleves, OH 45002 / 513-941-5682; FAX: 513-941-7970 triustraps@fuse.net www.triustraps.com
Trooper Walsh, 2393 N. Edgewood St., Arlington, VA 22207
Trotman, Ken, 135 Ditton Walk, Unit 11, Cambridge, CB5 8PY ENGLAND / 01223-211030; FAX: 01223-212317 www.kentrolman.com
Tru-Balance Knife Co., P.O. Box 140555, Grand Rapids, MI 49514 / 616-647-1215
True Flight Bullet Co., 5581 Roosevelt St., Whitehall, PA 18052 / 610-262-7630; FAX: 610-262-7806
Truglo, Inc., P.O. Box 1612, McKinna, TX 75070 / 972-774-0300; FAX: 972-774-0323 www.truglosights.com
Trulock Tool, P.O. Box 530, Whigham, GA 31797 / 229-762-4678; FAX: 229-762-4050 trulockchokes@hotmail.com trulockchokes.com
Tru-Nord Compass, 1504 Erick Lane, Brainerd, MN 56401 / 218-829-2870; FAX: 218-829-2870 www.trunord.com
Tru-Square Metal Products, Inc., 640 First St. SW, P.O. Box 585, Auburn, WA 98071 / 253-833-2310; or 800-225-1017; FAX: 253-833-2349 t-tumbler@qwest.net
Tucker, James C., P.O. Box 366, Medford, OR 97501 / 541-664-9160 jctstocker@yahoo.com
Tucson Mold, Inc., 930 S. Plumer Ave., Tucson, AZ 85719 / 520-792-1075; FAX: 520-792-1075
Turk's Head Productions, Mustafa Bilal, 908 NW 50th St., Seattle, WA 98107-3634 / 206-782-4164; FAX: 206-783-5677 info@turkshead.com www.turkshead.com
Turnbull Restoration, Doug, 6680 Rts. 5 & 20, P.O. Box 471, Bloomfield, NY 14469 / 585-657-6338; FAX: 585-657-6338 turnbullrest@mindspring.com www.turnbullrestoration.com
Tuttle, Dale, 4046 Russell Rd., Muskegon, MI 49445 / 616-766-2250

U

U.S. Importer-Wm. Larkin Moore, 8430 E. Raintree Ste. B-7, Scottsdale, AZ 85260
U.S. Optics, A Division of Zeitz Optics U.S.A., 5900 Dale St., Buena Park, CA 90621 / 714-994-4901; FAX: 714-994-4904 www.usoptics.com
U.S. Repeating Arms Co., Inc., 275 Winchester Ave., Morgan, UT 84050-9333 / 801-876-3440; FAX: 801-876-3737 www.winchester-guns.com
U.S. Tactical Systems (See Keng's Firearms Specialty, Inc.)
Ugartechea S. A., Ignacio, Chonta 26, Eibar, SPAIN / 43-121257; FAX: 43-121669
Ultra Dot Distribution, P.O. Box 362, 6304 Riverside Dr., Yankeetown, FL 34498 / 352-447-2255; FAX: 352-447-2266
Ultralux (See U.S. Importer-Keng's Firearms Specialty, Inc.)
UltraSport Arms, Inc., 1955 Norwood Ct., Racine, WI 53403 / 414-554-3237; FAX: 414-554-9731
Uncle Bud's, HCR 81, Box 100, Needmore, PA 17238 / 717-294-6000; FAX: 717-294-6005
Uncle Mike's (See Michaels of Oregon, Co.)
Unertl Optical Co., Inc., 103 Grand Avenue, P.O. Box 895, Mars, PA 16046-0895 / 724-625-3810; FAX: 724-625-3819 unertl@nauticom.net www.unertloptics.net
UniTec, 1250 Bedford SW, Canton, OH 44710 / 216-452-4017
United Binocular Co., 9043 S. Western Ave., Chicago, IL 60620
United Cutlery Corp., 1425 United Blvd., Sevierville, TN 37876 / 865-428-2532; or 800-548-0835; FAX: 865-428-2267 www.unitedcutlery.com
United States Products Co., 518 Melwood Ave., Pittsburgh, PA 15213-1136 / 412-621-2130; FAX: 412-621-8740 sales@us-products.com www.usporepaste.com
Universal Sports, P.O. Box 532, Vincennes, IN 47591 / 812-882-8680; FAX: 812-882-8680
Upper Missouri Trading Co., P.O. Box 100, 304 Harold St., Crofton, NE 68730-0100 / 402-388-4844 www.uppermotradingco.com
USAC, 4500-15th St. East, Tacoma, WA 98424 / 206-922-7589
Uselton/Arms, Inc., 842 Conference Dr., Goodlettsville, TN 37072 / 615-851-4919
Utica Cutlery Co., 820 Noyes St., Utica, NY 13503 / 315-733-4663; FAX: 315-733-6602

V

V. H. Blackinton & Co., Inc., 221 John L. Dietsch, Attleboro Falls, MA 02763-0300 / 508-699-4436; FAX: 508-695-5349
Valdada Enterprises, P.O. Box 773122, 31733 County Road 35, Steamboat Springs, CO 80477 / 970-879-2983; FAX: 970-879-0851 www.valdada.com
Valtro USA, Inc., 1281 Andersen Dr., San Rafael, CA 94901 / 415-256-2575; FAX: 415-256-2576
VAM Distribution Co. LLC, 1141-B Mechanicsburg Rd., Wooster, OH 44691 www.rex10.com
Van Gorden & Son Inc., C. S., 1815 Main St., Bloomer, WI 54724 / 715-568-2612
Van Horn, Gil, P.O. Box 207, Llano, CA 93544
Van Patten, J. W., P.O. Box 145, Foster Hill, Milford, PA 18337 / 717-296-7069
Vann Custom Bullets, 2766 N. Willowside Way, Meridian, ID 83642
Van's Gunsmith Service, 224 Route 69-A, Parish, NY 13131 / 315-625-7251
Varmint Masters, LLC, Rick Vecqueray, P.O. Box 6724, Bend, OR 97708 / 541-318-7306; FAX: 541-318-7306 varmintmasters@bendcable.com www.varmintmasters.net
Vecqueray, Rick. See: VARMINT MASTERS, LLC
Vector Arms, Inc., 270 W. 500 N., North Salt Lake, UT 84054 / 801-295-1917; FAX: 801-295-9316 vectorarms@bbscmail.com www.vectorarms.com
Vega Tool Co., c/o T. R. Ross, 4865 Tanglewood Ct., Boulder, CO 80301 / 303-530-0174 clanlaird@aol.com www.vegatool.com
Venco Industries, Inc. (See Shooter's Choice Gun Care)
Venus Industries, P.O. Box 246, Sialkot-1, PAKISTAN FAX: 92 432 85579
Verney-Carron, 54 Boulevard Thiers-B.P. 72, 42002 St. Etienne Cedex 1, St. Etienne Cedex 1, FRANCE / 33-477791500; FAX: 33-477790702 email@verney-carron.com www.verney-carron.com
Vest, John, 1923 NE 7th St., Redmond, OR 97756 / 541-923-8898
VibraShine, Inc., P.O. Box 577, Taylorsville, MS 39168 / 601-785-9854; FAX: 601-785-9874 rdbeke@vibrashine.com www.vibrashine.com
Vibra-Tek Co., 1844 Arroya Rd., Colorado Springs, CO 80906 / 719-634-8611; FAX: 719-634-6886
Vic's Gun Refinishing, 6 Pineview Dr., Dover, NH 03820-6422 / 603-742-0013
Victory Ammunition, P.O. Box 1022, Milford, PA 18337 / 717-296-5768; FAX: 717-296-9298
Victory USA, P.O. Box 1021, Pine Bush, NY 12566 / 914-744-2060; FAX: 914-744-5181
Vihtavuori Oy, FIN-41330 Vihtavuori, FINLAND, / 358-41-3779211; FAX: 358-41-3771643
Vihtavuori Oy/Kaltron-Pettibone, 1241 Ellis St., Bensenville, IL 60106 / 708-350-1116; FAX: 708-350-1606
Viking Video Productions, P.O. Box 251, Roseburg, OR 97470
Village Restorations & Consulting, Inc., P.O. Box 569, Claysburg, PA 16625 / 814-239-8200; FAX: 814-239-2165 www.villagerestoration@yahoo.com
Vincent's Shop, 210 Antoinette, Fairbanks, AK 99701
Viper Bullet and Brass Works, 11 Brock St., Box 582, Norwich, ON N0J 1P0 CANADA
Viramontez Engraving, Ray Viramontez, 601 Springfield Dr., Albany, GA 31721 / 229-432-9683 sgtvira@aol.com
Viramontez, Ray. See: VIRAMONTEZ ENGRAVING
Virgin Valley Custom Guns, 450 E 800 N. #20, Hurricane, UT 84737 / 435-635-8941; FAX: 435-635-8943 vvcguns@infowest.com www.virginvalleyguns.com
Visible Impact Targets, Rts. 5 & 20, E. Bloomfield, NY 14443 / 716-657-6161; FAX: 716-657-5405
Vitt/Boos, 1195 Buck Hill Rd., Townshend, VT 05353 / 802-365-9232
Voere-KGH GmbH, Untere Sparchen 56, A-6330 Kufstein, Tirol, AUSTRIA / 0043-5372-62547; FAX: 0043-5372-65752 voere@aon.com www.voere.com
Volquartsen Custom Ltd., 24276 240th Street, P.O. Box 397, Carroll, IA 51401 / 712-792-4238; FAX: 712-792-2542 vcl@netins.net www.volquartsen.com
Vorhes, David, 3042 Beecham St., Napa, CA 94558 / 707-226-9116; FAX: 707-253-7334
VSP Publishers (See Heritage/VSP Gun Books), P.O. Box 887, McCall, ID 83638 / 208-634-4104; FAX: 208-634-3101 heritage@gunbooks.com www.gunbooks.com
VTI Gun Parts, P.O. Box 509, Lakeville, CT 06039 / 860-435-8068; FAX: 860-435-8146 mail@vtigunparts.com www.vtigunparts.com
Vulpes Ventures, Inc., Fox Cartridge Division, P.O. Box 1363, Bolingbrook, IL 60440-7363 / 630-759-1229

W

W. Square Enterprises, 9826 Sagedale Dr., Houston, TX 77089 / 281-484-0935; FAX: 281-464-9940 lfdw@pdq.net www.loadammo.com
W. Waller & Son, Inc., 2221 Stoney Brook Rd., Grantham, NH 03753-7706 / 603-863-4177 www.wallerandson.com
W.B. Niemi Engineering, Box 126 Center Road, Greensboro, VT 05841 / 802-533-7180; or 802-533-7141
W.C. Wolff Co., P.O. Box 458, Newtown Square, PA 19073 / 610-359-9600; or 800-545-0077 mail@gunsprings.com www.gunsprings.com
W.E. Birdsong & Assoc., 1435 Monterey Rd., Florence, MS 39073-9748 / 601-366-8270
W.E. Brownell Checkering Tools, 9390 Twin Mountain Cir., San Diego, CA 92126 / 858-695-2479; FAX: 858-695-2479
W.J. Riebe Co., 3434 Tucker Rd., Boise, ID 83703
W.R. Case & Sons Cutlery Co., Owens Way, Bradford, PA 16701 / 814-368-4123; or 800-523-6350; FAX: 814-368-1736 jsullivan@wrcase.com www.wrcase.com
Wagoner, Vernon G., 2325 E. Encanto St., Mesa, AZ 85213-5917 / 480-835-1307
Waldron, Herman, Box 475, 80 N. 17th St., Pomeroy, WA 99347 / 509-843-1404
Walker Arms Co., Inc., 499 County Rd. 820, Selma, AL 36701 / 334-872-6231; FAX: 334-872-6262
Wallace, Terry, 385 San Marino, Vallejo, CA 94589 / 707-642-7041
Walls Industries, Inc., P.O. Box 98, 1905 N. Main, Cleburne, TX 76033 / 817-645-4366; FAX: 817-645-7946 www.wallsoutdoors.com
Walters Industries, 6226 Park Lane, Dallas, TX 75225 / 214-691-6973
Walters, John. See: WALTERS WADS
Walters Wads, John Walters, 500 N. Avery Dr., Moore, OK 73160 / 405-799-0376; FAX: 405-799-7727 www.tinwadman@cs.com
Walther America, P.O. Box 22, Springfield, MA 01102 / 413-747-3443 www.walther-usa.com
Walther GmbH, Carl, B.P. 4325, D-89033 Ulm, GERMANY
Walt's Custom Leather, Walt Whinnery, 1947 Meadow Creek Dr., Louisville, KY 40218 / 502-458-4361
WAMCO-New Mexico, P.O. Box 205, Peralta, NM 87042-0205 / 505-869-0826
Ward & Van Valkenburg, 114 32nd Ave. N., Fargo, ND 58102 / 701-232-2351
Ward Machine, 5620 Lexington Rd., Corpus Christi, TX 78412 / 512-992-1221
Wardell Precision Handguns Ltd., P.O. Box 391, Clyde, AZ 79510-0391 / 602-465-7995
Warenski Engraving, Julie Warenski, 590 E. 500 N., Richfield, UT 84701 / 435-896-5319; FAX: 435-896-8333 julie@warenskiknives.com
Warenski, Julie. See: WARENSKI ENGRAVING
Warne Manufacturing Co., 9057 SE Jannsen Rd., Clackamas, OR 97015 / 503-657-5590; or 800-683-5590; FAX: 503-657-5695 info@warnescopemounts.com www.warnescopemounts.com
Warren Muzzleloading Co., Inc., Hwy. 21 North, P.O. Box 100, Ozone, AR 72854 / 501-292-3268
Washita Mountain Whetstone Co., P.O. Box 20378, Hot Springs, AR 71903 / 501-525-3914 www.@hsnp.com
Wasmundt, Jim, P.O. Box 130, Powers, OR 97466-0130
Watson Bros., 39 Redcross Way, London Bridge SE1 1H6, London, ENGLAND FAX: 44-171-403-336
Watson Bullets, 231 Allies Pass, Frostproof, FL 33843 / 863-635-7948 cbestbullet@aol.com
Wayne Specialty Services, 260 Waterford Drive, Florissant, MO 63033 / 413-831-7083

MANUFACTURER'S DIRECTORY

WD-40 Co., 1061 Cudahy Pl., San Diego, CA 92110 / 619-275-1400; FAX: 619-275-5823
Weatherby, Inc., 3100 El Camino Real, Atascadero, CA 93422 / 805-466-1767; FAX: 805-466-2527 www.weatherby.com
Weaver Products ATK, P.O. Box 39, Onalaska, WI 54650 / 800-648-9624; or 608-781-5800; FAX: 608-781-0368
Weaver Scope Repair Service, 1121 Larry Mahan Dr., Suite B, El Paso, TX 79925 / 915-593-1005
Webb, Bill, 6504 North Bellefontaine, Kansas City, MO 64119 / 816-453-7431
Weber & Markin Custom Gunsmiths, 4-1691 Powick Rd., Kelowna, BC V1X 4L1 CANADA / 250-762-7575; FAX: 250-861-3655 www.weberandmarkinguns.com
Webley and Scott Ltd., Frankley Industrial Park, Tay Rd., Birmingham, B45 0PA ENGLAND / 011-021-453-1864; FAX: 0121-457-7846 guns@webley.co.uk www.webley.co.uk
Webster Scale Mfg. Co., P.O. Box 188, Sebring, FL 33870 / 813-385-6362
Weems, Cecil, 510 W. Hubbard St., Mineral Wells, TX 76067-4847 / 817-325-1462
Weigand Combat Handguns, Inc., 1057 South Main Rd., Mountain Top, PA 18707 / 570-868-8358; FAX: 570-868-5218 sales@jackweigand.com www.jackweigand.com
Weihrauch KG, Hermann, Industriestrasse 11, 8744 Mellrichstadt, Mellrichstadt, GERMANY
Welch, Sam. See: SAM WELCH GUN ENGRAVING
Wellington Outdoors, P.O. Box 244, 1140 Monticello Rd., Madison, GA 30650 / 706-342-4915; FAX: 706-342-7568
Wells, Rachel, 110 N. Summit St., Prescott, AZ 86301 / 928-445-3655 wellssportstore@cableone.net
Wells Creek Knife & Gun Works, 32956 State Hwy. 38, Scottsburg, OR 97473 / 541-587-4202; FAX: 541-587-4223
Welsh, Bud. See: HIGH PRECISION
Wenger North America/Precise Int'l., 15 Corporate Dr., Orangeburg, NY 10962 / 800-431-2996; FAX: 914-425-4700
Wenig Custom Gunstocks, 103 N. Market St., P.O. Box 249, Lincoln, MO 65338 / 660-547-3334; FAX: 660-547-2881 gustock@wenig.com www.wenig.com
Werth, T. W., 1203 Woodlawn Rd., Lincoln, IL 62656 / 217-732-1300
Wescombe, Bill (See North Star West)
Wessinger Custom Guns & Engraving, 268 Limestone Rd., Chapin, SC 29036 / 803-345-5677
West, Jack L., 1220 W. Fifth, P.O. Box 427, Arlington, OR 97812
Western Cutlery (See Camillus Cutlery Co.)
Western Mfg. Co., 550 Valencia School Rd., Aptos, CA 95003 / 831-688-5884 lotsabears@eathlink.net
Western Missouri Shooters Alliance, P.O. Box 11144, Kansas City, MO 64119 / 816-597-3950; FAX: 816-229-7350
Western Nevada West Coast Bullets, P.O. BOX 2270, DAYTON, NV 89403-2270 / 702-246-3941; FAX: 702-246-0836
Westley Richards & Co. Ltd., 40 Grange Rd., Birmingham, ENGLAND / 010-214722953; FAX: 010-214141138 sales@westleyrichards.com www.westleyrichards.com
Westley Richards Agency USA (See U.S. Importer
Westwind Rifles, Inc., David S. Sullivan, P.O. Box 261, 640 Briggs St., Erie, CO 80516 / 303-828-3823
Weyer International, 2740 Nebraska Ave., Toledo, OH 43607 / 419-534-2020; FAX: 419-534-2697
Whildin & Sons Ltd., E.H., RR 2 Box 119, Tamaqua, PA 18252 / 717-668-6743; FAX: 717-668-6745
Whinnery, Walt (See Walt's Custom Leather)
White Barn Wor, 431 County Road, Broadlands, IL 61816
White Pine Photographic Services, Hwy. 60, General Delivery, Wilno, ON K0J 2N0 CANADA / 613-756-3452
White Rifles, Inc., 234 S. 1250 W., Linden, UT 84042 / 801-932-7950 www.whiterifles.com
White Rock Tool & Die, 6400 N. Brighton Ave., Kansas City, MO 64119 / 816-454-0478
Whitestone Lumber Corp., 148-02 14th Ave., Whitestone, NY 11357 / 718-746-4400; FAX: 718-767-1748 whstco@aol.com
Wichita Arms, Inc., 923 E. Gilbert, Wichita, KS 67211 / 316-265-0661; FAX: 316-265-0760 sales@wichitaarms.com www.wichitaarms.com
Wick, David E., 1504 Michigan Ave., Columbus, IN 47201 / 812-376-6960
Widener's Reloading & Shooting Supply, Inc., P.O. Box 3009 CRS, Johnson City, TN 37602 / 615-282-6786; FAX: 615-282-6651
Wideview Scope Mount Corp., 13535 S. Hwy. 16, Rapid City, SD 57702 / 605-341-3220; FAX: 605-341-9142 wvdon@rapidnet.com www.wideviewscopemount.com
Wiebe, Duane, 5300 Merchant Cir. #2, Placerville, CA 95667 / 530-344-1357; FAX: 530-344-1357 wiebe@d-wdb.com
Wiest, Marie. See: GUNCRAFT SPORTS, INC.
Wilcox All-Pro Tools & Supply, 4880 147th St., Montezuma, IA 50171 / 515-623-3138; FAX: 515-623-3104
Wilcox Industries Corp., Robert F. Guarasi, 53 Durham St., Portsmouth, NH 03801 / 603-431-1331; FAX: 603-431-1221
Wild Bill's Originals, P.O. Box 13037, Burton, WA 98013 / 206-463-5738; FAX: 206-465-5925 wildbill@halcyon.com billcleaver@centurytel.net
Wild West Guns, 7521 Old Seward Hwy., Unit A, Anchorage, AK 99518 / 800-992-4570; or 907-344-4500; FAX: 907-344-4005 wwguns@ak.net www.wildwestguns.com
Wilderness Sound Products Ltd., 4015 Main St. A, Springfield, OR 97478
Wildey F. A., Inc., 45 Angevin Rd., Warren, CT 06754-1818 / 860-355-9000; FAX: 860-354-7759 wildeyfa@optonline.net www.wildeyguns.com
Wildlife Research Center, Inc., 1050 McKinley St., Anoka, MN 55303 / 763-427-3350; or 800-USE-LURE; FAX: 763-427-8354 www.wildlife.com
Will-Burt Co., 169 S. Main, Orrville, OH 44667
William E. Phillips Firearms, 38 Avondale Rd., Wigston, Leicester, ENGLAND / 0116 2886334; FAX: 0116 2810644 william.phillips2@tesco.net
William Powell Agency, 22 Circle Dr., Bellmore, NY 11710 / 516-679-1158
Williams Gun Sight Co., 7389 Lapeer Rd., Box 329, Davison, MI 48423 / 810-653-2131; or 800-530-9028; FAX: 810-658-2140 williamsgunsight.com
Williams Mfg. of Oregon, 110 East B St., Drain, OR 97435 / 503-836-7461; FAX: 503-836-7245
Williams Shootin' Iron Service, The Lynx-Line, Rt. 2 Box 223A, Mountain Grove, MO 65711 / 417-948-0902; FAX: 417-948-0902
Williamson Precision Gunsmithing, 117 W. Pipeline, Hurst, TX 76053 / 817-285-0064; FAX: 817-280-0044
Willow Bend, P.O. Box 203, Chelmsford, MA 01824 / 978-256-8508; FAX: 978-256-8508
Wilsom Combat, 2234 CR 719, Berryville, AR 72616-4573 / 800-955-4856; FAX: 870-545-3310
Wilson Arms Co., The, 63 Leetes Island Rd., Branford, CT 06405 / 203-488-7297; FAX: 203-488-0135
Wilson Case, Inc., P.O. Box 1106, Hastings, NE 68902-1106 / 800-322-5493; FAX: 402-463-5276 sales@wilsoncase.com www.wilsoncase.com
Wilson Combat, 2234 CR 719, Berryville, AR 72616-4573 / 800-955-4856
Winchester Consultants, George Madis, P.O. Box 545, Brownsboro, TX 75756 / 903-852-6480; FAX: 903-852-5486 gmadis@earthlink.com www.georgemadis.com
Winchester Div. Olin Corp., 427 N. Shamrock, E. Alton, IL 62024 / 618-258-3566; FAX: 618-258-3599
Winchester Sutler, Inc., The, 270 Shadow Brook Lane, Winchester, VA 22603 / 540-888-3595; FAX: 540-888-4632
Windish, Jim, 2510 Dawn Dr., Alexandria, VA 22306 / 703-765-1994
Winfield Galleries LLC, 748 Hanley Industrial Ct., St. Louis, MO 63144 / 314-645-7636; FAX: 314-781-0224 info@winfieldgalleries.com www.winfieldgalleries.com
Wingshooting Adventures, 0-1845 W. Leonard, Grand Rapids, MI 49544 / 616-677-1980; FAX: 616-677-1986
Winter, Robert M., P.O. Box 484, 42975-287th St., Menno, SD 57045 / 605-387-5322
Wise Custom Guns, 1402 Blanco Rd., San Antonio, TX 78212-2716 / 210-828-3388
Wise Guns, Dale, 1402 Blanco Rd., San Antonio, TX 78212 / 210-734-9999
Wiseman and Co., Bill, P.O. Box 3427, Bryan, TX 77805 / 409-690-3456; FAX: 409-690-0156
Wisners, Inc., P.O. Box 58, Adna, WA 98522 / 360-748-4590; FAX: 360-748-6028 parts@wisnersinc.com www.wisnersinc.com
Wolf Performance Ammunition, 2201 E. Winston Rd., Ste. K, Anaheim, CA 92806-5537 / 702-837-8506; FAX: 702-837-9250
Wolfe Publishing Co., 2625 Stearman Rd., Ste. A, Prescott, AZ 86301 / 928-445-7810; or 800-899-7810; FAX: 928-778-5124
Wolverine Footwear Group, 9341 Courtland Dr. NE, Rockford, MI 49351 / 616-866-5500; FAX: 616-866-5658
Woodleigh (See Huntington Die Specialties)
Woods Wise Products, P.O. Box 681552, Franklin, TN 37068 / 800-735-8182; FAX: 615-726-2637
Woodstream, P.O. Box 327, Lititz, PA 17543 / 717-626-2125; FAX: 717-626-1912
Woodworker's Supply, 1108 North Glenn Rd., Casper, WY 82601 / 307-237-5354
Woolrich, Inc., Mill St., Woolrich, PA 17701 / 800-995-1299; FAX: 717-769-6234/6259
World of Targets (See Birchwood Casey)
World Trek, Inc., 7170 Turkey Creek Rd., Pueblo, CO 81007-1046 / 719-546-2121; FAX: 719-543-6886
Worthy Products, Inc., RR 1, P.O. Box 213, Martville, NY 13111 / 315-324-5298
Wright's Gunstock Blanks, 8540 SE Kane Rd., Gresham, OR 97080 / 503-666-1705 doyal@wrightsguns.com www.wrightsguns.com
WTA Manufacturing, P.O. Box 164, Kit Carson, CO 80825 / 719-962-3570; or 719-962-3570 wta@rebeltec.net http://www.members.aol.com/ductman249/wta.html
Wyant Bullets, Gen. Del., Swan Lake, MT 59911
Wyoming Custom Bullets, 1626 21st St., Cody, WY 82414
Wyoming Knife Corp., 101 Commerce Dr., Fort Collins, CO 80524 / 303-224-3454

X

XS Sight Systems, 2401 Ludelle St., Fort Worth, TX 76105 / 888-744-4880; FAX: 800-734-7939
X-Spand Target Systems, 26-10th St. SE, Medicine Hat, AB T1A 1P7 CANADA / 403-526-7997; FAX: 403-528-2362

Y

Yankee Gunsmith "Just Glocks", 2901 Deer Flat Dr., Copperas Cove, TX 76522 / 817-547-8433; FAX: 254-547-8887 ed@justglocks.com www.justglocks.com
Yavapai College, 1100 E. Sheldon St., Prescott, AZ 86301 / 520-776-2353; FAX: 520-776-2355
Yavapai Firearms Academy Ltd., P.O. Box 27290, Prescott Valley, AZ 86312 / 928-772-8262; FAX: 928-772-0062 info@yfainc.com www.yfainc.com
Yearout, Lewis E. (See Montana Outfitters)
Yellowstone Wilderness Supply, P.O. Box 129, West Yellowstone, MT 59758 / 406-646-7613
Yesteryear Armory & Supply, P.O. Box 408, Carthage, TN 37030
York M-1 Conversion, 12145 Mill Creek Run, Plantersville, TX 77363 / 936-894-2397; FAX: 936-894-2397 bmf25years@aol.com
Young Country Arms, William, 1409 Kuehner Dr. #13, Simi Valley, CA 93063-4478

Z

Zabala Hermanos S.A., P.O. Box 97, Elbar Lasao, 6, Elgueta, Guipuzcoa, 20600 SPAIN / 34-943-768076; FAX: 34-943-768201 imanol@zabalahermanos.com www.zabalabermanos.com
Zander's Sporting Goods, 7525 Hwy. 154 West, Baldwin, IL 62217-9706 / 800-851-4373; FAX: 618-785-2320
Zanotti Armor, Inc., 123 W. Lone Tree Rd., Cedar Falls, IA 50613 / 319-232-9650 www.zanottiarmor.com
Zeeryp, Russ, 1601 Foard Dr., Lynn Ross Manor, Morristown, TN 37814 / 615-586-2357
Zero Ammunition Co., Inc., 1601 22nd St. SE, P.O. Box 1188, Cullman, AL 35056-1188 / 800-545-9376; FAX: 205-739-4683 zerobulletco@aoz.com www.zerobullets.com
Ziegel Engineering, 1390 E. Bunnett St. "F", Signal Hill, CA 90755 / 562-596-9481; FAX: 562-598-4734 ziegel@aol.com www.ziegeleng.com
Zim's, Inc., 4370 S. 3rd West, Salt Lake City, UT 84107 / 801-268-2505
Z-M Weapons, 203 South St., Bernardston, MA 01337 / 413-648-9501; FAX: 413-648-0219

Numbers

100 Straight Products, Inc., P.O. Box 6148, Omaha, NE 68106 / 402-556-1055; FAX: 402-556-1055
3-Ten Corp., P.O. Box 269, Feeding Hills, MA 01030 / 413-789-2086; FAX: 413-789-1549 www.3-ten.com
4-D Custom Die Co., 711 N. Sandusky St., P.O. Box 889, Mt. Vernon, OH 43050-0889 / 740-397-7214; FAX: 740-397-6600 info@ch4d.com ch4d.com